Lecture Notes in Computer Science

Edited by G. Goos and J. Hartmanis

85

Automata, Languages and Programming

Seventh Colloquium
Noordwijkerhout, the Netherlands
July 14–18, 1980

Edited by
J. W. de Bakker and J. van Leeuwen

Springer-Verlag
Berlin Heidelberg New York 1980

199719

Editors

Jaco de Bakker
Mathematical Centre, Kruislaan 413
1098 SJ Amsterdam, the Netherlands

Jan van Leeuwen
Dept. of Computer Science, University of Utrecht
P.O.Box 80.002
3508 TA Utrecht, the Netherlands

AMS Subject Classifications (1979): 68-XX
CR Subject Classifications (1974): 4.1, 4.2, 5.2, 5.3

ISBN 3-540-10003-2 Springer-Verlag Berlin Heidelberg New York
ISBN 0-387-10003-2 Springer-Verlag New York Heidelberg Berlin

Printed in Germany

Printing and binding: Beltz Offsetdruck, Hemsbach/Bergstr.
2145/3140-543210

PREFACE

ICALP is the acronym of the annual International Colloquium on Automata, Languages and Programming sponsored by the European Association for Theoretical Computer Science (EATCS). It is a broad-based conference covering all aspects of the foundations of computer science, including such topics as automata theory, formal language theory, analysis of algorithms, computational complexity, computability theory, mathematical aspects of programming language definition, semantics of programming languages, program verification, theory of data structures and theory of data bases. Previously ICALP conferences were held in Paris (1972), Saarbrücken (1974), Edinburgh (1976), Turku (1977), Udine (1978) and in Graz (1979).

ICALP 80 is the 7th conference of EATCS, covering once again a broad spectrum of theoretical computer science. ICALP 80 was organized by the University of Utrecht and the Mathematical Centre at Amsterdam and was held July 14-18, 1980, in Noordwijkerhout, the Netherlands. The program committee consisted of J.W. de Bakker (Amsterdam, chairman), A. Blikle (Warsaw), C. Böhm (Rome), H.D. Ehrich (Dortmund), S. Even (Haifa), P. van Emde Boas (Amsterdam), I.M. Havel (Prague), J. van Leeuwen (Utrecht), H. Maurer (Graz), L.G.L.T. Meertens (Amsterdam), K. Mehlhorn (Saarbrücken), A.R. Meyer (MIT), R. Milner (Edinburgh), U. Montanari (Pisa), M. Nivat (Paris), M. Paterson (Coventry), G. Rozenberg (Leiden), A. Salomaa (Turku), J.W. Thatcher (Yorktown Heights), J. Vuillemin (Paris). We wish to thank the members of the program committee for their arduous job of evaluating the record number of 169 papers that were submitted to the conference. On their behalf we extend our gratitude to the referees which assisted this process (see next page).

ICALP 80 has been made possible by the support from a number of sources. We thank the Dutch Ministry for Education and Sciences (The Hague), the Mathematical Centre (Amsterdam), the University of Utrecht, the University of Leiden, CDC-the Netherlands and IBM-the Netherlands for sponsoring the conference. A special tribute goes to Mrs. S.J. Kuipers of the Mathematical Centre (Amsterdam) for her expert assistance in all organizational matters related to the conference.

We feel that ICALP 80 has succeeded in bringing together a variety of important developments in modern theoretical computer science. The need for a thorough investigation of the foundations of computer science evidently is increasing rapidly, as computer science moves on to ever more complex and diverse systems and applications. We hope that the ICALP conferences will continue to be an exponent of this trend in the years to come.

J.W. de Bakker and J. van Leeuwen

I C A L P 80

REFEREES FOR ICALP 80

H. Alblas
V. Ambriola
P. Ancilotti
K.R. Apt
A. Arnold
P.R.J. Asveld
G. Ausiello

R.J. Back
J. Bergstra
E. Börger
D.P. Bovet
F.J. Brandenburg
A. de Bruin
J.A. Brzozowski
R.M. Burstall

D. de Champeaux
M.P. Chytil
E.M. Clarke jr.
A.B. Cremers
K. Culik II

P. Degano
G. Degli Antoni
P. Della Vigna
P. Dembinski
M. Dezani- Ciancaglini
G. Dittrich

H. Edelsbrunner
E. Edens
J. Engelfriet

G. Filè
P. Flajolet
N. Francez

S. Gal
Z. Galil
H.J.M. Goeman
S.L. Graham
S.A. Greibach
G. Guiho
J.V. Guttag

D. Harel
T. Harju
M.A. Harrison

W. Imrich
A. Itai

J.M. Jaffe
T.M.V. Janssen
H. Janssens
K. Jensen
P. Jirků
N. Jones

J. Karhumäki
O. Kariv
H.C.M. Klein
S.R. Kosaraju
D.C. Kozen

J.K. Lenstra
G. Levi
S. Levialdi
M.R. Levy
M. Linna
E. Lipeck
M.H. Löb
G. Longo
R. Loos
B.E. Lub

A. Machi
A. Maggiolo-Schettini
J. Małuszyński
Z. Manna
A. Martelli
A. Mazurkiewicz
B. Mayoh
E. Meineche Schmidt
B. Melichar
W. Merzenich
C. Montangero
P.D. Mosses
K. Müller

M. Nielsen
A. Nijholt

Th. Ottmann
M.H. Overmars

P. Paolini
M. Penttonen
J. Pittl
G.D. Plotkin
A. Poigné
V.R. Pratt
G.A. Prini
H. Prodinger

M.O. Rabin
J.C. Reynolds
M.M. Richter
M. Rodeh
F. Romani
K. Ruohonen
P. Ružička

A. Salwicki
W.J. Savitch
W.L. Scherlis
G. Schlageter
A. Shamir
E. Shamir
Y. Shiloach
M. Sintzoff
M. Sipser
A. Skowron
M. Steinby

A. Tang
A. Tarlecki
J. Tiuryn
P.R. Torregiani
J.V. Tucker

F.J. Urbanek

M. Venturini-Zilli
R. Verraedt
P.M.B. Vitányi

R.W. v.d. Waall
W.W. Wadge
E.G. Wagner
M. Wand
L. Wegner
J. Winkowski

A. Yehudai

CONTENTS

W. Ainhirn
How to get rid of pseudoterminals 1

J. Albert and K. Culik II
Test sets for homomorphism equivalence on context free languages 12

J. Albert and L. Wegner
Languages with homomorphic replacements 19

H. Alt
Functions equivalent to integer multiplication 30

E. Astesiano and G. Costa
Languages with reducing reflexive types 38

R.-J. Back
Semantics of unbounded nondeterminism 51

R.I. Becker, Y. Perl and St.R. Schach
A shifting algorithm for min-max tree partitioning 64

J.A. Bergstra and J.V. Tucker
A characterisation of computable data types by means of a finite equational specification method 76

P. Berman
A note on sweeping automata 91

D. Bini
Border rank of a pxqx2 tensor and the optimal approximation of a pair of bilinear forms 98

L. Boasson
Derivations et réductions dans les grammaires algébriques 109

P. Cousot and R. Cousot
Semantic analysis of communicating sequential processes 119

E. Ehrenfeucht and G. Rozenberg
DOS systems and languages 134

H. Ehrig, H.-J. Kreowski and P. Padawitz
Algebraic implementation of abstract data types: concept, syntax, semantics and correctness 142

H. Ehrig, H.-J. Kreowski, J. Thatcher, E. Wagner and J. Wright
Parameterized data types in algebraic specification languages 157

E.A. Emerson and E.M. Clarke
Characterizing correctness properties of parallel programs using fixpoints . . 169

J. Engelfriet and G. Filè
Formal properties of one-visit and multi-pass attribute grammars 182

S. Even and Y. Yacobi
Cryptocomplexity and NP-completeness 195

Ph. Flajolet and J.-M. Steyaert
On the analysis of tree-matching algorithms 208

G.N. Frederickson and D.B. Johnson
Generating and searching sets induced by networks 221

M. Fürer
The complexity of the inequivalence problem for regular expressions with intersection 234

Z. Galil
An almost linear time algorithm for computing a dependency basis in a relational data base 246

H.J. Genrich and P.S. Thiagarajan
Bipolar synchronization systems 257

A. Goralcíková, P. Goralcík and V. Koubek
Testing of properties of finite algebras 273

J. Gray
A transaction model (Invited address) 282

M. Hennessy and R. Milner
On observing nondeterminism and concurrency 299

G. Hornung and P. Raulefs
Terminal algebra semantics and retractions for abstract data types 310

Th.-D. Huynh
The complexity of semilinear sets 324

J.R. Kennaway and C.A.R. Hoare
A theory of nondeterminism 338

D. Kozen
*A representation theorem for models of *-free PDL* 351

H. Langmaack and E.-R. Olderog
Present-day Hoare-like systems for programming languages with procedures: power, limits and most likely extensions 363

H.R. Lewis and Ch.H. Papadimitriou
Symmetric space-bounded computation 374

A. de Luca and A. Restivo
On some properties of local testability 385

M.E. Majster-Cederbaum
Semantics: algebras, fixed points, axioms 394

J.A. Makowsky
Measuring the expressive power of dynamic logics: an application of abstract model theory 409

K. Mehlhorn
Pebbling mountain ranges and its application to DCFL-recognition 422

E. Meineche Schmidt
Space-restricted attribute grammars 436

P. Mosses
A constructive approach to compiler correctness 449

Ch.H. Papadimitriou and J.L. Bentley
A worst-case analysis of nearest neighbor searching by projection 470

J.-E. Pin
Propriétés syntactiques du produit non ambigu 483

K.-J. Räihä and E. Ukkonen
On the optimal assignment of attributes to passes in multi-pass attribute evaluators 500

J.C. Raoult and J. Vuillemin
Optimal unbounded search strategies 512

R. Reischuk
A "fast implementation" of a multidimensional storage into a tree storage . . 531

A. Salomaa
Grammatical families (Invited address) 543

P. Schlichtiger
Partitioned chain grammars 555

J. Schmidt and E. Shamir
An improved program for constructing open hash tables 569

A. Shamir
On the power of commutativity in cryptography (Invited address) 582

S. Sippu and E. Soisalon-Soininen
Characterizations of the LL(k) property 596

M.B. Smyth

Computability in categories 609

M. Snir

On the size complexity of monotone formulas 621

T. Toffoli

Reversible computing 632

V.F. Turchin

The use of metasystem transition in theorem proving and program optimization . 645

P.M.B. Vitányi

On the power of real-time Turing machines under varying specifications 658

M.A. Frumkin, G.V. Gens, Ju.I. Hmelevskii and E.V. Levner

On reducibility among extremal combinatorial problems (paper not received)

HOW TO GET RID OF PSEUDOTERMINALS

W. Ainhirn
Institut für Informationsverarbeitung
Technische Universität Graz
Steyrergasse 17
A-8010 Graz/Austria

Abstract

We investigate the role of pseudoterminals for EOL forms. This leads us to the definition of m - interpretation which avoids pseudoterminals. We solve the problem of m - completeness of short and simple EPOL forms and finally consider the validity of some basic results on EOL forms under m - interpretation.

Introduction and Preliminaries

Investigations of EOL forms in [AiM], [CM], [CMO] and [MSW2] have shown in the past that we actually deal with three (rather than two!) alphabets: the terminal, the pseudoterminal and the nonterminal alphabet. The pseudoterminal alphabet contains those symbols which are explicitely specified as terminal symbols but never occur in the language generated by the system. It seems that pseudoterminals sometimes act rather pathologically. For this reason we define a new type of interpretation, so - called marvellous interpretation (m - interpretation for short) which does not allow the existence of pseudoterminals. As a consequence of the modification of the interpretation mechanism we are able to give necessary and sufficient conditions for the m - completeness of short and simple EPOL forms. Finally the fact that many fundamental results also hold under m - interpretation shows the close relation to the ordinary interpretation mechanism whereas complications in carrying over the technique of isolation to m - interpretation gives a good feeling of what really happens when avoiding pseudoterminals.

We will denote an EOL system G by $G = (V,\Sigma,P,S)$ where V is the total, Σ the terminal alphabet, P the set of productions and S the startsymbol. G is called <u>short</u> if $\alpha \to x \in P$ implies $|x| \leq 2$, <u>simple</u> if $\mathrm{card}(V - \Sigma) = \mathrm{card}(\Sigma) = 1$, <u>synchronized</u> if $a \stackrel{+}{\Longrightarrow} x$ implies $x \notin \Sigma^*$ for every $a \in \Sigma$ and <u>looping</u> if $\alpha \stackrel{+}{\Longrightarrow} \alpha$ holds for some $\alpha \in V$.

For a precise definition of the notions used we refer to [H], [RS] and [MSW1]. However, we would like to give the fundamental definition of L form theory:

An EOL form F is an EOL system, $F = (V,\Sigma,P,S)$. An EOL system $F' = (V',\Sigma',P',S')$ is called an interpretation of F (modulo μ), if μ is a finite substitution defined on V and (i) to (v) hold:

(i) $\mu(A) \subseteq V' - \Sigma'$ for each $A \in V - \Sigma$;

(ii) $\mu(a) \subseteq \Sigma'$ for each $a \in \Sigma$;

(iii) $\mu(\alpha) \cap \mu(\beta) = \phi$ for all $\alpha \neq \beta$ in V;

(iv) $P' \subseteq \bigcup_{\alpha \to x \in P} \{\beta \to y \mid \beta \in \mu(\alpha),\ y \in \mu(x)\}$;

(v) $S' \in \mu(S)$.

In this case we write $F' \triangleleft F(\mu)$. $\mathcal{L}(F) := \{L(F') \mid F' \triangleleft F\}$ is the family of languages generated by F.

Examples of EOL systems are specified by listing the productions where small letters are used to denote terminals, capital letters to denote nonterminals and S to indicate the startsymbol. Many results in this paper are only sketched. A detailed version is available as [Ai] and has been submitted for publication elsewhere.

Underlying Philosophy

Rewriting systems have originally been introduced by Thue. Thue did not make a distinction between a terminal and a nonterminal alphabet as it has become customary in formal language theory. This distinction is due to three reasons: firstly, the introduction of nonterminals has a linguistic motivation since nonterminals can be viewed as representations of syntactic classes. Secondly, the variety of languages obtained by grammars is essentially increased with the use of nonterminals, cf. [MSW3] where pure grammars (that are grammars without nonterminal symbols) are investigated. Thirdly, nonterminals are necessary to obtain strong closure properties, e.g. one can show that the class of pure CF languages is an anti - AFL, whereas it is well - known that the class of CF languages (which differs from the first one only in the existence of nonterminal symbols) is a full AFL.

When considering parallel rewriting we may observe similar conditions: originally parallel rewriting has been introduced in [L] to describe the development of cell growth in simple organisms. These rewriting systems, so - called L systems, do not use nonterminals. However, it turned out that the introduction of nonterminal symbols in [He] involves similar advantages concerning the increase of languages obtainable and closure properties as mentioned above in the case of grammars, cf. [S] and [He]. The extension of OL systems to EOL systems by introducing nonterminals was found mathematically tractable and interesting. Moreover, we can justify the notion of extended OL systems from a biological point of view pointed out in [HR]: the family of languages of recurrence systems, which is of biological interest, equals the family of EOL languages. A final argument for considering EOL systems is the equivalence of the class of EOL languages and the class of codings of OL languages, cf. [ER], and the significance of codings for biological observations.

EOL systems differ from CF grammars in two ways: parallel rewriting is used rather than sequential rewriting and in EOL systems there exist productions also for terminal symbols. One could suspect that the latter is a natural consequence of the constraint of parallel rewriting: if there are no productions for terminal symbols, any derivation in an EOL system will stop whenever a terminal symbol is generated. Note that this situation is simulated exactly by synchronized EOL systems. Thus, as far as the generated languages are concerned, the existence of terminal productions is quite insignificant since it is well - known that for any EOL language L there exists a synchronized EOL system F such that L(F) = L, cf. [HR]. However, when working with EOL families, it turns out that terminal productions indeed lead to additional language families as shown in [MSW1].

When introducing nonterminal symbols for CF grammars, the character of all symbols not contained in the set of nonterminals is really "terminal" in the sense that each of these symbols actually occurs in some word of the generated language, provided the grammar is reduced. Clearly, this is due to sequential rewriting in CF grammars. The situation becomes more complicated in the case of EOL systems as demonstrated by the following example: let F be defined by the productions $S \to aS$, $S \to b$, $a \to b$ and $b \to b$. Clearly, $L(F) = b^+$. Although the symbol a is explicitely specified as member of the terminal alphabet, it does not occur in any word of the language which is caused by the parallel mode of rewriting.

<u>Definition:</u> Let $F = (V,\Sigma,P,S)$ be an EOL system. A symbol $a \in \Sigma$ is called a pseudoterminal iff $a \notin alph(L(F))$. PS(F) denotes the set of pseudoterminals of F.

The existence of pseudoterminals has been observed in a number of proofs in the past, cf. [MSW2] and [AiM]. In these cases pseudoterminals often lead to rather nasty complications. However, pseudoterminals play an important role for some results concerning the completeness of

EOL forms settled in [CM] and [CMO]. Also the quite surprising and somewhat pathological result of Theorem 3.4 in [AiM] seems to depend essentially on the existence of pseudoterminals. The aim of this paper, namely to consider EOL forms with restricted occurrence of pseudoterminals, is due to two reasons: the first one is to avoid complications as mentioned above and is a rather pragmatic one. The second reason becomes obvious when analysing the proofs of Theorem 2.4 and Theorem 2.5 in [CM]. These theorems establish the existence of complete EOL forms which do not contain a nonterminal chain - production, i.e. a production of the type $A \rightarrow B$ where A and B are nonterminals. This result is shown by a construction which uses pseudoterminals, i.e. terminal symbols with nonterminal character, to generate necessary nonterminal chains, thus veiling and falsifying in a certain way our knowldge about the structure of derivation trees which are necessary to generate all EOL languages. Indeed, Theorem 1 shows that such nonterminal chain - productions are necessary for completeness when suppressing pseudoterminals. We think that the mentioned results in [AiM], [CM] and [CMO] are not due to the structure of EOL systems in the first place but due to a weakness in the definition of EOL systems.

<u>Definition:</u> An EOL system $F = (V,\Sigma,P,S)$ is called <u>marvellous</u> if Σ contains no pseudoterminals.

The following lemma, which is easy to prove, shows that the generative capacity of EOL systems is not affected by this definition.

<u>Lemma 1:</u> For every EOL language L there exists a marvellous EOL system F such that $L(F) = L$. □

When dealing with EOL forms one easily checks that the form being marvellous is not sufficient to assume that all interpretations are marvellous. A general relation beween the sets of pseudoterminals of the form and its interpretations, respectively, is established by the following lemma.

<u>Lemma 2:</u> Let $F = (V,\Sigma,P,S)$ be an EOL form. For every interpretation $F' = (V',\Sigma',P',S') \lhd F(\mu)$ there holds: $\mu(PS(F)) \subseteq PS(F')$. □

We next present two examples. The first one shows that the inclusion of Lemma 2 may be proper; the second on shows that despite Lemma 2 interpretations of forms containing pseudoterminals may be marvellous (due to the fact that $\mu(PS(F)) = \phi$ may hold).

<u>Example 1:</u>

F: $S \rightarrow aS \mid a \mid b;\ a \rightarrow b;\ b \rightarrow b.$

F': $S \rightarrow aS \mid b;\quad a \rightarrow b;\ b \rightarrow b.$

Clearly, $F' \lhd F(\mu)$, $PS(F) = \phi$ and $PS(F') = \{a\}$.

Example 2:

F: $S \to a \mid bS;\ a \to a;\ b \to S.$

F': $S \to a;\ a \to a.$

Again, $F' \lhd F(\mu)$, and $PS(F) = \{b\}$, $PS(F') = \phi$.

Note that the generation of pseudoterminals via interpretation is crucial to the proof of the normal form result for EOL systems in [CM]. For example, the complete form G specified by the productions $S \to a \mid aS \mid Sa$, $a \to a \mid S \mid SS$ clearly does not contain pseudoterminals. However, the construction used in the proof of Theorem 2.5 in [CM] uses pseudoterminals which are interpretations of the terminal symbol a. By Lemma 2 and the above example it becomes obvious that the definition of marvellous systems does not suffice for the consideration of EOL forms. Indeed, we also have to modify the mechanism of interpretation, thus getting what we call marvellous or m - interpretation. Before presenting our definition we want to briefly discuss an alternative and why we feel that this alternative is not suitable: the idea of the modification is to allow interpretations of terminals to be nonterminals in the case that the interpreted terminal would have been a pseudoterminal. Thus, we could call an EOL system $F' = (V',\Sigma',P',S')$ a marvellous interpretation of the EOL system $F = (V,\Sigma,P,S)$ modulo μ (in symbols: $F' \lhd_m F(\mu)$) if μ is defined as usual except point (ii) which is altered to:

(ii) for all $a \in \Sigma$ and all $\alpha \in \mu(a)$

$$\alpha \in \begin{cases} V' - \Sigma' & \text{if for all } x' \in SF(F')\ \alpha \in alph(x') \text{ implies } alph(x') \\ & \quad \cap\ \mu(V - \Sigma) \neq \phi \\ \Sigma' & \text{otherwise.} \end{cases}$$

Clearly, the definition guarantees that every interpretation is marvellous. The main drawback of this kind of definition is that it blures the relation between the form and its interpretations. This fact greatly decreases the possibility of using complete forms as normal form results which, however, is one of the main objects in considering completeness of EOL forms. By Lemma 1 one easily checks that for each EOL form F there holds $\mathcal{L}(F) = \mathcal{L}_m(F)$. Thus, even under marvellous interpretation as defined above the form G with productions listed above remains complete. But, although G does not contain nonterminal chain - productions, that result does not imply that every EOL language can be generated by a marvellous EOL system containing no nonterminal chain - production as shown by Theorem 1. Indeed, this type of definition suppresses pseudoterminals in a merely formal way. The character of pseudoterminal symbols is not taken into consideration and thus the main complications which lead to the modification of the interpretation mechanism do not disappear. Let us now define m - interpretation:

Definition: Let $F = (V,\Sigma,P,S)$ and $F' = (V',\Sigma',P',S')$ be marvellous EOL systems. Then F' is called a marvellous interpretation (m - interpretation for short) of F (modulo μ), symbolically $F' \underset{m}{\lhd} F(\mu)$, iff $F' \lhd F(\mu)$. Additionally, $\mathcal{L}_m(F)$ and m - completeness are defined as usual but with respect to m - interpretation.

Remarks: Note that it also has been customary in the past to put constraints on the involved systems when defining interpretations for EOL forms. Since an EOL system must have a complete set of productions, i.e. there has to exist at least one production for each symbol, it follows that not each rewriting system F' obtained from an EOL form by a substitution μ is an EOL system again. In this case we do not have $F' \lhd F(\mu)$ even if μ satisfies conditions (i) to (v) since an interpretation is defined only for EOL systems. In our case additionally to the necessity of considering rewriting systems with a complete set of productions, e.g. EOL systems, we have to take care that F and F' are marvellous. Since it is decidable for every EOL system wether it is marvellous as will be shown in Lemma 3 our definition of m - interpretation is meaningfull and the relation $\underset{m}{\lhd}$ remains decidable. Note further that our definition exactly avoids the introduction of additional pseudoterminals via interpretation. For example, let $\mathcal{M}(F) = \{L(F') \mid F' \lhd F(\mu)$ and $\mu(PS(F)) = PS(F')\}$. Clearly, every language in $\mathcal{M}(F)$ can be generated by an interpretation (of F) which does not introduce additional pseudoterminals. Using the technique of Lemma 1 it can be shown that for every EOL form F there exists a marvellous EOL form F_1 such that $\mathcal{M}(F) = \mathcal{M}(F_1)$. This and the result of Lemma 1 show that our solution, which is somewhat more elegant, suffices since neither the generative power of EOL systems nor that of EOL forms (via interpretation) is decreased by considering marvellous forms only.

We want to mention that clearly $\mathcal{L}_m(F) \subseteq \mathcal{L}(F)$ holds for every EOL form F and that the inclusion may be proper. An example for the latter is the form F specified in Example 1. Finally we give the following decidability - result which is easily proved:

Lemma 3: Let $F = (V,\Sigma,P,S)$ be an EOL system. It is decidable for every $a \in V$ wether it is a pseudoterminal. □

Results

Lemma 4: Let $F = (V,\Sigma,P,S)$ be a marvellous EPOL system such that $L(F) = \{a^n b^n a^n b^n \mid n \geq 1\}$. Then $P \cap (V - \Sigma) \times (V - \Sigma) \neq \phi$.

Sketch of proof: We show that the following assumptions lead to a contradiction:

(1) F is a marvellous EPOL system and $L(F) = \{a^n b^n a^n b^n \mid n \geq 1\}$;

(2) $P \cap (V - \Sigma) \times (V - \Sigma) = \phi$.

It is well - known that every EPOL system generating L(F) must be looping. By condition (2) we can show that looping symbols in F must be terminal symbols, i.e. are elements of {a,b} since F is marvellous. Let us choose a to be looping, then at the same time b being looping implies $L(F) \in \mathcal{L}(CF)$. This is a contradiction and thus a is the only looping symbol in F. Intuitively it is clear that the fact that every loop of F has to use the terminal symbol a is too restrictive to allow the generation of a language like L(F). In particular, we show that in any F - derivation tree for a word $a^n b^n a^n b^n \in L(F)$ there occurs a path leading from the root labelled S to a leaf labelled b and containing no node with label a. Since a is the only looping symbol in F the above fact bounds the length of successfull derivations in F which leads to the final contradiction as in [CMO]. □

Lemma 5: Let $F = (V,\Sigma,P,S)$ be a short and marvellous EPOL system such that $L(F) = \{a^{5^n} \mid n \geq 1\}$. Then $P \cap (V - \Sigma) \times (V - \Sigma)^2 \neq \phi$.

Proof: We assume the contrary, i.e. P contains no production of the type $A \to BC$, $\{A,B,C\} \subseteq V - \Sigma$. Note that this implies that every length - increasing production in F involves the terminal symbol a since F is marvellous and thus $\Sigma = \{a\}$. Consider $x = a^5 \in L$. By the above observation and since F is short we have $S \overset{+}{\underset{F}{\Rightarrow}} x_1 a x_2 \overset{+}{\underset{F}{\Rightarrow}} a^5$ where $x_1 x_2 \in V^+$. The subderivation $a \overset{+}{\underset{F}{\Rightarrow}} a$ is impossible since it would imply $L(F) \in \mathcal{L}(CF)$ and we have left $a \overset{+}{\underset{F}{\Rightarrow}} a^j$, $2 \leq j \leq 4$ since $x_1 x_2 \neq \varepsilon$ and F is propagating. This immediately implies a contradiction since $a^{5j} \notin L(F)$ for $2 \leq j \leq 4$. □

Theorem 1: A simple and short EPOL form $F = (\{S,a\},\{a\},P,S)$ is m - complete iff P contains all of the productions $S \to a$, $S \to S$ and $S \to SS$ and at least one of the productions $a \to S$, $a \to aS$, $a \to Sa$ and $a \to SS$.

Proof: By Example 5.1 in [MSW1] the EPOL form G with productions $S \to a$, $S \to S$, $S \to SS$ and $a \to S$ is complete. When analysing the proof one easily checks that productions for terminal symbols are only used to block the derivation after having generated a terminal symbol in the interpretations of G. By Lemma 1 this implies that G is m - complete, too. It is clear that we may use interpretations of the productions $a \to aS$, $a \to Sa$ or $a \to SS$ also only for blocking if the form contains $S \to a$, $S \to S$ and $S \to SS$. Thus, we may assume that those productions do not cause pseudoterminals in the interpretations of the form. By the above observations, Proposition 1.2 in [CMO] and the Lemmas 4 and 5 the theorem follows immediately. □

Consequences

For a given EOL form $F = (V,\Sigma,P,S)$ let $N = \{x_i \in V^* \mid 1 \leq i \leq n\}$ be a finite set of words such that F contains the derivation $\alpha \overset{+}{\underset{F}{\Longrightarrow}} x$ for a fixed symbol $\alpha \in V$ and every $x \in N$. Then it is possible for every $M \subseteq N$ to construct an interpretation F' such that whenever a derivation (α) starts with α and ends with a word over V then (α) contains a word $y \in M$, i.e. the derivations $\alpha \overset{+}{\underset{F}{\Longrightarrow}} y$, $y \in M$ have been "isolated". The idea is to rename all symbols occurring in the intermediate steps of the derivations such that the new symbols differ from each other and all of the new symbols differ from the symbols of the form F, cf. the Isolation Lemma in [W]. This renaming is easily done in the case of ordinary interpretation when viewing the renamed symbols as interpretations of the original ones: it does not matter wether the original symbol is a terminal or a nonterminal. Obviously, this changes in the case of m - interpretation. Whenever an intermediate word of the derivation which we want to isolate contains both, terminal and nonterminal symbols, the renaming required in general leads to the introduction of pseudoterminals in the interpretation. Moreover, even the possible context of the intermediate words according to F must be taken into consideration. The basic difficulties which occur when isolating via m - interpretation are the following ones:

(i) Introduction of pseudoterminals caused by renaming.

This may happen inside the isolated derivation if an intermediate word of the derivation which contains a terminal symbol occurs together with a nonterminal symbol in any word generated by the form; outside the isolated derivation pseudoterminals may be introduced if a terminal symbol occurs only together with a nonterminal outside the derivation and thus becomes a pseudoterminal in the interpretation since all other occurrences of the symbol have been renamed.

(ii) Introduction of pseudoterminals caused by eliminating productions.

If we isolate a derivation $\alpha \overset{+}{\underset{F}{\Longrightarrow}} x$ then clearly any production for

α except the first one used in this derivation has to be removed from the production set of the interpretation. This may lead to a situation where the terminal context, which is generated by the form for some terminal, cannot be generated in the interpretation.
The following obvious lemma is very usefull for proving $F' \underset{m}{\lhd} F$ in many cases:

Lemma 6: Let $F = (V,\Sigma,P,S)$ be a marvellous EOL system. If for an arbitrary EOL system $F' = (V',\Sigma',P',S')$ we have $L(F) \subseteq L(F')$ and $\Sigma' \subseteq \Sigma$, then F' is marvellous. □

As indicated by the complications in the case of m - isolation words of the sentential form language of an EOL form are predestinated for the generation of pseudoterminals in an interpretation if they contain both, terminal and nonterminal symbols. This is also expressed by the fact that nonterminal derivations do not suffice to prove the Expansion Simulation Lemma but we need the following stronger definition:

Definition: Let $F = (V,\Sigma,P,S)$ be an EOL system. We say a derivation $x_o \overset{\ell}{\underset{F}{\Longrightarrow}} x_\ell$ is marvellous nonterminal [total marvellous nonterminal] and write $x_o \overset{\ell}{\underset{mtF}{\Longrightarrow}} x_\ell$ [$x_o \overset{\ell}{\underset{tmtF}{\Longrightarrow}} x_\ell$] if for some [any] sequence of words $x_1, x_2, \ldots, x_{\ell-1}$ with $x_i \underset{F}{\Longrightarrow} x_{i+1}$ for $i = 0,1,2,\ldots,\ell-1$ we have $x_1x_2 \ldots x_{\ell-1} \in (V - \Sigma)^*$.

The Simulation Lemmas for m - Interpretation are proved similar as in [MSW1] or [W], finally using Lemma 6 to conclude $F' \underset{m}{\lhd} F$ from $F' \lhd F$.

Expansion Simulation Lemma for m - Interpretation: Let $F = (V,\Sigma,P,S)$ and $F_1=(V_1,\Sigma_1,P_1,S_1)$ be two marvellous EOL forms and $\ell \geq 1$ be an integer such that for all $\alpha \to x$ in P there exists a derivation $\alpha \overset{\ell}{\underset{mtF_1}{\Longrightarrow}} x$. Then $\mathcal{L}_m(F) \subseteq \mathcal{L}_m(F_1)$. □

Note that the mt - condition is indeed necessary. For example, let F be defined by the productions $S \to S$, $S \to SS$, $S \to a$, $a \to S$ and F_1 by $S \to S$, $S \to aS$, $S \to a$, $a \to S$. We know that F is both complete and m - complete by Theorem 1. F and F_1 fulfil the conditions of the Expansion Simulation Lemma (for ordinary interpretation), cf. Lemma 3.3 in [MSW1], and thus F_1 is complete, too. However, Theorem 1 shows that F_1 is not m - complete. We want to mention that the proof of the above lemma shows us the power of Lemma 6. The proof uses the technique of isolation and does not care about the possible introduction of pseudoterminals. Only at the end of the proof it turns out that isolating indeed did not introduce pseudoterminals which is shown by Lemma 6.
The Contraction Simulation Lemma holds also for m - interpretation and therefore we only refer to Lemma 3.4 in [MSW1] in this case.

Before stating our next theorem we recall that an EOL form $F = (V,\Sigma,P,S)$ is called <u>seperated</u> if $\alpha \to x \in P$ implies (i) $x \in \Sigma \cup (V - \Sigma)^*$ and (ii) $\alpha \in \Sigma$ implies $x \notin \Sigma$. F is called <u>binary</u> if each production in P is of one of the types $A \to \varepsilon$, $A \to a$, $A \to B$, $A \to BC$ or $a \to A$, where $a \in \Sigma$ and $\{A,B,C\} \subseteq V - \Sigma$.

<u>Theorem 2:</u> For every EOL form F a seperated and short EOL form F_1 can be constructed such that $\mathcal{L}_m(F) = \mathcal{L}_m(F_1)$. If F is synchronized an m - form equivalent, synchronized, binary and propagating EOL form F_1 can be constructed.

<u>Sketch of proof:</u> The result is proved for ordinary interpretation in [MSW1] by a number of lemmas. Apart from constructions which obviously preserve m - form equivalence, too, there are two types of proofs. The first one uses the Simulation Lemmas and in this case it is easy to see that the constructions also satisfy the Simulation Lemmas for m - interpretation. The second type directly proves form equivalence and the validity for m - interpretation is shown by use of Lemma 6. □

Our last result which is proved by using isolation carries over an important nonreduction result from [MSW1]:

<u>Lemma 7:</u> Let $F = (\{S,a\},\{a\},\{S \to a,\ a \to a^2\},S)$ be an EOL form. Then $\mathcal{L}_m(F) \neq \mathcal{L}_m(H)$ for every synchronized EOL form H. □

Comparing Lemma 7 with the analogous result in [MSW1], i.e. Lemma 4.3, shows the peculiarity of m - interpretation in some sense. In particular, there exists a synchronized EOL form G which is m - form equivalent to the form F specified in [MSW1]:

F: $S \to aa$, $a \to b$, $b \to N$, $N \to N$.

G: $S \to aa$, $S \to bb$, $a \to Nb$, $b \to Na$, $N \to N$.

The reason for the above fact is that you have to interprete both productions existing for S in G. For example, if you do not interprete the production $S \to bb$ then the symbols of $\mu(b)$ are pseudoterminals and $\mu(b)$ is not empty due to the production $a \to Nb$.

<u>Acknowledgement:</u> I would like to thank Hermann A. Maurer for suggesting to investigate interpretations of EOL forms avoiding pseudoterminals. Further I want to thank the referees for their detailed comments on this paper.

References

[Ai] W. Ainhirn, How to get rid of pseudoterminals, Report No. 34, Institut für Informationsverarbeitung TU Graz (1979).

[AiM] W. Ainhirn, H. A. Maurer, On ε productions for terminals in EOL forms, Discrete Applied Mathematics 1 (1979), 155 - 166.

[CM] K. Culik II, H. A. Maurer, Propagating chain - free normal forms for EOL systems, Information and Control 36 (1978), 309 - 319.

[CMO] K. Culik II, H. A. Maurer, Th. Ottmann, Two - symbol complete EOL forms, Theoretical Computer Science 6 (1978), 69 - 92.

[ER] A. Ehrenfeucht, G. Rozenberg, The equality of EOL languages and codings of OL languages, International Journal of Computer Mathematics 4, Section A (1974), 95 - 104.

[H] M. A. Harrison, Introduction to formal language theory, Addison-Wesley, Reading (1978).

[He] G. T. Herman, Closure properties of some families of languages associated with biological systems, Information and Control 24 (1974), 101 - 121.

[HR] G. T. Herman, G. Rozenberg, Developmental systems and languages, North Holland Publishing Company, Amsterdam (1975).

[L] A. Lindenmayer, Mathematical modells for cellular interactions in development, Journal of Theoretical Biology 18 (1968), 280 - 315.

[MSW1] H. A. Maurer, A. Salomaa, D. Wood, EOL forms, Acta Informatica 8 (1977), 75 - 96.

[MSW2] H. A. Maurer, A. Salomaa, D. Wood, On generators and generative capacity of EOL forms, Acta Informatica 13 (1980), 87 - 107.

[MSW3] H. A. Maurer, A. Salomaa, D. Wood, Pure grammars, Mc Master University TR No. 79 - CS - 7 (1979).

[RS] G. Rozenberg, A. Salomaa, The mathematical theory of L systems, Academic Press, New York, to appear.

[W] D. Wood, Grammar and L forms, Springer Verlag, New York, to appear.

TEST SETS FOR HOMOMORPHISM EQUIVALENCE ON CONTEXT FREE LANGUAGES*

J. Albert+
Institut für Angewandte Informatik
und Formale Beschreibungsverfahren
Universität Karlsruhe
Karlsruhe, West Germany

and

K. Culik II
Department of Computer Science
University of Waterloo
Waterloo, Ontario, Canada N2L 3G1

Abstract

We show that for every context free language L over some alphabet Σ there effectively exists a test set F, that is a finite subset of L such that, for any pair (g,h) of homomorphisms on Σ^*, $g(x) = h(x)$ for each x in F implies $g(x) = h(x)$ for all x in L.

This result is then extended from homomorphisms to deterministic generalized sequential machine mappings defined by machines with uniformly bounded number of states.

1. Introduction

Problems concerning homomorphism equivalence have been intensively studied recently. Specifically, the homomorphic equivalence problem for a language family $\mathcal{L}$ is the following: Given a language L in $\mathcal{L}$ and two homomorphisms g and h determine whether g and h are equivalent on L, i.e. whether or not $g(w) = h(w)$ holds for all words w in L. It has been shown in Culik and Salomaa (1978) that there exists a uniform algorithm answering this question for any context free language L. In Culik and Richier (1979) the problem has been shown decidable also for ETOL languages over two-letter alphabets. It was conjectured in Culik and Salomaa (1978) that the problem is decidable for indexed languages, however at the present time it is open even for DOL languages (over at least three-letter alphabets). Actually, the homomorphic equivalence problem for DOL languages can be easily shown to be equivalent to the HDOL sequence equivalence problem, a well-known open problem. The homomorphic equivalence problem for (deterministic) context sensitive languages has been shown undecidable in Culik and Salomaa (1978). The decidability of homomorphic equivalence has many applications, the most important is probably in the proof of the DOL equivalence problem, Culik and Fris (1977). For applications to transducers, see Culik (1979), where the main result is the decidability of the equivalence problem between

---

*This research was supported by the National Sciences and Engineering Council of Canada, under Grant No. A7403.

+This paper was written during the first author's visit at the University of Waterloo, Waterloo, Ontario, Canada.

an unambiguous pushdown (algebraic) transducer and a functional finite (rational) transducer.

In the terminology of equality sets, see Salomaa (1978), the homomorphisms g and h are equivalent on language L iff $L \subseteq E(g,h)$. For a number of additional references on equality sets and other topics discussed here see the survey, Culik (1980).

Older than the above results but closely related is the following "Ehrenfeucht's conjecture": Every language L has a finite subset F such that, for any pair of homomorphisms (g,h), g and h are equivalent on L iff they are equivalent on F. Such a finite set was called test set in Culik and Salomaa (1979) where it has been shown that the conjecture holds true for languages over a two-letter alphabet. It is also clear from the arguments in Culik and Salomaa (1978) that the conjecture holds for regular sets over any alphabet, and that in this case a finite test set can be effectively constructed. On the other hand it follows from the undecidability result mentioned above that for context sensitive languages finite test sets cannot exist effectively since that would, clearly, imply the decidability of homomorphic equivalence for this family.

Our main result (Theorem 1) is that a finite test set exists, and effectively so, for any context free language (given by a context free grammar). This result clearly implies the main result of Culik and Salomaa (1978), Theorem 4.1, namely the decidability of homomorphic equivalence for context free languages. Our stronger result does not follow from the proof of Theorem 4.1 in Culik and Salomaa (1978), nevertheless we use a similar basic technique ("generalized pumping").

We actually prove a somewhat stronger result, namely, that given a context free grammar G with n nonterminals and maximum m letters at the right side of productions, the set of all words of L of the length at most m^{3n+1} form a test set which does not otherwise depend on G.

We conjecture that finite test sets effectively exist even for all indexed languages, however it follows from the above discussion that to show this even for DOL languages - a very special case of indexed languages - seems to be very hard.

In the last section we extend our results from homomorphisms to deterministic generalized sequential machines (with accepting states) with uniformly bounded number of states. It is not difficult to see that even further extension to unambiguous rational transducers with uniformly bounded number of states is possible.

Finally, we note that our Lemma 1 is an extension of Theorem 1 of Blattner and Head (1979). The main result (Theorem 2) of Blattner and Head (1979) gives implicitly a finite subset of the common domain for testing of equivalence for "deterministic finite transducers". However, they do not consider the restriction to a context free language without which the problem is considerably easier. Compare also with the above mentioned problem between an unambiguous pushdown transducer and a functional finite transducer.

2. Preliminaries

We study homomorphisms over free monoid Σ^* generated by finite set (alphabet) Σ. The unit of Σ^* (the empty word) is denoted by ε. The length of w in Σ^* is denoted by $|w|$, the cardinality of a set S by card S. For the other elementary notions of formal language theory we refer the reader to Harrison (1978), Hopcroft and Ullman (1969) or Salomaa (1973).

3. Finite Test Sets For Context Free Languages

We will show that whenever two homomorphisms agree on all "short" strings of a context free language (CFL) they must agree on the whole language. This bound on the size of strings is expressed by means of the pumping lemma.

Intuitively spoken, for deciding homomorphism equivalence it is sufficient to compare the homomorphic images of those words generated with at most "two nested loops". Hence, the set of strings to be considered is independent of the homomorphisms. It should be noted that it is not enough to test all strings derived with at most one loop as it is shown by the following example.

Consider the context free grammar (CFG) given by productions $S \to aSb \mid c$, i.e. $L(G) = \{a^n cb^n \mid n \geq 0\}$, and homomorphisms g,h given by

$$g(a) = 0 \qquad h(a) = 01$$
$$g(b) = 100 \qquad h(b) = 00$$
$$g(c) = \varepsilon \qquad h(c) = \varepsilon$$

Here, we have $g(c) = h(c) = \varepsilon$, $g(acb) = h(acb) = 0100$, however $g(a^2cb^2) \neq h(a^2cb^2)$.

The following lemma is crucial for the proof of our main theorem and might also have applications in the study of systems of equations over free monoids.

It reflects the initial steps in a pumping situation and shows that the equivalence of two homomorphisms cannot be destroyed by words containing at least three nested loops.

Definition: Let Σ be an alphabet and $\alpha, \beta, \gamma, \bar{\alpha}, \bar{\beta}, \bar{\gamma} \in \Sigma^*$. The set of pairs $M = \{(\varepsilon,\varepsilon), (\alpha,\bar{\alpha}), (\beta,\bar{\beta}), (\gamma,\bar{\gamma}), (\alpha\beta,\overline{\beta\alpha}), (\alpha\gamma,\overline{\gamma\alpha}), (\beta\gamma,\overline{\gamma\beta})\}$ is then called an initial loop set.

Lemma 1: Let M be an initial loop set as above and $u,w,y \in \Sigma^*$. If for any two homomorphisms $g,h : \Sigma^* \to \Delta^*$

(1) $$g(uvwxy) = h(uvwxy)$$

holds for all $(v,x) \in M$ then (1) also holds for $(v,x) = (\alpha\beta\gamma,\overline{\gamma\beta\alpha})$, i.e. $g(u\alpha\beta\gamma w\overline{\gamma\beta\alpha}y) = h(u\alpha\beta\gamma w\overline{\gamma\beta\alpha}y)$.

Since the proof of this lemma consists of a lengthy discussion of cases and subcases, we will omit it here. Readers interested in details are referred to Albert and Culik (1979).

As there were no restrictions on the strings and homomorphisms occurring in the above lemma, we can reformulate it equivalently in the following manner and relate it to a theorem given by Blattner and Head (1979).

Let $t_i, t_i', i \in \{1,\ldots,9\}$, be elements of a free monoid Δ^*.

If

$$t_1t_5t_9 = t_1't_5't_9' ,$$
$$t_1t_2t_5t_8t_9 = t_1't_2't_5't_8't_9' ,$$
$$t_1t_3t_5t_7t_9 = t_1't_3't_5't_7't_9' ,$$
$$t_1t_4t_5t_6t_9 = t_1't_4't_5't_6't_9' ,$$
$$t_1t_2t_3t_5t_7t_8t_9 = t_1't_2't_3't_5't_7't_8't_9' ,$$
$$t_1t_2t_4t_5t_6t_8t_9 = t_1't_2't_4't_5't_6't_8't_9' ,$$
$$t_1t_3t_4t_5t_6t_7t_9 = t_1't_3't_4't_5't_6't_7't_9'$$

then

$$t_1t_2t_3t_4t_5t_6t_7t_8t_9 = t_1't_2't_3't_4't_5't_6't_7't_8't_9' .$$

Considering now the special case

$$t_3 = t_3' = t_4 = t_4' = t_6 = t_6' = t_8 = t_8' = \varepsilon$$

just gives Theorem 1 of Blattner and Head (1979).

Now we are ready to prove our main result.

Theorem 1: For every context free language $L \subseteq \Sigma^*$ (given by a CFG) there exists an effectively constructible finite subset $L' \subseteq L$, such that for any two homomorphisms g,h on Σ^*, $g(x) = h(x)$ for all $x \in L'$ implies $g(x) = h(x)$ for all $x \in L$.

Proof: Assume L is generated by some ε-free context free grammar $G = (N,\Sigma,P,S)$. Let D' be the set of all terminal derivation trees generated by G such that on each path from the root to a leaf at most three nodes are labelled by the same nonterminal from N. L' is now defined as the set of terminal words generated by D' (the yield of D'). Clearly, L' is finite and $L' \subseteq L$.

Assume that there is a string z in $L - L'$ such that $g(z) \neq h(z)$ and let z be a minimal string in the sense that for each z' in L where $|z'| < |z|$, we have $g(z') = h(z')$. By the construction of L' there is a derivation tree for z of the form shown in Figure 1, for some nonterminal A, some words u, w, y and pairs of strings in Σ^* $(\alpha,\bar{\alpha})$, $(\beta,\bar{\beta})$, $(\gamma,\bar{\gamma})$ distinct from $(\varepsilon,\varepsilon)$.

Thus, by taking out any of these A-loops here, we get derivation trees generating words shorter than z. Now, clearly Lemma 1 applies and

$$g(u\alpha\beta\gamma w\overline{\gamma\beta\alpha}y) = h(u\alpha\beta\gamma w\overline{\gamma\beta\alpha}y) ,$$

completing the proof of Theorem 1. □

Definition: Let $L \subseteq \Sigma^*$. We say that F is a test set for L if $F \subseteq L$ and for any homomorphisms $g, h : \Sigma^* \to \Delta^*$, $g(x) = h(x)$ for all $x \in F$ implies $g(x) = h(x)$ for all $x \in L$.

Corollary 1: Let $G = (N,\Sigma,P,S)$ be a context free grammar with $n = \text{card } N$ and $m = \max(|X| : A \to X \in P)$. Let $F = \{w \in L(G) : |w| \leq m^{3n+1}\}$. Then F is a (finite) test set for $L(G)$.

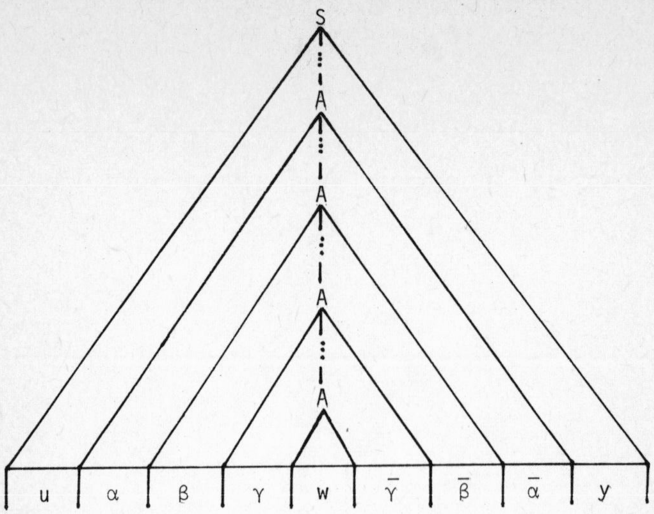

Figure 1

Proof: Clear by the proof of Theorem 1. □

Obviously, Corollary 1 implies the main result of (Culik and Salomaa, 1979, Theorem 4.1), namely, that given a CFL L and homomorphisms g, h, it is decidable whether $g(x) = h(x)$ for all x in L.

4. Extension to gsm

Now, we will extend our result from homomorphisms to the mappings defined by deterministic generalized machines (gsm's) (with accepting states). We will construct a single test set for all deterministic gsm with bounded number of states.

Theorem 2: For every context free language $L \subseteq \Sigma^*$ (given by a CFG) and for each natural number q there exists a finite subset $L' \subseteq L$ such that for any two functions $f_1, f_2 : \Sigma^* \to \Delta^*$ given by deterministic gsm's with at most q states, $f_1(x) = f_2(x)$ for all x in L' implies $f_1(x) = f_2(x)$ for all x in L.

Note: The above theorem clearly does not hold, if the numbers of states are arbitrary.

Proof of Theorem 2: Let $G = (N,\Sigma,P,S)$ be an ε-free CFG generating L, where $n = \text{card } N$, $d = \text{card } \Sigma$, $m = \max (|X| \mid A \to X \in P)$ and k is defined as $k := 2q^4(n+d)+1$. Let $L' = \{w \in L(G) \mid |w| \leq m^{3k+1}\}$.

Consider any two deterministic gsm's $S_i = (Q_i,\Sigma,\Delta,\delta_i,q_i,F_i)$, $i = 1,2$ (c.f. Hopcroft and Ullman (1969) or Salomaa (1973)) such that card $Q_i \leq q$. Let D_i be the domain of S_i, $i = 1,2$. For $x \in \Sigma^*$ and $i = 1,2$, define

$$f_i(x) := \begin{cases} y & \text{where } x \in D_i,\ \delta_i(q_i,x) = (p_i,y) \\ & \text{for some } p_i \in F_i \\ \text{undefined otherwise} & \end{cases}$$

i.e. f_i is the mapping defined by machine S_i. Furthermore, let $M = L \cap (D_1 \cup D_2)$ and $M' = L' \cap (D_1 \cup D_2)$. Then, proving that $f_1(x) = f_2(x)$ for all $x \in M'$ implies $f_1(x) = f_2(x)$ for all $x \in M$, clearly establishes Theorem 2.

We proceed as follows: f_1, f_2 are decomposed into one injective, length preserving function g and two homomorphisms h_1, h_2, such that for all $x \in D_1 \cup D_2$: $f_1(x) = f_2(x)$ iff $h_1(g(x)) = h_2(g(x))$, and furthermore: $h_1(y) = h_2(y)$ for all $y \in g(M')$ implies $h_1(y) = h_2(y)$ for all $y \in g(M)$. This function g operates on strings $x = a_1a_2 \ldots a_r \in D_1 \cup D_2$ as follows. For $i = 1,2,\ldots,r$, the letter a_i of x is indexed by the states reached in S_1 and S_2 just after reading $a_1a_2 \ldots a_{i-1}$; and the last letter is barred if x is accepted by exactly one of the gsm's S_1, S_2. In more detail, for $x = a_1a_2 \ldots a_{r-1}a_r \in D_1 \cup D_2$ let $g(x) = a_1(m_1,n_1)a_2(m_2,n_2) \ldots a_{r-1}(m_{r-1},n_{r-1})\tilde{a}_r(m_r,n_r)$ where $m_1 = q_1$, $n_1 = q_2$, $\delta_1(q_1,a_1 \ldots a_{i-1}) = (m_i,y_1)$ for some $y_1 \in \Delta^*$, $\delta_2(q_2,a_1 \ldots a_{i-1}) = (n_i,y_2)$ for some $y_2 \in \Delta^*$, and

$$\tilde{a}_r = \begin{cases} a_r & \text{if } x \in D_1 \cup D_2 \\ \bar{a}_r & \text{if } x \in (D_1 - D_2) \cup (D_2 - D_1)\ . \end{cases}$$

Clearly, g is length-preserving and injective and can be provided effectively by a deterministic gsm.

Since the family of context free languages is effectively closed under gsm-mappings, we can construct a context free grammar $G' = (N',\Sigma',P',S')$ such that $L(G') = g(M) = g(L(G) \cap (D_1 \cup D_2))$. Since the construction of G' is just a straightforward variant of the well-known construction with new nonterminals being triples from $Q_i \times N \times Q_i$, we omit the details for P' and consider only N'. It is obvious that the choice of

$$N' := \{(p,q,X,p',q'),(p,q,\bar{X},p',q') \mid X \in N \cup \Sigma,\ p,p' \in Q_1, q,q' \in Q_2\} \cup \{S'\}$$

is sufficient for our construction.
is sufficient for our construction.

Since, card $N' \leq 2 \cdot q^4 \cdot (n + d) + 1 = k$, by Corollary 1 it holds for any two homomorphisms h_1, h_2 on Σ'^* that $h_1(y) = h_2(y)$ for all $y \in g(M')$ implies $h_1(y) = h_2(y)$ for all $y \in g(M)$. Specifically, for any $a \in \Sigma$, $p \in Q_1$, $q \in Q_2$ let $h_1(a(p,q)) = y_1$, where $\delta_1(p,a) = (p',y_1)$ for some $p' \in Q_1$, $h_1(\bar{a}(p,q)) = \#_1$, for some new symbol $\#_1$. Analogously, let $h_2(a(p,q) = y_2$, where $\delta_2(q,a) = (q',y_2)$ for some $q' \in Q_2$, $h_2(\bar{a}(p,q) = \#_2$, for some new symbol $\#_2 \neq \#_1$. Since $g : M \to L(G')$ is bijective and length-preserving, we conclude: $h_1(g(x)) = h_2(g(x))$ for all $x \in M'$

implies $h_1(g(x)) = h_2(g(x))$ for all $x \in M$, which proves Theorem 2, because of $h_1(g(w)) = f_1(x)$, $h_2(g(x)) = f_2(x)$ for all $x \in L \cap D_1 \cap D_2$ and $h_1(g(x)) \in \Delta^*\{\#_1\}$, $h_2(g(x)) \in \Delta^*\{\#_2\}$ for all $x \in L \cap ((D_1 - D_2) \cup (D_2 - D_1))$. □

Finally we note that the proof of Theorem 2 suggests that Theorem 2 might be possibly extended to a larger family of languages L, e.g. even indexed languages, if the effective existence of finite test sets were shown for L and if L has some other properties like the family of CFL.

References

Albert, J. and Culik, K. II (1979), Test sets for homomorphisms equivalence on context free languages, Inf. and Control, to appear, also Res. Rep. CS-79-39, Department of Computer Science, University of Waterloo, Waterloo, Ontario, Canada.

Blattner, M. and Head, T. (1979), The decidability of equivalence for deterministic finite transducers, J. Computer Syst. Sci. 19, 45-49.

Culik, K. II (1977), On the decidability of the sequence equivalence problem for DOL-systems, Theoretical Computer Sci. 3, 75-84.

Culik, K. II (1979), Some decidability results about regular and push down translations, Information Processing Letters 8, 5-8.

Culik, K. II (1980), Homomorphisms: Decidability, Equality and Test Sets, Proceedings of the International Symposium on Formal Languages Theory, Santa Barbara, California, Dec. 1979, to appear, also Res. Rep. CS-80-02, Department of Computer Science, University of Waterloo, Waterloo, Ontario, Canada.

Culik, K. II and Fris, I. (1977), The decidability of the equivalence problem for DOL systems, Inform. Control 35, 20-39.

Culik, K. II and Richier, J.L. (1979), Homomorphism equivalence on ETOL languages, Int. J. Computer Math. Section A, 7, 43-51.

Culik, K. II and Salomaa, A. (1978), On the decidability of homomorphism equivalence for languages, J. Computer Syst. Sci. 17, 163-175.

Culik, K. II and Salomaa, A. (1979), Test sets and checking words for homomorphism equivalence, J. Computer Syst. Sci., to appear, also Res. Rep. CS-79-04, Department of Computer Science, University of Waterloo, Waterloo, Ontario, Canada.

Harrison, M.A. (1978), "Introduction to Formal Language Theory", Addison-Wesley, Reading, Massachusetts.

Hopcroft, J.E. and Ullman, J.D. (1969), "Formal Languages and Their Relation to Automata", Addison-Wesley, Reading, Massachusetts.

Salomaa, A. (1973), "Formal Languages", Academic Press, New York.

Salomaa, A. (1978), Equality sets for homomorphisms on free monoids, Acta Cybernetica, vol. 4, 127-139.

LANGUAGES WITH HOMOMORPHIC REPLACEMENTS

J. Albert and L. Wegner
Institut für Angewandte Informatik
und Formale Beschreibungsverfahren
Universität Karlsruhe (TH), D-7500 Karlsruhe
W.Germany

Abstract We introduce H-systems as language generators using the concept of homomorphic replacement of variables by words from metalanguages. This is a generalization of the hypernotion construct in van Wijngaarden grammars with a number of hard open problems. Here we concentrate on the generative power of the language families which result from varying the sets of axioms, resp. the sets of replacements, from ONE through the metalinear languages to CF.

0. Introduction

The languages whose properties we shall examine here are obtained by first deriving a word v in some metalanguage and then replacing consistently each symbol A in v by a word w from some replacement language L_A.

Applications of this type of languages occur in connection with W-Grammars (van Wijngaarden Grammars, Two-level Grammars), where a so-called "hypernotion" and the set of "strict notions" which it may yield can be considered as a particular class in our hierarchy with the metalanguage being a singleton language and each L_A a context-free language.

Recently, investigations have been started into "regular based"W-Grammars" [3,7,14], i.e. W-Grammars where each L_A is restricted to the class of regular languages. In [14] the question of decidability for the cross-reference problem for regular based W-Grammars was first posed and shown to be a hard open problem. In our discussion this question arises naturally as the intersection problem for H-systems with ONE and REG as underlying language classes. Even after the solvability of the famous "string unification problem", which is a special case of the intersection question, was shown by Makanin [9], the above problem remains open.

We generalize this method of generating a language by admitting various classes of metalanguages and replacement languages. This usage of homomorphisms seems very natural to us and it is surprising that it has not been examined as an independant concept before. Our task here will be to show how this homomorphic replacement differs from the iterated deterministic substitution of Asveld/Engelfriet [2] and parallel rewriting (Indian Parallel, L-Systems) as discussed by Skyum [12] and others.

1. Preliminaries

We assume that the reader is familiar with the notation and basic results of Formal Language Theory as contained in e.g. [10].

Definition 1.1. An H-system is a quadruple $H = (V_1, V_2, L_1, \varphi)$ with metaalphabet V_1, terminal alphabet V_2, $V_1 \cap V_2 = \emptyset$, metalanguage $L_1 \subseteq V_1^*$, and a function $\varphi\colon V_1 \to 2^{V_2^*}$ which assigns to each $A \in V_1$ a language $\varphi(A) \subseteq V_2^*$.

Instead of $\varphi(A)$ we shall also write L_A.

Definition 1.2. The language of an H-system $H = (V_1, V_2, L_1, \varphi)$ is defined as $L(H) = \{h(v) \mid v \in L_1, h \text{ a homomorphism with } h(A) \in \varphi(A) \text{ for all } A \in V_1\}$.

Thus, words in $L(H)$ are concatenations of words from $L_{A_1}, \ldots, L_{A_n}$ according to a template (axiom) v from the metalanguage. Note that all occurrences of A_i in v have to be replaced by identical words $h(A_i)$. It should further be noted that one might as well let L_1 range over $V_1 \cup V_2$ as with W-Grammars in which case φ acts as identity function on V_2.

Definition 1.3. Let $\mathcal{L}_1$, $\mathcal{L}_2$ be two language families. Then $\mathcal{H}(\mathcal{L}_1, \mathcal{L}_2)$ is to denote the family of H-system languages of $\mathcal{L}_1$, $\mathcal{L}_2$ formally defined as $\mathcal{H}(\mathcal{L}_1, \mathcal{L}_2) = \{L \mid L = L(H) \text{ for some H-system } H = (V_1, V_2, L_1, \varphi)$ with $L_1 \in \mathcal{L}_1$ and $\varphi(A) \in \mathcal{L}_2$ for all $A \in V_1\}$.

Furthermore, we shall denote the class of context-free (m-linear, regular, finite, singleton, resp.) languages by CF (m-LIN, REG, FIN, ONE, resp.). It is also assumed that L_1 and $L_{A_1}, \ldots, L_{A_n}$ are specified in a suitable way, e.g. for $L_1 \in$ REG, L_1 is specified by a right-linear grammar or a deterministic finite state automaton or a regular expression, etc.

We list a few examples of H-systems which should help to give the reader a more intuitive idea of the scope of H-system languages in relation to $\mathcal{L}_1$ and $\mathcal{L}_2$.

Examples 1.4. Let H_1 be specified by $L_1 = (AB)^+$, $V_1 = \{A,B\}$, $V_2 = \{a,b\}$, $\varphi_1(A) = a^+$, $\varphi_1(B) = b$. Then $L(H_1) = \{(a^n b)^m \mid n,m \geq 1\}$ and $L(H_1) \in \mathcal{H}(\text{REG}, \text{REG})$.

We see immediately that the homomorphic replacement of Def. 1.2 is more powerful than ordinary substitution as $L(H_1) \notin$ CF but REG closed under regular substitution. Even when limiting L_1 to ONE, powerful languages result.

Consider the H-system $H_2 = (\{A,B\}, \{a,b\}, \{ABABA\}, \varphi_2)$, where $\varphi_2(A) = a^+$, $\varphi_2(B) = b$.

Clearly, $L(H_2) = \{a^n b a^n b a^n \mid n \geq 1\} \in \mathcal{H}(\text{ONE}, \text{REG})$ which is a well-known non-context-free language.

For another language in $\mathcal{H}$(REG,REG) consider $H_3 = (\{A,B\},\{a,b,\#\},(AB)^+,\varphi_3)$ with $\varphi_3(A) = \{a,b\}^+, \varphi_3(B) = \#$. Again $L(H_3) = \{(w\#)^m \mid w \in \{a,b\}^+, m \geq 1\}$ is a non-context-free language and indeed non-EOL, but is an EDTOL language.

A interesting case are the H-system languages over a one-letter alphabet V_2. The H-system $H_4 = (\{A\},\{a\},A^+A,\varphi_4)$ with $\varphi_4(A) = a^+a$ generates the set of all non-prime numbers which is also non-context-free and $L(H_4) \in \mathcal{H}$(REG,REG). This is contrasted by the fact that if in $\mathcal{H}(\mathcal{L}_1, \mathcal{L}_2)$ one allows $\mathcal{L}_1$ to be at most FIN, then $\mathcal{H}(\mathcal{L}_1, \mathcal{L}_2) \subseteq$ REG for a one-letter alphabet V_2 [14]. Furthermore, it is immediately seen that the well-known L-systems language $\{a^{2^n} \mid n \geq 0\}$ is not in $\mathcal{H}$(CF,CF).

Finally consider any language $\bar{L}$ in CF-EDTOL, e.g. the Dyck language over an alphabet of at least eight letters [4]. In [6] it is shown that if a language $\bar{L} \in$ CF-EDTOL then $L' = \{w\#w\#w \mid w \in \bar{L}\}$ is not an outside-in macro language or equivalently not an indexed language. But L' is easily recognized as the $\mathcal{H}$(ONE,CF) language $L(H_5)$ for $H_5 = (\{A,B\},\bar{V} \cup \{\#\},ABABA,\varphi_5)$ with $\varphi_5(A) = \bar{L} \subseteq \bar{V}^*$ and $\varphi_5(B) = \#$.

It is obvious from the above examples that languages in $\mathcal{H}(\mathcal{L}_1, \mathcal{L}_2)$ have strong copying powers but that growth of word length cannot exceed the order of growth of the $\mathcal{L}_1, \mathcal{L}_2$ constituents. In particular, growth is at most linear for $\mathcal{H}$(CF,CF) but the Parikh-mappings do not remain semilinear, as shown by example H_4.

2. Homomorphic replacements

The type of homomorphic replacement we discuss here appears under various names within different context. In W-Grammars it is called "consistent substitution" or "consistent replacement". In connection with Macro Grammars [5] it is called "IO (inside-out)-substitution" and in the algebraic approach to Formal Language Theory it even appears as "call by value substitution" [13]. As with W-Grammars, homomorphic replacements have in these contexts been considered as part of a larger language generating system but not as separate (set-of-axioms, set-of-replacements)-systems.

Furthermore, the parallel rewriting of L-systems, even in the deterministic case, seems to be quite different as shown by $\{a^{2^n} \mid n \geq 0\}$ which is not in $\mathcal{H}$(CF,CF) and by H_5 above.

Equally, the homomorphic type of replacement occurs with Indian Parallel Grammars (see e.g. [12]) but there each replacement is given through a production from a finite set and - in contrast to CF grammars - all symbols are replaced in parallel by the same right-hand side of one chosen production.

The closest relative of H-systems in the family of language generating devices is the "deterministic K-iteration grammar" [2]. In that context the homomorphic replacement is called "deterministic substitution" and if the class K is explicitly mentioned for the language from which the replacement is chosen, then it is called deterministic K-substitution (short dK-substitution). However, K-substitutions (deterministic and nondeterministic) have always been examined in connection with iterations [8,11] which is not the case here.

The discussion above is also an indication as to where the difficulty in proofs about H-systems stems from. Clearly, the rewriting is not completely parallel in nature and thus length arguments which are often used with L-systems, do not work. On the other hand derivations are not context-free either and pumping arguments must take into account that for certain $\mathcal{H}(\mathcal{L}_1, \mathcal{L}_2)$ systems we may pump on the metalevel, i.e. within L_1, and within each L_A on the lower level.

However, there is one basic proof technique which can be used in most cases.

Lemma 2.1. Let $\mathcal{L}_1$, $\mathcal{L}_2 \subseteq CF$ and $\mathcal{L}_1$ be closed under finite deterministic substitution. Let furthermore $\mathcal{L}_1$, $\mathcal{L}_2$ be closed under product. If $L' \in \mathcal{H}(\mathcal{L}_1, \mathcal{L}_2)-CF$, $L' = L((V_1, V_2, L_1, \varphi))$, then there exists a $w \in L_1$ s.t. $w = w_1Xw_2Xw_3$, with $w_1, w_2, w_3 \in V_1^*$, $X \in V_1$ and $\varphi(X)$ infinite.

Proof: Assume the contrary, i.e. for all $w \in L_1$, w contains any $X \in V_1$ at most once (case i)) or $w = w_1Xw_2Xw_3$ and $\varphi(X)$ finite (case ii)).

i) For all $w \in L_1$, $w \neq w_1Xw_2Xw_3$. But then L_1 is finite and with Def. 1.2

$$L' = \bigcup_{w \in L_1} L'_w \text{, where for } w = A_1A_2 \ldots A_k,$$

$$L'_w = \{h(A_1A_2\ldots A_k) \mid h(A_i) \in \varphi(A_i)\} = \varphi(A_1)\cdot\varphi(A_2)\cdot\ldots\cdot\varphi(A_k).$$

Clearly, since L' is the finite union of finite products of $\mathcal{L}_2$-languages and $\mathcal{L}_2 \subseteq CF$ we have a contradiction.

ii) For all $w = w_1Xw_2Xw_3$, $\varphi(X)$ is finite. Now let $V' := \{X \in V_1 \mid \text{there is a } w = w_1Xw_2Xw_3 \in L_1\}$, $V'' := V_1 - V'$ and define a deterministic finite substitution on V_1 by

$$\psi'(A) := \begin{cases} \varphi(A) & A \in V' \\ \{A\} & \text{otherwise} \end{cases}$$

and a nondeterministic substitution on $V'' \cup V_2$ by

$$\psi''(A) := \begin{cases} \varphi(A) & A \in V'' \\ \{A\} & \text{otherwise} \end{cases}$$

Then, $\psi'(L_1)$ as well as $\psi''(\psi'(L_1))$ are context-free languages since CF is closed under deterministic finite substitutions and nondeterministic substitutions with CF-languages.

But obviously, $L' = \psi''(\psi'(L_1))$ which contradicts the assumption $L' \notin CF$. □

The next lemma (marker lemma) is straightforward but useful in cases where statements about the nature of L_1 are to be made.

Lemma 2.2. If $L(H_\#) \subseteq N^*\{\#\}N^*$ is an H-system language with $H_\# = (V_1, \{\#\} \cup N, L_1, \varphi)$, $\# \notin N$ then $V_1 = V_\# \cup M$, $V_\# \cap M = \emptyset$, and $L_1 \subseteq M^* V_\# M^*$.

Proof: Note that if each word in $L(H_\#)$ contains exactly once the special marker # then each word w in L_1 must be of the form $w = w_1 X w_2$ where X generates a word containing that #.

Furthermore, it should be obvious that no variable may generate both a word with # and a word without #.
Otherwise, by Def. 1.2 $H_\#$ generates a word with at least two markers or no marker at all. □

A stronger version (splitting lemma) can be used in reducing proofs about properties of complex H-system classes to simpler H-system classes such as $\mathcal{H}(\text{ONE}, \mathcal{L}_2)$.

Lemma 2.3. Let $L \in \mathcal{H}(\mathcal{L}_1, \mathcal{L}_2)$ be an H-system language s.t. Lemma 2.2 applies and let $\mathcal{L}_1$, $\mathcal{L}_2$ be closed under gsm-mapping.
Then $L' = \{u \mid \exists v\colon u\#v \in L\}$ and $L'' = \{v \mid \exists u\colon u\#v \in L\}$ are both in $\mathcal{H}(\mathcal{L}_1, \mathcal{L}_2)$.
The proof is left to the reader.

3. A Hierarchy of H-system families

Our aim is to build a grid of H-system families by varying the language classes $\mathcal{L}_1$, $\mathcal{L}_2$ in $\mathcal{H}(\mathcal{L}_1, \mathcal{L}_2)$. The number of proofs for the complete set of incomparability, resp. strict inclusion relations is kept at a minimum. The reader might wish to consult from time to time the diagram at the end of this chapter where each arrow from language class $\mathcal{L}$ to $\mathcal{L}'$ implies $\mathcal{L} \subsetneq \mathcal{L}'$.

For getting started we note that substituting ONE languages, resp. FIN languages, into words from L_1 does not change the class of languages as compared to $\mathcal{L}_1$, provided $\mathcal{L}_1$ is closed under homomorphism, resp. finite deterministic substitution.

Lemma 3.1. For any language family $\mathcal{L}_1$ which is closed under deterministic finite substitution we have $\mathcal{H}(\mathcal{L}_1,\mathrm{FIN}) = \mathcal{L}_1$.

Secondly, we note that inclusion row- and columnwise is trivially given while strict inclusion has to be proved separately.

Lemma 3.2. For language families $\mathcal{L}_1$, $\mathcal{L}_2$, $\mathcal{L}_3$ we have

$\mathcal{L}_1 \subseteq \mathcal{L}_3$ implies $\mathcal{H}(\mathcal{L}_1, \mathcal{L}_2) \subseteq \mathcal{H}(\mathcal{L}_3, \mathcal{L}_2)$,

$\mathcal{L}_2 \subseteq \mathcal{L}_3$ implies $\mathcal{H}(\mathcal{L}_1, \mathcal{L}_2) \subseteq \mathcal{H}(\mathcal{L}_1, \mathcal{L}_3)$.

We now start to show proper inclusion beginning with $\mathcal{H}(\mathrm{ONE}, \mathcal{L}_2) \subsetneq \mathcal{H}(\mathrm{FIN}, \mathcal{L}_2)$.

Theorem 3.3. There exists a language in $\mathcal{H}(\mathrm{FIN,REG})$ which is not in $\mathcal{H}(\mathrm{ONE,CF})$.

Proof. Consider $L = \{a^n\#a^n\#a^n \mid n \geq 1\} \cup \{c\}$. Let {ABABA,C} be the metalanguage and $\varphi(A) = a^+$, $\varphi(B) = \#$, $\varphi(C) = c$. If follows that $L \in \mathcal{H}(\mathrm{FIN,REG})$. Assume $L \in \mathcal{H}(\mathrm{ONE,CF})$. Since $L \notin \mathrm{CF}$ we conclude from Lemma 2.1 that $\{w\}=L_1$ contains at least two occurrences of a variable X with L_X infinite. Clearly, c does not occur in any $v \in L_X$, else is would appear at least twice in at least one word in L. Thus, there exists a $Y \neq X \in V_1$ s.t. $c \in L_Y$. But then there exists a homomorphism h(w) (Def. 1.2) with $h(X) \neq \varepsilon$ and $h(Y) = c$, h arbitrary otherwise, and $h(w) = z_1cz_2 \in L$, $z_1z_2 \neq \varepsilon$ - a contradiction. □

The theorem is also a hint at the fact that the $\mathcal{H}(\mathrm{ONE}, \mathcal{L}_2)$ families have extremely poor closure properties (cf [14]) since $\{a^n\#a^n\#a^n \mid n \geq 1\} \cup \{c\}$ is the union of an $\mathcal{H}(\mathrm{ONE,REG})$ and a regular language.

Next we show strict inclusion between the second and third row from the bottom of Figure 1 at the end of this section.

Theorem 3.4. There exists a language in $\mathcal{H}(\mathrm{REG,REG})$ which is not in $\mathcal{H}(\mathrm{FIN,CF})$.

Proof. Consider $L = \{(a^nb)^m \mid n,m \geq 1\} \in \mathcal{H}(\mathrm{REG,REG})$.

Assume $L \in \mathcal{H}(\mathrm{FIN,CF})$. Thus, there exists an H-system $H' = (V_1', V_2', L_1', \varphi')$ with $L_1' = \{w_1, w_2, \ldots, w_r\} \in \mathrm{FIN}$ and for each $A \in V_1'$: $L_A \in \mathrm{CF}$. Our argument is then that while m may be arbitrarily large, the $w_i \in L_1'$ $(1 \leq i \leq r)$ have a bounded length and that for sufficiently large m at least one L_A must generate subwords of L which contain at least four b's which in turn would imply that an infinite set of words of the form $a^i(ba^n)^kba^j$ with $i,j,n \geq 0$, $k \geq 3$ is CF, which is of course not the case.

First note that there exists a constant c_o, s.t. for each $L_A \in CF$, $A \in V_1$, and each $X \in L_A$ of the form $X = a^i(ba^j)^k ba^l$ either $j \leq c_o$ or $k \leq 2$ holds.

Then let $t_o := \max_{1 \leq i \leq r} \{|w_i| : w_i \in L_1\}$ and let n be an arbitrary, but fixed integer s.t. $n > c_o + 2t_o$. For $(a^n b)^n \in L$ there exists then a $w_\mu \in L_1$ $(1 \leq \mu \leq r)$ s.t. $(a^n b)^n = h(w_\mu) = h(A_1 A_2 \ldots A_t) = V_1 V_2 \ldots V_t$, $V_\nu \in L_{A_\nu}$, $1 \leq \nu \leq t \leq t_o$.

Each V_ν is of the form $a^{i_\nu}(ba^n)^{k_\nu} ba^{l_\nu}$ and, since $n > c_o$, we have $k_\nu \leq 2$.

Thus, the number of b's in $V_1 V_2 \ldots V_t$ is less or equal to $2t \leq 2t_o$, but $(a^n b)^n$ contains $n > 2t_o$ b's - a contradiction. □

Working our way up, we consider $\mathcal{H}$(1-LIN,REG). The metalinear languages have been included in our investigation because they give rise to an infinite hierarchy if used as $\mathcal{L}_1$ component. Surprisingly the use as $\mathcal{L}_2$ component does not work and the classes collapse to $\mathcal{H}(\mathcal{L}_1$, 1-LIN) as shown in Theorem 3.8.

Theorem 3.5. There exists a language in $\mathcal{H}$(1-LIN,REG) which is not in $\mathcal{H}$(REG,CF).

Proof. Clearly, $L = \{(a^n b)^m \# (a^n b)^m | m,n \geq 1\}$ is an $\mathcal{H}$(1-LIN,REG) language. By an application of the regular pumping lemma we can reduce the assumption $L \in \mathcal{H}$(REG,CF) to $L \in \mathcal{H}$(FIN,CF). Then Lemma 2.3 yields $L' = \{(a^n b)^m | m,n \geq 1\} \in \mathcal{H}$(FIN,CF), giving the desired contradiction. □

Proving the m-LIN case was certainly the technically most difficult part in our hierarchy investigation.

Theorem 3.6. For each $m \geq 1$ there exists a language L_{m+1} in $\mathcal{H}$((m+1)-LIN,REG) which is not in $\mathcal{H}$(m-LIN,CF).

We have chosen the languages

$$L_{m+1} = \{w_1^{i_1} \# w_1^{i_1} \# w_2^{i_2} \# w_2^{i_2} \ldots \# w_{m+1}^{i_{m+1}} \# w_{m+1}^{i_{m+1}} \# \mid$$
$$| w_\nu \in a_\nu^+ b_\nu,\ i_\nu \geq 1 \text{ for each } \nu \in \{1,\ldots,m+1\}\},$$

and refer the reader to [1] for details.

Since the class of m-linear languages is properly contained in CF the following corollary is an immediate consequence of Theorem 3.6.

Corollary 3.7. For each $m \geq 1$ there exists a language in $\mathcal{H}$(CF,REG) which is not in $\mathcal{H}$(m-LIN,CF).

This infinite hierarchy result for $\mathcal{H}(\text{m-LIN}, \mathcal{L}_2)$ cannot be carried over to the case $\mathcal{H}(\mathcal{L}_1, \text{m-LIN})$. The reason is that very weak closure-properties of $\mathcal{L}_1$ are sufficient to simulate the first derivationsteps in m-linear grammars. The following derivations are linear and thus, these language families are identical to $\mathcal{H}(\mathcal{L}_1, \text{1-LIN})$.

<u>Theorem 3.8.</u> Let $\mathcal{L}_1$ be a family of languages closed under homomorphism and union, then $\mathcal{H}(\mathcal{L}_1, \text{m-LIN}) = \mathcal{H}(\mathcal{L}_1, \text{1-LIN})$ for each $m \geq 1$.

For a proof cf. [1].

Let us continue now by proving the columnwise proper inclusion in our diagram. In 1.4 we gave a language in $\mathcal{H}(\text{ONE,REG})$ which was not in $\text{CF} = \mathcal{H}(\text{CF,FIN})$. Thus, the strict inclusions $\mathcal{H}(\mathcal{L}_1, \text{FIN}) \subsetneq \mathcal{H}(\mathcal{L}_1, \text{REG})$ for $\mathcal{L}_1 \in \{\text{ONE,FIN,REG,m-LIN,CF}\}$ hold trivially.

<u>Theorem 3.9.</u> There exists a language in $\mathcal{H}(\text{ONE,1-LIN})$ which is not in $\mathcal{H}(\text{CF,REG})$.

<u>Proof.</u> Consider $L = \{a^n b^n a^n b^n \mid n \geq 1\}$, which is generated by the H-system $H = (\{A\},\{a,b\},\{AA\},\varphi)$ where $\varphi(A) = \{a^n b^n \mid n \geq 1\} \in \text{1-LIN}$. For $L \notin \mathcal{H}(\text{CF,REG})$ note that L is obviously not context-free. Using Lemma 2.1 we can apply the regular pumping lemma. □

For columnwise strict inclusion it remains to be shown that there is a language in $\mathcal{H}(\text{ONE,CF}) - \mathcal{H}(\text{CF, 1-LIN})$. Here we proceed in the following way. First we show inclusion of $\mathcal{H}(\text{CF,1-LIN})$ in the family of ETOL languages and then give a language which is apparently in $\mathcal{H}(\text{ONE,CF})$ but not in ETOL by results in [4] and [6].

<u>Theorem 3.10.</u> $\mathcal{H}(\text{CF,1-LIN})$ is contained in the family of ETOL languages.

<u>Proof.</u> Generate L_1 with one table and then simulate consistent substitution by "deterministic" tables (cf. [1]). □

<u>Theorem 3.11.</u> There exists a language in $\mathcal{H}(\text{ONE,CF})$ which is not in $\mathcal{H}(\text{CF,1-LIN})$.

<u>Proof.</u> Let D_8 be the Dyck-language on 8 symbols (cf. Examples 1.4). Obviously, $\{w\#w\#w \mid w \in D_8\} \in \mathcal{H}(\text{ONE,CF})$. But by results in [4] and [6] $\{w\#w\#w \mid w \in D_8\}$ is not even an outside-in-macro language and because of

$$\text{OI} \supsetneq \text{ETOL} \supsetneq \mathcal{H}(\text{CF,1-LIN})$$

we get $\{w\#w\#w \mid w \in D_8\} \notin \mathcal{H}(\text{CF,1-LIN})$. □

In Figure 1 below, the strict inclusion of $\mathcal{H}(\text{CF,CF})$ in $\eta(\text{CF})$, i.e. in the iterated deterministic substitution languages with substitutions from CF, follows trivially from the definition of $\eta(\text{CF})$ ([2]) and from the fact that $\{a^{2^n} \mid n \geq 1\} \in \text{EDTOL} \subseteq \eta(\text{CF})$ is not in $\mathcal{H}(\text{CF,CF})$ as mentioned a number of times before. In [2], the inclusion of $\eta(\text{CF})$ in IO ("inside-out-macro languages") is shown as well.

Furthermore, the inclusions

(REG =)	$\mathcal{H}$(REG,FIN)	$\subsetneq$	$\mathcal{H}$(ONE,REG)
(1-LIN =)	$\mathcal{H}$(1-LIN,FIN)	$\subsetneq$	$\mathcal{H}$(ONE,1-LIN)
((m+1)-LIN =)	$\mathcal{H}$((m+1)-LIN,FIN)	$\subsetneq$	$\mathcal{H}$(FIN,1-LIN)
(CF =)	$\mathcal{H}$(CF,FIN)	$\subsetneq$	$\mathcal{H}$(ONE,CF)

are straightforward and the proofs are left to the reader (cf. Lemma 3.1, Theorem 3.8 and [14]).

Theorem 3.12. In Figure 1 $\mathcal{H}(\mathcal{L}_1, \mathcal{L}_2) \subsetneq \mathcal{H}(\mathcal{L}_3, \mathcal{L}_4)$ iff there is a path from the node corresponding to $\mathcal{H}(\mathcal{L}_1, \mathcal{L}_2)$ leading to the node corresponding to $\mathcal{H}(\mathcal{L}_3, \mathcal{L}_4)$. Furthermore, two language families are incomparable iff there is no path connecting their corresponding nodes.

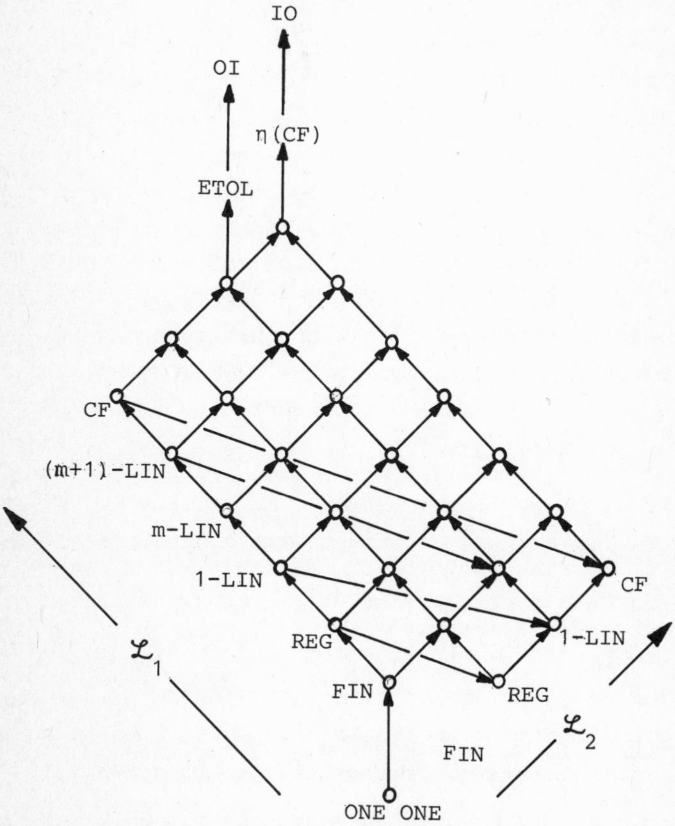

Figure 1

Proof. In addition to Theorems 3.3 - 3.11 we need the following four results, which can easily be verified:

1) $\{a^n ¢ b^n \mid n \geq 0\} \in \mathcal{H}(\text{1-LIN,FIN}) - \mathcal{H}(\text{REG,REG})$;

2) $\{a^i b^i a^j b^j \mid i,j \geq 1\} \cup \{c\} \in \mathcal{H}(\text{2-LIN,FIN}) - \mathcal{H}(\text{ONE,1-LIN})$;

3) $\{a^{i_1} b^{i_1} a^{i_2} b^{i_2} \ldots a^{i_{m+1}} b^{i_{m+1}} \mid i_\nu \geq 1\} \in$

$\mathcal{H}((m+1)\text{-LIN,FIN}) - \mathcal{H}(m\text{-LIN,REG}),\ m \geq 1$;

4) D_8 = Dyck-language on 8 letters $\in$
$\mathcal{H}(\text{CF,FIN}) - \mathcal{H}((m+1)\text{-LIN,1-LIN})$. □

4. Conclusion

We hope to have demonstrated that non-iterated homomorphic replacement is a concept in its own right. Its predominant aspect is the copying power. The results presented here should be looked at as a contribution to a classification of "rewriting modes" of which the (nested, iterated, controlled, tabled, etc.)-cases can be considered as particular variations. What has not been investigated are closure properties of H-systems. Only for the classes $\mathcal{H}$(ONE,REG) and $\mathcal{H}$(ONE,CF) complete results are given in [14].

The most interesting - and most difficult - questions arise in connection with decidability problems. Again for $\mathcal{H}$(ONE,REG) and $\mathcal{H}$(ONE,CF) some results are known but most problems remain open, e.g. the "Intersection problem for $\mathcal{H}$(ONE,REG)" (see [14]) of which the string unification problem is a particular case. Just as finding a matching notion for a given hypernotion in van Wijngaarden Grammars can be seen as solving the wordproblem for a language in $\mathcal{H}$(ONE,CF), a number of pattern matching problems may be viewed as intersection-, equivalence- and wordproblems in H-system languages.

References

[1] J. Albert und L. Wegner, Languages with homomorphic replacements, University Karlsruhe, Report No. 88, (1980).

[2] P.R.J. Asveld and J. Engelfriet, Iterated deterministic substitution, Acta Informatica 8, 3 (1977) 285-302.

[3] P. Dembiński and J. Małuszyński, Two level grammars: CF-grammars with equation schemes, Proc. 6th ICALP, Graz, LNCS 71, (1979) 171-187.

[4] A. Ehrenfeucht, G. Rozenberg and S. Skyum, A relationship between ETOL and EDTOL languages, Theoretical Computer Science 1 (1976) 325-330.

[5] J. Engelfriet and E.M. Schmidt, IO and OI, Part I : Journal of Comp. System Sciences 15 (1977) 328-353);

Part II: Journal of Comp. Syst. Sciences 16 (1978) 67-99.

[6] J. Engelfriet and S. Skyum, Copying theorems,Inf. Processing Letters, Vol. 5, No. 5 (1976) 157-161.

[7] S. Greibach, Some restrictions on W-grammars, International Journal of Computer and Information Sciences, Vol. 3, No. 4 (1974) 289-327.

[8] J. van Leeuwen, F-iteration languages, University of California, Berkeley, Memorandum (1973).

[9] G.S. Makanin, The problem of solvability of equations in a free semigroup, Russian Matematiceskij sbornik 103 (145), No. 2(6) (1977) 147-236; english summary in: Dokl.Akad.Nauk SSSR, Soviet Math.Dokl., Vol. 18, No. 2 (1977) 330-334.

[10] A. Salomaa, Formal Languages, (Academic Press, New York and London, 1973).

[11] A. Salomaa, Macros, iterated substitution and Lindenmayer-AFL's, University of Aarhus, Denmark, DAIMI PB-18 (1973).

[12] S. Skyum, Decomposition theorems for various kinds of languages parallel in nature, SIAM Journal on Computing, Vol. 5, No. 2 (1976) 284-296.

[13] M. Wand, Mathematical foundations of formal language theory, Mass. Institute of Technology, Report MAC TR-108 (1973).

[14] L. Wegner, Analysis of Two-Level Grammars, Ph.D.Thesis, (Hochschulverlag, Stuttgart, 1977).

FUNCTIONS EQUIVALENT TO INTEGER MULTIPLICATION

H. Alt
Department of Computer Science
The Pennsylvania State University
University Park, Pennsylvania 16802

Introduction

Two integer functions f and g are called computationally equivalent, if the computation of f is reducible to that of g and vice versa. This means that from a given network (= straight line program with bit-operations) computing $f(x)$ for n-bit integers of size $T(n)$ one can construct a network of size $O(T(n))$ for g and vice versa.

In this paper a large class of functions is shown to be computationally equivalent to integer multiplication.

There are two important reasons to deal with this problem:

1. "Fast" algorithms for all of these functions can be found by giving a fast algorithm for one of them. For example, Toom [10] found a fast multiplication algorithm by using the reduction of multiplication to squaring of integers. Conversely, the even faster algorithm of complexity $O(n \log n \log\log n)$ for integer multiplication by Schönhage/Strassen [9], gives us algorithms of this complexity for all functions equivalent to multiplication.
2. A lower bound for one of the multiplication equivalent functions is a lower bound for all of them. So the difficult problem of finding lower bounds for integer multiplication (cf. [6]) can be attacked by looking for lower bounds for one of these functions.

It has been known that squaring, inversion and division are functions which are computationally equivalent to multiplication (cf. [1]).

A recent paper of the author [3] shows that square rooting belongs to this class of functions too. This paper generalizes that result, showing that every nonlinear "algebraic function" is computationally equivalent to multiplication. The detailed proofs can be found in [4].

Main result

Definition: The class of algebraic functions is the smallest class of functions on the real numbers which contains the identity and the constants and is closed under multiplication, addition and exponentiation with a rational constant.

So for instance all polynomials, all rational functions, all roots and all compositions of these functions are algebraic.

As mentioned above, we assume that the inputs to our algorithms are integers in binary representation, the size of an input is its number of bits.

Since generally the binary representation of the result of an algebraic function is infinite we can only compute it with a certain precision and have to define what is meant by this.

Definition: We say that a program π computes an algebraic function f with precision k if π computes the binary representation of $f(x)$ up to an error $O(x^{-k})$ for every input x.

So an algorithm of precision k gives the result exactly up to about $k \cdot n$ digits right to the decimal point, where n is the number of digits of the input.

Definition: A function f is said to be computable with complexity $O(T(n))$ if for every integer k there exists a program of complexity $O(T(n))$ computing f with precision k.

f is said to be reducible to g $(f \leftarrow g)$ if to every algorithm of complexity $T(n)$ for f we can find an algorithm of complexity $O(T(n))$ for g.

f, g are called computationally equivalent, if $f \leftarrow g$ and $g \leftarrow f$.

Now we can formulate the main result of this paper.

Theorem: Every algebraic function f, which is nonlinear (i.e. f is not of the form $f(x) = ax + b$) is computationally equivalent to multiplication.

Useful reductions

For the proof of the main theorem two directions have to be shown: The reduction of multiplication to the evaluation of f and vice versa. This section provides some methods by which these reductions can be done.

We combine these techniques with others like substituting, composing functions and forming linear combinations which can be regarded as "free", since the costs of multiplying with constants and addition are linear which is obviously less than or equal to the costs of every multiplication algorithm.

The first method is to approximate algebraic functions by a linear combination of roots, i.e. functions of the form x^{α} where $\alpha \in Q$. Conversely every algorithm which evaluates an algebraic function can be used to compute a root.

More precisely, algebraic functions have the following properties.

Lemma 1: Let f be an algebraic function. Then for every $k > 0$ there exists an $n \geq 0$ and $a_0, \ldots, a_n, \alpha_0, \ldots, \alpha_n \in Q$ such that

$$f(x) = \sum_{i=0}^{n} a_i x^{\alpha_i} + O(x^{-k}).$$

Sometimes it will be useful to have the following "weaker" version of lemma 1:

<u>Lemma 2</u>: Let f be an algebraic function. Then there exist $a, \alpha \in Q$, $\beta > 0$ such that

$$f(x) = ax^{\alpha}(1 + O(x^{-\beta})).$$

Lemma 1 can be shown by induction on the number of additions, multiplications and exponentiations which are necessary to express f in terms of x and constants. The idea of the proof is to develop $f(x)$ in a Taylor series. It turns out that only finitely many terms are not $O(x^{-k})$, so the series has the form given in lemma 1.

Lemma 2 follows easily from lemma 1 if you take ax^{α} the term in L with the maximal exponent and $k < \alpha$.

Obviously α is unique, we call it the <u>degree</u> of f.

A consequence of lemma 2 is the following lemma which states that to every algebraic function f there exists a root whose evaluation is reducible to that of f.

<u>Lemma 3</u>: Let f be a nonlinear algebraic function. Then there exists an $\alpha \in Q - \{0, 1\}$ such that

$$x^{\alpha} \leftarrow f(x).$$

<u>Idea of the proof</u>: Consider the output of an algorithm computing f. Lemma 2 says that a certain portion of the digits coincide with the corresponding digits of $c \cdot x^{\alpha}$. We increase this portion by computing

$$\frac{f(x \cdot 2^d)}{2^{\alpha d}} \quad \text{by the algorithm for } f$$

where d is suitably high. It turns out that a d of size $O(n)$, where n is the number of digits of x is high enough to get all the correct digits of $c \cdot x^{\alpha}$ we want. So if an algorithm for f has complexity $T(n)$, we can construct one for $c \cdot x^{\alpha}$ with complexity $T(O(n))$, which is $O(T(n))$ for a "reasonable" complexity function T.

The next lemma allows us to decrease the degree of an algebraic function f, by 1, i.e. to find an algebraic function g which is reducible to f and has lower degree.

Lemma 4: Let f be an algebraic function. Then an algebraic function g can be found with

1) $g \leftarrow f$

2) $\deg(g) = \deg(f) - 1$.

g is a polynomial if f is one.

We simply use $g(x) = f(x + 1) - f(x)$ which is obviously reducible to f. Besides this $\deg(g) = \deg(f) - 1$. Actually g is an approximation of the derivative of f.

Reduction of multiplication to the evaluation of an algebraic function

Let us assume that f is a nonlinear algebraic function. We want to show one direction of the main theorem, namely: multiplication $\leftarrow f$.

If f is a polynomial of degree ≥ 2, we can apply lemma 4 $\lfloor \deg f \rfloor - 2$ times and get a polynomial f_2 of degree 2 which is reducible to f. Now we can get squaring from f_2 by subtraction of a linear function and multiplication by a constant so squaring is reducible to f and multiplication is reducible to squaring as shown in the introduction.

So assume that f is not a polynomial. By lemma 3 there exists some $\alpha \in Q - \{0, 1\}$ such that x^α is reducible to f. If $\alpha = -1$ we are done, since we know (cf. introduction) how to reduce multiplication to inversion.

If α is another negative number apply the function x^α twice which gives us $f_1(x) = x^{\alpha^2}$, a root with positive exponent $\neq 0, 1$ which is reducible to f. If α^2 is an integer then f_1 is a polynomial and we have our reduction by the considerations above.

So the remaining case is $f_1(x) = x^\beta$ for some $\beta > 0$ which is not an integer. By applying lemma 4 $\lfloor \beta \rfloor$ times we get a function $f_2(x) = x^\gamma$ where $0 < \gamma < 1$ which is reducible to f.

The next argument is the most difficult and important one in our proof.

Lemma 5: Let $f(x) = x^\gamma$ where $0 < \gamma < 1$, $\gamma \in Q$. Then there exists an integer $s < 0$ such that

$x^s \leftarrow f(x)$.

Idea of the proof: The functions $f_k(x)$, $k = 1, 2, \ldots$ defined by

$f_1 = f$

$f_k(x) = f(x + f_{k-1}(x))$

(i.e. $f_k(x) = \underbrace{(x + (x + \ldots\ldots (x + x^\gamma)^\gamma) \ldots\ldots)^\gamma)^\gamma}_{\text{depth } k}$

are obviously reducible to f and so are the functions

$$F_k(x) := f_{k+1}(x) - f_k(x).$$

Now one can show, that

$$F_k(x) = cx^{(\alpha-1)k+1}\,(1 + O(x^{\alpha-1}))$$

i.e. $Q_k(x) = x^{(\alpha-1)k+1}$ is reducible to F_k and so to f. Now choose k such that $(\alpha - 1)k + 1$ is an integer different from 1 and 0 so $Q_k(x) = x^{-n}$ for some integer $n \geq 2$. Therefore

$$p_k(x) := Q_k(Q_k(x)) = x^{n^2}$$

is a (nonlinear) polynomial which is reducible to Q_k and so to f.

By lemma 5 we have a negative integer s such that $f_3(x) = x^s$ is reducible to $f_2(x)$ from above. Now $f_4(x) = x^{s^2}$ is a polynomial of degree ≥ 2 which is reducible to f_3 and multiplication is reducible to the evaluation of such polynomials as we saw in the beginning of this proof.

Evaluation of an algebraic function by means of multiplication

In order to show the other direction of the main theorem fix an algebraic function f and an integer k. Assume that we have an algorithm for multiplication of complexity $T(n)$. We have to show that it can be used to evaluate f with precision k and the order of the complexity remains the same.

In [1] this result is already proven for division such that we can use division in our algorithm. The idea is the same as in that proof namely approximating f by Newton iteration.

By lemma 1 computing $f(x)$ with precision k is the same as computing $\sum_{i=1}^{n} a_i x^{\alpha_i}$ for some $n \in N$, a_i, $\alpha_i \in Q$.

Since the "linear" operations are free it is sufficient to show that any root x^α for $\alpha \in Q$ can be computed with precision k and complexity $O(T(n))$. So let $\alpha = p/q$ with $p,q \in Z$. Then $x^{p/q}$ for some input x is the root of the function

$$f(t) = t^q - x^p.$$

Applying Newton's iteration formula

$$x_{i+1} = x_i - \frac{f(x_i)}{f'(x_i)}$$

to this function we get

$$x_{i+1} = x_i(1 - \frac{1}{q}) + \frac{x^p}{qx_i^{q-1}}.$$

So one step of the iteration algorithm uses a finite number of multiplications, divisions.

Now computing x^α up to an error $O(x^{-k})$ means determining αn correct digits of this result left to the decimal point and kn correct digits right to the decimal point, where n is the number of digits of x. Altogether the result should have $(\alpha + k)n$ correct digits. (Obviously also for negative α).

Now Newton iteration converges quadratically--in other words the number of correct digits is doubled in every step of the iteration. So in order to get $(\alpha + k)n$ correct digits we need

$$\log((\alpha + k)n) = \log n + O(1)$$

steps.

Now it is reasonable to execute the i-th step only with those digits which are correct. So the multiplications, divisions in the i-th step are executed for 2^i-digit numbers.

So altogether the complexity of the iteration algorithm is

$$Q(n) = \sum_{i=1}^{\log n + O(1)} c \cdot T(2^i)$$

where c is the number of multiplications/divisions one step requires.

Now

$$Q(n) = \sum_{i=1}^{\log n + O(1)} c \cdot T(2^{\log n + O(1) - i})$$

$$= \sum_{i=1}^{\log n + O(1)} c \cdot T(dn/2^i)$$

for some constant d. Since for every "reasonable" complexity function T (e.g. for every continuous T growing at most polynomially)

$$T(n/2) \leq e \cdot T(n) \quad \text{for some} \quad e < 1,$$

we have

$$Q(n) = T(dn) \cdot c \cdot \sum_{i=1}^{\log n+O(1)} e^{i}$$

$$\leq T(dn) \cdot c' \quad \text{where} \quad c' = c \cdot \sum_{i=1}^{\infty} e^{i}$$

$$= O(T(n)) \quad \text{for "reasonable"} \quad T.$$

So our iteration algorithm determines x^{α} with precision k and the same order of complexity as that of the multiplication algorithm used in it.

More detailed reductions giving the resulting algorithms explicitly can be found in [1] and [2] for the cases $q = -1$ (inversion) and $q = 1/2$ (square rooting) respectively.

Conclusion

Presumably the algebraic functions form a proper subclass of multiplication equivalent functions, such that the complete characterization of these is an interesting open problem. The proof of lemma 1 essentially makes use of the fact that the exponents of the Taylor expansion of f do not exceed a certain maximum. Is this a characterization of all multiplication equivalent functions?

It is an interesting feature of these considerations, that results from real analysis are applied, whereas most of the previous results in computational complexity were proven by algebraic methods (cf. [5]).

Another interesting problem in this context is to show that certain functions are harder than multiplication. Presumably $\gcd(x, y)$, $f(x) = \alpha^{x}$ (α constant), radix conversion, and logarithm to some fixed base are examples for such functions (cf. [1], [7]).

References

[1] Aho A. V., Hopcroft J. E., Ullman J. D.: "The Design and Analysis of Computer Algorithms" Addison-Wesley, 1974.

[2] Alt H.: "Algorithms for Square Root Extraction" Report A77-12, Fachbereich Angew. Mathematik und Informatik, Saarbrücken, 1977.

[3] Alt H.: "Square Rooting is as Difficult as Multiplication" Computing 21, 221-232, (1979).

[4] Alt H.: "Functions Equivalent to Integer Multiplication," Report CS-80-8, The Pennsylvania State University, (1980).

[5] Borodin A., Munroe I.: "The Computational Complexity of Algebraic and Numeric Problems" Elsevier Comp. Sc. Library, 1975.

[6] Cook S. A., Anderaa S. O.: "On the minimum complexity of functions" Trans. Amer. Math. Soc. 142, 291-314, (1969).

[7] Knuth D. E.: "The Art of Computer Programming" Vol. 2, Addison-Wesley, 1969.

[8] Schönhage A.: "Schnelle Berechnung von Kettenbruchentwicklungen" Acta Informatica 1, 139-144, (1971).

[9] Schönhage A., Strassen V.: "Schnelle Multiplikation grosser Zahlen" Computing 7, 281-292, (1971).

[10] Toom A. L.: "The Complexity of a Scheme of Functional Elements Realizing the Multiplication of Integers" Soviet Math. Dokl. 4, 714-716, (1963).

LANGUAGES WITH REDUCING REFLEXIVE TYPES

Egidio ASTESIANO - Gerardo COSTA

Istituto di Matematica dell'Università di Genova

Via L.B.Alberti, 4 - 16132 Genova - Italy

ABSTRACT. *We consider a class of languages of typed λ-expressions with first-order primitives and reflexive types and investigate which types it is useful and consistent to allow, when the meaning of a term is defined by its behaviour as a part of programs. We define the class of reducing types and show that it is irrelevant to allow the non-reducing ones in our languages. Moreover we prove that, for any language with reducing types and a sufficiently rich set of primitives there is a fully abstract model, in the sense of Milner.*

1. INTRODUCTION.

It is well known that, following the work of Scott, there is a nice way of introducing "typed" via "untyped" using retractions /S/ or transformations, as in /E/, or both, as in /F/. On the other hand there are valid motivations for considering typed languages, as it has been argued, for example, by Milner et al. in /MMN/. Apart from theoretical motivations, types do exist in many popular programming languages and are also required for some new languages to come.

Here we look at the problem from a different point of view. The concept of full abstraction introduced by Milner in /M1/, to express full correspondence between operational and denotational semantics, seems to require the concept of type. Indeed, a distinction is needed between programs, on which a computation can be performed, and objects of higher type, whose behaviour is defined by considering how they act as parts of programs. A question arises, whether this concept of full abstraction can be generalized to untyped languages (see /M2/, pg. 3). We have no full answer to this question, neither we know of an existing one. Our approach towards a possible partial answer starts from the remark that "untyped" can be regarded as a particular reflexive type: σ s.t. $\sigma = \sigma \to \sigma$; then the idea is to keep the notion of type, so that we can talk about programs, and allow types of any kind, both finite and reflexive. Then we study which reflexive types it is useful and consistent to consider in a language whose semantics is required to be fully abstract. Here we begin this investigation, presenting a solution for the class of languages of typed λ-expressions with first order primitives and reflexive (functional) types. In this framework, the concept of reducing (reflexive) type, introduced in this paper, characterizes the class of useful and consistent types. We show indeed that if σ is a non-reducing type, any two terms M and N of type σ are identified in all fully abstract (extensional) models. Moreover, for any set A of reducing types, satisfying some decidability and closure properties (see Section 2), if a language L has types in A and its primitives are sufficiently expressive (rougly as in PCF, see /P,M2/), then L admits a fully abstract (extensional) model.

In the following lines we try to give an intuitive idea of the main concepts involved in this paper. Let us first consider an example. In Algol 60 one can write the following procedure for the factorial function /Ld/:

```
integer procedure  fact(n);  integer  n ;
   begin  integer procedure  f(g,m) ;  integer procedure g ; integer m ;
             f := if  m = 0  then  1  else  (m * g(g,m)) ;
      fact := f(f,n)    end
```

In this procedure, the identifiers f and g have type σ =(σ × integer) → integer, which is an example of a reducing type. Essentially, a term M has a reducing type when it can act as a function on tuples of terms producing a ground term; conversely, if M has a non-reducing type, then it can produce a ground term only behaving as an argument. The distinction above is motivated, roughly speaking, by the intuition that only a primitive function (of appropriate non-finite type) can transform two different terms, M and M', of the same non-reducing type, into two different terms of finite type. Hence, if in a language all the primitives are of finite type, all terms of a given non-reducing type behave the same way and have the same effect as parts of a program. It follows that, whenever the semantics of a term M is characterized by the behaviour of M as a part of programs (and this is the meaning of an intrinsicly fully abstract semantics /M2/), all the terms of a given non-reducing type are identified.

In this paper we restrict ourselves to consider languages with first order primitives; the motivation is twofold. Firstly, in this case we can obtain one of the main results (Corollary 4.6) as an immediate consequence of a theorem (Theorem 4.3) which generalizes the First Context Lemma of /M2/ and is established working in a framework similar to the one in /Lv,B2,B3/ (see Section 3). Secondly, this restriction is essential to the construction of fully abstract models of Section 5. This construction, which extends the results in /M2/, is based on Theorem 4.3 quoted above.

We intend to discuss the more general case (primitives of arbitrary finite type) in a further paper, giving a detailed direct proof of a stronger form of Corollary 4.6. In the concluding remarks (Section 6) we mention other directions for further investigations and connections to other works.

2. TYPES AND TERMS.

In general, reflexive types are defined by a set of equations; for decidability concerns, we shall consider only types defined by a finite set (system) of rational equations (rational types for short).

We assume the reader familiar with the concepts of: (universal) algebras, free algebras, ordered/continuous algebras, free continuous algebras, systems of rational (= polynomial = regular) equations on an algebra (see e.g. /ADJ,AC1/).

Let $K = \{ \kappa_1, \kappa_2, \ldots, \kappa_n \}$ be a set of ground types and $X = \{x_1, \ldots, x_n, \ldots\}$ be a set of indeterminates. We denote by $T(K,X)$ the free algebra generated by K, X and the bynary operation symbol $\rightarrow$ and by $T^\infty(K)$ the free continuous algebra generated by K and $\rightarrow$. We shall picture the elements in $T^\infty(K)$ as possibly infinite partial bynary trees. A system of rational equations on $T(K,X)$, $s: \{ x_i = t_i ,\ 1 \leq i \leq n,\ t_i \in T(K,X),$ is an admissible system if each of the terms t_i contains at least one symbol $\rightarrow$ and it does not contain indeterminates other than $x_1, \ldots, x_n$. It is well known that the system s has a unique solution in $T^\infty(K)$, namely an n-tuple of elements of $T^\infty(K)$, that we denote by $<s>$; $<s>_j$ indicates its j-th component.

Consider now a family S of admissible systems; then $B = B(S,K)$ is the set $\{ \sigma \in T^\infty(K) \mid \exists\, s \text{ in } S, \exists\, j \text{ such that } \sigma = <s>_j \}$. The set B, together with K, provides the basis for the definition of our types.

Definition 2.1. The set of types generated by B and K, $RT = RT(K,B)$, is the smallest subset of $T^\infty(K)$ such that:

i) $K \cup B \subseteq RT$;

ii) RT is closed w.r.t. the operation $\rightarrow$;

iii) if σ is in RT, then the solution of the equation $x = x \rightarrow \sigma$ is in RT (see the remark below for motivations). //

It is clear that RT contains all the usual functional types generated from K, that we shall call finite types (they indeed correspond to finite maximal trees in $T^\infty(K)$).

Lemma 2.2. a) Each type in RT is a rational element in $T^\infty(K)$, i.e. it is defined by an admissible system.

b) If $\sigma \to \tau$ is in RT, then σ and τ are in RT. //

By definition, types in RT are (possibly) infinite trees. For instance, if S contains the equations $x = x \to x$ and $x = x \to \kappa$, then RT contains the trees

$\sigma_1 =$ 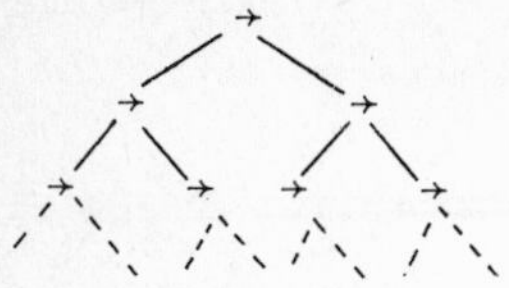 and $\sigma_2 =$ 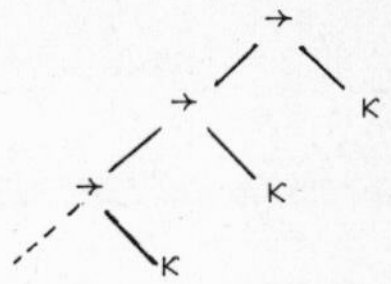

Obviously, a reflexive type has infinitely many different denotations, e.g. σ_1 above could also be denoted by $\sigma_1 \to \sigma_1$, $\sigma_1 \to (\sigma_1 \to \sigma_1), \ldots$ (this could be formalized by introducing type expressions). It is decidable whether two different denotations correspond to the same type, see e.g. /CKV,AC1/.

Notice the difference with the introduction of reflexive types in /MMN/, where types are equivalence classes w.r.t. a congruence induced by a relation.

In what follows, we shall use the letters σ and τ to indicate general elements in RT, reserving κ for ground types. In writing types (as terms) we shall usually omit redundant parenthesis, assuming association to the right;e.g. $\kappa \to \kappa \to \kappa$ stands for $(\kappa \to (\kappa \to \kappa))$. Finally, we allow ourselves to write, for instance, " $\sigma = \sigma \to \kappa$ " instead of " σ is the solution of the equation $x = x \to \kappa$ ".

Let now $C = \{c_1,\ldots,c_n,\ldots\}$, typical element c, and $F = \{f_1,\ldots,f_p\}$, typical element f, be, respectively, a set of <u>ground constant symbols</u> and a set of <u>first order function symbols</u> (i.e. symbols of type $\kappa_1 \to \ldots \to \kappa_n \to \kappa$). Moreover, let VAR=VAR(K,B) be a set of variables, $\{x^\sigma, y^\sigma, z^\sigma, \ldots, x_1^\sigma, y_1^\sigma, z_1^\sigma, \ldots \mid \sigma \in RT\}$. Then <u>L = L(K,B,C,F) is the set of all terms</u> constructed in the standard way from C,F and VAR, using typed λ-abstraction and application; moreover, L^σ is the set of terms of type σ.

We shall adopt some standard conventions in writing terms, suppressing redundant parenthesis (association is to the left) and using, for instance, $\lambda x^\sigma y^\tau.M$ instead of $\lambda x^\sigma(\lambda y^\tau M)$. The letters M and N ($M^\sigma$ and N^σ) will denote terms (of type σ) in L, while the letter P will be reserved for <u>programs</u> (i.e. closed terms of ground type).

<u>Remark</u>. For every σ in RT, $L^{(\sigma \to \sigma) \to \sigma}$ contains the term Y_σ, where, if $\tau = \tau \to \sigma$, $Y_\sigma = \lambda x^{\sigma\to\sigma}((\lambda y^\tau . x^{\sigma\to\sigma}(y^\tau y^\tau))(\lambda y^\tau . x^{\sigma\to\sigma}(y^\tau y^\tau)))$. Y_σ acts as a recursion operator, i.e. for every M of type $\sigma \to \sigma$, $Y_\sigma M \equiv M(Y_\sigma M)$, where $\equiv$ denotes equality in a sense to be defined in Section 3. //

<u>Example</u>. Let K,C and F be, respectively: $\{\iota, o\}$, where ι stands for integer and o for boolean, $\{tt,ff,0,1,\ldots,n,\ldots\}$ and $\{(+1)^{\iota\to\iota}, (-1)^{\iota\to\iota}, Z^{\iota\to o}, IF_\kappa^{o\to\kappa\to\kappa\to\kappa}\}$. For

every B, the associated language is an extension of PCF /P/ that we call PCF(B). Consider B_1 which contains $\sigma = \sigma \to \iota \to \iota$. Then we are able to write in PCF(B_1) a term FACT corresponding to the definition of the factorial function considered in Section 1. FACT = $\lambda x^\iota((NN)x^\iota)$, where N can be informally written as $\lambda y^\sigma\, x^\iota.$ <u>if</u> $x^\iota = 0$ <u>then</u> 1 <u>else</u> $x^\iota * ((y^\sigma\, y^\sigma)(x^\iota - 1))$, the symbol * denoting multiplication which can be easily defined recursively.

As a curiosity, consider now B_2 which contains $\tau = \tau \to \iota$. Then in PCF(B_2) we have the term, of type τ , $M = \lambda x^\tau.$ <u>if</u> $(x^\tau\, x^\tau) = 0$ <u>then</u> 1 <u>else</u> 0 , which would be a functional version of Russel's paradox if MM produced a result. //

3. MODELS AND SEMANTICS.

We briefly recall some well known concepts and results, due to Wadsworth, Lévy and Berry /W,Lv,B1,B2,B3/, in order to introduce the definition of model and some technical tools. This approach allows us to cut on proofs, by using well known results and extending some proof techniques. A more direct approach (i.e. starting from a notion of model which does not refer to the concept of syntactic approximation) would have been possible; this is, for example, the way taken in /M2,AC2/.

On the language L we consider the usual β-reduction (which preserves types), we assume α-conversion and denote by $\xrightarrow{*}$ the relation generated by β-reduction and α-conversion.

We extend L by introducing a family of primitive symbols, $\{\Omega^\sigma \mid \sigma \in RT\}$, and denote by L_Ω the language thus obtained and by L_Ω^σ the set of terms of type σ. Then the set $N = N(K,B,C,F)$ of <u>ω-β-normal forms</u> is given by: $N = \cup\{N^\sigma \mid \sigma \in RT\}$, where N^σ is the smallest subset of L_Ω^σ s.t.

i) $\Omega^\sigma \in N^\sigma$;

ii) if $M = \lambda x_1 \ldots x_m . s a_1 \ldots a_n$ is in L_Ω^σ , with s in $C \cup F \cup VAR$, $m,n \geq 0$ and a_i in N , $1 \leq i \leq n$, then M is in N^σ.

On N we define the relation $\prec$ as the coarsest order relation satisfying:

i) $\Omega^\sigma \prec a$, for all a in N^σ;

ii) $\lambda x_1 \ldots x_m . s a_1 \ldots a_n \prec \lambda x_1 \ldots x_m . s b_1 \ldots b_n$ iff $a_i \prec b_i$, $1 \leq i \leq n$.

We thus have that N^σ is a poset, with least element Ω^σ , whose elements are all isolated. Then N^σ can be completed in standard fashion to obtain an ω-algebraic cpo, $N^{\sigma\infty}$. We denote by N^∞ the set $\cup\{N^{\sigma\infty} \mid \sigma \in RT\}$ and by ≡ the equality in N^∞ .

The relation between L and N , N^∞ is given via the concept of <u>approximation</u> and we use head-normal-forms (hnf's) to define it.

A term in L is in hnf if it has the form $\lambda x_1 \ldots x_m . sM_1 \ldots M_n$, with $m,n \geq 0$, s in $C \cup F \cup VAR$ and the M_i's in L ; otherwise it has the form $\lambda x_1 \ldots x_m .((\lambda xM)N)M_1 \ldots M_n$. Then, if M is in L^σ its direct approximant, $\omega(M)$, is the term in N^σ given by:

i) $\omega(M) = \Omega^\sigma$ if M is not in hnf;

ii) $\omega(M) = \lambda x_1 \ldots x_m . s\omega(M_1) \ldots \omega(M_n)$ if $M = \lambda x_1 \ldots x_m . sM_1 \ldots M_n$.

Finally: $\mathcal{A}(M) = \{ \omega(M') \mid M \xrightarrow{*} M' \}$.

Lemma 3.1. a) If $M \xrightarrow{*} M'$ then $\omega(M) \prec \omega(M')$.

b) $\mathcal{A}(M)$ is directed in N^σ (by the Church-Rosser property). //

This lemma justifies the following definition:

Definition 3.2. If M is in L^σ, the syntactic value of M, val(M), is the l.u.b. of $\mathcal{A}(M)$ in $N^{\sigma\infty}$. //

An interpretation A for K,C and F is given by:

i) a cpo D^A_κ for each κ in K;

ii) an element $A(c)$ in D^A_κ for each c in C of type κ;

iii) a continuous function $A(f)$ for each f in F, s.t. if f has type $\kappa_1 \to \ldots \to \kappa_n \to \kappa$, then $A(f) : D^A_{\kappa_1} \times \ldots \times D^A_{\kappa_n} \longrightarrow D^A_\kappa$.

For the example of PCF(B), we shall refer to the natural interpretation: $D^A_\iota = \mathbb{N}_\perp$, $D^A_o = \{ \perp, \text{true}, \text{false}\}$, $A(tt) = \text{true}$, ..., $A(Z)$ = test for zero, ...

Definition 3.2. An (ω-algebraic, order-extensional) model for L and A, M , is given by the four clauses below:

i) Domains. For each σ in RT, we have an ω-algebraic cpo D_σ , where $D_\kappa = D^A_\kappa$, for every κ in K.

ii) Application maps. For each couple of types σ and τ , we have a continuous map $-.- : D_{\sigma\to\tau} \times D_\sigma \longrightarrow D_\tau$ such that:

- if d is in D_σ then $\perp_{\sigma\to\tau} . d = \perp_\tau$;
- (if (for every d in D_σ , $g.d \sqsubseteq g'.d$) then $g \sqsubseteq g'$) for any g, g' in $D_{\sigma\to\tau}$.

Notice that here we could have $\sigma = \sigma \to \tau$.

iii) Meanings. Let Env be the cpo of type preserving maps from VAR into $\cup\{ D_\sigma \mid \sigma \in RT\}$. Then it is possible to associate to each M^σ in L a continuous function $[\![M^\sigma]\!] : \text{Env} \longrightarrow D_\sigma$ such that, for each ρ in Env:

$[\![x^\sigma_i]\!]\rho = \rho(x^\sigma_i)$; $\qquad [\![c]\!]\rho = A(c)$;

if f has type $\kappa_1 \to \ldots \to \kappa_n \to \kappa$, then, for all $(d_1,\ldots,d_n)$ in $D_{\kappa_1} \times \ldots \times D_{\kappa_n}$:

$([\![f]\!]\rho).d_1 \ldots d_n = A(f)(d_1,\ldots,d_n)$;

$[\![MN]\!]\rho = ([\![M]\!]\rho).([\![N]\!]\rho)$;

$([\![\lambda x^\sigma M]\!]\rho).d = [\![M]\!](\rho[d/x^\sigma])$, for every d in D_σ , where: $(\rho[d/x^\sigma])y =$ if $y = x^\sigma$ then d else $\rho(y)$.

iv) Continuity w.r.t. approximants. If we extend $[\![\ ]\!]$ to N by setting $[\![\Omega^\sigma]\!]\rho = \bot_\sigma$, then $[\![M^\sigma]\!]\rho = \bigsqcup\{ [\![a]\!]\rho \mid a \in \mathcal{A}(M^\sigma)\}$, where the l.u.b. is taken in D_σ.

For a given model M , we write $M \sqsubseteq_M N$ whenever $[\![M]\!] \sqsubseteq [\![N]\!]$ in the model; $\sqsubseteq_M$ is a pre-order relation and we denote by $\equiv_M$ the associated equivalence.

We collect in a lemma some useful properties; the proof is straigtforward. Here and in what follows $[D \dashrightarrow D']$ denotes the space of continuous functions from D into D'.

Lemma 3.3. i) If $[\![M]\!] = \bigsqcup H$, $H = \{ [\![M_n]\!] \mid n \in \mathbb{N}\}$ directed in $[Env \dashrightarrow D_\sigma]$, then for every context $C[\ ]$, $[\![C[M]]\!] = \bigsqcup\{ [\![C[M_n]]\!] \mid n \in \mathbb{N}\}$.

ii) If P is a program of type κ , then $[\![P]\!]\rho = A^\infty(val(P))$, where A^∞ is the unique continuous extension of A to closed elements in $N^{\kappa\infty}$ s.t. $A^\infty(\Omega)=\bot$.

iii) If $M_1 \equiv M_2$ in $N^{\sigma\infty}$, then $[\![M_1]\!] = [\![M_2]\!]$. //

From well known results of Scott, see e.g. /S,R/, we know that there exist functional models for L and A . It is also known that, in general, these models are "too large", in the sense that there are terms M_1^σ , M_2^σ s.t. $[\![M_1^\sigma]\!] \neq [\![M_2^\sigma]\!]$, while they behave the same way in any operational context. This problem is the object of the next section.

4. FULL ABSTRACTION AND REDUCING REFLEXIVE TYPES.

Here we show that, as long as we are mainly interested in operational results, hence in programs, there is a class of reflexive types of no use in the languages we consider. This depends crucially on the fact that our primitives take their arguments in domains of finite type. We formalize this idea using the concept of full abstraction introduced by Milner.

Definition 4.1. Let M_1 , M_2 be two terms in L_σ ; then:

i) $M_1 \sqsubseteq_{pc} M_2$ iff $P[M_1] \sqsubseteq_M P[M_2]$, for every context $P[\ ]$ such that $P[M_1]$ and $P[M_2]$ are programs;

ii) assume that M_1 and M_2 have their free variables in $\{x_1,\ldots,x_n\}$ and set $\bar{M}_i = \lambda x_1 \ldots x_n . M_i$, i=1,2, then: $M_1 \sqsubseteq_{ac} M_2$ iff $\bar{M}_1 N_1 \ldots N_r \sqsubseteq_M \bar{M}_2 N_1 \ldots N_r$, for every $N_1,\ldots,N_r$ such that $\bar{M}_i N_1 \ldots N_r$, i=1,2, is a program. //

The relations $\sqsubseteq_{pc}$ and $\sqsubseteq_{ac}$ are preorders on L^σ; we denote by $\equiv_{pc}$ and $\equiv_{ac}$ the induced equivalences.

Definition 4.2. A model M for L is intrinsicly fully abstract (shortly i.f.a.) iff $\equiv_M$ and $\equiv_{pc}$ coincide. //

We recall that originally Milner introduced in /M1/ the concept of full abstraction w.r.t. an operational semantics, just to denote complete equivalence between operational and denotational semantics. It should be clear that, for an i.f.a. model M to be fully abstract w.r.t. an operational semantics it is enough that the last one agrees on programs with M. On the other hand, for the languages we consider here, the value of programs in M depends only on the interpretation A; hence it is up to the computation rules to be well designed to get the right value on programs. This stresses, we believe, the importance of intrinsic full abstraction.

Remark. It is well known /P/ that functional models are not f.a. in general. This is the case for PCF: to get full abstraction one should alter its sequential character by adding, for example, a parallel conditional. It should not be difficult to show that, adding reflexive types does not change the sequential nature of the language (this is true indeed both of the typed and the untyped λ-calculus /B1,B2,B3/).

The following theorem is a generalization to L of the First Context Lemma in /M2/; the proof can be done following a technique due to Lévy and used by Berry /Lv,B2,B3/.

Theorem 4.3. Let M and N be in L^σ; then: $M \sqsubseteq_{pc} N$ iff $M \sqsubseteq_{ac} N$. //

Notice that this result does not hold if we relax the restriction that primitives are first order.

Definition 4.4. A type σ in RT is reducing iff there exists a ground type κ s.t. $\sigma = \sigma_1 \to \dots \to \sigma_n \to \kappa$, for some $\sigma_1, \dots, \sigma_n$ in RT. Moreover: B, RT, is reducing iff every type in B, RT, is reducing. (We recall that RT = RT(K,B).) //

We do not insist here on the intuitive meaning of this definition, referring to Section 1 for it. We simply mention that the types used in the examples in Section 2 are reducing. It is not difficult to obtain, through a careful analysis of the definitions, the following lemma:

Lemma 4.5. i) RT is reducing iff B is reducing.

ii) RT is reducing iff every type in RT can be generated by a system of equations s.t. every r.h.s. t_i has the form $t'_1 \to \dots \to t'_n \to \kappa$, for some $t'_1, \dots, t'_n$ and κ.

iii) It is decidable whether B is reducing, for the class of finite B. //

We now show that we are justified in restricting our languages to admit only reducing types (if we are interested in f.a. models and the primitives are first order).

Indeed, if σ is non-reducing the condition $M \equiv_{ac} N$ is trivially (vacuously) verified for any M and N in L ; thus from Theorem 4.3 we obtain:

Corollary 4.6. If σ is non-reducing, $M \equiv_{pc} N$, for every M and N in L^{σ} ; hence: $M \equiv_{M} N \equiv_{M} \bot_{\sigma}$ for every i.f.a. model M . //

We have stated here this result as a corollary of Theorem 4.3 to minimize the lack of proofs. Actually it could be stated as an independent result and in a stronger form asserting that val(M) $\equiv$ val(N) in $N^{\sigma\infty}$. Moreover a direct proof is quite instructive on the role the primitives play in this result. At this point we can conclude that we can restrict ourselves to consider only languages with reducing reflexive types, without weakening their power in expressing programs.

5. FULLY ABSTRACT MODELS FOR A CLASS OF LANGUAGES WITH REDUCING TYPES.

In this section we assume B reducing and show in outline the existence of a fully abstract model for a wide class of languages with reducing types. The result is an extension of a beautiful result of Milner /M2/ for finitely typed λ-calculi; but here we adopt a nice variant of his technique due to Berry ; we refer to /B3/ for the general framework of the proof. The only important and distinguishing point here is the way our assumption about reducing types and the structure of RT allow us to define a suitable set of projections (of course this involves a number of minor changes).

If $D = \langle D, \sqsubseteq, \bot \rangle$ is a poset with minimum, a finite projection on D is a monotonic map $\phi : D \dashrightarrow D$ s.t. $\phi(d) \sqsubseteq d$, $\phi \circ \phi = \phi$, $\phi[D]$ is a finite set. D is an SFP-poset if there exists a sequence of finite projections on D, $\{ \phi_i \mid i \in \mathbb{N}\}$, s.t. $\phi_i \sqsubseteq \phi_{i+1}$ and, for any d in D, $d = \bigsqcup\{\phi_i(d) \mid i \in \mathbb{N}\}$. D is an SFP-cpo if it is an SFP-poset with continuous projections. If D is an SFP-poset, denote by $\bar{D}^{\infty}$ the completion by ideals of $\bar{D} = \{\phi_i(d) \mid i \in \mathbb{N}, d \in D\}$. If D is an SFP-poset and D' is a cpo, then $f : D \dashrightarrow D'$ is precontinuous if it is monotonic and, for every d in D, $f(d) = \bigsqcup\{f(\phi_i(d)) \mid i \in \mathbb{N}\}$. It is easy to show that:

Lemma 5.1. /B3/ If D is an SFP-poset, then $\bar{D}^{\infty}$ is an SFP-cpo and every precontinuous function h: D $\dashrightarrow$ D' can be extended in a unique way to a continuous function $\bar{h}: \bar{D}^{\infty} \dashrightarrow D'$, setting $\bar{h}(I) = \bigsqcup\{h(d) \mid d \in I\}$ for any ideal I in D. //

Definition 5.2. An interpretation A for L is SFP iff the domains D_{κ}^{A} are SFP with projections ϕ_i^{κ} which are definable, in the sense that there are terms $\underline{\phi}_i^{\kappa}$ in $L^{\kappa\to\kappa}$ s.t. for any P in L^{κ} ; $\phi_i^{\kappa}(A^{\infty}(\mathrm{val}(P))) = A^{\infty}(\mathrm{val}(\underline{\phi}_i^{\kappa} P))$. //

When A is SFP, it is easy to define, inductively from the $\underline{\phi}_i^{\kappa}$, a family of terms

$\underline{\phi}_i^{\sigma}$, for finite σ ,which behave as projections in any model for L and A , setting: $\underline{\phi}_i^{\sigma\to\tau} = \lambda x^{\sigma\to\tau} y^{\sigma} . \underline{\phi}_i^{\tau} (x^{\sigma\to\tau} (\underline{\phi}_i^{\sigma} y^{\sigma}))$. This is no longer possible with reducing reflexive types; we illustrate the problem and the solution on the reducing type $\sigma = \sigma \to \kappa$, to avoid clumsiness for heavy notation.

We would like to have $\underline{\phi}_i^{\sigma\to\kappa} = \lambda x^{\sigma\to\kappa} y^{\sigma} . \underline{\phi}_i^{\kappa}(x^{\sigma\to\kappa}(\underline{\phi}_i^{\sigma} y^{\sigma}))$. Hence, as $\sigma=\sigma\to\kappa$, $\underline{\phi}_i^{\sigma}=Y_{\sigma\to\sigma} M_{i\sigma}$, where $M_{i\sigma}$ is the term $\lambda w^{\sigma\to\sigma} x^{\sigma\to\kappa} y^{\sigma} . \underline{\phi}_i^{\kappa}(x^{\sigma\to\kappa}(w^{\sigma\to\sigma} y^{\sigma}))$. Remembering that we want finite projections, we can take the syntactic approximants $\underline{\phi}_{in}^{\sigma} = Y^{(n)}_{\sigma\to\sigma} M_{i\sigma} = (\lambda z.z^n \Omega^{\sigma\to\sigma})M_{i\sigma}$, where z is of type $(\sigma\to\sigma) \to (\sigma\to\sigma)$.

Then we can easily check, for example, that $\underline{\phi}_{in}^{\sigma}(\underline{\phi}_{in}^{\sigma} M) = \underline{\phi}_{in}^{\sigma} M$, by induction on n and remembering that $\underline{\phi}_i^{\kappa}(\underline{\phi}_i^{\kappa} N) = \underline{\phi}_i^{\kappa} N$; indeed: $\underline{\phi}_{in}^{\sigma}(\underline{\phi}_{in}^{\sigma} M) = \lambda y^{\sigma} . \underline{\phi}_i^{\kappa}(\underline{\phi}_{in}^{\sigma} M(\underline{\phi}_{i\,n-1}^{\sigma} y^{\sigma})) = \lambda y^{\sigma} . \underline{\phi}_i^{\kappa}(\underline{\phi}_i^{\kappa}(M(\underline{\phi}_{i\,n-1}^{\sigma}(\underline{\phi}_{i\,n-1}^{\sigma} y^{\sigma}))) = \lambda y^{\sigma} . \underline{\phi}_i^{\kappa} (M(\underline{\phi}_{i\,n-1}^{\sigma} y^{\sigma})) = \underline{\phi}_{in}^{\sigma} M$.

Then to get a sequence, one can diagonalize, choosing $\{\underline{\phi}_{ii}^{\sigma} , i \in \mathbb{N}\}$ (but there is no real need for having a sequence instead of a denumerable directed set).

What we can do now for the general case should be clear, if we remember that a type in RT can be defined by a finite system of recursive equations, with second members of the form $t = t_1 \to \ldots \to t_n \to \kappa$ (recall we have assumed RT reducing). Simply remark thath Böhm's technique (see e.g. /Bh/ pg. 186) for solving , syntactically, a system of recursive equations in λ-calculus, through the use of Y (Θ in that paper), n-tuples and projections $U_i^{(n)}$, works nicely on reducing types (i.e. all the formulas used are expressible in L, due to the closure properties of RT).

Following Berry, we now define: $[M^{\sigma}]_{pc} = \{N^{\sigma} \mid N^{\sigma} \equiv_{pc} M^{\sigma}\}$; $L_c^{\sigma} = \{M \mid M \text{ is closed in } L^{\sigma}\}$; $[L_c^{\sigma}] = \{[M^{\sigma}]_{pc} \mid M^{\sigma} \in L_c^{\sigma}\}$; $[L^{\sigma}] = \{ [M^{\sigma}]_{pc} \mid M^{\sigma} \in L^{\sigma}\}$; $\phi_i^{\sigma} : [L^{\sigma}] \dashrightarrow [L^{\sigma}]$ by $\phi_i^{\sigma} [M^{\sigma}]_{pc} = [\underline{\phi}_{ii}^{\sigma} M^{\sigma}]_{pc}$.

We shall drop the subscript pc in what follows.

Lemma 5.3. If A is an SFP-interpretation, then for every σ and τ :

i) $A_{\sigma} = < [L_c^{\sigma}] , \sqsubseteq_{pc}, [\Omega^{\sigma}]>$ and $E_{\sigma} = <[L^{\sigma}] , \sqsubseteq_{pc}, [\Omega^{\sigma}]>$ are SFP-posets;

ii) let $\overline{A}_{\sigma}^{\infty}$ and $\overline{E}_{\sigma}^{\infty}$ denote their completions defined by Lemma 5.1 and let the maps $-.-$ and $-_{\circ}-$ be defined as follows:

$-.- : A_{\sigma\to\tau} \times A_{\sigma} \dashrightarrow \overline{A}_{\tau}^{\infty}$, $[M].[N] = [MN]$;

$-_{\circ}- : E_{\sigma} \times \widetilde{Env} \dashrightarrow \overline{A}_{\sigma}^{\infty}$, $[M']_{\circ} \rho = [M' [\rho(x_1)/x_1,\ldots, \rho(x_n)/x_n]]$, where $\widetilde{Env}$ is the SFP-poset of type preserving maps from VAR into $\cup_{\sigma} A_{\sigma}$ and $\{x_1,\ldots,x_n\}$ is the set of free variables of M'; then the maps $-.-$ and $-_{\circ}-$ are precontinuous. //

If we assume now the definability of isolated points in the D_{κ}^{A} 's (and then D_{κ}^{A}

$\cong \overline{A}^{\infty}_{\kappa}$), we get in turn that also the isolated points in $\overline{A}^{\infty}_{\sigma}$ are definable. Milner has shown in /M2/ that the definability of isolated points of all the domains guarantees full abstraction of extensional algebraic models. This should help to understand the next theorem.

Theorem 5.4. Consider L = L(K,B,C,F), with B reducing, and an SFP-interpretation A for L s.t. the isolated points in the D^{A}_{κ}'s are definable. Then the following clauses define a fully abstract (order-extensional, ω-algebraic) model for L and A :

- domains: $D_{\sigma} = \overline{A}^{\infty}_{\sigma}$;
- application maps: the continuous extension of the maps -.- in Lemma 5.3;
- meanings: $[\![M]\!]\rho = [M]_{\circ}\rho$, where $-_{\circ}-$ is the continuous extension of the map $-_{\circ}-$ of Lemma 5.3. //

It is well known that the assumptions of the theorem are satisfied by the natural interpretation associated to PCF; hence we obtain immediately:

Corollary 5.5. For every reducing B, PCF(B) admits a fully abstract model. //

6. CONCLUDING REMARKS.

The concept of reducing type we have introduced here seems to be rather sound to be used in any applicative language,with functional types, which we want both typed and flexible enough to possess some features of untyped languages. The essential idea of the paper is that the maximum of flexibility can be reached without leaving the set of reducing types, as long as we are interested in programs and allow only first order primitives. This raises some questions. Does Corollary 4.6 still hold if the primitives are of arbitrary finite type? Does it hold also in a stronger form? We conjecture that this is indeed the case and that for any context $C[\ ]$ such that $C[M_i]$ is of finite type and closed, $val(C[M_1]) \equiv val(C[M_2])$, for any couple of non-reducing M_1 and M_2. (We intend to investigate this problem in a future paper.) What happens if we allow primitives to act on domains of reflexive type? Certainly the result above is no longer true, but can we define exactly the relationships between the functionalities of the primitives and the behaviour of terms w.r.t. $\equiv_{pc}$? Answering all these questions could also help to identify the reflexive types and primitive operations effectively needed in talking about semantics and correctness, as in /MMN/.

We have repeatedly pointed out that this paper deals with applicative languages and functional types; it seems interesting to extend this investigation to structured types (i.e. types built not only from $\rightarrow$, but also from $\times$, +, etc.). Apart from its intrinsic interest, this should be of some help when one considers non-applicative languages, where, for instance, a procedure declared of type $\sigma = \sigma \to \sigma$, has actually type $\sigma = \sigma \to (\sigma \times \kappa)$, because of side-effects. Of course in that case we should reserve the concept of reducing type for the actual types, i.e. those which take into account side-effects.

A paper in which the importance of reflexive structured types (not only functional) is emphasized in /Lh/, where an informal discussion reaches the conclusion that introducing "circularly defined modes" à la Scott provides a unifying and elegant approach to the semantics of modes in Algol 68. In that paper one can also find the remark that some legal reflexive types are obviously useless, but the thesis is mainly that the distinction between legal and illegal modes lacks a sound semantic basis. In the present paper we have discussed a criterion to discriminate, in a particular case, useful from useless, no matter how easily and elegantly a type can be given a semantics. In our opinion, of course, only the useful types, and possibly not all of them, should be legal in a programming language.

Finally, we mention two topics which have been completely left out of this presentation: polymorphism and assignment of reducing types to untyped expressions. It is not clear to us, at the moment, how the most general notion of polymorphism could fit in the framework proposed here. As for the second topic , it could be interesting to investigate the relationship with some recent work on systems of assignment of types (particularly /CDS/ and related papers), in order to generalize the concept of full abstraction.

ACKNOWLEDGEMENT. The autors would like to thank the referees for their valuable remarks and Mariangela Dezani-Ciancaglini for a very fruitful discussion.

REFERENCES

AC1 E.Astesiano, G.Costa, On algebraic semantics of polyadic recursive schemas, 2me Coll. Les Arbres en Algèbre et en Programmation, Univ.of Lille, 1977, 29-83.

AC2 === Fully abstract semantics for nondeterministic λ-s-calculi, 1979, to appear.

ADJ J.A.Goguen, J.W.Thatcher, E.G.Wagner, J.B.Wright, Initial algebra semantics and continuous algebras, JACM, 24 (1977) 68-95.

B1 G.Berry, Séquentialité de l'évaluation formelle des λ-expressions, in B.Robinet ed. Trasformations des programmes (3me Coll. Int. sur la Programmation, Paris, 1978) Dunod, Paris 1978.

B2 === Stable models of typed λ-calculi, 5th ICALP, Udine 1978, Lecture Notes in C.S. 62, Springer, 72-89.

B3 G.Berry, Modèles complètement adéquats et stables des λ-calculs typés, Thèse d'Etat, Univ. Paris VII, 1977.

Bh C.Böhm, the CUCH as a formal and description language, in T.B.Steel ed. Formal language description languages for computer programming, North Holland, Amsterdam 1966, 179-197.

CDS M.Coppo, M.Dezani-Ciancaglini, P.Sallé, Functional characterization of some semantic equalities inside λ-calculus, 6th ICALP, Graz 1979, Lecture Notes in C.S. 71, Springer.

CKV B.Courcelle, G.Kahn, J.Vuillemin, Algorithmes d'équivalence et de réduction à des expressions minimales dans une classe d'équations récursives simples, Rapport IRIA n. 37, 1973.

E E.Egli, Typed meanings in Scott's λ-calculus models, Symp. on λ-calculus and computer science theory, Rome 1975, Lecture Notes in C.S. 37, Springer.

F E.Fehr, Lamda-calculus as control structures of programming languages, Report n.57, RWTH-Aachen, 1980.

Ld H.F.Ledgard, Ten mini-languages: a study of topical issues in programming languages, Comp. Surv. 3 (1971) 115-146.

Lh D.J.Lehmann, Modes in Algol Y, in Implementation and design of algoritmic languages, J.André, J.P.Banâtre eds. IRIA, 1977, 111-123.

Lv J.J.Lévy, Reductions correctes et optimales dans le λ-calcul, Thèse d'Etat, Univ. Paris VII, 1978.

MMN R.Milner, L.Morris, M.Newey, A logic for computable functions with reflexive and polymorphic types, in Proving and improving programs, G.Huet, G.Kahn eds. (Coll. IRIA, Arc et Senans, 1975), IRIA, 1975.

M1 R.Milner, Processes, a mathematical model for computing agents, Studies in Logic 80, North Holland, 1975, 157-174.

M2 === Fully abstract models of typed λ-calculi, TCS 4 (1977) 1-22.

P G.Plotkin, LCF as a programming language, TCS 5 (1977) 223-255.

R J.C.Reynolds, Notes on a lattice theoretic approach to the theory of computation, Syracuse University, 1972.

S D.Scott, Data types as lattices, SIAM J. Comput. 5 (1976) n.3.

W C.P.Wadsworth, The relation between computational and denotational properties of Scott's D_∞ model of the λ-calculus, SIAM J. Comput. 5 (1976) 488-521.

SEMANTICS OF UNBOUNDED NONDETERMINISM

Ralph-Johan Back
Mathematisch Centrum,
Amsterdam

ABSTRACT. A program construct is proposed, for which the assumption of bounded nondeterminism is not natural. It is shown that the simple approach of taking the powerdomain of the flat cpo does not produce a correct semantics for programs in which nondeterminism is unbounded. The powerdomain approach is then extended to computation paths, resulting is an essentially operational semantics for programs of unbounded nondeterminism.

1. INTRODUCTION

Nondeterminism is usually introduced into a programming language in the form of a new control structure. One possibility is to define a binary construct, S_1 *or* S_2, which has the effect of selecting either S_1 or S_2 (but not both) for execution. The choice between the two alternatives is made nondeterministically. Another possibility, introduced by DIJKSTRA [76], is to generalise the conditional statement. The effect of the guarded command *if* $B_1 \rightarrow S_1 \,\square\, \ldots \,\square\, B_n \rightarrow S_n$ *fi* is to execute some statement S_i for which the corresponding guard B_i is true. Nondeterminism is possible in this case, because the guards are not required to be mutually exclusive.

There is, however, another way in which nondeterminism can be introduced into a sequential programming language. This is by allowing the basic statements to be nondeterministic. This can be achieved by generalising the ordinary assignment statement to a *nondeterministic assignment statement*. Such a construct has been used in HAREL [77] and in BACK [78], and in a somewhat different form, in BAUER [77]. A nondeterministic assignment statement has the form

$$x: = x'.Q$$

and has the effect of assigning to x some value x' that satisfies the condition Q, in which both x and x' (and also other variables) may occur free. Nondeterminism can occur, because there may be more than one x' that satisfies the condition Q for a given value of x. In this case some x' satisfying Q is choosen nondeterministically, and assigned to x. If no x' satisfies Q, then the effect of the statement is undefined.

This latter form of nondeterminism is actually very common, although in a somewhat disguised form. Consider a program S which calls a procedure p, and assume that p is specified by giving the entry and exit conditions for the procedure. Usually we will try to understand the way in which S works by only considering the information about p given in the specification of this procedure. The exit condition, however, may not define a unique final result of calling p. In understanding S, we then have to consider all possible final states which can result from the call, i.e.

we will in effect be looking upon S as a program with an nondeterministic basic statement p. The nondeterminism here results from lack of information as to the effect of calling p, rather than from the fact that S is executed by a nondeterministic machine. Somebody observing only the working of S and knowing only the specification of p, cannot, however, tell the difference between these two views. (One could argue that in the first case, because the procedure p actually is executed by a deterministic mechanism, the same result will always be choosen for the same initial state. On the other hand, it is possible that a nondeterministic mechanism executing p would choose to give the same result for the same initial state in all observed calls, but still could give some other result for some future call on p.)

We will here consider a simple iterative language embodying this kind of nondeterminism. For this purpose, let Var be a nonempty set of variables. Assume that certain function, predicate and constant symbols are given, and let Form be the set of all first-order formulas built out of variables and these symbols. We will let x,y and z range over variables and B,P,Q,R range over first-order formulas in Form.

Let Stat be the set of program statements, recursively defined by

$$S ::= \quad x:=x'.Q \mid S_1;S_2 \mid \textit{if } B \textit{ then } S_1 \textit{ else } S_2 \textit{ fi} \mid \textit{while } B \textit{ do } S_1 \textit{ od}.$$

Here S, S_1 and S_2 range over program statements. The effect of the first construct was already explained above. The other constructs have their usual meaning of composition, selection and iteration.

Our purpose here is to discuss how the semantics of programming languages such as Stat, containing nondeterministic basic statements, is to be defined. The semantics of nondeterministic control structures have been successfully defined in PLOTKIN [76]. This definition, however, makes essential use of the assumption that the nondeterminism is *bounded*. This means that execution of a program component for a given initial state either can only produce a finite number of different results, or then it must be possible that execution never terminates. The possibility that execution for some initial state will be guaranteed to terminate and at the same time may produce infinitely many different results is thus excluded.

The assumption of bounded nondeterminacy, also made and discussed in DIJKSTRA [76], is intuitively justified for nondeterministic control structures such as those given above. In these cases the choice of how to proceed is made between a finite number of alternatives. The set of all possible executions of a program from a given initial state will therefore form a finitely branching tree. If this tree contains infinitely many terminal nodes then the tree itself must be infinite. By Königs lemma, this means that there must be an infinite branch in the tree, i.e. an infinite execution starting from the given initial state is possible.

There does not, however, seem to be any intuitive reason for not considering *basic statements* of unbounded nondeterminacy. In his book Dijkstra e.g. rejects the basic statement "set x to any positive integer", because it cannot be implemented using guarded commands. While this is true, there is on the other hand nothing wrong intuitively in calling a procedure p, with the specification

proc p; *entry* true; *exit* x > 0;

This corresponds to using the nondeterministic assignment statement

x:=x.(x > 0)

in the program. The fact that this statement cannot be implemented is of no concern here, the purpose of the statement is only to express the information available about the effect of calling the procedure. Moreover, from the point of understanding a program, there is no difference between basic statements of bounded and unbounded nondeterminacy, both seem to be equally well defined and easy to understand. (This same point has also been made by BOOM [78]).

The nondeterministic assignment statement is more powerful that the nondeterministic control statements given above, because nondeterministic control structures can be simulated using nondeterministic assignment statements, while the converse does not necessarily hold. Thus e.g. the binary choice construct S_1 *or* S_2 can be expressed in our language by the statement

c:=c.(c=1 or c=2); *if* c=1 *then* S_1 *else* S_2 *fi*.

The assignment statement can also be expressed using the nondeterministic assignment statement. The assignment statement x:=t is expressed by the nondeterministic assignment

x :=x'.(x' = t).

E.g. x := x+1 corresponds to the statement x := x'.(x' = x+1).

An obvious generalisation of this nondeterministic assignment statement is to allow simultaneous assignment to several variables, i.e. we would allow nondeterministic assignment statements of the form

$x_1,\ldots,x_n:=x'_1,\ldots,x'_n.\Omega$.

We will only treat the single variable form below, for reasons of simplicity.

2. FUNCTIONAL SEMANTICS BASED ON $P(\Sigma_\perp)$

We will start by defining the semantics of Stat using the powerdomain $P(\Sigma_\perp)$ introduced in PLOTKIN [76].

Let D be a nonempty set, serving as the domain of interpretation for the formulas in Form. The set of proper program states is defined to be $\Sigma = \mathrm{Var} \to D$, while $\Sigma_\perp = \Sigma \cup \{\perp\}$ is the set of all program states, including the ***undefined state*** $\perp$. An ordering of approximation is defined in $\Sigma_\perp$ as usually, by the condition

$s \sqsubseteq s'$ iff $s = \perp$ or $s = s'$,

for any $s, s' \in \Sigma_\perp$. It is easily shown that $\Sigma_\perp$ is a complete partial order (cpo) with respect to this ordering. The undefined state is used to indicate nontermination, as usual.

The meaning of a nondeterministic program will be a function from the initial states to the set of possible final states for the given initial state. We therefore need the powerset of $\Sigma_\perp$. Let us define the set of possible results

$$P(\Sigma_\perp) = \{A \subset \Sigma_\perp \mid A \neq \emptyset\}.$$

A subset A of $\Sigma_\perp$ is *bounded*, if $|A| < \infty$ or $\perp \in A$ ($|A|$ is the cardinality of A). The set of possible bounded results is

$$P_B(\Sigma_\perp) = \{A \subset \Sigma_\perp | A \neq \emptyset \text{ and A is bounded}\}.$$

An ordering of approximation is defined between elements of $P(\Sigma_\perp)$ as follows:

$$A \sqsubseteq A' \text{ iff } \forall s{\in}A.\exists s'{\in}A'.s \sqsubseteq s' \text{ and } \forall s'{\in}A'.\exists s{\in}A.s \sqsubseteq s',$$

for any A, A' $\in P(\Sigma_\perp)$. An equivalent formulation for $P(\Sigma_\perp)$ is

$$A \sqsubseteq A' \text{ iff either } \perp \in A \text{ and } A - \{\perp\} \subset A'$$
$$\text{or } \quad \perp \notin A \text{ and } A = A'.$$

We then have that both $P(\Sigma_\perp)$ and $P_B(\Sigma_\perp)$ are cpo's with respect to this ordering.

We define the set of state transformations by $M(\Sigma_\perp) = \Sigma \to P(\Sigma_\perp)$ and the set of bounded state transformations by $M_B(\Sigma_\perp) = \Sigma \to P_B(\Sigma_\perp)$.

An ordering of approximation between state transformations is defined by

$$m \sqsubseteq m' \text{ iff } m(s) \sqsubseteq m'(s) \text{ for all } s \in \Sigma,$$

for any m, m' $\in M(\Sigma_\perp)$. We then have that $M(\Sigma_\perp)$ and $M_B(\Sigma_\perp)$ are both cpo's with respect to this ordering.

To define the meaning of the statements in Stat, we will also need the set of truth values T = {tt,ff} and the set of predicates on Σ, $W(\Sigma) = \Sigma \to T$.

Let $m \in M(\Sigma_\perp)$. The extension of m to $m^\dagger : P(\Sigma_\perp) \to P(\Sigma_\perp)$ is defined as follows. First, let $m' : \Sigma_\perp \to P(\Sigma_\perp)$ be defined by

$$m'(s) = \begin{cases} m(s), & \text{if } s \in \Sigma \\ \{s\}, & \text{if } s = \perp . \end{cases}$$

Then $m^\dagger$ is defined by

$$m^\dagger(A) = \cup\{m'(s) \mid s \in A\}.$$

The same construction extends $m \in M_B(\Sigma_\perp)$ to $m^\dagger : P_B(\Sigma_\perp) \to P_B(\Sigma_\perp)$.

Composition and selection is now easy to define. Let m and m' be elements of $M(\Sigma_\perp)$, and let b be an element of $W(\Sigma)$. The composition m;m' of m and m', defined by

$$(m;m')(s) = m'^\dagger(m(s)), \text{ for } s \in \Sigma,$$

will then be an element of $M(\Sigma_\perp)$. Similarly, the selection of m or m' by b, $(b \to m,m')$, defined by

$$(b \to m,m')(s) = \begin{cases} m(s), & \text{if } b(s) = tt \\ m'(s), & \text{if } b(s) = ff \end{cases}$$

will also be an element of $M(\Sigma_\bot)$.

The same construction defines composition and selection in $M_B(\Sigma_\bot)$; $M_B(\Sigma_\bot)$ will also be closed with respect to these operations. Composition and selection will be monotonic in both $M(\Sigma_\bot)$ and $M_B(\Sigma_\bot)$. In $M_B(\Sigma_\bot)$ these operations will also be continuous. However, composition in $M(\Sigma_\bot)$ is not continuous. This is the main technical reason for requiring bounded nondeterminacy, i.e. the requirement is needed to guarantee continuity of the control structures used.

We will finally define the iteration operator. Let Δ and Ω be two special elements of $M(\Sigma_\bot)$, defined for any $s \in \Sigma$ by $\Delta(s) = \{s\}$ and $\Omega(s) = \{\bot\}$. Let $b \in W(\Sigma)$ and let $m \in M(\Sigma_\bot)$. The approximates $(b*m)^n \in M(\Sigma_\bot)$ are then defined for $n = 0,1,2,\ldots$ by

$$(b*m)^0 = \Omega$$
$$(b*m)^{n+1} = (b \to m;(b*m)^n, \Delta),\ n = 0,1,\ldots \quad .$$

Because composition and selection is monotonic, it is easily proved that $(b*m)^0 \sqsubseteq (b*m)^1 \sqsubseteq (b*m)^2 \sqsubseteq \ldots$, so the least upper bound of this sequence exists, as $M(\Sigma_\bot)$ is a cpo. Thus we may define the iteration of m while b by

$$(b * m) = \bigsqcup_{n=0}^{\infty} (b * m)^n.$$

Before giving the meanings of the statements in Stat, we give one last technical definition. Let $s \in \Sigma$. Then $s[d/x] \in \Sigma$, defined by

$$s[d/x](y) = \begin{cases} d, & \text{if } x = y \\ s(y), & \text{otherwise.} \end{cases}$$

Let first $\mathcal{W}$: Form $\to W(\Sigma)$ be a function that assigns a predicate on Σ to each formula of Form. The function $\mathcal{W}$ is defined using the interpretation function for the predicate, function and constant symbols of Form. The definition is omitted here.

The meaning of unbounded nondeterministic statements could now be given by the function $\mathcal{M}$:Stat $\to M(\Sigma_\bot)$, defined as follows:

(i) $\mathcal{M}(x:=x'.Q)(s) = \begin{cases} \{s[d/x] \mid d \in D_s\}, & \text{if } D_s \neq \emptyset \\ \{\bot\}, \text{ if } D_s = \emptyset. \end{cases}$

where $D_s = \{d \in D \mid \mathcal{W}(Q)(s[d/x']) = tt\}$

(ii) $\mathcal{M}(S_1;S_2) = \mathcal{M}(S_1);\mathcal{M}(S_2)$

(iii) $\mathcal{M}(\textit{if } B \textit{ then } S_1 \textit{ else } S_2 \textit{ fi}) = (\mathcal{W}(B) \to \mathcal{M}(S_1),\mathcal{M}(S_2)]$

(iv) $\mathcal{M}(\textit{while } B \textit{ do } S_1 \textit{ od}) = (\mathcal{W}(B) * \mathcal{M}(S_1))$.

If the nondeterministic assignment statements $x:=x'.Q$ are restricted in a way which guarantees that only a finite number of values x' satisfying Q exist for any state $s \in \Sigma$ (i.e. $|D_s| < \infty$), then $\mathcal{M}(x:=x'.Q)(s) \in P_B(\Sigma_\bot)$. In this case the range of $\mathcal{M}$ is actually $M_B(\Sigma_\bot)$, and $\mathcal{M}$ gives the intuitively correct meaning to statements in Stat. If, however, no such restrictions are made, then the interpretation $\mathcal{M}$ is counterintuitive, as we will show in the next section.

3. WEAK AND STRONG TERMINATION

The problem with the meaning function M, defined above, is that it does not treat termination correctly. To see the problem, we will consider an example taken from DIJKSTRA [76,p.77]. Let S be the statement

$$S:\ \textit{while}\ x \neq 0\ \textit{do if}\ x \geq 0\ \textit{then}\ x := x-1\ \textit{else}\ x := x.(x \geq 0)\ \textit{fi od}\ .$$

Let S_1 denote the body of this loop.

Intuitively, this program must terminate for any initial value of x, be it positive, zero or negative. However, for negative initial values of x, the meaning function M says that termination is not guaranteed. To see this, let us compute

$$M(\textit{while}\ x \neq 0\ \textit{do}\ S_1\ \textit{od})(-1).$$

For simplicity, we here identify the state with the value of x in the state (we may assume that Var = {x}).

Let us denote $b = \mathcal{W}(x \neq 0)$ and $m_1 = M(S_1)$. We have that $b(x) = tt$ iff $x \neq 0$ and

$$m_1(x) = \begin{cases} \{x-1\}, & x \geq 0 \\ N, & x < 0, \end{cases}$$

where $N = \{0, 1, 2, \ldots\}$. Let further $m^i = (b * m_1)^i$, for $i = 0,1,\ldots$.

We have that for $x \geq 0$,

$$m^i(x) = \begin{cases} \{0\}, & x < i \\ \{\perp\}, & x \geq i \end{cases} .$$

Using this, we compute

$$m^0(-1) = \Omega(-1) = \{\perp\}$$
$$m^1(-1) = (b \to m_1;m^0, \Delta)(-1) = m_1;m^0(-1) = m^{0\dagger}(N) = \{\perp\}$$
$$m^2(-1) = (b \to m_1;m^1, \Delta)(-1) = m_1;m^1(-1) = m^{1\dagger}(N) = \{0,\perp\}$$
$$m^3(-1) = (b \to m_1;m^2, \Delta)(-1) = m_1;m^2(-1) = m^{2\dagger}(N) = \{0,\perp\},\ldots$$

We get that $m^i(-1) = \{0,\perp\}$, for $i \geq 2$. Consequently,

$$M(S)(-1) = \bigsqcup_{i=0}^{\infty} m^i(-1) = \{0,\perp\} .$$

Thus $M(S)(-1)$ contains $\perp$, stating that the loop S is not guaranteed to terminate for $x = -1$ initially. This contradicts our intuition about the behaviour of the loop S for this initial state.

The meaning function M actually formalises *strong termination* of while loops, instead of the usual, intuitive notion of termination. A loop

$$\textit{while}\ B\ \textit{do}\ S_1\ \textit{od}$$

is said to be strongly terminating if for each initial state s there is an integer n_s such that the loop is guaranteed to terminate in less than n_s iterations

(DIJKSTRA [78]). We will call termination that is not strong *weak termination*.

We therefore have to reinterpret the meaning of the undefined state. We have that $\perp \in M(S)(s)$ iff either it is possible that S does not terminate for the initial state s, or that S is guaranteed to terminate for s, but that the termination is weak. Thus the meaning function M does not distinguish between possible nontermination and weak termination.

Termination is always strong when the nondeterminism of a program is bounded. This is again a consequence of Königs lemma. The set of all executions of a program from some given initial state will then form a finitely branching tree. If the program is guaranteed to terminate for the given initial state, then each branch will be finite. By Königs lemma, this means that the tree itself must be finite, and therefore there is only a finite number of different branches in the tree. Thus there is a maximum number of iteration that any branch needs before termination, i.e. the termination is strong.

However, when we allow the branching of the execution tree to be infinite, Königs lemma is no longer applicable. I.e. it is possible that each branch of the tree is finite but that no longest branch exists in the tree, because there are infinitely many branches. An example is provided by the execution tree of the example treated above, for the initial state x = -1:

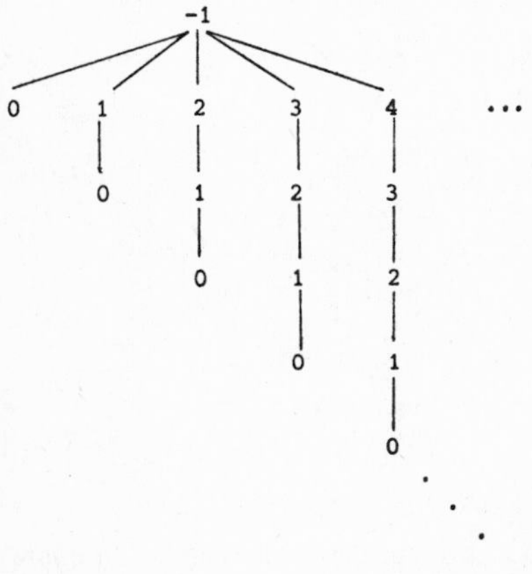

The failure of the powerdomain $P(\Sigma_\perp)$ to capture the correct notion of termination in the presence of unbounded nondeterminacy can thus be explained by noting that it is built on an erroneous inference: The fact that there after any number of iterations of a loop still could be unfinished computations going on, does not justify the conclusion that there could be a nonterminating computation of the loop.

One might hope that the right notion of termination could be captured by changing the approximation ordering, without changing $P(\Sigma_\perp)$. However, the following program will give the same sequence of approximations $\{0,\perp\}$ for x=-1 as the previous program, but will not be guaranteed to terminate:

while x≠0 *do* x:=x.(x=0 or x=1) *od*

We therefore conclude that the set $P(\Sigma_\perp)$ does not give enough information to decide between weak termination and nontermination.

The condition that we try to capture is that no branch in the execution tree of a program, for a given initial state, is infinitely expanded. This again means that we have to distinguish between different unfinished execution paths in the approximates of the loop, i.e. we are essentially forced into an operational semantics. This will be the subject of the next section.

4. OPERATIONAL SEMANTICS BASED ON $H(\Sigma_\omega)$

We will here show how the approach to nondeterminacy based on $P(\Sigma_\perp)$, explained above, can be adapted to provide a semantic definition for programs of unbounded nondeterminacy. Basically the adaption consists in considering sets of sequences of states in stead of just sets of states as is done in $P(\Sigma_\perp)$. The fact that we use sequences of states in defining the semantics of our programming language, where the sequences roughly correspond to the execution sequence of programs, is the reason for calling the semantic definition operational.

Let Σ as before be the set of states. We will have three different kinds of *execution paths*:

(i) *Terminal paths*, which are sequences of the form $\langle s_1,\ldots,s_n\rangle$, where $n \geq 1$ and $s_i \in \Sigma$ for $i = 1,\ldots,n$.

(ii) *Unfinished paths*, which are sequences of the form $\langle s_1,\ldots,s_n,\perp\rangle$, where $\perp$ is a special bottom element not in Σ, $n \geq 0$ and $s_i \in \Sigma$ for $i = 1,\ldots,n$.

(iii) *Infinite paths*, which are infinite sequences of the form $\langle s_1,s_2,\ldots\rangle$, where $s_i \in \Sigma$ for $i = 1, 2, \ldots$.

The set of all execution paths will be denoted Σ_ω.

Intuitively, a terminal path corresponds to an execution which has terminated, an infinite path corresponds to a nonterminating execution and unfinished paths correspond to executions which have not been completed. The bottom element is used to indicate that the path in question can be extended, by continuing the execution.

An approximation relation is defined in Σ_ω as follows: For paths h and h' in Σ_ω,

$$h \sqsubseteq h' \text{ iff either } h \text{ is terminal or infinite and } h = h',$$
$$\text{or } h \text{ is unfinished and } \bar{h} < h'.$$

Here $\bar{h}$ denotes the path h with the possible trailing element $\perp$ deleted. We use the notation $h \leq h'$ to express that h is an initial segment of h'($h < h'$ when h is a proper initial segment of h').

<u>LEMMA 1</u>. Σ_ω is a cpo with respect to $\sqsubseteq$.□ (Proofs of theorems and lemmas are given in BACK [79].)

The meaning of a nondeterministic program S will be a function $\mathcal{N}(S)$, which assigns to each initial state $s \in \Sigma$ the set of all possible execution paths, by which the execution can continue from s. As an example, consider the program

S': *while* x ≠ 0 *do* x := x.(x = 0 or x = 1) *od*.

The execution tree of this program, for initial state x = -1, is

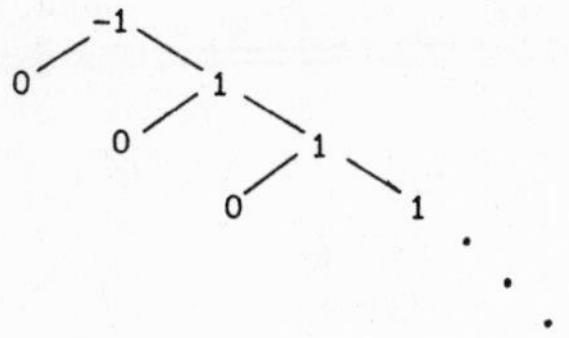

Thus we have that

$\mathcal{N}(S')(-1) = \{<0>, <1,0>, <1,1,0>, \ldots, <1,1,1,\ldots>\}$

This set contains, besides all finite paths of form <1,1,...,0> also the infinite path <1,1,...>, reflecting the fact that execution of the program does not necessarily terminate.

The set $\mathcal{N}(S')(-1)$ will actually be computed as the limit of an approximation sequence. The elements of this sequence are formed by performing only a certain number of iterations and then aborting the computation. Thus we get the set $\mathcal{N}(S)(-1)$ as the limit of the sequence

$H_0 = \{<\bot>\}$

$H_1 = \{<0>, <1,\bot>\}$

$H_2 = \{<0>, <1,0>, <1,1,\bot>\}$.

...

This corresponds to the sequence of execution trees below:

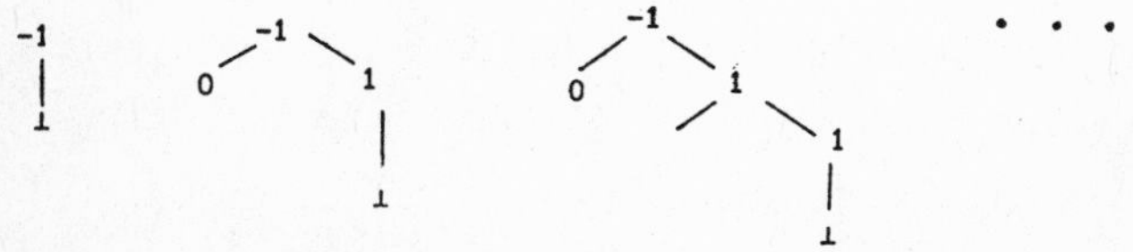

The next tree in the sequence is constructed by replacing the bottom element at the end of the unfinished path by the two possible successor states. The new unfinished path is then marked as such, by adding the bottom element to it.

The idea of constructing a new execution tree from another tree by extending some unfinished branches of the tree underlies the notion of approximation between sets of execution paths. For two sets of execution paths, H and H', approximation is defined in the same way as in $P(\Sigma_\bot)$, i.e.

$$H \sqsubseteq H' \text{ iff } \forall h \in H.\exists h' \in H'.\ h \sqsubseteq h' \text{ and}$$
$$\forall h' \in H'.\exists h \in H.\ h \sqsubseteq h'.$$

It turns out, however, that the sets of execution paths do not form a complete partial order under this ordering relation. In fact, they are not even partially ordered by the approximation relation defined. In order to get a cpo, we will need to put some restrictions on the sets of execution paths allowed.

The appropriate restrictions can be found by considering the way in which the execution trees are constructed. We start from an initial tree which only contains the path $<\bot>$. This tree is then extended step by step, by extending each unfinished branch of the tree by all its immediate successor nodes (of which there might be a finite or an infinite number). In this way we construct the finite approximations of the executions tree. Finally the execution tree itself is constructed by taking the limits of all paths in the finite approximations. In other words, if there is a growing path sequence $h_0 \sqsubseteq h_1 \sqsubseteq h_2 \sqsubseteq \ldots$ in the finite approximations, then the limit must contain the least upper bound of this path sequence. Conversely, any path in the limit must be the least upper bound of some growing path sequence in the finite approximations.

Any set of execution paths corresponding to an execution tree constructed in this manner must satisfy the following three requirements. First, the set cannot be empty. This is because the initial execution tree has the execution path $<\bot>$, and all other execution trees are constructed by extending this unfinished path.

A second property shared by all sets of execution paths generated in this way is *flatness*. This is defined as follows: A set H of execution paths is *flat* if $\bar{h} \leq h' \Rightarrow h = h'$ holds for any two paths h and h' in H. Thus, if H is flat and $h = <s_1, s_2, \ldots>$ and $h' = <s'_1, s'_2, \ldots>$ are two execution paths in H, then $s_i \neq s'_i$ for some $i \geq 1$, where both s_i and s'_i are elements of Σ. This is a consequence of the way in which unfinished paths are extended. The new paths created by extending an unfinished path are all different, because they have different last states.

The third property shared by all sets of execution paths generated by nondeterministic programs is *closedness*. A set H of execution paths is said to be *closed*, if the following holds: Let $h_0 \sqsubseteq h_1 \sqsubseteq h_2 \sqsubseteq \ldots$ be a sequence of unfinished paths of unbounded length (i.e. there is no upper bound of the lengths of the paths in the sequence). Assume that for each h_i is this sequence, there is some path h'_i in H such that $h_i \sqsubseteq h'_i$. Then the infinite path $\sqcup h_i = h$ belongs to the set H. This property is a consequence of the way in which the limit of the sequence of finite approximations is constructed: In the sequence of finite approximations of H there must be a sequence of unfinished paths of unbounded lengths growing along the path h. Otherwise the paths h'_i in H could not be constructed. But this means that the least upper bound of this sequence of unfinished paths, which also is h, must belong to the set H.

Let us now define the set $H(\Sigma_\omega)$ by

$$H(\Sigma_\omega) = \{H \subset \Sigma_\omega \mid H \text{ is nonempty, flat and closed}\}.$$

We then have the following result:

<u>THEOREM 1</u>. $H(\Sigma_\omega)$ is a cpo with respect to the ordering $\sqsubseteq$. The least upper bound of a sequence $H_0 \sqsubseteq H_1 \sqsubseteq H_2 \sqsubseteq \ldots$ of elements in $H(\Sigma_\omega)$ is

$$\bigsqcup_{i=0} H_i = \{ \bigsqcup_{i=0} h_i \mid h_i \in H_i,\ i = 0,1,2,\ \ldots \text{ and } h_0 \sqsubseteq h_1 \sqsubseteq h_2 \sqsubseteq \ldots \}. \ \square$$

$H(\Sigma_\omega)$ will now be taken as the set corresponding to $P(\Sigma_\perp)$. Analogous with the treatment of $P(\Sigma_\perp)$, we introduce the set $N(\Sigma_\omega) = \Sigma \to H(\Sigma_\omega)$, in which approximation is defined in the same way as in $M(\Sigma_\perp)$, i.e.

$$n \sqsubseteq n' \text{ iff } n(s) \sqsubseteq n'(s) \text{ for every } s \in \Sigma,$$

for $n, n' \in N(\Sigma_\omega)$. As before, $N(\Sigma_\omega)$ will be a cpo with respect to this ordering.

Continuing as before, we define the extension of $n: \Sigma \to H(\Sigma_\omega)$ to $n^\dagger: H(\Sigma_\omega) \to H(\Sigma_\omega)$. Let $n': \Sigma_\omega \to H(\Sigma_\omega)$ be defined for $h \in \Sigma_\omega$ by

$$n'(h) = \begin{cases} \{h \cdot h' \mid h' \in n(\mathrm{last}(h))\}, & \text{if } h \text{ is terminal} \\ \{h\} & \text{otherwise} \end{cases}$$

Here $h \cdot h'$ denotes the sequence h concatenated with the sequence h'. We then define

$$n^\dagger(H) = \cup \{n'(h) \mid h \in H\},$$

for $H \in H(\Sigma_\omega)$. The fact that $n^\dagger$ is well-defined is established by the lemma:

<u>LEMMA 2</u>. For any $n \in N(\Sigma_\omega)$, if $H \in H(\Sigma_\omega)$, then $n^\dagger(H) \in H(\Sigma_\omega)$. $\square$

Composition and selection in $N(\Sigma_\omega)$ is then defined as before, i.e.

$$(n_1;n_2)(s) = n_2^\dagger(n_1(s)), \text{ for } s \in \Sigma, \text{ and}$$

$$(b \to n_1,n_2)(s) = \begin{cases} n_1(s), & \text{if } b(s) = tt \\ n_2(s), & \text{if } b(s) = ff \end{cases} \quad \text{for } s \in \Sigma.$$

<u>LEMMA 3</u>. Composition and selection is monotonic in $N(\Sigma_\omega)$. $\square$

Let Δ' and Ω' be two elements in $N(\Sigma_\omega)$, defined by

$$\Delta'(s) = \{\langle s\rangle\}, \text{ for each } s \in \Sigma, \text{ and}$$

$$\Omega'(s) = \{\langle\perp\rangle\}, \text{ for each } s \in \Sigma.$$

Here <s> denotes the sequence with s as the only element.

Let $b \in W(\Sigma)$ and $n \in N(\Sigma_\omega)$. We then define $(b * n)$ as before. First, let

$$(b * n)^0 = \Omega', \text{ and}$$

$$(b * n)^{i+1} = (b \to n;(b * n)^i, \Delta'), \text{ for } i = 0,1,2,\ldots\ .$$

As before, $(b * n)^0 \sqsubseteq (b * n)^1 \sqsubseteq \ldots$ follows from the monotonicity of composition and selection. Iteration is then defined as

$$(b * n) = \bigsqcup_{i=0}^{\infty} (b * n)^i.$$

We are now ready to define the semantics of unbounded nondeterministic statements.

We assume that the function $\mathcal{W}$ is given as before. The meaning of statements in Stat is then given by the function N:Stat $\to N(\Sigma_\omega)$, defined as follows:

(i) $N(x:=x'.Q)(s) = \begin{cases} \{\langle s[d/x]\rangle \mid d \in D_s\} & \text{, if } D_s \neq \emptyset \\ \{\langle\bot\rangle\} & \text{, if } D_s = \emptyset \end{cases}$

where $D_s = \{d \in D \mid \mathcal{W}(Q)(s[d/x']) = tt\}$.

(ii) $N(S_1;S_2) = N(S_1);N(S_2)$

(iii) N(*if* B *then* S_1 *else* S_2 *fi*) $= (\mathcal{W}(B) \to N(S_1), N(S_2))$

(iv) N(*while* B *do* S_1 *od*) $= (\mathcal{W}(B) * N(S_1))$

It is easy to check that this definition does give the correct semantics for the example program in the previous section, i.e. the definition agrees with our intuition, treating both strong and weak termination as proper termination.

The domain $N(\Sigma_\omega)$ can also be used for defining the semantics of recursive programs. In order to do this, we require the following theorem.

<u>THEOREM 2</u>. Composition and selection is continuous in $N(\Sigma_\omega)$. □

Recursion can be introduced into our language by defining a new set Svar of statement variables, and adding two new productions to the recursive definition of statements:

$$S ::= \ldots X \mid \mu X.S \;.$$

Here $\mu X.S$ has the effect of executing S, with X recursively bound to S, i.e. any call on X is replaced with the execution of the statement S (X is a statement variable).

To defined the semantics of the recursive statements, we need environments E = Svar $\to N(\Sigma_\omega)$. The meaning function will now be of the type N': Stat $\to (E \to N(\Sigma_\omega))$. The semantic equations are then the following:

(i) $N'(x:=x'.Q)(\eta)(s) = N(x:=x'.Q)(s)$

(ii) $N'(S_1;S_2)(\eta) = N'(S_1)(\eta);N'(S_2)(\eta)$

(iii) N'(*if* B *then* S_1 *else* S_2 *fi*)$(\eta) = (\mathcal{W}(B) \to N'(S_1)(\eta),\ N'(S_2)(\eta))$

(iv) N'(*while* B *do* S_1 *od*)$(\eta) = (\mathcal{W}(B) * N'(S_1)(\eta))$

(v) $N'(X)(\eta) = \eta(X)$

(vi) $N'(\mu X.S)(\eta) = \mu n.N'(S_1)(\eta[n/X])$.

Here η ranges over elements of E. The notation $\eta[n/X]$ means the environment η with the value at X changed to $n \in N(\Sigma_\omega)$. The existence of the least fixed point in (vi) is guaranteed by theorem 2.

A domain similar to $H(\Sigma_\omega)$, using trees and the powerset ordering by PLOTKIN [76] has also been discussed in FRANCEZ [79], with the aim of providing a denotational semantics for nondeterministic, communicating sequential processes. Another, somewhat similar approach, has also been made by KOSINSKI [78], who is concerned with defining the denotational semantics of data flow languages.

6. SUMMARY

The mathematical semantics of nondeterministic programs has been defined in

PLOTKIN [76] using powerdomains. This definition, however, only works when the nondeterminism of the program is bounded. We have above argued that unbounded nondeterminism, introduced by a nondeterministic assignment statement, is a meaningful construct in a programming language. We have shown how to define the semantics of programs with unbounded nondeterminism using an extension of Plotkins construction $P(\Sigma_\omega)$. This extension considers sets of sequences of states (execution sequences) instead of just sets of states. This provides a richer structure, in which it is possible to give the correct semantics of unbounded nondeterminism. It was shown that the sets of execution sequences form a complete partially ordered set, provided that we restrict ourselves to sets which are nonempty, flat and closed. The reasonableness of these assumptions was also shown.

ACKNOWLEDGEMENT. I would like to thank Jaco de Bakker for pointing out the problem with unbounded nondeterminism to me, and Edger W. Dijkstra for his explanation of the difference between weak and strong termination. I am grateful to Lambert Meertens, David Park, Gordon Plotkin, Maarel Karttunen and Ari de Bruin for discussions on this subject.

REFERENCES

[78] BACK: *On the correctness of refinement steps in program development*. Dept. of Computer Science, Univ. of Helsinki, Report A-1978-4.

[79] BACK: *Semantics of unbounded nondeterminism*. Computing Centre of Univ. of Helsinki, Res. Rep. No 8, 1979.

[77] de BAKKER: *Semantics of infinite processes using generalised trees*. Math. Centrum Report IW 82/77.

[78] BAUER: *Design of a programming language for a program transformation system*. GI-8. Jahrestagung, Informatik Fachbereich 16, Springer Verlag.

[78] BOOM: *A weaker precondition for loops*. Mathematisch Centrum report IW 104/78.

[76] DIJKSTRA: *A discipline of programming*. Prentice-Hall, 1976.

[78] DIJKSTRA: Private communication.

[79] FRANCEZ & AL: *Semantics of nondeterminism, concurrency and communication*. Journal of Computer and System Sciences. Vol. 19, No. 3, December 1979, pp. 290-308.

[77] HAREL & AL: *A complete axiomatic system for proving deductions about recursive programs*. Proc. 9th annual ACM Symp. on the Theory of Computing, Boulder, Colorado, May 1977.

[78] KOSINSKI: *A straightforward denotational semantics for nondeterminant data flow programs*. 5th Annual ACM Symposium on Principles of Programming languages, Tucson, January 1978.

[76] PLOTKIN: *A powerdomain construction*. SIAM J. of Computing 5, 3, September 1976.

A SHIFTING ALGORITHM FOR MIN-MAX TREE PARTITIONING

Ronald I. Becker, University of Cape Town, South Africa
[1,2] Yehoshua Perl, Bar-Ilan University, Israel
[2] Stephen R. Schach, University of Cape Town, South Africa

1. INTRODUCTION

Let $T = (V,E)$ be an (unrooted) tree with n edges. We associate a non-negative weight $w(v)$ with every vertex $v \in V$. A q-partition of T into q connected components $T_1, T_2, \ldots, T_q$ is obtained by deleting $k = q - 1$ edges of T, $1 \leqslant k \leqslant n$. The weight $W(T_i)$ of a component T_i is then the sum of the weights of its vertices.

In this paper we present an algorithm for the following partition problem:

(a) Min-max q-partition: find a q-partition of T minimizing $\max_{1 \leqslant i \leqslant q} W(T_i)$.

We use the notation $W_{max} = \max_{1 \leqslant i \leqslant q} W(T\ )$ in a min-max q-partition of T.

A related problem is :

(b) Minimal partition bounded above: for a given bound U, find a partition of T into the minimum number of components satisfying $W(T_i) \leqslant U$.

Applications of these two problems arise in paging and over-laying techniques. Problems (a) and (b) are applied for bounding the size of a page and the number of pages respectively. Another tree-partitioning problem, that of minimizing the average number of pages accessed in a search is solved by Hosken [5] .

---

[1] Supported in part by the National Council for Research and Development of Israel

[2] Supported in part by the Council for Scientific and Industrial Research of South Africa

Both problems (a) and (b) defined for a general graph are NP-hard, even in their unweighted version, since their corresponding decision problems are NP-complete [2,3,6] . The reductions are from partitioning a graph into paths of length 2 [3].

The complexity of problem (a) for the partition of a general unweighted graph into a fixed number of components q (e.g. q = 2) is not known to us. However for a general weighted graph this problem is NP-Hard. The straightforward reduction for the weighted problem when q = 2 is from the partition problem [6].

Hadlock [4] gives a polynomial algorithm for problem (b). Kundu and Misra [7] describe a linear bottom up scanning algorithm for the same problem, for a rooted tree. Every partition of a rooted tree induces a partition, satisfying the same conditions, for the corresponding unrooted tree (and vice versa). So an algorithm for solving any partition problem for a rooted tree also provides a solution to the same problem for the corresponding unrooted tree. We shall use this property in our solution for problem (a).

The linear algorithm of Kundu and Misra [7] can be applied in a binary search procedure for the value W_{max} of a min-max q-partition problem. The complexity of the implied algorithm for a min-max q-partition problem depends on the range of the given weights.

In this paper we present a polynomial algorithm for min-max q-partitioning of a tree, whose complexity is independent of the given weights. An arbitrary terminal vertex is chosen as a root of the tree and then we use a top-down approach. The k cuts are initially assigned to the edge incident with the root. Then shifts of cuts from an edge to an adjacent edge improving the current partition are performed until no further improving shift is possible. Actually there are two kinds of shifts: down-shifts improving the partition, and side-shifts changing some previous shifts which are now wrong because of the last down-shift.

This algorithm is in the same spirit as our simpler Shifting Algorithm [8] for the related max-min q-partition problem which requires only down shifts.

2. DEFINITIONS AND STATEMENT OF THE SHIFTING ALGORITHM

Transform the given tree into a rooted directed tree by choosing an arbitrary terminal vertex as root, and imposing a top-down direction on the edges. In this paper we use the usual terminology of Graph Theory. If e is a directed edge incident from v_1 and incident to v_2, denoted by $(v_1 \to v_2)$, then we will refer to v_1 as tail(e) and to v_2 as head(e). Edge e is said to be the father of edge e_1 if head(e) = tail(e_1), and in this case e_1 is said to be the son of edge e. Edges e_1 and e_2 are said to be brothers if tail(e_1) = tail(e_2). For convenience, if a cut c is assigned to an edge $e = (v_1 \to v_2)$ then we shall use head(c), tail(c) for head(e), tail(e) respectively. We shall also refer to e as a son-edge of v_1 and to cut c as incident from v_1.

A cut is said to be down-shifted if it is moved from its present edge to a son-edge. It is said to be side-shifted at vertex v if it is moved from its present edge e_1 to a brother edge e_2, and v = tail(e_1)(=tail(e_2)).

We further require the notions of partial and complete rooted subtrees: a subtree T^1 of T is a partial (complete) subtree of T rooted at a vertex v if v is the root of T^1, and T^1 contains one (every) son of v together with all the latter's descendents.

Let A be an arbitrary assignment of the k cuts to the edges of T. We define a cut tree $C = C(T,A)$ to be a rooted tree with $k + 1$ vertices representing r, the root of T, and the k cuts of A. A cut c_1 is the son of r (of a cut c_2) if there exists a (unique) path from r (from head(c_2)) to tail(c_1) containing no cuts.

The down-component of a vertex v is obtained from the complete subtree of T rooted at v by deleting the complete subtrees rooted at the heads of all cuts of T immediately below v, if any. The down-component of a cut c is the down-component of head(c), and c is called the top cut of that component. The down-component of an edge e is the down-component of head(e). The root-component of T is the component obtained by deleting the complete subtrees rooted at the heads of the sons of r in C. The up-component of a cut is the down-component of its father in the cut tree if its father is not the root, else it is the root component. A bottom cut of a component is a son of the top cut of the component in the cut tree, if the component has a top cut, else it is a son of the root of the cut tree. The root of a component is head(c) for the top cut c, if the component has a top cut, else it is the root of the tree. A component T_i is lighter than another component T_j (or T_j is heavier than T_i) if

$W(T_i) < W(T_j)$.

The general idea of the algorithm presented below is as follows. We start with all k cuts lying on a single leaf of the tree and we regard the tree as being rooted at the terminal vertex of the leaf. We then move the cuts one at a time in such a way that the largest remaining component is decreased (see Step 3 below). In this sense it can be regarded as being a method of "steepest descent" to the state where the maximum component is smallest. These shifts are down shifts. However, as in many such methods, there are situations in which "steepest descent" does not lead to an optimal solution. It is possible that errors are made and it is then necessary that certain cuts be diverted to other branches before again moving downwards. It is fortunate that it is possible to recognize when such a wrong turn has been made before the cut makes any further progress, and to rectify the error by means of a side-shift (see Step 4 below).

We now present the algorithm

<u>The Shifting Algorithm: Min-max q-partition of a tree</u>

1. Place all k cuts on the edge incident with the root. Set BEST_MINMAX_SO_FAR ← ∞, and set BEST_PARTITION_SO_FAR equal to the starting configuration.
2. While the root component is not a heaviest component, perform steps 3 , 4 and 5 .
3. Find a cut with a heaviest down-component, and down-shift it from its current edge e to a vacant son-edge having heaviest down-component. If no such vacant edge exists then halt.
4. Traverse the path from tail(e) to the root in the bottom-up direction until a vertex v , which is the head of a cut, is encountered. For each vertex w on that path having a cut incident from w, perform the following:

   If the down-component of a cut incident from w is lighter than the down-component of the vacant son-edge e_s of w on the path, then side-shift that cut to edge e_s. If more than one cut incident from w can be side-shifted, choose a cut with a lightest down-component.
5. Set LARGESTWT equal to the weight of the largest component in the current partition A. If LARGESTWT < BEST_MINMAX_SO_FAR then set BEST_MINMAX_SO_FAR ← LARGESTWT, and set BEST_PARTITION_SO_FAR ← A.

We define a <u>terminating position</u> to be a partition at which

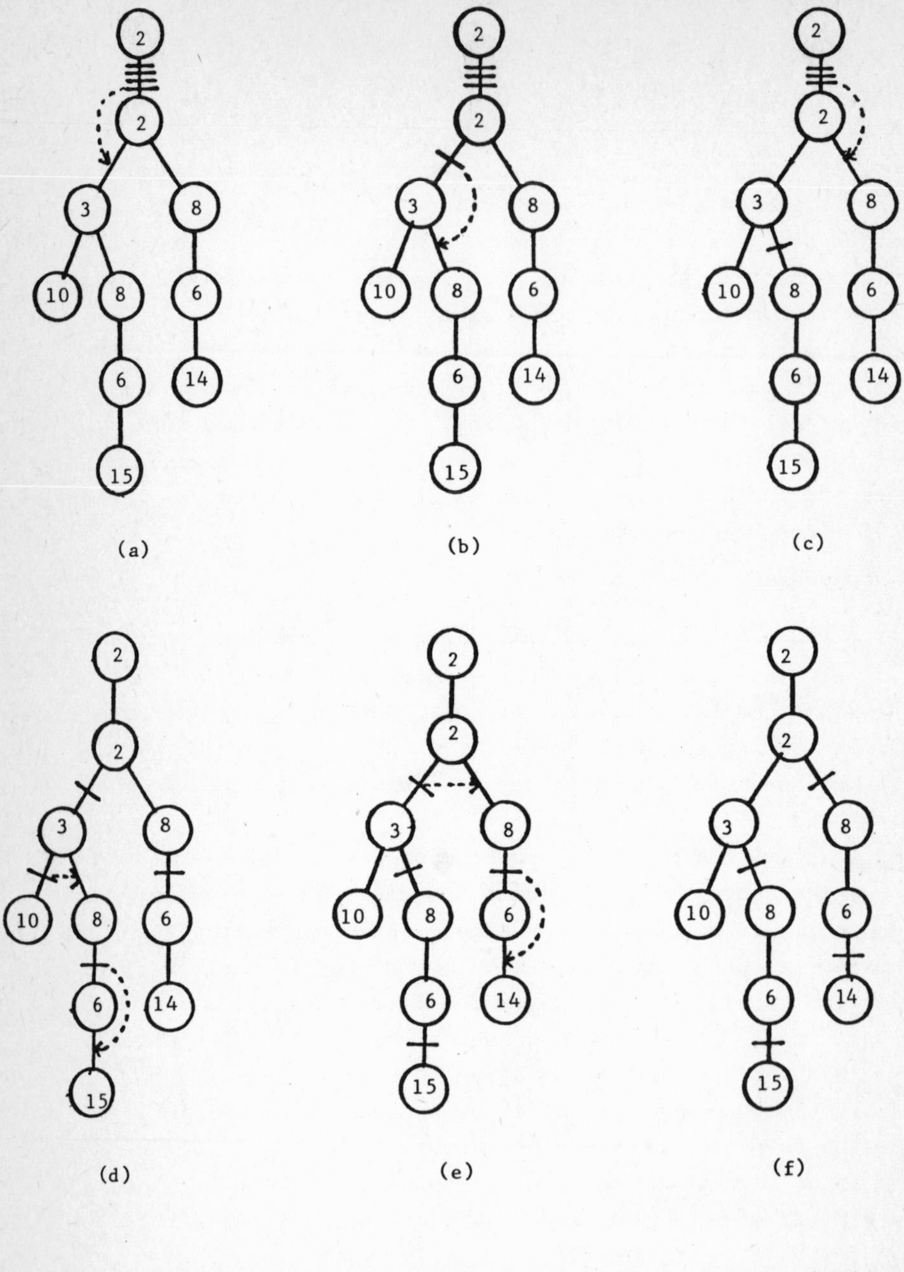

Figure 1: Illustration of the Shifting Algorithm (arrows indicate the next shift to be performed). (a) Initial partition (b) 2nd partition (c) 3rd partition (d) 9th partition, showing side-shift following next down-shift (e) 10th partition. Again a side-shift will occur. (f) 11th partition, the terminating position (as well as the resulting partition).

the algorithm terminates. A final value of BEST_PARTITION_SO_FAR is called a resulting partition of the algorithm. (The terminating partition is different from the resulting partition if some previous partition had lighter heaviest component than the terminating partition.) Figure 1 illustrates the operation of the algorithm.

3. VALIDITY PROOF OF THE SHIFTING ALGORITHM

We need the following additional definitions for the proof of the algorithm:

An algorithm partition A is a partition reached during the execution of the algorithm, while an optimal partition Q is one of minimum weight, i.e. a min-max q-partition. In what follows, the symbol A will always denote an algorithm partition, and Q an optimal partition.

For any given algorithm and optimal partition we define the following:

An exceptional algorithm cut is a top-cut in a partial subtree having one more algorithm cut than optimal cut, and the edge assigned the top-cut does not contain an optimal cut. (In Figure 2, cuts c_1 and c_2 are exceptional.)

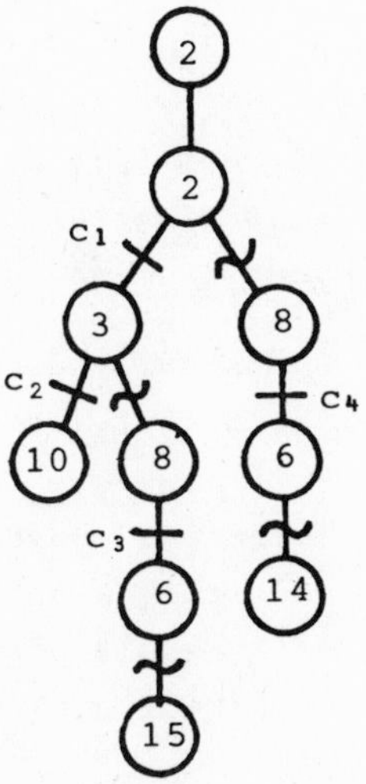

Figure 2: The partition A of Figure 1(d) (denoted by horizontal lines) is above the optimal partition Q (denoted by tildes).

A partition A is said to be above a partition Q (written A → Q) if for each vertex v of T

(i) The complete subtree rooted at v satisfies

$$\#(A \text{ cuts}) \leq \#(Q \text{ cuts})$$

(ii) Any partial subtree of v has at most one more algorithm cut than optimal cut, and a top-cut of the partial subtree is incident from v.

This definition is illustrated in Figure 2.

Proposition 1: *Let* A → Q. *Then the top-cut of a partial subtree with one more algorithm cut than optimal cut is an exceptional cut.*

Proof: From (i) of the definition of the relation "above", it follows that the top-cut in such a partial subtree has no optimal cut on the same edge. Q.E.D.

Let h(T) denote the height of tree T. We define h'(T) to be h(T) - 1.

Lemma 1: *The shifting algorithm terminates. The total number of down-shifts cannot exceed* kh'(T) *and the overall number of shifts (down and sideways) is bounded by* $k^2h'(T)$.

Proof: Since the number of possible down-shifts of each of the k cuts is bounded by h'(T), there can be at most kh'(T) down-shifts. After any one down-shift there can be at most k-1 side-shifts and the total number of down-shifts is at most k(k-1)h'(T). Hence the overall number of shifts is bounded by $k^2h'(T)$, and the algorithm terminates.

Lemma 2: *The following condition is always satisfied when the algorithm enters step 3:*

The down-component of a cut is not ***lighter*** *than the down-component of a vacant brother-edge. (Or* ***equivalently****: a side-shift of any vertex would not increase the down component of the cut shifted).*

Proof: The proof is technical and heavily uses Step 4, and Step 3. Since the result is fairly easy to accept, we omit the proof and refer the reader to [1] for details.

The following lemma has as immediate consequences Corollary 1: Mistakes do not move more than one wrong step and Corollary 2: The algorithm cannot terminate as a result of the "while" condition of Step 2 being violated without an optimal position being reached at some point. We give the proofs in full.

Lemma 3: *Let* A → Q, *and let* A *be non-optimal. Suppose that the root of some component of* A *has a complete subtree satisfying*

$$\#(\text{A cuts}) = \#(\text{Q cuts}) .$$

then this component is not a heaviest component of A.

Proof: Suppose that the root s of component D has the above property (see Figure 3). We will show below that the following property holds:

<u>Property 1</u>: It is possible to side-shift exceptional algorithm cuts lying below s thus obtaining a new component rooted at s, D' say, in such a way that no optimal cuts be on paths connecting s to the bottom cuts of D' (i.e. the cuts below s are algorithm cuts). Also, once a side-shift is made from an edge e in this process no other cut is side-shifted back to e.

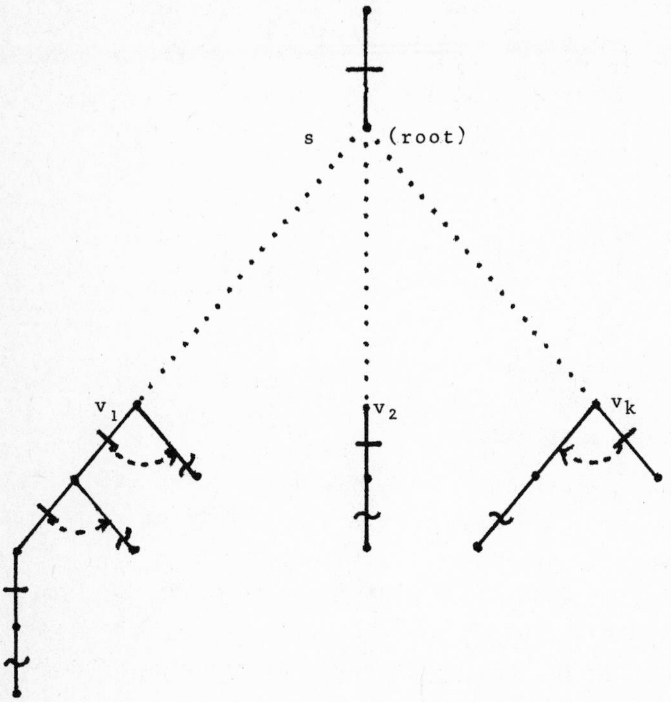

Figure 3

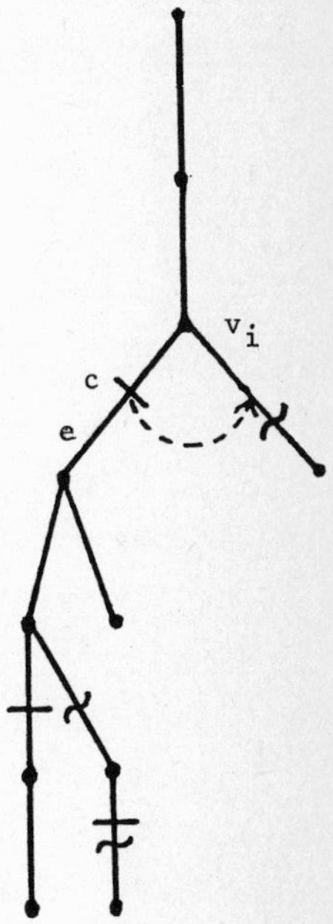

Figure 4

The horizontal lines denote the algorithm cuts of A, the tildes the optimal cuts of Q.

Assuming this, we note that by Lemma 2, no such side-shift will decrease the weight of component D. But after these side-shifts have been performed the (algorithm) cuts of D will all lie within or on the borders of an optimal component. Hence we deduce that

$$W(\text{maximum optimal component}) \geqslant W(D') \geqslant W(D) .$$

So if the original down-component D of s was the largest in A, then A must be optimal. This establishes the result.

We now prove Property 1. Consider the algorithm bottom cuts of D. Let $v_1, \ldots, v_\ell$ be the vertices incident to these cuts. By the first part of the definition of "above", the complete subtree at each v_i

must satisfy

$$\#(\text{A cuts below } v_i) \leq \#(\text{Q cuts below } v_i) \tag{1}$$

But since by assumption we have that

$$\#(\text{A cuts below } s) = \#(\text{Q cuts below } s),$$

we must have equality in (1) for each v_i, i.e.

$$\#(\text{A cuts below } v_i) = \#(\text{Q cuts below } v_i), \quad i=1, \ldots, \ell \tag{2}$$

Now by the second part of the definition of "above", a partial subtree of v_i can have at most one additional algorithm cut, which is then incident from v_i. Further, a partial subtree having as top cut an optimal cut with no algorithm cut on the same edge must have (possibly many) more optimal cuts than algorithm cuts (since in the complete subtree at any vertex v_i, $i=1,2,\ldots\ell$, $\#(\text{Q cuts}) = \#(\text{A cuts})$). Hence by (2) the number of partial subtrees rooted at v_i having an exceptional algorithm cut is greater than or equal to the number of partial subtrees at v_i with an unmatched optimal cut as top cut. Thus we have sufficient exceptional algorithm cuts to side-shift and so cover all unmatched optimal top cuts of partial subtrees of $v_i, \ldots, v_\ell$. Perform these side shifts.

Once an exceptional algorithm cut c has been side-shifted from edge e incident from v_i (see Figure 4), the son-cuts of c become bottom cuts of D'. We must now show that there are sufficient exceptional algorithm cuts below head(e) to side-shift in order to cover all unmatched optimal top cuts incident from head(e).

As in the above argument, it is sufficient to show that

$$\#(\text{A cuts below head}(e)) = \#(\text{Q cuts below head}(e)).$$

By definition of $A \to Q$, we have

$$\#(\text{A cuts below head}(e)) \leq \#(\text{Q cuts below head}(e)) \tag{3}$$

Since e is an exceptional algorithm cut, we have

$$\#(\text{A cuts below tail}(e)) = \#(\text{Q cuts below tail}(e)) + 1.$$

The desired equality therefore holds. Perform the side-shifts at head(e), etc.

The above process can be continued until no optimal cuts lie between s and the bottom cuts of D'.

<u>Corollary 1</u>: *Let* $A \to Q$ *and let* A *be non-optimal. Then no exceptional algorithm cut is down-shifted by the shifting algorithm.*

<u>Proof</u>: As in the proof of Lemma 3, starting at equation (3), the head of the exceptional algorithm cut (i.e. the root of the component below

the exceptional cut) has complete subtree with

$$\#(\text{A cuts}) = \#(\text{Q cuts}) .$$

Hence by Lemma 3 the component below the exceptional algorithm cut is never the largest and hence is never down-shifted.

Corollary 2: *Let* $A \to Q$, *and let* A *be non-optimal. Then the top component is not the largest component.*

Proof: The root of the tree is the root of the top component, and its complete subtree clearly satisfies

$$\#(\text{A cuts}) = \#(\text{Q cuts})$$

at all times. The result then follows by application of Lemma 3.

Theorem 1: *The resulting position of the Shifting Algorithm is optimal.*

Proof: If at any stage an algorithm partition is optimal, then the resulting partition is optimal (by definition of resulting, and Step 5 of the algorithm). So suppose that at no stage is the algorithm partition optimal. By Lemma 1, the algorithm terminates. It terminates either at Step 3, or when the "while" condition of Step 2 is not satisfied. Suppose firstly that termination is at Step 3. Then the heaviest down-component contains only one vertex, v say. Thus $W_{max} \leq w(v)$. But for every vertex v, $W_{max} \geq w(v)$. Hence $W_{max} = w(v)$ and the partition is an optimal partition. Suppose now that termination occurs because the "while" condition of Step 2 is not satisfied. Then the largest component of the terminating position is the root component. By Corollary 2, if we can show that the terminating position A^T satisfies $A^T \to Q$ for some optimal Q, we would have a contradiction. We therefore now show that under the above non-optimality assumption we have $A \to Q$ for every algorithm partition A and optimal partition Q.

The starting position is above any optimal partition Q. We show that if A^* is a partition obtained by some operation of the algorithm from partition A, then $A \to Q$ implies $A^* \to Q$; the result then follows by induction.

By Corollary 1, condition (ii) of the definition of "above" is always satisfied by A^*. (Intuitively, once a partial subtree has one algorithm cut too many, the extra cut "blocks" other cuts from entering the partial subtree.) It remains to be demonstrated that condition (i) also holds for A^*.

Consider firstly a side-shift at a vertex v from an edge e_1 to an edge e_2. The only complete subtrees containing e_1 or e_2 are rooted at v, and at the predecessors of v in the tree. If (ii) holds at v before the side-shifts, then clearly it holds after, and the same is true for the predecessors of v.

Next, consider a down-shift. By Lemma 3 and Step 3 of the algorithm, a cut on an edge e is not down-shifted if the complete subtree at head(e) satisfies

(A cuts below head(e)) = # (Q cuts below head(e)).

Hence, since $A \rightarrow Q$, we may assume that before the cut on edge e is down-shifted we have

(A cuts below head(e)) < # (Q cuts below head(e)).

So after the down-shift, the complete subtree at head(e) will satisfy

(A cuts at head(e)) ⩽ # (Q cuts at head(e));

As in the case of side-shifts, the only other possible vertices affected are those above head(e), and the numbers of cuts of complete subtrees of these vertices are clearly not altered. Q.E.D.

4. COMPLEXITY ANALYSIS OF THE ALGORTIHM

The algorithm can be efficiently implemented using a number of data structures. For each cut we maintain a pointer to its father in C, a list of its sons in C, and the weight of its down-component. In addition, we maintain for each cut the path it has traversed from the root. An additional edge incident with the centre of T is added to T and its terminal vertex is chosen as the root of T. Thus h'(T) = rd(T) where rd(T) denotes the number of edges in the radius of T.

A detailed implementation having complexity $O(k^3\, rd(T) + kn)$ (omitted for brevity) appears in [1]. The complexity analysis in [1] uses Lemma 1 and shows that at most O(k) operations are required for each downshift or sideshift and an additional O(n) operations are required for downshifting each of the k cuts during the execution of the algorithm as a whole.

In the introduction we mentioned an alternative solution based on a binary search procedure combined with the linear scanning algorithm of Kundu and Misra [7]. The complexity of this solution is O(n lg nc), where the weights are integers bounded by c. Thus the Shifting Algorithm is recommended for partitioning into a relatively small number of components (which is often the case in practice) while the binary search approach is superior for a large number of components. Note that for fixed k, the algorithm is linear. From examples we have examined, it appears that the average behaviour of the Shifting Algorithm is much lower than in the worst case, while for the binary search approach, the average and worst case behaviours are the same.

REFERENCES

[1] BECKER, R.I., PERL, Y. and SCHACH, S.R. A shifting algorithm for min-max tree partitioning, Technical Report, Computer Science Department, University of Cape Town, Rondebosch, South Africa.

[2] COOK, S.A. The complexity of theorem proving procedures. Proc. Third ACM Symp. on Theory of Computing, 1971, pp. 151-159.

[3] GAREY, M.R. and JOHNSON, D.S. Computers and Intractability: A Guide to the Theory of NP-Completeness, W.H. Freeman and Co., San Francisco, 1979.

[4] HADLOCK, F. Minimum spanning forests of bounded trees. Proc. Fifth S.E. Conf. on Combinatorics, Graph Theory, and Computing, 1974, pp.449-460.

[5] HOSKEN, W.H. Optimum partitions of tree addressing structures, SIAM J. Computing, 4, 3(1975), pp. 341-347.

[6] KARP, R.M. Reducibility among combinatorial problems. In Complexity of Computer, Computations, R.E. Miller and J.W. Thatcher, Eds., Plenum Press, New York, 1972, pp. 85-104.

[7] KUNDU, S. and MISRA, J. A linear tree partitioning algorithm. SIAM J. Computing, 6,1(1977), pp.151-154.

[8] PERL, Y. and SCHACH, S.R. Max-min tree partitioning. To appear in JACM.

A CHARACTERISATION OF COMPUTABLE DATA TYPES BY MEANS OF A FINITE EQUATIONAL SPECIFICATION METHOD

J.A. BERGSTRA

Department of Computer Science,
University of Leiden,
Wassenaarseweg 80, 2300 RA LEIDEN,
The Netherlands

J.V. TUCKER

Department of Computer Science,
Mathematical Centre,
2e Boerhaavestraat 49, 1091 AL AMSTERDAM,
The Netherlands

INTRODUCTION

By redefining the construction of finite equational hidden function specifications of data types, as these are made with the initial algebra methodology of the ADJ Group, we are able to give an algebraic characterisation of the computable data types and data structures. Our technical motivation are the simple notions of strong and weakly normalised Church-Rosser replacement systems studied in the λ-Calculus, and in plain mathematical terms the theorem we prove is this.

<u>THEOREM</u>. *Let* A *be a many-sorted algebra finitely generated by elements named in its signature. Then the following statements are equivalent:*
1. A *is computable.*
2. A *possesses a finite, equational hidden enrichment replacement system specification which is Church-Rosser and strongly normalising.*
3. A *possesses a finite, equational hidden enrichment replacement system specification which is Church-Rosser and weakly normalising.*

The unexplained concepts are carefully defined in Section 2, on replacement system specifications, and in Section 3, on computable algebras. In Sections 4 and 5 we prove the theorem. Section 1 explains in detail the theoretical issues to do with data types which the theorem attempts to resolve.

This paper continues our studies on the adequacy and power of definition of algebraic specification methods for data types which we began in [1], see also [5]. (It is an edited version of [2]; subsequent papers are [3,4].) Here the reader is assumed well versed in the initial algebra specification methods of the ADJ Group [6], see also KAMIN [7]; knowledge of our [1] is desirable but not, strictly speaking, essential. Prior exposure to the λ-calculus is not required, of course, but hopefully the reader is acquainted with the Church-Rosser property from ROSEN [11].

1. INITIAL ALGEBRA SEMANTICS AND DATA TYPES

A *data structure* is defined to be a many-sorted algebra A finitely generated from initial values $a_1,\ldots,a_n \in A$ named in its signature Σ. A *data type* is defined to be any class K of such data structures of common signature. At the heart of the ADJ Group's theory of data types is the idea that the semantics which characterise a data type K should be invested in the construction of an initial algebra I_K for K with the result that every data structure $A \in K$ is uniquely definable, up to isomorphism, as an epimorphic image of I_K. In its turn, this initial algebra I_K is uniquely definable, again up to isomorphism, as a factor algebra of the syntactic algebra $T(\Sigma)$ of all terms over Σ because $T(\Sigma)$ is initial for the class $ALG(\Sigma)$ of all Σ-algebras. Let $I_K \cong T(\Sigma)/\equiv_K$ where $\equiv_K$ is a congruence for which $t \equiv_K t'$ means that the terms t and t' are identical syntactic expressions as far as the semantics of K is concerned. Observe that in these circumstances we may plausibly call a data type (semantics for) K *computable* when $\equiv_K$ is decidable on $T(\Sigma)$. And the problem of syntactically specifying the data type K can be investigated through the problem of specifying the congruence $\equiv_K$.

The preferred method of prescribing $\equiv_K$ is to use a finite set of equations or conditional equations E over $T(\Sigma)$ to establish a basic set of identifications $D_E \subset T(\Sigma) \times T(\Sigma)$ and to take $\equiv_K$ as the smallest congruence $\equiv_E$ on $T(\Sigma)$ containing D_E. With reference to our [1], it is known that this method will not define all computable data types, but that it is able to define many non-computable ones. Enriching the method to allow the use of a finite number of hidden functions *does* enable it to specify *any* computable data type, but can be shown to expand the number of non-computable data types it defines.

Our proposal here is to determine the congruences for initial algebras by means of *replacement systems*. A replacement system is intended to formalise a system of deductions, governed by simple algebraic substitution rules, within which a deduction $t \to t'$ says that the rôle of t can be played by t' as far as the semantics of K is concerned, meaning $t \to t'$ implies $t \equiv_K t'$, but not conversely. What we do is to make an analysis of the congruence $\equiv_K$ through the structural behaviour of algebraically styled "proof systems" for it and from this, and an appropriate specification machinery, we are able to guess the classification theorem for computable data types. That this is *precisely* the theorem stated in the Introduction comes from the reflection that the semantics of a type K is *supposed* to be uniquely determined up to isomorphism with an initial algebra I_K, and not by a particular syntactical construction. Since the computability of $\equiv_K$ means the computability of the algebra $T(\Sigma)/\equiv_K$ under our definition and, in particular, since this notion of an algebra's computability is an isomorphism invariant, we can erase all mention of syntax in the semantical concept of a computable data type and identify these with the computable algebras.

So with regard to the content of our theorem, the reader may care to consider the ease with which statement (3) implies (1) is proved as evidence for the natural significance of strong and weakly normalised Chruch-Rosser replacement system specifications while the implication (1) implies (2) may be considered as the hard won answer to the question about adequacy: *Do these specifications define all the data types one wants*?

Because of the novelty of the specification technique and the involved proof of the theorem we shall work out the material in the case of a *single-sorted algebra* after which it becomes much easier for us to explain, and the reader to understand, the proof of the theorem in the many-sorted case.

In what follows ω denotes the set of natural numbers.

2. REPLACEMENT SYSTEMS AND THEIR SPECIFICATION

The technical point of departure is the idea of a traversal for an equivalence relation. Let A be a set and $\equiv$ an equivalence relation on A. A *traversal* for $\equiv$ is a set $J \subset A$ wherein

(i) for each $a \in A$ there is some $t \in J$ such that $t \equiv a$; and

(ii) if $t,t' \in J$ and $t \neq t'$ then $t \not\equiv t'$.

Consider an initial algebra specification (Σ,E) for a data type K where Σ gives the signature of K and E is some formula or other for axiomatising its properties so that the defining congruence $\equiv_K$ is $\equiv_E$. The choice of a traversal J for $\equiv_E$ fixes an operational view of the type as it is specified: given $t,t' \in T(\Sigma)$, to decide $t \equiv_E t'$ one imagines having to use E to calculate their prescribed "normal forms" $n,n' \in J$ and on completing these deductions $t \to_E n$, $t' \to_E n'$ one checks $n = n'$. The following bit of theory about algebraic replacement systems is made up with this in mind and is meant to abstract the bare essentials of such an operational view of data type specification.

Let A be a set and let R be a reflexive, transitive binary relation on A. We write R as $\to_R$ so to display membership $(a,b) \in R$ by $a \to_R b$ and say a *reduces* (under R or $\to_R$) to b or that b is a *reduct* (under R or $\to_R$) of a; and we shall call R and $\to_R$ a *reduction system* or a *replacement system* on the set A. Following the terminology of the λ-Calculus we make these distinctions:

An element $a \in A$ is a *normal form* for $\to_R$ if there is no $b \in A$ so that $a \neq b$ and $a \to_R b$; the set of all normal forms for $\to_R$ is denoted NF(R).

The reduction system $\to_R$ is *Church-Rosser* if for any $a \in A$ if there are $b_1,b_2 \in A$ so that $a \to_R b_1$ and $a \to_R b_2$ then there is $c \in A$ so that $b_1 \to_R c$ and $b_2 \to_R c$.

The reduction system $\to_R$ is *weakly normalising* if for each $a \in A$ there is some normal form $b \in A$ so that $a \to_R b$.

The reduction system $\to_R$ is *strongly normalising* if there does not exist an infinite chain

$$a_0 \to_R a_1 \to_R \dots \to_R a_n \to_R \dots$$

wherein for $i \in \omega$, $a_i \neq a_{i+1}$.

A reduction system is Church-Rosser and weakly normalising if, and only if, every element reduces to a unique normal form. Clearly strong normalisation entails weak normalisation.

Let $\equiv_R$ denote the smallest equivalence relation on A containing $\to_R$. It is an easy exercise to show that for $a,a' \in A$

$$a \equiv_R a' \iff \text{there is a sequence } a = b_1,\dots,b_k = a' \text{ such that for each pair } b_i,b_{i+1} \text{ there exists a common reduct } c_i,\ 1 \le i \le k-1.$$

Schematically:

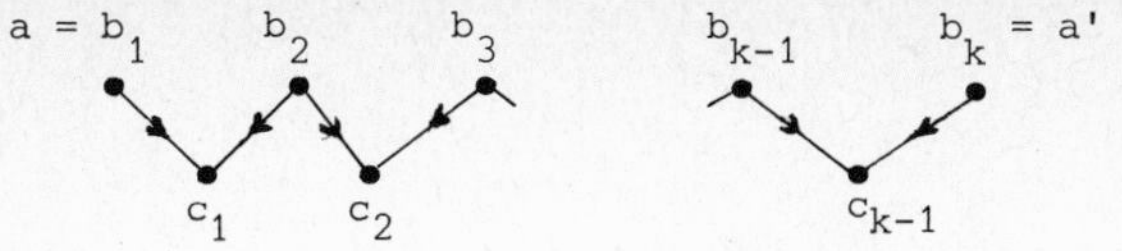

Using this characterisation of $\equiv_R$ it is straightforward to prove these facts.

2.1. LEMMA. *The replacement system* $\to_R$ *on* A *is Church-Rosser if, and only if, for any* $a,a' \in A$ *if* $a \equiv_R a'$ *then there is* $c \in A$ *so that* $a \to_R c$ *and* $a' \to_R c$.

2.2. LEMMA. *Let* $\to_R$ *be a Church-Rosser weakly normalising replacement system on* A. *Then the set of normal forms* NF(R) *is a traversal for* $\equiv_R$.

Suppose now that A is an algebra. Then by an *algebraic replacement system* $\to_R$ on the algebra A we mean a replacement system $\to_R$ on the domain of A which is closed under its operations in the sense that for each k-ary operation σ of A,

$$a_1 \to_R b_1,\ldots,a_k \to_R b_k \quad \text{implies } \sigma(a_1,\ldots,a_k) \to_R \sigma(b_1,\ldots,b_k).$$

2.3. BASIC LEMMA. *If* $\to_R$ *is an algebraic replacement system on an algebra* A *then* $\equiv_R$ *is a congruence on* A. *If* $\to_R$ *is, in addition, Church-Rosser and weakly normalising then the set of normal forms of* $\to_R$ *is a traversal for* $\equiv_R$.

To achieve our goal of constructing algebraic replacement systems on the algebra $T(\Sigma)$ we need to explain how a replacement system is generated by a set of one-step reductions and, furthermore, how these sets of one-step reductions can be determined from quite arbitrary sets. We must built up this equipment for both set-theoretic and algebraic replacement systems.

Let $\to_R$ be a replacement system on a set A. $S \subset A \times A$ is said to *generate* $\to_R$ *as a set of one-step reductions* if S is reflexive and $\to_R$ is the smallest transitive set containing S, the so called *transitive closure of* S.

Let $\to_R$ be an algebraic replacement system on an algebra A. $S \subset A \times A$ is said to *generate* $\to_R$ *as a set of algebraic one-step reductions* if S is reflexive, S is closed under *unit substitutions* in the following sense: writing $(a,b) \in S$ as $a \to_S b$, for any k-ary operation σ of A, for any $1 \le i \le k$ and $a_1,\ldots,a_{i-1},a_{i+1},\ldots,a_k \in A$, and $a \to_S b$ it follows that $\sigma(a_1,\ldots,a_{i-1},a,a_{i+1},\ldots,a_k) \to_S \sigma(a_1,\ldots,a_{i-1},b,a_{i+1},\ldots,a_k)$. And $\to_R$ is the transitive closure of S.

In the set-theoretic case any reflexive set determines a replacement system in its transitive closure. In the algebraic case any reflexive set, closed under unit substitutions, can be shown to determine an algebraic replacement system in its transitive closure. Thus, in either case, starting with an arbitrary set $D \subset A \times A$ one can close it up to the smallest one-step reduction relation containing it, which we write $\to_{D(1)}$, and hence to the set-theoretic or algebraic replacement system $\to_D$ which is its transitive closure.

Let us now apply these ideas to specify algebraic replacement systems on $T(\Sigma)$.

Let $T_\Sigma[X_1,\ldots,X_n]$ be the set of all polynomials over Σ in indeterminates $X_1,\ldots,X_n$. Let $T_\Sigma[X] = \bigcup_{n\in\omega} T_\Sigma[X_1,\ldots,X_n]$.

Given a set $E \subset T_\Sigma[X] \times T_\Sigma[X]$ first notice that if $(t,t') \in E$ then without loss of generality we can assume $t,t' \in T_\Sigma[X_1,\ldots,X_n]$ for sufficiently large n. Then we can define a set $D_E \subset T(\Sigma) \times T(\Sigma)$ by

$$D_E = \{(t(s_1,\ldots,s_n),\ t'(s_1,\ldots,s_n)) : (t,t') \in E \ \&\ s_1,\ldots,s_n \in T(\Sigma)\}$$

and so obtain the smallest set of algebraic one-step reductions containing D_E, which we write $\to_{E(1)}$, and from it the algebraic replacement relation it generates, denoted $\to_E$. In these circumstances we denote by $NF(\Sigma,E)$ the set of all normal forms of $\to_E$ and by $\equiv_E$ the congruence associated to $\to_E$. Let $T(\Sigma,E) = T(\Sigma)/\equiv_E$. Finally, if $(t(X_1,\ldots,X_n),\ t'(X_1,\ldots,X_n)) \in E$ then we prefer to write $t(X_1,\ldots,X_n) \geq t'(X_1,\ldots,X_n) \in E$, which we refer to as a *reduction equation*.

From these definitions we see how to equationally specify algebraic replacement systems which in turn specify algebras.

An algebra A of signature Σ_A is said to have a *finite equational replacement system specification* (Σ,E) if $\Sigma = \Sigma_A$ and E is a finite set of reduction equations over $T(\Sigma)$ such that the reduction system $\to_E$ on $T(\Sigma)$ defines a congruence $\equiv_E$ which specifies A by $T(\Sigma,E) \cong A$.

Recall that if A is an algebra of signature Σ_A and $\Sigma \subset \Sigma_A$ then $A|_\Sigma$ is the algebra obtained from A by deleting the constants and operations of A not named in Σ. $\langle A\rangle_\Sigma$ is smallest Σ-algebra contained in A.

An algebra A of signature Σ_A is said to have a *finite, equational hidden enrichment replacement specification* (Σ,E) if $\Sigma_A \subset \Sigma$ and E is a finite set of reduction equations over $T(\Sigma)$ such that the reduction system $\to_E$ on $T(\Sigma)$ determines the algebra $T(\Sigma,E)$ and

$$T(\Sigma,E)|_{\Sigma_A} = \langle T(\Sigma,E)\rangle_{\Sigma_A} \cong A.$$

Since the algebras which model data structures are finitely generated by elements named in their signatures, any such algebra A is automatically *minimal* in the sense that $A|_{\Sigma_A} = \langle A\rangle_{\Sigma_A}$.

The structural properties of a specification (Σ,E), such as the Church-Rosser and normalisation properties, are taken from those of its replacement relation $\to_E$. To gain acquaintance with the specification method, we leave to the reader the proof of this proposition.

2.4. LEMMA. *If* A *is a finite algebra then* A *possesses a finite, equational replacement system specification which is Church-Rosser and strongly normalising.*

And we conclude with a technical fact about set-theoretic replacement systems of use later on. Let A be a set. A set of one-step reductions $\to_{R(1)}$ which generates a reduction system $\to_R$ on A is said to be *finitely branching* if for each $a \in A$ the set $\{b \in A: a \to_{R(1)} b\}$ is finite.

The reduction system $\to_R$ on A together with its generating set of one-step reductions $\to_{R(1)}$ is said to be *weakly Church-Rosser* if for any $a \in A$, if $a \to_{R(1)} b_1$ and $a \to_{R(1)} b_2$ then there is $c \in A$ such that $b_1 \to_R c$ and $b_2 \to_R c$.

2.5. LEMMA. *Let $\to_R$ be a strongly normalising system on A generated by a finitely branching set of one-step reductions $\to_{R(1)}$. If $\to_R$ is weakly Church-Rosser with respect to $\to_{R(1)}$ then $\to_R$ is Church-Rosser.*

PROOF. By a chain of non-trivial one-step reductions from $a \in A$ of length k we mean a sequence $a = a_0 \to_{R(1)} a_1 \to_{R(1)} \dots \to_{R(1)} a_k$ wherein $a_i \neq a_j$ $0 \leq i,j \leq k$. Define $\|a\|$ = maximum length of any such chain from a. This $\|\cdot\|: A \to \omega$ is a total function thanks to *König's Infinity Lemma* and the hypothesis of strong normalisation. We prove the proposition by induction on the value of $\|a\|$.

The basis case is automatic because $\|a\| = 0$ iff a is a normal form.

As induction hypothesis assume the Church-Rosser property true of all reducts of $b \in A$ such that $\|b\| < \|a\|$. Let $a \to_R b_1$ and $a \to_R b_2$. We take the non-trivial case where a, b_1, b_2 are mutually distinct.

Since $\to_{R(1)}$ generates $\to_R$ choose a_1, a_2 such that for $i = 1,2$ $a \to_{R(1)} a_i \to_R b_i$ and notice that $\|a_i\| \leq \|a\|$. Let c_0 be a common reduct of a_1, a_2 supplied by the weak Church-Rosser property. By the induction hypothesis applied to a_1, a_2 we can choose c_1, c_2 as common reducts of c_0, b_1 and c_0, b_2 respectively. Moreover since $\|c_0\| < \|a\|$ we can apply the induction hypothesis again to obtain c as a common reduct of c_1, c_2. Clearly c is also a common reduct of b_1, b_2. Q.E.D.

3. COMPUTABLE ALGEBRAS

Our definition of a *computable algebra* is taken from M.O. RABIN [10] and A.I. MAL'CEV [9], independent papers devoted to founding a general theory of computable algebraic systems and their computable morphisms.

An algebra A is said to be *computable* if there exists a recursive set of natural numbers Ω and a surjection $\alpha: \Omega \to A$ such that to each k-ary operation σ of A there corresponds a recursive *tracking function* $\bar{\sigma}: \omega^k \to \omega$ which commutes the following diagram,

$$\begin{array}{ccc} A^k & \xrightarrow{\sigma} & A \\ \uparrow{\scriptstyle \alpha^k} & & \uparrow{\scriptstyle \alpha} \\ \Omega^k & \xrightarrow{\bar{\sigma}} & \Omega \end{array}$$

wherein $\alpha^k(x_1,\dots,x_k) = (\alpha x_1,\dots,\alpha x_k)$. And, furthermore, the relation $\equiv_\alpha$, defined on Ω by $x \equiv_\alpha y$ iff $\alpha(x) = \alpha(y)$ in A, is recursive. In case this relation $\equiv_\alpha$ is recursively enumerable we say A is *semicomputable*.

Both notions, in these formal definitions, become so called *finiteness conditions* of Algebra: isomorphism invariants possessed of all finite structures. And also noteworthy is this other invariance property from MAL'CEV [9]:

If A is a finitely generated algebra computable or semicomputable under both $\alpha: \Omega_\alpha \to A$ and $\beta: \Omega_\beta \to A$ then α and β are *recursively equivalent* in the sense that there exist recursive functions f,g which commute the diagram:

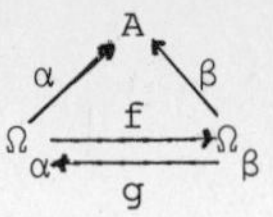

See MAL'CEV [9].

Given A computable under α then combining the associating tracking functions on the domain Ω makes up a recursive algebra of numbers from which α is an epimorphism to A. Applying the recursiveness of $\equiv_\alpha$ to this observation it is easy to prove this useful fact.

3.1. LEMMA. *Every computable algebra* A *is isomorphic to a recursive number algebra* Ω *whose domain is the set of natrual numbers,* ω, *if* A *is infinite, or else is the set of the first* m *natural numbers,* ω_m, *if* A *is finite of cardinality* m.

We proved this in its many-sorted version in [1]. Obviously, no such isomorphic representation is possible for the semicomputable algebras for otherwise they would be computable.

If A is computable under α then a set $S \subset A^n$ is (α-)*computable* or (α-)*semicomputable* accordingly as $\alpha^{-1}(S) = \{(x_1,\ldots,x_n)\in\Omega^n : (\alpha x_1,\ldots,\alpha x_n)\in S\}$ is recursive or r.e.

3.2. LEMMA. *Let* A *be a computable algebra and* $\equiv$ *a congruence* A. *If* $\equiv$ *is computable or semicomputable then the factor algebra* A/$\equiv$ *is computable or semicomputable accordingly.*

The algebras T(Σ) are always computable under any of their standard gödel numberings. Of course, it was this fact we had in mind when we spoke of a data type K being computable when its defining congruence $\equiv_K$ is decidable. Wherever $\equiv_K$ is syntactically determined by some specification mechanism (Σ,E) it is customary to speak of the *word* or *term problem* for (Σ,E) and mean the decidability of $\equiv_K$. In any case, through Lemma 3.2 and isomorphism invariance, we can now redefine a data type to be computable when its initial algebra is computable.

Relying on the reader's experience in constructively manipulating syntax, we set him or her the proofs of these last lemmas as easy, though instructive, exercises.

3.3. LEMMA. *Let* (Σ,E) *be a finite, equational replacement system specification. Then the basis set* D_E, *the one-step reduction relation* $\to_{E(1)}$, *the replacement system* $\to_E$, *the set of normal forms* NF(Σ,E), *and the congruence* $\equiv_E$ *are all semicomputable. In particular,* T(Σ,E) *is a semicomputable algebra.*

3.4. PROPOSITION. *Let* (Σ,E) *be a finite, equational replacement system specification which is Church-Rosser and weakly normalising. Then* T(Σ,E) *is a computable algebra.*

3.5. LEMMA. *Let* A *be a semicomputable algebra with semicomputable congruence* $\equiv$. *If there exists a semicomputable traversal for* $\equiv$ *then the factor algebra* A/$\equiv$ *is a computable algebra.*

4. PROOF OF THE THEOREM

A strongly normalising reduction system specification is at the same time a weakly normalising reduction system specification so statement (2) automatically implies statement (3). Since computability is an isomorphism invariant, Proposition 3.4 proves (3) implies (1). Thus this section is devoted to proving statement (1) implies statement (2). The case where A is finite the reader has proved as Lemma 2.4 and so we assume A to be infinite.

By Lemma 3.1, we can take A isomorphic to a recursive number algebra R = $(\omega; f_1,\ldots,f_p, c_1,\ldots,c_q)$ and concentrate on building a replacement system specification for R. First we shall build a complicated recursive number algebra R_0 by adding to R a variety of recursive functions.

Given a total recursive function f: $\omega^k \to \omega$ then, by the *Kleene Normal Form Theorem*, this may be written $f(x) = U(\mu z.T(e,x,z))$ where U and T are the so called *Kleene computation function* and *T-predicate*, respectively, and e is some index for f. Since U and T are primitive recursive so are the functions

$$h(z,x) = U(\mu z' \le z.[z' = z \vee T(e,x,z')])$$

$$g(z,x) = \begin{cases} 0 & \text{if } \exists z' \le z.\ T(e,x,z) \\ 1 & \text{otherwise.} \end{cases}$$

From these functions we can define a recursive function

$$t(z,x,0) = h(z,x)$$
$$t(z,x,y+1) = t(z+1,x,g(z+1,x))$$

so that f is factorised into t,h,g in the sense that $f(x) = t(0,x,1)$. (The uninitiated reader should consult M. MACHTEY & P. YOUNG [8].)

R_0 is constructed by adding 0 and the successor function x+1 on ω to R and, for each recursive operation f of R, adding the corresponding factorising functions h,g,t along with the list Δ of all primitive recursive functions used in the primitive recursive definitions of h and g.

Clearly, $R_0|_\Sigma = \langle R_0\rangle_\Sigma = R$ and so it is sufficient to show R_0 has a finite, equational replacement system specification which is Church-Rosser and strongly normalising. Let Σ_0 be the signature of R_0. The specifying reduction equations E_0 in mind are defined as follows. For each operation f,t,h,g of R_0, of the kind last mentioned, if $\underline{f},\underline{t},\underline{h},\underline{g}$ are their corresponding function symbols in Σ_0, then we take with X = $(X_1,\ldots,X_k)$

$$(-1)\quad \underline{f}(X) \ge \underline{t}(\underline{0},X,S(\underline{0}))$$

$$(0)\quad \underline{t}(Z,X,\underline{0}) \ge \underline{h}(Z,X)$$
$$\underline{t}(Z,X,S(Y)) \ge \underline{t}(S(Z),X,\underline{g}(S(Z),X))$$

For each function symbol $\underline{\lambda} \in \Sigma_0$ corresponding to a primitive recursive function λ in the list $\Delta \cup \{h,g\}$ we add equations determined by these case distinctions.

(1) If $\lambda(x_1,\ldots,x_k) = x_i$ then add $\underline{\lambda}(X_1,\ldots,X_k) \ge X_i$

(2) If $\lambda(y) = y+1$ then add $\underline{\lambda}(Y) \ge S(Y)$.

(3) If $\lambda(x) = \mu(\mu_1(x),\ldots,\mu_n(x))$ then add $\underline{\lambda}(X) \ge \underline{\mu}(\underline{\mu}_1(X),\ldots,\underline{\mu}_n(X))$ where here $x = (x_1,\ldots,x_k)$ and $X = (X_1,\ldots,X_k)$.

(4) If $\lambda(0,x) = \mu_1(x)$
$\lambda(y+1,x) = \mu_2(y,x,\lambda(y,x))$
then add
$\underline{\lambda}(\underline{0},X) \geq \underline{\mu}_1(X)$
$\underline{\lambda}(S(Y),X) \geq \underline{\mu}_2(Y,X,\underline{\lambda}(Y,X))$
where, again, x and X are possibly vectors.

Finally, we must take care of the constants of Σ in Σ_0. If $\underline{c}$ names the numerical constant c then add $\underline{c} \geq S^c(\underline{0})$. We number this as equation (5).

Thus (Σ_0,E_0) is a finite, equational replacement system specification and it remains to verify the Church-Rosser property and strong normalisation, and to show $T(\Sigma_0,E_0) \cong R_0$.

Call a term $t \in T(\Sigma)$ *strongly normalising* (with respect to E_0) if there does not exist an infinite chain $t = t_0 \to t_1 \to \ldots \to t_n \to \ldots$ where for $i,j \in \omega$ $t_i \neq t_j$ and $\to$ is the reduction relation determined by E_0. Most of the theorem is proved on showing

4.1. LEMMA. *If* t *is strongly normalising then it possesses a unique normal form of the kind* $S^n(0)$ *for some* $n \in \omega$.

4.2. LEMMA. *Every term in* $T(\Sigma)$ *is strongly normalising.*

The proof of Lemma 4.1 verifies the Church-Rosser property and combined with Lemma 4.2 shows our specification (Σ_0,E_0) to be of the required type. Given these lemmas, we know from Basic Lemma 2.3 that $\{S^n(\underline{0}): n \in \omega\}$ is a traversal for $T(\Sigma_0,E_0)$, and to prove this algebra isomorphic to R_0 we can use the map $\phi(n) = [S^n(\underline{0})]$. Since ϕ is known to be a bijection $R_0 \to T(\Sigma_0,E_0)$, all that must be verified is that ϕ is a homomorphism. This requires an inductive argument on the complexity of terms along the lines of the proof of Lemma 4.2. Because the reasoning is much simpler than that for Lemma 4.2, and routine for any reader with a little algebraic experience, we take the liberty of omitting it. Thus, to complete the theorem it remains for us to prove Lemmas 4.1 and 4.2.

PROOF OF LEMMA 4.1. For $t \in T(\Sigma_0)$ the restriction of $\to$ defines a replacement system on the set $Red(t) = \{s \in T(\Sigma_0): t \to s\}$ which is generated by any set of one-step reductions $\to_1$ for $\to$ also restricted to Red(t). If t is strongly normalising with respect to $\to$ then $(Red(t),\to)$ is a strongly normalising set-theoretic replacement system. It is a routine matter to check that $\to$ is weakly Church-Rosser with respect to $\to_1$ by considering term complexity and to see that $\to_1$ is finitely branching. So we may apply Lemma 2.4 to deduce that $(Red(t),\to)$ is Church-Rosser as well as strongly normalising. (This together with Lemma 4.1 proves our specification Church-Rosser!) A corollary of this is the fact that t has a normal form with respect to $\to$ and it is unique.

Now we argue that $NF(\Sigma_0,E_0) = \{S^n(\underline{0}): n \in \omega\}$. It is easy to see that $\{S^n(0): n \in \omega\} \subset NF(\Sigma_0,E_0)$ because a term $S^n(\underline{0})$ cannot be further reduced by equations from E_0. On the other hand we can rule out all other terms as normal forms by these case distinctions. Let $t \in T(\Sigma_0)$.

If $t = \underline{c} \in \Sigma_0$, a constant naming $c \neq 0$, then equation (5) permits a reduction to $S^c(\underline{0})$ and so since $\underline{c}$ can be reduced it is not a normal form.

If $t = \underline{\lambda}(s_1,\ldots,s_k)$ where $\underline{\lambda}$ is any function symbol of Σ_0 *except* S then, again, there is a reduction to a distinct term to be had from the equations written down for $\underline{\lambda}$ in the construction of E_0.

Finally, if $t = S^n(r)$, where r is a term of the first two kinds, then since r has been seen to possess some non-trivial reduction so does t (as $\to$ is an algebraic replacement system). Q.E.D.

PROOF OF LEMMA 4.2. We prove that each $t \in T(\Sigma_0)$ is strongly normalising by induction on the complexity of t.

As basis consider all constants. Let $\underline{c} \in \Sigma_0$ name the numerical constant c. By inspection of E_0, there is at most one reduction possible from t and this leads to a normal form, *viz.* $\underline{c} \geq S^c(\underline{0})$.

The induction step is precisely this lemma.

4.3. LEMMA. *Let* $s_1,\ldots,s_k \in T(\Sigma_0)$ *be strongly normalising and let* $\underline{\lambda}$ *be a k-ary function symbol of* Σ_0. *Then* $\underline{\lambda}(s_1,\ldots,s_k)$ *is strongly normalising.*

PROOF. First we order the signature Σ_0. For each operation f_i of R let h_i, g_i, t_i be the functions factoring f_i and let Δ_i be the list of primitive recursive functions used in the definitions of the h_i and g_i, those of h_i preceeding those of g_i and each of these two lists ordered by the complexity of the primitive recursive definitions of the h_i and g_i respectively. Thus we order the constants and operations of R_0 into the list

$$0, c_1,\ldots,c_q,\ x+1, \Delta_1,\ldots,\Delta_p,\ h_1,\ldots,h_p, g_1,\ldots,g_p, t_1,\ldots,t_p, f_1,\ldots,f_p$$

and let the signature Σ_0 of R_0 be ordered in this way. We shall now prove the lemma by induction on the position of $\underline{\lambda}$ in the ordering of Σ_0. One general remark, for any term $t = \underline{\lambda}(s_1,\ldots,s_k)$, is that an infinite reduction sequence from t which does not involve a reduction from E_0 determined by $\underline{\lambda}$ would require an infinite reduction sequence from one of its subterms in contradiction to the assumption that they are strongly normalising. Thus in the argument *we need only consider reduction sequences from* $t = \underline{\lambda}(s_1,\ldots,s_k)$ *which apply the reduction equations in* E_0 *written down for* $\underline{\lambda}$.

For this reason the basis $\underline{\lambda} = S$ is obvious. If $t = S(r)$ then inspection of E_0 confirms no reduction from t determined by S to be possible since r is irreducible.

So assume as induction hypothesis that $\underline{\mu}(s_1,\ldots,s_k)$ is strongly normalising for all function symbols $\underline{\mu}$ preceeding $\underline{\lambda}$ in Σ_0. The proof of the induction step divides into 6 cases conveniently distinguished by λ (rather than $\underline{\lambda}$). The first 3 cases

$$\lambda(x_1,\ldots,x_k) = x_i \qquad \lambda(y) = y+1 \qquad \lambda(x) = \mu(\mu_1(x),\ldots,\mu_k(x))$$

where $x = (x_1,\ldots,x_k)$ are straightforward and are omitted.

CASE 4. $\lambda(0,x) = \mu_1(x)$

$\lambda(y+1,x) = \mu_2(y,x,\lambda(y,x))$

Let $t = \underline{\lambda}(r,s)$ where $s = (s_1,\dots,s_k)$ corresponding to $x = (x_1,\dots,x_k)$. Now by Lemma 4.1 any strongly normalising term τ reduces to a unique normal form $S^n(\underline{0})$ from which we can define the value of τ to be $val(\tau) = n$. We do this case by an induction argument on the value of r.

First of all observe that at the stage in a reduction from t at which (4) is applied r must have been reduced to $\underline{0}$ or to some $S(\tau)$. In the former case we are in the basis of the induction for $val(r) = 0$. The next term in the sequence has leading function symbol $\underline{\mu}_1$ which preceeds $\underline{\lambda}$ and so we are done by the main induction hypothesis.

Consider $val(r) = n > 0$ and assume as induction hypothesis that for all strongly normalising terms τ with $val(\tau) < n$ then $\underline{\lambda}(\tau,s)$ is strongly normalising. Since $val(r) \neq 0$ we know that on the first application of equation (4) in a reduction sequence from t that r has been reduced to some $S(\tau)$. And that the next element in the sequence is $\underline{\mu}_2(\tau,s',\lambda(\tau,s'))$ where $s' = (s'_1,\dots,s'_k)$ and $s_i \to s'_i$, $1 \le i \le k$. Now since s and r are strongly normalising so are s' and τ. Moreover, since $val(\tau) < n$, by our latest induction hypothesis $\underline{\lambda}(\tau,s')$ is strongly normalising. Since $\underline{\mu}_2$ preceeds $\underline{\lambda}$ in Σ_0, the main induction hypothesis shows the reduct strongly normalising and the sequence to terminate.

Remember this case covers function symbols corresponding to h_i, g_i as well as those functions in Δ_i.

CASE 5. $\lambda(z,x,0) = h(z,x)$

$\lambda(z,x,y+1) = \lambda(z+1,x,g(z+1,x))$

Let $t = \underline{\lambda}(r,s,u)$ where $s = (s_1,\dots,s_k)$ corresponding to $x = (x_1,\dots,x_k)$. As before, observe that at the first stage in a reduction sequence from t at which equation (0) is applied it must have been reduced to $\underline{0}$ or to some $S(\tau)$. The first possibility does not permit an infinite continuation of the sequence because the next element is some $\underline{h}(r',s')$ where r' and s' are strongly normalised reducts of r and s and this term is strongly normalising by the induction hypothesis since $\underline{h}$ preceeds $\underline{\lambda}$ in Σ_0. Therefore only sequences of the second kind need careful consideration.

Let $val(\tau)$, for τ a strongly normalising term, be just as in Case 4. Define for any term of the kind $t = \underline{\lambda}(r,s,u)$ the number

$$\chi(r,s) = (\mu z)[g(z,val(s)) = 0] \dot{-} val(r)$$

wherein val(s) abbreviates $(val(s_1),\dots,val(s_k))$.

We do this case by a concise induction on the value $\chi(r,s)$. As basis we have t with $\chi(r,s) = 0$. Consider a reduction sequence from t in which the first application of equation (0) produces $\underline{\lambda}(S(r'),s',\underline{g}(S(r),s'))$ from $\underline{\lambda}(r',s',S(\tau))$. Since $r \to r'$, $s \to s'$ we have $\chi(r',s') = 0$ and

$$val(r') \ge (\mu z)[g(z,val(s)) = 0].$$

And, thanks to the main induction hypothesis, we know that all the subterms of $\underline{\lambda}(S(r'),s',\underline{g}(S(r'),s'))$ are strongly normalising. From this information we can deduce $val(\underline{g}(S(r'),s')) = 0$ so if a second application of equation (0) is made in the sequence then we will have a sequence of the kind considered, and proved finite, at the opening of this case; whereas if no second application of (0) is made in the sequence then the reductions must be made to the known strongly normalising subterms and so it must terminate as observed in the opening of the induction argument of Lemma 4.3. The calculation required is this

$$\begin{aligned} val(\underline{g}(S(r'),s')) &= g(val(r')+1,val(s')) \\ &= g((\mu z)([g(z,val(s')) = 0], val(s'))) \\ &= 0. \end{aligned}$$

Consider $t = \underline{\lambda}(r,s,u)$ with $\chi(r,s) = n > 0$ and assume as induction hypothesis that if r_1,s_1,u_1 are strongly normalising and $\chi(r_1,s_1) < n$ then $\underline{\lambda}(r_1,s_1,u_1)$ is strongly normalising. Consider a reduction sequence from t in which the first application of equation (0) produces $\underline{\lambda}(S(r'),s',\underline{g}(S(r'),s'))$ from $\underline{\lambda}(r',s',S(\tau))$. By our assumptions and the main induction hypothesis all subterms of the new reduct are strongly normalising. Moreover, $\chi(S(r'),s') < \chi(r',s') = \chi(r,s) = n$ and therefore by the latest induction hypothesis $\underline{\lambda}(S(r'),s',\underline{g}(S(r'),s'))$ is strongly normalising and the reduction sequence must terminate.

CASE 6. $\lambda(x) = f(x)$.

This is, by now, obvious.

Having concluded the proof of Lemma 4.3 we have also concluded the argument for Lemma 4.2. Q.E.D.

5. THE MANY SORTED CASE

We assume the reader thoroughly acquainted with the technical foundations of the algebra of many-sorted structures for which no reference can better substitute for the ADJ's basic paper [6].

In notation consistent with our [1], we assume A to be a many-sorted algebra with domains $A_1,\ldots,A_{n+m}$ and operations of the form

$$\sigma^{\lambda,\mu} = \sigma^{\lambda_1,\ldots,\lambda_k;\mu} : A_{\lambda_1}\times\ldots\times A_{\lambda_k} \longrightarrow A_\mu$$

where $\lambda_i,\mu \in \{1,\ldots,n+m\}$, $1 \le i \le k$.

The concepts and machinery of Section 2 must be reformulated, but this is not difficult: An *algebraic replacement system* R on A consists of a collection of set-theoretic replacement systems $R_1,\ldots,R_n$ on its domains which satisfy the property that for each operation $\sigma^{\lambda,\mu}$ of A, with arguments $a_{\lambda_1},\ldots,a_{\lambda_k}$ and $b_{\lambda_1},\ldots,b_{\lambda_k}$, where $a_{\lambda_i},b_{\lambda_i} \in A_{\lambda_i}$, if $a_{\lambda_1} \rightarrow_{R_1} b_{\lambda_1},\ldots,a_{\lambda_k} \rightarrow_{R_k} b_{\lambda_k}$ then $\sigma^{\lambda,\mu}(a_{\lambda_1},\ldots,a_{\lambda_k}) \rightarrow_{R_\mu} \sigma^{\lambda,\mu}(b_{\lambda_1},\ldots,b_{\lambda_k})$. The classification of replacement systems and the definitions of the associated congruence, one-step reductions and so on as *families* of single sorted relations proceed along the lines established for generalising algebraic ideas from single-sorted to many-sorted algebras; this is true of their properties and of the mechanisms for specifying replacement systems.

To lift Section 3 to computable many-sorted algebras is also quite straightforward and, in fact, has been virtually written out already in our [1]. Those lemmas pertaining to replacement system specifications require only the appropriate introduction of sort indices into their proofs.

Up to and including the proofs that (2) implies (3), and (3) implies (1), for the full theorem in its many-sorted case, it may be truly said that no new ideas or techniques are required.

Consider the proof that (1) implies (2). With the help of a trick (the real subject of this section) we are able to construct this proof with the toolkit of Section 4. Dispensing with an easy case where all the domains of A are finite, we assume A to be a many-sorted computable algebra with at least one domain infinite.

Without loss of generality we can take these domains to be $A_1,\ldots,A_n$, $B_1,\ldots,B_m$ where the A_i are infinite and the B_i are finite of cardinality $b_i + 1$. The generalised Lemma 3.1 provides us with a recursive many-sorted algebra of numbers R with domains $\Omega_1,\ldots,\Omega_n$ and $\Gamma_1,\ldots,\Gamma_m$ where $\Omega_i = \omega$ for $1 \le i \le n$, $\Gamma_i = \{0,1,\ldots,b_i\}$ for $1 \le i \le m$, and R is isomorphic to A. When not interested in the cardinality of a domain of R we refer to it as R_i, $1 \le i \le n+m$. The aim is to give R a finite equational hidden function replacement system specification.

The first task is to build a recursive number algebra R_0 by adding to R new constants and functions. The main idea is to code the many-sorted algebra R into its first infinite sort Ω_1 by means of functions $R_i \to \Omega_1$ and $\Omega_1 \to R_i$ and recursive tracking functions on Ω_1 associated to the multisorted operations of R. At the same time we shall dissolve the finite sorts by adding them as sets of constants. Here is the formal construction.

For each infinite sort i we add as a new constant of sort i the number $0 \in \Omega_i$ and the successor function x+1. For each finite sort i we add *all* the elements of Γ_i as *new* constants.

Each domain R_i is coded into Ω_1 by adding the function $\mathit{fold}^i(x) = x$, and is recovered by adding the function $\mathit{unfold}^i\colon \Omega_1 \to R_i$, defined for infinite sorts i by $\mathit{unfold}^i(x) = x$, and for finite sorts i by

$$\mathit{unfold}^i(x) = \begin{cases} x & \text{if } x \le b_i \\ b_i & \text{otherwise.} \end{cases}$$

Next we add for each operation $f = f^{\lambda,\mu}$ of R a recursive tracking function $\hat{f}\colon \Omega_1^k \to \Omega_1$ which commutes the following diagram:

$$\begin{array}{ccc} R_{\lambda_1}\times\ldots\times R_{\lambda_k} & \xrightarrow{\ f\ } & R_\mu \\ \mathit{fold}^{\lambda_1}\times\ldots\times\mathit{fold}^{\lambda_k} \big\downarrow & & \big\uparrow \mathit{unfold}^\mu \\ \Omega_1\times\ldots\times\Omega_1 & \xrightarrow{\ \hat{f}\ } & \Omega_1 \end{array}$$

And, just as in the single-sorted case, we factorise $\hat{f}$ into functions t,h,g and add these along with all the primitive recursive functions arising from the primitive recursive definitions of h and g. That is all. Observe $R_0|_\Sigma = \langle R_0 \rangle_\Sigma = R$, so it remains to give a finite equational replacement system specification for R_0 which is Church-Rosser and strongly normalising. Let Σ_0 be the signature of R_0 in which ${}^i\underline{0}$, ${}^i\underline{S}$, $FOLD^i$, $UNFOLD^i$ name the zero, successor function, and coding maps associated to sort i; for convenience we drop the sort superscript in case i = 1. Here are the requisite set of equations E_0, beginning with the operations of R.

Let $f = f^{\lambda,\mu}$ be an operation of R named by function symbol $\underline{f} \in \Sigma \subset \Sigma_0$ and let $\hat{f}$ be its associated tracking map on Ω_1 named by $\hat{\underline{f}} \in \Sigma_0$. First, following the procedure of Section 4, write out all the equations assigned to $\hat{f}$ and its factorisation. Secondly, add this equation to "eliminate" $\underline{f}$

$$\underline{f}(X_{\lambda_1},\ldots,X_{\lambda_k}) \geq UNFOLD^{\mu}(\hat{\underline{f}}(FOLD^{\lambda_1}(X_{\lambda_1}),\ldots,FOLD^{\lambda_k}(X_{\lambda_k}))$$

where X_{λ_i} is a variable of sort λ_i. Do this for every operation of R.

Turning to the coding machinery, consider first the folding functions. For each infinite sort i add the equations,

$$FOLD^i({}^i\underline{0}) \geq \underline{0}$$
$$FOLD^i({}^iS(X_i)) \geq S(FOLD^i(X_i))$$

where X_i is a variable of sort i.

For each finite sort i, if ${}^i\underline{\underline{c}} \in \Sigma_0 - \Sigma$ is a new constant of sort i denoting number $c \in \Gamma_i$ then add

$$FOLD^i({}^i\underline{\underline{c}}) \geq S^c(\underline{0}).$$

Secondly consider the unfolding functions. For each infinite sort i add the equations,

$$UNFOLD^i(\underline{0}) \geq {}^i\underline{0}$$
$$UNFOLD^i(S(X)) \geq {}^iS(UNFOLD^i(X))$$

where X is a variable of sort 1.

For each finite sort i, if ${}^i\underline{\underline{c}}$ is as before then add the equations

$$UNFOLD^i(S^c(\underline{0})) \geq {}^i\underline{\underline{c}} \qquad \text{if } c < b_i$$
$$UNFOLD^i(S^c(X)) \geq \underline{\underline{b}}_i \qquad \text{if } c \geq b_i$$

where b_i is the last element of Γ_i and is named in $\Sigma_0 - \Sigma$ by $\underline{\underline{b}}_i$; and X is a variable of sort 1.

And finally we consider the equations for the constants. For each infinite sort i, if ${}^i\underline{c} \in \Sigma$ denotes the number $c \in \Omega_i$ then add ${}^i\underline{c} \geq {}^iS^c(\underline{0})$. For each finite sort i, if ${}^i\underline{c} \in \Sigma$ denotes the number $c \in \Gamma_i$ and ${}^i\underline{\underline{c}} \in \Sigma_0 - \Sigma$ is its new constant symbol then we remove the duplication by adding ${}^i\underline{c} \geq {}^i\underline{\underline{c}}$.

This completes the construction of E_0.

What remains of the proof follows closely the arguments of Section 4. Here the sets of normal forms are, of course, $\{{}^{i}S^{c}({}^{i}\underline{0}) : c \in \omega\}$ when i is an infinite sort, and $\{{}^{i}\underline{\underline{c}} : c \in \Gamma_i\}$ when i is a finite sort. And the arguments which lift Lemma 4.1 and 4.2 are *in all essential respects the same*. Given, then, that (Σ_0, E_0) is Church-Rosser and strongly normalising, the normal forms being a traversal for $\equiv_{E_0}$, we can prove $R_0 \cong T(\Sigma_0, E_0)$ by using the mappings ϕ^i defined $\phi^i(c) = [{}^{i}S^{c}({}^{i}\underline{0})]$ for i an infinite sort and $\phi^i(c) = {}^{i}\underline{\underline{c}}$ for i a finite sort.

REFERENCES

[1] BERGSTRA, J.A. & J.V. TUCKER, *Algebraic specifications of computable and semi-computable data structures*, Mathematical Centre, Department of Computer Science Research Report IW 115, Amsterdam, 1979.

[2] ———, *A characterisation of computable data types by means of a finite, equational specification method*, Mathematical Centre, Department of Computer Science Research Report IW 124, Amsterdam, 1979.

[3] ———, *Equational specifications for computable data types: six hidden functions suffice and other sufficiency bounds*, Mathematical Centre, Department of Computer Science Research Report IW 128, Amsterdam, 1980.

[4] ———, *On bounds for the specification of finite data types by means of equations and conditional equations*, Mathematical Centre, Department of Computer Science Research Report IW 131, Amsterdam, 1980.

[5] ———, *On the adequacy of finite equational methods for data type specification*, ACM-SIGPLAN Notices 14 (11) (1979) 13-18.

[6] GOGUEN, J.A., J.W. THATCHER & E.G. WAGNER, *An initial algebra approach to the specification, correctness and implementation of abstract data types*, in R.T. YEH (ed.) *Current trends in programming methodology* IV, *Data structuring*, Prentice-Hall, Engelwood Cliffs, New Jersey, 1978, 80-149.

[7] KAMIN, S., *Some definitions for algebraic data type specifications*, SIGPLAN Notices 14 (3) (1979) 28-37.

[8] MACHTEY, M. & P. YOUNG, *An introduction to the general theory of algorithms*, North-Holland, New York, 1978.

[9] MAL'CEV, A.I., *Constructive algebras*, I., Russian Mathematical Surveys, 16 (1961) 77-129.

[10] RABIN, M.O., *Computable algebra, general theory and the theory of computable fields*, Transactions American Mathematical Society, 95 (1960) 341-360.

[11] ROSEN, B.K., *Tree manipulating systems and Church-Rosser theorems*, J. Association Computing Machinery, 20 (1973) 160-187.

A NOTE ON SWEEPING AUTOMATA

Piotr Berman
Mathematical Institute of PAS
Nowowiejska 10/50, 00 653-Warszawa
Poland

1. Introduction

Last year at the Eleventh Annual ACM Symposium on Computing (May 1979) Michael Sipser presented his paper: "Lower Bounds on the Size of Sweeping Automata". In this paper he stated a new question concerning automata size arised during efforts at solving the L = ?NL problem. Namely, this problem is related to the minimal size of two-direction finite automata for certain languages in cases when they are deterministic and nondeterministic (2dfa and 2nfa respectively). For details see [1] and [2] .

In his paper M. Sipser defined sweeping automata, denoted sa, as such 2dfa which do not change the direction of motion except at the ends of the input tape. He proved the theorem that the relationship between the minimal size of sa and 2nfa for certain languages implies an aswer to the L = ?NL problem (in fact he claims that his proof is the same as that given by Lingas on a similar theorem in [1], and it really is). Moreover Sipser proved that for the series of regular languages B_n the minimal sizes of 1nfa and sa which recognize B_n are n and 2^n respectively. He also conjectured that there is a series of languages for which minimal sizes of 2dfa and sa are O(n) and 2^n respectively. The proof of this fact is the subject of this work.

2. Main result

DEFINITION. Sweeping automaton is such a 2dfa that changes the direction of motion from rightward to leftward only over the letter $\dashv$ and from leftward to rightward only over the letter $\vdash$.

Let Σ be a finite alphabet, $\{\vdash, \dashv\} \cap \Sigma = \emptyset$, and A is a sa. Then the recognizing of $L \subset \Sigma^*$ by A means that A halts on the input $\vdash w \dashv$ in the accepting state iff $w \in L$.

THEOREM. There is a series of regular languages C_n and $c > 0$ that for any n the minimal sizes of 2dfa and sa recognizing C_n are less than cn, and at least 2^n respectively. Symbols of the alphabet of C_n are nonnegative integers not greater than 2^n:

$$\Sigma_n = \{0, 1, 2, \ldots, 2^n\}$$
$$C_n = -(\Sigma_n^* \, 012 \ldots (2^n - 1) \, \Sigma_n^*)$$

3. Proof of 2dfa's upper bound

C_n may be recognized by a $(4n + 3)$-state 2dfa which will check whether two consecutive letters represent two consecutive numbers by comparison of their binary digits. Say that $s + 1 = t$ and digits of s and t are $\alpha_1, \ldots, \alpha_n$ and $\beta_1, \ldots \beta_n$ respectively. It is easy to see that then there is a number i such tat:

(i) $1 < i \leqslant n$

(ii) $\bigwedge_{1 \leqslant j < i} \alpha_j = \beta_j$

(iii) $\alpha_i = 0$ and $\beta_i = 1$

(iv) $\bigwedge_{i < j \leqslant n} \alpha_j = 1$ and $\beta_j = 0$

Obviously the existence of such i implies also that $s + 1 = t$.

Now it is easy to design a $(4n + 3)$-state 2dfa which recognizes C_n. First in the initial state it seeks the letter 0. If 0 is found the automaton subsequently checks (using 4n states) whether consecutive letters represent consecutive numbers. Another state is needed to make the transition from one checking to another. If the last letter for which this test will succeed is the $(2^n - 1)$ one the automaton will reject the word. If not it will be again in the initial state.

4. Proof of sa lower bound

The proof will be similar to Sipser's one in 3 , it differs mainly in an example of a series of languages. C_n has three properties of B_n that enable us to proof that it has the same lower bound for sa size, i.e. 2^n. These properties are the following:

1° There is $x \in \sum_n$ that $w \in C_n$ and $v \in C_n$ iff wxv C_n (this x is 2^n).

2° There is $t \in \sum^*$ that $t \notin C_n$, $|t| = 2^n$ and $uvw = t$ and $|v|>0$ implies $uw \in C_n$ (this t is $012\ldots(2^n - 1)$).

3° If $u \notin C_n$ then for any v and w $vuw \notin C_n$.

Now we will describe an automata model which is used in the proof.

DEFINITION. A parallel finite automaton P is a string of 1dfa, called components, and an accepting set of state strings $F \subset Q_1 \times \ldots \times Q_k \times Q_1 \times \ldots \times Q_k$, where Q_i is the state set of A_i.

P recognizes L means that $w \in L$ iff $\langle A_1(w), \ldots, A_k(w), A_1(w^r), \ldots \ldots, A_k(w^r) \rangle \in F$, where $A_i(w)$ is the state reached by running A_i on w and where w^r is the reverse of w.

The lower bound proof is divided into two lemmas.

LEMMA 1. If for a language L there is a k-state sa recognizing L then there is a parallel automaton accepting L whose components all have k states.

For the proof see [3].

LEMMA 2. If a parallel automaton recognizes C_n then one of its components has at least $2^n - 1$ states.

In the proof of lemma 2 some notations are used. If q is a state of a 1dfa then q(s) denotes the state reached by starting at state q and applying an input word s. For S a set of words and R a set of states let R(S) denote $\{q(s) : q \in R \text{ and } s \in S\}$. $\# K$ denotes the cardinality of the set K. A word over $\sum_n$ will be called j-word if it belongs to C_n, otherwise it will be called s-word.

DEFINITION. Let A be a 1dfa with a state set Q_A. A j-word g is A-generic if $\# Q(g) \leqslant \# Q(t)$ for any j-word t. Say g is k-generic if it is A-generic for every 1dfa A with at most k states. Say g is k^r-generic if g is j-word and for any j-word t and k-state A holds $\# Q_A(g^r) \leqslant \leqslant \# Q_A(t^r)$.

SUBLEMMA. There are k-generic and k^r-generic words.

Proof. For every 1dfa A let $f_A : C_n \to N$, $f(w) = \# Q_A(w)$.
If $m = \min f(C_n)$, than any member of $f^{-1}(m)$ is A-generic. Next, if w is A-generic and vw and wu are j-words then vw and wu are also A-generic (because A is deterministic and $\# Q_A(s)$ cannot increase during scanning a word). Since the number of different k-state 1dfa's is finite, one can list them $A_1, A_2, \ldots, A_p$.
If w_i is A_i-generic for $i = 1, 2, \ldots, p$, then $w = w_1 x w_2 x \ldots x w_p$ is k-generic. The case of k^r-generic word is similar.

Let us assume that $P = \langle\langle A_1, \ldots, A_k\rangle, F\rangle$ recognizes C_n, Q_i is the state set of A_i, $m = \max(\# Q_1, \ldots, \# Q_k)$, g is m-generic, w is m^r-generic and s is the shortest s-word $01\ldots(2^n - 1)$.

Now some remarks. It is easy to see that if a word t is m-generic (m^r-generic) then $2^n t 2^n$ is also m-generic (m^r-generic). Thus we may assume that the words g and w are of the $2^n t 2^n$ form. For $i = 1, \ldots, k$ let $R_i = Q_i(g)$ and $S_i = S_i = Q_i(w^r)$. Three facts are to be established.

1) For any word v $\quad R_i(vg) \subset R_i$

$\quad S_i(v^r w^r) \subset S_i$

2) If vg is j-word then $R_i(vg) = R_i$ and
if wv is j-word then $S_i(v^r w^r) = S_i$

3) If v is s-word then exists such i that
$R_i(wvg) \neq R_i$ or $\quad S_i(g^r v^r w^r) \neq S_i$

Statement 1) holds since $R_i(vg) = (R_i(v))(g) \subset Q_i(g) = R_i$

$$S_i(v^r w^r) = (S_i(v^r))(w^r) \subset Q_i(w^r) = S_i$$

Statement 2) holds since $Q_i(gvg) = R_i(vg) \subset R_i = Q_i(g)$ and $\# Q_i(gvg) \geqslant \# Q_i(g)$, because g is m-generic and gvg j-word (as the concatenation of two j-words with the first one ended by 2^n). The case of S_i is similar.

With regard to statement 3) let us assume by contradiction that for any i $R_i(wvg) = R_i$ and $S_i(g^r v^r w^r) = S_i$. Then $\pi(q) = q(wvg)$ is a permutation on R_i (for any i) and $\tau(q) = q(g^r v^r w^r)$ is a permutation on S_i.
Hence for any i $A_i(gw) = q_o^i(gw) = q_o^i(g(wvg)^{m!}w) = A_i(g(wvg)^{m!}w)$ and similarly $A_i((gw)^r) = A_i([g(wvg)^{m!}w]^r)$, what yields the contradiction because P cannot distinguish j-word gw from s-word $g(wvg)^{m!}w$.

Let i be such that $R_i(wsg) \neq R_i$ or $S_i(g^r s^r w^r) \neq S_i$. To simplify the proof let us assume that $R_i(wsg) \neq R_i$ (we know that $R_i(wsg) \subset R_i$). By applying the more sophisticated reasoning of Sipser from [3] we may prove that $\# Q_i \geqslant 2^{n/2} - 1$.

We know that $f: R_i \to R_i$, $f(q) = q(wsg)$ is not one-one, hence there are $q_1, q_2 \in R_i$ that $q_1(wsg) = q_2(wsg)$ and $q_1 \neq q_2$. Then there are x, y such that $0 \leqslant x < y \leqslant 2^n - 1$ and $\langle q_1(w01\ldots x), q_2(w01\ldots y)\rangle =$ $= \langle q_1(w01\ldots y), q_2(w01\ldots y)\rangle$ or $\# Q_i \geqslant 2^{n/2} - 1$ (otherwise we have 2^n different members of a set which has at most $(2^{n/2} - 1)^2 < 2^n$ members). The latter is our thesis and first yields a contradition.
Indeed, then we have $q_1(w01\ldots x(y+1)\ldots(2^n - 1)g) = q_1(w01\ldots y(y+1)\ldots$ $\ldots(2^n - 1)g) = q_2(w01\ldots y(y+1)\ldots(2^n - 1)g) = q_2(w01\ldots x(y+1)\ldots$ $\ldots(2^n - 1)g)$ what means that for j-word $t = w01\ldots x(y+1)\ldots(2^n - 1)g$ holds $q_1(t) = q_2(t)$, so $R_i(t) \neq R_i$ what contradicts the statement 2).

With this weaker proof the Theorem holds for $\overline{C}_n = C_{2n}$ and $c = 8 + \varepsilon$, while the stronger method yields $c = 4 + \varepsilon$.

5. Final remarks

For any n the language C_n may be recognized by a (4n - 2)-state 1nfa*). Hence the upper bounds for sa recognizing C_n yields a relationship between 1nfa and sa which is similar to Sipser's one although weaker. Unfortunately these relationship do not imply any answer to L = ?NL question because the length of words that are used in the proof is exponential with respect to n. If somebody proved a similar relationship for a series of languages with a polynomial length of words then he would obtain a negative answer to the L = ?NL question.

---

*) The design of (4n - 2)-state 1nfa recognizer of C_n is based upon the following observation. For a string of n-digit binary numbers $s_1 \ldots s_p$ it holds

$$s_1 \ldots s_p = 01 \ldots (2^n - 1) \text{ iff}$$

(i) $s_1 = 0$ and $s_p = (2^n - 1)$

(ii) $s_i(n) = 1 - s_{i+1}(n)$ for $i = 0, 1, \ldots, p-1$

(iii) $s_i(j) = s_{i+1}(j)$ and $s_i(j+1) = s_{i+1}(j+1)$
or
$s_i(j+1) + 2s_i(j) + 1 = s_{i+1}(j+1) \mod 4$
for $i = 0, 1, \ldots, p-1$ and
$j = 1, 2, \ldots, n-1$

(iv) $s_i \neq 0$ for $i = 2, 3, \ldots, p$

To accept a word w as a j-word it is necessary to know that this statement does not hold for any subword of w. This means that after each letter 0 there is another 0 or 2^n before any $(2^n - 1)$, or no $(2^n - 1)$ at all, or (and this case is most important) there is a place between this 0 and the nearest $(2^n - 1)$ that is in contradiction with point (ii) or (iii). Such place can be found nondeterministically using 4n - 4 states. If the recognizer does not find such place it will reject the whole word.

REFERENCES

[1] Berman P. and A. Lingas, On the complexity of regular languages in terms of finite automata, ICS PAS Report no 304, 1977, Warszawa.

[2] Sakoda W.J. and M. Sipser, Nondeterminism and the size of two-way finite automata, Tenth Annual STOC, 1978.

[3] Sipser M., Lower Bounds on the size of sweeping automata, Eleventh Annual ACM Symposium on Theory of Computing, May 1979.

BORDER RANK OF A pxqx2 TENSOR AND THE OPTIMAL APPROXIMATION OF A PAIR OF BILINEAR FORMS

D. Bini

Istituto Matematico dell'Università di Pisa

Abstract. The border rank t_B over the field $\mathbb{F}$ of the non degenerate pxqx2 tensor $\mathbb{A} = [B,C]$ is such that $\max(p,q) \leqslant t_B \leqslant \max(p,q)+\delta$, with $\delta=0$ if the invariant polynomials of $B+\lambda C$ have roots in the closure of $\mathbb{F}$, $\delta=1$ otherwise. A pair of non degenerate pxq bilinear forms can be approximated with at most max(pxq)+1 non scalar multiplications over any field.

1. Introduction.

The problem of computing a set of bilinear forms with the least number of non scalar multiplications (1) over a field $\mathbb{F}$ is connected to a problem of linear algebra, namely to find the rank of a third order tensor [13]. In few cases this problem has been solved completely, see for example [9] concerning Toeplitz matrices, [12], [14] for 2x2 matrix multiplication, [7] for the computation of quarternions product.

Recently Ja'Ja' [8] has faced, analyzed and completely solved a problem which includes a wider class of cases, namely the problem of the evaluation of a pair of bilinear forms. In other words the rank of a pxqx2 tensor has been completely determined in terms of the elementary divisor of a suitable matrix.

In a recent paper [4] it has been pointed out that a set of bilinear forms can be evaluated with a multiplicative complexity lower than the rank of the associated tensor by allowing an arbitrarily small error. The complexity of such an approximate algorithm equals the border rank of the associated tensor (see sect. 2). Approximate algorithms and the border rank have been used to

(1) A multiplication axb is non scalar over $\mathbb{F}$ if $a,b \notin \mathbb{F}$. For the sake of brevity we use the term "multiplication" instead of "non scalar multiplication".

approximate nxn matrix product with $O(n^{\alpha})$ complexity, $\alpha \simeq 2.7799$ [3], to compute nxn matrix product with $O(n^{\alpha} \log n)$ complexity, $\alpha \simeq 2.7799$ [2], $\alpha \simeq 2.52$ [11], [10].

In this paper we consider the problem of finding the border rank of a pxqx2 tensor over a field $\mathbf{F}$ using the Kronecker's theory of pencils. Our main result is expressed by proposition 4.4, namely the border rank t_B of $\mathbb{A}=[B,C]$ is such that $\max(p,q) \leq t_B \leq \max(p,q)+\delta$ with $\delta=0$ if the polynomial $\det(\tilde{B}+\lambda\tilde{C})$ has roots in the closure of the field $\mathbf{F}$, $\delta=1$ otherwise, where $\tilde{B}+\lambda\tilde{C}$ is the regular kernel of the pencil $B+\lambda C$. An analogous result holds when $\mathbf{F}$ is finite. From the computational complexity point of view this fact implies that any pair of pxq bilinear forms can be approximated over $\mathbf{F}$ by $\max(p,q)+1$ multiplications. Other consequences are exposed in section 3, (namely: the product of two polynomial modulo a n-degree polynomial can be approximated with n multiplications over $\mathbf{C}$; the product of complex numbers cannot be approximated with less than three multiplications over the real field $\mathbf{R}$; the result about a topological property of triangular Toeplitz matrices, exposed in [1] is improved in a very simple way).

2. Definitions and notations.

Let $\mathbf{F}$ be a numeric field, of cardinality f. If $f=\infty$ we endow $\mathbf{F}$ with the topology induced by the distance $d(x,y)=|x-y|$, $x,y \in \mathbf{F}$ and we set $\bar{\mathbf{F}}$ for the topological closure of $\mathbf{F}$ so that we have $\mathbf{R}=\bar{\mathbf{Q}}$ where $\mathbf{Q}$ and $\mathbf{R}$ are respectively the rational and the real field. We denote with $\mathbf{C}$ the complex field.

Let $\mathbf{F}[\varepsilon]$, $\mathbf{F}(\varepsilon)$ be respectively the ring of polynomials over $\mathbf{F}$ and the field of rational functions over $\mathbf{F}$ in the variable ε.

Let $\mathbb{A}=\{a_{ijk}\}$, $a_{ijk} \in \mathbf{F}$, $i=1,\dots,p$, $j=1,\dots,q$, $k=1,\dots,m$, be a pxqxm third order tensor. $\mathbb{A}$ is a degenerate tensor if one of the following three sets of matrices $\{A_k : A_k \equiv \{a_{ijk}\}, k=1,\dots,m\}$, $\{B_j : B_j \equiv \{a_{ijk}\}, j=1,\dots,q\}$, $\{C_i : C_i \equiv \{a_{ijk}\}, i=1,\dots,p\}$, consists of linearly dependent matrices. The corresponding sets of bilinear forms $\{x^T A_k y: k=1,\dots,m\}$, $\{x^T B_j z: j=1,\dots,q\}$, $\{y^T C_i z: i=1,\dots,p\}$ are said to be degenerate if $\mathbb{A}$ is degenerate. The matrices A_k, B_j, C_i are the slabs of $\mathbb{A}$ and when it occurs we denote $\mathbb{A}$ by its slabs, namely $\mathbb{A}=[A_1,\dots,A_m]$. Let us recall some definitions and properties of the rank and the border rank of a tensor [4]

[5].

<u>Definition 2.1</u>. The <u>rank</u> of $\mathbb{A}$ over $\mathbf{F}$ is the minimal integer t such that there are u_{is}, v_{js}, w_{ks} $\in \mathbf{F}$, s=1,...,t, with

$$\mathbb{A}=\left\{\sum_{s=1}^{t} u_{is} v_{js} w_{ks}\right\}. \tag{2.1}$$

<u>Definition 2.2</u>. Let $f=\infty$, the <u>border rank</u> of $\mathbb{A}$ is the minimal integer t_B such that $\forall\ \delta>0$ there exists a tensor $\mathbb{E}=\{e_{ijk}\}$, $e_{ijk} \in \mathbf{F}$ such that $|e_{ijk}|<\delta$ and $\mathbb{A}+\mathbb{E}$ has rank t_B, namely

$$\mathbb{A}+\mathbb{E}=\left\{\sum_{s=1}^{t_B} \tilde{u}_{is} \tilde{v}_{js} \tilde{w}_{ks}\right\}. \tag{2.2}$$

In the case in which $\mathbf{F}$ is finite we need to give a different definition of border rank which, in the infinite case, would be a strong restriction (see proposition 3.4).

<u>Definition 2.3</u>. The <u>algebraic border rank</u> of $\mathbb{A}$ is the minimal integer t_o such that there exists a tensor $\mathbb{E}=\{e_{ijk}(\varepsilon)\}$, $e_{ijk}(\varepsilon)\in\mathbf{F}[\varepsilon]$, $e_{ijk}(0)=0$ and $\mathbb{A}+\mathbb{E}$ has rank t_o over $\mathbf{F}(\varepsilon)$, namely

$$\mathbb{A}+\mathbb{E}=\left\{\sum_{s=1}^{t_o} u_{is}(\varepsilon)\, v_{js}(\varepsilon) w_{ks}(\varepsilon)\right\}, \tag{2.3}$$

$u_{is}(\varepsilon)$, $v_{js}(\varepsilon)$, $w_{ks}(\varepsilon) \in \mathbf{F}(\varepsilon)$. The integer d=max degree $e_{ijk}(\varepsilon)$ is the <u>degree of the correction</u> $\mathbb{E}$.

Trivially we have

$$t_o \leqslant t \tag{2.4}$$
$$t_B \leqslant t_o \text{ if } f=\infty .$$

In [2] it is shown that $t \leqslant (1+d)t_o$. Examples of tensors with border rank lower than the tensorial rank are presented in [1], [3], [4]. In all these cases the upper bounds to the border rank are all obtained with a polynomial correction $\mathbb{E}$. That is, the upper bounds hold for the algebraic border rank. In section 3 we shall show an example of a tensor for which $t_o > t_B$.

With the following remarks we enunciate some properties of the rank, border rank and algebraic border rank which will be useful throughout the paper.

Remark 1. If $\mathbb{A}$ is a non degenerate tensor then $t, t_o, t_B \geq \max\{p,q,m\}$ [4].

Remark 2. If $\mathbb{A}=[A_1,\dots,A_m]$ is such that $A_i=\mathrm{diag}\{A_{i1},\dots,A_{ik}\}$, with A_{ij} $p_j x q_j$ matrices, $j=1,\dots,k$, $i=1,\dots,m$, then we have [5]

$$t(\mathbb{A}) \leqslant \sum_{j=1}^{k} t(\mathbb{A}_j), \quad \mathbb{A}_j=[A_{1j},\dots,A_{mj}].$$

Hence by the definitions 2.2, 2.3 we get $t_B(\mathbb{A}) \leqslant \sum_{j=1}^{k} t_B(\mathbb{A}_j)$, $t_o(\mathbb{A}) \leqslant \sum_{j=1}^{k} t_o(\mathbb{A}_j)$.

Remark 3. The rank and hence the (algebraic) border rank are invariant under the transformations

$$a_{i_1 i_2 i_3} \longrightarrow a_{i_{\sigma_1} i_{\sigma_2} i_{\sigma_3}}, \ \sigma \text{ permutation of 3 indices;}$$

$$a_{ijk} \longrightarrow \sum_{r=1}^{p} b_{ir} \sum_{s=1}^{q} c_{js} \sum_{h=1}^{m} d_{kh} a_{rsh};$$

where $\{b_{ir}\}, \{c_{js}\}, \{d_{kh}\}$ are nonsingular matrices over $\mathbb{F}$ of appropriate dimension [5].

Remark 4. The set of bilinear forms

$$f_k(x,y) = \sum_{i=1}^{p} \sum_{j=1}^{q} x_i \, a_{ijk} \, y_j, \quad k=1,\dots,m,$$

can be computed with t multiplications and can be approximated, with arbitrary precision, using t_B (respect. t_o) multiplications, where t is the rank of $\mathbb{A}=\{a_{ijk}\}$ t_B (respect. t_o) is the border rank (respect. algebraic border rank) of $\mathbb{A}$, by the following algorithms, obtained from the relations (2.1),(2.2),(2.3),

$$\sum_{s=1}^{t} \Big(\sum_{i=1}^{p} u_{is} x_i\Big)\Big(\sum_{j=1}^{q} v_{js} y_j\Big) w_{ks} = f_k(x,y);$$

$$\sum_{s=1}^{t_B} \Big(\sum_{i=1}^{p} \tilde{u}_{is} x_i\Big)\Big(\sum_{j=1}^{q} \tilde{v}_{js} y_j\Big) \tilde{w}_{ks} = f_k(x,y) + \sum_{i=1}^{p} \sum_{j=1}^{q} x_i \, e_{ijk} \, y_j \simeq f_k(x,y), \text{ with small } \delta;$$

$$\sum_{s=1}^{t_o} \Big(\sum_{i=1}^{p} u_{is}(\varepsilon) x_i\Big)\Big(\sum_{j=1}^{q} v_{js}(\varepsilon) y_j\Big) w_k(\varepsilon) = f_k(x,y) + \sum_{i=1}^{p} \sum_{j=1}^{q} x_i \, e_{ijk}(\varepsilon) y_j \simeq f_k(x,y),$$

with small ε ($f=\infty$).

The rank of a pxqx2 tensor $\mathbb{A}=[B,C]$ has been studied in [8] by using the Kronecker's theory of pencils of matrices [6] applied to $B+\lambda C$. We now use this theory to investigate the (algebraic) border rank of $\mathbb{A}$. We need to recall some basic definitions and results [6], [8].

Given B,C pxq matrices over $\mathbb{F}$ such that $(B+\lambda C)x$ and $(B+\lambda C)^T y$ do not annihilate identically in λ for any vectors x and y (that is $B+\lambda C$ is a <u>nondegenerate pencil</u>), there are nonsingular matrices P, Q over $\mathbb{F}$ of appropriate dimension such that [6]

$$P(B+\lambda C)Q=\mathrm{diag}\left\{L_{p_1},\dots,L_{p_l},\ L^T_{q_1},\dots,L^T_{q_h},\ \tilde{B}+\lambda\tilde{C}\right\} \tag{2.5}$$

$$0<p_1\leq p_2\leq\dots\leq p_l,\quad 0<q_1\leq q_2\leq\dots\leq q_h$$

where $\tilde{B}+\lambda\tilde{C}$ is a <u>regular pencil</u>, that is $\tilde{B}$, $\tilde{C}$ are square matrices with $\det(\tilde{B}+\lambda\tilde{C})\neq 0$, and $L_n=(l_{ij})$ is the nx(n+1) matrix such that $l_{ii}=\lambda$, $l_{ii+1}=1$, $l_{ij}=0$ elsewhere. Obviously, if $B+\lambda C$ is regular, then $l=h=0$.

3. <u>Regular Pencil</u>.

Let $\mathbb{A}=[B,C]$, $B+\lambda C$ nxn regular pencil, then there exists a $\hat{\lambda}\in\mathbb{F}$ such that $\det(B+\hat{\lambda}C)\neq 0$. From remark 3 we have $t_B(\mathbb{A})=t_B([B+\hat{\lambda}C,\ C])=t_B([I,(B+\hat{\lambda}C)^{-1}C])$, so, without loss of generality we can restrict our investigation to the case $\mathbb{A}=[I,A]$. Moreover we can assume $\mathbb{A}$ to be in the first normal form [6] that is $A=\mathrm{diag}\{A_1,\dots,A_l\}$ where $A_i\equiv\{a^{(i)}_{rs}\}$ is a companion matrix of dimension $n_i x n_i$, such that $a^{(i)}_{rr+1}=1$, $a^{(i)}_{n_i s}=\alpha^{(i)}_{s-1}$, $a^{(i)}_{rs}=0$ elsewhere. The monic polinomial $P_i(\lambda)$ whose j-th degree term is $\alpha^{(i)}_j\lambda^j$ is the characteristic and minimal polynomial of A_i and $P_i(\lambda)$ divides $P_j(\lambda)$ whenever $i<j$ [6]. The polynomials $P_i(\lambda)$ are the <u>invariant polynomials</u> of A.

We have the following

<u>Lemma 3.1</u> [8]. $t(\mathbb{A})=n$ if and only if A is similar to a diagonal matrix.

Lemma 3.2 [8]. If $l=1$ and $f \geq n$ then $t(\mathbb{A})=n$ if and only if the characteristic polynomial of A factors into n distinct linear factors; otherwise $t(\mathbb{A})=n+1$

We can now prove the following

Proposition 3.1. Let $f=\infty$, $l=1$, then $t_B(\mathbb{A})=n$ if and only if $sp(A) \subseteq \bar{\mathbf{F}}$, where $sp(A)$ is the spectrum of A that is $sp(A)=\{\lambda_1,\dots,\lambda_n : \lambda_i$ is an eigenvalue of $A\}$ moreover if $sp(A) \not\subseteq \bar{\mathbf{F}}$ then $t_B(\mathbb{A})=n+1$.

Proof. Suppose $sp(A) \subseteq \bar{\mathbf{F}}$ and let $a_j^{(k)} \in \mathbf{F}$ be such that $\lim a_j^{(k)} = \lambda_j$, $a_j^{(k)} \neq a_i^{(k)}$ if $i \neq j$. Put

$$\prod_{j=1}^{n} (\lambda - a_j^{(k)}) = \lambda^n + \sum_{j=0}^{n-1} \beta_j^{(k)} \lambda^j ;$$

Obviously $\beta_j^{(k)} \in \mathbf{F}$ and $\lim\ (\alpha_j - \beta_j^{(k)})=0$. Now, since the companion matrix B_k defined by the elements $\beta_j^{(k)}$ has distinct eigenvalues in $\mathbf{F}$, from Lemma 3.1 we have $t(\mathbb{B}_k)=n$ where $\mathbb{B}_k=[I,B_k]$. Hence, from the relation $\mathbb{A}=\mathbb{B}_k+(\mathbb{A}-\mathbb{B}_k)$, $\lim (\mathbb{A}-\mathbb{B}_k)=0$, we get from definition 2.2 and remark 1 that $n \leq t_B(\mathbb{A}) \leq t(\mathbb{B}_k)=n$, that is $t_B(\mathbb{A})=n$. Suppose now $t_B(\mathbb{A})=n$, then there exist matrices $E_1^{(k)}$, $E_2^{(k)}$ such that $\lim E_1^{(k)} = \lim E_2^{(k)}=0$ and $t([I+E_1^{(k)}, A+E_2^{(k)}])=n$. Now, using Gerschgorin theorem it is easy to show that $\exists\ k_o : \forall k > k_o$ $\det(I+E_1^{(k)}) \neq 0$. We have, from remark 3, $t([I+E_1^{(k)}, A+E_2^{(k)}])=t([I,(I+E_1^{(k)})^{-1}(A+E_2^{(k)})])$, hence from lemma 3.1 $A_k=(I+E_1^{(k)})^{-1}(A+E_2^{(k)})$ must have eigenvalues $\lambda_i^{(k)} \in \mathbf{F}$, but $\lim A_k=A$ and so $\lim \lambda_i^{(k)} = \lambda_i$ that is $\lambda_i \in \bar{\mathbf{F}}$. For the last part of the proposition we point out that, if $sp(A) \not\subseteq \bar{\mathbf{F}}$, then $t_B(\mathbb{A})=n$, hence because of lemma 3.2, $n \leq t_B \leq t \leq n+1$ and then we have $t_B(\mathbb{A})=n+1$.

Now suppose that $sp(A) \subseteq \mathbf{F}$ and let $P(\lambda)=\prod_{i=1}^{h} (\lambda-\lambda_i)^{m_i}$ be the irreducible factorization of the characteristic polynomial of A over $\mathbf{F}$. Let $m=\max m_i$.

Proposition 3.2. Let $l=1$; if $sp(A) \subseteq \mathbf{F}$ then $t_o(\mathbb{A})=n$. Moreover if $f > m$ then $d=n$ and if $f \leq m$ then $d\ n \leq \log n/\log f$.

Proof. Let $d_i \in \mathbf{F}$ be such that $d_i \neq d_j$ for $i \neq j$, $i,j=1,\dots,m$, $f>m$. The polynomial

$$\sum_{i=0}^{n-1} \beta_i \lambda^i + \lambda^n = \prod_{i=1}^{h} \prod_{j=1}^{m_i} (\lambda-\lambda_i-d_j\varepsilon),\ \beta_i \in \mathbf{F}[\varepsilon],\ \text{degr. } \beta_i \leq \sum_{j=1} m_j=n,$$

has n distinct roots over $\mathbf{F}[\varepsilon]$. Then by lemma 3.1, the companion matrix B defined by the elements β_i is such that $t(\mathbb{B})=n$, over $\mathbf{F}(\varepsilon)$, where $\mathbb{B}=[I,B]$. Hence, since the elements of $\mathbb{B}-\mathbb{A}$ are polynomials with null constant term from the relation $\mathbb{A}=\mathbb{B}+(\mathbb{B}-\mathbb{A})$ we get $n \leq t_o(\mathbb{A}) \leq t(\mathbb{B})=n$, that is $t_o(\mathbb{A})=n$. If $f \leq m$ we order the elements $\varphi_i \in \mathbf{F}[\varepsilon]$ in such a way that degree $(\varphi_i) \leq$ degree (φ_j) if $i \leq j$. We have $f^i(f-1)$ polynomials of degree i. Now it suffices to put

$$\sum_{i=0} \beta_i \lambda^i + \lambda^m = \prod_{i=1}^{h} \prod_{j=1}^{m_i} (\lambda - \lambda i - \varepsilon \varphi_i)$$ obtaining a degree $d \leq \sum_{i=1}^{h} m_i \frac{\log(m/(f-1))}{\log f} \leq$

$n \frac{\log n}{\log f}$.

If $l = 1$, applying the preceding technique to each block of A, in the light of remark 1 and remark 2, we get the following

Corollary 3.1. Let $f=\infty$. $t_B(\mathbb{A})=n$ if and only if $sp(A) \subseteq \bar{\mathbf{F}}$.

Corollary 3.2. If $sp(A) \subseteq \mathbf{F}$ then $t_o(\mathbb{A})=n$.

Now consider the following matrix $\tilde{A}=A+\text{diag}\{\varepsilon I_{n_1}, \ldots, \varepsilon^l I_{n_l}\}$, where I_{n_i} is the $n_i x n_i$ identity matrix. We have $sp(A_i+\varepsilon^i I_{n_i}) \cap sp(A_j+\varepsilon^j I_{n_j})=\phi$, if $i \neq j$, and so the minimal and the characteristic polynomial of A coincide. Hence there is a nonsingular matrix P with elements in $\mathbf{F}(\varepsilon)$ such that PAP^{-1} is a companion matrix with elements in $\mathbf{F}(\varepsilon)$, whence $t_B(\mathbb{A}) \leq t([I,A])=t([I,PAP^{-1}]) \leq n+1$ (for lemma 2.2) and $t_o(\mathbb{A}) \leq t([I,A])=t([I,PAP^{-1}]) \leq n+1$. So we can obtain the following

Proposition 3.3. Let $B+\lambda C$ be a regular pencil. We have $n \leq t_B([B,C]) \leq n+\delta_1$, $n \leq t_o([B,C]) \leq n+\delta_2$, where $\delta_1=0$ (respect. $\delta_2=0$) if the polynomial $\det(B+\lambda C)$ has roots on $\bar{\mathbf{F}}$ (respect. on $\mathbf{F}$), otherwise $\delta_1=1$, $\delta_2=1$.

Proof. Let $\hat{\alpha} \in \mathbf{F}$ be such that $\det(B+\hat{\alpha}C) \neq 0$ and put $A=(B+\hat{\alpha}C)^{-1}C$. Suppose that rank C=r, then A has n-r null eigenvalues and $P(\lambda)=\det(B+\lambda C)$ is a r-degree polynomial. If $\lambda \neq 0$ is an eigenvalue of A then $P(\hat{\alpha}-1/\lambda)=0$. In fact if $\det(A-\lambda I)=0$ then $(\lambda(B+\hat{\alpha}C)-C)x=0$ where x is the eigenvector of A corresponding to λ. Hence $Bx=(1/\lambda-\alpha)Cx$, whence $(B+(\hat{\alpha}-1/\lambda)C)x=0$. Because the number of non-null eigenvalues of A equals the number of roots of $P(\lambda)$ we can say that $P(\lambda)$ has roots in $\bar{\mathbf{F}}$ (respect. in $\mathbf{F}$) if and only if A has eigenvalues in $\bar{\mathbf{F}}$ (respect. in $\mathbf{F}$). The proof is complete since $t_B([B,C])=t_B([I,A])$, $t_o([B,C])=t_o([I,A])$.

It is worth stressing that the additive decomposition (2.1) obtained in lemma 3.1 is such that u_{is} (respect. v_{js}) is the matrix whose columns are the eigenvectors of A (respect. of A^T) corresponding to the eigenvalues $\lambda_1,\ldots,\lambda_n$ and $w_{1s}=1$ $w_{2s}=\lambda_s$, s=1,...,n. The nxnxn tensor with slabs $I,A,\ldots,A^{n-1}$, still has rank n. In fact (2.1) holds with t=n and u_{is}, v_{js} still being the matrices of the eigenvectors of A and A^T but with $w_{ks}=(\lambda_s)^{k-1}$, k=1,...,n.

This fact allows to state a corollary to propositions 3.1 and 3.2.

<u>Corollary 3.3</u>. If $sp(A)\subseteq \mathbf{F}$ then $t_o([I,A,\ldots,A^{n-1}])=n$ and if $sp(A)\subseteq\bar{\mathbf{F}}$ then $t_B([I,A,\ldots,A^{n-1}])=n$.

It is interesting to note that (in the case $sp(A)\subseteq\mathbf{F}$) if E is the matrix with elements on $\mathbf{F}[\varepsilon]$ such that A+E is similar to a diagonal matrix D, namely $S(A+E)S^{-1}=D$, then $S(A^i+E_i)S^{-1}=D^i$ where $E_i=(A+E)^i-A^i$ has elements on $\mathbf{F}[\varepsilon]$. That is, the product (and the inversion) in the matrix algebra generated by A can be evaluated through n multiplications (divisions) by an approximated algorithm. As the algebra generated by A over $\mathbf{F}$ is isomorphic to the algebra of polynomials over $\mathbf{F}$ with the product modulo $\mathbf{P}_n$, where $\mathbf{P}_n$ is the characteristic polynomial of A, we can say that the product modulo $\mathbf{P}_n$ of two polynomials can be evaluated through n multiplications over $\mathbf{C}$ by an approximate algorithm.

The nxnx2 tensor $\mathbb{A}=[I,A]$, $A\equiv\{a_{ij}\}$, $a_{ii+1}=1$, $a_{ij}=0$ elsewhere, has algebraic border rank $t_o=n$ over any field $\mathbf{F}$. If f>n the A+E can be diagonalized with $E=\varepsilon\,\mathrm{diag}\{d_1,\ldots,d_n\}$, $d_i\neq d_j$ for i≠j. So the degree of the correction is d=1 and hence the tensor $[I,A,\ldots,A^{n-1}]$ has algebraic border rank $t_o=n$ with a correction of degree n-1. This improves the result given in [1] where the value $t_o=n$ is obtained with a correction of degree 2^n.Moreover over the complex field we have $t_o=n$, d=1 by putting $E\equiv\{e_{ij}\}$, $e_{n1}=\varepsilon$, $e_{ij}=0$ elsewhere.

From proposition 3.1 it follows that the product of complex numbers cannot be evaluated by an approximate algorithm with less than three multiplications over $\mathbf{R}$, since the associated 2x2x2 tensor is $\mathbb{A}=[I,A]$, $A=\begin{bmatrix}0 & 1\\ -1 & 0\end{bmatrix}$ and $sp(A)\not\subseteq\mathbf{R}$.

It is worth pointing out the difference between the algebraic and the topological aspect of approximate algorithms. Not every approximate algorithms can be expressed in algebraic way in terms of algebraic border rank. An example can be given in the case in which $\mathbf{F}\neq\bar{\mathbf{F}}$ as shown in the following

Proposition 3.4. In the case $f=\infty$ the border and the algebraic border rank may have different values.

Proof. let $\mathbb{A}=[I,A]$, $A=\begin{bmatrix}0 & 1\\ 2 & 0\end{bmatrix}$, $\mathbf{F}=\mathbf{Q}$. We have $sp(A)=\{\sqrt{2}, -\sqrt{2}\}$, and from proposition 3.3 $t_B(\mathbb{A})=2$. Suppose $t_o(\mathbb{A})=2$, then there exist matrices E_1, E_2 with polynomial elements with null constant term such that $t([I+E_1, A+E_2])=2$. That means that there are two values of $\lambda\in\mathbf{F}(\varepsilon)$ such that $\det(\lambda(I+E_1)+A+E_2)=0$, that is $\lambda^2+p(\varepsilon)\lambda -2+q(\varepsilon)=0$ with $p(\varepsilon), q(\varepsilon)\in\mathbf{F}[\varepsilon]$. We find that $\lambda=(-p(\varepsilon)\pm(p(\varepsilon)^2-4q(\varepsilon)+8)^{1/2})/2 \notin\mathbf{F}(\varepsilon)$ since $p(\varepsilon)^2-4q(\varepsilon)+8$ cannot be the square of any polynomial over $\mathbf{F}$.

4. General Case.

Let $\mathbb{A}=\{a_{ijk}\}=[B,C]$, $B+\lambda C$ non degenerate pencil of pxq matrices . Without loss of generality, for remark 3, we can assume that $B+\lambda C$ is in its canonical form (2.5).

Proposition 4.1. If $B+\lambda C=\operatorname{diag}\{L_n, L_m^T\}$ then $t_o([B,C])=n+m+1$ and if $f=\infty$ then $t_B([B,C])=n+m+1$.

Proof. We have $t_o([B,C])=t_o([B+C,C])\leq t([B+C+E, C+(B+C+E)\tilde{E}])$, where $E\equiv\{e_{ij}\}$ and $e_{n+1\ n+1}=\varepsilon$, $e_{ij}=0$ elsewhere. If $f>\max(n,m+1)$ then we put $\tilde{E}=\varepsilon\operatorname{diag}\{d_1,\dots,d_n, d_1,\dots,d_{m+1}\}$ where $d_i\in\mathbf{F}$ and $d_i\neq d_j$ for $i\neq j$, $i,j=1,\dots,\max(n,m+1)$. If $f\leq\max(n,m+1)$ then we put $\tilde{E}=\operatorname{diag}\{\varepsilon,\dots,\varepsilon^n,\varepsilon,\dots,\varepsilon^{m+1}\}$. Now $t([B+C+E,C+(B+C+E)\tilde{E}])=t([I,(B+C+E)^{-1})C+\tilde{E}])$, but $(B+C+E)^{-1}C+\tilde{E}$ is upper triangular with different elements on the main diagonal. Hence, from lemma 3.1, $t([B+C+E,C+(B+C+E)\tilde{E}])=n+m+1$. Whence $t_o([B,C])\leq n+m+1$. Now, because of the slabs $A_i\equiv\{a_{ijk}\}$ $i=1,\dots,n+m+1$ are linearly independent, we have from remark 1, that $t_B([B,C])\geq n+m+1$ and $t_o([B,C])\geq n+m+1$, which completes the proof.

Proposition 4.2. If $B+\lambda C=L_n$, then $t_o([B,C])=n+1$, $t_B([B,C])=n+1$.

Proof. Since the slabs $A_i\equiv\{a_{ijk}\}$, $i=1,\dots,n+1$, are linearly independent we have $t_o([B,C])\geq n+1$, $t_B([B,C])\geq n+1$. But $t([B,C])=n+1$ (see [8] theorem 2.1) and hence (2.4) completes the proof.

An analogous result holds for L^T.

Proposition 4.3. If $B+\lambda C=\mathrm{diag}\{L_{p_1},\dots,L_{p_1},L_{q_1},\dots,L_{q_h}\}$ is a pxq pencil then $t_o([B,C])=\max(p,q)$ and if $f=\infty$ then $t_B=\max(p,q)$.

Proof. It suffices to consider the case $p\geqslant q$, that is $h\geqslant 1$. From remark 2 we have $t_o([B,C])\leqslant\sum_{i=1}^{h} t_o([B_i,C_i])$, where $B_i+\lambda C_i=\mathrm{diag}\{L_{p_i},L_{q_i}^T\}$ if $i\leqslant 1$, and $B_i+\lambda C_i=L_{q_i}^T$ if $i>1$. From propositions 4.1 and 4.2 we get $t_o([B,C])\leqslant\sum_{i=1}^{1}p_i+\sum_{j=1}^{h}q_j+h=p$

Now, since the slabs $A_i\equiv\{a_{ijk}\}$, $i=1,\dots,p$, are linearly independent, we have from remark 1 that $t_o([B,C])\geqslant p$. Analogously we proced for t_B.

We can now conclude with the main result.

Proposition 4.4. Let $A=[B,C]$ be a pxqx2 non degenerate tensor. Let $\tilde{B}+\lambda\tilde{C}$ be the regular kernel of the Kronecker canonical form of $B+\lambda C$. Then $B+\lambda C$ is a non degenerate pencil and $\max(p,q)\leqslant t_B(A)\leqslant\max(p,q)+\delta_1$, $\max(p,q)\leqslant t_o(A)\leqslant\max(p,q)+\delta_2$, where $\delta_1=0$ (respect. $\delta_2=0$) if the polynomial $\det(\tilde{B}+\lambda\tilde{C})$ has roots in $\bar{\mathbf{F}}$ (respect. in $\mathbf{F}$) and $\delta_1=1$ ($\delta_2=1$) otherwise.

Proof. If $B+\lambda C$ were degenerate there would exist a vector $x\equiv\{x_j\}$ or a vector $y\equiv\{y_i\}$ such that $Bx=Cx=0$ or $B^Ty=C^Ty=0$, that is $\sum_{j=1}^{q}a_{ijk}x_j=0$ or $\sum_{i=1}^{p}a_{ijk}y_i=0$ and hence A is degenerate. We can consider $B+\lambda C$ in the canonical form (2.5). From remark 2 we have $t_o([B,C])\leqslant t_o([B_1,C_1])+t_o([\tilde{B},\tilde{C}])$, where $B_1+\lambda C_1=\mathrm{diag}\{L_{p_1},\dots,L_p,L_{q_1}^T,\dots,L_{q_h}^T\}$. Hence from propositions 4.3 and 3.3 we have $t_o(A)\leqslant\max(p,q)+\delta_1$. Analogously for $t_B(A)$.

It is interesting to point out that the cardinality of $\mathbf{F}$ does not play any role either for the border rank or the algebraic border rank whereas it does for the tensor rank [8]. When f is "small" we have a greater value for the degree of the correction.

If $\mathbf{F}$ is the complex field then $t_B(A)=t_o(A)=\max(p,q)$.

It is interesting to compare the bound of proposition 4.4 and the bound for the tensorial rank obtained in [8]. We have $t(A)\leqslant p+1+\delta=q+h+\delta$, where δ is the number of invariant polynomials of $B+\lambda C$ which do not factor into distinct linear factors over $\mathbf{F}$. This bounds holds if f is large enough. The highest value of t, obtained in the case p=q=n is t=3/2 n (see [8]).

Remark 6. We can check whether $\det(\tilde{B}+\lambda\tilde{C})$ has roots in $\mathbf{F}$ or in $\bar{\mathbf{F}}$ either by computing the Kronecker canonical form of $B+\lambda C$ and evaluating the regular pencil, or by computing directly only the first invariant polynomial of $B+\lambda C$ $i_1(\lambda)=D_r(\lambda)/D_{r-1}(\lambda)$. Here r is the size of the largest minor of $B+\lambda C$ not identically equal to zero in λ and $D_i(\lambda)$, $i=r,r-1$, is the greatest common divisor of all the minors of order i. In fact $i_1(\lambda)$ and $\det(\tilde{B}+\lambda\tilde{C})$ have the same roots with different multiplicities [6].

From remark 4 we get a corollary to proposition 4.4.

Corollary 4.1. A non degenerate pair of pxq bilinear forms B,C can be approximated over any infinite field $\mathbf{F}$ with t_B multiplications, where $\max(p,q)\leq t_B \leq \max(p,q)+\delta$, $\delta=0$ if the invariant polynomial of $B+\lambda C$ have roots in $\bar{\mathbf{F}}$, $\delta=1$ otherwise.

REFERENCES

1. Bini D., Border Tensorial Rank of Triangular Toeplitz Matrices, Nota Interna B78-26, I.E.I. del C.N.R., Pisa 1979.
2. Bini D., Relations Between Exact and Approximate Bilinear Algorithms, Applications, (to appear in Calcolo).
3. Bini D., Capovani M., Lotti G., Romani F., $O(n^{2.7799})$ Complexity for nxn Approximate Matrix Multiplication, Information Processing Letter vol 8 n° 5, June 1979.
4. Bini D., Lotti G., Romani F., Approximate Solution for the Bilinear Form Computational Problem, (to appear in SIAM J. Comp.).
5. Brockett D., Dobkin D., On the Optimal Evaluation of a Set of Bilinear Forms, Linear Algebra Appl. 19, 207-235 (1978).
6. Gantmacher F. R., The Theory of Matrices, vol. 1 and 2, Chelsea Publishing Company, New York 1959.
7. Howell T., Lafon J. C., The Complexity of the Quaternion Product, Tech. Rep. 75-245, Dept. of Comput. Sci. Cornell Univ. (1975).
8. Ja' Ja' J., Optimal Evaluation of Pairs of Bilinear Forms, SICOMP 8 (1979) 443-462.
9. Lafon J. C., Base Tensorielle des Matrices de Hankel (ou de Toeplitz) Applications, Numer. Math. 23, 349-361 (1975).
10. Pan V., Ya., Winograd S., Personal Communication.
11. Schonage A., Total and Partial Matrix Multiplication, Technical Report, Mathematisches Institute of Universitat Tubingen, June 1979.
12. Strassen V., Gaussian Elimination is not Optimal, Numer. Math. 13, 354356 (1969).
13. Strassen V., Vermeidung von Divisionen, J. Reine Angew Math. Vol. 246, 184-202 (1975).
14. Winograd S., On Multiplication of 2x2 Matrices, Linear Algebra Appl. 4, 381-388 (1971).

DERIVATIONS ET REDUCTIONS DANS LES GRAMMAIRES ALGEBRIQUES

L. BOASSON

U.E.R. de Mathématiques - Université Paris VII

et

L.A. 248 du C.N.R.S. "Informatique Théorique et Programmation"

INTRODUCTION

Nous nous proposons d'étudier ici une extension de l'usage des règles d'une grammaire algébrique : précisément, nous étudions l'effet produit par l'usage de celles-ci dans les deux sens. Les raisons d'une telle étude sont essentiellement au nombre de trois :

a. La première raison est en quelque sorte la plus élémentaire : il est classique d'utiliser les règles d'une grammaire de la droite vers la gauche. C'est l'une des façons utilisées pour décrire l'analyse syntaxique ascendante. On peut aussi expliquer ainsi le fonctionnement d'un automate à pile [20]. Ce point de vue soulève déjà quelques problèmes comme celui de l'existence de grammaires à membres droits uniques (backwards deterministic grammars). En outre, dans de nombreux cas, l'analyse syntaxique s'avère plus facile à conduire via des stratégies mixtes, mélangeant les technique ascendantes et descendantes [1]. Il est donc naturel d'étudier ce qui se passe si l'on utilise aussi les règles d'une grammaire dans les deux sens pour engendrer des mots.

b. Notre deuxième raison est complètement différente. On dispose essentiellement de trois méthodes pour définir un langage ou une famille de langages : donner un mécanisme engendrant le langage (grammaire), donner une machine reconnaissant le langage (automate), donner une description algébrique du langage (le plus souvent par classe de congruence). Les liens entre grammaires et automates ont été largement étudiés et ce dès l'origine de la théorie [11, 15, 16]. Les quelques tentatives pour relier les définitions par congruences à l'une ou l'autre des définitions classiques n'ont pas vraiement réussies. Elles ont surtout montré que le problème est très difficile [7, 9]. L'approche proposée ici a au moins le mérite de fournir de nombreuses familles de langages pour lesquelles les définitions classiques peuvent être utilisées aussi bien que les définitions par congruences. En outre, toutes les familles connues être congruentielles se trouvent prises en compte ici : ainsi trouvons nous les langages de Dyck, les langage parenthètiques, les langages rationnels, les langages très simples...

c. Notre troisième et dernière raison est en fait à l'origine de cette étude ; c'est elle qui en a fourni l'idée. Bon nombre des problèmes soulevés par l'étude des schémas de programmes et de la sémantique algébrique sont très similaires à ceux posés par les grammaires algébriques. Il n'y a là rien d'étonnant, puisque les schémas de programme ne sont que des grammaires algébriques d'arbres un peu spéciales [13]. Les relations entre ces deux domaines deviennent d'ailleurs encore plus évidentes si l'on étudie les schémas non déterministes. Pour prouver que des programmes sont équivalents aussi bien que pour transformer un programme en un autre qui lui soit équivalent, Burstall et Darlington ont mis au point et implanté un système de transformations. Celui-ci utilise un ensemble de transformations élémentaires assez simples parmi lesquelles figure celle-ci : on peut remplacer une occurrence du corps d'une procédure (membre droit de règle) par son nom (membre gauche de règle). On sait [18] que cette règle de transformation est effectivement correcte. Cependant, il est évident que l'étendre au cas non déterministe exige que des conditions très particulières soient satisfaites. Il est alors naturel de regarder d'abord dans quels cas une telle extension ne change rien pour les grammaires de mots afin de se faire une idée de ce que peuvent être ces conditions.

Cette communication est divisée en deux sections : la première donne quelques résultats généraux sur les familles de langages engendrés par des grammaires algébriques utilisées dans les deux sens. La seconde est entièrement consacrée à l'étude de sous-classes de la famille des grammaires algébriques où cet usage généralisé des règles ne change pas le langage engendré. Cette dernière section se termine par quelques problèmes ouverts.

I. DÉRIVATIONS ET RÉDUCTIONS :

On considère ici une grammaire algébrique comme un triplet $G = \langle X,V,P \rangle$ où X désigne l'alphabet terminal, V celui des variables (disjoint de X) et P l'ensemble des règles. Les notions de dérivation et de dérivation directe sont définies de façon classique et notées $\xrightarrow{*}$ et $\longrightarrow$ respectivement. Nous introduisons la notion de réduction.

et de réduction directe comme étant les relations symmétriques des dérivations et dérivations directes ; ainsi on notera

$$f \xleftarrow{*} g \text{ ssi } g \xrightarrow{*} f \quad \text{et} \quad f \longleftarrow g \text{ ssi } g \longrightarrow f.$$

Enfin, on considère la relation $\longleftrightarrow$ qui n'est rien d'autre que l'union de la dérivation directe et de la réduction directe :

$$f \longleftrightarrow g \text{ ssi } f \longrightarrow g \text{ ou } g \longrightarrow f.$$

On désigne par $\xleftrightarrow{*}$ la fermeture réflexive et transitive de $\longleftrightarrow$. On peut alors, étant donné un langage A sur $(X \cup V)$, définir les langages :

$$D(G,A) = \{f \in X^* \mid \exists\, a \in A \quad a \xrightarrow{*} f\}.$$

Si A se réduit à une variable, on retrouve le langage engendré par G avec cette variable pour axiome.

$$\hat{D}(G,A) = \{f \in (X \cup V)^* \mid \exists\, a \in A \quad a \xrightarrow{*} f\}.$$

Comme d'habitude, on a alors $D(G,A) = \hat{D}(G,A) \cap X^*$.

On définit aussi

$$R(G,A) = \{f \in X^* \mid \exists\, a \in A \quad a \xleftarrow{*} f\}$$

$$\hat{R}(G,A) = \{f \in (X \cup V)^* \mid \exists\, a \in A \quad a \xleftarrow{*} f\}.$$

On notera que $R(G,A) = A \cap X^*$; cet ensemble de mots n'est donc pas très intéressant. Au contraire, $\hat{R}(G,A)$ peut permettre d'énoncer le problème de l'analyse syntaxique aisément :

décider si f est dans L(G,v), c'est décider si v est dans $\hat{R}(G,\{f\})$.

Enfin, si l'on utilise aussi bien les réductions que les dérivations, on obtient

$$DR(G,A) = \{f \in X^* \mid \exists\, a \in A \quad a \xleftrightarrow{*} f\}$$

$$\widehat{DR}(G,A) = \{f \in (X \cup V)^* \mid \exists\, a \in A \quad a \xleftrightarrow{*} f\}.$$

Exemple : Soient $X = \{a,b\}$, $V = \{S\}$; la grammaire G ayant les trois règles

$$S \longrightarrow aSb \quad S \longrightarrow aS \quad S \longrightarrow ab .$$

On voit que

$$D(G,S) = \{a^n\, b^m \mid n \geq m \geq 1\}$$

$$\hat{D}(G,S) = D(G,S) \cup \{a^n\, Sb^m \mid n \geq m \geq 0\}$$

(Il ne s'agit là que des dérivations usuelles).

Désignant par A le langage $\{a^n\, b^n \mid n \geq 1\}$, on aura

$$R(G,A) = A$$

$$\hat{R}(G,A) = A \cup \{a^n\, Sb^m \mid m \geq n \geq 0\}$$

La seconde égalité résulte immédiatement de ce que l'on peut écrire

$$p \geq q,\ a^p b^q \overset{*}{\longleftarrow} S \text{ et donc } a^{q+p}\, b^{q+p} = a^q.a^p b^q.b^p \overset{*}{\longleftarrow} a^q S b^p .$$

On vérifie aussi que

$$DR(G,S) = a^+\, b^+$$

$$\widehat{DR}(G,S) = a^+\, b^+ \cup a^* S b^*$$

Ainsi, par exemple

$$S \overset{*}{\longrightarrow} a^3\, b^3 \longleftarrow a^2 Sb^3 \longleftarrow aSb^2 \longleftarrow Sb^2 \longrightarrow ab^3$$

et de façon générale

$$S \overset{*}{\longrightarrow} a^n\, b^n \overset{*}{\longleftarrow} Sb^n \longrightarrow ab^{n+1}$$

Nous pouvons maintenant énoncer nos premiers résultats :

Théorème 1 : Un langage L sur X est récursivement énumérable ssi on peut trouver un langage algébrique A sur $Z = X \cup \overline{X}$ et une grammaire algébrique $G = \langle X, \overline{X} \cup \{\sigma\}, P\rangle$ tels que

$$L = DR(G,A).$$

Ce résultat n'a rien de surprenant. Il provient en fait de ce que deux piles simulent une machine de Türing. On peut le prouver sans peine en utilisant un résultat de Stanat (Théorème 6.3 de [21]) qui permet de montrer un résultat légèrement plus précis : la grammaire G de l'énoncé peut être choisie toujours la même ; ce sera celle engendrant D'^*_n si Card X = n.

On remarquera cependant que dans cet énoncé, la grammaire G n'est pas réduite : elle peut contenir des variables v telles que D(G,v) = ϕ. On peut d'ailleurs s'assurer que si l'on impose à G d'être réduite, le résultat ne vaut plus : en effet, si l'on définit un langage congruentiel comme un langage qui est union finie de classes d'une congruence finiement présentée, on a :

<u>Théorème 2</u> : Un langage L sur X est congruentiel ssi il existe une grammaire algébrique réduite G = <X,V,P> et une partie finie F tel que

$$L = DR(G,F).$$

Si l'on revient alors au théorème 1, on constate que si la grammaire considérée dans ce premier énoncé est réduite, on a

- soit A est un langage algébrique infini et DR(G,A) contient le langage algébrique infini D(G,A)
- soit A est un langage fini et DR(G,A) est congruentiel.

Or il existe des langages récursivement énumérables qui ne sont pas congruentiels et qui ne contiennent aucun langage algébrique infini. Tel est le cas, par exemple, de

$$L = \{a^n \mid n \text{ est un nombre premier}\} .$$

Nous terminons cette section par une remarque :

<u>Proposition 1</u> : Etant donnée une grammaire algébrique réduite G = <X,V,P> engendrant A = D(G,v), il se peut que $\hat{R}(G,A)$ ne soit pas algébrique.

Considérons, par exemple, sur l'alphabet X = {a,b,c,x}, la grammaire suivante :

$$S \longrightarrow S_1 + S_2 + S_3$$

$$S_1 \longrightarrow aS_1a + bS_1b + bS_1'b$$

$S_1' \longrightarrow cS_1'c + cxc$

$S_2 \longrightarrow cS_2b + cb$

$S_3 \longrightarrow aS_3b + ab$

On voit facilement que

$$D(G,S_3) = \{a^n\ b^n \mid n \geq 1\} = L_3$$

$$D(G,S_2) = \{c^n\ b^n \mid n \geq 1\} = L_2$$

$$D(G,S_1) = \{fbc^n\ x\ c^n b\tilde{f} \mid n \geq 1\ ;\ f \in \{a,b\}^*\} = L_1$$

Si l'on regarde alors $L = \hat{R}(G,D(G,S))$, on vérifie sans peine que $L \cap S_3^+\ c^+\ x\ S_2\ S_3^*\ a^+$ est exactement le langage $\{S_3^p\ c^n\ x\ S_2\ S_3^{p-1}\ a^n \mid n,\ p \geq 1\}$. Ce dernier langage n'est pas algébrique et la proposition est donc établie.

II. LANGAGES N.T.S. :

Ce dernier paragraphe est consacré à l'étude d'une sous-famille particulière des langages algébriques. Nous disons qu'une grammaire algébrique $G = \langle X,V,P \rangle$ est à Non-Terminaux Séparés (abrégé en N.T.S.) si, quel que soit la variable v de V, on a $\hat{D}(G,v) = \hat{DR}(G,v)$. Comme à l'accoutumée, un langage algébrique sera dit N.T.S. si il peut être engendré par une grammaire N.T.S.

Exemple : Sur l'alphabet $X = \{a,\bar{a}\}$, la grammaire $\langle S \longrightarrow SS + aS\bar{a} + 1 \rangle$ engendre $D_1'^*$. Elles est N.T.S.. Pour vérifier cette dernière propriété, on utilise la caractérisation des grammaires N.T.S.

(1) $\quad \forall\ v,w \in V \quad \alpha,m,\beta \in (X \cup V)^* \quad v \xrightarrow{*} \alpha m \beta\ ,\ w \xrightarrow{*} m \Longrightarrow v \xrightarrow{*} \alpha v \beta.$

Cette propriété caractéristique permet de voir que si deux variables distinctes d'une grammaire N.T.S. engendrent un même mot, elles engendrent le même langage. On peut alors les confondre, si bien que dans une grammaire N.T.S., on peut supposer que des variables distinctes engendrent des langage disjoints. C'est là l'origine du nom choisi ici. Poussant un peu plus loin l'analyse, on voit aussi que le langage engendré par chaque variable est une classe syntaxique. C'est de ce point de vue que cette classe de langage a été abordée dans [17].

On sait bien que, le plus souvent, une propriété définie sur les grammaires n'est pas partagée par toutes les grammaires équivalentes. Il en va bien ici de même : la grammaire <S $\longrightarrow$ aSaS + 1> engendre $D_1'^*$ et n'est pas N.T.S.

Cette dernière grammaire a pourtant une propriété très voisine : elle satisfait DR(G,S) = D(G,S), soit aussi, la propriété (1) sur X^* qui s'énonce

(2) $\forall$ v,w $\in$ V α,m,β $\in X^*$ $v \xrightarrow{*} \alpha m\beta$, $w \xrightarrow{*} m \Longrightarrow v \xrightarrow{*} \alpha w\beta$.

L'une des propriétés remarquables de la famille des langages N.T.S. est que, si une grammaire satisfait (2), il en existe une équivalente qui satisfait (1), ce que l'on peut énoncer:

Théorème 3 : Etant donnée une grammaire algébrique G = <X,V,P> telle que pour toute variable v, D(G,v) = DR(G,v), elle engendre un langage N.T.S.

La première propriété des langages N.T.S. résulte directement du théorème 2.

Théorème 2' : Tout langage N.T.S. est congruentiel.

On en déduit facilement que la famille des langages N.T.S. est strictement incluse dans celle des langages algébriques. En effet, un langage comme $\{a^n b^m \mid n \geq m \geq 1\}$ est algébrique non congruentiel. Il n'est donc pas N.T.S.. On vérifie d'ailleurs sans peine que

Proposition 2 : Tout langage N.T.S. est déterministe.
Il existe des langages déterministe qui ne sont pas N.T.S..

Pour ce qui concerne les propriétés de cloture, on vérifie que

Proposition 3 : La famille des langages N.T.S. est fermée par miroir, intersection rationnelle et morphisme inverse.
Elle ne l'est ni par union marquée, ni par produit marqué, ni par étoile marquée, ni par morphisme.

Ainsi cette famille constitue-t-elle un cylindre [2] qui n'est pas un A.F.D.L. [8]. De ce point de vue, on peut énoncer les deux

Conjecture 1 : La famille des langages N.T.S. est un cylindre non principal.

Conjecture 2 : La famille des langages N.T.S. est fermée par applications séquentielle inverse ("inverse g.s.m. mapping").

Si l'on cherche maintenant quels langages classiques sont N.T.S., on vérifie

Proposition 4 : Les familles suivantes ne contiennent que des langages N.T.S. :

- les langages rationnels,
- les (multi-) parenthétiques [12,19],
- les langages très simples [7,10],
- les langages de Dyck (restreints ou non),
- les classes de congruences confluentes basiques [9].

Cette proposition conduit naturellement à la question de savoir si notre théorème 2' admet une réciproque. Celle-ci est en général fausse car l'on vérifie que la classe de z dans la congruence engendrée par

$$z = axb = ayb^2 \; ; \; axb = a^2xb^2 \; ; \; ayb^2 = a^2yb^4 \; ; \text{ et}$$

$$s\alpha = \alpha s \quad \alpha \in \{a,b\}, \quad s \in \{x,y\}$$

est à la fois algébrique et non déterministe.

Le problème reste ouvert cependant. On peut ainsi se poser la

Questions : Existe-t-il une congruence confluente dont une classe soit algébrique sans être un langage N.T.S. ?

(Les congruence confluentes sont celles qui satisfont la propriété "Church-Rosser". On trouvera dans [3] les principaux résultats connus sur les rapports entre congruences et langages algébriques).

Nous terminerons cette communication par un bref retour à des problèmes différents concernant les langages algébriques. On dit qu'un langage est I.R.S. s'il ne contient aucun langage rationnel infini [14]. Il a été conjecturé [14] qu'un langage I.R.S. expansif était générateur. On sait que cela n'est pas vrai [4]. Cependant, cette conjecture vaut pour les langages parenthétiques [5] et pour les langages très simples [10]. Au vu de la proposition 3, on peut alors énoncer la

Conjecture 3 : Tout langage expansif I.R.S., N.T.S. est générateur.

BIBLIOGRAPHIE

[1] AHO A.V. and J.D. ULLMAN : The Theory of Parsing, Translation and Compiling. Prentice-Hall (1972).

[2] AUTEBERT J.M. : Non-Principalité du Cylindre des Langages à Compteur. Math.System Theory 11 (1977), p. 157-167.

[3] BERSTEL J. : Congruences Plus que Parfaites et Langages Algébriques. Séminaire d'Informatique Théorique. L.I.T.P. (1975-77) p. 123-147.

[4] BOASSON L. : Un Langage Particulier. R.A.I.R.O. - Informatique Théorique 13 (1979), p. 203-215.

[5] BOASSON L. et M. NIVAT : Parenthesis Generators. 17th Annual I.E.E. Symposimm (F.O.C.S.) (1976), p. 253-257.

[6] BURSTALL R. and J. DARLINGTON : A Transformation System for Developping Recursive Programs. Jour. of A.C.M. 24 (1977), p. 44-67.

[7] BUTZBACH P. : Une famille de Congruences de Thue pour lesquelles l'Equivalence est Décidable. 1st I.C.A.L.P. North-Holland (1973) p. 3-12.

[8] CHANDLER W.J. : Abstract Families of Deterministic Languages. 1st A.C.M. S.I.G.A.C.T. (1969), p. 21-30.

[9] COCHET Y. et M. NIVAT : Une Généralisation des Ensembles de Dyck. Israel Jour. of Math. 9 (1971), p. 389-395.

[10] FROUGNY C. : Langages très simples Générateurs. R.A.I.R.O. Informatique Théorique 13 (1979), p. 69-86.

[11] GINSBURG S. and S.A. GREIBACH : Abstract Families of Languages. Memoirs of the Amer. Math. Soc. 87 (1969), p. 1-32.

[12] GINSBURG S. and M. HARRISON : Bracketed Context-Free Languages. Jour. of Computer and System Science 1 (1967), p. 1-23.

[13] GREIBACH S.A. : Theory of Program Structures : Schemes, Semantics, Verification. Lecture Notes in Computer Science 36 (1975), Springer.

[14] GREIBACH S.A. : One-Counter Languages and the I.R.S. Condition. Jour. of Computer and System Science 10 (1975), p. 237-247.

[15] GREIBACH S.A. and S. GINSBURG : Multitape A.F.A. Jour. of A.C.M. 19 (1972), p. 193-221.

[16] HOPCROFT J. and J.D. ULLMAN : Formal Languages and their Relationship to Automata. Addison-Wesley (1969).

[17] HOTZ G. : Uber die Darstellbarkeit des Syntaktischen Monoides Kontext-Freier Spracher. Rapport de l'Université de Saarbruck.

[18] KOTT L. : About a Transformation System : a Theoretical Study. 3ème Colloque International sur la Programmation. Paris (1978), B. Robinet Ed.

[19] Mc NAUGHTON R. : Parenthesis Grammars. Jour. of A.C.M. 14 (1967), p. 490-500.

[20] SALOMAA A. : Formal Languages. Academic Press (1973).

[21] STANAT D.F. : Formal Languages and Power Series. 3rd A.C.M. S.I.G.A.C.T. (1971) p. 1-11.

Mailing Adress :

L. Boasson
5, Allée Georges Rouault
75020 PARIS FRANCE.

SEMANTIC ANALYSIS OF COMMUNICATING SEQUENTIAL PROCESSES

(Shortened Version)

Patrick Cousot* and Radhia Cousot**

1. *INTRODUCTION*

We present *semantic analysis techniques for concurrent programs* which are designed as networks of nondeterministic sequential processes, communicating with each other explicitly, by the sole means of synchronous, unbuffered message passing. The techniques are introduced using a version of Hoare[78]'s programming language CSP (*Communicating Sequential Processes*).

One goal is to propose an *invariance proof method* to be used in the development and verification of correct programs. The method is suitable to *partial correctness*, *absence of deadlock* and *non-termination proofs*. The design of this proof method is formalized so as to prepare the way to possible alternatives.

A complementary goal is to propose an *automatic technique for gathering information about CSP programs* that can be useful to both optimizing compilers and program partial verification systems.

2. *SYNTAX AND OPERATIONAL SEMANTICS*

2.1 *Syntax*

The set sCSP of syntactically valid programs is informally defined so as to capture the essential features of CSP.

- Programs $\underline{Pr}$: $[\underline{P}(1) \parallel \underline{P}(2) \parallel \ldots \parallel \underline{P}(\underline{\pi})]$ where $\underline{\pi} \geq 2$
  (A program consists of a single parallel command specifying concurrent execution of its constituent disjoint processes).

- Processes $\underline{P}(i)$, $i \in [1,\underline{\pi}]$: $\underline{P\ell}(i) :: \underline{D}(i);\underline{\lambda}(i,1):\underline{S}(i)(1);\ldots;\underline{\lambda}(i,\underline{\sigma}(i)):\underline{S}(i)(\underline{\sigma}(i))$ where $\underline{\sigma}(i) \geq 1$
  (Each process $\underline{P}(i)$ has a unique name $\underline{P\ell}(i)$ and consists of a sequence of simple commands prefixed with declarations $\underline{D}(i)$ of local variables).

- Process labels $\underline{P\ell}(i)$, $i \in [1,\underline{\pi}]$.

- Declarations $\underline{D}(i)$, $i \in [1,\underline{\pi}]$: $\underline{x}(i)(1):\underline{t}(i)(1);\ldots;\underline{x}(i)(\underline{\delta}(i)):\underline{t}(i)(\underline{\delta}(i))$ where $\underline{\delta}(i) \geq 1$.

- Variables $\underline{x}(i)(j)$, $i \in [1,\underline{\pi}]$, $j \in [1,\underline{\delta}(i)]$.

- Types $\underline{t}(i)(j)$, $i \in [1,\underline{\pi}]$, $j \in [1,\underline{\delta}(i)]$.

- Program locations $\underline{\lambda}(i,j)$, $i \in [1,\underline{\pi}]$, $j \in [1,\underline{\sigma}(i)]$.
  (Each command has been labeled to ease future references).

- Simple commands $\underline{S}(i)(j)$, $i \in [1,\underline{\pi}]$, $j \in [1,\underline{\sigma}(i)]$:
  - . Null commands $\underline{S}(i)(j)$, $i \in [1,\underline{\pi}]$, $j \in \underline{N}(i)$: <u>skip</u>
  - . Assignment commands $\underline{S}(i)(j)$, $i \in [1,\underline{\pi}]$, $j \in \underline{A}(i)$: $\underline{x}(i)(\underline{\alpha}(i,j)) := \underline{e}(i,j)(\underline{x}(i))$ where $\underline{\alpha}(i,j) \in [1,\underline{\delta}(i)]$

---

* Université de Metz, Faculté des Sciences, Ile du Saulcy, 57000 Metz, France.
** CRIN Nancy - Laboratoire Associé au CNRS n°262.
This work was supported by INRIA (SESORI-78208) and by CNRS (ATP Intelligence Artif.).

(The pattern-matching feature introduced in Hoare[78] is treated using dynamic type checking. Multiple assignments or assignments to parts of structured variables are realized using global assignments to variables).

- Test commands $\underline{S}(i)(j)$, $i \in [1,\underline{\pi}]$, $j \in \underline{T}(i)$:
  $\underline{if}\ \underline{b}(i,j)(\underline{x}(\overline{i}))\ \underline{go}\ \underline{to}\ \underline{\lambda}(i,\underline{\eta}(i,j))$ where $\underline{\eta}(i,j) \in [1,\underline{\sigma}(i)]$.

- Stop commands $\underline{S}(i)(j)$, $i \in [1,\underline{\pi}]$, $j \in \underline{H}(i)$: $\underline{stop}$
  (Specify termination of process $\underline{P}(i)$).

- Communication commands $\underline{S}(i)(j)$, $i \in [1,\underline{\pi}]$, $j \in \underline{C}(i)$:
  $[\underline{G}(i,j,1) \to \underline{\lambda}(i,\underline{\eta}(i,j,1)) \ [\!]\ \ldots\ [\!]\ \underline{G}(i,j,\underline{\gamma}(i,j)) \to \underline{\lambda}(i,\underline{\eta}(i,j,\underline{\gamma}(i,j)))]$
  where $(\underline{\gamma}(i,j) \geq 1) \wedge (\forall k \in [1,\underline{\gamma}(i,j)],\ \underline{\eta}(i,j,k) \in [1,\underline{\sigma}(i)])$
  (The execution of the command $\underline{S}(i)(j)$ is delayed until one arbitrary but successfully executable input-output guard $\underline{G}(i,j,k)$ $(k \in [1,\underline{\gamma}(i,j)])$ is selected and executed. Next the command labeled $\underline{\lambda}(i,\underline{\eta}(i,j,k))$ is executed. If all input-output guards fail the process $\underline{P}(i)$ fails in deadlock).

  $\{\underline{N}(i),\underline{A}(i),\underline{T}(i),\underline{H}(i),\underline{C}(i)\}$ is a partition of $[1,\underline{\sigma}(i)]$.

- Input-Output guards $\underline{G}(i,j,k)$, $i \in [1,\underline{\pi}]$, $j \in \underline{C}(i)$, $k \in [1,\underline{\gamma}(i,j)]$:
  - Input guards $\underline{G}(i,j,k)$, $i \in [1,\underline{\pi}]$, $j \in \underline{C}(i)$, $k \in \underline{I}(i,j)$:
    $\underline{b}(i,j,k)(\underline{x}(\overline{i}));\underline{P\ell}(\theta(i,j,k))?\underline{x}(i)(\underline{\alpha}(i,j,k))$
    where $(\underline{\theta}(\overline{i},j,k) \in ([1,\underline{\pi}]-\{i\})) \wedge (\underline{\alpha}(i,j,k) \in [1,\underline{\delta}(i)])$.
  - Output guards $\underline{G}(i,j,k)$, $i \in [1,\underline{\pi}]$, $j \in \underline{C}(i)$, $k \in \underline{O}(i,j)$:
    $\underline{b}(i,j,k)(\underline{x}(\overline{i}));\underline{P\ell}(\underline{\theta}(i,j,k))!\underline{e}(i,j,k)(\underline{x}(i))$ where $\underline{\theta}(i,j,k) \in ([1,\underline{\pi}]-\{i\})$.

  $\{\underline{I}(i,j),\underline{O}(i,j)\}$ is a partition of $[1,\underline{\gamma}(i,j)]$.
  (Pure signals are transmitted using typed variables).

- Expressions $\underline{e}(i,j)(\underline{x}(i))$, $i \in [1,\underline{\pi}]$, $j \in \underline{A}(i)$
  $\underline{e}(i,j,k)(\underline{x}(i))$, $i \in [1,\underline{\pi}]$, $j \in \underline{C}(i)$, $k \in \underline{O}(i,j)$
  ($\underline{e}(i,j)$ maps $dom(\underline{e}(\overline{i},j)) \subseteq \underline{t}(i)$ into $\underline{t}(\overline{i})(\underline{\alpha}(i,j))$ and $\underline{e}(i,j,k)$ maps $dom(\underline{e}(i,j,k)) \subseteq \underline{t}(i)$ into $\cup\{\underline{t}(\underline{\theta}(i,j,k))(\ell) : \ell \in [1,\underline{\delta}(\underline{\theta}(i,j,k))]\}$).

- Boolean expressions $\underline{b}(i,j)(\underline{x}(i))$, $i \in [1,\underline{\pi}]$, $j \in \underline{T}(i)$
  $\underline{b}(i,j,k)(\underline{x}(i))$, $i \in [1,\underline{\pi}]$, $j \in \underline{C}(i)$, $k \in [1,\underline{\gamma}(i,j)]$
  ($\underline{b}(i,j)$ (resp. $\underline{b}(i,j,k)$) maps $dom(\underline{b}(i,j))$ (resp. $dom(\underline{b}(i,j,k))$) into truth values).

- The following abbreviations will be used :
  $\underline{P\ell}(\underline{\theta}(i,j))?\underline{x}(i)(\underline{\alpha}(i,j)) = [\underline{true};\underline{P\ell}(\underline{\theta}(i,j,1))?\underline{x}(i)(\underline{\alpha}(i,j,1)) \to \underline{\lambda}(i,j+1)]$
  $\underline{P\ell}(\underline{\theta}(i,j))!\underline{e}(i,j)(\underline{x}(i)) = [\underline{true};\underline{P\ell}(\underline{\theta}(i,j,1))!\underline{e}(i,j,1)(\underline{x}(i)) \to \underline{\lambda}(i,j+1)]$

This syntax is not intended to be of practical use. The syntax of some examples freely deviates from the above definition when the correspondence is obvious.

2.2 *Operational Semantics*

Roughly an operational semantics defines for each syntactically valid program a set St of states and a transition relation $tr \in [[St \times St] \to B]$ which is *true* between each state and its possible successors. $B=\{true, false\}$ is the uniquely complemented complete lattice of truth values with ordering *false* $\Rightarrow$ *true*, infimum *false*, supremum *true*, join $\vee$, meet $\wedge$, complement $\neg$.

2.2.1 *Operational Semantics of Individual Processes*

The semantics of each process $\underline{P}(i)$, $i \in [1,\underline{\pi}]$ can be defined independently of the other processes as long as no communication command is involved.

- Program locations : $\underline{L} = \Pi\{\{\underline{\lambda}(i,j) : j \in [1,\underline{\sigma}(i)]\} : i \in [1,\underline{\pi}]\}$
  (If $\{E(i) : i \in I\}$ is a family of sets, the cartesian product $\Pi\{E(i) : i \in I\}$ is defined as the subset of $I \to \cup\{E(i) : i \in I\}$ of all functions f for which $f(i) \in E(i)$ for all $i \in I$).

- States : $S(i) = \underline{t}(i) \times \underline{L}(i),\ i\in[1,\underline{\pi}]$.

- Transition relation :

$\tau(i) \in [[S(i)\times S(i)]\to B],\ i\in[1,\pi]$

$\tau(i) = \lambda((xa,ca),(xb,cb)).[\exists j,k\in[1,\underline{\sigma}(i)]:\ ca=\underline{\lambda}(i,j) \wedge cb=\underline{\lambda}(i,k) \wedge [(\mathit{Null}(i,j)(xa,xb) \wedge k=j+1)\vee(\mathit{Assign}(i,j)(xa,xb) \wedge k=j+1)\vee(\mathit{Test}(i,j,k)(xa,xb))]]$

$\mathit{Null}(i,j) \in [[\underline{t}(i)\times\underline{t}(i)]\to B],\ i\in[1,\underline{\pi}],\ j\in[1,\underline{\sigma}(i)]$

$\mathit{Null}(i,j) = \lambda(xa,xb).[j\in\underline{N}(i) \wedge xa=xb]$

$\mathit{Assign}(i,j) \in [[\underline{t}(i)\times\underline{t}(i)]\to B],\ i\in[1,\underline{\pi}],\ j\in[1,\underline{\sigma}(i)]$

$\mathit{Assign}(i,j) = \lambda(xa,xb).[(j\in\underline{A}(i))\wedge(\forall q\in([1,\underline{\delta}(i)]-\{\underline{\alpha}(i,j)\}),\ xb(q)=xa(q)) \wedge (xa \in \mathit{dom}(\underline{e}(i,j))) \wedge xb(\underline{\alpha}(i,j))=\underline{e}(i,j)(xa)]$

$\mathit{Test}(i,j,k) \in [[\underline{t}(i)\times\underline{t}(i)]\to B],\ i\in[1,\underline{\pi}],\ j,k\in[1,\underline{\sigma}(i)]$

$\mathit{Test}(i,j,k) = \lambda(xa,xb).[(j\in\underline{T}(i))\wedge(xa=xb)\wedge(xa \in \mathit{dom}(\underline{b}(i,j))) \wedge [(\underline{b}(i,j)(xa) \wedge k=\underline{\eta}(i,j))\vee(\neg\underline{b}(i,j)(xa) \wedge k=j+1)]]$

2.2.2 *Characterization of the States that a Process can Reach after a Communication*

When process $\underline{P}(i)$ is at location c with values x of its local variables, the output guard $\underline{G}(i,j,k)$ is successfully executable only if $\mathit{Ogse}(i,j,k)(x,c)$ is *true* :

$\mathit{Ogse}(i,j,k) \in [S(i)\to B],\ i\in[1,\underline{\pi}],\ j\in\underline{C}(i),\ k\in\underline{O}(i,j)$

$\mathit{Ogse}(i,j,k) = \lambda(x,c).[c=\underline{\lambda}(i,j) \wedge x \in \mathit{dom}(\underline{b}(i,j,k)) \wedge \underline{b}(i,j,k)(x) \wedge x \in \mathit{dom}(\underline{e}(i,j,k))]$.

If tr is a relation then tr^* denotes its reflexive transitive closure.

The states (xb,cb) that process $\underline{P}(i)$ can reach after execution of output guard $\underline{G}(i,j,k)$ in state (xa,ca) and before meeting a communication or stop command are such that $\mathit{Rsao}(i,j,k)((xa,ca),(xb,cb))$ is *true* :

$\mathit{Rsao}(i,j,k) \in [[S(i)\times S(i)]\to B],\ i\in[1,\underline{\pi}],\ j\in\underline{C}(i),\ k\in\underline{O}(i,j)$

$\mathit{Rsao}(i\ j,k) = \lambda((xa,ca),(xb,cb)).[\mathit{Ogse}(i,j,k)(xa,ca) \wedge \tau[i]^*[(xa,\underline{\lambda}(i,\underline{\eta}(i,j,k))),(xb,cb)]]$

When process $\underline{P}(i)$ is at location c with values x of its local variables the input guard $\underline{G}(i,j,k)$ is successfully executable only if $\mathit{Igse}(i,j,k)(x,c)$ is *true* :

$\mathit{Igse}(i,j,k) \in [S(i)\to B],\ i\in[1,\pi],\ j\in\underline{C}(i),\ k\in\underline{I}(i,j)$

$\mathit{Igse}(i,j,k) = \lambda(x,c).[c=\underline{\lambda}(i,j) \wedge x \in \mathit{dom}(\underline{b}(i,j,k)) \wedge \underline{b}(i,j,k)(x)]$

If $\{E(i):i\in I\}$ is a family of sets and $x\in\Pi\{E(i):i\in I\}$, $j\in I$, $v\in E(j)$ then $\mathit{subst}(x)(j/v)$ equals y such that $y(j)=v$ whereas $y(k)=x(k)$ for all $k\in I$ such that $k\neq j$. If $n>1$, $j_1,\ldots,j_n \in I$ and $v_1\in E(j_1),\ldots,v_n\in E(j_n)$ then $\mathit{subst}(x)(j_1/v_1,\ldots,j_n/v_n) = \mathit{subst}[\mathit{subst}(x)(j_1/v_1)][j_2/v_2,\ldots,j_n/v_n]$

The states (xb,cb) that process $\underline{P}(i)$ can reach after execution in state (xa,ca) of input guard $\underline{G}(i,j,k)$ which assigns the transmitted value $v \in \underline{t}(i)(\underline{\alpha}(i,j,k))$ to variable $\underline{x}(i)(\underline{\alpha}(i,j,k))$ and before meeting a communication or stop command are such that $\mathit{Rsai}(i,j,k)((xa,ca),(xb,cb))$ is *true* :

$\mathit{Rsai}(i,j,k) \in [[S(i)\times\underline{t}(i)(\underline{\alpha}(i,j,k))\times S(i)]\to B],\ i\in[1,\underline{\pi}],\ j\in\underline{C}(i),\ k\in I(i,j)$

$\mathit{Rsai}(i,j,k) = \lambda((xa,ca),v,(xb,cb)).[\mathit{Igse}(i,j,k)(xa,ca) \wedge \tau[i]^*[(\mathit{subst}(xa)(\underline{\alpha}(i,j,k)/v),\underline{\lambda}(i,\underline{\eta}(i,j,k))),(xb,cb)]]$

2.2.3 *Operational Semantics of Communicating Processes*

We introduce the transition relations ι and μ which describe the cooperation of concurrently operating processes. Concurrency in the execution of a program is modeled by global nondeterminism in the selection of successor states. The resolution of the global nondeterminism is left unspecified since CSP definition specifies no scheduling policy whether fair or unfair.

2.2.3.1 *States*

$S = \underline{t} \times \underline{L}$

(When a process is willing to accept a rendez-vous, the states of all other processes may have to be checked in order to determine which processes are ready to communicate or have terminated and next which data are exchanged).

2.2.3.2 *Transition Relations*

- $\underline{C\ell}(i) = \underline{C}(i) \cup \underline{H}(i),\ i \in [1,\underline{\pi}]$

  (The only program locations relevant to cooperation between processes are those corresponding to communication or stop commands).

- $\iota \in [[S \times S] \rightarrow B]$

  $\iota = \lambda((xa,ca),(xb,cb)).[\forall i \in [1,\underline{\pi}],\ (ca(i)=cb(i)=\underline{\lambda}(i,1) \wedge xa(i)=xb(i)) \vee (ca(i)=\underline{\lambda}(i,1) \wedge \tau[i]^{*}[(xa(i),ca(i)),(xb(i),cb(i))] \wedge cb(i) \in \underline{\lambda}(i,\underline{C\ell}(i))]]$

  (If E, E1, E2 are sets, $f \in [E1 \rightarrow E2]$ and $E \subseteq E1$ then $f(E)$ is defined as $\{f(x) : x \in (dom(f) \cap E)\}$. The transition relation ι defines the "ready to communicate" or "stop" states which are possible successors of the "entry" states. As far as cooperation between processes is concerned, a process which is never willing to communicate and never terminates does not progress).

- $\underline{Ch} = \{\langle i,j,k \rightarrow \ell,m,n \rangle : i,\ell \in [1,\underline{\pi}] \wedge j \in \underline{C}(i) \wedge k \in \underline{O}(i,j) \wedge m \in \underline{C}(\ell) \wedge n \in \underline{I}(\ell,m) \wedge i=\underline{\theta}(\ell,m,n) \wedge \ell=\underline{\theta}(i,j,k) \wedge \{\underline{e}(i,j,k)(x) : x \in dom(\underline{e}(i,j,k))\} \cap \underline{t}(\ell)(\underline{\alpha}(\ell,m,n)) \neq \emptyset\}$.

  (The set $\underline{Ch}$ of communication channels is isomorphic with the set of statically matching pairs of input-output guards).

- $\mu \in [[S \times S] \rightarrow B]$

  $\mu = \lambda((xa,ca),(xb,cb)).[\exists \langle i,j,k \rightarrow \ell,m,n \rangle \in \underline{Ch} :$
  $[\forall q \in ([1,\underline{\pi}]-\{i,\ell\}),\ (ca(q)=cb(q)) \wedge (xa(q)=xb(q))]$
  $\wedge [Rsao(i,j,k)((xa(i),ca(i)),(xb(i),cb(i))) \wedge cb(i) \in \underline{\lambda}(i,\underline{C\ell}(i))]$
  $\wedge [\underline{e}(i,j,k)(xa(i)) \in \underline{t}(\ell)(\underline{\alpha}(\ell,m,n))]$
  $\wedge [Rsai(\ell,m,n)((xa(\ell),ca(\ell)),\underline{e}(i,j,k)(xa(i)),(xb(\ell),cb(\ell))) \wedge cb(\ell) \in \underline{\lambda}(\ell,\underline{C\ell}(\ell))]]$

  (The transition relation μ defines the "ready to communicate" or "stop" states which are the possible successors of "ready to communicate" states. The dynamic discrimination of input messages is modeled by dynamic type checking. When several rendez-vous are possible the selection is free. Hence μ specifies all possible orderings of the communications between processes).

3. FIXPOINT CHARACTERIZATION OF CORRECTNESS PROPERTIES

3.1 Fundamental Theorem

Let $\underline{Pr}$ be any syntactically correct sCSP program. Its operational semantics defines a set S of states and transition relations ι and μ. Let $P=[S \rightarrow B]$ be the set of predicates describing properties of initial, communication or termination states. It is a uniquely complemented complete lattice $P(\Rightarrow, false, true, \vee, \wedge, \neg)$ for the pointwise ordering $\Rightarrow$ (thus the meaning of symbols $\Rightarrow$, *false*, *true*, $\vee$, $\wedge$ and $\neg$ is context-dependent). Let E be the set of possible entry specifications for the program $\underline{Pr}$. The meaning of these specifications is described by $Init \in [E \rightarrow P]$ such that $Init(\phi)$ characterizes the set of possible initial states corresponding to the entry specification $\phi \in E$:

- $P = [S \rightarrow B]$

  $E = \Pi\{[\underline{t}(i) \rightarrow B] : i \in [1,\underline{\pi}]\}$

- $Init \in [E \rightarrow P]$

  $Init = \lambda\beta.[Post(\iota)(\lambda(x,c).[\forall i \in [1,\underline{\pi}],\ x(i) \in dom(\beta(i)) \wedge \beta(i)(x(i)) \wedge c(i)=\underline{\lambda}(i,1)])]$

  where the predicate transformer *Post* is defined as :

- $Post \in [[[S \times S] \rightarrow B] \rightarrow [P \rightarrow P]]$

  $Post = \lambda\theta.[\lambda\beta.[\lambda sb.[\exists sa \in S : \beta(sa) \wedge \theta(sa,sb)]]]$

By definition the set of states which may be reached during any execution of program $\underline{Pr}$ starting with an initial value of the variables satisfying the entry specification $\overline{\phi \in E}$ is characterized by $Post(\mu^*)(Init(\phi))$. Notice that when programs are non-deterministic *Post* characterizes possible but not necessarily certain descendants of the entry states. The following fixpoint characterization of $Post(\mu^*)(Init(\phi))$ is the basis of our approach (Cousot[79]) :

- $f \in [E \to [P \to P]]$
  $f = \lambda\phi.[\lambda\beta.[Init(\phi) \vee Post(\mu)(\beta)]]$
- $Lfp \in [[P \to P] \to P]$ is the least fixpoint operator for isotone operators on the complete lattice P (Cousot & Cousot[79b]).

Theorem 3.1.1

$\forall\phi\in E,\ Post(\mu^*)(Init(\phi)) = Lfp(f(\phi))$

The above fixpoint theorem leads to sound and complete invariance proof methods (Cousot[79]) and to automatic program analysis techniques (Cousot & Cousot[79a]). However in order to put these methods into practice one or several applications of the following step are required.

3.2 (Pre)homomorphic Image of the Predicate Algebra

Let $A(\Rightarrow, false, true, \vee, \wedge, \neg)$ be a uniquely complemented complete lattice of "assertions". The meaning of A is defined by a *false*-strict $\vee$-complete morphism from $P(\Rightarrow, false, true, \vee, \wedge, \neg)$ into $A(\Rightarrow, false, true, \vee, \wedge, \neg)$. $\rho(\beta)$ is the representation of a "Predicate" $\beta\in P$ by an "assertion" belonging to A. Corresponding to f, let us introduce $F\in[E \to [A \to A]]$ defined as $\lambda\phi.[\lambda\alpha.[INIT(\phi) \vee POST(\alpha)]]$ where $INIT\in[E \to A]$ and $POST\in[A \to A]$. F is said to be equivalent to (resp. an upper approximation of) f up to ρ if and only if $\forall\phi\in E$, $F(\phi)$ is isotone and $\rho\circ f(\phi)$ equals (resp. implies) $F(\phi)\circ\rho$. Let $LFP\in[[A \to A] \to A]$ be the least fixpoint operator. The following theorem shows that whenever F is equivalent to (resp. an upper approximation of) f, $\rho(Lfp(f(\phi)))$ equals (resp. implies) $LFP(F(\phi))$:

Theorem 3.2.1

Let f and F be respectively isotone operators on the complete lattices $P(\Rightarrow, false, true, \vee, \wedge)$ and $A(\Rightarrow, false, true, \vee, \wedge)$, ρ be a *false*-strict $\vee$-complete morphism from P into A such that $\rho\circ f = F\circ\rho$ (resp. $\rho\circ f \Rightarrow F\circ\rho$) then $\rho(Lfp(f)) = LFP(F)$ (resp. $\rho(Lfp(f)) \Rightarrow LFP(F)$).

The importance of this theorem is that it shows that whenever F is equivalent to (resp. an upper approximation of) f up to the $\vee$-morphism ρ, results about the considered program $\underline{Pr}$ obtained using P and f are equivalent to (resp. correctly approximated by) the results obtained using A and F. For example a set of assertions interleaved at appropriate places in the program can be used instead of a single global invariant.

3.3 Associating Assertions with Communication Channels

Let us introduce a *Proj* homomorphic image $Ag(false, \vee, INITg, POSTg)$ of $P(false, \vee, Init, Post(\mu))$:

- $Ag = [\underline{Ch} \to [S \to B]]$
- $Proj \in [P \to Ag]$
  $Proj = \lambda\beta.[\lambda\langle i,j,k \to \ell,m,n\rangle.[\lambda(x,c).[Ogse(i,j,k)(x(i),c(i)) \wedge$
  $\wedge\ Igse(\ell,m,n)(x(\ell),c(\ell)) \wedge \beta(x,c)]]]$

The following auxiliary definition is used for describing the behavior of process $\underline{P}(i)$ between locations $\underline{\lambda}(i,j)$ and $\underline{\lambda}(i,k)$ as long as no communication or stop command is encountered :

- $Tr\ell(i)(j,k) \in [[\underline{t}(i) \times \underline{t}(i)] \to B],\ i \in [1,\underline{\pi}],\ j \in [1,\underline{\sigma}(i)]$
  $Tr\ell(i)(j,k) = \lambda(\overline{xa,xb}).[\tau[i]^{*}[(xa,\underline{\lambda}(\overline{i,j})),(xb,\overline{\underline{\lambda}}(i,k))]]$

- $INITg \in [E \to Ag]$
  $$INITg = \lambda\phi.[\lambda\langle i,j,k \to \ell,m,n\rangle.[\lambda(x,c).[(\exists y \in \underline{t}(i):\ \phi(i)(y) \wedge Tr\ell(i)(1,j)(y,x(i)) \wedge Ogse(i,j,k)(x(i),c(i))) \wedge (\exists z \in \underline{t}(\ell):\ \phi(\ell)(z) \wedge Tr\ell(\ell)(1,m)(z,x(\ell)) \wedge Igse(\ell,m,n)(x(\ell),c(\ell))) \wedge (\forall p \in ([1,\underline{\pi}]-\{i,\ell\}),(\phi(p)(x(p)) \wedge c(p)=\underline{\lambda}(p,1)) \vee (\exists u \in \underline{t}(p), \exists q \in \underline{C\ell}(p):\ \phi(p)(u) \wedge Tr\ell(p)(\overline{1},q)(u,x(p)) \wedge \overline{c}(p)=\underline{\lambda}(p,\overline{q})))]]]$$

- $POSTg \in [Ag \to Ag]$
  $$POSTg = \lambda\alpha.[\lambda\langle i,j,k \to \ell,m,n\rangle.[\lambda(x,c).[Ogse(i,j,k)(x(i),c(i)) \wedge Igse(\ell,m,n)(x(\ell),c(\ell)) \wedge [\exists\langle p,q,r \to s,t,u\rangle \in \underline{Ch},\ y \in \underline{t}(p),\ z \in \underline{t}(s):\ \alpha(\langle p,q,r \to s,t,\overline{u}\rangle)(\overline{subst}(x)(\overline{p/y},s/z),subst(c)(p/\underline{\lambda}(p,q),s/\underline{\lambda}(s,t))) \wedge \underline{e}(p,q,r)(y) \in \underline{t}(s)(\underline{\alpha}(s,t,u)) \wedge (\overline{\exists v \in \underline{C\ell}}(p):\ c(\overline{p})=\underline{\lambda}(\overline{p},v) \wedge Tr\ell(p)(\underline{\eta}(p,q,r),v)(y,x(p))) \wedge (\exists w \in \overline{\underline{C\ell}}(s):\ c(s)=\overline{\underline{\lambda}}(s,w) \wedge Tr\ell(\overline{s})(\underline{\eta}(s,t,u),w)(subst(z)(\underline{\alpha}(s,t,u)/\underline{e}(p,q,r)(y)),x(s)))]]]]$$

- $Fg \in [E \to [Ag \to Ag]]$
  $Fg = \lambda\phi.[\lambda\alpha.[INITg(\phi) \vee POSTg(\alpha)]]$

Lemma 3.3.1

$\forall\phi \in E,\ Proj \circ f(\phi) = Fg(\phi) \circ Proj$

Theorem 3.3.2

$\forall\phi \in E,\ Proj(Lfp(f(\phi))) = LFP(Fg(\phi))$

3.4 Analysis of the Behavior of Individual Processes

A global assertion about the states of process $\underline{P}(i)$ can be replaced by a set of assertions about the values of the process variables preceding each command :

- $A\ell = \Pi\{\Pi\{[\underline{t}(i) \to B]:\ j \in [1,\underline{\sigma}(i)]\}:\ i \in [1,\underline{\pi}]\}$

- $Proj\ell(i) \in [[S(i) \to B] \to A\ell(i)],\ i \in [1,\underline{\pi}]$
  $Proj\ell(i) = \lambda\alpha.[\lambda j.[\lambda x.[\alpha(x,\underline{\lambda}(i,j))]]]$

3.4.1 Analysis of the Behavior of Individual Processes Independently of Communications

By definition $Tr\ell(i)(j,k)(xa,xb)$ is *true* if and only if execution of process $\underline{P}(i)$ starting from location $\underline{\lambda}(i,j)$ with the initial state xa of the variables $\underline{x}(i)$ can reach location $\underline{\lambda}(i,k)$ with $\underline{x}(\overline{i})$=xb and without encountering communication commands. The following characterization of $Tr\ell(i)(j,k)$ as a fixpoint together with Cousot & Cousot[77b] shows that the computation of $Tr\ell(i)(j,k)$ looks like symbolic execution with this difference that all paths are followed simultaneously and infinite paths are handled by induction.

- $Post\ell(i) \in [[[\underline{t}(i) \times \underline{t}(i)] \to B] \to [[\underline{t}(i) \to B] \to [\underline{t}(i) \to B]]],\ i \in [1,\underline{\pi}]$
  $Post\ell(i) = \lambda\theta.[\lambda\beta.[\overline{\lambda}xb.[\exists xa \in \underline{t}(i):\ \beta(xa) \wedge \theta(\overline{xa},xb)]]]$

- $F\ell(i) \in [A\ell(i) \to [A\ell(i) \to A\ell(i)]],\ i \in [1,\underline{\pi}]$
  $$F\ell(i) = \lambda\beta.[\lambda\alpha.[\lambda j.[\beta(j) \vee Post\ell(i)(Null(i,j-1))(\alpha(j-1)) \vee Post\ell(i)(Assign(i,j-1))(\alpha(j-1)) \vee (\exists k \in \underline{T}(i):\ Post\ell(i)(Test(i,k,j))(\alpha(k)))]]]$$

Theorem 3.4.1.1

$\forall i \in [1,\underline{\pi}],\ j,k \in [1,\underline{\sigma}(i)],$
$Tr\ell(i)(j,k) = \overline{\lambda}(xa,xb).[LFP[F\ell(i)(\lambda m.[\lambda x.[(m=j) \wedge x=xa]])][k][xb]]$

3.4.2 *Analysis of the Behavior of Individual Processes taking Communications into Account*

We define $Desc\ell(\phi)(i)(j)$ characterizing the possible values that local variables $\underline{x}(i)$ can possess at run-time when location $\underline{\lambda}(i,j)$ of process $\underline{P}(i)$ is reached during an execution of the program starting from an initial state of the local variables $\underline{x}(k)$, $k\in[1,\underline{\pi}]$ satisfying the entry specification $\phi\in E$:

- $Desc\ell \in [E \to A\ell]$

$$
\begin{array}{l}
Desc\ell = \lambda\phi.[\lambda i.[\lambda j.[\lambda x.[\{Post\ell(i)(\tau(i)^{*})(\lambda(y,c).[\phi(\underline{i})(y) \wedge c=\underline{\lambda}(i,1)])(x,\underline{\lambda}(i,j))\} \\
\quad \vee\{\exists<\ell,m,n \to p,q,r>\in \underline{Ch}, y\in\underline{t}, c\in\underline{L}:\ Proj[Post(\mu^{*})(Init(\overline{\phi}))][<\ell,m,n\to p,q,r>][y,c] \\
\quad\quad \wedge[\{(\ell=i) \wedge Rsao(i,\overline{m},n)((\overline{y(i)},c(i)),(x,\underline{\lambda}(i,j)))\} \vee \\
\quad\quad\quad \{(p=i) \wedge (\underline{e}(\ell,m,n)(y(\ell))\in\underline{t}(i)(\underline{\alpha}(i,q,\overline{r})) \\
\quad\quad\quad\quad \wedge Rsai(i,q,r)((y(\overline{i}),c(\overline{i})),\ \underline{e}(\ell,m,n)(y(\ell)),(x,\underline{\lambda}(i,j)))\}]\}]]]]
\end{array}
$$

Since the local descendants of the entry states are either direct descendants of the entry states or the descendants of the states following either an output or an input, the meaning of each separate process can be completely determined only when an initial state for the local variables is provided and the input-output requests from other processes (as determined at paragraph 3.3) are known.

If a state of the program is known before a communication then the corresponding state of the communicating processes after this communication is given by :

- $Postoc \in [Ag \to A\ell]$

$$
\begin{array}{l}
Postoc = \lambda\alpha.[\lambda i.[\lambda j.[\lambda x.[\exists<\ell,m,n\to p,q,r>\in\underline{Ch}, y\in\underline{t}, c\in\underline{L}:\ (\ell=i)\wedge(m+1=j)\wedge \\
\quad \alpha(<i,m,n\to p,q,r>)(subst(y)(i/\overline{x}),\overline{subst}(\overline{c})(i/\underline{\lambda}(i,m)))\wedge \\
\quad Ogse(i,m,n)(x,\underline{\lambda}(i,m))]]]]
\end{array}
$$

- $Postic \in [Ag \to A\ell]$

$$
\begin{array}{l}
Postic = \lambda\alpha.[\lambda i.[\lambda j.[\lambda x.[\exists<\ell,m,n\to p,q,r>\in\underline{Ch}, y\in\underline{t}, c\in\underline{L}:\ (p=i)\wedge(q+1=j)\wedge \\
\quad \alpha(<\ell,m,n\to i,q,r>)(y,subst(c)(\overline{i/\underline{\lambda}(i,q)}))\wedge\underline{e}(\ell,m,n)(y(\ell))\in\underline{t}(i)(\alpha(i,q,r))\wedge \\
\quad Igse(i,q,r)(x,\underline{\lambda}(i,q))\ \wedge\ x=\overline{subst}[y(i)][\overline{\underline{\alpha}}(i,q,r)/\underline{e}(\ell,m,\overline{n})(y(\overline{\ell}))]]]]]
\end{array}
$$

The following theorem gives a fixpoint characterization of the local descendants of the entry states :

Theorem 3.4.2.1

$\forall\phi\in E,\ \forall i\in[1,\underline{\pi}],$

$$
\begin{array}{l}
Desc\ell(\phi)(\overline{i}) = LFP[F\ell[i][\lambda m.(\lambda x.((m=1)\wedge\phi(i)(x)))\vee Postoc(LFP(Fg(\phi)))(i) \\
\qquad\qquad\qquad\qquad\qquad\qquad\qquad \vee Postic(LFP(Fg(\phi)))(i)]]
\end{array}
$$

3.5 *Example*

```
[P1 :: x:integer; 11: x:=10;
       12: loop 13: exit when x≤0; 14: P2!x; 15: P2?x; 16: end loop;
       17: P2!x; 18: stop

||P2 :: y:integer;
       21: loop 22: P1?y; 23: exit when y=0; 24: P1!y-1; 25: end loop;
       26: stop
]
```

3.5.1 *Analysis of the Behavior of Individual Processes*

The systems of equations $X = F\ell(i)(\beta)(X)$, $i=1,2$ are the following :

$$\left[\begin{array}{l}
X(11)=\beta(1)\\
X(12)=\lambda x.[\beta(2)(x)\vee\exists x'\in\text{integer}:X(11)(x')\wedge x=10]\\
X(13)=\beta(3)\vee X(12)\vee X(16)\\
X(14)=\lambda x.[\beta(4)(x)\vee(X(13)(x)\wedge x>0)]\\
X(15)=\beta(5)\\
X(16)=\beta(6)\\
X(17)=\lambda x.[\beta(7)(x)\vee(X(13)(x)\wedge x\leq 0)]\\
X(18)=\beta(8)
\end{array}\right.$$

$$\left[\begin{array}{l}
X(21)=\beta(1)\\
X(22)=\beta(2)\vee X(21)\vee X(25)\\
X(23)=\beta(3)\\
X(24)=\lambda y.[\beta(4)(y)\vee(X(23)(y)\wedge y\neq 0)]\\
X(25)=\beta(5)\\
X(26)=\lambda y.[\beta(6)(y)\vee(X(23)(y)\wedge y=0)]
\end{array}\right.$$

Using theorem 3.4.1.1 we compute :

$$\left[\begin{array}{l}
\mathit{Tr}\ell(1)(1,4)(xa,xb)=(xb=10)\\
\mathit{Tr}\ell(1)(5,5)(xa,xb)=(xb=xa)\\
\mathit{Tr}\ell(1)(6,4)(xa,xb)=(xa>0\wedge xb=xa)\\
\mathit{Tr}\ell(1)(6,7)(xa,xb)=(xa\leq 0\wedge xb=xa)\\
\mathit{Tr}\ell(1)(8,8)(xa,xb)=(xb=xa)
\end{array}\right.$$

$$\left[\begin{array}{l}
\mathit{Tr}\ell(2)(1,2)(ya,yb)=(yb=ya)\\
\mathit{Tr}\ell(2)(3,4)(ya,yb)=(ya\neq 0\wedge yb=ya)\\
\mathit{Tr}\ell(2)(3,6)(ya,yb)=(ya=0\wedge yb=ya)\\
\mathit{Tr}\ell(2)(5,2)(ya,yb)=(yb=ya)
\end{array}\right.$$

3.5.2 *Analysis of the Communications*

The channels of communications are $<14\rightarrow 22>$, $<24\rightarrow 15>$, $<17\rightarrow 22>$. Assume $\phi=(\lambda x.[\mathit{true}],\lambda y.[\mathit{true}])$ then the system of equations $X=Fg(\phi)(X)$ is constructed using the results of 3.5.1 :

$$\left[\begin{array}{lll}
X(<14\rightarrow 22>) & = & \lambda((x,y),(c1,c2)).[c1=14\wedge c2=22\wedge[(x=10)\vee(\exists x'\in\text{integer}:\\
 & & \quad X(<24\rightarrow 15>)(x',y,15,24)\wedge x=y-1\wedge x>0)]]\\
X(<24\rightarrow 15>) & = & \lambda((x,y),(c1,c2)).[c1=15\wedge c2=24\wedge(\exists y'\in\text{integer}:\\
 & & \quad X(<14\rightarrow 22>)(x,y',14,22)\wedge y=x\wedge y\neq 0)]\\
X(<17\rightarrow 22>) & = & \lambda((x,y),(c1,c2)).[c1=17\wedge c2=22\wedge(\exists x'\in\text{integer}:\\
 & & \quad X(<24\rightarrow 15>)(x',y,24,15)\wedge x=y-1\wedge x\leq 0)]
\end{array}\right.$$

The least solution P is computed by successive approximations (Cousot[77]) :

$$\left[\begin{array}{lll}
P(<14\rightarrow 22>) & = & \lambda((x,y),(c1,c2)).[c1=14\wedge c2=22\wedge[(x=10)\vee(1\leq x\leq 9\wedge y=x+1)]]\\
P(<24\rightarrow 15>) & = & \lambda((x,y),(c1,c2)).[c1=15\wedge c2=24\wedge 1\leq x=y\leq 10]\\
P(<17\rightarrow 22>) & = & \lambda((x,y),(c1,c2)).[c1=17\wedge c2=22\wedge x=0\wedge y=1]
\end{array}\right.$$

3.5.3 *Local descendants of the entry States*

The systems of equations $X=F\ell[i][\lambda m.(\lambda z.(m=1))\vee \mathit{Postoc}(P)(i)\vee \mathit{Postic}(P)(i)][X]$, $i=1,2$ are now :

$$\left[\begin{array}{l}
X(11)=\lambda x.[\mathit{true}]\\
X(12)=\lambda x.[\exists x':X(11)(x')\wedge x=10]\\
X(13)=X(12)\vee X(16)\\
X(14)=\lambda x.[X(13)(x)\wedge x>0]\\
X(15)=\lambda x.[1\leq x\leq 10]\\
X(16)=\lambda x.[0\leq x\leq 9]\\
X(17)=\lambda x.[X(13)(x)\wedge x\leq 0]\\
X(18)=\lambda x.[x=0]
\end{array}\right.$$

$$\left[\begin{array}{l}
X(21)=\lambda y.[\mathit{true}]\\
X(22)=X(21)\vee X(25)\\
X(23)=\lambda y.[0\leq y\leq 10]\\
X(24)=\lambda y.[X(23)(y)\wedge y\neq 0]\\
X(25)=\lambda y.[1\leq y\leq 10]\\
X(26)=\lambda y.[X(23)(y)\wedge y=0]
\end{array}\right.$$

$\mathit{Desc}\ell(\phi)(i)$, $i=1,2$ equals the least solutions to the above equations (Th.3.4.2.1):

$$\left[\begin{array}{l}
P(11)=\lambda x.[\mathit{true}]\\
P(12)=\lambda x.[x=10]\\
P(13)=\lambda x.[0\leq x\leq 10]\\
P(14)=P(15)=\lambda x.[1\leq x\leq 10]\\
P(16)=\lambda x.[0\leq x\leq 9]\\
P(17)=P(18)=\lambda x.[x=0]
\end{array}\right.$$

$$\left[\begin{array}{l}
P(21)=P(22)=\lambda y.[\mathit{true}]\\
P(23)=\lambda y.[0\leq y\leq 10]\\
P(24)=P(25)=\lambda y.[1\leq y\leq 10]\\
P(26)=\lambda y.[y=0]
\end{array}\right.$$

In general the least solutions to the systems of equations associated with non-trivial programs are not mechanically computable. Even by hand such calculations cannot be worked out since they are amazingly complex. The solution to this intricacy is the idea of approximation which is central to proof methods and automatic program analysis techniques.

4. INVARIANCE PROOF METHODS

4.1 Outline of Our Approach

$\psi \in P$ is said to be invariant during execution of program Pr starting with any state satisfying the entry specification $\phi \in E$ if and only if $\overline{Post}(\mu^*)(Init(\phi)) \Rightarrow \psi$.

4.1.1 Fundamental Invariance Proof Method

The fixpoint characterization of $Post(\mu^*)(Init(\phi))$ given by theorem 3.1.1 leads to a *sound* and *complete* invariance proof method :

Theorem 4.1.1.1

$$\forall \phi \in E, \forall \psi \in P, \ [\exists I \in P: (f(\phi)(I) \Rightarrow I) \wedge (I \Rightarrow \psi)] \Leftrightarrow [Post(\mu^*)(Init(\phi)) \Rightarrow \psi]$$

This invariance proof method fits for use in *partial correctness, abscence of deadlock* and *non-termination proofs* (the only difference is with respect to the choice of ψ).

4.1.2 (Pre)homomorphic Variants of the Fundamental Proof Method

(Pre)homomorphic images of the predicate algebra (as described at paragraph 3.2) have to be introduced in order to put the fundamental invariance proof method into practice. The soundness or soundness and completeness of these variants of the fundamental proof method follow from the following :

Theorem 4.1.2.1

Let f and F be respectively isotone operators on the complete lattices $P(\Rightarrow, \mathit{false}, \mathit{true}, \vee, \wedge)$ and $A(\Rightarrow, \mathit{false}, \mathit{true}, \vee, \wedge)$, ρ be a *false*-strict $\vee$-complete morphism from P into A such that $\rho \circ f \Rightarrow F \circ \rho$ (resp. $\rho \circ f = F \circ \rho$), $\overline{F}$ be an isotone operator on A such that $F \Rightarrow \overline{F}$ (resp. $F = \overline{F}$) then $\forall \psi \in A$, $[\exists I \in A: \overline{F}(I) \Rightarrow I \wedge I \Rightarrow \psi]$ implies (resp. implies and reciprocally) that $\rho(Lfp(f)) \Rightarrow \psi$.

4.2 A Sound and Complete Invariance Proof Method

For example using the homomorphic image of the predicate algebra described at paragraph 3.3 we get the following particular invariance proof method :

Corollary 4.2.1

$$\forall \phi \in E, \forall \psi \in Ag, \ [\exists I \in Ag: (INITg(\phi) \Rightarrow I) \wedge (POSTg(I) \Rightarrow I) \wedge (I \Rightarrow \psi)] \Leftrightarrow [Proj(Post(\mu^*)(Init(\phi))) \Rightarrow \psi]$$

Theorem 4.1.2.1 also shows that we can replace $Tr\ell(i)(j,k)$, $i \in [1,\underline{\pi}]$, $j,k \in [1,\underline{\sigma}(i)]$ by upper bounds in the definitions of *INITg* and *POSTg*. By theorems 3.4.1.1 and 4.1.2.1 the correctness of these upper bounds can be shown using an invariance proof method. Hence, proof method 4.2.1 follows the lines drawn by example 3.5 (except that no fixpoint computation is involved and equations are replaced by inequations understood as verification rules).

4.3 *A Sound Variant Without Program Location Counters*

For the sake of completeness in the invariance proof method 4.2.1 the assertions $I \in Ag$ may have to take the values of the program location counters into account. Yet, on grounds of methodology, reasonings about program location counters are usually ruled out. In order to get rid of program location counters let us introduce :

- $Ags = [\underline{Ch} \rightarrow [\underline{t} \rightarrow B]]$, $Epcg \in [Ag \rightarrow Ags]$, $Apcg \in [Ags \rightarrow Ag]$

- $Projs \in [P \rightarrow Ags]$
  $Projs = Epcg \circ Proj$

- $Fs \in [E \rightarrow [Ags \rightarrow Ags]]$
  $Fs = \lambda\phi.[Epcg \circ Fg(\phi) \circ Apcg]$

For example one can choose :

- $Epcg = \lambda\alpha.[\lambda ch.[\lambda x.[\exists c \in L: \alpha(ch)(x,c)]]]$
  $Apcg = \lambda\alpha.[\lambda ch.[\lambda(x,c).[\alpha(ch)(x)]]]$

The soundness of the corresponding invariance proof method is shown in a general setting by the following :

Theorem 4.3.1

If *Epcg* is a *false*-strict $\vee$-complete morphism, *Apcg* is upper semi-continuous, $Es \subseteq E$, $It = Lfp(\lambda X.[\{false\} \cup \{Init(\phi) \vee Post(\mu)(\alpha) : \phi \in Es \wedge \alpha \in X\}])$ and $(\forall \alpha \in It, Proj(\alpha) \Rightarrow Apcg(Projs(\alpha)))$ then :
$\forall \phi \in Es, Projs[Post(\mu^*)(Init(\phi))] \Rightarrow LFP(Fs(\phi))$

Corollary 4.3.2

If moreover $\forall \phi \in Es$, $\overline{Fs}(\phi) \in [Ags \rightarrow Ags]$ is isotone and such that $Fs(\phi) \Rightarrow \overline{Fs}(\phi)$, then : $\forall \phi \in Es, \forall \psi s \in Ags, [\exists I \in Ags: (\overline{Fs}(\phi)(I) \Rightarrow I) \wedge (I \Rightarrow \psi s)] \Rightarrow [Projs[Post(\mu^*)(Init(\phi))] \Rightarrow \psi s]$

Completeness can only be established for programs involving only one or two processes (i.e. when $\underline{\pi} = 2$).

4.4 *Introducing Auxiliary Variables for Completeness*

In general the reciprocal of theorem 4.3.2 is not true for programs involving more than two processes. A completeness result can nevertheless be obtained using history variables. The use of history variables (Apt, Francez & de Roever[79b], Clarke[78], Clint[73], Owicki & Gries[76]) has several drawbacks. For example, it is difficult to guess which auxiliary variables must be introduced. Only partial solutions are known (i.e. either incomplete or for restricted classes of programs (Clarke[79])) and this may be a major disadvantage for program verification systems. Another drawback is that for some proofs the number of auxiliary variables is greater than the number of variables in the original program (e.g. Gries[79]). Our invariance proof method for sCSP avoids these difficulties. A completeness result is obtained by adding a single local auxiliary variable to each process which is assigned a different value at initialization and prior to reach each communication or stop command.

4.4.1 *Soundness*

Let $\underline{Prx}$ be a program augmented with auxiliary variables which can only appear in assignments to auxiliary variables. "x" will be postfixed to the definitions of paragraph 2 and 3 when concerning $\underline{Prx}$. The set $\underline{tx}$ of values of the program variables will be understood as the product of the sets $\underline{tv}$ of values of the main variables and $\underline{ta}$ of values of the auxiliary variables. Assignments to auxiliary variables only involve total functions. Therefore whenever $\alpha=\iota x$ or $\alpha=\mu x$ we have :

$$(\forall x1,x2\in \underline{tv},\ c1,c2\in \underline{Lx},$$
$$[\exists a1,a2\in\underline{ta}:\alpha(((x1,a1),c1),((x2,a2),c2))]\Rightarrow[\forall a1\in\underline{ta},\exists a2\in\underline{ta}:\alpha(((x1,a1),c1),((x2,a2),c2))])]$$

Assume the program Prx is transformed into a program Pr by replacing all assignments to auxiliary variables by null statements and by deleting all declarations of auxiliary variables. The operational semantics of Pr defines a set of program locations $\underline{L}=\underline{Lx}$, a set of states $S=(\underline{tv}\times\underline{L})$ and transition relations $\iota,\mu\in[S\rightarrow B]$ such that :

- $\iota = \lambda((x1,c1),(x2,c2)).[\exists a1,a2\in\underline{ta}:\ \iota x(((x1,a1),c1),((x2,a2),c2))]$
- $\mu = \lambda((x1,c1),(x2,c2)).[\exists a1,a2\in\underline{ta}:\ \mu x(((x1,a1),c1),((x2,a2),c2))]$

A correspondance can be established between the entry specifications $\phi x\in Ex$ for Prx and $\phi\in E$ for Pr by elimination of the auxiliary variables :

- $Eave \in [Ex\rightarrow E]$ $\quad Eave = \lambda\phi x.[\lambda i.[\lambda x.[\exists a\in\underline{ta}(i):\phi x(i)(x,a)]]]$
- $Aave \in [E\rightarrow Ex]$ $\quad Aave = \lambda\phi.[\lambda i.[\lambda(x,a).[\phi(i)(x)]]]$

The same way assertions $\psi x\in Agx$ interleaved in Prx can be connected to assertions $\psi\in Ag$ interleaved in Pr by eliminating auxiliary variables :

- $Eavg \in [Agx\rightarrow Ag]$ $\quad Eavg = \lambda\alpha.[\lambda ch.[\lambda(x,c).[\exists a\in\underline{ta}:\alpha(ch)((x,a),c)]]]$
- $Aavg \in [Ag\rightarrow Agx]$ $\quad Aavg = \lambda\alpha.[\lambda ch.[\lambda((x,a),c).[\alpha(ch)(x,c)]]]$

Proofs about Prx using Fsx (hence refering to auxiliary variables but not to program counters) can safely be used for proving invariance properties of Pr :

Theorem 4.4.1.1

If $Epcgx$ is a *false*-strict $\vee$-complete morphism, $Apcgx$ is upper semi-continuous, $Es\subseteq E$, $Itx=Lfp(\lambda X.[\{false\}\cup\{Initx(Aave(\phi))\vee Postx(\mu x)(\alpha):\ \phi\in Es\ \wedge\ \alpha\in X\}])$, $(\forall\alpha\in Itx,$ $Projx(\alpha)\Rightarrow Apcgx(Projsx(\alpha)))$, $(\forall\phi\in Es, Fsx(Aave(\phi))\in[Agsx\rightarrow Agsx]$ is isotone and such that $Fsx(Aave(\phi))\Rightarrow Fsx(Aave(\phi)))$ then :
$\forall\phi\in Es, \psi x\in Agsx,$
$[\exists I\in Agsx:(Fsx(Aave(\phi))(I)\Rightarrow I)\wedge(I\Rightarrow\psi x)]\Rightarrow[Proj(Post(\mu^*)(Init(\phi)))\Rightarrow Eavg(Apcgx(\psi x))]$

4.4.2 Completeness

The reciprocal of theorem 4.4.1.1 is not true in general. Nevertheless the completeness of the invariance proof method employing auxiliary variables transformations can be understood in the following sense :

Theorem 4.4.2.1

Given an arbitrary program, let Pr be the equivalent transformed program such that every command is preceded by a null command. Assume $\phi\in E$, $\psi\in Ag$ and Pr is such that $[Proj(Post(\mu^*)(Init(\phi)))\Rightarrow\psi]$.
Then it is possible to transform Pr into Prx by adding auxiliary simple variables and assignments to Pr such that there exist $Epcgx$ and $Apcgx$ verifying $[\exists\phi x\in Ex,$ $\psi sx\in Agsx:\ (Eave(\phi x)=\phi)\wedge(Eavg(Apcgx(\psi sx))=\psi)\wedge(\exists I\in Agsx:(Fsx(\phi x)(I)\Rightarrow I)\wedge(I\Rightarrow\psi sx))]$.

We do not have to worry about assertion languages and interpretations which fail to be expressive since "assertions" are regarded as functions into $\{true,false\}$. The proof of theorem 4.4.2.1 clearly indicates that auxiliary variables in Prx exactly correspond to program location counters in Pr : the declaration $\underline{a}(i):\underline{ta}(i)$ of a single auxiliary variable is added to each process $\underline{P}(i)$ of Pr. $\underline{ta}(i)$ is such that there exists a one to one map $\underline{a\ell}(i)$ from $\underline{ta}(i)$ onto the set $\{\underline{\lambda}(i,1)\}\cup\underline{\lambda}(i,\underline{C\ell}(i))$ of locations preceding an entry, communication or stop command. Each null command "$\underline{\lambda}(i,j-1):\underline{skip}$" preceding a communication or stop command "$\underline{\lambda}(i,j):\underline{S}(i)(j)$" is replaced by an assignment "$\underline{\lambda}(i,j-1):\underline{a}(i):=\underline{a\ell}(i)^{-1}(\underline{\lambda}(i,j))$". No other command is changed (although the functions with domain $\underline{tv}(i)$ in $\underline{P}(i)$ are extended to domain $\underline{tv}(i)\times\underline{ta}(i)$ in $\underline{Px}(i)$). The fact that auxiliary variables simulate program counters is clear from the definitions of :

- $Epcgx = \lambda\alpha.[\lambda ch.[\lambda(x,a).[\alpha(ch)((x,a),\underline{a\ell}(a))]]]$
- $Apcgx = \lambda\alpha.[\lambda ch.[\lambda((x,a),c).[\alpha(ch)(x,\overline{a}) \wedge c=\underline{a\ell}(a)]]]$
- $\phi x = \lambda i.[\lambda(x,a).[\phi(i)(x) \wedge a=\underline{a\ell}(i)^{-1}(\underline{\lambda}(i,\overline{1}))]]$
- $\psi sx = \lambda ch.[\lambda(x,a).[\psi(ch)(x,\underline{a\ell(a)})]]$

4.5 *Examples of Proofs*

Given two disjoint sets of integers S_0 and T_0, $S_0 \cup T_0$ has to be partitionned into two subsets S and T such that $|S|=|S_0|$, $|T|=|T_0|$ and every element of S is smaller than any element of T :

- Entry specifications : $\phi_1(x,mx,S)=[S=S_0 \wedge S_0 \cap T_0=\emptyset \wedge S_0 \neq \emptyset]$, $\phi_2(y,mn,T)=[T=T_0 \wedge S_0 \cap T_0=\emptyset]$ (To cut it short the conventions that $min(\emptyset)=+\infty$ and $+\infty \notin (S_0 \cup T_0)$ have not been incorporated in the entry specifications).
- Exit specifications : $\psi(x,mx,S,y,mn,T)=[|S|=|S_0| \wedge |T|=|T_0| \wedge S \cup T=S_0 \cup T_0 \wedge max(S)<min(T)]$

The following version of a program given by Apt,Francez & de Roever[79b] uses two parallel processes P1 and P2 which exchange the current maximum of S with the current minimum of T until $max(S)<min(T)$.

```
P1 ::      mx, x:portion; S:set of portion;
       11: repeat 12: mx:=max(S); 13: S:=S-{mx}; 14: P2!mx; 15: P2?x; 16: S:=Su{x};
       17: until mx=x;
       18: stop
```

--- We first obtain the following descriptions $Tr\ell(1)(i,j)$ of the transformation of the values of the variables of P1 when P1 is executed starting at entry point or after communication point i and ending at stop point or before communication point j without intermediate communications. Since no loop is involved no inductive assertion is necessary and the equations of theorem 3.4.1.1 can be solved exactly.

$$\begin{cases} Tr\ell(1)(1,4)(mx1,x1,S1,mx2,x2,S2)=[mx2=max(S1) \wedge x2=x1 \wedge S2=S1-\{mx2\}] \\ Tr\ell(1)(5,5)(mx1,x1,S1,mx2,x2,S2)=[mx2=mx1 \wedge x2=x1 \wedge S2=S1] \\ Tr\ell(1)(6,4)(mx1,x1,S1,mx2,x2,S2)=[mx2=max(S1\cup\{x1\}) \wedge x2=x1 \wedge x1\neq mx1 \wedge S2=((S1\cup\{x1\})-\{mx2\})] \\ Tr\ell(1)(6,8)(mx1,x1,S1,mx2,x2,S2)=[mx2=mx1=x2=x1 \wedge S2=(S1\cup\{x1\})] \end{cases}$$

The independent analysis of P2 is similar :

```
P2 ::      mn, y:portion; T:set of portion;
       21: loop 22: mn:=min(T); 23: P1?y; 24: exit when y<mn; 25: T:=(T-{mn})u{y};
                26: P1!mn;
       27: end loop;
       28: P1!y; 29: stop
```

$$\begin{cases} Tr\ell(2)(1,3)(mn1,y1,T1,mn2,y2,T2)=[mn2=min(T1) \wedge y2=y1 \wedge T2=T1] \\ Tr\ell(2)(4,6)(mn1,y1,T1,mn2,y2,T2)=[mn2=mn1 \wedge y2=y1 \wedge y1\geq mn1 \wedge T2=((T1-\{mn1\})\cup\{y1\})] \\ Tr\ell(2)(4,8)(mn1,y1,T1,mn2,y2,T2)=[mn2=mn1 \wedge y2=y1 \wedge y1<mn1 \wedge T2=T1] \\ Tr\ell(2)(7,3)(mn1,y1,T1,mn2,y2,T2)=[mn2=min(T1) \wedge y2=y1 \wedge T2=T1] \\ Tr\ell(2)(9,9)(mn1,y1,T1,mn2,y2,T2)=[mn2=mn1 \wedge y2=y1 \wedge T2=T1] \end{cases}$$

--- The assertions I(ch1), I(ch2), I(ch3) respectively associated with the communication channels $ch1=<1,4,1\rightarrow 2,3,1>$, $ch2=<2,6,1\rightarrow 1,5,1>$ and $ch3=<2,8,1\rightarrow 1,5,1>$ of program [P1 || P2] are the following :

$$\begin{cases} I(ch1)(mx,x,S,mn,y,T)=[|S|+1=|S_0| \wedge |T|=|T_0| \wedge mx>max(S) \wedge S\cup\{mx\}\cup T=S_0\cup T_0 \\ \qquad \wedge (S\cup\{mx\})\cap T=\emptyset \wedge mn=min(T)] \\ I(ch2)(mx,x,S,mn,y,T)=[|S|+1=|S_0| \wedge |T|=|T_0| \wedge mn\notin T \wedge S\cup T\cup\{mn\}=S_0\cup T_0 \\ \qquad \wedge (S\cap(T\cup\{mn\}))=\emptyset \wedge y=mx] \\ I(ch3)(mx,x,S,mn,y,T)=[|S|+1=|S_0| \wedge |T|=|T_0| \wedge max(S)<mx=y<min(T) \wedge S\cup\{y\}\cup T=S_0\cup T_0] \end{cases}$$

The verification conditions given by theorem 4.2.1 are the following (universal quantification is implicit) :

$$\left[\begin{array}{l}
I(ch1)(mx,x,S,mn,y,T) \Leftarrow [[(\exists mx',x',S':\phi_1(mx',x',S') \wedge \mathit{Tr\ell}(1)(1,4)(mx',x',S',mx,x,S)) \wedge \\
\qquad (\exists mn',y',T':\phi_2(mn',y',T') \wedge \mathit{Tr\ell}(2)(1,3)(mn',y',T',mn,y,T))] \vee \\
\qquad [\exists mx',x',S',mn',y',T':I(ch2)(mx',x',S',mn',y',T') \wedge \\
\qquad \mathit{Tr\ell}(1)(6,4)(mx',mn',S',mx,x,S) \wedge \mathit{Tr\ell}(2)(7,3)(mn',y',T',mn,y,T)]] \\
I(ch2)(mx,x,S,mn,y,T) \Leftarrow [\exists mx',x',S',mn',y',T':I(ch1)(mx',x',S',mn',y',T') \wedge \\
\qquad \mathit{Tr\ell}(1)(5,5)(mx',x',S',mx,x,S) \wedge \mathit{Tr\ell}(2)(4,6)(mn',mx',T',mn,y,T)] \\
I(ch3)(mx,x,S,mn,y,T) \Leftarrow [\exists mx',x',S',mn',y',T':I(ch1)(mx',x',S',mn',y',T') \wedge \\
\qquad \mathit{Tr\ell}(1)(5,5)(mx',x',S',mx,x,S) \wedge \mathit{Tr\ell}(2)(4,8)(mn',mx',T',mn,y,T)]
\end{array}\right.$$

--- Finally the verification of the exit specification consists in proving that :

$$\psi(mx,x,S,mn,y,T) \Leftarrow [\exists mx',x',S',mn',y',T': I(ch3)(mx',x',S',mn',y',T') \wedge \mathit{Tr\ell}(1)(6,8)(mx',y',S',mx,x,S) \wedge \mathit{Tr\ell}(2)(9,9)(mn',y',T',mn,y,T)]$$

5. *AUTOMATIC PROGRAM ANALYSIS TECHNIQUES*

Automatic program analysis techniques can be used to gather information about programs in order to enhance program efficiency and reliability.

5.1 *Outline of Our Approach*

The design of a variety of automatic program analysis techniques (Cousot & Cousot[79a]) is tantamount to defining for each program Pr∈sCSP a prehomomorphic image $A(\bot,\sqcup,F)$ of $P(\mathit{false},\vee,f)$ using an approximation operator $\rho\in[P\to A]$ which is a strict join-complete morphism. In addition to the hypotheses of paragraph 3.2, the elements of A are chosen to be computer-representable and F must be such that $\forall\phi\in E$, $\mathit{LFP}(F(\phi))$ is either iteratively computable (using any chaotic iteration strategy, Cousot[77]) or approximable from above (using a widening operator which speeds up the convergence of the iterates, Cousot & Cousot[77a]).

Once understood in this way the numerous global flow analysis algorithms which have been developped in the literature for sequential programs can be generalized to sCSP. The main difficulty of these generalizations has been solved at paragraphs 3.3 and 3.4 which show how to use a system of equations obtained in a natural manner from the program text. Program locations counters can be dispensed with, but for programs involving more than two communicating processes more accurate results are obtained by introducing auxiliary variables as indicated at paragraph 4.4.2. When the approximate assertions of A can describe relationships among the values of the program variables the analysis schema can follow the three steps of paragraph 3.5 since information can be propagated through individual processes at step 1 once for all (it is sound and sometimes more accurate to intersect the results of step one with the ones obtained by a preliminary analysis of individual processes viewed as classical sequential programs by treating inputs as assignments of unknown values and outputs as null commands). When the approximate assertions cannot describe relationships among the values of variables, the first step based on theorem 3.4.1.1 is ineffective. Then during the evaluation of $\mathit{LFP}(F(\phi))$, information must be propagated through individual processes by fixpoint computations as many times as F is evaluated.

5.2 *Example*

The analysis of Hoare[78]'s bounded buffer example (modified using output guards and explicit termination signals) considering only linear equality or inequality relationships among integer variables (as in Cousot & Halbwachs[78]) is the following (booleans are mapped onto {0,1}, n is a global symbolic constant greater than 0) :

```
{n≥1}
[Producer :: output:(0..n-1)portion; i:integer; 1:i:=0;
       while i≠n do {0≤i<n} 3:X!output(i);i:=i+1 od; 6:X!true; 7:stop

||X ::   buffer:(0..9)portion; in,out:integer; Pe:boolean; 1:in:=0;out:=0;Pe:=false;
         {n≥1 ∧ in=out=Pe=0}
      2:*[¬Pe ∧ in<out+10 ∧ Producer?buffer(in mod 10) →
            {in<n ∧ 0≤out≤in<out+10 ∧ Pe=0} in:=in+1;
          □out<in; Consumer!buffer(out mod 10) →
            {in≤n ∧ 0≤out<in≤out+10 ∧ 0≤Pe≤1} out:=out+1
          □¬Pe; Producer?Pe →
            {1≤in≤n ∧ 0≤out≤in≤out+10 ∧ Pe=1} skip
          □Pe ∧(in=out); Consumer!true →
            {1≤in=out≤n ∧ Pe=1} 7:stop]

||Consumer :: input:(0..n-1)portion; j:integer; Xe:boolean; 1:j:=0; Xe:=false;
         {n≥1 ∧ j=Xe=0}
      2:*[¬Xe; X?input(j) → {0≤j<n ∧ Xe=0} j:=j+1
          □¬Xe; X?Xe → {1≤j≤n ∧ Xe=1} 5:stop]                              ]
```

The assertions I(ch1),...,I(ch4) respectively associated with the communication channels ch1=<1,3,1→2,2,1>, ch2=<1,6,1→2,2,3>, ch3=<2,2,2→3,2,1> and ch4=<2,2,4→3,2,2> are the following :

```
[I(ch1)=λ(n,i,in,out,Pe,j,Xe,c1,c2,c3).[i<n ∧ 0≤out=j≤i=in<out+10 ∧ Pe=0 ∧ Xe=0 ∧ c1=3 ∧
         c2=2 ∧ c3=2]
 I(ch2)=λ(n,i,in,out,Pe,j,Xe,c1,c2,c3).[1≤i≤n ∧ 0≤out=j≤i=in≤out+10 ∧ Pe=0 ∧ Xe=0 ∧
         c1=6 ∧ c2=2 ∧ c3=2]
 I(ch3)=λ(n,i,in,out,Pe,j,Xe,c1,c2,c3).[0≤out=j<i=in≤out+10 ∧ Pe≥0 ∧ Xe=0 ∧
         3n-3i+c1-6-Pe≥0 ∧ c1-4Pe≥3 ∧ c1-Pe≤6 ∧ 3≤c1≤7 ∧ c2=2 ∧ c3=2]
 I(ch4)=λ(n,i,in,out,Pe,j,Xe,c1,c2,c3).[1≤i=in=out=j≤n ∧ Pe=1 ∧ Xe=0 ∧ c1=7 ∧ c2=2 ∧ c3=2]
```

6. *CONCLUSIONS*

Our proof method differs from the ones introduced by Apt, Francez & de Roever[79a] (who use trees to record communications and account for nondeterminism as in Francez, Hoare, Lehmann & de Roever[78]), Apt, Francez & de Roever[79b] (who use a global invariant) and by Chandy & Misra[79] (who use assertions over message sequences). More interestingly the design of our proof method has been formalized so as to open the way to alternatives. For example one variant we have considered consists in choosing :

- Ag = Π{[t(i)×t(ℓ) → B] : <i,j,k → ℓ,m,n>∈Ch}
- *Proj* = λβ.[λ<i,j,k → ℓ,m,n>.[λ(xi,xℓ).[*Ogse*(i,j,k)(xi,λ(i,j)) ∧ *Igse*(ℓ,m,n)(xℓ,λ(ℓ,m)) ∧ (∃x∈t,c∈L: β(*subst*(x)(i/xi,ℓ/xℓ),*subst*(c)(i/λ(i,j),ℓ/λ(ℓ,m)))]]].

so that the assertion associated with any channel between two processes involve only the values of the local variables of these two processes. This is sound and leads to simpler verification conditions than the ones of paragraphs 3.3 and 3.4 but unfortunately this is not complete (e.g. for blocking states involving more than two processes).

We have said little about program analysis techniques since paragraph 3 together with Cousot & Cousot[79a] allow for an easy generalization of the now classical methods for sequential programs. By the way, the particular problem of data flow analysis for concurrent processes has also been considered by Reif[79] in the different context of asynchronous communications via buffers. His algorithm cannot be adapted to CSP since the size and number of elements in the buffers are not taken into account. In particular, CSP rendez-vous concept cannot be modeled. Another annoying thing is that communication histories are completely ignored. For example, his algorithm cannot discover that x and y are constants in the following trivial program :

```
[P1 :: P2!1; P2!2 || P2 :: x,y:integer; x:=1; y:=2; P1?x; P1?y ]
```

This is easily determined using constant propagation generalized along the lines of paragraph 3.

Several generalizations are in progress. On one hand, we are considering other homomorphic images of the predicate algebra leading to different (although formally equivalent) verification conditions and richer language constructs such as distributed termination of repetitive commands, families of processes and nested parallel commands. It might also be interesting to investigate other language features (such as automatic buffering, unbounded process activation, process valued variables, shared variables) which have not been incorporated to CSP. We are curious to know if these constructions have properties which are sufficiently simple to prove for justifying their inclusion in a programming language. On the other hand, we are considering other correctness properties of CSP that can be characterized using fixpoints and which are more difficult to prove than the invariance properties considered here.

7. REFERENCES

Apt K.,Francez N. & de Roever W.P.[1979a], *Semantics for concurrently communicating finite sequential processes, based on predicate transformers*, Progress Report, Vakgroep inf., Rijksuniversiteit Utrecht, The Netherlands, (June 1979).

Apt K., Francez N. & de Roever W.P.[1979b], *A proof system for communicating sequential processes*, Tech. Rep. RUU-CS-79-8, Vakgroep Inf., Rijkuniv. Utrecht, NL., (Aug. 79).

Chandy K.M. & Misra J.[1979], *An axiomatic proof technique for networks of communicating processes*, TR 98, Univ. of Texas at Austin, (May 79).

Clarke E.M.Jr[1978], *Proving correctness of coroutines without history variables*, TR-CS-1978-4, Dept. of Comp. Sci., Duke Univ., USA, (1978).

Clarke E.M.Jr[1979], *Synthesis of resource invariants for concurrent programs*, 6th ACM-POPL, (Jan. 1979), 211-221.

Clint M.[1973], *Program proving : coroutines*, Acta Informatica 2(1973), 50-63.

Cousot P.[1977], *Asynchronous iterative methods for solving a fixed point system of monotone equations in a complete lattice*, Rap. de Recherche n°88, Laboratoire IMAG, Univ. Grenoble, (Sept. 1977).

Cousot P.[1979], *Analysis of the behavior of dynamic discrete systems*, Rapport de Recherche n°161, Laboratoire IMAG, Univ. Grenoble, (Jan. 1979).

Cousot P. & Cousot R.[1977a],*Abstract interpretation: a unified lattice model for static analysis of programs by construction or approximation of fixpoints*, 4th ACM-POPL, (Jan. 1977), 238-252.

Cousot P. & Cousot R.[1977b], *Automatic synthesis of optimal invariant assertions : mathematical foundations*, ACM-Symp. on Artificial Int. & Prog. Languages, SIGPLAN Notices 12, 8(Aug. 1977), 1-12.

Cousot P. & Cousot R.[1979a], *Systematic design of program analysis frameworks*, 6th ACM-POPL, (Jan. 1979), 269-282.

Cousot P. & Cousot R.[1979b], *Constructive versions of Tarski's fixed point theorems*, Pacific J. Math. 82(1979), 43-57.

Cousot P. & Halbwachs N.[1978], *Automatic discovery of linear restraints among variables of a program*, 5th ACM-POPL, (Jan. 1978), 84-97.

Francez N., Hoare C.A.R., Lehmann D.J. & de Roever W.P.[1978], *Semantics of nondeterminism, concurrency and communication*, Lect. Notes Comp. Sci. 64, Springer Verlag, Extended abstract, (Sept. 1978), 191-200.

Gries D.[1979], *Yet another exercise: using two shared variables in two processes to provide starvation-free mutual exclusion*, TR 79-372, Dept. Comp. Sci., Cornell Univ., N.Y., (1979).

Hoare C.A.R.[1978], *Communicating sequential processes*, Comm. ACM 21, 8(1978), 666-677.

Owicki S. & Gries D.[1976], *An axiomatic proof technique for parallel programs I*, Acta Informatica 6(1976), 319-340.

Reif J.H.[1979], *Data flow analysis of communicating processes*, 6th ACM-POPL, (Jan. 1979), 257-268.

DOS SYSTEMS AND LANGUAGES

A. Ehrenfeucht
Dept. of Computer Science
University of Colorado at Boulder
BOULDER, COLORADO 80309
U.S.A.

and

G. Rozenberg
Institute of Applied Mathematics
and Computer Science
University of Leiden
2300 RA LEIDEN
THE NETHERLANDS

INTRODUCTION

There are several possible approaches to a systematic build-up of formal language theory or various fragments of it. An example of such an approach is the mathematical theory of L systems (see, e.g., [R] and [RS]). Its basic component is a DOL system which is essentially an iterated homomorphism on a free monoid. A DOL system is generalized to a OL system by allowing an iteration of a finite substitution rather than the iteration of a homomorphism. Then to either a DOL system or to a OL system nonterminals can be added giving rise to EDOL and EOL systems respectively. These four classes of systems (DOL,OL,EDOL and EOL) form the basic framework for the systematic development of the theory of L systems.

In an attempt to build-up a systematic theory of context free languages one can look for an analogue of the above situation in the framework of context free grammars. Obviously, context free grammars correspond to EOL systems, and, roughly speaking, context free grammars without nonterminals correspond to OL systems. In recent years context free (and other "classical") grammars without nonterminals were quite extensively investigated (see, e.g., [B1],[BPR],[HP],[MSW] and [S1]). What is missing at this moment is the sequential analogue of a DOL system, which, in the above outlined approach, forms the very essential element of the theory.

In this paper we introduce such a sequential analogue of a DOL system, called a DOS system, and we believe it will play the same role in the theory of context free languages, as DOL systems play in the theory of EOL languages. We think that our belief is supported already by the initial results of our investigation which we present in this paper. One of the essential advantages of DOS systems is (in our opinion) the fact that they allow for the first time to formalize the notion of "grammatical determinism" in the framework of "context-free-like" sequential grammars.

We assume the reader to be familiar with the rudiments of the theory of context free languages. We use mostly the standard notation and terminology. Perhaps only the following points require an additional explanation.

(1). Λ denotes the empty word.

(2). For a class X of rewriting systems, $L(X)$ denotes the class of languages generated by elements of X.

(3). A weak identity is a homomorphism which maps a letter into a letter of into the empty word.

I. BASIC DEFINITIONS AND RESULTS

In this section DOS systems and languages are introduced. Our first notion is that of a sequential homomorphism, which is like a homomorphism except that it is applied "sequentially", that is one occurrence in a string is replaced in one application of the sequential homomorphism.

Definition. Let Σ be a finite alphabet. A sequential homomorphism (abbreviated s-homomorphism) on Σ^* is a mapping h from Σ^* into 2^{Σ^*} defined inductively as follows:

(1). $h(\Lambda) = \{\Lambda\}$

(2). for each $b \in \Sigma$ there exists a $\beta \in \Sigma^*$ such that $h(b) = \{\beta\}$,

(3). for each $\alpha \in \Sigma^+$,

$h(\alpha) = \{\alpha_1\beta\alpha_2 : \alpha = \alpha_1 b \alpha_2$ for some $b \in \Sigma^*, \alpha_1\alpha_2 \in \Sigma^*$ and $h(b) = \{\beta\}\}$.

The s-homomorphism h is extended to 2^{Σ^*} by letting $h(K) = \bigcup_{\alpha \in K} h(\alpha)$ for each $K \subseteq \Sigma^*$. □

As usual, we assume that an s-homomorphism on Σ^* is given by providing its values for all letters from Σ. To simplify the notation, in the sequel we will often identify a singleton $\{x\}$ with its element x.

Definition. A DOS system is a construct $G = (\Sigma, h, \omega)$ where Σ is a finite nonempty alphabet, $\omega \in \Sigma^*$ and h is an s-homomorphism on Σ^*. The language of G, denoted L(G), is defined by $L(G) = \{x : x \in h^n(\omega)$ for some $n \geq 0\}$, and referred to as a DOS language. If for no $a \in \Sigma$, $h(a) = \Lambda$ then we call G propagating and refer to it as a PDOS sytem (in this case L(G) is called a PDOS language). □

Example. Let $G = (\{a,b,c,\}, h, abc$ be a DOS sytem where $h(a) = a^2$, $h(b) = abc$ and $h(c) = c$. Then $L(G) = \{a^m bc^n : m \geq n \geq 1\}$. □

We end this section by establishing two quite basic results. The first one settles the role of erasing in DOS systems.

Theorem 1. There exists a finite language which is in $\mathcal{L}(DOS) \setminus \mathcal{L}(PDOS)$.

The second result establishes the role of nonterminals in (a possible extension of) DOS systems. A standard language-theoretic method to increase the language generating power of a class X of rewriting systems is to equip the elements of X with the mechanism of nonterminal symbols. Surprisingly enough, adding nonterminals to DOS systems does not alter the class of languages generated.

Definition. An EDOS system is a construct $G = (\Sigma,h,\omega,\Delta)$ where $U(G) = (\Sigma,h,\omega)$ is a DOS system and $\Delta \subseteq \Sigma$ (elements of Δ are called terminal symbols and elements of $\Sigma \setminus \Delta$ are called nonterminal symbols). The language of G is defined by $L(G) = L(U(G)) \cap \Delta^*$. □

Theorem 2. $\mathcal{L}(DOS) = \mathcal{L}(EDOS)$. □

II. ON THE STRUCTURE OF DOS LANGUAGES

In this section we provide a result on the combinatorial structure of DOS languages and investigate some of its consequences.
We also take a look at the closure properties of $\mathcal{L}(DOS)$.

First of all we need the following terminology: if (α,β) is a pair of words such that either $|\alpha| = 1$ or $|\beta| = 1$ then (α,β) is called unary.

Theorem 3. Let K be a DOS language. For every $\alpha,\beta \in K$ there exist a positive integer n and words $\alpha_1,\dots,\alpha_n,\beta_1,\dots,\beta_n$ such that $\alpha = \alpha_1\dots\alpha_n$, $\beta = \beta_1\dots\beta_n$, (α_i,β_i) is unary for $1 \le i \le n$ and $\gamma_1\dots\gamma_n \in K$ for all words $\gamma_1,\dots,\gamma_n$ such that, for every $1 \le i \le n$, either $\gamma_i = \alpha_i$ or $\gamma_i = \beta_i$. □

The following result demonstrates that Theorem 3 cannot be strengthened into the "if and only if" result.

Theorem 4. There exists a nonrecursive language K satisfying the conclusion of Theorem 3. □

Even if we consider only languages K "quite close" to DOS languages, the condition of Theorem 3 would not suffice to characterize the class of DOS languages as illustrated by the following. Let us call a unary pair of words (α,β) from K strong if whenever $\gamma \in \{\alpha,\beta\}$ and $|\gamma| = 1$ then $\delta_1\gamma\delta_2 \in K$ implies that $\delta_1\beta\delta_2 \in K$ if $\gamma = \alpha$ and $\delta_1\alpha\delta_2 \in K$ if $\gamma = \beta$. Let us refer to the conclusion of Theorem 3 where we replace the word "unary" by "strong and unary" as the "modified conclusion of Theorem 3".
Following our proof of Theorem 3 one easily sees that the modified conclusion of Theorem 3 holds. A OS system is a "nondeterministic version of a DOS system" - that is the s-homomorphism in a DOS system is replaced, in the obvious way, by a sequential finite substitution. OS systems generate OS languages.

We can state now our second "negative" result about the possibility of turning Theorem 3 into an "if and only if" result.

Theorem 5. There exists a OS language K satisfying the modified statement of Theorem 3 such that K is not a DOS language. □

On the "positive side" we have the following corollary of Theorem 3 that allows one to provide numerous examples of languages that are not in L(DOS).

Corollary 1. Let $K \in L(\text{DOS})$.

(1). Let α,β in K be such that $|\alpha| \geq 2$ and $|\beta| \geq 2$.
Then there exist words $\alpha_1,\alpha_2,\beta_1,\beta_2$ such that $\alpha = \alpha_1\alpha_2, \beta = \beta_1\beta_2$, $\alpha_1\beta_1 \neq \Lambda$, $\alpha_2\beta_2 \neq \Lambda$, $\alpha_1\beta_2 \in K$ and $\beta_1\alpha_2 \in K$.

(2). Let $K \subseteq \Sigma^*$ and let (Σ_1,Σ_2) be a partition of Σ. If there exist α,β in K such that $|\alpha| \geq 2$, $|\beta| \geq 2$, $\alpha \in \Sigma_1^+$ and $\beta \in \Sigma_1^+$ then there exists a word γ in K such that $\gamma \in \Sigma_1^+\Sigma_2^+$. □

We conclude this section by establishing the closure properties of (DOS).

Theorem 6. For each of the following operations

(i). union,
(ii). intersection,
(iii). concatenation,
(iv). the star operation,
(v). intersection with a regular set,
(vi). Λ-free homomorphism,
(vii). inverse homomorphism,

there exists a finite DOS language, or finite DOS languages if the operation is binary, such that the application of the given operation to the given language or languages produces a language which is not a DOS language. □

III. REPRESENTATION THEOREMS USING DOS LANGUAGES.

Although DOS languages form a "rather small" subclass of the class of context free languages, they possess a surprising power in representing languages from various language families. This is one of the aspects supporting our belief that DOS languages will play a central role in the theory of context free languages.

First of all we establish a representation theorem for the class of context free languages that is analogous to the well known Chomsky-Schützenberger Theorem (see, e.g., [S2]) except that it uses DOS languages rather then Dyck languages.

Theorem 7. A language K is context free if and only if there exists a PDOS language L, a regular language R and a weak identity h such that $K = h(L \cap R)$.□

To put the above result in a proper perspective we observe the following.

Example. Let $n \geq 2$ and let D_n be the Dyck language over n letters. Then $D_n \notin L(\text{DOS})$. □

We turn now to the representation of classes of languages using intersections of DOS languages.

Theorem 8. For every context free language K there exist a weak identity h and PDOS languages M_1, M_2 such that $K = h(M_1 \cap M_2)$. □

The class of languages of the form $h(M_1 \cap M_2)$ where h is a weak identity and M_1, M_2 are DOS languages is larger than the class of context free languages, as shown by the following example.

Example. Let $G_1 = (\Sigma, h_1, \omega)$ and $G_2 = (\Sigma, h_2, \omega)$ be DOS systems where $\Sigma = \{a,b,c,A,B\}$, $h_1(a) = a$, $h_1(b) = b$, $h_1(c) = c$, $h_1(A) = aAb$, $h_1(B) = Bc$, $h_2(a) = a$, $h_2(b) = b$, $h_2(c) = c$, $h_2(A) = aA$, $h_2(B) = bBc$ and $\omega = aAbBc$. Then $L(G_1) \cap L(G_2) = \{a^nAb^nBc^n : n \geq 1\}$ - a well known example of a language that is not context free. □

We do not know whether the class of languages of the form $h(M_1 \cap M_2)$, where h is a weak identity and M_1, M_2 are DOS languages, forms a subclass of the class of recursive languages. However we can show that if this is the case then such an inclusion cannot be effective in the following sense.

Theorem 9. Let C be an effective enumeration of a recursive subclass of the class of recursive languages. There does not exist a total recursive function f such that, given a weak identity h and DOS systems G_1, G_2, $f(h,G_1,G_2) = n$ where n is the index of $h(L(G_1) \cap L(G_2))$ in C. □

Finally we have the following representation of the class of recursively enumerable languages.

Theorem 10. A language K is recursively enumerable if and only if there exist PDOS languages M_1, M_2, M_3 and a weak identity h such that $K = h(M_1 \cap M_2 \cap M_3)$. □

IV. ON INTERSECTIONS OF DOS LANGUAGES

The results of the last section demonstrated that the class of languages consisting of intersections of (several) DOS languages is worth investigating. Such an investigation is carried on in this section.

Let, for $n \geq 1$, $\bigcap_n \mathcal{L}(DOS)$ denote the class of languages resulting from the intersection of n DOS languages and let $\bigcap \mathcal{L}(DOS) = \bigcup_{n \geq 1} \bigcap_n \mathcal{L}(DOS)$.

First of all we establish the infinite hierarchy of classes of languages.

Theorem 11. For every $n \geq 2$ there exist a finite language K such that $K \in \bigcap_n \mathcal{L}(DOS)$ and $K \notin \bigcap_{n-1} \mathcal{L}(DOS)$. □

The upper bound for the above hierarchy is provided by the following result.

Theorem 12. $\bigcap \mathcal{L}(DOS)$ is strictly included in the class of context sensitive languages. □

V. A COMPARATIVE STUDY OF DOS AND DOL SYSTEMS

DOS systems allow for the first time to formalize and to study the notion of "generative determinism" in the framework of sequential rewriting systems. In this sense they form a very natural counterpart of DOL systems, and so the comparative study of DOS and DOL systems sheds a light on basic similarities and differences between sequential and parallel rewriting systems. Such a study is presented in this section.

One of the basic properties of a DOL language is that the number of different subwords of length k in it is bounded by the quadratic function $C \cdot k^2$ where C is a constant (see, e.g., [RS]). DOS languages are not subject to such a restriction.

Theorem 13. There exists a DOS language K over a two letter alphabet Σ, such that for each $n \geq 0$ all words over Σ of length n appear as subwords in K. □

An instructive way of investigating the relationship between parallel and sequential rewriting systems is to consider a DOL system as a DOS system (that is to apply the homomorphism involved sequentially) and, the other way around, to consider a DOS system as a DOL system (that is to apply the involved s-homomorphism in the parallel fashion).

Definition. Let $G = (\Sigma, h, \omega)$ be a DOL system and $\overline{G} = (\overline{\Sigma}, \overline{h}, \overline{\omega})$ be a DOS system. We say that G and $\overline{G}$ are twins if $\Sigma = \overline{\Sigma}$, $h = \overline{h}$ and $\omega = \overline{\omega}$ (and we write G = twin $\overline{G}$ = twin G)[(1)]. □

Theorem 14.
(1). There exist DOL systems G_1, G_2 such that $L(G_1) = L(G_2)$ but $L(\text{twin } G_1) \neq L(\text{twin } G_2)$.
(2). There exist DOS systems G_1, G_2 such that $L(G_1) = L(G_2)$ but $L(\text{twin } G_1) \neq L(\text{twin } G_2)$. □

We discuss now a situation in which knowing a property of a DOL system G we can infer a property of the language L(twin G). (We refer the reader to [ER 1] or to [RS] for the notion of rank of a DOL system.)

Theorem 15. Let G be a DOL system with rank. Then L(twin G) is a context free language of finite index. □

A quite fundamental result concerning DOL systems is the following one (see [ER 2]).

Theorem 16. It is decidable whether or not $L(G_1) \cap L(G_2) = \emptyset$ where G_1, G_2 are arbitrary DOL systems sharing the same homomorphism ($G_1 = (\Sigma, h, \omega_1)$ and $G_2 = (\Sigma, h, \omega_2)$ for some $\omega_1, \omega_2 \in \Sigma^*$). □

It is instructive to compare the above result with the following theorem.

Theorem 17. It is undecidable whether or not $L(G_1) \cap L(G_2) \neq \emptyset$ for arbitrary two DOS systems sharing the same s-homomorphism. □

We would like to remark here that we have proved the above result using the undecidability of the word problem for groups (see, e.g., [Br]) rather than, as usual, the Post Correspondence Problem (it is not clear at all how the latter can be "coded" into DOS systems *!!!*).

Finally we have the following result.

Theorem 18. It is undecidable whether or not $L(G_1) \cap L(G_2) = \emptyset$ where G_1 is an arbitrary DOS system and G_2 is an arbitrary DOL system. □

VI. THE SEQUENCE EQUIVALENCE PROBLEM

A natural "computational" point of view is to consider a rewriting system as a generator of a set of "derivation" sequences - in a derivative sequence each next word results from the previous one by applying a single rewriting step in the given grammar. Then we say that two grammars are computationally equivalent if they generate the same set of derivation sequences. We consider now the sequence equivalence problems (do two OS systems generate the same sets of derivation sequences?) for the class of OS systems. Recall from Section II that a OS system differs from a DOS system by the fact that it has a sequential finite substitution rather than a sequential homomorphism. Given a OS system G we use E(G) to denote the set of sequences it generates.

We get the following result which we believe is quite fundamental in the theory of sequential rewriting systems.

Theorem 19. It is decidable whether or not $E(G_1) \subseteq E(G_2)$ for arbitrary OS systems G_1 and G_2. □

This result has two interesting corollaries.

Corollary 2. It is decidable whether or not $E(G_1) \subseteq E(G_2)$ for arbitrary DOS systems G_1 and G_2. □

Corollary 3. It is decidable whether or not $E(G_1) \subseteq E(G_2)$ for arbitrary context free grammars G_1 and G_2. □

Corollary 4. The sequence equivalence problem is decidable for OS systems and for context free grammars. □

REFERENCES

[Bl] M. Blattner, Sentential forms of context-free grammars, Ph.D.Thesis, University of California, Los Angeles, 1973.

[Br] J.L. Britton, The word problem, Ann.Math., 77, 16-32, 1963.

[BPR] H.W. Buttelmann, A. Pyster and L.M. Reeker, Grammars without syntactic variables, University of Oregon, Dept. of Comp. Science, Technical Report 74-1, 1974.

[ER1] A. Ehrenfeucht and G. Rozenberg, On the structure of polynomially bounded DOL systems, Fundamenta Informatica, II, 187-197, 1979.

[ER2] A. Ehrenfeucht and G. Rozenberg, Simplifications of homomorphisms, Information and Control, 38, 298-309, 1978.

[HP] T. Harju and M. Penttonen, Some decidability problems of sentential forms, Int. Journal of Comp. Mathematics, 7, 95-108, 1979.

[MSW] H. Maurer, A. Salomaa and D. Wood, Pure grammars, McMaster University, Comp. Science Techn. Report no. 79-CS-7, 1979.

[R] G. Rozenberg, A systematic approach to formal language theory through parallel rewriting, Lecture Notes in Comp. Science, 71, 471-478, Springer-Verlag, Berlin-Heidelberg, 1979.

[RS] G. Rozenberg and A. Salomaa, The mathematical theory of L systems, Academic Press, New York - London, to appear.

[S1] A. Salomaa, On sentential forms of context free grammars, Acta Informatica, 2, 40-49, 1973.

[S2] A. Salomaa, Formal languages, Academic Press, New York - London, 1973.

FOOTNOTES

(1). As usual to simplify the notation we consider a finite substitution on Σ^* yielding a singleton image for each element of Σ to be a homomorphism on Σ^*.

ACKNOWLEDGEMENTS

The authors greatfully acknowledge the financial support of NSF grant number MCS 79-03838.

ALGEBRAIC IMPLEMENTATION OF ABSTRACT DATA TYPES: CONCEPT, SYNTAX, SEMANTICS AND CORRECTNESS

H. Ehrig

H.-J. Kreowski

P. Padawitz

TU Berlin, FB Informatik (20)

ABSTRACT

A new concept for the implementation of abstract data types is proposed: Given algebraic specifications SPECO and SPEC1 of abstract data types ADTO and ADT1 an implementation of ADTO by ADT1 is defined separately on the syntactical level of specifications and on the semantical level of algebras. This concept is shown to satisfy a number of conceptual requirements for the implementation of abstract data types. Several correctness criteria are given and illustrating examples are provided.

1. INTRODUCTION

While there are powerful algebraic concepts for specification of abstract data types, the problem to find an adequate notion for the implementation of abstract data types seems to be much more difficult. For first approaches we refer to Guttag /Gut 76/, ADJ /ADJ 76/, Goguen-Nourani /GN 78/, Ehrich /Eh 78 a+b/, Wand /Wa 77/, Lehmann-Smyth /LS 77/ and our own paper /EKP 78/ which more or less turn out to be special cases of our new concept. In contrast to most of these papers we propose a clear distinction between the syntactical and the semantical level and corresponding correctness criteria, which is well-known for specifications but not for implementations up to now. This distinction is a necessary step towards an implementation concept which can be used in a specification language for stepwise refinement (cf. e.g. /BG 77, Ko 79/) which is one of the main problems in software engineering. In the algebraic framework proposed by ADJ /ADJ 76/ a specification SPEC=$\langle S,\Sigma,E\rangle$ of an abstract data type consists of sorts S, operations[+)] Σ and equations E. Sorts denote data domains, operations declare data access and manipulation facilities and equations determine the effect of the operations. The semantics of a specification SPEC is defined by the corresponding quotient term algebra T_{SPEC} (or any isomorphic algebra initial in the category of all SPEC-algebras). In the terminology of universal algebra a specification is an equational presentation of T_{SPEC}. There are several good reasons widely discussed in /ADJ 76/ to consider any initial algebra T_{SPEC} as an abstract data type and vice versa. Data correspond to elements of the algebra and operations in the interface of an abstract data type to those of an algebra. Based on this concept, our problem is the following: Given two such abstract data types ADT1 and ADTO (of specifications SPEC1 and SPECO) what does it mean and how to describe that the operations of ADTO are simulated by those of ADT1 or in our terminology that "ADT1 implements ADTO"? Having in mind the software engineering and also the theoretical point of view, let us state the following informal conceptual requirements:

1.1. <u>SYNTACTICAL LEVEL</u>: The implementation of an abstract data type ADTO by an abstract data type ADT1 should be given on a syntactical level as an implementation of the corresponding specifications SPECO and SPEC1 respectively, IMPL:SPEC1$\Rightarrow$SPECO, where SPECO-sorts and -operations are synthezised by those of SPEC1.

1.2. <u>SEMANTICAL LEVEL</u>: There should be a construction on the semantical level transforming ADT1 into ADTO which allows to represent data and operations in ADTO

+) we use the notation "operations" instead of "operation symbols" also on the syntactical level.

and to simulate compound operations in ADT0 by corresponding data and operations synthezised from those in ADT1, SEM_{IMPL}: ADT1 $\Rightarrow$ ADT0. More detailed, the semantical requirements are

1.3. DATA REPRESENTATION: Data of ADT0 should be represented by data synthezised from ADT1. Each one may have different representations. In any case different data are to be represented differently. However, there may be synthezised data which do not correspond to data of ADT0.

1.4. SIMULATION OF COMPOUND OPERATIONS: Each operation and compound operation in ADT0 should be simulated by operations synthezised from those in ADT1. The computation of operation calls in ADT0 should lead to the same results (up to data representation) as the evaluation of the simulating operations.

1.5. TYPE PROTECTION: The synthesis of data should be restricted in such a way that the components used from ADT1 are not destroyed. In other words ADT1 should be protected by this construction.

1.6. PARAMETER PROTECTION: There may be a common parameter part ADT of ADT1 and ADT0 which should be protected by the semantical construction.

In Section 2 and 4 we introduce syntax and semantics of our new concept which satisfies the conceptual requirements 1.1. - 1.6. as shown in Section 5. Moreover, we give correctness criteria for the semantical requirements and a result concerning the power of different implementation techniques (including that of /Eh 78 a+b/). A comparative study with other approaches mentioned above is given in Section 6.

This paper is based on ADJ /ADJ 76/ in the notation (resp. /EKP 78/). A simple typical example - the implementation of sets by strings - is discussed in detail to illustrate the syntactical and semantical constructions. The correctness criteria are applied to show the correctness of this implementation. Some other examples like implementation of stacks by arrays with pointers, implementation of symbol tables by stacks of arrays, the implementation of sets by hash tables and the design of an airport schedule are sketched in Section 3.

2. SYNTACTICAL LEVEL OF IMPLEMENTATIONS

Let us assume that we have two specifications SPEC0 and SPEC1 together with a common subspecification SPEC which can be considered as common parameter part of SPEC0 and SPEC1. Hence we assume to have the following algebraic specifications SPEC0=SPEC+$\langle S0,\Sigma 0,E0\rangle$, SPEC1=SPEC+$\langle S1,\Sigma 1,E1\rangle$, SPEC=$\langle S,\Sigma,E\rangle$ where the former ones are combinations in the following sense: SPEC+$\langle S0,\Sigma 0,E0\rangle$ is called combination if SPEC=$\langle S,\Sigma,E\rangle$ and SPEC0=$\langle S+S0,\Sigma+\Sigma 0,E+E0\rangle$ are algebraic specifications (where + stands for disjoint union), but $\langle S0,\Sigma 0,E0\rangle$ is not assumed to be an algebraic specification. That means the operations in $\Sigma 0$ may use sorts belonging to S+S0 and the equations E0 may use operations of $\Sigma+\Sigma 0$. Due to the intention that SPEC is a common parameter part we assume that SPEC0 and SPEC1 are both extensions of SPEC. That means we have the following isomorphisms $(T_{SPEC0})_{SPEC} \cong T_{SPEC} \cong (T_{SPEC1})_{SPEC}$ where we are using the following notation: For each SPEC0-algebra A the SPEC-algebra A_{SPEC} is the restriction of A to sorts and operations of SPEC. In other words A_{SPEC} is the result of applying the forgetful functor to A. Especially we allow SPEC to be empty: SPEC=$\langle\emptyset,\emptyset,\emptyset\rangle$. In this case we only have two specifications SPEC0 and SPEC1 without additional assumptions.

Now we are able to define the syntactical level of an implementation, called weak implementation, which becomes an implementation if additional semantical properties - given in Section 4 - are satisfied:

2.1. DEFINITION
Given algebraic specifications SPEC0 and SPEC1 as above a weak implementation of of SPEC0 by SPEC1 is a triple IMPL=(ΣSORT,ESORT,EOP) of operations ΣSORT, called sorts implementing operations, and equations ESORT, called sorts implementing

equations, EOP, called operations implementing equations, such that SORTIMPL=SPEC1+<S0,ΣSORT,ESORT> and OPIMPL=SORTIMPL+<Σ0,EOP> are combinations, called sort implementation and operation implementation level respectively.

2.2. NOTATION

We use the following diagrammatic notation IMPL:SPEC1⟹SPEC0 or - especially for examples - the syntactical schema

SPEC1 impl SPEC0 by

sorts impl opns: ... (operations of ΣSORT)

sorts impl eqns: ... (equations of ESORT)

opns impl eqns: .... (equations of EOP)

where the lists of operations and equations can be written as usual in algebraic specifications (see below).

2.3. REMARKS

1. Sorts in S0 and operations in Σ0 are used ambiguously in different specification and implementation levels. First they name data domains and operations of the abstract data type specified by SPEC0. On the other hand they refer to the corresponding realizations of these domains and operations in the implementation levels. Whereas in the former case the semantics of S0 and Σ0 is given by T_{SPEC0}, in the latter case data of S0-sorts are considered to be generated by sorts implementing operations (and identified by sorts implementing equations) applied to data of T_{SPEC1}. The effect of the Σ0-operations is determined by the operations implementing equations. (Confer the synthesis step in 4.1.) Hopefully, it is not confusing for the reader that we use the same names for corresponding sorts and operations in different levels (which is done frequently in programming).

2. Without any additional technical problem we can allow that some auxiliary (hidden) sorts, in addition to ΣSORT and ESORT are used to generate the S0-sorts and some auxiliary (hidden) operations with (hidden) equations in addition to EOP are used to define the Σ0-operations. Implementation in this sense becomes a 6-tuple

IMPL=(ΣSORT,ESORT,EOP,SHID,ΣHID,EHID).

Based on the present paper this extended concept is used in /EM 80/ to consider composition of implementations and their complexity.

3. Restricting the form of sorts implementing operations, we can classify implementations by their type of sort implementation. The most simple case seems to be renaming of sorts by copy operations c:s1→s0 where s1 is a sort of SPEC1 and s0 of SPEC0. Most of the known implementation concepts /Gut 76, ADJ 76, GN 78, Eh 78, Wan 77, LS 77/ belong to this type. More complex than copy are constructions like cartesian products, unions, free monoids and power sets. Each of these constructions and each combination defines a special class, sometimes called device of the implementation, provided that all sorts implementing operations (and possibly equations) belong to this class. To be more specific we give some examples of sorts

implementing operations with s0, s1,...,sn$\in$(S+S1) and s$\in$S0: COPY={c:s0$\to$ s}, UNION={in_i:si$\to$ s / i=1,...,n}, TUPLE={TUP:s1...sn$\to$s}, TABLE={NIL:$\to$s,TAB:s s1...sn$\to$s}, BINTREE={EMPTY:$\to$s, BIN:s s s1...sn$\to$ s}.

3. STRINGS IMPLEMENT SETS, AND OTHER EXAMPLES

Let us point out why the implementation of sets by strings is adequate for demonstrating our new concept:

- First of all the example is small enough to give the complete specifications and implementation within the scope of this paper.
- On the other hand this example is powerful enough to include the main syntactical and semantical features in a non-trivial way.
- Finally this example is also typical in the following sense: In practical examples we often have the situation that elements have to be inserted into some data structure where the order of insertion is irrelevant. But using a computer to solve the problem - this is the aim of implementation in any case - the order is significant because a computer usually accepts only sequentialized information. But one sequential representation of sets are strings.

3.1. EXAMPLE

We want to implement sets of natural numbers by strings where each set is represented by those strings containing the elements in arbitrary order but without repetition.

```
set(nat)
    nat +
    sorts: set
    opns:  Ø:→ set
           INSERT: nat set → set
    eqns:  INSERT(n,INSERT(n,M))=INSERT(n,M)
           INSERT(n,INSERT(m,M))=INSERT(m,INSERT(n,M))

string(nat1)
    nat1 +
    sorts: string
    opns:  λ: → string
           ADD: nat string → string
```

nat1 is an extension of nat and bool which are the well-known specifications of natural numbers and boolean values respectively.

```
nat1
    nat + bool +
    opns:  EQ: nat nat → bool
    eqns:  EQ(0,0)=TRUE
           EQ(0,SUCC(n))=EQ(SUCC(m),0)=FALSE
           EQ(SUCC(m),SUCC(n))=EQ(m,n)
```

The common parameter part of SPEC0=set(nat) and SPEC1=string(nat1) is SPEC=nat.

Then a weak implementation is given by

string(nat1) impl set(nat) by

sorts impl opns: c: string→ set

c': set → string

if-then-else: bool set set→ set

sorts impl eqns: c'(c(S))=S

if TRUE then S1 else S2=S1

if FALSE then S1 else S2=S2

opns impl eqns: ∅=c(λ)

INSERT(n,c(λ))=c(ADD(n,λ))

INSERT(m,c(ADD(n,S)))=

if EQ(m,n) then c(ADD(n,S))

else c(ADD(n,c'(INSERT(m,c(S)))))

3.2. REMARK

Note, that the sorts implementing operation c:string→ set is a simple copy operation. Particularly, set does not refer to the power set of natural numbers but to that sort in the implementation level which contains the representatives of sets, namely copied strings (cf. 2.3.1.). The opposite operation c':set→ string is necessary to have a syntactically correct notation for the recursive INSERT-equation. The sorts implementing equation c'(c(S))=S makes sure that the inverse operation c' does not lead to new data of sort string (see 4.4. for the semantics).

3.3. FURTHER EXAMPLES

1. In general the sorts implementing operations may be much more complex (see 2.3.3.). Especially interesting are the following two cases which are used in /EKW 78/ to generate tuples and tables:

1) TUP:s1...sn→ s where data of sorts s become n-tuples (d1,...,dn) of data of sorts s1,...,sn.

2) NIL:→ s, TAB: s s1...sn→ s where data of sort s are strings of n-tuples (d1,...,dn) which can be considered as tables with entries (d1,...,dn) for each row. In /EKW 78/ flight schedules are defined as tables with flight number, destination and start time as entries:

NIL:→ flight schedule

TAB: flight schedule flight number destination start time→ flight schedule

Using a similar construction for plane schedules both are combined to an airport schedule by a pairing operation

TUP: flight schedule plane schedule → airport schedule

The construction so far corresponds to the sorts implementation part of a weak implementation. But there is also an analogon to operations implementing equations for the flight, plane and airport schedules. Data base access and manipulation operations are defined like CHANGE-START-TIME for given flight number, SEARCH-FLIGHT, CANCEL-FLIGHT and so on.

2. Goguen and Nourani /Gog 77, GN 78/ consider an implementation of stacks by arrays with pointers. Due to the limitations of their implementation concept they have pair(array,pointer) as implementing specification SPEC1 so that the sort stack can be implemented by a copy operation c:pair(array,pointer)→ stack. We believe that it is more adequate to consider array and pointer rather than their pair as SPEC1 and to include the pairing as sort implementation in the implementation PAIR: array pointer → stack. This allows (in a next implementation step) to implement array and pointer separately.
To simplify the error handling, all pairs with incorrect arrays are identified by the sorts implementing equation PAIR(error,m)=PAIR(error,n). This leads to a modified tuple construction. For details see our extended version /EKP 79/ of this paper.
3. Another interesting example is Guttag's /Gut 76/ implementation of symbol tables by stacks of arrays. Apart from its more realistic size the basic syntactic features are similar to those in our example 3.1. Especially, the sorts implementing part is obtained from 3.1. if string is replaced by stack and set by symbol table. Handling this example within our framework, however, we have a well-defined syntax, semantics, and correctness criteria.
4. In /EM 80/ we give an extended implementation of sets by strings. In addition to the generating operations ∅ and INSERT also a DELETE operation and some tests are included so that the full power set specification in /TWW 78 / for the actual parameter of natural numbers is implemented. Moreover, sets are not simply implemented by copies of strings but by m-tuples or bounded arrays of strings which are addressed by a hash function. Hence, sets can be represented by hash tables.
5. In /EKP 80b/ histograms, that record the number of equal entries in string files are implemented by pairs of hash-addressed arrays.

4. SEMANTICAL LEVEL OF IMPLEMENTATIONS

Now we are going to define the semantical constructions SYNTHESIS, RESTRICTION, and IDENTIFICATION and three additional semantical properties for weak implementations to become implementations such that the requirements of Section 1 are satisfied.

4.1. DEFINITION

Given a weak implementation IMPL=(ΣSORT,ESORT,EOP) of SPEC0 by SPEC1 the semantical construction SEM_{IMPL} is the composition (to be applied from right to left)

$$SEM_{IMPL}=\text{IDENTIFICATION}\circ\text{RESTRICTION}\circ\text{SYNTHESIS}$$

where each of the component constructions is defined below.

The SPEC0-algebra $S_{IMPL}=SEM_{IMPL}(T_{SPEC1})$, the result of the semantical construction applied to T_{SPEC1}, is called semantics of the weak implementation IMPL.

1. SYNTHESIS is the composition of SORT- and OP-SYNTHESIS, where

$SORT\text{-}SYNTHESIS(T_{SPEC1})=T_{SORTIMPL}$

$OP\text{-}SYNTHESIS(T_{SORTIMPL})=T_{OPIMPL}$ and hence

$SYNTHESIS(T_{SPEC1}) = T_{OPIMPL}$

and SORTIMPL and OPIMPL are the implementation levels of the weak implementation IMPL.

2. RESTRICTION is the composition of FORGETTING and REACHABILITY where

$FORGETTING(T_{OPIMPL})=(T_{OPIMPL})_{SPECO'}$

is the SPECO'=SPEC+<SO,ΣO> restriction of T_{OPIMPL} and

$REACHABILITY((T_{OPIMPL})_{SPECO'})=REP_{IMPL}$

is the image $REP_{IMPL}=eval(T_{\Sigma+\Sigma O})$ of the evaluation-homomorphism

$eval:T_{\Sigma+\Sigma O} \to (T_{OPIMPL})_{SPECO'}$.

Note that eval is a Σ+ΣO-homomorphism evaluating (Σ+ΣO)-terms in T_{OPIMPL} and it is uniquely defined by initiality of $T_{\Sigma+\Sigma O}$. REP_{IMPL} is called <u>representation</u> of the implementation.

Combining FORGETTING and REACHABILITY we have

$RESTRICTION(T_{OPIMPL})=REP_{IMPL}$.

3. IDENTIFICATION is defined by

$IDENTIFICATION(REP_{IMPL})=S_{IMPL}$

where REP_{IMPL} factored through the Σ+ΣO-congruence generated by EO yields S_{IMPL}, i.e.

$S_{IMPL}=REP_{IMP}/\equiv_{EO}$.

4.2. <u>REMARKS</u>

1. SORT- and OP-SYNTHESIS defined in step 1 are not yet necessarily extensions (resp. enrichment) in the sense of ADJ /ADJ 76/. But due to the conceptual requirement 1.5. (resp. 1.4.) we will assume corresponding protection properties as additional semantical properties for implementations. (See 4.5.)

2. All the constructions defined above make sense for all algebras of the corresponding specifications. In fact, all these constructions are adjoint functors in the sense of category theory. This observation enables us to generalize the implementation concept to implementations of parameterizations because their semantics is defined functorial (cf. /TWW 78/). This aspect will be handled in a forthcoming paper.

4.3. <u>INTERPRETATION</u>

The SORT-SYNTHESIS-construction generates new data for each sort in SO from the given data in SPEC1. These new data are generated by the sorts implementing operations in such a way that the sorts implementing equations are satisfied. The OP-SYNTHESIS-construction defines the ΣO-operations using the operations implementing equations such that we obtain the initial algebra T_{OPIMPL} of the operation implementation level. In the FORGETTING-construction the data of S1-sorts and all Σ1-

and ΣSORT-operations are forgotten. In the SPECO'-algebra REP_{IMPL} only those data of SO-sorts are left which are reachable by Σ- and ΣO-operations of SPECO and hence which are exactly the representatives of SPECO-data in the implementation level. This justifies the notation REP_{IMPL}. In general, however, REP_{IMPL} does not satisfy the equations EO. But this is forced for S_{IMPL} by the IDENTIFICATION construction.

4.4. EXAMPLE

For the (weak) implementation string(nat1) implements set(nat) of Section 3 we have the following semantical constructions:

Starting with strings of natural numbers $\mathbb{N}^*$ in SPEC1=string(nat1) we obtain by SORT-EXTENSION copies of all these strings as data of sort set in the sort implementation level. The algebra $T_{SORTIMPL}$ contains in addition the copy operations c and c' and if-then-else which are auxiliary operations for the implementation because they are not used in SPECO. The ΣO-operations $\emptyset$ and INSERT of SPECO are added by the OP-EXTENSION-construction. By the FORGETTING-construction we forget all data of sorts string and bool and the operation EQ of nat1, TRUE and FALSE of bool, and the sorts implementing operations c, c' and if-then-else. In $(T_{OPIMPL})_{SPECO'}$ the data of sort set are still all strings of natural numbers including those with repeated elements. But strings with repeated elements cannot be generated by the ΣO-operations $\emptyset$ and INSERT. Hence all these strings are removed by the REACHABILITY-construction in REP_{IMPL}. But we still have different representations in REP_{IMPL} like n1n2n3 and n1n3n2 for each set $\{n1,n2,n3\}$. These different representations are identified by the IDENTIFICATION-construction in S_{IMPL}. But S_{IMPL} is isomorphic to the set of all finite subsets of natural numbers which is the mathematical model of set(nat) isomorphic to T_{SPECO}. This weak implementation is already "type protecting", "ΣO-complete" and "RI-correct" and hence an implementation in the following sense:

4.5. DEFINITION

A weak implementation IMPL of SPECO by SPEC1 is called

(i) type protecting, if SORTIMPL is an extension of SPEC1, i.e.

$$(T_{SORTIMPL})_{SPEC1} \cong T_{SPEC1}$$

(ii) ΣO-complete, if ΣO-operations are completely specified on Σ(SORTIMPL)-terms, i.e. $REP_{IMPL} \subseteq opsynt(T_{SORTIMPL})$

where $opsynt: T_{SORTIMPL} \longrightarrow (T_{OPIMPL})_{SORTIMPL}$ is the initial homomorphism defined by $opsynt([t]_{E(SORTIMPL)}) = [t]_{E(OPIMPL)}$

(iii) RI-correct, if

$$S_{IMPL} := SEM_{IMPL}(T_{SPEC1}) \cong T_{SPECO}$$

Finally a weak implementation is called implementation if it is type protecting, ΣO-complete and RI-correct.

4.6. INTERPRETATION

Type protection means that data and operations of SPEC1 are protected in the sort implementation level but not necessarily in the operation implementation level unless we have canonical implementations (see 5.3.). ΣO-completeness means that each $(\Sigma+\Sigma O)$-term in T_{OPIMPL} is equivalent to (at least one) Σ(SORTIMPL)-term. This makes sure that ΣO-operations can be simulated by synthezised $(\Sigma+\Sigma 1)$-operations (see 1.4). RI-correctness means that the semantical construction SEM_{IMPL} actually leads to the abstract data type T_{SPEC0} as required in 1.2. Moreover we will see in Section 5 that RI-correctness is equivalent to the existence of an abstraction function.

4.7. REMARK (IR-SEMANTICAL CONSTRUCTION AND IR-CORRECTNESS)

If in our semantical construction SEM_{IMPL} of 4.1. the last two steps are performed in opposite order (that means first SYNTHESIS, then IDENTIFICATION from OPIMPL to EQIMPL=OPIMPL+E0 and then RESTRICTION to the SPEC0 part) we obtain another semantics, called IR-semantical construction $IR\text{-}SEM_{IMPL}$. At first glance it seems that both constructions lead to the same result, which is used for a special case in /GN 78/. But we will show in 5.4. that this is not true in general. There is only a surjective homomorphism $f:SEM_{IMPL}(T_{SPEC1}) \rightarrow IR\text{-}SEM_{IMPL}(T_{SPEC1})$. Let us call a weak implementation IMPL IR-correct if $IR\text{-}SEM_{IMPL}(T_{SPEC1}) \cong T_{SPEC0}$. Then IR-correctness implies RI-correctness but not vice versa. Hence the IR-semantical construction is more restrictive. But such a restriction is not assumed in our conceptual requirements.

5. CORRECTNESS OF IMPLEMENTATIONS

In this section we will give sufficient criteria for type protection and ΣO-completeness and characterizing conditions for RI- and IR-correctness. Moreover we show the latter ones are not equivalent and we will verify the conceptual requirements of Section 1.

5.1. LEMMA (TYPE-PROTECTION)

A weak implementation IMPL=(ΣSORT,ESORT,EOP) of SPEC0 by SPEC1 is type protecting if the following conditions (i) and (ii) are satisfied:

(i) For all $\sigma: s1 \ldots sn \rightarrow s$ in ΣSORT we have $s \in SO$ and in the case $n \geq 1$ there is an $m<n$ such that $s1,\ldots,sm \in SO$ and $s(m+1),\ldots,sn \in (S+S1)$.

(ii) ESORT is empty.

Proof: Condition (i) means that SORTIMPL-terms are either SPEC1-terms or they are of SO-sorts. Condition (ii) makes sure that SPEC1-terms are SORTIMPL-equivalent if they are SPEC1-equivalent (and conversely). Hence, restricting $T_{SORTIMPL}$ to SPEC1, we obtain T_{SPEC1}, what proves the stated type protection.
Moreover, by assumption (i) and (ii) terms of SO-sorts are equivalent if and only if they are equal up to SPEC1-equivalence of SPEC1-subterms. This proves the following construction correct, too. For examples see Remark 2.3.3.

5.2. COROLLARY (DATA-REPRESENTATION)

Given a weak implementation as in 5.1. satisfying (i) and (ii), the initial algebra $T_{SORTIMPL}$ is isomorphic to the following SORTIMPL-algebra $TREE_{IMPL}$ of totally SPEC1-colored trees: $(TREE_{IMPL})_{SPEC1} := T_{SPEC1}$ and $(TREE_{IMPL})_s$ for $s \in \Sigma SORT$ is defined by

- $\sigma \in (TREE_{IMPL})_s$ for all $\sigma : \rightarrow s \in \Sigma SORT$
- $\sigma(t1,\dots,tm/t(m+1),\dots,tn) \in (TREE_{IMPL})_s$ for all $\sigma : s1\dots sn \rightarrow s \in \Sigma SORT$, $ti \in (TREE_{IMPL})_{si}$ for $i=1,\dots,m$ and $tj \in (T_{SPEC1})_{sj}$ for $j=m+1,\dots,n$

and $\sigma_T := \sigma$ for $\sigma : \rightarrow s \in \Sigma SORT$, and for $\sigma : s1\dots sn \rightarrow s \in \Sigma SORT$

$\sigma_T : (TREE_{IMPL})_{si} x\dots x (T_{SPEC1})_{sn} \rightarrow (TREE_{IMPL})_s$

is defined by

$$\sigma_T(t1,\dots,tn) = \sigma(t1,\dots,tm/t(m+1),\dots,tn)$$

for all $ti \in (TREE_{IMPL})_{si}$ for $i=1,\dots,m$ and $tj \in (T_{SPEC1})_{sj}$ for $j=m+1,\dots,n$.

5.3. REMARK (CANONICAL IMPLEMENTATIONS)

If we have in addition

(iii) OPIMPL is enrichment of SORTIMPL,

then the elements of the representation algebra REP_{IMPL} are totally SPEC1-colored trees, and T_{SPEC} is protected, i.e.

$$(REP_{IMPL})_s \subseteq (TREE_{IMPL})_s \text{ for all } s \in S+SO \text{ and } (REP_{IMPL})_{SPEC} \cong T_{SPEC}.$$

Implementations satisfying (i)-(iii) (cf. 5.1.), called canonical implementations, may turn out to be of special interest, because there is a canonical data representation of REP_{IMPL}. This is very useful in order to define an explicit abstraction or representation homomorphism $rep: REP_{IMPL} \rightarrow T_{SPECO}$. But the existence of rep is equivalent to RI-correctness (see 5.5.4.).

5.4. LEMMA (ΣO-COMPLETENESS)

A weak implementation IMPL=(ΣSORT,ESORT,EOP) of SPECO by SPEC1 is ΣO-complete if the following conditions (i)-(iii) are satisfied:

(i) All equations $(L,R) \in EOP$ are ΣO-normal, i.e. $L=\sigma(t1,\dots,tn)$ where $\sigma \in \Sigma O$ and ti contains no ΣO-operation for $i=1,\dots,n$.

(ii) EOP is ΣO-generating, i.e. for all $\sigma : s1,\dots,sn \rightarrow s \in \Sigma O$ and all $(\Sigma+\Sigma 1+\Sigma SORT)$-terms t_i of sort si there are equivalent $(\Sigma+\Sigma 1+\Sigma SORT)$-terms t_i' with $weight(t_i') \leq weight(t_i)$ such that $\sigma(t1',\dots,tn')$ is the left hand side of an equation in EOP, where variables are replaced by terms.

(iii) EOP is ΣO-weight-decreasing, i.e. there is a map $deg: \Sigma O \rightarrow \mathbb{N}$ such that for each $(L,R) \in EOP$ with σ-rooted L we have $varR \subseteq varL$ and

$$weight(R_{\sigma'}) < weight(L)$$

for all $\sigma' \in \Sigma O$ with $deg(\sigma') \geq deg(\sigma)$ where $R_{\sigma'}$ is an σ'-rooted subterm of R and all those subterms are disjoint in R.

Remark: Regarding a term t as a tree weight(t) denotes the number of nodes of that tree.

Proof: (given in /EKP 80/)

Now we will characterize RI- and IR-correctness:

5.5. THEOREM (CHARACTERIZATION OF RI-CORRECTNESS)

Given a weak implementation IMPL of SPEC0 by SPEC1 together with the semantical construction SEM_{IMPL} in Section 4 then the following conditions are equivalent:

0. IMPL is RI-correct.
1. $SEM_{IMPL}(T_{SPEC1})$ is an initial SPEC0-algebra.
2. The unique SPEC0-homomorphism $l:T_{SPEC0} \longrightarrow SEM_{IMPL}(T_{SPEC1})$ is injective.
3. There is a surjective SPEC0'-homomorphism $rep:REP_{IMPL} \rightarrow T_{SPEC0}$. (rep is called representation homomorphism or abstraction function.)
4. In the operation implementation level we have for $(\Sigma+\Sigma 0)$-terms t and t' that OPIMPL-equivalence implies SPEC0-equivalence:

   $t \equiv_{OPIMPL} t'$ implies $t \equiv_{SPEC0} t'$

   where $\equiv_{SPEC}$ is the congruence generated by the equations in SPEC.

Proof: By construction 4.1. there are natural homomorphisms $nat:REP_{IMPL} \rightarrow SEM_{IMPL}(T_{SPEC1})$ and $nat0:T_{\Sigma+\Sigma 0} \rightarrow T_{SPEC0}$ as well as a surjective homomorphism $e:T_{\Sigma+\Sigma 0} \rightarrow REP_{IMPL}$. A unique homomorphism $l:T_{SPEC0} \rightarrow SEM_{IMPL}(T_{SPEC1})$ exists by initiality of T_{SPEC0}. Moreover, we have $nat \circ e = l \circ nat0$ because $T_{\Sigma+\Sigma 0}$ is initial. The surjectivity of the left composition implies that also l is surjective. Hence injectivity of l implies that l is an isomorphism. Since initiality is closed under isomorphisms, properties 0., 1. and 2. above are equivalent.
If l is an isomorphism, the composition of its inverse function and nat defines a homomorphism $rep:REP_{IMPL} \rightarrow T_{SPEC0}$ satisfying the condition (+) $rep \circ e = nat0$ using the initiality of $T_{\Sigma+\Sigma 0}$. Especially, property 0. implies 3. Translated to equivalence of terms, (+) becomes property 4. Conversely, 4. guarantees that the relation rep defined by (+) turns out to be a function and hence a homomorphism (as required for property 3.) because e and nat0 are homomorphic and e is surjective. Finally, if rep exists, then the quotient construction of $SEM_{IMPL}(T_{SPEC1})$ induces a homomorphism $l':SEM_{IMPL}(T_{SPEC1}) \rightarrow T_{SPEC0}$ with $rep = l' \circ nat$. As T_{SPEC0} is initial, the composition $l' \circ l$ is the identity and hence l is injective. Hence property 3. implies 2. which completes the proof.
A similar result for IR-correctness is the following where, however, IR-correctness is only sufficient for RI-correctness but not vice versa.

5.6. THEOREM (CHARACTERIZATION OF IR-CORRECTNESS)

Given a weak implementation IMPL of SPEC0 by SPEC1 then the following conditions are equivalent:

0. IMPL is IR-correct.
1. IMPL is RI-correct and $SEM_{IMPL}(T_{SPEC1}) \cong IR\text{-}SEM_{IMPL}(T_{SPEC1})$.
2. The unique SPEC0-homomorphism $f: T_{SPEC0} \rightarrow IR\text{-}SEM_{IMPL}(T_{SPEC1})$ is injective.
3. There is a SPEC0-homomorphism $g: IR\text{-}SEM_{IMPL}(T_{SPEC1}) \rightarrow T_{SPEC0}$.
4. In EQIMPL=OPIMPL+E0 for $\Sigma+\Sigma 0$-terms t and t' EQIMPL-equivalence implies SPEC0-equivalence

$$t \equiv_{EQIMPL} t' \text{ implies } \equiv_{SPEC0} t'.$$

Proof: Except for the equivalence of 0. and 1. Theorem 5.6. is proved analogously to Theorem 5.5. Property 1. implies 0. simply by composition of the two given isomorphisms. Conversely, the situation is more complicate. By $h \circ e = e'$ a homomorphism $h: REP_{IMPL} \rightarrow IR\text{-}SEM_{IMPL}(T_{SPEC1})$ is defined where e is the surjective homomorphism given in the proof of Theorem 5.5. and e' exists by initiality of $T_{\Sigma+\Sigma 0}$. The composition of h and the isomorphism which exists by definition of IR-correctness satisfies requirement 3. of Theorem 5.5. Hence we have RI-correctness. Combining the isomorphisms given by IR- and RI-correctness, both semantical constructions turn out to be isomorphic (second part of property 1.).

To show that IR-correctness is not equivalent to RI-correctness let us consider the following:

5.7. COUNTEREXAMPLE

The specification of a 2-element set

```
SPEC0
    sorts: 2
    opns: ZERO: → 2
          NEXT: 2 → 2
    eqns: NEXT(x)=NEXT²(x)
```

can be implemented by the empty specification ∅ in the following way:

```
∅ impl SPEC0 by
    sorts impl opns: 0:→ 2
                     SUCC, PRED: 2→ 2
    sorts impl eqns: SUCC(PRED(x))=x
                     PRED(SUCC(x))=x
    opns impl eqns:  ZERO = 0
                     NEXT(x)=SUCC(x)
```

In the second implementation level T_{OPIMPL} is isomorphic to the integers with usual successor SUCC and predecessor PRED. By the equation $NEXT(x)=NEXT^2(x)$ all integers are identified such that $T_{EQIMPL} \cong IR\text{-}SEM_{IMPL}(T_{SPEC1}) \cong \{0\}$.
On the other hand we have $RESTRICTION(T_{OPIMPL}) \cong \mathbb{N}$ and hence $SEM_{IMPL}(T_{SPEC1}) \cong \{0,1\} \cong T_{SPEC0}$. Hence IMPL is RI-correct but not IR-correct because RESTRICTION and IDENTIFICATION are not commutable in this case.

Finally we will verify the conceptual requirements of Section 1:

5.8. VERIFICATION OF CONCEPTUAL REQUIREMENTS

Given an implementation IMPL of SPEC0 by SPEC1 in the notation of Section 2 the abstract data types ADT0 and ADT1 used in Section 1 are given by the initial algebras T_{SPEC0} and T_{SPEC1} respectively. The conceptual requirements of Section 1 are verified as follows:

Syntactical and Semantical Level: The definition of implementation 2.1. and 4.1. together with RI-correctness in 4.5. (iii) takes into account the syntactical and semantical requirements 1.1. and 1.2. obviously.

Data Representation: Since REP_{IMPL} is a restriction of T_{OPIMPL} (4.1.) and the representation morphism rep:$REP_{IMPL} \rightarrow T_{SPEC0}$ (given by Theorem 5.5.) is surjective but not injective in general, requirement 1.3. is satisfied. REP_{IMPL}-data are considered to be synthezised from T_{SPEC1} because of Σ0-completeness in 4.5. (ii).

Simulation of Compound Operations: Since rep is a homomorphism, it is compatible with operations. But this implies compatibility with compound operations in the sense of requirement 1.4.

Type Protection: T_{SPEC1} is protected in $T_{SORTIMPL}$ because the implementation is type protecting. (4.5. (i)).

Parameter Protection: The designated common parameter part of T_{SPEC1} and T_{SPEC0} is T_{SPEC}. This is protected because SPEC1 and SPEC0 are extensions of SPEC by assumption in Section 2.

Finally we will show the correctness of our main example string(nat1) impl set(nat) while the correctness of the implementation of stacks by arrays with pointers is given in /EKP 79/.

5.9. CORRECTNESS OF EXAMPLE 3.1.

The weak implementation string(nat1) impl set(nat) given in 3.1. is type protecting, Σ0-complete, RI-correct and hence an implementation.

Proof: Using Lemma 5.1. for SPEC'=SPEC1+$<\{set\},\{c\},\emptyset>$ (cf. 3.1.), we have $(T_{SPEC'})_{SPEC1} \cong T_{SPEC1}$. Obviously, c' and if-then-else are enrichment operations of SPEC', this means $(T_{SORTIMPL})_{SPEC'} \cong T_{SPEC'}$. The composite isomorphism yields type protection. $\emptyset$ is defined as derived operation. The operations implementing equations for INSERT satisfy conditions (i)-(iii) of Lemma 5.4. so that INSERT is completely specified. It is also consistently specified and hence an enrichment operation because the left hand sides of SORTIMPL-equations do not overlap (cf. /EKP 78/). Altogether our sample OPIMPL is an enrichment of SORTIMPL and especially Σ0-complete.

Therefore, by Corollary 5.2. the OPIMPL-data can be considered as SPEC1-colored trees, which are nothing else but copies of SPEC1-data in case of a copy operation c:string$\rightarrow$ set. As to the INSERT-equations of our weak implementation, REP_{IMPL} consists exactly of those strings of natural numbers where all items occur at most once. This allows to define a representation function rep:$REP_{IMPL} \rightarrow T_{SPECO}$ assigning to each string the set of all occurring numbers. Hence RI-correctness follows from Theorem 5.5.

6. COMPARISON WITH OTHER APPROACHES

Wand /Wa 77/ and Lehmann and Smyth /LS 77/ assume that the data types ADT1 and ADTO are already of the same type. Hence ADT1 corresponds to our REP_{IMPL} and the implementation consists only of a surjective homomorphism (our representation homomorphism) in the IDENTIFICATION step.

Goguen, Nourani, Thatcher and Wagner /ADJ 76, Gog 77, GN 78/ are using the derivor concept. This restricts the SORT-SYNTHESIS to copy operations (see 3.3.2.) and the OP-SYNTHESIS to nonrecursive enrichment equations. An implementation in their sense is a congruence on a derived (and restricted) algebra. This corresponds to our semantical constructions RESTRICTION and IDENTIFICATION where our congruence, however, is automatically generated by the SPECO-equations EO. The possibility to consider arbitrary algebras in their implementation concepts forces to leave the level of abstract data types. This is the reason why they cannot give a syntactical level of implementation. Our concept, however, allows stepwise implementation and refinement within the same concept.

Two basic features of our new implementation concept were sketched already by Guttag in /Gut 75/: Recursive equations for (Σ+ΣO)-operations using (Σ+Σ1)-operations of the given specification SPEC1 and the idea of implementations on the specification level. Unfortunately, syntax and semantics of implementations is more or less informal in /Gut 75/: It seems to be restricted to copying in the SORT-SYNTHESIS level and to exclude nontrivial RESTRICTION and IDENTIFICATION. It was one of our main intentions to find a well-defined syntax and semantics compatible with the (slightly corrected) symbol-table-implementation given in /Gut 76/ because this seem to be a typical small practical example (see 3.3.3.).
Closely related to our concept is that of Ehrich in /Ehr 78 a+b/ where an implementation of DO by D1 is a triple I=(D2,f,t) with suitable specification morphisms f:D1$\rightarrow$ D2 and t:DO$\rightarrow$ D2. Actually his D2 corresponds to our EQIMPL (see 5.6.), f:D1$\rightarrow$ D2 "Ω-embedding and full wrt t" corresponds to our ΣO-completeness where, however, our SORT-SYNTHESIS is restricted to copy operations only.
Finally his condition "true embedding" on t:DO$\rightarrow$ D2 corresponds to our IR-correctness. Since the IR- semantical construction is less general than our RI-semantics (see 5.6. + 7.) and copying is only a very special case of SORT-SYNTHESIS Ehrich's implementation concept turns out to be a special case of our's although the concept of specification morphisms seems to be more general at first glance.

Similar to our first approach to implementation in /EKP 78/ our semantics is given by a functor, actually a composition of adjoint functors (see 4.2.2.). But we have avoided categorical terminology in this paper to be understandable for a wider audience. Actually we have given a syntactical description of the semantical functor SEM_{IMPL} in this paper. A similar situation is given by our algebraic specification schemes in / EKW 78 /. In both cases the syntax completely determines the semantical construction. The main conceptual difference is that we implement SPECO by SPEC1 and connection specifications (similar to our SORT- and OP-SYNTHESIS).

ACKNOWLEDGEMENTS

For several fruitful discussions of the implementation concept having a major influence on our new concept we are grateful to the ADJ-group, H.-D. Ehrich, C. Floyd (including the software engineering group at TU Berlin), B. Mahr, H. Weber and several students in our course "Theory of Data Structures". Thanks also to H. Barnewitz for excellent typing.

REFERENCES

/ADJ 76/ Goguen, J.A.-Thatcher, J.W.-Wagner, E.G.: An Initial Algebra Approach to the Specification, Correctness and Implementation of Abstract Data Types, IBM Research Report RC-6487, 1976; and in: Current Trends in Programming Methodology, IV: Data Structuring (R.Yeh Ed.), Prentice Hall, New Jersey, 1978, 80-144

/BG 77/ Burstall, R.M.-Goguen, J.A.: Putting Theories together to Make Specifications, Proc.Int.Conf. Artif.Intelligence, Boston, 1977

/Eh 78a/ Ehrich, H.-D.: Extensions and Implementations of Abstract Data Type Specifications, Proc.Conf.MFCS'78, Zakopane, Springer Lect.Not. in Comp. Sci. 64, 1978, 155-163

/Eh 78b/ ---: On the Theory of Specification, Implementation and Parametrization of Abstract Data Types, Forschungsbericht Uni. Dortmund, 1978

/EKP 78/ Ehrig, H.-Kreowski, H.-J.-Padawitz,P.: Stepwise Specification and Implementation of Abstract Data Types, Proc.5.Int.Colloq.on Automata, Languages and Programming, Udine 1978

/EKP 79/ ---: Algebraische Implementierung abstrakter Datentypen, Forschungsbericht Nr. 79-3, TU Berlin, FB 20, 1979

/EKP 80a/ ---: Completeness in Algebraic Specifications, to appear in Bull. EATCS no. 11, 1980

/EKP 80b/ ---: A Case Study of Abstract Implementations and Their Correctness, to appear in Proc. Int. Symp. on Programming, Paris 1980

/EKW 78/ Ehrig, H.-Kreowski, H.-J.-Weber, H.: Algebraic Specification Schemes for Data Base Systems, Proc.4, Int.Conf.on Very Large Data Bases, Berlin, 1978

/EM 80/ Ehrig, H.-Mahr, B.: A Complexity of Implementations on the Level of Algebraic Specifications, to appear in Proc. STOC'80

/Gog 77/ Goguen, J.A.: Abstract Errors for Abstract Data Types, Proc.IFIP Working Conf. on Formal Description of Programming Concepts, St.Andrews, New Brunswick, Aug.1977, and in: Formal Description of Progr. Concepts, ed.by E.J.Neuhold, North-Holland, 1978, 491-522

/GN 78/ Goguen, J.A.-Nourani, F.: Some Algebraic Techniques for Proving Correctness of Data Type Implementation, Extended Abstract, Comp. Sci. Dept., UCLA, Los Angeles, 1978

/Gut 76/ Guttag, J.V.: Abstract Data Types and the Development of Data Structures Supplement to Proc. Conf. on Data Abstraction, Definition, and Structure, SIGPLAN Notices 8, March 1976

/Ko 79/ Koch, W.: SPEZI - eine Sprache zur Formulierung von Spezifikationen, Proc. GI-9.Jahrestagung, Bonn 1979, Informatik-Fachberichte 19, Springer-Verlag, 1979, 132-138

/LS 77/ Lehmann, D.H.-Smyth, M.B.: Data Types, Univ.of Warwick, Dept. of Comp. Sci., Report No.19, 1977, and Proc.18th IEEE Symp.on Found.of Computing, Providende, R.I., Nov. 77, 7-12

/TWW 78/ Thatcher, J.W.-Wagner, E.G.-Wright, J.B.: Data Type Specification: Parameterization and the Power of Specification Techniques, Proc. 10 SIGACT Symp.on Theory of Computing, San Diego, 1978, 119-132

/Wa 77/ Wand, M.: Final Algebra Semantics and Data Type Extensions, Indiana Univ., Comp. Sci. Dept., Technical Report No. 65, 1977

PARAMETERIZED DATA TYPES IN ALGEBRAIC SPECIFICATION LANGUAGES

(SHORT VERSION)

Hartmut Ehrig and Hans-Jörg Kreowski

Technische Universität Berlin
Fachbereich Informatik (20)
Institut für Software und Theoretische Informatik
Otto-Suhr-Allee 18/20
D-1000 Berlin 10, Germany

James Thatcher, Eric Wagner and Jesse Wright

IBM Research Center
Mathematical Sciences Department
P.O. Box 218, Yorktown Heights 10598
New York, USA

1. INTRODUCTION

Procedural abstraction has been around a long time both in practice and in theory, although the semantic theory for procedures taking procedures as parameters is relatively recent, c.f. Scott [22]. A practical analog of procedural abstraction for data definition ("parameterized types", "type generators") is relatively new (for example see [14], [16], [20], [21], [23], and [24]). The semantic theory for parameterized types is the subject of this paper. There has been precious little work on the mathematics of parameter passing for parameterized types. Burstall and Goguen tackle it for the mathematical semantics of CLEAR; procedures in CLEAR correspond to parameterized types ([6], [7] [8]). Also Ehrich [10] studies parameterization on a syntactic level, as a relationship between specifications. Although ADJ [4] provides us with an algebraic formulation for parameterized types, they barely touch the question of parameter passing.

The problem of parameter passing for data abstractions is an important one. Hierarchical design of large programming systems depeds on the use of parameterized data abstractions (even familiar ***array( )*** or ***structure( )***) and an understanding of the semantics of parameter passing is a prerequisite to the understanding of the mathematical semantics of the hierarchical design.

In this paper we introduce an approach to algebraic (parameterized) data type specification using universal Horn sentences. This generalizes earlier work by ADJ and eliminates some of the problems therein. In particular the present treatment handles "side conditions" in a more natural manner. The main results, however, concern the treatment of parameter passing for parameterized types. First of all, we give a precise mathematical definition of what it means to insert a parameter into a parameterized type (e.g, inserting ***int*** into ***array( )***). Our approach is very general; it provides the necessary apparatus for treating several related problems. We provide the machinery for inserting of non-parameterized specifications into parameterized specifications, for composing parameterized types or specifications, for demonstrating the compatibility of different "call by name" strategies and of "call by name", and "call by value" interpretations. We are also able to conclude proofs of correctness; for example, if the specifications for ***int*** and ***array( )*** are correct, then the specification (obtained for) ***array(int)*** is correct. We will not treat all of these subjects in detail within this short version; we will focus on presenting (without proof) the Main Theorem (or Lemma) which is the keystone for our approach and leave the remaining topics and the proof of the Main Theorem to the long version [5].

2. PRELIMINARIES

We shall assume the algebraic background of ADJ [1], [2], [3], [4] or of Ehrig, Kreowski and Padawitz, [11], [12], [13]. We review that background here as we shall make one essential change in the form of axioms. A *data type* is regarded as (the isomorphism class of) a many-sorted (heterogeneous) algebra. A many-sorted algebra consists of an indexed family of sets (called *carriers*) with an indexed family of operations between those carriers. The indexing system is called a *signature* and consists of a set S of *sorts* which indexes the carriers and a family $<\Sigma_{w,s} \mid w \in S^*$ and $s \in S>$ of operation names (Σ is called the *operator domain*); a symbol $\sigma \in \Sigma_{w,s}$ with $w=s_1 \ldots s_n$ names an operation $\sigma_A : A_{s_1} \times \ldots \times A_{s_n} \to A_s$ in an algebra A with signature Σ. The pair $<S,\Sigma>$ determines the category $\mathbf{Alg}_{<S,\Sigma>}$ of all S-sorted Σ-algebras with Σ-homomorphisms between them.

Following Guttag and Zilles [16], [17], [18] [24], a signature (sorts and operations) is the syntactic part of a specification. Using their terminology, the "semantic part" of the specification consists of "axioms" which in general form ([4]) are universally quantified implications:

$$(*) \qquad e_1 \ \& \ e_2 \ \& \ \ldots \ \& \ e_n \Rightarrow e_{n+1},$$

where each e_i is an equation or inequation written in the operator symbols Σ together with variables. In the simplest and most widely accepted case, the axioms are equations (n=0 and e_1 an equation), c.f. [3]. More generally, the axioms are "positive conditional" (or "universal Horn" according to Cohn [9]), c.f. [2]. But in dealing with parameterized types, ADJ [4] thought it necessary to permit axioms of the general form above to specify formal parameters. This is highly undesirable since standard algebraic results (*a la* Cohn [9] and Graetzer [15]) do not hold for classes of algebras characterized by such general axioms.

We have found that there is a happy medium, a form for the axioms that is sufficient for characterizing formal parameters while necessary in order to get agreement between the model and the specification (correctness). That form requires all the antecedents of (*) to be equations (positive) while the consequent can be either an equation or an inequation. Differing from Cohn [9], Graetzer [15] calls *these* axioms *universal Horn* and we will use that terminology. Note that in the case of n=0 (no antecedents), we can assert inequations, like T≠F, which is in fact the kind of thing we want to do. We can not, however, as in [4], require X≠Y⇒EQUAL?(X,Y)=F because this axiom is *not* universal Horn.

Definition 2.1. A *specification*, SPEC = <S, Σ, E>, is a triple where <S, Σ> is a signature and E is a set of universal Horn axioms. $\mathbf{Alg}_{SPEC}$ is the category of all SPEC-algebras, i.e., all S-sorted Σ-algebras satisfying the axioms E. When we write the *combination* SPEC′ = SPEC + <S′, Σ′, E′> we mean that S and S′ are disjoint, that Σ′ is an operator domain over S∪S′ which is disjoint from Σ, and that E′ is a set of axioms over the signature <S∪S′, Σ∪Σ′>. □

Although, as indicated above, some see the axioms as "semantics," we follow [3] in saying that the semantics of a specification SPEC is the (isomorphism class of the) algebra T_{SPEC} which is initial in $\mathbf{Alg}_{SPEC}$. For parameterization, this becomes more complicated as we shall see, but at least we need to know:

Theorem 2.2. If SPEC is a specification and if $\mathbf{Alg}_{SPEC}$ is non-empty then there exists an algebra, T_{SPEC}, which is initial in $\mathbf{Alg}_{SPEC}$. □

We repeat the definition of correctness as given in Ehrig and Kreowski [11] which allows for "hidden functions," since this is the kind of correctness we need for parameterized types.

Definition 2.3. A specification $SPEC' = \langle S', \Sigma', E' \rangle$ is correct with respect to an $\langle S, \Sigma \rangle$-algebra A (called a *model*) iff $\langle S, \Sigma \rangle \subseteq \langle S', \Sigma' \rangle$ and the $\langle S, \Sigma \rangle$-reduct of $T_{SPEC'}$ is isomorphic to A.[†] □

Example 2.1. MODEL (SPEC = $\langle S, \Sigma \rangle$): ***int***

sorts (S): *int*, *bool*

opns (Σ): T,F: → *bool*

0: → *int*

PRED, SUCC: *int* → *int*

EQUAL?: *int int* → *bool*

The model SPEC-algebra A has $A_{int} = \mathbb{Z}$ (the integers) and $A_{bool} = \{0,1\}$, with the obvious definitions of the operations. In particular $EQUAL?_A$ is the Boolean valued function which corresponds to the identity relation on $\mathbb{Z}$.

SPECIFICATION (SPEC′ = SPEC + $\langle \Sigma', E' \rangle$): ***int′*** = ***int*** +

opns (Σ′): LE?: *int int* → *bool*

∧: *bool bool* → *bool*

axioms (E′):

(E′.1) F ∧ Y = F (E′.2) X ∧ F = F (E′.3) T ∧ T = T

(E′.4) PRED(SUCC(X)) = X (E′.5) SUCC(PRED(X)) = X

(E′.6) LE?(X, X) = T (E′.7) LE?(SUCC(X), X) = F

(E′.8) LE?(X, Y)=T ⇒ LE?(X, SUCC(Y))=T

(E′.9) LE?(X, Y)=F ⇒ LE?(SUCC(X), Y)=F

(E′.10) EQUAL?(X, Y) = LE?(X, Y) ∧ LE?(Y, X) □

Proposition 2.4. From Example 2.1, the specification ***int′*** is correct relative to the ***int***-algebra described in the example.[‡] □

[†] If $\langle S,\Sigma \rangle \subseteq \langle S',\Sigma' \rangle$, then the $\langle S,\Sigma \rangle$-*reduct* of an $\langle S',\Sigma' \rangle$-algebra A is that algebra which is obtained from A by forgetting all the sorts in S′-S and all the operations in Σ′-Σ.

[‡] In the first version of this paper, we conjectured that $EQUAL?_A$ on $\mathbb{Z}$ was not specifiable without additional "hidden" functions such as LE?. Shortly after the appearance of that version (August 15, 1979), Nicholas Pippenger outlined a proof of that conjecture to two of us (JWT, EGW). At about the same time H-JK (Kreowski [19]) was proving that the predicate ISZERO? cannot be specified with a finite set of *equations* over the signature ***int***. Of course, the former result implies the latter.

3. PARAMETERIZED TYPES

Definition 3.1. A *parameterized data type* PDAT = <SPEC,SPEC1,T> consists of the following data:

PARAMETER DECLARATION $\quad$ SPEC = <S, Σ, E>

TARGET SPECIFICATION $\quad$ SPEC1 = SPEC + <S1, Σ1, E1>

and a functor $T:\mathbf{Alg}_{SPEC} \to \mathbf{Alg}_{SPEC1}$, equipped with a (natural) family of homomorphisms $<I_A:A \to U(T(A))>$ where U is the forgetful functor from SPEC1 to SPEC-algebras.[†] PDAT is called *persistent* (*strongly persistent*) if T is, i.e., for every SPEC-algebra A, I_A is an isomorphism (I_A is the identity). □

It is perhaps not surprising that parameter passing for parameterized types and specifications is in large part a problem of "naming." With the obvious application of Definition 3.1 (and that of [4]) one can only apply PDAT to an algebra named exactly by SPEC. Let's immediately look at an example.

Example 3.1.

PARAMETER DECLARATION (SPEC = <S, Σ, E>): ***data***

sorts (S): *data, bool* $\quad$ opns (Σ): T,F: → *bool*

EQ?: *data data* → *bool*

axioms (E):

(E.1) $T \neq F$

(E.2) EQ?(X,X) = T $\quad$ (E.3) EQ?(X,Y) = EQ?(Y,X)

(E.4) EQ?(X,Y)=T & EQ?(Y,Z)=T ⇒ EQ?(X,Z)=T

Note that the parameter specification differs from that given in ADJ [4]: EQ? is included as an operator and is required (by E.2-E.4) to be an equivalence relation. This change has a significant effect on the mathematics of the specification. Our "model" and the specified construction will agree whereas this agreement was achieved in [4] only through the undesirable use of negative conditions.

TARGET SPECIFICATION (SPEC1 = SPEC + <S1, Σ1>): ***set(data)* = *data*** +

sorts (S1): *set* $\quad$ opns (Σ1): CREATE: → *set*

INSERT, DELETE: *data set* → *set*

MEMBER?: *data set* → *bool*

EMPTY?: *set* → *bool*

The (strongly persistent) model functor $SET:\mathbf{Alg}_{SPEC} \to \mathbf{Alg}_{SPEC1}$ is defined just as it was in [4], except that we are dealing with equivalence classes of data rather than data elements. SET takes a SPEC-algebra A $= < A_{data}, A_{bool}, T_A, F_A, EQ?_A>$ to the SPEC1-algebra (also denoted A) with $A_{set} = \mathcal{P}_\omega(A_{data}/EQ?_A)$ (finite subsets of equivalence classes of A_{data} modulo the equivalence relation $EQ?_A$). The operations in SET(A) are defined by T1-T5 below.

---

† The functor U forgets the new sorts S1 and the new operations Σ1. Forgetful functors will be assumed and used somewhat loosely in what follows. As discussed in [4], the family I tells how to find each parameter algebra A in the result of the construction T(A). That each type must be equipped with such a natural transformation will be glossed over in the sequel. The motivation for persistence is given in [4]; the idea is that the parameter algebra "persists" (up to isomorphism) in the result of the construction T.

(T1) $CREATE_A = \emptyset$

(T2) $INSERT_A(a, s) = \{[a]\} \cup s$

(T3) $DELETE_A(a, s) = s - \{[a]\}$

(T4) $MEMBER?_A(a, s) = (\text{If } [a] \in s \text{ then } T_A \text{ else } F_A)$

(T5) $EMPTY?(s) = (\text{If } s = \emptyset \text{ then } T_A \text{ else } F_A)$ □

We *can not* apply the functor SET to the data type ***int*** (Example 2.1) because the name of one of the sorts (and one of the operations) in the source signature differs from that in the signature for ***int*** *and* there are operations (0, PRED, SUCC) in the signature for ***int*** which do not occur (and we do not want) in the specification for the formal parameter for SET.

In order to "use" the parameterized type ***set*** we must do the following things: (1) rename the *int*-carrier of ***int***, calling it *data*; (2) forget the extra operations on the integers, namely 0, PRED and SUCC; and, (3) rename the operation EQUAL? on the integers, calling it EQ?. Now we have a ***data***-algebra, call it I. After checking that it satisfies the parameter axioms, the functor SET can be applied resulting in the algebra SET(I). We are not done! We must reverse steps (1), (2) and (3), above, renaming the *data* carrier, and the operation EQ?, and reinstating the integer operations to their rightful place.

There is an obvious morphism h:***data***→***int*** which identifies the sort *data* with the sort *int* in ***int*** and EQ? in ***data*** with EQUAL? in ***int***. These morphisms are the subject of Section 5; it is with them and the results of Section 6 that the manipulation described above is accomplished.

Before considering the necessary mathematics behind the parameter morphisms informally discussed above, we pause to define parameterized specifications and continue the "set" example.

4. PARAMETERIZED SPECIFICATIONS

Definition 4.1. A *parameterized specification* PSPEC = <SPEC, SPEC1> consists of the following data:

PARAMETER DECLARATION	$SPEC = \langle S, \Sigma, E\rangle$
TARGET SPECIFICATION	$SPEC1 = SPEC + \langle S1, \Sigma 1, E1\rangle$

The semantics of the specification is the free construction (see [4]), $T: \mathbf{Alg}_{SPEC} \to \mathbf{Alg}_{SPEC1}$, i.e., the parameterized type PDAT = <SPEC, SPEC1, T>. □

We will talk about the "parameterized type SPEC⊆SPEC1" and mean the type whose (model) functor is the free construction from SPEC-algebras to SPEC1-algebras.

In Example 3.1 we have the parameterized type ***set***; now we want a parameterized specification. The notation for the type in 3.1 was ***<data, set(data)***, SET>. We will use the notation ***<data′, set′(data′)>*** for the specification. As is usually the case in specifying a type, the primed specifications contain the unprimed ones, the differences being, in effect, the hidden functions required by the specification. In general the form of the information will be a type SPEC⊆SPEC1 (with its associated functor) and a specification SPEC′⊆SPEC1′. But also we will have (see Definition 4.2) SPEC⊆SPEC′ and SPEC1⊆SPEC1′ with SPEC1′ = SPEC′∪SPEC1 + <S1′,Σ1′,E1′>; the S1′ and Σ1′ being "hidden" sorts and operations and E1′ being the real "guts" of the specification. Note that this is consistent with the notation of Definition 4.1; it is just that we don't want to rewrite all the sorts and operations of SPEC1.

Example 4.1.

PARAMETER DECLARATION (SPEC′ = SPEC + <Σ′, E′>):

***data′* = *data* +**

opns (Σ′): IF__THEN__ELSE__:*bool bool bool* → *bool*

axioms (E′):

(E′.1) IF T THEN X ELSE Y = X (E′.2) IF F THEN X ELSE Y = Y

TARGET SPECIFICATION (SPEC1′ = SPEC′ ∪ SPEC1 + <S1′, Σ1′, E1′>):

***set′ (data′)* = *data′* ∪ *set(data)* +**

opns (Σ1′): IF__THEN__ELSE__:*bool set set* → *set*

axioms (E1′):

(E1′.1) IF T THEN X ELSE Y = X

(E1′.2) IF F THEN X ELSE Y = Y

(E1′.3) INSERT(D, INSERT(D′, X)) = IF EQ?(D, D′) THEN INSERT(D, X)
ELSE INSERT(D′, INSERT(D, X))

(E1′.4) DELETE(D, CREATE) = CREATE

(E1′.5) DELETE(D, INSERT(D′, X)) = IF EQ?(D, D′) THEN DELETE(D, X)
ELSE INSERT(D′, DELETE(D, X))

(E1′.6) MEMBER?(D, CREATE) = F

(E1′.7) MEMBER?(D, INSERT(D′, X)) = IF EQ?(D, D′) THEN T
ELSE MEMBER?(D, X)

(E1′.8) EMPTY?(CREATE) = T

(E1′.9) EMPTY?(INSERT(D, X)) = F □

Definition 4.2. Let PDAT = <SPEC, SPEC1, T> be a parameterized type and let PSPEC′ = <SPEC′, SPEC1′> be a parameterized specification. Then PSPEC′ is *correct* with respect to PDAT if SPEC⊆SPEC′, SPEC1⊆SPEC1′ and

$$\begin{array}{ccc} \mathbf{Alg}_{\mathrm{SPEC}} & \xrightarrow{T} & \mathbf{Alg}_{\mathrm{SPEC1}} \\ U_0 \downarrow & & \downarrow U_1 \\ \mathbf{Alg}_{\mathrm{SPEC'}} & \xrightarrow[T']{} & \mathbf{Alg}_{\mathrm{SPEC1'}} \end{array}$$

commutes up to isomorphism where U_0 and U_1 are the indicated forgetful functors and T′ is the functor obtained as the semantics of the specification (see Definition 4.1). □

Theorem 4.3: The parameterized specification <***data′***, ***set′ (data′)***> (Example 4.1) is correct with respect to the parameterized type <***data***, ***set(data)***, SET> (Example 3.1). □

5. PARAMETER MORPHISMS

We return now to the development of the morphisms needed to allow us to insert data types in for the parameters in parameterized data types (and/or specifications in for the parameters in parameterized specifications, etc.). The intuitive idea was sketched in Section 3. Recall that we pointed out that there is an "obvious" morphism h:***data***→***int*** which identifies the sort *data* with the sort *int* in ***int*** and EQ? in ***data*** with EQUAL? in ***int***. It is not hard to see (intuitively) that this morphism h "tells us" how we want to modify the parameterized type ***set(data)*** to get the desired data type ***set(int)*** with sorts *bool*, *int* and *set*, operations T, F, 0, PRED, SUCC, EQUAL?, CREATE, INSERT, DELETE, MEMBER?, and EMPTY? and with the evident three-sorted algebra A in which A_{int} = the integers, $A_{bool} = \{0,1\}$, and A_{set} all finite sets of (singleton equivalence classes of) integers, together with the evident operations on these carriers.

Now lets look at the same process but in a more abstract setting: let ***para*** = <SPEC, SPEC1, T> be a strongly persistent parameterized data type with SPEC = <S, Σ, E> and SPEC1 = SPEC + <S1, Σ1, E1>, and let ***item*** = <SPEC′, A′> be a (non-parameterized) data type, where SPEC′ = <S′, Σ′, E′>. Then intuitively what we want for ***para(item)*** is some appropriate (SPEC′+<S1, $\overline{\Sigma 1}$, $\overline{E1}$>)-algebra $\bar{A}$, where $\overline{\Sigma 1}$, $\overline{E1}$ are suitable reformulations of Σ1 and E1, respectively (see Theorem 6.1 (ii)). Which reformulation depends, of course, on how we "insert" A′ in for the parameters of ***para***. Again what we need is a means for assigning each sort in SPEC a sort in SPEC′ and each operator in SPEC an operator in SPEC′. This can not be just done any-which-way for this process must extract from the SPEC′-algebra A′, a SPEC-algebra A to which we can apply the functor T from ***para***. What we need is a pair of mappings $<h_S:S\to S', h_\Sigma:\Sigma\to\Sigma'>$ such that the resulting forgetful functor $V_h:\mathbf{Alg}_{S',\Sigma'}\to\mathbf{Alg}_{S,\Sigma}$ takes A′ to a SPEC-algebra A (i.e., a Σ-algebra satisfying the axioms in E). The desired (SPEC′+<S1, $\overline{\Sigma 1}$, $\overline{E1}$>)-algebra $\bar{A}$ is then constructed by putting together the appropriate pieces of A′ and T(A). That is, for each $s \in S'$, $\bar{A}_s = A'_s$, and for each $s \in S1$, $\bar{A}_s = T(A)_s$. Note that the strong persistency of T together with the definition of A as $V_h(A')$ ensures that if $s \in S$, then $T(A)_s = A_s = A'_{h(s)}$ so $\bar{A}_s$ is well-defined. In a similar manner we define the operations of $\bar{A}$ from those of A′ and T(A). (When h is an inclusion, this corresponds to the construction in the proof of Theorem 10, ADJ [4].) However there is another, rather neat, way to describe $\bar{A}$ abstractly. Speaking informally (for now), the morphism h given above together with the "inclusions" s:SPEC⊆SPEC1 and $\bar{s}$:SPEC′ ⊆ SPEC′+<S1, $\overline{\Sigma 1}$, $\overline{E1}$ > induce a similar morphism $\bar{h}$ from SPEC1 to SPEC′+<S1, $\overline{\Sigma 1}$, $\overline{E1}$ > yielding a "commuting diagram"

$$\begin{array}{ccc} \text{SPEC} & \xrightarrow{s} & \text{SPEC1} \\ \downarrow h & & \downarrow \bar{h} \\ \text{SPEC}' & \xrightarrow{\bar{s}} & \text{SPEC}'+\langle S1, \Sigma 1, E1\rangle \end{array}$$

(we make this precise below and indeed establish that it is a pushout diagram). The morphisms $\bar{s}$ and $\bar{h}$ again induce forgetful functors $V_{\bar{s}}$ and $V_{\bar{h}}$ respectively. The algebra $\bar{A}$ is characterized by the fact that $V_{\bar{s}}(\bar{A}) = A'$ and $V_{\bar{h}}(\bar{A}) = T(A)$ $(= T(V_h(A')))$.

To pull this together we must make it more precise. This we shall now do. In this section we will introduce the necessary morphism in a precise manner, this will allow us to give a precise statement of the theorem suggested by the above discussion. In the next section we shall present a *much* more general version of the theorem which will not only cover the insertion of actual parameters for formal parameters but all the other examples listed in the introduction as well.

There is one possibly confusing step in what we are going to do, namely that we shall push everything up to the level of parameterized types (viewing a non-parameterized type as a parameterized type with a trivial parameter). The advantage of this is that it allows us to put the necessary conditions on the morphism in a very clean and uniform way and state all results within the category of parameterized types.

Definition 5.1. A *specification morphism* $h:<S, \Sigma, E> \to <S', \Sigma', E'>$ consists of a mapping $h_S:S \to S'$ and an $(S^* \times S)$-indexed family of mappings, $h_\Sigma:\Sigma \to \Sigma'$ (where $h_{\Sigma(w,s)}:\Sigma_{w,s} \to \Sigma_{h_S(w),h_S(s)}$). This data is subject to the condition that every axiom of E, is, when translated by h, true of every $<S', \Sigma', E'>$-algebra.† □

Proposition 5.2. If h:SPEC→SPEC′ is a specification morphism, then there is a forgetful functor $V_h:\mathbf{Alg}_{SPEC'} \to \mathbf{Alg}_{SPEC}$. □

Definition 5.3. Given a parameterized specification PSPEC = <SPEC, SPEC1> with SPEC = $<S, \Sigma, E>$ and SPEC1 = SPEC + $<S1, \Sigma1, E1>$, define the *body specification* of PSPEC to be

$$BODY = <S, \Sigma> + <S1, \Sigma1, E1>$$

(so SPEC1 = BODY + $<\emptyset, \emptyset, E>$). If PSPEC′ is another parameterized specification with body BODY′, then a *body morphism* h:PSPEC → PSPEC′ is a specification morphism h:BODY → BODY′. The body morphism is *simple* if SPEC = SPEC′ and SPEC1 ⊆ SPEC1′ so that the specification morphism is given by the inclusion of sorts and operation symbols. □

Definition 5.4. Let PDAT = <PSPEC, T> and PDAT′ = <PSPEC′, T′> be two parameterized data types. A *parameter morphism* h:PDAT → PDAT′ is a body morphism h:PSPEC → PSPEC′ with the *preservation property* that for every parameter algebra $A' \in \mathbf{Alg}_{SPEC'}$, there exists a parameter algebra $A \in \mathbf{Alg}_{SPEC}$ such that $V_h(T'(A')) = T(A)$. (We are viewing $\mathbf{Alg}_{SPEC1} \subseteq \mathbf{Alg}_{BODY}$ and $\mathbf{Alg}_{SPEC1'} \subseteq \mathbf{Alg}_{BODY'}$ and not naming these inclusions.) A parameter morphism h is *simple* if h is a simple body morphism. □

What we are doing in introducing parameter morphisms here is pushing everything up in functionality to the level of parameterized types (see Figure 7.1). Our objects become parameterized types (or specifications with their semantic functors) and the morphisms are parameter morphisms. We want to see how to retrieve standard data types in this setting and reconsider the discussion at the end of Section 3. Let ∅ denote the empty parameter declaration (no sorts or operations or axioms). If <∅⊆SPEC, T> is a parameterized type, then T is a functor from the one point category (**1**) to the category of SPEC-algebras and the image of T is a data type. On the other hand we can identify the parameterized type SPEC⊆SPEC and the accompanying identity functor (which is the free construction) with all SPEC algebras.

Now, in particular, lets look at the parameter morphism from ***data***⊆***data*** to ∅⊆***int***. The specification part is the morphism h referred to at the end of Section 3. This is because the body specification for ***data***⊆***data*** is just the signature for ***data***. The parameter preservation property requires the existence of exactly the ***data***-algebra I.

---

† Ehrich [10] has a extensive treatment of the category **Spec** of specifications and morphisms between them which are only required to preserve *constant* equations. When all axioms are equations Ehrich's definition would correspond to ours with the requirement that the translated axioms hold in the initial $<S', \Sigma', E'>$-algebra. What we have here determines a *signed many-sorted theory morphism* as needed by Burstall and Goguen [7].

Continuing, the parameterized data type here is ***data⊆set(data)*** and the relationship between ***data*** and this parameterized data type is clearly captured by the evident simple parameter morphism

$$s{:}\mathbf{data} \subseteq \mathbf{data} \rightarrow \mathbf{data} \subseteq \mathbf{set(data)}$$

Putting these together we get the diagram

$$\begin{array}{ccc} \mathbf{data} \subseteq \mathbf{data} & \xrightarrow{s} & \mathbf{data} \subseteq \mathbf{set(data)} \\ \downarrow h & & \\ \emptyset \subseteq \mathbf{int} & & \end{array}$$

It remains now to give a general method for "filling-in" the lower right-hand corner of such diagrams in the desired manner. In this example, the desired manner means filling it in with the appropriate data type $\emptyset \subseteq$ ***set(int)***.

6. THE MAIN THEOREMS

In this section we will present the "Main Lemmas" of our approach. We state them in a very general form. This has the advantage of capturing many cases at the same time but the disadvantage that the intuitive content is hidden. To help remedy this problem, we have split the main result into two parts: the syntax of parameter passing in Theorem 6.1 and the semantics of parameter passing in Theorem 6.2. The general form of the lemmas corresponds to "generalized parameter passing" to be explained in the more detailed technical report [5]. It might seem to the reader that it would be more intuitive to start with "standard parameter passing" where an actual parameter (e.g. ***int***) is inserted into a parameterized specification (e.g. ***set(data)***). However, to show some general results about iterated types we need the level of "generalized parameter passing." Also, this level of generality is the cleanest and the most symmetric one from the mathematical point of view. We do include the specialization to standard parameter passing; it is here as Corollary 6.3.

Theorem 6.1. (Syntax of Parameter Passing) Let PSPECi (i = 1,2,3) be given parameterized specifications; PSPEC4 will be constructed:

$$\begin{aligned} PSPECi &= \langle SPEC, SPECi \rangle \quad \text{for } i = 1,2 \\ PSPECi &= \langle SPEC', SPECi \rangle \quad \text{for } i = 3,4. \end{aligned}$$

Let s:PSPEC1 → PSPEC2 and h:PSPEC1 → PSPEC3 be body morphisms with s simple.

$$\begin{array}{ccc} PSPEC1 & \xrightarrow{s} & PSPEC2 \\ \downarrow h & & \Downarrow \overline{h} \\ PSPEC3 & \xRightarrow{\overline{s}} & PSPEC4 \end{array}$$

Then there is a parameterized specification PSPEC4, called the *value specification* and body morphisms $\overline{s}$:PSPEC3 ⇒ PSPEC4 (simple) and $\overline{h}$:PSPEC2 ⇒ PSPEC4 such that:

(i) $\langle \overline{h}, \overline{s} \rangle$ is a pushout for $\langle h, s \rangle$ in the category of parameterized specifications and body morphisms.

(ii) $\overline{s}$ is injective so, in particular, we can take

$$SPEC4 = SPEC3 + \langle S4, \Sigma 4, E4 \rangle$$

where $S4 = S2$, $\Sigma 4 = \overline{h}(\Sigma 2)$ and $E4 = \overline{h}(E2)$, with $SPEC2 = SPEC1 + \langle S2, \Sigma 2, E2 \rangle$ and

$\overline{h}_S(s)$ = if s $\in$ S2 then s else $h_S(s)$, and

$\overline{h}_\Sigma(\sigma)$ = if $\sigma \in \Sigma 2$ the σ else $h_\Sigma(\sigma)$. □

Theorem 6.2. (Semantics of Parameter Passing) Let PDATi (i = 1,2,3) be given parameterized data types; PDAT4 will be constructed;

PDATi = <PSPECi, Ti> for i = 1,2,3,4

with parameterized specifications PSPECi as in Theorem 6.1. Let s:PDAT1 $\rightarrow$ PDAT2 and h:PDAT1 $\rightarrow$ PDAT3 be parameter morphisms with s simple.

$$\begin{array}{ccc} \text{PDAT1} & \xrightarrow{s} & \text{PDAT2} \\ \downarrow h & & \Downarrow \overline{h} \\ \text{PDAT3} & \xRightarrow{\overline{s}} & \text{PDAT4} \end{array}$$

Further let $F:\mathbf{Alg}_{BODY1} \rightarrow \mathbf{Alg}_{BODY2}$ be strongly persistent with respect to V_s (i.e., $F \circ V_s = 1$ (the identity on $\mathbf{Alg}_{SPEC1}$)). Let $\overline{Ti}$ be Ti followed by a suitable forgetful functor to the corresponding BODYi-algebras, for i = 1,2,3,4. Finally, assume that F has the property that $\overline{T1} \circ F = \overline{T2}$. Then there exists a parameterized data type PDAT4, called the *value data type*, a persistent functor

$$F':\mathbf{Alg}_{BODY3} \rightarrow \mathbf{Alg}_{BODY4}$$

with $\overline{T4} = \overline{T3} \circ F'$ and parameter morphisms $\overline{s}$:PDAT3 $\Rightarrow$ PDAT4 (simple) and $\overline{h}$:PDAT2 $\Rightarrow$ PDAT4 such that

(i) PSPEC4 is the value specification and $\overline{s}$, $\overline{h}$ are the body morphisms constructed in Theorem 6.1.

(ii) <$\overline{h}$, $\overline{s}$> is a pushout for <h, s> in the category of parameterized data types and parameter morphisms.

(iii) F' is strongly persistent, i.e. $F' \circ V_{\overline{s}} = 1$ (the identity on $\mathbf{Alg}_{BODY3}$).

(iv) F' is *passing compatible*, i.e., $F' \circ V_{\overline{h}} = V_h \circ F:\mathbf{Alg}_{BODY3} \rightarrow \mathbf{Alg}_{BODY2}$.

(v) F' is universal with respect to (iii) and (iv) above, i.e., for all $Ai \in \mathbf{Alg}_{BODYi}$ (i = 3,4) if $V_{\overline{s}}(A4) = A3$ and $V_{\overline{h}}(A4) = F(V_h(A3))$ then $F'(A3) = A4$.

(vi) If F is free (left adjoint to V_s), then F' is free (left adjoint to $V_{\overline{s}}$.) □

Corollary 6.3. (Standard Parameter Passing) Let SPEC = SPEC1 and SPEC$'$ = $\emptyset$ in Theorem 6.1. This means that we have a parameterized specification <SPEC, SPEC2> with an actual parameter SPEC3. The body morphism h becomes a specification morphism h:<S, Σ> $\rightarrow$ SPEC3, because the body part of SPEC$\subseteq$SPEC is just <S, Σ>. The value specification becomes a (non-parameterized) specification SPEC4 = SPEC3 + <S4, Σ4, E4> as defined in 6.1 (ii). Semantically we have two cases to consider.

1. *All Ti are free constructions.*

This means T1 is the identity, $T2 = F:\mathbf{Alg}_{SPEC} \rightarrow \mathbf{Alg}_{SPEC2}$, the free construction, and $Ti:\mathbf{Alg}_{\emptyset} \rightarrow \mathbf{Alg}_{SPECi}$ picks out the initial algebra T_{SPECi} for i = 3,4. Moreover we have $V_h(T_{SPEC3}) \in \mathbf{Alg}_{SPEC}$ and $V_{\overline{h}}(T_{SPEC4}) \in \mathbf{Alg}_{SPEC2}$ because h and $\overline{h}$ are parameter morphisms. T_{SPEC4} is uniquely defined by $V_{\overline{s}}(T_{SPEC4}) = T_{SPEC3}$ and $V_{\overline{h}}(T_{SPEC4}) = F(V_h(T_{SPEC3}))$ (see 6.2 (iii) and (iv) using $F'(T_{SPEC3}) = T_{SPEC4}$ by 6.2).

2. *The Ti are not necessarily free constructions.*

Again take T1 to be the identity, $F:\mathbf{Alg}_{SPEC} \rightarrow \mathbf{Alg}_{SPEC2}$ is an arbitrary persistent functor and T3 picks out an arbitrary SPEC3-algebra A3 such that $V_h(A3) \in \mathbf{Alg}_{SPEC}$. Due to 6.2 (iii) and (iv), $F':\mathbf{Alg}_{SPEC3} \rightarrow \mathbf{Alg}_{SPEC4}$

becomes a persistent extension of the functor F.

The First case above means correctness of parameter passing while the second case is used to show induced correctness of the value specification (see [5]). □

7. ITERATED TYPES AND SPECIFICATIONS

In the diagram below, all the "fat" arrows are given by the main theorem, the "slim" one are given by specifications. In each case correctness of the specification of the slim arrow implies correctness for the corresponding fat arrow.

				par ⊆ ***par***	→	***par*** ⊆ ***queue(par)***
				↓		⇓
		attr ⊆ ***attr***	→	***attr*** ⊆ ***stack(attr)***	⇒	***attr*** ⊆ ***queue(stack(attr))***
		↓		⇓		⇓
data ⊆ ***data***	→	***data*** ⊆ ***set(data)***	⇒	***data*** ⊆ ***stack(set(data))***	⇒	***data*** ⊆ ***queue(stack(set(data)))***
↓		⇓		⇓		⇓
∅ ⊆ ***int***	⇒	∅ ⊆ ***set(int)***	⇒	∅ ⊆ ***stack(set(int))***	⇒	∅ ⊆ ***queue(stack(set(int)))***

Figure 7.1

The "call by name" strategy of constructing first ***stack(set( ))*** (i.e., ***data*** ⊆ ***stack(set(data))***) and then inserting the actual parameter ***int*** (i.e. ∅ ⊆ ***int***) leads to the same specification as the "call by value" strategy of constructing first ***set(int)*** and then inserting this as an actual parameter in ***stack( )*** (i.e., ***attr*** ⊆***stack(attr)***). This follows from the push-out composition properties resulting from the Theorem 6.2. For a general formulation of these results we refer to [5].

BIBLIOGRAPHY

ADJ (Authors: J. A. Goguen, H. Ehrig, H.-J. Kreowski, J. W. Thatcher, E. G. Wagner and J. B. Wright)

[1] ADJ (JAG, JWT, EGW, JBW). "Abstract data types as initial algebras and correctness of data representations," *Proceedings*, Conference on Computer Graphics, Pattern Recognition and Data Structure, May 1975, pp. 89-93.

[2] ADJ (JWT, EGW, JBW) "Specification of abstract data types using conditional axioms," IBM Research Report RC-6214, September 1976.

[3] ADJ (JAG, JWT, EGW) "An initial algebra approach to the specification, correctness, and implementation of abstract data types," IBM Research Report RC-6487, October 1976. *Current Trends in Programming Methodology, IV: Data Structuring* (R. T. Yeh, Ed.) Prentice Hall, New Jersey (1978) 80-149.

[4] ADJ (JWT, EGW, JBW) "Data Type Specification: parameterization and the power of specification techniques," *Proceedings*, SIGACT 10th Annual Symposium on Theory of Computing, May, 1978, pp. 119-132.

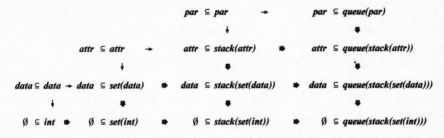

[5] ADJ (HE, H-JK, JWT, EGW, JBW) "Parameter passing in algebraic specification languages," Technical Report to appear, 1980.

[6] Burstall, R.M. and Goguen, J. A. "Putting Theories together to make Specifications," *Proceedings* 1977 IJCAI, MIT, Cambridge, MA., August, 1977.

[7] Burstall, R.M. and Goguen, J.A. "Semantics of CLEAR," Working Note - Draft version, Department of Artificial Intelligence, Edinburgh University, January, 1979.

[8] Burstall, R.M. and Goguen, J.A. "The semantics of CLEAR, A specification Language," Working Draft, Edinburgh University, January, 1980. To appear, *Proceedings*, 1979 Copenhagen Winter School on Abstract Software Specification.

[9] Cohn, P.M. *Universal Algebra*, Harper and Row, New York, 1965.

[10] Ehrich, H.-D. "On the theory of specification, implementation and parameterization of abstract data types," Research report, Dortmund, 1978. Short version, *Lecture Notes in Computer Science 64* (1978) 155-164.

[11] Ehrig, H. and Kreowski, H.-J. "Some remarks concerning correct specification and implementation of abstract data types," Technical University of Berlin, Report 77-13, August 1977.

[12] Ehrig, H., Kreowski, H.-J. and Padawitz, P. "Stepwise specification and implementation of abstract data types," Technical University of Berlin, Report, November 1977. Proceedings 5th ICALP, Udine, July 1978: *Lecture Notes in Computer Science* (1978).

[13] Ehrig, H., Kreowski, H.-J. and Padawitz, P. "Algebraic implementation of abstract data types: concept, syntax, semantics, correctness," This volume.

[14] Goguen, J.A. and Tardo, J. "OBJ-0 preliminary users manual," UCLA, Los Angeles, CA. 1977.

[15] Graetzer, G. *Universal Algebra*, Van Nostrand, Princeton, NJ, 1968.

[16] Guttag, J.V. "The specification and application to programming of abstract data types," Univ. of Toronto, Computer Systems Research Group, Technical Report CSRG-59, September, 1975.

[17] Guttag, J.V. "Abstract data types and the development of data structures," supplement to Proc. Conf. on Data Abstraction, Definition, and Structure, *SIGPLAN Notices 8*, March, 1976.

[18] Guttag, J.V. "The algebraic specification of abstract data types," USC Computer Science Department, Draft Manuscript, April, 1977.

[19] Kreowski, Hans-Jörg. "Notes on the power of equational specification: an example," Manuscript, Technical University Berlin. September, 1979.

[20] Liskov, Barbara, Snyder, Alan, Atkinson, Russel, and Schaffert, Craig. "Abstraction mechanisms in CLU," *CACM 20*, Nr. 8 (1977) 564-576.

[21] Liskov, Barbara and Zilles, Stephen. "Programming with abstract data types," *SIGPLAN Notices 9*, Nr.4 (1977) 50-59.

[22] Scott, Dana. "Mathematical concepts in programming language semantics," *Proceedings*, AFIPS Spring Joint Computer Conference, 1962, pp. 225-234.

[23] Wulf, W.A., London, R.L., and Shaw. M. "An introduction to the construction and verification of Alphard programs," *IEEE Transactions on Software Engineering SE-2* 4 (1976)253-265.

[24] Zilles, S.N. "An introduction to data algebras," working draft paper, IBM Research, San Jose, September, 1975.

CHARACTERIZING CORRECTNESS PROPERTIES OF PARALLEL PROGRAMS USING FIXPOINTS

E. Allen Emerson
Edmund M. Clarke
Aiken Computation Laboratory
Harvard University
Cambridge, Mass. 02138 USA

1. Introduction

1.1 Background. Dijkstra [DI76] proposes the use of weakest precondition predicate transformers to describe correctness properties. A typical example of such a predicate transformer is the weakest precondition for total correctness wp(π,Q) which gives a necessary and sufficient condition on initial states to ensure that program π terminates in a final state satisfying predicate Q. Dijkstra defines the wp predicate transformer on a do-od program as the least fixpoint of a simple predicate transformer which is derivable directly from the program text. Basu and Yeh [BY75] and Clarke [CL76] extend Dijkstra's fixpoint characterization of weakest preconditions to arbitrary sequential programs with "regular" control structures. In addition, Clarke argues that soundness and (relative) completeness of a Hoare-style [HO69] axiom system are equivalent to the existence and extremality of fixpoints for appropriate predicate transformers. Related results appear in the work of de Bakker [DE77a] and Park [PA69].

Many important properties of parallel programs can also be described using fixpoints. Flon and Suzuki [FS78] give fixpoint characterizations of certain correctness properties including freedom from deadlock, invariance, absence of logical starvation, and inevitability under pure nondeterministic scheduling. They also give proof rules which allow the construction of a sound and (relatively) complete proof system for any correctness property with an appropriate fixpoint characterization (e.g. as the least fixpoint of a continuous predicate transformer or as the greatest fixpoint of a monotonic transformer). This reduces the task of designing a proof system for a specified correctness property to the problem of giving a fixpoint characterization for the property. Developing the initial fixpoint characterization can still be quite difficult, however, for correctness properties such as fair inevitability.

A valuable attribute of a correctness property is the existence of a "continuous" fixpoint characterization (i.e. one in terms of extremal fixpoints of continuous transformers). Such a characterization is desirable because the extremal fixpoints are defined as the limit of a natural sequence of approximations. The approximations can be useful in applications, particularly in mechanical efforts to develop reliable and efficient parallel programs. Sintzoff and Van Lamsweerde [SV76] use continuous fixpoint characterizations of certain correctness properties to show how a given

---

This work was partially supported by NSF Grant MCS-7908365

program can be transformed into another program with the specified correctness properties. Clarke [CL78] shows how a widening operator [CO76] can be used to synthesize resource invariants from a continuous fixpoint characterization of the set of reachable states in a computation. Continuous fixpoint characterizations are also used by Reif [RE79] for parallel program optimization.

1.2 New results of this paper. We investigate the problem of characterizing correctness properties of parallel programs using fixpoints and, in particular, using "continuous" fixpoints. In this paper, a parallel program is treated as a nondeterministic sequential program at an appropriate level of granularity. A program's semantics is defined in terms of computation trees recording all possible execution sequences for the program starting in a particular state. In order to make precise statements about computation trees, we introduce the language of computation tree formulae (CTF). The advantage of this approach is that many correctness properties for parallel programs have a natural description in terms of computation trees. Thus, with CTF's we can define in a straightforward manner most correctness properties of interest for parallel programs, including invariance, deadlock freedom, absence of actual starvation, and inevitability under fair scheduling assumptions. We also define the language of fixpoint formulae, FPF, and give an effective procedure for translating CTF's into FPF's. A practical consequence of this procedure is that we can derive an FPF characterization of a correctness property from its CTF description in a uniform manner. Since it is often easier to give an operational (CTF) characterization than a fixpoint characterization, this can make the Flon and Suzuki proof rule technique considerably easier to apply. We then give conditions on a correctness property's CTF description which ensure that it has an FPF characterization using only continuous transformers. Finally, we show how our results can be interpreted in a modal logic where the computation trees determine Kripke structures.

One consequence of our findings is that, while inevitability under fair scheduling can be characterized as the least fixpoint of a monotonic noncontinuous predicate transformer, it cannot be characterized in terms of fixpoints of continuous transformers (nor can it be meaningfully characterized as the greatest fixpoint of a monotonic transformer). We also show that inevitability under fair scheduling, over the natural numbers, is not expressible by a formula of 1st order arithmetic (see also [CH78]). These facts strongly suggest that it is impossible to formulate a useful, sound and (relatively) complete proof system for this correctness property.

1.3 Outline of paper. The paper is organized as follows: Section 2 gives preliminary information about the model of computation and the lattice of total predicates. Sections 3 and 4 informally discuss the syntax and semantics of computation tree formulae (CTF) and fixpoint formulae (FPF), respectively. Section 5 describes the main results on the existence of fixpoint characterizations for parallel programs. Section 6 discusses the relationship with modal logic. Finally, Section 7 presents some concluding remarks and suggests some remaining open questions.

2. Model of Computation.

We represent parallel programs as nondeterministic sequential programs using Dijkstra's do-od construct:

$$\underline{do}\ B_1 \rightarrow A_1\ [\,]\ B_2 \rightarrow A_2\ [\,]\ \ldots\ [\,]\ B_k \rightarrow A_k\ \underline{od}.$$

Let Σ be the set of program states (for this paper, we can assume that $\Sigma = \omega$, the set of natural numbers). Each guard B_i is a total recursive predicate on Σ. Each action A_i is a total recursive function from Σ to Σ. The pair $B_i \rightarrow A_i$ is called a command. Intuitively, we may describe the operation of the do-od construct as follows: repeatedly perform the body of the do-od loop. On each trip through the loop, nondeterministically select a command whose guard B_i evaluates to True and execute the corresponding action A_i. If all guards B_i evaluate to False, execution of the loop halts.

Given a state σ in Σ and a do-od program π we define the computation tree $\mathcal{T}(\pi,\sigma)$. Each node of the tree is labelled with the state it represents, and each arc out of a node is labelled with the guard indicating which nondeterministic choice is taken, i.e., which command having a true guard is executed next. The root is labelled with the start state σ. Thus, a path from the root through the tree represents a possible computation sequence of program π starting in state σ. A fullpath of $\mathcal{T}(\pi,\sigma)$ is a path which starts at the root and which is not a proper "subpath" of any other path. Any infinite path starting at the root is a fullpath. A finite path is a fullpath only when its last node is labelled with a state in which all guards are false. A segment of $\mathcal{T}(\pi,\sigma)$ is a (finite or infinite) contiguous initial portion of a fullpath. Similar uses of computation trees appear in the work of de Bakker [DE77b], Meyer and Winklmann [MW79], and Flon and Suzuki [FS78].

We now describe how to transform cobegin-coend programs with conditional critical regions into do-od programs. We let the underlying domain of states Σ be the set of all tuples of the form

$$(pc_1,\ldots,pc_n,v_1,\ldots,v_m)$$

where $pc_1,\ldots,pc_n$ are explicit location counters and $v_1,\ldots,v_m$ are all the variables which appear in the cobegin-coend program. The transformation is essentially the same as that used by Flon and Suzuki [FS78] and will only be illustrated by example:

```
x:=0;
cobegin
    repeat produce; when true do x:=x+1 end forever
     //
    repeat when x > 0 do x:=x-1 end; consume forever
coend
```

is transformed into

```
pc1:=pc2:=0; x:=0;
do
     pc1 = 0              -> produce; pc1:=(pc1+1) mod 2 []
     pc1 = 1 and TRUE     -> x:=x+1; pc1:=(pc1+1) mod 2 []
     pc2 = 0 and x > 0    -> x:=x-1;pc2:=(pc2+1) mod 2 []
     pc2 = 1              -> consume; pc2:=(pc2+1) mod 2
od
```

Finally, we use PRED(Σ) to denote the lattice of total predicates where each predicate is identified with the set of states in Σ which make it true and the ordering is set inclusion.

2.1 Definition

Let τ: PRED(Σ) -> PRED(Σ) be given; then

(1) τ is monotonic provided that $P \subseteq Q$ implies $\tau[P] \subseteq \tau[Q]$

(2) τ is $\cup$-continuous provided that $P_1 \subseteq P_2 \subseteq \ldots$ implies $\tau[\bigcup_i P_i] = \bigcup_i \tau[P_i]$

(3) τ is $\cap$-continous provided that $P_1 \supseteq P_2 \supseteq \ldots$ implies $\tau[\bigcap_i P_i] = \bigcap_i \tau[P_i]$. []

A monotonic functional τ on PRED(Σ) always has both a least fixpoint, $\text{lfpX}.\tau[X]$, and a greatest fixpoint, $\text{gfpX}.\tau[X]$ (see Tarski [TA55]): $\text{lfpX}.\tau[X] = \bigcap\{X:\tau[X]=X\}$ whenever τ is monotonic, and $\text{lfpX}.\tau[X] = \bigcup_i \tau^i[\text{False}]$ whenever τ is also $\cup$-continuous; $\text{gfpX}.\tau[X] = \bigcap\{X:\tau[X]=X\}$ whenever τ is monotonic, and $\text{gfpX}.\tau[X] = \bigcap_i \tau^i[\text{True}]$ whenever τ is also $\cap$-continuous.

3. Computation Tree Formulae

Given a program π and an initial state σ, a computation tree formula (CTF) makes a statement about the occurence of nodes and arcs satisfying certain correctness predicates in the computation tree $\mathcal{T}(\pi,\sigma)$. When presenting the syntax of CTF's we will use the notation:

$$\begin{bmatrix} \text{choice } 1 \\ \cdot \\ \cdot \\ \text{choice } n \end{bmatrix}$$

to indicate that one item may be selected from among n alternatives. A fixed but arbitrary $k > 1$ is chosen. Our discussion of CTF semantics will assume a fixed interpretation $I = (\pi,\langle R_i\rangle,\sigma)$ consisting of: 1) a do-od program π with k commands over domain of states Σ, 2) an assignment of predicates $R_i \subseteq \Sigma$ to each predicate symbol X_i, and 3) an initial state σ.

A CTF is a boolean combination of predicate symbols, guard symbols, and constructs of the following form:

$$\begin{bmatrix} \exists \\ \forall \end{bmatrix} \begin{bmatrix} \text{fullpath} \\ \text{segment} \end{bmatrix} \quad \langle\text{body}\rangle$$

The body is a boolean combination of one or more terms. Each term makes a statement about a particular path p of $\mathscr{T}(\pi,\sigma)$ and has the form:

$$\begin{bmatrix}\exists\\ \forall\\ \overset{\infty}{\exists}\\ \overset{\infty}{\forall}\end{bmatrix} \quad \begin{bmatrix}\text{node } \langle\text{CTF}\rangle\\ \text{arc } \langle\text{guard symbol set}\rangle\end{bmatrix}$$

$\exists$ and $\forall$ have their usual meanings. $\overset{\infty}{\exists}$ means "there exist infinitely many" and $\overset{\infty}{\forall}$ means "for all but a finite number". Each predicate symbol is interpreted by one of the predicates R_i from I. Similarly, each guard symbol is interpreted by one of the guards B_i in the program π. A guard symbol set corresponds to a subset $\{B_{i_1},\dots,B_{i_n}\}$ of the actual guards of π. Examples of CTF's together with their intuitive meanings are given below:

1) " $\forall$fullpath $\exists$ node R_1" which means "for every fullpath p of $\mathscr{T}(\pi,\sigma)$, there is a node v on p labelled with a state satisfying predicate R_1" (this describes the correctness property inevitability of R_1 [under pure nondeterministic scheduling]).

2) "$R_1 \wedge \exists$ segment $\exists$ arc $\{B_1,B_3\}$" which means "σ satisfies predicate R_1 and there is a segment of $\mathscr{T}(\pi,\sigma)$ having an arc labelled with guard B_1 or guard B_3".

3) " $\forall$fullpath ($\overset{\infty}{\exists}$ node $B_1 \Rightarrow \overset{\infty}{\exists}$ arc $\{B_1\}$)" which means "for every fullpath p of $\mathscr{T}(\pi,\sigma)$ if there are infinitely many states along p at which the guard B_1 is true, then there are infinitely many arcs labelled with guard B_1 (i.e., if process 1 is enabled infinitely often, it is executed infinitely often)".

4) " $\exists$fullpath $\exists$ node ($\forall$ fullpath $\overset{\infty}{\forall}$ node R_1)" which means "there exists a fullpath p of $\mathscr{T}(\pi,\sigma)$ and there is a node v on p labelled with state σ' such that for every fullpath q of $\mathscr{T}(\pi,\sigma')$ all but a finite number of nodes on q are labelled with a state satisfying R_1".

Each of the above CTF's will be either true or false depending on the particular interpretation I that is chosen.

CTF's define predicate transformers for correctness properties of parallel programs. Let $e(X_1,\dots,X_n)$ be a CTF involving predicate symbols $X_1,\dots,X_n$. Then e defines the mapping e': $\mathrm{PROG}(\Sigma) \times (\mathrm{PRED}(\Sigma))^n \rightarrow \mathrm{PRED}(\Sigma)$ such that $e'(\pi,R_1,\dots,R_n) = \{\sigma \in \Sigma : e(X_1,\dots,X_n)$ is true when interpreted with program π, start state σ, and X_i assigned R_i for $i \in [1{:}n]\}$.

4. The Language of Fixpoint Formulae

A fixpoint formula (FPF) is interpreted with respect to a program π (with k commands) and domain Σ. Each FPF is built up from predicates $R_1,R_2,R_3,\dots$ over Σ, guards $B_1,B_2,B_3,\dots$ of the program π, and "sub-FPF's" using

(1) the logical connectives $(\wedge,\vee,\sim)$,

(2) the weakest preconditions for the actions A_i of π $(A_1^{-1}, A_2^{-1}, A_3^{-1}\dots)$, and

(3) the least fixpoint and greatest fixpoint operators (lfp, gfp).

We write $E[X_i]$ to indicate that the predicate R_i in the fixpoint formula E is viewed as a variable ranging over $\mathrm{PRED}(\Sigma)$. $E[X_i]$ defines a mapping E': $\mathrm{PRED}(\Sigma) \rightarrow \mathrm{PRED}(\Sigma)$ in the obvious way; for example, $(\sim B_1 \wedge R_2) \vee (B_3 \wedge A_3^{-1}X_1)$ sends each predicate $R \subseteq \Sigma$ to $((\Sigma \setminus B_1) \cap R_2) \cup (B_3 \cap wp(A_3,R))$. We use $lfpX_i.E[X_i]$ and $gfpX_i.E[X_i]$ to denote the least fixpoint and the greatest fixpoint, respectively, of E' where $E[X_i]$ is required to be (formally) monotonic; i.e. all occurrences of X_i in E must be in an even number of distinct negated "sub-FPF's". Examples of FPF's are

$$gfpX_1.[(B_1 \wedge R_2) \vee (B_3 \wedge A_3^{-1}X_1)]$$

$$lfpX_1.[(R_1 \wedge {\sim}B_1 \wedge {\sim}B_2) \vee ((B_1 \wedge A_1^{-1}X_1) \vee (B_2 \wedge A_2^{-1}X_1))].$$

We shall be interested in "Continuous FPF's" where we only allow least fixpoint formation on (formally) $\cup$-continuous transformers and greatest fixpoint formation on (formally) $\cap$-continuous transformers. We say that an FPF E is formally $\cup$-continuous ($\cap$-continuous) in X provided that its normal form E' (obtained by driving all negations "inward" using DeMorgan's laws and the fact that ${\sim}gfpX.t[X,Y] = lfpX.{\sim}t[{\sim}X,Y]$) satisfies two conditions: (i) E' is monotonic in X and (ii) E' contains no free occurrence of X inside a subFPF of the form gfpY.E''[...Y,...,X...] (lfpY.E''[...Y,...,X...]). Given that E is in normal form, we can say the following: if E contains no occurrences of lfp or gfp, then E is a Continuous FPF. If E contains no occurrences of lfp or gfp, and no negated occurrences of X, then lfpX.E[X] and gfpX.E[X] are Continuous FPF's. On the other hand, if E involves an "alternation" of lfp and gfp operators (entailing the situation disallowed in (ii)), then E is not a Continuous FPF.

5. Results

Our main results are summarized below (and proved in the appendix):

5.1 Theorem: There is an effective procedure to translate CTF definitions of correctness properties into FPF definitions. Any correctness property defined in CTF without use of the $\overset{\infty}{\exists}$ and $\overset{\infty}{\forall}$ quantifiers is translated into a Continuous FPF. []

5.2 Theorem: Any correctness property definable as a Continuous FPF is Δ_1^1 over the natural numbers. []

5.3 Theorem: The correctness property definable in CTF as "$\forall$ fullpath $\overset{\infty}{\forall}$ node R" is Π_1^1-complete on the domain of natural numbers. []

5.4 Corollary: "$\forall$ fullpath $\overset{\infty}{\forall}$ node R" is not definable as a Continuous FPF, nor as a CTF without use of the $\overset{\infty}{\exists}$ or $\overset{\infty}{\forall}$ quantifiers. []

A formula $F(x_1,\ldots,x_n)$ of 1st order arithmetic with free variables $x_1,\ldots,x_n$ defines, in a natural way, an n-ary relation over ω. For example, the formula $F(x) \equiv \exists y\ x=2y$ defines the set of even natural numbers. A relation definable by a formula of 1st order arithmetic is called an arithmetical relation. The class of all arithmetical relations can be organized in a hierarchy based on the number of alternations of existential and universal quantifiers required in the defining formulae: Let $\Sigma^0_0 = \Pi^0_0$ = the class of all recursive relations over ω. For all m > 0, let Σ^0_m be the class of all relations R definable as $R(x_1,\ldots,x_n) \equiv \exists y\ S(y,x_1,\ldots,x_n)$ where S belongs to Π^0_{m-1}, and let Π^0_m be the class of all relations whose complements belongs to Σ^0_m. By induction, we can show that each relation in Σ^0_m can be defined by a formula of the form: $\exists x_1\ \forall x_2\ \exists x_3 \ldots Qx_m\ R(z,x_1,\ldots,x_m)$ where R is recursive and Q denotes $\exists$ for odd m, $\forall$ for even m. Similarly, each relation in Π^0_n can be defined by a formula of the form: $\forall x_1\ \exists x_2 \ldots Qx_m\ R(z,x_1,\ldots,x_m)$ where R is recursive and Q denotes $\forall$ for odd m, $\exists$ for even m. It can be shown that the arithmetical hierarchy is indeed a hierarchy ($\Sigma^0_m \cup \Pi^0_m \subsetneq \Sigma^0_{m+1} \cap \Pi^0_{m+1}$ for all m) which covers the arithmetical relations. Also, for each class in the hierarchy there are "complete" relations ("hardest" relations in the class). For example, the class Σ^0_1 (which coincides with the class of all recursively enumerable relations) has a complete relation K = "the set of encodings of Turing machines which halt on their own encodings".

There are also relations whose arguments include "2nd order" objects such as predicates (i.e. total functions $\omega \to \{0,1\}$). For instance, if P is a variable ranging over 2^ω, then we could have a relation $R(x_1,\ldots,x_n,P) \subseteq \omega^n \times 2^\omega$. To say that such a relation R is recursive means that there is an "oracle Turing machine" which (i) takes as input $x_1,\ldots,x_n$, (ii) uses a read-only, one-way infinite oracle tape encoding the graph of P, and (iii) always halts (for all inputs and all possible oracle tape contents). This notion leads to the analytical hierarchy which is a classification for relations definable in 2nd order arithmetic based on the alternation of 2nd order quantifiers. We are interested in two classes at the bottom of the analytical hierarchy: Π^1_1 and Σ^1_1. Π^1_1 consists of all relations $R(x_1,\ldots,x_n,P_1,\ldots,P_p)$ over the natural numbers which are definable by a formula of 2nd order arithmetic of the form $\forall F\ \exists y\ \forall z\ Q(x_1,\ldots,x_n,y,z,F,P_1,\ldots P_p)$ where $F,P_1,\ldots,P_p$ range over 2^ω, $x_1,\ldots,x_n,y,z$ range over ω, and Q is a recursive relation. Σ^1_1 = the class of all relations whose complements are in Π^1_1. $\Delta^1_1 = \Sigma^1_1 \cap \Pi^1_1$ is called the class of hyperarithmetical relations and contains the class of arithmetical relations. (See [RO67] and [HI78] for discussions of hierarchy theory.)

When we say that a correctness property such as "$\forall$ fullpath $\overset{\infty}{\forall}$ node R" is, e.g., Π^1_1, we mean that the <u>representing relation</u> $\{(\pi,\sigma,R): \forall$ fullpath of $\mathcal{T}(\pi,\sigma)\ \overset{\infty}{\forall}$ node $R\} \subseteq \omega^2 \times 2^\omega$ is Π^1_1. Since a Π^1_1-complete relation cannot be hyperarithemetical, it follows that " $\forall$ fullpath $\overset{\infty}{\forall}$ node R" cannot be characterized in Continuous FPF. Using some additional machinery from recursive function theory, it can also be shown that "$\forall$ fullpath $\overset{\infty}{\forall}$ node R" cannot be characterized as the greatest fixpoint of any monotonic transformer of any degree of complexity lower than Π^1_1. These conclusions hold for inevitability under fair scheduling as well. (Here we use "weak eventual fairness": there is no process which is active almost everywhere yet executed only finitely often; "strong eventual fairness" would also work.) Inevitability under fair scheduling can be characterized in CTF as

"$\forall$ fullpath [path_is_unfair $\vee$ $\exists$ node R]"

where path_is_unfair abbreviates

"$\forall$ node ($\bigvee_i B_i$) $\wedge$ [($\overset{\infty}{\forall}$ node B_1 $\wedge$ $\sim\overset{\infty}{\exists}$ arc $\{B_1\}$)$\vee$ ... $\vee$ ($\overset{\infty}{\forall}$ node B_k $\wedge$ $\sim\overset{\infty}{\exists}$ arc $\{B_k\}$)]".

Since this has the form " $\forall$ fullpath (... $\overset{\infty}{\forall}$ node B_1 ...)" it can be shown that it is at least as hard to describe as "$\forall$ fullpath $\overset{\infty}{\forall}$ node R". In the appendix we show how to apply the effective translation procedure to derive a monotonic, noncontinuous FPF characterization for fair inevitability from the above CTF formula.

6. Relationship to Modal Logic

CTF may be viewed as a modal logic. The computation trees determine Kripke structures where the accessibility relation R between states is given by σ_1 R σ_2 iff there is a path in the computation tree from a node labelled with state σ_1 to a node labelled with state α_2. Since each CTF formula $E(R_1,\ldots,R_n)$ defines a modality, there are an infinite number of modalities in this logic. However, in the proof that CTF is translatable into FPF, we show that all these modalities can be expressed in terms of four basic types of modalities: α , ξ , ι , and ν . Thus, these modalities are expressively complete for CTF.

7. Conclusion

We have shown that correctness properties of parallel programs can be described using computation trees and that from these descriptions fixpoint characterizations can be generated. We have also given conditions on the form of computation tree descriptions to ensure that a correctness property can be characterized using continuous fixpoints. A consequence is that a correctness property such as inevitability under fair scheduling can be characterized as the least fixpoint of a monotonic, noncontinuous transformer, but cannot be characterized using fixpoints of continuous transformers (nor as the greatest fixpoint of a monotonic transformer of any degree of complexity lower than fair inevitability itself). Hence, currently known proof rules are not applicable (see however [FS80]). We are now investigating whether useful proof rules can exist for correctness properties having only a monotonic, noncontinuous least fixpoint characterization. In addition, we are examining alternate notions of fairness which do have continuous fixpoint characterizations.

8. References

[BY75] Basu, S.K. and Yeh, R.T., Strong Verification of Programs. IEEE Trans. on Software Engineering, v. SE-1. no. 1, pp.339-354, September 1975.

[CH78] Chandra, A. K., Computable Nondeterministic Functions. 19th Annual Symp. on Foundations of Computer Science, 1978.

[CL77] Clarke, E. M., Program Invariants as Fixpoints. 18th Annual Symp. on Foundations of Computer Science, 1977.

[CL79] Clarke, E. M., Synthesis of Resource Invariants for Concurrent Programs, 6th POPL Conference, January, 1979.

[CO76] Cousot, P. and Cousot R., Static Determination of Dynamic Properties of Programs. Proc. 2nd Int. Symp. on Programming, (B. Robinet, ed.), Dunod, Paris, April 1976.

[DE77a] de Bakker, J. W., Recursive Programs as Predicate Transformers. Mathematical Centre, Amsterdam, 1977.

[DE77b] de Bakker. J. W., Semantics of Infinite Processes Using Generalized Trees. Mathematical Centre, Amsterdam, 1977.

[DI76] Dijkstra, E. W., A Discipline of Programming, Prentice-Hall, 1976.

[FS78] Flon, L. and Suzuki, N., Consistent and Complete Proof Rules for the Total Correctness of Parallel Programs. 19th Annual Symp. on Foundations of Computer Science, 1978.

[FS80] Flon, L. and Suzuki, N., The Total Correctness of Parallel Programs. SIAM J. Comp., to appear

[HI78] Hinman, P. G., Recursion-Theoretic Hierarchies, Springer-Verlag,Berlin, 1978.

[HO69] Hoare, C. A. R., An Axiomatic Approach to Computer Programming CACM, v.10. no 12., pp.322-329, October 1969.

[MW79] Meyer, A. R. and Winklmann, K., On the Expressive Power of Dynamic Logic. Proceedings of the 11th Annual ACM Symp. on Theory of Computing, 1979.

[PA69] Park, D., Fixpoint Induction and Proofs of Program Properties, in Machine Intelligence 5, (D. Mitchie, ed.) Edinburgh University Press, 1970.

[RE79] Reif, J. H., Data Flow Analysis of Communicating Processes. 6th POPL Conference, January 1979.

[RO67] Rogers, H. R., Theory of Recursive Functions and Effective Computability, McGraw-Hill, New York, 1967.

[SV76] Sintzoff, M. and Van Lamsweerde, A., Formal Derivation of Strongly Correct Parallel Programs, M. B. L. E. Research Lab., Brussels, Report R338, October 1976.

[TA55] Tarski, A., A Lattice-Theoretical Fixpoint Theorem and Its Applications. Pacific J. Math.,5, pp.285-309 (1955).

9. Appendix

Proof outline for 5.1

We outline the main steps of the effective procedure for translating CTF into FPF. Note that if there are no path quantifiers present in the CTF, then it is already a legitimate FPF. (To simplify notation we adopt these conventions: symbols such as G, G_1, G_2^3, etc. denote guardsets chosen from $\{B_1,\ldots, B_k\}$ and the corresponding lower case symbols g, g_1, g_2^3, etc. denote the corresponding set of indices; e.g., if G_2^3 represents $\{B_1,B_3,B_5\}$ then g_2^3 denotes $\{1,3,5\}$. We use,e.g., $\bar{R}^2$ and $\bar{G}^2$ to denote vectors $(R_1^2,\ldots,R_n^2)$ and $(G_1^2,\ldots,G_n^2)$, respectively. Finally, we use BB to abbreviate $B_1 \vee \ldots \vee B_k$.)

(1) Reduce to translating CTF's with at most one path quantifier by recursively applying the translation procedure to nested CTF sub-expressions. For example:

Let e(R,S) = "$\exists$ fullpath $\forall$ node [$\forall$ fullpath $\exists$ node R $\wedge$ $\exists$ fullpath $\overset{\infty}{\exists}$ node S]" be the CTF to be translated.

Let f1(R), f2(S), f3(T) denote the FPF translations of " $\forall$ fullpath $\exists$ node R", "$\exists$ fullpath $\overset{\infty}{\exists}$ node S", and "$\exists$ fullpath $\forall$ node T", respectively.

Then the FPF translation is $f3(f1(R) \wedge f2(S))$.

(2) Reduce to translating CTF's with one <u>existential</u> path quantifier by use of duality. The <u>dual</u> of a correctness property $C(R_1,\ldots,R_n)$ is $C^*(R_1,\ldots,R_n) = {\sim}C({\sim}R_1,\ldots,{\sim}R_n)$. The following facts about fixpoints of duals are useful (see [PA69]):

$$lfpR_1.C^*(R_1,\ldots,R_n) = {\sim}gfpR_1.C(R_1,{\sim}R_2,\ldots,{\sim}R_n)$$
$$gfpR_1.C^*(R_1,\ldots,R_n) = {\sim}lfpR_1.C(R_1,{\sim}R_2,\ldots,{\sim}R_n)$$

For example, let $C(R)$ = "$\forall$ fullpath $\exists$ node R" be the CTF to be translated. Its dual $C^*(R)$ = " $\sim\forall$ fullpath $\exists$ node $\sim$R" = "$\exists$ fullpath $\forall$ node R" is in the desired form with a single existential quantifier. The remaining steps of the procedure will show that the FPF translation of $C^*(R)$ is

$$gfpX.D[X,R] \text{ where } D[X,R] = R \wedge [\ {\sim}(\bigvee_i B_i) \vee \bigvee_i (B_i \wedge A_i^{-1}X)\ ]$$

To get the FPF translation of $C(R) = (C^*)^*(R)$ we again dualize to get

$$\begin{aligned} &{\sim}gfpX.D[X,{\sim}R] \\ &= lfpX.D^*[X,R] \\ &= lfpX.{\sim}({\sim}R \wedge [{\sim}(\vee\ B_i) \vee \bigvee_i (B_i \wedge A_i^{-1}({\sim}X))]) \\ &= lfpX.R \vee [\bigvee_i B_i \wedge \bigwedge_i ({\sim}B_i \vee {\sim}A_i({\sim}X))] \\ &= lfpX.R \vee [\bigvee_i B_i \wedge \bigwedge_i (B_i \Rightarrow A_i^{-1}X)] \end{aligned}$$

(3) Reduce to translating a <u>disjunction of CTF's</u>. First, place the body in the following general form:

$$\bigvee(\forall\text{-PART} \wedge \exists\text{-PART} \wedge \overset{\infty}{\forall}\text{-PART} \wedge \overset{\infty}{\exists}\text{-PART})$$

where each $\forall$-PART has the form " $\bigwedge\forall$ node P $\wedge$ $\bigwedge\forall$ arc G ",

each $\exists$-PART has the form " $\bigwedge(\bigvee\exists$ node P $\vee$ $\bigvee\exists$ arc G)",

each $\overset{\infty}{\forall}$-PART has the form " $\bigwedge\overset{\infty}{\forall}$ node P $\wedge$ $\bigwedge\overset{\infty}{\forall}$ arc G", and

each $\overset{\infty}{\exists}$-PART has the form " $\bigwedge(\bigvee\overset{\infty}{\exists}$ node P $\vee\bigvee$ $\overset{\infty}{\exists}$ arc G)".

There may be more than one specific form for the body consistent with the above general form, but there is always at least one: Disjunctive Normal Form (DNF may be obtained by having certain appropriate inner disjunctions of $\exists$-PART and $\overset{\infty}{\exists}$-PART be vacuous). However, more concise FPF translations often result from keeping $\exists$-PART and $\overset{\infty}{\exists}$-PART in true "product of sums" form with the sums as large as possible. We use the fact that $\vee$ "commutes" with $\exists$ to separate into a disjunction of CTF's, e.g.:

$$\exists \text{ fullpath } (\bigvee_i (\forall\text{-PART}_i \vee \exists\text{-PART}_i \vee \overset{\infty}{\forall}\text{-PART}_i \vee \overset{\infty}{\exists}\text{-PART}_i))$$
$$\equiv \bigvee_i \exists \text{ fullpath}(\forall\text{-PART}_i \vee \exists\text{-PART}_i \vee \overset{\infty}{\forall}\text{-PART}_i \vee \overset{\infty}{\exists}\text{-PART}_i\ )$$

Each of the disjuncts is then translated separately by the remaining step.

(4) Put the CTF in a <u>standard form</u> which can be translated via the tables below. Note that $\wedge$ and $\cap$ "commute" with $\forall$ and $\overset{\infty}{\forall}$ and that $\vee$ and $\cup$ "commute" with $\exists$ and $\overset{\infty}{\exists}$. For example, $\bigwedge_i \overset{\infty}{\forall}$ node $R_i \equiv \overset{\infty}{\forall}$ node $\bigwedge_i R_i$ and $\bigvee_i$ $\exists$ arc $G_i \equiv \exists$ arc $\bigcup_i G_i$. Using these facts we obtain the standard form:

$$\exists \begin{bmatrix} \text{fullpath} \\ \text{segment} \end{bmatrix} \left(\begin{array}{l} \overbrace{(\forall \text{ node } R^1 \wedge \forall \text{ arc } G^1)}^{(1)} \wedge (\bigwedge_i \overbrace{(\exists \text{ node } R^2 \vee \exists \text{ arc } G^2)}^{(2)}) \wedge \\ \underbrace{(\overset{\infty}{\forall} \text{ node } R^3 \wedge \overset{\infty}{\forall} \text{ arc } G^3)}_{(3)} \wedge (\bigwedge_i \underbrace{(\overset{\infty}{\exists} \text{ node } R_i^4 \vee \overset{\infty}{\exists} \text{ arc } R_i^4)}_{(4)}) \end{array} \right)$$

Any (nonempty) combination of clauses (1) - (4) may be "present" (i.e., have at least one term for nodes or at least one term for arcs present). The tables below show how to translate any combination of clauses (1) - (4) by an appropriate composition of the basic correctness properties (a) - (d) below:

(a) $\alpha(R,G)$ which means "along some fullpath, R holds of all nodes and G holds of all arcs."

(b) $\xi(R,G,S)$ which means "along some (finite) segment, R holds of all nodes and G holds of all arcs upto (and including) the last node at which S holds"

(c) $\iota(R^1,G^1,\bar{R}^2,\bar{G}^2)$ which means "along some (infinite) fullpath, R_1 holds of all nodes, G_1 holds of all arcs, and for each $i \in [1:m]$ there are infinitely many occurrences of a node where R_i^2 holds or infinitely many occurrences of an arc where G_i^2 holds."

(d) $\nu(R^1,G^1,\bar{R}^2,\bar{G}^2,S)$ which means " along some (finite) segment, R^1 holds of all nodes, G^1 holds of all arcs, for each $i \in [1:m]$ there is on the segment either a node satisfying R_i^2 or an arc satisfying G_i^2, and then at the last node of the segment , S holds.

These basic correctness properties may be defined directly in FPF:

(a) $\alpha(R,G) = \text{gfp}X.R \wedge (\sim \bigvee_j B_j \vee \bigvee_{i \in g} (B_i \wedge A_i^{-1}X))$

(b) $\xi(R,G,S) = \text{lfp}X.R \wedge (S \vee \bigvee_{i \in g} (B_i \wedge A_i^{-1}X))$

(c) $\iota(R^1,G^1,\bar{R}^2,\bar{G}^2) =$

$$\text{gfp}X. \bigwedge_{j=1}^{m} \xi(R^1,G^1, (R_j^2 \wedge \bigvee_{i \in g^1} (B_i \wedge A_i^{-1}X)) \vee \bigvee_{i \in g^1 \cap g_j^2} (B_i \wedge A_i^{-1}X))$$

(d) $\nu(R^1,G^1,\bar{R}^2,\bar{G}^2,S) =$

$$\bigvee \{ \gamma_{i_1} \circ \cdots \circ \gamma_{i_m} \circ \varepsilon(R^1,G^1,S) : (i_1,\ldots,i_m) \text{ is a permutation of } \{1,2,\ldots,m\} \}$$

where for $j \in [1:m]$ $\gamma_j(P) = \xi(R^1,G^1, (R_j^2 \wedge P) \vee \bigvee_{i \in g^1 \cap g_j^2} (B_i \wedge A_i^{-1}P))$

Note that while the notation looks formidable, the idea in (4) is simple. Each permutation records a possible order of occurrence of nodes satisfying each of the R_i^2 (or arcs satisfying the G_i^2). It is necessary to consider all permutations since the definition of ν does not specify an order. Verification of the correctness of the above FPF characterizations and the table entries below is straightforward and is left to the reader.

Table	for fullpath	for segment
$1\bar{2}\bar{3}\bar{4}$:	$\alpha(R^1,G^1)$	$R^1 \wedge G^1_1 \wedge \ldots \wedge G^1_n$ where $G^1 = \{G^1_1,\ldots,G^1_n\}$
$1\bar{2}\bar{3}4$:	$\iota(R^1,G^1,\bar{R}^4,\bar{G}^4)$	$\iota(R^1,G^1,\bar{R}^4,\bar{G}^4)$
$1\bar{2}3\bar{4}$:	$\xi(R^1,G^1,\sim BB \vee \alpha(R^1 \wedge R^3, G^1 \cap G^3))$	$R^1 \wedge G^1_1 \wedge \ldots \wedge G^1_n$
$1\bar{2}34$:	$\xi(R^1,G^1,\iota(R^1 \wedge R^3, G^1 \cap G^3, \bar{R}^4,\bar{G}^4))$	$\xi(R^1,G^1,\iota(R^1 \wedge R^3, G^1 \cap G^3, \bar{R}^4,\bar{G}^4))$
$12\bar{3}\bar{4}$:	$\nu(R^1,G^1,\bar{R}^2,\bar{G}^2,\alpha(R^1,G^1))$	$\nu(R^1,G^1,\bar{R}^2,\bar{G}^2,True)$
$12\bar{3}4$:	$\nu(R^1,G^1,\bar{R}^2,\bar{G}^2,\iota(R^1,G^1,\bar{R}^4,\bar{G}^4))$	$\nu(R^1,G^1,\bar{R}^2,\bar{G}^2,\iota(R^1,G^1,\bar{R}^4,\bar{G}^4))$
$123\bar{4}$:	$\nu(R^1,G^1,\bar{R}^2,\bar{G}^2,\sim BB \vee \alpha(R^1 \wedge R^3, G^1 \cap G^3))$	$\nu(R^1,G^1,\bar{R}^2,\bar{G}^2,True)$
1234:	$\nu(R^1,G^1,\bar{R}^2,\bar{G}^2,\iota(R^1 \wedge R^3, G^1 \cap G^3, \bar{R}^4,\bar{G}^4))$	$\nu(R^1,G^1,\bar{R}^2,\bar{G}^2,\iota(R^1 \wedge R^3, G^1 \cap G^3, \bar{R}^4,\bar{G}^4))$

Note that 2 indicates clause 2 is present, and $\bar{2}$ indicates clause 2 is absent, etc. If clause (1) is absent, we translate just as when it is present but let R^1 = True, $G^1 = \{B_1,\ldots,B_k\}$. If clause (i) is present but there are no node conditions, we let R^i = True. If clause (i) is present but there are no arc conditions, let $G^i = \{B_1,\ldots,B_k\}$. For example, the segment table entry for $1\bar{2}\bar{3}4$ indicates that $\exists$ segment ($\forall$ node $R^1 \wedge \forall$ arc $G^1 \wedge \bigwedge_i$ ($\overset{\infty}{\exists}$ node $R^4_i \vee \overset{\infty}{\exists}$ arc G^4_i) $= \iota(R^1,G^1,\bar{R}^4,\bar{G}^4)$, which follows directly from the definition of ι and the fact that any infinite segment is a fullpath.

We now derive an FPF characterization of fair inevitability starting with the CTF description $\forall$ fullpath [path_is_unfair $\vee \exists$ node R]:

1. Dualize to obtain

   $\exists$ fullpath [$\forall$ node R $\wedge \sim$path_is_unfair]

2. Use the definition of path_is_unfair to obtain

   $\exists$ fullpath [$\forall$ node R $\wedge$ [$\exists$ node ($\sim$BB) $\vee \bigwedge_j$ ($\overset{\infty}{\exists}$ node $\sim B_j \vee \overset{\infty}{\exists}$ arc $\{B_j\}$)]]

3. Use the distributive law and then split apart disjuncts to obtain

   $\exists$ fullpath [$\forall$ node R $\wedge \exists$ node ($\sim$BB)] $\vee$

   $\exists$ fullpath [$\forall$ node R $\wedge \bigwedge_j$ ($\overset{\infty}{\exists}$ node $B_j \vee \overset{\infty}{\exists}$ arc $\{B_j\}$)]]

4. Use the translation procedure to obtain:

   $\xi(R,\{B_1,\ldots,B_k\},\sim BB) \vee \iota(R,\{B_1,\ldots,B_k\}, B_1,\ldots, B_k,\{B_1\},\ldots,\{B_k\})$

5. Dualize again to obtain

   $\xi^*(R,\emptyset,BB) \wedge \iota^*(R,\emptyset,\{B_2,\ldots,B_k\},\ldots,\{B_1,\ldots,B_{k-1}\})$

Finally, observe that any CTF defined without using the quantifiers $\overset{\infty}{\exists}$ or $\overset{\infty}{\forall}$ is translated using only α and ξ which are Continuous FPF's. []

<u>Proof outline for 5.2</u>

We outline a proof by induction on the structure of correctness properties definable in Continuous FPF that any such correctness property is hyperarithmetical (i.e. Δ_1^1): Since $gfpX.t[X] = \sim lfpX.t^*[X]$ and $\{\vee,\sim\}$ is a complete set of boolean connectives, the following steps suffice:

<u>Basis</u>: $t[R_1,\ldots,R_n] = R_i$ $(1 \leq i \leq n)$ is Δ_1^1 immediately.
$t[R_1,\ldots,R_n] = B_i$ $(1 \leq i \leq k)$ is Δ_1^1 since guard B_i is Δ_1^0.

<u>Induction</u>: $t[R_1,\ldots,R_n] = t_1[R_1,\ldots,R_n] \vee t_2[R_1,\ldots,R_n]$ is Δ_1^1 since Δ_1^1 is closed under finite union.
$t[R_1,\ldots,R_n] = \sim t_1[R_1,\ldots,R_n]$ is Δ_1^1 since Δ_1^1 is closed under complementation.
$t[R_1,\ldots,R_n] = A_i^{-1}t_1[R_1,\ldots,R_n]$ $(1 \leq i \leq k)$ is Δ_1^1 since action A_i is Δ_1^0.
$t[R_1,\ldots,R_n] = lfpR.t_1[R,R_1,\ldots,R_n]$ is Δ_1^1 since Δ_1^1 is closed under inductive definitions with closure ordinals $\leq \omega$. (See [HI78]). []

<u>Proof outline of 5.3</u>

We show that $Q = \{(\pi,\sigma,R)\colon \exists$ fullpath $\overset{\infty}{\exists}$ node R is true of $\mathcal{T}(\pi,\sigma)\}$ is Σ_1^1-complete. It follows that (the reprepresenting relation of the) dual correctness property "$\forall$ fullpath $\overset{\infty}{\forall}$ node R" is Π_1^1-complete.

<u>Q is Σ_1^1-hard</u>: Let S be an arbitrary Σ_1^1 set. then for some recursive relation $P \subseteq \omega^3 \times 2^\omega$, $x \in S \Leftrightarrow \exists F \forall y \exists z\, P(x,y,z,F)$ (see [RO67]). We can construct a <u>do-od</u> program π_s which on input x, guesses F and attempts to find for each y some z so that P holds. We design π_s so that for each distinct y = 1,2,3,... when (and if) the appropriate z is found, π_s sets (for one step) a special flag q_0 to true before proceeding to check the next y value. There is a possible computation of π_s starting in state x for which q_0 becomes true infinitely often iff $x \in S$. Thus, the question "Is $x \in S$?" has been effectively reduced to "Is $(\pi_s, x, \{q_0=\text{True}\}) \in Q$?". So Q is Σ_1^1-hard.

<u>Q is in Σ_1^1</u>: We use $\langle x,y\rangle$ to indicate a (recursive) pairing function establishing a bijection $\omega^2 \to \omega . (\langle x,y\rangle_0 = x$ and $\langle x,y\rangle_1 = y)$. We define the recursive functional <u>state</u>: $\omega^3 \times 2^\omega \to \omega$ by $\underline{state}(\pi,\sigma,n,F) = \langle 1, A_{F(n)} \circ A_{F(n-1)} \circ \ldots \circ A_{F(1)}(\sigma)\rangle$ if $F(1),\ldots,F(n)$ encodes a legitimate initial segment in $\mathcal{T}(\pi,\sigma)$ where π = <u>do</u> $A_1 \to B_1$ [\]...[\] $A_k \to B_k$ <u>od</u> and each $F(i) \in [1:k]$ and gives the index of the command chosen on the ith trip through the loop. Otherwise, $\underline{state}(\pi,\sigma,n,F) = \langle 0,0\rangle$.

Then Q is defined by the Σ_1^1 formula of 2nd order arithmetic:

$$\exists F \forall i \exists j\, (j > i \wedge (\underline{state}(\pi,\sigma,j,F))_0 = 1 \wedge P(\, (\underline{state}(\pi,\sigma,j,F))_1\,) = \text{True}).\ []$$

<u>proof outline for 5.4</u>

If "$\forall$ fullpath $\overset{\infty}{\forall}$ node R" were definable as a Continuous FPF, it would be Δ_1^1 by Theorem 5.2. But this contradicts Theorem 5.3 since no Δ_1^1 relation can be Π_1^1-complete. If it were definable as a CTF without using the $\overset{\infty}{\exists}$ or $\overset{\infty}{\forall}$ quantifiers, it would be definable as a Continuous FPF by Theorem 5.1. But, we just saw that this is impossible. []

FORMAL PROPERTIES OF ONE-VISIT AND MULTI-PASS ATTRIBUTE GRAMMARS

(extended abstract)

Joost Engelfriet and Gilberto Filè
Twente University of Technology
Enschede, The Netherlands

Abstract. The purpose of this paper is to study the formal power of certain classes of attribute-grammars (AG). We first consider the class of 1S-AG and extend a result of [DPSS]. Then we compare the formal power of "one-visit" AG with that of related types of AG. Finally, using a partial characterization of the formal power of arbitrary AG we prove some results on deciding whether an AG is (left-to-right) multi-pass.

In Section 1 we give some necessary definitions about AG and related concepts. Section 2 consists of the study of 1S-AG. In Section 3 we extend some of the results of Section 2 to "one-visit" AG and we finally summarize the relations existing among all the classes of AG we considered. In Section 4 we show that the multi-pass problem for AG is complete in exponential time. No complete proofs are given, they can be found in [EF1] and [EF2].

1. Preliminaries

Attribute-grammars (AG) were introduced by Knuth [Kn] as a means of defining the semantics of context-free languages. For the purpose of studying their formal power, for each AG G we explicitly give, together with the usual specifications, its semantic domain D consisting of an ordered pair (Ω,Φ), where Ω contains the sets of allowed attribute values of all the attributes of G and Φ contains all functions (on these sets) which may be used in the semantic rules of G. We shortly give now the definition of AG[Kn] and of some useful concepts related to them.

Definition 1.1. An attribute-grammar G over semantic domain $D = (\Omega_D,\Phi_D)$ consists of the following four parts:

1) G has a context-free grammar (CFG), $G_0 = (N,T,P,Z)$, called the underlying CFG of G. We always assume G_0 to be reduced in the usual sense. Throughout the paper we will denote a production $p \in P$ of G_0 (and of G) as, $p : F_0 \to w_0F_1w_1 \dots w_{n_p-1}F_{n_p}w_{n_p}$, where $n_p \geq 0$, $F_i \in N$ and $w_i \in T^*$ for all $i \in [0,n_p]$. We denote with DT(G) the set of the derivation-trees of G (of G_0), where we assume a derivation tree to have all leaves labeled by terminals. A complete derivation-tree is a derivation-tree whose root is labeled by Z. The set of complete derivation-trees of G is indicated with CDT(G).

2) Each nonterminal F of N of G_0 has two associated finite sets, denoted S(F) and

I(F), of synthesized and inherited attributes, respectively (shortly s- and i-attributes). The initial nonterminal Z does not have any i-attribute and one of its s-attributes is designated to hold the translation of any complete derivation-tree in G. We indicate the set of all the attributes of nonterminal F with $A(F) = I(F) \cup S(F)$ and with b(F) we denote an attribute $b \in A(F)$.

3) For each attribute b of G, Ω_D contains a set V(b) of the possible values of b.

4) With each production $p \in P$ is associated a set r_p of semantic rules which have the following form: $a_0(F_{i_0}) \leftarrow f(a_1(F_{i_1}),\ldots, a_m(F_{i_m}))$ where $i_j \in [0,n_p]$ and f is a mapping in Φ_D from $V_1 \times V_2 \ldots \times V_m$ to V_0 such that $V_j = V(a_j(F_{i_j}))$, $\forall j \in [1,m]$. When the identity of the nonterminals is not important we indicate it simply by $a_0 \leftarrow f(a_1,\ldots,a_m)$ and we say that a_0 depends on $a_1,\ldots,a_m$ in p. We assume that the semantic rules in r_p define all and only the attributes in $S(F_0)$ and $I(F_j)$ using as arguments only attributes in $I(F_0)$ and $S(F_j)$, $j \in [1,n_p]$. □

We define the translation realized by an AG G, denoted by T(G), as the mapping which assigns to each complete derivation-tree t of G the value of the designated s-attribute of the root of t. The output-set of G, denoted OUT(G), is the range of T(G). Two AG G_1 and G_2 are <u>equivalent</u> if they are defined over the same semantic domain and $T(G_1) = T(G_2)$.

It is useful, when working with AG, to visualize the dependencies among attributes by means of graphs. Given an AG G, for each production $p : F_0 \to w_0F_1w_1\ldots w_{n_p-1}F_{n_p}w_{n_p}$, the production-graph of p (pg(p)) is the graph having as nodes the attributes of all nonterminals F_j of p, $j \in [0,n_p]$, and in which there is an edge running from attribute a_1 to attribute a_2 iff a_2 depends on a_1 in p, (see also [Kn] and [KW]). It is also useful to define for each production p of G the brother-graph of p (bg(p)) as the graph which has one node for each F_j, $j \in [1,n_p]$, and such that there is an edge from node F_i to node F_j iff some i-attribute of F_j depends on an s-attribute of F_i, i and $j \in [1,n_p]$. Recall from point (4) of Definition 1.1 that this is the only type of dependency possible among attributes of nonterminals of the right-hand side of a production (brothers).

Because of the obvious fact that derivation-trees consists of productions pasted together, for each derivation-tree t of G we obtain a graph, called derivation-tree graph of t (dtg(t)) by pasting together the pg(p)'s of all the productions p used in t, (see [Kn], [KW]). Troughout the paper we will consider only noncircular AG, where an AG G is noncircular if there is no $t \in DT(G)$ such that dtg(t) contains an oriented cycle [Kn].

Two particular semantic domains, called STRINGS and TREES, are especially interesting for us because it is possible to connect classes of output sets of AG defined on them with classes of languages already known in formal language theory.

The domain STRINGS is defined to contain all possible strings on some denumerable alphabet with string-concatenation as only allowed operation. This means that, for any AG on STRINGS, the attributes will take strings as values and the semantic rules will have the form: $a_0 \leftarrow \alpha = w_0 a_1 w_1 \ldots w_{n-1} a_n w_n$, where w_i are strings and a_i are attribute names, $i \in [0,n]$; the value of a_0 is computed by substituting in α the corresponding values (strings) for the attribute names. In [DPSS] such semantic rules are "simple-word functions".

The domain TREES is defined to contain all possible labeled trees over some denumerable ranked alphabet and whose only allowed operation is "top-concatenation" of trees. This means that in any AG defined on TREES the values of the attributes are trees and the semantic rules have the form: $a_0 \leftarrow t(a_2,\ldots,a_n)$, where $t(a_1,\ldots,a_n)$ is a tree t having one or more occurrence of each of the attribute names $a_1,\ldots,a_n$ at some of its leaves. If the value of attribute a_i is tree t_i, $\forall i \in [1,n]$; then the value of a_0 is the tree t' obtained from t by substituting t_i for each occurrence of a_i, $\forall i \in [1,n]$.

The notation we will use in order to indicate particular classes of AG is the following: for a given property X, the class of AG having this property is indicated with X-AG. For example, the class of AG whose nonterminals have at most one s-attribute (and an arbitrary number of i-attributes) is 1S-AG, that of the AG having only s-attributes is OnlyS-AG, and with Only1S-AG we indicate the intersection of the previous two. For a class X-AG of AG over a particular semantic domain D, we indicate with T(X-AG,D) and OUT(X-AG,D) its classes of translations and of output-sets, respectively.

To define certain classes of AG we need the following concept concerning attribute evaluation.

Definition 1.2. Consider an AG G and a derivation-tree t in G. A one-visit strategy (1V-strategy) for attribute-evaluation in t is any way of walking through t in which each subtree t' of t is visited at most once and in such a way that when entering t' some i-attributes of the root n of t' are computed and when exiting it some s-attributes of n are computed. □

An important class of AG is that of the "one-pass left-to-right evaluatable "AG (denoted L-AG) defined in [B]. Here we give two equivalent definitions of L-AG as follows.

Definition 1.3.

(1) An AG G is L iff for each production p of G the brother-graph of p has an edge from F_i to F_j only if $i < j$, j and $i \in [1,n_p]$.

(2) An AG G is L iff for each complete derivation-tree t in G there is a 1V-strategy for t which computes all attributes of t and traverses it from left-to-right (in a depth-first fashion). □

Point (1) of the definition is what we call a static characterization of the L-property because it is based on the structure of G and it is practically the same as the original definition of [B]. Point (2) of the definition is, instead, what we call a dynamic characterization of the L-property. The fact that the two parts of the definition are equivalent is shown in [B].

2. Attribute-grammars with one s-attribute only

The start point of our study of the formal power of AG is a recent result of [DPSS] which can be stated as follows:

(*) OUT(L-1S-AG,STRINGS) = IO

where L-1S-AG is the class of AG satisfying Definition 1.3 and having only one s-attribute and IO is the class of IO-macrolanguages [Fi]. In practically the same way it is easy to prove a similar result for the domain TREES:

OUT(L-1S-AG,TREES) = IOT, where IOT is the class of macro-tree languages [ES].

Here we extend these results by showing that for any semantic domain D:

(**) OUT(1S-AG,D) = OUT(L-1S-AG,D).

This means that the L-restriction in (*) can be dropped. In order to prove this result we examine the class of 1S-AG. Because of the restriction of having at most one s-attribute for each nonterminal, it is not difficult to understand that 1S-AG satisfy the following property.

Definition 2.1. An AG G is translationally one-visit (t1V) iff for every t $\in$ CDT(G), there exists a 1V-strategy computing the translation of t, (that is the value of the designated s-attribute of the root of t). □

The fact that any 1S-AG is t1V is clear from the following simple observation. In general, if we are interested only in computing the translation, a visit to a subtree is sensible only if some s-attribute of its root is evaluated during the visit. Thus, in a 1S-AG, each subtree needs at most one visit to compute the only s-attribute of its root.

Comparing Definition 2.1 with Definition 1.3(2), we see that there are two differences between them:

Difference (a). The 1V-strategy of an L-AG computes all attributes of t, whereas for a t1V-AG we require only the computation of the translation of t.

Difference (b). The 1V-strategy of an L-AG visits t in a left-to-right order, whereas no order is fixed for t1V-AG.

We will now show that, as far as output-sets are concerned, these two differences do not change the power of the class 1S-AG with respect to that of L-1S-AG. To get rid of Difference (a) we will prove that, given any 1S-AG we can construct an equivalent 1S-AG which satisfies the following property.

Definition 2.2. An AG is one-visit (1V) iff for each complete derivation-tree t in G, there is a 1V-strategy computing all attributes of t. □

Since the 1V-property is very similar to the dynamic characterization of the L-property of Definition 1.3(2), it will not be surprising that also for the 1V-property we have a static characterization similar to that of the L-property (Definition 1.3(1)).

Definition 2.3. An AG G is 1V iff no brother-graph of a production p of G contains an oriented cycle. □

Lemma 2.1. The dynamic (Definition 2.2) and the static (Definition 2.3) characterizations of the 1V-property are equivalent.

Proof: (a) 2.2 ⇒ 2.3.
An arc from F_i to F_j in bg(p) implies that F_i has to be visited before F_j. Hence, if there is a cycle in bg(p), no 1V-strategy can exist.

(b) 2.3 ⇒ 2.2.
For any AG G, satisfying Definition 2.3 we can construct an attribute-evaluation algorithm which is a 1V-strategy satisfying Definition 2.2 for every $t \in CDT(G)$. In fact, since, for any production p of G, bg(p) does not contain cycles, there is at least one way of visiting the nonterminals $F_1,\dots,F_{n_p}$, such that when F_i is visited all the F_j which in bg(p) have out-edges entering F_i have already been visited. If the order of the visits is $F_{i_2},\dots,F_{i_{n_p}}$, $i_j \in [1,n_p]$, $j \in [1,n_p]$, we say that p has visiting sequence $v_p = <i_1,\dots,i_{n_p}>$. From the v_p's of all productions of G we construct the following one-visit attribute-evaluation algorithm, which we call the Static-Algorithm.

Static-Algorithm

```
            procedure evaluate node (m)
      << assume that production p is applied to node m and that it
         has visiting-sequence  v_p = <i_1,...,i_np>      >>
            begin
                for j = 1 to n_p do
            compute all attributes of I(F_ij)
            evaluate node (F_ij)
                                  od
            compute all attributes of S(m)
            end
```

□

We now return to 1S-AG and consider the problem of "when a 1S-AG does not satisfy the 1V-property". By the static characterization of the 1V-property, this happens when some productions p of G has an oriented cycle in bg(p). The existence of such a cycle in bg(p) has a particular implication for a 1S-AG. Assume that production p is $F_0 \rightarrow F_1F_2$ and that the cycle in bg(p) is generated because $i_1(F_1)$ depends on $s(F_2)$ and $i_1(F_2)$ depends on $s(F_1)$. Then, by our assumption to consider only non-circular AG, there cannot be two derivation-trees of G t_1 and t_2, rooted in F_1 and F_2, respectively, and such that in $dtg(t_1)$ there is a path from $i_1(F_1)$ to $s(F_1)$ and in $dtg(t_2)$ one from $i_1(F_2)$ to $s(F_2)$: there would be a cycle in dtg $(F_0(t_1,t_2))$. This means that either $i_1(F_1)$ is never used to compute $s(F_1)$ and/or $i_1(F_2)$ is never used to compute $s(F_2)$. We call such an i-attribute useless. From the circularity algorithm of [Kn], it should be clear that there is an effective way of detecting the useless i-attributes. Assume that, in our case, $i_1(F_1)$ is useless. Then we can break the cycle in bg(p) by replacing the semantic rule defining it in p by one of the form $i_1(F_1) \leftarrow c$, where c is any constant value in the domain of $i_1(F_1)$. This transformation will clearly never affect the value of the translation. We state this result formally in the following Lemma.

Lemma 2.2. For any 1S-AG there is an effective way of constructing an equivalent 1S-AG which is 1V.

This Lemma and the fact that 1V-1S-AG is a subclass of 1S-AG proves the next Theorem.

Theorem 2.1. For any semantic domain D, T(1S-AG,D) = T(1V-1S-AG,D).

With this last result we have overcome Difference (a) between 1S-AG and L-1S-AG. To show that also Difference (b) does not influence output-sets is easier because we can now use 1V-1S-AG instead of 1S-AG. Recall from the proof of Lemma 2.1 the concept of visiting-sequence of a production. Given a 1V-1S-AG G, assume that the v_p of production p of G is $v_p = \langle i_1,\ldots,i_{n_p}\rangle$. Clearly if we permute the nonterminals of the right-hand side of p following v_p, that is, if we construct $p' : F_0 \rightarrow w_0 F_{i_1} w_1 \ldots w_{n_p-1} F_{i_{n_p}} w_{n_p}$, then v_p is a left-to-right visiting sequence for p'. This means that from G and all its visiting-sequences we can construct a 1S-AG G' whose productions are obtained from those of G as described above, whose semantic rules are equal to those of G, and such that for any derivation-tree t in G' the static-algorithm for G would be a 1V-strategy for t which visits it from left-to-right. This obviously implies that G' is L-1S.

The transformation which gave us G' from G can clearly be viewed as a syntax-directed-translation scheme in the sense of [AU], cf. [P]. Thus, we can view each 1V-1S-AG as related to a L-1S-AG through a syntax-directed translation scheme (sdts). For a class X-AG, we indicate with Π(X-AG) the class of AG related to X-AG by an sdts. From this we have immediately the following results.

Lemma 2.3. 1V-1S-AG = Π(L-1S-AG)

From the preceding Lemma, Theorem 2.1 and the fact that output sets of AG related by sdts are equal we have:

Theorem 2.2. For any semantic domain D,

(1) T(1S-AG,D) = T(Π(L-1S-AG),D)

(2) OUT(1S-AG,D) = OUT(L-1S-AG,D)

This Theorem, for D equal to STRINGS and TREES, gives us the results of (**) (which extends that of [DPSS] (*)) which we were looking for at the beginning of this Section.
We state these results in the next Theorem.

Theorem 2.3. (1) OUT(1S-AG,STRINGS) = OUT(L-1S-AG,STRINGS) = IO.
(2) OUT(1S-AG,TREES) = OUT(L-1S-AG,TREES) = IOT.

3. One-visit attribute grammars

In the previous Section we defined the t1V-and 1V-properties of AG and applied them to the class 1S-AG. We will now study the classes t1V-AG and 1V-AG in general, that is, with no limitation on the number of the s-attributes.

We first consider the class 1V-AG and easily extend to it some results of the previous Section; then we show that also in this case it is possible to fill the gap between t1V and 1V, but not as easily as for 1S-AG.

The result of Lemma 2.3 can be extended to 1V-AG and L-AG by the same arguments we used there.

Lemma 3.1. 1V-AG = Π(L-AG).

As an immediate consequence of this result we have the following Theorem.

Theorem 3.1. For any semantic domain D,
(1) T(1V-AG,D) = T(Π(L-AG),D).
(2) OUT(1V-AG,D) = OUT(L-AG,D).

Observe that this Theorem differs from Theorem 2.2 because of the fact that there we had already overcome the difference between t1V (1S-AG) and 1V. We now turn to this problem in general. Given a t1V-AG G which is not 1V, we know that there must be a production p of G such that bg(p) contains a cycle. Assume, as we did before, that p is $F_0 \rightarrow F_1F_2$ and that the cycle is originated becase $i_1(F_1)$ depends on $s_1(F_2)$ and $i_1(F_2)$ depends on $s_1(F_1)$, the argument we used for 1S-AG can no longer be used, but, because G is t1V, the following is true: there is no complete derivation-tree t in G which contains an occurrence of production p and in which both $i_1(F_1)$ and $i_1(F_2)$ are needed to compute the translation of t. This means that either $i_1(F_1)$ and/or $i_1(F_2)$ is useless in the following (new) sense: given any complete derivation-tree t in G an attribute of a node of t is useless in t if it is not needed to compute the translation of t, otherwise it is useful in t. Observe now that if we have an AG G such that in each complete derivation-tree t of G only useful attributes are present, then, if G is t1V it is also 1V. Such an AG will be called reduced. The following Lemma is easy to prove using noncircularity.

Lemma 3.2. An AG G is reduced iff

(i) Its start-symbol has only one s-attribute.

(ii) For every production p of G all attributes of $I(F_0)$ and $S(F_i)$, $i \in [1,n_p]$, are used as arguments in some semantic rule of p.

Proof. If G satisfies (i) and (ii), then it is possible to show by induction on the height of derivation-tree t that all attributes of t are useful in t. □

Theorem 3.2. Given any AG G, there is an effective way of constructing a reduced AG G' over the same semantic domain such that OUT(G) = OUT(G') and such that, if G was t1V then also G' is t1V.

Proof. Roughly G' is constructed as follows: For any nonterminal F of G, G' contains nonterminals (F,A_0) for all possible subsets A_0 of A(F) in G. For each production $p : F_0 \rightarrow w_0F_1w_1 \ldots w_{n_p-1}F_{n_p}w_{n_p}$ of G, G' has all productions of the form $p' : (F_0,A_0) \rightarrow w_0(F_1,A_1)w_1 \ldots w_{n_p-1} \quad (F_{n_p},A_{n_p})w_{n_p}$, such that p' has in G' the obvious corresponding subset of semantic rules of p and moreover satisfies (ii) of Lemma 3.2. The fact that G' is reduced comes directly from Lemma 3.2. The derivation-trees of G' are extactly the derivation-trees of G such that to every occurrence of a nonterminal in a derivation-tree of G its subset of useful attributes is added; moreover the semantics concerning these attributes is the same. □

Corollary 3.1. For any semantic domain D, OUT(t1V-AG,D) = OUT(1V-AG,D).

We now return to 1V-AG and show that on the domain TREES and STRINGS, for its class of output-languages, as for that of 1S-AG, it is possible to show a relation with known concepts of formal language theory: the translation realized by a 1V-AG on TREES can be decomposed into a translation realized by a 1S-AG also on TREES and a deterministic top-down tree transducer (DT) [ERS]. Using $R_1 \circ R_2$ t denote "R_1 first, then R_2"; the result can be stated as follows.

Theorem 3.3. T(1V-AG,TREES) = T(1S-AG,TREES) ∘ DT.

Proof. In what follows we call G_1 the 1V-AG, G_2 the 1S-AG and M the DT.

(a) ⊆ Since the proof is very involved, we simply give the following intuition. In G_1 the attribute-evaluation can be performed in such a way that all the s-attributes of every node are computed simultaneously, see the static-algorithm. This allows to simulate many s-attributes with one, by tupling them with top-concatenation. From this we may say that G_2 has the same underlying CFG as G_1 and that, for a production p, the semantic rule computing the only s-attribute of F_0 in G_2, is obtained by top-concatenating all the right-hand sides of the semantic rules defining the s-attributes of F_0 in G_1, in which special symbols are added in order to indicate symbolically which are the needed operations of selection from the tuples representing the s-attributes of the F_j, $j \in [1,n_p]$ in G_1. M will, then, just interprete these selection symbols.

(b) $\supseteq$ Observe that the translation of any derivation-tree in G_2 is a tree composed by right-hand sides of semantic rules of G_2 (the same is true for any AG on TREES). Therefore, the transformation of this tree by M can be simulated substituting the right-hand side t of each semantic rule of G_2 with the tree t' generated by M with input t. If M has m states, then for each attribute of G_2, G_1 has m corresponding attributes. □

From Theorems 3.3, 3.2, 3.1 and 2.3 we have:

Theorem 3.4. OUT(t1V-AG,TREES) = OUT(1V-AG,TREES) = OUT(L-AG,TREES) = = DT(OUT(1S-AG,TREES)) = DT(IOT).

Analogous results for STRINGS can be obtained by applying the yield operation.

Corollary 3.2.

(1) T(1V-AG,STRINGS) = T(1S-AG,TREES) $\circ$ DT $\circ$ yield

(2) OUT(t1V-AG,STRINGS) = OUT(1V-AG,STRINGS) = OUT(L-AG,STRINGS) = = yield(DT(OUT(1S-AG,TREES))) = yield(DT(IOT)).

So far we have established relationships between translations and output-sets of 1V-AG on one side and those of L-AG and 1S-AG on the other side. These results enable us to show that the following diagrams characterize the power of the considered classes of AG with respect to their translations and output-sets. The shown inclusions hold for an arbitrary domain D, and there is a domain (viz: TREES) for which the diagrams cannot be reduced.

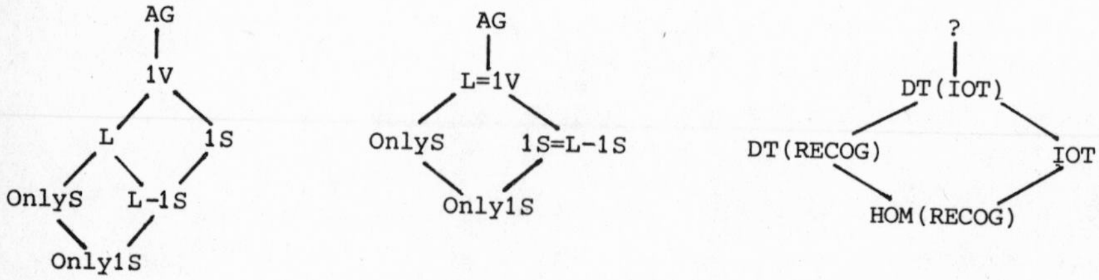

(a) Translations (X stands for T(X-AG,D))

(b) Output sets (X stands for OUT(Y-AG,D))

(c) diagram (b) for D=TREES in terms of tree transducers and tree grammars.

Figure 1.

In diagram (c) of figure 1 RECOG is the class of recognizable tree languages and HOM is the class of tree homomorphism, i.e., DT with one state only. The equalities DT(RECOG) = OUT(OnlyS-AG,TREES) and HOM(RECOG) = OUT(Only1S-AG,TREES) can be intuitively understood by viewing each state of the DT as an s-attribute (of all nodes) and vice versa.

In order to prove the correctness of the diagrams we have to show that the following classes are non empty.

(1) OUT(OnlyS-AG,TREES)-OUT(1S-AG,TREES)

(2) T(1S-AG,TREES)-T(L-AG,TREES)

(3) OUT(L-1S-AG,TREES)-OUT(OnlyS-AG,TREES)

(4) OUT(AG,TREES)-OUT(1V-AG,TREES)

Point (1) can be proved by giving a tree language which is easily producable by an OnlyS-AG but which is not in IOT. Point (2), which regards translations only, can be shown by providing a counter-example with a combinatorial proof. For points (3) and (4), instead, we use "the path approach", i.e., we determine the class of path-languages corresponding to the involved classes of output tree languages. For a tree t, we denote by $\Pi(t)$ the set of paths through t which lead from the root to some leaf. For a tree language L and a class of tree languages X, $\Pi(L) = \cup\{\Pi(t) \mid t \in L\}$ and $\Pi(X) = \{\Pi(L) \mid L \in X\}$.

It is either well known or easy to see that Π(DT(RECOG)) = Π(HOM(RECOG)) = the class of regular languages and that Π(DT(IOT)) = Π(IOT) = the class of context-free languages. From this point (3) immediately follows. To prove point (4) we observe that an AG can be easily constructed which produces the non-context-free language $\{w\#w \mid w \in \{a,b\}^*\}$ as path-language, (using two visits to each node).

4. Multi-pass attribute grammars

Although in Section 3 we were not able to express OUT(AG,TREES) in terms of known concepts (see the ? in fig. 1 (c)), we can do so for the corresponding class of path-languages Π(OUT(AG,TREES)). It turns out that Π(OUT(AG,TREES)) is related to output string languages of finite-copying top-down tree transducers (T_{fc}) [ERS], where finite copying means that there is a bound on the number of copies the transducer can make of each input subtree. In order to show this result, we introduce the concept of dependency-path language (dpl) of an AG G as follows: let every edge in pg(p) for each production p of G be labeled by a unique name. The dpl of G is the set containing all strings which label an oriented path ph in the dtg(t) of any t $\in$ CDT(G) and such that, ph is connected in dtg(t) with the designated s-attribute of G and there is no other path in dtg(t) containing ph as a suffix.

It is easy to see that for an AG G on TREES, because of the form of the semantic rules, Π(OUT(G)) can be obtained from dpl of G through a gsm-mapping. The following Theorem can now be stated.

Theorem 4.1. Π(OUT(AG,TREES)) = yield(T_{fc}(RECOG)).

Proof. (a) $\subseteq$ From the above observation and the fact that the class yield (T_{fc} (RECOG)) is closed under gsm-mapping [ERS], it is sufficient to prove that for any AG G we can construct a T_{fc} M which produces dpl of G. We only sketch the construction of M. Let F be a nonterminal of G, then each s-attribute of F and each possible pair (i,s), where $i \in I(F)$ and $s \in S(F)$, will correspond to a state of M. For every production p of G, consider the graph g_p obtained from pg(p) by adding to it all possible edges running from an i- to an s-attribute of nonterminal $F_j, \forall j \in [1,n_p]$. M has as many rules, corresponding to production p, as there are paths in g_p connected to some s-attribute of F_0. It is not difficult, then, to see that the number of rules of M is exponential in the size of G. Since a path visits each subtree a bounded number of times, M is finite copying.

(b) $\supseteq$ For this direction of the proof we note that it becomes simpler using the fact that yield (T_{fc}(RECOG)) = yield(DT_{fc}(RECOG)). The construction of the AG corresponding to a given DT_{fc} M is practically a backwards version of the one in part (a).

□

We now show what the consequences of the above result are for multi-pass AG. An AG G is multi-pass if there is a $K > 0$ such that for any derivation-tree t of G all the attributes of t can be evaluated by at most K consecutive depth-first (left-to-right) passes through t. It was recently observed by Alblas [A] that the algorithm of [B] does not decide the multi-pass property but a restricted version of it, in which all occurrences of an attribute can be evaluated during the same pass. Whereas the algorithm in [B], works in polynomial time we have the following results on the time complexity of deciding the multi-pass property of AG.

Theorem 4.2.

(1) The multi-pass property of AG is decidable in exponential time.

(2) There is no polynomial algorithm deciding it (in fact, it is complete in exponential time).

(3) The K-pass property of AG is decidable in polynomial time for any fixed $K > 0$.

Proof. (1) Given an AG G, consider a production p of G of the usual form. In a left-to-right pass, F_1 is visited before F_2 and so on. This means that if attribute i of F_K depends on attribute s of F_j, $K \le j$, K and $j \in [1,n_p]$, i can be evaluated only at a later pass than s. We call the edge in pg(p) corresponding to this dependency an R-edge. Consider now $t \in CDT(G)$ and an occurrence of attribute a in dtg(t), assume also that all the nodes in dtg(t) which have out-edges entering a are $a_1,\dots,a_m$. Then, a can be evaluated in t only when $a_1,\dots,a_m$ are already evaluated and moreover the number of the pass in which a can be evaluated is Max { pass of a_j plus 1 if (a_j,a) is an R-edge, plus 0 otherwise, $\forall j \in [1,m]$}. From this it is easy to see that G is multi-pass iff there is a bound on the number of R-edges of any path in dtg(t) for any $t \in CDT$. We call R-language of G the set L containing strings on the alphabet $\{R\}$ and such that R^n is in L iff there is a path in dtg(t) of some $t \in CDT(G)$ containing n R-edges. By slightly modifying the construction of the proof of Theorem 4.1, we can construct a T_{fc} M producing the R-language of G. At this point, to decide whether G is multi-pass, it is sufficient to test if the language produced by M is finite and this problem is decidable in polynomial time in the size of M which is exponential in that of G by Theorem 4.1.

(2) A slight modification of the proof given in [JOR] for showing the intrinsical exponentiality of the circularity problem for AG, allows us to show the following. Let K be an exponential-time language (problem). For every word w of length n we can construct an AG G_w such that, (i) it is an L-AG, (ii) the size of G_w is O(nlogn), (iii) there is a nonterminal F of G_w having i-attributes $i_1,\ldots,i_n$ and s-attributes $s_1,\ldots,s_n$ and such that $w \in K$ iff there is $t \in DT(G_w)$, with root F such that in dtg(t) there is a path from i_j to s_j for all $j \in [1,n]$. From this it is not difficult to construct an AG such that for deciding whether it is multi-pass we must decide the above problem. Hence, any exponential-time language may be reduced to the multi-pass problem of AG.

(3) As for point (1) we can use the construction of the proof of Theorem 4.1 to test whether a given AG G is K-pass for a fixed $K > 0$. However in this case the size of the constructed T_{fc} M can be made polynomial in that of G, (instead of exponential as in Theorem 4.1) because, when we check whether G is K-pass we do not have to look at all paths but only at those which visit a subtree at most K + 1 times. The number of such paths, and so also of rules of M, in the graph g_p of the proof of Theorem 4.1 is polynomial in the number of the attributes of p. □

References

[A] H. Alblas; The limitations of attribute-evaluation in passes, Memorandum, Twente University of Technology, 1979.

[AU] A.V. Aho and J.D. Ullman: The theory of parsing, translation and compiling, Vols. 1 and 2; Prentice-Hall, Englewood Cliffs, N.J., 1972.

[B] G.V. Bochmann; Semantic evaluation from left-to-right, Comm. of the ACM 19 (1976), 55-62.

[DPSS] J. Duske, R. Parchmann, M.Sedello and J. Specht; IO-macro languages and attributed translations, Inf. and Control 35 (1977),87-105.

[EF1] J. Engelfriet and G. Filè; The formal power of one-visit attribute grammars; Memorandum 286, Twente University of Technology, 1979.

[EF2] J. Engelfriet and G. Filè; work in progress.

[ERS] J. Engelfriet, G. Rozenberg and G. Slutzki; Tree transducers, L systems and two-way machines; Memorandum 187, Twente University of Technology, 1977 (also in: Proc. 10-th Ann. ACM Symp. on Theory of Computing, San Diego, 1978), to appear in J. Comp. Syst. Sci.

[ES] J. Engelfriet and E. Meineche Schmidt; IO and OI, J. Comp. System Sci. 15 (1977), 328-353, and J. Comp. System Sci. 16 (1978), 67-99.

[Fi] M.J. Fischer; Grammars with macro-like productions, Ph. D.Thesis, Harvard University, 1968 (see also the 9-th Conference on Switching and Automata Theory, pp. 131-142).

[JOR] M. Jazayeri, W.F. Ogden and W.C. Rounds; The intrinsically exponential complexity of the circularity problem for attribute grammars; Comm. of the ACM 18 (1975), 697-706.

[Kn] D.E. Knuth; Semantics of context-free languages, Math. Syst. Theory 2 (1968), 127-145, Correction: Math. Syst. Theory 5 (1971), 95-96.

[Kw] K. Kennedy and S.K. Warren; Automatic generation of efficient evaluators for attribute grammars, Conf. Record of the Third Symp. on Principles of Programming Languages, 1976, 32-49.

[P] R. Parchmann; Grammatiken mit Attributschema und zweistufige Auswertung attributierter Grammatiken, Bericht nr. 46, Technische Hochschule Aachen, Informatik, 1978.

CRYPTOCOMPLEXITY AND NP-COMPLETENESS*

by

S. Even** and Y. Yacobi***

ABSTRACT

In view of the known difficulty in solving NP-hard problems, a natural question is whether there exist cryptosystems which are NP-hard to crack. In Section 1 we display two such systems which are based on the knapsack problem. However, the first one, which is highly "linear" has been shown by Lempel to be almost always easy to crack. This shows that NP-hardness of a cryptosystem is not enough. Also, it provides the only natural problem we know of, which is NP-hard and yet almost always easy to solve. The second system is a form of a "double knapsack" and so far has resisted the cryptanalysis efforts.

In Section 2 a Public-Key Crypto-System (PKCS) is defined, and evidence is given that no such system can be NP-hard to break. This relates to the work of Brassard, et al. [2, 11], but the definition of PKCS leads us to a different cracking problem, to which Brassard's technique still applies, after proper modification.

---

* This paper is based on two research reports, written by the authors in July 1979. It was supported in part by the Army Research Office under Grant No. DAAG29-79-C-0054.

** Computer Science Department, Technion, Haifa, Israel. Part of this research was done while the author visited the E.E. Department-Systems, University of Southern California, Los Angeles, CA., U.S.A.

*** Graduate student, Electrical Engineering Department, Technion, Haifa, Israel.

1. CONVENTIONAL NP-HARD CRYPTOSYSTEMS

1.1 A Description of the General System

The system is a form of a running key cipher, or stream cipher. The information is assumed to be in binary words of length m. The cleartext word at time t, M_t, is added to the key-word at this time, K_t, in a bit by bit mod 2 fashion to yield the cryptogram C_t; i.e.,

$$C_t = M_t \oplus K_t \quad . \tag{1}$$

The receiver, who knows K_t, and gets C_t through the channel, can simply compute M_t by

$$M_t = C_t \oplus K_t \quad . \tag{2}$$

It remains to be shown how K_t is generated. Let X be the secret key, which remains fixed for a relatively long time. Every unit of time, t, the transmitter generates a word R_t which is transmitted openly to the receiver. This word may be generated randomly, pseudorandomly, may be a serial number or a date, or some combination of the above. F is a function known to all parties concerned including possibly some eavesdroppers. F is easy to compute, and it yields for every X and R_t the key-word K_t; i.e.,

$$K_t = F(X,R_t) \quad . \tag{3}$$

Clearly K_t must be a binary m-vector. The length of X, R_t and the nature of F remain to be defined. Clearly, K_t must change with t, as R_t changes; it must be hard to compute K_t without the knowledge of X; repeated observations of past key-words must not allow an easy determination of future key-words, and therefore should not allow an easy determination of the secret key (X).

Thus, F is similar to a one-way function, as discussed by Diffie and Hellman [1], however is not necessarily one to one. Even if X is uniquely determined by K_t and R_t, no trap-door is necessary and probably none exists. Also, the result of Brassard, Fortune and Hopcroft [2] is not applicable.

In this section we discuss a family of F's, which is based on the knapsack problem. Let $A = (a_1,a_2,\ldots,a_n)$ be an n-vector of positive integers. It is assumed to be known to all parties concerned. $G(X,R_t)$ is a known function whose image is a binary n-vector. Now F is defined by

$$F(X,R_t) = [A \cdot G(X,R_t)], \tag{4}$$

that is, if $G(X,R_t) = (g_1,g_2,\ldots,g_n)$ then

$$F(X,R_t) = \left[\sum_{i=1}^{n} a_i \cdot g_i\right]$$

where the brackets denote the binary representation of the integer, and where the number of digits to be used, m, satisfies

$$m = \lceil \log_2 (\sum_{i=1}^{n} a_i + 1) \rceil . \qquad (5)$$

($\lceil x \rceil$ denotes the least integer greater than or equal to x.)

Before we proceed to discuss particular realizations of G let us define the cracking problem.

The adversary is assumed to know A, G (and therefore F, n and m). We also assume he eavesdrops on R_t and C_t. Furthermore, he may have access to many (M_i, C_i, R_i) triples. The question is whether he can use this information to efficiently compute M_t?

Clearly, the knowledge of X compromises the system immediately. But we do not define the cracking problem to be the computation of X, since the knowledge of X may not be necessary. Thus, we define the cracking problem to be the computation of M_t, which is directly the information we want to conceal.

Since C_t is assumed known to the adversary, the knowledge of K_t is equivalent to the knowledge of M_t (see (2)). Also the information about the system which is contained in (M_i, C_i, R_i) is also included in (K_i, R_i). Thus we define a history of length ℓ to be a sequence of pairs: $(K_1, R_1), (K_2, R_2), \ldots, (K_\ell, R_\ell)$. Note that in this system, as long as the adversary has no control over R_t (we may assume that the legitimate transmitter does not control it either) a "chosen plaintext attack" is equivalent to a "known plaintext attack".

Since we consider an algorithm efficient only if its time complexity is bounded by a polynomial in the message length, m, clearly the length of the allowed history should be bounded by some polynomial p(m). In our formulation this is necessary since the history is part of our input-data and the complexity is measured in terms of the input length; if we allowed a history exponentially long (in terms of m), then the cracking problem would be easy to solve in terms of the input length. (For an introduction to the complexity concepts see, for example, [3], [4] or [5].) [Brassard [14] did not impose this restriction, and therefore could "prove" that"Public-key cryptosystems do not exist". The same method could be used to "prove" that "Finite key cryptosystem does not exist".]

Since a given history may not determine X uniquely, we consider a system cracked if an X is found which is consistent with the history; i.e., it satisfies

$$K_i = [A \cdot G(X, R_i)] \quad , \qquad \text{for } i = 1,2,\ldots,\ell \ .$$

Furthermore, since we do not insist on finding X, we consider the system cracked if for a given R, a K is computed, which is consistent with the history; i.e., an X exists such that

$$K_i = [A \cdot G(X,R_i)] \qquad \text{for } i = 1,2,\ldots,\ell \quad \text{and}$$
$$K = [A \cdot G(X,R)]. \tag{6}$$

Thus the cracking problem is defined as follows:

INPUT: A,G,R and history $\{(K_i, R_i) \mid i = 1,2,\ldots,q\}$ where $q \leq p(m)$. (p is a fixed polynomial.)

GOAL: Find a K consistent with the given history.

We proceed to discuss two particular G's.

1.2 System I

System I is defined by

$$G(X,R_t) = X \oplus R_t, \tag{7}$$

where both X and R_t are binary n-vectors, and the addition mod 2 is carried out bit by bit.

Our first goal is to prove that for this particular G, the cracking problem is NP-hard. Following Aho, Hopcroft and Ullman [5,6] we say that a problem is NP-hard if the existence of a polynomially bounded algorithm for its solution implies that P = NP. We shall use the 0-1 knapsack decision problem, which is known to be NP-complete:

INPUT: A,b (A is an n-vector of distinct positive integers and b is a nonnegative integer).

QUESTION: Is there a binary n-vector X such that $A \cdot X = b$?

This problem is NP-complete even with our restriction that A does not contain repeated numbers. (This follows from the reduction from the exact cover problem.) Let us define now the 0-1 knapsack construction problem:

INPUT: A,b .

GOAL: Find a binary n-vector X which satisfies $A \cdot X = b$.

Even if we assume that the constructive problem is applied only to data for which an X exists, the problem is NP-hard. For if we had an algorithm AL with time complexity $p(\ell)$, where ℓ is the input length, which solves the constructive problem, we could use it to solve the decision problem as follows: Given A and b, apply AL to this data, allowing it to run $p(\ell)$ units of time. If AL stops within $p(\ell)$ units of time, check if $A \cdot X = b$. If so, answer the decision problem positively. If AL does not stop in $p(\ell)$ units of time, or if its output X does not satisfy $A \cdot X = b$, answer the decision problem negatively.

THEOREM 1: The cracking problem of System I is NP-hard.

PROOF: Assume there exists a polynomial algorithm AL which solves the cracking of System I problem; i.e., Given A,R and a history $\{(K_i, R_i) \mid i=1,2,\ldots,q\}$ where $q \leqslant p(m)$ (p is a preassigned polynomial); AL finds in polynomial time a K (if one exists) consistent with the data; that is there exists an X such that

$$K_i = [A \cdot (X \oplus R_i)] \qquad \text{for } i = 1,2,\ldots,q \quad \text{and}$$

$$K = [A \cdot (X \oplus R)].$$

Let A,b specify the input of an instance of the constructive knapsack problem. Define the following instance of the cracking problem: A is unchanged, $R = \bar{1} = (1,0,0,\ldots,0)$ and the history consists of one pair $(B,\bar{0})$, where $\bar{0}$ denotes the all-zero vector and B is the m-bit binary representation of b. Now apply AL to find a K_1 for which an X exists which satisfies:

$$B = [A \cdot (X \oplus \bar{0})] \qquad \text{and}$$

$$K_1 = [A \cdot (X \oplus \bar{1})] \quad .$$

It is easy to see that $x_1 = 0$ (x_1 is the first component of X) if and only if $b < k_1$ (where k_1 is the numeric value represented by K_1). Thus, we find x_1 for some X which is consistent with $\{(\bar{0},B)\}$.

Now define a new constructive knapsack problem with:

$$A_1 = (a_2, a_3, \ldots, a_n)$$

$$b_1 = b_1 - x_1 \cdot a_1 .$$

Clearly there is an (n-1)-vector X_1 which satisfies $A_1 \cdot X_1 = b_1$ if and only if $X = (x_1, X_1)$ satisfies $A \cdot X = b$. We can use the same technique to find x_2 (the first component of X_1) etc. Thus, by applying AL n times we find an X which satisfies $A \cdot X = b$, if one exists.

Q.E.D.

In spite of the fact that System I is NP-hard to break, it was shown by A.Lempel [7] that in most cases the system is easily broken. The equation

$$K_t = [A \cdot (X \oplus R_t)]$$

can be written as follows:

$$k_t = \sum_{i=1}^{n} a_i \cdot (x_1 \oplus r_{ti}) \quad . \tag{7}$$

Since $u \oplus v = u+v-2uv$, for $u,v \in \{0,1\}$, equation (7) can be written as

$$k_t = \sum_{i=1}^{n} a_i \cdot (x_i + r_{ti} - 2x_i r_{ti}) \quad \text{or}$$

$$k_t - \sum_{i=1}^{n} a_i \cdot r_{ti} = \sum_{i=1}^{n} x_i \cdot (a_i - 2a_i r_{ti}) \quad . \tag{8}$$

Since K_t, A and R_t are known, this is a linear equation with unknowns $x_1, x_2, \ldots, x_n$. Given a system of such n linearly independent equations (which correspond to n R's which happen to produce an independent system) it is a simple matter to find (the unique) X in polynomial time. Lempel showed that if the R's are randomly generated then the probability of getting an independent system of n equations is high, and the probability that in N trials there will be n independent equations approaches unity rapidly, as N-n increases. Thus, System I is very insecure.

The moral of this result is that, even if P≠NP, there are natural NP-hard problems for which an algorithm exists which solves most instances in polynomial time. An interesting open problem is whether such algorithms exist for all NP-hard problems.

We have found a few more G's for which the cracking problem is NP-hard and yet almost always is easy to break, but all maintain the "linear" behavior of limiting the operations between the x_i's and r_{ti}'s to be a bit by bit operation through a two variable Boolean function which depends on each of its two variables.

1.3 System II

The system to be described in this section is also NP-hard to break. However, the operation G between X and R is not of a bit-by-bit nature. We believe that this is a "stronger" system since no "linearization" seems feasible, and so far, it has resisted all attempts to crack it. However we cannot prove that it is "safe". System II is defined by

$$G(X,R) = [X \cdot R] \quad , \tag{9}$$

where X is a p-vector of positive integers, R is a binary p-vector and the binary representation uses n bits, where

$$n = \lceil \log_2 (\sum_{i=1}^{p} x_i + 1) \rceil .$$

Clearly $F(X,R) = [A \cdot [X \cdot R]]$ where the second binary representation uses m bits. Let $p(\ell)$ be a polynomial. The <u>cracking problem of System II</u> is therefore:

<u>INPUT</u>: A,R and $\{(K_i,R_i) \mid i = 1,2,\ldots,q\}$ where $q \leqslant p(\ell)$ (where ℓ is the input length of A,R).

<u>GOAL</u>: Find a K consistent with the data. i.e., there exist an X such that

$$K_i = [A \cdot [X \cdot R_i]] \qquad \text{for } i = 1,2,\ldots,q \quad \text{and}$$
$$K = [A \cdot [X \cdot R]] \quad .$$

The <u>restrictive 0-1 knapsack decision problem</u> is defined as follows:

<u>INPUT</u>: A,b,m.

<u>QUESTION</u>: Is there a binary n-vector X, with exactly m components equal to 1, which satisfies $A \cdot X = b$?

Clearly, this problem is in NP. Also, it is NP-hard. For if there were a polynomial algorithm AL which solved it, then by at most n applications of it, with $m = 1,2,\ldots,n$, we could solve the unrestricted version. (This is an example of establishing NP-completeness by using a Cook reduction [8], rather than Karp's [3]. We do not know if a Karp reduction can be used.)

The <u>restrictive 0-1 knapsack construction problem</u> is defined as follows:

<u>INPUT</u>: A,b,m.

<u>GOAL</u>: Find a binary n-vector X, with exactly m components equal to 1, which satisfies $A \cdot X = b$.

Again, by an argument similar to the one used in the previous section, the NP-completeness of the decision problem implies the NP-hardness of the constructive problem.

<u>THEOREM 2</u>: The problem of cracking System II is NP-hard.

<u>PROOF</u>: Let us assume that there is a polynomial algorithm, AL, which solves the cracking problem of System II. We shall show that by using AL to solve n instances of the cracking problem we can solve the restrictive 0-1 knapsack construction problem. Thus, proving the NP-hardness of the cracking problem.

Let A,b and m be the input data of an instance of the restrictive knapsack construction problem, where $A = (a_1,a_2,\ldots,a_n)$. Let $\alpha = \sum_{i=1}^{n} a_i$.

Define an instance of the cracking problem as follows:

$$A' = ((n+1)\alpha+1,\ \alpha+a_1,\ \alpha+a_2,\ldots,\alpha+a_n),$$

$$R = (1,1) \qquad \text{and}$$

$$\{((1,0),\ [m\alpha+b]),\ ((0,1),\ [\alpha+a_1])\}.$$

Now use AL to produce a K_1, for which an $X' = (x,y)$ exists which satisfies the following three equations:

$$m\alpha+b = A' \cdot [(x,y) \cdot (1,0)],$$

$$\alpha+a_1 = A' \cdot [(x,y) \cdot (0,1)],$$

$$K_1 = [A' \cdot [(x,y) \cdot (1,1)]].$$

First, let us show that if the knapsack problem has a solution then an (x,y) and K_1 exist which satisfy all three equations.

Let X be a binary n-vector with exactly m components equal to 1, which satisfies $A \cdot X = b$. Let x be the integer whose binary representation is X, and $y = 2^{n-1}$. In this case

$$A' \cdot [(x,y) \cdot (1,0)] = A' \cdot (0,X) = m\alpha+b,$$

$$A' \cdot [(x,y) \cdot (0,1)] = A' \cdot (0,1,0,0,\dots 0) = \alpha+a_1 ,$$

and the value of K_1 is determined by $A' \cdot [x+2^{n-1}]$.

If $x \geq 2^{n-1}$ then $k_1 \geq (n+1)\alpha+1$, but if $x < 2^{n-1}$ then $k_1 < (n+1)\alpha+1$. Furthermore, if (x,y) and K_1 satisfy all three equations then the following conclusions can be drawn:

(a) $A' \cdot [x] = m\alpha+b < (n+1)\alpha+1$. Thus the first component of $[x]$ is 0, and the number of components which are equal to 1 is exactly m. Therefore, the binary representation of x in n digits, yields an X with exactly m ones, which satisfies the knapsack condition: $A \cdot X = b$.

(b) $A' \cdot [y] = \alpha+a_1$. Since the a's are distinct, $y = 2^{n-1}$.

(c) The first component of X, x_1, is determined by:

$$x_1 = 0 \text{ if and only if } k_1 < (n+1)\alpha+1.$$

Namely, we know that there exists an X, whose first component is x_1 (as determined above), with exactly m ones, which satisfies $A \cdot X = b$. Let us look, then, for a solution of the following restricted knapsack problem:

$$A_1 = (a_2,a_3,\dots,a_n) ,$$

$$b_1 = b - x_1 \cdot a_1,$$

$$m_1 = m - x_1 .$$

Clearly, an $(n-1)$-vector X_1 with exactly m_1 ones satisfies $A_1 \cdot X_1 = b_1$ if and only if $X = (x_1,X_1)$ with exactly m ones satisfies $A \cdot X = b$. By the same method we can use AL to find an x_2, and then x_3, etc.

Q.E.D.

Other G's for which a similar result follows and which also have "carry" and therefore are not a "bit by bit" operations are:

$$G(X,R) = x+r \mod 2^n$$

or

$$G(X,R) = x \cdot r \mod 2^n$$

where X and R are binary n-vectors and $X = [x]$, $R = [r]$. Clearly many others exist. However, we believe that our "double knapsack" system is probably "safer". So far we have not been able to prove that System II is hard to crack in most cases, but attempts to cryptanalyse the system have failed too.

2. THE COMPLEXITY OF PUBLIC KEY SYSTEMS

2.1 Definition of the PKCS Cracking Problem

Let us describe, for definiteness purposes, a simple structure of a PKCS (public key crypto-system).

The diagram shows the basic layout.

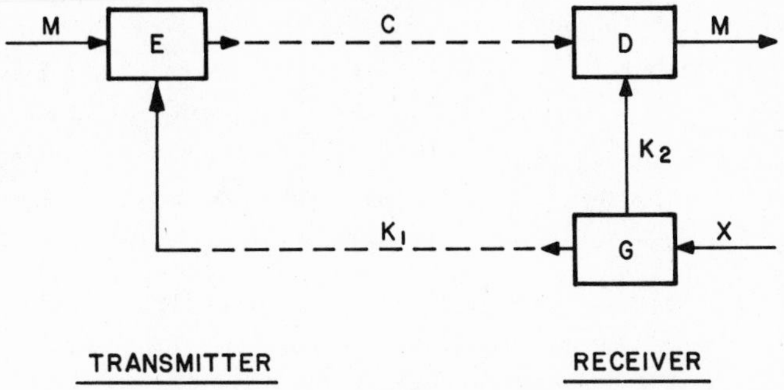

M, C, K_1, K_2, X are binary words, called the message, cryptogram, encryption key, decryption key, and trap-door, respectively. For simplicity, we assume that n, the length of M, is equal to q, the length of C. The length of K_1, k(n), is polynomially bounded (in n), and the lengths of K_2 and X are also polynomially bounded.

E, D, and G are fixed and publically known deterministic algorithms of time complexities polynomial in n. Thus, n is a parameter. E is the encryption algorithm, D is the decryption algorithm and G is the key generator. X is generated, say randomly, by the receiver, who does not reveal it to anyone. He uses G to compute K_1 and K_2. He makes K_1 publically known but does not reveal K_2 to anyone. This encryption-decryption key pair, (K_1,K_2), is used for encoding and decoding purposes for a relatively long time. When a transmitter wants to send M, confidentially, to the receiver, he computes C by

$$C = E(K_1,M), \qquad (1)$$

and transmits C in the open channel. The receiver, knowing his secret decryption key, K_2, reconstructs M by

$$M = D(K_2,C). \qquad (2)$$

It is assumed that for every X the system works, in the sense that for every M, when the corresponding K_1, K_2 are used, the C which is computed by (1) will satisfy (2). Thus, $E(K_1,\cdot)$ is a one-one onto function from the space of messages to the space of cryptograms. Also, we assume that every word of length k(n) is generated as a K_1, for some X and therefore the mapping from X to K_1 is onto.

We shall discuss later the consequences of weakening this requirement, but our ideas are best explained, first, with this assumption.

Note that in a conventional system $K_1 = K_2$ and is known only to the two communicants, while in a PKCS, K_1 is publically known and K_2 is only known to the receiver. Thus, it allows anyone in the network to send messages to the receiver which only he can decrypt. For more details on PKCS's and their applications see references 1, 9 and 10.

The system would be considered safe, if an eavesdropper, who knows the structure of E, D and G, and listens to K_1 and C, must spend an exuberantly long computation to find M. Note, that in a PKCS this is the only meaningful cracking problem: the eavesdropper, knowing E and K_1, can prepare for himself a long list of messages and their corresponding cryptograms, and therefore, there is no difference between a "passive" cryptanalysis and a "chosen plaintext attack".

The basic question, we relate to, is this: Is there a PKCS, of the simple type we have defined, for which the determination of M from K_1 and C is NP-hard? We want to show evidence that no such PKCS exists.

One may criticize this approach since it deals with worst-case analysis, rather than the complexity for almost all cases. However, if a cryptosystem, for which the cracking problem is hard, does not exist when the worst-case approach is taken, then certainly it does not exist when the average or most-cases approach is used.

The cracking problem (for known and fixed E, D, and G) is: Given K_1 and C, find M. We define a related decision problem which we call the cracking problem (CP):

INPUT: K_1, C, M'.

PROPERTY: $M' \geq M$, where M is the message which satisfies $C = E(K_1,M)$.

Since we assume that $E(K_1,\cdot)$ is a one-one onto function, for a given C and K_1, there is one, and only one M which satisfies (1). Thus, the question whether the numerical value of M' is greater or equal to the numerical value of M is always meaningful, and has a positive or negative answer.

Clearly, if the constructive cracking problem (find M) can be solved in polynomial time then so can the decision problem: Simply check whether $M' \geq M$. Also, if the decision problem is solvable in polynomial time, then we can use it to find M by using binary search, and the algorithm would still be polynomially bounded.

2.2 Both the Cracking Problem and its Complement are in NP

A nondeterministic algorithm for solving CP can be constructed as follows: Guess M. Compute $E(K_1,M)$. If it is equal to the given C, then compare M' with M. If both tests yield positive results ($C = E(K_1,M)$ and $M' \geq M$) then halt with a 'yes' answer. If either test fails, halt with an 'undecided' answer. It is easy to see that the algorithm runs in polynomial time, and the property holds if and only if there is a computational path (determined by the guess of M) which yields a 'yes' answer. Thus, the cracking problem is in NP.

The complementary property is: "$M' < M$, where M is the message which satisfies $C = E(K_1,M)$". One can use a similar argument to show that the problem complementary to the cracking problem ($\overline{CP}$), is also in NP.

Thus $CP \in NP \cap CoNP$. Now, if $CP \notin P$ then $NP \cap CoNP \neq P$. Also, if $CP \in NPC$ then $NP = CoNP$, a very unlikely event. Thus, we see this as evidence that no simple PKCS is NP-hard to break.

This result is clearly similar to that of Brassard, et al. [2, 11], and in fact our work is the result of attempts to understand the implications of their work on the likelihood of existence of a PKCS which is hard to break. Let us quote their Proposition [2]:

> "Suppose f has the following properties: $|f(i)| = |i|$, f is one-one and onto, f is computable in polynomial time and f^{-1} is not polynomial time computable. Then the set $S = \{\langle n,m\rangle \mid f^{-1}(n) > m\}$ is in $NP \cap CoNP - P$. Moreover, if f^{-1} is NP-hard then $NP = CoNP$."

First, a function f, as in the premise of the proposition, is of no use as an encryption function of a PKCS, since the decryption is impractical. There must be a trap-door, and therefore a decryption key, which makes the decryption easy. And if such a key exists, the f^{-1} cannot be hard to compute, since there is an efficient algorithm (one which uses the decryption key) to compute it.

Second, and more important, the proposition tells us that no f, as in its premise, is likely to exist. Yet, this does not rule out the possibility of existence of a PKCS which is NP-hard to break, since a cracking algorithm must handle all possible ecryption keys, while f is one and fixed function with no such varying parameter.

2.3 Extensions of the Model

So far we have used the simple model, in which M and C are of the same length and every K_1, of length $k(n)$, is generated for some X (by G).

If we remove the condition that q, the length of C, satisfies $q = n$, and assume $q \neq n$, then for $E(K_1,\cdot)$ to be one-one, clearly $q > n$. Now, $E(K_1,\cdot)$ cannot be onto, and the input (K_1, C and M') may be a sham if the given C is not the image of any M. We need a "promise" that the C is legitimate.

Also, the removal of the condition that every K_1, of length $k(n)$, is generated for some X, creates a similar problem. We need a "promise" that the K_1 is legitimate.

This gives rise to an unconventional type of problem. In order to understand it better, first consider a conventional problem:

INPUT: x.

PROPERTY: P(x).

Where P is a predicate. A solution is an algorithm AL, which halts with a 'yes' or 'no' answer such that:

$$\forall x[AL(x) = \text{'yes'} \Leftrightarrow P(x)].$$

A problem with a promise has the following structure:

INPUT: x,

PROMISE: Q(x),

PROPERTY: P(x).

Where P and Q are predicates. Now, a solution is an algorithm AL such that

$$\forall x[Q(x) \Rightarrow (AL(x) = \text{'yes'} \Leftrightarrow P(x))] .$$

Namely, AL is guaranteed to yield the right answer if Q(X) holds.

This is similar to what S. Ginsburg [12] calls a "birdy problem" (see also Ullian [13]). Now, we can remove all the restrictions on the lengths of the words, provided that all are polynomially bounded (in n), and the cracking problem (CP) gets the following form:

INPUT: K_1, C and M'.

PROMISE: There exists an X for which G produces K_1 (and a proper K_2) and there exists a M such that $C = E(K_1,M)$.

PROPERTY: $M' \geqslant M$, where M is the message which satisfies $C = E(K_1,M)$.

As in the previous section, we can show that both this more general CP and its complementary problem, $\overline{CP}$, (same input and promise, but the complementary property) are computable by nondeterministic algorithms, whose time complexities are bounded polynomially. It is not obvious whether the NP-hardness of CP implies that NP = CoNP, since CP is not a conventional decision problem. However, the same reasons that lead to the belief that if a problem is in NP∩ CoNP then it cannot be NP-hard, lead us to believe that since both CP and $\overline{CP}$ are nondeterministically computable in polynomial time then CP cannot be NP-hard.

A more detailed account of promise problems and their study will be given in Yacobi's forthcoming Ph.D. thesis.

ACKNOWLEDGEMENT

The authors wish to express their gratitude to L. Adleman, A. Lempel, E. Shamir and J. Ziv for their helpful comments.

REFERENCES

[1] Diffie, W. and Hellman, M.E., "New Directions in Cryptography", IEEE Transactions on Information Theory, Vol. 22, 1976, pp. 644-654.

[2] Brassard, G., Fortune, S., and Hopcroft, J., "A Note on Cryptography and NP $\cap$ CoNP-P", TR78-338, Dept. of Comp. Sci., Cornell University.

[3] Karp, R.M., "Reducibility Among Combinatorial Problems", in R.E. Miller and J.W. Thatcher (eds.), Complexity of Computer Computations, Plenum Press, 1972, pp. 85-104.

[4] Garey, M.R., and Johnson, D.S., Computers and Intractability: A Guide to the Theory of NP-Completeness, W.H. Freeman, 1979.

[5] Aho, A.V., Hopcroft, J.E. and Ullman, J.D., The Design and Analysis of Computer Algorithms, Addison-Wesley, 1974.

[6] Even, S., Graph Algorithms, Computer Science Press, 1979.

[7] Lempel, A., "Cryptology in Transition", Computing Surveys, December 1979.

[8] Cook, S.A., "The Complexity of Theorem Proving Procedures", Proceedings 3rd Am. ACM Symposium on Theory of Computing, ACM, 1971, pp. 151-158.

[9] Rivest, R.L., Shamir, A., and Adleman, L., "A Method for Obtaining Digital Signatures and Public-Key Cryptosystems", Comm. ACM 21, February 1978, pp. 120-126.

[10] Merkle, R., and Hellman, M., "Hiding Information and Signatures in Trapdoor Knapsack". IEEE Transactions on Information Theory. Vol. IT-24, September 1978, pp. 525-530.

[11] Brassard, G., "A Note on the Complexity of Cryptography", IEEE Transactions on Information Theory. Vol. IT-25, March 1979, pp. 232-233.

[12] Ginsburg, S., private communication.

[13] Ullian, J.S., "Partial Algorithm Problems for Context Free Languages". Information and Control, Vol. 11, 1967, pp. 80-101.

[14] Brassard, G., "Relativized Cryptography". Proceedings of 20th FOCS, Puerto Rico 1979.

ON THE ANALYSIS OF TREE-MATCHING ALGORITHMS

Philippe FLAJOLET
IRIA - B.P. 105
78150 LE CHESNAY (France)

Jean-Marc STEYAERT
Ecole Polytechnique
91128 PALAISEAU Cédex
(France)

0 - INTRODUCTION : This paper deals with the average case performance analysis of *tree-matching* algorithms. The trees we consider here are planar labelled trees as occurs in programming experience under the form of syntax trees, expression trees or tree-representation of structured objects (records). More specifically, we are interested in methods of estimating the average time of matching algorithms as a function of the pattern size and the tree size, under a wide class of statistics on the imputs.

Until recently, analysis of (planar) tree algorithms has received rather little attention. The basic results appear in [KNUTH ; 1968] and other problems are considered, for example in [de BRUIJN, KNUTH ; RICE ; 1972] and [FLAJOLET, ODLYZKO ; 1980] (stack size in exploration of trees), [FLAJOLET ; 1979] (binary tree matching) or [KEMP ; 1979] and [FLAJOLET, RAOULT, VUILLEMIN ; 1979] (register allocation problems). These works deal almost exclusively with the *Catalan statistics** where the average performance of an algorithm is determined over the set of all possible shapes of trees of a given size.

We consider here more general statistics corresponding to various classes of labelled trees, the purpose of which is to closely model particular applications. Following [MEIR, MOON ; 1978], a *simply generated* family of trees is informally defined by specifying a finite set of admissible labels for each node-degree. Instances of simply generated families of trees include :

- expression trees where each node has degree 0, 1 or 2 ; nodes of degree 0 are labelled var ("variable"), nodes of degree 1 are labelled e.g. +, -, log, exp, sin, nodes of degree 2 are labelled +, -, ×, ÷.
- trees where the nodes of degree 0 are labelled var, nodes of degree 1 are labelled +, -, log, sin, nodes of degree 2 are labelled +, -, ×, ÷, ← ; nodes of degree 3 are labelled cond, iter... ; this is a simply generated family as can be defined to approximate syntax trees in a structured programming language.
- unlabelled trees (binary or general) that appear in this framework as trees with at most one possible label for each degree. Thus, simply generated families of trees include the classical families of binary and general trees as subcases.

We can now formulate our initial problem as follows : given a tree-matching A, let

---

* The shapes of trees of size n+1 and the shapes of binary trees of size n are *counted* by the Catalan number $\frac{1}{n+1}\binom{2n}{n}$.

$T_A(P\ ;\ T)$ be the execution time of algorithm A applied to the pattern tree P and text tree T. Let $\mathscr{S}$ and $\mathscr{R}$ be simply generated families of text and pattern trees (the sets of admissible text and pattern inputs) ; we wish to determine the behaviour of the algorithm A applied to inputs in $\mathscr{S}$ and $\mathscr{R}$, as measured by the *average execution times* :

$$\overline{T}_A(P;t) = \frac{1}{\mathrm{card}\{T/|T|=t\}} \sum_{|T|=t} T_A(P;T) \quad \text{(average over texts)}$$

$$\overline{\overline{T}}_A(p;t) = \frac{1}{\mathrm{card}\{P/|P|=p\}} \sum_{|P|=t} \overline{T}_A(P;t) \quad \text{(average over texts and patterns).}$$

Section 1 of this paper is devoted to the study of occurrences of patterns in trees ; it contains the generating functions related to the enumeration of occurences, together with exact expressions derived via the Lagrange-Bürmann inversion theorem for analytic functions (1.1) and (1.2). Then follow some asymptotic estimates based on the study of the algebraic singularities of these generating functions by means of the Darboux-Polya method (1.3). As a consequence, it is shown that the probability of occurrence of a pattern tree at a node of a (large) text tree decreases approximatively as an exponential, in the size of the pattern. This result which is valid for classes of simply generated families of trees, is the basis of the linearity of the average time of most commonly used tree matching algorithms.

Section 2, as a showcase, presents the complete analysis of the simplest sequential matching algorithm : in (2.1), (2.2), we estimate the $T_A(P,t)$ for fixed patterns P, and in (2.3), we show that

$$\overline{\overline{T}}_A(p,t) = ct(1 + O(\tfrac{1}{p}))\ (1 + O(\tfrac{1}{t^{1-\varepsilon}})) \quad \text{for arbitrary } \varepsilon > 0\ ;$$

here c is a constant depending explicitly on the set of inputs and on the particular implementation constants. It is to be noted that this linear expected time strongly contrasts with the worst case which is obviously quadratic.

Section 3 is devoted to a few specific applications including the cases of unlabelled binary and general trees which belong to the Catalan domain. In § 3.4, we discuss some of the possible extensions and implications of our work. The following conclusions can be drawn :

a) the analysis of tree algorithms under the Catalan statistics provides a rough estimate of the performance of algorithm yielding (at least in our case) the actual order of magnitude of the parameters. Thus, this analysis is interesting as far as orders of magnitude are concerned ;

b) a detailed analysis is feasible under very general statistical hypotheses that can be made to approximate many practical conditions of application. The techniques here involved are probably general enough to be of intrisic interest ;

c) these analysis can be supported by simulation results showing very good agreement to the theoretical estimates. Although the variance analysis seems to be a harder problem, empirical evidence shows a very low dispersion of the characteristics which justifies the usefulness of the analysis.

1 - ENUMERATION OF TREES AND OCCURRENCES OF PATTERNS

1.1 - The generating series - Trees are recursively defined combinatorial structure for which systematic schemes allows translation of inductive definitions into equations over generating functions. This fact is rather well known in the theory of context-free languages and is treated in detail by [FLAJOLET : 1979] and [BERSTEL, REUTENAUER ; 1980].

Let $\Sigma = \Sigma_0 \cup \Sigma_1 \cup \Sigma_2 \ldots$ be a ranked alphabet, and let $\mathcal{S}$ be the set of all trees over Σ, i.e. such that a node of out-degree n is labelled with a symbol in Σ_n ; in other words Σ_n is the set of symbols with arity n. We let s_n be the cardinality of Σ_n. Throughout this paper, we shall make an extensive use of the generating function associated to the sequence $\{s_n\}_{n>0}$ and we set $\Phi(t) = \sum_{n>0} s_n t^n$ *. Given s_0 and Φ, we are able to compute the number of trees in $\mathcal{S}$ with exactly n nodes ; let A_n be the number of trees of size n and let $A(z) = \sum_{n>0} A_n z^n$ be the corresponding generating functions. A is given by

PROPOSITION : The generating function for trees in $\mathcal{S}$ satisfies

$$(1) \qquad A(z) = s_0 z + \sum_{n>0} s_n z A^n(z) = s_0 z + z \Phi(A(z)).$$

In a quite similar way, let $A_{n,f}$ be the number of trees in $\mathcal{S}$ with n nodes, f of them being leaves and let $A(z,u)$ be the corresponding double generating series $A(z,u) = \sum_{n,f} A_{n,f} z^n u^f$. $A(z,u)$ satisfies

$$(2) \qquad A(z,u) = s_0 zu + z \Phi(A(z,u)).$$

Notice that $A(z,1) = A(z)$, which justifies our notation.

We can now remark that the power series $\left.\frac{\partial A}{\partial u}\right|_{u=1}$ counts the number of trees in $\mathcal{S}$, with exactly one leaf marked. Actually,

$$\frac{\partial A}{\partial u} = \sum_{n,f} f A_{n,f} z^n u^{f-1}$$

and taking its values in $u = 1$ sums all coefficients with constant n. Some formal computations on series give the equality :

$$(3) \qquad \left.\frac{\partial A}{\partial u}\right|_{u=1} = s_0 \frac{z^2 \, dA(t)}{A(t) dz} = s_0 \frac{z^2}{A} A' \quad \text{for short.}$$

The set of possible patterns is given in the same way by a subset $\Sigma' = \Sigma'_0 \cup \Sigma'_1 \cup \Sigma'_2 ..$ of Σ, with the convention that there is only one symbol of arity 0 : indeed with the notion of matching we have in mind this one symbol is a "don't-care" symbol that can match any subtree of a text tree. We shall thus have $|\Sigma'_0| = 1$, and we shall usually take $\Sigma'_j = \Sigma_j$ for all $j > 1$, although our treatment is general enough to allow different statistics to be applied to texts and patterns.

Let Ψ denote the power series associated to Σ', i.e. $\Psi(t) = \sum_{n>0} s'_n t^n$ with $s'_n = \text{card } \Sigma'_n$. The generating power series R for the set of patterns satisfies

---

* If $\Psi(z) = \sum_{n\geq 0} \Psi_n z^n$ is a power series, we denote its n-th coefficient Ψ_n by $[z^n] \Psi(z)$.

the equations

(4) $R(z) = z + z\,\Psi(R(z))$, and (5) $R(z,u) = zu + z\,\Psi(R(z,u))$.

for the double generating power series (notice that in most cases, we shall have $\Phi = \Psi$).

We now need to compute the number of occurrences of a pattern P in a family $\mathscr{S}$. This amounts to computing the number of ways of splitting a tree T (or size t) in $f+2$ subtrees $T_0, P, T_1, \ldots, T_f$ as shown by the diagram :

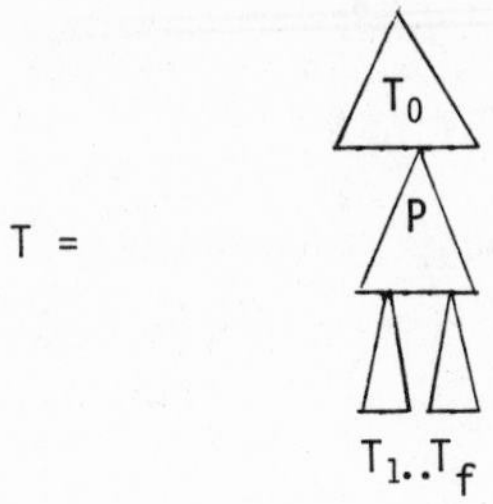

when P has exactly f leaves. In the sequel, we let m be the number of internal nodes of P (hence P has a total of $p = m - f$ nodes).

Define $\mathcal{O}^P(z)$ as the generating series for the number of occurences $\mathcal{O}^P_t$ of P in trees of size t ; we have, corresponding to the above splitting :

(6) $$\mathcal{O}^P(z) = \frac{1}{s_0 z} \left.\frac{\partial A}{\partial u}\right|_{u=1} \cdot z^m \cdot A^f(z).$$

Now, using (3), (6) can be reshapped as

<u>*PROPOSITION*</u> *: The generating series of occurrences is given by :*

(6') $$\mathcal{O}^P(z) = z^{n+1} A' A^{f-1} = z^{n+1} \frac{d}{dz}\left(\frac{A^f}{f}\right).$$

We shall also need another variety of occurrences, on subtrees of a pattern P. Let us traverse the internal nodes of P in prefix order from left to right and number these nodes according to traversal order (see example on figure 1). For $1 \leq k \leq m$, the k-segment of P is the subtree obtained from P by pruning all internal nodes of rank greater than k.

We shall say that P has a *k-vanishing occurrence* in T at some node is its (k-1)-segment occurs in T at that node but not its k-segment ; in other words, a mismatch occurs precisely on the kth internal node in a preorder comparison procedure of P and T.

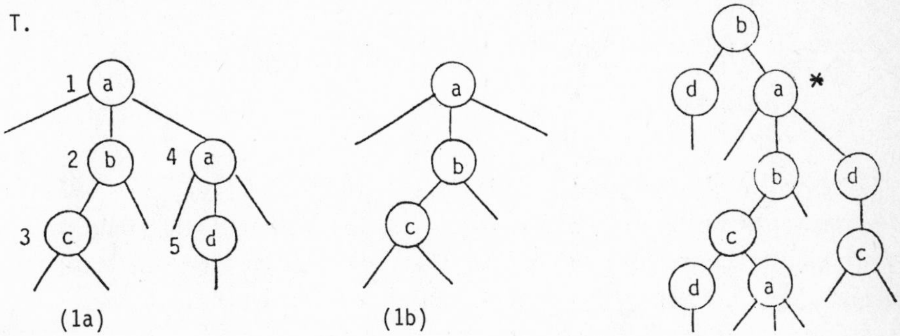

(1a) (1b) (1c)

Figure 1 above represents a pattern (1a), its 3-segment (1b), and a text with a 3-vanishing occurrence of pattern at node marked* (1c).

In order to count the k-vanishing occurrences, we define a function on patterns $g_p : \{1,2,..,n+1\} \to \{0,1,2,...,f-1\}$ such that $g_p(k)$ = the number of leaves of the (k-1)-segment of P, e.g. $g_p(1) = 0$, $g_p(n+1) = f-1$. One can see that

(7) $g_p(k) = g_p(k-1) + \text{degree (k-th node)} - 1,$

and g_p can be defined inductively on the subtrees of P. Now, the generating power series of k-vanishing occurrences of P, $E^{p,k}$, is expressible as :

(8) $E^{p,k}(z) = \frac{1}{s_0 z} \left.\frac{\partial A}{\partial u}\right|_{u=1} z^m A^{g_p(k)}(A - z^{d(k)} A^{d(k)}),$

where d(k) stands for the degree of the kth node. Combining (3), (7) and (8) yields

PROPOSITION : The generating series for k-vanishing occurrences of P is given by :

(8') $E^{p,k}(z) = z^k A' A^{g_p(k)} - z^{k+1} A' A^{g_p(k+1)}.$

1.2 - Exact enumeration formulae - The equation satisfied by A(z) can in some cases be solved explicitly when Φ is of low degree (see examples later), whence exact enumeration results using Taylor expansions. The Catalan numbers are usually obtained in this way. However, when Φ has a degree > 2, this method proves intractable if not impossible. We can however derive expressions for $[z^n]\ A(z)$ by means of the Lagrange-Bürmann inversion theorem for analytic functions.

THEOREM : Given the equation $y = z\,\phi(y)$ *defining implicitly* y *as a function of* z, *where* ϕ *is a power series s.t.* $\phi(0) \neq 0$, *the Taylor coefficients of* y *are expressible in terms of those of the powers of* ϕ *by :*

$$[z^n]\ y = \frac{1}{n} [y^{n-1}](\phi(y))^n .$$

Furthermore the coefficients of the powers of y *are given by*

$$[z^n]\ y^k = \frac{k}{n} [y^{n-k}]\ (\phi(y))^n .$$

These results can be derived either from purely combinatorial considerations [RANEY ; 1960] or by means of Cauchy's residue theorem. The theorem yields explicit formulae for the coefficients of series A^k and R^k defined by equations (1) and (4) :

(9) $[z^n]\ A^k = \frac{k}{n} [y^{n-k}](s + \Phi(y))^n$;

(10) $[z^n]\ R^k = \frac{k}{n} [y^{n-k}](1 + \Psi(y))^n.$

PROPOSITION : The enumerations of occurrences are given by :

(11) $[z^n]O_n^p = [y^{n-m}](s + \phi(y))^{n-m-f}$;

(12) $[z^n]E_n^{p,k} = [y^{n-k+1}](s_0 + \phi(y))^{n-k-g_p(k)} - [y^{n-k}](s_0 + \Phi(y))^{n-k-1-g_p(k+1)}.$

This proposition is of interest since Φ usually has a much simpler form than A. In simple cases, (11) and (12) lead to non trivial closed form expressions (see section 3 for applications).

1.3 - Asymptotic estimations - The most general treatment of tree and occurrence enumerations is by means of complex analysis. It is largely independent of the particular form of Φ and is thus of very general applicability. To that purpose we shall make the following further assumptions on Φ :

(i) $\forall\ i \in N,\ s_i \in N$;

(ii) $\exists\ M, \forall\ i,\ s_i \quad M$;

(iii) $\gcd\ \{i > 0/s_i \neq 0\} = 1$.

(i) is justified by the nature of the problem, (ii) and (iii) are little restrictive conditions that can actually be weakened to include most of the cases of interest in applications. From these assumptions follows that Φ has either radius of convergence 1 or ∞

The growth of the Taylor coefficients of a function is known to be largely determined by the position and nature of its singularities. Since A is implicitly defined in terms of Φ, we thus need investigate the points where the implicit function theorem fails to apply and determine the infinitesimal behaviour of A around these points. This is essentially the Darboux-Polya method [POLYA ; 1937] ; we present here a sketch of the method as can be seen in [MEIR, MOON ; 1978]. (General formulations of the result can be found in [COMTET ; 1970] and [HENRICI ; 1978]).

Starting from the equation that implicitly defines $A(z)$ in terms of Φ, we see that $A(z)$ is analytic as long as $\frac{dz}{dA} \neq 0$ (this is nothing but the implicit function theorem). A simple computation shows that when this condition ceases to be true, $A(z)$ is still defined and has value τ given by the equation :

$$s_0 = \tau\,\Phi'(\tau) - \Phi(\tau) \qquad 0 < \tau \leqslant 1,$$

and the corresponding value of z, which gives the radius of convergence of A is

$$(13) \qquad \rho = \frac{\tau}{s_0 + \Phi(\tau)} = \frac{1}{\Phi'(\tau)}, \quad \text{with} \quad \rho < \tau \leqslant 1.$$

It can be checked that these equations always have a solution, and that $z = \rho$ is the unique singularity of $A(z)$ on its circle of convergence. Using a local expansion of $\Phi(y)$ around τ and expanding, we see that $A(z)$ satisfies

$$(14) \qquad z - \rho = -\frac{1}{2}\,\frac{\Phi''(\tau)}{\tau(\Phi'(\tau))^2}\,(A(z) - \tau)^2 + O((A(z) - \tau)^3).$$

Solving for $A(z)$ and neglecting smaller order terms, we see that $A(z)$ behaves locally like

$$\tau - \beta\left(1 - \frac{z}{\rho}\right)^{\frac{1}{2}} \quad \text{with} \quad \beta = \sqrt{\frac{2\tau\Phi'(\tau)}{\Phi''(\tau)}}$$

These developments can be justified formally, and the Darboux-Polya theorem asserts that the n-th Taylor coefficient of $A(z)$ asymptotically behaves like the n-th coefficient of its approximation ; so that :

$$[z^n]\ A(z) \sim [z^n] - \beta\left(1-\frac{z}{\rho}\right)^{\frac{1}{2}} \sim + \frac{\beta}{2n}\binom{2n-2}{n-1} 4^{-n}\ \rho^{-n}$$

$$\sim \frac{\beta}{2\sqrt{\pi}}\ \rho^{-n}\ n^{-3/2}$$

using the standard Newton expansion of $(1-z)^{\frac{1}{2}}$ and the Stirling approximation for factorials.

The count occurrences, we also need a uniform approximation for the coefficient of powers of $A(z)$. Locally $A^k(z)$ behaves as $\tau^k - k\,\tau^{k-1}\,\beta(1-\frac{z}{\rho})^{\frac{1}{2}}$ from which estimates for its coefficients can be derived. Hence :

PROPOSITION : The number of trees A_n *satisfies*

(15) $A_n = \frac{\beta}{2\sqrt{\pi}}\,\rho^{-n}\,n^{-3/2}(1 + O(\frac{1}{n}))$.

For $k = O(\log^2 n)$, the coefficients of $A^k(z)$ satisfy

(16) $[z^n]\,A^k(z) = k\,\tau^{k-1}\,\frac{\beta}{2\sqrt{\pi}}\,\rho^{-n}\,n^{-3/2}(1+O(\frac{1}{n^{1-\varepsilon}}))$ for any $\varepsilon > 0$.

We can now derive equivalents for $[z^n]\,O^P$ and $[z^n]\,E^{P,k}$. We have

PROPOSITION

(17) $[z^n]\,O^P = \frac{\beta}{2\sqrt{\pi}}\quad \tau^{f-1}\,\rho^m\,n^{-\frac{3}{2}}(1 + O(\frac{1}{n^{1-\varepsilon}}))\,\rho^{-n}$

(18) $[z^n]\,E^{P,k} = \frac{\beta}{2\sqrt{\pi}}\quad (\tau^{g_P(k)}\,\rho^{k-1} - \tau^{g_P(k+1)}\,\rho^k)\,n^{-\frac{3}{2}}(1 + O(\frac{1}{n^{1-\varepsilon}}))\,\rho^{-n}$

as long as f *and* k *are* $O(\log^2 n)$.

Thus, within a certain range of value of f, the probability of occurrence of a pattern of size $m+f$ at a node of a tree of size n decreases exponentially in the size of the pattern, being equivalent to

$\tau^{f-1}\,\rho^m$ (with $\rho < \tau \leqslant 1$).

2 - THE SEQUENTIAL ALGORITHM

The results of the last section are fairly general. As a showcase, we shall prove their use by obtaining a complete analysis of the sequential tree matching algorithm.

2.1 - The algorithm

This algorithm consists of two basic procedures : the procedure VISIT explores the nodes of the text tree in some definite order - here preorder - , at each node of the text tree, the procedure COMPARE sequentially tries to match the pattern with the subtree of the text rooted at that node.

```
Boolan procedure COMPARE (P,T) ;
    A : if degree (root (P)) = 0,  then return (true) fi
    B : if root (P) ≠ root (T),    then return (false) fi
    C : for i from 1 to degree (root (P)) do
    D : if COMPARE (P_i, T_i)       then return (false) fi
        od
        return (true)
end proc
Procedure  OCCUR (P,T)
    MATCH (P,T)
    if degree (root (T)) = 0, then return fi
    for i from 1 to degree (root (T)) do
```

MATCH (P,T_i)

od

end proc

In the above procedures, A_i denotes the ith subtree of the root in tree A. The cost of the comparison procedure depends on the success or failure of the match. In case of success, the whole pattern has been explored and the cost is seem to be $\alpha + \beta f + \gamma m$. In case of failure on the k-th internal node, the only leaves explored are those located on the left of this k^{th} node. So we introduce the function $f_p : \{1,2,\ldots, m+1\} \to \{0,1,\ldots, f\}$ such that $f_p(k)$ counts that number of leaves. One can observe that $f_p(1) = 0$ and $f_n(m+1) = f$ and that f_p can be defined *inductively* on subtrees of P. With these notations, the cost of the matching procedure in case of failure on the kth node (P has then a k-vanishing occurrence) reads :

$$\alpha' + \beta f_p(k) + \gamma k.$$

Here, the constants α, α', β, γ, depend solely upon the implementation.

PROPOSITION : The total time required for matching P *to all trees of size* n *is*

$$(19)\quad T(P,n) = \delta n\, [z^n]\, A + (\alpha + \beta f + \gamma m)\, [z^n]\, \mathcal{O}^P + \sum_{1 \leq k \leq m} (\alpha' + \beta f_p(k) + \gamma k)\, [z^n]\, E^{p,k}.$$

where the terms of the sum correspond respectively to the exploration of the texts, the cost of successfull matches and the cost of unsuccessfull one

2.2 - The average cost

From (19), we derive a formula for the average cost of the matching of a pattern P. We have

$$(20)\quad \overline{T}(P,n) = dn + (\alpha + \beta f + \gamma m) \frac{[z^n]\, \mathcal{O}^P}{[z^n]\, A} + \sum_{1 \leq k \leq m} (\alpha' + \beta f_p(k) + \gamma k) \frac{[z^n] E^{p,k}}{[z^n]\, A}.$$

It is even more convenient to study $\frac{\overline{T}(P,n)}{n}$ so that we need now give estimates for $\frac{[z^n]\, \mathcal{O}^P}{n[z^n]\, A}$ and $\frac{[z^n] E^{p,k}}{n[z^n] A}$. There are derived from (15), (17) and (18) :

$$(21)\quad \frac{[z^n]\, \mathcal{O}^P}{n[z^n]\, A} = \tau^{f-1} \rho^m (1 + \mathcal{O}(\frac{1}{n^{1-\varepsilon}})),$$

$$(22)\quad \frac{[z^n] E^{p,k}}{n[z^n] A} = (\tau^{g_p(k)} \rho^{k-1} - \tau^{g_p(k+1)} \rho^k)(1 + \mathcal{O}(\frac{1}{n^{1-\varepsilon}})),$$

with the hypotheses that f and k keep smaller that $\log^2 n$.

$$(22')\quad \frac{\overline{T}(P,n)}{n} = \delta + (\alpha + \beta f + \gamma m)\, \tau^{f-1} \rho^m (1 + \mathcal{O}(\frac{1}{n^{1-\varepsilon}}) + \sum_{1 \leq k \leq n} (\alpha' + \beta f_p(k) + \gamma k)(\tau^{g_p(k)} \rho^{k-1} - \tau^{g_p(k+1)} \rho^k)(1 + \mathcal{O}(\frac{1}{n^{1-\varepsilon}})).$$

Since $\tau,\rho < 1$, the second term vanishes as $f,m,n \to \infty$ and the sum is bounded above by some constant. Therefore we have the following

PROPOSITION : *There exists constants* K,L *such that the average search time is linearly bounded*

$$\overline{T}(P,n) < K.n + L, \quad \textit{uniformly in } P \textit{ and } n.$$

2.3 - Average searchtime for typical texts and patterns

We now need to estimate the value of the coefficient of n in $\overline{T}(P,n)$ averaged over all pattern trees of a given (large) size. This coefficient represents the cost of the COMPARE procedure weighted by probabilities of occurrences of segments of the pattern. The rather unwieldy expressions appearing there can be simplified by expressing them as valuations on patterns inductively defined on subtrees. This presentation makes them amenable to the generating function approach.

The second term in (22') tends to zero as $m,f \to \infty$ so that we are left with estimating the value

$$\sum_{1 \leq k \leq m} (\alpha' + \beta f_p(k) + \gamma k)(\tau^{g_p(k)} \rho^{k-1} - \tau^{g_p(k+1)} \rho^{k}).$$

averaged over all P of size p. The expression splits into three sums

$$s_1 = \sum_{1 \leq k \leq m} (n_k - n_{k+1}), \quad s_2 = \sum_{1 \leq k \leq m} f(n_k - n_{k-1}), \quad s_3 = \sum_{1 \leq k \leq m} f_p(k)(n_k - n_{k+1}),$$

where $n_k = \tau^{g_p(k)} \rho^{k-1}$. We first simplify the expressions using Abel's transformation so that we are left with five new expressions

$$\rho^m \tau^{f-1}, \quad f\,\tau^{f-1} \rho^m, \quad m\,\tau^{f-1} \rho^m.$$

$$v(P) = \sum_{1 \leq k \leq m} \tau^{g_p(k)} \rho^{k-1}, \quad w(P) = \sum_{2 \leq k \leq m+1} (f_p(k) - f_p(k-1))\, \rho^{k-1} \tau^{g_p(k)}.$$

The average value of the first three quantities tends to 0 as $|P|$ tends to infinity. In order to evaluate the average value of $v(P)$, we first define it inductively on trees.

$$\begin{cases} v(\square) = 0 & (\square \text{ denotes a leaf}) \\ v\left(\overset{\circ}{\wedge}_{P_1 .. P_q}\right) = 1 + \tau^{q-1} \displaystyle\sum_{1 \leq j \leq q} (\tau^{f_1 + .. + f_{j-1}})\, \rho^{m_1 + ... + m_{j-1}}\, v(P_j). \end{cases}$$

Let $V(z)$ be the generating function whose p^{th} coefficient is the total valuation of patterns of size P : $V_p = \sum_{|P|=P} v(P)$. $V(z)$ is defined by the equation

$$\begin{aligned} V(z) &= (R(z)-z) + \sum_{q>0} c_q z^q \sum_{1 \leq j \leq q} \tau^{q-j}\, V(z)\, R^{j-1}(\rho z, \tau/\rho)\, R^{q-j}(z) \\ &= (R(z)-z) + V(z) \frac{\rho z}{\tau R(z) - R(\rho z, \rho)} (\Psi(\tau R(z)) - \Psi(R(\rho z, \tau/\rho))), \end{aligned} \tag{23}$$

A similar but more complex treatment applies to $w(P) = \sum \eta_k[f_p(k) - f_p(k-1)]$ leading to a series $W(z)$. Hence :

<u>*LEMMA*</u> *: The generating series for the valuations on patterns satisfy*

(24) $V(z) = \dfrac{R(z) - z}{1 - U(z)}$; $W(z) = \tau z \dfrac{U(z)}{1 - U(z)}$,

where $U(z) = \rho z \dfrac{\Psi(\tau R(z)) - \Psi(R(\rho z, \frac{\tau}{\rho}))}{\tau R(z) - R(\rho z, \frac{\tau}{\rho})}$.

The methods of section 1, show that $R(z)$, the generating function of patterns, has a radius of convergence $\rho' \geqslant \rho$, and that around ρ', $R(z)$ behaves as $\tau' - \beta'(1 - \frac{z}{\rho'})^{\frac{1}{2}}$; hence again the asymptotic equivalent

$$R_n = [z^n]\, R(z) \sim \frac{\beta'}{2\sqrt{\pi}} \rho'^{-n}\, n^{-3/2} .$$

A detailed study of the expressions of V and W shows that their radius of convergence is also ρ', and that around ρ', they behave like $\lambda + \mu(1 - \frac{z}{\rho'})$. Hence

<u>*PROPOSITION*</u> *: Let* $V_n = \sum_{|P|=n} v(P)$ *and* $W_n = \sum_{|P|=n} w(P)$. *There exist constants* $\overline{v}$ *and* $\overline{w}$ *such that*

$$\frac{V_n}{R_n} \to \overline{v} \quad \textit{and} \quad \frac{W_n}{R_n} \to \overline{w} \quad \textit{when} \quad n \to \infty .$$

The limit values $\overline{v}, \overline{w}$ can in each particular case be explicitly computed from the infinitesimal expansions of V and W around ρ'. Plugging this result into (22') we get :

<u>*THEOREM*</u> *: For each simply generated $\mathcal{S}$, there exists a constant σ, depending only on the family, such that the average time for searching an occurrence of a pattern* P *of size* p *in a text* T *of size* t *is*

$$\sigma\, t(1 + O(\tfrac{1}{p}) + O(\tfrac{1}{t^{1-\varepsilon}})).$$

3 - APPLICATIONS

We shall briefly sketch here some of the possible applications of the results to specific families of trees.

3.1 - <u>Planar trees</u> (Catalan statistics)

Let G be the family of unlabelled planar trees of arbitrary specification. Here $\Phi(t) = t + t^2 + t^3 + \ldots = \frac{t}{1-t}$, and $A(z) = \frac{1 - \sqrt{1-4z}}{2}$ whence $A_n = \frac{1}{n}\binom{2n-2}{n-1} \sim \frac{1}{4\sqrt{\pi}} 4^n\, n^{-3/2}$. The algebraic singularity at $\rho = \frac{1}{4}$ is explicit on the expression of A.

A pattern P of type (m,f) has number of occurrences given by

$$O_n^P = z^{n-m} \frac{1}{1-z}^{n-m-f} = \binom{2n-2m-f-1}{n-m}$$

and the probability that P occurs at a node of a tree is essentially $2^{1-f}\, 4^{-m}$.

3.2 - Unary - Binary trees (Motzkin statistics)

We consider here the family M of trees in which every node has degree 0, 1 or 2. Hence $\Phi(t) = t + t^2$ and $A(z)$ satisfies $A(z) = z(1 + A(z) + A^2(z))$. Solving, we get

$$A(z) = \frac{1 - z - \sqrt{(1-3z)(1+z)}}{2z}, \text{ and } \quad \tau = 1, \rho = \frac{1}{3}.$$

The coefficient satisfy

$$M_n = [z^n]\, M \sim \frac{3}{2}\, \frac{1}{\sqrt{3\pi}}\, 3^n\, n^{-\frac{1}{2}},$$

and the probability of occurrences of a pattern P of type (m,f) is asymptotically 3^{-n}.

3.3 - Binary trees (Catalan statistics)

Let B denote the family of binary trees with B_n the number of trees with n internal nodes. Then $B(z) = \Sigma\, B_n z^n$ satisfies

$$B(z) = z + z\, B^2(z), \quad B(z) = \frac{1 - \sqrt{1-4z}}{2z} \quad \text{and} \quad B_n = \frac{1}{n+1}\binom{2n}{n}.$$

The number of occurrences of a pattern P with m internal nodes (and $m+1$ external nodes) is

$$O_n^p = \binom{2p-m+1}{p+1},$$

and the probability of occurrence of P in a large tree is approximately 2^{1-m}.

The two valuations v and w reduce in that case to one, and we have

PROPOSITION : The average cost of the sequential matching algorithm is given by

$$t(\sigma + \bar{v}\,\sigma')(1 + O(\tfrac{1}{m}))$$

where t *is the size of the text,* m *the size of the pattern,* σ *and* σ' *constants depending on the implementation and*

$$\bar{v} = 6 - 4\sqrt{2}.$$

A simulation corresponding to this analysis is displayed in figure 2.

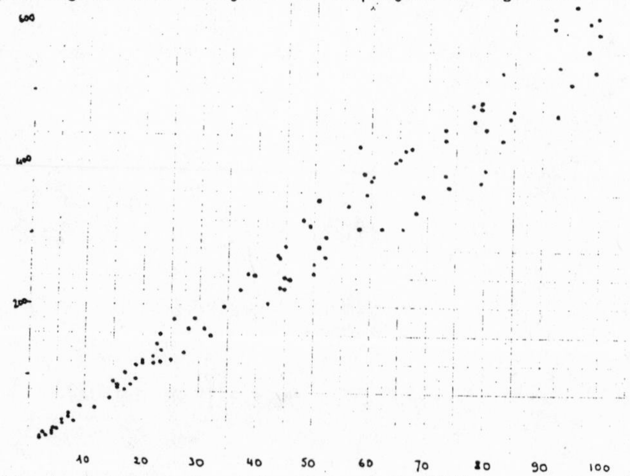

Figure 2 : Cost of 100 simulations of match, when $p \leq t \leq 100$, as a function of text size ; all elementary operations are taken with unit cost.

5 - REFERENCES

[de BRUIJN, KNUTH, RICE ; 1972], *The average height of planted plane trees*, in Graph Theory and Computing ; R.C. Read Editor, Academic Press, New York, 1972, pp. 15-22.

[BERSTEL, REUTENAUER ; 1980], *Séries formelles reconnaissables d'arbres et applications*, in 5° CLAAP, Lille (1980).

[COMTET ; 1970], *Analyse combinatoire*, 2 vol., PUF, Paris, 1970.

[FLAJOLET ; 1979], *Analyse d'algorithmes de manipulation d'arbres et de fichiers*, Thèse, Université de Paris XI-Orsay, 1979.

[FLAJOLET, ODLYZKO ; 1980], *The Average height of binary trees and other simple trees*, manuscript, 1980.

[FLAJOLET, RAOULT, VUILLEMIN ; 1979], *The number of registers required for evaluating arithmetic expressions*, Theoretic Comp. Sc. 9 (1979), pp. 99-125.

[HENRICI ; 1978], *Applied and computational complex analysis*, 2 vol., J. Wiley & Sons, New York, 1978.

[KEMP ; 1978], *The average number of registers to evaluate a binary tree optimally*, Acta Informatica, 1979.

[KNUTH ; 1968], *The art of computer programming : fundamental algorithms*, Addison Wesley, Reading, 1968.

[MEIR, MOON ; 1978], *On the altitude of nodes in random trees*, Can. J. Math. XXX, N° 5 (1978), pp. 997-1015.

[POLYA ; 1937], *Kombinatorische Anzahlbestimmungen für Gruppen, Graphen und chemische Verbindungen*, Acta Mathematica 68 (1937), pp. 145-254.

[RAMEY ; 1960], *Functional composition patterns and power series reversion*, Trans. A.M.S., 94 (1960), pp. 441-451.

GENERATING AND SEARCHING SETS INDUCED BY NETWORKS

(Preliminary Version)

Greg N. Frederickson* and Donald B. Johnson†

Computer Science Department
The Pennsylvania State University
University Park, Pennsylvania 16802 USA

Introduction

Let a network be an undirected connected graph $G = (V,E)$ with a nonnegative cost function c on E and a nonnegative distance function d on $V \times V$ representing the cost of shortest paths. Certain problems on networks can be solved efficiently if a succinct representation of the set of all shortest distances in the network can be generated and searched efficiently. One such problem of practical significance which meets this criterion is the location of p-centers in networks with simple topologies. A p-center consists of p supply points chosen so that the largest distance from a demand point to its nearest supply point is minimized [H1]. We present algorithms for locating p-centers in simple networks which improve upon known results. Moreover, our searching methods relate to those of selection in succinctly represented sets, which we have considered in [FJ1,FJ2]. Besides set representation and set searching, we also address interesting problems of graph decomposition and graph searching.

For the p-center problem, we assume that the sets of supply and demand points may include not only vertices but also points lying on the edges, taking each edge as a line segment of length equal to its cost and thereby extending the distance function d to all points in E taken as the union of these lines. We also call the set of all these points E when no confusion can result. Let S represent a set of supply points and D the set of demand points. We define the <u>radius</u> $r(S,D)$ of a network with sets S and D as

$$r(S,D) = \max_{v \in D}\{\min_{w \in S}\{d(v,w)\}\}.$$

We define the p-<u>radius</u> $r_p(D)$ of a network with demand set D as

$$r_p(D) = \min_{|S|=p}\{r(S,D)\}.$$

A p-<u>center</u> is a supply set S that realizes the p-radius. We distinguish four types of problems with the notation $X/D/p$, where $S \subset X$ and X and D may be either the set V of vertices or the set of all points E.

*Work of this author partially supported by the National Science Foundation under grant MCS 7909259.

†Work of this author partially supported by the National Science Foundation under grant MCS 77-21092.

For general networks, the problem of finding p-centers appears difficult [KH]. We thus limit our consideration to networks with tree or "near-tree" topologies. We first consider trees. For $p = 1$ and $p = 2$, $O(n)$ algorithms, where $n = |V|$, are known for locating p-centers [G1,G2,Hr1,Hr2,KH]. For $p > 2$, our general approach is the following: Generate a set X that is known to contain the p-radius. Search X for the p-radius, which will be the smallest value in X that satisfies a feasibility test. The feasibility test for a value t involves attempting to find a set S of no more than p supply points such that $r(S,D) \leq t$.

For the problem V/V/p, a set containing the p-radius is the set of all intervertex distances. Hence a straightforward procedure [KH] would generate X in $O(n^2)$ time and then sort X in $O(n^2 \log n)$ time. Since each feasibility test can be done in $O(n)$ time [KH], X may be searched and values tested in $O(n \log n)$ time. A more refined approach [MTZC] does not generate all the elements of X explicitly, and hence does not sort X in its entirety. Instead, a more involved search strategy is employed to achieve an overall time of $O(n(\log n)^2)$.

It is possible to do better if a convenient representation R of the set X of potential p-radii is used. Our choice for R allows both for efficient generation of the representation and for efficient searching. We organize R as a set of subsets, where each subset is represented by what we refer to as a <u>sorted Cartesian matrix</u> (or <u>sorted matrix</u>). By sorted Cartesian matrix we mean $A+B = \{a+b \mid a \in A \text{ and } b \in B\}$ with A and B being multisets of numbers in sorted order. While the cardinality of sorted A+B is $|A| \cdot |B|$, we note that only $|A| + |B|$ elements are needed to represent it. Hence A+B admits a succinct representation. As we shall see in the next section, a representation consisting of a set of such sorted matrices is a natural way to represent all intervertex distances in a tree.

We show how to decompose a tree and generate a representation R as a set of matrices in the above form in $O(n \log n)$ time. We also show how to search R efficiently, using methods similar to those described in [FJ2] for finding the k-th shortest path in a tree. For V/V/p, V/E/p, and E/V/p, we achieve a time of $O(n \log n)$, and for E/E/p we achieve $O(qn \log(2pn/q^2))$ where $q = \min\{n,p\}$. When $p \leq n$ this bound is $O(pn \log(2n/p))$. We also consider two other network topologies, a tree with $s \ll n$ leaves, and a network in which each edge is contained in at most one cycle. Our solutions to these additional problems demonstrate extensions to our basic strategies for decomposition, searching, and feasibility testing.

<u>Tree Decomposition and Set Generation</u>

Let v be a vertex in a tree T. If v is replaced by new vertices v' and v", and each edge (v,w) is replaced by (v',w) or (v",w) as appropriate, then two trees T_1 and T_2 result. Thus any vertex v induces one or more decompositions of the form (v,T_1,T_2). Let $T_1 = (V_1,E_1)$ and $T_2 = (V_2,E_2)$, with $v' \in V_1$ and $v'' \in V_2$. We may generate a representation R of the set X of all intervertex distances by finding a decomposition (v,T_1,T_2) of T, forming the set of all distances for pairs in $(V_1-\{v'\}) \times (V_2-\{v''\})$, and then applying the procedure recursively to T_1 and T_2. It is easy to see that X can thus be partitioned into a set of Cartesian matrices.

In order to achieve a reasonable time complexity, we require that each decomposition vertex be a centroid. A <u>centroid</u> v of a tree T is a vertex that minimizes over all vertices the size of the largest connected component of $T - v$. A decomposition of a tree of n vertices induced by a centroid will be called a <u>centroid decomposition</u> if $1/3(n-1)+1 \leq |V_1| \leq 2/3(n-1)+1$.

<u>LEMMA 1</u>. Let T be a tree with $n > 2$ vertices. A centroid decomposition (v,T_1,T_2) of T exists, and can be found in $O(n)$ time.

<u>Proof</u>: For $n = 3$, there is a unique tree and it can be verified that the lemma holds. For $n \geq 4$, we argue as follows: If v is a centroid, then the size of the largest component of $T - v$ is no larger than $n/2$. For $n \geq 4$, $n/2 \leq 2/3(n-1)$. Hence if some component of $T - v$ is of size b, $1/3(n-1) \leq b \leq n/2$, then this component may serve as the basis for T_1, and all other components as the basis for T_2. Otherwise, all components are smaller than $1/3(n-1)$, and they may be combined in any order until the combined size is b, for $1/3(n-1) \leq b \leq 2/3(n-1)$. The remaining components form the basis for T_2.

A centroid v and the size of the components in $T - v$ may be computed in $O(n)$ time using a centroid algorithm in [G,KH]. □

Our decomposition based on a centroid is similar to that in [MTZC]. However their decomposition uses three subtrees and produces a set of sorted subsets, which may be viewed essentially as unrelated rows of our Cartesian matrices. Also, as we shall see, our algorithm distributes the steps of a number of carefully organized merge sorts over the generation of our representation. This allows us to generate all of our sorted lists more efficiently.

We generate our representation $R(T) = R$ for the set X of intervertex distances of $T = (V,E)$ recursively as follows:

$$R(T) = R(T_1) \cup R(T_2) \cup (v,L_1(v),L_2(v)) \quad \text{for } |V| > 2,$$

$$R(T) = (v,(\langle v,0\rangle),(\langle w,c(v,w)\rangle)) \quad \text{for } V = \{v,w\},$$

where (v,T_1,T_2) is a centroid decomposition of T, $L_1(v)$ is a list of ordered pairs $(\langle v_i,d(v,v_i)\rangle | v_i \in V_1-\{v'\})$ sorted on $d(v,v_i)$ and representing distances from all vertices v_i in $T_1 - v'$ to v, and $L_2(v)$ is similarly defined. Of course, the pair of lists $L_1(v)$ and $L_2(v)$ associated with vertex v implicitly define a sorted Cartesian matrix $L_1(v) + L_2(v)$.

We now show how to generate the sorted lists $L_1(v)$ and $L_2(v)$ from information generated at deeper levels of recursion for a tree T with more than two vertices.

Let (v,T_1,T_2) be a centroid decomposition of T. We generate $L_1(v)$ with a call to a recursive list building procedure LISTBUILD with $T_J = T_1$ and $v^* = v'$ as arguments. Procedure LISTBUILD performs as follows: If T_J contains exactly two vertices u and v^* (one must be the replacement of v in T_1), then return the list $(\langle u,c(v^*,u)\rangle)$. Otherwise T_J contains more than two vertices, and we let (v_J,T_{J1}, T_{J2}) be the centroid decomposition of T_J used to generate $R(T_J)$. If $v_J = v^*$, then return the result of merging $L_1(v_J)$ and $L_2(v_J)$. Otherwise, if v^* is in T_{J2}, then return the result of merging two lists: One of these is the result of adding $d(v_J,v^*)$ to each distance in $L_1(v_J)$, and the other is the list returned by a recursive call to LISTBUILD with T_{J2} and v^*. If v^* is in T_{J1}, an analogous strategy is employed. We generate $L_2(v)$ by a call to LISTBUILD with $T_J = T_2$ and $v^* = v''$. We omit the details since they are similar to those for $L_1(v)$.

We assume that this method for generating a representation $R(T)$ of set X is embodied by a procedure REPGEN.

LEMMA 2. Let T be a tree with $n \geq 2$ vertices. Procedure REPGEN will correctly generate the representation $R(T)$ of the set of intervertex distances in T.

Proof: We proceed by induction on n. If $n = 2$, then $R(T)$ is correctly computed. For $n > 2$, let (v,T_1,T_2) be the centroid decomposition of T used by REPGEN, and let IH1 be the hypothesis that the lemma holds for trees of smaller size. By IH1, REPGEN correctly generates $R(T_1)$ and $R(T_2)$. We must show that $L_1(v)$ and $L_2(v)$ are correctly generated by LISTBUILD.

We require LISTBUILD to return a sorted list of the distances to v^* from all vertices in any T_J generated by REPGEN and containing v^*. We proceed by induction on m, the number of vertices in T_J. If $m = 2$, then the appropriate list is returned. For $m > 2$, let (v_J,T_{J1},T_{J2}) be the centroid decomposition of T_J employed by REPGEN, and let IH2 be the hypothesis that LISTBUILD performs correctly for trees of size less than m. If $v_J = v^*$, then by IH1, $L_1(v_J)$ and $L_2(v_J)$ are correctly computed as a part of $R(T_J)$. Merging these yields the desired ordered list of distances from vertices in T_J to v^*.

If $v_J \neq v^*$, then assume without loss of generality that v^* is in T_{J2}. By IH1, $L_1(v_J)$ is correctly computed as a part of $R(T_J)$. Adding $d(v_J,v^*)$ yields distances from vertices in T_{J1} to v^*. By IH2, the list resulting from calling LISTBUILD with argument T_{J2} yields all distances from vertices in T_{J2} to v^*. Merging these two lists will give all distances from vertices in T_J to v^*. This completes the induction for LISTBUILD.

Thus $L_1(v)$ and $L_2(v)$ are generated correctly, and the outer induction follows. □

LEMMA 3. Procedure LISTBUILD runs in time proportional to the length of the list that it returns.

Proof: We proceed by induction on m, the number of vertices in T_J. If $m = 2$, then constant time is required. For $m \geq 3$, let (v_J,T_{J1},T_{J2}) be the centroid decomposition of T_J used by REPGEN, and assume that LISTBUILD requires time cm', for trees with $m' < m$ vertices. If $v_J = v^*$, then LISTBUILD will use time proportional to m to merge two available lists. If $v_J \neq v^*$, then LISTBUILD will be called on a tree of size no greater than $2/3(m-1)+1 < m$. Adding a value to each element of an extant list and then merging also costs time no more than $c_1 m$ for some constant c_1. Hence total time will be no more than $(2/3(m-1)+1)c + c_1 m$, which is at most cm for sufficiently large c. □

THEOREM 1. Let T be a tree with $n \geq 2$ vertices. Procedure REPGEN will generate the representation R of the set of intervertex distances in time $O(n \log n)$.

Proof: Correctness follows from Lemma 2. The work done by the algorithm may be described recursively, using Lemma 3:

$$T(n) \leq T(g(n)) + T(n+1-g(n)) + c_1 n \quad \text{for } n > 2,$$

$$T(2) = c_2,$$

where $1/3(n-1)+1 \leq g(n) \leq 2/3(n-1)+1$. It may be verified that $T(n)$ is $O(n \log n)$. □

Searching Collections of Sorted Matrices

In the previous section, we saw how to generate a representation R in the form of a set of sorted Cartesian matrices for the set X of intervertex distances in a tree. In this section we show how to search this set to find the value of the p-radius. We note that the techniques used to search in the set of sorted matrices are similar to those of selecting the k-th largest element in such a set [FJ2].

The algorithm proceeds by choosing representative elements from R and testing them for feasibility. The feasibility test involves finding a supply set S of minimum cardinality p' such that the radius does not exceed the value of the representative element. Given a test radius, such a minimum cardinality supply set may be found in $O(n)$ time [KH].

If the number p' of supply points needed to realize the test radius exceeds p, then the test value is too small, and all values in R less than or equal to it may be discarded. If p' is less than or equal to p, then the test radius need be no larger than p, and all larger values may be discarded. Thus a binary search on R, using feasibility testing, is sufficient to identify the p-radius. However, to achieve a favorable time complexity in searching a set of sorted Cartesian matrices, the search for test values must be made over carefully chosen subsets of R.

In choosing a representative for feasibility testing, not all values in R are considered. In fact some matrices are ignored until late in the search. The algorithm performs a sequence of iterations including matrices of increasingly smaller size on each iteration. The matrices that are active are divided into submatrices called cells. On each iteration certain cells are discarded from further consideration, on the basis of the value of a representative element. For simplicity, we assume that the matrices are padded out so that they will be square in shape, with the dimension of the matrix being a power of 2. This can be done by concatenating elements with large distance values onto the ends of the lists that define the matrices of R. Since the matrices are almost square to begin with, the padding will increase only the multiplicative constant in the running time.

We now show how to choose the test values. Initially make all matrices inactive, and let the cell dimension be equal to the dimension of the largest matrix. At the beginning of an iteration, change from inactive to active all matrices whose dimension is equal to the current cell dimension, and designate these newly active matrices as new cells. For all new and remaining cells, divide each into four square cells of equal size. Select the upper median element x_s (ranking $h/2+1$ among h elements) from the set consisting of the smallest element from each of the h cells. Select the lower median x_ℓ (ranking $h/2$) from the set consisting of the largest element from each cell. Both values are then tested for feasibility. If x_s is feasible, then discard all cells whose smallest elements are greater than or equal to x_s except one cell for which the smallest element is equal. Otherwise, discard all cells whose largest elements are less than or equal to x_s. Perform the same operations with regard to x_ℓ. When cells consist of single elements, all matrices have been made active. No further cell division is done, but the search continues until a single element remains.

We show that the number of cells does not increase too quickly as the iterations progress. Let b_{ij} be the ratio of the dimension of matrix M_j to the current cell dimension if M_j is active on the i-th iteration, and zero otherwise. Let $B_i = 4\Sigma_j b_{ij} - 1$.

LEMMA 4. The number of cells remaining at the end of the i-th iteration is no greater than B_i.

Proof: We proceed by induction on i. At the end of the first iteration, no cells need to have been discarded to satisfy the lemma. For $i > 1$, we assume that the lemma holds for iteration $i-1$. Then there are at most $4B_{i-1} + 4N$ cells after cell division on the i-th iteration where N is the number of newly active matrices. If x_s is feasible, or x_ℓ is infeasible, then no more than $1/2(4B_{i-1} + 4N) + 1 \leq 4\Sigma_j b_{ij} - 1$ cells will remain. Suppose x_s is infeasible and x_ℓ is feasible, and let the number of cells be h. In any matrix M_j, at most $2b_{ij} - 1$ cells have smallest element less than x_s, and largest element greater than x_s. Hence at least $h/2 - \Sigma_j(2b_{ij}-1)$ cells have all elements less than or equal to x_s. By similar reasoning at least $h/2 - \Sigma_j(2b_{ij}-1)$ cells have all elements greater than or equal to x_ℓ. Hence at least $h - 2\Sigma_j(2b_{ij}-1) - 1$ cells are discarded, leaving no more than $2\Sigma_j(2b_{ij}-1) + 1 \leq 4\Sigma_j b_{ij} - 1$ cells. □

LEMMA 5. Let T be a tree with n vertices, and its set of intervertex distances be represented as the set R of sorted Cartesian matrices. Then the time required to search R for the p-radius is O(n log n).

Proof: From the preceding lemma, the number of cells remaining at the end of iteration i-1 is no more than B_{i-1}. Hence no more than $O(B_i)$ work is done in dividing and selecting among cells on the i-th iteration [Bℓ]. The work over all iterations in which cell divisions occur may be distributed over all matrices so that matrix M_j accounts for $O(b_{ij})$ work on iteration i, or O(dimension of matrix M_j) work over all such iterations. Thus the total work for dividing and selecting cells may be described by the recurrence in Theorem 1, which is O(n log n). Iterations with no cell division will begin when there are O(n log n) elements (as may be seen using the same recurrence). Iterations will decrease the number of elements remaining by half each time, yielding O(n log n) for the succession of such selections ultimately giving a least feasible element. For feasibility testing, O(log n) iterations of the first type are performed, and O(log n) iterations of the second type are performed. Hence all feasibility testing is O(n log n). □

THEOREM 2. The p-center problem V/V/p on a tree of n vertices may be solved in O(n log n) time.

Proof: From Theorem 1 the set of intervertex distances can be generated in O(n log n) time. The time for searching is established as O(n log n) in Lemma 5. Correctness for searching follows from the fact that elements in R are discarded only when a discarded element is infeasible or when the discarded element is feasible and there is an element equal to it or smaller that is feasible and is retained. It is clear that the set X of intervertex distances must contain the p-radius for any $p < n$. When $p = n$, the problem is trivial. □

Continuous p-Centers

We now consider the cases where either or both of the supply set and the demand set may be points on the edges. As in the case of V/V/p, O(n) algorithms are known for testing the feasibility of a test radius r (See [KH] for E/V/p and [CT2] for V/E/p and E/E/p). As we have seen, a set of relevant values for V/V/p is the set of intervertex distances $\{d(v,w) \mid v,w \in V\}$. For E/V/p, [KH] have shown a set of relevant values to be $\{1/2d(v,w) \mid v,w \in V\}$. For V/E/p, [CT1] have shown such a set to be $\{d(v,w), 1/2d(v,w) \mid v,w \in V\}$. For E/E/p, [CT2] have shown a relevant set to be $\{1/(2k)d(v,w) \mid v,w \in V \text{ and } k=1,\dots,p\}$. It is easy to see that the sets for V/E/p and E/V/p can be generated and searched in the same time as for V/V/p.

LEMMA 6. The p-center problems V/E/p and E/V/p on a tree of n vertices may each be solved in O(n log n) time. □

Both results are improvements over the $O(n(\log n)^2)$ algorithms presented in [MTZC].

We note from the preceding that we can solve E/E/p within a bound of $O(pn \log n)$. To do so we first generate the representation R of the set of intervertex distances, and then generate for each matrix in R the p-1 additional matrices corresponding to $k = 2,\dots,p$. The searching algorithm is as before. The total time of $O(pn \log n)$ is an improvement on the result in [MTZC] for all cases in which $p = o(n)$. By carefully managing the search we can do even better.

As before we generate the representation R of the set of intervertex distances. For simplicity, we pad these matrices out to be square with dimension a power of 4, and round p up to a power of 4. For each matrix of dimensions $m \times m$ from R, we generate implicitly p matrices of dimensions $m \times m$ if $m \geq p$, or generate m matrices of dimensions $m \times p$ otherwise. Let R_p be the representation so generated, where each matrix consists of a triple of pointers to the relevant portions of the generator lists, i.e. the lists in R and the list $(1,\dots,p)$. Given R, the triples for R_p can be obtained in time dominated by $O(n \log n)$, the time to generate R.

The searching algorithm involves cells as before, but the cells are handled somewhat differently. The cells are the same shape as their parent matrices, up until the width (the smaller dimension) of a cell equals one. When a cell (called a thin cell) has width one, cell division is realized by dividing the cell into four cells along the longer dimension. As before, an inactive matrix will be made active when its size is that of the current cell size.

As in the last section, we show that the number of cells does not grow too quickly as the iterations progress. Let b_{ij} be the ratio of the width of M_j to the width of its current cell size on the i-th iteration if M_j is active, and zero otherwise. Let $B_i = 4\Sigma_j b_{ij} - 1$.

LEMMA 6. The number of cells remaining at the end of the i-th iteration is no greater than B_i.

Proof: The proof proceeds as in Lemma 4. When a matrix has only thin cells remaining, then at most b_{ij} (rather than $2b_{ij}-1$) cells have smallest element less than or equal to x_s. Hence the proof still goes through. □

THEOREM 3. Let T be a tree with n vertices. The time required to solve an E/E/p problem on T is $O(qn \log(2pn/q^2))$, where $q = \min\{n,p\}$.

Proof: As indicated, R_p can be generated in $O(n \log n)$, which is within the required time bound. For the search of R_p, as in Lemma 5 we may distribute the work of dividing and selecting among cells over the matrices, charging matrix M_j with $O(\Sigma_i b_{ij})$ work. If matrix M_j has width m_j and is square, then this is $O(m_j)$. If M_j is not square then this work is $O(m_j \log(2p/m_j))$. Thus total work for dividing and selecting among cells in all matrices is described by the recurrence:

$$T(m) = T(g(m)) + T(n+1-g(m)) + f(p,m) \quad \text{for } m > 2,$$

$$T(2) = c \log p,$$

where $1/3(m-1)+1 \leq g(m) \leq 2/3(m-1)+1$, and $f(p,m) = pm$ for $p \leq m$ and $m^2\log(2p/m)$ for $p > m$. For $p > m$, it can be shown that $T(m) \leq am^2\log(2p/m)$ for some constant a. Using this result, it can be shown that for $p \leq m$, $T(m) \leq bmp \log(2m/p)$ for some constant b. Combining these yields $T(n) = O(qn \log(2pn/q^2))$, where $q = \min\{n,p\}$, as the total work for cell division and selection. Iterations with no cell division will similarly begin with $O(qn \log(2pn/q^2))$ elements, as may be seen from the same recurrence. As before the cost of selection on all remaining iterations will be $O(qn \log(2pn/q^2))$. For feasibility testing, $O(\log n)$ iterations of the first type and $O(\log n)$ of the second type are performed, for a total of $O(n \log n)$. □

Our result improves on the time complexity of $O(\min\{pn(\log n)^2, n^2\log(2p)\})$ achieved by [MTZC]. For the case of $p \leq n$, we note that our algorithm is $O(pn \log(2n/p))$, which ranges between $O(n \log n)$ and $O(n^2)$, depending on the value of p.

Trees with Few Leaves

We consider the problem of locating a p-center in a tree in which the number s of leaves is considerably smaller than the number of vertices. For the V/V/p, V/E/p, and E/V/p problems with values of p and s that are $o(n)$, we find that there is an algorithm that is $o(n \log n)$. The E/E/p problem with $s = o(n)$ can be reduced in $O(n)$ time to a problem for which the number n' of vertices is $\Theta(s)$. The first three problems are more interesting, however, since our algorithms involve further refinements in generating representations and testing feasibility.

We generate a representation of the set that contains the set X of all intervertex distances in $O(n \log s)$ time. In order to achieve this, we use on alternate levels of recursion, (normal) centroid decomposition and leaf-centroid decompositions. A <u>leaf-centroid</u> of a tree with s leaves is a vertex whose removal leaves a forest in which no tree has more than $s/2$ of the leaves from the original tree. A <u>leaf-centroid decomposition</u> (v,T_1,T_2) is a decomposition induced by a leaf-centroid v such that the number s_1 of leaves in T_1 satisfies $s/3 \leq s_1 \leq 2s/3$.

<u>LEMMA 7</u>. Let T be a tree with $s > 2$ leaves. A leaf-centroid decomposition of T exists and can be found in $O(n)$ time. □

For a tree with 2 leaves and n vertices, a sorted Cartesian matrix containing the set of all intervertex distances can be generated in $O(n)$ time. Let the vertices be labeled $v_1,v_2,\ldots,v_n$ in order of appearance in the tree. Let $y_i = d(v_1,v_i)$, $i = 1,\ldots,n$, and let $Y = (y_1,y_2,\ldots,y_n)$. Then the required Cartesian matrix is $Y \dot{-} Y^r$, where $\dot{-}$ is proper subtraction, and Y^r is the sequence Y in reverse order. By using proper subtraction, we have padded out the set of intervertex distances with zeroes. As in the second section, a Cartesian matrix not generated at a lowest level of recursion can be generated in time proportional to the size of the subtree from which it is drawn. Let R^s be the representation defined above.

LEMMA 8. Let T be a tree with n vertices and s leaves. The time to generate R^s is $O(n \log s)$.

Proof: Let $T(n,s)$ be the time required to generate R^s if a normal centroid decomposition is first applied, and $T^{\ell}(n,s)$ the time if a leaf-centroid decomposition is applied first. The time required is thus

$$T(n,s) \leq T^{\ell}(g(n),x+1) + T^{\ell}(n+1-g(n),s+1-x) + cn \quad \text{for } s > 2,$$

$$T^{\ell}(n,s) \leq T(y,h(s)+1) + T(n+1-y,s+1-h(s)) + cn \quad \text{for } s > 2,$$

$$T(n,2) = T^{\ell}(n,2) \leq cn,$$

where $g(n)$ is as in Theorem 1, $1/3s \leq h(s) \leq 2s/3$, c is some constant, and x and y are integers such that $0 < x < s$ and $0 < y < n+1$. It can be shown that $T(n,s)$ and $T^{\ell}(n,s)$ are $O(n \log s)$. □

The time to search R^s, exclusive of the time to perform the feasibility tests, is also $O(n \log s)$, as can be seen by analysis similar to that of the previous sections. However, the use of the $O(n)$ feasibility test from the previous sections forces a total time of $O(n \log n)$ over the $O(\log n)$ search iterations. We now present a better feasibility test that binary searches the paths of the tree.

A tree with s leaves can be partitioned into a set of no more than $2s$ paths, where the internal vertices on the paths are all of degree 2 in the tree. We represent each path as a sorted array of distances from one of the endpoints of the path. In our feasibility test, we proceed from the subtrees upward, as in the feasibility test cited above, except that we use a one-sided binary search to locate a point at which to place a supply point, or the farthest demand point that can be supplied from an already placed supply point. A one-sided binary search [BY] finds a value v in a sorted array $x(1{:}n)$ by determining $i = 2^k$ such that $x_i \leq v < x_{2i}$ and then finding q such that $x_q \leq v < x_{q+1}$. The search may be carried out in $O(\log q)$ time.

LEMMA 9. Let T be a tree with n vertices and s leaves. The above procedure tests for feasibility of a test radius in time $O(s + p \log(2n/p))$ for $p < n$.

Proof: The supply points plus the points of furthest extent will partition no more than $2s$ paths into no more than $2s + 2p$ subpaths. If subpath i contains z_i vertices, then the subpath may be determined in $O(\log z_i)$ time. At most $2p$ of these paths are searched. Hence the total search time for the paths is $O(s + \Sigma_{i=1,2p} \log z_i)$, where $\Sigma_{i=1,2p+2s}\, z_i = n + 2s$. The search time is thus $O(s + p \log(2n/p))$. □

THEOREM 4. Let T be a tree with n vertices and s leaves. The time to locate a p-center of T is $O(n \log s + p \log n \log(2n/p))$.

Proof: From Lemma 8, the time to generate a set of sorted matrices containing all intervertex distances is $O(n \log s)$. The time for searching these matrices exclusive of feasibility testing is also $O(n \log s)$. From Lemma 9, the feasibility test takes $O(s + p \log(2n/p))$ time. The feasibility test must be performed $O(\log n)$ times. Since $s \log n$ is $O(n \log s)$, the result follows. □

Networks with Independent Cycles

In this section, we relax the constraints on the topology of a network to allow graphs that are more general than trees. We define a cycle tree C to be a simple graph in which each edge is contained in at most one cycle. Cycle trees appear to be a natural generalization of trees with properties which still allow our techniques to be applied. For example, depth-first search can be applied to a cycle tree in a straightforward manner if each cycle is treated as a "super vertex."

The notion of centroid decomposition is extended to cycle trees in the following manner. If there is a vertex v such that no connected component in $C - v$ has more than $n/2$ vertices, then v is a centroid of C and we generate a centroid decomposition analogous to those for trees. Otherwise, there is a cycle whose removal satisfies the same condition when treated as a super vertex. We identify a pair of edges on the cycle whose removal leaves no connected component with more than $2n/3$ vertices, and leaves two path segments from the cycle, neither of which is longer than one half the cycle length. We identify a vertex v incident from one of the edges identified and in one component, and a vertex w incident from the other edge and in the other component, and base a centroid set decomposition $(\{v,w\},C_1,C_2)$ on these vertices. As before v is replaced by v' in C_1 and v'' in C_2, and w is handled similarly. Further, all vertices except v and w from one component are in C_1, and similarly for the other component and C_2.

LEMMA 10. Let C be a cycle tree with $n > 2$ vertices. If C does not have a centroid, then it has a centroid set decomposition $(\{v,w\},C_1,C_2)$, which can be found in $O(n)$ time. □

We generate a representation R^c in the form of a set of sorted Cartesian matrices for a set that contains all shortest intervertex distances in our cycle tree C. The procedure is similar to that for generating R for a tree T. If the centroid set of C is of cardinality one, then the same recursive rule as in the second section is applied. If the centroid set is of cardinality two, then the following is applied:

$$R(C) = R(C_1) \cup R(C_2) \cup (v,L_1(v),L_2(v)) \cup (w,L_1(w),L_2(w)),$$

where L_1 and L_2 are as in the second section. The set so generated will actually have more values than what is needed, since every pair of vertices in $V_1 \times V_2$ will have values for two paths between them in $R(C)$.

We generate $L_1(v)$ with a call to LISTBUILDC with $C_J = C_1$ and $v^* = v'$ as arguments. If C_J has a centroid, it is handled in a fashion similar to the tree procedure. If C_J has a centroid set decomposition $(\{v_J,w_J\},C_{J1},C_{J2})$, then we proceed as follows. If $v^* = v_J$ (and without loss of generality $d(v'_J,w'_J) \geq d(v''_J,w''_J)$), then add $d(v''_J,w''_J)$ to each element in $L_1(w_J)$, merge with $L_1(v_J)$ and $L_2(v_J)$, and delete second entries for any repeated vertex u. The case with $v^* = w_J$ is handled similarly. Otherwise if v' is in C_{J2}, for instance, then add $d(v^*,v''_J)$

to each element in $L_1(v_J)$ and $d(v^*,w''_J)$ to each element in $L_1(w_J)$, merge these lists and eliminate second entries. This list is then merged with the result of a recursive call to LISTBUILDC with arguments C_{J2} and v^*. $L_2(v)$, $L_1(w)$, and $L_2(w)$ are handled similarly.

We assume that the preceding method for generating R^c is realized by procedure REPGENC. With arguments analogous to those employed in Lemmas 2 and 3, we can establish that REPGENC correctly computes a representation that includes all shortest intervertex distances, and that LISTBUILDC runs in time proportional to the length of the list that it returns.

LEMMA 11. Let C be a cycle tree with n vertices. Procedure REPGENC will generate representation R^c in $O(n \log n)$ time. □

The time to search R^c exclusive of feasibility testing can also be seen to be $O(n \log n)$.

We indicate briefly how to conduct a feasibility test in a cycle tree in $O(n)$ time. The test is embedded in a depth-first search of the cycle tree taking cycles as super vertices. As in feasibility testing in a normal tree, we locate supply points in subtrees, passing back up the tree either a requirement to cover some vertices in a subtree by a supply vertex yet to be placed, or the information that vertices already covered can cover one or more vertices above it in the depth-first order. Information returned to a super vertex is returned to the attach vertices on the cycle, the vertices to which the respective subtrees attach. When all the attach vertices of a cycle have received information, we proceed as follows. If any attach vertex is labeled with information that it is covered from below, the cycle can be split at this attach vertex and the search may continue as if being performed on a normal tree. Otherwise each attach vertex demands that a supply vertex be placed in some interval of the cycle (which could be the entire cycle and include part of the tree above). In a traversal of the cycle in, say, the clockwise direction, the initial points of these intervals are encountered in the same order as the attach vertices with which they are associated, if we ignore intervals wholly containing other intervals.

We can therefore perform such a traversal, assigning to each vertex on the cycle a pointer to a preceding vertex in the clockwise ordering which is the furthest vertex which can cover it as a supply point. In similar fashion, we may identify the furthest point that the vertex may cover. Then a search in the opposite direction can be performed, also in time linear in the number of vertices on the cycle, which locates sets of supply points of minimum cardinality at their maximal spread. From among these sets, we choose a minimal cycle cover, which has a supply vertex closest to the entry point of the cycle. The search continues, with the information of the furthest vertex not covered transmitted upwards.

LEMMA 12. Let C be a cycle tree with n vertices. Feasibility testing can be done in O(n) time. □

THEOREM 5. Let C be as above. A V/V/p p-center may be located in C in O(n log n) time. □

References

[BY] Bentley, J. L. and A. C. Yao, An almost optimal algorithm for unbounded searching, Inf. Proc. Letters 5 (1976) 82-87.

[Bℓ] Blum, M., R. W. Floyd, V. R. Pratt, R. L. Rivest, and R. E. Tarjan, Time bounds for selection, J. Comput. Sys. Sci. 7 (1972) 448-461.

[CD] Chandrasekaran, R. and A. Daughtey, Problems of location on trees, Disc. Paper 357, Ctr. for Math. Studies in Econ. and Mgmt. Sci., Northwestern U., 1978.

[CT1] Chandreskaran, R. and A. Tamir, Polynomially bounded algorithms for locating P-centers on a tree, Disc. Paper 358, Ctr. for Math. Studies in Econ. and Mgmt. Sci., Northwestern U., 1978.

[CT2] Chandrasekaran, R. and A. Tamir, An $O((n\log P)^2)$ algorithm for the continuous P-center problem on a tree, Disc. Paper 367, Ctr. for Math. Studies in Econ. and Mgmt. Sci., Northwestern U., 1978.

[FJ1] Frederickson, G. N. and D. B. Johnson, Optimal algorithms for generating quantile information in X+Y and matrices with sorted columns, Proc. 13th Ann. Conf. on Inf. Sci. and Sys., The Johns Hopkins U. (1979) 47-52.

[FJ2] Frederickson, G. N. and D. B. Johnson, Generalized selection and ranking, Proceedings 12th Ann. ACM Symp. Theory Comput., April 1980, (to appear).

[G1] Goldman, A. J., Optimal center location in simple networks, Transp. Sci. 5 (1971) 212-221.

[G2] Goldman, A. J., Minimax location of a facility in an undirected tree graph, Transp. Sci. 6 (1972) 407-418.

[H1] Hakimi, S. L., Optimum locations of switching centers and the absolute centers and medians of a graph, Opns. Res. 12 (1964) 450-459.

[H2] Hakimi, S. L., Optimal distribution of switching centers in a communications network and some related graph theoretic problems, Opns. Res. 13 (1965) 462-475.

[Hr1] Handler, G. Y., Minimax location of a facility in an undirected tree graph, Transp. Sci. 7 (1973) 287-293.

[Hr2] Handler, G. Y., Finding two-centers of a tree: the continuous case, Transp. Sci. 12 (1978) 93-106.

[KH] Kariv, O. and S. L. Hakimi, An algorithmic approach to network location problems, SIAM J. Appl. Math. 37 (Dec. 1979) 513-538.

[MTZC] Megiddo, N., A. Tamir, E. Zemel, and R. Chandrasekaran, An $O(n\log^2 n)$ algorithm for the kth longest path in a tree with applications to location problems, Disc. Paper 379, Ctr. for Math. Studies in Econ. and Mgmt. Sci., Northwestern U., 1979.

THE COMPLEXITY OF THE INEQUIVALENCE PROBLEM FOR REGULAR EXPRESSIONS WITH INTERSECTION

Martin Fürer
Department of Computer Science
University of Edinburgh
Edinburgh, Scotland.

Abstract

The nondeterministic lower space bound $\sqrt{n}$ of Hunt, for the problem if a regular expression with intersection describes a non-empty language, is improved to the upper bound n. For the general inequivalence problem for regular expressions with intersection the lower bound c^n matches the upper bound except for the constant c. And the proof for this tight lower bound is simpler than the proofs for previous bounds. Methods developed in a result about one letter alphabets are extended to get a complete characterization for the problem of deciding if one input-expression describes a given language. The complexity depends only on the property of the given language to be finite, infinite but bounded, or unbounded.

1. Introduction and previous results

Semi-extended regular expressions are built as regular expressions, but in addition they contain the intersection. The problem if two regular-like expressions describe different languages (inequivalence problem) is of interest in connection with pattern-matching algorithms. The inequivalence problem for semi-extended regular expressions has an upper space bound d^n, because it is easy to build a nondeterministic finite automaton with 2^n states, which accepts the language described by a semi-extended regular expression E of length n. A product construction can be used for every intersection.

Hunt [1973] has given a lower space bound $c^{\sqrt{n/\log n}}$ for the inequivalence problem. This theorem which also appeared in Aho, Hopcroft and Ullman [1974], has a pretty complicated proof. The better lower bound $(c^{n/\log n})$ of Stockmeyer [1974] does not change the proof techniques. We give a tight lower space bound (c^n) by a proof, which is easier to understand.

The general method to prove lower bounds for word problems of regular-like expressions introduced by Meyer and Stockmeyer [1972] is to describe computations or their complement by regular-like expressions. Here a computation is a sequence of subsequent ID's (instantaneous descriptions) of a Turing machine. In describing such a computation we have in particular to compare the jth position in an ID with the jth position in the following ID. But especially for regular-like expressions which contain intersections it would be much easier to compare the first position of one ID with the last position of the other ID and so on. This idea was used in

Fürer [1978] to improve the lower bound of the inequivalence problem for star-free expressions. So we change the code of a computation, instead of trying to find a better description of a fixed code.

The method is well illustrated by the following example:

Describe the set $L_n = \{ww \mid w \in \Sigma^* , |w| = n\}$ by a short semi-extended regular expression!

This can easily be done by a semi-extended regular expression of length $O(n^2)$. With a dive-and-conquer approach, we get an expression of length $O(n \log n)$ and our conjecture is: It cannot be done better.

To the contrary it is not hard to describe the set

$L'_n = \{w^R w \mid w \in \Sigma^* , |w| = n\}$ by a semi-extended regular expression of linear size:

We define the expression E_n which describes L'_n inductively by

$E_0 = \lambda$

$E_{i+1} = \Sigma E_i \Sigma \cap \bigcup_{\sigma \in \Sigma} \sigma\Sigma^*\sigma$

Strictly speaking, the right side of E_{i+1} is not an expression, but a notation to describe an expression. For example, for $\Sigma = \{0,1\}$ the expression E_1 looks more like $((0 \cup 1)\cdot\lambda\cdot(0 \cup 1)) \cap (0\cdot(0 \cup 1)^*\cdot 0 \cup 1\circ(0 \cup 1)^*\cdot 1)$, in fact even with more parenthesis.

Instead of comparing the regular languages described by two expressions, we can take one particular regular language L_0, and decide if a semi-extended regular expression given as input describes this language. If we choose L_0 to be Σ^* we get the problem $NEC(\Sigma,\{\cup,\cdot,*,\cap\})$ (non-empty complement), if L_0 is empty we get the problem $NE(\Sigma,\{\cup,\cdot,*,\cap\})$ (non-empty). In general we get the problem $SINEQ(\Sigma,L_0)$ (semi-extended inequivalence).

For $|\Sigma| \geq 2$ $NEC(\Sigma,\{\cup,\cdot,*,\cap\})$ has the same complexity as the general inequivalence problem, but $NE(\Sigma,\{\cup,\cdot,*,\cap\})$ is CSL-complete. Hunt [1973] has shown that this problem is POLYSPACE-complete by showing that every nondeterministic Turing machine M needs at least space $c\sqrt{n}$ (for some constant $c > 0$ depending on M) to decide this problem. We get cn for the same bound. This implies a nontrivial lower time bound.

We want to give a characterization of the complexity of $SINEQ(\Sigma,L_0)$ for every regular L_0 . It is easy to see that for finite L_0, the problem has the same difficulty as for L_0 empty, and that L_0 unbounded (see section 2) is as difficult as $L_0 = \Sigma^*$. The easiest case with L_0 infinite but bounded is $L_0 = \{0\}^*$. So we have to deal with regular-like expressions over one letter alphabets. The periodicity of these languages yields polynomial space upper bounds for most of the inequivalence problems. The lower bound for the inequivalence problem for regular expressions over a singleton alphabet is nondeterministic polynomial time by Stockmeyer and Meyer [1973]. It is an open problem to improve this lower bound for semi-extended regular expressions. But for $|\Sigma| \geq 2$ we have a polynomial space lower bound for SINEQ $(\Sigma,\{0\}^*)$, because it is hard to decide if a semi-extended regular expression describes also words containing other letters than 0 .

It is very complicated to show that SINEQ (Σ,L_0) has about the same difficulty for every infinite but bounded regular language L_0. This proof needs other techniques than the proof by Hunt, Rosenkrantz and Szymanski [1976] of the corresponding classification for regular expressions (without intersection).

2. Notation

The notation is mostly the same as in Aho, Hopcroft and Ullman [1974] and Stockmeyer [1974].

$\leq_{log-lin}$-complete means that a transformation can be computed in logarithmic space and the length of the output is linear. CSL-complete means $\leq_{log-lin}$-complete in NSpace $(n+1)$. Hence by Seiferas, Fischer and Meyer [1973] every CSL-complete set really needs linear space to be recognized.

Subsets of the operators $\{\cup,\cdot,*,\cap,\neg,^2\}$ are denoted by ψ. $\{\cup,\cdot,*\}$ are the regular operators: union, concatenation and Kleene star, $\cap$ is the intersection, $\neg$ is the complement relative to Σ^*, and ^{2} is the squaring operator defined by $L(E^2) = L(EE)$. NEC (Σ,ψ) (resp. NE (Σ,ψ)) is the set of those regular-like expressions over the alphabet Σ, built with the operators in ψ, which don't describe Σ^* (resp. ϕ). INEQ (Σ,ψ) is the set of pairs (E,E') of regular-like ψ-expressions which describe different languages (i.e. $L(E) \neq L(E')$). SINEQ (Σ, L_0) is the set of semi-extended regular expressions which don't describe L_0.

Definition: A language is bounded if it is contained in $W_1^* \ldots W_k^*$ for some words $W_1,\ldots,W_k$.

3. The non-empty problem

Theorem 1

NE $(\{0,1\}, \{\cup,\cdot,*,\cap\})$ is CSL-complete.

Proof

a) NE $(\{0,1\}, \{\cup,\cdot,*,\cap\}) \in$ CSL.
This result of Hopcroft is an exercise in Aho, Hopcroft and Ullman [1974, p.424]. In fact the powerset of the parenthesis-positions in a semi-extended regular expression can be used as the set of states of a nondeterministic finite automaton which accepts the language described by the expression. (A state in $(E_1 \cap E_2)$ is determined by a pair of states, one in E_1 and one in E_2.)

b) Given a lba M (linear-bounded automaton = nondeterministic $n+1$ space-bounded Turing machine) with the tape alphabet T, the state set S, the accepting states

F, the start state q_o and the input word x of length $|x| = n$, we construct a semi-extended regular expression which describes the set of accepting computations of M with input x . For this theorem we define a <u>computation</u> as a word of the following kind:

$$\& \; ID_1^R \# ID_1 \& ID_2^R \# ID_2 \;\ldots\ldots\; \& ID_{k-1}^R \# ID_{k-1} \& ID_k^R \# ID_k \;\&$$

w^R is the reversed of the word w . $ID_1, ID_2, \ldots, ID_k$ are subsequent instantaneous descriptions ($ID_j \vdash ID_{j+1}$) of the lba M . All ID's have length $n+2$ ($n+1$ tape symbols and 1 state).

Let Σ be the alphabet $S \cup T \cup \{\&,\#\}$. We describe the set of accepting computations by the semi-extended regular expression $E = \bigcap_{i=1}^{4} E_i$.

<u>E_1: Reflection</u>

We define the subexpressions RE_j by

$RE_o = \#$

$RE_{j+1} = \Sigma \, RE_j \Sigma \cap \bigcup_{\sigma \in S \cup T} \sigma \Sigma^* \sigma$ for $j \in N$ $\quad N = \{0,1,2,\ldots\}$

$E_1 = \& \, (RE_{n+2} \&)^*$

With E_1 we demand the correct format (positions of the separating symbols & and #) and the reflection at the symbols # .

<u>E_2: Computation Step</u>

We define the subexpression CS_j by

$CS_1 = T \& T$

$CS_2 = \Sigma \, CS_1 \, \Sigma$

$CS_{j+1} = \Sigma \, CS_j \, \Sigma \cap \bigcup_{Next} \sigma_1\sigma_2\sigma_3\Sigma^*\sigma_6\sigma_5\sigma_4$ for $j = 2,3,\ldots$

Where $Next = \{(\sigma_1\sigma_2\sigma_3, \sigma_4\sigma_5\sigma_6) \mid$ there exist $u,u',v,v' \in (S \cup T)^*$ such that $u\sigma_1\sigma_2\sigma_3 v \vdash u'\sigma_4\sigma_5\sigma_6 v'\}$

$CS = CS_{n+2} \cap (\Sigma^* T \cup (S \cup \Sigma S)\Sigma^* S)$ (No head is allowed to walk in from the left end.)

$E_2 = (\Sigma - \{\#\})^* \# (CS \#)^* (\Sigma - \{\#\})^*$. $L(E_1 \cap E_2)$ is the set of computations (of the lba M) which start and stop with any ID's.

<u>E_3: ID_1 is the Start-ID</u>

$E_3 = (\Sigma - \{\#\})^* \# q_o \, x \, b \;\& \Sigma^*$ where x is the input.

<u>E_4: Accepting Computation</u>

$E_4 = \Sigma^* F \Sigma^*$

where $F \subseteq \Sigma$ is the set of accepting states of the lba M .

Given any lba M , the transformation from an input x to the corresponding semi-extended regular expression $E = \bigcap_{i=1}^{4} E_i$ can be done by a Turing machine with a two-way read-only input tape in linear time without using any space on the work tapes.

In particular the length of E is linear in the length of the input x .

Since the size of Σ is constant (independent of the input x) there is no problem in changing the expression E to an expression which describes a binary encoding of $L(E)$. □

Corollary

$NE(\{0,1\},\{\cup,\cdot,*,\cap\}) \not\in D\,Time(cn)$

Proof

$D\,Time(t) \subseteq D\,Space(t/\log t)$ by Hopcroft, Paul and Valiant [1977]. □

4. The non-empty complement problem

Definition: A marked binary number x is a word (over the four letter alphabet $\{0,\underline{0},1,\underline{1}\}$) described by the regular expression

$$(0\cup 1)^*\ \underline{1}\underline{0}^* \cup \underline{0}^* .$$

Example: $0100\underline{1}\underline{0}\underline{0}$ is a marked binary number of length 7. Note that, if i has the binary representation 0100100 (of length 7), then $i-1 \bmod 2^7$ has the binary representation 0100011 . The representations of i and $i-1 \bmod 2^7$ differ in the underlined digits. For two marked binary numbers the successor relation can be tested locally.

Theorem 2

$NEC(\{0,1\},\{\cup,\cdot,*,\cap\})$ is $\leq_{\text{log-lin}}$ - complete in EXPSPACE.

Proof

a) It is well known that $NEC(\{0,1\},\{\cup,\cdot,*,\cap\})$ is in EXSPACE.

b) Let M be a nondeterministic 2^n-2 space-bounded Turing machine. We choose another code for sequences of subsequent ID's of M , and call this code a computation of M . Here we combine an idea of Stockmeyer [1974] (numbering positions helps to "find" them with regular-like expressions) with an idea of Fürer [1978] (a reflection is easier to describe by regular-like expressions than a translation).

Let $ID_1, ID_2, \ldots, ID_k$ be a sequence of subsequent instantaneous descriptions of the Turing machine M, where ID_1 is the initial ID corresponding to the input x and ID_k is an accepting ID. We define a_{ij} to be the jth symbol in ID_i $(i = 1,2,\ldots,k\ ;\ j = 1,2,\ldots,2^n-1)$.

Let $[j]$ be the marked binary number j of length n and $[j]^R$ be the reversed word of it.

Then we define (for this proof) the word

$$\& [0]^R \# [0] \& [1]^R a_{11} [1] \& [2]^R a_{12} [2] \& \ldots$$
$$\ldots [2^n - 1]^R a_{1,2^n-1} [2^n - 1] \& [0]^R \# [0] \& [1]^R a_{21} [1] \& \ldots\ldots$$
$$\ldots\ldots [2^n - 1]^R a_{k,2^n-1} [2^n - 1] \& [0]^R \# [0] \&$$

to be <u>an accepting computation</u> of the Turing machine M with input x .

To define a transformation from the language accepted by M in the set of semi-extended regular expressions which do not describe Σ^* , we map each input x of M in an expression E describing the complement of the accepting computations of the Turing machine M with input x . With our code of computations this can be done in a straightforward way, by enumerating the mistakes which imply that a word is not a computation of M with input x . Each mistake is described by a semi-extended regular expression E_i and $E = \bigcup_{i=1}^{10} E_i$.

The possible mistakes are:

1. Two symbols with distance n + 1 do not match.

$$E_1 = \Sigma^* (\bigcup_{\sigma \in \Sigma} \sigma\ \Sigma^n(\Sigma\text{-match}(\sigma)))\Sigma^*$$

with match (σ) defined by

σ	match(σ)
$0,\underline{0},1,\underline{1}$	$\{0,\underline{0},1,\underline{1}\}$
&	$S \cup T \cup \{\#\}$
$\sigma \in S \cup T \cup \{\#\}$	$\{\&\}$

2. The word does not start correctly.

$$E_2 = (\Sigma \cup \lambda)^{n+1} \cup (\Sigma - \{\&\})\Sigma^*$$
$$\cup\ \Sigma\ (\Sigma \cup \lambda)^{n-1}\ (\Sigma - \{\underline{0}\})\Sigma^*$$
$$\cup\ \Sigma^{n+1}\ (\Sigma - \{\#\})\Sigma^*$$

So all words in $\Sigma^* - L(E_2)$ start with $\&\ \underline{0}^n \#$

3. The word does not end correctly. E_3 is symmetric to E_2 .

4. A subword of length $\le 2n+1$ with an a_{ij} or $\#$ in the middle is not symmetric:

Let $SY_0 = \{\#\} \cup S \cup T$

$$SY_{j+1} = \Sigma\ SY_j \Sigma \cup SY_0 \quad \text{for } j \in N.$$

Then $E_4 = \Sigma^* (SY_n \cap \bigcup_{\sigma\in\Sigma} \sigma\,\Sigma^*(\Sigma - \{\sigma\}))\Sigma^*$

5. A binary number is not correctly marked.

$$E_5 = \Sigma^* (S \cup T \cup \{\#\})(0 \cup 1 \cup \underline{0} \cup \underline{1})^* [(0 \cup 1)(\underline{0} \cup \&) \cup (\underline{0} \cup \underline{1})(\underline{1} \cup 0 \cup 1)]\Sigma^*$$

6. A subword of length $2n+1$ with & in the middle is not of the form $[j] \& [j+1]^R$ with $0 \le j \le 2^n - 1$ and addition mod 2^n.

$$E_6 = \Sigma^* \, (CN_n \cap \bigcup_{\sigma \in \{0,1,\underline{0},\underline{1}\}} \sigma \, \Sigma^* (\Sigma - succ(\sigma)))\Sigma^*$$

with $CN_0 = \&$

$$CN_{j+1} = \Sigma \; CN_j \; \Sigma \cup CN_0 \quad \text{for } j \in N$$

and $succ(0) = succ(\underline{0}) = \{0, \underline{1}\}$

$succ(1) = succ(\underline{1}) = \{1, \underline{0}\}$

The remaining mistakes are:

7. # or [0] appear not only as a pair #[0] .

8. The initial ID is wrong.

9. A computation step is wrong, i.e. two triples $a_{ij-1}\; a_{ij}\; a_{ij+1}$ and $a_{i+1,j-1}\; a_{i+1,j}\; a_{i+1,j+1}$ are not in the relation "Next". All pairs of such triples are found, because a_{ij} is to the left of $[j]$, $a_{i+1,j}$ is to the right of $[j]^R$, and there is exactly one # between them.

10. No ID is accepting.

The reader can find similar expressions for these mistakes.

As in the previous theorem the length of the expression $E = \bigcup E_i$ is $O(n)$ and the transformation from an input to the corresponding expression E can be computed on a Turing machine without using the work tapes. □

Corollary

The inequivalence problem for semi-extended regular expressions is $\le_{\text{log-lin}}$-complete in EXPSPACE.

5. Regular-like expressions over a one letter alphabet

Known results are:

a) $INEQ(\{0\},\{\cup,\cdot,\neg\}) \in P$

b) $INEQ(\{0\},\{\cup,\cdot,*\})$ is NP-complete

c) $INEQ(\{0\},\{\cup,\cdot,{}^2,\neg\})$ is POLYSPACE-complete

d) $INEQ(\{0\},\{\cup,\cdot,*,\neg,{}^2\}) \in$ EXPSPACE

b) is proved and c) is claimed in Stockmeyer and Meyer [1973]. In both cases, the lower bound is difficult.

d) follows from the fact that there is a bound for the length of the initial segment and the period (of the described ultimately periodic languages) which is only squared with each operation. A double exponential time bound is implicit in Rangel [1974].

We extend the list by

e) NE $(\{0\},\{\cup,\cdot,*,\cap\})$ is NP-complete

f) INEQ $(\{0\},\{\cup,\cdot,*,\cap,^2\}) \in$ POLYSPACE

The proof of the upper bound in e) is not presented here. The lower bound is very similar to the lower bound of b). f) is the next theorem.
Open problems suggest themself by the incompleteness of the list.

For regular-like expressions E over a one letter alphabet, let $i(E)$ be the length of the shortest initial segment and let $p(E)$ be the length of the shortest period of the language $L(E)$. I.e. $i(E) \geq 0$ and $p(E) > 0$ are the smallest integers such that for all $j \geq i(E)$ $0^j \in L(E) \Leftrightarrow 0^{j+p(E)} \in L(E)$.

For $i_j \geq i(E_j)$, and p_j a positive multiple of $p(E_j)$ $(j=1,2)$, we define i and p by the following table (depending on E, i_j and p_j).

E	i	p
$E_1 \cup E_2$, $E_1 \cap E_2$	$\max(i_1,i_2)$	$\mathrm{lcm}(p_1,p_2)$
E_1E_2	$i_1+i_2+\mathrm{lcm}(p_1,p_2)$	$\mathrm{lcm}(p_1,p_2)$
E_1^2	$2i_1+p_1$	p_1
E_1^* for $L(E_1)$ infinite	$(i_1+p_1)p_1/p(E_1^*)$	p_1
E_1^* for $L(E_1)$ finite	$i_1^2 / p(E_1^*)$	$p(E_1^*)$

i is an initial segment length and p is a period of $L(E)$ (maybe not the smallest). ($\mathrm{lcm}\ (s,t)$ is the least common multiple of s and t.)

Lemma 1

For E equal to $E_1 \cup E_2$, $E_1 \cap E_2$, E_1E_2 or E_1^2 we have $i(E) \leq i$ and $p(E) | p$.
This Lemma can be checked easily.

Lemma 2

For $E = E_1^*$ and $L(E_1)$ infinite, p is a positive multiple of $p(E_1^*)$ and $i(E_1^*) \leq i$.

Proof

The smallest period $p(E_1^*)$ of $L(E_1^*)$ is the greatest common divisor of all lengths of words in $L(E_1)$. Furthermore $L(E_1^*)$ is contained in $P = \{0^{jp(E_1)} \mid j \in N\}$ and $P - L(E_1^*)$ is finite.

Let 0^k be any word of $L(E_1)$ with $i_1 < k \leq i_1 + p_1$, and let E_2 be $0^k(0^{p_1})^*E_1{}^*$. Then $L(E_2) \subseteq L(E_1^*) \subseteq P$ and $P - L(E_2)$ is finite too. Therefore $i(E_2) \geq i(E_1^*)$.
So it is enough to show that $i = (i_1+p_1)p_1/p(E_1^*) \geq i(E_2)$. If $0^j \in L(E_2)$ then also $0^{j+p_1} \in L(E_2)$. We want to investigate, where words of new lengths modulo p_1

come to the set L(E).

Let S be the set of new word lengths modulo p_1 in $L(E_2)$, i.e.

$$S = \{j \mid 0^j \in L(E_2) \text{ but } 0^{j-p_1} \notin L(E_2)\}$$

Then S has the properties:

1) $k \in S$ and the difference between any two adjacent elements of the ordered set S is less than $i_1 + p_1$.

2) $|S| = p_1/p(E_1^*)$

To see property 1), assume $j \in S$ and $j \neq k$.

$0^j \in L(E_2)$ and $j \neq k$ imply that there exist j_1, j_2, j_3 with

a) $j = j_1 + j_2 + j_3$

b) $j_1 = k + np_1$ for some $n \in N$

c) $0^{j_2} \in L(E_1^*)$

d) $0^{j_3} \in L(E_1)$ and $j_3 > 0$

$j \in S$ and b) imply $j_1 = k$

$j \in S$ and c) imply $k + j_2 \in S$

$j \in S$ and d) imply $j_3 - p_1 \notin L(E_1)$ and therefore

$j_3 \leq i_1 + p_1$.

Hence we have shown, if $j \in S$ then either $j = k$ or there exists j_2 with $k + j_2 \in S$ and $1 \leq j - (k+j_2) \leq i_1 + p_1$.

Property 2) of S follows from the definition of S, and the fact that modulo p_1 exactly the multiples of $p(E_1^*)$ appear as word lengths in $L(E_2)$.

The properties 1) and 2) of S imply that

$$i(E_2) \leq k + (|S|-1)(i_1 + p_1) \leq |S|(i_1 + p_1) \leq (i_1 + p_1)\, p_1/p(E_1^*)$$

□

<u>Lemma 3</u>

For $E = E_1^*$ and $L(E_1)$ finite $p(E_1^*) \leq \max(i_1, 1)$ and $i(E_1^*) \leq 2i$.

<u>Proof</u>

The Lemma is trivial for $L(E_1) \subseteq \{\lambda\}$. Otherwise choose p_2 such that $0 < p_2 \leq i_1$ and $0^{p_2} \in L(E_1)$. Let E_2 be $(0^{p_2})^* E_1$. Then $L(E_2^*) = L(E_1^*)$, but $L(E_2)$ is infinite with $p(E_2) \leq p_2 \leq i(E_1)$ and $i(E_2) \leq i(E_1)$. Now Lemma 2 is applied to E_2. (A direct proof would give the bound $i = i_1^2 / p(E_1^*)$ (instead of 2i) for $i(E_1^*)$.

We want to show that $i(E)$ and $p(E)$ are bounded by $2^{c|E|}$. But the star operation makes difficulties in our induction proof. E.g. for $L(E) = \{0^j, 0^{j+1}\}, i(E^*) \approx (i(E))^2$. We avoid these difficulties by proving bounds for the product $i(E)p(E)$.

Lemma 4

If E is an expression with the operators $\{\cup,\cdot,*,\cap,^2\}$ over the alphabet $\{0\}$ then

$p(E) \le 2^{\frac{1}{2}|E|}$ and $i(E)p(E) \le 2^{|E|}$.

Proof

The induction step for $f(E) \le c^{|E|}$ is to show for each unary operation op_1 and each binary operation op_2:

$$f(E_1^{op}) \le c\, f(E_1)$$

$$f(E_1 \text{ op } E_2) \le c\, f(E_1) f(E_2)$$

This is trivial, except for the case "E_1^* for $L(E_1)$ finite", where the induction does not go through and a separate proof is necessary. But this problem has a surprisingly elegant solution.

Every ultimately periodic language L can be represented by three sets P,A,B, where P is periodic, A and B are disjunct finite sets and $L = (P-B) \cup A$. Let $\max(A)$ be the length ℓ of the longest word 0^ℓ in L. By induction on the structure of a regular-like expression E (without $\neg$), it is easy to see that $\max(A) \le 2^{|E|}$ (for A corresponding to $L(E)$). Without the operation ^{2}, $\max(A)$ is even less than n. □

Problem: Can $\max(B)$ grow faster than $2^{|E|}$? Otherwise the upper bound of Theorem 3 would hold for the operation $\neg$ too.

Theorem 3

$\text{INEQ}(\{0\}, \{\cup,\cdot,*,\cap,^2\})$ is in POLYSPACE.

Proof

If $L(E_1) \nsubseteq L(E_2)$ then an integer $k \le \max(i(E_1),i(E_2)) + \text{lcm}(p(E_1),p(E_2))$ exists such that $0^k \in L(E_1) - L(E_2)$. By Lemma 4, $k \le 2^n$ (for $n = |E_1| + |E_2|$).

An $O(n^2)$ time bounded alternating Turing machine (see Chandra and Stockmeyer [1976] or Kozen [1976]) can guess a binary representation of such a k and check if it has this property. The only difficult case is to check for a number p and a subexpression E^* if $0^p \in L(E^*)$. This is done by

```
if p = 0 then accept and stop
guess an exponent e = 2^j < 2p such that 0^p ∈ L((E ∪ λ)^e)
for i := j down to 1 do
        choose universally q with 0 ≤ q ≤ p
        choose universally p := q or p := p - q
if p = 0 then accept and stop
check if 0^p ∈ L(E)
```

Note: To guess q with $0^q \in L(E)$ and $0^{p-q} \in L(E^*)$ needs too much time. □

6. Equivalence to a fixed language

Theorem 4

SINEQ $(\{0,1\}, L_0)$ is

a) CSL-complete for L_0 finite

b) POLYSPACE-complete for L_0 infinite but bounded (Definition in Section 2).

c) $\leq_{\text{log-lin}}$-complete in EXPSPACE for L_0 unbounded.

Proof

Let E_0, $\bar{E}_0$ be semi-extended regular expressions with $L(E_0) = L_0$ and $L(\bar{E}_0) = \{0,1\}^* - L_0$.

From $L(0^*E \cup E_0) \neq L_0 \Leftrightarrow L(E) \neq \emptyset$ and Theorem 1 follows that all three cases (except for $L_0 = \{0,1\}^*$) are CSL-hard. Also the containment problem $L(E) \subseteq L_0$ is CSL-hard.

The EXPSPACE lower bound for L_0 unbounded follows from Theorem 2 and the fact that an unbounded L_0 contains a homomorphic image of $\{0,1\}^*$. This method was used by Hunt, Rosenkvantz and Szymanski [1976] to show that the same problem for regular expressions is CSL-hard.

To get the upper bounds, we use $L(E) \neq L_0 \Leftrightarrow L(E) \nsubseteq L_0 \vee L_0 \nsubseteq L(E)$ and give upper bounds for both containment problems.

From $L(E) \nsubseteq L_0 \Leftrightarrow L(E \cap \bar{E}_0) \neq \emptyset$ and Theorem 1 follows that the first containment problem is in CSL for all L_0. The upper bounds of $L_0 \nsubseteq L(E)$ depend on L_0.

a) $\{E \mid L_0 \nsubseteq L(E)\} \in P$ for L_0 finite by Stockmeyer and Meyer [1973]. To test membership of a word x in the language described by a regular-like expression, a list of all memberships of subwords of x in languages described by subexpressions is built bottom-up.

c) From $L_0 \nsubseteq L(E) \Leftrightarrow L(E \cup \bar{E}_0) \neq \{0,1\}^*$ and Theorem 2 follows the EXPSPACE upper bound.

b) This is by far the most difficult part, and only the main points are sketched here. The bounded language L_0 is contained in $w_1^* \ldots w_k^*$ with $w_i = a_{i1} \ldots a_{i\ell_i}$.

We call $L \cap a_{ij}\, a_{ij+1} \ldots a_{i\ell_i}\, w_i^* w_{i+1}^* \ldots w_{i'-1}^* w_{i'}^* a_{i'1}, \ldots a_{i'j'}$ the (i,j,i',j')-part of the language L. For all subexpressions E' of E, all parts of $L(E')$ are represented by the corresponding set of $(i'-i+1)$-tuples of exponents for $w_i, \ldots, w_{i'}$. These sets of $(i'-i+1)$-tuples are ultimately periodic, and in a way similar to Theorem 3, it is shown that the initial segment length and periods are not too big (only $2^{c|E|\log|E|}$).

Difficult to handle are those operations which involve more than one part of the language, namely the concatenation and especially the Kleene star. Here Kleene's method of constructing a regular expression from a finite automaton is used to get a survey of all possible decompositions of one part of L(E*) in finitely many parts of L(E). □

Open problem

What is the complexity of the containment problem $\{E \mid E$ is a semi-extended regular expression with $L_0 \not\subseteq L(E)\}$ for L_0 infinite but bounded? The upper bound is polynomial space, the lower bound is nondeterministic polynomial time.

This problem is closely related to the easier problem about the complexity of $INEQ(\{0\},\{\cup,\cdot,*,\cap\})$ (also between NP and POLYSPACE).

References

Aho, A.V., J.E. Hopcroft and J.D. Ullman, "The Design and Analysis of Computer Algorithms", Addison-Wesley, Reading, Mass., 1974.

Chandra, A.K. and L.J. Stockmeyer, "Alternation", Proc. 17th Annual IEEE Symposium on Foundations of Comp. Sci., 98-108, 1976.

Fürer, M., "Non-elementary lower bounds in automata theory", (in German), Diss. ETH 6122 (Ph.D. Thesis), Zürich, 1978.

Hopcroft, J.E., W.J. Paul and L.G. Valiant, "On Time Versus Space", Journal of the Association for Computing Machinery 24, 332-337, 1977.

Hunt III, H.B., "The equivalence problem for regular expressions with intersection is not polynomial in tape", Tech. Report TR 73-161, Dept. of Computer Science, Cornell University, 1973.

Hunt III, H.B., D.J. Rosenkrantz and T.G. Szymanski, "On the Equivalence, Containment, and Covering Problems for the Regular and Context-Free Languages", J. of Computer and System Sciences 12, 222-268, 1976.

Kozen, D., "On parallelism in Turing machines", Proc. 17th Annual IEEE Symposium on Foundations of Comp. Sci., 89-97, 1976.

Meyer, A.R. and L.J. Stockmeyer, "The equivalence problem for regular expressions with squaring requires exponential space", Proc. 13th Annual IEEE Symposium on Switching and Automata Theory, 125-129, 1972.

Rangel, J.L. "The Equivalence Problem for Regular Expressions over One Letter is Elementary", 15th Annual Symposium on Switching and Automata Theory, 24-27,1974.

Sieferas, J.I., M.J. Fischer and A.R. Meyer, "Refinements of the Nondeterministic Time and Space Hierarchies", Proc. 14th Annual IEEE Symposium on Switching and Automata Theory, 130-137, 1973.

Stockmeyer, L.J., "The complexity of decision problems in automata theory and logic". Report TR-133, M.I.T., Project MAC, Cambridge, Mass., 1974.

Stockmeyer, L.J. and A.R. Meyer, "Word Problems Requiring Exponential Time: Preliminary Report", Proc. 5th Annual ACM Symposium on the Theory of Computing, 1-9, 1973.

AN ALMOST LINEAR TIME ALGORITHM FOR COMPUTING A DEPENDENCY BASIS IN A RELATIONAL DATA BASE

Zvi Galil

Department of Mathematical Sciences
Computer Science Division
Tel Aviv University
Tel Aviv, Israel

ABSTRACT: We describe an algorithm that constructs for a given set of (functional and multivalued) dependencies Σ and a set of attributes X, the dependency basis of X. The algorithm runs in time $O(\min(k,\log p)|\Sigma|)$, where p is the number of sets in the dependency basis of X and k is the number of dependencies in Σ. A variant of the algorithm tests whether a dependency σ is implied by Σ in time $O(\min(k,\log \bar{p})|\Sigma|)$, where $\bar{p}$ is the number of sets in the dependency basis of the left-hand side of σ that intersect the right-hand side of σ. Whenever all the dependencies in $\Sigma \cup \{\sigma\}$ are functional dependencies these algorithms are linear time.[††]

[†]The work reported in this paper was done while the author visited the IBM San Jose Research Laboratory.

[††]logx will stand for $\max(1,\log_2 x)$.

1. INTRODUCTION

The relational model for data bases uses dependencies to express constraints that the data must satisfy. The most common type of dependencies are the functional and multivalued dependencies. Two computational problems that deal with these dependencies are:

Problem 1: Given a set of dependencies Σ and a set of attributes X, construct the dependency basis of X.

Problem 2 (Membership Test): Given a set of dependencies Σ and a dependency σ , find whether Σ implies σ.

Solutions to these problems (especially the first one) are useful in designing relation data base schemes in certain normal forms. (A data base scheme is often required to be in normal form in order to avoid certain anomalies.) Problem 2 is an easier problem, because given a solution to Problem 1 one can solve Problem 2 in linear time.

In Ref. 1, Beeri gives an $O(|\Sigma|^4)$ algorithm that solves Problem 1, where $|\Sigma|$ is the length of Σ. It was later refined by four Japanese[5] to an $O(\min\{k^2|U|,|\Sigma|^2)$ algorithm, where U is the set of attributes in Σ, $|U|$ is the size of U, and k is the number of dependencies in Σ. Recently, Sagiv[7] used a somewhat different approach and solved Problem 2 in time $O(|\Sigma||Y|)$ where Y is the right-hand side of σ. He also used this solution to derive an $O(|\Sigma|p)$ algorithm for Problem 1, where p is the number of sets in the dependency basis of X. These last time bounds are incomparable. In the worst case (and in many other cases) Sagiv's algorithm is better because it is $O(|\Sigma||U|)$ compared to $O(|\Sigma|^2)$ in the case of the four Japanese. But both algorithms are essentially quadratic. Note that in the very special case that k is a small constant, the four Japanese algorithm is linear.

In this paper we first give an $O(\min(k,\log p)|\Sigma|)$ algorithm for solving Problem 1. Its worst case is $O(|\Sigma|\log|U|)$ and is superior to the previous algorithms. It is never worse than the other algorithms. (Note that $k^2|U|\geq k|\Sigma|$.) It ties the four Japanese algorithm only in the very special case when k is constant (in which cases both are linear), and it ties Sagiv's algorithm only in the very special case when p is constant (in which case both are linear).

In the restricted case when only functional dependencies occur, a very simple linear time algorithm is given in Ref. 3. Our algorithm has the nice feature that is not shared by the earlier algorithms; it is linear in this case. Obviously the other algorithms could be augmented so that they solve this case in linear time.

Our algorithm can be slightly modified to solve Problem 2. If the right- and left-hand sides of σ are X and Y, the modified algorithm solves Problem 2 in time $O(\min(k,\log \bar{p})|\Sigma|)$, where $\bar{p}$ is the number of sets in the dependency basis of X that have nonempty intersection with Y. This should be compared to Sagiv's $O(|\Sigma|\bar{p})$ algorithm. (Sagiv gives the bound of $O(|\Sigma||Y|)$ but the slightly better $O(|\Sigma|\bar{p})$ bound obviously holds.)

The structure of the paper is the following. Section 2 gives basic definitions and results and is borrowed almost completely from Ref. 7, where additional details and motivation can be found. In Section 3 we describe the algorithm that solves Problem 1. In Section 4 we prove some of the properties of the algorithm. Section 5 describes the modified algorithm that solves Problem 2.

2. BASIC DEFINITIONS AND RESULTS

The relational model for data bases assumes that the data is stored in tables called relations. The columns of a table correspond to attributes, and the rows to records or tuples. Each attribute has an associated domain of values. It is convenient to regard the tuples as mappings from the attributes to their domains, since no canonical ordering of the attributes is needed in this way. Given a tuple μ of a relation r and a set of attributes X, $\mu[X]$ denotes the values of μ for the attributes of X. We call $\mu[X]$ an X-value (in r). If tuples μ and ν agree on all the attributes of the set X, then we write $\mu[X] = \nu[X]$.

A relation scheme is a set of attributes labeling the columns of a table. We often use the relation scheme itself as the name of the table. A relation is just the "current value" of a relation scheme.

We use the letters A,B,C,... to denote attributes, and the letters ...,X,Y,Z to denote sets of attributes. A string of attributes (e.g., ABCD) denotes the set containing these attributes, and the union of two sets X and Y is written as XY. The set of all the attributes is denoted by U.

Example 1: Suppose that the attributes are P (part-number), Q (quantity), S (supplier), and C (city). Figure 1 shows a relation that might be a current value of the relation scheme PQSC. (Note that multiple copies of the same tuple are not allowed.) This relation represents information about parts, their quantities, the suppliers who supply these parts, and the cities in which a supplier has a distribution center. It is assumed that a supplier may have a distribution center in more than one city, and all these centers supply all the parts that are produced by the supplier.

P	Q	S	C
438	1300	Smith	New York
341	50	Smith	Chicago
438	1300	Smith	Chicago
341	50	Smith	New York
108	200	Jones	Boston
204	150	Jones	Boston

Figure 1. An example of a relation.

A <u>functional</u> <u>dependency</u> is a statement of the form $X \to Y$, where both X and Y are sets of attributes. A relation r <u>satisfies</u> the functional dependency $X \to Y$ (or $X \to Y$ <u>holds</u> in r) if and only if for all tuples μ and ν of r, if $\mu[X] = \nu[X]$, then $\mu[Y] = \nu[Y]$. That is, if tuples μ and ν agree on all the columns for X, then they also agree on all the columns for Y. Note that the functional dependency $P \to Q$ holds in the relation of Figure 1.

A <u>multivalued</u> <u>dependency</u> is a statement of the form $X \to\to Y$, where X and Y are sets of attributes. Let Z be the set of all the attributes that are neither in X nor in Y (i.e., $Z=U-X-Y$). The multivalued dependency $X \to\to Y$ <u>holds</u> in r if and only if for every XZ-value xz

$$\{y \mid \text{for some tuple } \mu \text{ in } r,\ \mu(XZ) = xz \text{ and } \mu(Y) = y\} =$$

$$= \{y \mid \text{for some tuple } \mu \text{ in } r,\ \mu(X) = x \text{ and } \mu(Y) = y\}.$$

In other words, $X \to\to Y$ means that the set of Y-values associated with a particular X-value must be independent of the values of the rest of the attributes. Note that the multivalued dependency $S \to\to PQ$ holds in the relation of Figure 1.

A dependency σ is a <u>consequence</u> of a set of dependencies Σ if for all relations r, σ holds in r if all the dependencies of Σ hold in r.

Let Σ be a set of dependencies and X be a set of attributes. Then the <u>dependency</u> <u>basis</u> of X is a partition of the set of attributes U into a pairwise disjoint subsets $W_1,\ldots,W_n$ such that (1) $X \to\to W_i$ is a consequence of Σ for all $1 \leq i \leq n$, and (2) $X \to\to Y$ is a consequence of Σ if and only if Y is a union of some of the W_i's. The existence and uniqueness of the dependency basis of X were proved in Ref. 4.

Beeri[1] made two observations that imply that any solution to the restricted version of Problem 1 or 2 that allows only multivalued dependencies can be used for the general version (allowing both dependencies) for essentially no extra cost. So without loss of generality we assume that σ is of the form $X \to\to Y$ in Problem 2. According to Beeri, the functional dependencies $S \to T$ in Σ can be replaced by $\{S \to\to A \mid A \in T\}$. We do not rewrite Σ using this transformation so that we do not unnecessarily increase the size of Σ considerably. So, Σ will contain functional dependencies.

3. THE ALGORITHM

Our algorithm implements the simple idea behind Beeri's algorithm.[1] We start with an initial partition which consists of U-X and a singleton for every attribute in X and iterate applying the following refinement rule. (We call a set in the current partition a block.) If there is a block P and a dependency $S \to\to T$ in Σ satisfying (1) $S \cap P = \phi$, and (2) $T \cap P \neq \phi$ and $T^c \cap P \neq \phi$, then split P into $P^1 = P \cap T$ and $P^2 = P \cap T^c$. The algorithm terminates when the refinement rule cannot be applied. The correctness of this method was proved in Ref. 1.

We assume that the dependencies in Σ are $\{S_i \to\to T_i\}_{i=1}^{k}$. We refer to a dependency by its index i. We say that (a dependency) i is alive with respect to (a block) P if $T_i \cap P \neq \phi$ and $T_i^c \cap P \neq \phi$, and we say that i is dead w.r.t. P otherwise. Note that if i is dead w.r.t. P, then P is contained either in T_i or in T_i^c. Consequently, i will be dead w.r.t. any subset of P. (In particular w.r.t. future blocks that are subsets of P.) We say that i is active [nonactive] w.r.t. P if it is alive w.r.t. P and in addition $P \cap S_i = \phi$ [$P \cap S_i \neq \phi$]. Note that by definition i is active w.r.t. P if and only if we can use the refinement rule with $T = T_i$. The remarks above explain why in case i is dead w.r.t. P, it will never be active w.r.t. subblocks of P. Also if there are no active dependencies w.r.t. a block P, there will be no active dependencies w.r.t. P in the future. So P will not be split any more.

The efficiency of the algorithm is due to the way we represent each block P, which we now describe. (See Figure 2.) The elements of P appear in a doubly linked list.[6] For every i which is alive w.r.t. P we maintain $P \cap T_i$ as a doubly linked list and also $P \cap S_i$ if i is nonactive w.r.t. P. These lists are doubly linked to each other, and the active i's appear first. Also for each attribute A in P we have a doubly linked list that starts in A and contains all occurrences of A in these small lists. (In Figure 2 A occurs in T_3, T_{10}, T_2 and S_4.) If i is nonactive and the i-th dependency is functional dependency, then its corresponding lists will be marked (e.g., $P \cap T_2$ and $P \cap S_2$ in Figure 2). We also maintain m_A the number of occurrences of A in these lists. Note that $m_A \leq \bar{m}_A$, where $\bar{m}_A$ is the number of occurrences of A in Σ. We also maintain $m_P = \sum_{A \in P} m_A$. We will also have a queue of blocks. The queue will contain all blocks P that have at least one active i w.r.t. P. The total space required is $O(|\Sigma|)$ because since P is a block in a

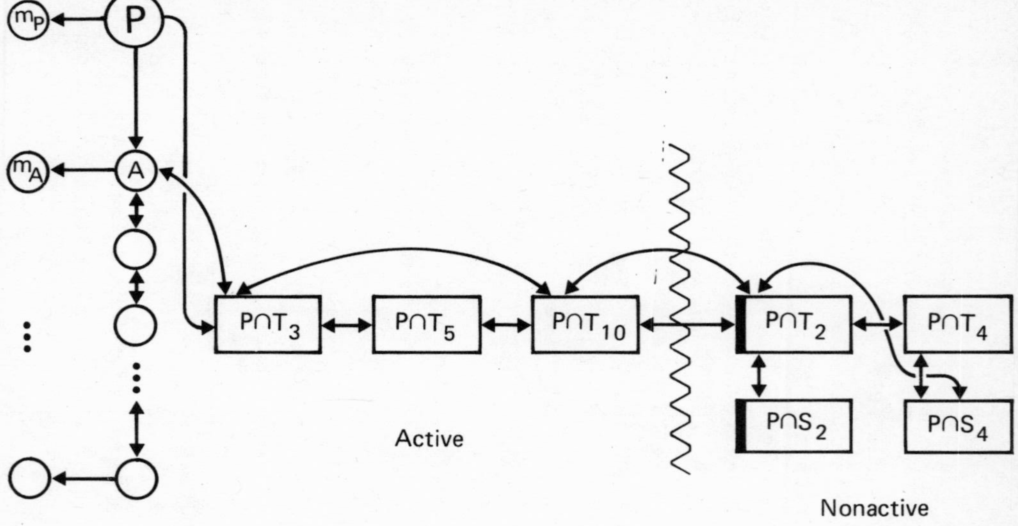

Figure 2. The construct that corresponds to P

partition, an occurrence of an attribute in Σ is represented in at most one construct that corresponds to some block P.

Initially we have only one clock namely U-X (the singletons can be ignored) and the structure above can be easily initialized using one pass over Σ. The complete algorithm now follows.

1. Initialize the construct corresponding to U-X.
2. Insert U-X into queue.
3. While queue is nonempty do 4-10.
4. Let P be the first block in queue.
5. Delete P from queue.
6. If there is an active i w.r.t. P do 7-10.
7. Use $P \cap T_i$ to split P into $P^1 = P \cap T_i$ and $P^2 = P \cap T_i^c$ and to compute m_{P1} and m_{P2}.
8. Without loss of generality let $m_{P1} \leq m_{P2}$. (Otherwise exchange P^1 and P^2 below.).
9. Delete the elements of P^1 from the construct that corresponds to P while generating the construct corresponding to P^1 and P^2. (The latter is what is left of the construct corresponding to P.)
10. Insert P^1 and P^2 into queue.

In step 9 we must watch for the following possibilities. If j is alive w.r.t. P it can be dead w.r.t. one of P^1 and P^2. j is dead w.r.t. P^k ($k \in \{1,2\}$) if $P^k \cap T_j = \phi$ or if $P^k \cap T_j^c = \phi$. The first case is taken care of automatically by deleting empty sets. The second case is taken care of my maintaining $|P \cap T_j|$ and testing if $|P^k| = |P^k \cap T_j|$. This equality holds if and only if $P^k \cap T_j^c = \phi$, and in this case $P^k \cap T_j$ is deleted from the construct that corresponds to P^k. Similarly a non-active j w.r.t. P can become active w.r.t. one of P^1 and P^2 (i.e., $P^1 \cap S_j$ or $P^2 \cap S_j$ becomes empty). In this case we have to move $P^1 \cap T_j$ (or $P^2 \cap T_j$) to the active part. If j becomes active and the j-th dependency is a functional dependency, then instead of moving $P \cap T_j$ to the active part we put every attribute in $P \cap T_j$ as a singleton in the active part. (Recall that the j-th dependency is just a short notation for the dependencies $S_j \twoheadrightarrow A$ for every A in T_j.) Step 9 can be implemented so that it requires only $O(m_{P1})$ time. The details are left to the reader.

4. SOME PROPERTIES OF THE ALGORITHM

Theorem 1: The algorithm is correct and has running time $O(\min(k,\log p)|\Sigma|)$.

Proof: The correctness of the algorithm is obvious. As for the running time, except for step 9 the total time of the other steps is $O(|\Sigma|)$. In particular step 7 costs $|P\cap T_i|$. To compute the total cost of step 7 we charge a cost of one to the occurrence of each A in $P\cap T_i$. The total charge is $O(\sum|T_i|) = O(|\Sigma|)$ since each occurrence is charged at most once, because i is dead w.r.t. P^1 and P^2.

The cost of step 9 is bounded by cm_{P1}, where c is a constant. Let f(P) be total cost of step 9 in computing the sets of the basis that cover P. It follows that (1) $f(P)\leq cm_{P1}+f(P^1)+f(P^2)$. Assume the number of sets in the basis that cover P, P^1 and P^2 is p, p_1 and p_2, respectively. We show by induction that $f(P) \leq cm_P\log p$. The basis of the induction follows by choosing an appropriate constant c. If $p_1 \leq p_2$ then $f(P)\leq cm_{P1}\log 2p_1+cm_{P2}\log p_2\leq cm_P\log p$ (since $2p_1\leq p$ and $m_{P1}+m_{P2}\leq m_P$). Otherwise $p_1\geq p_2$ and since $m_{P1}\leq m_{P2}$,

$f(P)\leq cm_{P2}+cm_{P1}\log p_1+cm_{P2}\log p_2\leq cm_{P1}\log p_1+cm_{P2}\log 2p_2\leq cm_P\log p$.

Since we start with P=U-X and $m_P\leq|\Sigma|$ we derive that $f(P)\leq c|\Sigma|\log p$. To show that the time is bounded by $k|\Sigma|$ we compute it differently. Assume i is a multivalued dependency and we split a block P according to T_i. The cost of step 9 is bounded by $c\bar{m}_{P1}$ and is now computed by charging a cost of c to each occurrence in Σ of an attribute A, $A\in P^1$. We say that each occurrence is charged due to i. Now, each occurrence is charged at most once due to a fixed i. This is because after the charge i is dead w.r.t. P^1 and P^2 and w.r.t. any of their future subblocks. Therefore each occurrence can be charged at most k times and the total charge is bounded by $ck|\Sigma|$. The total cost of splitting according to functional dependencies is $O(|\Sigma|)$. This follows from the proof of Theorem 2 below. □

Theorem 2: If Σ contains only functional dependencies the algorithm runs in time $O(|\Sigma|)$.

Proof: In this case if i is active w.r.t. P, then $P\cap T_i = \{A\}$. The cost of step 9 is bounded by cm_A, and is charged to A. No attribute is charged twice because from now on every dependency j is dead w.r.t. the new block {A}. Therefore the total cost is bounded by $c\sum_A m_A\leq c|\Sigma|$. □

Obviously for the special case allowing functional dependencies only, the algorithm of Ref. 3 will have a smaller constant because our algorithm is designed for the more general case.

5. AN ALGORITHM FOR MEMBERSHIP TEST

We make several small changes in the previous algorithm to give a solution for Problem 2. For every block P we maintain $|P|$ and $|P \cap Y|$. We change the algorithm so it finds only the sets in the basis that have nonempty intersection with Y. In step 5 when we delete a block P from the queue (i.e., we know that P will not be refined) we compare $|P|$ and $|P \cap Y|$ and if these differ we stop with a negative answer. (Y is not covered exactly by sets of the basis.) We also delete from the queue in step 5 if $|P \cap Y| = 0$. Also we add step 11 that announces a positive answer.

Theorem 3: The modified algorithm correctly solves Problem 2 and runs in time $O(\min(k, \log \bar{p})|\Sigma|)$.

Proof: Correctness if immediate. The bound $k|\Sigma|$ holds as for the original algorithm. To prove the other bound we need (as before) to compute the total cost of step 9. We distinguish between two types of splits. A split is of type 1 if $P^1 \cap Y = \phi$ or $P^2 \cap Y = \phi$, and a split is of type 2 otherwise. Assume the split is of type 1 and $P^j \cap Y = \phi$, $j \in \{1,2\}$. The cost of the split is bounded by cm_{P^j} and each occurrence of an attribute of P^j in Σ is charged by c. The total charge is $O(|\Sigma|)$ because P^j is going to be deleted from queue and the occurrences of its attributes will not be charged again. The total cost of type 2 splits is $O(|\Sigma| \log \bar{p})$. It follows immediately from the following observation: Inequality (1) of the previous section holds for type 2 splits and a similar inductive proof follows by focussing attention to type 2 splits only. □

Finally we make some remarks on Sagiv's solution of Problem 2. It is the first solution that solves Problem 2 directly without finding first the basis. He uses an elegant way to represent multivalued dependencies as propositional formulas that was described in Ref. 8. However, once you replace the propositional logic in Sagiv's algorithm by the corresponding original objects it turns out that Sagiv's algorithm FIND(B), that finds the set of the basis that contains B, is just applying Beeri's refinement rule always keeping the block that contains B. (More specifically the only change is to replace the condition "S is true" by "$W \cap S = \phi$".) Moreover, the use of propositional logic in this case is unnecessary (except to make the proof self contained) and as a result the correctness proof in Ref. 7 is quite long. In comparison, without the use of propositional logic, a correctness proof immediately follows from the correctness proof of Beeri's algorithm.[1] That is not to say that the approach using propositional logic is not useful. Possibly, using it one may come up with a linear time algorithm for Problem 2.

ACKNOLWEDGMENT

The author is indebted to Ron Fagin for introducing him to the subject of relational data bases and for many discussions.

REFERENCES

1. C. Beeri, "On the Membership Problem for Multivalued Dependencies in Relational Databases," to appear in ACM Trans. on Database Systems.
2. C. Beeri, "On the Role of Data Dependencies of Relational Database Schemas," Report No. 43, Dept. of Comp. Sci., The Hebrew University, Jerusalem, Israel, January 1979.
3. C. Beeri and P.A. Bernstein, "Computational Problems Related to the Design of Normal Form Relational Schemas," ACM Trans. on Database Systems, Vol. 4, No. 1 (March 1979), pp. 30-59.
4. R. Fagin, "Multivalued Dependencies and a New Normal Form for Relational Databases," ACM Trans. on Database Systems, Vol. 2, No. 3 (September 1977), pp. 262-278.
5. K. Hagihara, M. Ito, K. Taniguchi and T. Kasami, "Decision Problems for Multivalued Dependencies in Relational Databases," SIAM J. Computing, Vol. 8, No. 2 (May 1979), pp. 247-264.
6. D.E. Knuth, The Art of Computer Programming: Fundamental Algorithms, Vol. 1, Addison-Wesley, Reading, Massachusetts, 1968.
7. Y. Sagiv, "An Algorithm for Inferring Multivalued Dependencies with an Application to Propositional Logic," Manuscript, Department of Computer Science, University of Illinois at Urbana-Champaign, to appear in JACM.
8. Y. Sagiv and R. Fagin, "An Equivalence Between Relational Database Dependencies and a Subclass of Propositional Logic," IBM Research Report RJ2500, March 1979.

BIPOLAR SYNCHRONIZATION SYSTEMS

H.J. Genrich and P.S. Thiagarajan
Institut für Informationssystemforschung (ISF)
Gesellschaft für Mathematik und Datenverarbeitung
Schloss Birlinghoven, D-5205 St.Augustin 1

0. Introduction

C. A. Petri initiated the net theory of systems and processes with his doctoral dissertation in 1962 [1]. Since then, various concepts, tools and techniques have been added to this theory [2]. The study of systems within this formal approach is based on the Condition-Event systems model. (A related but quite different entity is the well known Petri net model.) The Condition-Event system model provides the most detailed and basic representation of systems that are the objects of study in net theory. In practice, a variety of net based models will have to be defined in order to obtain descriptions of systems at different levels of detail and to represent different aspects of system behaviour. Place-Transition systems, information flow graphs, channel-agency systems and predicate-transition systems are - to name a few - some of the net models that have been so far proposed and investigated. One of the key ideas of net theory is that it is as important to inter-relate the various net based models as it is to formulate them in the first place. The formal basis for developing such inter-relationships is provided by (net) morphism diagrams within a suitably chosen category of nets. The role of the Condition-Event system model is then to serve as a connecting bridge, when necessary.

With this background in mind, we present here a net based model called bipolar synchronization systems. We have formulated this model in order to isolate and study an important organizational principle which is often - implicitly or explicitly - employed in the construction and use of complex information processing systems. This principle consists of recognizing that the absence of effects, signals and entities can be frequently used together with the presence of effects, signals and entities to achieve the desired coordination among a group of concurrently acting agents. Consequently, we will, in our model, explicitly represent the executions of the actions that are committed due to the outcome of a decision and the non-executions of the actions that are omitted due to the outcome of a decision. In fact, we will go one step further and demand that in our systems, the executions of the actions that are commissioned by a decision be synchronized with the non-executions of the actions that are omitted (because of the decision), before this decision is permitted to be made again. Since ours is a preliminary attempt in this direction, we have carried out our study for a class of systems which exhibit a rather restricted form of decision-making capability and concurrency in their behaviour.

The contents of this paper have have been presented at the Advanced Course on General Net Theory of Systems and Processes and is part of the (unreviewed) course material of this course [2].

1. The Model

Our model is founded upon the notion of a live and safe marked graph. The theory of marked graphs is well understood as evidenced in [3,4,5]. We will, for most parts, assume the main results concerning marked graphs.

Definition: A directed graph is a quadruple $G=(V,A;Q,Z)$ where:

1) V is a finite set of nodes
2) A is a finite set of arcs ($V \cap A = \emptyset$)
3) $Q:A \to V$ and $Z:A \to V$ are the source and target functions respectively.

In diagrams we will represent the nodes as boxes. If $a \in A$, $Q(a)=v_1$ and $Z(a)=v_2$ then we will draw a directed arc from v_1 to v_2 labelled with the symbol a. Let $v \in V$. Then,

$I(v)=\{a \in A \mid Z(a)=v\}$ is the set of input arcs of v.

$O(v)=\{a \in A \mid Q(a)=v\}$ is the set of output arcs of v.

We will represent directed paths as a sequence of arcs and assume standard terminology concerning directed circuits, directed elementary circuits etc. In fact, we will have little occasion to deal with undirected paths as such. Hence we shall from now on drop the qualifying "directed" where ever it is clear from the context that it is a directed entity under consideration.

Definition: A marked graph is a 5-tuple $MG=(V,A;Q,Z,M)$ where:

1) $(V,A;Q,Z)$ is a directed graph.
2) $M: A \to \{0,1,2,...\}$ is the initial marking of MG.

Let MG=(V,A;Q,Z,M) be a marked graph and $a \in A$. If M(a)=k, then a is said to carry k tokens under M. In diagrams we will indicate this by placing k tokens on a. Let $\Pi=a_1,a_2,..,a_n$ be a path. Then $M(\Pi)=M(a_1)+M(a_2)+..+M(a_n)$. Π is said to be a token free path at M if $M(\Pi)=0$.

Let Π be an elementary circuit of MG. Then Π is called a basic circuit of MG if $M(\Pi)=1$. Basic circuits play a crucial role in the development of our results.

The initial marking of a marked graph can be transformed into a new marking through node firings. Crudely stated, a node can fire at M, whenever every one of its input arcs carries at least one token. When a node fires, one token is removed from each of its input arcs and one token is added to each of its output arcs to yield a new marking. If the set of markings thus reached is 'strongly connected' w.r.t. node firability (for every node) then the marked graph is said to be live . If every marking reached through node firings puts at most one token on every arc then the marked graph is called safe. The results of this paper depend heavily on the following well known characterization of live and safe marked graphs.

Theorem: (See [3,4]) Let MG=(V,A;Q,Z,M) be a marked graph. MG is live and safe iff

1) For every elementary circuit Π of MG, $M(\Pi)>0$,

2) For every $a \in A$, a is contained in a basic circuit of MG.

In this paper we will deal with (live and) safe marked graphs only. Let MG be a safe marked graph and let [M> denote the set of markings reached,starting from M, through node firings. Since MG is safe, $\forall a \in A$ and $\forall M' \in [M>$, M'(a)=0 or M'(a)=1. Hence we can view M' as a subset of (marked) arcs. In other words,
$M'=\{a \in A | M'(a)=1\}$.

From now on we will adopt this convention for dealing with markings. We obtain our model by extending the concept of a live and safe marked graph along two directions. Essentially, we shall distinguish between two types of nodes and introduce two types of tokens.

Definition: A bipolar synchronization graph (bp-graph) is a 5-tuple $BP = (V_\nabla, V_\&, A; Q, Z)$ where:

1) $V_\nabla \cup V_\& \neq \emptyset$ and $V_\nabla \cap V_\& = \emptyset$

2) $(V_\nabla \cup V_\&, A; Q, Z)$ is a directed graph.

V_∇ is the set of <u>∇-nodes</u> and $V_\&$ is the set of &-nodes.

<u>Defintion</u>: Let $BP=(V_\nabla, V_\&, A; Q, Z)$ be a bp-graph. A <u>marking</u> of BP is an ordered pair of arcs (M_H, M_L) such that:

1) $M_H, M_L \subseteq A$ and $M_H \cap M_L = \emptyset$.

2) $(V_\nabla \cup V_\&, A; Q, Z, M)$ is a live and safe marked graph where:

$$\forall a \in A,\ M(a) = \begin{cases} 1, & \text{if } a \in M_H \cup M_L \\ 0, & \text{otherwise.} \end{cases}$$

If $a \in M_H$ (M_L) we will say that a carries a <u>h-token</u> (<u>l-token</u>) under (M_H, M_L). In diagrams we will indicate this by placing a darkened (plain) token on a. Briefly stated, a h-token(l-token) passing through an arc models the execution(omission) of the action associated with the arc. An example of a bp-graph together with a marking is shown in fig. 1.

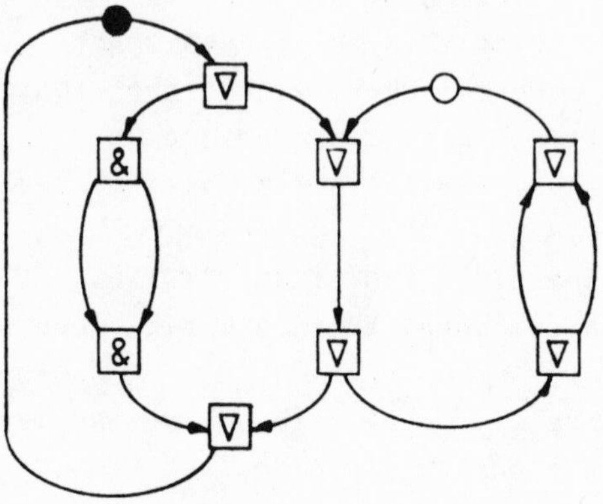

Fig. 1

A marking of a bp-graph can be transformed into a new marking through node firings. We will now state the rules for node firings.

Let $BP = (V_\nabla, V_\&; A; Q, Z)$ be a bp-graph and (M_H, M_L) a marking of BP. The material that follows, unless stated otherwise, is developed w.r.t. this bp-graph and the marking (M_H, M_L).

Let v be a ∇-node of BP. Then v is <u>firable</u> at (M_H, M_L) if:

1) $I(v) \subseteq M_H \cup M_L$

2) $|I(v) \cap M_H| \leq 1$.

When v <u>fires</u> a new marking (M_H', M_L') is reached which is given by,

1) $M_H' \cup M_L' = ((M_H \cup M_L) - I(v)) \cup O(v)$

2) $|M_H' \cap O(v)| = |M_H \cap I(v)|$.

Roughly speaking, one token is removed from each input arc of v and one token is added to each output arc of v. After v has fired, some output arc of v will carry a h-token (and the remaining output arcs of v l-tokens) iff some input arc of v carries a h-token under (M_H,M_L). That (M_H',M_L') is indeed a marking of BP can be shown easily using the theory of marked graphs.

Let u be a &-node of BP. u is <u>firable</u> at (M_H,M_L) if:

1) $I(u) \subseteq M_H \cup M_L$
2) $I(u) \subseteq M_H$ or $I(u) \subseteq M_L$.

When u fires, a new marking (M_H',M_L') is reached which is given by:

1) $M_H' \cup M_L' = ((M_H \cup M_L)-I(u)) \cup O(u)$
2) $O(u) \subseteq M_H' \ (M_L')$ iff $I(u) \subseteq M_H (M_L)$.

Thus ∇-nodes represent the choices (IF-THEN-ELSE) and &-nodes the concurrency (PARBEGIN-PAREND) that arise in the behavior of the system under study. If (M_H,M_L) can be transformed to (M_H',M_L') through a node firing we will indicate this as $(M_H,M_L) \rightarrow (M_H',M_L')$.

If the second part of the conditions imposed on the firability of a node is violated we will say that the node is in deadlock. Specifically, let v be a ∇-node of BP. Then v is in <u>deadlock</u> at (M_H,M_L) if $|I(v) \cap M_H| > 1$. Let u be a &-node of BP. Then u is in <u>deadlock</u> at (M_H,M_L) if $I(u) \cap M_H \neq \emptyset$ <u>and</u> $I(u) \cap M_L \neq \emptyset$. A node which is in deadlock can never fire again. This is a firing rule convention that we shall adopt.

We can now define two sets of reachable markings associated with a marking of a bp-graph. In doing so, as also through the remaining part of this material, we will adopt a convenient notation for dealing with markings. If (M_H,M_L) is a marking of BP we will often write this as simply M and (M_H',M_L') as M' etc. Only when necessary we will explicitly indicate the partitioning of the arcs into those that carry a h-token (M_H) and those that carry a l-token (M_L) under M.

<u>Definition</u>: Let $BP = (V_\nabla, V_\&, A; Q, Z)$ be a bp-graph and M a marking of BP. Then the <u>forward marking class</u> of BP <u>defined by</u> M is denoted as [M> and is the smallest set of markings of BP given by:

1) $M \in [M>$
2) If $M' \in [M>$ and $M' \rightarrow M''$ then $M'' \in [M>$.

<u>Definition</u>: Let $BP = (V_\nabla, V_\&, A; Q, Z)$ be a bp-graph and M a marking of BP. Then the <u>full marking class</u> of BP <u>defined by</u> M is denoted as [M] and is the smallest set of markings of BP given by:

1) $M \in [M]$

2) If $M' \in [M]$ and $M' \rightarrow M''$ then $M'' \in [M]$

3) If $M' \in [M]$ and M'' is a marking of BP such that $M'' \rightarrow M'$ then $M'' \in [M]$.

We are now prepared to define our system model called bipolar synchronization system (bp-system).

Definition: A bipolar synchronization system is a 6-tuple $S = (V_{\nabla}, V\ , A; Q, Z, [M])$ where:

1) $BP = (V_{\nabla}, V_{\&}, A; Q, Z)$ is a bp-graph
2) $M = (M_H, M_L)$ is a marking of BP
3) $[M]$ is the full marking class of BP defined by M.

In diagrams, we will indicate the underlying BP and a representative member of [M]. Fig. 1 may now be viewed as an example of a bp-system.

We conclude this section by formulating the notion of good behaviour.

Definition: Let $S = (V_{\nabla}, V_{\&}, A; Q, Z, [M])$ be a bp-system. S is well behaved if

1) $\forall a \in A$ and $\forall M' \in [M]$, $\exists M'' \in [M'\rangle$ such that $a \in M''$;
2) $\forall w \in V_{\nabla} \cup V_{\&}$ and $\forall M' \in [M]$, w is not in deadlock at M'.

Intuitively, in a well-behaved system, independent of the "initial marking", we can execute the action associated with any arc as often as desired. There are a number of equivalent formulations of this notion. One of them will be of particular interest to us. To state this, we need:

Definition: Let $S = (V_{\nabla}, V_{\&}, A; Q, Z, [M])$ be a bp-system and v (u) a ∇-node (&-node) and $M' \in [M]$. v (u) is h-firable at M' if v (u) is firable at M' and $|I(v) \cap M'_H| = 1$ $(I(u) \subseteq M'_H)$.

If w is h-firable at M' and fires, we will say that w h-fires at M'. From the definitions it is easy to derive,

Proposition: Let $S = (V_{\nabla}, V_{\&}, A; Q, Z, [M])$ be a bp-system. S is well behaved iff $\forall w \in V_{\nabla} \cup V_{\&}$ and $\forall M' \in [M]$, $\exists M'' \in [M\rangle$ such that w is h-firable at M".

To conclude, there is a stronger behavioral property of bp-systems which is also of interest. This property can be stated as:

Definition: Let $S = (V_\nabla, V_\&, A; Q, Z, [M])$ be a bp-system and let $S' = (V_\nabla, V_\&, A; Q', Z', [M])$ be the bp-system with $Q'=Z$ and $Z'=Q$. S is strongly well behaved if both S and S' are well-behaved.

2. The Synthesis Problem

In the study of bp-systems, we have, to date, concentrated on the problem of systematically constructing well behaved systems. Our solution to this problem consists of starting with some 'simple' well behaved systems and then obtaining from them, through repeated applications of a small set of transformation rules, more complex well-behaved systems. The simple bp-systems that we start with are called elementary systems and they are essentially of two types.

Definition: A ∇-elementary bp-system is a bp-system of the form $S = (V_\nabla, \emptyset, A; Q, Z, [M])$ where:

1) $|V_\nabla| = 1$
2) $|M_H| = 1$ (and $M_L = A - M_H$).

Definition: A &-elementary system is a bp-system of the form $S = (\emptyset, V_\&, A; Q, Z, [M])$ where:

1) $|V_\&| = 1$
2) $M_H = A$ (and $M_L = \emptyset$).

Clearly, all elementary bp-systems are well-behaved. We now state a set of rules using which a class of bp-systems called well formed bp-systems can be generated. Due to lack of space these rules are given in a pictorial form in fig. 2. In this diagram, on the whole 10 transformation rules have been shown. They are basically just 5 transformations together with their 'inverses'. For generating well formed systems we use the rules 1 through 7. Hence we will often refer to them as production rules. Each of the rules indicate the way in which a local (sub)structure of a bp-system is transformed to yield a new bp-system. For each rule, the source of the arrow is the bp-system - called the source system - to which the rule is applied. The identifying number of the rule is indicated within enclosing parantheses directly above the arrow. The target of the arrow, for each rule, is the resulting bp-system called the target system. In the material that follows, the source system will be denoted as S and the target system as S'. For a production rule to be applicable the

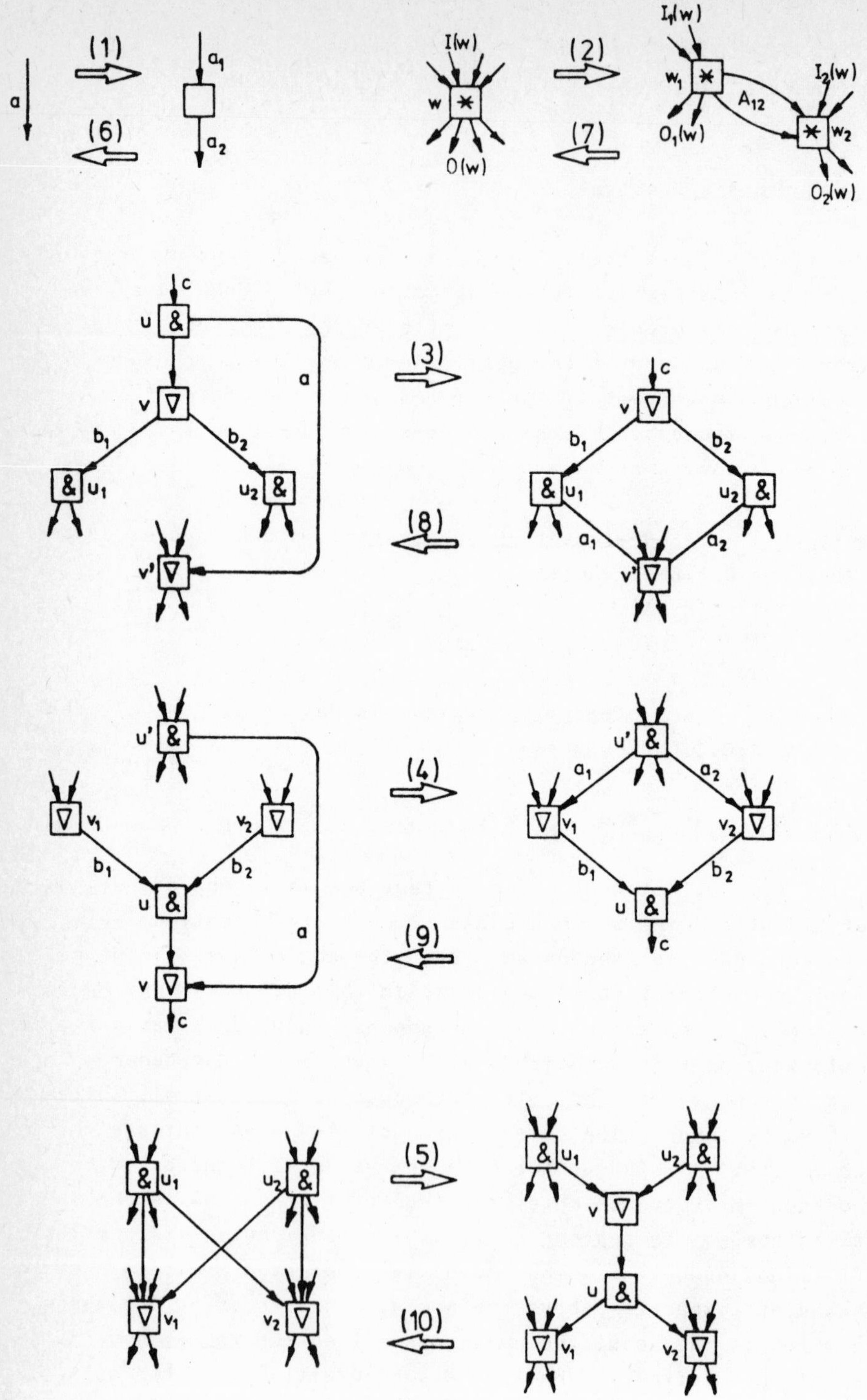
(1)
(6)
a
a1
a2
I(w)
w
O(w)
(2)
(7)
I1(w)
w1
A12
I2(w)
O1(w)
w2
O2(w)
c
u
&
v
∇
a
b1
b2
u1
u2
v'
(3)
(8)
a1
a2
u'
v1
v2
(4)
(9)
(5)
(10)

Fig. 2

structure of S and the marking M of S at which the rule is applied, should satisfy certain restrictions. They are:

For rule 2, $I(w)$ should be split into $I_1(w)$ and $I_2(w)$ and $O(w)$ should be split into $O_1(w)$ and $O_2(w)$ in such a way that in S, there is at least one basic circuit passing through some arc in $I_1(w)$ and some arc in $O_2(w)$. And there should be no basic circuit passing through some arc in $I_2(w)$ and some arc in $O_1(w)$. In S', $A_{12} \neq \emptyset$. Finally, if w is a ∇-node (&-node) in S, then both w_1 and w_2 are ∇-nodes (&-nodes) in S'.

To apply rule 3 (rule 4), the environment of the node v (u) in S as shown must be complete. In other words, in S, $I(v)=\{b\}$ and $O(v)=\{b_1,b_2\}$ ($O(u)=\{b\}$ and $I(u)=\{b_1,b_2\}$).

To apply rule 7, in S, there should be a non-empty set of arcs directed from w_1 to w_2. These two nodes must of the same type. At the marking M of S at which the rule is to be applied, there should be no token free path of length greater than 1 from w_1 to w_2. Finally, if w_1 and w_2 are ∇-nodes (&-nodes) in S then w is a ∇-node (&-node) in S'.

Now for the restrictions on the markings: For rules 1 and 6 there are no restrictions on the marking M of S at which the rules are applied. For the remaining rules, M should be such that an arc in S is marked under M only if it appears in S' also.

For each of the production rules we will now specify the means for obtaining M', a marking of S' from M the marking of S at which the rule is applied. For all the rules, if an arc b appears in S and S' then b is marked at M' in the same way in which it is marked at M. For all the rules except rules 1 and 6, if b' appears in S' but not in S then it is unmarked at M'. For rule 1, a_1 is marked at M' with a h-token (l-token) iff a is marked with a h-token (l-token) at M. In any case a_2 is not marked at M'. For rule 6, a is marked with a h-token (l-token) at M' iff a_1 or a_2 is marked with a h-token (l-token) at M.

Using these production rules, subject to the conditions stated above, the class of well formed bp-systems is obtained by:

<u>Definition</u> : The class of <u>well formed bp-systems</u> is denoted as WF and is the smallest class of bp-systems given by:

1) If S is an elementary bp-system then $S \in WF$.
2) If $S \in WF$ and S' is obtained by applying one of the production rules to S, then $S' \in WF$.

Some remarks are in order at this stage regarding the production rules.

Remark 1: Rules 3 and 4 have been stated w.r.t. a 1-in 2-out ∇-node and a 2-in 1-out &-node respectively. Instead of generalizing these rules we get the same effect by combining them with rules 6 and 7 in a suitable fashion.

Remark 2: In a preliminary version of the paper [2], rule 5 was not included as a production rule. We had thought that the effect of having this rule can be obtained by a suitable combination of the remaining rules. We still believe this to be the case. But unfortunately, we have since then discovered a flaw in our original proof of this fact. Hence in this paper, we have explicitly included rule 5 as a production rule.

Remark 3: Starting from the class of elementary bp-systems by using rules 1 and 2 alone, we can generate a class of systems called well structured bp-systems. We can prove that this class is precisely the class of strongly well behaved bp-systems [6]. In addition, we can also show that this a proper subclass of the class of well behaved bp-systems. Due to lack of space we will not develop these results here.

Remark 4: For the same reason, many of the (intermediate) results in the body of the paper will be stated with a skeleton of a proof or with none at all. Detailed proofs appear in [6].

The first result concerning the class WF is:

Theorem 1: Let S ∈ WF. Then S is well behaved.

Proof: Let S' be well formed and well behaved. Let S" be obtained from S' by applying one of the seven production rules to S'. We claim that S" is also well behaved. To establish the claim, one can develop a scheme ([6]) using which S' is made to follow the behavior of S" with a certain bounded 'delay'. This scheme is somewhat detailed and relies heavily on the fact that the underlying marked graphs of S' and S" are live and safe. Having done this, it is easy to show that if M" is a marking of S" at which some node x" is in deadlock then there is a marking M' of S' at which some node x' of S' is in deadlock. This would then imply that S" is also well behaved.

To establish the theorem, we argue: Since S ∈ WF, there exists a finite seqence of elements in WF of the form $S_0, S_1, .., S_n$ such that

1) S_0 is elementary (and hence is well behaved).

2) $S_n = S$ and for $1 < i \le n$, S_i is obtained by applying one of the production rules to S_{i-1}. The theorem then follows by induction on n.

□

What is appealing about WF is that the converse of theorem 1 is also true. To show this, we need to first define five reduction rules which are the 'inverses' of the rules 1 through 5. We will then show that, starting from a well behaved system, by repeatedly applying these reduction rules, we will always end up with an elementary system. The reduction rules also are shown in fig. 2. They are the rules 6 through 10. Thus rules 6 and 7 are both production and reduction rules. But this should cause no confusion because in what follows we will use them only in contexts where they function as reduction rules. As before, the structure of S and the marking M at which the reduction rule is to be applied should satisfy, for each rule certain restrictions. They are:

Rules 6 and 7 have been dealt with already. For applying rules 8,9 and 10 there are no structural restrictions. We should point out though, that they have been stated w.r.t. nodes having restricted indegree and out-degree. Hence in general, they will have to be combined with rules 1 and 2 in a suitable fashion to become applicable. But this is a mere technicality and as can be seen from one of the results that follow(lemma 1).

For rules 8,9, and 10 the marking M of S at which they are to be applied should be such that if an arc appears in S and not in S' then it should not be marked at M. A representative marking M' of S' is obtained from M in the obvious way.

Let S be a bp-system and let S' be a bp-system obtained by applying one of the reduction rules to S. Then S' is called a reduction of S. Let S be a bp-system to which none of the reduction rules can be applied. Then S is said to be an irreducible bp-system.

Lemma 1: Let S be be a well behaved bp-system and S' a reduction of S. Then

1) S' is well behaved.

2) If S' $\in$ WF then S $\in$ WF.

Proof The first part of the lemma can be proved by using the simulation idea outlined in the proof of theorem 1. The second part of the lemma follows from the definitions. □

Lemma 2: Let S be a bp-system, u a &-node and v a ∇-node of S. Let $\Pi_1=a_1,a_2,..,a_n$ and $\Pi_2=b_1,b_2,..,b_m$ be two distinct paths in S such that at some marking M' of S,

1) u is h-firable at M' and $M'(\Pi_1)=M'(\Pi_2)=0$,

2) $Q(a_1)=Q(b_1)=u$ and $Z(a_n)=Z(b_m)=v$,

3) for $1 \leq i < n$ and $1 \leq j < m$, $Z(a_i) \neq Z(b_j)$.
Then S is not well behaved.

Proof By induction on Max(n,m). □

We will now introduce three bi-polar graphs and argue that they can not be substructures of a well behaved bp-system. Once again,we specify these graphs pictorially as shown below.

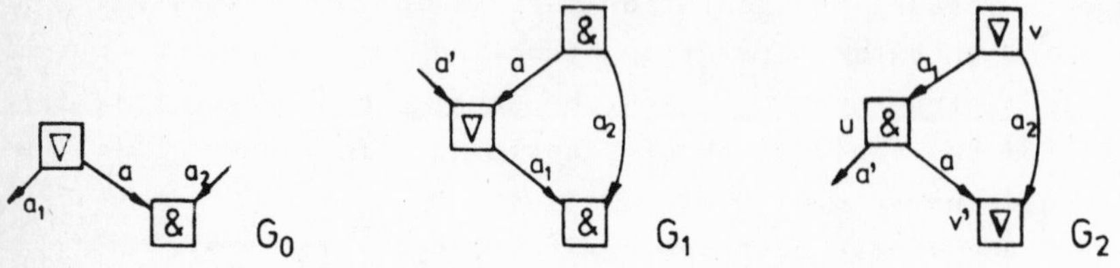

Lemma 3: Let S be a bp-system. If S contains G_0, G_1, or G_2 as a proper substructure then S is not well behaved.

Proof: It is quite easy to show that if S contains G_0 or G_1, then it can not be well behaved. To deal with G_2 is more difficult and we will merely outline the proof idea here. Assume that S contains G_2 as a proper substructure. Suppose that S is well behaved. Consider a pair of basic circuits Π, Π' passing through a and a' respectively (see diagram below). Clearly $I(u) = \{a_1\}$.Otherwise S would contain G_0 as a substructure and S could not be well behaved. Now Π and Π' part ways at u and come together at or before v. Hence Π and Π' can be expressed as Π = Π1,Π2 and Π' = Π1',Π2' where $Π1 = a, c_1, c_2, .., c_n$ and $Π2 = a', d_1, d_2, .., d_m$ such that:

1) $Z(c_n) = Z(d_m) = u'$

2) for $1 \leq i < n$ and $1 \leq j < m$, $Z(c_i) \neq Z(d_j)$.

Due to lemma 2, u' must be a &-node (see diagram). We assume that Π and Π' have been so chosen that lg(Π1)+lg(Π1') is minimum. Consider a marking M_0 at which v is h-firable. At M_0, we h-fire v towards a_2 and then l-fire u to obtain M_1. At M_1, a' will carry a l-token. Starting from M_1, without disturbing the token on a', we can reach a marking M_2 at which v' will be h-firable. At M_2, we h-fire v' to get M_3. At M_3, a' will carry a l-token and c_1 will carry a h-token. Now starting from M_3, we argue that the l-token on a' can be pushed along Π1' <u>and</u> the h-token on c_1 can be pushed along Π1 to eventually obtain a marking M_4 at which u' will be in deadlock. To account for the cases where the l-token on Π1', in its journey towards

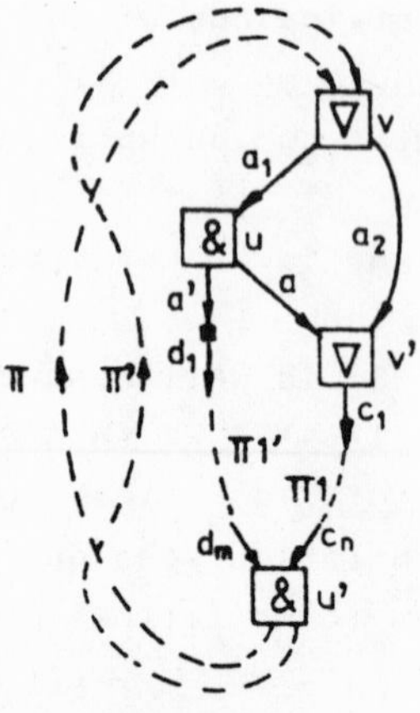

u', turns into a h-token, we appeal to

1) a variation of lemma 2, for the case where an 'external' h-token provides the required help,

2) the fact that $lg(\Pi 1)+lg(\Pi 1')$ is minimum for the case where the h-token on $\Pi 1$ provides the required help. □

Next we show that a well-behaved irreducible bp-system which is not already elementary must contain a specific substructure.

Let S be a bp-system and Π a basic circuit of S. Π is called a <u>maximal</u> basic circuit of S if for every basic circuit Π' of S, $lg(\Pi)\geq lg(\Pi')$.

<u>Lemma 4</u>: Let S be a well behaved irreducible bp-system which is not elementary. Let Π be a maximal basic circuit of S. Then Π passes through at least on ∇-node v and one &-node u such that, $|I(u)|>1$ and $|O(v)|>1$.

<u>Proof</u>: The result follows easily from lemma 2 and the characterization of live and safe marked graphs. □

<u>Lemma 5</u>: Let S be a well-behaved, irreducible bp-system which is not elementary. Let Π be a maximal basic circuit of S. Then Π can be expressed as $\Pi = a_1,a_2,a_3,\ldots,a_n$ where:

1) $Q(a_1)=v$ is a ∇-node and $|O(v)|>1$,

2) $Z(a_1)=u$ is a &-node and $|I(u)|=1$ and $|O(u)|>1$,

3) $Z(a_2)=v'$ is a ∇-node and $|I(v')|>1$ and $|O(v')|=1$,

4) $Z(a_3)=u'$ is a &-node and $|I(u')|>1$.

<u>Proof</u>: Follows easily from lemmas 3 and 4 and the fact that S is irreducible and well-behaved. □

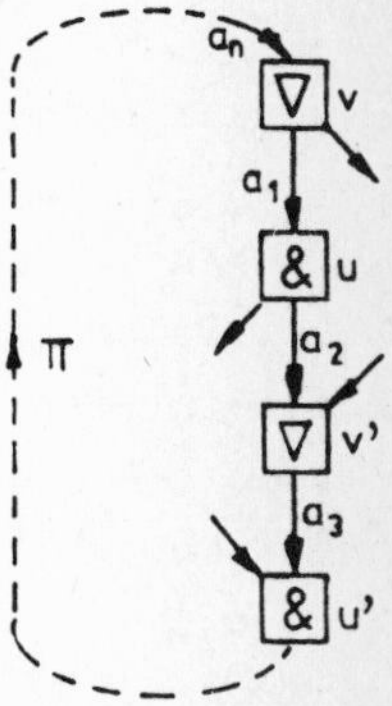

<u>Lemma 6</u>: Let S be a well behaved and irreducible bp-system. Then S is elementary.

<u>Proof</u>: Assume that S is not elementary. Let Π be a maximal basic circuit of S. Then along Π, we can find a substructure of the form shown above (lemma 5). With reference to the labels associated with this diagram, let M_0 be a marking of S at which v is h-firable.

<u>Claim</u>: At M_0, <u>either</u> there is a token free path Π_1 from v to v' which does not pass through a_2 <u>or</u> there is a token free path Π_2 from u to u' which does not pass through a_3.

To prove this claim, assume that neither Π_1 nor Π_2 exists. Then starting from M_0, we can, without firing v, reach M_1 at which every arc in $I(v')-\{a_2\}$ is marked. Every such arc must be marked with a l-token. (Otherwise, at M_1 we can h-fire v towards a_1, h-fire u to produce M' at which v' will be in deadlock.) Now there are two cases to consider;

Case 1: Suppose that at M_1 there is no token free path from v to u' which does not pass through a_3. Starting from M_1, we can, without firing v, reach M_2 at which some arc, say $b_n \in I(u')-\{a_3\}$, carries a token. If this token is a h-token (l-token), then at M_2, we can h-fire v away from a_1 (towards a_1), l-fire (h-fire) u, l-fire (h-fire) v', to obtain M_3 at which u' will be in deadlock.

Case 2: Suppose that M_1, there is a token free path $\Pi'=b_1,b_2,\ldots,b_n$ such that $Q(b_1)=v$, $Z(b_n)=u'$ and $b_n \neq a_3$. Since Π_2 does not exist, $b_1 \neq a_1$. Now at M_1, we can h-fire v towards b_1, l-fire u, l-fire v' to reach M_2 at which a_3 will carry a l-token and b_1 a h-token. Starting from M_3, we can push the h-token on b_1 along Π' to eventually reach a marking M_3 at which a_3 will carry l-token and b_n a h-token. This implies that u' is in deadlock at M_3 and hence the claim is established.

Returning to the proof of the lemma, assume that Π_1 exists. Since Π_1 is (at M_0) token free, $lg(\Pi_1)>0$. If $lg(\Pi_1)=1$, then S contains G_2 as a substructure and hence is not well-behaved. If $lg(\Pi_1)>2$ then Π is not a maximal basic circuit. Hence $lg(\Pi_1)=2$. Let $\Pi_1=c_1,c_2$ where $Q(c_1)=v$ and $Z(c_2)=v'$. If $Z(c_1)=Q(c_2)$ is a ∇-node then either node reduction can be applied to S, or Π_1 is not maximal and hence Π is not a maximal basic circuit. Hence $Z(c_1)$ is a &-node. But this implies that rule 8 (see fig. 2) can be applied to S and hence S is not irreducible. A similar argument (using G_1) applies in the case where we assume that Π_1 does not exist, but Π_2 exists. Hence S must be elementary. □

Theorem 2 (Main Result): A bp-system is well behaved iff it is well formed.

Proof: Let S be a well behaved bp-system. Then considering the effects that the various reduction rules have on the lengths of basic circuits we can show that there exists a finite sequence of bp-systems of the form $S_0,S_1,\ldots,S_n$ where $S_0=S$, for $0 \le i<n$, S_{i+1} is a reduction of S_i, and $S_n=S'$ is irreducible. Now by induction on n it is immediate (lemma 1, part 1) that S' is well behaved. Hence due to lemma 6, S' is elementary, which implies it is well formed. But then due to part 2 of lemma 1, S is also well formed. The second half of the theorem is theorem 1. □

3. Summary

We have presented here a net based model for studying a specific organizational principle. This principle of representing and exploiting the absence of effects has been pursued, in a more general context, by Holt [7]. An application of Holt's idea in this direction has been developed by Shapiro [8].

As mentioned in the introductory section, we view bp-systems as a higher level net model. What this means is we can systematically translate (if we wish) a bp-system specification into a basic Condition-Event system specification. Hence our synthesis results, in effect, outline a technique for constructing a class of Condition-Event systems which have some attractive behavioral properties. To date a number of attempts have been made to synthesize restricted classes of nets or net like structures. In this setting, our research is also related to the efforts of Yoeli [9], Jodwani and Jump [10] and Valette [11]. We feel that a good deal of the graph-based studies on structured programming have implications for (and can perhaps benefit from) future work on bp-systems. Obtainig a suitable interpretation will be the first step towards building a bridge to aid in this process and we hope to accomplish this in the near future.

References

1. Petri, C. A.: Kommunikation mit Automaten. Institut für Intrumentelle Mathematik, Schriften des IIM Nr. 2, Bonn, 1962.
2. Genrich, H. J.; Lautenbach, K.; Thiagarajan, P.S: An overview of Net Theory. Course Material of the Advanced course on General Net Theory of Systems and Processes, Hamburg, 1979. (Published by GMD, St. Augustin)
3. Genrich, H. J.; Lautenbach, K.: Synchronisationsgraphen. Acta Informatica 2, pp 143-161, 1973.
4. Commoner, F.; Holt, A. W.; Even, S.; Pnueli, A.: Marked Directed Graphs. J. Computer and System Sc. 5, pp 511-523, 1973.
5. Jump, J. R.; Thiagarajan, P. S.: On the Equivalence of Asynchronous Control Structures. SIAM Journal on Computing, 2, pp 67-87, 1973.
6. Genrich, H. J.; Thiagarajan, P. S.: Bipolar Synchronization Systems. ISF-Report 80.02, GMD, St.Augustin, West Germany (1980).

7. Holt, A. W.: Roles and Activities. Unpublished Monograph, Boston University Academic Computing Centre, 1979.
8. Shapiro, R. M.: Calculating Logical and Probabilistic Dependencies in a Class of Net Models. Internal Report, Meta Information Applications, Inc., Wellfleet, MA, U.S.A, 1975.
9. Yoeli, M.: A Structured Approach to Parallel Programming and Control. Proceedings of the First European Conference on Parallel and Distributed Processing (J. C. Syre, Editor), Toulouse, France, pp 163-170, 1979.
10. Jodwani, N. D; Jump, J. R.: Top-down Design in the Context of Parallel Programs. Information and Control 40, pp 241-257, 1979.
11. Valette, R.: Analysis of Petri Nets by Stepwise Refinement. J. Computer and System Sc., 18, pp 35-46, 1979.

TESTING OF PROPERTIES OF FINITE ALGEBRAS

A. Goralčíková, P. Goralčík, V. Koubek
Faculty of Mathematics and Physics
Charles University, Prague
118 00 Praha 1, Czechoslovakia

0. Introduction

After graphs and like, a new generation of combinatorial structures, more complex ones, start to penetrate into the field of discrete modelling of concrete situations, namely, finite algebras, especially well fit to capture the deterministic aspects of the situations ranging from physics and biology to the social sciences.

Let us bring, as an example, the possibility, suggested by Z. Hedrlín, of representing the result of choices, in a situation where every couple of members of a social group chooses a member of the group (to meet some purpose of the group), in the form of the multiplication table of a groupoid. With such a representation in hand, we may establish various algebraic properties of the groupoid obtained and try to connect them with the sociological characteristics of the group in question. For example associativity might mean a high degree of coherency (unanimity) of the choice.

Unlike graphs, algebraic structures involving binary (and of higher arity) operatons can hardly be visualized. The more we do need efficient means of handling their basic properties.

Among most important properties of algebras are those which are preserved under passage to products, subalgebras, and homomorphic images of algebras. Satisfaction of various identities belongs to the most well-known examples of such properties. The reason may be seen in that these fundamental algebraic constructions enable us to reduce the algebraic structure by the so called subdirect reduction, which also may often lead to quicker algorithms testing the "varietal" properties mentioned above.

Suppose we are given a class C of objects of finite size and a property P to be tested for the objects of C. Let there further be a reduction algorithm processing any object $A \in C$ of size n in $O(n^k)$ time which, for a given object A, either decides whether A has or has not the property P or constructs a couple A_1, A_2 of objects, both of size at most $\frac{n}{q}$, where $q > \sqrt[k]{2}$, such that A has

P if and only if both A_1 and A_2 have P. Then there exists an algorithm deciding in (the same) $O(n^k)$ time whether an object $A \in C$ of size n has or has not the property P. We get such an algorithm just by reiteration of the previous reduction algorithm. The time estimate will remain the same because the sizes of the objects which may occur in the process decrease very quickly. Summing up the times needed we get

$$O\left(n^k + 2\left(\frac{n}{q}\right)^k + 4\left(\frac{n}{q^2}\right)^k + \dots \right) =$$
$$O\left(n^k\left(1 + \frac{2}{q^k} + \left(\frac{2}{q^k}\right)^2 + \dots \right)\right) = O(n^k) .$$

If C is a class of finite algebras of a given type and P a property of algebras preserved under passage to finite products, subalgebras, and homomrphic images we can, sometimes, obtain a quick reduction algorithm based on the process of subsequent subdirect reduction. If we want to subdirectly reduce a given algebra A, we have to find a separating couple π, ρ of proper congruences on A ("separating" means that $(a,b) \in \pi \cap \rho$ iff $a = b$) and to construct the corresponding quotients $A_1 = A/\pi$ and $A_2 = A/\rho$. There may exist no such couple of congruences, the algebra A is then called subdirectly irreducible. For any separating couple π, ρ of congruences on A we have an embedding $a \to (\pi(a), \rho(a))$ of A into the product $A_1 \times A_2$ of its homomorphic images, therefore A has the property P if and only if both A_1 and A_2 have the property P.

Suppose we would like to construct an algorithm deciding in $O(n^k)$ time whether or not an algebra $A \in C$ of size n has the property P. The way we suggest is to make sure that the following two steps can be done in $O(n^k)$ time:

Step 1. Decide whether A is subdirectly irreducible with the property P.

Step 2. If A is not subdirectly irreducible then either decide that A has not the property P or construct a separating couple π, ρ of proper congruences such that the quotients A/π, A/ρ have sizes at most $\frac{n}{q}$, $q > \sqrt[k]{2}$, and, construct the quotients.

These two steps obviously constitute an $O(n^k)$ reduction algorithm. Step 1 depends very much upon the description of the subdirectly irreducible algebras with P, Step 2 then on the description of congruences on the algebras with P.

We want to demostrate the usefulness of the above method by showing that it is possible to decide in $O(n^2)$ time whether a groupoid is an abelian group or whether a bigroupoid is a distributive lattice. In both cases the description of subdirectly irreducibile algebras and congruences is very simple: an abelian group is subdirectly irreducible if and only if it is cyclic of order (= size) p^m with p prime, a distributive lattice is subdirectly irreducible if and only if it has at most two elements.

The class of modular lattices, however close to the distributive ones, seems to be much harder because there is no satisfactory description of finite subdirectly irreducible modular lattices. On the other hand, the semilattices have, like the distributive lattices, also only at most two-point subdirectly irreducible members. However the congruences seem not to be as transparent in semilattices as in the distributive lattices. For the groups (and also for the rings) Step 2 works quite well, whereas it seeems to be difficult to recognize among groupoids (bigroupoids) a subdirectly irreducible group (ring) in $O(n^2)$ time.

In the case of abelian groups the result is not new. Tarjan [8] had given an $O(n^2)$ algorithm deciding whether a groupoid is a solvable (in particular, abelian) group based on the particularities of generation in groups.

Technically, our objects - the finite algebras with at most two binary operations - will be presented by lists and tables and dealt with by algorithms executed an a RAM with uniform cost of operations [1].

1. Groupoids

Let $(X,\cdot)$ be a <u>groupoid</u>, i.e. an algebra with just one operation of multiplication, given by a table.

A subset $Y \subseteq X$ is called a subgroupoid of $(X,\cdot)$ if it is closed under multiplication, in the sense that $a,b \in Y \Rightarrow ab \in Y$. For every subset $M \subseteq X$, there exists the smallset subgroupoid of X containing M : it is the intersection $\langle M \rangle$ of all subgroupoids of X containing M as a part. We call $\langle M \rangle$ the subgroupoid of X generated by M.

Given $M \subseteq X$, we can count $\langle M \rangle$ by forming successively the sets $M_0 \subseteq M_1 \subseteq \ldots \subseteq M_i \subseteq \ldots$, $M_0 = M$, $M_1 = \{ab \; ; \; a,b \in M_0\} \cup M_0$ ..., $M_{i+1} = \{ab \; ; \; a,b \in M_i$ and $(a \notin M_{i-1}$ or $b \notin M_{i-1})\} \cup M_i$, until we find M_k with $M_k = M_{k+1}$. Then obviously $M_k = \langle M \rangle$. Note that for finding $\langle M \rangle$ by this procedure we need to inspect at most once each entry of the multiplication table.

Lemma 1. Given a subset M of a groupoid $(X,.)$ of size n, there exists an algorithm computing the subgroupoid $\langle M \rangle$ generated by M in $O(n^2)$ time.

A partition π of X into a disjoint union $X = \coprod_{i=1}^{m} A_i$ is a congruence on $(X,.)$, if for every couple (i,j), $i,j = 1,\dots,m$, there exists k such that

(1) $A_iA_j = \{ab \; ; \; a \in A_i \text{ and } b \in A_j\} \subseteq A_k$.

If π is a congruence on X, we can turn the set $X/\pi = \{A_1,\dots,A_m\}$ of blocks of π into the quotient groupoid $(X/\pi,\bullet)$ defining the $\bullet$ -multiplication of blocks by

(2) $A_i \bullet A_j = A_k$ iff $A_iA_j \subseteq A_k$.

Again, the testing of a given partition π for a congruence essentially requires to go once through the multiplication table. Each time $A_iA_j \subseteq A_k$ is confirmed we get the entry $A_i \bullet A_j = A_k$ in the multiplication table for $(X/\pi,\bullet)$.

Lemma 2. Given a groupoid $(X,.)$ of size n and a partition π of X, there exists an algorithm testing π for congruence and, if so, computing the quotient groupoid $(X/\pi,\bullet)$ in $O(n^2)$ time.

Suppose we want to test $(X,.)$ for associativity and we know some particular set M of size m generating $X = \langle M \rangle$. Then we need not inspect all ordered triples of X but only $m.n^2$ of them, using an easy observation [3], that $(X,.)$ is associative iff $x(ay) = (xa)y$ for all $x,y \in X$ and for all $a \in M$. We have then

Lemma 3. If there is an algorithm computing, for every groupoid $(X,.)$ of size n belonging to some class C, a set of at most $g(n)$ generators in a time $O(f(n))$, then there exists an algorithm testing $(X,.)$ from C for associativity in $O(f(n) + n^2g(n))$ time.

This lemma is completely worthless for the class of all groupoids, since there are groupoids without any proper set of generators (e.g. the groupoids in which $ab \in \{a,b\}$ for all $a,b \in X$). However, satisfaction of other identities, such as commutativity or idempotency

$x^2 = x$,

may immediately place the groupoid into a class for which Lemma 3 gives a non-trivial estimate.

Perhaps the most important example, as noted by Tarjan [8], is that of groups. Any group of size n has a set of at most $\log n$ generators which can be found in $O(n^2)$ time, hence by Lemma 3 we get

Theorem 1. There exists an algorithm deciding in $O(n^2 \log n)$ time whether a given groupoid $(X,.)$ of size n is a group.

2. Abelian groups

A groupoid $(X,.)$ is an abelian group if it satisfies the following conditions

A1. $x(yz) = (xy)z$ (associativity)

A2. $xy = yx$ (commutativity)

A3. $\exists e \,\forall x\, (ex = x)$ (existence of an identity)

A4. $\forall a,b \,\exists c\, (ac = b)$ (division)

Condition A4, in view of finiteness of X, means that any row of the multiplication table for $(X,.)$ contains all elements of X, which can be checked in $O(n^2)$ time, and so can be A2 and A3. This done, let us further compute, for every $x \in X$, the set $x_1, x_2, \ldots$ by $x_1 = x$, $x_{k+1} = xx_k$, until we find the first x_k with $k \le n$ and $x_k = e$. If there is no such x_k for some x then $(X,.)$ is not abelian group. If it works for all x, we can assign the order $o(x) = k$ and the cycle $C(x) = \{x_1,\ldots,x_k\}$ to every $x \in X$ in $O(n^2)$ time. If $(X,.)$ is an abelian group, then $C(x)$ is a subgroup of order k and the sets $aC(x)$, $a \in X$, form a congruence on X. So we can proved further as follows: For a selected point $b \in X$, form a partition $\pi(b)$ of X by building up its blocks $A_1 = C(b)$, $A_2 = a_2A_1$ for some $a_2 \notin A_1$, ..., $A_{k+1} = a_{k+1}A_k$ for some $a_{k+1} \notin A_1 \cup A_2 \cup \ldots \cup A_k$, simultaneously checking that $\{A_1 \cup \ldots \cup A_k\} \cap A_{k+1} \neq \emptyset$. This procedure either fails or gives a partition in at most $O(n)$ time. If it fails then $(X,.)$ is not abelian group. If we get a partition $\pi(b)$, we can test it for congruence and pass to the quotient $X/\pi(b)$ in $O(n^2)$ time, by Lemma 2. Since the sizes of all blocks of $\pi(b)$ are equal to the order $o(b)$ of b, the size of $X/\pi(b)$ is $\frac{n}{o(b)}$.

If there is another element $c \in X$ yielding a congruence $C(c)$ on $(X,.)$ and $|C(b) \cap C(c)| = 1$, then $\pi(b)$ and $\pi(c)$ are separating congruences (in the sense that any two distinct points of X are either in two different blocks of $\pi(b)$ or in two different blocks of $\pi(c)$), therefore $(X,.)$ is a subgroupoid of $X/\pi(b) \times X/\pi(c)$ (by the embedding $a \to (a/\pi(b), a/\pi(c))$, where $a/\pi(b)$ is the block of $\pi(b)$ containing a and $a/\pi(c)$ is the block of $\pi(c)$ containing a).

From the theory of finite abelian groups [6,7] we know that if such a group is not cyclic, then it must contain two elements b,c of prime orders with $|C(b) \cap C(c)| = 1$ (here of course $C(x) = \langle x\rangle$).

Putting all the pieces together, we get

Theorem 2. There exists an algorithm deciding in $O(n^2)$ time whether a given groupoid $(X,.)$ of size n is an abelian group.

Proof. Assume that A2, A3 and A4 are checked and that every element $a \in X$ is assigned its order $o(a)$ yet. If there is some element a of order n, then it generates $(X,.)$ and using it, we can check associativity in $O(n^2)$ time, by Lemma 3. If there is no element of order n, choose an element b of the least possible order $\neq 1$ and an element c of the least possible order in $X-C(b)$ and check if $|C(b) \cap C(c)| = 1$. If so, form the congruences $\pi(b), \pi(c)$ and pass to quotients $X/\pi(b), X/\pi(c)$. Till now either everything has gone through or $(X,.)$ is not an abelian group. We have thus reduced our problem in $O(n^2)$ time to the same problem about $X/\pi(b)$ and $X/\pi(c)$, two groupoids of size at most $\lceil \frac{n}{2} \rceil$.

The idea of repeated subdirect reduction has been suggested by T. Kepka, which we gladly acknowledge.

3. Modular lattices

Let (X,E) be a relation, i.e. a set X structured by a set of oriented edges $E \subseteq X \times X$. It can be presented either by the characteristic function of E (given by an $n \times n$ matrix with entries 0 or 1 and rows and columns labeled by the elements of X) or as a collection of lists of elements of the sets

$$xE = \{y \in X ; (x,y) \in E\} , \quad Ey = \{x \in X ; (x,y) \in E\} .$$

Any subset $M \subseteq X$ determines a relation $(M, (M \times M) \cap E)$ called a full subrelation of (X,E) and denoted shortly by M.

An element $a \in X$ is a minimal element of (X,E) if $Ea - \{a\} = \emptyset$.

A sequence $(a_1, \ldots, a_k)$ of distinct elements of X is a cycle of (X,E) if $(a_1,a_2), (a_2,a_3), \ldots, (a_{k-1},a_k), (a_k,a_{k+1}) \in E$. If there is no cycle in (X,E), the relation is called acyclic.

Construct successively, for a given relation (X,E), a sequence of disjoint sets $L(0) = \min X , \ldots , L(k+1) = \min (X - \bigcup_{i=0}^{k} L(i))$ for $k \geq 0$. Let $L(s)$ be the last non-void memeber of the sequence. Then clearly (X,E) is acyclic iff $X = \bigcup_{i=0}^{s} L(i)$. The sets $L(0), \ldots , L(s)$ then form a partition of X into levels and define a height function $h: X \to \{0, \ldots, s\}$, $h(x) = k$ iff $x \in L(k)$, with the property that $(x,y) \in E$ implies $h(x) < h(y)$. The following statement has been proved in [5]:

Lemma 4. There is an algorithm deciding in $O(n^2)$ time, for a given relation (X,E), whether it is acyclic, and, if so, computes the decomposition of X into levels $L(0), \ldots, L(s)$ and the corresponding height function h.

A *lattice* can be defined either as a partially ordered set $(X, \leq)$ in which for every couple $a,b \in X$ there exist the smallest upper bound $\sup\{a,b\}$ and the biggest lower bound $\inf\{a,b\}$, or equivalently, as a bigroupoid $(X,\vee,\wedge)$ satisfying the lattice identities:

$a \vee (b \vee c) = (a \vee b) \vee c \qquad a \wedge (b \wedge c) = (a \wedge b) \wedge c$

(associativity)

$a \vee b = b \vee a \qquad a \wedge b = b \wedge a$ (commutativity)

$a \vee a = a \qquad a \wedge a = a$ (idempotency)

$a \vee (a \wedge b) = a \qquad a \wedge (a \vee b) = a$. (absorption)

The passage from $(X,\leq)$ to $(X,\vee,\wedge)$ is done by defining the operations $\vee$, $\wedge$, called *join* and *meet*, as suprema and infima. The passage backwards recovers the ordering from the operations by

either $x \leq y \Leftrightarrow x \vee y = y$

or $x \leq y \Leftrightarrow x \wedge y = x$.

For a given lattice $(X,\vee,\wedge)$, we shall be interested in two additional identities:

$x \vee (y \wedge (x \vee z)) = (x \vee z) \wedge (x \vee y)$ (modularity)

$(x \vee y) \wedge z = (x \wedge z) \vee (y \wedge z)$ (distributivity)

Modularity is equivalent with the following condition:

$a \leq b \Rightarrow (a \vee c) \wedge b = a \vee (c \wedge b)$.

A straightforward testing by inspection of triples requires $O(n^3)$ time. In [4], an algorithm for verifying modularity in time $O(n^{2,79})$ was proposed. The most time consuming part of the algorithm is a construction of the transitive reduction of the relation $\leq$ induced by operation $\wedge$.

Lemma 5. A lattice $(X,\vee,\wedge)$ is modular iff the height function h associated with the level decomposition of $(X,\leq)$ satisfies the identity $h(x \vee y) + h(x \wedge y) = h(x) + h(y)$.

Proof. Observe first that $h(x)$ is the maximal length of a chain from 0 to x. Thus if X is modular h must satisfy the identity ([2], Theorem 16, p. 41).

If X is not modular, then for some $a,b,c \in X$ we have $a < b$ and $a \vee c = b \vee c$, $a \wedge c = b \wedge c$ ([2], Theorem 12, p. 13).

If $h(a \vee c) + h(a \wedge c) = h(a) + h(c)$,

$$h(b \vee c) + h(b \wedge c) = h(b) + h(c) ,$$

then $h(a) = h(b)$ - a contradiction.

Lemmas 4 and 5 easily yield

Theorem 3. There exists an algorithm deciding in $O(n^2)$ time whether a given lattice $(X,\vee,\wedge)$ is modular.

4. Distributive lattices

In the class of distributive lattices the subdirect reduction nicely works to decide in a quadratic time whether a given bigroupoid $(X,\vee,\wedge)$ (not assumed to be a lattice) is a distributive lattice. We do not know if the same is true for modular lattices.

Lemma 6. Let $(X,\vee,\wedge)$ be a bigroupoid, let for an element $a \in X$ the following four properties hold for any $x,y \in X$:

(1) $a \vee (x \wedge y) = (a \vee x) \wedge (a \vee y)$

$a \vee (x \vee y) = (a \vee x) \vee (a \vee y)$

(2) $a \wedge (x \wedge y) = (a \wedge x) \wedge (a \wedge y)$

$a \wedge (x \vee y) = (a \wedge x) \vee (a \wedge y)$

(3) $\left.\begin{array}{l} a \vee x = a \vee y \\ a \wedge x = a \wedge y \end{array}\right\} \Rightarrow x = y$

(4) both $a \vee X = \{a \vee x ; x \in X\}$ and $a \wedge X = \{a \wedge x ; x \in X\}$ are distributive sublattices of $(X,\vee,\wedge)$.

Then $(X,\vee,\wedge)$ is a distributive lattice. Conversely, if $(X,\vee,\wedge)$ is a distributive lattice, then every $a \in X$ has the properties (1) - (4).

Proof. The first three properties exactly mean that the assignments $x \to a \vee x$, $x \to a \wedge x$ define a separating couple of endomorphisms of $(X,\vee,\wedge)$ with images $a \vee X$, $a \wedge X$, thus $(X,\vee,\wedge)$ is a subdirect product of the images, hence the first assertion. The converse statement is obvious.

If we want to put this lemma to an effective use we have to choose $a \in X$ so that both $a \vee X$ and $a \wedge X$ are about half the size of X . But this is clearly possible if $(X,\vee,\wedge)$ is a lattice, because of the following

Lemma 7. Let $(X,\leq)$ be a partially ordered set of size n . hen there exists $a \in X$ such that

$$\max (|\{x ; x \leq a\}| , |\{x ; x \geq a\}|) \leq \left\lceil \frac{n+1}{2} \right\rceil .$$

Proof. Let $x_o < x < \dots < x_m$ be some maximal chain in $(X,\le)$. Then clearly for $k = \max \{i ; |\{x ; x \le x_i\}| \le \lceil \frac{n+1}{2} \rceil\}$ the element $a = x_k$ has the required property.

Indeed, if $k = m$ then $a = x_m$ has the property. Let $k < m$. If $|\{x ; x \ge x_k\}| > \lceil \frac{n+1}{2} \rceil$ then $\{x ; x \le x_{k+1}\} \cap \{x ; x \ge x_k\} = \{x_k, x_{k+1}\}$, from the maximality of the chain, thus $|\{x ; x \le x_{k+1}\}| + |\{x ; x \ge x_k\}| \ge \lceil \frac{n+1}{2} \rceil + \lceil \frac{n+1}{2} \rceil + 2 \ge n + 3$, a contradiction.

Theorem 4. There exists an algorithm deciding in $O(n^2)$ time whether a given bigroupoid $(X,\vee,\wedge)$ of size n is a distributive lattice.

Proof. The reduction step consists in finding an element $a \in X$ with $\max (|a \vee X|, |a \wedge X|) \le \lceil \frac{n+1}{2} \rceil$ and checking up the four properties of Lemma 6. If some part of it fails then the answer is no. If we get through we next reduce the two half-size bigroupoids obtained, and so forth. A successful complete reduction is achieved in $O(n^2)$ time, by a similar computation as in the case of abelian groups.

Remark. If a subclass of the class of all distributive lattices is defined by a condition testable in $O(n^2)$ time then clearly members of the subclass can be recognized by an algorithm in $O(n^2)$ time. As an important example let us note the class of boolean lattices, defined as distributive lattices with the property of complementation:

$$\forall x \ \exists y \ (x \wedge y = 0 \text{ and } x \vee y = 1) .$$

References

[1] A. V. Aho, J. E. Hopcroft, J. D. Ullman, The Design and Analysis of Computer Algorithms, Addison-Wesley, 1974.

[2] G. Birkhoff, Lattice Theory, Amer. Math. Soc. vol. XXV (1967).

[3] A. H. Clifford, G. B. Preston, The Algebraic Theory of Semigroups Amer. Math. Soc. Math. Surveys 7 (1964).

[4] M. Demlová, J. Demel, V. Koubek, Several Algorithms for Finite Algebras, Proceedings of FCT'79, Akademie-Verlag, Berlin (1979), 99-104.

[5] A. Goralčíková, V. Koubek, A Reduct - and - Closure Algorithms for Graphs, Proceedings of MFCS'79, Springer-Verlag Berlin, Heidelberg, New York (1979), 301-307

[6] L. Ja. Kulikov, On Abelian Groups of an Arbitrary Cardinality, Mat. Sbornik 9(1941), 165-182 (in Russian).

[7] B. M. Schein, On Subdirectly Irreducible Semigroups, Doklady, 144(1962), 999-1002 (in Russian).

[8] R. E. Tarjan, Determining Whether a Groupoid Is a Group, Inf. Proc. Letters 1(1972), 120-124.

A TRANSACTION MODEL

Jim Gray

IBM Research San Jose Research Laboratory
San Jose, California. 95193

February 1980

ABSTRACT: This paper is an attempt to tersely restate several theoretical results about transaction recovery and concurrency control. A formal model of entities, actions, transactions, entity failures, concurrency and distributed system is required to present these results. Included are theorems on transaction undo and redo, degrees of consistency, predicate locks, granularity of locks, deadlock, and two-phase commit.

CONTENTS

- Definition of transaction
- Reliability
  - Model of failures
  - Transaction restart
  - System restart
  - Checkpoint and volatile entity reconstruction
- Concurrency
  - Motivation for serializable history
  - Locking protocol for serializable histories
  - Locking and recovery
  - Degrees of consistency
  - Predicate locks
  - Granularity of locking
  - Deadlock
- Issues in distributed systems
  - Model of distributed system
  - Validity of serial history
  - Reliability
  - Concurrency
- Transaction concept in a programming language
- References

ACKNOWLEDGMENTS: This paper draws heavily from the models of Charlie Davies, Janusz Gorski, Butler Lampson and Howard Sturgis, and from discussions with Dieter Gawlick, Bruce Lindsay, Ron Obermarck, and Irv Traiger. Critical readings by Bruce Lindsay and Anita Jones clarified several aspects of the presentation.

DEFINITION OF TRANSACTION

A **database state** is a function from names to values. Each <name,value> pair is called an **entity.** The system provides **operations** each of which manipulates one or more entities. The execution of an operation on an entity is called an **action.** Record and terminal are typical entity types and read and write are typical operations.

Associated with a database is a predicate on entities called the **consistency constraint.** A database state satisfying the consistency constraint is said to be **consistent.**

Transactions are the mechanism which query and transform the database state. A **program** P is a static description of a transaction. The consistency constraint of the database is the minimal precondition and invariant of the program. The program may have a desired effect which is expressed as an additional postcondition C'. Using Hoar's notation:

$$C \{ P \} C \& C'.$$

The execution of such a program on a database state is called **transaction** on the state. The exact execution sequence of a program is a function of the database state but we model a transaction as a fixed sequence of actions:

$$T = \langle\langle t, Ai, Ni \rangle | i=1,\ldots n\rangle$$

where t is the transaction name, Ai are operations and Ni are entity names.

The system may interleave the execution of the actions of several transactions. The execution of a set of transactions by the system starting from some database state is called a **history** and is denoted by the sequence:

$$H = \langle\langle ti, Ai, Ni \rangle | i=1,\ldots,m\rangle$$

which is an order preserving merge of the actions of the transactions. (A later section will show that even multiple nodes executing actions may be modeled by a single execution sequence.)

The users of the system author programs and invoke them as transactions. They are assured that each invocation:

- Will be executed exactly once (reliability).
- Will be isolated from temporary violations of the consistency constraint introduced by actions of concurrently executing transactions (consistency).

The transaction may attempt to commit with the consistency constraint violated or the program itself may detect an error. In this case the effects of the transaction are undone and the system or program issues an error message as the transaction output.

This paper presents a model of reliability and concurrency issues associated with such systems.

RELIABILITY

Model of failures

Reliability is a goal which may only be approached by the careful use of redundancy. One never has a reliable system, if everything fails then there is no hope of reconstructing which transactions executed or the final system state. Hence one needs a model of failures in order to discuss reliability.

There are three kinds of entities:

- **Real** entities initially have null values and their values cannot be changed once they are non-null. They may spontaneously change (in which case they are **real input** messages). Or they may be written once (in which case they are **real output** messages). If a transaction gives away a 100$ bill, that piece of paper exists and is beyond the control of the system.

- **Stable** entities are have values which may be changed by the system and which survive system restart. Pages of duplexed disk or tape (two independent copies) are examples of stable storage. Pages of disk with an associated duplexed log of changes from a stable (archive) base version of the pages is another example of stable storage.

- **Volatile** entities have values which may be changed by the system and which are reset to null at system restart.

Two kinds of failures are considered:

- **Transaction restart:** for some reason a transaction needs to be restarted; however, its current state and the current state of the system exists (deadlock is an example of such a failure).

- **System restart:** for some reason the state of all volatile entities spontaneously change to null. However, all actions on stable and real entities prior to a certain instant will complete and all actions after that instant will have no effect until the system restarts.

The third kind of failure in which stable entities spontaneously change is not considered.

Transaction restart

A transaction may experience a finite number of transaction restarts. The system must have some way to undo such partially executed transactions. It would be nice to postulate:

- Every action <t,A,E> has an undo-action ¬<t,A,E> which cancels the effect of the action.

Thus if T =<<t,Ai,Ei>|i=1,...,n> executes actions <<t,Ai,Ei>|i=1,...,k> for some k<n then the system executes the actions: <¬<t,Ai,Ei>|i=k,...,1> and the transaction is undone.

Unfortunately, some entities are real and actions on them cannot be undone. The action <John,Eat,Cake> has no undo-action ¬<John,Eat,Cake>. You can't have your cake and eat it too.

Hence transactions are partitioned into two parts delimited by a **commit action, c:**

T = <<t,Ai,Ei>|i=1,...,c-1> <<t,Ai,Ei>|i=c,...,n>

where <t,Ac,Ec> is the first action of T which has no undo-action. The first part of the transaction is called the **prelude** and the second is called the **commitment.**

The commitment is not undoable (precludes transaction undo). So the actual execution of a transaction will be of the form:

P1 ¬P1 P2 ¬P2 ... Pj ¬Pj T

where each Pi is a prefix of the prelude of T, and ¬Pi is the corresponding undo of that prefix. The transaction finally runs to completion without any more restarts. This backtracking of the transaction is transparent to the programmer who wrote T and will only be visible to the user of T if some Pi sends messages to the user which are subsequently undone.

In order to support transaction restart [3,4,5,6],

- Before executing any action on an entity, the system records the corresponding undo-action in an entity called the transaction UNDO log.

- When a transaction is restarted, the actions in the transaction's UNDO log are applied (in last-in first-out order) to reverse the effects of the transaction.

A program may fail at any time or may attempt to commit with the consistency constraint violated. In this case the system must undo the transaction and commit it with an error message. Thus the system cannot allow a transaction to enter the commitment phase until the the program issues its last action (recall that commitment cannot be undone). Hence a special operation, the **commit operation,** is introduced which signals the end of the program.

Prior to the commit action, the effects of all actions which modify real entities are **deferred** and placed into an entity called a **REDO log** or **intentions list** for the transaction. When the transaction issues an action <t,A,e> on real entity e, a **redo action** denoted #<t,A,e> is inserted into the REDO log and the action itself is deferred (thereby making the action undoable). The commit action of the transaction requests the system to make a stable copy of the REDO log and then perform all the deferred actions in the REDO log.

Some systems defer all actions until commit and thereby avoid the need for transaction undo. A formal definition of this is complex since one must define the values of volatile and stable entities which have deferred actions pending against them. (i.e. are the changes visible before commit?) Real entities are initially null and, as will be explained below, changes to them are deferred until they are committed. **System restart**

If there were no volatile entities, system restart would be of no consequence. However, current and anticipated hardware and software, provide microsecond access times to volatile storage and millisecond access times to stable storage. This gap is likely to persist. Hence the state of the transaction and of many entities are represented in volatile storage.

There are four kinds of transactions at system restart:

1. Those which have all their committed actions reflected in real and stable entities.
2. Those which were in the commitment phase at the instant of system restart.
3. Those which were in the prelude at the instant of the system restart.
4. Those which had not yet begun.

System restart transforms transactions of type 3 to transactions of type 4 because the (volatile) transaction state has been lost. System restart transforms transactions of type 2 to transactions of type 1 because committing transactions cannot be undone.

When the restart process completes, all transactions will be either committed or not-yet-started and the database state will satisfy the consistency constraint. The processing of the not-yet-started transactions is then begun. (The next section discusses reconstruction of volatile entities at restart.)

The previous section described two things necessary for transaction restart:

- When performing an action on a volatile or stable entity, record the undo action in the transaction's undo log.

- Defer all actions which have no undo action into a REDO log of actions until a transaction commits.

In order to accomplish system restart three more things must be done during normal operation of the system (in addition to the logging required for transaction restart) [5,6,8]:

- Before performing an uncommitted action on a stable entity, record the undo of the action in stable storage (in a stable UNDO log).

- As the first step of the commit of a transaction, record the (committed) REDO log of a transaction as a stable object.

- As the second step of the commit of a transaction, perform all the deferred actions in the REDO log and mark them done in the REDO log.

The first rule (called the **write ahead log** protocol) allows any uncommitted action on stable storage to be undone by applying the undo actions in the UNDO log. There is one problem: recording the undo record and performing the operation on the stable entity are two separate actions. If the system restarts after the undo record is recorded but before the uncommitted operation is performed on the stable entity then the undo action will be applied to the old value (not to the new value) of the stable entity. Further, if a system restart occurs during transaction undo then the transaction may be only partially undone. To solve these problems,

- all undo actions ¬<t,A,E> must be **restartable** (or **idempotent**):
  <t,A,E>¬<t,A,E> is equivalent to <t,A,E>¬<t,A,E>,...,¬<t,A,E>

is equivalent to ¬<t,A,E>,...,¬<t,A,E>

(i.e. DO-UNDO equals UNDO equals DO-UNDO-UNDO-...-UNDO). Restartability is an additional requirement if UNDO is to be part of restart. One way to avoid this problem is to defer all stable updates to the commitment phase and thereby eliminate UNDO at restart.

Deferring all actions which have no undo action allows the transaction to be undone at any time prior to that step (maximally defers commitment). The requirement that the REDO log be made a stable object at the commit step of the transaction allows the system to continue the execution of transaction commit at system restart (by simply applying the REDO log of the transaction). Once a deferred action is actually performed, the redo action may be marked as "done" in the REDO log. But again there is the problem that performing the operation and marking it "done" in the REDO log are two separate actions. At restart one cannot be sure whether the last deferred action is done or not. Hence, one concludes that:

- redo actions #<t,A,E> must be **restartable:**
  <t,A,E> is equivalent to <t,A,E>,#<t,A,E>,...,#<t,A,E>
  is equivalent to #<t,A,E>,...,#<t,A,E>

(i.e. DO equals REDO equals DO-REDO-REDO-...-REDO). Thus if restart redoes already-done actions, they will do no harm.

The most common technique for achieving restartability of redo and undo actions is to put a version number in the entity and in the undo or redo action. The redo (or undo) step tests the version number of the entity against the desired version number and does nothing if the version numbers match, otherwise the undo or redo step is actually performed. For example, message sequence numbers are used in this way to detect and discard duplicate (redo) messages and to cancel messages which have been sent (undo).

Checkpoint and volatile entity reconstruction

In the discussion above, only the state of stable and real entities is reconstructed at system restart. The state of volatile entities is lost at system restart.

If the state of some volatile entity is to be reconstructed at system restart then the system must keep a REDO log of all actions on such entities and either:

- redo all actions on the entity since the beginning of time (using the REDO logs), or

- record a stable copy of the volatile entity at some time and then (using the REDO logs) redo all actions since that time.

Such a stable copy is called a checkpoint and is used to minimize redo work at restart [5,6].

The system allows the declaration of **recoverable volatile** entities. All entities appearing in the system invariant should be recoverable. The system periodically checkpoints recoverable volatile entities to stable objects. At restart *all actions* subsequent to the checkpoint on these entities are redone (including undo-actions).

Recoverable volatile entities are stable entities which have the fast access times of volatile entities. Their cost is periodic checkpoints, long term maintenance of REDO logs and extra work at system restart.

CONCURRENCY

Motivation for serializable history

The initial database state satisfies the consistency constraint. Although each transaction preserves the consistency constraint, the constraint may be violated while the transaction is in progress. For example, if a transaction transfers funds from one account to another, the constraint that "money is preserved" may be violated between the debit of one account and the credit of another account.

If there is no concurrency then each transaction begins with a consistent state and produces a consistent state. However, one transaction may see inconsistencies introduced by another if transactions execute concurrently.

It is difficult to write programs which work correctly in the presence of such inconsistencies. Therefore the system prevents such inconsistencies. Clearly a history without any concurrency (e.g. the history T1•T2•...•Tn) has no concurrency anomalies. Such histories are called **serial histories.**

Concurrency is allowed, only if it does not introduce inconsistencies. The simplest definition of this is to insist that any allowable history be equivalent to a serial history. Several different equivalence relations have been defined. Perhaps the most intuitive is developed as follows: Two operations on entities are recognized:

- READ: reads the value of a named entity but does not change it.

- WRITE: writes the value of a named entity.

Given this interpretation, we define the **dependency relation of history:**

$$H = \langle \ldots, \langle t1, A1, e\rangle, \ldots, \langle t2, A2, e\rangle, \ldots \rangle$$

where $t1 \neq t2$ as:

$$\begin{aligned} DEP(H) = \{ \langle t1,e,t2\rangle \mid\ & (A1 = \text{WRITE and } A2 = \text{WRITE}) \text{ or} \\ & (A1 = \text{WRITE and } A2 = \text{READ}) \text{ or} \\ & (A1 = \text{READ and } A2 = \text{WRITE}) \} \end{aligned}$$

DEP(H) tells "who gave what to whom". Two histories are **equivalent** if they have the same dependency relation. A history equivalent to a serial history is variously called **serializable, consistent,** and **degree 3 consistent.**

Intuitively, if H has the same "who gave what to whom" relationship as some serial history, then transactions cannot distinguish H from that serial history. **Locking protocol for serializable histories**

Locking is one technique for controlling concurrency (the interleaving of actions of several transactions). Used properly it can assure that all histories are equivalent to a serial history. Four new operations are introduced:

- LOCK_S: lock the named entity in shared mode.
- LOCK_X: lock the named entity in exclusive mode.
- UNLOCK_S: unlock the named entity from shared mode.
- UNLOCK_X: unlock the named entity from exclusive mode.

We say a lock action (S or X) by a transaction on the entity named E **covers** all actions up to the next unlock action (S or X respectively) action by that transaction on entity E.

The system will ensure that no LOCK_X action is performed on an entity while another transaction has that entity locked and conversely that no LOCK_S action on an entity is performed while another transaction has that entity locked in exclusive mode. More formally, the history H is **legal**

if H = <...<t1,A1,e>...<t2,A2,e>....> and t1 ≠ t2

and <T1,A1,e> is a lock action covering action <t2,A2,e> then:

if A1 = LOCK_S implies A2 ≠ LOCK_X

if A1 = LOCK_X implies (A2 ≠ LOCK_S and A2 ≠ LOCK_X).

A transaction is said to be **well-formed** if

- Each READ action is covered by a LOCK_S action on the entity name to be read, and
- Each WRITE action is covered by a LOCK_X action on the entity to be written, and
- Nothing is covered beyond the last action of the transaction (i.e. it unlocks everything).

A transaction is said to be **two-phase** if it does not perform a lock action after the first unlock action.

The definition of DEP(H) and of equivalence given before must be amended to treat LOCK_S and UNLOCK_S actions as READ actions and LOCK_X and UNLOCK_X actions as WRITE actions. Given that amendment, the central theorem of this development is:

THEOREM [2,10,11,12]:

(1) If all transactions are two-phase and well-formed
then any legal history is equivalent to a serial history.

(2) If some nontrivial§ transaction T is not two-phase or well-formed
then there is a transaction T' such that
T,T' have a legal history not equivalent to any serial history.

§Excluded are the null transaction, transactions which consist of a single read action and associated locks, and transactions which have locks which do not cover any action.

By automatically inserting LOCK_S and LOCK_X actions into a transaction prior to each READ and WRITE the system can guarantee a consistent execution of the transactions. Further, if the set of transactions is not known in advance all these precautions are required. However, if the set of transactions is known in advance, then some of the locks may be superfluous. For example, if there is only one transaction in the system then no locks are required. These observations have lead to many variations of the theorem. Another source of variations is possible by giving the operations an interpretation (e.g. we interpreted read, write and lock).

Locking and recovery

Consistency requires that a transaction be two-phase. We now argue that support of transaction restart requires that the second locking phase be deferred to transaction commit.

The first argument is based on the observation that UNLOCK_X generally does not have an undo action (and hence must be deferred). If transaction T1 unlocks an entity E which T1 has modified, entity E may be subsequently read or modified by another transaction T2. Restarting transaction T1 requires that the action of T1 on E be undone. This may invalidate the read or write of T2. One might suggest undoing T2, but T2 may have committed and hence cannot be undone. This argues that UNLOCK_X actions are not undoable and must be deferred.

A second argument observes that both UNLOCK_S and UNLOCK_X actions must be deferred to the commit action if the system automatically acquires locks for transactions. Suppose the system released a lock held by transaction T on entity E prior to the commit of T. Subsequent actions by T may require new locks. The acquisition of such locks after an unlock violates the two-phase lock protocol.

Summarizing:

- Consistency combined with transaction restart requires that UNLOCK_X actions be deferred until the transaction executes the commit action.

- Consistency combined with automatic locking requires that all locks be held until the transaction executes the commit action.

Degrees of consistency

Most systems do not provide consistency. They fail to set some required locks or release them prior to the commit point. The resulting anomalies can often be described by the the notions of degrees of consistency [4]. (A more appropriate term would be degrees of inconsistency.)

In order to support transaction restart, all systems acquire X-mode locks to cover writes and hold them to transaction commit. This is called the degree 1 consistency lock protocol.

If the system additionally acquires S-mode locks to cover reads but releases the locks prior to commit then it provides degree 2 consistency.

Both of these protocols are popular. Initially this was because system implementors did not understand the issues. Now some argue that the "lower" consistency degrees are more efficient than the degree 3 lock protocol. In the experiments we have done, degree 3 consistency has a cost (throughput and processor overhead) indistinguishable from the lower degrees of consistency.

Predicate locks

Some transactions want to access many entities. Others want only a few. It is convenient to be able to issue one lock specifying a set of desired entities. Such locks are called **predicate locks** and are represented as <T,P,M> where T is the name of the requesting transaction, P is the predicate on entities, and M is a mode: either S (for shared) or X (for exclusive) [2]. A typical predicate is:

VARIETY = CABERNET and VINTNER = FREEMARK_ABBY and YEAR = 1971

This should reserve all entities satisfying this predicate. Two predicate locks <T1,P1,M1> and <T2,P2,M2> **conflict** (and hence cannot be granted concurrently) if:

- They are requested by different transactions (T1≠T2) and,
- The predicates are mutually satisfiable (P1&P2) and,
- The modes are incompatible (not both S-mode).

Predicate locks are an elegant idea. (People have tried to patent them!). Unfortunately, no one has proposed a acceptable implementation for them. (Predicate satisfiability was one of the first problems to be proven NP complete).

Another problem with predicate locks is that satisfiability is too weak a criterion for conflict. For example the predicate:

VARIETY = CABERNET and SEX = FEMALE

is only formally satisfiable (I think). But the predicate locks:

<T1,VARIETY=CABERNET,X> and <T2,SEX=FEMALE,X>

formally conflict. A theorem prover might sort this out, but theorem provers are suspected to be very expensive.

Granularity of locking

The granularity of locks scheme captures the intent of predicate locks and avoids their high cost. It does this by choosing a *fixed* set of predicates.

Let P be a set of predicates on entities including the predicate TRUE and all predicates of the form: "ENTITY_NAME=e" for each entity <e,v>. Assume that for each pair Q, Q' of predicates in P:

either Q implies Q' or Q' implies Q. (*)

Define the binary relation on → on P:

Q → Q' iff for all entities e: Q'(e) implies Q(e).

The relation → is the set containment relation and because of assumption (*) above it orders P into a tree with root predicate TRUE.

Let the graph $G(P) = <P,E>$ be the Hesse diagram of this partial order. That is P is the set of vertices and E is the set of edges such that:

$$E = \{ <A,B> \mid A \rightarrow B \text{ and there is not } C \text{ in } P: A \rightarrow C \rightarrow B \}$$

A new lock mode is introduced: **Intention mode (I-mode)** which is compatible with I-mode but not with S-mode or X-mode. Using this new mode, the following lock protocol allows transactions to lock any predicate Q in P:

- Before locking Q in S-mode or X-mode, acquire I-mode locks on all parents of Q on graph G(P).

If this protocol is followed, acquiring an S-mode or X-mode lock on a node Q **implicitly** acquires an S-mode or or X-mode lock on all entities e such that Q(e).

THEOREM [4]: Suppose locks granted on graph G(P) are:

$$L = \{ <T,Q,M> \}.$$

Define the **intent** of these locks to be:

$$L' = \{ <T,Q',M> \mid <T,Q,M> \text{ is in } L \text{ and } Q \text{ implies } Q' \text{ and } M \neq \text{I-mode} \}.$$

Then if no locks in L conflict, no locks in L' will conflict.

Since L' contains all the entity locks which are children of the predicate locks this indicates that the predicate locks prevent undesired concurrency. Here we have restricted the graph to a tree (by constraint (*) on P). These results generalize to an arbitrary set of predicates which in trun generate an arbitrary directed acyclic graph G. The generalization is useful but notationally complex. A more detailed development would also resolve I-mode into three modes IS, IX, and SIX for greater concurrency. see [4] for a development of these generalizations.

Deadlock

A locking system must have some strategy for treating lock requests which conflict with already-granted locks. The simplest schemes either restart transactions which make such requests (no wait) or restart them if the request is ungranted for a certain time period (timeout).

Both of these approaches are subject to a phenomenon known as **livelock** in which two or more transactions repeatedly cause each other to be restarted. On the other hand, if transactions are allowed to wait indefinitely then they are subject to **deadlock** in which each member of a set of transactions is waiting for another member of the group to release a lock.

An approach which avoids such waiting allocates all desired resources to the transaction when it starts. This avoidance scheme has notorious performance because the resources potentially needed by a transaction are frequently much greater than those actually used.

Data management systems generally allow deadlock to occur. Deadlock appears as a cycle in the who-waits-for-whom graph. Deadlocks are resolved by choosing a minimal cost node set which breaks all cycles. Transactions corresponding to nodes of the set are undone and their locks preempted. The choice of preempted transactions must avoid livelock.

Fortunately, the mechanism for transaction restart is already present and so deadlock is simply another source of transaction restart. Further, deadlock is quite rare in practice (e.g. one transaction in one thousand) and the deadlock detection and resolution is comparatively simple (three pages of code compared to thirty for transaction restart).

We have observed that the probability a transaction deadlocks rises linearly with concurrency. A crude argument for this goes as follows: Let there be N+1 transactions each of which request r resources from a universe of R ($r \ll R$). The expected fraction of resources locked by others is $(Nr)/(2R)$ because each transaction holds about r/2 resources. Since a transaction makes r requests, the probability that it ever waits for a lock is: $(Nr^2)/(2R)$. Thus the probability that a request by a transaction will wait is proportional to N. Deadlocks are of the form "T waits for T' waits for T" or "T waits for T' waits for T'' waits for T", . . . The probability of a cycle of length two involving T and T' is

$$P(T \text{ waits for } T')P(T' \text{ waits for } T).$$

which is:

$$(r^2/2R)(r^2/2R).$$

Since there are N possible T', the probability that T deadlocks with some T' in a cycle of length 2 is:

$$N(r^2/2R)^2.$$

Generalizing, the probablility of a cycle of any length is:

$$N(r^2/2R)^2 + N^2(r^2/2R)^3 + N^4(r^2/2R)^3 + \ldots$$

Assuming that the probability a transaction waits is much less than one (typically .1 to .01):

$$(Nr^2)/(2R) \ll 1$$

we may drop the higher order terms and conclude that the probability of deadlock is approximately the probability of cycles of length 2:

$$Nr^4/4R^2.$$

The conclusions from all this arithmatic are:

- The probability a transaction experiences deadlock is proportional to the degree of concurrency (N).
- The rate of deadlocks is proportional to N^2.
- The propability a waiting transaction deadlocks is not sensitive to the degree of concurrency.

These results have been observed in practice and in several analytic models but no convincing proof of the result are known [7].

ISSUES IN DISTRIBUTED SYSTEMS

Model of distributed system

A distributed system partitions the set of entities into disjoint sets called **nodes.** Transactions may execute at several nodes but at any instant, a transaction **resides** at a particular node. Initially a transaction resides at the node of its input message. In order for a transaction at node N1 to execute an action on an entity at node N2 the transaction must **migrate** to that node by executing the operation MIGRATE_TO(N2) at node N1 and then execute the operation MIGRATE_FROM(N1) at node N2. Each node participating in a transaction keeps a REDO an UNDO log for the transaction's actions on entities at that node.

In a distributed system, nodes may fail independently. This introduces a new kind of failure:

- **node restart:** for some reason all volatile entities at the node spontaneously change to null.

Validity of serial history

Let T1,...,Tn be a set of transactions which execute on a system of m nodes. Each node has a history of the actions it executes, H1,...,Hm. To generalize the results for a single node system to a multi-node system we must exhibit a single schedule H such that:

- Each Hi is a subsequence of H and,

- Each Ti is a subsequence of H.

Among other things, the dependency set of H will be the same as the union of the dependency sets of H1,...,Hm. So H will be a single node history with the same who-gave-what-to-whom relation as the union of the Hi.

H may be demonstrated constructively by associating an initially zero counter with each node. Each time a node executes an action of transaction T the node and transaction counters are set to the maximum of the node and transaction counters plus 1. If the actions are sorted major by their counter value and minor by their node index then the resulting ordering is a schedule H for all actions. This ordering has the desired properties [10,11].

Reliability

Node restart in a distributed system is much like system restart in a single node system with the exception of transactions which have migrated among several nodes. Transactions which migrate complicate both node restart and transaction restart. The simplest approach to transaction restart is to adopt the rule [12]:

- Only the node of residence can initiate transaction restart.

This rule implies that when transaction, T, migrates from node, N1, node N1 abdicates the right to restart T. This in turn means that the MIGRATE_TO(N2) operation at node N1 must prevent a restart of node N1 from restarting T. Hence, as part of the MIGRATE_TO(N2) operation, node N1 must make a stable copy of the state of T. At a minimum, this state includes REDO and UNDO logs of transaction T along with all locks and the state of all volatile entities belonging to T (recall that T may migrate back to N1 and expect its program state to be preserved). Until the transaction commits or restarts, each node restart at N1 must reconstruct the state of T at node N1 from this information.

The commit operation broadcasts commit to each node participating in the transaction. The transaction restart operation broadcasts restart to each such participant. When all participants have acknowledged that they have performed their part of the commit or restart, the node of residence can terminate the transaction or reinitiate it.

This commit protocol has the virtue of simplicity and may become the most commonly used algorithm. It has to properties which have caused a search for alternate algorithms. These two problems are:

- It requires a node to be able to record the entire state of a migrated transaction in stable storage.
- It prevents a node from unilaterally aborting a transaction which has migrated from that node. This may tie up the resources of one node for a long time if the transaction migrates to a node which subsequently fails.

The **two-phase commit** protocol is designed to eliminate the first problem and minimize the second. The two-phase commit protocol implements the commit action as follows: As part of the commit action, one participant of the transaction is appointed the **commit coordinator.**

The coordinator obeys the following protocol:

- Phase 1: Each participant of T is polled to see if it is prepared to commit.
- The coordinator enters phase 2 when it *recoverably* makes the decision to commit or abort.
  - If all participants agree to commit, the coordinator records the commit decision in T's stable REDO log and then broadcasts the commit message to each participant.
  - If any node does not agree to commit or does not respond within a time limit, the commit coordinator records the decision in T's stable UNDO log and then broadcasts the restart message to each participant.
  - The broadcast message is periodically re-broadcast to each participant until it acknowledges that it has acted on the message.
  - When the coordinator has received all the phase 2 acknowledgments it either terminates (commit) or reinitiates (restart) transaction T.

The participants obey the following protocol:

- Phase 0: Prior to agreeing to commit, any node may unilaterally undo all actions of the transaction at that node and broadcast transaction restart.

- Phase 1: Upon receiving a prepare to commit request,

  - If the node has unilaterally restarted T it responds with transaction restart,

  - Otherwise, the participant records the REDO and UNDO log of the transaction at the node in stable storage and responds with an agree to commit message.

- Phase 2: The participant then waits for the coordinator's decision.

  - If the coordinator broadcasts commit then the participant commits its part of T and then acknowledges completion to the coordinator.

  - If the coordinator broadcasts restart, the the participant undoes its part of T and then acknowledges completion to the coordinator.

The two-phase commit algorithm avoids saving the volatile parts of the transaction state. Node restart can restart any transaction not in phase two of the commit operation. Such transactions are described as **in-doubt.** At node restart, the node must reestablish all X-mode locks belonging to in-doubt transactions as well as maintain the UNDO and REDO logs of such transactions. The two-phase commit protocol also minimizes the period during which a node cannot unilaterally restart the transaction.

There are many variations of the two-phase commit protocol. There are almost no proofs about the properties of these protocols. The central theorem is:

THEOREM: If all participants observe the two-phase commit protocol then
either all participants eventually enter the commit state
without passing through the transaction restart state.
or all participants eventually enter the restart state
without passing through the commit state.

Lindsay 99 has the most careful presentation of this result.

Concurrency

Concurrency is inherent in a distributed system (each node executes autonomously). The existence of a global history implies that the theorems about locking generalize to distributed systems. The node can acquire locks for actions on entities at that node. If all transactions are well-formed and two phase then the system will provide the illusion of a centralized serial history.

A problem with this approach is that each node has only a portion of the who-waits-for-whom graph. In order to detect deadlock cycles, someone must glue the pieces of the graph together. Otherwise, deadlock detection in a distributed system is analogous to deadlock detection in a centralized system.

TRANSACTION CONCEPT IN A PROGRAMMING LANGUAGE

The transaction concept is a fundamental notion. It already appears in data definition and data manipulation languages associated with data management systems. It is likely to appear in more conventional languages in the future. This is a proposal for what such a language extension might include.

The language provides an abstraction for something like a **module type** which appears to the user as a collection of operations on entities. When a **module instance** is created it may be given the attributes **real, stable, recoverable volatile** or **volatile** which indicate whether REDO and UNDO records need to be kept for the instance and whether or not the actions must be deferred. If the instance is to be shared then (Note that monitors are inappropriate for the transaction notion. They violate the two phase lock protocol by releasing locks at procedure exit rather than at transaction commit.) it may be given the attribute **shared** which will cause the operations on the instance to acquire appropriate locks prior to manipulating the instance.

Each operation of the module must have corresponding undo and redo operations based on the UNDO and REDO log.

The language also supports two verbs COMMIT and ABORT which commit the transaction or undo it and commit it with an error message.

This is the view of the *user of a module*. The implementor of a module type needs to have an interface to a *lock management facility* which will handle lock requests and do deadlock detection. He also needs an interface to the *log management facility* which will accept log records and return them on request. Transaction undo and redo appears to the module as calls from *recovery manager* which invokes the undo and redo operation passing the the undo or redo log record [5,6].

REFERENCES

[1] Davies, C.T., "Recovery Semantics for a DB/DC System," Proceedings ACM National Conference, 1973, pp. 136-141.

[2] Eswaran, K.E., J.N. Gray, R.A. Lorie, I.L. Traiger, "On the Notions of Consistency and Predicate Locks in a Relational Database System," Communications of the ACM, Vol. 19, No. 11, Nov. 1976, pp. 624-634.

[3] Gorski J., "A Formal Model for Transaction Back-up in a Database Environment", Institute of Informatics, Technical University of Gdansk, Poland, Draft, March 1979, pp. 13.

[4] Gray, J.N., R.A. Lorie, G.F. Putzolu, I.L. Traiger, "Granularity of Locks and Degrees of Consistency in a Shared Data Base", *Modeling in Data Base Management Systems.* G.M. Nijssen editor, North Holland, 1976, pp. 365-394. Also IBM Research Report: RJ 1606.

[5] Gray, J.N., "Notes on Data Base Operating Systems", *Operating Systems - An Advanced Course,* R. Bayer, R.M. Graham, G. Seegmuller editors, Springer Verlag, 1978, pp. 393-481. Also IBM Research Report: RJ 2188, Feb. 1978.

[6] Gray J.N., P. McJones, M. W. Blasgen, R. A. Lorie, T. G. Price, G. F. Putzolu, I. L. Traiger, "The Recovery Manager of a Data Management System", IBM Research Report RJ 2623, August 1979. pp. 23.

[7] Korth H., Homan P. This is a brief discussion of work done by Hank Korth (of Stanford) and myself in 1978 and of discussions with Pete Homan (of IBM Hursley).

[8] Lampson B.W., H. E. Sturgis. "Crash Recovery in a Distributed Data Storage System", Xerox Research Report: ?, To appear in Communications of the ACM. April 1979, pp. 23.

[9] Lindsay B. G., P. G. Selinger, C. A. Galtieri, J. N. Gray, R. A. Lorie, T. G. Price, G. F. Putzolu, I. L. Traiger, B. W. Wade, "Notes on Distributed Databases", IBM Research Report: RJ 2571, July 1979. pp. 57.

[10] Papadimitriou C. H., "The Serializability of Concurrent Database Updates", Journal of the ACM, Vol. 26, No. 4, October 1979, pp. 631-653.

[11] Traiger I. L., Galtieri C. A., Gray J. N., Lindsay B. G., "Transactions and Consistency in Distributed Database Systems", To appear in ACM Transactions on Database Systems. also IBM Research Report: RJ 2555, June 1979, pp. 17.

[12] Rosenkrantz D. J., R. E. Sterns, R. E. Lewis, "System Level Concurrency Control for Distributed Database Systems", ACM Transactions on Database Systems, Vol. 3, No. 2, June 1978, pp. 178-198.

On Observing Nondeterminism and Concurrency

Matthew Hennessy and Robin Milner
University of Edinburgh

1. Introduction

The denotational approach to the semantics of programming languages has been well-developed in recent years (see [1],[6]) and applied successfully to many non-trivial languages. Even languages with parallel constructs have been treated in this way, using the powerdomain constructions of [2],[5],[7]. Indeed for such languages there is no shortage of possible denotational models. For example there are several simple variations on the model for processes, introduced in [3].

Faced with such an abundance it is best to recall the motivation for seeking such models. They provide a useful mathematical framework for the analysis of programs, and for developing logical systems for proving their properties. However if either the mathematics or the logic is to have any relevance a link must be made between the denotational model and the behaviour, or operational semantics, of the programs.

What exactly is meant by the behaviour of non-deterministic or concurrent programs is far from clear and in this paper we put forth one possible definition. The essence of our approach is that the behaviour of a program is determined by how it communicates with an observer. We begin by assuming that every program action is observable in this way; later we allow that some actions (in particular, internal communications between concurrent components) are not observable.

We apply our definition to a sequence of simple languages for expressing finite behaviours, and show that in each case it can be characterised by algebraic axioms. This leads automatically to fully abstract models. Moreover, a proper understanding of the finite case seems a necessary prelude to a study of programs with infinite behaviour. Such programs may be gained simply by adding recursion to our languages.

In fact with the addition of recursion, and with a natural extension to allow data values to be communicated between concurrently active agents, the simple algebra described here becomes a language for writing a specifying concurrent programs and for proving their properties. This language was introduced in [4]; it was partly the need for a firm basis for the algebraic laws discussed there which led to the present study of observation equivalence.

In section 2 we present our general framework. In section 3 we outline and summarize our results for the languages considered. The proofs will appear in a technical report.

2. Observational Equivalence of Processes

Let us start with the idea that two programs are operationally congruent if it is impossible to distinguish between them operationally. Thus, if they are considered as modules, one can be exchanged for the other in a larger program, without affecting the behaviour of the latter.

In the deterministic case the behaviour of a program is usually taken to mean its input-output relation. To summarise: two programs p,q are behaviourly equivalent, written $p \sim q$, if $IO(p) = IO(q)$; the operational congruence generated by $\sim$ is defined by $p \sim_c q$ if for every suitable programming environment $\mathcal{C}[\,]$, $\mathcal{C}[p] \sim \mathcal{C}[q]$. If the language is defined algebraically, i.e. by operations for constructing new programs from ones already defined, $\sim_c$ is the largest congruence contained in $\sim$.

However, any satisfactory comparison of the behaviour of concurrent programs must take into account their intermediate states as they progress through a computation, because differing intermediate states can be exploited in larger programming environments to produce different overall behaviour (e.g. deadlock). With this in mind, we now outline a more general notion of behaviour equivalence between programs, called observational equivalence.

Let P be a set of objects called programs, or agents, which are capable of some form of communication. An atomic experiment on p can be considered as an attempt to communicate with p. Since the act of communication can change the nature of an agent, and can change it in various different ways depending on its internal structure, the effect of an atomic experiment can be captured by a binary relation over P. Since in general there may be various means of communication we have a set of relations $\{R_i \subseteq P \times P,\ i \in I\}$. Using these atomic experiments, we define a sequence of equivalence relations $\sim_n$ over P as follows:

Let $p \sim_o q$ if $p,q \in P$

$p \sim_{n+1} q$ if

i) $\forall i \in I$, $\langle p,p'\rangle \in R_i$ implies $\exists q'.\ \langle q,q'\rangle \in R_i, p' \sim_n q'$

and ii) $\forall i \in I$, $\langle q,q'\rangle \in R_i$ implies $\exists p'.\ \langle p,p'\rangle \in R_i, p' \sim_n q'$

Then p is observationally equivalent to q, written $p \sim q$, if $p \sim_n q$ for every n. Before discussing $\sim$ we give some of its properties. For any $S \subseteq P \times P$ let $E(S)$ be defined by

$\langle p,q\rangle \in E(S)$ if $\forall i \in I$

i) $\langle p,p'\rangle \in R_i \Rightarrow \exists q'.\ \langle q,q'\rangle \in R_i,\ \langle p',q'\rangle \in S$

ii) $\langle q,q'\rangle \in R_i \Rightarrow \exists p'.\ \langle p,p'\rangle \in R_i,\ \langle p',q'\rangle \in S$

We say that a relation R is image-finite if for each p, $\{p' \mid \langle p,p'\rangle \in R\}$ is finite.

Theorem 2.1

If each R_i is image-finite then $\sim$ is the maximal solution to $S = E(S)$. ☒

More complicated experiments can be carried out by applying sequences of atomic experiments. Let s be the sequence $i_1, \ldots, i_n$ in $I\ (n \geq 1)$. An <u>s-experiment on p</u> is a sequence $p_1, \ldots, p_{n+1}$ where $p_1 = p$ and $\langle p_k, p_{k+1} \rangle \in R_{i_k}$. Thus if $p \sim q$ and we perform an experiment on p which consequently changes to p', then when the same experiment is performed on q it can change to a q' which is equivalent to p'.

If we consider a computation as a sequence of experiments (or communications) then the above remarks show that intermediate states are compared. In fact if p is to be equivalent to q there must be a strong relationship between their respective intermediate states. For example it is not sufficient to say that for every s, p has an s-experiment iff q has an s-experiment. At each intermediate stage in the computations the respective "potentials" must also be the same. To indicate more clearly when two programs are equivalent we give a little language for talking about programs. It is designed in such a way that two programs are equivalent iff the set of sentences true of one is identical with the set of sentences true of the other.

Let that language $\mathcal{L}$ of formulae be the least set such that

i) $T \in \mathcal{L}$

ii) $A, B \in \mathcal{L} \Rightarrow A \wedge B \in \mathcal{L},\ \neg A \in \mathcal{L}$

iii) $A \in \mathcal{L}$ and $i \in I \Rightarrow \langle i \rangle A \in \mathcal{L}$

The satisfaction relation $\models \subseteq P \times \mathcal{L}$ is the least relation such that

i) $p \models T$ for all $p \in P$

ii) $p \models A \wedge B$ iff $p \models A$ and $p \models B$

iii) $p \models \neg A$ iff not $p \models A$

iv) $p \models \langle i \rangle A$ iff for some i-experiment $\langle p, p' \rangle$, $p' \models A$

For convenience let

F	stand for	$\neg T$
$A \vee B$	" "	$\neg(\neg A \wedge \neg B)$
$\langle s \rangle A$	" "	$\langle i_1 \rangle \ldots \langle i_n \rangle A$, where $s = i_1 \ldots i_n,\ n \geq 1$
$[s] A$	" "	$\neg \langle s \rangle \neg A$.

We say p is <u>s-deadlocked</u> if there are no s-experiments on p.

<u>Examples</u>

a) $p \models \langle s \rangle T$ - it is possible to carry out an s-experiment on p.

b) $p \models [s] F$ - p is s-deadlocked.

c) $p \models \langle s_1 \rangle ([s_2] F \vee [s_3] F)$ - it is possible, via an s_1-experiment, to get into a state which is either s_2-deadlocked or s_3-deadlocked.

d) $p \models [s_1] (\langle s_2 \rangle [s_3] F)$ - at the end of any s_1-experiment an s_2-experiment is possible which will leave the program in a state which is s_3-deadlocked.

Note that it is the interleaving to arbitrary depth of the two modal operators $\langle\ \rangle$,

$\Box$ that gives the language its power. Although we do not here develop $\mathcal{L}$ into a logic for reasoning about programs, it is worth noting that as a language it is endogenous by Pnueli's classification [8]. This means that a formula states something about the 'world' of a single program, in contrast to exogenous logics such as Dynamic Logic [9] where parts of programs may be constituents of formulae.

Theorem 2.2 Assume that each R_i is image-finite.

Let $\mathcal{J}(p) = \{A \in \mathcal{L} \mid p \models A\}$. Then $p \sim q$ iff $\mathcal{J}(p) = \mathcal{J}(q)$. ⊠

This characterization theorem, together with our examples which indicate that in $\mathcal{L}$ it is possible to discuss deadlocking properties of programs, encourages us to believe that our notion of observation equivalence is natural. Moreover each connective of $\mathcal{L}$ is important; by removing first negation, then conjunction, from $\mathcal{L}$ we obtain characterizations of progressively weaker equivalences.

In the remainder of the paper we study the observational equivalence (and the observational congruence it generates) of finite programs. We will consider two different types of atomic experiment and in each case we show that the congruence can be algebraically characterised.

3. Algebraic Characterization

In the previous section we showed how to define observational equivalence over an arbitrary set P of programs or agents, in terms of an indexed family $\{R_i \mid i \in I\}$ of binary relations over P with the finite image property.

Here we wish to introduce structure over P, by considering it to be the word algebra W_Σ for a variety of signatures Σ. In each case, we shall define the observation relations R_i in two different ways, and hence obtain observational equivalence relations $\sim$ over W_Σ .

Now in general $\sim$ may not be a congruence with respect to the operations of W_Σ ; this is to say that a pair of words w and w' may satisfy $w \sim w'$, but there may be a context $\mathcal{C}[\,]$ (that is, a word with a hole in it, or equivalently a derived unary operation over W) for which $\mathcal{C}[w] \not\sim \mathcal{C}[w']$. ($\sim$ is a congruence iff $w \sim w'$ implies $\mathcal{C}[w] \sim \mathcal{C}[w']$ for every $\mathcal{C}[\,]$.) Thus observational equivalence of w and w' does not guarantee that one may be exchanged for the other without observable difference.

We therefore define observational congruence $\sim_c$ over W_Σ as follows:

$w \sim_c w'$ iff for all contexts $\mathcal{C}[\,]$. $\mathcal{C}[w] \sim \mathcal{C}[w']$

It is easy to check that this is a congruence, and is moreover the largest congruence contained in $\sim$.

Our aim is to find alternative characterization of this congruence relation of "indistinguishability by observation in all contexts"; specifically, we aim to show that it is exactly the congruence induced by a set of equational axioms over Σ . By this means we obtain an algebraic theory, of which $W_\Sigma/\sim_c$ is the initial algebra.

In the rest of this section we present three signatures Σ_1, Σ_2 and Σ_3 , define the experiment relations R_i for each of them in two distinct ways, and summarise our main results. These results state, for each of the six cases, a set of equational axioms which induce exactly the observational congruence determined by the relations.

3.1 The signature $\Sigma_1 = M \cup \{NIL,+\}$

M is an arbitrary set of unary operators, whose members μ we shall call labels. NIL is a nullary operator and + is a binary operator. Our programs are W_{Σ_1} , and our experiment relations $\{R_\mu \mid \mu \in M\}$ are the smallest relations satisfying the following conditions (we write $\overset{\mu}{\rightarrow}$ for R_μ).

($\rightarrow$1) $\mu(w) \overset{\mu}{\rightarrow} w$

($\rightarrow$2) if $u \overset{\mu}{\rightarrow} u'$ then $u + v \overset{\mu}{\rightarrow} u'$

($\rightarrow$3) if $v \overset{\mu}{\rightarrow} v'$ then $u + v \overset{\mu}{\rightarrow} v'$

W_{Σ_1} may be regarded as perhaps the simplest possible language for finite nondeterministic programs, built from the null program NIL, the atomic actions M (represented by the unary operators M, which may be thought of as prefixing an atomic action to a program) and the binary choice (or ambiguity) operator + . An atomic experiment consists in the observation of an atomic action; the experiment fails if the program cannot perform the action.

Axioms

(A1) $x + (y + z) = (x + y) + z$

(A2) $x + y = y + x$

(A3) $x + x = x$

(A4) $x + NIL = x$

Theorem 3.1 The observational congruence $\sim_c$ over W_{Σ_1} is exactly the congruence induced by (A1) - (A4). ☒

In this particularly simple case the observational equivalence $\sim$ turns out to be already a congruence, and therefore $\sim_c = \sim$. Note the absence of the distributive law $\mu(x + y) = \mu(x) + \mu(y)$ from the axioms. That this is natural may be explained as follows. In view of our axioms, the set $W_{\Sigma_1}/\sim_c$ is isomorphic with set of finite, rooted, unordered trees whose arcs are labelled by members of M. Thus we have two distinct (incongruent) programs $w_1 = \mu_1(\mu_2(NIL) + \mu_3(NIL))$, $w_2 = \mu_1(\mu_2(NIL)) + \mu_1(\mu_3(NIL))$ represented by the distinct trees

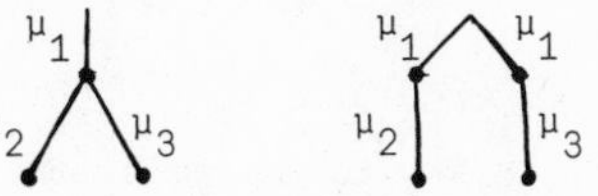

Indeed, in terms of our language $\mathcal{L}$ we have

$$w_1 \models A, \quad w_2 \not\models A$$

where A is $\langle\mu_1\rangle(\langle\mu_2\rangle T \wedge \langle\mu_3\rangle T)$. By contrast, if B is $\langle\mu_1\rangle[\mu_2]F$ then

$$w_1 \not\models B, \quad w_2 \models B.$$

3.2 Unobservable atomic actions in Σ_1

In the above system every atomic action is observable; a program cannot proceed without being observed. Let us now suppose that among M there are atomic actions which cannot be observed; for such an atomic action we shall have no corresponding atomic experiment. Intuitively, we may consider these actions as beyond the observer's control. But their presence may have a bearing upon the observable behaviour of a program, as the following example shows. Suppose that τ is an unobservable atomic action, and consider the programs $w_1 = \mu_1(\mu_2(\text{NIL} + \tau(\text{NIL})), \; w_2 = \mu_1(\mu_2(\text{NIL}))$.

w_1 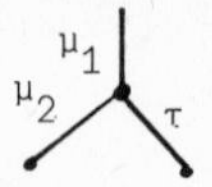

w_2 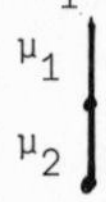

When we have redifined the notion of μ-experiment to allow it to be accompanied by unobservable actions, then one possible result of a μ_1-experiment on w_1 is NIL (since τ may occur unobserved), while the only possible result of the experiment on w_2 is $\mu_2(\text{NIL})$. Thus we have

$$w_1 \models A, \quad w_2 \not\models A$$

where A is $\langle\mu_1\rangle(\neg\langle\mu_2\rangle T)$. Notice however that both w_1 and w_2 satisfy $\langle\mu_1\rangle\langle\mu_2\rangle T$.

For simplicity we assume that τ is the only unobservable atomic action. (This may be formally justified; if there were two such, τ_1 and τ_2, we would arrive at an axiom $\tau_1(x) = \tau_2(x)$ - indicating that the replacement of τ_1 by τ_2 can affect no observation.) We therefore assume $M = \Lambda \cup \{\tau\}$ $(\tau \notin \Lambda)$, and we define a new set $\{R_\lambda \mid \lambda \in \Lambda\}$ of experiment relations as follows. First, define $\overset{s}{\rightarrow}$ over W_{Σ_1}, for any $s = \mu_1 \ldots \mu_n \in M^*$ $(n \geq 0)$, by

$$w \overset{s}{\rightarrow} w' \text{ iff } w = w_0 \overset{\mu_1}{\rightarrow} w_1 \overset{\mu_2}{\rightarrow} \ldots \overset{\mu_n}{\rightarrow} w_n = w'$$

Then, writing R_λ as $\overset{\lambda}{\Rightarrow}$, we define for each $\lambda \in \Lambda$

$$w \overset{\lambda}{\Rightarrow} w' \text{ iff } w \xrightarrow{\tau^m \lambda \tau^n} w' \text{ for some } m,n \geq 0$$

Thus our new atomic observation $\overset{\lambda}{\Rightarrow}$ may absorb any finite sequence of unobservable actions before or after the action λ. It is easy to check that each $\overset{\lambda}{\Rightarrow}$ is image-finite.

We obtain now a new observational equivalence relation $\approx$ over W_{Σ_1}, using the definition of section 2 with the relations $\{\overset{\lambda}{\Rightarrow} \mid \lambda \in \Lambda\}$.

This induces, as before, an observational congruence $\approx_c$ (the largest congruence contained in $\approx$), but this is not identical with $\approx$. Indeed, the latter is not a congruence. For example, it is easy to check that $\tau(\text{NIL}) \approx \text{NIL}$; but if we place each of these programs in the context $\mathcal{C}[\;] = \lambda_1(\lambda_2(\text{NIL}) + [\;])$ we obtain $\mathcal{C}[\tau(\text{NIL})] \not\approx \mathcal{C}[\text{NIL}]$ as may be readily checked (this is in effect the pair w_1, w_2 discussed earlier).

Axioms

(A5) $x + \tau x = \tau x$

(A6) $\mu(x + \tau y) = \mu(x + y) + \mu y \quad (\mu \in M)$

(We will often, as here, omit parentheses and write $\mu(x)$ as μx .)

Theorem 3.2 The observational congruence $\approx_c$ over W_{Σ_1} is exactly the congruence induced by (A1)-(A6). ⊠

This theorem is not so immediate as the previous one, partly because $\approx$ is not a congruence. It involves defining a normal form for programs in W_{Σ_1} ; the most important step in deriving a normal form is the use of (A6) to eliminate most occurrences of τ in a program.

3.3 The Signature $\Sigma_2 = \Sigma_1 \cup \{|\}$

We now add a binary operator "|" to our signature; it is one of a variety of operators which may be chosen to represent the combination of a pair of programs which may proceed concurrently and may also communicate with one another. These two properties are reflected by separate new conditions upon the experiment relations $\xrightarrow{\mu}$. One condition (in two parts) expresses that the program $u|v$ admits all the experiments which u and v admit separately. (Since an atomic experiment corresponds to a single atomic action, the simultaneous activity of u and v cannot be observed.)

($\rightarrow$4) if $u \xrightarrow{\mu} u'$ then $u|v \xrightarrow{\mu} u'|v$

($\rightarrow$5) if $v \xrightarrow{\mu} v'$ then $u|v \xrightarrow{\mu} u|v'$

To express communication we introduce a little structure over M . We assume $M = \Lambda \cup \{\tau\}$ as before, and also that $\Lambda = \Delta \cup \overline{\Delta}$ where Δ is a possibly infinite alphabet of names, and that the alphabet $\overline{\Delta}$ of conames is disjoint from Δ and in bijection with it. We represent the bijection and its inverse by overbar ($\bar{\ }$), and use $\{\alpha,\beta,\gamma\}$ to range over Δ . Thus $\bar{\alpha} \in \overline{\Delta}$, and $\bar{\bar{\alpha}} = \alpha$. We continue to use λ to range over Λ , and μ,ν to range over $M = \Lambda \cup \{\tau\}$. Communication between u and v may occur when u admits a λ-experiment and v admits a $\bar{\lambda}$-experiment, for some λ ; the result is a τ-action of $u|v$.

($\rightarrow$6) if $u \xrightarrow{\lambda} u'$ and $v \xrightarrow{\bar{\lambda}} v'$ then $u|v \xrightarrow{\tau} u'|v'$

This choice to represent communication between components of a program by a τ-action will allow us in section 3.4 to treat internal communications as unobservable.

Now taking $\{\overset{\mu}{\rightarrow} \mid \mu \in M\}$ to be the smallest relations over W_{Σ_2} satisfying $(\rightarrow 1)$ - $(\rightarrow 6)$, we obtain an observational equivalence $\sim$ over W_{Σ_2} as in Section 2. As before, this turns out to be a congruence, so that $\sim_c$ is identical with $\sim$.

Since axioms (A1) - (A4) are satisfied by $\sim_c$, we may adopt the notation, for any $n \geq 0$,

$$\sum_{1\leq i\leq n} \mu_i x_i = \begin{cases} \mu_1 x_1 + \ldots + \mu_n x_n & \text{if } n > 0 \\ \text{NIL} \quad \text{if } n = 0 \end{cases}$$

Now we add an axiom for "|":

(A7) if u is $\sum \mu_i x_i$ and v is $\sum \nu_j y_j$ then

$$u|v = \sum_i \mu_i (x_i|v) + \sum_j \nu_j (u|y_j) + \sum_{\mu_i = \bar{\nu}_j} \tau(x_i|y_j)$$

<u>Examples</u> Instances of (A7) are (for distinct names α, β and γ)

$$(\alpha x_1 + \beta x_2) | \gamma y = \alpha(x_1|\gamma y) + \beta(x_2|\gamma y) + \gamma((\alpha x_1 + \beta x_2)|y)$$
$$(\alpha x_1 + \beta x_2) | \bar{\beta} y = \alpha(x_1|\bar{\beta} y) + \beta(x_2|\bar{\beta} y) + \bar{\beta}((\alpha x_1 + \beta x_2)|y) + \tau(x_2|y)$$
$$(\sum \mu_i x_i)|\text{NIL} = \sum \mu_i (x_i|\text{NIL}) + \text{NIL} + \text{NIL}$$

Note that (A7) allows | to be eliminated from any word in W_{Σ_2} .

<u>Theorem 3.3</u> The observational congruence $\sim_c$ over W_{Σ_2} is exactly the congruence induced by (A1) - (A4) and (A7). ☒

<u>Remark</u> The following laws for "|" may be proved to hold over W_{Σ_2} by induction on the structure of terms (though they are not deducible from (A1) - (A4), (A7) by equational reasoning):

$$x | (y|z) = (x|y) | z$$
$$x | y = y | x$$
$$x | \text{NIL} = x$$

3.4 <u>Unobservable actions in</u> Σ_2

We now repeat for Σ_2 what we did for Σ_1 ; we wish to treat τ as an unobservable atomic action (in particular, the intercommunication of u and v in $u|v$ is not an observable action). If we define the experiment relations $\{\overset{\lambda}{\Rightarrow} \mid \lambda \in \Lambda\}$ as previously then we gain again an observational congruence $\approx_c$ over W_{Σ_2} . We then might expect this to be exactly the congruence induced by the axioms (A1) - (A7), but this is not the case, since (A6) is not satisfied by $\approx_c$ over W_{Σ_1} . We shall demonstrate, in particular that the following instance of (A6) is false

$$\alpha(\beta\,\text{NIL} + \tau\,\text{NIL}) \approx_c \alpha(\beta\,\text{NIL} + \text{NIL}) + \alpha\,\text{NIL}$$

For this would imply the observational equivalence (not congruence)

$$\gamma NIL \mid \alpha(\beta NIL + \tau NIL) \approx \gamma NIL \mid (\alpha(\beta NIL + NIL) + \alpha NIL) \qquad (1)$$

Calling the left and right sides of (1) u and v respectively, we have

$$u \stackrel{\alpha}{\Rightarrow} u' = \gamma NIL \mid (\beta NIL + \tau NIL)$$

while $v \stackrel{\alpha}{\Rightarrow} v'$ implies that $v' = v_1$ or $v' = v_2$ where

$$v_1 = \gamma NIL \mid (\beta NIL + NIL)$$
$$v_2 = \gamma NIL \mid NIL$$

Now if (1) holds, then by definition of $\approx$ we must have $u' \approx v_1$ or $u' \approx v_2$. The second is impossible since $u' \stackrel{\beta}{\Rightarrow} \gamma NIL|NIL$, while $v_2 \stackrel{\beta}{\Rightarrow} v_2'$ is impossible. Hence $u' \approx v_1$. But

$$u' \stackrel{\gamma}{\Rightarrow} NIL|NIL$$

while the only γ-experiment for v_1 is

$$v_1 \stackrel{\gamma}{\Rightarrow} NIL \mid (\beta NIL + NIL)$$

Hence we must have $NIL|NIL \approx NIL \mid (\beta NIL + NIL)$, which is easily false.

Axiom (A6) fails for W_{Σ_2} because the operator "|" provides a richer class of contexts in which to perform experiments. We therefore hope to characterise $\approx_c$ over W_{Σ_2} by replacing (A6) by something weaker.

<u>Axioms</u>

(A 6.1) $\quad \mu(x + \tau y) = \mu(x + \tau y) + \mu y$

$(\mu \in M)$

(A 6.2) $\quad \mu \tau y = \mu y$

These axioms are indeed implied by (A1) - (A6). First observe that (A6.2) follows by placing $x = NIL$ in (A6) and using the other axioms. Then to get (A6.1) place τy for y in (A6).

$$\mu(x + \tau\tau y) = \mu(x + \tau y) + \mu \tau y$$

and use two instances of (A6.2).

<u>Theorem 3.4</u> The observational congruence $\approx_c$ over W_{Σ_2} is exactly the congruence induced by (A1) - (A5), (A6.1), (A6.2) and (A7). ☒

This theorem is the central result of our paper, since the method not only generalises in a routine manner to the corresponding theorem for our next signature $\sum_3$, but also applies we believe - with minor adjustments - to many other signatures and experiment relations representing concurrent and communicating activity. The axioms (A1) - (A5), (A6.1) and (A6.2) seem to be what is required for the operators in $\sum_1$ in the presence of extra operators for communication and concurrency.

3.5 The signature $\sum_3 = \sum_2 \cup \mathcal{S}$

In [4] we considered operations over behaviours corresponding to $\sum_2$, together with two other families of operations called relabelling and restriction; in the present context, these operations may be described as changing (bijectively) the labels for atomic experiments (i.e. permutations of Λ), and restricting the class of atomic experiments to a subset of Λ . The approach in [4] was to classify behaviours into sorts; a sort L was a subset of Λ, and the behaviours B_L of sort L were those which employed only members of L as labels.

Here we do not consider sorts; these may be later introduced, and are indeed useful in providing a stronger basis for reasoning about realistic programs. Moreover, we can treat relabelling and restriction as subclasses of a wider family of operations indexed by a subset of the partial functions $M \rightharpoonup M$ from M to M. To this end we add to the signature $\sum_1$ the operators

$$\mathcal{S} = \{[S] \mid S \in M \rightharpoonup M,\ S\tau = \tau\}$$

We shall postfix these operators. We characterise them operationally by adding a further condition for the production relations $\overset{\mu}{\rightarrow}$:

$(\rightarrow 7)$ If $w \overset{\mu}{\rightarrow} w'$ and $S\mu$ is defined then $w[S] \overset{S\mu}{\rightarrow} w'[S]$

Now we take $\{\overset{\mu}{\rightarrow} \mid \mu \in M\}$ to be the smallest relations over W_{Σ_3} satisfying $(\rightarrow 1)$ - $(\rightarrow 7)$, and again obtain an observational equivalence $\sim$ over W_{Σ_3} , which is a congruence, so that again $\sim_c$ is identical with $\sim$.

The axioms needed to characterise $\mathcal{S}$ are the obvious ones:

(A8) $(\mu x)[S] = S\mu(x[S])$ if $S\mu$ is defined, NIL otherwise

(A9) $(x + y)[S] = x[S] + y[S]$

(A10) $NIL[S] = NIL$

Theorem 3.5 The observational congruence $\sim_c$ over W_{Σ_3} is exactly the congruence induced by (A1) - (A4) and (A7) - (A10). ☒

The treatment of experiment relations $\{\overset{\lambda}{\Rightarrow} \mid \lambda \in \Lambda\}$ and the corresponding observational congruence $\approx_c$ over W_{Σ_3} is exactly as it was for W_{Σ_2} , and by trivially adapting the proof of Theorem 3.4 we obtain

Theorem 3.6 The observational congruence $\approx_c$ over W_{Σ_3} is exactly the congruence induced by (A1) - (A5), (A6.1), A(6.2) and (A7) - (A10). ☒

3.6 Summary

We have characterised observational congruence in six cases by equational axioms. There are three signatures, and in each case two classes of experiment relations: $\{\overset{\mu}{\rightarrow} \mid \mu \in M\}$ when the atomic action τ is observable, and $\{\overset{\lambda}{\Rightarrow} \mid \lambda \in \Lambda\}$ when τ is not directly observable but may "occur" a finite number of times during any atomic experiment. The axioms for each case may be tabulated as follows ((A1) - (A4) are needed in every case):

Signature	$\Sigma_1 = M \cup \{NIL,+\}$	$\Sigma_1 = \Sigma_1 \cup \{\|\}$	$\Sigma_3 = \Sigma_2 \cup \mathcal{S}$
Production rules	$(\rightarrow 1)$ - $(\rightarrow 3)$	$(\rightarrow 1)$ - $(\rightarrow 6)$	$(\rightarrow 1)$ - $(\rightarrow 7)$
Axioms for $\sim_c$	-	(A7)	(A7)-(A10)
Axioms for $\approx_c$	(A5),(A6)	(A5),(A6.1),(A6.2),(A7)	(A5),(A6.1),(A6.2),(A7)-(A10)

Furthermore, we believe that the replacement of (A6) by two axioms (A6.1) and (A6.2) will be needed with the introduction of any operator representing concurrent activity, in place of "|", and that this replacement persists with the addition of any reasonable family of partial relabelling operators (even multi-valued ones, though we restricted consideration to single valued relabelling).

References

[1] Gordon, M.J., "The Denotational Description of Programming Languages", Springer-Verlag, 1979.

[2] Hennessy, M. and Plotkin, G.D., "Full Abstraction for a Simple Parallel Programming Language", Proc. 8th MFCS Conference, Olomouc, Czechoslovakia, Springer-Verlag Lecture Notes in Computer Science, Vol.74, pp. 108-121, 1979.

[3] Milne, G. and Milner, R., "Concurrent Processes and their Syntax", to appear in J.A.C.M., 1979.

[4] Milner, R., "Synthesis of Communicating Behaviour", Proc. 7th MFCS Conference, Zakopane, Poland, Springer-Verlag Lecture Notes in Computer Science, Vol.64, pp. 71-83, 1978.

[5] Smyth, M., "Powerdomains", J.C.S.S. 15, Vol.1, 1978.

[6] Stoy, J.E., "Denotational Semantics: The Scott Strachey Approach to Programming Language Theory", MIT Press, 1977.

[7] Plotkin, G.D., "A Powerdomain Construction", SIAM Journal on Computing 5, Vol.3, pp. 452-487, 1976.

[8] Pnueli, A., "The Temporal Logic of Programs", Proc. 19th Annual Symposium on Foundations of Computer Science, Providence, R.I., 1977.

[9] Pratt, V.R., "Semantical Considerations on Floyd-Hoare Logic", Proc. 17th IEEE Symp. on Foundations of Comp. Sci, pp.109-121, 1976.

Terminal Algebra Semantics and Retractions for Abstract Data Types

Günter Hornung and Peter Raulefs

Institut für Informatik III
Universität Bonn
Postfach 2220
D-5300 Bonn 1, West Germany

Abstract.

Very often, the *terminal* algebra semantics of an algebraic specification of an abstract data type is more important than the initial algebra semantics. This paper develops a theory of terminal algebra semantics. The notion of terminal (t-) abstract data type is introduced, and it is shown that a t-abstract data type is a terminal object in the categories of terminal models and implementations of an abstract data type specification. Many, but not all notions and properties of initial algebra semantics have their dual analogue in terminal algebra semantics.

The connection between t-abstract data types and Scott's notation of a data type being a retract on a universal domain is explored. The main result is that for the class of *recognizable t-specifications* retracts constituting terminal models of respective t-specifications can be explicitly constructed.

0. Introduction

The meaning associated with an algebraic data type specification Sp is usually taken to be the initial algebra in the category of algebras satisfying Sp [ADJ 73, 75, 76, 78]. However, there are observations suggesting to consider *terminal algebras* as the appropriate semantics of algebraic specifications.

In the initial algebra satisfying a specification Sp, terms are identified only if their equality is implied by the equational axioms of Sp. It has been suggested that the design of data type specifications, particularly when "implementing" an abstract data type in terms of others, should be done systematically by stepwise extensions [GUT 75, GHM 76a,b, EKP 79]. Let Sp' be an extension of Sp. Inserting terms t,t' of a newly introduced sort in Sp' into all appropriate contexts of sorts in Sp may result in terms identified by the initial congruence relation although t,t' are distinct in the initial algebra.
To obtain this from the initial algebra semantics, it is often necessary to introduce new axioms into the specification. This is not only unpleasant, but may also have unwanted side-effects such as destroying the Church-Rosser property of some operational semantics imposed on the axioms (see [WAN 78]). Hence, the initial algebra semantics of algebraic specifications may lead to redundant and even unwanted inequalities impairing the systematic design of data type specifications.

These difficulties are avoided by considering an appropriately defined terminal algebra to be the meaning of an algebraic specification. Except for preliminary investigations [GUT 75, WAN 78, BDPPW 79], there has been no approach to defining a notion of terminal algebra semantics, and developing a theory that, similarly as for the initial algebra semantics, provides tools to algebraic software specification techniques.

This paper presents first results of an investigation in this direction. As specifications with *conditional equations* are hardly avoidable [ADJ 76, GUT 75, GHM 76a,b], our exposition assumes specifications with conditional equations. After briefly reviewing the initial algebra semantics in Section 1, Section 2 introduces terminal algebra semantics based on a *terminal congruence relation*. We need to assume that specifications contain a sort having at least two distinct elements, which serve to discriminate between objects meant to be unequal (*t-specifications)*. Under this assumption we can define a *terminal* (or *t-*) *abstract data type* and show it is indeed a terminal object in the categories of *t-models* and *t-implementations*. It turns out that many notions and properties of initial algebra semantics have their dual analogue in terminal algebra semantics.

In Section 3, we explore connections between t-abstract data types and Scott's notion of a data type being a retract on a universal domain. Our main result is that for the class of *recognizable t-specifications* we can explicitly construct retracts constituting a model of a respective t-specification. Because of space restrictions, we could not present all results in due detail. The interested reader is referred to the full version of this paper in [HR 79] and its precursor [HOR 79] with results concerning t-specifications as rewrite- systems.

Notation. $\omega := \{0,1,2,\ldots\}$ $\qquad \omega_+ := \{1,2,\ldots\}$

For any $n\in\omega$, (n) denotes *both* the set $\{1,2,\ldots,n\}$ *and* the sequence $\langle 1,\ldots,n\rangle$, and $[n]$ denotes *both* the set $\{0,1,\ldots,n\}$ *and* the sequence $\langle 0,1,\ldots,n\rangle$.

Analogously, for any $n\in\omega$,

$t_{(n)}$ denotes *both* $\{t_1,\ldots,t_n\}$ *and* $\langle t_1,\ldots,t_n\rangle$, and

$t_{[n]}$ denotes *both* $\{t_0,t_1,\ldots,t_n\}$ *and* $\langle t_0,t_1,\ldots,t_n\rangle$.

1. Algebraic Specifications and Initial Algebra Semantics with Conditional Terms

1.1. Algebraic specification This section briefly reviews basic notions and properties about specifications of algebras, following [ADJ 77, EKP 78]. As our exposition deals with conditional instead of "simple" equations, this review simultaneously serves to extend the usual mathematical machinery to conditional equations.

1.1.1. Definition [conditional equation] Given a signature (S,Σ), we define for each sort s in S the set of *conditional equations of sort* s to be $T^2_{\Sigma(X),s} \times (\bigcup_{s' \in S} T^2_{\Sigma(X),s'})^*$, where T_Σ $(T_{\Sigma(X)})$ denotes the Σ-algebra of Σ-terms (with variables from X).

Notation. "*if* $l_1=r_1$ *&...&* $l_n=r_n$ *then* L=R" stands for $((L,R),(l_1,r_1),\ldots,(l_n,r_n))$.

L=R stands for $((L,R),\varepsilon)$.

1.1.2. Definition [specification] (S,Σ,E) is a *specification* iff (1) (S,Σ) is a signature, and (2) $E \subseteq \bigcup_{s \in S}(T^2_{\Sigma(X),s} \times [\bigcup_{s' \in S} T^2_{\Sigma(X),s'}]^*)$.

1.1.3. Definition [assignment, interpretation, (Σ,E)-algebra] For any signature (S,Σ) and Σ-algebra A, an A-*assignment* is a function $assn_A$: $X \to \cup\{A_s \mid s \in S\}$ mapping s-sorted variables to elements of A_s for any sort s in S. Any A-assignment $assn_A$ induces an *interpretation* $int_{assn_A}: T_{\Sigma(X)} \to \cup\{A_s \mid s \in S\}$ in an obvious way. For Σ-algebras A, $Assn_A$ denotes the set of all A-assignments. For any specification (S,Σ,E), a Σ-algebra A is a (Σ,E)-*algebra* iff A is Σ-generated and satisfies all equations in E.

1.1.4. Definition [$Alg_{\Sigma,E}$] For any specification (S,Σ,E), $Alg_{\Sigma,E}$ denotes the category given by

- objects: $|Alg_{\Sigma,E}| := \{A \mid A \text{ is } (\Sigma,E)\text{-algebra}\}$
- morphisms: $/Alg_{\Sigma,E}/ := \{H:A \to B \mid H \text{ is } \Sigma\text{-homomorphism } \& \ A,B \in |Alg_{\Sigma,E}|\}$.

1.1.5. Definition/Lemma [congruence relation $\equiv_E$] Any specification (S,Σ,E) induces the following Σ-congruence $\equiv_E = \{\equiv_{E,s} \mid s \in S\}$ on T_Σ:

Let $Kon(T_\Sigma)$ be the set of all Σ-congruences on the term algebra T_Σ. For any $\equiv \in Kon(T_\Sigma)$, let

[A] $\forall((L,R),C) \in E.\ \forall assn \in Assn_{T_\Sigma}.\ C=\varepsilon \Rightarrow int_{assn}(L) \equiv int_{assn}(R)$.

[B] $\forall n \in \omega.\ \forall s \in S, s_{[n]} \subseteq S.\ \forall e \in E.\ \forall assn \in Assn_{T_\Sigma}.\ \forall l,r \in T_{\Sigma(X),s}.$

$\forall l_{[n]}, r_{[n]} \in T_{\Sigma(X),s_0} \times \ldots \times T_{\Sigma(X),s_n}.$

$\{e = \textit{if } l_1=r_1 \ \&\ldots\&\ l_n=r_n \textit{ then } l=r \ \ \& \ \ \forall i \in [n].\ int_{assn}(l_i) \equiv int_{assn}(r_i)\}$

$\Rightarrow int_{assn}(l) \equiv int_{assn}(r)$.

Let $K_E := \{\equiv \mid \ \equiv \in Kon(T_\Sigma) \ \ \& \equiv \text{ satisfies [A] and [B]}\}$, and we define $\forall s\in S.\ \equiv_{E,s} := \cap\{\equiv_s \mid \equiv\in K_E\}$.

Then, $\equiv_E$ is a Σ-congruence satisfying [A] and [B].

Remark. Intuitively, $\equiv_E$ is the congruence identifying exactly all terms in T_Σ the equality of which is deducible from E.

1.1.6. Definition [initial quotient term algebra] For any specification (S,Σ,E),

$$T_{\Sigma,E} := T_{\Sigma/\equiv_E}$$

is the *initial quotient term algebra* of (S,Σ,E).

1.1.7. Theorem Let $Sp=(S,\Sigma,E)$ be a specification.

(1) For any specification (S',Σ',E') with $S\subseteq S'$, $E\subseteq E'$, and $\forall w\in S^*, s\in S.\ \Sigma_{w,s}\subseteq\Sigma'_{w,s}$:
$\forall s\in S.\ \equiv_{E,s} \subseteq \equiv_{E',s}$.

(2) For any (Σ,E)-algebra A: $\forall s\in S.\ \equiv_{E,s} \subseteq \equiv_{A,s}$.

Note. For specifications with conditional equations, the converse
$(\forall A\in Alg_\Sigma.\equiv_E\subseteq\equiv_A \Rightarrow A\in Alg_{\Sigma,E})$ does not hold!

(3) $T_{\Sigma,E}$ is initial in $Alg_{\Sigma,E}$,
where $\forall A\in|Alg_{\Sigma,E}|.H:T_{\Sigma,E} \to A$ is a unique Σ-epimorphism.

Proof: This is an extension of well-known results to specifications with conditional equations observing Definition 1.1.5. The proofs are done by straightforward structural induction.

1.2. Initial algebra semantics Next, we extend familiar notions of initial algebra semantics to specifications with conditional equations, and introduce concepts later allowing us to compare initial and terminal algebra semantics.

1.2.1. Definition [i-abstract data type] For any specification (S,Σ,E), $T_{\Sigma,E}$ is called the *i-abstract data type* specified by (S,Σ,E).

1.2.2. Definition [i-extension, i-enrichment, i-complete, i-consistent]
For any two specifications $Sp=(S,\Sigma,E)$, $Sp'=(S',\Sigma',E')$ with
(1) $S\subseteq S'$, $E\subseteq E'$, and (2) $\forall w\in S^*, s\in S.\ \Sigma_{w,s}\subseteq\Sigma'_{w,s}$, we define:

A. Sp' is an *i-extension* of Sp iff $T_{\Sigma,E}$ is Σ-isomorphic to $T_{\Sigma',E'}|\Sigma$.

B. Sp' is an *i-enrichment* of Sp iff Sp' is an i-extension of Sp and S=S'.

C. Sp' is *i-complete* on Sp iff

$$\forall s\in S.\ \forall t\in T_{\Sigma',s}.\ \exists t'\in T_{\Sigma,s}.\ t\equiv_E t'.$$

D. Sp' is *i-consistent* on Sp iff

$$\forall s\in S.\ \forall t,t'\in T_{\Sigma,s}.\ t\equiv_{E'}t' \Rightarrow t\equiv_E t'.$$

1.2.3. Theorem Let $Sp=(S,\Sigma,E)$, $Sp'=(S',\Sigma',E')$ be specifications s.t. $S\subseteq S'$, $E\subseteq E'$, and $\forall w\in S^*, s\in S.\ \Sigma_{w,s}\subseteq\Sigma'_{w,s}$. Then,

1. Sp' is i-consistent on Sp iff $T_{\Sigma,E}$ is Σ-isomorphic to a subalgebra of $T_{\Sigma',E'}$.
2. Sp' is an i-extension of Sp iff Sp' is i-complete and i-consistent on Sp.

Proof: These results extend those of [EKP 78] to specifications with conditional equations. The proof consists of a rather tedious structural induction (omitted).

2. Terminal Algebra Semantics

2.1. Introductory Remarks

The initial algebra semantics of specifications identifies terms iff their equality is deducible from the equations. This, however, admits that terms are not considered equal although in all "contexts of interest" their "behaviour" is not distinguishable, which would allow implementations implementing such terms in the same way to be agreeable. To capture this idea we need to make precise what is meant by "context of interest" and "behaviour".

We require specifications to contain a special sort dis (to distinguish objects) s.t. there are at least two dis-constants tt, ff (obtaining *t-specifications)* which must not be identified by the initial congruence relation $\equiv$ *(consistency)*. For any sorts s, s' a context $t\in C(s',s)$ is a term of sort s with a "hole" for plugging in terms of sort s'. We have to make sure that terms of sort dis can be evaluated to either tt or ff *(completeness)*. Then, any terms p,q of some sort s have the same behaviour in all contexts of interest iff p and q are exchangeable in all dis-contexts $t\in C(s,dis)$, i.e. both tp and tq evaluate to either tt or ff.

This idea is formalized by defining, for any t-specification (S,Σ,E), a *terminal congruence relation* $\sim_{E'}$ and it is justified to call the Σ-isomorphism class of the terminal quotient algebra $T_{\Sigma/\sim_E}$ a *terminal* (or *t-)abstract data type*. This section shows that much of the theory of initial algebra semantics has its dual analogue in the terminal algebra semantics of t-specifications. We develop a notion for implementations of t-abstract data types and present results which are useful when developing terminal extensions and implementations of t-abstract data types. Finally, we give a sufficient criterion for t-specifications to admit exactly one semantics so that initial and terminal algebra semantics collapse into one.

2.2. T-Specifications and Their Terminal Congruence Relation

2.2.1. Definition [t-specification] A specification (S,Σ,E) is called *t-specification*

iff
(1) $dis \in S$, (2) $tt, ff \in \Sigma_{\varepsilon,dis}$, and (3) $\forall((L,R),C)\in E.\ C \in (T^2_{\Sigma(X),dis})^*$.

A t-specification (S,Σ,E) is
(a) *consistent* iff $tt \not\equiv_E ff$, and
(b) *complete* iff $\forall t\in T_{\Sigma,dis}.\ \exists tv\in\{tt,ff\}.\ t \equiv_E tv$.

<u>2.2.2. Definition [context category C_Σ]</u> For any signature (S,Σ) the *context category* C_Σ is defined by: $|C_\Sigma| := S$

$$/C_\Sigma/ := \{t:s\to s' \mid s,s'\in S\ \&\ t\in T_{\Sigma(X),s'}\ \&\ t \text{ contains exactly one variable } x_s \text{ of sort } s\}.$$

For any two morphisms $t_1:s_1\to s_2$, $t_2:s_2\to s_3$, the composition is defined by

$$t_2t_1:s_1\to s_3 := t_2[t_1/x_{s_2}]$$

Notation. $\forall s,s'\in S.\ C_\Sigma(s,s') := \{t:s\to s' \mid t\in /C_\Sigma/\}$.

<u>2.2.3. Definition [t-congruence relation $\sim_E$]</u> Let $Sp = (S,\Sigma,E)$ be a t-specification. The family $\sim_E = \{\sim_{E,s} \mid s\in S\}$ of relations on T_Σ defined by

$$\forall s\in S.\ \forall p,q\in T_{\Sigma,s}.\ (p\sim_{E,s}q\ :\Longleftrightarrow\ \forall t\in C_\Sigma(s,dis).\ t[p/x_s] \equiv_{E,dis} t[q/x_s])$$

is called the *t-congruence relation* specified by Sp.
Intuitively, $\sim_E$ distinguishes exactly those terms which behave differently in a dis-context.
Our first lemma shows that the relation $\sim_E$ is indeed a congruence relation which coarsens the initial congruence relation $\equiv_E$:

<u>2.2.4. Lemma</u> Let $Sp=(S,\Sigma,E)$ be a t-specification and $\sim_E$ as defined in definition 2.2.2
(1) $\sim_E$ is a Σ-congruence.
(2) $\equiv_E \subseteq \sim_E$.

The following lemma suggests an equivalent version of the t-congruence relation which is helpful in proofs by structural induction:

<u>2.2.5. Lemma</u> Let $Sp = (S,\Sigma,E)$ be a t-specification defining the t-congruence relation $\sim_E$.
The family $\dot\sim_E = \{\dot\sim_{E,s} \mid s\in S\}$ of relations on T_Σ is defined by

(1) $\forall n\in\omega.\ \overset{n}{\sim}_{E,dis} := \equiv_{E,dis}$.

(2) $\forall s\in S-\{dis\}.\ \forall p,q\in T_{\Sigma,s}.$

$$p \overset{0}{\sim}_{E,s} q :\Longleftrightarrow \forall n\in\omega_+.\ \forall s_{(n)}\subseteq S.\ \forall\sigma\in\Sigma_{s_1..s_n,dis}.\ \forall t_{(n)}\in_{i\in(n)}T_{\Sigma,s_i}.\ \forall j\in(n).$$

$$\{s_j=s \Rightarrow \sigma(t_1,..,t_{j-1},p,t_{j+1},..,t_n) \overset{0}{\sim}_{E,dis} \sigma(t_1,..,t_{j-1},q,t_{j+1},..,t_n)\}.$$

(3) $\forall s\in S-\{dis\}.\ \forall i\in\omega.\ \forall p,q\in T_{\Sigma,s}.$

$$p \overset{i+1}{\sim}_{E,s} q \ :\Longleftrightarrow\ 1.\ p \overset{i}{\sim}_{E,s} q$$
$$\&\ \ 2.\ \forall n\in\omega_+.\ \forall s'\in S.\ \forall s_{(n)}\subseteq S.\ \forall\sigma\in\Sigma_{s_1..s_n,s'}.\ \forall t_{(n)}\in\bigtimes_{i\in(n)} T_{\Sigma,s_i}.\ \forall j\in(n).$$
$$\{s_j=s \Rightarrow \sigma(t_1,..,t_{j-1},p,..,t_n) \overset{i}{\sim}_{E,s'} \sigma(t_1,..,t_{j-1},q,..,t_n)\}.$$

(4) $\forall s\in S.\ \dot{\sim}_{E,s} := \bigcap_{i\in\omega} \overset{i}{\sim}_{E,s}.$

Then, $\dot{\sim}_E = \sim_E$.

Next, in analogy to Definition 1.1.6., we consider the terminal quotient term algebra:

2.2.6. Definition/Lemma [terminal quotient term algebra]

For any t-specification (S,Σ,E), $T_{\Sigma,\sim} := T_{\Sigma/\sim_E}$ denotes the *terminal quotient term algebra.*

$T_{\Sigma,\sim}$ is a (Σ,E)-algebra.

When extending a specification (S,Σ,E) to (S',Σ',E') s.t. $S\subseteq S'$, $E\subseteq E'$, and $\forall s\in S, w\in S^*.\ \Sigma_{w,s}\subseteq\Sigma'_{w,s}$, it is known that $\equiv_E\subseteq\equiv_{E'}$, (i.e. $\forall s\in S.\ \equiv_{E,s}\subseteq\equiv_{E',s}$). As might be expected, the terminal congruence relation behaves conversely:

2.2.7. Lemma Let (S,Σ,E) and (S',Σ',E') be consistent and complete t-specifications with $S\subseteq S'$, $E\subseteq E'$, $\forall w\in S^*$, $s\in S$. $\Sigma_{w,s}\subseteq\Sigma'_{w,s}$. Then

$$\forall s\in S.\ \forall p,q\in T_{\Sigma,s}.\ p\sim_{E'}q \Rightarrow p\sim_E q, \qquad \text{i.e.}\quad \sim_{E'} \subseteq \sim_E.$$

2.2.8. Definition [$\sim_A$] Let (S,Σ,E) be a t-specification, and A a Σ-algebra. The family $\sim_A$ of relations on T_Σ is defined by

$$\forall s\in S.\ \forall p,q\in T_{\Sigma,s}.\ (p\sim_A q \ :\Longleftrightarrow\ \forall t\in C_\Sigma(s,dis).\ t[p/x_s] \equiv_A t[q/x_s])$$

Intuitively, $\sim_A$ identifies terms whose corresponding objects in A behave equally.

2.2.9. Lemma Let (S,Σ,A) be a t-specification, A a Σ-algebra. Then $\sim_A$ is a Σ-congruence.

2.3. Terminal Models and Implementations

For any consistent t-specification $Sp=(S,\Sigma,E)$, we consider a (Σ,E)-algebra A to be a t-model iff A interprets $T_{\Sigma,E,dis}$ as $\{tt_A,ff_A\}$. However, t-imlementations of Sp need not necessarily satisfy the axioms E of Sp. Instead, we require any t-implementation $A\in Alg_\Sigma$ to induce a congruence relation $\sim_A$ on T_Σ which coarsens $\sim_E$, i.e. $\sim_E \subseteq \sim_A$:

2.3.1. Definition [t-models/t-implementations]

For any consistent t-specification $Sp=(S,\Sigma,E)$:

1. $t\text{-Mod}_{\Sigma,E}$ is the category defined by

   $|t\text{-Mod}_{\Sigma,E}| := \{A \in Alg_{\Sigma,E} |\ A_{dis}=\{tt_A, ff_A\}\ \&\ tt_A \neq ff_A\}$

   $/t\text{-Mod}_{\Sigma,E}/ := \{H:A \to B |\ H \text{ is } \Sigma\text{-homomorphism}\ \&\ A,B \in |t\text{-Mod}_{\Sigma,E}|\}$

2. $t\text{-Imp}_{\Sigma,E}$ is the category given by:

   (1) $\forall A \in |Alg_\Sigma|.\ A \in |t\text{-Imp}_{\Sigma,E}|$ iff

   (a) A is Σ-generated.

   (b) $A_{dis}=\{tt_A, ff_A\}\ \&\ tt_A \neq ff_A$.

   (c) $\forall s \in S.\ \forall p,q \in T_{\Sigma,s}.\ p \sim_E q \Rightarrow p \sim_A q$.

   (2) $/t\text{-Imp}_{\Sigma,E}/ := \{H:A \to B |\ H \text{ is } \Sigma\text{-homomorphism}\ \&\ A,B \in |t\text{-Imp}_{\Sigma,E}|\}$.

Algebras in $t\text{-Mod}_{\Sigma,E}$ resp. $t\text{-Imp}_{\Sigma,E}$ are called *t-models* resp. *t-implementations*.
The following lemma shows that t-models are also t-implementations:

2.3.2. Lemma. For any consistent t-specification (S,Σ,E)

$|t\text{-Mod}(\Sigma,E)| \subseteq |t\text{-Imp}(\Sigma,E)|$.

2.3.3. Theorem Let (S,Σ,E) be a consistent and complete t-specification. Then, $T_{\Sigma,\sim}$ is terminal in both $t\text{-Imp}_{\Sigma,E}$ and $t\text{-Mod}_{\Sigma,E}$.

Lemma 2.2.6. and Theorem 2.3.3. justify the following definition:

2.3.4. Definition [t-abstract data type]

For any complete and consistent t-specification $Sp=(S,\Sigma,E)$, the isomorphism class of $T_{\Sigma,\sim}$ is called the *t-abstract data type* specified by Sp. Objects of $t\text{-Mod}_{\Sigma,E}$ and $t\text{-Imp}_{\Sigma,E}$ are called t-models resp. t-implementations of $T_{\Sigma,\sim}$.

Given a t-specification (S,Σ,E) and a t-abstract data type $T_{\Sigma,\sim}$, a t-model A of $T_{\Sigma,\sim}$ with terminal Σ-homomorphism $H_A : A \to T_{\Sigma,\sim}$ may model a data object t by two different elements a and a', i.e. $H_A(a)=H_A(a')=t$ but $a \neq a'$, although A satisfies the equations E. A t-implementation B of $T_{\Sigma,\sim}$ with terminal Σ-homomorphism $H_B:B \to T_{\Sigma,\sim}$ and initial Σ-homomorphism $H'_B:T_\Sigma \to B$ does not necessarily satisfy the equations of E. In other words, there may be terms t,t' in T_Σ s.t. $t \equiv_E t'$ but $H'_B(t) \neq H'_B(t')$ (although $t \sim_B t'$). However, the following lemma shows that $\equiv_B$ coarsens $\equiv_E$ as far as objects of sort dis are concerned:

2.3.5. Lemma Let (S,Σ,E) be a consistent and complete t-specification and B be a t-implementation of $T_{\Sigma,\sim}$. Then

$\forall t,t' \in T_{\Sigma,dis}.\ t \equiv_E t' \Rightarrow t \equiv_B t'$.

2.4. Terminal Extensions and Enrichments

In this section, we show that properties about extensions and enrichments of the initial algebra semantics to some extent carry over to dual properties in the terminal algebra semantics.

2.4.1. Definition [t-extension, t-enrichment] Let $Sp=(S,\Sigma,E)$ and $Sp'=(S',\Sigma',E')$ be complete and consistent t-specifications.

1. Sp' is a *t-extension* of Sp iff
   (1) $S \subseteq S'$, $E \subseteq E'$ and $\forall w\in S^*, s\in S.\ \Sigma_{w,s} \subseteq \Sigma'_{w,s}$.
   (2) $T_{\Sigma,\sim}$ is Σ-isomorphic to $T_{\Sigma',\sim|\Sigma}$.
2. Sp' is a *t-enrichment* of Sp iff Sp' is t-extension of Sp and S=S'.

2.4.2. Definition [t-consistent, t-complete] Let $Sp=(S,\Sigma,E)$ and $Sp'=(S',\Sigma',E')$ be t-specifications with $S\subseteq S'$, $E\subseteq E'$ and $\forall w\in S, s\in S.\ \Sigma_{w,s}\subseteq\Sigma'_{w,s}$.

(1) Sp' is *t-consistent* on Sp iff $\forall s\in S.\ \forall p,q\in T_{\Sigma,s}.\ p\sim_E q \Rightarrow p\sim_{E'} q$.
(2) Sp' is *t-complete* on Sp iff $\forall s\in S.\ \forall p\in T_{\Sigma',s}.\ \exists q\in T_{\Sigma,s}.\ p\sim_{E'} q$.

Remark. Note that t-completeness is a weaker notion than i-completeness. By i-completeness, new terms of old sorts are derivable to old terms. t-completeness only ensures that for any new term of an old sort there is an old term behaving equally in all contexts of interest ("old" refers to Sp, "new" to Sp'). Nevertheless, dual properties hold for the terminal notions.

2.4.3. Theorem Let $Sp=(S,\Sigma,E)$ and $Sp'=(S',\Sigma',E')$ be t-specifications s.t. $S \subseteq S'$, $E \subseteq E'$, and $\forall w\in S^*, s\in S.\ \Sigma_{w,s} \subseteq \Sigma'_{w,s}$. Then:

1. Sp' is t-consistent on Sp iff $T_{\Sigma,\sim_E}$ is Σ-isomorphic to a subalgebra of $T_{\Sigma',\sim_{E'}}$.
2. *If* Sp is consistent and Sp' is t-consistent on Sp *then* Sp' is consistent.
3. *If* Sp is complete and Sp' t-complete on Sp *then* Sp' is complete.

An immediate consequence of the previous theorem is

2.4.4. Corollary Let $Sp=(S,\Sigma,E)$ and $Sp'=(S',\Sigma',E)$ be complete and consistent t-specifications.
If Sp' is a t-extension of Sp *then* Sp' is t-consistent on Sp.
Theorem 2.4.3.1. is the terminal dual to Theorem 1.2.3.1. The dual property to Theorem 1.2.3.2. is shown next:

2.4.5. Theorem Let $Sp=(S,\Sigma,E)$ and $Sp'= (S'\Sigma',E')$ be two consistent and complete t-specifications with $S\subseteq S'$, $E\subseteq E'$, and $\forall w\in S^*, s\in S.\ \Sigma_{w,s} \subseteq \Sigma'_{w,s}$. Then,
Sp' is t-consistent and t-complete on Sp *iff* Sp' is a t-extension of Sp.

2.4.6. Theorem Let $Sp=(S,\Sigma,E)$ and $Sp'=(S',\Sigma',E)$ be consistent and complete t-specifications, and A be a t-implementation of $T_{\Sigma,\sim}$ so that Sp' is t-extension of Sp. Then, there is a t-implementation A' of $T_{\Sigma',\sim}$ with

1. A is subalgebra of A'.
2. $\forall s \in S.\ A'_s = A_s$.

For the constructive proof the reader is referred to the full version in [HR 79].

2.5. Categorical t-Specifications

2.5.1. Definition [categorical]

A t-specification (S,Σ,E) is *categorical* iff $\equiv_E = \sim_E$.

By Lemma 2.2.3.(2), (S,Σ,E) is categorical iff $\sim_E \subseteq \equiv_E$.

2.5.2. Fact For any consistent and complete categorical t-specification (S,Σ,E), $t\text{-Mod}_{\Sigma,E}$ contains exactly one object, the initial (terminal) (Σ,E)-algebra.

2.5.3. Definition [anti-congruent]

Let $Sp = (S,\Sigma,E)$ be a specification, $s,s' \in S$, $t \in C_\Sigma(s,s')$.

t is *anti-congruent* iff $\forall p,q \in T_{\Sigma_{1,s}}$. *if* $t[p/x_s] \equiv_E t[q/x_s]$ *then* $p \equiv_E q$.

2.5.4. Lemma [Categoricity Lemma]

Let $Sp = (S,\Sigma,E)$ be a t-specification.

If $\forall s \in S-\{dis\}.\exists\ t \in C(s,dis)$. t is anti-congruent

then Sp is categorical.

3. Retractions for Algebraic Data Type Specifications

3.1. Introductory Remarks

This section connects the terminal algebra semantics of algebraic data type specifications with Scott's approach of considering data types to be retracts on a universal domain. This appears useful when considering recent programming languages centred around "module type" constructs such as scripts in CSSA [BFR 77], forms in ALPHARD [LSW 78], clusters in CLU [LZ 74], or classes in SIMULA 67 [BDMN 73]. We require a module type construct to denote as its mathematical semantics a retract on a universal domain with instances of the module type (e.g. CSSA-agents or SIMULA-class instances) being elements of the retract. Due to space restrictions we can only briefly outline our ideas. They are fully worked out in [HR 79].

A module type specifies a set of characteristic operations s.t. each object of this type is capable of performing only operations of this set. Software design techniques require that module type instances are (up to implementation details) entirely determined by their *behaviours*, i.e. their "outwardly visible" reactions to requests for carrying out operations. This suggests a particular style of writing module type instances in the form

λop:Op. *if* $op=op_1$ *then* λin_1. $reaction_1$
if $op=op_2$ *then* λin_2. $reaction_2$
⋮
where Op is a discrete domain of operation symbols.

An operation request is done by presenting a module type instance an operation symbol (e.g. op_i), and some information bound to in_i s.t. $reaction_i$ is carried out. This style reflects the fact that module type instances are "clusters" of "operation capabilities", and retractions for module types can be written accordingly.

3.2. Retraction Systems on Universal Domains

Taking domains to be, say, coherent continuous cpo's, we assume U to be a *universal domain* in the sense that any domain is isomorphic to a retract of U [PLO 77, SCO 76]. For convenience, we let U be $\mathbb{T}^{\omega}$. $\underline{c}$ and uu denote the partial order and bottom element of U. For any retraction f in U (i.e. $f \circ f = f$), dom f := $(\{x \mid fx=x\}, \underline{c})$. We use Plotkin's LAMBDA-notation (cf. [PLO 77]). $\lambda x{:}f.t$ is our abbreviation for $\lambda x.t[f(x)/x]$.

3.2.1. Definition [retraction system]

For any signature Sig=(S,Σ), $(\{r_s \mid s \in S\}, \{op_f \mid f \in \Sigma\})$ is a retraction system on Sig iff

(1) $\forall s \in S.\ r_s$ is a retraction.

(2) $\forall n \in \omega_+.\ \forall s,s_1,..,s_n \in S.\ \forall f \in \Sigma_{s_1..s_n,s}.\ \forall i \in (n).\ \forall e_{(n)} \in \bigtimes_{k \in (n)} dom(r_{s_k}).$

$op_f \in dom(Op)\ \ \&\ \ e_1 op_f e_2 \ldots e_n \in dom(r_s).$

(3) $\forall s \in S.\ \forall f \in \Sigma_{\varepsilon,s}.\ op_f \in dom(r_s).$

3.2.2. Definition/Lemma [Σ-algebra generated by a retraction system]

For any retraction system RS = $(\{r_s \mid s \in S\}, \{op_f \mid f \in \Sigma\})$ on a signature Sig=(S,Σ), we define:

(1) $\forall s \in S.\ M_{s,o} := \{op_f \mid f \in \Sigma_{\varepsilon,s}\}.$

(2) $\forall s \in S.\ \forall i \in \omega.$

$$M_{s,i+1} := \{e_1 op_f e_2 .. e_k \mid k \in \omega_+\ \&\ s_{(k)} \in S^k\ \&\ f \in \Sigma_{s_1..s_k,s}\ \&\ \forall j \in (k).e_j \in \bigcup_{n \in [i]} M_{s_j,n}\}.$$

(3) $\forall s \in S.\ \forall f \in \Sigma_{\varepsilon,s}.\ g_f := op_f.$

(4) $\forall n \in \omega_+.\ \forall s,s_1,..,s_n \in S.\ \ \forall f \in \Sigma_{s_1..s_n,s}.\ g_f := \lambda x_1{:}r_{s_1} \ldots \lambda x_n{:}r_{s_n}.r_s(x_1 op_f x_2 .. x_n).$

(5) $\forall s \in S.\ M_s := \bigcup_{n \in \omega} M_{s,n}.$

We call $A(RS) := (\{M_s \mid s \in S\}, \{g_f \mid f \in \Sigma\})$ the *Σ-algebra generated by* RS.

A (RS) is Σ-generated.

We are interested in an algorithm *constructing* from a consistent and complete t-specification (S,Σ,E) a system of retracts whose generated Σ-algebra is a t-model of $T_{\Sigma,\sim}$. This problem is solved for the class of *recognizable t-specifications* (*rec-specifications*), yielding retractions written in the style indicated in 3.1. Most common data type specifications (such as stack, queue, set) can be written as rec-specifications. Our full paper [HR 79] gives the transformation algorithm from a rec-specification RS to a retraction system modelling RS and proves its correctness.

4. References

[ADJ 73] Goguen, J.A., Thatcher, J.W., Wagner, E.G., Wright, J.B. (ADJ-authors). A junction between computer science and category theory. IBM Research Report RC-4525, Sept. 1973.

[ADJ 75] (ADJ authors). Initial algebra semantics and continuous algebras. IBM Research Report RC-5701, Nov. 1975 and JACM:24 (1977)68-95.

[ADJ 76] (ADJ authors). Specification of abstract data types using conditional axioms. IBM Research Report RC-6214, Sept. 1976.

[ADJ 78] (ADJ authors). Data type specification: parametrization and the power of specification techniques. Proc. SIGACT 10th Ann. Symp.Thy. of Comp. (78).

[BDMN 73] Birtwistle, Dahl, Myhrhaug, Nygaard. SIMULA Begin. Studentlitteratur. Stockholm 1973.

[BFR 77] Böhm, H.P., Fischer, H.L., Raulefs, P. CSSA:Language concepts and programming methodology. Proc. Symp. PL & AI (Rochester 77)100-109.

[BDPPW 79] Broy, M., Dosch,W., Partsch, H., Pepper, P., Wirsing, M. Existential Quantifiers in Abstract Data Types. Proc. 6thICALP (Graz 1979).

[EKP 79] Ehrig, H., Kreowski, H.-J., Padawitz, P., Algebraische Implementierung abstrakter Datentypen. Bericht Nr. 79-3. TU Berlin, Inst.Software&Theor.Inf.

[GUT 75] Guttag, J.V.Specification and application to programming of abstract data types. Tech. Rept. CSRG-59 (1975), University of Toronto.

[GHM 76a] Guttag, J.V., Horowitz, E., Musser, D.R. Abstract data types and software validation. Tech. Rept. ISI/RR-76-48. Inform. Sci. Inst./USC.

[GHM 76b] Guttag, J.V., Horowitz, E., Musser, D.R. The design of data type specifications, Tech. Rept. ISI/RR-76-49. USC Information Sciences Institute.

[HOR 79] Hornung, G. Einige Probleme der Algebrasemantik abstrakter Datentypen. SEKI-Projekt, Memo SEKI-BN-79-7(1979)

[HR 79] Hornung, G., Raulefs, P. Terminal Algebra Semantics and Retractions for Abstract Data Types. SEKI-Projekt, Memo SEKI-BN-79-6(1979).

[LSW 76] London, R., Shaw, M., Wulf, W. An informal definition of Alphard. Tech. Rept. Dept. of Computer Science, Carnegie-Mellon U (1976).

[LZ 74] Liskov, B., Zilles, S. Programming with abstract data types. Proc. ACM/ SIGPLAN Symp. Very High Level Languages. SIGPLAN Notices:9(74)50-59.

[PLO 77] Plotkin, G. T^{ω} as a universal domain. Research Rept. No. 28. Dept. of Artificial Intelligence, Univ. of Edinburgh (1977).

[SCO 76] Scott, D. Data types as lattices. SIAM J. of Computing:5(1976)522-587.

[WAN 78] Wand, M. Final algebra semantics and data type extensions (revised). Tech. Rept. No. 65, Comp. Sci. Dept., Indiana Univ. (1978).

THE COMPLEXITY OF SEMILINEAR SETS

Thiet-Dung Huynh
Fachbereich Informatik
Universität Saarbrücken

Abstract: In this paper we shall characterize the computational complexity of two decision problems: the inequality problem and the uniform word problem for semilinear sets. It will be proved that the first problem is log-complete in the second class (Σ_2^p) of the polynomial-time hierarchy and the second problem is log-complete in NP. Moreover we shall show that these problems restricted to the 1-dimensional case have the 'same' computational complexity as the general case.

0. Introduction. Recently, G. Hotz has begun his investigations on invariants of formal languages. He pointed out in [7,8] that necessary criteria for the basic decision problems in language theory such as the equivalence problem, the word problem ... are useful. Considering context-free languages the oldest invariant seems to have appeared in Parikh's theorem, which states that the commutative images of context-free languages are semilinear sets. On the other side semilinear sets play an important role in other research areas of theoretical computer science. Thus it is interesting to study the complexity of the inequality problem and the uniform word problem for semilinear sets.

In section 2 basic definitions and some necessary auxiliary results will be presented. In section 3 we shall derive some results on semilinear sets, especially we shall prove a lemma which gives us some information about the complement of a semilinear set. In the last section we shall prove our main results, which state that the inequality problem resp. the equality problem for semilinear sets is log-complete in Σ_2^p resp. Π_2^p in the polynomial-time hierarchy studied in [11,12].

1. Preliminaries. In this section we review commonly known definitions and give some notations which will be used later.

Let Σ be a finite alphabet. Σ^* denotes the free monoid generated by Σ. Σ^+ is Σ^* without the empty word ε. #w denotes the length of the word w. Let DTIME(C( )) resp. NTIME(C( )) be the class of languages, which are recognizable on TM's resp. NTM's in time C( ). Let DSPACE(C( )) resp. NSPACE(C( )) be the class of languages which are recognizable on TM's resp. NTM's in space C( ).

Notation 1.1. $P := \bigcup_{k=1}^{\infty} \mathrm{DTIME}(n^k)$, $NP := \bigcup_{k=1}^{\infty} \mathrm{NTIME}(n^k)$, $\mathrm{PSPACE} := \bigcup_{k=1}^{\infty} \mathrm{DSPACE}(n^k)$. LOGSPACE denotes the class of functions computable in logarithmic space (logspace).

Definition 1.2. Let Σ and Δ be two finite alphabets, $L_1 \subset \Sigma^*$ and $L_2 \subset \Delta^*$ be two languages. $L_1 \leq_{log} L_2 :\Leftrightarrow [\exists f \in \text{LOGSPACE} : w \in L_1 \Leftrightarrow f(w) \in L_2]$. $\leq_{log}$ is reflexive and transitive.It is called reduction in logspace.

Let L be a language and Ω be a class of languages.$\Omega \leq_{log} L :\Leftrightarrow \forall L' \in \Omega : L' \leq_{log} L$. L is called log-complete in $\Omega :\Leftrightarrow L \in \Omega$ and $\Omega \leq_{log} L$.

Definition 1.3.Let A be a language.NP(A) denotes the class of languages accepted by nondeterministic oracle machines M^A in polynomial time. Let Ω be a class of languages. $NP(\Omega) := \bigcup_{A \in \Omega} NP(A)$.The polynomial-time hierarchy studied in [11,12,14] is the following hierarchy:

Σ_o^p , Π_o^p , Σ_1^p , Π_1^p , Σ_2^p , Π_2^p , ... , where $\Sigma_o^p = \Pi_o^p = P$ and $\Sigma_{k+1}^p = NP(\Sigma_k^p)$, $\Pi_{k+1}^p = \text{co-}NP(\Sigma_k^p)$ for all $k \geq o$.(co-$\Omega := \{\bar{A} \mid A \in \Omega\}$).

Remark 1.4.In [10,11] Meyer and Stockmeyer defined integer expressions and showed that the inequivalence problem for integer expressions is log-complete in Σ_2^p. Our result presents a new combinatorial problem which is log-complete in this class of the polynomial-time hierarchy.

2.Basic definitions and auxiliary results.In this section we give the basic definitions and reproduce some auxiliary results without proofs.

In the following let Z be the set of integers,N_o be the set of nonnegative integers and N the set $N_o - \{O\}$.We first define the notion of semilinear sets by the following

Definition 2.1.Let C and Π be two finite subsets of N_o^k and $C \neq \emptyset$.

$L(C;\Pi) := \{c + \sum_{i=1}^{n} \lambda_i p_i \mid c \in C, \lambda_i \in N_o$ and $\Pi = \{p_1, \ldots, p_n\}\}$.A subset L of N_o^k is called a linear set,iff $L = L(\{c\};\Pi)$ for some $\{c\}$ and Π of N_o^k. c is called the constant,Π the period system,$p \in \Pi$ a period of L.A subset SL $\subset N_o^k$ is called a semilinear set (s.l.),iff SL is a finite union of linear sets.If $L = L(c;\Pi)$ $(=L(\{c\};\Pi))$ is a linear set,so we call $(c;\Pi)$ a representation of L.If $SL = L(c_1;\Pi_1) \cup \ldots \cup L(c_m;\Pi_m)$ is a s.l. set,so we call $(c_1;\Pi_1) \cup \ldots \cup (c_m;\Pi_m)$ a representation of SL.Let SL_1 and SL_2 be two s.l. set representations.SL_1 and SL_2 are called equivalent,iff SL_1 and SL_2 define the same s.l. set.

Convention 2.2.W.l.o.g. we consider s.l. set representations as words over the finite alphabet $\Sigma := \{O,1,\{,\},(,),,,\cup,;\}$.On our computation models nonnegative integers have binary representations without leading zeros.We now formulate the two decision problems which we shall study.

The equality problem for s.l. sets :It is to decide,whether two s.l. set representations are equivalent,i.e.whether they define the same s.l. set.In a similar way we can formulate the inequality problem for s.l.sets.

The uniform word problem for s.l. sets :For a vector v with nonnegative integer entries and a s.l. set representation SL it is to decide, whether v is a member of the set defined by SL.

Notation 2.3.We define the languages describing these decision problem over the alphabet $\Sigma \cup \{\int\}$:

EQ:={$SL_1 \int SL_2$ | SL_1 and SL_2 are equivalent s.l. set representations},
INEQ:={$SL_1 \int SL_2$ | SL_1 and SL_2 are inequivalent s.l. set representations}.
Further let UWP denote the uniform word problem for s.l. sets.

For the proofs of our theorems we shall use some known results which are given here without proofs.The interested reader is referred to [3,6].

Auxiliary results.The auxiliary results used later concern:

-Bounds on the minimal positive integer solutions of a linear diophantine equation system.

-Aggregating linear diophantine equations with nonnegative coefficients to a single one without affecting the nonnegative integer solution set.

Let $A=(a_{ij})$, $1\le i\le k$, $1\le j\le m$, be a kxm matrix with entries in Z, where $k\le m$. Let $B=(b_i)\in Z^k$, $1\le i\le k$ and $X=(x_i)$, $1\le i\le m$, be two column vectors. Consider the linear diophantine equation system $A\cdot X=B$ (I). Let S(A,B) denote the set of nonnegative integer solutions of the system (I), i.e. $S(A,B)=\{v\in N_o^m \mid A\cdot v=B\}$. We first show the following lemma.

Lemma 2.4. S(A,B) is a s.l. set in N_o^m of the form $S(A,B)=L(\{c_1,..,c_r\};\{v_1,..,v_s\})$ for some $r,s\in N_o$.

Proof. With the usual partial order relation $\le$ on N_o^m we can define the notion "minimality" of the elements of some subset of N_o^m. From the well-known theorem on the finiteness of the minimal element number of a set $S\subset N_o^m$ it follows that there are only a finite number of minimal solutions in S(A,B). Let these solutions be $c_1,...,c_r$. Consider the solution set S(A,O), i.e. the solution set of the homogenous system $A\cdot X=O$. It is not hard to show that S(A,O) is a submonoid of the commutative monoid N_o^m. Let $v_1,..,v_s$ be the minimal elements of the set $S(A,O)-\{O\}$. One can easily prove the following fact : $S(A,B)=L(\{c_1,..,c_r\};\{v_1,..,v_s\})$. This completes the proof of the lemma. □

Notation 2.5. For a vector $w\in N_o^m$ let $\|w\|$ be $Max\{w_i \mid w=(w_1,...,w_m)\}$. For a finite set $C=\{c_1,...,c_r\}\subset N_o^m$ we denote by $\|C\|$ the maximum $\underset{1\le i\le r}{Max}\{\|c_i\|\}$.

We now give an upper bound for $\|C\|$, where $C=\{c_1,...,c_r\}$ is the minimal solution set of the system (I). Analysing the proof of [3] we get

Theorem 2.6. Let α be the rank of A and M be the maximum of the absolute values of the $\alpha\times\alpha$ subdeterminants of the extended matrix (A|B). The following inequality holds : $\|C\| \le (m+1)M$. □

Corollary 2.7. With $S(A,B)=L(\{c_1,..,c_r\};\{v_1,..,v_s\})$ the following inequality holds: $\|\{c_1,..,c_r,v_1,..,v_s\}\| \le (m+1)M$. □

As in the case of s.l. sets we can represent linear diophantine equation systems on TM's in an analogous manner. Thus we can define the size of such an equation system and we denote by #(A,B) the size of the equasystem (I). We can now prove the following

Lemma 2.8. Let S(A,B) be $L(\{c_1,..,c_r\};\{v_1,..,v_s\})$. Then the inequality

$\# \| \{c_1,..,c_r,v_1,..,v_s\} \| \leq d\#(A,B) \cdot \ln(\#(A,B))$ holds, where d is some constant and ln is the logarithm to base 2.

Proof. For an arbitrary real nxn matrix G the following Hadamard's formula holds: $\det(G)^2 \leq \prod_{i=1}^{n} (\sum_{k=1}^{n} g_{ik}^2)$. A simple calculation yields the inequality stated in the lemma. □

The following theorem was proved in [6] .

Theorem 2.9. Let $\sum_{j=1}^{m} a_{1j}x_j = b_1$, $\sum_{j=1}^{m} a_{2j}x_j = b_2$ (II) be a system of two linear diophantine equations, where the a_{ij}'s and b_i's are nonnegative integers and $b_i>0, i=1,2$. Let $t_1,t_2 \in N$ be two natural numbers with the following properties:

(1) $\gcd(t_1,t_2)=1$, (2) $t_1 \nmid b_2$ and $t_2 \nmid b_1$,

(3) $t_1>b_2-a_1$ and $t_2>b_1-a_2$, where $a_i := \min_{1 \leq j \leq m} \{a_{ij}>0\}$ for i=1,2 .

Then the nonnegative integer solution set of (II) is the same as the nonnegative integer solution set of the equation

$$\text{(III)} \quad t_1 \cdot \sum_{j=1}^{m} a_{1j}x_j + t_2 \cdot \sum_{j=1}^{m} a_{2j}x_j = t_1b_1 + t_2b_2 . \quad □$$

3. Some results on semilinear sets. In this section we prove some properties of s.l. sets which are essential in the proof of the upper bounds for the complexity of EQ and INEQ. Especially we are interested in the computing of the complement for a s.l. set. In [5] there is an algorithm due to Ginsburg & Spanier for this problem. Our method is different from theirs and allows us to obtain the derised upper bounds.

For our argument some notions in the theory of convex bodies are needed. A detailed presentation of this topic in connection with the theory of linear inequalities can be found in [12] .

Definition 3.1. Let $L=L(c;\{p_1,..,p_n\}) \subset N_0^k$ be a linear set. The cone K(L) defined by L is the set $K(L) := \{c+\sum_{i=1}^{n} \lambda_i p_i \mid \lambda_i \in Q_+^k\}$, where Q_+ is the set of nonnegative rational numbers.

In the following we are only concerned with linear sets whose constants are the origin O of the space N_0^k. For those cones defined by such linear sets we simply write $K(p_1,..,p_n) := K(L) = \{\sum_{i=1}^{n} \lambda_i p_i \mid \lambda_i \in Q_+\}$.

Remark 3.2. Our definition of cones is not general. On the other side the reader should verify that we can work in the space Q^k instead of R^k as in [12]. All theorems in [12] used later in this paper remain valid in this case.

Definition 3.3. A subset E of Z^k is called a generating system of a cone K, iff K(E)=K holds. A generating system E of a cone K is called minimal, iff no element of E can be presented as a linear combination of the rest with coefficients in Q_+.

From the above definition one gets easily the following

Lemma 3.4. For every cone K=K(E) there exists a minimal generating system $E' \subset E$ for K and E' is unique up to multiplications with some factors, i.e. if E' and E" are minimal generating systems, the following holds : For every $p' \in E'$ there is exactly one $p'' \in E''$ such that $p' = \lambda p''$ for some $\lambda \in Q_+$

Definition 3.5. If E is a minimal generating system of a cone K, then the cardinality of E is called the rank of K. For a cone $K = K(p_1, .., p_n)$ we define the dimension of K as the dimension of the subspace generated by $p_1, .., p_n$ in the vector space Q^k and we write dim K. Let $A \in Z^k$ be a vector. A hyperplane $H = \{v \in Q^k \mid A \cdot v = 0\}$ is called a boundary plane of the cone K, iff $\sup_{v \in K} A \cdot x = 0$ holds (where v is written as a column vector). A point $v \in K$ is called a boundary point of K, iff $x \in H$ for some boundary plane H of K. The set of all boundary points of K forms the boundary or the frame of K and is denoted by $R(K)$. A point $v \in K - R(K)$ is then an interior point of K. The set of all interior points of K is denoted by $\dot{K}$. A subset S of Q^k is called a face of K, iff $S = K \cap H$ for some boundary plane H. The face of K induced by a boundary plane H is denoted by $S_K(H)$ or shortly $S(H)$.

Remark 3.6. Admitting a cone to be a face of itself the set of faces of K forms a finite complete lattice under set inclusion and we denote it by $F(K)$. One notes that a face of a cone is itself a cone. Therefore dim(s) is well defined for $s \in F(K)$.

A face s' of K covers the face s , iff $s \subsetneq s'$ and there exists no other face $s'' \in F(K)$ such that $s \subsetneq s'' \subsetneq s'$. Let $s, s' \in F(K)$ be two faces of K and $s' \subsetneq s$ Then there exist faces $s_1, .., s_l$ such that $s_1 = s, s_l = s'$ and s_i covers s_{i+1} for $i = 1, .., l-1$.

We now give another definition of cones, namely the notion of polyhedral cones which will be used later.

Definition 3.7. Let $A \in Z^{m \times k}$ be a mxk matrix with integer entries. The polyhedral cone defined by A is the following set $G(A) := \{v \in Q^k \mid A \cdot v \leq 0\}$. (Let A_i, $1 \leq i \leq m$, be the i-th row of the matrix A. Then there exists a subset $I \subset \{1, .., m\}$ such that the hyperplanes $H_i := \{v \in Q^k \mid A_i \cdot v = 0\}$ are boundary planes of $G(A)$, if we consider $G(A)$ as a cone).

Remark 3.8. Definition 3.7 is also a restriction of the general one. In accordance with our definition of cones we have only to consider such polyhedral cones. It is sufficient for our argument.

Remark 3.9. There is an equivalence between cones and polyhedral cones stated by the theorems of H. Weyl and Minskowski. Weyl's theorem says that every cone is a polyhedral cone. (cf. [12])

Definition 3.10. Let K be a cone with dim $K = k'$, $k' \leq k$. A face s of K is called proper, iff dim $s = k' - 1$.

The proper faces of a cone K form the boundary of K. Every vector in a minimal generating system of K lies in the boundary of K. Now we are interested in computing the number of the proper faces of K. The inductive proof of Weyl' theorem yields a too large upper bound. Using the properties of the lattice F(K) we are able to derive a smaller upper bound for the proper face number of K.

Fact 3.11. Let $K=K(p_1,..,p_n)$ be a cone with minimal generating system $\{p_1,..,p_n\}$ and H be a boundary plane of K. Then we have:

$$S(H) = K(H \cap \{p_1,...,p_n\}) .$$

Let K be a cone and H be a boundary plane of K which induces the proper face S(H) of K.H decomposes the space Q^k into two halfspaces denoted by H^l and H^r with the property that $K \subset H^r$.Now let $H_1,...,H_m$ be all boundary planes of K which induce the proper faces of K.Consider the sets G_i, $1 \leq i \leq m$,of points in the first octant which lie in the halfspaces H_i^l, i.e. $G_i = Q_+^k \cap H_i^l$.With these notations we get the following

Lemma 3.12. It holds the equality $\bigcup_{i=1}^m G_i = Q_+^k - \dot{K}$. Moreover, $H_i^l \cap Q_+^k$ is a cone , $1 \leq i \leq m$.

Proof. Trivial. □

In the following we only need to consider cones with dimension k in the space Q^k. The results can be generalized in a straight-forward manner.Before presenting the method for computing the complement of a linear set resp. a s.l. set we show that the cone $Q_+^k \cap H_i^k$ can be generated by a minimal generating system whose vectors have small entries.

Let E_j, j=1,..,k,be the hyperplanes $Q^{j-1} x \{0\} x Q^{k-j}$.It is clear that the boundary planes of a cone $Q_+^k \cap H_i^l$ are certain hyperplanes E_j and the hyperplane H_i.This suggests the following lemma.

Lemma 3.13. Let H_i's he the hyperplanes $\{v \in Q^k \mid A_i \cdot v = 0\}$, $1 \leq i \leq m$,where A_i's are vectors in Z^k.Then the cone $Q_+^k \cap H_i^l$, $1 \leq i \leq m$,has a minimal generating system E with the property $\|E\| \leq (k+1) \cdot \|A\|$.

Proof. Consider some fixed cone $Q_+^l \cap H_i^l$.This cone has as boundary planes the hyperplane H_i and some E_j's.Thus $Q_+^k \cap H_i^l$ can be generated by unit vectors in the E_j's and certain vectors in the intersections $H_i \cap E_j = \{v \in Q^k \mid A_i \cdot v = 0$ and $e_j \cdot v = 0\}$,where e_j is the unit vector whose j-th entry is 1. Now the above formula follows from theorem 2.7. □

Let $K=K(p_1,..,p_n)$ be a cone with minimal generating system $\{p_1,..,p_n\}$ and dim K=k.We are going to give an upper bound for the proper face number of K which depends on n.

Let $K^p := \{v \in Q^k \mid \forall w \in K: w^T \cdot v \leq 0\}$ be the polar cone defined by K.If $K=K(p_1, ...,p_n)$,one gets the following fact:

$$K^p = K(p_1,...,p_n)^p = \{v \in Q^k \mid \begin{pmatrix} p1 \\ \vdots \\ p_n \end{pmatrix} \cdot v \leq 0\} ,$$

where the p_i's are written as row vectors. Thus K^p has at most n proper faces.Further it was proved in [12] that there exists an antiisomorphism between the face lattice of K and the face lattice of K^p. Hence an upper bound for the number of the 1-dimensional faces of K^p is also an upper bound for the proper face number of K. From this fact it is sufficient to derive an upper bound for the number of the 1-dimensional faces of K^p.

In order to achieve this upper bound we show the following claim.

Claim 3.14. Let s and s' be two proper faces of a cone K. Then there exist different proper faces $s_1,..,s_l$, $l \geq 0$, and (k-2)-dimensional faces $t_1,...,t_{l+1}$ such that $s \cap s_1 = t_1$; $s_i \cap s_{i+1} = t_{i+1}$, $1 \leq i \leq l-1$; and $s_l \cap s' = t_{l+1}$. That is we have the diagram:

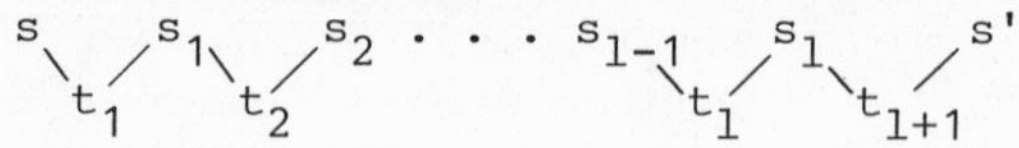

Proof. Let s and s' be two different proper faces of K. Then the intersection $s \cap s'$ is again a face of K. If $\dim(s \cap s') = k-2$, we are finished. So we assume that $\dim(s \cap s') \leq k-2$.

Consider the boundary planes H and H' generated by s and s'. The intersection of H and H' is a linear subspace of dimension k-2. Let $q_1,..,q_{k-2} \in Z^k$ be a minimal generating system for $H \cap H'$ which is contained in a halfspace defined by certain boundary plane. Let $\{p_{i,1},..,p_{i,k-1}\}$ resp. $\{p_{j,1},..,p_{j,k-1}\}$ be the generating system for s resp. s'. Look at the cone generated by $\{q_1,..,q_{k-2}\} \cup \{p_{i,1},..,p_{i,k-1}\} \cup \{p_{j,1},..,p_{j,k-1}\}$ we see that H and H' induce two proper faces $\bar{s}$ and $\bar{s}'$. Further $\bar{s}$ and $\bar{s}'$ are generated by $\{q_1,..,q_{k-2}\}$ plus a vector of $\{p_{i,1},..,p_{i,k-1}\}$ resp. of $\{p_{j,1},...,p_{j,k-1}\}$. Thus there are k-2 vectors of $\{p_{i,1},..,p_{i,k-1}\}$ resp. of $\{p_{j,1},..,p_{j,k-1}\}$ which are interior points of $\bar{s}$ resp. $\bar{s}'$. W.l.o.g. let these sets be $\{p_{i,1},...,p_{i,k-2}\}$ and $\{p_{j,1},...,p_{j,k-2}\}$. Thus we have the following diagrams in the face lattice F(K) :

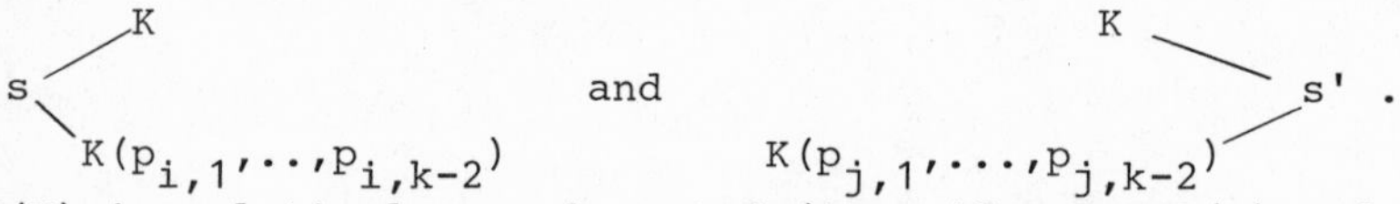

Because F(K) is relatively complemented (i.e. if $H,F,G \in F(K)$ and $H \subset F \subset G$, then there exists an $\bar{F} \in F(K)$ such that $F \wedge \bar{F} = H$ and $F \vee \bar{F} = G$ and $\dim F + \dim \bar{F} = \dim H + \dim G$), we can complete the diagrams above :

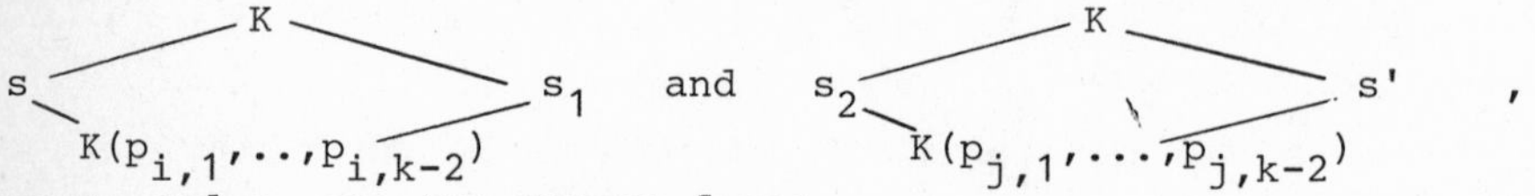

where s_1 and s_2 are two proper faces.

On the other side the new generating vector for s_1 resp. s_2 is an interior point of $K(\{q_1,..,q_{k-2}\} \cup \{p_{i,1},..,p_{i,k-1}\} \cup \{p_{j,1},..,p_{j,k-1}\})$. Otherwise s resp. s' would be no proper faces of K. Continuing this process we get the situation stated in the claim . □

On the other hand we know that the proper faces of K^p contain all vectors of a minimal generating system of K^p. So we can conclude from claim 3.14 that K^p can be generated by at most n+k-2 vectors. Thus one gets the following

Lemma 3.15. A cone $K=K(p_1,..,p_n)$ possesses at most n+k-2 proper faces and each of them can be generated by k-1 linearly independent vectors of

$\{p_1,\ldots,p_n\}$. □

One can easily prove the following lemma.

Lemma 3.16. Let $K=K(p_1,..,p_n)$ be a cone with minimal generating system $\{p_1,..,p_n\}\subset N_o^k$. Let $s_1,\ldots,s_m$ be all proper faces of K and v be an interior point of K. Then we have $K = \bigcup_{i=1}^{m} K(v,s_i)$ □

For a cone $K=K(p_1,..,p_n)$ consider the grid points contained in K. The following lemma gives us a property of these points.

Lemma 3.17. Let $K=K(p_1,..,p_n)$ be a cone. Then there exists a constant $h\in N_o$ with the property that $\forall x\in K\cap N_o^k$: $hx \in L(O;\{p_1,\ldots,p_n\})$. Moreover, the size of h fulfills the inequality $\#h \leq d(\#(p_1,..,p_n))^2$, for some constant d.

Proof. Let $s_1,..,s_m$ be all proper faces of K and $\{p_{i,1},\ldots,p_{i,k-1}\}$, $1\leq i\leq m$, a minimal generating system for s_i, i.e. $K(p_{i,1},\ldots,p_{i,k-1})=s_i$. According to lemma 3.16 let $v\in\dot{K}$ be an interior point, $v\in N_o^k$, with the property that $K=\bigcup_{i=1}^{m} K(v,p_{i,1},\ldots,p_{i,k-1})$. $v,p_{i,1},\ldots,p_{i,k-1}$ are linearly independent in the vector space Q^k for all i, $1\leq i\leq m$.

For a fixed i, $1\leq i\leq m$, consider the cone $K(v,p_{i,1},\ldots,p_{i,k-1})$. If x is a grid point in $K(v,p_{i,1},..,p_{i,k-1})$, then from lemma A.2 in [5] there exists a constant $h_i'\in N_o$ such that $h_i'x\in L(O;\{v,p_{i,1},..,p_{i,k-1}\})$. Analysing the proof of this lemma we see that for h_i' one can choose the absolute value of the determinant of the matrix $(v\ p_{i,1}\ldots p_{i,k-1})$, where v and the $p_{i,j}$'s are written as column vectors.

Let h_i be the absolute value of $\det(v\ p_{i,1}\ldots p_{i,k-1})$ for $1\leq i\leq m$. Define $h:=\prod_{i=1}^{m} h_i$. One can verify that h has the desired property stated in the lemma above. Now we derive an upper bound for the size of h. From the previous lemmas we have the following facts:

-The proper face number of K is less than 2n.

-$\forall i$, $1\leq i\leq m$: $\#\det(v\ p_{i,1}\ldots p_{i,k-1}) \leq d'\#(v\ p_{i,1}\ldots p_{i,k-1})$ for some constant d'.

On the other hand we can choose a vector $v\in L(O;\{p_{i,1},\ldots,p_{i,k-1}\})$ with small entries. From these observations lemma 3.17 follows. □

Now we derive an upper bound for the generating vectors of the inverse image of a s.l. set under a linear mapping.

Lemma 3.18. Let $K=K(p_1,..,p_n)$ be a cone, $p_1,\ldots,p_n\in N_o^k$, and $h\in N$ be some constant. Let $\mu_h:N_o^k\to N_o^k$ be the mapping defined by $x\mapsto hx$. Then for any linear set $L\subset N_o^k$, $\mu_h^{-1}(L)$ is a s.l. set and an upper bound for the entries of generating vectors of $\mu_h^{-1}(L)$ can be obtained by the inequality $\#(\|\bigcup_{i=1}^{l}\{c_i\}\cup\bigcup_{i=1}^{l}\Pi_i\|) \leq d(\ln\#L)(\#L+k\#h)$ for some constant d, where $\mu_h^{-1}(L) = \bigcup_{i=1}^{l} L(c_i;\Pi_i)$.

Proof. Because of the linearity of μ_h, $\mu_h^{-1}(L)$ is a s.l. set. We derive the upper bound stated in the lemma.

Consider the space $N_o^k x N_o^k$. Let M_k be the linear set $M_k:=\{(x,\mu_h(x)) \mid x \in N_o^k\} = L(O;\{(e_1,he_1),\ldots,(e_k,he_k)\})$, where the e_i's are unit vectors of N_o^k.

Then we have: $\mu_h^{-1}(L)=\pi_k(M_k \cap N_o^k xL)$, where π_k is the projection on the first k components. W.l.o.g. let be $L=L(0;\{q_1,..,q_m\})$.It follows that $N_o^k xL = L(0;\{(e_1,0),..,(e_k,0),(0,q_1),..,(0,q_m)\})$.From lemma 2.9 we know that the minimal positive integer solutions of the following linear diophantine equation system

$$\begin{bmatrix} 1 & & 0 \\ & \ddots & \\ 0 & & 1 \\ h & & 0 \\ & \ddots & \\ 0 & & h \end{bmatrix} \begin{bmatrix} z_1 \\ \cdot \\ \cdot \\ \cdot \\ z_k \end{bmatrix} = \begin{bmatrix} 1 & & & & \\ & \ddots & & & 0 \\ & & 1 & & \\ & 0 & & q_{11} & \cdots & q_{m1} \\ & & & \vdots & & \vdots \\ & & & q_{1k} & \cdots & q_{mk} \end{bmatrix} \begin{bmatrix} y_1 \\ \cdot \\ y_k \\ y_{k+1} \\ \vdots \\ y_{k+m} \end{bmatrix}$$

have entry size smaller than $\ln(2k+m).(k\#h+d'\#(q_1...q_m))$ for some constant d'. A simple calculation yields the desired upper bound. □

It is not hard to show the following lemma.

Lemma 3.19. Let $K=K(p_1,..,p_n)$ be a cone.Then the set L of grid points contained in K,$L=K\cap N_o^k$,is a linear set and the size of the entries of generating vectors for L can be estimated as follows : $\#(\|\{c,q_1,..,q_m\}\|) \leq \#(\|\{p_1,..,p_n\}\|)$, where $L=L(c;\{q_1,..,q_m\})$. □

From the previous lemma the following corollary holds.

Corollary 3.20. Let $K=K(p_1,..,p_n)$ be a cone and $s=K(p_1,..,p_{k-1})$ be a proper face of K.Then the set $SL:=N_o^k \cap (K-s)$ is s.l. and the size of the entries of generating vectors for SL can be estimated as follows : $\#(\|C\cup\Pi\|) \leq \#(\|\{p_1,..,p_n\}\|)$, where $SL=L(C;\Pi)$. □

And we get the following theorem.

Theorem 3.21. Let $K=K(p_1,..,p_n)$ be a cone. Then the set $SL:=N_o^k\cap(Q_+^k-K)$ is s.l. and the entry size of generating vectors for SL can be estimated as follows: $\#(\|\{c_1,..,c_l\}\cup\bigcup_{i=1}^{l}\Pi_i\|) \leq \#\|\{p_1,...,p_n\}\|$. □

Theorem 3.19 gives us an upper bound for the maximal size of the vectors in certain representation for the complement of a linear set where this complement is outside the cone induced by this linear set.We have not yet derived an upper bound for the size of the vectors of some generating system for the complement inside the induced cone.This will be done in the following theorem.

Theorem 3.22. Let $L=L(0;\{p_1,..,p_n\})$ be a linear set.Then the set $\bar{L} := N_o^k\cap K(L) - L$ is a s.l. set and we have an upper bound for the size of the generating vectors for $\bar{L}$ as follows : $\#\|\{c_1,..,c_l\}\cup\bigcup_{i=1}^{l}\Pi_i\| \leq d\#(p_1,..,p_n)^4$ for some constant d,where $\bar{L}=\bigcup_{i=1}^{l}L(c_i;\Pi_i)$.

Proof. W.l.o.g. we assume that $\dim K(L)=k$ and $\{p_1,..,p_n\}$ is a minimal generating system of K(L).Let h be the constant given in lemma 3.17. Consider the set $N_o^k x N_o^n$. For all i,$1\leq i\leq n$,define the vectors $\bar{p}_i$'s by $\bar{p}_i := (p_i,0,..,0,\underset{(k+i)\text{-th position}}{1},0,..,0)\in N_o^k x N_o^n$.The following facts are evident:

(a) As vectors in Q^{k+n} , $\bar{p}_1,..,\bar{p}_n$ are linearly independent .

(b) $x=\sum_{i=1}^{n}\lambda_i p_i \in L(0;\{p_1,..,p_n\}) \subset N_0^k \Leftrightarrow (x,\lambda_1,..,\lambda_n) \in L(0;\{\bar{p}_1,..,\bar{p}_n\})$.
Let $\bar{L}_h$ be the set $\bar{L}_h:=L(0;\{\bar{p}_1,..,\bar{p}_n\})-L(0;\{h\bar{p}_1,..,h\bar{p}_n\})$.

Claim. $\mu_h^{-1}(\pi_k(\bar{L}_h)) = \bar{L}$, where μ_h is the linear mapping defined in lemma 3.18.

Proof of the claim. We have : $x\in\bar{L} \Leftrightarrow x \in (N_0^k \cap K(L))-L$

$\Leftrightarrow \exists\lambda_1,..,\lambda_n \in N_0$: $hx=\sum_{i=1}^{n}\lambda_i p_i$ and $\forall\beta_1,..,\beta_n \in N_0$: $x\neq \sum_{i=1}^{n}\beta_i \bar{p}_i$

$\Leftrightarrow \exists\lambda_1,..,\lambda_n \in N_0$: $(hx,\lambda_1,..,\lambda_n) = \sum_{i=1}^{n}\lambda_i\bar{p}_i$ and $\forall\beta_1,..,\beta_n\in N_0$:
$(hx,h\beta_1,..,h\beta_n) \neq \sum_{i=1}^{n}\beta_i(h\bar{p}_i)$

$\Leftrightarrow$ $hx \in \pi_k((L(0;\{\bar{p}_1,..,\bar{p}_n\}) - L(0;\{h\bar{p}_1,..,h\bar{p}_n\}))$ $\Leftrightarrow$ $x\in \mu_h^{-1}(\pi_k(\bar{L}_h))$.

This completesthe proof of the claim . □

Now define the following linear mapping $\varphi:N_0^n \longrightarrow N_0^{n+k}$ by : $\forall i, 1\leq i\leq n$: $e_i \longmapsto \bar{p}_i$, where the e_i's are unit vectors in N_0^n. It is evident that φ is a bijection from N_0^n onto $L(0;\{\bar{p}_1,..,\bar{p}_n\})$ and $\bar{L}_h=\varphi(N_0^n-hN_0^n)$.

Let $C=\{c_1,..,c_s\}$ be the set $\{x\in N_0^n \mid 0<x<(h,h,..,h)\}$. One can easily verify that $\bigcup_{i=1}^{s} c_i+hN_0^n = N_0^n-hN_0^n$. Hence we have :

$$\bar{L} = \mu_h^{-1}(\pi_k(\varphi(N_0^n-hN_0^n))) \quad .$$

From this fact we conclude that L is a s.l. set,because semilinearity is closed under linear mappings,inverse linear mappings and projections.

From lemma 3.18 one gets the desired upper bound.This completes the proof of the theorem . □

From theorem 3.21 and theorem 3.22 we obtain the following

Theorem 3.23. Let $L=L(0;\{p_1,..,p_n\})$ be a linear set.Then the complement $\bar{L}=N_0^k-L$ of L is a s.l. set and $\bar{L}$ can be generated by vectors whose maximal entry size is bounded by $\#(\|\{c_1,..,c_m\}\cup\bigcup_{i=1}^{m}\Pi_i\|) \leq d\#(p_1,..,p_n)^4$, for some constant d,where $\bar{L}=\bigcup_{i=1}^{m}L(c_i;\Pi_i)$. □

From the previous theorem the following corollary holds.

Corollary 3.24. Let $L=L(c;\{p_1,..,p_n\})$ be a linear set.Then the complement $\bar{L}=N_0^k-L$ is a s.l. set and $\bar{L}$ can be generated by vectors whose maximal entry size is bounded by $\#(\|\{c_1,..,c_m\}\cup\bigcup_{i=1}^{m}\Pi_i\|) \leq d\#(p_1,..,p_n)^4$ for some constant d,where $\bar{L} =\bigcup_{i=1}^{m}L(c_i;\Pi_i)$.

Proof. This corollary follows directly from theorem 3.21 and the proof of lemma A.5 in [5] . □

Until now we have derived an upper bound for generating vectors of the complement of a linear set and we are going to do that for the general case,i.e. the case of s.l. sets. This is done in the following

Theorem 3.25. Let $SL=L_1\cup L_2\cup ... \cup L_n$ be a s.l. set,where $L_i=L(c^i;\{p_1^i, ...,p_{m_i}^i\})$ for $1\leq i\leq n$. Then the complement $\overline{SL}:=N_0^k-SL$ of SL is a s.l. set and $\overline{SL}$ can be generated by vectors whose maximal entry size is bounded by $\#(\|\{c_1,..,c_l\}\cup\bigcup_{i=1}^{l}\Pi_i\|) \leq P(\#SL)$ for some fixed polynomial P,where $\overline{SL} = \bigcup_{i=1}^{l}L(c_i;\Pi_i)$.

Proof. We have $SL=L_1\cup ... \cup L_n$. Because of the semilinearity of the

L_i's it follows that $\overline{SL}$ is s.l.,too.(Semilinearity is closed under intersections). From corollary 3.24. the following fact holds :

$$(*)\quad \bar{L}_i=\bar{L}_1^i\cup\dots\cup\bar{L}_{l_i}^i \text{ and } =(\|\{\bar{c}_1^i,\dots,\bar{c}_{l_i}^i\}\cup\bigcup_{j=1}^{l_i}\bar{\Pi}_j^i\|)\le d(\#(p_1^i,\dots,p_{m_i}^i))^4$$

for some constant d,where $\bar{L}_j^i=L(\bar{c}_j^i;\bar{\Pi}_j^i)$, $1\le j\le l_i$, $1\le i\le n$.

Now we want to derive an upper bound for the maximal entry size of the generating vectors for $\overline{SL}$. From (∗) it follows that the cardinality $t_{i_j}=|\bar{\Pi}_j^i|$ of the period system of $\bar{L}_j^i$, $1\le j\le l_i$, $1\le i\le n$, is bounded by $\left[2^{d[\#(p_1^i,\dots,p_{m_i}^i)]^4}\right]^k$ .In order to determine generating vectors for $\overline{SL}$ $=\bar{L}_1\cap\dots\cap\bar{L}_n$ we consider the minimal positive integer solutions of the following linear diophantine equation system

$$\begin{bmatrix} \bar{\Pi}_{j_1}^1 & -\bar{\Pi}_{j_2}^2 & & & & \\ & \bar{\Pi}_{j_2}^2 & -\bar{\Pi}_{j_3}^3 & & 0 & \\ & & \ddots & \ddots & & \\ & 0 & & \ddots & \ddots & \\ & & & & \bar{\Pi}_{j_{n-2}}^{n-2} & -\bar{\Pi}_{j_{n-1}}^{n-1} & \\ & & & & & \bar{\Pi}_{j_{n-1}}^{n-1} & -\bar{\Pi}_{j_n}^{n} \end{bmatrix} \begin{bmatrix} x_1 \\ \vdots \\ x_{t_{1j_1}} \\ \vdots \\ \vdots \\ x_{\sum_{i=1}^{n} t_{ij_i}} \end{bmatrix} = \begin{bmatrix} b_1 \\ \vdots \\ b_k \\ \vdots \\ \vdots \\ b_{(n-1)\cdot k} \end{bmatrix} \qquad (**)$$

where $1\le j_i\le l_i$, $1\le i\le n$, the vectors of $\bar{\Pi}_{j_i}^i$ are written as column vectors, $-\{v_1,\dots,v_n\}$ means $\{-v_1,\dots,-v_n\}$ for a subset $\{v_1,\dots,v_n\}$ of N_0^k , and for $0\le r\le n-1$:

(i) to determine the constants for $\overline{SL}$ we set

$$\begin{bmatrix} b_{rk+1} \\ \vdots \\ b_{rk+k} \end{bmatrix} = \begin{bmatrix} \bar{c}_{j_{r+1},1}^{r+1} - \bar{c}_{j_r,1}^{r} \\ \\ \bar{c}_{j_{r+1},k}^{r+1} - \bar{c}_{j_r,k}^{r} \end{bmatrix}$$

(ii) to determine the periods for $\overline{SL}$ we set

$$\begin{bmatrix} b_{rk+1} \\ \vdots \\ b_{rk+k} \end{bmatrix} = \begin{bmatrix} 0 \\ \vdots \\ 0 \end{bmatrix}$$

The determinants of the $[(n-1)k \times (n-1)k]$ submatrices of the extended matrix defined by (∗∗) can be estimated by the Hadamard's formula.The maximal length of their binary representations is bounded by

$$k\cdot\underbrace{\ln[(n-1)k]}_{\le\,\#SL}\cdot\underbrace{\sum_{i=1}^{n} d(\#(p_1^i,\dots,p_{m_i}^i,c_{m_i}^i))^4}_{\le d'(\#SL)^4 \text{ for some } d'} \le d''\cdot(\#SL)^6 \text{ for some constant } d''.$$

On the other hand we have $\sum_{i=1}^{n} t_{ij_i} \le \sum_{i=1}^{n}\left[2^{d(\#(p_1^i,\dots,p_{m_i}^i))^4}\right]^k$

Hence : $\#(\sum_{i=1}^{n} t_{ij_i}) \le \ln(n) + dk[\max_{1\le i\le n}\{\#(p_1^i,\dots,p_{m_i}^i)\}]^4 \le d'''(\#SL)^5$

for some constant d''' .

Thus the maximal entry size of generating vectors for $\overline{SL}$ can be bounded as follows : $\#(\|\{\tilde{c}_1,\ldots,\tilde{c}_l\}\cup\bigcup_{i=1}^{l}\tilde{\Pi}_i\|) \leq \tilde{d}(\#SL)^8$, for some constant $\tilde{d}$. This completes the proof of theorem 3.24 . □

Remark 3.26. In order to classify the complexity of EQ resp. INEQ , we have deriveda number of upper bounds and did not pay any attention to the optimality of these bounds.The reader should note that we have repeatedly used lemma 2.8 which is not sharp.For our purpose it suffices to obtain polynomial bounds.

4.The complexity of the equality problem for s.l. sets. As the main result of this paper we shall show in this section that the inequality problem resp. the equality problem for s.l. sets is log-complete in Σ_2^p resp. in Π_2^p .

We first prove that INEQ is in Σ_2^p by the following lemma .

Lemma 4.1. INEQ is in Σ_2^p .

Proof. Let $SL_1=L(c_1^1;\Pi_1^1)\cup\ldots\cup L(c_m^1;\Pi_m^1)$ and $SL_2=L(c_1^2;\Pi_1^2)\cup\ldots\cup L(c_n^2;\Pi_n^2)$ be two s.l. set representations.(It is not hard to see that a TM can verify in polynomial time,whether a word $w \in (\Sigma\cup\{\int\})^*$is syntactically correct,i.e.whether it is of the form $SL_1\int SL_2$,where SL_1 and SL_2 are two representations of s.l. sets in N_o^k for some $k \in N$).

Now we have : $(c_1^1;\Pi_1^1)\cup\ldots\cup(c_m^1;\Pi_m^1)\int(c_1^2;\Pi_1^2)\cup\ldots\cup(c_n^2;\Pi_n^2) \in INEQ \Leftrightarrow$ $SL_1-SL_2 \neq \emptyset$ or $SL_2-SL_1 \neq \emptyset \Leftrightarrow$ (*) $SL_1\cap(N_o^k-SL_2)\neq\emptyset$ or $SL_2\cap(N_o^k-SL_1)\neq\emptyset$. Consider the set $SL_1\cap(N_o^k-SL_2)$.(The case $SL_2\cap(N_o^k-SL_1)$ is symmetric).From theorem 3.23 it follows that $N_o^k\cap SL_2$ is s.l. and it can by generated by vectors of which the maximal entry size is bounded by $P(\#SL_2)$ for some fixed polynomial P.Let $N_o^k-SL_2=\overline{SL}_2=L(\bar{c}_1^2;\bar{\Pi}_1^2)\cup\ldots\cup L(\bar{c}_{\bar{n}}^2;\bar{\Pi}_{\bar{n}}^2)$ be some representation for $\overline{SL}_2$ and $\#(\|\{\bar{c}_1^2,\ldots,\bar{c}_{\bar{n}}^2\}\cup\bigcup_{i=1}^{\bar{n}}\bar{\Pi}_i^2\|) \leq P(\#SL_2)$. We have :

$$SL_1\cap(N_o^k-SL_2) = [L(c_1^1;\Pi_1^1)\cup\ldots\cup L(c_m^1;\Pi_m^1)]\cap[L(\bar{c}_1^2;\bar{\Pi}_1^2)\cup\ldots\cup L(\bar{c}_{\bar{n}}^2;\bar{\Pi}_{\bar{n}}^2)]$$
$$= \bigcup_{\substack{1\leq i\leq m\\ 1\leq j\leq\bar{n}}} L(c_i^1;\Pi_i^1)\cap L(\bar{c}_j^2;\bar{\Pi}_j^2) .$$

Now the intersection $L(c_i^1;\Pi_i^1)\cap L(\bar{c}_j^2;\bar{\Pi}_j^2)$, $1\leq i\leq m, 1\leq j\leq n$, are s.l. sets and they can be represented by vectors of which the maximal entry size is bounded by : $\#(\|\{\text{generating vectors for } L(c_i^1;\Pi_i^1)\cap L(\bar{c}_j^2;\bar{\Pi}_j^2)\}\|)$ $\leq d\cdot Max(\#(c_i^1,\Pi_i^1),\#(\bar{c}_j^2,\bar{\Pi}_j^2))^5 \leq P'(Max(\#SL_1,\#SL_2))$ for some fixed polynomial P'.(The intersection of two linear sets can be computed in the usual way.One has to solve certain linear diophantine equation system again). Thus we have the following facts :

$(SL_1\int SL_2)\in INEQ \Leftrightarrow$ There exists a vector $v\in N_o^k$ with $\#v \leq P'(Max(\#SL_1,\#SL_2))$ such that ($v\in SL_1$ and $v\notin SL_2$) or ($v\in SL_2$ and $v\notin SL_1$).

On the other side we have : $v \in SL_1$ and $v \notin SL_2$ $\Leftrightarrow$

[There exist some i,$1\leq i\leq m$,and some coefficient vector Λ with $\|\Lambda\| \leq \|v\|$ such that $v=c_i^1+\Pi_i^1\cdot\Lambda$ and for all j,$1\leq j\leq n$,for all coefficient vector Δ with $\|\Delta\|\leq\|v\|$ it holds : $v \neq \bar{c}_j^2+\bar{\Pi}_j^2\cdot\Delta$].

Thus INEQ is in Σ_2^p and the proof is complete . □

Corollary 4.2. EQ is in Π_2^p. □

Modifying the proof of Stockmeyer in [11] for the Log-completeness of the inequivalence problem for integer expressions in Σ_2^p we can prove the following lemma.

Lemma 4.3. INEQ is $\leq_{\log}$-hard for Σ_2^p .

Proof. We omit the proof. □

From lemma 4.1 and lemma 4.3 one obtains the main

Theorem 4.4. INEQ is log-complete in Σ_2^p . □

and the following corollary.

Corollary 4.5. EQ is log-complete in Π_2^p . □

With 1-EQ resp. 1-INEQ we denote the sublanguages of EQ resp. INEQ, which describe the equality problem and the inequality problem for s.l. sets in N_o.Using theorem 2.9 the following result can be proved.We omit the proof .

Theorem 4.6. 1-INEQ resp. 1-EQ is log-complete in Σ_2^p resp. Π_2^p . □

For the uniform word problem for s.l. sets we have the following results.

Theorem 4.7. UWP is log-complete in NP . □

Theorem 4.8. UWP in N_o is log-complete in NP . □

Remark. Recently,E.M. Gurari and O.H. Ibara have achieved an $2^{2^{c \cdot N^2}}$ upper bound for the equality problem,where c is some constant and N is the input size.(E.M. Gurari and O.H. Ibara:"The Complexity of the Equivalence Problem for Counter Machines,Semilinear Sets,and Simple Programs", Proc. of the 11-th Annual ACM Symposium on the Theory of Computing,1979, pp.142-152) From our main theorem in this paper one can verify that EQ and INEQ are in PSPACE.Thus we can recognize EQ resp. INEQ in DTIME($2^{P(N)}$) where P is a fixed polynomial and N is the input size.

Acknowledgements. The author wishes to thank Prof. G. Hotz for valuable suggestions concerning this paper.

References.

1. E.Cardoza,R.Lipton and A.R.Meyer: "Exponential Space Complete Problem for Petri Nets and Commutative Semigroups",in "Proc. of the 8-th Annual ACM Symposium on the Theory of Computing" (1976),pp.50-54.
2. S.Eilenberg and M.P.Schützenberger:"Rational Sets in Commutative Monoids",Journal of Algebra,No 13,1969,pp.173-191.
3. J.Von Zur Gathen and M.Sieveking:"A bound on Solutions of Linear Integer Equalities and Inequalities",Proc. of the AMS,Vol.72,No1, 1978,pp.155-158.
4. M.Gerstenhaber:"Theory of Convex Polyhedral Cones",in Proc. of a Conference on "Activity Analysis of Production and Allocation",Ed.

T.C.Koopmans,John Willey & Sons - Chapman & Hall,1951.

5. S.Ginsburg:"The Mathematical Theory of Context-free Languages",Mc Graw-Hill,1966.
6. F.Glover and R.E.D.Woolsey:"Aggregating Diophantine Equations",Zeitschrift für Operations Researchs,Vol.16,1972,pp.1-10.
7. G.Hotz:"Eine Neue Invariante Kontext-freier Grammatiken",1978,to appear in Theoretical Computer Science.
8. G.Hotz:"Verschränkte Homomorphismen Formaler Sprachen",1979,to appear in RAIRO.
9. W.J.Paul:"Komplexitätstheorie",Teubner Verlag,1979.
10. L.Stockmeyer and A.R.Meyer:"Word Problem Requiring Exponential Time", in Proc. of the 5-th Annual Symposium on the Theory of Computing, 1973,pp.1-9.
11. L.Stockmeyer:"The Polynomial-Time Hierarchy",Theoretical Computer Science,Vol.3,1977,pp.1-12.
12. J.Stoer and C.Witzgall:"Convexity and Optimization in Finite Dimension I",Springer Verlag,1970.
13. C.Wrathall:"Complete Sets and the Polynomial-Time Hierarchy",Theoretical Computer Science,Vol.3,1977,pp.23-33.

A THEORY OF NONDETERMINISM

J.R. Kennaway, Department of Computer Science, Edinburgh University
C.A.R. Hoare, Programming Research Group, Oxford University

Abstract

A construction is described which takes an arbitrary set of machines, an arbitray set of tests, and an arbitrary relation on machines and tests defining which machines pass which tests. It produces a domain of specifications, which is a retract of the lattice of sets of tests (with the subset ordering), and a domain of nondeterministic machines (ndms), which is a retract of the lattice of sets of machines (with the superset ordering). These two domains are isomorphic. Simple conditions ensure that they are ω-algebraic.

Functions on such domains may be defined equivalently either as transformations of ndms (an operational definition) or as transformations of specifications (an axiomatic definition). Conditions for the "realism" of such functions are formulated.

Keywords: axiomatic semantics; operational semantics; complementary definitions; nondeterminism; powerdomains.

1. The Construction

1.1 Deterministic Machines

We start with a set $\mathcal{M}$ of deterministic machines. These machines may be subjected to tests drawn from a set $\mathcal{T}$. There is a relation $\mathcal{S} \subseteq \mathcal{M} \times \mathcal{T}$ specifying which machines pass which tests.

Definition 1.1.1 For m in $\mathcal{M}$, $s(m) = \{t \in \mathcal{T} \mid \mathcal{S}mt\}$
For t in $\mathcal{T}$, $i(t) = \{m \in \mathcal{M} \mid \mathcal{S}mt\}$

Tests may be combined into sets. A machine satisfies a set of tests if and only if it passes every test which is a member of it. So we extend the definition of $\mathcal{S}$.

Definition 1.1.2 For any subset T of $\mathcal{T}$ and m in $\mathcal{M}$,

$$\mathcal{S}mT \Leftrightarrow \forall t \in T.\ \mathcal{S}mt$$

For any m, s(m) is the largest set of tests which m satisfies.

1.2 Nondeterministic Machines

We extend the discussion to nondeterministic machines (ndms) by identifying an ndm as a certain kind of set of deterministic machines. An ndm M contained in $\mathcal{M}$, will behave like some m in M but the choice of M cannot be known in advance or influenced from outside in any way. We postpone a discussion of which subsets of $\mathcal{M}$ are admissible representations of ndms, first considering how to extend $\mathcal{S}$ to ndms.

When does an ndm M pass a test t? There are two main alternative definitions. We might consider M to pass t if and only if some member of M passes t. Even if the actual outcome of the test is failure (the m M that is chosen fails t), perhaps M would have passed t if the choice had been different (some m M does pass t). Adopting this definition makes $\mathcal{S}Mt$ mean "M might pass t" and would lead to a theory of partial or conditional correctness of machines.

But we shall pursue the other alternative, analogous to total correctness. If users of machines are interested only in certainties, they refuse to agree that M passes t unless they can be sure that every member of M passes t. In this case $\mathcal{S}Mt$ means "M will pass t" and the other definitions are extended accordingly.

<u>Definition 1.2.3</u> For $M \subseteq \mathcal{M}$, $t \in \mathcal{T}$, $\mathcal{S}Mt \quad \forall m \in M.\ \mathcal{S}mt$

For $M \subseteq \mathcal{M}$, $T \subseteq \mathcal{T}$, $\mathcal{S}MT \quad \forall m \in M. \forall t \in T.\ \mathcal{S}mt$

For $M \subseteq \mathcal{M}$, $sM = \{t \mid \mathcal{S}Mt\} \quad \{sm \mid m \in M\}$

For $T \subseteq \mathcal{T}$, $iT = \{m \mid \mathcal{S}mT\} \quad \{it \mid t \in T\}$

Three simple examples illustrate these definitions.

<u>Example 1</u> $\mathcal{M} = \mathcal{T} = N$ (the natural numbers)

$\mathcal{S}mt \Leftrightarrow m \geq t$

(m may be thought of as the length of time a machine continues to operate before breaking. t is the length of time a user wishes to interact with a machine. A machine satisfies a user if it lasts as long as the user wants.)

$sm = \{0..m\}$ $\quad it = \{t, t+1, ..\}$

$sM = \{0..\min(M)\}$ for $M \neq \emptyset$ $\quad iT = N$ for $T = \emptyset$

$s\emptyset = N$ $\quad iT = \{\max(T), \max(T)+1, ...\}$ for T nonempty and finite

$iT = \emptyset$ for infinite T

<u>Example 2</u> $\mathcal{M} = \mathcal{T} = N \quad \mathcal{S}mt \Leftrightarrow m \leq t$

(The dual of ex.1. m is the length of time a machine takes to produce a result. t is the length of time a user is prepared to wait for a result. s and i can be calculated by interchanging s with i and m with t in ex.1.)

<u>Example 3</u> $\mathcal{M} = \mathcal{T} = N \cup \{\omega\} \quad \mathcal{S}mt \Leftrightarrow m \geq t$

This is the same as ex.1 except that we now have an infinite machine ω and an infinite test ω. This will have important consequences later.

1.3 <u>Equivalence of Machines and Tests</u>

Two ndms M and M' may be different as sets but pass exactly the same tests. Such machines are for all practical purposes indistinguishable. We wish to identify machines which are in this sense equivalent.

There are two ways of proceeding. We may consider the equivalence classes of ndms as single objects, or we may seek canonical members of these equivalence classes. We follow the latter course. Among all the ndms equivalent to a given ndm M there is a largest one, which contains every deterministic machine which passes all the tests that M passes: i(sM) (or isM — we omit parentheses whenever there is no ambiguity). Machines M and M' are equivalent if and only if isM=isM'.

We may apply the same argument to sets of tests. Two sets of tests which are passed by exactly the same machines are equivalent; and among all the sets of tests equivalent to a set T there is a largest one, namely siT.

These observations and some other properties of s and i are confirmed in the next proposition. We define $c = s \circ i$ and $\hat{c} = i \circ s$.

Proposition 1.3.4

1.	$T \subseteq T' \Rightarrow iT \supseteq iT'$	$M \subseteq M' \Rightarrow sM \supseteq sM'$
2.	$T \subseteq T' \Rightarrow cT \subseteq cT'$	$M \subseteq M' \Rightarrow \hat{c}M \subseteq \hat{c}M'$
3.	$s \circ i \circ s = s$	$i \circ s \circ i = i$
4.	c and $\hat{c}$ are idempotent	
5.	$iT=iT' \Leftrightarrow cT=cT'$	$sM=sM' \Leftrightarrow cM=cM'$
6.	$i(\bigcup_j T_j) = \bigcap_j iT_j$	$s(\bigcup_j M_j) = \bigcap_j sM_j$
7.	$c(\bigcap_j T_j) = c(\bigcap_j cT_j)$	$\hat{c}(\bigcup_j M_j) = \hat{c}(\bigcup_j \hat{c}M_j)$
8.	$\bigcap_j cT_j = c(\bigcap_j cT_j)$	$\bigcap_j \hat{c}M_j = \hat{c}(\bigcap_j \hat{c}M_j)$

In what follows we assume familiarity with the following concepts: lattice, complete lattice, continuous lattice, ω-algebraic lattice, continuous function, domain.

We note from part 1 of the proposition that the larger a set of tests is the more demanding it is, and the fewer machines pass it. But the larger an ndm is, the more unpredictable it is, and the fewer the tests it passes. We therefore define information orderings on the powersets $P\mathcal{M}$ and $P\mathcal{T}$ in opposite senses.

Definition 1.3.5 $\langle P\mathcal{M}, \sqsubseteq \rangle = \langle P\mathcal{M}, \supseteq \rangle$

$\langle P\mathcal{T}, \sqsubseteq \rangle = \langle P\mathcal{T}, \subseteq \rangle$

Because c and $\hat{c}$ are idempotent their images are the same as their sets of fixed points. Let S (specifications) and I (implementations) denote the images of c and $\hat{c}$ respectively. and define $\sqsubseteq$ on S and I as the orderings induced from those on $P\mathcal{T}$ and $P\mathcal{M}$. Since c and $\hat{c}$ are monotonic, Tarski's theorem [6] implies that S and I are complete lattices. Ndms and specifications must be members, respectively, of I and S. These are in fact the same domain.

Proposition 1.3.6 I and S are isomorphic.

Example 1 (cont.)

$\hat{c}M = \{\min(M), \min(M)+1, ..\}$ for $M \neq \emptyset$

$\hat{c}\emptyset = \emptyset$

$c\emptyset = \{0\}$

$cT = \{0..\max(T)\}$ for nonempty finite T

$cT = N$ for infinite T

Example 3 (cont.)

$\hat{c}M = \{\min(M)..\omega\}$ for $M \neq \emptyset$

$\hat{c}\emptyset = \{\omega\}$

$c\emptyset = \{0\}$

$cT = \{0..\max(T)\}$ for nonempty finite T

$cT = \{0..\omega\}$ for infinite T

Example 4

Let $\mathcal{M}$ be a domain. Let $\mathcal{T}$ be the set of finite nonempty sets of finite elements of $\mathcal{M}$.

$\mathcal{S}mt \Leftrightarrow \exists x \in t.\ x \sqsubseteq m$

$sm = \{t \mid \exists x \in t. x \sqsubseteq m\}$ $it = \{m \mid \exists x \in t. x \sqsubseteq m\}$

$sM = \{t \mid \forall m \in M. \exists x \in t. x \sqsubseteq m\}$ $iT = \{m \mid \forall t \in T. \exists x \in t. x \sqsubseteq m\}$

i(t) is the right-closure of t, that is, the smallest subset of $\mathcal{M}$ containing t and every member of $\mathcal{M}$ larger (in the ordering of $\mathcal{M}$) than any member of itself.

I is the weak powerdomain of $\mathcal{M}$, $P_o(\mathcal{M})$.

Proof

(See [4] for definitions of the terms used here.) Both I and $P_o(\mathcal{M})$ are sub-posets of $<P\mathcal{M}, \sqsubseteq>$. So we need only prove their equality as sets.

$P_o(\mathcal{M})$ is the set of right-closed finitely generable subsets of $\mathcal{M}$. Every member t of $\mathcal{T}$ is a finitely generable subset of $\mathcal{M}$. Therefore i(t), the right-closure of t, is right-closed and finitely generable. So I is contained in $P_o(\mathcal{M})$.

For the reverse inclusion, let $x \in P_o(\mathcal{M})$. Let $\{X_n \mid n \in N\}$ be the sequence of cross-sections of a strict generating tree for X. Each X_n is a member of $\mathcal{T}$ and

$$X = \bigcap_n \text{right-closure}(X_n)$$

$$= \bigcap_n iX_n$$

$$= \bigcap_n iX_n$$

$$= i\bigcup_n X_n \qquad \text{(proposition 1.3.4.(6))}$$

$$\in I$$

So $P_0(\mathcal{M})$ is contained in I.

Example 5

Let L be the language of first-order predicate calculus.

$\mathcal{M}$ = the set of all L-structures

$\mathcal{T}$ = the set of sentences of L

$\mathcal{S}mt \Leftrightarrow m \models t$ (m is a model for t, or m satisfies t)

sm = the set of sentences true in m

sM = the set of sentences true in every model in M

it = the set of models of t

iT = the set of models of T

The members of I are known [1] as the generalised elementary classes of models. Those members of the form i(t) are the elementary classes of models. Let $(B,\leq)$ be the Lindenbaum algebra of L. S is the completion of $(B,\geq)$.

Because of the soundness theorem, every member of S is deductively closed, that is, is a theory. The completeness theorem implies that for $T \subseteq \mathcal{T}$, cT is the deductive closure of T; any sentence which is satisfied by every model of T is derivable from T. So every theory is a member of S.

2. Global Restrictions

The construction described in section 1 may be applied to any sets $\mathcal{M}$ and $\mathcal{T}$ and relation $\mathcal{S}$. However, the domains I and S we arrive at may be unsuitable as models of nondeterministic computation, for reasons we discuss in this section.

2.1 Finiteness and Continuity

Our intuitive picture of a test is that of a series of one or more actions and observations that a user may carry out on a machine. However, it is reasonable to assume that in practice a user can engage in only countably many different actions or sequences of actions. Our set $\mathcal{T}$ of tests can therefore be assumed to be countable. Furthermore, in a finite time a user can engage in only finitely many different actions. If there are infinitely many different actions this implies that they can be, in some sense, arbitrarily large. That is, there should be some measure of "size" on $\mathcal{T}$ such that every test in $\mathcal{T}$ has a finite size, and such that there are only finitely many tests smaller than any given finite size.

Now suppose that $M_0 \sqsubset M_1 \sqsubset \ldots$ is a strictly ascending sequence in I. Then $sM_0 \supset sM_1 \supset \ldots$ Thus successive members of the sequence of ndms pass successively more and more tests. The tests in $sM_j - sM_{j-1}$ introduced at the jth stage must become larger and larger as j increases. This implies that the difference between M_j and M_{j-1} requires larger and larger tests to reveal. A test passed by the limit machine $\bigsqcup_j M_j$ but not by any M_j would, intuitively, have to be infinitely large. Such a test could not be guaranteed to produce a result within any finite time. It is reasonable to deny the existence of any such test.

Assumption

For any ascending sequence $M_0 \sqsubseteq M_1 \sqsubseteq \ldots$ in I and any test t in $\mathcal{T}$,

$$\mathcal{S}(\bigsqcup_j M_j)t \Longrightarrow \exists j.\, \mathcal{S} M_j\ t$$

Noting that the reverse implication is always true (by the monotonicity of s), this assumption is equivalent to requiring that $s|I$ is continuous. We state without proof three alternative formulations of this condition.

Proposition 2.1.1

The following are equivalent.

(i) $s|I$ is continuous

(ii) c is continuous

(iii) $c|S$ is continuous

We may use the second formulation to prove something about the structures of I and S.

Proposition 2.1.2

S is ω-algebraic; its isolated elements are the set $\{cT | T$ is a finite subset of $\mathcal{T}\}$.

Proof

c is continuous (by the preceding proposition), idempotent (prop 1.3.4(4)), and stronger than the identity on $P\mathcal{T}$; and we have assumed that $\mathcal{T}$ is countable. Therefore c is a closure operator [3]. The proposition follows by an application of theorem 5.1 of [3]. By the isomorphism of S and I we also have:

Corollary 2.1.3

I is ω-algebraic; its isolated elements are the set $\{iT | T$ is a finite subset of $\mathcal{T}\}$.

Examples 1 and 2 (cont)

s is continuous.

Example 3 (cont)

Let $M_j = \{j,j+1,\ldots,\omega\}$. Then $\bigsqcup_j M_j = \{\omega\}$, which satisfies the test ω. None of of the M_j satisfy ω. The presence of the infinite test ω makes $s|I$ discontinuous.

Example 5 (cont)

c is continuous. For let $T_0 \subseteq T_1 \subseteq \ldots$ be an ascending sequence of theories and let $t \in c(\bigsqcup_j T_j)$. Then t is derivable from $\bigsqcup_j T_j$, and hence derivable from a finite subset of $\bigsqcup_j T_j$. There must be some j for which $T \subseteq T_j$, so t is derivable from T_j. Therefore $t \in cT_j$ and c is continuous.

2.2 Miracles

The top element of I, $\top_I$, is $\hat{c}\emptyset$. Since $s\top_I = \top$, if $\top_I \neq \emptyset$ then there is some deterministic machine which satisfies every test. But then there is scarcely any point in considering any less satisfactory machine and the theory becomes trivial. One may choose some m in $c\emptyset$, use only it, and ignore all other members of $\mathcal{M}$ and all of $P\mathcal{M}$.

But in practice no such machine can be built and $\top_I = \emptyset$. $\top_I$ is then the "miraculous" machine which trivially passes every test by exhibiting no behaviour at all — in fact, by not existing.

In such circumstances, when $\top_I$ is a paradoxical machine, it would be undesirable if it were to be approachable as a limit of more reasonable ndms(e.g. as the result of a recursive definition). We therefore require that $\top_I$ be an isolated element of I.

Proposition 2.2.1

$\top_I$ is isolated $\Leftrightarrow \exists T.$ T is a finite subset of $\top \wedge cT = \top$

Proof

by proposition 2.1.2.

Example 5 (cont)

$\top_S$ is the inconsistent theory which contains every sentence. $\top_S$ is isolated since it is equal to $c\{t, {\sim}t\}$ for any t in $\top$.

3. Nondeterministic Functions

3.1. Realism Conditions

We are interested in methods of constructing complex machines from simpler component machines. Let $f:I \to I'$ be a function on ndms (our discussion will apply equally to functions of more than one argument). In this section we consider conditions which f must satisfy in order to be a "realistic" method of constructing the machine fM from a machine M.

1. Continuity The ordering on I is one of information. The smaller a set of machines is, the less uncertainty there is about its possible behaviour. Therefore in order for f to be computable at all, it must be continuous. A clear explanation of the reasons for this is given in [5] and applies generally, not just to functions on domains resulting from the construction of section 1. We outline here how the argument applies in the present situation.

Consider an ascending chain of machines $M_0 \sqsubseteq M_1 \sqsubseteq \ldots$ We suppose that the cost of these machines is increasing and that the cost of the limit machine $\bigsqcup_j M_j$ is infinite. If we wish to construct $f(\bigsqcup_j M_j)$ but cannot construct $\bigsqcup_j M_j$ we may proceed as follows. Construct fM_0. If this passes all the tests we require, well and good. If not, replace fM_0 by fM_1, then fM_2, ... We must be sure that any test which the limit $f(\bigsqcup_j M_j)$ satisfies is passed by some fM_j. So we require that $\bigsqcup_j s(fM_j) = sf(\bigsqcup_j M_j)$. The fact that s and i are isomorphisms implies that this condition is equivalent to the continuity of f.

2. Backtracking Continuity is usually all that is required of "good" functions. But our view of nondeterminism leads us to make more stringent requirements. If an implementation of nondeterministic processes is required to explore every branch of every nondeterministic choice encountered in the course of a computation, then execution time or space will grow exponentially or faster with the number of such choices. This is impractical. We will suppose the opposite: that an implementation is only required to follow one branch of the computation. Whenever a choice arises, a single choice is made, irrevocably. No backtracking is allowed. This is in line with our definition in 1.2 of $\mathcal{S}$ on nondeterministic machines, where we rejected the view that possible success is of any use.

This view imposes a strong restriction on f. Suppose $m,m' \in \mathcal{M}$, and for simplicity suppose that $\{m\}$, $\{m'\}$, and $\{m,m'\}$ are all in I. Consider the calculation of $f\{m,m'\}$. By the above discussion, either m or m' is chosen, then f is applied. The set $fm \cup fm'$ of possible results so obtained must be indistinguishable from $f\{m,m'\}$. That is, we must have:

$$s(fm \cup fm') = sf\{m,m'\}$$

More generally, for any $M \in I$ we can calculate fM by applying f to any single element of M; we therefore require that f have the following property:

$$\forall M \in I . s(\bigsqcup\{fm \mid m \in M\}) = s(fM)$$

Note that this condition implies monotonicity of f (but not continuity). We will refer to this property as the no-backtracking property.

3. Nonmiraculousness A realistic function should not be able to perform miracles - that is, for $M \neq \top_I$, $fM \neq \top_I$. For functions satisfying the preceding condition, this is true if and only if for all m in $\mathcal{M}$, $fm \neq \emptyset$.

A function satisfying these three conditions will be called realistic.

3.2 Equivalence of Definitions

The isomorphisms of I with S and I' and S' induce an isomorphism of $I \to I'$ with $S \to S'$:

$$f: S \to S' \quad \to \quad f' = s' \circ f \circ i : I \to I'$$

$$f: I \to I' \quad \to \quad f' = i' \circ f \circ s : S \to S'$$

Functions f and f' which correspond under this isomorphism may be thought of as, respectively, an "axiomatic" definition, in terms of specifications, and an "operational" definition, in terms of machines. The conditions of continuity and non-miraculousness take the same form for functions on specifications as for functions on ndms, since they are defined only in terms of the order structure of I. The no-backtracking condition for $f: S \to S'$ is:

$$\forall T \in S \;.\; s(\bigsqcup\{i(f(s(m))) \mid m \in iT\}) = s(i(fT))$$

which may be simplified to

$$\forall T \in S \;.\; \bigsqcap \{f(s\{m\}) \mid m \in iT\} = fT$$

That is, fT is equal to the meet of all fT', where T' is the specification of a single machine in i(T). Note that T is the meet of all such T'; so the no-backtracking property is satisfied by any completely multiplicative function (one which commutes with $\bigsqcap$ over arbitrary families).

Example 7

$\lambda M.\lambda M'.M \cap M'$ is the nondeterministic composition operator — the meet in I. It is continuous because I is a continuous lattice. It clearly satisfies the other two conditions. The corresponding function on S is the meet on S.

Example 8

Let $\mathcal{T}' \subseteq \mathcal{T}$, $\mathcal{M}' = \mathcal{M}$, $S' = S | (\mathcal{M}' \times \mathcal{T}')$. Similarly define s', i', etc. Let $f = \lambda T \in S.(T \cap \mathcal{T}')$. This is a "forgetting" operator, which restricts the range of tests to $\mathcal{T}'$. In terms of machines, it describes putting a machine into a box which conceals some of the lights and buttons by which it interacts with the environment.

f is well-defined.

Proof:

We must show that $\forall T.c'(fT)=fT$.

But $c'(fT) = c(fT) \cap \mathcal{T}' = c(T \cap \mathcal{T}') \cap \mathcal{T}'$.

Since $T \cap \mathcal{T}' \subseteq c(T \cap \mathcal{T}')$ and $T \cap \mathcal{T}' \subseteq \mathcal{T}'$, $T \cap \mathcal{T}' \subseteq c'(fT)$.

Conversely, $T \cap \mathcal{T}' \subseteq T$

$$\Rightarrow c(T \cap \mathcal{T}') \subseteq cT$$
$$= T$$
$$\Rightarrow c'(fT) \subseteq T \cap \mathcal{T}'.$$

f is non-miraculous if and only if $c\,\mathcal{T}' = \mathcal{T}$.

Proof:

If $c\,\mathcal{T}' = \mathcal{T}$ then $fT = \mathcal{T}' \Leftrightarrow c(T \cap \mathcal{T}') \supseteq \mathcal{T}'' \Leftrightarrow c(T \cap \mathcal{T}') = \mathcal{T} \Leftrightarrow T = \mathcal{T}$

The converse follows from the fact that $f(c\,\mathcal{T}') = \mathcal{T}' = \tau_S$.

f is completely multiplicative, hence non-backtracking; continuity is obvious.

The corresponding function on I is $\lambda M \in I.i(\mathcal{T}' \cap sM)$; it is derived from the function on deterministic machines $\lambda m \in \mathcal{M}.i(\mathcal{T}' \cap sm)$.

Example 5 (cont)

The propositional connectives $\wedge$, $\vee$, $\supset$, and $\sim$ give operations on theories which are, respectively, $\bigsqcup$, $\bigsqcap$, $\lambda T.\lambda T'.T'$, and $\lambda T.\tau_S$. Notice that although $\supset$ (in its first argument) and $\sim$ are anti-monotonic on tests, they nonetheless induce continuous operations on theories.

4. Examples

4.1 Outputting automata

In this section we consider outputting automata, that is, machines whose behaviour can only be observed, not influenced, from outside. The communication between a machine and a user is one-way: from the machine to the user.

4.1.1

We describe a general family of domains of outputting automata. A machine outputs some object drawn from a class O; a test is the set of those objects which are acceptable (in some undefined sense) to a user. We assume O to be infinite.

$$\mathcal{M} = O \qquad \mathcal{T} \subseteq PO \qquad \mathcal{S}mt \Leftrightarrow m \in t$$
$$sm = \{t \mid m \in t\} \qquad it = t$$
$$sM = \{t \mid M \subseteq t\} \qquad iT = \bigcap T$$

So I is the closure of $\mathcal{T}$ under intersections.

In a sense, this example is the most general possible, for any $\mathcal{M}$, $\mathcal{T}$, $\mathcal{S}$ can be transformed into this form by replacing $\mathcal{T}$ with $\{it \mid t \in \mathcal{T}\}$ and $\mathcal{S}$ by $\lambda mt.m \in t$. The resulting I and S are isomorphic to the original I and S (indeed, I is unchanged). We consider two special cases.

(i) $\mathcal{T}$ = PO. Then $\hat{c}M = M$, $cT = c(\bigcap T)$, and $I = \mathcal{T}$. Every machine is closed, every specification corresponds to some single test, and each test corresponds to a different ndm. c is not continuous. To see this, let $O_0, O_1, \ldots$ be an enumeration of an infinite subset of O. Let $t_j = \{O_j, O_{j+1}, \ldots$, $T = \{t_0, \ldots t_j\}$.

Then $\bigsqcup_j c(T_j) = \{t \mid \exists\, n. \forall m \geq n, O_m \in t\}$

but $c(\bigsqcup_j T_j) = \mathcal{T}$.

This is only to be expected, since there are infinite tests, contrary to the discussion of 2.1. So we amend $\mathcal{T}$ to get our second example.

(ii) $\mathcal{T}$ = {finite subsets of O}

$\mathcal{M}$, $\mathcal{S}$ as in ex. 1

$\hat{c}M$ = <u>if</u> M is finite <u>then</u> M <u>else</u> $\mathcal{M}$

$I = \mathcal{T} \cup \{O\}$

c is continuous (proof omitted), and $\top$ is isolated since $\top_S = c\{\emptyset\}$ (not to be confused with $c\emptyset$ which is $\bot_S$).

<u>4.1.2</u>

A more concrete example. A machine outputs a string of symbols drawn from a finite alphabet Σ. A test is a finite set of finite strings over Σ. A machine passes a test if at some stage the output it has produced so far is a member of the test (whether or not the machine will produce any more output).

$\mathcal{M} = \Sigma^* \cup \Sigma^\infty$

$\mathcal{T}$ = finite subsets of Σ^*

$\mathcal{S}\, mt \Leftrightarrow \exists\, s \in t. s \geq m$

where the ordering on strings is the initial substring ordering: $s \leq s'$ if s' begins with s.

$sm = \{t \mid \exists\, s \leq m. s \in t\}$ $\quad$ $it = \{m \mid \exists\, s \leq m. s \in t\}$

$sM = \{t \mid \forall m \in M. \exists\, s \leq m. s \in t\}$ $\quad$ $iT = \{m \mid \forall t \in T. \exists\, s \leq m. s \in t\}$

$\hat{c}M = \{m \mid \exists\, m' \leq m. m' \in M\}$

cT is too complicated to describe briefly. We will therefore use the method described in 4.1.1 and replace $\mathcal{T}$ by $\{it \mid t \in \mathcal{T}\}$ and $\mathcal{S}$ by $\lambda mt.m \in t$. We now have:

$\mathcal{M} = \Sigma^* \cup \Sigma^\infty$

$\mathcal{T}$ = {t | t is a right-closed subset of $\Sigma^* \cup \Sigma^\infty$

$\wedge$ every minimal element of t is finite

$\wedge$ there are only finitely many minimal elements of t}

$\mathcal{S}\, mt \Leftrightarrow m \in t$

$sm = \{t \mid m \in t\}$ $\qquad$ $it = t$

$sM = \{t \mid M \subseteq t\}$ $\qquad$ $iT = \bigcap T$

I is the closure of $\mathcal{T}$ under intersections. Note that $\bigcap T$ is a member of $\mathcal{T}$ if T is finite, but not necessarily if T is infinite.

$\hat{c}M = \{m \mid \exists\, m' \leq m. m' \in M\}$ $\qquad$ (as before)

$cT = \{t \mid t \supseteq \bigcap T\}$

c is continuous (proof omitted) and $\top$ is isolated ($\top_S = c\{\emptyset\}$).

4.2 Inputting automata

This is, roughly speaking, the dual of 4.1. A test consists of a single piece of behaviour which the machine chooses to accept (in some undefined way) or not. Communication is one-way: from the user to the machine.

A general family of inputting automata is obtained as in 4.1.1 by:

$\mathcal{M} \subseteq PO \qquad \mathcal{T} = O \qquad \mathcal{S}\, mt \Leftrightarrow t \in m$

$sm = m$ $\qquad$ $it = \{m \mid t \in m\}$

$sM = \bigcap M$ $\qquad$ $iT = \{m \mid T \subseteq m\}$

S is the closure of $\mathcal{M}$ under intersections. If $\mathcal{M}$ is already closed under intersections then S = $\mathcal{M}$ and there are no intrinsically nondeterministic machines - every ndm is indistinguishable from some deterministic machine. c is continuous if and only if $\mathcal{S}$ is a directed-complete subset of PO (with the subset ordering). If c is continuous, $\top$ is isolated iff there is a finite subset of O which is not contained in any deterministic machine.

This is another most general example, for any $\mathcal{M}$, $\mathcal{T}$, $\mathcal{S}$ may be put into this form by replacing $\mathcal{M}$ by $\{sm \mid m \in \mathcal{M}\}$ and $\mathcal{S}$ by $\lambda mt.t \in m$. The resulting version of S is identical to the orginal one.

4.3 Machines as functions from states to states

Let A be a set of <u>machine states</u>. We write FPA for the set of finite subsets of A.

$\mathcal{M} = A \times A \qquad \mathcal{T} = FPA \times FPA$

$\mathcal{S}\, m \langle t_0, t_1\rangle \Leftrightarrow dom(m) \subseteq t_0 \wedge \forall x \in t_0 . mx\ t_1$

A test $\langle t_0, t_1\rangle$ may be considered as a precondition-postcondition pair: a machine passes the test if whenever it starts in a state in t_0 it will finish in a state in t_1. We do not bother to write out formulae for i, s, c, and $\hat{c}$. c is continuous and $\top$ is isolated in I and S.

Note that 1. $\{\langle t_0, t_1\rangle\} \simeq \{\langle\{x\}, t_1\rangle \mid x \in t_0\}$

2. $\{\langle\{x\}, X_j\rangle \mid j \in J\} \simeq \{\langle\{x\}, \bigcap\{X_j \mid j \in J\}\rangle\}$

It follows that every set of tests T is equivalent to one of the form $\{\langle\{x\}, X_x\rangle \mid x \in X\}$ where X is a subset of A and each X_x is a finite subset of A. This may equivalently be regarded as a partial function (which we denote by $\tilde{T}$) from A to PA. $\mathcal{S}$ may be extended to such functions as follows:

$$\mathcal{S}\, mT \Leftrightarrow dom(m) \supseteq dom(T) \wedge \forall x \in dom(m).mx \in \tilde{T}x$$

But we can simplify this by adjoining A to FPA, producing the set B, and considering total functions from A to B, which are clearly in 1-1 correspondence with partial functions from A to FPA. A partial function F from A to FPA corresponds to the function

$$\lambda x \in A.\ \underline{if}\ x \in dom(F)\ \underline{then}\ F(x)\ \underline{else}\ A$$

For any set of tests T we redefine $\tilde{T}$ as $\lambda x \in A. \quad \{X \mid \langle\{x\},X\rangle \in T\}$. The extension of $\mathcal{S}$ to $A \to B$ is now

$$\mathcal{S}\, mT \Leftrightarrow \forall x \in dom(m).mx \in \tilde{T}x$$

Any function F in $A \to B$ corresponds to the set of tests

$$\tilde{F} = \{ \langle\{x\},X\rangle \mid Fx \subseteq X \in FPA\}$$

In particular, $\tilde{\tilde{T}} = \{ \langle\{x\},X\rangle \mid \bigcap\{X' \mid \langle\{x\},X'\rangle \in T\} \subseteq X \in FPA\}$

Routine calculation shows this to be just cT. Further calculation shows that for distinct F,F' in $A \to B$, F and F' are also distinct. To sum up, $A \to B$ is in 1-1 correspondence with S. The ordering on S induces the following ordering on $A \to B$:

$$F \sqsubseteq F' \Leftrightarrow \forall x \in A.Fx \supseteq F'x$$

This is the same ordering as that obtained by extending the superset ordering on B pointwise to $A \to B$.

($\langle B, \supseteq \rangle$ is isomorphic (and almost identical) to $P_0(A_\perp)$, the weak powerdomain of the flat cpo obtained by adding a bottom element to A. The only difference is that $\perp_B = A$ whereas $\perp_{P_0(A_\perp)} = A_\perp$.)

The isomorphism of I and S makes F $A \to B$ correspond to

$$\{m \mid \forall x \in dom(m).mx \in Fx\}$$

Conversely, the function in $A \to B$ corresponding to a set of machines M in I is

$$\lambda x \in A.\{mx \mid m \in M\}$$

It may be argued that the domain $A \to B$, of functions from states to sets of states, more intuitively captures the idea of a nondeterministic function than does the domain I, of sets of functions from states to states. The purpose of the above discussion is to show that these two concepts are, at least in this example, equivalent.

References

1. Bell, J.L. and Slomson, A.B., "Models and ultraproducts" (North-Holland, 1969).
2. Milne, R.E. and Strachey, C., "A theory of programming language semantics", (Chapman & Hall, 1976).
3. Scott, D., "Data types as lattices", SIAM J. Computing 5, 522-587 (1976).
4. Smyth, M.J., "Powerdomains", J. Computer System Science 16, 23-36 (1978).
5. Stoy, J.E., "Denotational Semantics", (M.I.T., 1977).
6. Tarski, A., "A lattice-theoretical fixpoint theorem and its applications", Pacific J. Math. 5, 285-309, (1955).

A REPRESENTATION THEOREM FOR MODELS OF *-FREE PDL

Dexter Kozen
IBM Thomas J. Watson Research Center
Yorktown Heights, New York 10598

Abstract. We introduce *dynamic algebras* and show how they can be used to give an algebraic interpretation to propositional dynamic logic (PDL). Dynamic algebras include all Kripke models, the standard interpretation of PDL. We give a simple algebraic condition on *-free dynamic algebras that is necessary and sufficient for representation by *-free Kripke models. In the presence of *, the condition is sufficient for representation by a nonstandard Kripke model. This result leads to a duality between certain topological Kripke models and dynamic algebras analogous to the duality between Boolean algebras and their Stone spaces.

1. Introduction

Propositional Dynamic Logic (PDL) is a logic for reasoning in situations in which truth is time-dependent, such as computer programs. PDL was first introduced by Fischer and Ladner [FL]. It is the propositional version of Dynamic Logic (DL), first introduced by Pratt [Pr1] and developed by Harel, Meyer, Pratt, and others (see [H] and references therein). DL bears strong resemblance to the Algorithmic Logic (AL) of Salwicki and others (see [Ba]) and the programming logic of Constable and O'Donnell [CO].

PDL has two types of objects: *programs* α, β,... and *propositions* X, Y,... . It has primitive symbols of each type, the usual propositional connectives $\wedge$, $\vee$, $\neg$, the program connectives $\cup$ (choice), ; (composition), * (iteration), and connectives $<>$ and [ ] by which programs and propositions interact. If α is a program and X is a proposition, then $<\alpha>X$ and $[\alpha]X$ are propositions. The intent of $<\alpha>X$ is, "it is possible for program α to halt in a state in which X is true," or simply, "α enables X," and the intent of $[\alpha]X$ is, "it is necessary that X is true upon termination of α." Thus $[\alpha]X$ is equivalent to $\neg<\alpha>\neg X$. PDL is a generalization of modal logic, since the latter is essentially PDL with a single program and no * operator. This connection is discussed in depth by van Emde Boas [vEB].

PDL is usually interpreted over a *standard Kripke model*, consisting of a set S of *worlds* or *states*, a family K of binary relations on S, and a Boolean algebra B of subsets of S. Each primitive program letter is assigned a binary relation in K and each primitive proposition is assigned an element of B. The interpretation of nonprimitive programs and propositions is then determined by induction on the syntactic structure of the program or proposition, where the Boolean connectives have their usual set theoretic interpretation, the connectives ;, $\cup$, * are interpreted as relational composition, set union, and reflexive transitive closure, and $<\alpha>X$ is interpreted as the set

$$\{ s \mid \exists t \in X \ (s,t) \in \alpha \} .$$

In other words, state s satisfies proposition $<\alpha>X$ (is contained in the set $<\alpha>X$) iff there is a state t satisfying X such that s can go to t under program α ($(s,t) \in \alpha$). The reader should consult [H,FL,Be] for a complete treatment.

Attempts to provide a complete axiomatization PDL and the propositional version of AL

[Se,Pa,G,N,Pr2,Ba,Be] have met with some difficulty. The primary obstacle is the * operator. In standard Kripke models, α^* is interpreted as α^{rtc}, the reflexive transitive closure of binary relation α. Consequently, the logic is not compact: the set

$$\{ <\alpha^*>X \} \cup \{ \neg X, \neg <\alpha>X, \neg <\alpha^2>X, \ldots \}$$

has no model, yet every finite subset does. Parikh [Pa] and Berman [Be] have considered relaxing the requirement $\alpha^* = \alpha^{rtc}$ to obtain *nonstandard* Kripke models, a more general class of models over which the logic is compact. They use these models as an intermediate step in proofs of the completeness of the Segerberg axioms of PDL [Se].

In this paper we introduce *dynamic algebras*, a class of algebraic structures that include the Kripke models. A *dynamic algebra* is a two-sorted algebra $D = (K,B,<>)$, where K is a *Kleene algebra* or relation algebra (see [C]) and B is a Boolean algebra, for which a scalar multiplication $<>:K \times B \rightarrow B$ is defined. The axioms for <> are reminiscent of those for scalar multiplication in vector spaces or modules. Dynamic algebras can be used to give PDL a more algebraic interpretation, exposing it to standard techniques of universal algebra and model theory. Some of the benefits of this approach are expounded by Pratt [Pr3,Pr4].

In §2 we give the axioms for dynamic algebras, prove some of their elementary properties, and give several examples. We also discuss a natural algebraic property satisfied by many common dynamic algebras called *separability*. This property has also been discussed by Pratt [Pr3,Pr4].

In §3 we prove a representation theorem for dynamic algebras: every separable dynamic algebra is represented by a nonstandard Kripke model. Separability is also necessary for representation by a standard Kripke model.

It is well known that every Boolean algebra is isomorphic to a Boolean algebra of sets. After McKinsey's [McK1] and Tarski's [T] axiomatization of relation algebras, several authors [EU,JT,McK2] searched for a similar representation result for relation algebras, with only partial success. This work culminated in in a counterexample of Lyndon [L]. In his conclusion, Lyndon discussed the possibility of a positive representation result in weaker systems; he mentioned specifically "relational rings", which are essentially Kleene algebras without *. Thus the development of PDL and dynamic algebra has prompted an answer to Lyndon's question.

The representation result of this paper raises the question: is separability a sufficient condition for a dynamic algebra to be represented by a *standard* Kripke model? In [K3], we give a negative answer. The construction of the counterexample uses topological concepts and motivates the definition of *topological Kripke models*. In [K2] we develop some properties of these structures. The main result of [K2] is a duality between separable dynamic algebras and certain topological Kripke models. This duality is completely analogous to the duality between Boolean algebras and their Stone spaces.

It is assumed that the reader is at least casually familiar with dynamic logic. If not, an introduction to the subject can be found in [H,FL,Be].

2. Elementary properties of dynamic algebras

Kleene algebras

The definition of *Kleene algebra* is meant to capture the notion of an algebra of binary relations (as in Tarski [T] and McKinsey [McK1]) with the inclusion of a unary operator * for reflexive transitive closure. An axiomatization of Kleene algebras was given by Conway [C]; in fact he gave five of them. Our axiomatization fits into Conway's spectrum between his S-algebras and R-algebras.

Definition. A *Kleene algebra* (or *relation algebra*) K is a structure

$$K = (K, \cup, 0, ;, \lambda, ^-, ^*)$$

such that $(K, \cup, 0)$ is an upper semilattice with identity 0, $(K, ;, \lambda)$ is a monoid, and $^-$ and * are unary operations satisfying the axioms below. The order of precedence of the operators is *, $^-$, ;, $\cup$, and $\alpha;\beta$ is abbreviated $\alpha\beta$.

$$\alpha(\beta \cup \gamma) = \alpha\beta \cup \alpha\gamma$$

$$(\alpha \cup \beta)\gamma = \alpha\gamma \cup \beta\gamma$$

$$\alpha 0 = 0\alpha = 0$$

$$(\alpha\beta)^- = \beta^-\alpha^-$$

$$(\alpha \cup \beta)^- = \alpha^- \cup \beta^-$$

$$\alpha^{--} = \alpha$$

(2.1) $$\alpha\beta^*\gamma = \sup_n \alpha\beta^n\gamma$$

where in 2.1, $\beta^0 = \lambda$, $\beta^{n+1} = \beta\beta^n$, and the supremum is with respect to the semilattice order $\leq$ in K:

$$\alpha \leq \beta \text{ iff } \alpha \cup \beta = \beta . \quad \square$$

The following are some examples of Kleene algebras:

(2.2) $$(R(S), \cup, \phi, \circ, \lambda, ^-, ^{rtc}),$$

where R(S) is the family of all binary relations on a set S, $\cup$ is set union in R(S), $\circ$ is relational composition

$$\alpha \circ \beta = \{ (s,t) \mid \exists u\ (s,u) \in \alpha \text{ and } (u,t) \in \beta \},$$

ϕ is the null set, λ is the identity relation on S, $^-$ is reversal

$$\alpha^- = \{ (s,t) \mid (t,s) \in \alpha \},$$

and ^{rtc} is reflexive transitive closure

$$\alpha^{rtc} = \bigcup_n \alpha^n ;$$

(2.3) $$(Reg, \cup, \phi, ;, \{\varepsilon\}, ^-, ^*),$$

where Reg is the family of regular sets over $\{0,1\}^*$, ε is the null string of $\{0,1\}^*$, ; is concatenation, and $^-$ is string reversal;

(2.4) $$(B, \vee, 0, \wedge, 1, ^-, ^*),$$

where $(B, \vee, 0, \wedge, 1, \neg)$ is a Boolean algebra, $^-$ is the identity on B, and $\alpha^* = 1$ for all α;

(2.5) $$(\mathbf{N} \cup \{\infty\}, \mathrm{MIN}, \infty, +, 0, ^*),$$

where **N** is the set of nonnegative integers, + is addition, and MIN is a function returning the minimum of two arguments. The operations in the last example are rather nonstandard. The example is useful in the study of shortest path problems [AHU].

See [Pr3,Pr4] for additional examples.

The following are some elementary properties of Kleene algebras:

λ is unique

0 is unique

$\alpha\alpha^* = \alpha^*\alpha$

$\alpha^*\alpha^* = \alpha^*$

$0^* = \lambda^* = \lambda$

$\alpha^* = \lambda \cup \alpha\alpha^*$

$\alpha^{**} = \alpha^*$

$\alpha^* \cup \beta = \sup_n \alpha^n \cup \beta$

if $\alpha \leq \beta$ then $\alpha\gamma \leq \beta\gamma$, $\gamma\alpha \leq \gamma\beta$, $\alpha^- \leq \beta^-$, and $\alpha^* \leq \beta^*$

$(\alpha^*)^- = (\alpha^-)^*$

$\lambda^- = \lambda$

$0^- = 0$.

Dynamic algebras

Definition. A *dynamic algebra* is a structure

$$D = (K,B,<>)$$

where K is a Kleene algebra, B is a Boolean algebra, and $<>: K \times B \to B$ is a scalar multiplication satisfying the following axioms:

$<\alpha \cup \beta>X = <\alpha>X \vee <\beta>X$

$<\alpha>(X \vee Y) = <\alpha>X \vee <\alpha>Y$

$<\alpha>(<\beta>X) = <\alpha\beta>X$

$<\alpha>0 = <0>X = 0$

$<\lambda>X = X$

(2.6) $X \leq [\alpha]<\alpha^->X$

(2.7) $$<\alpha^*>X = \sup_n <\alpha^n>X$$

where $[\alpha]X$ denotes $\neg<\alpha>\neg X$ in 2.6, and the supremum in 2.7 is with respect to the lattice order $\leq$ in B. Axiom 2.7 says that scalar multiplication is **-continuous*. □

The first five axioms are reminiscent of the axioms for scalar multiplication in vector spaces or modules. In fact, dynamic algebras are quite similar to *semimodules*, a structure of considerable importance in algebraic automata theory (see [SS]).

The following are some elementary properties of dynamic algebras:

$$\text{if } X \leq Y \text{ then } <\alpha>X \leq <\alpha>Y$$
$$\text{if } \alpha \leq \beta \text{ then } <\alpha>X \leq <\beta>X$$
$$[\lambda]X = <\lambda>X = X$$
$$[\alpha]X \wedge [\alpha]Y = [\alpha](X \wedge Y)$$
$$X \leq [\alpha^-]<\alpha>X .$$

(2.8) $$[\alpha]X \wedge <\alpha>Y \leq <\alpha>(X \wedge Y) .$$

In addition, dynamic algebras satisfy all the Segerberg axioms for dynamic logic [Se,Pa]. We prove the *induction axiom* as an example.

Proposition. In all dynamic algebras,

$$X \wedge [\alpha^*](X \supset [\alpha]X) \leq [\alpha^*]X .$$

Proof. Dually, we need to show

$$<\alpha^*>X \leq X \vee <\alpha^*>(\neg X \wedge <\alpha>X) .$$

First note that for all $n \geq 0$,

(2.9) $$\begin{aligned} \neg<\alpha^n>X \wedge <\alpha^{n+1}>X &= [\alpha^n]\neg X \wedge <\alpha^n><\alpha>X \\ &\leq <\alpha^n>(\neg X \wedge <\alpha>X) \text{ by 2.8} \\ &\leq <\alpha^*>(\neg X \wedge <\alpha>X) . \end{aligned}$$

It follows purely from the axioms of Boolean algebra that

$$\begin{aligned} 1 = X &\vee (\neg X \wedge <\alpha>X) \\ &\vee (\neg<\alpha>X \wedge <\alpha^2>X) \\ &\vee (\neg<\alpha^2>X \wedge <\alpha^3>X) \\ &\dots \\ &\vee (\neg<\alpha^{n-1}>X \wedge <\alpha^n>X) \\ &\vee \neg<\alpha^n>X . \end{aligned}$$

By 2.9,

$$1 = X \vee \langle\alpha^*\rangle(\neg X \wedge \langle\alpha\rangle X) \vee \neg\langle\alpha^n\rangle X$$

or

$$\langle\alpha^n\rangle X \leq X \vee \langle\alpha^*\rangle(\neg X \wedge \langle\alpha\rangle X) .$$

The result follows from axiom 2.7. □

Kripke models

The *standard Kripke models*, which form the usual interpretation of PDL (see [H,FL,Be]), give rise to dynamic algebras in a natural way. A *standard Kripke model* is a structure

$$A = (S,K,B)$$

where S is a nonempty set of *states*, B is a Boolean algebra of subsets of S with the set-theoretic Boolean algebra operations, and K is a Kleene algebra of binary relations on S in which the operators are interpreted as in example 2.2, for which the set

(2.11) $$\langle\alpha\rangle X = \{ s \mid \exists t \in X \ (s,t) \in \alpha \}$$

is in B whenever $\alpha \in K$ and $X \in B$. If 2.11 is taken as the definition of scalar multiplication $\langle\rangle$, then the structure $(K,B,\langle\rangle)$ is a dynamic algebra, called the *characteristic algebra* of A and denoted $C(A)$.

In any standard Kripke model, $\alpha^* = \alpha^{rtc}$ for any $\alpha \in K$, where

$$\alpha^{rtc} = \bigcup_n \alpha^n$$

is the reflexive transitive closure of α. Following Parikh [Pa] and Berman [Be], let us relax this restriction and say that * need only satisfy axioms 2.1 and 2.7. Then α^* is a reflexive transitive relation containing α^{rtc}, and is the least such element of K, but need not equal α^{rtc}. Such Kripke models will be called *nonstandard*. Henceforth the term *Kripke model* will encompass both standard and nonstandard models.

Separability

An important property of some dynamic algebras and Kleene algebras is *separability*. This property says that distinct elements of K can be distinguished by their action as scalars. Pratt [Pr3,Pr4] has also discussed the importance of this property.

Definition. A dynamic algebra $D = (K,B,\langle\rangle)$ is *separable* if for every $\alpha, \beta \in K$, $\alpha \neq \beta$, there exists an $X \in B$ such that $\langle\alpha\rangle X \neq \langle\beta\rangle X$. A Kleene algebra K is *separable* if there exists a separable dynamic algebra over K. □

Not all Kleene algebras are separable; for example, 2.5 is not. This fact follows immediately from the following proposition, which clearly does not hold in 2.5.

Proposition. In any separable K, if $\alpha \leq \lambda$, then $\alpha^2 = \alpha$.

Proof. Certainly $\alpha \leq \lambda$ implies $\alpha^2 \leq \alpha$. To show $\alpha \leq \alpha^2$, let $(K,B,\langle\rangle)$ be any separable dynamic algebra over K. Then $\alpha \leq \lambda$ implies $\langle\alpha\rangle X \leq X$ for all X, or dually, $X \leq [\alpha]X$ for all X. In particular, $\langle\alpha\rangle X \leq [\alpha]\langle\alpha\rangle X$ for all X, and $\langle\alpha\rangle X \leq \langle\alpha\rangle 1$, thus for all X

$$\begin{aligned}\langle\alpha\rangle X &\leq [\alpha]\langle\alpha\rangle X \wedge \langle\alpha\rangle 1\\ &\leq \langle\alpha\rangle\langle\alpha\rangle X \quad \text{by 2.8,}\end{aligned}$$

and $\alpha \leq \alpha^2$ follows from separability. □

3. The representation of dynamic algebras

In this section we show that separability of K is necessary for a dynamic algebra $(K,B,\langle\rangle)$ to be the characteristic algebra of a standard Kripke model and sufficient for $(K,B,\langle\rangle)$ to be the characteristic algebra of a nonstandard Kripke model. Thus in the *-free case, separability is necessary and sufficient for representation.

Necessity of separability for representation by a standard model

Proposition 3.1. If Kripke model (S,K,B) is standard, then K is separable.

Proof. Let B′ be the Boolean algebra of all subsets of S. Then (S,K,B′) is a standard Kripke model. Moreover, its characteristic algebra is separable, since if $\alpha \neq \beta$, and if $(s,t) \in \alpha - \beta$, then $s \in \langle\alpha\rangle\{t\} - \langle\beta\rangle\{t\}$, so $\langle\alpha\rangle\{t\} \neq \langle\beta\rangle\{t\}$. □

Sufficiency of separability for representation by a nonstandard model

We now turn to the task of constructing, for a given separable K and dynamic algebra $D = (K,B,\langle\rangle)$, a (possibly nonstandard) Kripke model A such that $C(A)$ is isomorphic to D.

Let U, V, W denote ultrafilters of B and let S denote the set of all ultrafilters. A set $E \subseteq B$ is *consistent* if the filter generated by E does not contain 0. Define

$$\begin{aligned}\langle\alpha\rangle V &= \{\, \langle\alpha\rangle X \mid X \in V \,\}\,,\\ \langle\alpha\rangle/V &= \{\, X \mid \langle\alpha\rangle X \in V \,\}\,.\end{aligned}$$

$[\alpha]V$ and $[\alpha]/V$ are defined similarly. It follows easily from the properties of dynamic algebras that

Lemma 3.2. $[\alpha]/U$ is either a proper filter or all of B, and the following are equivalent:

(i) $[\alpha]/U = B$

(ii) $\langle\alpha\rangle/U = \phi$

(iii) $[\alpha]0 \in U$

(iv) $[\alpha]/U \not\subseteq \langle\alpha\rangle/U$. □

The following construction gives a family K' of binary relations on S and a family B' of subsets of S. Later we will give B' the Boolean algebra operations and K' the Kleene algebra operations as in example 2.2, except for *, which will have a nonstandard definition.

Definition. For each $X \in B$ and $\alpha \in K$, define

$$X' = \{ U \mid X \in U \},$$
$$\alpha' = \{ (U,V) \mid <\alpha>V \subseteq U \}.$$

Let B' and K' be the sets of all X' and α' respectively. The triple (S,K',B') is denoted $S(D)$. □

With the set-theoretic Boolean algebra operations, B' is isomorphic to B under the map $'$; this is just the Stone representation theorem for Boolean algebras (see e.g. [BS]).

The following are some technical lemmas that will allow us to prove that the Kleene algebra operations can be defined on K' so that $K \rightarrow K'$ becomes a homomorphism. The first lemma has some intrinsic interest. It says that the V for which $<\alpha>V \subseteq U$ are exactly the maximal consistent extensions of $[\alpha]/U$.

Lemma 3.3. $<\alpha>V \subseteq U$ iff $[\alpha]/U \subseteq V$.

Proof.

$$\begin{aligned} <\alpha>V \subseteq U \quad &\text{iff} \quad \forall X \; X \in V \rightarrow <\alpha>X \in U \\ &\text{iff} \quad \forall X \; [\alpha]\neg X \in U \rightarrow \neg X \in V \\ &\text{iff} \quad [\alpha]/U \subseteq V . \quad \Box \end{aligned}$$

Lemma 3.4. Let $E, F \subseteq B$.

(i) If $E \cup [\alpha]/U$ is consistent, then $\exists V \; E \subseteq V \subseteq <\alpha>/U$.

(ii) If F is a filter and $F \subseteq <\alpha>/U$, then $\exists V \; F \subseteq V \subseteq <\alpha>/U$.

(iii) If $X \in <\alpha>/U$ then $\exists V \subseteq <\alpha>/U$ with $X \in V$.

Proof. (i) Since $E \cup [\alpha]/U$ is consistent, by Zorn's lemma it extends to an ultrafilter V. Since $[\alpha]/U \subseteq V$, $V \subseteq <\alpha>/U$ by Lemma 3.3. (ii) By (i), it suffices to show that if F is a filter and $<\alpha>F \subseteq U$, then $F \cup [\alpha]/U$ is consistent. Suppose $F \cup [\alpha]/U$ were inconsistent. Since both F and $[\alpha]/U$ are filters, $\exists X \in F$, $Y \in [\alpha]/U$ with $X \wedge Y = 0$. But $<\alpha>X \in U$ and $[\alpha]Y \in U$ so by 2.8, $<\alpha>(X \wedge Y) = 0 \in U$, a contradiction. (iii) Consider the principal filter generated by X and use (ii). □

Now let K' have the Kleene algebra operations of example 2.2, except *.

Theorem 3.5. If $(K,B,<>)$ is separable, then the operation * can be defined on K' so that K' is a Kleene algebra and $K \rightarrow K'$ is an isomorphism.

Proof. First we show that if $(K,B,<>)$ is separable then

$$\text{(3.6)} \qquad \alpha' = \beta' \text{ iff } \alpha = \beta ,$$

i.e. $'$ is one-to-one. Suppose $\alpha' = \beta'$. Then for all U, V, $<\alpha>V \subseteq U$ iff $<\beta>V \subseteq U$. It follows from the properties of ultrafilters that for all X, $<\alpha>X = <\beta>X$, therefore $\alpha = \beta$ by separability.

Next we show that $K \to K'$ is a homomorphism for all operations except *. For this we need to show

(3.7) $(\alpha \cup \beta)' = \alpha' \cup \beta'$

(3.8) $(\alpha\beta)' = \alpha' \circ \beta'$ where $\circ$ is relational composition

(3.9) $\lambda' =$ the identity relation

(3.10) $0' = \phi$

(3.11) $\alpha^{-\prime} = \alpha^{\prime -}$.

Each of the statements (3.7)-(3.11) is equivalent to one of the statements (3.7′)-(3.11′) below:

(3.7′) $<\alpha \cup \beta>V \subseteq U$ iff either $<\alpha>V \subseteq U$ or $<\beta>V \subseteq U$

(3.8′) $<\alpha\beta>V \subseteq U$ iff $\exists W$ $<\alpha>W \subseteq U$ and $<\beta>V \subseteq W$

(3.9′) $<\lambda>V \subseteq U$ iff $V = U$

(3.10′) for all U, V, $<0>V \not\subseteq U$

(3.11′) $<\alpha^->V \subseteq U$ iff $<\alpha>U \subseteq V$.

To prove 3.7′: ($\leftarrow$) follows from the fact that both $<\alpha>X, <\beta>X \leq <\alpha \cup \beta>X$. ($\rightarrow$) Suppose $<\alpha \cup \beta>V \subseteq U$ but there are $X, Y \in V$ such that $<\alpha>X \notin U$, $<\beta>Y \notin U$. Then $X \wedge Y \in V$ so $<\alpha \cup \beta>(X \wedge Y) = <\alpha>(X \wedge Y) \vee <\beta>(X \wedge Y) \in U$, so either $<\alpha>(X \wedge Y) \in U$ or $<\beta>(X \wedge Y) \in U$, say $<\alpha>(X \wedge Y) \in U$. Since $<\alpha>(X \wedge Y) \leq <\alpha>X$, $<\alpha>X \in U$, a contradiction.

To prove 3.8′: ($\leftarrow$) $<\alpha>W \subseteq U$ and $<\beta>V \subseteq W$ implies that $<\alpha><\beta>V \subseteq <\alpha>W \subseteq U$, so $<\alpha\beta>V \subseteq U$. ($\rightarrow$) $<\alpha\beta>V = <\alpha><\beta>V \subseteq U$, so by Lemma 3.2, $[\alpha]/U$ is a proper filter. By Lemma 3.4, it suffices to show that $<\beta>V \cup [\alpha]/U$ is consistent. Suppose it were not consistent. Then there would be a finite set $E \subseteq V$ and a $Y \in [\alpha]/U$ such that $\wedge_{Z \in E} <\beta>Z \wedge Y = 0$. Let $X = \wedge_{Z \in E} Z$. Then $<\beta>X \leq <\beta>Z$ for all $Z \in E$, so $<\beta>X \leq \wedge_{Z \in E} <\beta>Z$, therefore $Y \wedge <\beta>X = 0$. Now $X \in V$, so $<\alpha><\beta>X \in U$; and $[\alpha]Y \in U$, so by 2.8, $<\alpha>(Y \wedge <\beta>X) = <\alpha>0 = 0 \in U$, a contradiction.

3.9′ and 3.10′ are trivial.

To prove 3.11′: Since $\alpha^{--} = \alpha$, we need only show the implication in one direction. Suppose the left side of 3.11′ holds. If $Y \in U$ then $[\alpha^-]<\alpha>Y \in U$, by 2.7. By Lemma 3.3, $<\alpha>Y \in V$.

It remains to define *. From 3.6 and 3.7 it follows that

$$\text{(3.12)} \qquad \alpha' \leq \beta' \text{ iff } \alpha \leq \beta .$$

Thus, if we define

$$\beta'^* = \beta^{*\prime} ,$$

then * is well-defined on K′ by 3.6, and moreover

$$\begin{aligned} \alpha'\beta'^*\gamma' &= \alpha'\beta^{*\prime}\gamma' \\ &= (\alpha\beta^*\gamma)' \text{ by 3.8} \\ &= (\sup(\alpha\beta^n\gamma))' \\ &= \sup((\alpha\beta^n\gamma)') \text{ by 3.12} \\ &= \sup(\alpha'\beta'^n\gamma') \text{ again by 3.8,} \end{aligned}$$

fulfilling 2.1. Thus K′ is a Kleene algebra and ′ is an isomorphism. □

Theorem 3.13. If D is separable then $C(S(D))$ is a dynamic algebra isomorphic to D under the map ′.

Proof. In light of the previous theorem, we need only verify that

$$(\langle\alpha\rangle X)' = \langle\alpha'\rangle X' .$$

By definition of scalar multiplication in S(D) (equation 2.11), this is equivalent to

$$U \in (\langle\alpha\rangle X)' \text{ iff } \exists V\ (U,V) \in \alpha' \text{ and } V \in X' ,$$

or in other words,

$$\langle\alpha\rangle X \in U \text{ iff } \exists V\ \langle\alpha\rangle V \subseteq U \text{ and } X \in V .$$

But (←) is trivial and (→) is exactly Lemma 3.4(iii). □

It remains to show that the assumption of separability of D can be replaced by the weaker assumption of separability of K.

Theorem 3.14. If K is separable and D = (K,B,<>), then there is a (possibly nonstandard) Kripke model A such that D is isomorphic to $C(A)$.

Proof. By definition, there exists a separable K-dynamic algebra D_0. Let D_1 be the direct product of D_0 and D in the category of K-dynamic algebras. Then D_1 is separable and contains D as a subalgebra. By Theorem 3.13, D_1 is isomorphic to $C(S(D_1))$, thus D is isomorphic to a substructure of $C(S(D_1))$. □

4. Conclusion and open problems

Like Boolean algebras of sets, Kripke models have a natural topology. In [K2] we define *dynamic spaces* to be topological Kripke models satisfying certain separation properties analogous to those of Boolean spaces. We arrive at a duality between separable dynamic algebras and dynamic spaces analogous to the duality between Boolean algebras and Boolean spaces. This allows us to characterize the discrepancy between standard and nonstandard Kripke models from a topological viewpoint. For example, we are able to prove that in a nonstandard model, although $\langle\alpha^*\rangle X - \langle\alpha^{rtc}\rangle X$ can be nonempty, it is always nowhere dense. The representation result of this paper accounts for one-half of the duality result. In [K3] we construct a separable dynamic algebra that is not represented by any standard Kripke model. The counterexample is built on the

Cantor space, a traditional source of counterexamples in topology, and makes essential use of the topological duality established in [K2].

Let D = (K,B,<>) be a separable dynamic algebra. An ultrafilter U is **-consistent* if $<\alpha^*>X \in U$ implies $<\alpha^n>X \in U$ for some n. The property

(4.1) any $Y \in B$, $Y \neq 0$ extends to a *-consistent ultrafilter

is not true in general; indeed, the counterexample of [K3] is constructed expressly not to satisfy 4.1. However any *countable* dynamic algebra satisfies 4.1. This is proved using the Tarski-Rasiowa-Sikorski Theorem [BS, Theorem 1.4.10], which states that if A_i are countably many subsets of a Boolean algebra, each with a supremum X_i, then any nonzero element Y extends to an ultrafilter U preserving these suprema, in the sense that $X_i \in U$ iff some element of A_i is in U. Thus any Y extends to a *-consistent ultrafilter, since there are only countably many *-consistency conditions.

These remarks raise the question:

(4.2) Is every *countable* separable dynamic algebra the characteristic algebra of some standard *A*?

In dynamic spaces, the elements of B are the clopen sets. The topological dual of 4.1 is the statement

(4.3) every clopen set contains a *-consistent point

where a **-consistent point* is one not contained in any $<\alpha^*>X - <\alpha^{rtc}>X$. The topological dual of the Tarski-Rasiowa-Sikorski Theorem is the Baire Category Theorem, which states that, for sufficiently well-behaved spaces, no open set can be meager. If D is countable then the set of *-inconsistent points is meager, therefore (4.3). Suppose (K,B,<>) is a countable separable dynamic algebra, and let (S,K,B) be the corresponding nonstandard Kripke model. Using the Tarski-Rasiowa-Sikorski Theorem, it can be shown that a meager set of points of S including all the *-inconsistent points can be removed without changing the characteristic algebra, but unfortunately the resulting Kripke model (S',K',B') is still nonstandard. (Here $B' = B \cap S'$ and $K' = K \cap S'^2$.) However, if K'' is the standard Kleene algebra generated from K' by taking all elements α^* as primitive, then K' is a homomorphic image of K'', and moreover the homomorphism is exactly reduction modulo the congruence relation of inseparability.

Any finite dynamic algebra is represented by a standard Kripke model, as shown by Pratt [Pr4] and Berman (private communication).

Proposition 3.1 says that the Kleene algebra of a standard Kripke model is separable.

(4.4) Can a nonstandard Kripke model be constructed with an inseparable Kleene algebra?

Acknowledgments

I sincerely thank David Harel, Rohit Parikh, and Vaughan Pratt for many stimulating discussions.

References

[AHU] Aho A.V., J.E. Hopcroft, and J.D. Ullman, *The Design and Analysis of Computer Algorithms*. Addison-Wesley, Reading, Mass., 1974.

[Ba] Banachowski, L., A. Kreczmar, G. Mirkowska, H. Rasiowa, and A. Salwicki, "An introduction to Algorithmic Logic," in: Mazurkiewicz and Pawlak, eds., *Math. Found. of Comp. Sci.*, Banach Center Publications, Warsaw, 1977.

[Be] Berman, F., "A completeness technique for D-axiomatizable semantics," *Proc. 11th ACM Symp. on Theory of Comp.* (May 1979), 160-166.

[BS] Bell, J.S. and A.B. Slomson, *Models and Ultraproducts.* North Holland, Amsterdam, 1971.

[C] Conway, J.H. *Regular Algebra and Finite Machines*. Chapman-Hall, London, 1971.

[CO] Constable, R.L. and M.J. O'Donnell. *A Programming Logic*. Winthrop, Cambridge, Mass., 1978.

[EU] Everett, C.J. and S. Ulam, "Projective algebra I," *Amer. J. Math.* 68:1 (1946), 77-88.

[FL] Fischer, M.J. and R.E.Ladner, "Propositional dynamic logic of regular programs," *J. Comput. Syst. Sci.* 18:2 (1979).

[G] Gabbay, D., "Axiomatizations of logics of programs," manuscript, Nov. 1977.

[H] Harel, D. *First-Order Dynamic Logic*. Lecture Notes in Computer Science 68, ed. Goos and Hartmanis, Springer-Verlag, Berlin, 1979.

[JT] Jonsson, B. and A. Tarski, "Representation problems for relation algebras," abstract 89t, *Bull. Amer. Math. Soc.* 54 (1948), 80.

[K1] Kozen, D., "A representation theorem for models of *-free PDL," Report RC7864, IBM Research, Yorktown Heights, New York, Sept. 1979.

[K2] Kozen, D., "On the duality of dynamic algebras and Kripke models," Report RC7893, IBM Research, Yorktown Heights, New York, Oct. 1979.

[K3] Kozen, D., "On the representation of dynamic algebras," Report RC7898, IBM Research, Yorktown Heights, New York, Oct. 1979.

[L] Lyndon, R.C., "The representation of relation algebras," *Ann. Math.* 51:3 (1950), 707-729.

[McK1] McKinsey, J.C.C., "Postulates for the calculus of binary relations," *J. Symb. Logic* 5:3 (1940), 85-97.

[McK2] -----, "On the representation of projective algebras," *Amer. J. Math.* 70 (1948), 375-384.

[N] Nishimura, H., "Sequential Method in Propositional Dynamic Logic," *Acta Informatica* 12 (1979), 377-400.

[Pa] Parikh, R., "A completeness result for PDL," *Symp. on Math. Found. of Comp. Sci.*, Zakopane, Warsaw, Springer-Verlag, May 1978.

[Pr1] Pratt, V.R., "Semantical considerations on Floyd-Hoare logic," *Proc. 17th IEEE Symp. on Foundations of Comp. Sci.* (Oct. 1976), 109-121.

[Pr2] -----, "A practical decision method for Propositional Dynamic Logic," *Proc. 10th ACM Symp. on Theory of Computing* (May 1978), 326-337.

[Pr3] -----, "Models of program logics," *Proc. 20th IEEE Symp. on Foundations of Comp. Sci.* (Oct. 1979), to appear.

[Pr4] -----, "Dynamic algebras: examples, constructions, applications," manuscript, July 1979.

[Se] Segerberg, K., "A completeness theorem in the modal logic of programs," *Not. AMS* 24:6 (1977), A-552.

[SS] Salomaa, A. and M. Soittala. *Automata Theoretic Aspects of Formal Power Series*. Springer-Verlag, New York, 1978.

[T] Tarski, A., "On the calculus of relations," *J. Symb. Logic* 6:3 (1941), 73-89.

[vEB] van Emde Boas, "The connection between modal logic and algorithmic logics," report 78-02, Univ. of Amsterdam, May 1978.

PRESENT-DAY HOARE-LIKE SYSTEMS

FOR PROGRAMMING LANGUAGES WITH PROCEDURES:

POWER, LIMITS AND MOST LIKELY EXTENSIONS

Hans Langmaack Ernst-Rüdiger Olderog
Institut für Informatik und Praktische Mathematik
Christian-Albrechts-Universität Kiel
Olshausenstr. 40-60, D-2300 Kiel 1

1. Introduction

The power of Hoare-like systems is reflected in completeness results on these systems. Since Clarke [Cl 77/79] it is known that there are programming languages for which there cannot be any sound and complete Hoare-like systems, even in the sense of Cook [Co 75/78] . On the other hand, there exist quite a few ALGOL-like programming languages for which there are sound and (relatively) complete Hoare-like systems.

An overview over other authors' and our own results indicates already that with respect to procedures Hoare-like systems in their presently known form cannot go beyond a certain limit: Roughly speaking, they can deal only with programs which have an "irrelevant" procedure nesting structure. Irrelevant means that these programs can effectively be transformed into formally equivalent ones without local procedures.

On the other hand, there exist ALGOL-like languages beyond that limit whose halting problems are solvable for all finite interpretations. According to a theorem of Lipton [Li 77] this is a first step towards Hoare-like systems for those languages. These extended systems must necessarily contain new types of inference rules. We think that approaches to find them will also develop tools and methods applicable for program transformation problems, for questions on how to elect good programming language constructs and for problems on tree generating structures and tree languages.

2. Basic Definitions

<u>An interpreted programming language</u> is defined to be a tuple $P = (T, L, St, \Sigma)$ where T is a decidable set of so-called <u>tokens</u> or <u>basic symbols</u> and L is decidable subset of T^*. The elements π of L are called <u>programs</u>. St is the set of <u>states</u> and the so-called semantics Σ of P is a mapping which assigns a partially defined function $\Sigma(\pi)|St \xrightarrow{part} St$ to every program $\pi \in L$. A program $\pi \in L$ is called <u>Σ-divergent</u> iff $\Sigma(\pi)(s)$ is undefined for all $s \in St$.

In this paper we are interested in special programming languages, namely interpreted <u>ALGOL-like languages</u> $A(L, \mathfrak{I}, \mathfrak{C})$. In this case there are several sorts of basic symbols: Among others, we distinguish between the sets VI of <u>variable identifiers</u> (<u>variables</u> for short) x, y, z, PI of <u>procedure identifiers</u> p, q, r, C of <u>constants</u>, Op of <u>operators</u> and Re of <u>relators</u>. The <u>full set L_f</u> of <u>ALGOL-like programs</u> consists of all proper blocks B generated by the following production system:

B ::= $\underline{\text{begin}}$ $\overline{\underline{\text{var}}\ x;}$ $\overline{\Delta}$ S $\underline{\text{end}}$ (blocks)

Δ ::= $\underline{\text{proc}}$ $p(\bar{x}:\bar{q})$; B; (procedures)

S ::= x := t | $\underline{\text{dummy}}$ | $\underline{\text{error}}$ | S_1; S_2 | $\underline{\text{if}}$ e $\underline{\text{then}}$ S_1 $\underline{\text{else}}$ S_2 $\underline{\text{fi}}$ |
$\underline{\text{while}}$ e $\underline{\text{do}}$ S $\underline{\text{od}}$ | $p(\bar{x}:\bar{q})$ | B (statements)

The subset L_0 of flowchart programs is obtained from L_f by disallowing procedures. By the flowchart language we mean $A(L_0, \mathcal{J}) = (T, L_0, St_D, \Sigma^0_{\mathcal{J}})$ where $\mathcal{J}$ is an interpretation of C, Op and Re over a certain domain $D \neq \emptyset$. $\mathcal{J}$ is called finite if $|D| < \infty$.

In order to extend the semantics $\Sigma^0_{\mathcal{J}}$ from L_0 to all programs in L_f we employ the notion of copy rule: Let a procedure statement $S = p(\bar{y}:\bar{r})$ with associated declaration proc $p(\bar{x}:\bar{q})$; B; occur (outside of all procedure declarations) in a program π. Then a copy rule $\mathcal{C}$ describes how to replace S by a modification $B_{\mathcal{C}}$ of B, thus generating an expanded program π': $\pi \vdash_{\mathcal{C}} \pi'$ [La 73, Ol 79] . Especially, $\mathcal{C}$ defines how to handle (1) clashes of local identifiers in B with the actual identifiers inserted for formal parameters and (2) clashes of global identifiers of B with identifiers global to S.

In our paper we consider the ALGOL 60 or static scope copy rule $\mathcal{C}_{60}$ [Na 63, Cl 77/79] the naive copy rule $\mathcal{C}_n$ [Ol 79], the dynamic scope copy rule $\mathcal{C}_{dyn}$ [Co 75/78 , Go 75, Cl 77/79] and the "most recent" copy rule $\mathcal{C}_{mr}$ [Ol 79]. Among these, only $\mathcal{C}_{60}$ avoids the deficiencies (1) and (2) by proper renaming of identifiers as opposed to $\mathcal{C}_n$ where no identifiers renaming is done and consequently both (1) and (2) can occur. $\mathcal{C}_{dyn}$ excludes (1) and $\mathcal{C}_{mr}$ avoids (1) and (2) for variable identifiers only.

A copy rule gives rise to an approximating semantics $\Sigma^j_{\mathcal{J}\mathcal{C}}(\pi)$ which is the meaning of π when we restrict ourselves to a copy-depth of at most j ($j \in \mathbb{N}_0$). The full semantics $\Sigma_{\mathcal{J}\mathcal{C}}$ is defined by $\Sigma_{\mathcal{J}\mathcal{C}}(\pi) = \bigcup_j \Sigma^j_{\mathcal{J}\mathcal{C}}(\pi)$. Now, an interpreted ALGOL-like language is defined to be the tuple $A(L, \mathcal{J}, \mathcal{C}) = (T, L, St_D, \Sigma_{\mathcal{J}\mathcal{C}})$ where L is a decidable subset of L_f with $L_0 \subseteq L$. Besides interpreted ALGOL-like languages we consider semi-interpreted ALGOL-like languages which are tuples $A(L, \mathcal{C}) = (T, L, \mathcal{C})$.

To investigate the computational behaviour of a program π independent of the actual operations on data, we study formal execution paths

$$\wp: \pi \vdash_{\mathcal{C}} \pi_1 \vdash_{\mathcal{C}} \dots \vdash_{\mathcal{C}} \pi_k$$

(where every program in $\wp$ has at most one innermost block $B_{\mathcal{C}}$ generated by $\mathcal{C}$). For each program $\pi'' \neq \pi$ in $\wp$ the predecessor π' of π'' contains exactly one procedure statement whose call generates π''. The set of all formal execution paths is represented by the formal execution tree $T_\pi(\mathcal{C})$ [La 73]. A statement S in $\pi'' \in T_\pi(\mathcal{C})$ is called formally reachable if it occurs outside all procedure declarations; a procedure p in π is formally reachable if a copy of p is called somewhere in $T_\pi(\mathcal{C})$; p is formally recursive if there are two calls of copies of p along some path in $T_\pi(\mathcal{C})$ [La 73].

Let Fo denote the set of first order formulae P, Q, R w.r.t. VI, C, Op and Re. We write $\mathcal{J} \models P$ iff P is valid under $\mathcal{J}$. The theory of $\mathcal{J}$ is given by $Th(\mathcal{J}) = \{P \mid \mathcal{J} \models P\}$. A Hoare assertion $P\{\pi\}Q$ is valid (w.r.t. $\mathcal{J}$ and $\mathcal{C}$) [$\mathcal{J}\mathcal{C} \models P\{\pi\}Q$ for short] iff $\Sigma_{\mathcal{J}\mathcal{C}}(\pi)(\tilde{P}) \subseteq \tilde{Q}$ where $\tilde{P}$ denotes the set of states $\in St_D$ expressed by P. Thus Hoare assertions can be used to describe the partial correctness of programs.

Remark 1. $\pi \in L_f$ is $\Sigma_{\mathcal{J}\mathcal{C}}$-divergent iff $\mathcal{J}\mathcal{C} \models$ true $\{\pi\}$ false.

A Hoare like system [Ho 69] is a formal proof system $\mathcal{H}$ for Hoare assertions $P\{\pi\}Q$ given by a finite collection of proof rules which are decidable relations over a set of so-called proof lines. Usually it is required that these proof rules reflect the syntactical structure of the programs. We write $\mathcal{H}, \mathcal{J} \vdash P\{\pi\}Q$ iff $P\{\pi\}Q$ can be formally proved in $\mathcal{H}$ with the help of an oracle for $Th(\mathcal{J})$.

In this paper we are interested in the question for which semi-interpreted ALGOL-like languages $A(L,\mathcal{C})$ there are Hoare-like systems which are sound (i.e. $\mathcal{H},\mathcal{J} \vdash P\{\pi\}Q$ implies $\mathcal{J}\mathcal{C} \models P\{\pi\}Q$ for all interpretations $\mathcal{J}$ and all $\pi \in L$) and relatively complete (i.e. $\mathcal{J}\mathcal{C} \models P\{\pi\}Q$ implies $\mathcal{H},\mathcal{J} \vdash P\{\pi\}Q$ for all interpretations $\mathcal{J}$ and all $\pi \in L$ provided Fo is expressive w.r.t. $\mathcal{J}$ and $\mathcal{C}$ [Co 75/78]) for $A(L,\mathcal{C})$. The notion of relative completeness was introduced by Cook [Co 75/78] in order to talk about completeness of Hoare-like systems independent of problems caused by the interpretation $\mathcal{J}$ [Wa 78]. We mention that relative completeness is a stronger property than arithmetical completeness [Ha 79].

Remark 2. [Cl 77/79] Let $\mathcal{H}$ be sound and relatively complete for $A(L,\mathcal{C})$. Then the set $\mathcal{A}$ of valid Hoare assertions $\mathcal{J}\mathcal{C} \models P\{\pi\}Q$ with $\pi \in L$ is recursively enumerable relative to Th $(\mathcal{J})$ provided Fo is expressive w.r.t. $\mathcal{J}$ and $\mathcal{C}$ for $A(L,\mathcal{C})$. Thus for all finite $\mathcal{J}$ it is decidable whether $\pi \in L$ is $\Sigma_{\mathcal{J}\mathcal{C}}$-divergent (by Remark 1).

3. Difficulties with Static Scope Semantics $\mathcal{C}_{60}$

Theorem 1. [La 73/74] Even for finite $\mathcal{J}$ it is undecidable whether $\pi \in L_f$ is $\Sigma_{\mathcal{J}\mathcal{C}_{60}}$-divergent.

Corollary 1. There is no sound and relatively complete Hoare-like system for $A(L_f,\mathcal{C}_{60})$.

Let L_{Pas} be the set of PASCAL-like programs (procedures which occur as actual procedure parameters are not allowed to have own formal procedures as parameters [JW 75]) and let L_{sh} denote the set of programs without formal sharing (All variables in the actual parameter list $\bar{x}$ of a formally reachable procedure statement $p(\bar{x}:\bar{q})$ are distinct and different from certain "global" variables determined by p [Cl 77/79].). Though formal reachability and sharing depend on the copy rule $\mathcal{C}$ we shall avoid additional indices in L_{sh}.

In general, restriction to programs without sharing causes problems: L_{sh} is an undecidable subset of L_f because for programs in L_f the formal reachability of procedures is undecidable when the copy rule $\mathcal{C}_{60}$ is applied [La 73]. Thus $A(L_{sh},\mathcal{C}_{60})$ would not be a proper ALGOL-like language (see Appendix). But $L_{Pas} \cap L_{sh}$ is a decidable subset of L_f because the formal reachability problem is solvable for PASCAL-like programs [La 78].

Theorem 2. [Cl 77/79] For all finite $\mathcal{J}$ with $|D| \geq 2$ it is undecidable whether $\pi \in L_{Pas} \cap L_{sh}$ is $\Sigma_{\mathcal{J}\mathcal{C}_{60}}$-divergent.

Corollary 2. [Cl 77/79] There is no sound and relatively complete Hoare-like system for $A(L_{Pas} \cap L_{sh},\mathcal{C}_{60})$.

Theorem 3. Theorem 2 cannot be extended to $|D| = 1$ [La 78, LLW 79] or to $L_{Pas} \cap L_{sh} \cap L_{gv} \subseteq L_{sa} \cap L_{gv}$ (see Theorem 10 later).

4. More Luck with Simplified Semantics

According to the last section we can only hope to prove relative completeness results for sublanguages $A(L,\mathcal{C}_{60})$ of $A(L_f,\mathcal{C}_{60})$ with $L \subsetneq L_f$.

The situation changes if we consider the copy rules $\mathcal{C}_n$, $\mathcal{C}_{dyn}$ and $\mathcal{C}_{mr}$. For $\mathcal{C}_{dyn}$ we have the following

Theorem 4. For the following subsets L of L_f there exit sound and relatively complete Hoare-like systems $\mathcal{H}$ for $A(L, \mathcal{C}_{dyn})$:

$L_{pp} \cap L_{sh} \cap L_{fr}$ [Co 75/78]

$L_{pp} \cap L_{sh}$ [Go 75]

L_{pp} [CO 78] $\qquad$ $L_5 = L_{sa} \cap L_{sh}$ [Cl 77/79]

L_f [Ol 79] (with $\mathcal{H} = \mathcal{H}(\mathcal{C}_{dyn})$)

L_{pp}: no procedures as parameters

L_{fr}: no formally recursive procedures

L_{sa}: no self-application of procedures [Cl 77/79], i.e. finite procedure modes in in the sense of ALGOL 68 [vW 75]

For $\mathcal{C}_n$ and $\mathcal{C}_{mr}$ we can state

Theorem 5. [Ol 79] The Hoare-like systems $\mathcal{H}(\mathcal{C}_n)$ and $\mathcal{H}(\mathcal{C}_{mr})$ are sound and relatively complete for $A(L_f, \mathcal{C}_n)$ resp. $A(L_f, \mathcal{C}_{mr})$.

Details about the Hoare-like systems $\mathcal{H}(\mathcal{C})$, $\mathcal{C}$ a copy rule, can be found in the sections 6 and 7 later.

5. Static Scope Semantics Revisited

In this section we are interested in relative completeness results for sublanguages $A(L, \mathcal{C}_{60})$ with $L \subseteq L_f$.

Claim 1. [Cl 77/79] There are sound and relatively complete Hoare-like systems $\mathcal{H}_i$ for $A(L_i, \mathcal{C}_{60})$ where $i \in \{2,3,4,6\}$.

According to [Cl 77/79] we define

$L_2 = L_{pp} \cap L_{sa} \cap L_{sh}$ [1], $L_3 = L_{fr} \cap L_{sa} \cap L_{sh}$

$L_4 = L_{gv} \cap L_{sa} \cap L_{sh}$ (L_{gv}: no global variables)

$L_6 = L_{pnes} \cap L_{sa} \cap L_{sh}$ (L_{pnes}: no procedure nesting)

Unfortunately the proof of Claim 1 is not worked out in [Cl 77/79], but Clarke states

Remark 3. The system $\mathcal{H}_i$ can be chosen similar to $\mathcal{H}_{dyn}$ where $\mathcal{H}_{dyn}$ denotes the Hoare-like system presented for $A(L_5, \mathcal{C}_{dyn})$ in [Cl 77/79] (cf. Theorem 4).

Claim 1 is partly verified by

Theorem 6. [Ol 79] The Hoare-like systems $\mathcal{H}(\mathcal{C}_{60})$ and $\mathcal{H}(\mathcal{C}_{mr})$ are sound and relatively complete for $A(L_{gf}, \mathcal{C}_{60})$ and $A(L_{mr}, \mathcal{C}_{60})$.

---

[1] Also $L_{sa} \cap L_{sh}$ is a decidable subset of L_f: The formal reachability problem is decidable for programs without self-application of procedures [La 78, LLW 79].

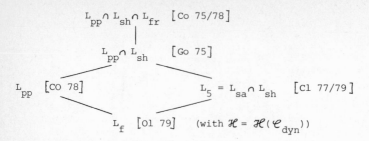

L_{gf}: no global formal procedure identifiers [La 73]

L_{mr}: the formal "most recent" property holds (A program π is said to have the formal "most recent" property if every call of a procedure in the formal execution tree of π is a call of the most recently declared copy of that procedure [McG 72, Ka 74].)

Because of $L_2, L_6 \subseteq L_{gf}$ and $L_2, L_3, L_6 \subseteq L_{mr}$ we have the following

Theorem 7. For the following subsets L of L_f there exist sound and relatively complete Hoare-like systems for $A(L, \mathcal{C}_{60})$:

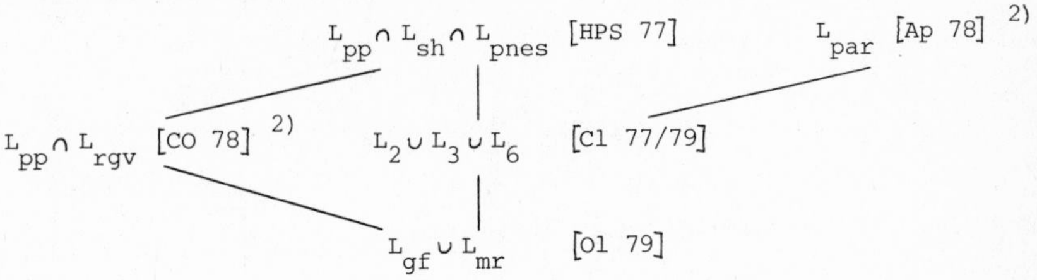

L_{par}: without formal parameters only

L_{rgv}: restricted use of global variables (see [CO 78])

Therefore we are left with the

Question 1. Is Clarke's claim true for the language $A(L_4, \mathcal{C}_{60})$?

Concerning Theorem 6 and 7 it is important to point out

Remark 4. Programs π in L_{gf} and L_{mr} can be effectively transformed into formally equivalent programs π' without procedure nesting [La 73 resp. Kl 77]. Formally equivalent means that the formal execution trees of π and π' become equal after erasing all procedure declarations and replacing each remaining procedure statement by error [La 73, LS 78]. (We mention that the proof of Theorem 6 works without using such program transformations).

6. The Hoare-like Systems $\mathcal{H}(\mathcal{C})$

Let us now give some idea of the Hoare-like systems $\mathcal{H}(\mathcal{C})$ [Ol 79] mentioned previously. Proof lines of these systems are of the form $H_1 \longrightarrow H_2$ where H_1 and H_2 are finite sets of Hoare formulae h which are either formulae P or Hoare assertions $P\{\pi\}Q$ or constructs $P\ (\overline{\Delta}|\ S)\ Q$. (Proof lines of the form $\emptyset \longrightarrow H$ and $\{h_1\} \longrightarrow \{h_2\}$ are abbreviated by H resp. $h_1 \longrightarrow h_2$.) Pairs $(\overline{\Delta}|\ S)$ - so-called units which correspond to programs begin $\overline{\Delta}$ S end - are used in order to talk about program segments instead of whole programs. The systems $\mathcal{H}(\mathcal{C})$ are based on the same simple notion of formal proof as Gentzen-like sequent calculi [Pr 65] for first order logic. (A different type of formal proof is employed in [Go 75], [Do 76], [Cl 77/79].) Two rules - here presented in a simplified form - are essential for the completeness results on $\mathcal{H}(\mathcal{C})$:

2) Besides the language constructs considered in our paper, [Ap 78] and [CO 78] treat also arrays.

(R) Rule of recursive procedure calls

$$\frac{P(\overline{\Delta}\mid p(\bar{y}:\bar{r}))Q \longrightarrow P(\overline{\Delta}\mid B_{\mathcal{C}})Q}{P(\overline{\Delta}\mid p(\bar{y}:\bar{r}))Q} \qquad \left(\frac{H_p \longrightarrow H_B}{H_p} \text{ for short }\right)$$

where proc $p(\bar{x}:\bar{q});B;$ occurs in $\overline{\Delta}$, the lengths of the actual and formal parameter lists agree and $B_{\mathcal{C}}$ is the modification of B according to the copy rule $\mathcal{C}$.

(S) Rule of substitution

$$\frac{H_1 \longrightarrow \{ P(\overline{\Delta}\mid S)Q \} \cup H_2}{H_1 \longrightarrow \{ P\sigma\,(\sigma(\overline{\Delta})\mid \sigma(S))\,Q\sigma \} \cup H_2}$$

where σ is a certain injective substitution of variable and procedure identifiers.

Rule (R) dates back in principle to Hoare [Ho 71] . Rule (S) is powerful enough to deal with the problem of sharing: Let call $(p,\bar{q},\overline{\Delta})$ be the set of all units of the form $(\overline{\Delta}\mid p(\bar{x}:\bar{q}))$ such that actual and formal parameter lengths agree. Rule (S) yields a partition of call $(p,q,\overline{\Delta})$ into sharing classes [Ol 79] . The fact that there are only *finitely many* sharing classes in call $(p,q,\overline{\Delta})$ leads to relative completeness results in the presence of sharing too (Theorem 8 later). The sharing restriction simply means to admit *only one* sharing class.

The soundness of $\mathcal{H}(\mathcal{C})$ for the full ALGOL-like language $A(L_f,\mathcal{C})$ is proved by means of an interpretation for proof lines which is defined - according to our copy rule approach to semantics - by the *approximating semantics* $\Sigma^j_{\mathcal{I}\mathcal{C}}$:
As abbreviations we write

$\mathcal{I}\mathcal{C}j \models P$ iff $\mathcal{I} \models P$

$\mathcal{I}\mathcal{C}j \models P\{\pi\}Q$ iff $\Sigma^j_{\mathcal{I}\mathcal{C}}(\pi)\ (\tilde{P}) \subseteq \tilde{Q}$

$\mathcal{I}\mathcal{C}j \models P(\overline{\Delta}\mid S)Q$ iff $\Sigma^j_{\mathcal{I}\mathcal{C}}(\overline{\Delta}\mid S)\ (\tilde{P}) \subseteq \tilde{Q}$

$\mathcal{I}\mathcal{C}j \models H$ iff $\mathcal{I}\mathcal{C}j \models h$ for all Hoare formulae $h \in H$

A proof line $H_1 \longrightarrow H_2$ is called valid (w.r.t. $\mathcal{I}$ and $\mathcal{C}$) [$\mathcal{I}\mathcal{C} \models H_1 \longrightarrow H_2$ for short] iff $\mathcal{I}\mathcal{C}j \models H_1$ implies $\mathcal{I}\mathcal{C}j \models H_2$ for all $j \in \mathbb{N}_0$ [Ap 79, Ol 79]. This definition is consistent with the validity of Hoare assertions as defined in section 2.

As an example let us prove the soundness of (R): Assuming the validity of the premise of (R) we have to show the validity of the conclusion of (R), i.e.

$\mathcal{I}\mathcal{C}j \models H_p$ for all $j \in \mathbb{N}_0$.

We proceed by induction on j. The case "j=0" is trivial since $\Sigma^0_{\mathcal{I}\mathcal{C}} = \emptyset$. Let us now consider the induction step "$j \longrightarrow j+1$". By induction hypothesis $\mathcal{I}\mathcal{C}j \models H_p$ holds. The premise of (R) yields $\mathcal{I}\mathcal{C}j \models H_B$, but $\mathcal{I}\mathcal{C}j \models H_B$ iff $\mathcal{I}\mathcal{C}j{+}1 \models H_p$ since $\Sigma^{j+1}_{\mathcal{I}\mathcal{C}}(\overline{\Delta}\mid p(\ldots)) = \Sigma^j_{\mathcal{I}\mathcal{C}}(\overline{\Delta}\mid B_{\mathcal{C}})$. Thus $\mathcal{I}\mathcal{C}j{+}1 \models H_p$ holds what was to be proved.

Several other papers need an additional argumentation to prove the soundness of the rule (R) for recursive procedures [ILL 75,GO 75,Do76,Cl 77/79,Ap 78]. Especially, the idea to use full semantics $\Sigma_{\mathcal{I}\mathcal{C}}$ instead of approximating semantics $\Sigma^j_{\mathcal{I}\mathcal{C}}$ - which is natural when denotational semantics methods are applied - leads to a complicated soundness proof [Ap 78]. This is not surprising because application of the copy rule occurs explicitly in rule (R). Further, the full semantics notion

$\mathcal{I}\mathcal{C} \models_{full} H_1 \longrightarrow H_2$ iff($\mathcal{I}\mathcal{C} \models H_1$ implies $\mathcal{I}\mathcal{C} \models H_2$)

of validity of a proof line is weaker than our notion $\mathcal{I}\mathcal{C} \models H_1 \longrightarrow H_2$ so that a more complex proof rule (R') is necessary. (Of course, both notions of validity coincide when restricted to proof lines with empty antecedents, especially to Hoare assertions in which we are finally interested.) Summarizing: In soundness and completeness proofs for Hoare-like systems a semantics definition should be employed which yields shortest proofs. The question of equivalence of partly operational and purely denotational semantics should be answered separately.

7. A Characterization of the Provability in $\mathcal{H}(\mathcal{C})$

Let π be a program in L_f. By a <u>reference chain</u> of length n in π we mean a sequence

Δ_1 = <u>proc</u> $p_1(\bar{x}_1:\bar{q}_1)$; B_1;, ..., Δ_n = <u>proc</u> $p_n(\bar{x}_n:\bar{q}_n)$; B_n;

of procedure occurences in π on static level 1 such that there is a *free* occurrence of p_{i+1} in B_i whose associated declaration is Δ_{i+1} and $p_i \neq p_j$ if $i \neq j$. π is said to be <u>$\mathcal{C}$-bounded</u> iff there is a constant k such that for all $\pi' \in T_\pi(\mathcal{C})$ the lenghts of the reference chains in π' are bounded by k. Now we can characterize the formal provability in $\mathcal{H}(\mathcal{C})$:

<u>Theorem 8</u>. [Ol 79] Let Fo be expressive w.r.t. $\mathcal{I}$ and $\mathcal{C}$. Then for all programs π in L_f the following assertions are equivalent:
(1) $\mathcal{H}(\mathcal{C}), \mathcal{I} \vdash P\{\pi\}Q$.
(2) $\mathcal{I}\mathcal{C} \models P\{\pi\}Q$ and π is $\mathcal{C}$-bounded.

The direction "(2) $\longrightarrow$ (1)" of Theorem 8 is a general completeness theorem (C) on the Hoare-like systems $\mathcal{H}(\mathcal{C})$, and the completeness results in Theorem 4-7 are corollaries of (C): For example, simply show that all programs in L_{gf} are $\mathcal{C}_{60}$-bounded.

<u>Remark 5</u>. $\mathcal{C}$-bounded programs can be effectively transformed into formally equivalent ones without procedure nestings, but the Hoare-like systems $\mathcal{H}(\mathcal{C})$, especially the rules (R) and (S), are powerful enough that the proof of Theorem 8 works without employing such additional program transformations.

8. Extensions of the Hoare-like System $\mathcal{H}(\mathcal{C}_{60})$

A program π is said to have a <u>depth k</u> for some constant k iff procedures which can only be "referenced by a reference chain" with length $> k$ in a program $\pi' \in T_\pi(\mathcal{C}_{60})$ are never called later on in a program π'' with $\pi' \vdash^{*}_{\mathcal{C}_{60}} \pi''$. Note that π need not be $\mathcal{C}_{60}$-bounded. For a computable function $K \mid L_f \longrightarrow \mathbb{N}$ let the <u>depth K language</u> $L_{(K)}$ consist of all programs π which have a depth $K(\pi)$. In particular, L_{pnes}, L_{gf} and L_{mr} are among these sets $L_{(K)}$. Define for example $K(\pi)$ to be the number of procedures in π. Then $L_{gf} \subseteq L_{(K)}$ holds. About depth K languages we can prove the following [Ol 80]:

(1) $L_{(K)}$ is a decidable subset of L_f.
(2) There is a sound and relatively complete Hoare-like system for $A(L_{(K)}, \mathcal{C}_{60})$ - namely an extension of $\mathcal{H}(\mathcal{C}_{60})$.
(3) Again, programs in $L_{(K)}$ can be effectively transformed into formally equivalent programs without procedure nesting.

9. Back to the Question on Clarke's Language L_4

In this section we investigate Question 1 more closely. Programs in L_4 may have the following procedure structure:

```
π̃: begin ...proc p(...:r); begin proc s(...:); begin...end;
                                  ...p(...:s)...r(...:)...
                            end;
            proc q(...:);   begin...end; ... p(...:q)...
    end
```

Note that $\tilde{\pi}$ is not $\mathcal{C}_{60}$-bounded. Moreover, $\tilde{\pi}$ can be completed in such a way that $\tilde{\pi}$ is not $\Sigma_{\mathcal{I}\mathcal{C}_{60}}$-divergent, but $\Sigma_{\mathcal{I}\mathcal{C}}$-divergent for all copy rules $\mathcal{C}$ for which $\tilde{\pi}$ is $\mathcal{C}$-bounded. Therefore we conclude by Theorem 8: There is no copy rule $\mathcal{C}$ such that $\mathcal{H}(\mathcal{C})$ is sound and relatively complete for $A(L_4, \mathcal{C}_{60})$. Thus

Remark 6. Remark 3 is false if we take "one of the systems $\mathcal{H}(\mathcal{C})$" as an explication of Clarke's phrase "similar to $\mathcal{H}_{dyn}$".

To overcome this difficulty, it was Clarke's idea [Cl 79] to use an effective transformation $T \mid L_4 \longrightarrow L_6 \subseteq L_{pnes}$ such that $\Sigma_{\mathcal{I}\mathcal{C}_{60}}(\pi) = \Sigma_{\mathcal{I}\mathcal{C}_{60}}(T(\pi))$ holds for all interpretations $\mathcal{I}$ and all $\pi \in L_4$. Then Question 1 could be solved by using $\mathcal{H}(\mathcal{C}_{60})$ augmented with T as additional proof rule (cf. Theorem 6).

Now let us study the formal execution tree $T_{\tilde{\pi}}(\mathcal{C}_{60})$ of $\tilde{\pi}$:

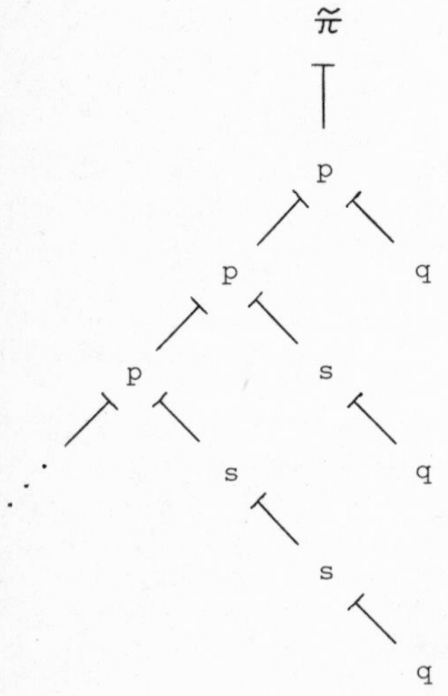

$T_{\tilde{\pi}}(\mathcal{C}_{60})$ shows that $\tilde{\pi}$ generates a contextfree path language $\mathcal{P}_{\tilde{\pi}} = \{ p^{n+1} s^n q \mid n \in \mathbb{N}_o \}$. On the other hand, programs $\pi \in L_{pnes}$ can only generate regular path languages $\mathcal{P}_{\pi}$ [DF 78]. Therefore there is no program $\pi' \in L_{pnes}$ which is formally equivalent to π. Thus it is hard to see how to establish such a transformation mentioned above [Cl 79].

Let us summarize the situation as follows: Present-day Hoare-like systems for languages $A(L, \mathcal{C})$ - which we think are essentially represented by the systems $\mathcal{H}(\mathcal{C})$ - are not powerful enough to deal with the language $A(L_4, \mathcal{C}_{60})$ (Theorem 8, section 8, difficulties with the transformation T). Therefore we regard Question 1 as a challenge to develop new tools and methods in the field of Hoare-like systems. First steps in this direction are presented in the next section.

10. Divergence and Relative Completeness

Lipton extended Remark 2 to the following

Theorem 9. [Li 77] Let $\mathcal{L}i = (T, L, \mathcal{I}nt)$ be an uninterpreted acceptable programming language in the sense of Lipton. Then the following assertions are equivalent:

(1) The set $\mathcal{A}$ of valid Hoare assertions $\mathcal{J}, \mathcal{I}nt \models P\{\pi\}Q$ with $\pi \in L$ is recursively enumerable relative to Th ($\mathcal{J}$) provided Fo is expressive w.r.t. $\mathcal{J}$ and $\mathcal{I}nt$ for $\mathcal{L}i$.

(2) For all finite $\mathcal{J}$ it is decidable whether $\pi \in L$ is $\Sigma_{\mathcal{J}\mathcal{I}nt}$-divergent.

($\mathcal{L}i$ is called acceptable [Li 77] iff the flowchart language is contained in $\mathcal{L}i$, $\mathcal{L}i$ is closed under so-called subroutine calls, and $\Sigma_{\mathcal{J}\mathcal{I}nt}$ is defined by a certain type of interpreter $\mathcal{I}nt$. The programs in L may use arbitrary first order formulae P as expressions in conditional and while statements.)

Though property (1) does not imply that $\mathcal{A}$ can be generated by a syntax-directed Hoare-like system, it can be understood as a first step in this direction.

Theorem 10. [La 79] For all finite $\mathcal{J}$ it is decidable whether $\pi \in L_{sa} \cap L_{gv}$ is $\Sigma_{\mathcal{J}\mathcal{C}_{60}}$-divergent.

The proof of Theorem 10 uses a technique introduced in [LLW 79] :
Let a finite $\mathcal{J}$ and $\pi \in L_{sa} \cap L_{gv}$ be given. All procedure calls $p(\bar{x}:\bar{q})$ in π are replaced by non-deterministic statements $[S_1 \,[]\, \ldots \,[]\, S_n]$ (cf. [Di 75]) such that the substatements S_i are essentially procedure calls $p(\bar{x}:\bar{q}_i)$ where the actual parameters $\bar{q}_i$ are so-called standard procedures which simulate the possible behaviour of the original procedures $\bar{q}$. (The number n of substatements S_i is bounded because $\mathcal{J}$ is finite and $p(\bar{x}:\bar{q})$ generates only finitely many sharing classes (see section 6).) This tranformation yields a non-deterministic program π' which is functionally equivalent to π. Therefore the divergence properties of π and π' are invariant. Since only standard procedures occur as actual procedure parameters, π' has the "most recent" property [McG 72, Ka 74] and consequently a decidable halting problem because the run time stack behaves like a regular stack system in the sense of [GGH 67].

Corollary 3. The valid Hoare assertions $\mathcal{J}\mathcal{C}_{60} \models P\{\pi\}Q$ with $\pi \in L_{sa} \cap L_{gv}$ are recursively enumerable relative to Th($\mathcal{J}$) prov. Fo expr. w.r.t. $\mathcal{J}, \mathcal{C}_{60}$ for $A(L_{sa} \cap L_{gv}, \mathcal{C}_{60})$.

Remark 7. Theorem 10 is also true for non-deterministic programs $\pi \in L_{sa} \cap L_{gv}$, but the proof of Theorem 9 requires determinate programs.

Corollary 3 and the proof of Theorem 10 lead us to the following

Conjecture 1. There exists a sound and relatively complete Hoare-like system for $A(L_{sa} \cap L_{gv}, \mathcal{C}_{60})$.

Conjecture 2. There exists a sound and relatively complete Hoare-like system for $A(L \cap L_{gv}, \mathcal{C}_{60})$ provided it is decidable whether $\pi \in L$ is $\Sigma_{\mathcal{J}\mathcal{C}_{60}}$-divergent for interpretations $\mathcal{J}$ with $|D| = 1$.

11. Conclusion

This paper indicates that presently known Hoare-like systems for ALGOL-like languages with static scope semantics can deal only with programs which can effectively be transformed into formally equivalent programs without procedure nesting (Remark 4 and 5 and Section 8).There are not yet methods to attack PASCAL-like programs (sample program $\tilde{\pi}$ in section 9), programs without self-application of procedures (Conjecture 1) and program classes for which the formal termination problem is solvable (Conjecture 2).

Appendix: Languages Discussed in this Paper

For each copy rule $\mathcal{C}$ we have the following diagram

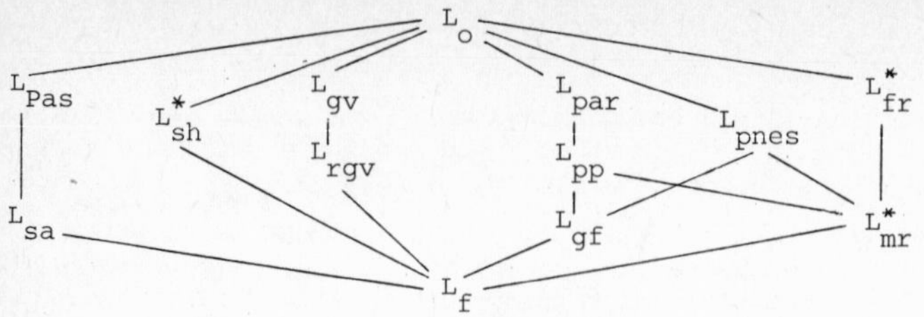

$L^*_2 = L_{pp} \cap L_{sa} \cap L^*_{sh}$, $L^*_3 = L^*_{fr} \cap L_{sa} \cap L^*_{sh}$

$L^*_4 = L_{gv} \cap L_{sa} \cap L^*_{sh}$, $L^*_5 = L_{sa} \cap L^*_{sh}$, $L^*_6 = L_{pnes} \cap L_{sa} \cap L^*_{sh}$

A star * indicates that this language varies with $\mathcal{C}$. $L^*_{sh} \subseteq L_f$ is undecidable if the copy rule $\mathcal{C}_{60}$ is applied, but decidable for $\mathcal{C}_n, \mathcal{C}_{dyn}$ and $\mathcal{C}_{mr}$.

References

[Ap 78] Apt, K.R.: A sound and complete Hoare-like system for a fragment of PASCAL, Math.Centrum IW 96/78, Amsterdam, 59 pp. (1978)

[Ap 79] Apt, K.R.: Ten years of Hoare's logic, a survey, Fac.Econom., Erasmus Univ. Rotterdam, 43 pp. (1979)

[CO 78] Cartwright, R., Oppen, D.: Unrestricted procedure calls in Hoare's logic, in: Proc. 5th Annual ACM Symposium on Principles of Programming Languages, 131-140 (1978)

[Cl 77/79] Clarke, E.M. Jr.: Programming Language constructs for which it is impossible to obtain good Hoare axiom systems, J.ACM 26, 1, 129-147 (1979)

[Cl 79] Clarke, E.M. Jr.: Private letter (1979)

[Cl 75/78] Cook, S.A.: Soundness and completeness of an axiomatic system for program verification. SIAM. J. Comp. 7, 1, 70-90 (1978)

[DF 78] Damm, W., Fehr, E.: On the power of selfapplication and higher type recursion, in: Aussiello, G., Böhm, C. (Ed.): Automata Languages and Programming, 5th Colloquium; Udine, July 1978, 177-191 (1979)

[Di 75] Dijkstra, E.W.: Guarded commands, non-determinacy and formal derivation of programs, Comm. ACM 18, 8, 453-457 (1975)

[DO 76] Donahue, J.E.: Complementary definitions of programming language semantics, Springer Lecture Notes in Computer Science 42, 172 pp. (1976)

[GGH 67] Ginsburg, S., Greibach, S.A., Harrison, M.A.: Stack automata and compiling, J. ACM 14, 172-201 (1967)

[GO 75] Gorelick, G.A.: A complete axiomatic system for proving assertions about recursive and non-recursive programs. Tech. Rep. 75, Dept. Comp. Sc. Univ. Toronto (1975)

[Ha 79] Harel, D.: First-order dynamic logic. Springer Lecture Notes in Computer Science 68, 133 pp. (1979)

[HPS 77] Harel, D., Pnueli, A., Stavi, J.: A complete axiomatic system for proving deductions about recursive programs, in: Proc. 9th ACM Symposium on Theory of Computing, 249-260 (1977)

[Ho 69] Hoare, C.A.R.: An axiomatic basis for computer programming, Comm. ACM 12, 576-580, 583 (1969)

[Ho 71] Hoare, C.A.R.: Procedures and parameters: An axiomatic approach, in: Engeler, E. (Ed.): Symposium on Algorithmic Languages, Springer Lecture Notes in Mathematics 188, 102-116 (1971)

[ILL 75] Igarashi, S., London, R.L. Luckham, D.C.: Automatic program verification I: A logical basis and its implementation. Acta Informatica 4, 145-182 (1975)

[JW 75] Jensen, K., Wirth, N.: PASCAL user manual and report. Springer, New York - Heidelberg - Berlin (1975)

[Ka 74] Kandzia, P.: On the "most recent" property of ALGOL-like programs, in: Springer Lecture Notes in Computer Science 14, Ed. J. Loeckx, 97-111 (1974)

[Kl 77] Klein, H.-J.: Untersuchungen im Zusammenhang mit der "most recent" Eigenschaft von Programmen. Bericht Nr. 8/77, Inst. Inform. Prakt.Math.Univ. Kiel, 41 pp. (1977)

[La 73] Langmaack, H.: On correct procedure parameter transmission in higher programming languages. Acta Informatica 2, 110-142 (1973)

[La 73/74] Langmaack, H.: On procedures as open subroutines I, II. Acta Informatica 2, 311-333 (1973) and Acta Informatica 3, 227-241 (1974)

[La 78] Langmaack, H.: On a theory of decision problems in programming languages, in: Blum, E.K., Takasu, S. (Ed.): Proceed. Internat. Conf. Math. Studies Information Processing, Kyoto 1978, Springer Lecture Notes in Computer Science 75, 538-558 (1979)

[La 79] Langmaack, H.: On termination problems for finitely interpreted ALGOL-like programs. Bericht Nr. 7904, Inst. Inf. Prakt. Math. Univ. Kiel, 42 pp. (1979)

[LLW 79] Langmaack, H., Lippe, W.M., Wagner, F.: The formal termination problem for programs with finite ALGOL 68-modes. Inf.Proc. Letters 9, 155-159 (1979)

[LS 78] Lippe, W.M., Simon, F.: A formal notion for equivalence of ALGOL-like programs, in: Proceedings of the 3rd International Symposium on Programming in Paris: Program Transformation, ed. by B. Robinet, Dunod-Paris, 141-158 (1978)

[Li 77] Lipton, R.J.: A necessary and sufficient condition for the existence of Hoare logics, in: 18th Symp. on Found. Comp. Science, ed. IEEE, 1-6 (1977)

[McG 72] McGowan, C.L.: The "most recent" error: its causes and correction. SIGPLAN Notices 7, 1, 191-202 (1972)

[Na 63] Naur, P. (ed.), et al.: Report on the algorithmic language ALGOL 60, Numer. Math. 4, 420-453 (1963)

[Ol 79] Olderog, E.-R.: Sound and complete Hoare-like calculi based on copy rules. Bericht 7905, Inst. Inf. Prakt. Math. Univ. Kiel, 57 pp. (1979); submitted for publication

[Ol 80] in preparation

[Pr 65] Prawitz, D.: Natural deduction - a proof-theoretic study. Stockholm, Almquist & Wiksell 1965

[vW 75] Wijngaarden, A. van, et al. (Ed.): Revised report on the algorithmic language ALGOL 68, Acta Informatica 5, 1-236 (1975)

[Wa 78] Wand, M.: A new incompleteness result for Hoare's system. J. ACM 25, 168-175 (1978)

SYMMETRIC SPACE-BOUNDED COMPUTATION
(Extended Abstract)

Harry R. Lewis[1]
and
Christos H. Papadimitriou[2]

ABSTRACT

A symmetric Turing machine is one whose "yields" relation between configurations is symmetric. The space complexity classes for such machines are found to be intermediate between the corresponding deterministic and nondeterministic space complexity classes. Certain natural problems are shown to be complete for symmetric space complexity classes, and the relationship of symmetry to determinism and nondeterminism is investigated.

1. INTRODUCTION

Computations can be performed by systems which are inherently symmetric or reversible in their operation. This idea goes back at least to Post's proof of the unsolvability of the word problem for Thue systems [Po,LP], which is the basis for the unsolvability of word problems for more structured algebraic systems such as groups. In Post's proof, a general (asymmetric) computational system is first reduced to a semi-Thue system; it is then shown that the operation of "symmetrically closing" this semi-Thue system to form a Thue system does not change its computational characteristics. The crux of the argument is (as we would now say) that the original computational system was *deterministic*. Of course, the determinism-nondeterminism distinction was unknown at the time, and in the classical theory of computability deterministic and nondeterministic computation are equally powerful. From the standpoint of complexity theory, however, the relationship between deterministic and nondeterministic computation is a deep and perplexing problem. Accordingly, we here reconsider, as a question of computational complexity, the computational power of symmetric formal systems. Specifically, we introduce a notion of *symmetric computation* which is shown to be intermediate, with respect to space bounds, between its deterministic and nondeterministic counterparts. The crucial step in Post's proof reappears at the heart of our proof that symmetry is no weaker than determinism. (The same combinatorial pattern is critical in [Ji].)

A second motivation for this work is the complexity analysis of certain graph problems. For many purposes undirected graphs can be regarded as special directed

[1]Aiken Computation Laboratory, Harvard University, Cambridge, Mass. 02138. Research supported by NSF Grant MCS76-09375-A01.

[2]Department of Electrical Engineering and Computer Science, Massachusetts Institute of Technology, Cambridge, Mass. 02139. Research supproted by NSF Grant MCS-77-01193.

graphs--ones representing symmetric relations. But problems which are hard for general directed graphs not uncommonly seem much easier in the undirected case. Examples are the homeomorphism problem for certain fixed graphs [FHW, LaPR, Sh, Cy] and the problem of finding an even-length path [LaP], which are NP-complete in the directed case but polynomial-time solvable in the undirected case. An instance of a slightly different type is the *graph accessibility problem* (GAP). Jones [Jo] proved that finding a path from one given node to another in a directed graph is complete for nondeterministic logarithmic space, a result implicit in [Sa], where GAP is called the "threadable maze" problem. In [JoLL] it was pointed out that the corresponding problem for undirected graphs (called UGAP) cannot so easily be shown hard for the same class. Motivated by UGAP, [AKLLR] were the first to question "the role of symmetry in the complexity of computation." While the exact deterministic and nondeterministic space complexity of UGAP remain unknown at present, we show that, with respect to the notion of symmetric computation here introduced, UGAP is a complete problem for logarithmic space. We also identify a Thue system problem complete for symmetric linear space.

Unlike determinism and nondeterminism, symmetry is *not* a natural *programming* concept; its main motivation comes from the symmetry inherent in classical formal systems and UGAP. Precisely for this reason, simulation and upper bound results which are routine for deterministic and nondeterministic computation do not easily generalize to symmetric computation. Indeed, it is not even obvious that symmetry can be captured by a *syntactic* restriction of the Turing machine model, as can determinism, nondeterminism, and the requirement that a tape be accessed only as a stack or pushdown store. We introduce a Turing machine model which differs from standard ones in a way which permits a purely syntactic definition of symmetry for Turing machines. A fundamental lemma (Lemma 1) is used to facilitate the programming of symmetric Turing machines; still, the symmetric counterparts of several standard arguments are surprisingly difficult.

The main contribution of this paper is some additional insight on the question of whether deterministic and nondeterministic space bounds are equivalent. We also investigate symmetry, determinism, and nondeterminism in the context of *simultaneous* space-time bounds (when time alone is considered, symmetry and nondeterminism are trivially equivalent) and restricted memory access.

Our computational model is specified in Section 2. Section 3 establishes the fundamental lemma on programming symmetric Turing machines. Section 4 shows that the symmetric space complexity classes have the invariance properties desired of any complexity measure--for example, closure under log-space reducibility. Section 5 deals with complete problems for symmetric space, such as UGAP. In Section 6 we further explore the power of symmetry by examining simultaneous space-time bounds, probabilistic computation, and stack automata. A few concluding observations are made in Section 7.

2. THE MODEL

Intuitively, a Turing machine is *symmetric* if its computation is at every step reversible, or, in other words, if the "yields" relation between configurations is a symmetric relation. We can formulate this condition syntactically by introducing a variant of the Turing machine model, whose tape heads are able to peek one square to the left or right before moving in that direction.

A *Turing machine* is a 7-tuple $M=(K,\Sigma,\Sigma_0,k,\Delta,s,F)$, where K is a finite set of states, Σ is a finite alphabet, $\Sigma_0 \subseteq \Sigma$ is the input alphabet, k is the number of tapes, s is a starting state, and F a set of final states. Δ is a set of *transitions*. A transition $\delta \in \Delta$ is of the form $\delta=(p,t_1,\ldots,t_k,q)$, where $p,q \in K$, and the t_j's are *tape triples*. Each tape triple is of the form (ab,D,cd), where $a,b,c,d \in \Sigma$ and $D=\pm 1$. Applying the transition δ to some configuration entails changing the state from p to q, and applying the tape triple t_j to the j-th tape, for $j=1,\ldots,k$. M applies $(ab,1,cd)$ to a tape by moving the tape head one square to the right, provided that the currently scanned square and the one to its right contain the symbols a,b. These two squares contain c and d after the application of the triple. Similarly, a triple $(ab,-1,cd)$ indicates leftward movement, provided that the scanned symbol is b and the one to its left is a.

Every triple $t_i=(ab,D,cd)$ has an inverse $t_i^{-1}=(cd,-D,ab)$; the inverse of a transition $\delta=(p,t_1,\ldots,t_k,q)$ is $\delta^{-1}=(q,t_1^{-1},\ldots,t_k^{-1},p)$. The inverse of the Turing machine M is $M^{-1}=(K,\Sigma,\Sigma_0,k,\Delta^{-1},s,F)$, where $\Delta^{-1}=\{\delta^{-1}\colon \delta \in \Delta\}$. M is *symmetric* if it is its own inverse. When a Turing machine is symmetric, then the yields relation $\vdash$ among its configurations is a symmetric relation. The machine $\bar{M}=(K,\Sigma,\Sigma_0,k,\Delta \cup \Delta^{-1},s,F)$ is called the *symmetric closure* of M. We shall consider in this paper only off-line Turing machines, in which the first tape is read-only. As usual, a Turing machine is deterministic if its yields relation is a function.

A Turing machine M accepts an input string w if it can pass from $I_M(w)$, the initial configuration with that input on its first tape, to a configuration with a final state. Let $S\colon \mathbb{N} \to \mathbb{N}$ be a function. Then we say that a Turing machine M accepts a language $L \subseteq \Sigma_0^*$ in space S provided that L is exactly the set of strings that M accepts, and that for every string $w \in \Sigma_0^*$, M on input w never uses more than $S(|w|)$ tape squares on any one of its work tapes. In addition to the standard DSPACE(S) and NSPACE(S) we can now define

$$\mathrm{SSPACE}(S) = \{L\colon \text{some symmetric Turing machine accepts } L \text{ in space } S\}.$$

3. THE MAIN LEMMA

In this Section we develop the main tool used to show that various computational tasks can be accomplished by symmetric Turing machines within give space bounds. This lemma is applied to yield symmetric Turing machines which simulate other Turing machines, or accept particular languages. In each case the idea is to construct a Turing machine M which is clearly not symmetric, but which is readily seen to solve the problem at hand. Provided that M satisfies the three hypotheses of the lemma, a symmetric machine accepting the same language in the same space is obtained in two steps. First, M is converted into its "normal form" Turing machine $M^{\#}$--still not symmetric. $M^{\#}$ is identical to M, except that it does not leave its final states, or reenter its initial state, or write a blank on its worktapes. It is easy to argue that M has such a well-defined normal form $M^{\#}$. Next, we obtain the symmetric closure of $M^{\#}$, $\overline{M^{\#}}$, which, we argue, is functionally equivalent to M.

The hypotheses on M which guarantee that $\overline{M^{\#}}$ accepts the same language as M in the same space are stated in terms of a set of *special configurations* $\mathcal{A}$. These hypotheses, stated informally, are the following:

(i) The nondeterminism of M is confined to these special configurations. To all other configurations, at most one transition applies. We say that all configurations outside $\mathcal{A}$ are *locally deterministic in the forward direction* (Condition (b) of Lemma 1 below).

(ii) Furthermore, all configurations outside $\mathcal{A}$ may have only a *limited* kind of *backwards nondeterminism*. More precisely, from any configuration of M there is at most one configuration in $\mathcal{A}$ to which M^{-1} can get without passing through other configurations of $\mathcal{A}$ (Condition (c) of Lemma 1).

(iii) Finally, M has a kind of *macroscopic symmetry*; if M can get from one configuration of $\mathcal{A}$ to another, then it can also get from the second to the first (Condition (a) of Lemma 1).

Figure 1 illustrates the configuration space of a typical machine to which hypotheses (i)-(iii) ((a)-(c) of Lemma 1) apply. Special configurations are dots; the paths may contain many configurations not in $\mathcal{A}$.

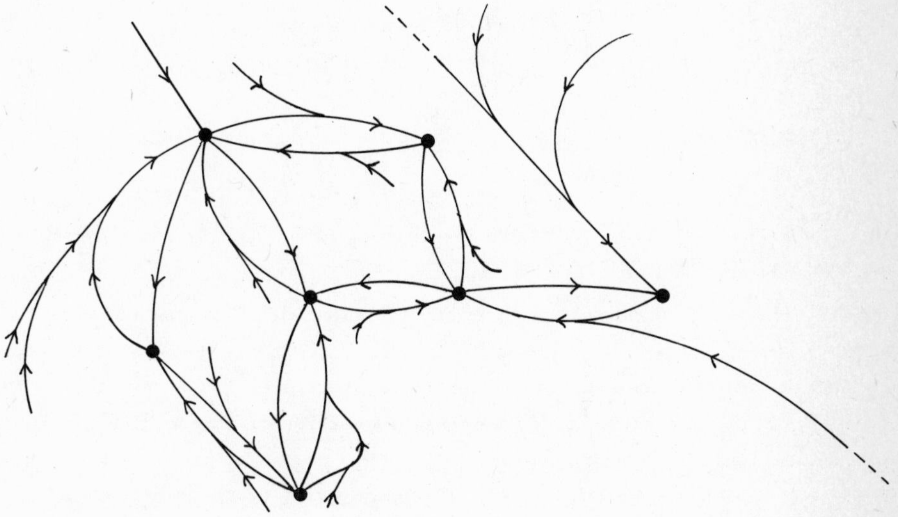

Figure 1

In order to state the Lemma, we need to introduce some notation. If M is a Turing machine, $\mathscr{C}(M)$ is the set of all configurations of M and $\mathscr{I}(M)$ the set of initial configurations of M. Let $\mathscr{A} \subseteq \mathscr{C}(M)$. If $n \geq 0$, $C_0,\ldots,C_n \in \mathscr{C}(M)$, $C_0 \vdash_M C_1 \vdash_M \cdots \vdash_M C_n$, $C_1,\ldots,C_{n-1} \notin \mathscr{A}$, and, if $n > 0$, at most one of C_0, C_n is in $\mathscr{A}$, then we write $C_0 \overset{*\mathscr{A}}{\vdash_M} C_n$ (or equivalently $C_n \overset{*\mathscr{A}}{\dashv_M} C_0$). Also, we write $A_1 \overset{+\mathscr{A}}{\vdash_M} A_2$ (or equivalently $A_2 \overset{+\mathscr{A}}{\dashv_M} A_1$) if $A_1, A_2 \in \mathscr{A}$, and there is a $B \in \mathscr{C}(M)$ such that $A_1 \overset{*\mathscr{A}}{\vdash_M} B \vdash_M A_2$.

We can now state Lemma 1:

LEMMA 1. *Let* $M = (K,\Sigma,\Sigma_0,k,\Delta,s,F)$ *be any Turing machine, and let* $\mathscr{A} \subseteq \mathscr{C}(M)$. *Suppose that*

(a) *For any* $A_1, A_2 \in \mathscr{A}$, *if* $A_1 \overset{+\mathscr{A}}{\vdash_M} A_2$ *then* $A_2 \overset{+\mathscr{A}}{\vdash_M} A_1$.

(b) *For any* $A \in \mathscr{A} \cup \mathscr{I}(M)$, *any* $B, C_1, C_2 \notin \mathscr{A}$, *and any* C_3, *if*

$$A \overset{*\mathscr{A}}{\vdash_M} C_1 \overset{*\mathscr{A}}{\dashv_M} C_2 \dashv_M B \vdash_M C_3, \text{ then } C_2 = C_3.$$

(c) *For any* $A_1 \in \mathscr{A} \cup \mathscr{I}(M)$, $A_2 \in \mathscr{A}$, *and* $B \notin \mathscr{A}$, *if* $A_1 \overset{*\mathscr{A}}{\vdash_M} B \overset{*\mathscr{A}}{\dashv_M} A_2$, *then* $A_1 = A_2$.

Then $\overline{M^{\#}}$ *accepts the same language as* M *in the same space.* □

4. SIMULATION THEOREMS

In this Section we show the following basic results.

THEOREM 1. *For any function* $S: \mathbb{N} \to \mathbb{N}$, $DSPACE(S) \subseteq SSPACE(S) \subseteq NSPACE(S)$.

Sketch of Proof. The second inclusion is trivial. For the first, it turns out that any deterministic Turing machine M vacuously satisfies Lemma 1, with $\mathscr{A} = \emptyset$. □

THEOREM 2. *For any function* $S: \mathbb{N} \to \mathbb{N}$, *and any* $\varepsilon > 0$, $SSPACE(S) = SSPACE(\varepsilon \cdot S)$. □

THEOREM 3. *If* L *is accepted by a* k*-tape Turing machine in space* S, *it is also accepted in space* S *by a Turing machine with two tapes (i.e., only one work tape).* □

Our notion of space-bounded reducibility is the ordinary, deterministic one (see [HU2], [Jo]).

THEOREM 4. *For any* $S \geq \log$ *and* $L_1, L_2 \subseteq \Sigma_0^*$, *if* L_1 *is reducible to* L_2 *in space* S *and* $L_2 \in SSPACE(S)$, *then* $L_1 \in SSPACE(S)$. □

All three theorems above are symmetric versions of quite routine results. Their proofs, however, are at times surprisingly complex, exactly because of the "programming awkwardness" apparently inherent in symmetric computation. In all three cases, we first construct a carefully designed version of the original (deterministic) construction, and we then apply Lemma 1.

We shall outline some of the details of the proof of Theorem 4. This proof follows the argument of [Jo], refined to reflect the intricacies of symmetric computation. Let M_2 be the symmetric Turing machine accepting L_2 in space S, and let T be the transducer which reduces L_1 to L_2 in space S. We construct a symmetric Turing machine M_1 which accepts L_1 in space S. The flow-chart of the operation of M_1 is shown in Figure 2. M_1 has the tapes of M_2, those of T, and two more tapes. These latter tapes always contain two integers in binary, denoted by h and j.

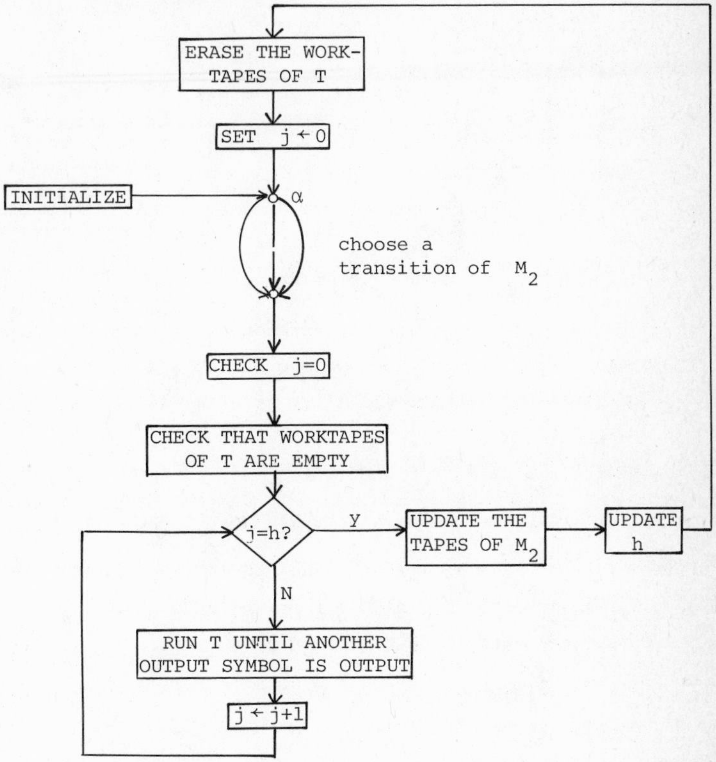

Figure 2

M_1 does *not* proceed, on input w, by simulating T, recording the output T(w) on some tape, and then simulating M_2 on input T(w); this would take too much space if $|T(w)| > S(|w|)$. Instead, M_1 keeps track, by a number h, of the head position of M_2 on a hypothetical tape containing T(w). Every time one step of M_2 is to be simulated, M_1 first chooses the next transition of M_1 to be performed, in its only nondeterministic step per simulated step of M_2 (α in Figure 2). M_1 then carries out from the beginning the computation of T on input w. Every time an output symbol is produced, it is discarded, and a counter j is advanced by one. When $j = h$, M_1 consults the most recent output of T and the tapes of M_2, and performs the nondeterministically chosen transition.

It is quite easy to argue, following [Jo], that $L_1 = L(M_1)$. What is harder to show is that Lemma 1 applies (with $\mathscr{A}$ the set of configurations at which

M_1 is at point α of the flowchart), and thus $L_1 \in SSPACE(S)$. This involves a complex argument, and the construction of such elementary components as a symmetric binary counter. Details are omitted.

We can also show the following (see [RF]):

THEOREM 5. *Let* $S_1, S_2 : \mathbb{N} \to \mathbb{N}$ *be functions such that:*

(i) $\log < S_1 < S_2$

(ii) $\forall n \exists m (S_1(m) = S_2(n))$.

Then $SSPACE(S_1) = NSPACE(S_1)$ *implies* $SSPACE(S_2) = NSPACE(S_2)$, *and* $DSPACE(S_1) = SSPACE(S_1)$ *implies* $DSPACE(S_2) = SSPACE(S_2)$. □

COROLLARY. *If* $SSPACE(\log n) = NSPACE(\log n)$, *then* $SSPACE(n) = NSPACE(n)$. *Similarly, if* $DSPACE(\log n) = SSPACE(\log n)$ *then* $DSPACE(n) = SSPACE(n)$. □

5. COMPLETE PROBLEMS

Consider the following symmetric version of the "graph accessibility problem" (GAP), shown in [Sa] and [Jo] to be log-space complete for $NSPACE(\log n)$.

UGAP (undirected graph accessibility problem) [JoLL].

Input: A graph $G = (\{1,2,\ldots,p\},E)$

Property: There is a path from node 1 to node p in G.

THEOREM 6. UGAP *is log-space complete for* $SSPACE(\log n)$.

Sketch of Proof. To show that $UGAP \in SSPACE(\log n)$, we first construct a (non-symmetric) Turing machine M which accepts UGAP in space $\log n$, and then apply Lemma 1. Completeness follows from the argument of [Sa]. □

COROLLARY. *These problems are log-space complete for* $SSPACE(\log n)$:

1) NONBIPARTITE GRAPHS

Input: A graph G.
Property: G has a cycle of odd length.

2) UNSAT - $\oplus$

Input: A set of clauses, each the exclusive-or of two literals.
Property: Their conjunction is unsatisfiable.

Proof. These problems are shown in [JoLL] to be log-space equivalent to UGAP. □

We now introduce a symmetric analog of context-sensitive recognition, which is complete for $SSPACE(n)$. A *Thue system* is a pair $T = (\Sigma, P)$, where Σ is a finite alphabet and P is a finite set of unordered pairs from Σ^*. For $\alpha, \beta \in \Sigma^*$ we write $\alpha \underset{T}{\sim} \beta$ if, for some $u,v,w_1,w_2 \in \Sigma^*$, $\alpha = uw_1v$, $\beta = uw_2v$, and $\{w_1,w_2\} \in P$; $\overset{*}{\underset{T}{\sim}}$ is the reflexive-transitive closure of $\underset{T}{\sim}$. A Thue system (Σ, P) is *balanced* if $|\alpha| = |\beta|$ whenever $\{\alpha, \beta\} \in P$. Consider the following problem.

WPBTS (Word Problem for Balanced Thue Systems)

Input: A balanced Thue system $T = (\Sigma, P)$; two strings $\alpha, \beta \in \Sigma^*$.

Property: $\alpha \overset{*}{\underset{T}{\sim}} \beta$.

THEOREM 7. WPBTS *is log-space complete for* SSPACE(n). □

6. ON THE RELATION OF SYMMETRY TO DETERMINISM AND NONDETERMINISM

The most intriguing question raised by the notion of symmetric space-bounded computation is its exact position with respect to its deterministic and nondeterministic counterparts. Understanding this position could shed light on the most perplexing problem of whether or not DSPACE(log n) = NSPACE(log n), and the LBA problem as well. Certainly, by Savitch's results [Sa] $\mathrm{SSPACE}(S) \subseteq \mathrm{DSPACE}(S^2)$, and also (by Theorem 1) $\mathrm{NSPACE}(S) \subseteq \mathrm{SSPACE}(S^2)$. Any improvement on either bound would be valuable evidence about whether symmetry is closer to determinism or to nondeterminism. Unfortunately, we have no conclusive results here. There are, however, some interesting insights of this sort, which can be gained indirectly, by considering *symmetric time bounds* and *symmetric stack automata*.

6.1 Symmetric Time Bounds

Let M be a Turing machine. By $\vdash_M^t$ we denote the t-th power of $\vdash_M$. Let $T: \mathbb{N} \to \mathbb{N}$ be a function. As usual, we say that M accepts a language $L \subseteq \Sigma_0^*$ *in time* T if for all $w \in \Sigma_0^*$, $w \in L$ iff $I_M(w) \vdash_M^t C$ for some $C \in \mathscr{I}(M)$ and $t \leq T(|w|)$. It is routine to define the complexity classes DTIME(T), NTIME(T), and STIME(T). The symmetric time complexity classes, however, are rather uninteresting, in view of the following:

THEOREM 8. *Let* $T: \mathbb{N} \to \mathbb{N}$. *Then* STIME(T) = NTIME(T).

<u>Sketch of Proof</u>. To show $\mathrm{STIME}(T) \supseteq \mathrm{NTIME}(T)$, any language in NTIME(T) can be recognized in time 2T by a "canonical" nondeterministic Turing machine which operates in two stages: a purely nondeterministic one--in which a "plan" for the computation is constructed--and a deterministic one, in which the plan guides the computation. The canonical Turing machine can be constructed in such a way that Lemma 1 is applicable. □

That symmetric time bounds are inconsequential, however, does not necessarily imply the same for *simultaneous* time-space bounds (notice that the symmetric machine in the above proof uses space T). Let NST(S,T) be the class of languages accepted simultaneously in space S and time T; DST(S,T) and SST(S,T) are defined as usual. What is known about inclusions of such classes? Savitch's simulation result [Sa] implies $\mathrm{NST}(S,T) \subseteq \bigcup_{c>1} \mathrm{DST}(S \log T, T^{cS})$. We may improve this somewhat by noting that in the log S deepest recursion levels in Savitch's simulation the guessed "midpoint" configuration will not differ from the "endpoint" ones in all tape squares--see [Sa], [HU2]. The inclusion thus becomes

$$\mathrm{NST}(S,T) \subseteq \bigcup_{c>1} \mathrm{DST}\left(S \log T, \left(c\,\frac{T}{S}\right)^{cS}\right) .$$

To our knowledge, this is the best such inclusion known. It is interesting to observe that when the simulating machine is symmetric instead of deterministic, the above result may be improved as follows:

THEOREM 9. *Let* $S,T: \mathbb{N} \to \mathbb{N}$ *be constructible functions, and let* $S(n) > \log n$. *Then* $NST(S,T) \subseteq SST(S \log T, T \log S)$.

Sketch of Proof. We can use the nondeterminism of symmetric machines to guess the midpoint configuration at each recursion level. □

Theorem 9 does suggest that symmetry may be stronger than determinism for simulating nondeterminism. Our next result--a direct consequence of the results in [AKLLR]--reveals one direction in which symmetry appears to be more manageable than nondeterminism.

We adapt the notion of *probabilistic computation* of Gill [Gi]. A language L is accepted by a Turing machine M in probabilistic space S and time T--notation $L \in RST(S,T)$--if M operates in space S, and $w \in L$ if and only if more than half of the computations of length $T(|w|)$ end up accepting w.

THEOREM 10. *Let* S *be a constructible function. Then* $SSPACE(S) \subseteq \bigcup_{c>1} RST(S,c^S)$.

Sketch of Proof. In [AKLLR] it is shown that a random walk on a connected undirected graph will with high probability visit all nodes in polynomial time. We apply this to the "yield" relation of an $S(n)$ space-bounded symmetric Turing machine. □

In contrast, it is doubtful that $NSPACE(S) \subseteq \bigcup_{c>1} RST(S,c^S)$.

6.2 Stack Automata

In search of evidence relating the computational power of symmetry to that of determinism or nondeterminism we may examine a number of computational models other than unrestricted Turing machines. For some, such as auxiliary pushdown automata, determinism and nondeterminism are equivalent and so the three concepts collapse. For others, such as two-way pushdown automata and linear (space-) bounded automata, it is an open question whether determinism and nondeterminism are equivalent; so while some useful insights may be gained by considering symmetry, no proper inclusion results may be expected without a significant methodological advance. (Here we should include as well the question of an exponential gap in the number of states in equivalent deterministic and nondeterministic two-way finite automata [Si,SaS]. For some other computational models--one-way pushdown automata and nonerasing stack automata [HU1]--nondeterminism is known to be more powerful than determinism, but the concept of symmetry is inherently inapplicable.

There remain the ordinary--i.e., erasing--stack automata. Let NSTACK, DSTACK and SSTACK be the classes of languages accepted by general, deterministic, and symmetric stack automata, respectively. Cook showed [Co], by extending the techniques of [HU1], that $DSTACK = \bigcup_{c>1} DTIME(c^{n \log n})$, whereas $NSTACK = \bigcup_{c>1} DTIME(c^{n^2})$; therefore $DSTACK \subsetneq NSTACK$. What is the exact position of SSTACK? We can show

THEOREM 11. SSTACK = DSTACK.

Sketch of Proof. By the argument of [HU1] as modified by Cook, the time complexity of a stack automaton may be related to the space required to store and modify upwards the "yields" relation among the surface configurations--those with the stack head on the top. The theorem follows from the fact that equivalence relations can be stored almost as space-efficiently as functions. □

7. CONCLUDING REMARKS

Symmetric computation is a natural idea, closely related to classical symmetric formal system and undirected graph traversal problems. It can be captured syntactically by the concept of a symmetric Turing machine, which is a natural restriction on ordinary Turing machines, though sometimes awkward to reason about and to program. In computational power, symmetry lies somewhere between determinism and nondeterminism, though its exact position seems to vary considerably with the criterion used. With respect to time bounds, it is the same as nondeterminism. With respect to stack access, it is the same as determinism. With respect to probabilistic computation, it seems to be weaker than nondeterminism, and with respect to simultaneous space-time bounds it seems to be stronger than determinism. Its power with respect to logarithmic space bounds is the major open question suggested by our work: the challenge is to improve Savitch's simulation results when either the simulated or the simulating machine is symmetric.

It is interesting to note in closing that another--also syntactically definable--restriction of determinism turns out to be equivalent to symmetry. Call a Turing machine M *Eulerian* if for each configuration C, the number of transitions of M applicable to C is equal to the number of transitions of M^{-1} applicable to C. Symmetric machines are always Eulerian, since $M = M^{-1}$ if M is symmetric. The converse fails on the syntactic level, but if M is Eulerian then $L(M) = L(\bar{M})$ (this follows from the fact that strong and weak connectivity coincide for Eulerian digraphs). Hence every Eulerian Turing machine can be simulated by a symmetric one. To put the point differently, the accessibility problem for Eulerian digraphs (EGAP) is also complete for SSPACE(log n). This special position of EGAP with respect to logarithmic space was hinted at in [AKLLR].

REFERENCES

[AKLLR] R. Aleliunas, R.M. Karp, R.J. Lipton, L. Lovasz, C. Rackoff: Random walks, universal sequences, and the complexity of maze problems, Proceedings of 20th Annual Symposium on Foundations of Computer Science, 1979, pp. 218-223.

[Co] S.A. Cook: Characterizations of pushdown machines in terms of time-bounded computers, Journal of the Association for Computing Machinery 18 (1971), pp. 4-18.

[Cy] A. Cypher: An approach to the k-paths problem, Proceedings of 12th Annual Symposium on Theory of Computing, 1980.

[FHW] S. Fortune, J.E. Hopcroft, J. Wyllis: The directed subgraph homeomorphism problem, Theoretical Computer Science 10 (1980), pp. 111-121.

[Gi] J. Gill: Computational complexity of probabilistic Turing machines, SIAM Journal on Computing 6 (1977), pp. 675-695.

[HU1] J.D. Hopcroft, J.E. Ullman: Nonerasing stack automata, Journal of the Association for Computing Machinery 18 (1971), pp. 4-18.

[HU2] J.D. Hopcroft, J.E. Ullman: *Introduction to Automata Theory, Languages, and Computation*, Addison-Wesley, 1979.

[Ji] H. Jia-wei: On some deterministic space complexity problems, Proceedings of 12th Annual Symposium on Theory of Computing, 1980.

[Jo] N.D. Jones: Space-bounded reducibility among combinatorial problems, Journal of Computer and Systems Sciences 11 (1972), pp. 68-85.

[JoLL] N.D. Jones, Y.E. Lien, W.T. Laaser: New problems complete for log space, Mathematical Systems Theory 10 (1976), pp. 1-17.

[LaP] A. LaPaugh: Private communication, November 1979.

[LaPR] A. LaPaugh, R.L. Rivest: The subgraph homeomorphism problem, Proceedings of 10th Annual Symposium on Theory of Computing, 1978, pp. 40-50.

[LP] H.R. Lewis, C.H. Papadimitriou: *Elements of the Theory of Computation*, Prentice-Hall, 1981 (to appear).

[Po] E.L. Post: Recursive unsolvability of a problem of Thue, Journal of Symbolic Logic 13 (1947), pp. 1-11.

[RF] S. Ruby and P.C. Fischer: Translational methods and computational complexity, IEEE Conference Record on Switching Circuit Theory and Logical Design, 1965, pp. 173-178.

[Sa] W.J. Savitch: Relations between nondeterministic and deterministic tape complexities, Journal of Computer and Systems Sciences 4 (1970), pp. 177-192.

[Sh] Y. Shiloach: The two paths problem is polynomial, Journal of the Association for Computing Machinery, to appear.

[SaS] W.J. Sakoda, M. Sipser: Nondeterminism and the size of two-way finite automata, Proceedings of 10th Annual Symposium on Theory of Computing, 1978, pp. 275-286.

[Si] M. Sipser: Lower bounds on the size of sweeping automata, Proceedings of 11th Annual Symposium on Theory of Computing, 1979, pp. 360-364.

ON SOME PROPERTIES OF LOCAL TESTABILITY

Aldo de Luca, Antonio Restivo

Istituto di Cibernetica del CNR, Arco Felice, Napoli, Italy.

1. INTRODUCTION.

In this paper we consider the family of strictly locally testable languages [7]. A subset L of a free semigroup A^+, generated by a finite set A, is strictly locally testable if there exist a positive integer k and three subsets U,V,W of A^k such that:

$$L \cap A^k A^* = (UA^* \cap A^* V) \setminus A^* W A^*,$$

where $A^* = A^+ \cup \{1\}$.

The family of strictly locally testable languages is not closed under the Boolean operations. Its Boolean closure is the class of locally testable languages. From the definition, a locally testable language L is recognizable; that is, its syntactic semigroup S(L) is finite [4].

In recent years many papers have been devoted to the study of locally testable languages. We recall, in particular, the following characterization of the syntactic semigroup S(L) of a locally testable language L : *a recognizable language* L *is locally testable if and only if, for all idempotents* $e \in S(L)$, $e\,S(L)e$ *is a semilattice* [1,6,12].

This result is of great interest since it gives, S(L) being finite, an algebraic decision procedure for local testability. More complex, however, seems the algebraic characterization of strictly local testability given by McNaughton [6] which makes use of six suitable conditions for the elements of S(L).

In this paper we present a simple characterization of strictly local testability in terms of the concept of *constant* introduced by Schützenberger [11]. More precisely we show (see theorem 1) *that a recognizable language* L *is strictly locally testable if and only if all the idempotents of its syntactic semigroup* S(L) *are constants for* $L\phi$, where $\phi : A^+ \to S(L)$ is the syntactic morphism.

This result gives an algebraic decision procedure for strictly local testability which seems more simple and manageable than that given by McNaughton.

In the last section some remarkable consequences of the previous theorem are derived concerning conditions under which, if L is strictly locally testable, then the subsemigroup L^+ generated by L is also strictly locally testable. As we shall see, similar results cannot be extended to the wider family of locally testable languages.

2. A CHARACTERIZATION OF STRICTLY LOCALLY TESTABLE LANGUAGES.

If S is a semigroup and X a subset of S, an element $c \in S$ is a *constant* for X if, for all $p,q,r,s \in S^1$:

$$pcq,\ rcs \in X \Rightarrow pcs \in X .$$

Let us denote by C(X) the set of constants of S for X. From the definition it follows that C(X) is a two-sided ideal of S. If $\phi : A^+ \to S(X)$ is the syntactic morphism, one easily derives that $C(X)\phi \subseteq C(X\phi)$ and $C(X\phi)\phi^{-1} \subseteq C(X)$, where $C(X\phi)$ is the set of constants of S(X) for $X\phi$.

<u>Theorem 1</u>. A recognizable language L is strictly locally testable if and only if all the idempotents of S(L) are constants for $L\phi$, where $\phi : A^+ \to S(L)$ is the syntactic morphism.

<u>Proof:</u>

(⇒). Let L be a k-strictly locally testable language. One has that

$$L \cap A^k A^* = (UA^* \cap A^* V) \setminus A^* W A^*$$

with U, V, W subsets of A^k. We prove first that all words $f \in A^k A^*$ are constants for L. Let $u_1, u_2, u_3, u_4 \in A^*$ be such that

$$u_1 f u_2 ,\ u_3 f u_4 \in L .$$

As $|f| \geq k$ one has that $u_1 f \in U A^*$, $f u_4 \in A^* V$ and $u_1 f u_4 \notin A^* W A^*$. Thus $u_1 f u_4 \in L$. This shows that f is a constant for L. Let now e be an idempotent of S(L) and $g \in A^k A^*$ be such that $g\phi = e$. Since g is a constant for L, it follows that e is a constant for $L\phi$.

(⇐). Let us now suppose that all the idempotents of S(L) are constants for $L\phi$. We shall first prove that there exists a positive integer k such that all the words of $A^k A^*$ are constants for L. Since the idempotents of S(L) are contained into the two-sided ideal $C(L\phi)$ as well known (see Eilenberg [4, Vol. B, p. 81]) one has that $[S(L)]^k \subseteq C(L\phi)$ with $k = |S(L) \setminus C(L\phi)| + 1$. This shows that all the words of $A^k A^*$ are constants for L. We denote by U_k (resp. V_k) the set of prefixes (resp. suffixes) of L of length k, and by T the set of the words of A^+

incompletable in L, i.e. $T = \{f \in A^+ \mid A^* f A^* \cap L = \emptyset\}$. Let us now prove that $L \cap A^k A^* = (U_k A^* \cap A^* V_k) \setminus T$. One has obviously that $L \cap A^k A^* \subseteq (U_k A^* \cap A^* V_k) \setminus T$. To prove the inverse inclusion let $g \in (U_k A^* \cap A^* V_k) \setminus T$. One can write

$$g = u h_1 = h_2 v \quad \text{with} \quad h_1, h_2 \in A^*, \ u \in U_k, \ v \in V_k .$$

Since $g \notin T$, there exist $f_1, f_2 \in A^*$ such that

$$f_1 g f_2 = f_1 u h_1 f_2 = f_1 h_2 v f_2 \in L .$$

Moreover, since $u \in U_k$ and $v \in V_k$ there exist $f', f'' \in A^*$ for which

$$u f', \ f''v \in L.$$

Since $|u| = |v| = k$, u and v are constants for L, so that from the previous relations it follows

$$f_1 h_2 v = f_1 u h_1 \in L$$

and then $u h_1 = g \in L$.

Let us finally prove that the ideal T is finitely generated. Let $W = T \setminus (A^* T A^+ \cup A^+ T A^*)$ be the base of the ideal T, i.e. $T = A^* W A^*$. We shall prove that the length of the words of W is less than or equal to k+1.

Let $w \in W$ and suppose $|w| \geq k+2$. We can then write $w = aub$ with $a, b \in A$ and $u \in A^k A^*$. Let us show that either $au \in T$ or $ub \in T$. In fact if $au \notin T$ and $ub \notin T$ there would exist $f_1, f_2, f_3, f_4 \in A^*$ such that

$$f_1 auf_2, f_3 ubf_4 \in L .$$

Since u is a constant for L it would follow

$$f_1 aubf_4 = f_1 wf_4 \in L,$$

which is absurd as $w \in T$. Thus either $W \cap AT \neq \emptyset$ or $W \cap TA \neq \emptyset$, which contradicts the fact that W is the base of T. Hence the length of the elements of W is $\leq k+1$.

This proves that L is strictly locally testable of order $\leq k+1$.

Q.E.D.

3. A CLOSURE PROPERTY OF STRICTLY LOCALLY TESTABLE LANGUAGES.

In this section some consequences of theorem 1 are derived concerning the invariance of the strictly local testability under the operation "+". It is well known that, if L is a strictly locally testable language, L^+ is not, in general, strictly locally testable. Our problem is here to find the conditions under which L^+ is again strictly locally testable. In order to state our results let us first recall the following definition.

Let L be a subsemigroup of A^+. L has a *bounded synchronization delay* if a positive integer q exists such that all the elements of L^q are constants for L. The minimal integer for which this condition is verified is called the *synchronization delay* of L.

Lemma. Let $L \subseteq A^+$ be a recognizable language and let u be an element of A^+.

i) If u is a constant for L^+ and L is the minimal generating set of L^+ then u^2 is a constant for L.

ii) If u is a constant for L and L^+ has a bounded synchronization delay, then there exists a positive integer k such that u^k is a constant for L^+.

Proof. Let us first prove i). Let u be a constant for L^+. We want to show that u^2 is a constant for L. Let $m_1, m_2, m_3, m_4 \in A^*$ be such that

$$m_1 u^2 m_2 \ , \ m_3 u^2 m_4 \ \in L \ .$$

Since u^2 is a constant for L^+, one has

$$m_1 u^2 m_4 \ \in L^+ \ .$$

If $m_1 u^2 m_4 \in L$, the result is achieved. Let us then suppose that $m_1 u^2 m_4 \in L^2 L^*$. By factorizing $m_1 u^2 m_4$ in terms of the elements of L, we have to consider two cases.

In the first case *there is a factorization line inside the word* u^2. Let us then suppose that $m_1 u' \in L^+$, $u'' u m_4 \in L^+$ with $u'u'' = u$. Since $m_1 u^2 m_2 \in L$, u being a constant for L^+, one has $u'' u m_2 \in L^+$. Thus $m_1 u^2 m_2 = (m_1 u')(u'' u m_2) \in L \cap (L^+)^2$ which is a contradiction.

One obtains a similar contradiction if there exist u' and u'' such that

$$m_1 u u' \in L^+ \quad \text{and } u'' m_4 \in L^+ \text{ with } u'u'' = u \ .$$

Let us consider now the case in which *does not exist a factorizazion line inside* u^2. One has then that either there exist $m'_1, m''_1 \in A^*$ such that

$$m'_1 m''_1 = m_1 \quad \text{and} \quad m'_1 \in L^+ , \ m''_1 u^2 m_4 \in L^+$$

or there exist $m'_4, m''_4 \in A^*$ such that

$$m'_4 m''_4 = m_4 \quad \text{and} \quad m_1 u^2 m'_4 \in L^+, \; m''_4 \in L^+ .$$

In the first case, since u is a constant for L^+ and $m_1 u^2 m_2 \in L$, it follows that $m''_1 u^2 m_2 \in L^+$ and $m_1 u^2 m_2 = (m'_1)(m''_1 u^2 m_2) \in L \cap (L^+)^2$ which is a contradiction. In a similar way one reaches a contradiction in the second case.

Let us now prove statement ii). Let u be a constant for L and k a positive integer such that $u^k \phi = e$ is an idempotent of $S(L^+)$. Let us denote $u^k = g$ and take $h > |g|$. If $e = 0$ the result is trivial. Let us then suppose that $e \neq 0$.

We have to distinguish two cases.

CASE 1. There exists a context $(v_1, v_2) \in A^* \times A^*$ such that $w = v_1 g^h v_2 \in L^+$ and, moreover, there exists a factorization of w in terms of the elements of L such that each g in w contains a factorization line.

In this case since $h > |g|$ two factorization lines will lie in the same position. This implies that words $g_1, g_2 \in A^*$ and nonnegative integers p, q, r exist such that:

$$v_1 g^p g_1 , \; (g_2 g_1)^{r+1} , \; g_2 g^q v_2 \in L^+ , \quad g_1 g_2 = g$$

$$p + q + r + 2 = h .$$

From these relations one derives:

$$(g_2 g_1)^{r+1} \phi = (g_2 g_1)^2 \phi \in L^+ \phi,$$

and $\quad (g_2 g_1)^2 \phi = f = f^2 .$

Since L^+ has a bounded synchronization delay the idempotent f is a constant for $L^+ \phi$. In fact let $h \in L^+$ be such that $f = h\phi$. Since f is an idempotent, $f = h^s \phi$ with s equal to delay of synchronization of L^+. Thus $e = (g_1 g_2)\phi = (g_1 (g_2 g_1)^2 g_2)\phi = g_1 \phi \, f \, g_2 \phi$ is a constant for $L^+ \phi$. It follows then that u^k is a constant for L^+.

CASE 2. For each context $(v_1, v_2) \in A^* \times A^*$ such that $w = v_1 g^h v_2 \in L^+$ any factorization of w in terms of the elements of L is such that a g, at least, in w is factor of a word of L.

We shall prove that in such a case g^h is a constant for L^+.

Let $m_1, m_2, m_3, m_4 \in A^*$ be such that

$$m_1 g^h m_2 , \; m_3 g^h m_4 \in L^+ .$$

By the made hypothesis integers $r, s \geq 1$, $p, q, m, n \geq 0$ and words $g_1, g_2, g_3, g_4, g'_1, g'_2, g'_3, g'_4 \in A^*$ have to exist such that:

$$m_1 g^p g_1, \quad g_4 g^q m_2 \in L^+, \quad g_2 g^r g_3 \in L$$

$$m_3 g^n g'_1, \quad g'_4 g^m m_4 \in L^+, \quad g'_2 g^s g'_3 \in L$$

$$g_1 g_2 = g_3 g_4 = g'_1 g'_2 = g'_3 g'_4 = g$$

$$p + q + r + 2 = n + m + s + 2 = h .$$

Since g is a constant for L, from the relations $g_2 g^r g_3$, $g'_2 g^s g'_3 \in L$ it follows $g_2 g^t g'_3 \in L$, where $t = \min\{r, s\}$. From this and the previous relations one derives:

$$m_1 g^p g_1 (g_2 g^t g'_3) g'_4 g^m m_4 = m_1 g^i m_4 \in L^+$$

with $i = p+t+m+2$. Since $g^h\phi = g^i\phi$ it follows, syntactically, that $m_1 g^h m_4 \in L^+$. Thus $g^h = u^{hk}$ is a constant for L^+.

Q.E.D.

Theorem 2. Let L be a strictly locally testable language. L^+ is strictly locally testable if and only if L^+ has a bounded synchronization delay.

Proof.

($\Rightarrow$). This implication is a trivial consequence of theorem 1 since if L^+ is strictly locally testable all the idempotents of $S(L^+)$ are constants for $L^+\phi$, and then, for $k = |S(L^+) \setminus C(L^+\phi)| + 1$, one has that

$$(L^+)^k \phi \subseteq (S(L^+))^k \subseteq C(L^+\phi).$$

This shows that L^+ has a bounded synchronization delay.

($\Leftarrow$). Let e be an idempotent of $S(L^+)$ and $g \in A^+$ such that $g\phi = e$. Let us denote by $\psi : A^+ \to S(L)$ the syntactic morphism of L. Let h be a positive integer such that $g^h\psi$ is an idempotent of $S(L)$. Since L is strictly locally testable, by theorem 1, $g^h\psi$ is a constant for $L\psi$ and then g^h a constant for L. Hence, from the previous lemma, there exists a positive integer p such that g^{hp} is a constant for L^+. This implies that $g^{hp}\phi = e$ is a constant for $L^+\phi$.

Q.E.D.

Thus if L is strictly locally testable and L^+ has a bounded synchronization delay then L^+ is strictly locally testable. We remark that a similar result has been given by Schützenberger for *aperiodic languages*. As shown in [11] *if* L^+ *has a bounded synchronization delay and* L *is aperiodic, then* L^+ *is also aperiodic*. The techniques of this proof cannot be, however, extended to our case: indeed the fact that the family of aperiodic languages is closed under product, which is not the case for strictly locally testable languages, plays an essential rôle in the proof.

We remark further that under the hypothesis that L is strictly locally testable, the properties of local testability in the strict sense and bounded synchronization delay for L^+ coincide also with the property of local parsability as shown in [3] .

Theorem 2 gives an answer to our initial problem. One can then pose the same problem for the more general class of locally testable languages. However, we shall prove that no non-trivial condition exists which assures the local testability of a subsemigroup L^+ under the hypothesis of local testability of its generator set L. This fact is a consequence of the two following propositions.

Proposition 1. If L^+ is a strictly locally testable subsemigroup of A^+ and L its minimal generating set, then L is also strictly locally testable.

Proof: Let e be an idempotent of $S(L)$ and $f \in A^+$ such that $f\psi = e$, where ψ is the syntactic morphism $\psi : A^+ \to S(L)$. Let h be a positive integer such that $f^h\phi$ is an idempotent of $S(L^+)$. Since L^+ is strictly locally testable, then $f^h\phi$ is a constant for $L^+\phi$ and f^h a constant for L^+. Since L is the minimal generating set of L^+, from the previous lemma f^{2h} is a constant for L. Thus $f^{2h}\psi = e$ is a constant for $L\psi$. From theorem 1, L is strictly locally testable.

Q.E.D.

Let us remark that the above proposition does not, generally, hold for locally testable languages, as shown by the following example. Let $A = \{a,b\}$. The subsemigroup $A^* a A^*$ of A^+ is locally testable, but not in the strict sense. Its minimal generating set is given by $b^*a b^*$, which is not a locally testable language as one can easily verify.

The next proposition states that, in the case of free subsemigroups of A^+, the notion of local testability coincides with that of strictly local testability:

Proposition 2. Let L be a free subsemigroup of A^+. L is locally testable if and only if it is strictly locally testable.

Proof: Let us suppose that L is locally testable. We shall prove that all the idempotents of $S(L)$ are constants for $L\phi$. Let e be an idempotent of S(L) and

$p, q, r, s \in [S(L)]^1$ be such that

$$peq, res \in L\phi .$$

Since $L\phi$ is a subsemigroup of $S(L)$, one has that

$$peqrespeqres \in L\phi .$$

Moreover, from the syntactic characterization of locally testable languages, $eS(L)e$ is a semilattice. So that one can write

$$peqrespeqres = pespeqreqres = pespeqres =$$

$$= peqrespes \in L\phi .$$

From a classical result of Schützenberger [10], since $peqres \in L\phi$ and $L\phi$ is free in $S(L)$, it follows that $pes \in L\phi$.

Q.E.D.

By these propositions we obtain then the following:

Corollary. Let L be the minimal generating set of L^+ and let L^+ be free. If L is locally testable, but not in the strict sense, then L^+ is not locally testable.

Example. Let $A = \{a,b,c,d,e\}$ and $L = \{ab^+c\} \cup \{db^+e\}$. L is locally testable but not in the strict sense. L^+ is a free subsemigroup of A^+ having a bounded synchronization delay but not locally testable.

REFERENCES

1. Brzozowski, J.A. and I. Simon, Characterizations of locally testable events, Discrete Math., 4 (1973) 243-271.

2. de Luca, A. and A. Restivo, Synchronization and maximality for very pure subsemigroups of a free semigroup, Lectures Notes in Computer Science, vol. 74, Springer-Verlag (1979).

3. de Luca, A. and A. Restivo, A characterization of strictly locally testable languages and its application to subsemigroups of a free semigroup (1980), Information and Control (to appear).

4. Eilenberg, S., "Automata, Languages and Machines", Academic Press, New York, vol. A (1974), vol. B (1976)

5. Hashiguchi, K. and N. Honda, Properties of code events and homomorphisms over regular events, J.Comput. System Sci. 12 (1976) 352-367.

6. McNaughton, R., Algebraic decision procedures for local testability, Math. Systems Theory, 8 (1974) 60-76.

7. McNaughton, R. and S. Papert, "Counter-Free Automata", MIT Press, Cambridge, Mass 1971.

8. Restivo, A., On a question of McNaughton and Papert, Information and Control, 25 (1974) 93-101.

9. Restivo, A., A combinatorial property of codes having finite synchronization delay, Theoretical Computer Science, 1 (1975), 95-101.

10. Schützenberger, M.P., Une théorie algébrique du codage, Séminaire Dubreil-Pisot (Algebre et Théorie des nombres), exposé no. 15, 1955/1956, Paris.

11. Schützenberger, M.P., Sur certaines opérations de fermeture dans les langages rationnels, Symposia Mathematica XV (1975) 245-253.

12. Zalcstein, Y., Locally testable semigroups, Semigroup Forum, 5 (1973) 216-227.

Semantics :Algebras,Fixed Points,Axioms

Mila E. Majster-Cederbaum
Institut für Informatik
Technische Universität München
Arcisstr.21 8000 München 2

1. Introduction

Syntactic aspects of programming languages have been well understood for a long time already. Syntactic features are uniformly discussed in terms of grammars and have been investigated in formal language theory. In contrast to this, semantic aspects of programming languages seem harder to understand and formalize. A variety of approaches have been suggested to describe the semantics of a language, including e.g. VDL |1,2,3,4| , attributed grammars |5| , state machines |6,7|, λ-calculus and SECD-machine |8,9|, denotational semantics |10-17|, flow-charts with inductive assertions|18|, axioms and inference rules |19,20|, predicate transformers | 21| , etc.. An attempt to classify these approaches to describe semantics resulted in the classification operational-denotational-assertion semantics.

The motivation for our studies of semantics is to find out what the inherent properties of semantics are. I.e. what are the properties shared by all semantic specifications, where do they differ? Can we find a common "structure" in all the different approaches?

This paper is concerned with the metatheory of semantics and has two aims:

I) To provide a formal language in which all the different approaches can be formulated.

II) Given that formal language, to investigate the inherent properties of semantic specifications and to study the relationships between different specifications techniques.

If we survey all the different approaches that have been proposed for the semantic description of a programming language we could make the following observation: Any semantic description of a programming language is heavily based on the way a program is composed of smaller components. Or stated differently: the meaning of a construct is determined by the meaning of its constituents. This observation suggests that the meaning function |16| which associates a meaning with a program has <u>homomorphical</u> character. Homomorphisms are mappings between general algebras. This is the reason why we chose the language of universal algebra in order to be able to provide a framework for investigating semantics. The necessary definitions and constructions are given in section 3. In section 4 we introduce a programming language PL($\mathcal{L}$) and show how in general operational, denotational and assertion semantics can be presented in our framework. Sections 4,5 are devoted to studying the relationship between the different semantic descriptions. A diagram showing some of the results obtained is shown at the end of section 5. We prove e.g. that Dijkstra's semantics and Scott's semantics are isomorphic. Some other results are obtained under the assumption that the assertion language is expressive: e.g. we prove that Scott's semantics is a homomorphic image of a Hoare semantics, etc.. Section 6 deals with the abstraction from a particular specification technique and is a first attempt to state axioms for a theory of semantic specifications. We show an interesting relationship between these axioms and the characterization of the meaning of programs as fixed points of operators on complete lattices.

2. Related work

First attempts to use an algebraic approach in dealing with semantics go back to |23|, |24|. Compare also |22|, |25|, |26|. In |28| an algebraic formulation of Knuth's attribute semantics is attempted. The notion of relative completeness goes back to |29|. A characterization of program invariants as fixed points can be found in |34|. Compare also |35| . A first account of our approach is given in |33|. Further results appear in |37|.

3. Definitons

In the following both syntactic and semantic aspects of a programming language will be discussed in terms of manysorted algebras.

Definition 1. Let Σ be a finite set (of signatures), S be a finite set (of sorts) and two mappings $r: \Sigma \to S$, $d: \Sigma \to S$. A S-sorted Σ-algebra is a pair

$$D = [\{D_s\}_{s \in S}, \quad \{O_\sigma\}_{\sigma \in \Sigma}]$$

where D_s is a set and O_σ a mapping

$$O_\sigma : D_{s_1} x \ldots D_{s_n} \to D_s$$

where $d(\sigma) = s_1 \ldots s_n$, $r(\sigma) = s$. A homomorphism between S-sorted Σ-algebras D,D' is a family of mappings $\{h_s\}_{s\in S}$

$$h_s: D_s \to D'_s$$

such that for each $\sigma\in\Sigma$, $x_i \in D_{s_i}$

$$h_s(O_\sigma(x_1 \ldots x_n)) = O'_\sigma(h_{s_1}(x_1), \ldots h_{s_n}(x_n))$$

where $D' = [\{D'_s\}_{s\in S}, \{O'_\sigma\}_{\sigma\in\Sigma}]$.

The syntax of a programming language will be given as a context-free grammar. With this grammar we associate a "syntactic algebra." A semantic algebra will then be defined to be a homomomorphical image of the syntactic algebra. (Compare |25|.)

Definition 2. Let G = (N,T,P,S) be a context-free grammar, where N denotes the set of nonterminals, T the set of terminals, P the set of productions and S the start symbol. Let for each $A\in N$

$$L_A = \{w\in T^*: A \stackrel{*}{\Rightarrow} w\}$$

For each production $p = (A, u_1A_1u_2A_2 \ldots u_nA_nu_{n+1})$ with $A, A_i \in N, u_i \in T^*$, let

$$O_p: L_{A_1} \ldots x \ldots L_{A_n} \to L_A \qquad O_p(x_1, \ldots, x_n) = u_1x_1 \ldots u_nx_nu_{n+1}$$

The N-sorted P-algebra

$$\mathfrak{A}_G = [\{L_A\}_{A\in N}, \{O_p\}_{p\in P}]$$

is called the syntactic algebra of G.

A semantic algebra for G is a N-sorted P-algebra that is a homomorhic image of $\mathfrak{A}_G$.

REMARK 1. Let G = (N,T,P,S) an unambiguous reduced[+] context-free grammar, $\mathfrak{A}$ a N-sorted P-algebra, then there is a unique homomorphism $h: \mathfrak{A}_G \to \mathfrak{A}$. Consequently every N-sorted P-algebra gives rise to exactly one semantic algebra for G.

The above-mentioned homomorphism can be thought of as the "meaning function." By the previous remark principally any N-sorted P-algebra can be taken to provide a "meaning" to a language.

[+] We call a grammar reduced if for every $A\in N$ there are $u,v\in \{N\cup T\}^*$ such that $S \stackrel{*}{\Rightarrow} uAv$.

In the following section 4 we show how Hoare's assertion semantics and Dijkstra's predicate transformer semantics can be viewed as semantic algebras.

For a given programming language only a few semantic algebras will be of interest. In section 6 we discuss how the class of semantic algebras can be restricted.

4. Algebraic Formulation of Assertion Semantics

In the following we want to present a simple programming language and show how Hoare's and Dijkstra's assertion semantics can be presented in the above framework. The programming language allows assignment, conditional, while and concatenated statements. We assume that the expressions are the terms of some first-order language $\mathcal{L}_1$. An extension language $\mathcal{L}_2$ of $\mathcal{L}_1$ will be used as assertion language for the assertion semantics. Let the nonlogical symbols of $\mathcal{L}_1$ be f,g,h... for functions and p,q,r... for predicates.

The syntax of the programming language is given by

```
<command>::= <id>:= <exp> | (<command>;<command>) |
             if <boolexp> then <command> else  <command>  |
             while <boolexp> do <command>  | skip
<exp>    ::= <id> | <const> | f(<exp>,...<exp>)
                               \______n______/
```

for every n-ary function symbol f in $\mathcal{L}_1$

```
<boolexp> := p(<exp>,...<exp>)| (<boolexp> ∨ <boolexp>)|
             ¬<boolexp>  |  (<boolexp>  → <boolexp>)| true
```

for every predicate symbol p in $\mathcal{L}_1$.

The constants and variables (identifiers) in the programming language are the constants and variables of $\mathcal{L}_1$.[+]

We denote the programming language generated by the above grammar by PL($\mathcal{L}_1$). The <u>syntactic algebra</u> associated with the above grammar $\mathfrak{A}(\mathcal{L}_1)$ contains the domains L_{co}, L_{exp}, $L_{boolexp}$, L_{id}, L_{cons} and an operation for each production.

Let $\mathcal{L}_2$ be an <u>extension</u> of $\mathcal{L}_1$, i.e. the set of symbols of $\mathcal{L}_1$ is contained in the set of symbols of $\mathcal{L}_2$. We call $\mathcal{L}_2$ the assertion language. A <u>Hoare-like specification</u> of the programming language PL($\mathcal{L}_1$) is a system for the deduction of formulas of the form $F_1\{X\}F_2$

[+] We assume that variables act as input to programs and have a value before the program is executed.

where F_1 and F_2 are formulas of the assertion language $\mathcal{L}_2$ and X is a program.

Let γ be a structure for the first-order language $\mathcal{L}_2$, i.e. γ consists of a nonempty set $|\gamma|$ together with a n-ary function for each n-ary function symbol in $\mathcal{L}_2$ and a n-ary relation for each n-ary relation symbol in $\mathcal{L}_2$.[+] A formula F in $\mathcal{L}_2$ is said to be <u>true</u> in the structure γ if its <u>universal</u> closure is true in γ. The universal closure of a formula is obtained by binding all free occurrences of variables in F by universal quantifiers.

In the following we derive two semantic algebras from a Hoare-like specification of PL($\mathcal{L}_1$). One algebra $\mathfrak{A}_H(\mathcal{L}_2,D)$ is based on a deductive system D for the data types of $\mathcal{L}_2$ and incorporates the usual rule of consequence |19|. The other $\mathfrak{A}_H(\mathcal{L}_2,\gamma)$ is constructed in order to be able to separate the issue of completeness of D. Given a structure[++] γ for the assertion language $\mathcal{L}_2$ we construct a semantic algebra for PL($\mathcal{L}_1$) from the usual rules of inference |19| and the true implications $F \to F'$. Let $\mathcal{F}(\mathcal{L})$ be the set of all formulas in the first-order language $\mathcal{L}$.

<u>Definition 3.</u> Let $\phi \subset \mathcal{F}(\mathcal{L}) \times \mathcal{F}(\mathcal{L})$, i.e. ϕ is a binary relation on formulas. The closure $CL(\phi,\gamma)$ of ϕ with respect to γ is the smallest binary relation Υ that contains ϕ and if $(F_1,F_2) \in \Upsilon$ and $G_1 \to F_1$, $F_2 \to G_2$ are true in γ, it also contains (G_1,G_2).

Let $\mathcal{L}_1$, an extension $\mathcal{L}_2$ of $\mathcal{L}_1$ and a structure γ for $\mathcal{L}_2$ be given. We define an algebra with domains:

$$A_{co} = \{\phi : \phi \text{ is a binary relation on } \mathcal{F}(\mathcal{L}_2)\}$$

$A_{exp} = L_{exp}$, $A_{boolexp} = L_{boolexp}$, $A_{cons} = L_{cons}$, $A_{id} = L_{id}$

and with operations:

$$O_{skip}: \to A_{co}, \quad O_{skip}(\,) = CL(\{(F,F): F \in \mathcal{F}(\mathcal{L}_2)\},\gamma)$$

$$O_{assign}: A_{id} \times A_{exp} \to A_{co}, \quad O_{assign}(x,E) = CL(\{(F_x^E,F): F \in \mathcal{F}(\mathcal{L}_2)\},\gamma)$$ [+++]

$$O_{concat}: A_{co} \times A_{co} \to A_{co}$$

$$O_{contact}(\phi_1,\phi_2) = \phi_1 \circ \phi_2 \text{ (product of binary relations)}$$

[+] We will assume for simplicity that the functions and predicates are total.

[++] Obviously, γ can also be viewed as providing a structure for the language $\mathcal{L}_1$.

[+++] F_x^E is the formula resulting by substituting all free occurrences of x by E.

$$O_{if}: A_{boolexp} \times A_{co} \times A_{co} \to A_{co}$$

$$O_{if}(B,\phi_1,\phi_2) = \{(F,G): (F \wedge B,G) \in \phi_1, (F \wedge \neg B,G) \in \phi_2\}$$

$$O_{while}: A_{boolexp} \times A_{co} \to A_{co}$$

$$O_{while}(B,\phi) = CL(\{(F,F \wedge \neg B): (F \wedge B,F) \in \phi\},\gamma)$$

The definition of the remaining operations is obvious. We define

$$\mathfrak{A}_H(\mathcal{L}_2,\gamma) = [\{M_{co},M_{exp}\ldots\}, \{O_{skip},\ldots O_{while}\ldots\}]$$

to be the unique subalgebra which is generated by the operations. $\mathfrak{A}_H(\mathcal{L}_2,\gamma)$ is the smallest subalgebra of the algebra $[\{A_{co},A_{exp}\ldots\}, \{O_{skip},\ldots O_{while}\ldots\}]$.

<u>REMARK 2.</u> Let γ be a structure for $\mathcal{L}_2$, then there is a unique homomorphism h from $\mathfrak{A}(\mathcal{L}_1)$ to $\mathfrak{A}_H(\mathcal{L}_2,\gamma)$. h is onto, hence $\mathfrak{A}_H(\mathcal{L}_2,\gamma)$ is a semantic algebra.

Let us now consider the case that we have a deductive system D for our assertion language $\mathcal{L}_2$, i.e. a set of axioms and inference rules. We define similarly the closure of a binary relation on formulas with respect to D. Let π be a binary relation on formulas, then $CL(\pi,D)$ is given as follows

1) $\pi \subset CL(\pi,D)$
2) if $(F_1,F_2) \in CL(\pi,D)$, $F_1' \vdash_D F_1$, $F_2 \vdash_D F_2'$ then $(F_1',F_2') \in CL(\pi,D)$

where $F_1' \vdash_D F_1$ means that F_1 can be proven in D under hypothesis F_1'.

As before we build an algebra with

$$B_{co} = \{\pi : \pi \text{ is r.e. bin. relation on } \mathcal{F}(\mathcal{L}_2)\}$$

$$B_{exp} = L_{exp}, B_{boolexp} = L_{boolexp}, A_{id} = L_{id}$$

$$A_{cons} = L_{cons}$$

and operations as before where the closure with respect to γ is substituted by the closure $CL(\pi,D)$ with respect to D. E.g.

$$O_{while}(B,\pi) = CL(\{(F,F \wedge \neg B) : (F \wedge B,F) \in \pi\},D)$$

Let $\mathfrak{A}_H(\mathcal{L}_2,D)$ denote the subalgebra generated by the operations. As before there is a unique homomorphism from $\mathfrak{A}(\mathcal{L}_1)$ onto $\mathfrak{A}_H(\mathcal{L}_2,D)$.

It should be clear by now, how any other semantic specification of $PL(\mathcal{L}_1)$ can be treated in the same way. If we take e.g. Dijkstra's weakest precondition approach then we proceed as follows: we consider Dijkstra's function wp as a function from programs X and sets of states U to sets of states. wp (X,U) is the largest set U' with: starting the program in a state $s \in U'$ garanties that X halts in a state of U.

Let γ be a structure for $\mathcal{L}_1$. The algebra associated with wp is built from

$$A_{co} = \{d: d \text{ is a mapping from } \mathcal{P}(S) \text{ to } \mathcal{P}(S)\}$$

where $\mathcal{P}(S)$ is the power set of the set of states S. A state+ is a mapping from variables to $|\gamma|$. Let $A_{exp} = \{m: m \text{ maps } S \text{ to } |\gamma|\}$ $A_{boolexp} = \{b: b \text{ maps to } S \text{ to } \{true, false\}\}$, $A_{id} = L_{id}$, A_{cons} = constants of $|\gamma|$. Then e.g. the meaning of the while construct is given by: Let U range over elements of $\mathcal{P}(S)$

$O_{while}(b,d) = \lambda U \{s \in S: \exists k : s \in H(k,U,b,d)\}$ where

$H(0,U,b,d) = \{s \in Def(b) : b(s) = false\} \cap U$, $H(k,U,b,d) =$

$(\{s \in Def(b) : b(s) = true \text{ implies } s \in d(H(k-1,U,b,d))\} \cap$

$\{s \in Def(b): b(s) = true\}) \cup H(0,U,b,d)$

The remaining operations are defined similarly. The subalgebra generated by the operations is a semantic algebra for $\mathfrak{A}(\mathcal{L}_1)$. It will be denoted by $\mathfrak{A}_D(\mathcal{L}_1, \gamma)$.

5. Comparing Semantics

In this section we want to study the relation between denotational and the different assertion semantics. To do so we briefly sketch a denotational algebra.

A denotational semantic description of the language $PL(\mathcal{L}_1)$ is given by a structure γ for $\mathcal{L}_1$ and by

$$A_{co} = |S_{\perp\top} \to S_{\perp\top}|$$

where $S_{\perp\top} = S \cup \{\perp,\top\}$ is the complete flat lattice of states and $|\to|$ denotes the domain of continuous functions.

$$A_{exp} = |S_{\perp\top} \to |\gamma|_{\perp\top}|$$

where $|\gamma|_{\perp\top}$ is the flat complete lattice constructed from the set $|\gamma|$.

$A_{boolexp} = |S_{\perp\top} \to \{true, false, \perp, \top\}|$, $A_{id} = L_{id}$, A_{cons} = constants of γ. The operations are defined as usual, e.g. the meaning of the while-loop is the least fixed point of

$\Omega(y) = O_{if}(b, O_{concat}(f,y), O_{skip})$, i.e.

+Remember that it is assumed that variables act as an input to programs and have a value before a program is executed

$O_{while}(b,f) = O_{if}(b, O_{concat}(f, O_{while}(b,f), O_{skip})$

The subalgebra generated from the operations will be denoted by $\mathfrak{A}_S(\mathcal{L}_1,\mathfrak{r})$. In the remainder of this section we are going to compare the given semantic algebras via homomorphisms. The following two lemmas are helpful for establishing the existence of homomorphisms.

LEMMA 3. Let G be an unambiguous reduced context-free grammar, $\mathfrak{A}_G$ the syntactic algebra of G, $\mathfrak{A}$, $\mathfrak{B}$ semantic algebras. If there is a homomorphism h from $\mathfrak{A}$ to $\mathfrak{B}$ then $h_A(z) = h_{\mathfrak{B},A}(h^{-1}_{\mathfrak{A},A}(z))$[+] $A\in N$ where $h_{\mathfrak{A}}:\mathfrak{A}_G \to \mathfrak{A}$, $h_{\mathfrak{B}}:\mathfrak{A}_G \to \mathfrak{B}$ are the unique homomorphisms existing according to REMARK 1.

LEMMA 4. Let G, $\mathfrak{A}_G$, $\mathfrak{A}$, $\mathfrak{B}$ be as in LEMMA 3. If for every nonterminal A of G the relation $\{(h_{\mathfrak{A},A}(x_A), h_{\mathfrak{B},A}(x_A)) : x_A \in L_A)\}$ is a mapping then $\{h_A\}_{A\in N}$ with $h_A(x) = h_{\mathfrak{B},A}(z)$ for some z with $h_{\mathfrak{A},A}(z) = x$ is a homomorphism from $\mathfrak{A}$ to $\mathfrak{B}$.

Let us now consider the language PL($\mathcal{L}_1$). The grammar of PL($\mathcal{L}_1$) is unambiguous and reduced hence LEMMAS 3 and 4 can be applied. We compare first the Dijkstra-like semantics with the Scott-like semantics. Using LEMMAS 3 and 4 we can prove

THEOREM 5. Scott's semantics and Dijkstra's semantics for PL($\mathcal{L}_1$) are isomorphic, i.e. $\mathfrak{A}_S(\mathcal{L}_1,\mathfrak{r})$ is isomorphic to $\mathfrak{A}_D(\mathcal{L}_1,\mathfrak{r})$.

REMARK 6. Let $f = h_{co}(X)$ be the denotational meaning of X, $U\subset S$. Let $d = \lambda U f^{-1}(U)$ and $s\in S$.[++] Let $\{U_i\}_{i\in I}$ be the family of subsets of S such that $s\in d(U_i)$. Then $\bigcap_{i\in I} U_i$ contains exactly one element or $I = \emptyset$.

By THEOREM 5 and REMARK 6 we can give the homomorphism from $\mathfrak{A}_D(\mathcal{L}_1,\mathfrak{r})$ to $\mathfrak{A}_S(\mathcal{L}_1,\mathfrak{r})$ by associating with each $d = g_{co}(X)$ (i.e. the Dijkstra-meaning of X) the following mapping f: $S_{\bot\top} \to S_{\bot\top}$

$$f(\bot) = \bot \qquad f(\top) = \top \qquad f(s) = \begin{cases} \bigcap_{s\in d(U)} U & \text{if } \exists U: s\in d(U) \\ \bot & \text{else} \end{cases}$$

The above shows that basically the Scott-like semantics for PL($\mathcal{L}_1$) and the Dijkstra-like semantics are the same; moreover it is shown how the Scott-meaning of a program is calculated from the Dijkstra-meaning and vice versa.

Let us now compare Scott-like and Hoare-like semantics.

Definition 4. Let $\mathcal{L}_2 \supset \mathcal{L}_1$ be first-order languages, $\mathfrak{r}$ a structure for $\mathcal{L}_2$. We say (F_1,F_2) holds for f, f: $S_{\bot\top} \to S_{\bot\top}$, iff whenever for $s\in S$

[+] For any function f: A → B, $f^{-1}(b) = \{a: f(a) = b\}$.

[++] $f^{-1}(U) = \{x\in S: f(x)\in U\}$.

$F_{1\,(y_1,\ldots y_n)}^{(s(y_1),\ldots s(y_n))}$ is true in γ then $f(s) = s'$ S implies that

$F_{2\,(z_1,\ldots z_m)}^{(s'(z_1),\ldots s'(z_m))}$ is true in γ. $y_1,\ldots y_n$ (resp. $z_1,\ldots z_m$)

are the free variables of F_1 (resp. F_2).

<u>LEMMA 7.</u> Let X be a program, i.e. $X \in L_{co}$, $h: \mathfrak{A}(\mathcal{L}_1) \to \mathfrak{A}_S(\mathcal{L}_1, \gamma)$
$i: \mathfrak{A}(\mathcal{L}_1) \to \mathfrak{A}_H(\mathcal{L}_2, \gamma)$

the unique homomorphism. Then $(F_1, F_2) \in i_{co}(X)$ implies that (F_1, F_2) holds for $h_{co}(X)$. (Compare |20|, |29|).

<u>Corollary 8</u>. Let $j: \mathfrak{A}(\mathcal{L}_1) \to \mathfrak{A}_H(\mathcal{L}_2, D)$ where D is a deductive system such that γ is a model. Then $(F_1, F_2) \in j_{co}(X)$ implies (F_1, F_2) holds for $h_{co}(X)$.

The relation between $\mathfrak{A}_S(\mathcal{L}_1, \gamma)$ and $\mathfrak{A}_H(\mathcal{L}_2, D)$ expressed in Corollary 8 if often phrased the "consistency of the axiomatic definition" |30| or the "consistency of axiomatic and denotational semantics" |20|. As the following results show this relation between semantic algebras is weaker than the existence of homomorphisms.

<u>THEOREM 9.</u> Let $\mathcal{L}_1 \subseteq \mathcal{L}_2$ be first-order languages, D a deductive system for $\mathcal{L}_2$ and γ a structure for $\mathcal{L}_2$ that is a model of D. Let $\{X_i\}_{i \in \mathbb{N}}$ be an effective enumeration of all programs X_i computing functions of one variable. If there is a recursive set of variable-free expressions $E_i \in L_{exp}$, $i \in \mathbb{N}$, such that

$$\{i: X_i \text{ does not halt for } x_i = E_i\}$$

is not recursively enumerable then there is no homomorphism from Scott's semantics $\mathfrak{A}_S(\mathcal{L}_1, \gamma)$ to a factor algebra $\mathfrak{A}_H(\mathcal{L}_2, D)/E$ with $(\phi_1 \; E_{co} \; \phi_2$ iff $\phi_1 = \phi_2)$.

<u>Corollary 10</u>. If $\mathcal{L}_1 = \mathcal{L}_{\mathbb{N}}$ with nonlogical symbols $\{0,1,+,\cdot,=,<\}$ and the restriction of γ to $\mathcal{L}_1$ is the standard model for the natural numbers then there is no homomorphism from $\mathfrak{A}_S(\mathcal{L}_1, \gamma)$ to $\mathfrak{A}_H(\mathcal{L}_2, D)$ or any factor algebra as above.

We investigate now the relationship between the semantic algebras $\mathfrak{A}_S(\mathcal{L}_1, \gamma)$ and $\mathfrak{A}_H(\mathcal{L}_2, \gamma)$. Similarly to |29|, we define when the language

$\mathcal{L}_2$ is expressive. The expressiveness of $\mathcal{L}_2$ guarantees the existence of homomorphisms.

<u>THEOREM 11</u>. If $\mathcal{L}_2$ is expressive relative to $\mathcal{L}_1$ and γ then there is a homomorphism from $\mathfrak{A}_H(\mathcal{L}_2,\gamma)$ to $\mathfrak{A}_S(\mathcal{L}_1,\gamma)$.

<u>COROLLARY 12</u>. Under the condition of THEOREM 11 there is a congruence relation $E = \{E_{co}, E_{exp} \ldots\}$ on $\mathfrak{A}_H(\mathcal{L}_2,\gamma)$ such that $\mathfrak{A}_S(\mathcal{L}_1,\gamma)$ and $\mathfrak{A}_H(\mathcal{L}_2,\gamma)/E$ are isomorphic. Moreover $\Pi_1 E_{co} \Pi_2$ iff $\Pi_1 = \Pi_2$.

<u>COROLLARY 13</u>. If $\mathcal{L}_2$ is expressive relative to $\mathcal{L}_1$ and γ and if γ is a model of D and D is semantically complete relative to γ then there is a congruence F on $\mathfrak{A}_H(\mathcal{L}_2, D)$ such that $\mathfrak{A}_S(\mathcal{L}_1,\gamma)$ and $\mathfrak{A}_H(\mathcal{L}_2,D)/F$ are isomorphic.

Some results of this section can be summarized in the following diagram.

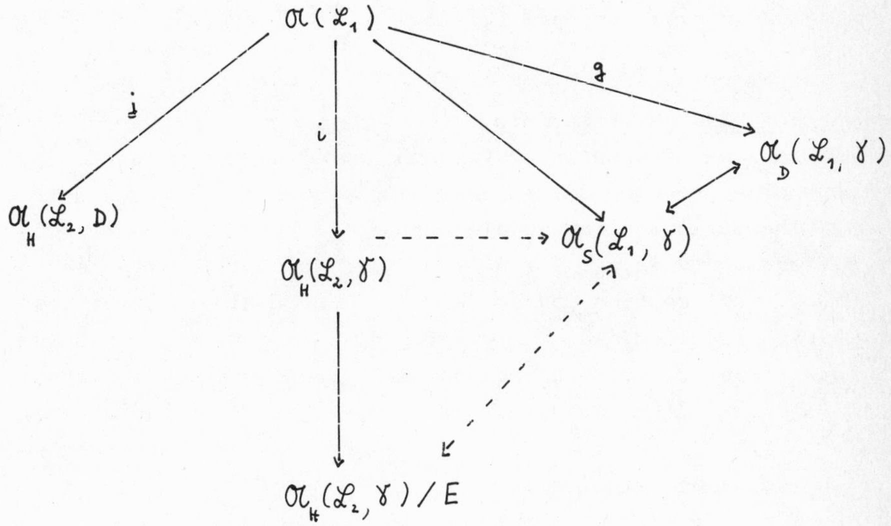

$$\Pi_1 E_{co} \Pi_2 \text{ iff } \Pi_1 = \Pi_2$$

Here a solid arrow expresses a homomorphism and a dotted arrow means a homomorphism if $\mathcal{L}_2$ is expressive.

In the previous results we considered one fixed deductive system for formulas of the form $F_1\{X\}F_2$, i.e. Hoare's original rules |19|. Let us now briefly consider the general case. Let $(H',D',\mathcal{L}_2)$ be a deductive system for formulas of the form $F_1\{X\}F_2$, i.e. H' consists of the rules for the language constructs of $PL(\mathcal{L}_1)$. D' is a deductive system for the data types expressed in the language $\mathcal{L}_2$. In analogy to section 4 we construct an algebra $\mathfrak{M}(H',D',\mathcal{L}_2) = [\{M'_{co},M'_{exp}\ldots\},\{O_{skip},\ldots\}]$. Let $\mathfrak{A}(H',D',\mathcal{L}_2)$ be its semantic subalgebra.

LEMMA 14. Let $\mathcal{L}_2 \supset \mathcal{L}_1$ and γ be a model for D'. Then $(H',D',\mathcal{L}_2)$ is sound and complete relative to the denotational semantics $\mathfrak{A}_S(\mathcal{L}_1,\gamma)$ iff the mapping $\rho : \mathfrak{A}_S(\mathcal{L}_1,\gamma) \to \mathfrak{M}$ where

$$\rho(f) = \{(P,Q): (P,Q) \text{ holds for } f\}$$

is a homomorphism from $\mathfrak{A}_S(\mathcal{L}_1,\gamma)$ to $\mathfrak{A}(H',D',\mathcal{L}_2)/E$. The congruence Ξ is defined as follows: $\phi_1 \; E_{co} \; \phi_2$ iff $\phi_1 = \phi_2$ and expressions are equivalent iff they induce the same mapping.

LEMMA 14 states that the notion of soundness and completeness of a deductive system for formulas $F_1\{X\}F_2$ can be characterized algebraically.

6. Abstraction, Axioms, Fixpoints

In the previous sections we have seen how different semantic specifications of a programming language can be presented in the same framework. The various semantic algebras which have been described before differ mainly in the formalism chosen to describe the meaning of a command. The question can be raised if one could abstract from the formalisms involved. We will briefly discuss the issue in the following. Let us consider the programming language $PL(\mathcal{L}_1)$. Every semantic algebra $\mathfrak{A}$ is by definition a homomorphic image of the syntactic algebra $\mathfrak{A}(\mathcal{L}_1)$, i.e. $\mathfrak{A} = \mathfrak{A}(\mathcal{L}_1)/E$ for a uniquely determined congruence relation E. Hence one might say

"semantics is a congruence relation on syntax"

As isomorphic algebras can be considered to be the "same" one could think of factor algebras of the syntactic algebra instead of those involving an additional formalism. The question arises how the desirable equivalence relations are characterized. We have seen before, that a semantic specification of $PL(\mathcal{L}_1)$ can be interpreted as a semantic algebra. But there are many semantic algebras and hence corresponding equivalence relations which we would have not been willing to accept as "semantics" for $PL(\mathcal{L}_1)$. This means that--in our mind-- we have some "axioms" that a semantic algebra must fulfill in order to be acceptable as semantics for $PL(\mathcal{L}_1)$. That is, there must be a theory of program meanings in our mind by which we distinguish reasonable semantic algebras from the others.

We attempt in the following to give some first axioms for such a theory. The language of the theory contains 1) variables for program meaning: χ, χ', 2) variables for the meaning of quantifier-free formulas of $_1$: β, β', 3) variables for the meaning of terms of L_1: ε, ε', 4) the function symbols for the program constructors O_{concat}, O_{while}, O_{if}, and some command symbols (=0-ary function symbols), e.g. O_{skip}, 5) an equality predicate = (for every type), 6) the logical connectives and quantifiers.

Some of the axioms all semantic algebras which where given in the previous sections fulfill are

TS1) $O_{concat}(\chi, O_{skip}) = O_{concat}(O_{skip},\chi) =$

TS2) $O_{concat}(\chi, O_{concat}(\chi',\chi'')) = O_{concat}(O_{concat}(\chi,\chi'),\chi'')$

TS3) $O_{if}(true,\chi,\chi') = \chi$

TS4) $O_{if}(\beta,\chi,\chi') = O_{if}(\neg\beta,\chi',\chi)$

TS5) $O_{while}(\beta,\chi) = O_{if}(\beta, O_{concat}(\chi, O_{while}(\beta,\chi)),O_{skip})$

In |37| a more elaborate list of axioms can be found. E.g. if we extended the language PL($\mathcal{L}_1$) to include procedures similar to |34| we would get some axioms about procedure calls (call(p) is a command) call(p) = ... where p is a procedure name. The right-hand side of the equation would be an expression involving the procedure body. If the procedure were recursive we would get TS6) call(P) = ... call(P) ...

The axioms we find for Pl($\mathcal{L}_1$) can be interpreted in two differnt ways. In the <u>first</u> place we can view the axioms as a <u>formalization</u> of our <u>intuitive understanding</u> of the constructs. Verifying that the various semantic algebras fulfill the laws proves that constructing formal semantics one has been <u>successful</u> in capturing our intuition. The <u>second</u> interpretation deals with fixed points. Let us consider TS5) and TS6). Both axioms can be considered as generic fixed point equations. TS5) e.g. states that the meaning of the program "while B do St" in a semantic algebra $\mathfrak{A} = [\{A_{co},...\},\{O_{skip},...\}]$ must be a fixed point of the operator

$$\Omega_{b,st}: A_{co} \to A_{co}$$

$$\Omega_{b,st}(y) = O_{if}(b, O_{concat}(st,y), O_{skip})$$

where b (resp.st) is the meaning of B (resp. St) in $\mathfrak{A}$.
It is known that this holds true for Scott's semantics by definition. In |37| we show that TS5) is true for all other kinds of semantics for PL($\mathcal{L}_1$). Moreover, some results of |34| can be obtained as corollaries of our investigations.

OPEN PROBLEM. How far can we get in finding axioms for semantics for Pl($\mathcal{L}_1$)? Is it possible to characterize the commonly used semantics axiomatically?

References

|1| Lucas, P.: Formal Definition of Programming Languages and Systems. IFIP Congress, 71, August 1971.

|2| Lucas, P., P. Lauer, H. Stigleither: Method and Notation for the Formal Definition of Programming Languages. Technical Report TR-250-87. IBM, Vienna Laboratories, 1970.

|3| Lucas, P., K. Walk: On the Formal Definition of PL/I. Annual Review in Automatic Programming 6. Eds: M. Halpern and C. Shaw. Pergamon Press, 1971.

|4| Wegner, P.: The Vienna Definition Language. Computing Surveys 4, 1. March 1972.

|5| Knuth, D.: Semantics of Context-free Languages. Mathematical Systems Theory 2, 1968.

|6| McCarthy, J.: A Formal Definition of a Subset of Algol. Formal Language Description Language for Computer Programming, Proceedings of IFIP Working Conference on Formal Language Description Language. North-Holland Publ., 1966.

|7| Lauer, P.: Consistent and Complementary Formal Definitions of Programming Languages. Techn. Report TR 25-121. IBM, Vienna Laboratory, 1971.

|8| Landin, P.: A Formal Description of Algol 60. Formal Language Description Language for Computer Programming. Proceedings of IFIP Working Conference on Formal Language Description Languages. North-Holland, 1966.

|9| Landin, P.: A Lambda-Calculus Approach. Advances in Programming and Nonnumerical Computation. Ed.: L. Fox., Pergamon Press, 1966.

|10| McCarthy, J.: Towards a Mathematical Theory of Computation. IFIP Congress 1962. North-Holland, 1962.

|11| McCarthy, J.: A Basis for a Mathematical Theory of Computation. Computer Programming and Formal Systems. Eds.: P. Braffort and D. Hirschberg. North-Holland, 1963.

|12| Strachey, C.: Towards Formal Semantics. Formal Language Description Language for Computer Programming. Proceedings of IFIP Working Conference on Formal Language Description Languages. North-Holland, 1966.

|13| Scott, D.: Outline of a Mathematical Theory of Computation. Proceedings of the Fourth Annual Princeton Conference on Information Science and Systems, 1970.

|14| Scott, D.: Continuous Lattices. Technical Monograph PR 6-7, Oxford University, August, 1971.

|15| Scott, D.: Lattice Theory, Data Types and Formal Semantics. NYU Symposium on Formal Semantics. Prentice Hall, 1972.

|16| Scott, D.: C. Strachey: Towards a Mathematical Semantics for Computer Languages. Computers and Automata. Ed.: J. Fox, John Wiley, 1972.

|17| Scott, D.: The Lattice of Flow Diagrams. Semantics of Algorithmic Languages. Ed.: E. Engeler. Springer Notes in Mathematics, vol. 188.

|18| Floyd, R.: Assigning Meaning to Programs. Proceedings of Symposia in Applied Mathematics, vol. 19, Mathematical Aspects of Computer Science, 1967.

|19| Hoare, C.A.R.: An Axiomatic Approach to Computer Programming. CACM 12, 10, October, 1969.

|20| Hoare, C.A.R., P.E. Lauer: Consistent and Complementary Formal Theories of The Semantics of Programming Languages. Acta Informatica, 3,2, 1974.

|21| Dijkstra, E.W.: A Simple Axiomatic Basis for Programming Language Constructs. EWD 72. Technological University, Eindhoven, 1973.

|22| Goguen, J.A.: Semantics of Computation. Proceedings of the First International Symposium on Category Theory Applied to Computation and Control. Lecture Notes in Computer Science 25. Springer, 1975.

|23| Burstall, R.M.: Proving Properties of Programs by Structural Induction. Computer Journal 12, 1969.

|24| Burstall, R.M., P.J. Laudin: Programs and their Proofs: an Algebraic Approach. Machine Intelligence, 4. Edinburgh Press, 1969.

|25| Goguen, J.A., J.W. Thatcher, E.E. Wagner, J.B. Wright: Initial Algebra Semantics and Continuous Algebras. JACM 24, 1 1977.

|26| Burstall, R.M.: An algebraic description of Programs with Assertions, Verification and Simulation. Proc. ACM Conference and Proving Assertions about Programs. Las Cruces, New Mexico, 1972.

|27| Reynolds, J.C.: Formal Semantics. Preliminary Draft for COSIRS, 1976.

|28| Chirica, L. D.F. Martin: An Algebraic Formulation of Knuthian Semantics. Proc. 17th Annual IEEE Symposium on Formulations of Computer Science, Houston, Texas, 1978.

|29| Cook, S.A.: Soundness and Completeness of an Axiom System for Program Verification. SIAM J. on Computing vol. 7, no. 1, 1978.

|30| Donahue, J.E.: Complementary Definitions of Programming Language Semantics. Springer Lecture Notes in Computer Science, 42, 1976.

|31| Majster, M.E.: Data Types, Abstract Data Types and their Specification Problem. Theoretical Computer Science, 8, 1979.

|32| Goguen, J.A., J.W. Thatcher, E.G. Wagner: An Initial Approach to the Specification Correctness and Implementation of Abstract Data Types. Corrent Trends in Programming Methodology, vol. 4, Data Structuring. Ed.: R. Yeh. Prentice Hall, 1978.

|33| Majster, M.E.: A unified view of semantics, Technical Report TR79-394, Cornell University (1979). Also submitted for publication.

|34| Clarke, E.M.: Program invariants as fixed points, Computing 19, 1, 1978.

|35| de Bakker, J.W.: Fixed point semantics and Dijkstra's fundamental invariance theorem, Mathematical Centre, January 1975.

|36| de Bakker, J.W., Meerteus, L.G.L.: On the completeness of the induction assertion method, Mathematical Centre, December 1975.

|37| Majster, M.E.: General properties of semantics. Technical Report in preparation.

MEASURING THE EXPRESSIVE POWER OF DYNAMIC LOGICS: AN APPLICATION OF ABSTRACT MODEL THEORY

J.A. Makowsky

2.Mathematisches Institut der Freien Universität Berlin

Königin-Luise-Str. 24-26, 1 Berlin 33, West Berlin

ABSTRACT: We compare two notions to measure the expressive power of various dynamic logics: Reducibility and AP-reducibility. With those and the techniques from model theory for infinitary and other generalized logics we solve some open problems in definability theory of dynamic logic.

0. Introduction

The following note introduces some concepts of abstract model theory (i.e. the model theory of infinitary and generalized first order logic [Ba,MSS]) and applies them in the study of the expressive power of dynamic logics.
This approach is the author's. In chapter 1 the abstract framework is outlined. A survey of some of the recent development in abstract model theory may be found in [Ba,MSS] . For dynamic logic we refer to [Ha]. In chapter 2 we present our main theorem: All dynamic first order logics presented in [Ha] are AP-equivalent, though not equivalent. Here logics are equivalent if they can be translated into each other, and AP-equivalent means that such a translation exists only with the help of auxiliary predicates. In the light of abstract model theory this is just a corollary to a theorem due to A.Meyer and R.Parikh [MP], and this chapter is actually due to R.Parikh and the author. While we

both were visiting the ETH-Zurich R. Parikh asked me to explain to him some aspects of weak second order logic, for he suspected that theorem 8 below could be generalized to weak second order logic. This is indeed possible if we allow AP-reducibility. In chapter 3 we draw some consequences of the general theory to the new operation loop added to dynamic logic. This was suggested to me by V. Pratt and R. Parikh during the same visit in Zurich. Chapter 4 finally gives characterization of logics which behave nicely with respect to occurrence of and dependency on relation or function symbols. For this we have to define what it means that a formula does not depend on a predicate or function symbol which does occur in it. The logic behaves nicely, if whenever such a situation occurs, then there is a formula, in which the symbol does not occur and which is equivalent to it. We shall call such logics occurrency normal. The main result then connects this property with the Δ-closure of logics as studied in [MSS]. The results of this chapter are even new in the context of abstract model theory. Consequences of this will be studied in further details in a different paper. The possibility of such a characterization was suggested to me by a question of M. Ziegler. It turns out, that there is, up to equivalence, only one dynamic logic which is occurency normal. This should be of some significance for the choice of dynamic logics. It is clear from our approach that the same methods can be applied to study various logics connected with programs, e.g. algorithmic logics as in [Pol]. This will also be presented at a different occasion.

During part of the work on this paper the author was supported by a MINERVA-Grant and enjoied the hospitality of the Hebrew University Jerusalem and the Forschungsinstitut fur Mathematik at the ETH-Zurich as a guest of Erwin Engeler . During the revision of this paper the author was visiting MIT, supported by AFOSR- contract no. F 4 9620-79-C-o174 as a guest of V.Pratt. I am also indebted to A.Meyer, R.Parikh and V.Pratt for answering all my questions on dynamic logic, for their criticism and stimulating discussions. Parts of 3.3 are independently due to A.Meyer and R.Parikh.

1. AP-Reducibility for Logics

1.1 Dynamic Logic

We denote by DL_o the regular dynamic logic described in [Ha] . If π is a new instruction we write $DL_o(\pi)$ for the dynamic logic obtained from DL_o by adjunction of π to the set of instructions. Similarily if σ is a new operation on formulas and/or programs. A dynamic logic D is a logic obtained from DL_o by adjunction of finitely many new instructions $\pi_1,\dots,\pi_n$ and operations $\tau_1,\dots,\tau_k$.

Examples:

Additional instructions possible are

ar the array assignment

rd the random assignment

rt rich test

An additional operation is

loop: Programs $\rightarrow$ Formulas defined in chapter 3.

We denote by DL^{rec} the dynamic logic with recursive programs and DL_f^{rec} the dynamic logic DL^{rec} with the restriction that only finitely many tests occur in a formula or program of DL^{rec} .

1.2 Logics

For this note we shall use a minimum of abstract model theory as developed in [Ba,MSS].

We do not need to know in general, what a logic is, but we shall need four examples, which are typical.

First order logic , denoted by FOL.

Recursive infinitary logic RIL, where infinite conjunctions and disjunctions over recursive sets of formulas are allowed iteratively.

Weak second order logic WSL, which is like FOL, but we allow quantification over finite sets.

Logics with extra quantifiers: We just give two examples: Let Q_o be a new unary quantifier symbol and $Q^{\omega f}$ a new binary quantifier symbol, i.e. Q_o binds one and $Q^{\omega f}$ binds two variables. $FOL(Q_o)$ and $FOL(Q^{\omega f})$ denote the logics obtained from FOL by adjunction of these quantifiers respectively. $Q_o x\varphi$ is interpreted by "there are only finitely x such that φ" and $Q^{\omega f} xy\,\varphi$ is interpreted by "the set of $\langle x,y\rangle$ such that $\varphi(x,y)$ is a well ordering of the domain of φ" .

In this note logics are either dynamic logics or one of the above examples.

1.3 AP-Reducibility

Let L_1, L_2 be two logics. L_1 is *AP-reducible* to L_2 $(L_1 \subset_{AP} L_2)$ if for every similarity type τ and every τ-formula φ of L_1 there is a similarity type τ' extending τ and a τ'-formula ψ of L_2 such that (i) every model of φ can be expanded to a model of ψ and (ii) every model of ψ is a model of φ . [In model theory we say that every projective class of L_1 is a projective class of L_2] L_1 and L_2 are *AP-equivalent*, $L_1 \cong_{AP} L_2$, if $L_1 \subset_{AP} L_2$ and $L_2 \subset_{AP} L_1$. [AP stands for Reducibility with Additional Predicates]. Clearly AP-reducibility is transitive and reflexiv. If $L_1 \subset_{AP} L_2$ and τ' is always equal to τ we say that L_1 is *reducible* to L_2 and write $L_1 \subset L_2$. Similarily $L_1 \cong L_2$ is called *equivalent* and defined by $L_1 \subset L_2$ and $L_2 \subset L_1$.

1.4 Finitely generated logics

A logic is *finitely* generated if it is generated by a finite number of finitary operations and instructions. It is *recursively* generated if there are recursive formation rules.

All the logics mentioned here are recursively generated.

$FOL, DL(\pi_1 \ldots \pi_n, \tau_1, \ldots, \tau_k)$, WSL, $FOL(Q_o, Q^{\omega f})$ are finitely generated, RIL, DL^{rec} and DL_f^{rec} are not.

1.5 The validity Problem

The validity problem for all dynamic logics considered here is Π^1_1 if we consider all the wff's. A theorem of Lindstrom will shed some light on this. First we observe that all logics we consider here here have the ***Löwenheim Property*** (LP) which states that every satisfiable formula is satisfiable in a finite or countable domain. It is also clear, that this LP is a reasonable assumption from a computer scientists point of view. Now Lindström proved [Li]:

THEOREM 1 (Lindström) Let L_1 be a logic satisfying LP and which is recursively generated. Then

(i) If the validity problem of L_1 is Σ^0_1 then $L_1 \simeq$ FOL.

(ii) If L_1 is not reducible to FOL, then the validity problem is at least Π^1_1.

This should be combined with

THEOREM 2 Let L_1, L_2 be recursively generated logics and $L_1 \simeq_{AP} L_2$. Let Val_1, Val_2 be the set of valid sentences of L_1, resp. L_2. Then for each $k \in \mathbb{N}$, $i = 0,1$ we have that $Val_1 \in \Pi^i_k$ (Σ^i_k) iff $Val_2 \in \Pi^i_k$ (Σ^i_k).

The proof is like in [MSS].

This together with theorem 9 below reproves all the results about the validity problem of dynamic logics concerning all wff's.

1.6 Some reduction results.

The main advantage of AP-reducibility is the transfer of many properties of the logics in question. Theorem 2 tells us this about the validity problem. In [MSS] this has been proved also for compactness and LP. But there are indications that AP-reducibility is too coarse. In particular most dynamic logics are not closed under substitutions of arbitrary formulas into tests. If they are this amounts to rich tests (rt) being present. But now we have the following

THEOREM 3 Let D be an arbitrary dynamic logic. Then $D \simeq_{AP} D(\underline{rt})$.

Proof: Let t be a test which occurs in a formula $\alpha(t)$. If t is β then $\alpha(\beta)$ is equivalent to $\alpha(R) \& \forall x(R \leftrightarrow \beta)$ where R has the same free variables as β. QED.

With this we can prove also

THEOREM 4 Let D_1 and D_2 be dynamic logics which contain rd and such that $D_1 \simeq_{AP} D_2$. Let π be a new instruction or operation on programs and/or formulas. Then $D_1(\pi) \simeq_{AP} D_2(\pi)$.

Outline of proof: We use the transitivity of AP-equivalence, theorem 3 and the fact that rich tests together with random assignment allows us to pass between formulas and programs. QED.

2. Measuring the expressive power of logics

2.1. *Equivalence vs. AP-equivalence*

Section 1.6 tells us something about the expressive power of dynamic logics, for they are AP- equivalent. The aim of this chapter is to show that most of them are AP-equivalent. This shows us that differencies in the expressive power of most dynamic logics are "accidental" in the sense that to show their equivalence one needs additional predicates. This means introducing "abbreviations" for certain procedures and is done freely in mathematics and programming. The results of this chapter are, unless otherwise stated the result of joint work of the author with R. Parikh.

2.2 *Some results from abstract model theory*

The following theorem is implicit in [Ba] and [MSS] .

THEOREM 5 (Barwise) Let L be a logic such that

(i) L is AP-reducible to RIL and

(ii) $FOL(Q_o)$ is AP-reducible to L

Then L is AP-equivalent to RIL .

COROLLARY 6 RIL and WSL are AP-equivalent.

THEOREM 7 (Folklore, [Ba,MSS]) For every logic L there is, up to equivalence, a unique logic $\Delta(L)$ such that (i) $\Delta(L)$ is AP-equivalent to L and (ii) . For every logic $L_1 \subset L$ L_1 and $L_1 \subset_{AP} L$ we have $L_1 \subset \Delta(L)$.

A further characterization of $\Delta(L)$ will follow in chapter 4 .

2.3 *A result of A.Meyer and R.Parikh*

A. Meyer and R. Parikh proved the following theorem, which is fundamental for much of our results.

THEOREM 8 (Meyer-Parikh [MP]) DL^{rec} is equivalent to RIL , but DL^{rec} is not reducible to DL_f^{rec} .

2.4 *The main theorem*

The result of this section was obtained jointly by R. Parikh and the author, while we were both visiting at the ETH-Zürich.

THEOREM 9 (Makowsky-Parikh) Let D be any dynamic logic AP-reducible to DL^{rec} and such that $DL_o \subset D$. Then D is AP-equivalent to both WSL and RIL .
Outline of proof: By corollary 6 it suffices to prove the result for RIL .
By theorem 5 we have to show that $FOL(Q_o)$ is AP-reducible to DL_o , i.e. we have to show that finiteness is expressible in DL_o with some additional predicates.
For this we write a program $\alpha = (n > o? \; ; \; n \leftarrow n-1)^* \; ; -n > 0 \; ?$ on the structure of the natural numbers and note that α is deterministic. So $\langle\alpha\rangle$ true says that α terminates always, hence n is finite. QED

COROLLARY 10 The validity of DL_o and all its extensions $D \subset DL^{rec}$ is Π^1_1 .

Proof: use theorem 9 and 1 and the fact that the validity problem of WSL is Π_1^1 QED

Corollary 10 gives a new proof of theorem 2.11 in [Ha].

Similar results can be obtained the same way for algorithmic logic [Pol.]

3. Loop in Dynamic logic

Some of the results and the main impetus for this chapter come from joint work with V. Pratt and R. Parikh.

3.1 Defining loop

Let α be a program of $DL^{rec}_{f'b}$ i.e. α is finitely branching. We define an operation

loop: programs $\rightarrow$ formulas by

loop α holds if there is an infinite executable sequence of instructions in , i.e. if α can loop.

LEMMA 11 (Harel and Pratt) The following defines

loop inductively for DL_o :

loop $(x \leftarrow t)$ is false

loop $(A?)$ is false

loop $(\alpha;\beta)$ is loop $\alpha \vee \langle\alpha\rangle$ loop β

loop $(\alpha \vee \beta)$ is loop $\alpha \vee$ loop β

loop (α^*) is $\langle\alpha^*\rangle$ loop $\alpha \vee \forall n \langle\alpha^n\rangle$ true

THEOREM 12 DL_o(loop) is AP-equivalent to DL_o and hence to DL^{rec} .

Proof: Lemma 11 gives us a translation of DL_o(loop) into RIL . QED

Note that recently A.Meyer and K.Winklmann have shown that $DL_o \simeq DL_o$(loop) .
Cf. [MW] for more results along these lines.

3.2 *Does the random assignment loop ?*

Does the random assignment loop? We shall examine both possibilities. Intuitively we would first say no. Now look at the following program

$\alpha = (y < x?; y \leftarrow ?; x \leftarrow y)$.

What could $\underline{loop}(\alpha^*)$ express? By lemma 11 we have

$\langle\alpha^*\rangle\ \underline{loop}\ \alpha \vee \forall n \langle\alpha^n\rangle\langle\alpha\rangle True$

If $\underline{loop}\ \alpha$ is false then $loop(\alpha^*)$ expresses that α^* loops, i.e. there are infinite descending sequences in the linear order $<$.

<u>THEOREM 13</u> If $\underline{loop}(x \leftarrow ?)$ is false then $FOL(Q^{\omega f})$ is A^P-reducible to $DL_o(\underline{loop}, \underline{rd})$.

Proof: We shall use the program α from above. Now $\underline{loop}(x \leftarrow ?)$ false implies $\underline{loop}\ \alpha$ false. So let φ be the axioms of a linear ordering $<$, and ψ be $\varphi \wedge - \underline{loop}(\alpha^*)$. Then ψ defines the class of well orderings. QED

In contrast to this we have

<u>THEOREM 14</u> If $\underline{loop}(x \leftarrow ?)$ is true then $DL_o(\underline{loop}, \underline{rd})$ is A^P-equivalent to DL_o . Outline of proof: Use lemma 11, theorem 8 and 9 . QED

3.3 *Well orderings and RIL*

To make more sense out of Theorem 13 we need a result due to Lopez-Escobar.

<u>THEOREM 15</u> (Lopez-Escobar [Ke]). $FOL(Q^{\omega f})$ is not AP-reducible to RIF .

<u>COROLLARY 16</u> If $\underline{loop}(x \leftarrow ?)$ is false, then $DL_o(\underline{rd}, \underline{loop})$ is not AP-reducible to DL^{rec} .

Proof: Theorem 9 again. QED

Corollary 16 contrasts sharply with theorem 13: If $loop(x \leftarrow ?)$ is true, then $\underline{loop}$ can be defined in DL^{rec} or even in $DL_o(\underline{rd})$ with additional predicates, if $\underline{\text{loop}}(x \leftarrow ?)$ is false, then no such definition is possible. It should be pointed out though, that in the first case the definition of loop is rather complicated, i.e. involves a coding of number theory. Another major difference of the two cases will become clear in the next chapter.

4. Occurrence of and dependence on predicate symbols

The content of this chapter is new even for abstract model theory. I am indebted to M. Ziegler and D. Giorgetta for man valuable remarks.

4.1 *Occurrence and dependency*

It is clear what we mean, when we say that a relation or function symbol occur in a formula φ of a logic L in our examples (and it can be made clear also in a abstract definition). Here we want to define what it means that φ does or does not depend on a relation or functionsymbol that does occur in φ. Let L be a logic and $\varphi(R)$ be a formula of L in which some relationsymbol R occures. We say that $\varphi(R)$ *does not depend on* R if the truth of $\varphi(R)$ in some structure does not change with changes of the interpretation of R (and similarily for functionsymbols or free variables). Now assume $\varphi(R)$ does not depend on R. Does there exist a formula ψ in L which has the same relation-symbols as φ, but for R, and such that (i) every model of φ is a model of ψ and (ii) every expansion of a model of ψ is a model of φ? If this is always the case, we say that L *occurrence normal*.

4.2 *Characterizing occurrence normality*

Remember the definition of $\Delta(L)$ for a given logic L in section 2.2.

THEOREM 17 A logic L is occurrence-normal if L is equivalent to $\Delta(L)$.

Proof: In [MSS] it was shown that $\Delta(L) \cong L$ iff the following property Δ holds:

Δ : If R,S are predicatesymbols, $\varphi(R)$, $\psi(S)$ formulas of L and R(S) does not occur in $\psi(\varphi)$ and $\varphi(R) \leftrightarrow \psi(S)$ is valid, then there is a Θ, a formula with all the symbols from φ, ψ but R and S do not occur in Θ, such that $\varphi \leftrightarrow \Theta$ and $\Psi \leftrightarrow \Theta$ are valid.

So we have to show that Δ is equivalent to occurrence-normality(N), which can be written as N : If $\varphi(R) \leftrightarrow \varphi(S)$ is valid (for all R,S) then there is Θ without R,S as in Δ such that $\varphi(R) \leftrightarrow \Theta$ is valid.

Clearly $\Delta \rightarrow N$. Now assume N. Without loss of generality R and S have the same arity. So suppose $\varphi(R) \leftrightarrow \psi(S)$ is valid. So $\varphi(R) \leftrightarrow \psi(R)$ and hence $\psi(R) \leftrightarrow \psi(S)$ are valid. Similarily for $\varphi(R) \leftrightarrow \varphi(S)$. So by N there are $\Theta_\varphi, \Theta_\psi$ satisfying the conclusion of N. But then also $\Theta_\varphi \leftrightarrow \Theta_\psi$ is valid and $\Theta = \Theta_\varphi$ will do. QED

<u>COROLLARY 18</u> If $L_1 \subset_{AP} L_2$ and L_2 occurence-normal then $L_1 \subset L_2$.

4.3 *Which logics are occurrence normal*

So theorem 7 tells us that up to equivalence there is for a given logic L only one logic L' AP-equivalent to L which is occurence normal, i.e. $\Delta(L)$.
It also tells us, with theorem 9 that

<u>THEOREM 19</u> Among all the dynamic logics D with $DL_o \subset D \subset DL^{rec}$ only DL^{rec} is occurrence normal.

Proof: It suffices to show that RIL is occurrence normal by theorem 9 and 7.
This follows from

<u>THEOREM 20</u> (Barwise [Ka]) RIL = Δ(RIL)

together with theorem 17. QED

The following theorem of A. Burgess [MSS] tells us more about <u>loop</u> in the case of theorem 13.

THEOREM 21 (Burgess) Let L be any recursively generated logic with Σ^1_1-satisfaction-predicate, such that $FOL(Q^{\omega f})$ is AP-reducible to L. Then L is not occurrence-normal.

COROLLARY 22 If $\underline{loop}(x \leftarrow ?)$ is false then no recursively generated dynamic logic AP-reducible to $DL_o(\underline{rd},\underline{loop})$ is occurrence-normal.

Proof: Clearly all satisfaction predicates of dynamic logics are Σ^1_1. So we apply theorem 20. QED

5. Conclusion

We think we have showed the following:

- Abstract model theory is a useful tool in the study of the expressive power of dynamic logic. It is clear that those methods can also be applied to algorithmic logic and related logics.
- AP-reducibility is a natural notion to compare expressive power of logics, eventually even more natural than reducibility. Their relationship is described in corollary 18.
- We have clarified the difference between $\underline{loop}(x \leftarrow ?)$ true and false
- And last but not least we solved in section 1.6 some open problems from [Ha], using the concepts of reducibility and AP-reducibility.

We shall present more of the details in a different paper, entitled "Applications of abstract model theory to various programming logics".

References

[Ba] Barwise, K.J., Axioms for abstract model theory, *Annals of mathematical logic, vol. 7* (1974) pp 221-265

[Ha] Harel, D. *First-order Dynamic logic*, Lecture Notes in Computer Science, vol. 68, Heidelberg 1979

[Ke] Keisler,H.J., *Model Theory for Infinitary Logic*, Studies in Logic vol 62, Amsterdam 1971

[MSS] Makowsky,J.A., Shelah,S. and Stavi,J., Δ-Logics and generalized quantifiers, *Annals of mathematical logic, vol 10* (1976) pp 155-192

[MP] Meyer,A. and Parikh,R., Definability in dynamic logic, MIT/LCS/TM-156, 198o

[Pol] Banachowski,L. et al., An Introduction to algorithmic logic; Metamathematical investigation in the theory of programs, In *Mathematical Foundations of Computer Science*, Mazurkiewicz et al.ed. Banach Center Publications, vol. 2, Warsaw 1977

[MW] A.Meyer and K.Winklmann, On the expressive power of dynamic logic, MIT/LCS/TM-157, Feb. 1980

[Li] P.Lindström , On extensions of elementary logic, *Theoria ,vol.35* (1969), pp 1 - 11.

Pebbling Mountain Ranges and its Application to DCFL-Recognition *

by Kurt Mehlhorn **

Abstract: Recently, S.A. Cook showed that DCFL's can be recognized in $O((\log n)^2)$ space and polynomial time simultaneously. We study the problem of pebbling mountain ranges (= the height of the pushdown-store as a function of time) and describe a family of pebbling strategies. One such pebbling strategy achieves a simultaneous $O((\log n)^2/\log \log n)$ space and polynomial time bound for pebbling mountain ranges. We apply our results to DCFL recognition and show that the languages of input-driven DPDA's can be recognized in space $O((\log n)^2/\log \log n)$. For general DCFL's we obtain a parameterized family of recognition algorithms realizing various simultaneous space and time bounds. In particular, DCFL's can be recognized in space $O((\log n)^2)$ and time $O(n^{2.87})$ or space $O(\sqrt{n} \log n)$ and time $O(n^{1.5} \log \log n)$ or space $O(n/\log n)$ and time $O(n(\log n)^3)$. More generally, our methods exhibit a general space-time tradeoff for manipulating pushdownstores (e.g. run time stack in block structured programming languages).

I. Introduction

Recently, S.A. Cook showed how to recognize DCFL's in $(\log n)^2$ space and polynomial time simultaneously. The proof is an ingenious application of the pebble game.

Consider the height of the pushdown store as a function of time, a mountain range. In order to simulate the move of a DPDA at time t one needs to know the state (which comes from time t-1) and the top pushdown symbol (which either comes from t-1 or from t' where t' is the last node with height(t') = height(t)). (cf. Fig. 1). This is in complete analogy to the pebble game: a pebble may be put on a node if all predecessors hold pebbles.

Of course, the mountain range is not given as an input. Rather, Cook's simulation consists of two coroutines: Pebbling a mountain range and constructing a mountain range.

---

* Full version of paper is available from author

** FB 10, Universität des Saarlandes, 6600 Saarbrücken, West Germany

Nevertheless, in section I of this paper we concentrate on the first aspect only: pebbling mountain ranges. This will allow us to considerably simplify Cook's construction on the one hand and to extend his results on the other hand.

Definition: A mountain range of length n is a directed graph $G = (V,E)$ with

$V = \{0,1,\dots,n-1\}$ and a function height: $V \to \mathbb{N} \cup \{0\}$ with

a) $\text{height}(x) > 0$ for all $x > 0$, $\text{height}(0) = 0$ and $|\text{height}(x) - \text{height}(x-1)| \le 1$.

b) $E = \{(x,x+1);\ 0 \le x < n\} \cup$

$$\{(x,y);\ x < y \text{ and } \text{height}(x) = \text{height}(y) < \text{height}(z) \text{ for all } x < z < y\}$$

Definition: If $\text{height}(x-1) \le \text{height}(x)$ then $x-1$ is the left neighbor of x, otherwise the unique y with $(y,x) \in E$ and $\text{height}(x) = \text{height}(y)$ is the left neighbor of x. Also x is the right neighbor of y in this case.
If x,y are nodes then x is visible from y if $x \le y$ and $\text{height}(x) < \text{height}(z)$ for all z with $x < z \le y$.

We assume that a mountain range is given by the sequence

$\{h(x) - h(x-1)\}_{x=1}^{n-1} \in \{-1,0,1\}^{n-1}$.

Our approach to pebbling mountain ranges is divide and conquer. (So is Cook's but in a disguised form). We feel that our approach is simpler. We describe a family (parameterized by function f) of pebbling strategies (f describes the division of a mountain range into subranges (e.g. a mountain range of length n could be divided in two pieces, or log n pieces or n pieces,...)),and analyse its space and time requirements. For one particular choice of f we obtain the following theorem :

Thm.: Mountain Ranges can be pebbled in space $O((\log n)^2/\log\log n)$ and polynomial time simultaneously.

It is easy to see that some mountain ranges require $\Omega(\log n)$ pebbles. Hence our strategy requires only $o(\log n)$ tape for recording positions of pebbles. Of course, this can only be achieved if pebbles are placed in a very regular fashion. This supports our intuitive feeling that our approach is simpler than Cook's.

In section II we apply our results to DCFL recognition. We first observe that for input-driven dpda's (= real time + input symbol determines the type of the move (i.e. push or pop)), Thm. 1 give the corresponding bounds for DCFL recognition.

Thm. 2: Let M be an input-driven dpda. Then L(M), the language accepted by M, can be recognized in space $O((\log n)^2/\log\log n)$ and polynomial time.

Then we consider general DCFL's. We derive a parameterized class of recognition algorithms for DCFL's, realizing different simultaneous space, time bounds for DCFL-recognition. In particular, we show that DCFL's can be recognized in

space	and	time	
$O((\log n)^2)$		$O(n^{2.87})$	(Cook)
$O(\sqrt{n}\cdot\log n)$		$O(n^{1.5}\log\log n)$	
$O(n/\log n)$		$O(n\cdot(\log n)^3)$	

simultaneously. This establishes a general time/space trade-off for DCFL-recognition. More generally, our methods are applicable to any deterministic manipulation of pushdownstores, e.g. run time stack in block structured programming languages (B. Schmidt, Swamy/Savage, Gurari/Ibarra).

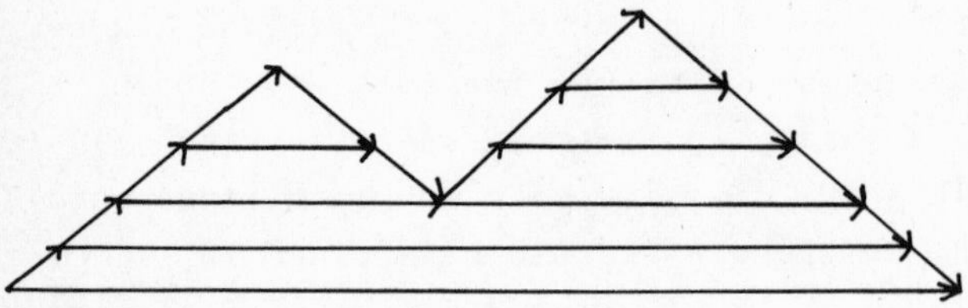

Figure 1: A mountain range.

Acknowledgement: Discussions with Bernd Schmidt are gratefully acknowledged.

I. The Algorithm

Our approach to pebbling mountain ranges is divide and conquer. The division is guided by function f.

Let $f : \mathbb{N} \cup \{0\} \to \mathbb{N}$ be any function with

1) $f(0) = 1$
2) $f(d+1) \geq 2f(d)$; in particular $f(d) \geq 2^d$
3) the binary representation of f(d) can be computed in space log f(d) (and hence in time p(f(d)) for some polynomial p) given the binary representation of d.

A d-order (d is the number of levels of the divide-and-conquer approach) strategy can be applied to a mountain range M of length m if $m \leq f(d+1)$. Let $v, v+1, \ldots, v+m-1$ be the nodes of M. The purpose of the strategy is to move a pebble on node $v+m-1$.

Any strategy uses two kinds of pebbles: recursion pebbles and ordinary pebbles. A d-order strategy uses d recursion pebbles, one for each d', $1 \leq d' \leq d$. Furthermore, for each d', $0 \leq d' \leq d$, it uses $\lceil f(d'+1)/f(d') \rceil$ ordinary pebbles of type d'. These pebbles are denoted by (d',0), (d',1),... . The second component of a pebble is called its index, the first component is its type.

We assume that a pebble of some type > d is on v initially. It will stay on v during the entire game.

A d-order strategy is played as follows. If $m \leq f(d)$ then it is identical to the (d-1)-order strategy on M. If d = 0, i.e. $m \leq f(1)$ then we put pebble (0,i) on node v+i one after the other. This will take m moves. Assume now that $d \geq 1$ and $m > f(d)$. Then range M is divided into subranges of length f(d). More precisely, the j-th subrange consists of points $v+j\cdot f(d), \ldots, v+\min(m-1, (j+1)\cdot f(d)-1)$. Then

$0 \leq j \leq \lceil m/f(d) \rceil - 1 \leq \lceil f(d+1)/f(d) \rceil - 1$.

The game is started by putting pebble (d,0) on node v. (Note that index 0 pebbles are always put on nodes which have already a pebble).

Assume now that we just placed pebble (d,j) on the first node of the j-th subrange, $j \geq 0$. Let $i = v+j\cdot f(d)$ be that node. Then the following statement holds (later refered to as Invariant).

a) let $j' \leq j$. If the j'-th subrange contains a point visible from i then pebble (d,j') is on the leftmost visible point in that subrange.

b) if a pebble is on node u, $u \leq i$, then u is visible from i. Furthermore, let w be any point visible from i and let d', $0 \leq d' \leq d$, be arbitrary. Let $u \leq w$ be the rightmost node holding a pebble of type d', if any. Then $w < u+f(d')$.

Remark: Our invariant captures the following idea : a pebble of type d' supports the exploration of a subrange of length at most $f(d')$. If w is visible and u is the rightmost point $\leq w$ holding a pebble then the pebble on u supports w.

□

Consider the j-th subrange in more detail. Let the sequence $v_o, v_1, \ldots, v_k$ of points in the j-th subrange be defined by

a) v_o is the first point in the j-th subrange

b) $v_{\ell+1} = \min\{w;\ v_\ell < w \text{ and height } (v_\ell) \geq \text{height}(w)\}$

Furthermore, v_{k+1} is the first point in the (j+1)-th subrange. Then either height $(v_\ell) \leq$ height $(v_{\ell+1})$ (= for $\ell < k$) or height $(v_{\ell+1})$ = height$(v_\ell)-1$ and $v_{\ell+1} = v_\ell + 1$. (cf. Fig. 2).
The j-th subrange is played as follows.

<u>for</u> $\ell = 0$ <u>to</u> k <u>do</u>

<u>begin</u> <u>co</u> pebble (d,j) is on node v_ℓ and the invariant holds with $i = v_\ell$;

<u>if</u> height $(v_\ell) \leq$ height $(v_{\ell+1})$

<u>then</u> let d' be minimal with $v_\ell + f(d') \geq v_{\ell+1}$;

<u>co</u> then $d' \leq d$;

remove all pebbles of type $\leq d' - 1$ from the graph;

(A) play $(d'-1)$-order strategy on mountain $v_\ell, v_\ell+1, \ldots, v_{\ell+1}-1$;

<u>co</u> at this point pebble (d,j) is still on v_ℓ and there is a pebble on $v_{\ell+1}-1$;

<u>fi</u>;

replace the pebble on node $v_{\ell+1}-1$ by the recursion pebble of type d

let t' be the left neighbor of $v_{\ell+1}$;

let $u \leq t'$ be the rightmost node which holds a pebble, let d' be the type of the pebble on u;

<u>co</u> by part b) of the Invariant $u+f(d') \geq t'$;
let d'' be minimal such that $u+f(d'') \geq t'$;
remove all pebbles of type $\leq d''-1$ from the graph;

(B) play $(d''-1)$-order strategy on $u,\ldots,t'$;

(C) move pebble (d,j) ($(d,j+1)$) on node $v_{\ell+1}$ if $\ell < k$ ($\ell=k$), and remove pebbles from points which are not visible from $v_{\ell+1}$;

<u>co</u> the invariant holds with $i = v_{\ell+1}$

<u>end</u>

This finishes the description of a d-order strategy given by function f. On an arbitrary mountain M we will always play a d-order strategy with the smallest possible d, i.e. $f(d) < \text{length } M \leq f(d+1)$.

<u>Definition:</u> Let f be any function as described above, let $m \in \mathbb{N}$. Define

$$d_o(m,f) := \min\{d;\ m \leq f(d+1)\}$$

$$N(m,f) := \sum_{d=0}^{d_o(m,f)} (1 + \lceil f(d+1)/f(d) \rceil)$$

□

<u>Remark:</u> $N(m,f) = \Omega(\log m)$ for all functions f.

<u>Lemma 1:</u> Let f be any function with $f(0) = 1$ and $f(d+1) \geq 2 \cdot f(d)$ for $d \geq 0$.

a) Let M be any mountain with m nodes. Then our strategy uses at most $N(m,f)$ pebbles on M.

b) An $O(N(m,f) \cdot \log m)$ space bounded Turing machine can play our strategy.

c) An $O(N(m,f) \cdot \log N(m,f) + d_o(m,f) \cdot \log m)$ space bounded TM can play our strategy.

<u>Proof:</u> part a) is an immediate consequence of the description of our strategy. Part b) follows from a) and the observation that space $O(\log m)$ suffices to record the position of a pebble. A proof of c) can be found in the full paper. It uses the fact that ordinary pebbles are placed in a very regular fashion and that it suffices to know the order in which the pebbles appear on the mountain from left to right in order to be able to compute their positions.

□

Next we turn to the timing analysis. We will first derive a bound on the number of moves.

Lemma 2: Let f be any function as described above. Let T(m,d) be the maximal number of moves in a d-order strategy on a mountain M of length m ($m \le f(d+1)$). Then

$$T(1,d) = 0 \qquad\qquad T(m,0) = m$$

$$T(m,d) \le m + T_A + T_B + T_C + (\lceil m/f(d)\rceil - 1)\, T(f(d-1),d-2) + (\lceil m/f(d)\rceil - 2)\, T(f(d),d-1)$$

where

$$T_A = \max\left\{ \sum_{i=0}^{k} T(y_i,e_i);\quad \begin{array}{l} 0 \le e_i \le d-1, \\ f(e_i) < y_i \le f(e_i+1) \\ y_o+\ldots+y_k \le m \end{array} \right\}$$

$$T_B = \max\left\{ \sum_{i=0}^{k'} T(f(h_i+1),h_i);\ \begin{array}{l} 0 \le h_i \le d-1, \\ f(h_o)+\ldots+f(h_{k'}) \le m \end{array} \right\}$$

$$T_C = \sum_{g=1}^{d-1} \left(\frac{\lceil m\rceil}{f(d)} - 1\right) \frac{\lceil f(d)\rceil}{f(d-1)} \cdots \frac{\lceil f(g+1)\rceil}{f(g)} \cdot T(f(g),g-1)$$

Proof: Let M be a mountain range of m points $v,v+1,\ldots,v+m-1$, $m \le f(d+1)$, such that a d-order strategy on M uses a maximal number of moves. If m = 1 then no move is required and hence T(1,d) = 0. If d = 0 then the number of moves is bounded by m, hence $T(m,0) \le m$.

Suppose now that $d \ge 1$. Let $x_o,x_1,\ldots,x_k$ be the set of points which receive pebbles of type d, let $x_{k+1} = v+m$. Then $x_o = v$.

Consider the description of our d-order strategy. We will count the moves in lines A, B and C of the algorithm separately.

line C: the number of moves in line C is certainly bounded by the number m of nodes of mountain M.

<u>line A:</u> in line A the games on subranges $x_i,\dots,x_{i+1}-1$ are played, $0 \le i \le k$; say an e_i order strategy is used. Then $f(e_i) < x_{i+1} - x_i \le f(e_i+1)$. The cost of an e_i-strategy on $x_i,\dots,x_{i+1}-1$ is at most $T(y_i,e_i)$ where $y_i := x_{i+1}-x_i$. Hence the total cost arising in line A is at most T_A where T_A is defined as above.

<u>line B:</u> For i, $0 \le i \le k$, let index (i) be the index of the type d pebble which was used on x_i. Then index (0) = 0 and index (1) = 1 since pebble (d,0) is only used on v. Furthermore, index(i) $\le$ index(i+1) and index(i) = index(i+1) implies height(x_i) $\ge$ height(x_{i+1}).

Let t_i be the left neighbor of x_i. Of course, a t_i is either identical to one of the x's (and then repebbling t_i in line B is free) or t_i lies properly between two x's. So let

$$Q = \{i; 1 \le i \le k,\ t_i \text{ is not one of the x's}\}$$

and for $i \in Q$ let int(i) be such that $x_{int(i)-1} < t_i < x_{int(i)}$.
Then int(i) $\le$ i, height($x_{int(i)-1}$) < height($x_{int(i)}$) and hence index(int(i)-1) < index(int(i)). Furthermore, for $i \in Q$ let

$$\text{left}(i) = \begin{cases} \max\{\ell; \ell < i \text{ and } \text{int}(\ell) = \text{int}(i)\} & \text{if such an } \ell \text{ exists} \\ \text{undefined} & \text{otherwise} \end{cases}$$

(cf. Figure 3). Note that left(i) undefined is equivalent to int(i) = i and that left(i) defined implies height($x_{left(i)}$)-1 = height (x_i). Note further that left is injective on the points on which it is defined.

The total cost of line B is

$$\sum_{i \in Q} \text{cost of repebbling } t_i \text{ in line B.}$$

We will split this cost in four parts.

<u>part 1:</u> Let Q_1 = {i; $i \in Q$ and left(i) undefined}. Then int(i) = i by the remark above. From index (int(i)-1) < index(int(i)) we conclude $Q_1 \le \lceil m/f(d) \rceil - 1$. Furthermore, t_i needs to be repebbled just after we finished pebbling the interval $x_{int(i)-1},\dots,x_{int(i)}-1$.

Hence the cost of repebbling t_i is bounded by T(f(d-1),d-2). This shows

$$\sum_{i\in Q_1} \text{cost of repebbling } t_i \leq (\lceil \frac{m}{f(d)} \rceil - 1)\cdot T(f(d-1),d-2)$$

<u>part 2:</u> Let $Q_2 \in \{i; i \in Q$ and left(i) defined and index(left(i)) $\neq$ index(i)}. Since the cost of repebbling t_i is certainly bounded by the cost of pebbling the entire interval $x_{int(i)-1},\ldots,x_{int(i)}-1$, and this in turn is bounded by T(f(d),d-1), we have

$$\sum_{i\in Q_2} \text{cost of repebbling } t_2 \leq |Q_2|\cdot T(f(d),d-1)$$

<u>claim 1:</u> $|Q_2| \leq \lceil m/f(d) \rceil - 2$

<u>proof:</u> It suffices to show $i_1, i_2 \in Q_2$, $i_1 \neq i_2$ implies index(left(i_1)) $\neq$ index(left(i_2)). (Note that $0 <$ index(left(i)) $\leq \lceil m/f(d) \rceil - 2$ for $i \in Q_2$).So assume i_1, $i_2 \in Q_2$, $i_1 \neq i_2$. Since left is injective on the points on which it is defined we may assume w.l.o.g. that left(i_1) < left(i_2). If $i_1 \leq$ left(i_2) then we are done. So suppose left(i_2) < i_1. Since height($x_{left(i_1)}$) = height(x_{i_1}) + 1 $\leq$ height(j) for all j with $x_{left(i_1)} \leq j \leq x_{i_1} - 1$ (this follows from int(left(i_1)) = int(i_1)) and height($x_{left(i_2)}$) = height(x_{i_2}) + 1 we conclude $i_2 < i_1$. Hence height(left(i_1)) < height(left(i_2)) and thus index(left(i_1)) < index(left(i_2)). This proves the claim.

□

Using claim 1 we get

$$\sum_{i\in Q_2} \text{cost of repebbling } Q_2 \leq (\lceil m/f(d) \rceil - 2)\cdot T(f(d),d-1)$$

<u>parts 3 and 4:</u> Let $Q_3 = \{i; i \in Q$ and left(i) defined and index(left(i)) = index(i)}. Let h_i be the maximal type ($\neq$ d) of pebble used in going from $x_{left(i)}$ to $x_i - 1$, i.e. $h_i = \max(e_{left(i)},\ldots,e_{i-1})$. Let g_i be the type of pebble which was used on $t_{left(i)}$, i.e. pebble (g_i, r), $r > 0$, was used on $t_{left(i)}$. Then $g_i \leq d-1$.

claim 2: A $\max(g_i-1,h_i)$-order strategy suffices to repebble t_i.

proof: When $x_{left(i)}$ was pebbled there was pebble (g_i,r) on $t_{left(i)}$. Let T_o be moment of time when pebble (g_i,r) was put on $t_{left(i)}$. At time T_o pebbles $(g_i,0)$, $(g_i+1,0),\ldots,(e_{int(i)-1},0)$ where also on the interval $x_{int(i)-1},\ldots,t_{left(i)}$. Since t_i is the rightmost point which is visible from $t_{left(i)}$, all these pebbles are to the left or at t_i. Hence at time T_o a (g_i-1)-order strategy would suffice to pebble node t_i, This is still true when $x_{left(i)}$ gets its pebble since (g_i,r) is still on $t_{left(i)}$ at that moment of time. When we proceed from $x_{left(i)}$ to x_i-1 all pebbles of type $> h_i$ stay where they are. Hence a $\max(g_i-1,h_i)$-order strategy suffices to play t_i. This proves claim 2.

□

Let $Q_{31} = \{i;i \in Q_3 \text{ and } g_i-1 \leq h_i\}$ and let $Q_{32} = \{i;i \in Q_3$ and $g_i-1 > h_i\}$

claim 3: $\sum_{i\in Q_{31}}$ cost of repebbling $t_i \leq T_B$

where T_B is defined as above.

proof: Since a pebble of type h_i is used in going from $x_{left(i)}$ to x_i-1 we have $x_i-x_{left(i)} > f(h_i)$ Hence claim 3 follows immediately from claim 4.

claim 4: Let i_1, $i_2 \in Q_3$, $i_1 \neq i_2$. Then the intervals $x_{left(i)},\ldots,x_{i_1}-1$ and $x_{left(i_2)},\ldots,x_{i_2}-1$ are disjoint.

proof: Assume $i_1,i_2 \in Q_3$, $i_1 \neq i_2$. Since $left(i_1)$ and $left(i_2)$ are defined we may assume w.l.o.g. that $left(i_1) < left(i_2)$. If $i_1 < left(i_2)$ then we are done. So suppose $left(i_2) < i_1$. As in the proof of claim 1 we conclude $index(left(i_1)) < index(left(i_2))$. But $left(i_2) < i_1$ implies $index(left(i_2)) \leq index(i_1)$. Hence $index(left(i_1)) < index(i_1)$ which contradicts $i_1 \in Q_3$. This proves claim 4 and 3.

□ □

claim 5: $\sum_{i\in Q_{32}}$ cost of repebbling $t_i \leq T_C$

where T_C is as defined above.

proof: If $i \in Q_{32}$ then the cost of repebbling t_i is bounded by $T(f(g_i), g_i - 1)$ where (g_i, r) is the pebble used on $t_{left(i)}$ $(r > 0)$. For g, $1 \leq g \leq d$, let $u(g) = |\{i \in Q_3 \text{ and } g_i = g\}|$. Then

$$\sum_{i \in Q_{32}} \text{cost of repebbling } t_i \leq \sum_{g=1}^{d-1} u(g) T(f(g), g-1) \text{ since } g_i \leq d-1$$

always. An induction argument can be used to show

$u(g) \leq (\lceil m/f(d) \rceil - 1) \cdot \lceil f(d)/f(d-1) \rceil \ldots \lceil f(g+1)/f(g) \rceil$.

□

Putting everything together we obtain

$$T(m,d) \leq m + T_A + T_B + T_C + \left(\frac{\lceil m \rceil}{f(d)} - 1 \right) T(f(d-1), d-2)$$

$$+ \left(\frac{\lceil m \rceil}{f(d)} - 2 \right) T(f(d), d-1)$$

□

Lemma 3: $T(m,d) \leq m \cdot \prod_{g=1}^{d} [3 + f(g)/f(g-1)]$

proof: by induction on d; we refer the reader to the full paper.

□

Better bounds can be obtained for specific functions f; e.g. for $f = 2^d$, one obtains $T(m,d) \leq m^{2.86}$.

Theorem 1: Mountain Ranges can be pebbled in space $O((\log n)^2/\log \log n)$ and polynomial time simultaneously.

proof: Use $f(d) = d!$. The space bound follows from Lemma 1, part c, the time bound follows from lemma 3 and the observation that a TM can simulate one move of the pebble game in polynomial time.

□

Applications: The methods of this paper show a general space, time tradeoff in manipulating pushdownstores; in particular they are applicable to space and time efficient realizations of run time stacks in block structured programming languages (cf. B. Schmidt, Swamy/Savage, Gurari/Ibarra) and to the simulation of deterministic pushdown automata. In this section we will sketch very briefly the application to DCFL-recognition.

Definition: A deterministic pushdown automaton is input-driven if the input symbol determines the type (push, pop, change of top pushdown symbol) of the move.

Theorem 2: Let N be an input driven dpda. Then L(N), the language accepted by N, can be recognized in space $O((\log n)^2/\log n)$ and polynomial time simultaneously on a multitape TM.

proof: Consider the height of the pushdown store as a function of time; this defines a mountain range. Store in each pebble state and top pushdown symbol. Then apply Theorem 1. □

For input driven dpda's the input string encodes a mountain range in a natural way. In the general case, one has to store in each pebble its position (the time of the move), the position of the largest visible node, a pointer to the current input symbol, state and top pushdown symbol. This will require space O(log n) per pebble.

Theorem 3: Let N be a dpda. Then L(N) can be recognized in

	space	time	
a)	$O((\log n)^2)$	$O(n^{2.87})$	[Cook]
b)	$O(\sqrt{n}\log n)$	$O(n^{1.5}\log\log n)$	
c)	$O(n/\log n)$	$O(n(\log n)^3)$	

simultaneously on a unit cost RAM.

proof: we sketch a proof of b). Let c be such that N uses at most cn moves on any input of length n. Let $h(m) = \lfloor\sqrt{m}\rfloor$. Let d_o be minimal such that $h^{(d_o+1)}(cn+1) = 1$. Then $d_o = O(\log\log n)$. Let $f(i) = h^{(d_o-i+1)}(cn+1)$. Then $N(n,f) = O(\sqrt{n})$. This gives the space bound.

For the time bound use Lemma 3 and observe that a unit cost RAM can simulate one move of the pebbling strategy in time $O(d_o)$. For part c) use $h(m) = (\log m)^2$.

□

References:

S.A. Cook : Deterministic CFL's are accepted simultaneously in polynomial time and log squared tape, 11th ACM Symposium on Theory of Computing, 1971, 338-345

E.M. Gurari, O.H. Ibarra : On the space complexity of recursive algorithm, Inf. Proc. Letters, Vol. 8, No. 5, 1979, 267-272

B. Schmidt : Ph.D. Thesis, Universität des Saarlandes, Fachbereich 10, 6600 Saarbrücken, in preparation

S. Swami, J. Savage : Space-Time Tradeoffs for linear Recursion, 6th ACM Symposium on Principles of Programming Languages, 1979, 135-142

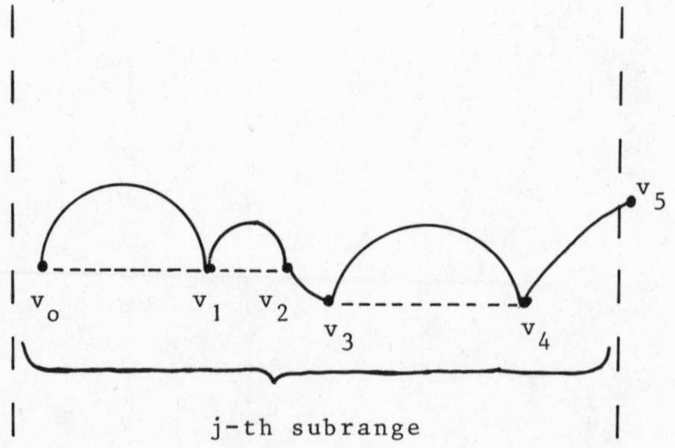

Figure 2: a subrange and its v-nodes

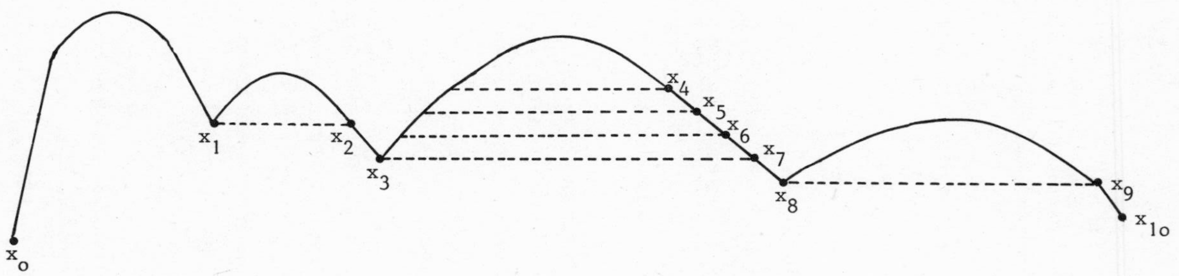

<u>Figure 3:</u> Assumption: index(0) = 0, index(1) = ... = index(3) = 1, index(4) = ... = index(10) = 2

Then Q = {1,3,4,5,6,7,8,10} int(1) = int(3) = int(8) = int(10) = 1, int(4) = int(5) = int(6) = 4, left(1) = left(4) = undef., left(5) = 4, left(6) = 5, left(3) = 1, left(8) = 3, left(10) = 8; Q_1 = {1,4}, Q_2 = {8}, Q_3 = {3,5,6,10}

Further assumptions: $c_1 = 5$, $e_8 = 8$; $g_3 = 6$, $g_{10} = 4$, $g_5 = g_6 = 1$.

Then Q_{31} = {3,10} , Q_{32} = {5,6}

Space-restricted attribute grammars

Erik Meineche Schmidt
Computer Science Department
Aarhus University
DK-8000 Aarhus C, Denmark

Abstract

Restricting the size of attribute values, relative to the length of the string under consideration, leads to a model of attribute grammars in which grammars with both inherited and synthesized attributes can be significantly more economical than grammars with synthesized attributes only.

1. Introduction

When Knuth introduced the notion of an attribute grammar ([Knu]) as a formalization of the concept of assigning meaning to strings generated by context-free grammars, the definition allowed any collection of sets as attribute values and any collection of functions over these sets as semantic functions. This generosity has the immediate consequence that there is no real need for inherited attributes, because any translation defined by an arbitrary attribute grammar can be defined by another attribute grammar which uses only synthesized attributes. Although this is a correct observation, one has the feeling (as also pointed out in [Knu]) that it doesn't tell the whole story and that there are many situation - handling declarations in a programming language for example - where the use of inherited attributes is both natural and advantageous. One way of turning this feeling into mathematical results is to restrict the use of semantic domains in such a way that one cannot "drag along" the whole derivation tree as an attribute value, and then apply a function at the root which maps the tree into whatever translation is wanted (this is the argument that makes inherited attributes obsolete).

There are several papers where this approach has been taken - we know of [Dus], [EF], [LRS] and [Ri], where translations defined by attribute grammars over fixed domains are analyzed and compared. It is common to these approaches that the restrictions on the domains are "syntactic" in nature, exemplified by [EF], where the main concern is with domains whose values are strings or trees, and whose operations are string- or tree-concatenation. We shall also restrict attention to domains whose values are strings, but instead of restricting the semantic functions, we take a more information theoretic approach in which we bound the size of the attribute values relative to the length of the word under consideration.

Inspired by the definition of spacebounds in complexity theory, we call an attribute grammar S(n)-spacebounded if there exists a constant c, such that for any word w generated by the underlying context-free grammar, all attribute values in all derivation trees for w are of length at most c $S(|w|)$. We repeat that attribute values are strings.

It follows that if the spacebound is sublinear, then the "drag along the whole tree"-approach to elimination of inherited attributes can only be used at the cost of expanding the bound. The question then becomes whether there is another, less expensive, way of eliminating inherited attributes. We answer the question by showing that if the attribute grammars are what we call determinate, then there exists a simple language, generated by a logn-bounded attribute grammar with inherited attributes, which requires more than space n/log n in any attribute grammars with synthesized attributes only. The logn-bounded grammar is L-attributed ([LRS]) and is the "natural" attribute grammar for the language.

The determinacy-requirement ensures that if a string has several derivation trees, then the attribute values in all the trees "make sense". This means that determinate grammars can't be used in a "guess-and-check" fashion, and this restriction is vital for our argument. On the other hand, the class of determinate attribute grammars is sufficiently large to include all well-defined grammars (in the sense of [Knu]) whose underlying context-free grammar is unambiguous.

2. Space-restricted attribute grammars

We follow [EF] in the definition of attribute grammars.

A semantic domain is a pair (Ω, Φ) where Ω is a set of sets (the sets of attribute values) and Φ is a collection of mappings (the semantic functions) of the form $f: V_1 \times V_2 \times \ldots \times V_m \rightarrow V_0$ where $m \geq 0$ and $V_i \in \Omega$ for $0 \leq i \leq m$.

An attribute grammar A over semantic domain (Ω, Φ) consists of 1)-4) as follows:

1) A reduced context-free grammar $G = (N, \Sigma, P, S)$ called the underlying context-free grammar of A.

2) Each nonterminal F in G has two associated finite sets, Sy(F) and In(F), called the synthesized and the inherited attributes of F, respectively. The startsymbol S has no inherited attributes, and one of its synthesized attributes is designated to hold the value or translation of the tree under consideration.

3) With each attribute a is associated a set in Ω, which contains a's values.

4) With each production in G of the form

$$p: F \rightarrow v_0 D_1 v_1 \ldots D_m v_m$$

where $F, D_1, \ldots, D_m$ are nonterminals, is associated a set of semantic rules which define the values of p's applied attributes $\mathrm{Apl}(p) = \mathrm{Sy}(F) \cup \bigcup_{j=1}^{m} \mathrm{In}(D_j)$,

in terms of the values of p's defining attributes $Def(p) = In(F) \cup \bigcup_{j=1}^{m} Sy(D_j)$.
A semantic rule is of the form

$$a \leftarrow f(a_1, \ldots, a_m)$$

where $a \in Apl(p)$, f is a semantic function and the a_i's are either domain values or attributes from Def(p). There is exactly one semantic rule for each applied attribute in every production.

In the following, whenever we refer to G, we always mean the underlying context-free grammar of the attribute grammar under consideration.

In what follows we are interested in viewing attribute grammars as language generators, and of all the different ways in which we can define the language generated by such a grammar (see [Ri]), we take the approach where the semantic rules associated with the nodes in a derivation tree, t, are viewed as a set of equations, E_t, in which the attributes are the unknowns. If we assume that the designated synthesized attribute of the grammar's startsymbol has only two values (which we can denote by true and false), then the language generated by the grammar can be defined as follows.

Definition 1 Let A be an attribute grammar over a semantic domain (Ω, Φ) and assume that the value-set associated with the designated synthesized attribute of the startsymbol, d(S), is (true, false). The language generated by the grammar is

$$L(A) = \{w \mid w \in L(G) \text{ and there exists a derivation tree for } w,\ t_w, \text{ such that } E_{t_w} \text{ has a solution in which } d(S) = \underline{true}\}$$

□

This definition allows for the possibility that a word in the language can have several derivation trees, some of whose equations have solutions where d(S) = true, some where d(S) = false and some where there are no solutions. As mentioned in the introduction, we shall restrict attention to the case, where it is sufficient to analyze just one derivation tree of a string, in order to find out whether the string is generated by the attribute grammar. Formally, we define the class of determinate attribute grammars, dAG, to be the class of grammars where, for each word w generated by the underlying context-free grammar, 1) each E_{t_w} has exactly one solution, and 2) the value of d(S) is the same in the solutions to all E_{t_w}'s.

The difference between dAG's, general AG's and socalled unambiguous AG's is discussed further in [Ri]. We now restrict attention to semantic domains (Ω_S, Φ) where Ω_S is the set of all strings over some finite alphabet.

Definition 2 Let $\mathfrak{a}$ be a class of attribute grammars and let $S: R_+ \to R_+$ be a function mapping nonnegative reals to nonnegative reals. An attribute grammar A (over some domain (Ω_S, Φ)) belongs to $\mathfrak{a}(S(n))$ if A is in $\mathfrak{a}$, and there exists a constant c such that for every word $w \in L(G)$ and every derivation tree for w, t_w, all attribute values, v(a), in all solutions to E_{t_w} satisfy $|v(a)| \leq c\, S(|w|)$.

□

In the rest of the paper we are only interested in the following two simple classes of attribute grammars:

S-AG: the class of grammars whose nonterminals have no inherited attributes.

L-AG: the class of grammars where an attribute associated with a nonterminal on the righthandside of a production does not depend on any attribute to its right (see [LRS]).

3. Space-restricted L-dAG's and S-dAG's

As described above, we now consider semantic domains (Ω_s, Φ) where Ω_s consists of strings over some finite alphabet. The following theorem shows that inherited attributes add power to space-restricted determinate attribute grammars.

Theorem 3 There exists a language L_0 such that

a) L_0 is generated by an attribute grammar in L-dAG(logn)

b) L_0 is not generated by any attribute grammar in S-dAG(n/logn)

□

L_0 consists of strings of the form $\$z_1\$\ldots\$z_n\$$ where $z_i \in \{0,1\}^*$. Each such string is interpreted as a sequence of binary numbers where the substring z_i represents the number $\bar{z}_i$ whose binary representation is $1z_i$. L_0 is defined as follows

$$L_0 = \{\$z_1\$\ldots\$z_n\$ \mid n \geq 2,\ n \text{ even},\ z_i \in \{0,1\}^*,\ \#\{i \mid \bar{z}_i > \tfrac{n}{2}\} \geq \tfrac{n}{2}\}$$

i.e. the language consists of sequences of integers, at least half of which are greater than half the length of the sequence (# M denotes the number of elements in the set M).

Proof of Theorem 3a)

Let A be an attribute grammar (over a domain to be specified later) whose underlying context-free grammar generates the language $(\$\{0,1\}^*\$\{0,1\}^*)^+\$$ in such a way that the derivation tree for the word $z = \$z_1\$\ldots\$z_n\$$ looks as follows

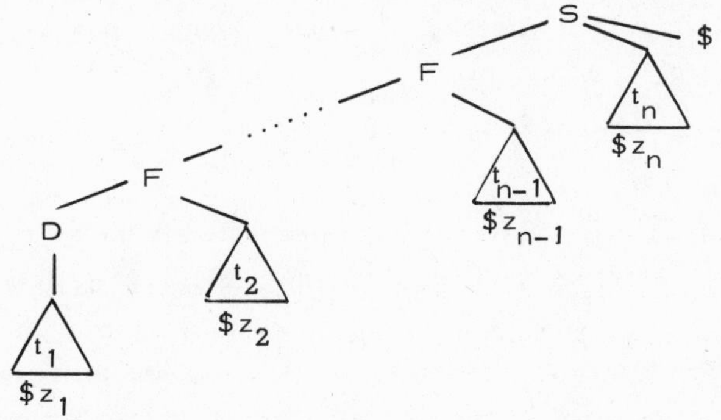

We can specify the semantic rules implicitly by the following top-down left-to-right pass over the tree, which evaluates the attributes.

1. Count the number of trees $t_n, t_{n-1}, \ldots, t_1$ using inherited attributes for F and D.
2. Check whether $\bar{z}_i$ is greater than $\frac{n}{2}$. Each time such a z_i is found, increase a counter (which is a synthesized attribute of D, F and S).
3. Set d(S) = <u>true</u> if the value of the counter is at least $\frac{n}{2}$, otherwise set d(S) = <u>false</u>.

It should be clear that we have specified an L-attributed grammar over some domain (Ω_S, Φ) where Φ contains functions which can compare two values, increase a value by 1 etc. It is also clear that the largest value of the counters is n, and since in step 2 only the $\lceil \log n \rceil$ most significant bits of z_i are needed in the comparison, no attribute in the tree requires more space than $\lceil \log n \rceil$. Since the length of the word z is at least n and since the grammar is obviously determinate, we have shown that L_0 is generated by an attribute grammar in L-dAG(logn). □

Notice that the reason attribute values could be kept small in the above grammar is that the total number of z_i's is known when "processing" each z_i locally. The proof of the second half of the theorem amounts to showing that, when inherited attributes are ruled out and when "guessing" is impossible (this is what determinacy prevents), then the nonterminals in the grammar have to "remember" which substring they generate. The proof is rather lengthy and we present it in the form of a sequence of lemmas.

First, we introduce the following notation. Let z be an arbitrary string of the form $z = \$z_1\$z_2 \ldots \$z_n\$$ (where $n \geq 2$). We shall refer to such strings as <u>sequences</u>, to the z_i's as <u>words</u> in z and to the $\bar{z}_i$'s as the <u>numbers</u> in z. Since we want to abstract away from the order in which the numbers in z occur, we define the <u>characteristic vector of z</u> to be the vector

$$\vec{v}(z) = (v_1(z), v_2(z), \ldots, v_{\bar{m}}(z))$$

where $\bar{m} = \max_{1 \leq j \leq n} \{\bar{z}_j\}$ and $v_i(z) = \#\{j \mid \bar{z}_j = i\}$. Hence $v_i(z)$ is the number of j's such that $\bar{z}_j = i$. Using $\vec{v}(z)$, we can characterize the elements of our language L_0 as the set of sequences z, for which

$$\sum_{i=\frac{n}{2}+1}^{\bar{m}} v_i(z) \geq \frac{n}{2}$$

Because of this characterization we are also interested in the <u>accumulated characteristic vector of z,</u> which is denoted by $\vec{s}(z) = (s_0(z), \ldots, s_{\bar{m}-1}(z))$ and defined by

$$s_i(z) = \sum_{j=i+1}^{\bar{m}} v_j(z) \quad \text{for } 0 \leq i \leq \bar{m}-1$$

Now, let, for some $S(n)$, A be an attribute grammar in S-dAG($S(n)$) which generates L_0. Because spacebounds are defined up to a constant factor, we can assume without loss of generality that A's underlying context-free grammar G only has productions of the form $F \to DE$, $F \to d$, $F \to \lambda$ where F, D, E are nonterminals, d is a terminal, and λ is the empty word. Since our proof is basically a pumping argument, we need the following "typical" constants. Let m be the number of nonterminals in G, r the number of productions, $k_G = 2^{9m+1}$ and let $k = \lceil (9m+1)k_G \rceil !$ be fixed for the rest of the paper.

We now introduce a structured subset of L_0 for which we can show that the attributes in the grammar must be used to distinguish many words with different characteristic vectors. Let, for each n which is a multiple of k and for which $\lceil \log 3 + \log n \rceil = \lceil \log 4 + \log n \rceil$, K_n be the set

$$K_n = \{ \$z_1\$\ldots\$z_{2n}\$ \mid 3n < \bar{z}_i \leq 4n \text{ for } 1 \leq i \leq 2n \}$$

i.e. K_n consists of sequences of length $2n$ in which each number lies between $3n$ and $4n$. It is clear that K_n is a subset of L_0 and it follows from the construction that all words in sequences in K_n are of length $\lceil \log n \rceil + 1$. We shall call sequences $z_1, z_2 \in K_n$ <u>separable</u> if there exists an $i \geq 0$ such that

$$|s_{ik}(z_1) - s_{ik}(z_2)| \geq 2 \qquad (1)$$

i.e. if there is a component (which is a multiple of k) in their accumulated characteristic vectors where they differ by more than 1. The following lemma shows that there are many separable vectors in K_n (the proof is outlined in the appendix).

<u>Lemma 4</u> There exists an integer n_1 and a constant $c_1 > 0$ such that for all $n \geq n_1$, the number of mutually separable sequences in K_n is at least $2^{c_1 n}$. □

The reason for calling sequences z_1 and z_2 in (1) separable should become clear when we now show that there exists a derivation in the grammar G of the form $S \overset{*}{\Rightarrow} \alpha = sFt$ (s and t are possibly empty terminal strings and F is a nonterminal) such that 1) sFt generates many mutually separable sequences, and 2) if $z_1 = sw_{z_1}t$ and $z_2 = sw_{z_2}t$ are separable then we can pump within s and t to obtain two words $s'w_{z_1}t'$ and $s'w_{z_2}t'$, exactly one of which belongs to L_0.

We construct the form $\alpha = sFt$ iteratively as the limit of a sequence $\alpha_1, \alpha_2, \ldots, \alpha_i, \ldots$ in the following way.

1. $\alpha_1 = S$, where S is the startsymbol of the grammar.
2. Assume that $\alpha_1, \alpha_2, \ldots, \alpha_i$ has been constructed and let $\alpha_i = s_iF_it_i$. Let z be a sequence in K_n generated by α_i, and assume the derivation looks like $\alpha_i = s_iF_it_i \overset{p}{\Rightarrow} s_iDEt_i \overset{*}{\Rightarrow} s_iw_Dw_Et_i = s_iw_zt_i = z$, where $p: F_i \to DE$ is the p'th production in G ($1 \leq p \leq r$). Let us for any such z define its <u>cutpoint</u> to be the length of w_D, and denote by $M(p,c)$ the set of mutually separable sequences in K_n which have cutpoint c and which are generated

by α in the above way (i.e. p is the first production used). Remove from the total collection of sets $M = \{M(p,c) \mid p \text{ is an } F_i\text{-production}, 0 \le c \le |w_z|\}$ all sets for which $c = 0$ ($c = |w_z|$) and the form $s_i E t_i$ ($s_i D t_i$) already occurs in the sequence $\alpha_1, \alpha_2, \ldots, \alpha_i$. Let the remaining collection of sets be M' and choose among these a set M(p,c) which con-contains as many elements as any other set in M'. Let $p(i): F_i \to DE$ and c(i) be the production and cutpoint associated with the chosen set.

3. There are three cases to consider

a) $c(i) \le (k_G+1)(1+\lceil \log n \rceil)$. The sequences in M(p(i),c(i)) are of the form $s_i w_D w_E t_i$ where $|w_D| = c(i)$. Choose w_D such that $s_i w_D E t_i$ generates as many sequences in M(p(i),c(i)) as for any other choice of w_D and let $\alpha_{i+1} = s_i w_D E t_i$. If $s_i w_D t_i$ contains more than $(9m+1)k_G$ \$'s then halt, otherwise go back to step 2.

b) $c(i) \ge |w_z| - (k_G+1)(1+\lceil \log n \rceil)$. The situation is analogous to a) with C and D interchanged.

c) $(k_G+1)(\lceil \log n \rceil + 1) < c(i) < |w_z| - (k_G+1)(1+\lceil \log n \rceil)$. Again the sequences in M(p(i),c(i)) are of the form $s_i w_D w_E t_i$. Choose among all w_D's and w_E's the one for which $s_i w_D E t_i$ or $s_i D w_E t_i$ generates most sequences in M(p(i),c(i)). Assuming the one chosen is a w_D, let $\alpha_{i+1} = s_i w_D E t_i$ and halt.

Let us say that the above procedure terminates normally if one of the halt-instructions in step 3 is executed.

Lemma 5 There exists an integer n_2 and a constant $c_2 > 0$ such that the procedure terminates normally for all $n \ge n_2$ and furthermore the resulting $\alpha = sFt$ generates at least $2^{c_2 n}$ mutually separable sequences in K_n. □

Proof

Let f(i) be the number of mutually separable sequences in K_n generated by α_i. It is clear that any such sequence $z = s_i w_z t_i$ belongs to at least one of the sets in the collection M in step 2 (provided $|w_z| \ge 2$). It is also easy to see that it belongs to at least one of the sets in M', because removing elements with cutpoint 0 (or $|w_z|$) whose "corresponding" sentential form already appeared in the sequence $\alpha_1, \alpha_2, \ldots, \alpha_i$ just amounts to eliminating useless derivations of the form $sFt \overset{*}{\Rightarrow} sFt$.

Since no cutpoint can be larger than $2n(\lceil \log n \rceil + 3)$ and since the grammar has at most r productions, the set M(p(i),c(i)) above contains at least $\frac{f(i)}{2rn(\lceil \log n \rceil + 3)}$ elements. If step 3a) or 3b) is executed, the string w_D (w_E) is of length at most $(k_G+1)(1+\lceil \log n \rceil)$ and since there are only 3 terminal symbols in the language, it follows that

$$f(i+1) \geq \frac{f(i)}{2rn(\lceil \log n \rceil + 3) \circ 3^{c}}$$

for some $c \leq (k_G+1)(1+\lceil \log n \rceil)$. If step 3c) is executed we "loose" at most the square-root of the sequences in M(p(i), c(i)), hence

$$f(i+1) \geq \left(\frac{f(i)}{2rn(\lceil \log n \rceil + 3)}\right)^{1/2}$$

Since step 3a) or 3b) is executed at most $i_{max} = m[(9m+1)k_G(\lceil \log n \rceil + 1)$ times, and step 3c) at most once, we conclude that if the procedure terminates normally then the resulting α generates at least

$$\left(\frac{f(1)}{[(2rn(\lceil \log n \rceil + 3)\, 3^{c}]^{i_{max}}}\right)^{1/2} \qquad (2)$$

mutually separable sequences in K_n. The dominating term in the denominator is of the form $(n\log n \cdot 3^{\log n})^{c' \log n}$ for some constant c'. But since we know from Lemma 4 that f(1) is (asymptotically) of the form $2^{c_1 n}$ then it follows that (2) is also asymptotically of the form $2^{c_2 n}$ for some $c_2 \geq 0$. Since this implies that each α_i generates lots of separable sequences, we have in fact also shown that the procedure terminates normally.

□

Next we show that if $z_1 = sw_{z_1}t$ and $z_2 = sw_{z_2}t$ are separable sequences from K_n generated by sFt then we can "pump within s and/or t" in such a way that exactly one of the resulting words $s'w_{z_1}t'$ and $s'w_{z_2}t'$ belongs to L_0.

Assume that the iterative procedure above stopped in step 3a) or 3b). We know that st contains at least $(9m+1)k_G$ \$'s and since no step in the construction introduced more than k_G \$'s (otherwise we would have stopped in step 3c)) the path $S = F_1, F_2, \ldots, F_i = F$ from the startsymbol to F contains at least 9m+1 nonterminals each of which generates \$'s. Among these nonterminals there are at least 10 occurrences of the same nonterminal. Choose the largest j such that $F_j, F_{j+1}, \ldots, F_i = F$ contains 10 occurrences of the same nonterminal (generating \$'s). This piece of the path is of the form B,...,B,...,F where B is the "repeating" nonterminal. Hence we have a derivation of the form

$$S \overset{*}{\Rightarrow} uBy \overset{*}{\Rightarrow} uvBxy \overset{*}{\Rightarrow} uvw'Fw''xy = sFt$$

where vx contains at least 9 and at most $(9m+1)k_G$ \$'s.

In the case where the iterative procedure stopped in step 3c), the string w_D added in the last step is itself sufficiently long to allow pumping within the subtree generated by the derivation $D \overset{*}{\Rightarrow} w_D$. The argument is similar to the one just given, which is in fact a trivial extension of the proof of Ogden's lemma found in [AU]. In the last situation we have a derivation of the form

$$S \overset{*}{\Rightarrow} uByFt \overset{*}{\Rightarrow} uvBxyFt \overset{*}{\Rightarrow} uvwxyFt = sFt \qquad (3)$$

where we now know that vx contains at least 9 and at most k_G \$'s.

In the following we shall assume that the derivation looks like (3), the argument in the other case being similar. Let $\alpha = uvwxyFt$ be the sentential form generated in (3) and consider for arbitrary $i \geq 0$ the form

$$\alpha(i) = uv^{i+2}w\, x^{i+2}yFt$$

which is also generated by the grammar. We know that vx contains at least 9 \$'s and we shall assume that both v and x contain at least one \$, the argument in the case where only one of them contains a \$ is similar. If we write v and x in the form $v = a\eta\,\$d$, $x = b\delta\,\$e$ where $\eta, \delta \in (\$\{0,1\}^*)^*$ and $a, b, d, e \in \{0,1\}^*$ then $\alpha(i)$ looks like

$$ua\eta\,\$d\,(a\eta\,\$d)^i a\eta\,\$d\,w\;\; b\delta\,\$e\,(b\delta\,\$e)^i\, b\delta\,\$e\,y\,Ft$$

which we can rewrite as

$$ua\,[\eta\,\$d\,(a\eta\,\$d)^i a]\,\eta\,\$d\,w\;\; b[\delta\,\$e\,(b\delta\,\$e)^i b]\,\delta\,\$\,e\,y\,Ft \qquad (4)$$

This string is equal to α with the brackets "inserted". We shall show that by choosing i appropriately and by pumping/contracting <u>within</u> the individual pieces $a\eta\,\$d \ldots b\delta\,\$e$,we can distinguish any two separable sequences from K_n generated by α. Let z_1 and z_2 be two such sequences and let $i_0 = ik$ be the index for which $|s_{i_0}(z_1) - s_{i_0}(z_2)| \geq 2$. Assume wlg that

$$s_{i_0}(z_1) > s_{i_0}(z_2) + 1 \qquad (5)$$

and consider the equations

$$\begin{aligned} s_{i_0}(z_1) + p &= i_0 \\ 2n + p + q &= 2i_0 \end{aligned} \qquad (6)$$

Let us call a number which is greater than i_0 a <u>big</u> number and a number which is smaller than or equal to i_0 a <u>small</u> number. If the derivations of z_1 and z_2 are as follows

$$\begin{aligned} S &\overset{*}{\Rightarrow} uvwxyFt \overset{*}{\Rightarrow} uvwxyw_1t = z_1 \\ S &\overset{*}{\Rightarrow} uvwxyFt \overset{*}{\Rightarrow} uvwxyw_2t = z_2 \end{aligned} \qquad (7)$$

and if we can choose i such that the two pieces

$$[\eta\,\$d\,(a\eta\,\$d)^i\, a] \text{ and } [\delta\,\$\,e\,(b\delta\,\$\,e)^i\, b]$$

together contain p+q words, then we only have to show that we can pump/contract within each of the pieces $a\eta\,\$d \ldots b\delta\,\$e$ in such a way that (almost) p of the words represent big numbers. Because then it follows from (6) that the resulting word $z_1' = uvv_1 \ldots v_i vwxx_i \ldots x_1 xyw_1t$ belongs L_0 whereas $z_2' = uvv_1 \ldots v_i vwxx_i \ldots x_1 xyw_2t$

does not. Notice that the second equation in (6) says that z_1' contains $2n+p+q = 2i_0$ numbers and that the first equation says that i_0 of these numbers are big. Taken together this means that $z_1' \in L_0$. z_2', on the other hand, also contains $2n+p+q = 2i_0$ numbers but, because of (5), less than i_0 of them are large, i.e. $z_2' \notin L_0$.

Now, the reason the difference in (5) has to be more than 1 is that we can't quite obtain p big and q small words, but as the following lemma says we can do almost as well (the proof is outlined in the appendix).

Lemma 6 There exists an integer n_3 and a constant $c_3 > 0$ such that for all $n \geq n_3$, if $z_1 \in K_n$ is derived as in (7) and if p, q satisfy (6) then there exists a derivation of a word z_1' of the form $z_1' = uvv_1 \ldots v_i vwxx_i \ldots x_1 xyw_1 t$ which contains $2n+p'+q'$ numbers, $s_{i_0}(z_1)+p'$ of which are big, and such that $p'+q' = p+q$ and $p+1 \geq p' \geq p$.

□

Now we can finally prove Theorem 3b).

Proof of Theorem 3b)

Assume that the language L_0 is generated by an attribute grammar in S-dAG(n/logn). Let c_0 be the constant such that for all words w generated by the underlying grammar, any attribute value v(a) in a solution to the equations E_{t_w} satisfies $|v(a)| \leq c_0 (|w|/\log(|w|))$. Let $l(n) = 2n(\lceil \log n \rceil + 2) + 1$ and choose n larger than any of the integers n_1, n_2, n_3 in lemmas 4, 5, 6 and such that $c_2 n > c_0 \log(g)$ $(l(n)/\log(l(n)))$ where g is the size of the grammar's attribute-alphabet (recall that attribute values are strings over a finite alphabet). Let $\alpha = sFt$ be the sentential form from Lemma 5 which generates at least $2^{c_2 n}$ mutually separable sequences from K_n. All these sequences are of length l(n), hence the attribute values v(a(F)) associated with the nonterminal F in all these derivations satisfy

$$|v(a(F))| \leq c_0\, l(n)/\log(l(n)) < \frac{c_2}{\log(g)} n$$

The total number of different values a string of length $|v(a(F))|$ can represent is

$$g^{|v(a(F))|} < g^{\frac{c_2 n}{\log g}} = 2^{c_2 n}$$

Hence there are at least two separable sequences in K_n, z_1 and z_2 such that the values of a(F) in the sets of equations $E_{t_{z_1}}$ and $E_{t_{z_2}}$ are equal. Now construct z_1' (and z_2') according to Lemma 6 and consider the corresponding equations $E_{t_{z_1'}}$ and $E_{t_{z_2'}}$. Since the grammar is S-attributed, the set of equations determining a(F) in $E_{t_{z_1'}}$ ($E_{t_{z_2'}}$) is the <u>same</u> as the set of equations determining a(F) in $E_{t_{z_1}}$ ($E_{t_{z_2}}$) because the subtrees with F as root are identical in the two cases. Hence the values of a(F) in $E_{t_{z_1'}}$ and $E_{t_{z_2'}}$ are equal. Since the remaining equations in $E_{t_{z_1'}}$ and $E_{t_{z_2'}}$

are identical, the values of the designated attribute of the startsymbol in the two sets of equations are equal. But that's impossible because z_1' is in the language whereas z_2' is not, and since the grammar is determinate the two values of d(S) must be different. Thus we have reached a contradiction, which shows that no grammar in S-dAG(n/logn) can generate L_0. □

4. Conclusion

Theorem 3 is obtained under very weak assumptions about the semantic domains involved. Indeed in the proof of part 3b) nothing is assumed about the semantic functions. It is also relevant to consider the situation where we, in addition to the restriction on the size of the attribute values, require that the semantic functions belong to some complexity class. The first steps in this direction has been taken in [Je], where semantic functions were measured in terms of the complexity of the RAM-programs used to implement them.

5. Appendix

Here we outline the proofs of Lemma 4 and Lemma 6.

Proof of Lemma 4

Each sequence z in K_n consists of 2n numbers in the range from 3n to 4n. Hence $\vec{v}(z)$ has at most n nonzero components, and the total number of vectors of this form can be computed as the number of ways to distribute 2n balls over n boxes, which is equal to

$$\binom{3n-1}{n-1} \qquad (8)$$

Let's say that the accumulated characteristic vectors associated with $z_1, z_2 \in K_n$ are similar if $s_{ik}(z_1) = s_{ik}(z_2)$ for $i \geq 0$. Given an arbitrary sequence $z \in K_n$, the number of vectors similar to $\vec{s}(z)$ is

$$\prod_{i=1}^{\frac{n}{k}} \binom{p_i+k-1}{k-1} \qquad (9)$$

where $p_i = s_{(i-1)k}(z) - s_{ik}(z)$, (i.e. $\sum_{i=1}^{\frac{n}{k}} p_i = 2n$).

(9) is maximal when $p_1 = p_2 = \ldots = p_{\frac{n}{k}} = 2k$, which means that the maximal number of vectors similar to any given vector is

$$\binom{3k-1}{k-1}^{\frac{n}{k}} \qquad (10)$$

Let's say that $\vec{s}(z_1)$ and $s(z_2)$ are almost similar if $|s_{ik}(z_1) - s_{ik}(z_2)| \leq 1$ for $i \geq 0$. We can bound the number of vectors which are almost similar to any given vector by

$$D_{\frac{n}{k}} \cdot \binom{3k-1}{k-1}^{\frac{n}{k}} \qquad (11)$$

where $D_{\frac{n}{k}}$ is a solution to the following difference equations

$$\begin{aligned} D_n &= D_{n-1} + 2\,C_{n-1} \\ C_n &= D_{n-1} + C_{n-1} \\ D_1 &= C_1 = 1 \end{aligned} \qquad (12)$$

which are obtained by systematically analyzing the ways in which almost similar vectors can be different at components which are multiples of k.

Dividing (8) by (11) gives a lower bound on the number of separate sequences in K_n. Since the solution to (12) is $D_n \approx (1+\sqrt{2})^n$ and since we can show (using Stirling's Formula) that (8) divided by (10) is asymptotically equal to $3^{\frac{n}{k}}$, we find that for sufficiently large n, the number of mutually separable sequences in K_n is at least $\left(\frac{3}{1+\sqrt{2}}\right)^{\frac{n}{k}}$ which is equal to $2^{c_1 n}$ for some $c_1 > 0$. □

Proof of Lemma 6

Assume that z_1, z_2, p and q satisfy (5) and (6). Since the sequences z_1 and z_2 only contain numbers between 3n and 4n, any index i_0 for which their s-vectors differ, satisfies $3n \leq i_0 < 4n$. Furthermore, the sequences both contain 2n numbers, which means that $0 \leq s_{i_0}(z_1) \leq 2n$. From this it follows that $n \leq p < 4n$, $4n \leq p+q < 6n$ and $\frac{q}{p} \geq \frac{1}{3}$. Finally, since both n and i_0 are multiples of k, so is p+q. Now, consider the piece

$$\ldots v \ldots x \ldots \; = \; \ldots a\eta \; \$ d \ldots b\delta \$ e \ldots \qquad (13)$$

which can be pumped according to (3) and (7). Assume that (13) contains h occurrences of a \$. We know that $9 \leq h \leq k_G$ and since $k = [(9m+1)k_G]!$, h is a divisor in k. Hence there exists a j such that $h \cdot j = (p+q)$, and it follows that the sequence

$$z_1' = uvv^{j-1}vwxx^{j-1}xyw_1t \qquad (14)$$

contains $2n+p+q = 2i_0$ words. Now we only have to show that we can make sure that exactly p' of the p+q added numbers are big, where $p+1 \geq p' \geq p$. This is shown by observing that when n is large, then the distance between consecutive \$'s in (13) is large, and since the number of \$'s in (13) is independent of n, we can pump within the piece (13) without changing the number of occurrences of \$'s.

To be precise, we can show the following observation, again by extending the proof of Ogden's Lemma (see [AU]).

Observation Let $G = (N, \Sigma, P, S)$ be a context-free grammar with m nonterminals whose productions are of the form $F \to DE$, $F \to d$, $F \to \lambda$, and let $\Sigma = \Sigma_1 \cup \Sigma_2$ be a partition of Σ (i.e. $\Sigma_1 \cap \Sigma_2 = \emptyset$). If G generates a word of the form $z = u'w'y'$ in which the total number of occurrences of symbols from Σ_2 is g, $w' \in \Sigma_1^*$, and $|w'| \geq 2^{2mg+3}$ then z can be written in the form $z = uvwxy$, where $vx \in \Sigma_1^*$, v (or x) is a nonempty substring of w' and each word of the form uv^iwx^iy ($i \geq 0$) is also generated by G. □

Using this observation, we can construct three new pumping pieces of the form

$$\ldots a'\eta'\$d' \ldots b'\delta'\$e'$$

one in which all words, except possibly a', d', b', e', are long (and thus represent big numbers), one in which they are all short (and thus represent small numbers), and one in which all but one or two are short. It is easy to show that we can replace $\ldots v^{j-1} \ldots x^{j-1} \ldots$ in (14) by properly chosen copies of these three pieces in such a way that p' words are long and the rest are short, and this proves the lemma. Notice that when using the pumping piece with long words, we might obtain 2 short words every time we get h-2 long ones. But since $\frac{q}{p} \geq \frac{1}{3}$ and $h \geq 9$, that many short words are needed anyway (this is the reason for the occurrence of the number 9 in our various constants). □

Acknowledgments

The initial inspiration for this work came up during discussions with Poul Jespersen. Ole Lehrmann Madsen's expertise on attribute grammars has also been very helpful.

References

[AU] A.V. Aho and J.D. Ullman [1972]. "The Theory of Parsing, Translation and Compiling" Vol. 1: Parsing, Prentice-Hall, Englewood Cliffs, N.J.

[Dus] J. Duske, R. Parchmann, M. Sedello and J. Specht [1977]. "IO-macrolanguages and attributed translations", Information and Control 35, 87-105.

[EF] J. Engelfriet and G. Filé [1979]. "The formal power of one-visit attribute grammars", Manuscript, Tech. Hoogeschool, Twente, Netherlands.

[Je] P. Jespersen [1979]. "Attributgrammatikker med begrænsede semantiske funktioner", Master's Thesis, Aarhus University, Denmark.

[Knu] D.E. Knuth [1968]. "Semantics of context-free languages", Math. Syst. Theory 2, 127-145.

[LRS] O.M. Lewis, P.J. Rosenkrantz and R.E. Stesrns [1974]. "Attributed translations", JCSS 9, 191-194.

[Ri] H. Riis [1980]. "Subclasses of attribute grammars", Master's Thesis, Aarhus University, Denmark.

A CONSTRUCTIVE APPROACH TO COMPILER CORRECTNESS *

Peter Mosses

Computer Science Department
Aarhus University
Ny Munkegade
DK-8000 Aarhus C, Denmark

Abstract

It is suggested that denotational semantic definitions of programming languages should be based on a small number of abstract data types, each embodying a fundamental concept of computation. Once these fundamental abstract data types have been implemented in a particular target language (e.g. stack-machine code), it is a simple matter to construct a correct compiler for any source language from its denotational semantic definition. The approach is illustrated by constructing a compiler similar to the one which was proved correct by Thatcher, Wagner & Wright (1979). Some familiarity with many-sorted algebras is presumed.

1. INTRODUCTION

There have been several attacks on the compiler-correctness problem: by McCarthy & Painter (1967), Burstall & Landin (1969), F.L. Morris (1973) and, more recently, by Thatcher, Wagner & Wright, of the ADJ group (1979). The essence of the approach advocated in those papers can be summarised as follows: One is given a source language L, a target language T, and their respective semantics in the form of models M and U. Given also a compiler to be proved correct, one constructs an encoder: M → U and shows that this diagram commutes:

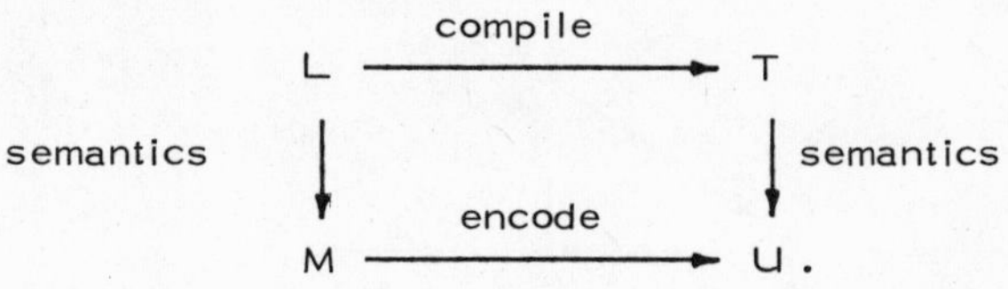

---

*) An earlier version of this paper is to appear in Proceedings of a Workshop on Semantics-Directed Compiler Generation, Aarhus, 1980 (Springer-Verlag).

It is assumed that the semantic and compiling functions are "syntax-directed". This amounts to insisting on denotational semantics in the style of Scott & Strachey (1971): "The values of expressions are determined in such a way that the value of a whole expression depends functionally on the values of its parts". ADJ (1979) reformulated this in the framework of initial algebra semantics, where the grammar, say G, of L is identified with "the" initial G-algebra. The advantage of this is that a semantic function: L → M can be seen to be a (by initiality, unique) homomorphism from L to a G-algebra based on the model M. Similarly, a compiling function: L → T is a homomorphism from L to a G-algebra derived from T, and then the semantics: T → U induces a G-algebra based on U.

So L, M, T and U can be considered as G-algebras, and the two semantics and the compiler are homomorphisms. A proof that encode: M → U is a homomorphism then gives the commutativity of the above diagram, by the initiality of L. (Actually, to interpret this as "compiler correctness", one should also show that encode is injective, or else work with decode: U → M.) ADJ (1979) illustrated the approach for a simple language L, including assignment, loops, expressions with side-effects and simple declarations. T was a language corresponding to flow charts with instructions for assignment and stacking. Their semantic definitions of L and T can be regarded as "standard" denotational semantics in the spirit (though not the notation!) of Scott & Strachey (1971). They succeeded in giving a (very!) full proof of the correctness of a simple compiler: L → T.

We shall take a somewhat different approach in this paper. The <u>semantics</u> of the source language L will be given in terms of an <u>abstract data type</u> S, rather than a particular model. The target language T will also be taken as an abstract data type. Then the correct <u>implementation</u> of S by T will enable us to <u>construct</u> a correct compiler (from L to T) from the semantic definition of L. The compiler to be constructed is actually the composition of the semantics and the implementation, as shown by the following diagram:

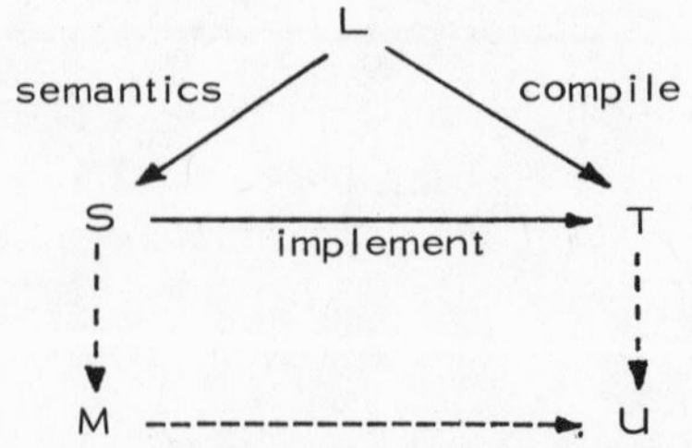

The models M and U are not relevant to the proof of the correctness of the implementation: S → T, but may aid the comparison of this diagram with the preceding one.

As with the earlier attacks on the compiler correctness problem, we shall regard the semantics and the compiler as homomorphisms on G-algebras, where G is the grammar of L. However, a crucial point is that with the present approach, the implementation of S by T can be proved correct before making S and T into G-algebras (one need only make T into an algebra with the same signature as S). Thus the proof is completely independent of the productions of G, in contrast to that of ADJ (1979). This allows us to generate correct compilers for a whole family of source languages - languages which are similar to L, in that their denotational semantics can be given in terms of S - without repeating (or even modifying) the proof that the implementation of S by T is correct.

The abstract data types S and T will be specified equationally, enabling the use of the work on initial algebras, such as that by ADJ (1976), in proving our implementation of S by T correct. It is important to establish the "correctness" of these equational specifications, in order to see that the semantics: L → S is the intended semantics. However, this problem will be considered only briefly here, as it is independent of the proof of correctness of our implementation.

The main concern of this paper is with the compiler-correctness problem. However, it is hoped that the example presented below will also serve as an illustration of on-going work on making denotational semantics "less concrete" and "more modular". It is claimed that there are abstract data types corresponding to all our fundamental concepts of computation - and that any programming language can be analyzed in terms of a suitable combination of these. "Bad" features of programming languages are shown up by the need for a complicated analysis - so long as the fundamental concepts are chosen appropriately. Of course, only a few of the fundamental concepts are needed for the semantics of the simple example language L (they include the sequential execution of actions, the computation and use of semantic values, and dynamic associations). An ordinary denotational semantics for L would make use of these concepts implicitly - the approach advocated here is to be explicit.

The use of abstract data types in this approach encourages a greater modularity in semantic definitions, making them - hopefully - easier to read, write and modify. It seems that Burstall & Goguen's (1977) work on "putting theories together" could form a suitable formal basis for expressing the modularity. However, this aspect of the approach is not exploited here.

It should be mentioned that the early paper by McCarthy & Painter (1967) already made use of abstract data types: the relation between storing and accessing values in variables was specified axiomatically. ADJ (1979) also used an abstract data type, but only for the operators on the integers and truth-values.

The approach presented here has been inspired by much of the early work on abstract data types, such as that of ADJ (1975, 1976), Guttag (1975), Wand (1977) and Zilles (1974). Also influential has been Wand's (1976) description of the application of abstract data types to language definition, although he was more concerned with definitional interpreters than with denotational semantics. Goguen's (1978) work on "distributed-fix" operators has contributed by liberating algebra from the bonds of prefix notation.

However, it is also the case that the proposed approach builds to a large extent on the work of the Scott-Strachey "school" of semantics, as described by Scott & Strachey (1971), Tennent (1976), Milne & Strachey (1976), Stoy (1977), and Gordon (1979). The success of Milner (1979) in describing concurrency algebraically has provided some valuable guidelines for choosing semantic primitives.

The rest of this paper is organized as follows. After the explanation of some notational conventions, the abstract syntax of the ADJ (1979) source language L is given. A semantic abstract data type S is described, possible models are discussed, and the standard semantics of L is given. The next section presents a "stack" abstract data type T, which needs extending before the implementation of S can be expressed homomorphically. The proof of the correctness of the implementation is sketched, and a compiler - corresponding closely to ADJ's - is constructed. Finally, the application of the approach to more realistic examples is discussed.

2. STANDARD SEMANTICS

The notation used in this paper differs significantly from that recommended by ADJ (1979) by remaining close to the notation of the Scott-Strachey school. This is not just a matter of following tradition. There are two main points of contention:

(i) The use of the semantic function explicitly in semantic equations. Although technically unnecessary, from an algebraic point of view, this allows us to regard the semantic function as just another equationally-defined operator in an abstract data type, and to forget about the machinery of homomorphisms and initial algebras (albeit temporarily!). Perhaps more important is that we apply the operators of the abstract syntax only to syntactic values, whereas in the pure algebraic notation, used by ADJ, one applies the semantic versions of the syntactic operators to semantic values - thereby hindering a "naive" reading of a semantic description.

(ii) The use of mixfix(*) notation for the operators of the abstract syntax. Mixfix notation is a generalization of prefix, infix and postfix notation: operator symbols

(*) called "distributed-fix" by Goguen (1978).

can be distributed freely around and between operands (e.g. if-then-else). ADJ used infix and mixfix notation ($f \circ g$, $[f,g,h]$) freely in their semantic notation, but stuck to postfix notation ((x)f) for the syntactic algebra. This made the correspondence between the abstract syntax and the "usual" concrete syntax for their language rather strained. Whilst not disastrous for such a simple and well-known language as their example, the extra burden on the reader would be excessive for more realistic languages.

Notational Conventions

The names of sorts are written starting with a capital, thus: A, Cmd. Algebraic variables over a particular sort are represented by the sort name, usually decorated with subscripts or primes, A, A_1, A'. Operator symbols are written with lower-case letters and non-alphabetic characters: tt, even( ), +, if then else. Families of operators are indicated by letting a part of the operator vary over a set, e.g. id := (id $\in$ Id) is a family of prefix operators indexed by elements of Id. It is also convenient to allow families of sorts (indexed by (sequences of) domain names from a set Δ; lower-case Greek letters (δ, σ, τ) are used for the indices.

The arity and co-arity of an operator in a signature are indicated by the notation

$$S \Leftarrow f(S_1,\ldots,S_n)$$

- here, the arity of f is $S_1 \cdots S_n$, the co-arity is S. Mixfix notation can be used here for the operator symbol, giving a pleasing similarity to BNF, e.g.

Cmd <= if BExp then Cmd else Cmd.

The term "theory" will here be used synonymously with "abstract data type". So much for notation.

Abstract Syntax (L)

The abstract syntax of the source language L is given in Table 1. It may be compared directly with that of ADJ (1979), although, as explained above, we shall not restrict ourselves to postfix notation for syntactic operators here. Id is taken to be a set, rather than a sort, following ADJ - in effect, this gives a parameterised abstract data type, and we need not be concerned about the details of Id.

Table 1. Abstract Syntax of L

sorts		
	Cmd	- commands
	AExp	- arithmetic expressions
	BExp	- Boolean expressions
	Id	- unspecified set of identifiers

operators		indices
Cmd <=	continue	
	id := AExp	id ∈ Id
	if BExp then Cmd else Cmd	
	Cmd; Cmd	
	while BExp do Cmd	
AExp <=	aconst	aconst ∈ {0, 1}
	id	id ∈ Id
	aop1 AExp	aop1 ∈ {−, pr, su}
	AExp aop2 AExp	aop2 ∈ {+, −, ×}
	if BExp then AExp else AExp	
	Cmd result AExp	
	let id be AExp in AExp	id ∈ Id
BExp <=	bconst	bconst ∈ {tt, ff}
	prop AExp	prop ∈ {even}
	AExp rel AExp	rel ∈ {≤, ≥, eq}
	bop1 BExp	bop1 ∈ {¬}
	BExp bop2 BExp	bop2 ∈ {∧, ∨}

Standard Semantic Theory (S)

The standard semantic theory presented in Table 2 may seem a bit daunting at first. Actually, the operators themselves (left-hand column) are quite simple, but the "book-keeping" concerned with indices (δ, σ, τ) of the sorts is somewhat cumbersome.

Table 2 could be regarded as a theory schema, or as an instantiation of a parameterised theory, where Δ is a formal parameter (as is Id). Whichever way one looks at it, the use of Δ gives a hint of modularity, as well as avoiding undue repetition in the specification.

Table 2. Semantic Theory S

sorts (indices: $\delta \in \Delta$; $\sigma, \tau \in \Delta^*$, where $\Delta = \{T, Z\}$)

A – actions, with source σA and target τA
Y – variables over actions, with source σY and target τY
V – values, with domain δV
X – variables over values, with domain δX

operators (indices: $id \in Id$; $n \in \{0, 1, \ldots\}$)

actions A	source σA		target τA
A <= skip	( )		( )
$A' ; A''$	$\sigma A' \cdot \sigma A''$		$\tau A' \cdot \tau A''$
$V!$	( )		δV
$X.A'$	$\delta X \cdot \sigma A'$		$\tau A'$
$A' \succ_n A''$	$\sigma A' \cdot s''$		$t' \cdot \tau A''$
	where $\sigma A'' = d_1 \cdots d_n \cdot s''$,	and	$\tau A' = d_1 \cdots d_n \cdot t'$
tt? A' / ff? A''	$T \cdot \sigma A'$		$\tau A'$
	where $\sigma A'' = \sigma A'$,	and	$\tau A'' = \tau A'$
fix Y.A'	σY		τY
	where $\sigma A' = \sigma Y$	and	$\tau A' = \tau Y$
Y	σY		τY
$contents_{id}$	( )		Z
$update_{id}$	Z		( )

action variables Y	source σA	target τY
Y <= a	( )	( )
a_n	( )	( )

values V	domain δV	conditions
V <= X	δX	
aconst	Z	
aop1 V'	Z	$\delta V' = Z$
V' aop2 V''	Z	$\delta V' = \delta V'' = Z$
bconst	T	
prop V'	T	$\delta V' = Z$
V' rel V''	T	$\delta V' = \delta V'' = Z$

value variables X	domain δX	
X <= z	Z	
z_n	Z	

The following informal description of S may help the reader.

The basic concept is that of <u>actions</u> (A). Actions not only have an "effect", but may also consume and/or produce sequences of values (V). These values can be thought of as belonging to the "semantic domains" in Δ, i.e. T and Z. The book-keeping referred to above mainly consists of keeping track of the number and sorts of values consumed (σ, for source) and produced (τ, for target). Note that a raised dot ($\cdot$) stands for concatenation of sequences in Δ^* and ( ) is the empty sequence.

Variables (X) are used to name computed values and to indicate dependency on these values (by actions and other computed values). Variables over actions (Y) allow the easy expression of recursion and iteration.

Table 2 continued

equations

1. $\text{skip} ; A = A$
2. $A ; \text{skip} = A$
3. $(A_1 ; A_2) ; A_3 = A_1 ; (A_2 ; A_3)$
4. $V! \succ (X.\ A) = A\ \{X \leftarrow V\}$
5. $(V! ; A_1) \succ_n A_2 = A_1 \succ_{n-1} (V! \succ_1 A_2)$
6. $tt! \succ (tt?\ A_1\ /\ ff?\ A_2) = A_1$
7. $ff! \succ (tt?\ A_1\ /\ ff?\ A_2) = A_2$
8. $\text{fix}\ Y.\ A = A\ \{Y \leftarrow \text{fix}\ Y.\ A\}$
9. $(V! \succ \text{update}_{id}) ; \text{contents}_{id} = (V! \succ \text{update}_{id}) ; V!$
10. $(V! \succ \text{update}_{id}) ; \text{contents}_{id'} = \text{contents}_{id'} ; (V! \succ \text{update}_{id})$ for $id \neq id'$
11. $A ; V! = V! ; A$ for $\tau A = (\ )$
12. $X.\ A = X'.\ A\ \{X \leftarrow X'\}$ for X' not free in A
13. $(tt?\ A_1\ /\ ff?\ A_2) ; A_3 = tt?\ (A_1 ; A_3)\ /\ ff?\ (A_2 ; A_3)$
14. $A_1 ; (tt?\ A_2\ /\ ff?\ A_3) = tt?\ (A_1 ; A_2)\ /\ ff?\ (A_1 ; A_3)$
15. $(X.\ A_1) ; A_2 = X.\ (A_1 ; A_2)$ for X not free in A_2
16. $A_1 ; (X.\ A_2) = X.\ (A_1 ; A_2)$ for X not free in A_1 and $\sigma A_1 = (\ )$
17. $V! ; (A_1 \succ X.\ A_2) = A_1 \succ X.\ (V! ; A_2)$ for X not free in V and $\tau A_1 = (\delta X)$
18. $\text{contents}_{id} \succ X.\ tt?\ A_1\ /\ ff?\ A_2 = tt?\ \text{contents}_{id} \succ X.\ A_1\ /\ ff?\ \text{contents}_{id} \succ X.\ A_2$

We consider the value operators first. They are taken straight from the "underlying" data type of ADJ (1979). It is assumed that bconst, prop, etc. vary over the same sets as in Table 1, thus giving families of operators. The Boolean operators ($\neg$, $\wedge$, $\vee$) are not needed in giving the semantics of L, and have been omitted from S (as have variables over truth values).

There is a domain name $\delta \in \Delta$ associated with each value of V; also, the domain name Z is associated with the variables used to name values in the sort Z. (This would be of more importance if we were to include variables naming T-values as well - the idea is just to make sure that a sort-preserving substitution can be defined.)

The <u>action operators</u> are perhaps less familiar. A <= skip is the null action, it is an identity for the sequencing operator A <= A' ; A''. Note that sequencing is additive in the sources and targets. For example, if A' and A'' both consume one value, then A' ; A'' consumes two values.

The most basic action operator producing a value is A <= V! . The consumption of a value is effected by A <= X. A', and X is bound to the consumed value in A'. To indicate that n values produced by one action are consumed by another, we have the operator $A <= A' \succ_n A''$, and it is the <u>first</u> n values produced by A' which get consumed by A''. ($\succ_n$ will be written simply as $\succ$ when the value of n can be deduced from the context.) For example, consider $V! \succ X.\ A'$. The value V is produced (by V!), consumed (by X. A') and then bound to X in A'. Free occurrences of X in A' just indicate where the consumed value is used.
In $(V_1! \ ; V_2!) \succ X_1.\ X_2.\ (X_2! \ ; X_1!)$, the values V_1, V_2 are produced, consumed and bound to X_1, X_2 and then produced again in reverse order - thus the net effect of the whole action is to produce two values.

A <= tt? A' / ff? A'' is a choice operator: it consumes a truth value (tt or ff) and reduces to A' or A''. The sources and targets of A' and A'' must be identical.

A <= fix Y. A' binds Y in A' and, together with A <= Y, allows the expression of recursively-defined actions. Actually, it is used here (in describing L) only in a very limited form, corresponding to iteration: $A <= \text{fix a. } (A' \succ \text{tt? } A''; \text{ a / ff? skip})$, where A' produces a truth-value, and the action variable, a, does not occur free in A' or A''.

Finally, there are two families of operators for storing and accessing computed values: $A <= \text{update}_{id}$, and $A <= \text{contents}_{id}$, for id $\in$ Id. Only integer values may be stored. Note that update_{id} consumes a value, contents_{id} produces a value.

Now for the equations of Table 2, specifying the laws which the operators of S are to satisfy. ADJ (1979) gave equations for the value operators - they are much as one might expect, and are not repeated here. The novelty of S lies in its action operators.

To avoid getting bogged down in irrelevant details, the equations for the binding operators of S (A <= X. A' and A <= fix Y. A') are given with the help of notation for syntactic substitution: for any action term A of S, $A\{X \leftarrow V\}$ is the term with all free occurrences of X replaced by the value term V (and with uniform changes of bound variables in A to avoid "capturing" free variables in V). Similarly for $A\{Y \leftarrow A'\}$. This syntactic substitution could have been added as an operator to S, and specified equationally. (This is not immediately obvious, because one cannot define an operator in S to test whether a variable is free in an action. Fortunately, Berkling's (1976) idea of adding an "unbinding" operator to the λ-calculus leads to an equational specification of syntactic substitution in S.) Another way of treating binding operators will be discussed below.

The equations should now be self-explanatory. What might not be obvious is that they are the "right" equations, and are neither inconsistent nor incomplete. It would delay us too much to go into all the details here, but the idea is to use a Scott-model for S to show consistency, and a so-called canonical term algebra to prove completeness. The canonical term algebra in effect specifies (possibly infinite) "normal forms" for arbitrary actions in S, and we are satisfied when these normal forms correspond to "fully evaluated" actions. (The potential infiniteness of actions suggests that the rational theories of ADJ (1976a) are the right setting for the meta-theory of abstract data types like S. The operator fix of S corresponds closely to the dagger of rational theories - when $\circ$ is substitution.)

The "obvious" Scott-model for S (corresponding to the M of ADJ (1979)) has a carrier for sort A, with $\sigma A = d_1 \cdots d_m$ and $\tau A = d_1' \cdots d_n'$ ($d_i, d_i' \in \{T, Z\}$), the domain of continuous functions

$$[Env \times d_1 \times \cdots \times d_m \to Env \times d_1' \times \cdots \times d_n'],$$

where Env = Id $\to$ Z. (Of course, one could also take a continuations-based model, or one with both static and dynamic environments, if preferred.)

However, S has binding operators, and terms can have "free" (semantic) variables. This raises the question of whether a modelling function from S to the Scott-model above could be expressed as a homomorphism, or whether one must allow the function to take an environment (giving the values of the semantic variables, not of the program variables). Robin Milner (1979) has suggested that one can regard a binding operator as a notational means for representing a family, indexed by the values which may be substituted for the bound variables. E.g. X. A represents the family $\langle A\{X \leftarrow v\}\rangle_{v \in \delta X}$, and in V! $\succ$ (X. A), the second operand of $\succ$ is a family. This enables the modelling function to be given as a homomorphism. One might wonder whether the introduction of operators acting on (in general) infinite families undermines the whole algebraic framework, but Reynolds (1977) shows that this is not the case. Anyway, modelling is not our main concern in this paper, so let us leave the topic there.

<u>Semantics (sem)</u>

The "standard" denotational semantics of L in terms of the abstract data type S is given in Table 3. The use of the "semantic equations" notation, with the explicit definition of the semantic function, was defended at the beginning of this section. To allow the omission of parentheses, it is assumed that the operator '.' binds as far to the right as possible (as in λ-notation). As in the specification of S, it is assumed that bconst, prop, etc. vary over the same sets as in Table 1, thus giving families of equations.

Note that sem⟦ ⟧ can be considered either as an operator in an extension of the theories L and S, or else as a homomorphism from L to a derived theory of S. Under the latter view, the composition of sem with the modelling function (from S to the Scott-model mentioned above) yields the semantics which ADJ (1979) gave for L. The differences in appearance between ADJ's semantics and ours are due largely to ADJ's reliance on the operators of algebraic theories (tupling, projections, composition, iteration), whereas our S provides us with binding operators.

Table 3. Standard Semantics for L using S

operators
A <= sem⟦Cmd⟧ $\sigma A = (\,)$, $\tau A = (\,)$
A <= sem⟦AExp⟧ $\sigma A = (\,)$, $\tau A = Z$
A <= sem⟦BExp⟧ $\sigma A = (\,)$, $\tau A = T$

sem⟦Cmd⟧ equations (id ∈ Id)

sem⟦continue⟧ = skip
sem⟦id := AExp⟧ = sem⟦AExp⟧ >– update$_{id}$
sem⟦if BExp then Cmd$_1$ else Cmd$_2$⟧ = sem⟦BExp⟧ >– tt? sem⟦Cmd$_1$⟧ / ff? sem⟦Cmd$_2$⟧
sem⟦while BExp do Cmd⟧ = fix a. sem⟦BExp⟧ >– tt? sem⟦Cmd⟧ ; a / ff? skip

sem⟦AExp⟧ equations

sem⟦aconst⟧ = aconst !
sem⟦id⟧ = contents$_{id}$
sem⟦aop1 AExp⟧ = sem⟦AExp⟧ >– z. (aop1 z) !
sem⟦AExp$_1$ aop2 AExp$_2$⟧ = sem⟦AExp$_1$⟧ >– z_1. sem⟦AExp$_2$⟧ >– z_2. (z_1 aop2 z_2) !
sem⟦if BExp then AExp$_1$ else AExp$_2$⟧ = sem⟦BExp⟧ >– tt? sem⟦AExp$_1$⟧ / ff? sem⟦AExp$_2$⟧
sem⟦Cmd result AExp⟧ = sem⟦Cmd⟧ ; sem⟦AExp⟧
sem⟦let id be AExp$_1$ in AExp$_2$⟧ = contents$_{id}$ >– z_1. (sem⟦AExp$_1$⟧ >– update$_{id}$);
sem⟦AExp$_2$⟧ >– z_2. (z_1 ! >– update$_{id}$); z_2 !

sem⟦BExp⟧ equations

sem⟦bconst⟧ bconst !
sem⟦prop AExp⟧ = sem⟦AExp⟧ >– z. (prop z) !
sem⟦AExp$_1$ rel AExp$_2$⟧ = sem⟦AExp$_1$⟧ >– z_1. sem⟦AExp$_2$⟧ >– z_2. (z_1 rel z_2) !
sem⟦¬ BExp⟧ = sem⟦BExp⟧ >– tt? ff! / ff? tt!
sem⟦BExp$_1$ ∧ BExp$_2$⟧ = sem⟦BExp$_1$⟧ >– tt? sem⟦BExp$_2$⟧ / ff? ff!
sem⟦BExp$_1$ ∨ BExp$_2$⟧ = sem⟦BExp$_1$⟧ >– tt? tt! / ff? sem⟦BExp$_2$⟧

3. STACK IMPLEMENTATION

We now take a look at the target language T for our compiler. Like the target language taken by ADJ (1979), T represents flow-charts over stack-machine instructions. The abstract syntax of T is given in Table 4.

Actually, our T is not as general as ADJ's: they considered flow-charts of arbitrary shape, whereas we shall make do with "regular" flow-charts, corresponding to the "algebraic" flow diagrams of Scott (1970). This loss of generality doesn't seem to matter in connection with compiling L, which has no goto-command.

Table 4. Stack Theory T

sorts (indices: $\delta \in \Delta$; $\tau \in \Delta^*$, where $\Delta = \{T, Z\}$)

- A – actions, with source σA and target τA
- Y – variables over actions, with source σY and target τY
- V – values, with domain δV

operators (indices: $id \in Id$; $n \in \{0, 1, \ldots\}$)

actions A	source σA	target τA
A <= skip	( )	( )
$A' ; A''$	$\sigma A' \cdot \sigma A''$	$\tau A' \cdot \tau A''$
V!	( )	δV
$A' \underset{n}{\rightarrow} A''$	$\sigma A' \cdot s''$ where $\sigma A'' = d_1 \cdots d_n \cdot s''$, and	$t' \cdot \tau A''$ $\tau A' = t' \cdot d_n \cdots d_1$
tt? A' / ff? A''	$T \cdot \sigma A'$ where $\sigma A' = \sigma A''$ and	$\tau A'$ $\tau A' = \tau A''$
fix Y.A'	σY where $\sigma A' = \sigma Y$ and	τY $\tau A' = \tau Y$
Y	σY	τY
$contents_{id}$	( )	Z
$update_{id}$	Z	( )
switch	$Z \cdot Z$	$Z \cdot Z$
prop	Z	T
rel	$Z \cdot Z$	T
aop1	Z	Z
aop2	$Z \cdot Z$	Z

action variables Y	source σY	target τY
Y <= a	( )	( )
a_n	( )	( )

values V	domain δV	
V <= aconst	Z	
bconst	T	

A comparison of Tables 2 and 4 shows that T is rather similar to S. However, this should not be too surprising: many of the same fundamental concepts of computation are being used, e.g. sequencing of actions, storing of values. Note that $A <= A' \underset{n}{\rightarrow} A''$ in T corresponds to $A <= A' \underset{n}{\succ} A''$ in S, but it is the last n values produced by A' which get consumed (in reversed order), by A'' in T. Also, the value terms V in T are restricted to be constants, and A <= V! represents pushing V onto the stack. The value operators (prop, rel, aop1, aop2) of S have become actions operating on the stack in T. A <= switch interchanges the top two values on the stack. Finally, there are no value variables X in T - and hence no A <= X. A' either.

However, T is to be more than just a language: it is to be an abstract data type! There are equations, very similar to those for S, which the operators of T must satisfy. The one equation which is crucially different is

(4.) $$(A_1 ; V!) \underset{n}{\rightarrow} A_2 = A_1 \underset{n-1}{\rightarrow} (V! \underset{1}{\rightarrow} A_2)$$

expressing a sort of associativity for $\rightarrow$, something which is lacking for $\succ$ in S. In fact it is this property which allows us to think of terms in T as representing ordinary flow-charts.

So the problem is now to implement one abstract data type (S) by another (T), and show that the implementation is correct. If imp: S $\rightarrow$ T, then let us say that imp is a correct implementation of S by T if it is an injective homomorphism (into the implicit derived algebra of T with the same signature as S). In other words, imp respects the equations of S: for any s, s' in S, $imp[\![s]\!] = imp[\![s']\!]$ iff s = s'. Having found such an imp, the composite imp $\circ$ sem: L $\rightarrow$ T is a correct compiler from L to T.

Unfortunately, it is actually impossible to implement S correctly by the T of Table 4! To see why, consider a term of S with free (value-) variables, such as z! . What could imp give in T as the implementation of this term? If one tries to answer this question, one discovers that free variables in S correspond to values at an unknown depth on the stack in T - and that there is no way of representing such values. (Considering binding operators as a means for representing families of terms without free variables doesn't help, as there is no means of representing such a family in T.)

This is annoying, because one can easily implement the closed terms of S by T: one knows the positions of all the values on the stack. Moreover, only closed terms were used in giving the semantics of L. One could argue that we could make do with an implementation of only the closed terms of S, and proceed with our compiler construction. However, to show that the implementation (and hence the compiler) is correct, we need it to be a homomorphism - and that means considering all the terms of S, including those with free variables.

Thus we are forced to extend T, before we can use it to give a homomorphic implementation of S. The most natural extension to take seems to be Tx, given in Table 5. The action A <= X. A' can be thought of as removing the top item from the stack and binding it to X in A'.

Table 5. Extension of T to Tx

sorts X - variables over values, with domain δV

operators

actions A		source σA	target τA
A <=	X.A'	$\delta X \cdot \sigma A'$	$\tau A'$

values V		domain δV	
V <=	X	δX	

value variables X		domain δX	
X <=	t	T	
	t_n	T	
	z	Z	
	z_n	Z	

equations

1. $V! \rightarrow (X.A) = A\{X \leftarrow V\}$
2. $\text{switch} = z_1.\ z_2.\ (z_2!\ ;\ z_1!)$

Now we are able to give a homomorphic implementation of S by Tx, and prove it correct. But how does that help us in constructing a compiler from L to T (rather than to Tx)? Recall that only closed terms of S are used in the semantics of L - and that they are implemented by closed terms in Tx. It just happens that any closed term of Tx is equivalent to a term of T, i.e. one without any value variables at all! This ensures that our compiler from L to Tx can be converted to one from L to T.

Actually, that is not quite true. We need to add a few derived operators to Tx: generalizations of A <= switch, for permuting the top values on the stack. (This is analogous to adding the combinators (S, K, etc.) to the λ-calculus, in using them to eliminate λ-abstractions.) The extra operators, extending Tx to Tx', are given in Table 6. It turns out that they do not occur in the compiler we construct for L, because of the lack of exploitation of the generality of S in giving the semantics of L. Table 6 also gives the (derived) equations which are used in converting closed terms in Tx' to ones without value variables. Note that these equations simplify considerably when the sources or targets of actions are empty: $up^{d}_{()}$ and $down^{d}_{()}$ have no effect, and may be removed.

Table 6. Extension of Tx to Tx'

operators (indices: d, $d_i \in \Delta$)

actions A	source σA	target τA
A <= pop	d	$()$
copy	d	$d \cdot d$
$up^{d}_{d_1 \cdots d_n}$	$d_n \cdots d_1 \cdot d$	$d_1 \cdots d_n \cdot d$
$down^{d}_{d_1 \cdots d_n}$	$d \cdot d_n \cdots d_1$	$d \cdot d_1 \cdots d_n$
$flip^{n}_{d_1 \cdots d_m}$	$d_m \cdots d_1$	$d_{n+1} \cdots d_m \cdot d_n \cdots d_1$

equations where $x_{(i)} = t_{(i)}$, if $d_{(i)} = T$
$z_{(i)}$, if $d_{(i)} = Z$

1. $pop_d = x.\ skip$
2. $copy_d = x.\ (x!\ ;\ x!)$
3. $up^{d}_{d_1 \cdots d_n} = x_n \cdots x_1.\ x.\ (x_1!\ ;\ \ldots\ ;\ x_n!\ ;\ x!)$
4. $down^{d}_{d_1 \cdots d_n} = x.\ x_n \cdots x_1.\ (x!\ ;\ x_1!\ ;\ \ldots\ ;\ x_n!)$
5. $flip^{n}_{d_1 \cdots d_m} = x_m \cdots x_1.\ (x_{n+1}!\ ;\ \ldots\ ;\ x_m!\ ;\ x_n!\ ;\ \ldots\ ;\ x_1!)$

---

6. $X.\ (X! \rightarrow A) = A$ when X not free in A
7. $X!\ ;\ A = X! \rightarrow down^{\delta X}_{\delta A} \rightarrow A$
8. $A\ ;\ X! = X! \rightarrow down^{\delta X}_{\delta A} \rightarrow A \rightarrow up^{\delta X}_{\tau A}$
9. $X! \rightarrow (X! \rightarrow A) = X! \rightarrow copy_{\delta X} \rightarrow A$
10. $A_1 \rightarrow (X! \rightarrow A_2) = X! \rightarrow down^{\delta X}_{\sigma A_1} \rightarrow A_1 \rightarrow up^{\delta X}_{\tau A_1} \rightarrow A_2$
11. $tt\,?\ (X! \rightarrow A_1)\ /\ ff\,?\ (X! \rightarrow A_2) = X! \rightarrow down^{\delta X}_{T} \rightarrow (tt\,?\ A_1\ /\ ff\,?\ A_2)$
12. $fix\ Y.\ (X! \rightarrow A) = X! \rightarrow (fix\ Y.\ copy_{\delta X} \rightarrow A) \rightarrow up^{\delta X}_{\tau A} \rightarrow pop_{\delta X}$
13. $A = X! \rightarrow (pop_{\delta X}\ ;\ A)$

Our implementation of S by T seems to have two rather independent aspects: (i) the "serialization" of value terms in S into action sequences in T; (ii) the representation of the binding action A <= X. A' of S in T. The second part caused us considerably more trouble than the first. Whilst it might be tempting to use this as an excuse to throw the binding operators out of S, it would be prefereble to find a way of implementing binding more systematically than by the introduction of combinators.

At last we can implement S, by Tx'. The implementation function, imp: S $\rightarrow$ Tx', is defined in Table 7, using the same notation as was used for defining the semantics of L. S-operators now occur inside $\llbracket\ \rrbracket$ (in contrast to Table 2). As one can see, the implementation itself is really quite trivial: most of the operators go straight over from S to Tx'. The exceptions are value transfers $A \Leftarrow A' \succ A''$, which cause some "shuffling" on the stack; and the production of compound values $A \Leftarrow V!$, which get sequentialized.

Table 7. Implementation of S by Tx'

operators

$A \Leftarrow \text{imp}\llbracket A' \rrbracket \qquad \sigma A = \sigma A', \quad \tau A = \tau A'$

$Y \Leftarrow \text{imp}\llbracket Y' \rrbracket \qquad \sigma Y = \sigma Y', \quad \tau Y = \tau Y'$

$A \Leftarrow \text{imp}\llbracket V \rrbracket \qquad \sigma A = (\,), \quad \tau A = \delta V$

$X \Leftarrow \text{imp}\llbracket X' \rrbracket \qquad \delta X = \delta X'$

imp⟦A⟧ equations

$\text{imp}\llbracket \text{skip} \rrbracket = \text{skip}$

$\text{imp}\llbracket A_1 ; A_2 \rrbracket = \text{imp}\llbracket A_1 \rrbracket ; \text{imp}\llbracket A_2 \rrbracket$

$\text{imp}\llbracket V! \rrbracket = \text{imp}\llbracket V \rrbracket$

$\text{imp}\llbracket X.A \rrbracket = \text{imp}\llbracket X \rrbracket .\ \text{imp}\llbracket A \rrbracket$

$\text{imp}\llbracket A_1 \underset{n}{\succ} A_2 \rrbracket = \text{imp}\llbracket A_1 \rrbracket \rightarrow \text{flip}^{n}_{\tau A_1} \underset{n}{\rightarrow} \text{imp}\llbracket A_2 \rrbracket$

$\text{imp}\llbracket \text{tt}?\ A_1 \,/\, \text{ff}?\ A_2 \rrbracket = \text{tt}?\ \text{imp}\llbracket A_1 \rrbracket \,/\, \text{ff}?\ \text{imp}\llbracket A_2 \rrbracket$

$\text{imp}\llbracket \text{fix}\ Y.A \rrbracket = \text{fix}\ \text{imp}\llbracket Y \rrbracket .\ \text{imp}\llbracket A \rrbracket$

$\text{imp}\llbracket Y \rrbracket = \text{imp}\llbracket Y \rrbracket$ (the Y on the left is an action)

$\text{imp}\llbracket \text{contents}_{id} \rrbracket = \text{contents}_{id}$

$\text{imp}\llbracket \text{update}_{id} \rrbracket = \text{update}_{id}$

imp⟦V⟧ equations

$\text{imp}\llbracket X \rrbracket = X!$

$\text{imp}\llbracket \text{aconst} \rrbracket = \text{aconst}!$

$\text{imp}\llbracket \text{aop1}\ V \rrbracket = \text{imp}\llbracket V \rrbracket \underset{1}{\rightarrow} \text{aop1}$

$\text{imp}\llbracket V_1\ \text{aop2}\ V_2 \rrbracket = (\text{imp}\llbracket V_1 \rrbracket ; \text{imp}\llbracket V_2 \rrbracket) \underset{2}{\rightarrow} \text{aop2}$

$\text{imp}\llbracket \text{bconst} \rrbracket = \text{bconst}!$

$\text{imp}\llbracket \text{prop}\ V \rrbracket = \text{imp}\llbracket V \rrbracket \underset{1}{\rightarrow} \text{prop}$

$\text{imp}\llbracket V_1\ \text{rel}\ V_2 \rrbracket = (\text{imp}\llbracket V_1 \rrbracket ; \text{imp}\llbracket V_2 \rrbracket) \underset{2}{\rightarrow} \text{rel}$

($\text{imp}\llbracket X \rrbracket$, $\text{imp}\llbracket Y \rrbracket$ are identities- equations omitted)

The rest of this section sketches the proof of the correctness of imp, and justifies the claim that value variables can be eliminated from closed terms of Tx'. The next section goes on to construct a correct compiler from L to T.

The proof of the correctness of imp: $S \rightarrow Tx'$ is quite routine, but unfortunately no shorter than that of ADJ (1979). Recall that we are to prove that for terms s, s' in S, $\text{imp}\llbracket s \rrbracket = \text{imp}\llbracket s' \rrbracket$ if and only if $s = s'$. The "if" part is the simpler: it is sufficient to show that for all equations $s = s'$ in the specification of S, $\text{imp}\llbracket s \rrbracket = \text{imp}\llbracket s' \rrbracket$ can be obtained from the equations of Tx'.

The "only if" part says that imp is injective. The easiest way to prove this seems to be to define an inverse for imp, abs: $Tx' \rightarrow S$. This is just as simple as defining imp, and only the few non-trivial cases of the definition are given in Table 8. Using the equations of S, one can show that $(\text{abs} \circ \text{imp})\llbracket s \rrbracket = s$ for all terms s in S. Furthermore, it can be shown that for all terms t, t' in Tx', $\text{abs}\llbracket t \rrbracket = \text{abs}\llbracket t' \rrbracket$ if $t = t'$ – this is just like the "if" part already proved for imp. But then, taking $t = \text{imp}\llbracket s \rrbracket$ and $t' = \text{imp}\llbracket s' \rrbracket$, it follows that $s = s'$ if $\text{imp}\llbracket s \rrbracket = \text{imp}\llbracket s' \rrbracket$, which is the desired result.

Table 8. Abstraction from Tx' to S

operators	$A \Leftarrow \text{abs}\llbracket A' \rrbracket$	$\sigma A = \sigma A'$, $\tau A = \tau A'$
	$Y \Leftarrow \text{abs}\llbracket Y' \rrbracket$	$\sigma Y = \sigma Y'$, $\tau Y = \tau Y'$
	$V \Leftarrow \text{abs}\llbracket V' \rrbracket$	$\delta V = \delta V'$
	$X \Leftarrow \text{abs}\llbracket X' \rrbracket$	$\delta X = \delta X'$

abs $\llbracket A \rrbracket$ equations (examples)

...

$$\text{abs}\llbracket A_1 \underset{n}{\rightarrow} A_2 \rrbracket = \text{abs}\llbracket A_1 \rrbracket \succ \text{flop}^n_{\tau A_1} \underset{n}{\succ} \text{abs}\llbracket A_2 \rrbracket$$

where $\text{flop}^n_{d_1 \cdots d_m} = x_m \ldots x_1 .\ (x_1! \ ; \ \ldots \ ; \ x_n! \ ; \ x_m! \ ; \ \ldots \ ; \ x_{n+1}!)$

$\text{abs}\llbracket V! \rrbracket = \text{abs}\llbracket V \rrbracket\ !$

$\text{abs}\llbracket \text{aop1} \rrbracket = z.\ (\text{aop1}\ z)\ !$

$\text{abs}\llbracket \text{aop2} \rrbracket = z_1 .\ z_2 .\ (z_1\ \text{aop}\ z_2)\ !$

$\text{abs}\llbracket \text{prop} \rrbracket = z.\ (\text{prop}\ z)\ !$

$\text{abs}\llbracket \text{rel} \rrbracket = z_1 .\ z_2 .\ (z_1\ \text{rel}\ z_2)\ !$

As for the elimination of value variables from closed terms of Tx', there is an algorithm, resembling the standard one for converting λ-calculus expressions to combinators. The algorithm proceeds as follows. Let A be a closed action term of Tx'. If A does not contain any occurrences of $X.\ A'$, then it cannot contain any occurrences of X (by closedness) and we are done. Otherwise, consider an innermost occurrence of $X.\ A'$ in A. If X does not occur free in A', then $X.\ A'$ can be replaced by $\text{pop}_{\delta X}$; A', by the equations in Table 6, and so this occurrence of $X.\ A'$ has been eliminated. On the other hand, if X does occur free in A', it must be as an action: $X!$. The equations of Table 6, interpreted as left-to-right replacement rules, allow A' to be transformed to the form X! → A'', where X does not occur in A''. But then X. A' can be replaced by A'', and again the occurrence of X. A' has been eliminated. As no extra occurrences have been introduced in the process (thanks to the use of the "combinators" pop, copy, up and down) the iteration of this process removes all occurrences of X. A' from A.

4. COMPILER CONSTRUCTION

We are now able to construct a correct compiler from L to T - or for any other source language whose semantics is given in terms of S. All we need to do is to take comp: L → Tx' as imp ∘ sem, and, using the fact that imp: S → Tx' is a homomorphism, combine the definitions of imp and sem to a definition of comp. The correctness of comp comes from the correctness of imp. This correctness is preserved under transforming the terms in Tx' in the definition, to terms of T, using the algorithm of the previous section. The finished product is shown in Table 9.

The process of transformation is not as painful as the equations of Table 6 (used as replacement rules) might suggest. This is because the only action sorts used in giving the semantics of L have an empty source and an empty or singleton target. Moreover, $A' \succ_n A''$ is only used for n = 1. It can be shown from the equations of Tx' that $flip^1_d$ can be omitted from the definition of imp, and that $down^d_{()}$ and $up^d_{()}$ are unnecessary in the equations in Table 6. In addition, up^z_z is equivalent to switch. These simplifications make the transformation from Tx' to T quite straightforward, and the only extra step necessary to obtain Table 9 is the removal of a couple of occurrences of switch; switch.

Conclusion

By using a form of denotational semantics based on abstract data types, we have seen how to construct correct compilers for a whole family of source languages directly from their semantic definitions.

For realistic source languages (such as Pascal, Clu, Ada), the feasibility of the approach presented here depends on the extent to which their denotational semantics can be given in terms of a small number of fundamental abstract data types. On the other hand, going to more realistic target languages should not present any major problems - except that it might prove rather difficult to exploit the "richness" of some machine codes!

Table 9. Compiler from L to T

<u>operators</u>

$A \Leftarrow comp[\![Cmd]\!] \qquad \sigma A = (\,), \quad \tau A = (\,)$

$A \Leftarrow comp[\![AExp]\!] \qquad \sigma A = (\,), \quad \tau A = Z$

$A \Leftarrow comp[\![BExp]\!] \qquad \sigma A = (\,), \quad \tau A = T$

comp[[Cmd]] equations

$comp[\![continue]\!] = skip$

$comp[\![id := AExp]\!] = comp[\![AExp]\!] \rightarrow update_{id}$

$comp[\![if\ BExp\ then\ Cmd_1\ else\ Cmd_2]\!] = comp[\![BExp]\!] \rightarrow tt?\ comp[\![Cmd_1]\!]\ /\ ff?\ comp[\![Cmd_2]\!]$

$comp[\![Cmd_1\ ;\ Cmd_2]\!] = comp[\![Cmd_1]\!]\ ;\ comp[\![Cmd_2]\!]$

$comp[\![while\ BExp\ do\ Cmd]\!] = fix\ a.\ comp[\![BExp]\!] \rightarrow tt?\ comp[\![Cmd]\!]\ ;\ a\ /\ ff?\ skip$

comp[[AExp]] equations

$comp[\![aconst]\!] = aconst!$

$comp[\![id]\!] = contents_{id}$

$comp[\![aop1\ AExp]\!] = comp[\![AExp]\!] \rightarrow aop1$

$comp[\![AExp_1\ aop2\ AExp_2]\!] = comp[\![AExp_1]\!] \rightarrow comp[\![AExp_2]\!] \rightarrow aop2$

$comp[\![if\ BExp\ then\ AExp_1\ else\ AExp_2]\!] = comp[\![BExp]\!] \rightarrow tt?\ comp[\![AExp_1]\!]\ /\ ff?\ comp[\![AExp_2]\!]$

$comp[\![Cmd\ result\ AExp]\!] = comp[\![Cmd]\!]\ ;\ comp[\![Aexp]\!]$

$comp[\![let\ id\ be\ AExp_1\ in\ AExp_2]\!] = contents_{id} \rightarrow comp[\![AExp_1]\!] \rightarrow update_{id};$
$\qquad comp[\![AExp_2]\!] \rightarrow switch \rightarrow update_{id}$

comp[[BExp]] equations

$comp[\![bconst]\!] = bconst!$

$comp[\![prop\ AExp]\!] = comp[\![AExp]\!] \rightarrow prop$

$comp[\![AExp_1\ rel\ AExp_2]\!] = comp[\![AExp_1]\!] \rightarrow comp[\![AExp_2]\!] \rightarrow rel$

$comp[\![\neg BExp]\!] = comp[\![BExp]\!] \rightarrow tt?\ ff!\ /\ ff?\ tt!$

$comp[\![BExp_1 \wedge BExp_2]\!] = comp[\![BExp_1]\!] \rightarrow tt?\ comp[\![BExp_2]\!]\ /\ ff?\ ff!$

$comp[\![BExp_1 \vee BExp_2]\!] = comp[\![BExp_1]\!] \rightarrow tt?\ tt!\ /\ ff?\ comp[\![BExp_2]\!]$

Finally, why did our constructed compiler turn out to be so similar to the one proved correct by ADJ (1979)? One might suspect that our construction was "rigged" to deal with just this example - but that is not the case. Another possibility is that ADJ themselves constructed their compiler systematically - albeit informally - from their semantic definition. It may also be that there is essentially only <u>one</u> correct compiler from L to T! In any case, for realistic source languages, one could conjecture that any compilers proved correct using the approach of ADJ (1979) will reflect the structure of the semantic definition of the source language, and in general be constructible by the method outlined here.

References

ADJ ($\subseteq$ {J.A. Goguen, J.W. Thatcher, E.A. Wagner, J.B. Wright})

(1975) "Initial algebra semantics and continuous algebras", IBM Res. Rep. RC-5701, 1975. JACM 24 (1977) 68-85.

(1976) "An initial algebra approach to the specification, correctness, and implementation of abstract data types", IBM Res. Rep. RC-6487, 1976. Current Trends in Programming Methodology IV (r. Yeh, ed.), Prentice Hall, 1979.

(1976a) "Rational algebraic theories and fixed-point solutions", Proc. 17th IEEE Symp. on Foundations of Computing, Houston, 1976.

(1979) "More on advice on structuring compilers and proving them correct", IBM Res. Rep. RC-7588, 1979. Proc. Sixth Int. Coll. on Automata, Languages and Programming, Graz, 1979.

Berkling, K.J.
(1976) "A symmetric complement to the lambda-calculus", Interner Bericht ISF-76-7, GMD-Bonn, 1976.

Burstall, R.M. & Goguen, J.A.
(1977) "Putting theories together to make specifications", Proc. Fifth Int. Joint Conf. on Artificial Intelligence, Boston, 1977.

Burstall, R.M. & Landin, P.J.
(1969) "Programs and their proofs: an algebraich approach", Machine Intelligence 4, 1969.

Goguen, J.A.
(1978) "Order sorted algebras: exceptions and error sorts, coercions and overloaded operators", Semantics and Theory of Comp. Rep. 14, UCLA, 1978.

Gordon, M.J.C.
(1979) The Denotational Description of Programming Languages, Springer-Verlag, 1979.

Guttag, J.V.
(1975) "The specification and application to programming of abstract data types", Tech. Rep. CRSG-59, Toronto University, 1975.

McCarthy, J. & Painter, J.
(1967) "Correctness of a compiler for arithmetic expressions", Proc. Symp. in Applied Math. 19 (1967) 33-41.

Milne, R.W. & Strachey, C.
1976) A Theory of Programming Language Semantics, Chapman & Hall (UK), John Wiley (USA), 1976.

Milner, R.
(1979) Algebraic Concurrency, unpublished lecture notes.

Morris, F.L.
(1973) "Advice on structuring compilers and proving them correct", Proc. ACM Symp. on Principles of Programming Languages, Boston, 1973.

Scott, D.S.
(1971) "The lattice of flow diagrams", Tech. Mono. PRG-3, Oxford Univ., 1971. Lect. Notes in Maths. 182: Semantics of Algorithmic Languages (E. Engeler, ed.), Springer, 1971.

Scott, D.S. & Strachey, C.
(1971) "Toward a mathematical semantics for computer languages", Tech. Mono. PRG-6, Oxford Univ., 1971. Computer and Automata (J. Fox, ed.), John Wiley, 1971.

Stoy, J.E.
(1977) Denotational Semantics, MIT Press, 1977.

Tennent, R.D.
(1976) "The denotational semantics of programming languages", CACM 19 (1976) 437-453.

Wand, M.
(1976) "First order identities as a defining language", Tech. Rep. 29, Indiana University, 1976, (revised: 1977).

(1977) "Final algebra semantics and data type extensions", Tech. Rep. 65, Indiana University, 1977. JCSS 19 (1979) 27-44.

Zilles, S.N.
(1974) "Algebraic specification of data types", Computation Structures Group Memo 119, MIT, 1974.

A Worst-Case Analysis of Nearest Neighbor Searching by Projection[1]

Christos H. Papadimitriou
Laboratory for Computer Science
Massachusetts Institute of Technology
Cambridge, Massachusetts 02139

Jon Louis Bentley
Departments of Computer Science and Mathematics
Carnegie-Mellon University
Pittsburgh, Pennsylvania 15213

Abstract -- The nearest neighbor searching problem (also called the post office problem) calls for organizing the set P of N points in k-space so that the nearest neighbor in P to a new point can be quickly found. Friedman, Baskett and Shustek describe an algorithm for nearest neighbor searching based on projecting the points onto the various coordinate axes; their analysis of this method shows that a nearest neighbor search can be performed in $O(N^{1-1/k})$ expected time, for any fixed dimension $k>1$ under a variety of probability distributions. In this paper we shall prove the stronger (worst-case) result that the total time required by (an extension of) their method to find the nearest neighbor of every point in any fixed k-dimensional point set is $O(N^{2-1/k})$, which immediately implies a result similar to theirs. The above results hold only for the L_∞ metric; we also investigate the Euclidean (L_2) metric. Our first result for that metric shows that the above analysis does not hold in general, and our second result then goes on to show that the analysis does in fact apply in practice, because of the finite word-length restrictions of real computers.

1. Introduction

A number of applications call for finding *nearest neighbors* in a multidimensional point set. Formally, point q in set P is the nearest neighbor of point p if no point in P is closer to p than q is; notice that this definition allows ties for nearest neighbor to be broken arbitrarily. We left undefined the metric that measures the distance between points; common metrics include the L_2 (Euclidean) and the L_∞ (Maximum Coordinate) metrics. There are two computational problems that involve finding nearest neighbors. We shall call the first *nearest neighbor searching*; in this problem we must organize the point set P so that the nearest neighbor in P to any new point can be found quickly. (This problem is often called the "post office" problem: given an address to receive mail, we want to find quickly the nearest post office.) A second problem is that of computing *all nearest*

---

[1]This research was supported in part by the Office of Naval Research under Contract N00014-76-C-0370 and in part by the National Science Foundation under Grant MCS-77-01193.

neighbors: we are given the point set P and must tell for each point in P what its nearest neighbor is (excluding, of course, the point itself). Both of these problems arise in a wide variety of applications (such as data analysis and document retrieval); the references contain many pointers to applications.

Much previous work has been done on nearest neighbor problems. Friedman, Baskett and Shustek [1975] were the first to describe an algorithm for nearest neighbor searching with probably sublinear search time (although only for the average case). They showed that the "projection" method requires O(N lg N) time to organize a file of N points in k-space, after which a nearest neighbor can be located in $O(N^{1-1/k})$ expected time, for a variety of underlying distributions. Lee, Chin and Chang [1976] later extended the projection algorithm to project on "principal component" directions in addition to coordinate axes. Knuth [1973] described the projection method in a database (rather than geometric) context under the name "inverted lists". Additional methods for nearest neighbor searching have been given by Friedman, Bentley and Finkel [1977] and Bentley, Weide and Yao [1979]; these techniques are faster than projection for very large problem sizes, but projection still does better when the number of points is small compared to the number of dimensions. A great deal of work has also been spent on worst-case algorithms for nearest neighbor problems. Shamos [1978] showed how the Voronoi diagram can be used to find all nearest neighbors in a planar point set, and Lipton and Tarjan used that structure to facilitate rapid nearest neighbor searching in the plane. Bentley [1979] used a technique called "multidimensional divide-and-conquer" to find all nearest neighbor pairs in a d-dimensional point set, and Zolnowsky [1978] gave a worst-case analysis of the nearest neighbor searching structure of Friedman, Bentley and Finkel that showed that it is very efficient on the average, regardless of the underlying probability distribution (his result is very similar to the result that we will see in Section 3.)

Even though many structures have been described that are demonstrably better for nearest neighbor problems than is projection, we shall study that structure in this paper for two reasons. First, it is an eminently practical structure: it is easy to code and relatively efficient, particularly in the (important) planar case. The second motivation for our study is the mathematical interest of the analysis: it is surprising that a structure proposed only for efficient expected times can be shown to perform well in the worst case also.

In Section 2 we will study an extension of Friedman, Baskett and Shustek's projection method for solving planar nearest neighbor problems, and then analyze its performance in an abstract combinatorial setting in Section 3. In Section 4 we will interpret the analysis and show how it can be extended to nearest neighbor problems in dimensions greater than two. All of this work is done for the well-behaved L_∞ metric; we turn to the more difficult L_2 metric in Section 5. Finally, conclusions are offered in Section 6.

2. The Algorithm

In this section we will examine various projection algorithms for performing nearest neighbor searches. (We will not explicitly study the all nearest neighbors problem, but rather solve that problem by repeatedly searching for the nearest neighbor of every point.) The simplest case of nearest neighbor searching is in one-dimensional space. If we have the point set in sorted order, we can find the nearest neighbor of point p by locating p's position in the order, finding its successor and predecessor in the order by "searching out", and taking the closest of those two points. Note that if the order is implemented as a sorted array or balanced binary tree, then point p's nearest neighbor in an N-point set can be found in time proportional to lg N.

We turn now to the two-dimensional case: suppose that we wish to perform nearest neighbor searches in a set, P, of N points in the plane. For ease of discussion, we will assume that we are using the L_∞ metric, in which the distance between two points is given by the maximum of the absolute values of their distances in all coordinates. The projection method keeps a sorted list of all points, *sorted in increasing order by x-value.* We can generalize the one-dimensional search described above to find nearest neighbors in the plane as follows. To find the nearest neighbor to point p, we locate p's position in the sorted list of x-values (which we assume is implemented as a sorted array), and then "search out", looking for p's nearest neighbor. In searching out, we will obey the simple rule of always next examining the point that is closer to p in x-distance, and remember the closest point to p so far observed (which we will call q). Note that we can "prune" this search as soon as we know that any other points we would visit are necessarily further from p than q is. Specifically, if the distance *in the x-direction only* from p to the next point to be searched is greater than the distance to q, then the search can be stopped and q can be reported as p's nearest neighbor. This process is illustrated pictorially in Figure 1; the dashed lines represent the sorted array, and the numbers on the points indicate the order in which they were searched. (Unnumbered points were not searched.)

We will now see how the intuitive procedure we saw above can be made more precise in pseudo-Pascal. We will assume that the point p is described by the variable p, with the two fields p.X and p.Y representing its two coordinate values. To preprocess a point set into a projection structure, we create an array P of points with the condition $P[i].X \leq P[i+1].X$, for all $1 \leq i < n$ (note that we assume here that the points have distinct

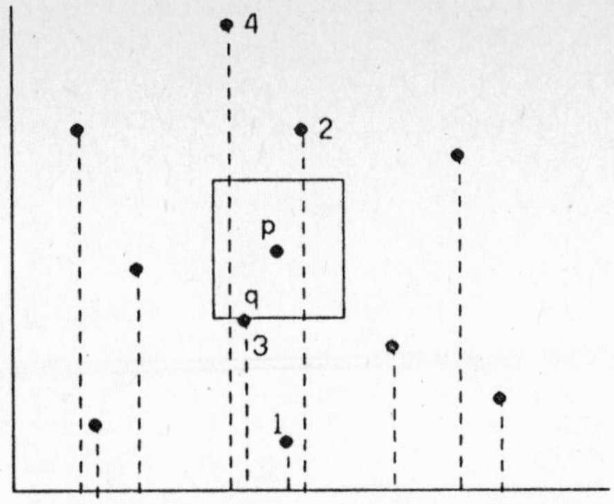

Figure 1. Nearest neighbor searching by projection on the x-axis.

x-values). Furthermore, we will assume that there are two "dummy" end points satisfying P[0].X=-∞ and P[N+1].X=∞, and that the function D returns the distance between the two points that are its arguments. We can now describe the search method precisely in the following code, which calculates the distance from p to its nearest neighbor, and stores that value in the variable QDist.

```
Use binary search to find the unique i satisfying
        P[i].X < p.X < P[i+1].X
NextLo ← i
NextHi ← i+1
QDist ← ∞
loop
    NextDist ← min{ p.X-P[NextLo].X, P[NextHi].X-p.X }
  while QDist < NextDist
    if p.X-P[NextLo].X  <  P[NextHi].X-p.X then
        QDist ← min{QDist, D(p,P[NextLo])}
        NextLo ← NextLo-1
     else
        QDist ← min{QDist, D(p,P[NextHi])}
        NextHi ← NextHi+1
  repeat
```

(The loop-while-repeat construct is used to loop "N-and-a-half times" by repeating until the while clause fails, at which point the loop terminates.) Although the procedure as written returns only the distance to point q (p's nearest neighbor), it is trivial to modify it to return also q itself. The running time of this procedure is proportional to lg N (for the binary search), plus the number of points visited in the loop.

The number of points visited by this simple projection nearest neighbor search is highly sensitive to the point set on which it is invoked. This fact is illustrated pictorially in Figure 2. In part a of that figure the search performs very well: it visits only two points before finding q as p's nearest neighbor. In part b, however, it performs very poorly, visiting all N points. This example shows that it is sometimes better to "search out" first in the horizontal direction, while other times it is better to search first in the vertical direction.

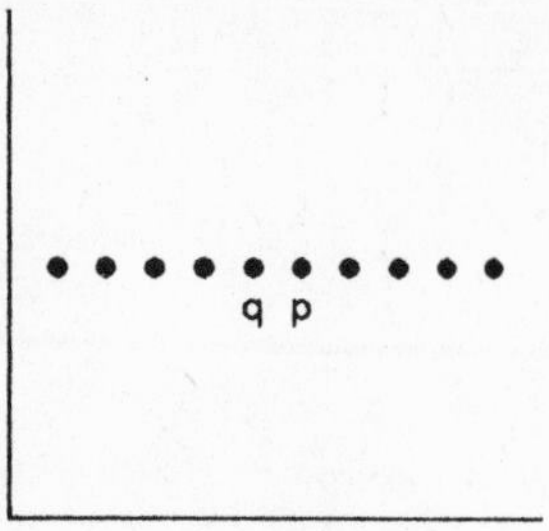

a.) A fast search.

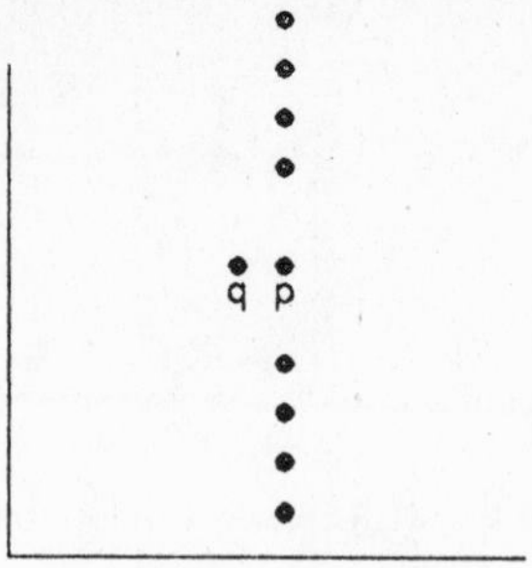

b.) A slow search.

Figure 2. Two nearest neighbor searches using projection on x-axis only.

With this example as motivation, we can modify projection to project the points onto both the x- and the y-axes, instead of only the x-axis. The search procedure is now substantially the same as before, except that we "search out" on the x- and y-axes *in parallel*. More precisely, we take the first step out on the x-axis (to whichever point is nearer p in the x-projection), the second step on the y-axis, the third step on the x-axis, and so forth. The search stops as soon as the search in either direction stops. We will call this method Algorithm A and not bother writing it formally; the code merely "interleaves" two copies of the program we saw earlier. Such a nearest neighbor search is illustrated in Figure 3.

It is easy to calculate the running time required by Algorithm A: it is proportional to lg N plus the number of points visited. Assume that the distance from p to its nearest neighbor, q, is d. To count the number of points visited during the search we shall consider a vertical strip of width 2d centered at p, and a horizontal strip of width 2d also centered at p. Let us call the number of points in the vertical strip a, and the number of points in the horizontal strip b. The number of points visited in the search is then at most $2 \cdot \min(a,b)$. Observe that the effect of this "pseudo-parallel" algorithm is that by interleaving the searches of the x- and y-projections, we always pay at most twice the cost of searching the best projection for that given search.

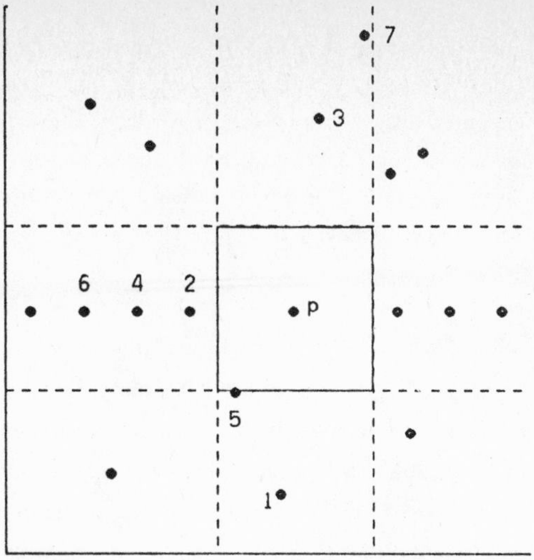

Figure 3. A nearest neighbor search using two projections.

3. A Combinatorial Theorem

In this section we will investigate properties of point sets in the plane from a combinatorial viewpoint, and prove a key theorem (Theorem 3). In Section 4 we will see how this theorem can be applied to analyze Algorithm A. Some terminology is needed for this study. We call the point set $P = \{p_1, \dots p_N\}$. For simplicity, we will assume that no two points in P share x- or y-values; this assumption could be removed by a slightly more complicated analysis. Let us call the distance from p_i to its nearest neighbor d_i, and define S_i as the *nearest neighbor square* or "nn-square" centered at p_i with edge length of $2d_i$ (note that the interior of S_i must be empty). With this background, we are ready for the first lemma leading to our main theorem.

Lemma 1:

There exists some constant, K, such that any point x in the plane (not necessarily an element of P) cannot be in the intersection of more than K nn-squares of the point set P.

Proof:

We will show that the lemma holds for K=9 and that this is the tightest possible result. The nine comes from placing four points in each quadrant of x, four points on the rays separating the quadrants, and one point on x itself; we will now consider each of these cases. We first observe that if point x is contained in S_i, and p_i is in quadrant 1 of x, then x is contained in no other nn-square S_j whose point p_j is in quadrant 1 of x. If this were the case, then p_i would lie in the interior of S_j, which is impossible. Similar reasoning applies to each of the three other quadrants. Likewise each of the four rays separating the quadrants can contain at most one point p_i; points further out on the ray are closer to p_i than to x. Finally, at most one point p_i could lie directly on x. These arguments together show that no more than nine squares S_i can contain x. That nine nn-squares can in fact contain S follows by placing a rectilinearly oriented three-by-three grid of points centered at x. (This proof is from Bentley [1976, Theorem 3.3-1].) QED.

We need some additional definitions to move on to our next lemma. We will let a_i be the number of points in P that lie in the vertical strip of width $2d_i$ centered at p_i. (Intuitively, a_i is the number of points examined if points were projected only on the x-axis.) Likewise, b_i denotes the number of points in the corresponding horizontal strip centered at p_i, and c_i is defined as the minimum of a_i and b_i. For any pair of points p_i and p_j, we define their two *phantoms* as $(p_i.x, p_j.y)$ and $(p_j.x, p_i.y)$; two points and their phantoms are shown in Figure 4. Let f_i be the number of phantoms in nn-square S_i; we can now prove the following lemma.

Lemma 2:

For every point p_i in P, $c_i \leq (f_i)^{1/2}$. That is, the minimum of the number of points in the vertical and horizontal strips defined by p_i is less than the square root of the number of phantoms in the nn-square S_i.

Proof:

The number of phantoms in S_i is $f_i = a_i \cdot b_i$ (because each of the a_i points in the vertical slab combines with each of the b_i points in the horizontal slab to yield a unique phantom in S_i, and no other phantoms exist in S_i). Because $c_i = \min\{a_i, b_i\}$, we have

$$c_i^2 \leq a_i \cdot b_i = f_i,$$

and taking the square root of this equation proves the lemma. QED.

We can now combine Lemmas 1 and 2 to prove the following theorem.

Theorem 3:

For any point set P,

$$\sum_{1 \leq i \leq N} c_i = O(N^{3/2}).$$

Proof:

There are precisely N(N-1) phantoms. Since each of these can lie in at most K

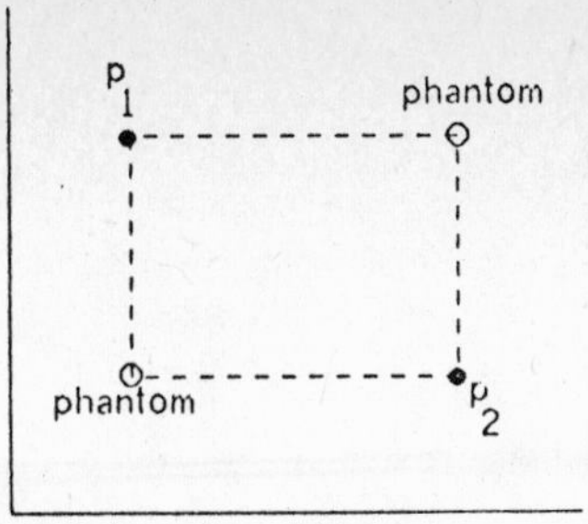

Figure 4. Two points and their phantoms.

nn-squares (by Lemma 1), we have

$$\sum_{1 \leq i \leq N} f_i \leq KN(N-1).$$

This inequality immediately implies that

$$\sum_{1 \leq i \leq N} (f_i)^{1/2} \leq N[K(N-1)]^{1/2} = O(N^{3/2}),$$

because the latter sum is maximized when $f_i = [K(N-1)]^{1/2}$ for all $1 \leq i \leq N$. By Lemma 2 we know that

$$\sum_{1 \leq i \leq N} c_i \leq \sum_{1 \leq i \leq N} (f_i)^{1/2},$$

and combining the last two inequalities establishes the theorem. QED.

4. Implications and Extensions

In this section we will use the combinatorial results of Section 3 to analyze the performance of the projection method for nearest neighbor searching. We will first consider the planar case using the L_∞ metric, and study its two aspects of finding all nearest neighbors and of searching. We will then consider the planar L_1 metric, and finally turn to the L_∞ metric in higher dimensions.

With Theorem 3 in hand we can easily analyze the time Algorithm A requires to find all nearest neighbors in an N-element point set. From Section 2 we know that the cost of searching for point p_i's nearest neighbor is proportional to lg N plus twice c_i. (Recall that c_i was defined in Section 3 as the minimum of the numbers of points in the smallest vertical and horizontal strips containing p_i's nn-square S_i.) In nearest neighbor searching for each of the N points in a set, the sum of the lg N terms is O(N lg N), and Theorem 3 shows that the sum of the c_i's is $O(N^{3/2})$. These observations immediately yield the following corollary of Theorem 3.

Corollary 4:

The time required by Algorithm A to find all nearest neighbors in any fixed planar point set is $O(N^{3/2})$.

Proof:

In the preceding text.

Corollary 4 is the tightest possible result in the sense that there exist planar sets on which Algorithm A requires $\theta(N^{3/2})$ time. For example, suppose that $N=n^2$ and consider the point set generated by mapping each integer i satisfying $1 \leq i \leq N$ to the point (i, ni mod(N-1)). Indeed, the analysis of Friedman, Baskett and Shustek [1975] shows that Algorithm A requires $\theta(N^{3/2})$ time on the average for point sets randomly drawn from several important planar distributions.

We turn now to consider the *average* cost of planar nearest neighbor searching using Algorithm A. Friedman, Baskett and Shustek asked the question "if set S is chosen randomly from distribution F, what is the expected time required by a search to locate the nearest neighbor of a new point drawn randomly from F?". We will now examine an expected-time result of a different flavor.

Corollary 5:

Let P be any planar set of N points. If one point, say p, of P is chosen at random (with each point having probability 1/N of being chosen), then the expected time to find p's nearest neighbor using Algorithm A is $O(N^{1/2})$.

Proof:

Corollary 4 shows that the total time required by N such searches is $O(N^{3/2})$. Since each of the N points in the set is equally likely to be chosen, we can divide the total time required in the set by N to yield this corollary. QED.

All the results that we have examined so far have been for the L_∞ metric. Results similar to Corollaries 4 and 5 can also be achieved for the planar L_1 (Manhattan or "taxicab") metric. The algorithm works as before, except that the points are projected onto the two lines x=y and x=-y. The analysis follows without change.

Algorithm A can be extended to find L_∞ nearest neighbors in k-space. The modified algorithm projects the set onto all k coordinate axes, and a search then performs k searches in parallel, until one finds the answer. Analysis of this algorithm yields the following theorem.

Theorem 6:

The projection method can be used to find all nearest neighbors in any fixed k-dimensional set of N points in $O(N^{2-1/k})$ time.

Sketch of Proof:

In direct analogy with Lemma 2, the minimum number c_j of points of P in any of the k strips $\{(x_1,...,x_k): |x_i - P_j \cdot x_i| \leq d_j\}$ is at most $(f_j)^{1/k}$, where f_j is the number of phantoms in the k-cube S_j. A phantom is now a point that has coordinates taken from k different points of P. There are at most $N \cdot (N-1) \cdot ... \cdot (N-k+1)$ phantoms. Thus

$$\sum_{1 \leq j \leq N} c_j \leq \sum_{1 \leq j \leq N} (f_j)^{1/k} .$$

It is also straightforward to extend Lemma 1 to k-dimensions, where K becomes now 3^k. Thus we must have

$$\sum_{1 \leq j \leq N} f_j \leq 3^k \cdot N \cdot (N-1) \cdot ... \cdot (N-k+1) .$$

It follows that

$$\sum_{1 \leq j \leq N} c_j \leq N(3^k (N-1) \cdot ... \cdot (N-k+1))^{1/k} = O(N^{2-1/k}) .$$

QED.

5. The Euclidean Metric

Our proof of the time bounds for the planar all-nearest-neighbors problem in the L_∞ metric relied on the following crucial fact: there exists a constant K such that, given any point set $P=\{p_1,...,p_N\}$, every point in the plane lies in at most K of the nn-squares $S_1,...,S_N$. Recall that, for point $p_j \in P$, d_j is the distance from p_j to its nearest neighbor (under the metric at hand) in p_j and that S_j is the nn-square of p_j, that is, the square with center p_j and sides of length $2d_j$, parallel to the axes. In this section we ask whether there is such a constant K for the planar Euclidean (L_2) metric. We will first prove that no such upper bound exists, and then go on to show that in practice such a bound *does* exist, and is in fact explicitly dependent on the precision of our computation.

Because of the space limitations of these proceedings, we are not able to include the results of this section. Readers interested in the details of these results are referred to the complete version of this paper, which is available as a Carnegie-Mellon University Computer Science Department Technical Report.

6. Conclusions

In this section we will briefly review the contents of this paper and then summarize its contributions. In Section 2 we examined the projection-based nearest-neighbor algorithm of Friedman, Baskett and Shustek and saw how it could be modified to interleave k searches. We then analyzed the performance of the algorithm in Section 3 and interpreted that analysis in Section 4. This analysis was performed for the well-behaved L_∞ metric; we then studied the L_2 (Euclidean) metric in Section 5. That section contains two primary results: the first shows that the analysis of Section 4 is not applicable to the L_2 metric, and the second shows that this objection can not in fact arise in practice.

The primary contribution of this paper is the modified algorithm and its analysis. The bound on running time shows that the expected-time bounds of previous analyses also hold for the worst case. This analysis is interesting from a theoretical viewpoint and also very practical: the projection method remains the best method for nearest neighbor searching in many practical contexts. The analysis of the Euclidean metric shares this flavor: the negative result is of primary theoretical interest, while the positive result (of a very novel flavor) shows that this can be ignored in practice.

Our analysis is novel for another reason. Selecting an instance of the nearest-neighbor problem can be viewed as consisting of two stages: in the first stage one chooses a point set P, and in the second stage a particular point $p \in P$ is chosen. In classical average-case analyses it is assumed that both stages are randomized, while classical worst-case analyses assume that both stages are performed by an adversary. In this paper we have considered a *hybrid* model, in which the first stage is carried out by a malevolent intelligence and the second by chance. Our analysis has shown that the performance of the projection algorithm in the hybrid model is as efficient as its performance in the average-case model (which is a stronger result). It may be that in other problems, in which purely worst-case or average-case models give weak results, a hybrid approach would yield something more interesting.

One natural question is, what happens to the projection algorithm in the "dual" hybrid model, in which a point set P is randomly chosen from, say, a uniform distribution on the unit square, and then we are asked to find the nearest neighbor of the least advantageous point $p \in P$. We argue briefly below that Algorithm A of Section 2 does not fare much worse in this model than it does in the reverse one. In particular, we can show that, with probability 1-o(1), Algorithm A of Section 2 requires $o(n^{1/2+\epsilon})$ steps (for all $\epsilon > 0$) for *all* points in the set P. In fact, we can show this for the simpler algorithm given in Section 2 in pseudo-Pascal, by the following argument: Suppose that this algorithm requires $C_1 n^{1/2+\epsilon}$ steps for some point $p \epsilon P$ (for some $\epsilon > 0$). Then it is immediate that one of the two following claims must be true for appropriate constants C_2, $C_3 > 0$. Either

a. some 1-by-$C_2 n^{(-1+\epsilon)/2}$ strip contains at least $C_1 n^{1/2+\epsilon}$ points of P, or

b. there is a $C_3 n^{(-1+\epsilon)/2} \times C_3 n^{(-1+\epsilon)/2}$ square which is empty of points of P.

It can be shown (see, for example, Lemma 7 of Papadimitriou [1979]) that the probability of either of these events occurring goes to zero as n goes to infinity. A more careful analysis may yield an exact $O(n^{1/2})$ bound.

A number of open problems are raised naturally by this work. The primary technique used in the new algorithm of Section 2 is that of *interleaving*. This technique is commonly used to show that if Algorithms A and B solve problem P in F(n) and G(n) time, respectively, then interleaving them yields an algorithm for P with running time of $2 \cdot \min\{F(n), G(n)\}$. Weide [1978, Section 4.2.2] has used interleaving to decrease the *expected* running time of certain programs. Is there some underlying theory of applying interleaving to yield efficient algorithms? A second open problem is to use techniques similar to those in this paper to analyze the worst-case costs of algorithms analyzed (so far) only for the average case; such analyses might be based on the hybrid model discussed above. Thirdly, the "positive" analysis of the Euclidean metric is performed in a "fixed word size" model of computation. This model seems to reflect accurately an important facet of real computation, and it would be interesting to investigate the complexities of various problems in this model.

Acknowledgements

The assistance of the Macsyma program at M.I.T. is gratefully acknowledged.

References

Bellman, R. [1957]. *Dynamic Programming*, Princeton University Press, Princeton, New Jersey.

Bentley, J. L. [1976]. "Divide and conquer algorithms for closest point problems in multidimensional space," unpublished Ph.D. Thesis, University of North Carolina, December 1976.

Bentley, J. L. [1979]. "Multidimensional divide-and-conquer," to appear in *Communications of the ACM*.

Bentley, J. L., B. W. Weide, and A. C. Yao [1979]. "Optimal expected-time algorithms for closest-point problems," Carnegie-Mellon University Computer Science Report CMU-CS-79-111.

Friedman, J. H., F. Baskett, and L. J. Shustek [1975]. "An algorithm for finding nearest neighbors," *IEEE Transactions on Computers C-24*, 10, pp. 1000-1006, October 1975.

Friedman, J. H., J. L. Bentley, and R. A. Finkel [1977]. "An algorithm for finding best matches in logarithmic expected time," *ACM Transactions on Mathematical Software* 3, pp. 209-226, September 1977.

Knuth, D. E. [1973]. *The Art of Computer Programming, volume 3: Sorting and Searching*, Addison-Wesley, Reading, Massachusetts.

Lee, R. C. T., Y. H. Chin, and S. C. Chang [1976]. "Application of principal component analysis to multikey searching," *IEEE Transactions on Software Engineering SE-2*, 3, pp. 185-193, September 1976.

Lipton, R. and R. E. Tarjan [1977]. "Applications of a planar separator theorem," *Eighteenth Symposium on the Foundations of Computer Science*, pp. 162-170, IEEE, October 1977.

Papadimitriou, C. H. [1979]. "Worst-case probabilistic analysis of a geometric location problem," submitted to *Mathematics of Operations Research*, November 1979.

Shamos, M. I. [1978]. "Computational geometry", unpublished Ph.D. Thesis, Yale University, May 1978.

Weide, B. W. [1978]. "Statistical methods in algorithm design and analysis," Ph.D. Thesis, Carnegie-Mellon University, Carnegie-Mellon University Computer Science Report CMU-CS-78-142.

Zolnowsky, J. E. [1978]. "Topics in computational geometry," Ph.D. Thesis, Stanford University. Stanford Computer Science Department Report STAN-CS-78-659.

PROPRIETES SYNTACTIQUES DU PRODUIT NON AMBIGU

Jean-Eric PIN

CNRS - Université Paris VI - Tour 55-65 - 4è étage

4 place Jussieu 75230 Paris Cedex 05

INTRODUCTION

Lorsque l'on étudie les langages rationnels, les deux opérations les plus importantes - hormis les opérations booléennes - sont l'étoile et le produit. On a par exemple cherché à donner une classification des langages rationnels basée sur la hauteur d'étoile (éventuellement restreinte) et, pour les langages de hauteur d'étoile 0, ou langages apériodiques ("star-free" en anglais), on a construit une classification basée sur l'opération produit : c'est la hiérarchie de Brzozowski ("dot-depth hierarchy"). Par ailleurs, on a cherché à déterminer les propriétés syntactiques de l'opération produit. Le premier résultat obtenu dans cette voie est le théorème de Schützenberger datant de 1965 qui affirme qu'un langage est apériodique ssi son monoïde syntactique est fini et sans groupe. La preuve originale de Schützenberger est algorithmique et se fait par récurrence sur le cardinal du monoïde syntactique. Une autre preuve, basée sur les propriétés du produit en couronne, a été trouvée indépendamment par Meyer [5] et Cohen-Brzozowski [1]. D'autres résultats ont suivi, mais nous ne mentionnerons ici que le récent théorème de Straubing [8] qui permet de donner une caractérisation syntactique des langages qui sont éléments de la fermeture par produit d'une variété de langages donnée. En fait Straubing démontre qu'à l'opération "fermeture par produit" définie sur les variétés de langages correspond une opération sur les variétés de monoïdes. La démonstration de Straubing utilise elle aussi des techniques issues de la théorie de la complexité des semigroupes.

Dans cet article, nous nous intéressons plus particulièrement au produit non ambigu. On sait en effet que tout langage rationnel est engendré à partir de l'ensemble vide et des lettres de l'alphabet à l'aide des 3 opérations rationnelles non ambiguës qui sont l'union disjointe, le produit non ambigu et l'étoile non ambiguë. Si l'étude de l'étoile non ambiguë - qui n'est autre que la théorie des codes - a été entreprise dès 1956, l'étude du produit non ambigu semble en revanche beaucoup plus récente. C'est en effet en 1976 que Schützenberger a donné une version "non ambiguë" de son théorème sur les apériodiques. Il a en effet trouvé une caractérisation syntactique de la plus petite classe de langages de X^* contenant les langages de la forme $\{x\}$ (avec $x \in X$) ou Y^*(avec $Y \subset X$) et qui soit fermée par union disjointe et par produit inambigu. Un langage rationnel est élément de cette classe ssi, dans son monoïde syntactique, toute $\mathcal{D}$-classe régulière est un semigroupe sans groupe. Cette classe de langages a été à nouveau étudiée par Fich et Brzozowski [3] d'un point de vue tout à fait différent.

Le but de cet article est de décrire les 4 opérations sur les variétés de semigroupes (ou de monoïdes) qui correspondent aux 4 opérations suivantes, définies sur les variétés de langages : fermeture par produit, produit non ambigu, produit déterministe, produit déterministe opposé. Les preuves que nous proposons sont constructives et reposent sur un algorithme de Schützenberger dont nous présentons ici une version améliorée (section 2). On obtient donc ainsi une preuve constructive et plus élémentaire du théorème de Straubing, qui correspond au cas du produit (section 3), et trois nouveaux résultats pour le produit non ambigu, déterministe et déterministe opposé (section 4). Enfin, la démonstration de ces théorèmes permet de retrouver au passage de nombreux résultats connus (section 5), dont les deux théorèmes de Schützenberger évoqués plus haut. Pour les démonstrations et la formulation des résultats, nous avons utilisé systèmatiquement la notion de morphisme relationnel de semigroupe dont diverses propriétés sont énoncées dans la section 1.

1. Préléminaires

Nous renvoyons le lecteur aux traités d'Eilenberg [2] et de Lallement [4] pour tous les termes non définis dans cet article. Par ailleurs, nous supposerons connue la théorie classique des relations de Green (chapitre 2 de [4]) La notation $|E|$ désignera le cardinal d'un ensemble fini E.

1.1. Variétés

Rappelons qu'un semigroupe S divise un semigroupe T si S est image homomorphe (ou quotient) d'un sous-semigroupe de T. Une variété de semigroupes (resp. de monoïdes) finis est une classe de semigroupes (resp. de monoïdes) fermée par division et par produit direct fini. Comme nous autorisons le produit indexé par l'ensemble vide, le semigroupe 1 (formé d'un seul élément) est élément de toute variété $\underline{V}$. Voici quelques exemples importants de variétés de monoïdes et de semigroupes

. $\underline{G}$ désigne la variété des monoïdes qui sont des groupes.

. $\underline{A}$, $\underline{R}$, $\underline{R}^r$ et $\underline{J}$ désignent respectivement la variété des monoïdes (resp. semigroupes) $\mathcal{H}$-triviaux (ou apériodiques), $\mathcal{R}$-triviaux, $\mathcal{L}$-triviaux et $\mathcal{J}$-triviaux.

. $\underline{J}_1$ désigne la variété des demi-treillis (i.e. des semigroupes idempotents et commutitifs.) Elle est engendrée par le monoïde U_1 formé d'une unité et d'un zéro.

. $\underline{DA}$ désigne la variété des monoïdes (resp. semigroupes) dont chaque $\mathcal{D}$-classe régulière est un semigroupe.

. $\underline{Nil}$ désigne la variété des semigroupes nilpotents

. $\underline{D}$ et $\underline{D}^r$ désigneront respectivement la variété des semigroupes S satisfaisant la condition $eS = e$ (resp $Se = e$) pour tout idempotent $e \in S$. Remarquons, en ce qui concerne $\underline{D}$ et $\underline{D}^r$, que nous avons interverti les notations utilisées par Eilenberg pour les raisons suivantes. Avec nos notations, on a les inclusions $\underline{D} \subset \underline{R}$ et $\underline{D}^r \subset \underline{R}^r$, ce qui donne des formules plus homogènes qu'avec la notation d'Eilenberg. Nous verrons d'autre part que la variété $\underline{D}$ est liée au produit déterministe alors que la variété $\underline{D}^r$ est liée au produit déterministe opposé. Là aussi notre notation parait plus homogène.

Si $\underline{V}$ est une variété de monoïdes, on note $\underline{LV}$ la variété de semigroupes S tels que pour tout idempotent $e \in S$, on ait $e\,Se \in \underline{V}$. Ainsi $L\{1\}$ désigne la variété des semigroupes S tels que $e\,Se = e$ pour tout idempotent $e \in S$ et $\underline{LG}$ désigne la variété des semigroupes dont tous les idempotents sont contenus dans l'idéal minimal.

Si $\underline{V}_1$ et $\underline{V}_2$ sont deux variétés de semigroupes (ou de monoïdes) on note $\underline{V}_1 v \underline{V}_2$ la plus petite variété contenant $\underline{V}_1$ et $\underline{V}_2$.

Si $L \subset X^+$ (resp X^*) est un langage rationnel, on note $S(L)$ (resp. $M(L)$) le semigroupe (resp. monoïde) syntactique de L.

Soit $\underline{V}$ une variété de semigroupes (resp. de monoïdes). A chaque alphabet X, on associe la classe $X^+\mathcal{V}$ (resp $X^*\mathcal{V}$) des langages de X^+ (resp. X^*) tels que $S(L) \in \underline{V}$ (resp. $M(L) \in \underline{V}$). On définit ainsi une + variété (resp. une *variété) de langages $\mathcal{V}$ et on dit que $\mathcal{V}$ est la + variété correspondant à $\underline{V}$ ou que $\underline{V}$ est la variété de semigroupes correspondant à $\mathcal{V}$ (car la correspondance $\underline{V} \leftrightarrow \mathcal{V}$ est bijective : c'est le théorème des variétés d'Eilenberg [2]). Signalons encore que pour chaque alphabet X, $X^+\mathcal{V}$ (resp. $X^*\mathcal{V}$) est une algèbre de Boole.

1.2. Morphismes relationnels

Nous empruntons à Tilson [9] la définition suivante : un morphisme relationnel entre deux semigroupes S et T est une relation $\tau : S \to T$ qui satisfait

(i) $s\tau \neq \emptyset$ pour tout $s \in S$

(ii) $(s_1\tau)(s_2\tau) \subset (s_1 s_2)\tau$ pour tout $s_1, s_2 \in S$.

Etant donné une variété de semigroupes finis $\underline{V}$, on dit qu'un morphisme (relationnel) $\tau : S \to T$ est un $\underline{V}$-morphisme (relationnel) si pour tout semigroupe T' de T élément de $\underline{V}$, $T'\tau^{-1}$ est aussi élément de $\underline{V}$.
On démontre qu'un $\underline{V}$-morphisme relationnel $\tau : S \to T$ peut se factoriser en $\tau = \alpha^{-1}\beta$ où $\alpha : R \to S$ est un morphisme surjectif et $\beta : R \to T$ est un $\underline{V}$-morphisme. Si $\underline{V}=\underline{A}$, un $\underline{V}$-morphisme (relationnel) est aussi appelé morphisme (relationnel) apériodique

Un morphisme relationnel $\tau : S \to T$ est dit injectif si pour tout $s_1, s_2 \in S$, $s_1 \neq s_2$ entraine $s_1\tau \cap s_2\tau = \emptyset$.

Nous allons donner à présent sans démonstration un certain nombre d'énoncés relatifs aux morphismes relationnels : certains sont classiques (cf. [8], [9], [10]), d'autres sont moins connus, voire originaux. Les preuves de ces énoncés constituent de bons exercices sur les relations de Green.

<u>Proposition 1.1</u> [10] Si $\tau_1 : S \to R$ et $\tau_2 : R \to T$ sont des $\underline{V}$-morphismes relationnels $\tau_1\tau_2 : S \to T$ est un $\underline{V}$-morphisme relationnel.

Proposition 1.2. [10] S divise T ssi il existe un morphisme relationnel injectif $\tau : S \to T$

Proposition 1.3. Soit $\underline{V}$ l'une des variétés de semigroupes $\underline{A}$, $\underline{R}$, $\underline{R}^r$, $\underline{J}$, $\underline{L\{1\}}$, $\underline{D}$, $\underline{D}^r$, $\underline{Nil}$, $\underline{LG}$. Alors $\tau : S \to T$ est un $\underline{V}$-morphisme relationnel ssi pour tout idempotent $e \in T, e\tau^{-1} \in \underline{V}$

Il est à remarquer que cette propriété n'est pas vraie pour toute variété $\underline{V}$ (contre exemple : $\underline{V} = \underline{LJ}$).

Rappelons qu'une $\mathcal{H}$-classe est dite régulière si elle est contenue dans une $\mathcal{D}$-classe régulière

Proposition 1.4. Soit $\tau : S \to T$ un morphisme relationnel. Alors τ est apériodique (resp. un $\underline{R}$, $\underline{R}^r$-morphisme) ssi la restriction de τ aux $\mathcal{H}$-classes (resp. $\mathcal{R}$-classes, $\mathcal{L}$-classes) régulières de S est injective.

Voici pour terminer un résultat dont l'énoncé m'a été suggéré par les travaux de E. et M. Le Rest.

Proposition 1.5. Soit $\tau : S \to T$ un $\underline{LG}$-morphisme relationnel. Alors si d(S) désigne le nombre de $\mathcal{D}$-classes régulières de S, on a $d(S) \leqslant d(T)$ avec égalité si τ est un $\underline{LG}$-morphisme surjectif de semigroupes.

Soient $\underline{V}$ et $\underline{W}$ deux variétés de semigroupes. On note $\underline{V}(\underline{W})$ la classe des semigroupes S tels qu'il existe un $\underline{V}$-morphisme relationnel $\tau : S \to T$ où $T \in \underline{W}$. On démontre alors (cf [10]) que $\underline{V}(\underline{W})$ est une variété de semigroupes. Cette définition s'étend au cas où $\underline{W}$ est une variété de monoides: $\underline{V}(\underline{W})$ est alors une variété de monoides. Voici quelques exemples classiques:

$\underline{Nil}(\underline{J}_1) = \underline{J}$ (cf[2])

$\underline{L\{1\}}(\underline{J}_1) = \underline{DA}$, $\underline{D}(\underline{J}_1) = \underline{R}$ $\underline{D}^r(\underline{J}_1) = \underline{R}^r$ (cf[7])

1.3. Produit de langages

Rappelons que le produit de concaténation (ou simplement produit) de n langages $A_1, A_2, \dots, A_n$ de X^*, pris dans cet ordre est défini par la formule :

$$A_1 \dots A_n = \{a_1 \dots a_n \in X^* \mid \forall i \in \{1, \dots, n\} \quad a_i \in A_i\}$$

On peut imposer diverses conditions restrictives à cette définition. Ainsi, on dira que le produit est non ambigu si les A_i sont tous non vides et si chaque mot du produit admet une seule factorisation de la forme $a_1 \dots a_n$ avec $a_i \in A_i$ pour $1 \leqslant i \leqslant n$.

Nous dirons avec Schützenberger [7] que le produit AB est déterministe si A et B sont vides et vérifient l'une des conditions suivantes

(a) A est préfixe ; (b) AB est préfixe et B est une partie de l'alphabet X Symétriquement, le produit de deux langages non vides A et B est déterministe opposé ssi (a) B est suffixe ou si (b) AB est suffixe et $A \subset X$.

Plus généralement, un produit $A_1 A_2 \dots A_n$ sera dit déterministe (resp. déterministe opposé) si chacun des produits $A_1A_2, (A_1A_2)A_3 \dots (A_1 \dots A_{n-1})A_n$ est déterministe (resp. si chacun des produits $A_{n-1}A_n, A_{n-2}(A_{n-1}A_n), \dots A_1(A_2 \dots A_n)$ est déterministe opposé). On voit facilement qu'un produit déterministe ou déterministe opposé est non ambigu.

Le résultat qui suit, du à Straubing [9], a permis de simplifier substantiellement l'étude du produit de concaténation.

Théorème 1.6. [9] Soient A et B deux langages rationnels de X^*. Il existe un morphisme relationnel apériodique $\tau : M(AB) \to M(A) \times M(B)$. Si le produit est non ambigu (resp. déterministe, déterministe opposé) τ est un $\underline{L}\{1\}$- (resp. un $\underline{D}$-, $\underline{D}^r$) morphisme relationnel.

2. L'algorithme de Schützenberger

En fait, Schützenberger a donné, non pas un, mais deux algorithmes ([6], [7]) permettant d'exprimer un langage reconnu par un monoïde M en fonction de langages reconnus par des diviseurs stricts de M uniquement à l'aide des opérations booléennes et du produit. Cette technique permet alors, comme nous le verrons, d'effectuer des raisonnements par récurrence sur le cardinal de M.

Nous présentons ici une version plus générale qui, d'une part, permet de regrouper les deux algorithmes et qui d'autre part est valable pour un monoïde fini quelconque, alors que Schützenberger imposait certaines conditions d'apériodicité. Faute de place nous n'indiquerons pas les preuves des énoncés qui vont suivre : elles sont calquées pour la plupart sur celles données par Schützenberger en [7].

Pour faciliter la compréhension de cet algorithme nous avons préféré le diviser en plusieurs cas. Dans toute la suite $\eta : X^* \to M$ désigne un morphisme du monoïde libre X^* dans un monoïde fini *ayant deux éléments au moins.* K désigne l'intersection des idéaux de M ayant au moins deux éléments. On voit que si $K \neq 0$, $D = K - 0$ (= K si M n'a pas de zéro) est une $\mathcal{D}$-classe de M.

Nous emprunterons à Schützenberger la notation $X^* \Delta M$ pour désigner l'ensemble des langages de X^* reconnus par un diviseur strict de M. m désigne un élément de M et H,R et L désignent respectivement la $\mathcal{H}$-classe, la $\mathcal{R}$-classe et la $\mathcal{L}$-classe de m.

Théorème 2.1. Si $m \in M-K$, alors $m\eta^{-1} \in X^* \Delta M$

Posons $L_o = 0\eta^{-1}$ si M a un zéro
$\quad = \emptyset$ si M n'a pas de zéro

On a alors les résultats suivants

<u>Théorème 2.2.</u> Supposons $m \in D$

(i) $(mM)\eta^{-1} = L_0 \cup L_1$ où L_1 s'exprime comme union disjointe finie de produits déterministes de la forme X^* ou $Ax\,X^*$ avec $A \in X^*\Delta M$ et $x \in X$

(ii) $(Mm)\eta^{-1} = L_0 \cup L_2$ où L_2 s'exprime comme union disjointe finie de produits déterministes opposés de la forme X^* ou $X^*x\,A$ avec $A \in X^*\Delta M$ et $x \in X$

(iii) $(mM \cap Mn)\eta^{-1} = L_0 \cup L_3$ où L_3 s'exprime comme union disjointe finie de produits non ambigus de la forme X^*, AxB ou $Ax\,X^*x'\,B$ avec $A,B \in X^*\Delta M$ et $x,x' \in X$.

Le théorème 2.2. est complété par le théorème suivant, qui fournit une expression du langage L_0.

<u>Théorème 2.3.</u> Si M a un zéro, le langage $0\eta^{-1}$ peut s'exprimer comme union finie (pas nécessairement disjointe) de langages de la forme $X^*x\,X^*$ ou $X^*x\,A\,x'\,X^*$ avec $x,x' \in X$ et $A \in X^*\Delta M$.

Dans le cas où $K^2 = 0$, on a un résultat plus précis :

<u>Théorème 2.4.</u> Si $K^2 = 0$ et si $m \in K$, on peut exprimer $m\eta^{-1}$ de deux façons différentes :

(a) Soit comme union disjointe finie de produits déterministes de la forme $A_0\,x_1\,A_1\,x_2 \ldots x_n\,A_n$ où $n \in \mathbb{N}$, $x_i \in X$ et $A_i \in X^*\Delta M$ pour $0 \leqslant i \leqslant n$

(b) Soit comme union disjointe finie de produits déterministes opposés de la même forme qu'au (a).

Si D est un semigroupe non vide, on peut également préciser les résultats précédents :

<u>Théorème 2.5.</u> Si $D^2 = D \neq \emptyset$, $M-0$ est un sous-monoïde de M, dont D est l'idéal minimal. De plus il existe une partie Y de X et un morphisme $\eta_0 : Y^* \to M - 0$ tels que le diagramme suivant soit commutatif

$$\begin{array}{ccc} Y^* & \xrightarrow{\ \eta_0\ } & M-0 \\ \downarrow & & \downarrow \\ X^* & \xrightarrow{\ \eta\ } & M \end{array}$$

<u>Corollaire 2.6.</u> Si $D^2 = D \neq \emptyset$, $0\eta^{-1}$ peut s'exprimer de deux façons différentes

(a) Soit comme union disjointe finie de produits déterministes de la forme $Y^*x\,X^*$ avec $Y \subset X$ et $x \in X-Y$.

(b) Soit comme union disjointe finie de produits déterministes opposés de la forme $X^*x\,Y^*$ avec $Y \subset X$ et $x \in X-Y$.

Corollaire 2.7. Supposons $D = D^2 \neq \emptyset$ et soit $m \in D$

(i) On peut exprimer $R\eta^{-1}$ comme union disjointe finie de produits déterministes de la forme Y^* ou $A x Y^*$ avec $A \in Y^* \Delta M$, $x \in Y$ et $Y \subset X$.

(ii) On peut exprimer $L\eta^{-1}$ comme union disjointe finie de produits déterministes opposés de la forme Y^* ou $Y^* x A$ avec $A \in Y^* \Delta M$, $x \in Y$ et $Y \subset X$.

(iii) On peut exprimer $H\eta^{-1}$ comme union disjointe finie de produits non ambigus de la forme Y^*, $A x B$, ou $A x Y^* x' B$ avec $A, B \in Y^* \Delta M$ $x, x' \in Y$ et $Y \subset X$

Les résultats qui précèdent s'adaptent facilement au cas des semigroupes. Il suffit de remarquer qu'une expression du type A^*B s'écrit aussi sous la forme $A^+B \cup B$. De plus, si le produit A^*B est non ambigu, le produit A^+B est non ambigu et l'union $A^+B \cup B$ est disjointe. A titre d'exemple, le corollaire 2.6 (a) devient "Si $D^2 = D \neq \emptyset$, $O\eta^{-1}$ peut s'exprimer comme union disjointe finie de produits déterministes de la forme $\{x\}$, Y^+x, $x X^+$ et $Y^+x X^+$ avec $Y \subset X$ et $x \in X-Y$".

3. Fermeture par produit d'une variété de langages

Soit $\mathcal{V}$ une $*$ variété (resp. une + variété) de langages.
Nous noterons $P(\mathcal{V})$ la plus petite variété $\mathcal{V}'$ contenant $\mathcal{V}$ et telle que pour tout alphabet X, $X^*\mathcal{V}'$ (resp $X^+\mathcal{V}'$) soit fermée par produit. Une variété $\mathcal{V}$ est dite fermée par produit si $\mathcal{V} = P(\mathcal{V})$. On notera d'autre part que pour toute variété $\mathcal{V}$, on a $P(P(\mathcal{V})) = P(\mathcal{V})$. Nous conviendrons d'accepter, dans le cas des $*$variétés, les produits indexés par l'ensemble vide. On a de ce fait $\{1\} \in X^* P(\mathcal{V})$ pour toute $*$variété $\mathcal{V}$ et pour tout alphabet X.

Signalons un premier résultat

Proposition 3.1 Toute variété fermée par produit est littérale (i.e. contient les langages de la forme $\{x\}$ où x est une lettre)

Preuve Soit X un alphabet non vide. Si $\mathcal{V}$ est une + variété, on a $X = X^+ - X^+X^+ \in X^+$ Or si $x \in X$, on a $S(\{x\}) = S(X)$ d'où $\{x\} \in X^+\mathcal{V}$ d'après le théorème d'Eilenberg.

Si $\mathcal{V}$ est une $*$variété, on a $\{1\} \in X^*\mathcal{V}$ d'après ce qui précède donc $X^+ = X^* - \{1\} \in X^*\mathcal{V}$ et on conclut comme dans le cas des + variétés en remplaçant S par M.

Remarque : sans la convention sur le produit vide, ce résultat n'est vrai que pour les $*$ variétés non triviales.

Le théorème de variétés établit une bijection entre les variétés de langages et les variétés de monoïdes (ou de semigroupes) et cette bijection permet d'associer à toute opération de fermeture définie sur les variétés de langages une opération de fermeture définie sur les variétés de monoïdes (ou de semigroupes). Dans le cas de la fermeture par produit, on connait exactement l'opération correspondante sur les variétés de monoïdes (ou de semigroupes) grâce au théorème de Straubing [8] dont voici l'énoncé précis.

Théorème 3.2. (Straubing) Soit $\mathcal{V}$ une $*$-variété (resp. une $+$-variété) de langages et soit $\underline{V}$ la variété de monoïdes (resp. de semigroupes) correspondant à $\mathcal{V}$. Alors $P(\mathcal{V})$ correspond à $\underline{A}(\underline{V})$.

Nous désignerons par $\mathcal{V}'$ la variété de langages correspondant à $\underline{A}(\underline{V})$. Pour établir l'inclusion $P(\mathcal{V}) \subset \mathcal{V}'$, la preuve originale de Straubing reposait sur les propriétés du produit de Schützenberger de deux semigroupes. Depuis Straubing a simplifié cette partie de la preuve, qui est maintenant basée sur le théorème 1.6. : c'est celle que nous donnons ici. Pour l'inclusion opposée - qui est plus difficile à obtenir-, la démonstration originale de Straubing utilisait des résultats assez profonds de théorie de la complexité. Nous proposons ici une nouvelle preuve, basée sur l'algorithme de Schützenberger.

Démonstration du théorème 3.2.

1. $P(\mathcal{V}) \subset \mathcal{V}'$

Soit X un alphabet. Si $A, B \in X^*\mathcal{V}'$ (resp. $X^+\mathcal{V}'$ si $\mathcal{V}'$ est une $+$-variété) le théorème 1.6. montre l'existence d'un morphisme relationnel apériodique $\tau : M(AB) \to M(A) \times M(B)$ (resp. $\tau : S(AB) \to S(A) \times S(B)$).
Comme $M(A) \times M(B) \in \underline{A}(\underline{V})$, on a $M(AB) \in \underline{A}(\underline{A}(\underline{V})) = \underline{A}(\underline{V})$ (resp. $S(AB) \in \underline{A}(\underline{V})$) et donc $AB \in X^*\mathcal{V}'$ (resp. $X^+\mathcal{V}'$). Si $\mathcal{V}'$ est une $+$-variété, on en déduit que $\mathcal{V}'$ est fermée par produit ce qui démontre l'inclusion $P(\mathcal{V}) \subset \mathcal{V}'$. Si $\mathcal{V}'$ est une $*$-variété il faut encore montrer que pour tout alphabet X, $\{1\} \in X^*\mathcal{V}$. Or un calcul évident montrer que $M(1) \in \underline{A} \subset \underline{A}(\underline{V})$ d'où le résultat.

2. $\mathcal{V}' \subseteq P(\mathcal{V})$.

Supposons tout d'abord que $\mathcal{V}$ soit une $*$ variété et soit X un alphabet.
Si $A \in X^*\mathcal{V}'$, alors $M = M(A) \in \underline{A}(\underline{V})$ par définition. On va montrer par récurrence sur $|M|$ que tout langage A de X^* reconnu par un monoïde $M \in \underline{A}(\underline{V})$ est élément de $X^*P(\mathcal{V})$. Notons dès maintenant que l'hypothèse de récurrence peut être ainsi traduite : pour tout alphabet X, $X^*\Delta M \subset X^*P(\mathcal{V})$. En effet, si N est un diviseur strict de M, on a $N \in \underline{A}(\underline{V})$ et $|N| < |M|$.

D'après l'hypothèse, il existe une partie P de M et un morphisme $\eta : X^* \to M$ tel que $A = P\eta^{-1}$. Si $|M| = 1$, alors $P = M$ ou $P = \emptyset$, d'où $A = X^*$ ou $A = \emptyset$ et $A \in X^*\mathcal{V} \subset X^* P(\mathcal{V})$ dans les deux cas.
Supposons $|M| \geqslant 2$. Comme $A = \bigcup_{m \in P} m\eta^{-1}$ et puisque $X^*P(\mathcal{V})$ est fermée par union, nous sommes ramenés au cas où $P = \{m\}$. Nous allons maintenant suivre la discussion de l'algorithme de Schützenberger dont nous reprendrons les notations.

(a) $m \notin K$

Le théorème 2.1. montre alors que $A = m\eta^{-1}$ est reconnu par un diviseur strict de M et donc $A \in X^*P(\mathcal{V})$ d'après l'hypothèse de récurrence.

(b) $m \in K$ et $K^2 = 0$

Le théorème 2.4. montre que A s'exprime comme union finie de langages de la forme $A_0 x_1 A_1 x_2 \dots x_n A_n$ où $n \in \mathbb{N}$ $x_i \in X$ et $A_i \in X^* \Delta M$ pour $0 \leqslant i \leqslant n$. Or $X^*\Delta M \subset X^*P(\mathcal{V})$ d'après l'hypothèse de récurrence. Comme d'autre part $P(\mathcal{V})$ est littérale d'après la proposition 3.1., on a finalement $L \in X^*P(\mathcal{V})$.

(c) $m = 0$

Le théorème 2.3. montre que A s'exprime comme union finie de langages de la forme $X^*x X^*$ ou $X^*x B x'X^*$ avec $x, x' \in X$ et $B \in X^*\Delta M$. On en déduit comme dans le cas (b) que $A \in X^*P(\mathcal{V})$.

(d) $m \in D = K-0$ et $D^2 \neq 0$

On va d'abord montrer que $H\eta^{-1} \in X^*P(\mathcal{V})$. On a en effet, avec les notations du théorème 2.2. :
$H\eta^{-1} = ((mM)\eta^{-1} \cap (Mm)\eta^{-1}) - L_0 = L_1 \cup L_2 - L_0$. Comme L_0, L_1 et L_2 s'expriment comme union de langages de la forme X^*, $Bx X^*$, $X^*x B$ ou $X^*x B x' X^*$ avec $x,x' \in X$ et $B \in X^*\Delta M$, on a $L_0, L_1, L_2 \in X^*P(\mathcal{V})$ d'où $H\eta^{-1} \in X^*P(\mathcal{V})$

Il reste à montrer que $A = m\eta^{-1} \in X^*P(\mathcal{V})$. Or d'après l'hypothèse $M \in \underline{A}(\underline{V})$. Il existe par conséquent un morphisme relationnel apériodique $\tau : M \to N$ où $N \in V$. Autrement dit, il existe un monoïde M' et des morphismes $\alpha : M' \to M$ et $\beta : M' \to N$ avec α surjectif et β apériodique. Le morphisme $\eta : X^* \to M$ admet donc une factorisation $\eta = \eta'\alpha$ avec $\eta' : M' \to M$. La situation est résumée par le schéma suivant, où on a posé $\varphi = \eta'\beta$

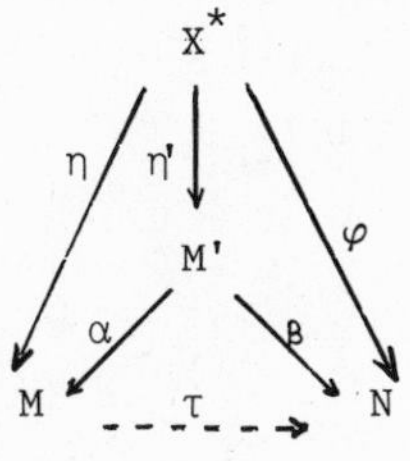

On a alors le

Lemme 3.3. $\{m\} = H \cap m\tau\tau^{-1}$

L'inclusion de gauche à droite est évidente. Réciproquement, soit $s \in H \cap m\tau\tau^{-1}$. Alors $s \in H$ et $s\tau \cap m\tau \neq \emptyset$. Comme τ est un morphisme relationnel apériodique, sa restriction aux $\mathcal{H}$-classes régulières -et en particulier à H- est injective. Donc $s = m$; ce qui conclut la preuve du lemme.

On déduit alors du lemme 3.3. la formule :

$m\eta^{-1} = H\eta^{-1} \cap m\tau\tau^{-1}\eta^{-1} = H\eta^{-1} \cap m\tau\,\beta^{-1}(\alpha^{-1})^{-1}\alpha^{-1}\eta'^{-1} = H\eta^{-1} \cap (m\tau)\varphi^{-1}$

Or $(m\tau)\varphi^{-1}$ est un langage reconnu par N, et comme $N \in V$, on a $(m\tau)\varphi^{-1} \in X^*\mathcal{V} \subset X^* P(\mathcal{V})$. Comme $H\eta^{-1} \in X^*P(\mathcal{V})$, il vient $m\eta^{-1} = H\eta^{-1} \cap (m\tau)\varphi^{-1} \in X^*P(\mathcal{V})$ ce qui achève la récurrence. On en déduit $\mathcal{V}' = P(\mathcal{V})$ et le théorème est démontré dans le cas des $*$-variétés.

On ferait la même démonstration dans le cas des +-variétés, en utilisant la version "semigroupe" de l'algorithme de Schützenberger.

4. Fermeture par produit non ambigu, déterministe, déterministe opposé.

Nous disons qu'un ensemble E de langages de X^* (resp. de X^+) est fermé par produit non ambigu (resp. déterministe, déterministe opposé) si pour toute famille finie $\{L_i\}\ 1 \leqslant i \leqslant n$ de langages de E telle que le produit $L_1 \ldots L_n = L$ soit non ambigu (resp. déterministe, déterministe opposé), on a $L \in E$.

Soit $\mathcal{V}$ une $*$-variété (resp. une +-variété) de langages. Nous noterons respectivement $PNA(\mathcal{V})$, $PD(\mathcal{V})$ et $PD^r(\mathcal{V})$ la plus petite variété littérale $\mathcal{V}'$ contenant $\mathcal{V}$ et telle que pour tout alphabet X, $X^*\mathcal{V}'$ ($X^+\mathcal{V}'$) soit fermée par produit non ambigu (resp. déterministe, déterministe opposé). Par définition $PNA(\mathcal{V})$, $PD(\mathcal{V})$ et $PD^r(\mathcal{V})$ sont respectivement la fermeture littérale de $\mathcal{V}$ par produit non ambigu, déterministe et déterministe opposé.

Il reste à déterminer les variétés de semigroupes (resp. de monoïdes) correspondantes

Théorème 4.1. Soit $\mathcal{V}$ une + variété et soit $\underline{V}$ la variété de semigroupes correspondant à $\mathcal{V}$. Alors $PNA(\mathcal{V})$ correspond à $\underline{L\{1\}}\ (\underline{V})$, $PD(\mathcal{V})$ correspond à $\underline{D}(\underline{V})$ et $PD^r(\mathcal{V})$ correspond à $\underline{D}^r(\underline{V})$.

Théorème (4.1)'. Soit $\mathcal{V}$ une $*$variété de langages et soit $\underline{V}$ la variété de monoïdes correspondant à $\mathcal{V}$. Alors $PNA(\mathcal{V})$ correspond à $\underline{L\{1\}}\ (\underline{J}_1 \vee \underline{V})$, $PD(\mathcal{V})$ correspond à $\underline{D}(\underline{J}_1 \vee \underline{V})$ et $PD^r(\mathcal{V})$ correspond à $\underline{D}^r(\underline{J}_1 \vee \underline{V})$

Démonstration du théorème 4.1.

Nous désignerons respectivement par $\mathcal{V}_1$, $\mathcal{V}_2$ et $\mathcal{V}_3$ les +variétés correspondant à $\underline{L\{1\}}\ (\underline{V})$, $\underline{D}(\underline{V})$ et $\underline{D}^r(\underline{V})$.

1. $PNA(\mathcal{V}) \subset \mathcal{V}_1$, $PD(\mathcal{V}) \subset \mathcal{V}_2$, $PD^r(\mathcal{V}) \subset \mathcal{V}_3$.

Soit X un alphabet, soient $A, B \in X^+\mathcal{V}_1$ (resp. $X^+\mathcal{V}_2$, $X^+\mathcal{V}_3$) et supposons que le produit AB soit non ambigu (resp. déterministe, déterministe opposé). D'après le théorème 1.1, il existe un $\underline{L\{1\}}$- morphisme relationnel (resp. un $\underline{D}$, $\underline{D}^r$-morphisme relationnel) : $S(AB) \to S(A) \times S(B)$. Comme $S(A) \times S(B) \in \underline{L\{1\}}\ (\underline{V})$, on a $S(AB) \in (\underline{L\{1\}}\ \underline{L\{1\}}\ (\underline{V})) = \underline{L\{1\}}\ (\underline{V})$ (resp. $\underline{D}(\underline{V})$, $\underline{D}^r(\underline{V})$).

On en déduit que $\mathcal{V}_1$ (resp $\mathcal{V}_2$, $\mathcal{V}_3$) est fermée par produit non ambigu (resp. déterministe, déterministe opposé). De plus, si $x \in X$, $S(\{x\}) \in \underline{Nil} \subset \underline{D} \cap \underline{D}^r$. Par conséquent, pour toute lettre $x \in X$, $\{x\} \in X^+\mathcal{V}_1$ (resp. $X^+\mathcal{V}_2$, $X^+\mathcal{V}_3$) et les variétés $\mathcal{V}_1, \mathcal{V}_2, \mathcal{V}_3$ sont littérales. Les inclusions cherchées résultent maintenant des définitions de $PNA(\mathcal{V})$, $PD(\mathcal{V})$ et $PD^r(\mathcal{V})$.

2. $\underline{\mathcal{V}_1 \subset PNA(\mathcal{V}),\ \mathcal{V}_2 \subset PD(\mathcal{V}),\ \mathcal{V}_3 \subset PD^r(\mathcal{V})}$

On va montrer par récurrence sur $|S|$ que tout langage A de X^+ reconnu par un semigroupe $S \in \underline{L\{1\}}(\underline{V})$ (resp. $\underline{D}(\underline{V})$, $\underline{D}^r(\underline{V})$) est élément de $X^+PNA(\mathcal{V})$ (resp $X^+PD(\mathcal{V})$, $X^+PD^r(\mathcal{V})$). Comme précédemment l'hypothèse de récurrence se traduit par l'inclusion $X^+\Delta S \subset X^+ PNA(\mathcal{V})$ (resp. $PD(\mathcal{V})$, $PD^r(\mathcal{V})$).

D'après l'hypothèse, il existe une partie P de S et un morphisme $\eta : X^+ \to S$ tel que $A = P\eta^{-1}$. Si $|S| = 0$ ou 1, on a $P = S$ ou $P = \emptyset$ d'où $A = X^+$ ou $A = \emptyset$ et $A \in X^+\mathcal{V}$ dans les deux cas. Supposons $|S| \geqslant 2$. Comme $A = \bigcup_{m \in P} m\eta^{-1}$ il suffit d'établir le résultat dans le cas où $P = \{m\}$. On va maintenant suivre la version "semigroupe" de l'algorithme de Schützenberger dont on reprendra les notations.

(a) $\underline{m \notin K}$

Le théorème 2.1. montre que $A = m\eta^{-1}$ est reconnu par un diviseur strict de S et donc $A \in X^+ PNA(\mathcal{V})$ (resp. $PD(\mathcal{V})$, $PD^r(\mathcal{V})$ d'après l'hypothèse de recurrence).

(b) $\underline{m \in K \text{ et } K^2 = 0}$

Le théorème 2.4. montre que A s'exprime comme union disjointe de produits déterministes (resp. déterministes opposés) de langages de la forme $A_0 x_1 A_1 x_2 \dots x_n A_n$ avec $x_i \in X$ et $A_i \in X^+\Delta M$ pour $0 \leqslant i \leqslant n$. On en déduit $A \in X^+PNA(\mathcal{V})$ (resp. $PD(\mathcal{V})$, $PD^r(\mathcal{V})$) d'après l'hypothèse de récurrence.

(c) $\underline{m = 0 \text{ et } D^2 = D \neq \emptyset}$

Nous aurons besoin d'un lemme qui sera utilisé à nouveau un peu plus loin :

Lemme 4.2. Si S contient au moins deux $\mathcal{D}$-classes régulières, alors

$Y^+ \in X^+\mathcal{V}$ pour toute partie Y de X.

Puisque $S \in \underline{L\{1\}}(\underline{V})$ (resp. $\underline{D}(V)$, $\underline{D}^r(\underline{V})$), il existe un $\underline{L\{1\}}$-morphisme relationnel $\tau : S \to T$ avec $T \in V$. D'après la proposition 1.5, T contient donc au moins deux $\mathcal{D}$-classes régulières. Il existe donc un idempotent e qui n'appartient pas à l'idéal minimal I de T. Soit $\gamma : T \to T/I$ le morphisme canonique. On voit que le semigroupe $\{e\gamma, J\gamma\}$ est isomorphe à U_1 et donc U_1 divise T, d'où $U_1 \in V$. Maintenant si $Y \subset X$, on a $S(Y^+) \prec U_1$ d'où $Y^+ \in X^+\mathcal{V}$. ■

Dans le cas c), les hypothèses du lemme 4.2 sont satisfaites et donc $Y^+ \in X^+\mathcal{V}$ pour toute partie Y de X. Or d'après le corollaire 2.6, A peut s'exprimer comme union disjointe de produits déterministes (resp. déterministes opposés) de langages de la forme $Y^+ \times X^+$, $x X^+$, Y^+x, $\{x\}$ (resp. $X^+ x X^+$ X^+x, xY^+, $\{x\}$) avec $Y \subset X$ et $x \in X-Y$. On en déduit que $A \in X^+ PNA(\mathcal{V})$ (resp $X^+ PD(\mathcal{V})$, $X^+ PD^r(\mathcal{V})$).

d) $\underline{D^2 = D \text{ et } m \in D}$

On va d'abord montrer que $H\eta^{-1} \in X^+ PNA(\mathcal{V})$ (resp. $R\eta^{-1} \in X^+ PD(\mathcal{V})$, $L\eta^{-1} \in X^+ PD^r(\mathcal{V})$). Nous distinguerons deux cas

d.1 $D = K$

Alors $mM = R$, $Mm = L$, $mM \cap Mm = H$ et il suffit d'appliquer le théorème 2.2. et l'hypothèse de récurrence pour conclure.

d.2 $D \neq K$

Dans ce cas, S a un zéro et contient donc au moins deux $\mathcal{D}$-classes régulières D'après le lemme 4.2, on a donc $Y^+ \in X^+\mathcal{V}$ pour toute partie Y de X.
Il suffit alors d'appliquer le corollaire 2.7 et l'hypothèse de récurrence pour conclure.

Il reste à démontrer que $A = m\eta^{-1} \in X^+ PNA(\mathcal{V})$ (resp. $X^+ PD(\mathcal{V})$, $X^+ PD^r(\mathcal{V})$). Or d'après l'hypothèse $S \in \underline{L\{1\}}(\underline{V})$ (resp. $\underline{D}(\underline{V})$, $\underline{D}^r(\underline{V})$). Il existe par conséquent un $\underline{L\{1\}}$-morphisme relationnel (resp. un $\underline{D}$, $\underline{D}^r$-morphisme relationnel) $\tau : S \to T$ où $T \in V$. Autrement dit, il existe un semigroupe S' et des morphismes $\alpha : S' \to S$ et $\beta : S' \to T$ avec α surjectif et β $\underline{L\{1\}}$-morphisme (resp. $\underline{D}$-morphisme, $\underline{D}^r$-morphisme). Le morphisme $\eta : X^+ \to S$ admet donc une factorisation $\eta = \eta'\alpha$ avec $\eta' : S' \to S$. La situation est résumée par le schéma suivant, où on a posé $\varphi = \eta'\beta$

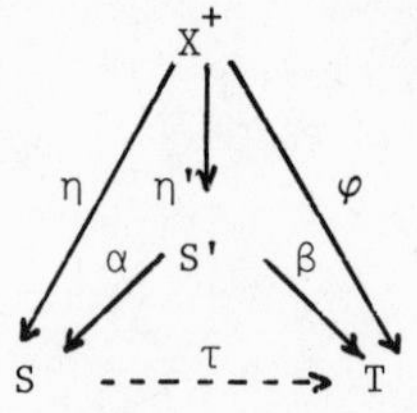

On a alors le résultat suivant, qui complète le lemme 3.3.

Lemme 4.3 (i) Si τ est un $\underline{R}$-morphisme relationnel, $\{m\} = R \cap (m\tau)\tau^{-1}$

(ii) Si τ est un $\underline{R}^r$- morphisme relationnel, $\{m\} = L \cap (m\tau)\tau^{-1}$

La démonstration se calque sur celle du lemme 3.3. ■

Puisqu'un $\underline{L\{1\}}$ (resp. $\underline{D}$, $\underline{D}^r$) -morphisme relationnel est en particulier un $\underline{A}$ (resp $\underline{R}$, $\underline{R}^r$)-morphisme relationnel, on déduit des lemmes 3.3 et 4.3 les formules $m\eta^{-1} = H\eta^{-1} \cap (m\tau)\varphi^{-1}$ (resp. $m\eta^{-1} = R\eta^{-1} \cap (m\tau)\varphi^{-1}$, $m\eta^{-1} = L\eta^{-1} \cap (m\tau)\varphi^{-1}$). Or $(m\tau)\varphi^{-1}$ est un langage reconnu par T, et comme $T \in V$, on a $(m\tau)\varphi^{-1} \in X^+\mathcal{V}$.
Comme $H\eta^{-1} \in X^+ PNA(\mathcal{V})$ (resp. $R\eta^{-1} \in X^+ PD(\mathcal{V})$, $L\eta^{-1} \in X^+ PD^r(\mathcal{V})$, il vient finalement $m\eta^{-1} \in X^+ PNA(\mathcal{V})$ (resp $PD(\mathcal{V})$, $PD^r(\mathcal{V})$)

e) $\underline{m \in D \text{ et } D \text{ est une } \mathcal{D}\text{-classe régulière telle que } D^2 \neq D}$

Ce cas particulier nécessite un lemme plus précis que le lemme 4.3

Lemme 4.4

(i) Si τ est un $\underline{L\{1\}}$ -morphisme relationnel, $\{m\} = m\tau\tau^{-1} \cap H = m\tau\tau^{-1} \cap (H \cup 0)$

(ii) Si τ est un $\underline{D}$-morphisme relationnel, $\{m\} = m\tau\tau^{-1} \cap R = m\tau\tau^{-1} \cap (R \cup 0)$

(iii) Si τ est un $\underline{D}^r$-morphisme relationnel, $\{m\} = m\tau\tau^{-1} \cap L = m\tau\tau^{-1} \cap (L \cup 0)$

(i) Il est clair que $\{m\} \subset m\tau\tau^{-1} \cap H \subset m\tau\tau^{-1} \cap (H \cup 0)$. Réciproquement, soit $u \in m\tau\tau^{-1} \cap (H \cup 0)$. Alors $u \in H \cup 0$ et $u\tau \cap m\tau \neq \emptyset$. Comme τ est un $\underline{L\{1\}}$-morphisme relationnel, $u\tau \cap m\tau \neq \emptyset$ entraine $u \mathcal{D} m$, donc en particulier $u \neq 0$ et finalement $u \in H$. Mais la restriction de τ aux $\mathcal{H}$-classes régulières est injective et donc $u = m$.

(ii) et (iii) se démontrent de manière analogue en utilisant le fait que la restriction d'un $\underline{D}$-morphisme relationnel (resp $\underline{D}^r$-morphisme relationnel) aux $\mathcal{R}$-classes (resp. $\mathcal{L}$-classes) régulières est injective. ∎

Revenons au cas e). On a, avec les notations du théorème 2.2. $(mM)\eta^{-1} = (R \cup 0)\eta^{-1} = L_0 \cup L_1$ avec $L_0 = 0\eta^{-1}$, d'où puisque $L_0 \cap R\eta^{-1} = \emptyset$, $R\eta^{-1} \subset L_1 \subset (R \cup 0)\eta^{-1}$. On trouve de la même façon $L\eta^{-1} \subset L_2 \subset (L \cup 0)\eta^{-1}$ et $H\eta^{-1} \subset L_3 \subset (H \cup 0)\eta^{-1}$. On déduit alors du lemme 4.4. que si τ est un $\underline{L\{1\}}$ -morphisme relationnel (resp un $\underline{D}$, $\underline{D}^r$-morphisme relationnel), on a l'égalité $m\eta^{-1} = (m\tau)\varphi^{-1} \cap L_3$ (resp. $m\eta^{-1} = (m\tau)\varphi^{-1} \cap L_1$, $m\eta^{-1} = (m\tau)\varphi^{-1} \cap L_2$). Or $(m\tau)\varphi^{-1}$ est un langage reconnu par $T \in V$, donc $(m\tau)\varphi^{-1} \in X^+\mathcal{V}$. De plus, l'expression de L_3(resp L_1, L_2) fournie par le théorème 2.2 montre, compte tenu de l'hypothèse de récurrence que $L_3 \in X^+\mathrm{PNA}(\mathcal{V})$ (resp $L_1 \in X^+\mathrm{PD}(\mathcal{V})$ $L_2 \in X^+\mathrm{PD}^r(\mathcal{V})$). On en déduit finalement $m\eta^{-1} \in X^+\mathrm{PNA}(\mathcal{V})$(resp. $m\eta^{-1} \in X^+\mathrm{PD}(\mathcal{V})$, $m\eta^{-1} \in X^+\mathrm{PD}^r(\mathcal{V})$)

f) $m = 0$ et D est une $\mathcal{D}$ -classe régulière telle que $D^2 \neq D$

Il suffit de remarquer que $0\eta^{-1} = X^+ - \bigcup_{m \neq 0} m\eta^{-1}$. Or si $m \neq 0$, On a $m\eta^{-1} \in X^+\mathrm{PNA}(\mathcal{V})$ (resp $X^+\mathrm{PD}(\mathcal{V})$, $X^+\mathrm{PD}^r(\mathcal{V})$) d'après les cas a) b) d) et e). Donc $0\eta^{-1} \in X^+\mathrm{PNA}(\mathcal{V})$ (resp $\mathrm{PD}(\mathcal{V})$, $\mathrm{PD}^r(\mathcal{V})$).

Ce dernier cas achève la récurrence, ce qui conclut la preuve du théorème 4.1.

Démonstration du théorème (4.1)'.

Nous désignerons respectivement par $\mathcal{W}_1, \mathcal{W}_2$ et $\mathcal{W}_3$ les $*$-variétés correspondant aux variétés $\underline{L\{1\}}\ (\underline{J}_1 \vee \underline{V})$, $\underline{D}(\underline{J}_1 \vee \underline{V})$ et $\underline{D}^r(\underline{J}_1 \vee \underline{V})$

1. $\mathrm{PNA}(\mathcal{V}) \subset \mathcal{W}_1$, $\mathrm{PD}(\mathcal{V}) \subset \mathcal{W}_2$, $\mathrm{PD}^r(\mathcal{V}) \subset \mathcal{W}_3$

On montre, par le même argument que dans le cas des + variétés, que $\mathcal{W}_1$ (resp $\mathcal{W}_2$, $\mathcal{W}_3$) est fermé par produit non ambigu (resp. déterministe, déterministe opposé). De plus si $x \in X$, on a $M\{x\} \in \underline{J} = \underline{\mathrm{Nil}}(\underline{J}_1) \subset \underline{D}(\underline{J}_1) \cap \underline{D}^r(\underline{J}_1) \subset \underline{D}(\underline{J}_1 \vee \underline{V}) \cap \underline{D}^r(\underline{J}_1 \vee \underline{V}) \subset \underline{L\{1\}}\ (\underline{J}_1 \vee \underline{V})$ ce qui démontre que $\mathcal{W}_1, \mathcal{W}_2$ et $\mathcal{W}_3$ sont littérales. Les inclusions cherchées résultent maintenant des définitions de $\mathrm{PNA}(\mathcal{V})$, $\mathrm{PD}(\mathcal{V})$ et $\mathrm{PD}^r(\mathcal{V})$.

2. $\mathcal{W}_1 \subset PNA(\mathcal{V})$, $\mathcal{W}_2 \subset PD(\mathcal{V})$, $\mathcal{W}_3 \subset PD\,(\mathcal{V})$.

Posons $\underline{W} = \underline{V} \vee \underline{J}_1$ et soit $\mathcal{W}$ la $\star$variété correspondant à W. Comme $PNA(\mathcal{V})$ (resp. $PD(\mathcal{V})$, $PD^r(\mathcal{V})$) est littérale, elle contient la variété correspondant à $\underline{J}_1$. Comme elle contient aussi $\mathcal{V}$ par définition elle contient $\mathcal{W}$. On en déduit les égalités $PNA(\mathcal{V}) = PNA(\mathcal{W})$ (resp. $PD(\mathcal{V}) = PD(\mathcal{W})$, $PD^r(\mathcal{V}) = PD^r(\mathcal{W})$).

Il suffit maintenant de reprendre la démonstration effectuée pour les +variétés en l'adaptant pour les $\star$-variétés. On notera d'ailleurs que la démonstration est légèrement simplifiée : en effet puisque les $\star$variétés $PNA(\mathcal{V})$, $PD(\mathcal{V})$ et $PD^r(\mathcal{V})$ sont littérales, on a pour tout alphabet X et pour toute partie Y de X, $Y^* \in X^*PNA(\mathcal{V})$ (resp. $X^*PD(\mathcal{V})$, $X^*PD^r(\mathcal{V})$) et on peut se dispenser du lemme 4.2.

On trouve finalement $\mathcal{W}_1 \subset PNA(\mathcal{W})$, $\mathcal{W}_2 \subset PD(\mathcal{W})$ et $\mathcal{W}_3 \subset PD^r(\mathcal{W})$, ce qui établit les inclusions cherchées. Ceci conclut la preuve du théorème (4.1)'. ■

5. Résultats complémentaires et problèmes ouverts

Voici tout d'abord une version légèrement plus précise du théorème de Schützenberger [6]

Corollaire 5.1 Pour tout alphabet X, $X^*\mathcal{A}$ est égal à la plus petite classe de langages de X^* contenant les lettres et fermée pour les opérations booléennes et pour les opérations $L \to Lx\,X^*$, $L \to X^*x\,L$ où $x \in X$.

Autrement dit, on n'a besoin d'utiliser que des produits très particuliers pour décrire X^* .

Preuve. Si on reprend la preuve du théorème 3.2 avec $V = \{1\}$, on s'aperçoit que dans le cas (d), on a $H = \{m\}$. On peut d'autre part regrouper les cas (b) et (d) et utiliser l'expression de $H\eta^{-1} = m\eta^{-1}$ obtenue en (d). On conclut en remarquant que les seules opérations utilisées sont maintenant celles indiquées dans l'énoncé du corollaire 5.1. ■

Voici maintenant un énoncé qui précise les théorèmes (4.1) et (4.1)' dans le cas où $\underline{V} \subset \underline{A}$. Commençons par le cas des + variétés

Théorème 5.2 Soit $\underline{V}$ une variété de semigroupes contenue dans $\underline{A}$ et soit $\mathcal{V}$ la + variété de langages correspondante. Soient $\mathcal{V}_1, \mathcal{V}_2, \mathcal{V}_3$ les + variétés correspondant respectivement à $\underline{L\{1\}}(\underline{V})$, $\underline{D}(\underline{V})$ et $\underline{D}^r(\underline{V})$. Alors, pour tout alphabet X, $X^+\mathcal{V}_1$ (resp $X^+\mathcal{V}_2$, $X^+\mathcal{V}_3$) est la plus petite classe de langages de X^* contenant $X^*\mathcal{V}$ et les lettres de l'alphabet qui soit fermée par union disjointe et produit non ambigu (resp. déterministe, déterministe opposé).

Preuve : Il suffit de reprendre la démonstration du théorème 4.1 en remarquant que l'hypothèse $\underline{V} \subset \underline{A}$ conduit à $H = \{m\}$.

Corollaire 5.3 (Eilenberg [2, chap. VIII]). Soit $L \subset X^+$

(a) $S(L) \in \underline{D}$ ssi L s'écrit $X^+A \cup B$ avec A et B finis

(b) $S(L) \in \underline{D}^r$ ssi L s'écrit $AX^+ \cup B$ avec A et B finis

(c) $S(L) \in \underline{L\{1\}}$ ssi L s'écrit $AX^+B \cup C$ avec A,B,C finis

Preuve Appliquons le théorème précédent avec $\underline{V} = \{1, \emptyset\}$. On trouve $\underline{L\{1\}}\ (\underline{V}) = \underline{L\{1\}}$ $\underline{D}(\underline{V}) = \underline{D}$ et $\underline{D}^r(\underline{V}) = \underline{D}^r$. D'autre part, pour tout alphabet X, on a $X^+\mathcal{V} = \{\emptyset, X^+\}$. Or la plus petite classe de langages de X^+ contenant $\emptyset$, X^+ et les lettres de X qui soit fermée par union disjointe et produit non ambigu (resp. déterministe, déterministe opposée) est précisément la classe des langages de la forme indiquée en c) (resp a), b)). ∎

Dans le cas des $*$ variétés, on obtient de la même façon les énoncés suivants :

Théorème (5.2)' Soit $\underline{V}$ une variété de monoïdes contenue dans $\underline{A}$ et soit $\mathcal{V}$ la $*$ variété de langages correspondante. Soient $\mathcal{W}_1$, $\mathcal{W}_2$ et $\mathcal{W}_3$ les $*$-variétés correspondant respectivement à $\underline{L\{1\}}\ (\underline{J}_1 \vee \underline{V})$, $\underline{D}(\underline{J}_1 \vee \underline{V})$ et $\underline{D}^r(\underline{J}_1 \vee \underline{V})$. Alors pour tout alphabet X, $X^*\mathcal{V}_1$ (resp $X^*\mathcal{V}_2$, $X^*\mathcal{V}_3$) est la plus petite classe de langages de X^* contenant $X^*\mathcal{V}$ et les lettres de l'alphabet et qui soit fermée par union disjointe et produit non ambigu (resp. déterministe, déterministe opposé).

Corollaire (5.3)'(Eilenberg [2, chap. X], Schützenberger [7]). Soit $L \subset X^*$

(a) $M(L) \in \underline{R}$ ssi L s'écrit comme union disjointe de langages de la forme

$$X_0^* x_1 X_1^* \ldots x_n X_n^* \qquad n \geq 0$$

avec $x_1, \ldots, x_n \in X$ $X_n \subseteq X$ et $X_i \subset X - \{x_{i+1}\}$ pour $1 \leq i \leq n$

(b) $M(L) \in \underline{R}^r$ ssi L s'écrit comme union disjointe de langages de la forme

$$X_0^* x_1 X_1^* \ldots x_n X_n^* \qquad n \geq 0 \quad \text{avec } x_1, \ldots x_n \in X,\ X_0 \subset X$$

et $X_i \subset X - \{x_i\}$ pour $1 \leq i \leq n$

(c) $M(L) \in \underline{DA}$ ssi L est élément de la plus petite classe de langages de X^* contenant les langages de la forme $\{x\}$ (avec $x \in X$) et Y^* (avec $Y \subset X$) et fermée pour l'union disjointe et le produit non ambigu.

Preuve Appliquons le théorème précédent avec $\underline{V} = \{1\}$. On a vu que $\underline{L\{1\}}\ (\underline{J}_1) = \underline{DA}$ $\underline{D}(\underline{J}_1) = \underline{R}$ et $\underline{D}^r(\underline{J}_1) = \underline{D}$. Il suffit donc de vérifier que les langages décrits en (a) et (b) forment respectivement la plus petite classe de langages de X^* contenant les lettres et les langages Y^* avec $Y \subset X$ qui soit fermée par produit déterministe (resp. déterministe opposé). Nous laisserons cette vérification (facile) aux soins du lecteur. ∎

Signalons pour finir un corollaire du à Schützenberger [7]. Soit $\underline{H}$ une variété de groupes. On peut démontrer que $\underline{L\{1\}}\ (\underline{J}_1 \vee \underline{H}) = \underline{DA}(\underline{H})$ (resp. $\underline{D}(\underline{J}_1 \vee \underline{H}) = \underline{R}(\underline{H})$,

$\underline{D}^r(\underline{J}_1 \vee \underline{H}) = \underline{R}^r(\underline{H}))$ et que cette variété est la variété des semigroupes dont chaque $\mathcal{D}$-classe régulière est un semigroupe isomorphe au produit direct d'un groupe $H \in \underline{H}$ par une bande rectangulaire (resp par une bande rectangulaire $\mathcal{R}$-triviale, $\mathcal{L}$-triviale). On a alors le

Corollaire 5.4. [7] Soit $L \subset X^*$. Alors $M(L) \in \underline{DA}(\underline{H})$ (resp $\underline{R}(\underline{H})$, $\underline{R}^r(\underline{H})$) ssi L est élément de la plus petite classe $\mathcal{C}$ de langages de X^* satisfaisant les conditions suivantes

(i) $\mathcal{C}$ contient les lettres et les langages Y^* avec $Y \subset X$

(ii) $\mathcal{C}$ est fermé par union disjointe et produit non ambigu (resp. déterministe, déterministe opposé).

(iii) Si $A \in \mathcal{C}$ et si $B \subset X^*$ vérifie $M(B) \in \underline{H}$ alors $A \cap B \in \mathcal{C}$.

Preuve : La démonstration du théorème (4.1)' comportait l'étude des monoïdes M de $\underline{L\{1\}}$ $(\underline{V})$ (resp. $\underline{D}(\underline{V})$, $\underline{D}^r(\underline{V})$) où $\underline{V}$ était une variété contenant $\underline{J}_1$. Il suffit de reprendre cette étude dans le cas où $M \in \underline{DA}(\underline{H})$ (resp. $\underline{R}(\underline{H})$, $\underline{R}^r(\underline{H})$). On voit que les cas (e) et (f) disparaissent. Par ailleurs, dans les cas restants, seule l'hypothèse $M \in \underline{A}(\underline{V})$ (resp. $\underline{R}(\underline{V})$, $\underline{R}^r(\underline{V})$) avait été utilisée et la démonstration était en fait valable pour une variété $\underline{V}$ quelconque. La démonstration s'adapte donc sans difficulté. Une dernière précision : puisque $X^* \in \mathcal{C}$ d'après (i), on a, pour tout $B \subset X^*$ vérifiant $M(B) \in \underline{H}$, $X^* \cap B = B \in \mathcal{C}$, ce qui démontre que $\mathcal{C}$ contient $X^*\mathcal{H}$ où $\mathcal{H}$ est la $\star$variété correspondant à $\underline{H}$. ∎

Questions ouvertes : il serait évidemment très intéressant de décrire les opérations de fermeture sur les +variétés de langages qui correspondent aux opérations $\underline{W} \to \underline{V}(\underline{W})$ pour diverses variétés de semigroupes $\underline{V}$. En particulier, le cas $\underline{V} = \underline{Nil}$, suggéré par H. Straubing, semble être d'une importance cruciale. En effet, puisque $\underline{J} = \underline{Nil}(\underline{J}_1)$, on pourrait espérer obtenir ainsi une nouvelle preuve du théorème de Simon sur les langages testables par morceaux (cf [2]).

Bibliographie

[1] COHEN R. et BRZOZOWSKI J.A., Proceedings of the Hawaii International Conference on System Sciences (1968), p 1-4, University of Hawaii Press, Honolulu, Hawaii.

[2] EILENBERG S., Automata, Languages and Machines, Academic Press, Vol B. (1976)

[3] FICH F.E. et BRZOZOWSKI J.A., A characterization of a dot-depth analogue of generalized definite languages. 6th Colloguium on Automata, Languages and Programming, Lecture Notes in Computer Science N° 71, (1979), 230-244.

[4] LALLEMENT G. Semigroups and Combinatorial applications. Interscience (1979).

[5] MEYER A.R., A note on star-free events. J. Assoc. Comput. Mach. 16 (1969), 220 -225.

[6] SCHÜTZENBERGER M.P. On finite monoïds having only trivial subgroups. Information and Control 8 (1965), 190-194.

[7] SCHÜTZENBERGER M.P. Sur le produit de concaténation non ambigu. Semigroup Forum 13, (1976), 47-75.

[8] STRAUBING H. Aperiodic homomorphisms and the concatenation product of recognizable sets. Journal of Pure and Applied Algebra, 15, (1979), 319-327.

[9] STRAUBING H. Relational morphisms and operations on recognizable sets. A paraitre dans la R.A.I.R.O.

[10] TILSON B. Chapitres 11 et 12 de la référence 2.

ON THE OPTIMAL ASSIGNMENT OF ATTRIBUTES TO PASSES IN MULTI-PASS ATTRIBUTE EVALUATORS

Kari-Jouko Räihä and Esko Ukkonen
Department of Computer Science, University of Helsinki
Tukholmankatu 2, SF-00250 Helsinki 25, Finland

ABSTRACT

The problem of constructing multi-pass evaluators for attribute grammars is studied. The algorithm used heretofore is demonstrated to be able to produce evaluators which perform almost twice as many passes through the parse tree as necessary. The problem of constructing a shortest possible evaluation order is then shown to be NP-complete. Based on a new characterization of multi-pass attribute grammars, a modified construction algorithm is then developed. The new heuristics is motivated by experience with real grammars.

1. INTRODUCTION

The first algorithm for constructing multi-pass evaluators for attribute grammars [9] was developed by Bochmann [2]. Although Bochmann considers only left-to-right passes, his algorithm forms the basis of further generalizations. We shall briefly sketch the approach of Bochmann.

The purpose of the construction algorithm is to assign attributes to passes in the following manner. For each pass, suppose initially that all attributes not evaluated on previous passes are evaluable during the next pass. Search through the semantic rules of the grammar and delete from the set of evaluable attributes all those which depend on unavailable attributes, these being the ones which have not been evaluated on previous passes, and either will not be evaluated on the present pass or will be encountered after the attribute which thus must be deleted. Repeat the process until the set of evaluable attributes has stabilized. Repeating this for every pass, either all attributes will be assigned to passes, or the grammar is not evaluable by a left-to-right multi-pass evaluator.

Note that an essential feature of multi-pass evaluators in Bochmann's sense is that *all* instances of an attribute are evaluated during the same pass. Such evaluators are in [1] called *simple* multi-pass evaluators in contrast with *pure* multi-pass evaluators, where different instances of the same attribute can be evaluated during different passes. In practice, simple multi-pass evaluators are more interesting, since their implementation is much simpler. Therefore we consider here only simple multi-pass evaluators.

As a generalization of Bochmann's evaluators, Jazayeri [4] suggested that right-to-left passes should alternate with left-to-right ones. Clearly, Jazayeri's evaluators (called alternating semantic evaluators or ASE, for short) contain Bochmann's evaluators as a special case. The change in the construction algorithm is small: the set of unavailable attributes is different depending on the direction of the pass.

It was soon realized [7] that the approach of [4] is wasteful, because some of the passes can be merged with neighbouring ones. Based on this observation, a new form of the construction algorithm was developed independently in [12] and [13]. The idea is to let the direction of each pass be either left-to-right or right-to-left regardless of the direction of the previous pass. This means that the algorithm has to find out the sets of evaluable attributes for both directions. If one is contained in the other, the larger set is chosen. If the sets are incommensurate, both [12] and [13] suggested letting the evaluator alternate its direction as originally proposed in [4].

If Bochmann's algorithm terminates successfully, it produces an optimal left-to-right evaluator: as many attributes as possible are evaluated on each pass. However, the possibility of choice introduced by right-to-left passes has the effect that the number of passes is not necessarily minimal. An example of this situation is given in Section 2.

The use of alternating semantic evaluators over more advanced methods (e.g. [3], [8]) accepting larger classes of grammars has often been motivated by the simplicity and efficiency of both the evaluator and the construction algorithm. Thus it comes as somewhat of a surprise that in our search for a construction algorithm which produces a minimal number of passes we found that the problem is in fact NP-complete. The proof of this result is outlined in Section 3.

The grammar used in the proof of the intractability result is certainly one which is not encountered in real life. Therefore it seemed possible to find an algorithm which, although nonoptimal in the general case, produces optimal evaluators for practical grammars. We approach the problem from two directions. In Section 4 we investigate the properties of real grammars from the point of view of multi-pass evaluation, whereas in Section 5 we provide a new characterization of the evaluation technique. Drawing from these results and observations we give a new construction algorithm for multi-pass evaluators in Section 6.

The following treatment is rather informal. A more rigorous treatment (with complete constructions and proofs of the results) can be found in [17].

2. NONOPTIMALITY OF THE PRESENT ALGORITHM

We say that a construction algorithm for multi-pass evaluators is *optimal* if it produces evaluators which use a minimum number of passes. This definition, though but one of many possibilities, is natural: in traditional implementations of multi-pass evaluators (e.g. [15]) a decrease in the number of passes results in savings in the overhead caused by traversing the tree. Even in approaches where the number of passes is not of equal importance [6] the optimality of the construction algorithm decreases the lifetime of attributes, which is good for storage allocation [11].

We demonstrate the behaviour of the ASE constructor using the following example grammar. Here x denotes the only terminal symbol. The superscripts L and R are used to distinguish two occurrences of the same nonterminal in a production.

Nonterminal	Inherited attributes	Synthesized attributes
Z	–	–
X_1	a_1, b_1, c_1, d_1	p_1, q_1, r_1
X_i, i=2,...,n-1	a_i, b_i, c_i	p_i, q_i, r_i

Productions with semantic rules

1° $Z \rightarrow X_1^L X_1^R$

$$a_1(X_1^L) \leftarrow q_1(X_1^R) \qquad a_1(X_1^R) \leftarrow \text{constant}$$
$$b_1(X_1^L) \leftarrow r_1(X_1^R) \qquad b_1(X_1^R) \leftarrow \text{constant}$$
$$c_1(X_1^L) \leftarrow \text{constant} \qquad c_1(X_1^R) \leftarrow p_1(X_1^L)$$
$$d_1(X_1^L) \leftarrow p_1(X_1^R) \qquad d_1(X_1^R) \leftarrow \text{constant}$$

2° $X_i \rightarrow X_{i+1}^L X_{i+1}^R$,
i=1,...,n-3

$$p_i(X_i) \leftarrow b_i(X_i) + c_i(X_i)$$
$$q_i(X_i) \leftarrow a_i(X_i) + p_{i+1}(X_{i+1}^R)$$
$$r_i(X_i) \leftarrow p_{i+1}(X_{i+1}^R)$$
$$a_{i+1}(X_{i+1}^L) \leftarrow q_{i+1}(X_{i+1}^R)$$
$$b_{i+1}(X_{i+1}^L) \leftarrow r_{i+1}(X_{i+1}^R)$$
$$c_{i+1}(X_{i+1}^L) \leftarrow \text{constant}$$
$$a_{i+1}(X_{i+1}^R) \leftarrow \text{constant}$$
$$b_{i+1}(X_{i+1}^R) \leftarrow \text{constant}$$
$$c_{i+1}(X_{i+1}^R) \leftarrow p_{i+1}(X_{i+1}^L)$$

3° $X_{n-2} \rightarrow X_{n-1}^L X_{n-1}^R$

like 2°, with the following exception: $b_{n-1}(X_{n-1}^L) \leftarrow \text{constant}$

4° $X_{n-1} \rightarrow x$

$$p_{n-1}(X_{n-1}) \leftarrow b_{n-1}(X_{n-1}) + c_{n-1}(X_{n-1})$$
$$q_{n-1}(X_{n-1}) \leftarrow a_{n-1}(X_{n-1})$$
$$r_{n-1}(X_{n-1}) \leftarrow \text{constant}$$

This grammar generates exactly one attributed parse tree, fragments of which are shown below. Inherited attributes are shown on the left and synthesized attributes on the right of each nonterminal. Attributes with no entering arcs are constants.

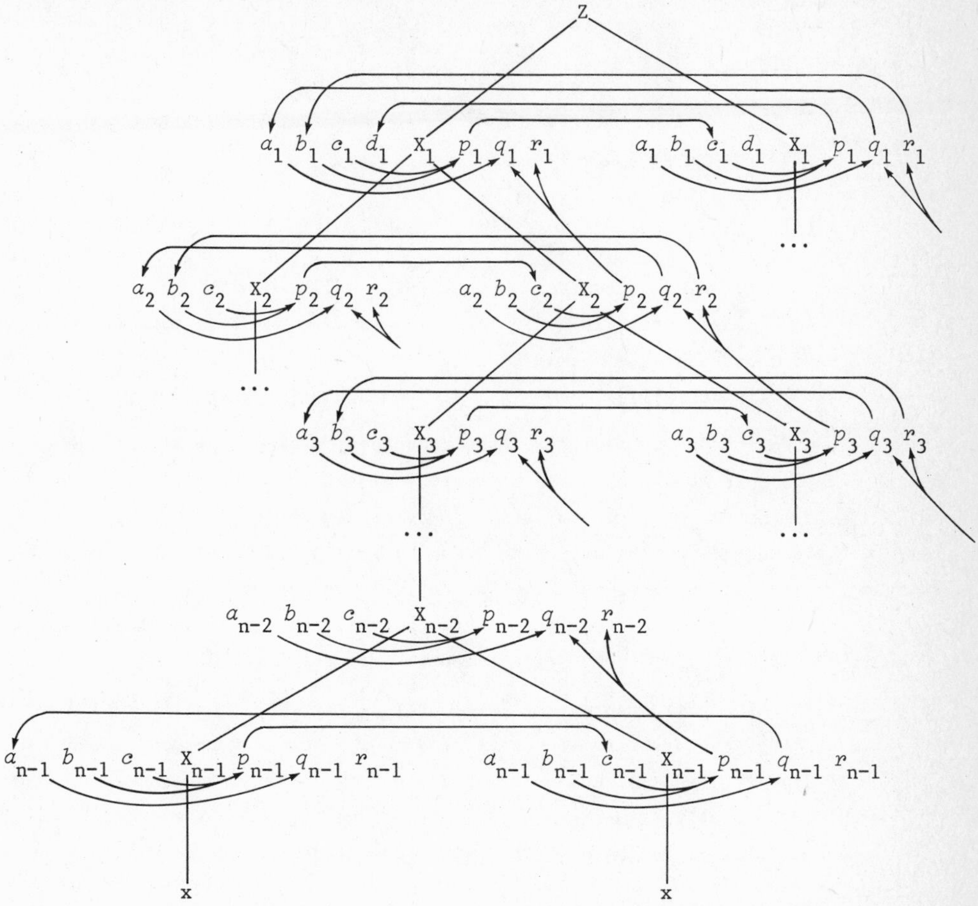

The evaluation order produced by the ASE constructor is the following:

pass	direction	attributes to be evaluated
1	left-to-right	b_{n-1}, c_{n-1}, p_{n-1}, r_{n-1}, r_{n-2}
2	right-to-left	a_{n-1}, q_{n-1}, a_{n-2}, b_{n-2}, q_{n-2}
3	left-to-right	c_{n-2}, p_{n-2}, r_{n-3}
4	right-to-left	a_{n-3}, b_{n-3}, q_{n-3}
⋮	⋮	⋮
2n-4	right-to-left	a_1, b_1, q_1
2n-3	left-to-right	c_1, p_1
2n-2	right-to-left	d_1

By inspecting the dependencies we note that none of the attributes a_i, q_i (i=1,...,n) contributes in the evaluation of the other attributes. Consequently, also the following evaluation order could be used:

pass	direction	attributes to be evaluated
1	left-to-right	b_{n-1}, c_{n-1}, p_{n-1}, r_{n-1}, r_{n-2}
2	left-to-right	b_{n-2}, c_{n-2}, p_{n-2}, r_{n-3}
3	left-to-right	b_{n-3}, c_{n-3}, p_{n-3}, r_{n-4}
⋮	⋮	⋮
n-1	left-to-right	b_1, c_1, p_1
n	right-to-left	a_i, q_i (i=1,...,n-1), d_1

This evaluation order, which is in fact optimal, uses n-2 fewer passes than the order produced by the ASE constructor. In general, it is possible to prove that if the shortest evaluation order uses k passes then the ASE constructor produces for the same grammar at most 2k-1 passes [17].

The basic reason for the nonoptimality of the construction algorithm is that we do not know which direction to choose when the corresponding sets of attributes are incommensurate. The algorithm follows the heuristics that the direction of the next pass is opposite to the direction of the preceding pass. Consequently, when an attribute becomes ready for evaluation, its evaluation is not delayed for more than one pass. Thus the algorithm tries to take new attributes into the evaluation process as soon as possible hoping that this would make other attributes evaluable.

A simple solution which yields an optimal evaluator is to delay the choice of direction if the corresponding sets are incommensurate, and to see how many passes each choice would produce. However, since each pass can contain only one attribute, such a recursive approach would clearly result in an exponential algorithm. On the other hand, the result of the next section indicates that in the general case there is not much hope for anything better.

3. INTRACTABILITY OF THE CONSTRUCTION OF OPTIMAL EVALUATORS

If we add nondeterminism to the algorithm proposed at the end of the previous section, so that the algorithm every time guesses the right choice, we obviously get an algorithm in NP. To show that the problem of constructing an optimal evaluator is actually NP-complete, we transform the shortest common supersequence problem in a binary alphabet into the optimal evaluator construction problem. The former problem has recently been shown to be NP-complete [16] based on a general result of Maier [10].

Suppose that we are given n sequences $S^1,\ldots,S^n$ in $(L \cup R)^+$. For this set of sequences we construct an attribute grammar. The set of nonterminals in the grammar is $\{Z\} \cup \{Y_i \mid 1 \leq i \leq n\} \cup \{X_i \mid 1 \leq i \leq n\}$. The Z and Y_i symbols have no associated attributes.

Suppose that $S^i = s_1^i s_2^i \ldots s_m^i$; then the set of attributes associated with X_i is $\{a_j^i \mid 1 \leq j \leq m\} \cup \{b_j^i \mid 1 \leq j \leq m\}$, where attributes a_j^i are inherited and attributes b_j^i are synthesized.

We will not give here the entire construction, but rather demonstrate the technique by an example. Suppose that S^3 = LRRLL. We interpret L as meaning a left-to-right pass, and R as meaning a right-to-left pass. The dependencies induced by the grammar have the following structure. Note that all the dependencies shown are induced by semantic rules associated with production $Y_3 \rightarrow X_3X_3$. The layering of the attributes reflects the distribution of the attributes over the evaluation passes.

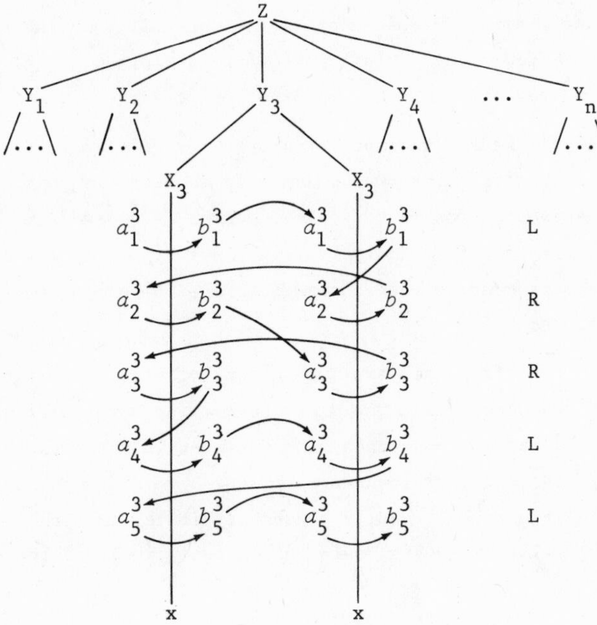

The attributes a_1^3 and b_1^3 can only be evaluated during the same pass from left to right. Furthermore, a_2^3 and b_2^3 must be evaluated on a right-to-left pass which follows the pass of a_1^3 and b_1^3. Continuing in this way we see that the evaluation order for the entire grammar must contain LRRLL as a subsequence. Since the Y_i subtrees are independent, the evaluation order must contain all the sequences S^i as subsequences. Thus an evaluation order is a supersequence of the sequences $S^1, \ldots S^n$ and vice versa. We conclude that a sequence is an optimal evaluation order for the attribute grammar if and only if it is a shortest common supersequence of $S^1, \ldots, S^n$. Noting [16], this proves the NP-completeness.

This result must not discourage us from searching for efficient algorithms which produce optimal evaluators for a class of grammars which is of practical importance. In the next section we examine what real grammars are like.

4. ATTRIBUTE GRAMMARS FOR PROGRAMMING LANGUAGES

Some statistics for a large set of attribute grammars have been presented in [11] and [14]. In the grammars the number of evaluation passes ranges from 1 to 5. These figures are very small. However, in all grammars the target language is very close to the source language, which partly explains their simplicity. Thus the grammars do not exhibit all the complications encountered in describing translation from a source language to an independent low-level target language. In particular, code optimization does not receive any attention in any of the grammars.

In compiling a program, information flows mainly from left to right. Thus most of the passes in a multi-pass evaluator are likely to be from left to right; this is confirmed by experience with existing grammars. Consequently, the optimality of the evaluation order depends on whether the few right-to-left passes are performed at the right moment. We can see mainly two reasons that require right-to-left passes.

First, the source language can have some inherent properties which are most conveniently described by right-to-left attributes. One example is identifiers which are used before declaration. Another source for right-to-left passes is code optimization. In particular, many grammars for data flow analysis (e.g. [5]) typically introduce right-to-left dependencies in the grammar, since information must be propagated from the end of the program towards its beginning.

These two causes for right-to-left passes are independent of each other. Thus there is no apparent reason why the computation could not be carried out during a single pass. On the other hand, a blind method such as the one used in the present construction algorithm can easily push the corresponding attributes to different passes. The reason for this is that the algorithm greedily grasps attributes into the evaluation process, even when waiting a little longer would considerably increase the size of the pass.

The number of right-to-left passes is small. The above observations lead us to the conclusion that adding a little ingenuity to the present algorithm can give us a method for producing optimal evaluators for practical grammars. To do this, we first distill from the attribute grammar the essential information required for assigning attributes to passes. This is accomplished in the next section.

5. CHARACTERIZATION OF ASE GRAMMARS

We construct a *dependency graph* whose vertices are the attribute symbols and whose arcs denote the dependencies. An arc goes from a to b if a is used in some semantic rule which defines b. Moreover, arcs are labeled by the symbols L, R, ANY and NO indicating the following: if the attributes connected by the arc are to be evaluated during the same pass, the direction of the pass must be left-to-right (L), right-to-left (R), or either one (ANY); NO indicates that the attributes must be assigned to separate passes.

The basic situations which cause each of these labels to be attached to an arc are given below. Here i denotes an inherited and s a synthesized attribute.

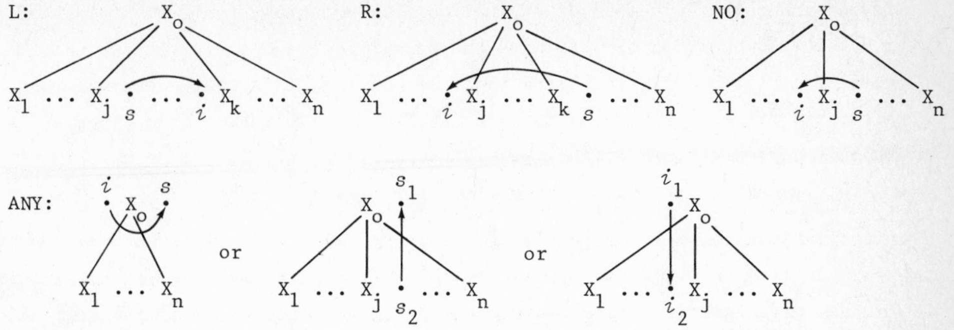

We assume that the grammar is in canonical form [4], i.e. attributes that are defined within a production are not used as arguments within the same production. It is well-known that all attribute grammars can be transformed into canonical form by simple textual substitution. In a canonical grammar all attribute dependencies are of one of the above forms. Thus we have a rule for finding for every dependence the label induced by it.

Different semantic rules may induce different labels to be attached to the same arc. However, we shall attach only one label to each arc. The following rule is used in combining a set of labels Δ into a single label $\delta(\Delta)$:

$$\delta(\Delta) = \underset{\sim}{\text{if}}\ \text{NO} \in \Delta \vee (\text{L} \in \Delta \wedge \text{R} \in \Delta)\ \underset{\sim}{\text{then}}\ \text{NO}\ \underset{\sim}{\text{else}}$$
$$\underset{\sim}{\text{if}}\ \text{L} \in \Delta\ \underset{\sim}{\text{then}}\ \text{L}\ \underset{\sim}{\text{else}}$$
$$\underset{\sim}{\text{if}}\ \text{R} \in \Delta\ \underset{\sim}{\text{then}}\ \text{R}\ \underset{\sim}{\text{else}}\ \text{ANY}\ \underset{\sim}{\text{fi}}\ \underset{\sim}{\text{fi}}\ \underset{\sim}{\text{fi}}$$

For instance, for the grammar of Section 2 we get the following graph.

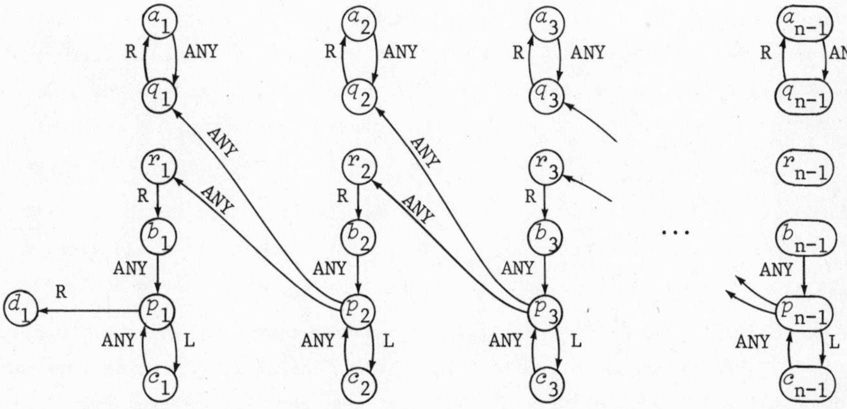

For any D in {L, R, ANY, NO}, we say that the dependency graph G has a *strongly connected D-component* C, if C is a strongly connected component of G, and D is the label obtained by compressing the labels of the arcs of C into one using the rule given above.

It is easy to see that it is an inherent property of simple multi-pass evaluators that all the attributes in a strongly connected component must be evaluated during the same pass. Furthermore, the direction of the pass must be in conformity with the labels of the arcs of the component. Thus it is fairly simple to show the following characterization for ASE grammars:

A grammar can be evaluated using an alternating semantic evaluator if and only if its dependency graph does not contain strongly connected NO-*components.*

A similar characterization has been independently developed by Alblas [1].

Our result is a solution to the invitation in [7] to find a characterization for ASE grammars which is on a higher level than the construction algorithm. Our characterization has also immediate appealing applications. It can be used as an efficient and direct test for ASE membership. The present algorithm requires the production of the entire evaluation order before it can decide whether the grammar belongs to the ASE class or not; in the negative case, a lot of work is wasted. More exactly, let π denote the number of attribute dependencies in the grammar and let $|A|$ denote the number of attribute symbols. The time requirement of the entire construction algorithm is $\mathcal{O}(\max(|A|^3,\pi))$ (for details, see [11]), whereas the membership test can be carried out in $\mathcal{O}(\max(|A|,\pi))$ steps [17].

Furthermore, in our characterization the labels of the arcs in the strongly connected component clearly reveal the reasons for possible ASE conflicts. This is useful when one considers the implementation of ASE grammars in a compiler writing system.

6. A NEW CONSTRUCTION ALGORITHM

We will use the dependency graph as the basis of the construction algorithm. We first check that the grammar belongs to the ASE class using the result of the previous section. Then we proceed by combining nodes into blocks. Each block will have a label indicating the direction to be used in the evaluation of the attributes in the block. Initially each node is labeled with ANY.

Since the attributes in a strongly connected component all have to be evaluated during the same pass, they can be combined into a single block. The label of the block is formed from the labels of the arcs in the component using the rule given in Section 5. As a result we get a directed acyclic graph with labels on both nodes and arcs. For instance, the graph of Section 5 is compressed to the form shown on the next page.

We go on by constructing the *L block* for the compressed graph. Initially the L block is empty. A node X can be added to the L block if the following conditions are satisfied: (a) the label of X is L or ANY; (b) all arcs entering X start from nodes already in the L block; (c) all arcs entering X are labeled with L or ANY. The construction of an *R block* is defined analogously.

These blocks correspond exactly to the sets of attributes used in the original

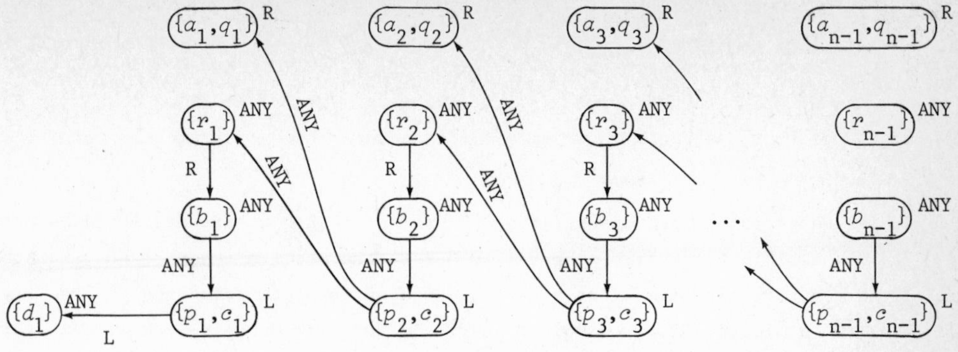

algorithm. We continue in the same way: if the attributes in either block are entirely contained in the other, the larger block is chosen. From the point of view of following passes, these attributes become available. Consequently, the block and all arcs starting from it can be deleted from the dependency graph. New versions of the L and R blocks can then be formed. By repeating the process, the entire evaluation order will eventually be constructed.

Our improvement of the original algorithm concerns the choice of the proper block when the sets are incommensurate. The observations in Section 4 indicate that left-to-right passes and right-to-left passes should not be treated equally. Instead, the evaluator should stick to the left-to-right direction until the R block has grown to its full size.

We first define the *extended L block* to consist of those nodes whose attributes can be evaluated using successive left-to-right passes with no intermediate right-to-left passes. The extended L block is constructed just like the L block, except that condition (c) does not have to be satisfied.

We go on to define the *maximal R block* as containing all those nodes whose attributes can be evaluated in a single right-to-left pass, provided that sufficiently many left-to-right passes are performed first. The maximal R block is formed like the R block, except that in condition (b) we also allow arcs with arbitrary label starting from the extended L block.

If the L and R blocks are incommensurate, we use the maximal R block for choosing the direction of the next pass in the following simple way. If the maximal R block equals the R block, the right-to-left direction is chosen, otherwise the left-to-right direction is preferred.

In the general case this heuristics obviously does not produce optimal evaluators. However, the arguments of Section 4 indicate that the special case where the attribute grammar has an evaluation order with only one right-to-left pass is particularly interesting. It is easy to see that in this situation our algorithm in fact produces optimal evaluators. Thus an optimal evaluation order is found for the example grammar of

Section 2, too. Some other heuristics are discussed in [11] and [17].

It is possible to let the algorithm output whether it has encountered a situation where no clear choice between L and R could be made. If the number of passes found is not too large, but not known to be optimal, it is possible to determine the optimal number by a systematic search.

It has recently been suggested that the evaluation of each attribute should be delayed as long as possible [11]. This proposal is due to the observation that such a change often shortens the lifetime of attributes, which in turn decreases the storage requirements of the evaluator. It is simple to define a dual for our algorithm which starts assigning attributes to passes from the other end of the dependency graph, thus having the effect suggested in [11].

7. CONCLUSIONS

We have demonstrated that the present algorithm used for constructing alternating semantic evaluators for attribute grammars produces nonoptimal evaluators. Furthermore, the problem of constructing optimal evaluators was shown to be NP-complete. However, based on an investigation of the structure of real-life attribute grammars and the class of ASE grammars, we were able to develop a new polynomial-time construction algorithm having the properties:

(a) It provides a direct and efficient test for ASE membership.

(b) For grammars not in the ASE class, the reasons for ASE conflicts are clearly revealed.

(c) The algorithm constructs optimal evaluators for a subclass of ASE grammars. This class strictly includes the grammars which have an optimal evaluation order containing only one right-to-left pass.

Because of these properties, the use of our algorithm in a compiler writing system makes life easier for the user of the system (because of improved diagnostics). It may also improve the efficiency of the compilers produced by the system.

ACKNOWLEDGEMENT

The work of Kari-Jouko Räihä was supported by the Academy of Finland.

REFERENCES

1. Alblas,H.: The limitations of attribute evaluation in passes. Manuscript, Department of Applied Mathematics, Twente University of Technology, Enschede, Dec. 1979.
2. Bochmann,G.V.: Semantic evaluation from left to right. CACM 19,2 (Feb. 1976), 55-62.
3. Cohen,R. and Harry,E.: Automatic generation of near-optimal linear-time translators for non-circular attribute grammars. Conf. Record of the Sixth ACM Symposium on Principles of Programming Languages, 1979, 121-134.

4. Jazayeri,M.: On attribute grammars and the semantic specification of programming languages. Report 1159, Jennings Computing Centre, Case Western Reserve University, Cleveland, Ohio, Oct. 1974.

5. Jazayeri,M.: Live variable analysis, attribute grammars, and program optimization. Manuscript, Dept. of Computer Science, Univ. of North Carolina, Chapel Hill, N.C., March 1975.

6. Jazayeri,M. and Pozefsky,D.: Algorithms for efficient evaluation of multi-pass attribute grammars without a parse tree. Report TR 77-001, Dept. of Computer Science, Univ. of North Carolina, Chapel Hill, N.C., Feb. 1977 (revised May 1979).

7. Jazayeri,M. and Walter,K.G.: Alternating semantic evaluator. Proc. of the ACM Annual Conference, Oct. 1975, 230-234.

8. Kennedy,K. and Warren,S.K.: Automatic generation of efficient evaluators for attribute grammars. Conf. Record of the Third ACM Symposium on Principles of Programming Languages, 1976, 32-49.

9. Knuth,D.E.: Semantics of context-free languages. Mathematical Systems Theory 2,2 (1968), 127-145. Correction in Mathematical Systems Theory 5,1 (1971), 95-96.

10. Maier,D.: The complexity of some problems on subsequences and supersequences. Journal of the ACM 25,2 (April 1978), 322-336.

11. Pozefsky,D.: Building efficient pass-oriented attribute evaluators. Report TR 79-006, Dept. of Computer Science, Univ. of North Carolina, Chapel Hill, N.C., 1979.

12. Pozefsky,D. and Jazayeri,M.: A family of pass-oriented attribute grammar evaluators. Proc. of the ACM Annual Conference, Dec. 1978, 261-270.

13. Räihä,K.-J.: On attribute grammars and their use in a compiler writing system. Report A-1977-4, Dept. of Computer Science, Univ. of Helsinki, Helsinki, Aug. 1977.

14. Räihä,K.-J.: Experiences with the compiler writing system HLP. Proc. of the Aarhus Workshop on Semantics-Directed Compiler Generation, Springer-Verlag, Berlin - Heidelberg - New York, 1980.

15. Räihä,K.-J., Saarinen,M., Soisalon-Soininen,E. and Tienari,M.: The compiler writing system HLP (Helsinki Language Processor). Report A-1978-2, Dept. of Computer Science, Univ. of Helsinki, Helsinki, March 1978.

16. Räihä,K.-J. and Ukkonen,E.: The shortest common supersequence problem over binary alphabet is NP-complete. Report C-1979-95, Dept. of Computer Science, Univ. of Helsinki, Helsinki, Sept. 1979.

17. Räihä,K.-J. and Ukkonen,E.: Minimizing the number of evaluation passes for attribute grammars. Report C-1979-121, Dept. of Computer Science, Univ. of Helsinki, Helsinki, Nov. 1979.

OPTIMAL UNBOUNDED SEARCH STRATEGIES

J.C. RAOULT, J. VUILLEMIN
Laboratoire de Recherche en Informatique
Université de Paris-Sud
Bât. 490 - 91405 ORSAY - France

Abstract: *We present here strategies for searching the (unique) zero of a real function, or its n-th derivative; we assume no a priori bound on the value x of this zero. The proposed strategy performs* $\log_r y + \log\log_r y + \ldots + 1 + \log_r^* y$ *evaluations of f to determine* $x = \varepsilon y$ *with error less than* ε *(here r depends only on n). An argument of slowly converning integrals shows that these strategies are essentially optimal.*

I. INTRODUCTION

Searching an ordered table of *bounded* size N can be done in $\lceil \log_2(N+1) \rceil$ probes, and this is optimal (see Knuth vol 3 [75]).

In this paper, we consider the problem of optimally searching *unbounded* ordered tables. An equivalent problem is that of finding the zero of a monotone real function $f : \mathbb{R} \to \mathbb{R}$, with $f(0).f(\infty) < 0$, using the minimal number of function evaluations; the zero of f is found to within ε once we can exhibit u and v such that $|u-v| \leq \varepsilon$ and $f(u).f(v) < 0$. Such a general problem can be met in many different settings:

- how should one search a (large but finite) ordered table when the cost measure is the item's distance from the origin (rather than the table size)?
- how can the integers be encoded with zeros and ones? More precisely, what is the shortest prefix code for $\mathbb{N}$?
- what is the most economical way of encoding blanks in data transmissions?
- how should we design circuitry to find the position of the leftmost one in a binary register?

All these questions are equivalent and have been addressed by Bentley-Yao [76], Elias [75], Even-Rodeh [78], etc... . The question even arises in Kolmogorov [68] randomness (see Martin-Löf [71] and Katseff [78]).

Generalizations of binary search have been proposed. Kiefer [53], Karp and Miranker [72] show the optimality of Fibonacci search for finding the maximum of a unimodular function. The general problem of finding the zero of the n-th derivative of a real function is solved by Hyafil [77] for n=2; n=4 and n odd. Applications to asynchronous parallel searching are shown by Kung [76] and Linn [73].

In this paper, we show that all known optimal bounded search techniques can be extended to the unbounded case. We also argue about the optimality of the proposed unbounded strategies. If we restrict ourselves to considering strategies which are "regular" enough, then our L^*E^* algorithm (similar to that of Even-Rodeh [78], Bentley-Yao [76] and Elias [75]) is optimal in a rather strong sense. Implications regarding short prefix codes for $\mathbb{N}$ are discussed. Section 3 generalizes the preceding results to n-ary search. In particular, we show an optimal unbounded strategy for finding the maximum of a unimodular function.

II. UNBOUNDED BINARY SEARCH

A way to formulate the problem, independantly of particular applications, is to consider the following two persons game : player A makes up a number, *any positive real number* a; player B must find a number b such that $|b-a| \leq \varepsilon$, by asking question of the form :"is number a strictly less than x ?". Player A gives yes/no answers, and the problem is to determine B's best strategy.

Definition 1: An ε-strategy ($\varepsilon > 0$) over an interval $[p,q[$ with $1 \leq p < q \leq \infty$ is a complete binary search tree such that

- each node of the tree is associated with an interval $[u,v[$ with $p \leq u < v \leq q$.
- the interval associated with the root is $[p,q[$.
- each internal node I is labelled by a real number q_I such that $u < q_I < v$, where $[u,v[$ is the associated interval; the intervals associated with the left and right sons of I are respectively $[u,q_I[$ and $[q_I,v[$.
- at external nodes, the measure of the associated interval is at most ε: $v-u \leq \varepsilon$.

The interval associated with each node is an interval of uncertainty in which the searched number is located. The label q_I of node I corresponds to the question: "is $x < q_I$". The *yes* answer reduces the interval of uncertainty down to $[u,q_I[$, associated with the left son, and similarly for the *no* answer. If $q=\infty$, we say that the strategy is *unbounded*. By an obvious translation, any unbounded strategy can be mapped into a strategy over $[1,\infty[$.

Definition 2 :The *cost* of an ε-strategy S is a mapping $c_S : [p,q[\to \mathbb{N}^+$ defined by $c_S(x)=d$ where d is the depth of the external node associated with an interval $[u,v[$ containing x : $p \leq u \leq x < v \leq q$.

2.1 Description of four particular strategies

Any ε-strategy can be transformed into a 1-strategy, merely called *strategy* by replacing $[u,v[$ and q by $[u/\varepsilon, v/\varepsilon[$ and q/ε throughout.

Definition 3 :An *integer strategy* is a strategy over $[p,q[$ with $p \in \mathbb{N}$, $q \in \mathbb{N} + \{\infty\}$, where all labels are integers.

*) Added in proof: Knuth [79] has obtained (independantly) most of the results in section II.

Extend this definition by saying that an ε-*strategy is integer* if the associated 1-strategy is integer. A redundant notation would represent internal nodes by

$$\text{(}[u,q,v[\text{)}$$

where $[u,v[$ is the associated interval , q the label, and external nodes by

$$\boxed{[u,v[}\ .$$

To simplify notations in the four strategies over $[1,\infty[$ described in this section,we represent internal nodes by their labels only, since this is sufficient to reconstruct such strategies.

Using this convention, the naïve *sequential search* SS is defined by SS (1) where :

$$SS(n) = (n+1) \searrow SS(n+1) \quad \text{(see figure 1 at the end).}$$

The cost c_{SS} of the sequential search is $c_{SS}(x) = \lfloor x \rfloor$.
More interesting is the *exponential-logarithmic* strategy EL(1) where

$$EL(n) = \quad (2n) \text{ with children } BS(n,n) \quad EL(2n)\ .$$

There, $BS(a,\ell)$ is the traditional (bounded) *binary search* :

$$BS(a,\ell) = \text{if } \ell > 1 \textit{ then } (a+\ell/2) \text{ with children } BS(a,\ell/2) \quad BS(a+\ell/2,\ell/2).$$

The cost of strategy EL is given by $c_{EL}(x) = 2\lfloor \log_2 x \rfloor + 1$.

In order to describe our next strategy, we introduce the following iterations of the exponential and logarithmic functions:

$$(1) \begin{cases} \exp_b(0,x) = x; \\ \exp_b(k+1,x) = \exp_b(k,b^x) = b^{\exp_b(k,x)}, \ k \in \mathbb{N}. \end{cases}$$

$$(2) \begin{cases} \log_b(0,x) = x; \\ \log_b(k+1,x) = \log_b(k,\log_b x) = \log_b \log_b(k,x), \quad k \in \mathbb{N}. \end{cases}$$

We also let $\log_b^* x$ denote (for $b > e^{1/e}$, otherwise see section 3.1) the unique integer satisfying the following equivalent conditions :

1) $\exp_b(\log_b^* x, 0) \le x < \exp_b(\log_b^* x, 1)$,

2) $0 \le \log_b(\log_b^* x, x) < 1$,

3) $\log_b^* x = \inf\{i \ ; \ \log_b(i,x) < 1\}$.

With these notations, we define the *exp*-log* strategy by* $E^*L^*(1)$ where

$$E^*L^*(n) = \quad \left(2^n\right)$$

$$B^*S(\log_2^* n, 0, 1) \qquad E^*L^*(2^n).$$

Here $B^*S(k,a,\ell)$ is a k-th order generalization of binary search defined by

$$B^*S(k,a,\ell) = \textit{if } \ell > 1 \quad \textit{then} \quad \left(\exp_2(k, a+\tfrac{\ell}{2})\right)$$

$$B^*S(k,a,\tfrac{\ell}{2}) \qquad B^*S(k,a+\tfrac{\ell}{2},\tfrac{\ell}{2})$$

$$\textit{else if } k > 0 \textit{ then } B^*S(k-1, 2^a, 2^{a+\ell}-2^a) .$$

The cost of the E^*L^* strategy is given by

$$c_{E^*L^*}(x) = \sum_{1 \le k \le \log^* x} \lfloor \log_2(k,x) \rfloor + \log_2^* x = \sigma\log_2^* x + \log^* x$$

with

$$\sigma\log_2 x = \lfloor \log_2 x \rfloor + \lfloor \log_2 \log_2 x \rfloor + \dots + \underbrace{\lfloor \log_2 \dots \log_2 x \rfloor}_{\log_2^* x \text{ times}} .$$

The last strategy considered here is defined as $E^*L(1)$ where

$$E^*L(n) = \quad \left(2^n\right) \qquad ;$$

$$BS(n, 2^n - n) \qquad E^*L(2^n)$$

here $BS(a,\ell)$ is the ordinary binary search used in the EL strategy.

The cost of the E^*L strategy can be expressed, for $x \ge 4$ by

$$c_{E^*L}(x) = \log_2^* x + \exp_2(\log_2^* x, 0) .$$

This is indeed a monotone step function, but note that the steps are huge: if θ satisfies $0 < \theta < 1$, then for $x = \exp_2(k,1) - \theta$ we have $c_{E^*L}(x) = \lfloor \log_2 x \rfloor + \log_2^* x$ while for $x = \exp_2(k,1) + \theta$, we have $c_{E^*L}(x) = x + \log_2^* x - 1$. Although E^*L looks like a fairly reasonable strategy, its cost has a rather erratic behaviour as a function of x, oscillating between $\log_2 x + \log_2^* x$ and $x + \log_2^* x - 1$.

2.2 Optimality considerations for unbounded binary search:

The natural question to be asked at this point is: can another strategy do significantly better than those of section 2.1?

Of course, $C_{SS} \gg C_{EL} \gg C_{E^*L^*}$ where $f \gg g$ means $g = o(f)$, so that E^*L^* is the best candidate so far (section 2.3 shows further improvements on E^*L^*). But comparison between E^*L^* and E^*L is more difficult : each strategy can be arbitrarily better than the other one for infinitely many integers. In the following section, we show that this is more or less the general situation to be expected.

2.2.1 Slow and fast strategies

An obvious way to make quantitative comparison between strategies hopeless, is to "tune" a strategy to a given subset of $\mathbb{N}$. For instance the strategy beginning with the two questions : "is $x < 733$? Is $x < 732$? " certainly is optimal when $x = 732$. To avoid such anomalies, we restrict ourselves to *only consider monotone strategies* S, *for which* $x \leq y$ *implies* $c_S(x) \leq c_S(y)$, and we get on immediate reward.

Proposition 1 : For any monotone ε-strategy S over $[0,q[$ we have $c_S(x) > \log_2(x/\varepsilon)$ where $0 < \varepsilon < x < q \leq \infty$.

Proof : The numbers x, $x-\varepsilon$, $x-2\varepsilon, \ldots, x-\lfloor x/\varepsilon \rfloor \varepsilon$ all belong to distinct external nodes of S; one of them must therefore be at depth greater that $\lceil \log_2(\lfloor x/\varepsilon \rfloor) \rceil$ and the result follows by nonotonicity. ■

This bound is the best possible for uniform bounded search. In the four unbounded strategies described in section 2.1, we see that some trade-off is taking place : in a first stage, one tries to obtain a bound on the answer; the seconde stage is a search in a bounded interval. If we go too fast in the first stage, the bound is loose and the second stage becomes costly; if we go too slow, the time spent in obtaining the bound becomes the dominant factor. To formalise this idea, we introduce the following definition.

Definition 4 : The *edge* of an unbounded strategy S is the increasing infinite sequence $A(1)$, $A(2)$, ... labelling the nodes of S associated with infinite intervals.

The only infinite path in an unbounded strategy is the edge. For example $A_{SS}(i) = i+1$, $A_{EL}(i) = 2^i$ and $A_{E^*L}(i) = A_{E^*L^*}(i) = \exp_2(i,1)$. Define also the (integer) reciprocal $a(x)$ of $A(i)$ by

$$i = a(x) \Leftrightarrow A(i) \leq x < A(i+1).$$

Then the intuitive trade-off between the bounding step and the bounded search can be quantified.

Proposition 2 : For any (monotone) strategy $c(x) \geq a(x/2) + \log_2(x/2)$.

Proof : Let $2A(i) \leq x < 2A(i+1)$. The path going down from the root of the tree to the leaf containing x has at least i nodes on the edge, leading to node $A(i)$. In the right subtree of node $A(i)$, there are at least $\lfloor x-A(i) \rfloor$ external nodes at the left of x, so that the path from $A(i)$ to x has length at least $\log_2(x-A(i))$:

$$c(x) \geq i + \log_2(a-A(i)) \geq a(x/2) + \log_2(x/2). \ ■$$

Corollary : If $A(i) \ll 2^i$, then there exists x_0 such that $c(x) > 2\log_2 x$ for all $x > x_0$ (hence $c(x) \geq c_{EL}(x)$).

<u>Proof</u> : $A(i) << 2^i$ means that $A(i) = f(i)2^i$ with $\lim_{i\to\infty} f(i) = 0$. Taking logarithms:

$\log_2 A(i) = \log_2 f(i) + i$. Hence, for $A(i-1) \le x < A(i)$:

$$\log_2 x + \log_2 1/f(i) < a(x) + 1.$$

Since $\lim f(i) = 0$, there exists x_0 such that $f(i) < 1/8$ for all $x > x_0$. Rewriting the above formula for $x/2$ yields

$$a(x/2) > (\log_2(x/2) + 2.$$

Replacing in proposition 2 gives the result. ■

This result allows us to discard *slow* strategies for which $A(i) << 2^i$ and to only consider *fast* strategies for which $A(i) >> 2^i$.

2.2.2 <u>Weak optimality of all fast strategies</u>

The cost $c_S(x)$ of any ε-strategy can be decomposed as the sum of the cost $i = a_S(x) + 1$ of finding an upper bound to x along the edge of S, defined by $A_S(i-1) \le x < A_S(i)$, and of the cost $b_S(x)$ of finding x in the bounded interval $[A_S(i-1), A_S(i)[$. For arbitrary S, we write $c_S = b_S + a_S + 1$. For fast strategies, b_S is the main contribution to the cost since

$$\lim_{x\to\infty} (\log_2 x - a(x)) = \infty \text{ and } \lim_{x\to\infty} (b_S - \log_2 x) = \infty.$$

<u>Definition 5</u> : An ε-strategy is *reasonable* if the interval $[u,v[$ associated with any extremal node has length $v-u \ge \varepsilon/2$.

In other words, reasonable strategies do not make silly cuts. In particular, integer strategies are reasonable.

<u>Proposition 3</u> : Let S be an ε-strategy over $[p,q[$, $0 \le p < q \le \infty$ of cost $c_S = b_S + a_S + 1$.

Then (1) $\int_p^q 2^{-c_S(x)}\, dx \le \varepsilon$;

(2) if S is reasonable, then $\int_p^q 2^{-c_S(x)}\, dx \ge \varepsilon/2$;

(3) if S is integer, then $\int_p^q 2^{-c_S(x)}\, dx = \varepsilon$;

(4) if S is reasonable and unbounded ($q=\infty$), then $\int_p^\infty 2^{-b_S(x)}\, dx = \infty$.

<u>Proof</u> : If S is the degenerate strategy consisting only of an external node $[p,q[$, assertions 1, 2 and 3 hold. If they hold of strategies S_1 and S_2 and if

S = 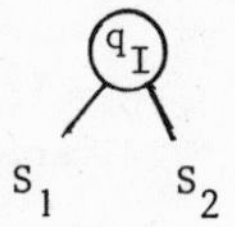

then $c_S(x) = \textit{if } x < q_I \textit{ then } 1 + c_{S_1}(x) \textit{ else } 1 + c_{S_2}(x)$.

Therefore

$$\int_p^q 2^{-c_S(x)}\,dx = \frac{1}{2}\int_p^{q_I} 2^{-c_{S_1}(x)}\,dx + \frac{1}{2}\int_{q_I}^{q} 2^{-c_{S_2}(x)}\,dx\ ,$$

so that 1, 2 and 3 also hold of S. By induction, they hold of any finite strategy, and letting q tend to infinity shows that they remain true of unbounded strategies.

Assertion 4 is perphaps less expected : consider the edge A(1), ..., A(i),... of S and let S_i be the substrategy induced by S over [A(i), A(i+1)[. Definition $c_{S_i}(x) = b_S(x)$. Assertion 2 shows that

$$\int_{A(i)}^{A(i+1)} 2^{-c_{S_i}(x)}\,dx \geq \frac{\varepsilon}{2}\ ,\ \text{which yields}$$

$$\int_p^{A(i)} 2^{-b_S(x)}\,dx \geq i\,\frac{\varepsilon}{2}\ ,\ \text{hence assertion 4.}\ \blacksquare$$

Combined with the analysis of section 1, this result provides unexpected ways of computing some integrals :

$$\text{for SS :}\quad \int_1^\infty \frac{dx}{2^{\lfloor x\rfloor}} = 1 \quad\text{and}\quad \int_p^{p+1} dx = 1\ ;$$

$$\text{for EL :}\quad \int_1^\infty \frac{dx}{4^{\lfloor \log_2 x\rfloor}} = 2 \quad\text{and}\quad \int_{2^p}^{2^{p+1}} \frac{dx}{2^{\lfloor \log_2 x\rfloor}} = 1\ ;$$

$$\text{for } E^*L^*\text{:}\quad \int_1^\infty \frac{dx}{2^{\sigma\log_2 x+\log_2^* x}} = 1 \ \text{and}\ \int_{\exp_2(p,0)}^{\exp_2(p,1)} \frac{dx}{2^{\sigma\log_2 x}} = 1\ ;$$

$$\text{for } E^*L\ :\ \frac{1}{2} < \int_1^\infty \frac{dx}{2^{\exp_2(\log_2^* x,0)+\log^* x}} \leq 1 \ \text{and}\ \frac{1}{2} < \int_{\exp_2(p,0)}^{\exp_2(p,1)} \frac{dx}{2^{\exp_2(\log^* x,0)}} \leq 1.$$

Of course, the integrands being step functions, these integrals are in fact discrete series.

Interesting consequences regarding optimal strategies can be drawn from proposition 4. Before stating them, we introduce the notion of *density* of a subset of $\mathbb{R}$: let P be a measurable subset of [0,∞[and $\mathbb{1}_P$ the characteristic function of P. We define :

$$\textit{inf-density}\ (P) = \liminf_{x\to\infty} \frac{1}{x}\int_0^x \mathbb{1}_P(t)\,dt,\ \text{and}$$

$$\textit{sup-density}\ (P) = \limsup_{x\to\infty} \frac{1}{x}\int_0^x \mathbb{1}_P(t)\,dt.$$

Note that $0 \leq$ inf-density (P) $\leq$ sup-density (P) ≤ 1, and

inf-density (P) = 1 − sup-density ($\bar{P}$), where $\bar{P}$ = [0,∞[−P.

Subsets which are dense enough are sufficient to test convergence or divergence of integrals .

Lemma : Let $P \subseteq \mathbb{R}_+$ be a measurable subset satisfying inf-density $(P) > 0$, and $f : \mathbb{R}_+ \to \mathbb{R}_+$ a monotone function. Then

$$\int_{\mathbb{R}_+} f(x)dx = \infty \Leftrightarrow \int_P f(x)dx = \infty.$$

Proof : Since $\int_P f(x)dx \le \int_{\mathbb{R}_+} f(x)dx$, the $\Leftarrow$ implication is clear. Conversely, inf-density $(P) > 0$ implies that there exist $a > 0$ and $x_0 \ge 0$ such that $x \ge x_0$ implies $\int_0^x {}_P(t)\, dt \ge ax$, and since $\int_0^{x_0} f(x)dx$ is bounded anyway we may just as well assume that $x_0=0$. Now sum by parts $f(x)dx$ over $(0,y)$.

$$\int_0^y f(x)dx = [xf(x)]_0^y - \int_0^y xdf(x) = [xf(x)]_0^y + \int_0^y x|df(x)|$$

(here the remaining sum is a Riemann-Stieltjes integral).

$$\int_0^x f(x)dx \le [\frac{1}{a} \int_0^x 1\!\!1_P(t)dt\ f(x)]_0^y + \int_0^y \frac{1}{a} \int_0^x 1\!\!1_P(t)dt|df(x)|, \text{ or}$$

$$\int_0^y f(x)dx \le \frac{1}{a} \{[\int_0^x 1\!\!1_P(t)dt\ f(x)]_0^y - \int_0^y \int_0^x 1\!\!1_P(t)dt\ df(x)\}.$$

The right-hand side is a summation by parts, so that

$$\int_0^y f(x)dx \le \frac{1}{a} \int_0^y 1\!\!1_P(x)f(x)dx.$$

Letting y tend to the infinity yields the result ∎

Proposition 4 : Let T be any reasonable strategy with cost $c_T = a_T+b_T+1$, where b_T is an increasing function. Then for any strategy S

$$\sup \text{density } \{x;\ c_S(x) > b_T(x)\} = 1.$$

Proof : By proposition 3(1), $\int_0^\infty 2^{-c_S(x)}\, dx \le \varepsilon$ while (4) $\int_0^\infty 2^{-b_T(x)}\, dx = \infty$.

Let $P = \{x \ge 0\ ;\ c_S(x) \le b_T(x)\}$. Thus $x \in P$ iff $2^{-c_S(x)} \ge 2^{-b_T(x)}$, so that

$$\int_P 2^{-b_T(x)}\, dx \le \int_P 2^{-c_S(x)}\, dx \le \int_0^\infty 2^{-c_S(x)}\, dx \le \varepsilon.$$

Since b_T is increasing, then inf-density $(P) = 0$ by the preceding lemma, hence the result. ∎

As a corollary, the cost c_S of any ε-strategy satisfies

$$\text{sup-density } \{x\ ;\ c_S(x) > \sigma \log_2 x\} = 1\ ,$$

and consequently for all x there exists y such that $c_S(y) > \sigma \log_2 y$. This last result has been obtained by Bentley-Yao [76] using a similar diverging integral argument. It is not however a very good indication of the optimality of E^*L^* since it applies just as well to any other reasonable strategy, and to E^*L in particular. In fact, an *ad hoc* argument shows that E^*L^* and E^*L are incomparable in the strong sense :

$$\text{sup-density } \{x \; ; \; c_{E^*L^*}(x) < c_{E^*L}(x)\} = \text{sup-density}\{x; c_{E^*L}(x) < c_{E^*L}(x)\} = 1.$$

2.2.3 Optimality of E^*L^* among regular strategies

One reason to be dissatisfied with strategies like E^*L is that the cost $c_{E^*L}(x)$ varies between $O(x)$ and $O(\log x)$. It has no asymptotic expansion in terms of ordinary "regular" functions. In this paragraph, we consider the implications of assuming that $c_S(x)$ does have such an asymptotic expansion.

A precise setting for introducing asymptotic expansion is that of a *Hardy field* (cf. Bourbaki [76]). A *function*(H) is a function obtained from real constants and the identity function by a finite number of sums, products, quotients, logarithms and exponentiations. A classical result is the following.

Proposition 5 : Any two *functions*(H) are comparable when x tends to infinity : either $f \ll g$ or $g \ll f$ or $f \sim ag$ for a real constant a.

Proof : see Bourbaki [76] . ∎

Definition 6 : A function c is *k-regular* if it admits an asymptotic expansion of order k:

$$c = f_1 + f_2 + \dots + f_k + r_k$$

where $f_1 \gg f_2 \gg \dots f_k \gg r_k$ and f_i is a function(H) for $i=1,\dots,k$.

A strategy is k-regular when its cost is k-regular.

Among the strategies of section 2.1, SS, EL, E^*L^* are k-regular for all k, but E^*L is not even 1-regular. It is now possible to state a strong form of the optimality of E^*L^*.

Proposition 6 : For any integer k and k-regular strategy S

$$c_S(x) > \sum_{1\leq i<k} \log_2(i,x)$$

for x large enough.

Proof : Consider the case $k=1$: $c_S \sim f_1$ where f_1 is a function(H). In this case $c_S(x) < tf_1(x)$ for all $t > 1$ and all x large enough :

$$(\exists x_0)\; x > x_0 \Rightarrow 2^{-tf_1(x)} < 2^{-c_S(x)}.$$

In fact, we prove a slightly more general result, replacing 2 by a constant $r > 1$ (in view of section 3). So we suppose that

$$\int_p^\infty r^{-tf_1(x)} dx \leq \int_p^\infty r^{-c_S(x)} dx \leq I.$$

Now, f_1 being a function (H), it is ultimately decreasing, constant or increasing.

Convergence of the integral rules out the first two cases. Let m(x) be the maximum of f_1 over (p,x).

$$I \geq \int_p^\infty r^{-tf_1(x)}dx \geq \int_p^x r^{-tf_1(y)}dy \geq \int_p^x r^{-tm(x)}dy = (x-p)r^{-tm(x)}.$$

Since f_1 is increasing and tends to infinity, ultimately $m(x) = f_1(x)$ so that $(x-p)r^{-tf_1(x)} \leq I$. Taking logarithms:

$$(*) \quad tf_1(x) \geq \log_r(x-P)-\log_r I = \log_r x-\log_r I + \log(1 \tfrac{P}{x}).$$

Recall now proposition 5. It is impossible that $f(x)>>\log_r x$, so that either $f(x)>>\log_r x$, in which case proposition 6 is clearly true, or there exists a constant s such that

$$tf_1(x) \sim s\log_r x ,$$

$$t_1(x) \sim \tfrac{s}{t}\log_r x.$$

Since t is arbitrarily near to 1, the inequality (*) forbids $\frac{s}{t} < 1$; so that here again, either $f_1 \sim \lambda\log_r x$ with $\lambda > 1$, in which case proposition 6 holds, or $f_1(x) \sim \log_r x$, in which case we may just as well take $f_1(x)=\log_r x$, since f_1 is defined up to equivalence.

Write now $c_S(x) = \log_r x - \log_r I + c'_S(x)$ in which $c'_S(x)$ must be a (k-1)-regular function.

$$\int_p^\infty r^{-c_S(x)}dx = \int_p^\infty r^{-c'_S(x)} I \frac{dx}{x} \leq I, \text{ thus } \int_p^\infty r^{-c'_S(x)} \frac{dx}{x} \leq 1.$$

The change of variable $u = \log_r x$ $(du = \frac{dx}{x} \log_r e)$ leads to:

$$\int_{\log_r P}^\infty r^{-c'_S(r^u)} du \leq \log_r e , \text{ hence}$$

$$c'_S(x) > \log_r\log_r x - \log_r\log_r e + \log_r(1 - \frac{\log_r P}{x}) \text{ for x large enough.}$$

By induction, we thus show

$$c_S(x) > \sum_{1\leq i<k} \log_r(i,x) + \log_r(k,x) - \log_r I - (k-1) \log_r\log_r e.$$

The conclusion follows by choosing x large enough to ensure

$$\log_r(k,x) - \log_r I - (k-1)\log_r\log_r e > 0 . \blacksquare$$

2.3 Implications for prefix binary codes for the integers

With each integer strategy S, we can associate a *prefix code* $\mathcal{C}_S$ for the integers $\mathbb{N} = \{1,2,\ldots\}$: each $n \in \mathbb{N}$ belongs to exactly one external node of S and the code $\mathcal{C}_S(n) \in \{0,1\}^*$ represents the path from the root of S to n with the convention that 1 correspond to right sons and 0 to left sons.

Let $UNA(n) = 1^{n-1}0$ represent the unary code for n and BIN(n) the traditional binary representation of n except for its leading leftmost one which is omitted; thus UNA(2) = 10, BIN(2) = 0, UNA(5) = 11110 and BIN(5) = 01. In general, $|UNA(n)| = n$ and $|BIN(n)| = \lfloor \log_2 n \rfloor$. The codes corresponding to the strategies of section 2.1 are :

$$\mathcal{C}_{SS}(n) = UNA(n) ;$$

$$\mathcal{C}_{EL}(n) = UNA(\lfloor \log_2 n \rfloor + 1) \; . \; BIN(n) ;$$

$$\mathcal{C}_{E^*L^*}(n) = UNA(k) \; . \; B_k \; . \; B_{k-1} \; \ldots \; B_1$$

with $k = \log_2^* n$, $B_1 = BIN(n)$ and $B_i = BIN(|B_{i-1}|)$ for $k \geq i > 1$.

For example the code E^*L^* for 12 is | 1 1 0 | 1 | 1 0 0 | and the code for 23 is | 1 1 1 0 | 0 | 0 0 | 0 1 1 1 | .

It is clear that, in general, the length of the code $\mathcal{C}_S$ associated with S is equal to the cost c_S of strategy S : $|\mathcal{C}_S(n)| = c_S(n)$. It is *not true* that every code for $\mathbb{N}$ can be constructed as the code associated with an integer unbounded strategy. A prefix code which is not the image of a strategy is the following :

$$\mathcal{C}(2p) = 0\,\mathcal{C}_S(p) \text{ and } \mathcal{C}(2p-1) = 1\,\mathcal{C}_S(p) \text{ where } p \geq 1 \text{ and } \mathcal{C}_S \text{ is the}$$

code associated with an integer strategy. There is however a direct analog of Proposition 3, generally attributed to Kraft and Mc Millan (cf. for example Eilenberg [74]):

<u>Proposition 3bis</u> : For any k-regular prefix code for $\mathbb{N}$,

$$\sum_{n \geq 1} 2^{-|\mathcal{C}(n)|} \leq 1$$

If we call k-*regular*, a code whose length is a k-regular function, the argument of Proposition 6 carries over easily .

<u>Proposition 6bis</u> : for any k-regular prefix code $\mathcal{C}$ for $\mathbb{N}$,

$$|\mathcal{C}_S(n)| > \sum_{1 \leq i \leq k} \lfloor \log_2(i,n) \rfloor \text{ for all n large enough.}$$

To conclude this (long) section, let us construct strategies which are asymptotically better than E^*L^* : the code $\mathcal{C}_{E^*L^*}(n) = UNA(\log^* n).W(n)$ can be "improved" by replacing the unary code for $\log^* n$ by the most efficient code so far, namely, $\mathcal{C}_{E^*L^*}$; we have thus defined

$$\mathcal{C}_{(E^*L^*)^*}(n) = \mathcal{C}_{E^*L^*}(\log^* n). \; W(n) \; , \text{ a code whose length is}$$

$$\sigma \log_2 n + \sigma \log_2(\log^* n) + \log^*(\log^* n).$$

This will in fact shorten the code word length for $n \geq \exp_2(7,1)$, an <u>enormous</u> number.

This process can obviously be repeated as far as we please, yielding asymptotically better and better codes. We leave it as an exercise to construct the strategies associated with such codes.

Again, unexpected results about very slowly converging or diverging series can be obtained. For example ,

$$\sum_{n\geq 1} 2^{-\sigma\log_2 n - \sigma\log_2(\log^* n) - \log^*(\log^* n)} = 1$$

$$\sum_{n\geq 1} 2^{-\sigma\log_2(n) - \sigma\log_2(\log n)} = \infty$$

where $\log_2 n$ means in fact $\lfloor \log_2 n \rfloor$.

III. UNBOUNDED n-ARY SEARCH

In this section, we generalize the preceding results to n-ary searching. Binary strategies correspond to n=2. Bounded ternary strategies solve the problem of finding the maximum of a unimodular (increasing, then decreasing) function; the optimal strategy is the well-known Fibonaccian search (Kiefer [1953]). General n-ary strategies have applications to finding the zero, assumed to be unique, of the (n-2)nd derivative of a function (Hyafil [1977]), and to several zero finding problems on parallel machines (Kung [1976]).

Definition 7 : A n-ary strategy over a real interval $[p,q[$ with $p < q \leq \infty$ is a complete binary tree such that :

1) each node of the tree is labelled with n+1 real nombers $p \leq q_0 < q_1 < \ldots < q_n \leq q$;
2) if an internal node is labelled with $q_0 < \ldots < q_n$, then $q_0 < \ldots < q_{n-1}$ are among its left son's labels, and $q_1 < \ldots < q_n$ are among its right son's labels ;
3) at he root $q_0 = p$, $q_n = q$;
4) at an external node, the "interval of uncertainty" has length less than ε : $q_n - q_0 \leq \varepsilon$.

The intuitive idea is that the unkown x is, at the beginning, in the interval of uncertainty $[p,q[$, and at each step in the interval $[q_0,q_n[$. Compared with binary search where each node represents the unary test $t_x(q)$ = "is $x < q$?", n-ary search may be viewed as a tree of (n-1)-ary tests $t_x(q_1,\ldots,q_{n-1})$, upon the answer of which all real numbers less than q_1(or greater than q_{n-1}) are rejected.

Again, an unbounded strategy is one with $q = \infty$; a strategy is specified once we know the full labelling of its root, plus one label for each internal node, namely the label which does not belong to its father's list. Given any "starting point" s_1 , the function $y = (x-p+s_1)/\varepsilon$ maps any ε-strategy over $[p,\infty[$ into a 1-strategy (or simply strategy) over $[s_1,\infty[$.

The 3-ary analog of strategy E^*L^* is described in fig. 2.

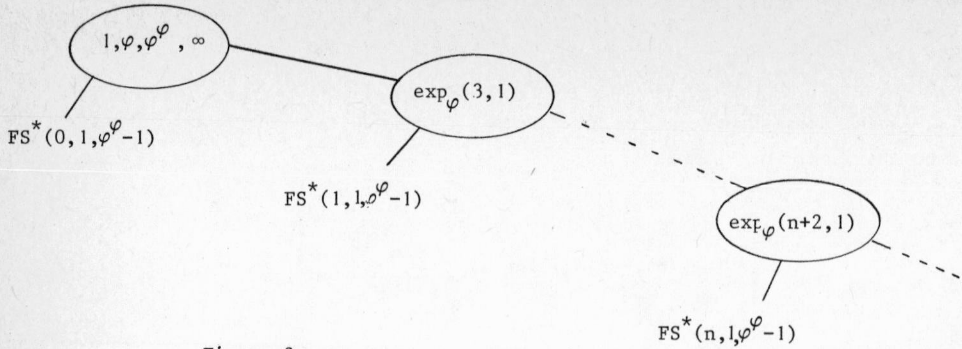

Figure 2.

Here $FS^*(k,a,\ell)$ is a k-th order generalization of Fibonaccian search defined by

$$FS^*(k,a,\ell) = \textit{if } \ell > \varepsilon \textit{ then } (\exp_{\varphi}(k,a),\ \exp_{\varphi}(k,a+\tfrac{\ell}{\varphi^2}),\ \exp_{\varphi}(k,a+\tfrac{\ell}{\varphi}),\ \exp_{\varphi}(k,a+\ell))$$

$$FS^*(k,a,\tfrac{\ell}{\varphi}) \qquad\qquad FS^*(k,a+\tfrac{\ell}{\varphi^2},\tfrac{\ell}{\varphi})$$

$$\textit{else if } k > 0 \textit{ then } FS^*(k-1,\varphi^{a},\varphi^{a}(\varphi^{\ell}-1)) .$$

Notice that the above tree is not, strictly speaking, an ε-strategy. Several nodes introduce two intermediate labels q_1 and q_2 instead of a single one : the first left son visited by the search, and each time the *else* clause is chosen in the definition of F^*S. Nevertheless we shall see that this is a minor extension of our definition, introducing a negligible amount of extra labels during one search.

For $n > 2$, there are in general many external nodes containing a given number x, and we introduce :

Definition 8 : The cost $c_S(x)$ of a n-ary strategy S at x is the length of the longest path from the root to an external node containing x in its labelling interval.

One may choose instead the number of labels encountered on this path. For an ε-strategy, this new cost is equal to the old one plus n+1, a constant independant of the unknown number x.

3.1 Description of some unbounded n-ary strategies

Optimal bounded strategies are known for n=3 (Kiefer [1953]), n=5 (Hyafil [1977]) and even n (Hyafil [1977] and Kung [1976]). We demonstrate here that all these strategies can be extended to unbounded intervals. In generalizing the strategies of section 2, one problem to be faced is that the sequence $x_0=1$, $x_{i+1}=r^{x_i}$

does not tend to infinity in all cases :

Proposition 7 : The sequence $x_{i+1}=r^{x_i}$ (with $1<r<e^{1/e}$ and e=2.718...) has a finite limit s_0 if $x_0<s_1$ and it tends to ∞ if $x_0>s_1$; the numbers s_0 and s_1 depend only on r .

Proof : By elementary calculus, one finds

$$1 < s_0 < e < s_1 < -2\log_e(\log_e(r)) / \log_e(r). \blacksquare$$

Conversely the sequence $y_{i+1} = \log_r y_i$ decreases until $y_i<0$ if $y_o<s_o$ and tends to s_1 if $y_0>s_0$.

Thus the starting point of our generalized strategies will be s_1 instead of 0 for iterating logarithms, when the basis r is less than $e^{1/e}$. Let us extend our definition of the $\log_r^*$ function.

Definition 9 : The integer function $\log_r^*$ for $1<r<e^{1/e}$ is defined by

$$\log_r^* x = \inf\{i \; ; \; \log_r(i,x) < s_1+1\}$$

Proposition 8 : Define $r>1$ by the condition : if n is even then $r=2^{2/n}$, else n=2p-1 and r is the unique solution of $r^p=r+1$. Then for n = 3,5 or $2m (m\in\mathbb{N}_+)$ there exists an unbounded search strategy S_n of cost

$$c_{S_n}(x) \le \sum_{1\le i\le \log_r^* x} \lfloor \log_r(i,x) \rfloor + \log_r^* x + d$$

where $d\le \exp(n-2,s_1+1)$ is a constant (dependant upon n).

Proof : **As** for dichotomy, the search divides in two steps; the first one finds a bound on x , and the second one searches x in a bounded interval. See a few values of r, s_1 and its upper bound $-2\log_e(\log_e(r))/\log_e(r)$ in fig. 3. Notice that $e^{1/e}=1,44...$, and therefore the above definition applies for $n\ge 4$; for n=3, one takes $s_1=0$, as in the binary case.

Step 1 : The sequence $\exp_r(i,s_1+1)$ tends to ∞ with i, and thus for some i , we have :

$$\exp_r(i,s_1+1) \le x < \exp_r(i+n-1,s_1+1) .$$

Indeed, the edge of the strategy is the following sequence of (n+1)-tuples :

$$(\exp_r(0,s_1+1), \ldots , \exp_r(n-1,s_1+1), \infty) ,$$

$$(\exp_r(1,s_1+1), \ldots , \exp_r(n,s_1+1), \infty) ,$$

....

$(\exp_r(i,s_1+1), \ldots , \exp_r(i+n-1,s_1+1), \infty)$, at which node the test says : turn left. According to the definition of a n-ary strategy, x satisfies the following inequalities :

$$\exp_r(i,s_1+1) \le x < \exp_r(i+n-1,s_1+1), \text{ or equivalently}$$

$$s_1+1 \le \log_r(i,x) < \exp_r(n-1,s_1+1) .$$

At this point, we known that $i < \log_r^* x \le i+n-1$.

Step 2 : Knowing that $a \le \log_r(i,x) < b$ with $b-a \le 1$, one can deduce that $a' \le \log_r(i-1,x) < b'$ where $b' - a' \le 1$ with at most $\lfloor \log_r(i,x) \rfloor$ (n-1)-ary tests, for all integer $i > 0$.

Indeed, $a \le \log_r(i,x) < b$ is equivalent to

$$r^a \le \log_r(i-1,x) < r^b .$$

The usual algorithm for the bounded case determines a' and b' with at most $\log_r(r^b - r^a)$ tests, or

$$\lceil \log_r r^a + \log(r^{b-a}-1) \rceil .$$

Now $b-a \le 1 \Rightarrow r^{b-a} \le r \Rightarrow r^{b-a}-1 \le r-1 \le 1/r$ (for $r \le \varphi$, that is $n \ge 3$) $\Rightarrow \log(r^{b-a}) \le -1$, so that the number of tests is bounded by $\lfloor a \rfloor \le \lfloor \log_r(i,x) \rfloor$.

Summing up, i+1 tests are sufficient to bound x ; then $\lceil \log_r(\exp_r(n-1,s_1+1)-(s_1+1)) \rceil$ to localise log(i,x) within 1 ; then

$\lfloor \log_r(i,x) \rfloor + \ldots + \lfloor \log_r(1,x) \rfloor$ to localise x within one.

That is :

$$c(x) \le i+1 + \lceil \log_r(\exp_r(n-1,s_1+1)-(s_1+1)) \rceil + \sum_{1 \le i \le k} \lfloor \log_r(i,x) \rfloor ,$$

$$c(x) \le \sum_{1 \le i \le \log^* x} \lfloor \log_r(i,x) \rfloor + \log_r^* x + d$$

with $d = i+1 + \lceil \log_r(\exp(n-1,s_1+1)-(s_1+1)) \rceil - \sum_{i \le k \le \log^* x} \lfloor \log_r(k,x) \rfloor - \log_r^* x$,

$d \le \exp(n-2,s_1+1)$, which is a constant, independant of x ∎

Remark : This is not exactly a n-ary strategy : whole sets of n-1 new labels are introduced at the beginning of every bounded search, instead of just one. Adding up the overall number of labels used during the search, one finds that the (new) cost is increased by $(n-2)(k+1) \le (n-2)\log^* x$, which is indeed negligible.

n	r	s_1	$-2l l_n(r)/l_n(r)$
2	2	-	- 1.0575
3	1.618033988	-	- 0.1712
4	1.414213562	4	6.115
5	1.324717957	6.835425356	9.023
6	1.259921050	9.93953514	12.682
7	1.220744085	12.76989337	16.165
8	1.189207115	16	20.230
9	1.167303978	19.05091099	24.128
10	1.148698355	22.44000568	28.507

Figure 3.

3.2 Optimality of such strategies

The key point in proving the optimality of the strategies described in the preceding section is the following.

Proposition 9 : For any n-ary ε-strategy S over $\lceil p,q\lceil$, $0 \le p < q < \infty$ of cost c_S, we have

$$I = \int_p^q r^{-c_S(x)} dx \le 2\varepsilon/r$$

where $1 < r \le 2$ satisfies : if n is even then $r^{n/2} = 2$ else $r^{(n+1)/2} = r+1$

Proof : We first prove the inequality for finite strategies by induction on the number of nodes in S. Let

$$p < q_1 < \dots < q_{n-1} < q$$

be the labels of the root of S, and $h = \lceil n/2 \rceil$. We argue by cases :

Case 1 : $q-p \le \varepsilon$. In that case, $I \le \varepsilon \le 2\varepsilon/r$.

Case 2 : $q-p > \varepsilon$, $q_h-p \le \varepsilon$, $q-q_h \le \varepsilon$. Since $q-p > \varepsilon$, we have $c_S(x) \ge 1$ for $p \le x < q$. Then

$$I \le \int_p^{q_h} r^{-1} dx + \int_{q_h}^q r^{-1} dx \le 2\varepsilon/r.$$

Case 3 : $q_h-p \le \varepsilon$, $q-q_h > \varepsilon$. Let R be the node of S obtained by starting at the root and taking h times the right son. The interval associated with R is necessarily of the form $\lceil u,q\lceil$ with $u \le q_h$. If c_R is the cost of the substrategy having root R, we have

$$c_S(x) \ge 1 \text{ for } p \le x < u \text{ , and}$$

$$c_S(x) \ge h + c_R(x) \text{ for } u \le x < q.$$

It follows that

$$I \le \int_p^u r^{-1} dx + r^{-h} \int_u^q r^{-c_R(x)} dx \le \frac{\varepsilon}{r} + \frac{2\varepsilon}{r^{h+1}} \le \frac{2\varepsilon}{r} \text{ .}$$

The last inequality holds since $r^h \ge 2$.

Case 4 : $q_h-p > \varepsilon$, $q-q_h \le \varepsilon$. This is symmetrical of case 3.

Case 5 : $q_h-p > \varepsilon$, $q-q_h > \varepsilon$. Let R (resp. L) be the nodes attained from the root by taking the right son (resp. left son) h times (resp. n-h times). The intervals associated with L and R are respectively of the form $[p,v[$ and $[u,q[$ with $u \le q_h \le v$. The costs c_S, c_L and c_R are related by

$$c_S(x) \ge n - h + c_L(x) \text{ for } p \le x < v \text{ , and}$$

$$c_S(x) \ge h + c_R(x) \text{ for } u \le x < q \text{ .}$$

It follows that

$$I = \int_p^q r^{-c_S(x)}\,dx \le \int_p^v r^{-c_S(x)}\,dx + \int_u^q r^{-c_S(x)}\,dx\ ,$$

$$I \le (r^{-n+h} + r^{-h})\,\frac{2\varepsilon}{r} = \frac{2\varepsilon}{r}\ .$$

This concludes the proof for bounded strategies. Letting q tend to infinity extends it to the unbounded case. The upper bound obtained for I is the best possible since one can construct strategies arbitrarily close to the bound. ■

Once convergence of $\int_1^\infty r^{-c_S(x)}\,dx$ is established, the argument of proposition 6 carries through without any modification and yields :

Proposition 10 : Let S be a n-ary unbounded strategy the cost c_S of which is a k-regular function. Then for all x large enough

$$c_S(x) > \sum_{1\le i<k} \log_r(i,x)$$

where $1 < r \le 2$ satisfies $r^{\lfloor n/2\rfloor} + r^{\lceil n/2\rceil} = r^n$.

IV. CONCLUSION

When optimal search strategies for bounded intervals are known, we have shown that it is possible to transform them into search strategies over unbounded intervals of the form $[p,+\infty[$.
Without *a priori* probability on the interval, there is no uniformly optimal strategy (see prop. 4). We introduce (cf. definition 7) a reasonable subclass of strategies, in which the cost is a "k-regular" function of the result.
A l.u.b. is given for all strategies in the class and optimal strategies are given, at least when the search is binary, ternary, 5-ary or 2m-ary. The existence of optimal n-ary strategies for odd n is an interesting open problem. Should strategies be discovered in this case over a bounded interval, and proved to be optimal (in the minimax sense), then the method given in this paper extends them into optimal unbounded strategies, optimal in the subclass of "regular" strategies.

On the other hand, a search strategy which has not been extended to the unbounded case is that of Rivest *et al.* [78] which copes with E errors, at most, during the search, and it would be interesting to also extend such strategies to the unbounded case.

REFERENCES

J.L. BENTLEY & A.C. YAO [76] : *An almost optimal algorithm for unbounded searching*, IPL, vol. 3, n° 3 (1976) pp. 82-87.

N. BOURBAKI [76] : *Théorie des fonctions de variables réelles*, ch. V, app. n° 8 (1976 3rd ed.), Hermann Paris.

S. EILENBERG [74] : *Automata, languages, and machines*, Vol. A, Academic Press (1974).

P. ELIAS [75] : *Universal codework sets and representation of the integers*, IEEE Trans. on Information theory, IT-21 (1975) pp. 194-203.

S. EVEN & M. RODEH [78] : *Economical encoding of commas between strings*, CACM, Vol. 21, n° 4 (1978) pp. 315-317.

L. HYAFIL [77] : *Optimal search for the zero of the $n^{\underline{th}}$ derivative*, IRIA/LABORIA, Rapport n° 247 (1977).

R.M. KARP & W.L. MIRANKER [72] : *Parallel minimax search for a maximum*, J. of Comb. Theory 4 (1972) pp. 19-35.

H.P. KATSEFF [78] : *Complexity dip in random infinite binary sequences*, SIGACT Newsletters (Winter 1978) pp. 22-23.

J. KIEFER [53] : *Sequential minimax search for a maximum*, Proc. Ameri. Soc. 4 (1953) pp. 502-506.

D.E. KNUTH [75] : *The art of computer programming*, Vol. 3, Sorting and searching, Addison-Wesley (1975).

D.E. KNUTH [79] : *Supernatural numbers*. (Dedicated to Martin Gardner).

A. KOLMOGOROV [68] : *Three approaches for defining the concept of information quantity*, Selected Translations in Math. Stat. and Prob., AMS Publication (1968).

H.T. KUNG [76] : *Synchronized and asynchronous parallel algorithms for multi-processors*, in Proc. of a Symp. on Algorithms and Complexity (1976). Edited by J.F. Traub, Academic Press, 1976, pp. 153-200.

J. LINN [73] : *General methods for parallel searching*, Tech. Rep. n° 61, Digital Systems Lab., Stanford University (1973).

P. MARTIN-LÖF [71] : *Complexity oscillations in infinite binary sequences*, Z. Wahrsheinlichkeitstheorie Verw. Geb. 19 (1971) pp. 225-230.

J.C. RAOULT, J. VUILLEMIN [79] : *Optimal unbounded search strategies*, Rapport LRI, n° 33 (1979).

R.L. RIVEST, A.R. MEYER, D.J. KLEITMAN, J. SPENCER, K. WINKLMAN [78] : *Coping with errors in binary search procedures*, Proc. of the $10^{\underline{th}}$ annual ACM Symposium on Theory of Computing, San Diego (1978) pp. 227-232.

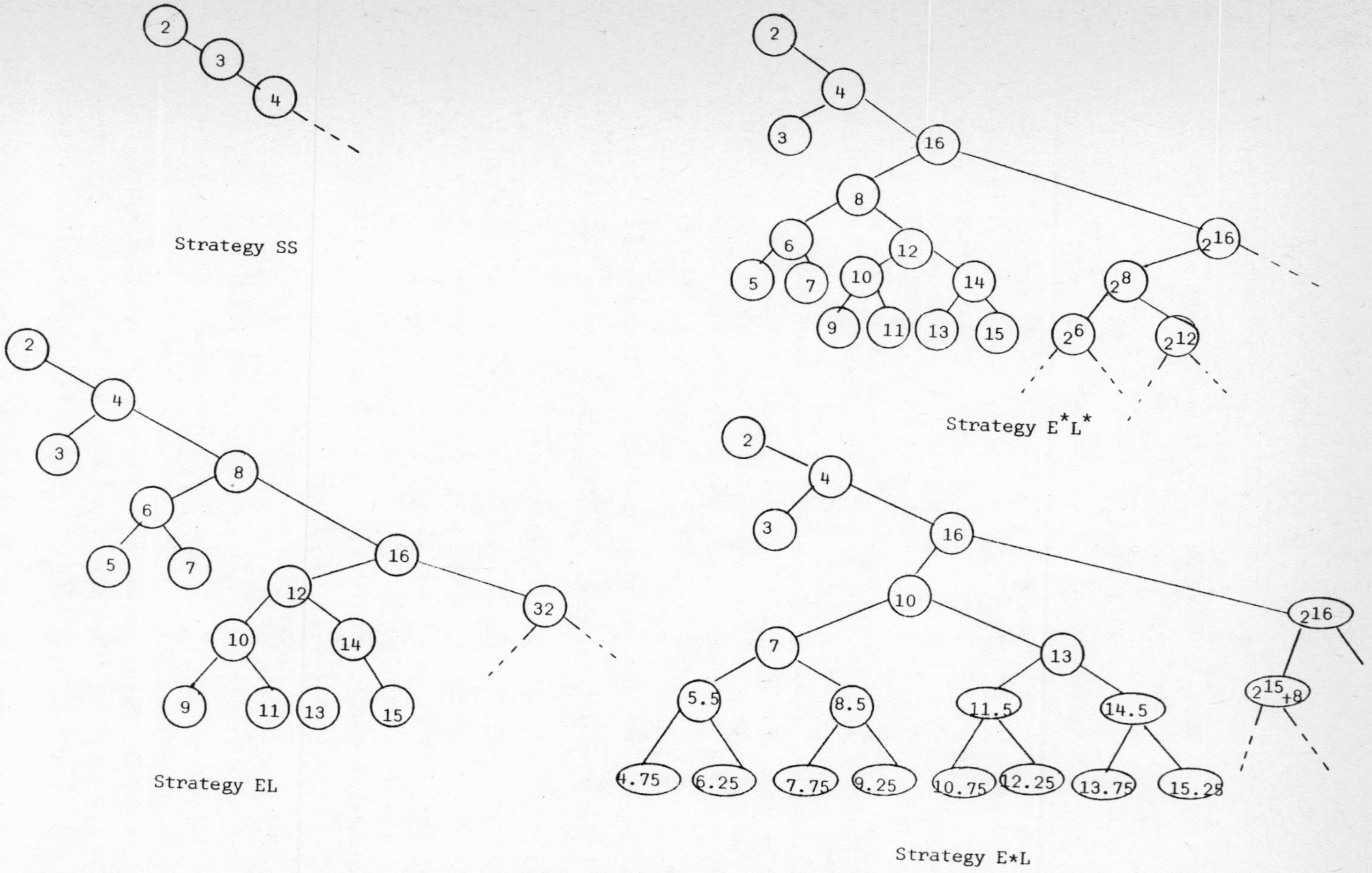

Figure 1

A "FAST IMPLEMENTATION" OF A MULTIDIMENSIONAL STORAGE INTO A TREE STORAGE

Rüdiger Reischuk
Fakultät für Mathematik
Universität Bielefeld
4800 Bielefeld 1
Germany

Abstract: Every multidimensional Turing-machine can be simulated on-line by a tree-tape Turing-machine in nearly the same amount of time.

1. Introduction

Many authors have extended Turing's original machine model [13] by considering possibly more powerful storage structures. For example instead of one-dimensional tapes multidimensional or tree tapes have been used to allow non-sequential access to the storage cells [5,10,12]. It is known that for space-bounded computations these storage structures make no difference whereas for time bounded computations one may have the feeling that the number of computation steps depends heavily on the storage structure. That this is indeed the case has been proved only under the strong restriction of on-line computations [5,10]. These papers compare d-dimensional and tree-tapes with one-dimensional tapes and yield exact upper and lower bounds for on-line simulation by machines with one-dimensional tapes: $\Theta(n^{2-1/d})$ for d-dimensional tapes and $\Theta(n^2/\log n)$ for tree-tapes.
In this paper we describe an on-line simulation of multidimensional machines by tree-tape machines.

The standard simulation techniques - using for each cell of a multidimensional tape one cell of a tree-tape - give an $O(t(n) \log t(n))$ - time bounded simulation of $t(n)$-time bounded multidimensional machines by tree-tape machines. This method doesn't seem to yield a better time bound because paths in a multidimensional tape may contain loops and therefore cells of the tree-tape corresponding to cells of the d-dimensional tape in a short distance may have a distance about $\log t(n)$.

That the above time bound is not optimal will be proved in the following by a "fast implementation" of a multidimensional tape into a tree-tape. This allows to simulate t steps of a machine with d-dimensional tapes in $O(t\cdot 5^{d\cdot \log^* t})$ steps by a tree-tape machine. Therefore multidimensional machines can be simulated by tree-tape machines spending only a very small amount of additional time.

In [9] space-efficient simulations of tree-tape and multidimensional Turing-machines are given. t steps of a tree-tape machine can be simulated in space $O(t/\log t)$ and t steps of a multidimensional machine in space $O(t \log\log t/\log t)$ by one-dimensional machines. Thus the above result also improves the space-bound for the simulation of multidimensional machines.

2. Definitions

The Turing-machines we consider consist of an one way read-only input tape, an one way write-only output tape and a storage. The storage has a finite number of work tapes with one head for each tape and each cell of a work tape can store one symbol of a finite alphabet. As usual such a machine has a finite number of states and a computation consists of a sequence of steps where in each step the state and the content of the visited tape cells may be changed and each head may move to an adjacent tape cell.

A work tape is called d-dimensional if there is a bijection between the set of tape cells and the vector-space $\mathbb{Z}^d$ such that two tape cells are adjacent iff their images differ in exactly one coordinate by one.

For a fixed bijection let us call the image of a cell its address.
We may assume that the address of the tape cell the head scans at the beginning of the computation is the zero vector.
In the following we consider work tapes as graphs - the nodes are the cells and edges connect adjacent nodes.

A tree-tape is a complete binary tree and the address of a node/tape cell is a word over $\{0,1\}$. The root is that cell where the head starts and gets the address Λ (the empty word). The two sons of a node with address x $(x \in \{0,1\}^*)$ have the addresses $x0$ and $x1$.
A storage is called d-dimensional (tree-tape storage) if all work tapes are d-dimensional (tree-tapes) and a Turing-machine is called a d-dimensional machine (tree-tape machine) if its storage is d-dimensional (tree-tape).

3. Theorem and idea of the proof

We'll prove the following

Theorem:

Every t(n)-time bounded d-dimensional Turing-machine can be simulated by an $O(t(n)\cdot 5^{d\cdot\log^* t(n)})$-time bounded tree-tape machine.

($\log^* t(n)$ is the smallest number k such that $2^{2^{\cdot^{\cdot^{2}}}}$ (k-times) is bigger or equal to t(n)).

Let M be a d-dimensional Turing machine $(d > 1)$ t(n)-time bounded and w be an input of M of length n . We may assume that $t = t(n)$ can be computed easily from w , otherwise try the simulation for $t = n, 2n, 4n, \dots$. We'll describe the behaviour of a tree-tape machine M' that simulates M step by step. Therefore it suffices to say how to simulate the read and write operations that are performed in one d-dimensional work-tape in a tree-tape. For this purpose we "embed" the part D of the d-dimensional tape that can be reached in t steps into a binary tree B , this means each cell of D is associated with some nodes of the tree. During the simulation these nodes/tape cells will be used to store the content of that cell/node and read and write operations in that cell will be simulated by executing the same operations in one of the associated nodes. In order to loose not too much time in the course of the simulation the following conditions must be satisfied:

1. For every pair of nodes of D in short distance there must be corresponding nodes in B such that their distance is also small.
2. If a write-operation in a cell of D has been simulated by the appropriate change of the content of one of its associated cells the content of the other associated cells have to be updated before they are used. This actualisation must not cost too much extra time.

The easiest sort of embedding is an injective mapping from the nodes of the lattice into those of the tree. But because a multidimensional lattice contains a lot of cycles whereas a tree none one runs into difficulties to fulfill the first condition. On the other hand the second condition is trivially satisfied. The embedding we choose associates to every node of D a lot of nodes of B (about $3^{\log^* t}$) and works recursively with the help of coverings by d-dimensional cubes.

4. Embedding of the d-dimensional lattice into a binary tree

In the following let u be an element of $\mathbb{Z}$ and $x = (x^1,\ldots,x^d)$, $y = (y^1,\ldots,y^d)$, $z = (z^1,\ldots,z^d)$ be vectors in $\mathbb{Z}^d$. $\underline{u}$ denotes the vector $(u,\ldots,u) \in Z^d$.

We write $x \leq y$ $(x < z)$ iff for all $1 \leq i \leq d$ holds: $x^i \leq y^i$ $(x^i < z^i)$.

Let W be a subset of Z^d. Then we define for $x \in Z^d$ $x + W := \{x + y \mid y \in W\}$.

W is called a <u>d-dimensional cube</u> with side-length u if $W = \{y \in Z^d \mid x \leq y < x + \underline{u}\}$ with $x \in Z^d$ and $u \in \mathbb{N}$.

First we recursively cover the lattice by overlapping d-dimensional cubes.

Assume t to be bigger than $2^{2^{2^2}}$ and define the following numbers:

$$a := \log^* t - 3,$$

$$u_o := 2^{\mu} \cdot 3 \cdot \underbrace{2^{2^{\cdot^{\cdot^{2}}}}}_{a+2\text{-times}},$$

where μ is the smallest natural number such that

$$6t \leq 2^{\mu} \cdot 3 \cdot \underbrace{2^{2^{\cdot^{\cdot^{2}}}}}_{a+2\text{-times}},$$

$$u_i := 3 \cdot \underbrace{2^{2^{\cdot^{\cdot^{2}}}}}_{a-(i-3)\text{-times}} \quad \text{for } 1 \leq i \leq a+1.$$

4.1 Remark

The u_i's satisfy the following inequalities:

1. $\log u_i = u_{i+1}/3 + \log 3$

   $< u_{i+1} - u_{i+2}$ for $1 \leq i < a$,

2. $\log u_o < \log 12t$

   $< \frac{u_1}{3} + \log 12$ as $u_1 \geq 3 \log t$

   $< u_1 - u_2$.

These numbers will be used as side-lengths of the d-dimensional cubes.

4.2 Definition

For $0 \le i \le a$ let us define

$$C_i := \{x \in Z^d / \underline{0} \le x < \underline{u_i}\}$$

$$C_i^* := \{x \in Z^d / \underline{u_{i+1}/3} \le x < \underline{u_i} - \underline{u_{i+1}/3}\}$$

$$C_i^{**} := \{x \in Z^d / \underline{u_i/3} \le x < \underline{2u_i/3}\}$$

$$C_i^! := \{x \in Z^d / \underline{0} < x < \underline{3u_{i-1}/u_i - 1}\} .$$

Now i-cubes are defined recursively in the following way:

Let $x_o := \underline{0}$ be the zero vector. There is one 0-cube $W(x_o)$ with side-length u_o and starting point $S(x_o) := \underline{-u_o/2}$. It is given by $W(x_o) := S(x_o) + C_o$. $W^*(x_o) := S(x_o) + C_o^*$ is called the interior of $W(x_o)$ and $W^{**}(x_o) := S(x_o) + C_o^{**}$ the center of $W(x_o)$.

For $0 \le i-1 \le a$ let the i-1-cube $W(x_o,\dots,x_{i-1})$ with starting point $S(x_o,\dots,x_{i-1})$ and side length u_{i-1} be defined by $W(x_o,\dots,x_{i-1}) = S(x_o,\dots,x_{i-1}) + C_{i-1}$.

Then for $x_i \in C_i^!$ we define the i-cube $W(x_o,\dots,x_{i-1},x_i)$ with the help of its starting point
$S(x_o,\dots,x_{i-1},x_i) := S(x_o,\dots,x_{i-1}) + u_i/3 \cdot (x_i - \underline{1})$ by
$W(x_o,\dots,x_{i-1},x_i) := S(x_o,\dots,x_{i-1},x_i) + C_i$ (see figure 1 and 2).

Its interior is $W^*(x_o,\dots,x_i) := S(x_o,\dots,x_i) + C_i^*$ and its center $W^{**}(x_o,\dots,x_i) := S(x_o,\dots,x_i) + C_i^{**}$.

$x_o,\dots,x_{i-1},x_i$ is called the address of $W(x_o,\dots,x_{i-1},x_i)$ and x_i the relative address (related to $W(x_o,\dots,x_{i-1})$).

For $0 \le j \le i \le a$ let $W_1 = W(x_o,\dots,x_j)$ and $W_2 = W(x_o,\dots,x_j,x_{j+1},\dots,x_i)$ be cubes. Then we say that W_2 is a subcube of W_1.

A cube $W_3 = W(x_o,\dots,x_{j-1},z_j) \neq W_1$ is a neighbourcube of W_1 if $W_1 \cap W_3 \neq \emptyset$ holds.

If $i > 0$ then for $x_i \in C_i^!$ let $\underline{b(x_i)}$ be an encoding of x_i of fixed length $O(\log u_{i-1})$ and $\overline{b(x_o,\dots,x_i)} := b(x_o)\, b(x_1) \dots b(x_i)$ an encoding of the address of $W(x_o,\dots,x_i)$ $(b(x_o) := \Lambda)$.

4.3 Remark

This covering has the following properties:

1. Every cube has at most 5^d-1 neighbourcubes.
2. Every node contained in an i-1-cube W is a member of at most 3^d i-subcubes of W.
3. $W^{**}(x_o)$, the center of $W(x_o)$, contains all nodes that can be reached in t steps starting at x_o.
4. For every i-1-cube $W(x_o,\ldots,x_{i-1})$ the set of centers of its i-subcubes is a disjoint decomposition of the interior of W, that is

$$W^*(x_o,\ldots,x_{i-1}) = \dot{\bigcup_{x_i \in C_i'}} W^{**}(x_o,\ldots,x_i) .$$

5. Starting at any node of the center of an i-cube W one stays in the interior of W for the next $(u_i-u_{i+1})/3$ steps.

Let $\tilde{B}$ be a complete binary tree. The nodes of $\tilde{B}$ are labelled by addresses as defined in paragraph 2. For $b \in \{0,1\}^*$ let T_b be the complete subtree of $\tilde{B}$ whose root has address b.

Then the d-dimensional lattice - exactly only the cube $W(x_o)$ - is embedded into $\tilde{B}$ in the following way:

A cube $W(x_o,\ldots,x_i)$ is embedded into $T_{b(x_o,\ldots,x_i)}$ by associating the nodes of an a-subcube $W(x_o,\ldots,x_i,x_{i+1},\ldots,x_a)$ to the node of $\tilde{B}$ with address $b(x_o,\ldots,x_a)$.

4.4 Remark

The embedding satisfies:

1. For any two neighbourcubes $W(x_o,\ldots,x_{i-1},x_i)$ and $W(x_o,\ldots,x_{i-1},y_i)$ the distance between their corresponding subtree - that is the distance between the roots of $T_{b(x_o,\ldots,x_{i-1},x_i)}$ and $T_{b(x_o,\ldots,x_{i-1},y_i)}$ - is proportional to their side-length u_i.
2. For every pair of nodes u,v of $W(x_o)$ with distance L from each other their exists a subcube $W(x_o,\ldots,x_i)$ containing these nodes such that the associated nodes in $T_{b(x_o,\ldots,x_i)}$ are

within a distance $O(L)$.

5. The simulation

The embedding of the d-dimensional lattice into a binary tree described above translates directly into an embedding of a d-dimensional tape D of M into a tree tape B of M'.

Over an appropriate alphabet A the inscription of the cells of an a-cube $W(x_o,...,x_a)$ of D can be encoded by one symbol because a-cubes consists of only $(3.2^{2^2})^d$ cells and this symbol is stored in the cell of B with address $b(x_o,...,x_a)$. The encoding can be chosen such that the blank symbol of A represents an inscription where all cells are empty.

5.1 Definition

If the p-th step of M started with input w is to be simulated by M' we say that an a-cube W is timely iff the content of the cell in B associated to W represents the actual inscription of W just before step p .
An i-cube W is timely iff all its a-subcubes are timely.

For $i < a$ the last condition is equivalent to: All its i+1-subcubes are timely.

By choice of the encoding all cubes are timely before simulation of the first step of M .

We now describe a recursive strategy $tsm[b(x_o,...,x_i),p]$ to simulate M , where $b(x_o,...,x_i)$ is the address of a cube $W(x_o,...,x_i)$ such that the head of M is in the center of $W(x_o,...,x_i)$ just before step p . To call $tsm[b(x_o,...,x_i),p]$ the following conditions must be satisfied:

5.2: $W(x_o,...,x_i)$ is timely and the head of the simulating machine M' scans the cell of B with address $b(x_o,...,x_i)$.

M' starts the simulation with $tsm[b(x_o),1]$.

<u>prodecure:</u> $tsm[b(x_o,\dots,x_i),p]$

```
if  i = a  then do
    simulate read and write operations of  M  in the cube
    W(x_o,...,x_a)  beginning with step  p  until the head tries to
    leave  W*(x_o,...,x_a) ; this is done by storing the actual inscrip-
    tion of the cells in  W(x_o,...,x_a)  in the cell of  B  with address
    b(x_o,...,x_a) .
    end
if  i < a  then do
    c ← p
α:  choose that  x_{i+1} ∈ C'_{i+1}  such that the head of  M  just before
    step  c  is in  W**(x_o,...,x_i,x_{i+1}) .
    go to that cell of  B  whose address is  b(x_o,...,x_i,x_{i+1}) .
    call  tsm[b(x_o,...,x_i,x_{i+1}),c] .
    let  q  be the last step simulated in this subprocedure.
    c ← q+1
    make  W(x_o,...,x_i)  timely.
    if  c ≤ t  and just before step  c  the head of  M  visits a cell
        in  W*(x_o,...,x_i)  then go back to  α .
    end.
end.
```

During the simulation M' must know in which cubes the head of M is. This can be computed quickly if the machine uses <u>relative addresses</u> of nodes. Let v be a cell of D with address $y \in Z^d$. Then the relative address of v with respect to a cube $W(x_o,\dots,x_i)$ is defined as

$$h(W(x_o,\dots,x_i),y) := y - S(x_o,\dots,x_i)$$

where $S(x_o,\dots,x_i)$ is the starting point of $W(x_o,\dots,x_i)$.

If v is in $W(x_o,\dots,x_i)$ $h(W(x_o,\dots,x_i),y)$ can be encoded by $O(\log u_i)$ bits. Because of the choice of the u_i's in $tsm[b(x_o,\dots,x_i),p]$ the head of M can be located with the help of relative addresses in $O(\log u_i)$ steps if we use an additional linear tape. We don't go into the technical details here.

For $i = a$ the tsm-strategy can simulate r steps of M in time $O(r)$.

In the other case let's suppose that in the subprocedures $tsm[b(x_o,\ldots,x_i,x_{i+1}^j),c^j]$ $(j = 1,\ldots,\ell)$ of $tsm[b(x_o,\ldots,x_i),p]$ r_j steps of M are simulated. By (4.3.5) we have

$$r_j \geq (u_{i+1}-u_{i+2})/3 \quad \text{and}$$

$$r = \Sigma r_j \geq (u_i-u_{i+1})/3 .$$

This implies

$$\ell \leq 3r/(u_{i+1}-u_{i+2}) .$$

If for a strategy $tsm[b(x_o,\ldots,x_i),p]$ $T(i,r)$ denotes the maximal time for simulation of r steps and $A(i+1,r_j)$ the maximal time for making an i-cube timely after having simulated r_j steps in one of its $i+1$-subcubes we get the following inequalities:

$$T(a,r) \leq O(r) \quad \text{and}$$

$$T(i,r) \leq \ell\cdot O(\log u_i) + \max_{\Sigma r_j = r} \Sigma\, T(i+1,r_j) + A(i+1,r_j)$$

for $i < a$.

6. Actualisation of cubes

It remains to say how to make the i-cube $W(x_o,\ldots,x_i)$ timely after simulation of r_j steps in $tsm[b(x_o,\ldots,x_i,x_{i+1}^j),c^j]$. As $W(x_o,\ldots,x_i)$ has been timely before it suffices to update the inscription of cells of B associated to those nodes of D which have been visited by M in the last r_j steps and belong to $W(x_o,\ldots,x_i)$. All these cells are elements of the at most 5^d-1 neighbourcubes of $W(x_o,\ldots,x_i,x_{i+1}^j)$.

If we store on an extra linear tape the headmovements of M and the symbols printed by the machine in the last r_j steps updating can be performed in less than $(5^d-1)\,T(i+1,r_j)$ steps.

This gives with the help of (4.1)

$$T(i,r) \leq O(r) + 5^d \max_{\Sigma r_j = r} \Sigma T(i+1,r_j) .$$

Now inductively one can prove

$$T(i,r) \leq C\cdot(5^{d(a-i)}-0.5)r$$

for an appropriate constant C .

This gives

$$T(0,t) \leq C\cdot(5^{d\cdot a}-0.5)\cdot t$$
$$\leq O(5^{d\cdot \log^* t}\cdot t) \ .$$

Therefore M can be simulated by M' in time $O(5^{d\cdot\log^* t(n)}\cdot t(n))$ which proves the theorem. □

Using the results in [9] we get as a

Corollary:

Every $t(n)$-time bounded d-dimensional Turing-machine can be simulated by an $O(t(n)5^{d\cdot\log^* t(n)}/\log t(n))$-space bounded Turing-machine.

7. Final remarks

The recurrence equations show that the time bound for the simulation decreases if the actualisation of the i-cubes can be performed faster. This is indeed possible if we modify the coverings by the d-dimensional cubes in such a way that the cubes overlap only outside their centers. Then every node of an i-cube W is contained in at most 2^d i+1-sub-cubes of W and if one estimates the time needed for the actualisation more carefully in this case it can be shown that the whole simulation can be done in time $O(2^{d\cdot\log^* t(n)}\cdot t(n))$.

It would be interesting to find out whether multidimensional machines can be simulated by tree-tape machines still faster. Is it possible without loss of time? If not where between $t(n)$ and $t(n)\cdot 2^{d\cdot\log^* t(n)}$ does the lower bound lie?

References

1. Cook and Aanderaa, *On the minimum computation time of functions*, Trans. AMS 142, August 1969, 291-314.

2. Fischer, Meyer and Rosenberg, *Real-time simulation of multihead tape units*, J. ACM 19, 4, 1972, 590-607.

3. Grigorjev, *Imbedding theorems for Turing-machines of differnet dimensions and Kolmogorov's algorithms, Soviet Math. Dokl. 18, 1977, 588-592.*

4. Grigorjev, *Time bounds of multidimensional Turing-machines*, 1979.

5. Hennie, *On-line Turing machine computations*, IEEE Trans. EC 15, 1, 1966, 34-44.

6. Hennie and Stearns, *Two-tape simulation of multihead tape units*, I. ACM 13, 4, 1966, 533-546.

7. Leong and Seiferas, *New real-time simulations of multihead tape units*, Proc. 9th ACM Symp. Theory of Computing, 1977, 239-248.

8. Paterson, Fischer and Meyer, *An improved overlap argument for on-line multiplication*, SIAM-AMS Proc. 7, 1974, 97-111.

9. Paul and Reischuk, *On time versus space II*, 20th IEEE-FOCS, 1979, 298-306.

10. Pippenger and Fischer, *Relations among complexity measures*, J. ACM 26, 2, 1979, 361-381.

11. Reischuk, *Beziehungen zwischen Rechenzeit, Speicherplatz und Speicherstruktur*, Preprint, Universität Bielefeld, 1979.

12. Stoss, *Zwei-Band Simulation von Turingmaschinen*, Computing 7, 1971, 222-235.

13. Turing, *On computable numbers with an application to the Entscheidungsporblem*, Proc. London Math. Soc. (2), 42, 1936, 230-265.

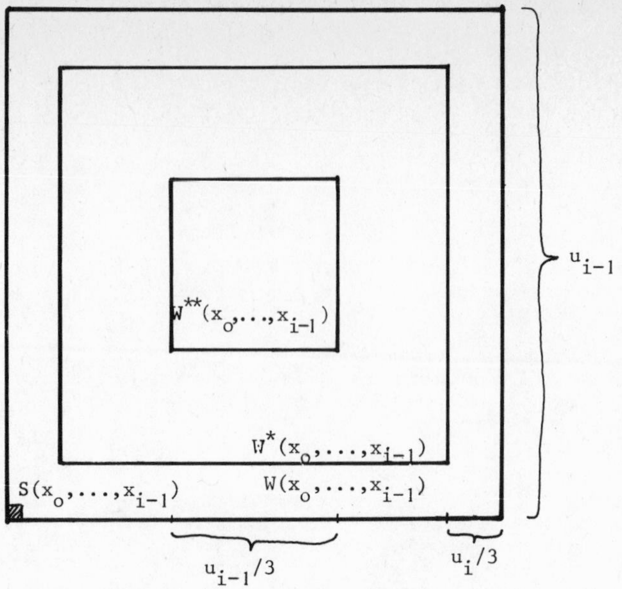

figure 1: the i-1-cube $W(x_o,\ldots,x_{i-1})$

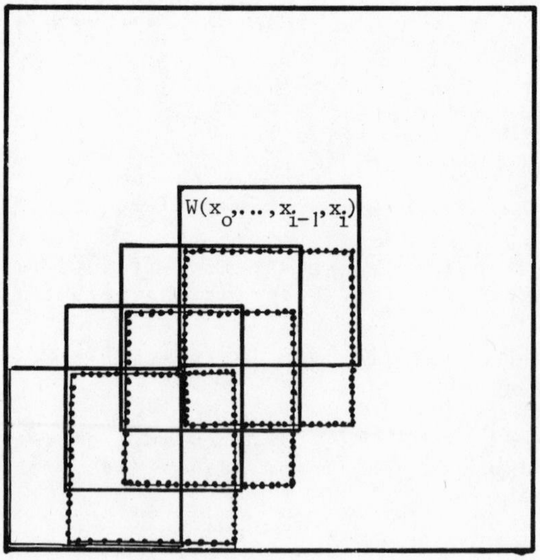

figure 2: i-subcubes

GRAMMATICAL FAMILIES

Arto Salomaa
Mathematics Department
University of Turku, Finland

1. Introduction. A family of languages is grammatical if it is generated by some grammar form. The definitions in this paper follow [2] - [4]. In particular, the interpretation mechanism is defined in the same way both for terminals and nonterminals - this is sometimes referred to as the "strict" interpretation.

The notion of a grammar form was originally introduced in [1] as an attempt to develop a theory of structurally similar grammars. During the past few years, grammar forms have been investigated quite vigorously from many angles. Moreover, an analogous model (L form) has been introduced for the study of grammatical similarity of L systems. The purpose of this paper is not to survey these by now quite vast areas - the reader is referred to [10] or [8], the latter only as regards L forms. We discuss in this paper only some particularly interesting recent results about completeness and density. Attention is restricted to context-free grammar forms.

We now give more formally the basic definitions.

A finite substitution μ defined on an alphabet V is said to be a dfl-substitution (a disjoint finite letter substitution) if, for any a in V, $\mu(a)$ is a finite set of letters and, moreover, $a \neq b$ implies $\mu(a) \cap \mu(b) = \phi$.

A (context-free) grammar form is a context-free grammar $G = (V, \Sigma, P, S)$. (Here V is the total alphabet, Σ the terminal alphabet, P the production set, and S the initial letter.) Given a dfl-substitution μ defined on V, we say that a context-free grammar $G' =$

(V', Σ', P', S') is an <u>interpretation</u> of G modulo μ, in symbols $G' \triangleleft G(\mu)$, if the following conditions (i) - (iv) obtain:

(i) $\mu(A) \subseteq V' - \Sigma'$ for all A in $V - \Sigma$,

(ii) $\mu(a) \subseteq \Sigma'$ for all a in Σ,

(iii) $P' \subseteq \mu(P)$, where $\mu(P) = \{B \to y : B$ is in $\mu(A)$, y is in $\mu(x)$, for some $A \to x$ in $P\}$,

(iv) S' is in $\mu(S)$.

The <u>language family</u> generated by the grammar form G is defined by

$$\mathcal{L}(G) = \{L(G') : G' \triangleleft G(\mu) \text{ for some } \mu\}.$$

Language families generated by grammar forms are referred to as <u>grammatical</u>.

Observe that μ^{-1} is always a length-preserving homomorphism. In fact, grammar forms fit nicely into the framework of the theory of morphisms defined on free monoids, a point further exploited in [9].

Consider the following examples of grammar forms. Each grammar form is given by listing the productions.

$F_1 : S \to ab, S \to ba;$

$F_2 : S \to aa;$

$F_3 : S \to aS, S \to a;$

$F_4 : S \to aSa, S \to a, S \to a^2;$

$F_5 : S \to aS, S \to Sa, S \to a;$

$F_6 : S \to A, S \to B, A \to A^2, A \to a^2, B \to aB, B \to Ba, B \to a;$

$F_7 : S \to SS, S \to a.$

Here F_1 and F_2 are finite forms: their language is finite and, consequently, every language in their language family is finite. The family of F_3 equals the family $\mathcal{L}(REG)$ of regular languages. (Indeed, we get only regular languages not containing λ. However, we make the customary convention that languages and language families are considered modulo λ.) Similarly, F_5 and F_7 generate the families $\mathcal{L}(LIN)$ and $\mathcal{L}(CF)$ of linear and context-free languages, respectively. It can also be shown that, for every $i \leq 6$, $L(F_i)$ is strictly contained in $L(F_{i+1})$. The reason why F_6 does not generate $L(CF)$ is that expansions are possible in the generation of even length words only - words of odd length are generated in a linear fashion. Similarly, the reason why F_4 does not generate the whole $L(LIN)$ is in the restricted capability for "pumping": for instance, the language

$$\{a^{2n}b^n \mid n \geq 1\}$$

is not in the family of F_4.

The above examples indicate some of the phenomena typical for the language families of grammar forms. With the exception of the form F_1, all of the forms are unary, i.e., have only one terminal letter. Forms with several terminal letters are, in general, more difficult to handle. In such cases it is often useful to consider a-restrictions F_a of a given form F. Such an a-restriction (where a is a terminal letter) is obtained from F by removing all productions containing terminals $b \neq a$.

We say that a grammatical family L is unary-complete, if, whenever a grammar form F satisfies $L(F) = L$, then F also possesses an a-restriction F_a satisfying $L(F_a) = L$.

Remark. The interpretation mechanism introduced in [1], referred to as the g-interpretation, differs from the definition above with respect to the following two points: (1) μ is a dfl substitution only on $V - \Sigma$, and μ is just a finite substitution on the entire V. (2) The condition (ii) in the definition above is replaced by: $\mu(a) \subseteq \Sigma'^*$ for all a in Σ. Intuitively, terminals carry very little information if g-interpretations are considered, for instance, the language family remains invariant if all terminals are identified. For g-interpretations, μ^{-1} is not in general a homomorphism.

2. Normal forms for regular, linear and context-free grammars. We begin with some further definitions and terminology. The families of finite, regular, linear and context-free languages are denoted by L(FIN), L(REG), L(LIN), L(CF), respectively.

A grammar form F is complete with respect to a family L of languages or, briefly, L-complete if

$$L(F) = L.$$

F is complete if it is L(CF)-complete. F is L-sufficient if

$$L(F) \supseteq L.$$

It is a nontrivial problem to determine necessary and sufficient conditions for L-completeness and L-sufficiency for specific families L. (In fact, the problem as regards completeness is still open, as will be seen below.) On the other hand, the solution of the problem of L-completeness for a specific family L gives a characterization of all possible "normal forms" of grammars for L. This follows because each L-complete form gives a "normal form" of grammars for L. For instance, each time we construct a complete form, we also give a normal form for context-free grammars.

The following three theorems from [2] settle these problems for the family L(REG). In the statement of the results, "self-embedding" and "reduced" have their customary meanings.

Theorem 2.1. A reduced grammar form F is L(REG)-complete if and only if (i) F is not self-embedding, and (ii) F possesses an L(REG)-complete a-restriction.

Theorem 2.2. The family L(REG) is unary-complete. It is decidable whether or not a given grammar form F is L(REG)-complete.

Theorem 2.3. The following conditions (i) - (iii) are equivalent for a grammar form F:

(i) F is L(FIN)-sufficient.

(ii) F is L(REG)-sufficient.

(iii) $L(F) \supseteq a^+$, for some terminal letter a.

The corresponding problems are essentially more difficult for the family $L(\mathrm{LIN})$. Some of the difficulties were already pointed out above in connection with the examples given. As another illustration we mention that the grammar form

$$S \to a^3S \mid Sa^4 \mid a \mid a^2 \mid a^3$$

is $L(\mathrm{LIN})$-complete.

The following notions are needed for the solution of the problems for the family $L(\mathrm{LIN})$.

We say that a nonterminal A in a unary reduced grammar form F is <u>left-pumping</u> (resp. <u>right-pumping</u>) if, for some fixed $m,n \geq 0$, there are infinitely many values i such that

$$A \Rightarrow^* a^{i+m} A a^n \quad (\text{resp. } A \Rightarrow^* a^m A a^{n+i}).$$

The nonterminal A is <u>pumping</u> if it is both left-pumping and right-pumping.

Let $A_1, \ldots, A_m$ be all the pumping nonterminals in a unary reduced grammar form F. For each i, the lengths j of the terminal words a^j generated by A_i constitute an almost periodic sequence. Denote its period by $p(A_i)$. Let p be the least common multiple of all the numbers

$$p(A_i),\ i = 1, \ldots, m.$$

Denote the residue classes modulo p by

$$R_0, R_1, \ldots, R_{p-1}.$$

We say that the residue class R_j is <u>A_i-reachable</u> if there are numbers r, s and t such that

$$S \Rightarrow^* a^r A_i a^s,\ A_i \Rightarrow^* a^{t+np},\ \text{for all } n \geq 0,\ j \equiv r + s + t\ (p).$$

The <u>pumping spectrum</u> of F consists of all numbers in all A_i-reachable residue classes, where i ranges over $1, \ldots, m$.

It should be emphasized that A_i-reachability as defined above implies that almost all of the numbers in the residue class R_j in question are reachable in the sense defined, i.e., the reachability of an "initial mess" does not count.

We are now in the position to settle the problems for the family $\mathcal{L}$(LIN). The solution is contained in the next three theorems. The proofs are quite complicated and can be found in [2].

Theorem 2.4. A unary reduced linear grammar form F is $\mathcal{L}$(LIN)-complete if and only if (i) $L(F) = a^+$, and (ii) the pumping spectrum of F consists of all numbers.

Theorem 2.5. A unary reduced grammar form F is $\mathcal{L}$(LIN)-complete if and only if each of the following conditions (i) - (iii) is satisfied. (i) $\mathcal{L}(F)$ is contained in $\mathcal{L}$(LIN). (ii) $L(F) = a^+$. (iii) The pumping spectrum of F consists of all numbers. Each of the conditions (i) - (iii) is decidable. In particular, (i) is equivalent to the nonexistence of a sentential form of F containing two occurrences of self-embedding nonterminals.

Theorem 2.6. A unary reduced grammar form F is $\mathcal{L}$(LIN)-sufficient if and only if $L(F) = a^+$ and the pumping spectrum of F consists of all numbers. The family $\mathcal{L}$(LIN) is unary-complete. It is decidable whether or not a given grammar form is $\mathcal{L}$(LIN)-complete.

Finally, we turn to the discussion of the family $\mathcal{L}$(CF). Here the notion corresponding to pumping spectrum is that of an expansion spectrum. (Cf. also F_6 among the examples above.)

We say that a nonterminal A is expansive if

$$A \Rightarrow^* x_1 A x_2 A x_3 ,$$

for some terminal words x_1, x_2, x_3 and, in addition, A derives some nonempty terminal word.

Let $A_1, \ldots, A_m$ be all the expansive nonterminals in a unary reduced grammar form F. For each i, the lengths j of the terminal words a^j generated by A_i constitute an almost periodic sequence.

Denote its period by $p(A_i)$. Let p be the least common multiple of all of the numbers

$$p(A_i), \quad i = 1, \ldots, m.$$

Denote the residue classes modulo p by

$$R_0, R_1, \ldots, R_{p-1}.$$

We say that the residue class R_j is <u>A_i-reachable</u> if there are numbers r, s and t such that

$$S \Rightarrow^* a^r A_i a^s, \quad A_i \Rightarrow^* a^{t+np}, \quad \text{for all } n \geq 0,\ j \equiv r+s+t\ (p).$$

The <u>expansion spectrum</u> of F consists of all numbers in all A_i-reachable residue classes, where i ranges over $1, \ldots, m$.

<u>Theorem 2.7.</u> Assume that F is a unary reduced complete grammar form. Then $L(F) = a^+$ and the expansion spectrum of F consists of all numbers.

Theorem 2.7 is established in [3]. The converse of this theorem, as well as the solution of the completeness and general normal form theorems for the family $\mathcal{L}(CF)$ depend on the validity of the following.

<u>Conjecture.</u> Assume that (i, j, k) is a triple of nonnegative integers. Then every context-free language L is generated by a grammar whose productions are of the two types (i) $A \to w$ and (ii) $A \to w_i B w_j C w_k$, where A, B, C are nonterminals and w's are terminals such that $|w_i| = i$, $|w_j| = j$, $|w_k| = k$. Moreover, $|w|$ in type (i) productions assumes values from the length set of L only.

If the last sentence ("Moreover ...") is removed from the above conjecture, then the resulting statement is known to be true.

Assuming the Conjecture, the converse of Theorem 2.7 holds for unary reduced grammar forms F. (Cf. [3].) Under this assumption, it also follows that the family $\mathcal{L}(CF)$ is unary-complete and that the completeness of a given grammar form is a decidable property. In fact, the decision method is not too complicated and amounts to the computing of an expansion spectrum.

3. Density. Perhaps the most interesting phenomena about grammatical families deal with density. In fact, no other collections of language families obtained by generative devices are known to possess such a density property. We now present some of the details.

Assume that L and L' are grammatical families such that $L \subsetneq L'$. The pair (L, L') is said to be dense if, whenever L_1 and L_2 are grammatical families satisfying

$$L \subseteq L_1 \subsetneq L_2 \subseteq L',$$

then there is a grammatical family L_3 such that

$$L_1 \subsetneq L_3 \subsetneq L_2.$$

Theorem 3.1. The pair $(L(\mathrm{REG}), L(\mathrm{CF}))$ is dense.

Theorem 3.1 is established in [4], where also other dense pairs are given and the question of the "maximality" of such pairs (for instance, whether $(L_1, L(\mathrm{CF}))$ is dense for some $L_1 \subsetneq L(\mathrm{REG})$) is investigated.

As regards finite forms, very interesting problems remain open. Moreover, these problems can be considered as basic problems about morphisms.

For instance, it is not known whether there are dense pairs whose components are generated by finite forms. (It is easy to see that if F is a finite and G an infinite form then the pair $(L(\mathrm{F}), L(\mathrm{G}))$ is not dense.) As regards the examples listed above,

$$(L(\mathrm{F}_1), L(\mathrm{F}_2))$$

is a reasonable candidate for such a dense pair. We can at least show that if L_3 is a grammatical family satisfying

$$L(\mathrm{F}_1) \subsetneq L_3 \subsetneq L(\mathrm{F}_2),$$

then there are grammatical families L_4 and L_5 such that

$$L(\mathrm{F}_1) \subsetneq L_4 \subsetneq L_3 \subsetneq L_5 \subsetneq L(\mathrm{F}_2).$$

It is no wonder that these problems are difficult because recently we have been able to exhibit close interconnections between these problems and those of graph theory. This will be discussed in the oral presentation of this paper.

The equivalence problem for (context-free) grammar forms is still open: no algorithm is known for deciding whether or not two grammar forms generate the same grammatical family. Intuitively, density results indicate that there are "many" grammatical families and, consequently, the decision of the equivalence problem is "hard". However, the results in [5] and [7] show that it is possible to have a dense collection of grammatical families and still a decidable equivalence problem.

4. MSW spaces. The notion of an MSW space was introduced in [6] to analyze further density properties of collections of language families. The definitions are quite general and give rise also to many collections not obtained using the mechanism of grammar forms.

Let L_1 and L_2 be languages over disjoint alphabets. Their superdisjoint union, denoted by $L_1 \dot{\cup} L_2$, is just the union of L_1 and L_2. Observe that the terminology "superdisjoint union" and the notation $\dot{\cup}$ serve to specify that the operation is defined only if the alphabets of the languages involved are disjoint.

We now define the operation of breaking as a kind of inverse of the operation superdisjoint union. Let L be a language over some alphabet Σ. The language L_1 is obtained from L by breaking (with respect to an alphabet $\Sigma_1 \subseteq \Sigma$) if $L_1 = L \cap \Sigma_1{}^*$ and $L - L_1$ contains no word containing a symbol of Σ_1. A language L is called coherent if it cannot be broken in a nontrivial fashion; more precisely, if L_1 is obtained from L by breaking then either $L_1 = L$ or $L_1 = \phi$ (the empty set).

For every language L and integer $i \geq 1$ we denote by $L(i)$ the language defined by $L(i) = \{x \in L \mid |x| \neq i\}$. I.e., $L(i)$ consists of all words of L whose length is different from i. Similarly, for an arbitrary language family $\mathcal{L}$ and integer $i \geq 1$ we denote by $\mathcal{L}(i)$ the language family $\mathcal{L}(i) = \{L(i) \mid L \in \mathcal{L}\}$ and we call $\mathcal{L}(i)$ an <u>extraction</u> of $\mathcal{L}$.

A language family $\mathcal{L}$ is closed under <u>covering</u> if for every infinite language L the fact that $L(i)$ is in $\mathcal{L}$ for infinitely many i implies that L itself is also in $\mathcal{L}$.

The <u>superdisjoint wedge</u> of two language families $\mathcal{L}_1$ and $\mathcal{L}_2$, in symbols $\mathcal{L}_1 \dot{\vee} \mathcal{L}_2$, is defined by $\mathcal{L}_1 \dot{\vee} \mathcal{L}_2 = \{L_1 \dot{\cup} L_2 \mid L_1 \in \mathcal{L}_1, L_2 \in \mathcal{L}_2\}$.

We now formulate the notion of dense collections of language families generalizing to some extent the definition in Section 3.

Let $\mathcal{M}$ be a collection of language families. $\mathcal{M}$ is called <u>dense</u> if for any two language families $\mathcal{L}_1$ and $\mathcal{L}_2$ in $\mathcal{M}$ with $\mathcal{L}_1 \subsetneq \mathcal{L}_2$ there exist a language family $\mathcal{L}_3 \in \mathcal{M}$ strictly in between, $\mathcal{L}_1 \subsetneq \mathcal{L}_3 \subsetneq \mathcal{L}_2$. Two language families $\mathcal{L}_1$, $\mathcal{L}_2$ of $\mathcal{M}$ with $\mathcal{L}_1 \subsetneq \mathcal{L}_2$ are called a <u>dense pair</u> (with respect to $\mathcal{M}$) if $\{\mathcal{L} \in \mathcal{M} \mid \mathcal{L}_1 \subseteq \mathcal{L} \subseteq \mathcal{L}_2\}$ is dense. $\mathcal{L}_1$ is called <u>density forcing</u> (with respect to $\mathcal{M}$) if $\{\mathcal{L} \in \mathcal{M} \mid \mathcal{L}_1 \subseteq \mathcal{L}\}$ is dense.

A collection $\mathcal{M}$ of language families is an <u>MSW space</u> if the following conditions (i) - (iii) hold:

(i) Each $\mathcal{L}$ in $\mathcal{M}$ is closed under superdisjoint union and breaking.

(ii) $\mathcal{M}$ is closed under superdisjoint wedge.

(iii) For each infinite language L occurring in some language family of $\mathcal{M}$ there exist subsets L_i of L for $i = 1, 2, \ldots$ such that (a) and (b) hold:

  (a) L is in a language family $\mathcal{L}$ of $\mathcal{M}$ iff L_i is in $\mathcal{L}$ for all i with $L_i \neq L$.

  (b) If L belongs to $\mathcal{L} \in \mathcal{M}$, then for every p with $L_p \neq L$ there exists an $\mathcal{L}_p \in \mathcal{M}$ such that $\mathcal{L}_p \subseteq \mathcal{L}$ and $\mathcal{L}_p$ contains L_p but does not contain L.

For instance, the collection of language families

$$\{\mathcal{L}(F) \mid F \text{ is a context-free grammar form}\}$$

is an MSW space. Similarly, collections defined by arbitrary grammar forms, by synchronized EOL forms, or by finite or by one-sided linear grammar forms constitute MSW spaces. However, the next theorem shows that "most" MSW spaces are obtained quite independently of form theory.

Theorem 4.1. Assume that $\mathcal{M}$ is a collection of language families such that each family $\mathcal{L}$ of $\mathcal{M}$ is closed under superdisjoint union, intersection with regular sets and covering. Let $\overline{\mathcal{M}}$ be the closure of $\mathcal{M}$ under superdisjoint wedge and extraction. Then $\overline{\mathcal{M}}$ is an MSW space.

Theorem 4.1 gives the following general method of constructing MSW spaces. Start with an arbitrary (finite or infinite) collection of languages. Close each language in the collection with respect to the operations $\dot{\cup}$, intersection with regular sets and covering, yielding a collection $\mathcal{M}$ of language families. Close $\mathcal{M}$ under superdisjoint wedge and extraction to obtain $\overline{\mathcal{M}}$. Then $\overline{\mathcal{M}}$ is an MSW space.

The main result about the density properties is the following theorem.

Theorem 4.2. Let $\mathcal{M}$ be an MSW space and let $\mathcal{F}$ be the collection of all finite languages occurring in language families of $\mathcal{M}$. If $\mathcal{L}$ is a family of $\mathcal{M}$ containing $\mathcal{F}$, then $\mathcal{L}$ is density forcing.

Theorem 4.2 can also be used to show that certain collections of language families, such as the collection of all AFL's, are not MSW spaces.

References

[1] A. CREMERS and S. GINSBURG. Context-free grammar forms. Journal of Computer and System Sciences 11 (1975) 86-116.

[2] H. MAURER, A. SALOMAA and D. WOOD. Context-free grammar forms with strict interpretations. Journal of Computer and System Sciences, to appear.

[3] H. MAURER, A. SALOMAA and D. WOOD. Strict context-free grammar forms: completeness and decidability. McMaster University Computer Science Technical Report 78-CS-19.

[4] H. MAURER, A. SALOMAA and D. WOOD. Dense hierarchies of grammatical families. ACM Journal, to appear.

[5] H. MAURER, A. SALOMAA and D. WOOD. Decidability and density in two-symbol grammar forms. Submitted for publication.

[6] H. MAURER, A. SALOMAA and D. WOOD. MSW spaces. Submitted for publication.

[7] TH. OTTMANN, A. SALOMAA and D. WOOD. Grammar and s-grammar forms: decidability and density. Submitted for publication.

[8] G. ROZENBERG and A. SALOMAA. The Mathematical Theory of L Systems. Academic Press (1980).

[9] A. SALOMAA. Morphisms on free monoids and language theory. Proceedings of the Conference on Formal Languages, Santa Barbara. Academic Press, to appear.

[10] D. WOOD. Grammar and L forms. Springer-Verlag, in preparation.

PARTITIONED CHAIN GRAMMARS

Peter Schlichtiger
Universität Kaiserslautern/FB Informatik
D-6750 KAISERSLAUTERN

currently: SIEMENS AG
D-8000 Munich 70

0. ABSTRACT

A new class of grammars, the partitioned chain grammars, is introduced. It is shown that such grammars are not only efficiently parsable, but also comparatively easy to construct. The combination of these two properties makes them very attractive for use in parser-generators.

1. INTRODUCTION

In parsing, the decision which action a parser is going to perform next largely depends on the already recognized part of the derviation tree. Thus, all derivations of a grammar will have to obey certain conditions if a particular parsing-scheme is to work in linear time. Consequently, the definition of those classes of grammars for which some parsing-scheme works in linear time is usually formulated in terms of restrictions on derivations. Derivations, however, are very complex structures, and this makes it very difficult for the constructor of a grammar to check whether the restrictions imposed on it by such a definition are really met. This must be considered a major drawback of all of the parser-generators which have so far been built for such grammars.

The partitioned chain grammars show that much simpler structures than derivations, namely chains (first introduced in [Nijholt 77]) and a partition of the nonterminal alphabet, suffice to define a large class of efficiently parsable grammars. Using only simple structures in the definition of a grammar class has two mayor advantages:

1. Testing whether a specific grammatical construct obeys the definition becomes much easier.
2. By increasing the intelligibility of the definition many faulty constructs can be avoided in the first place.

Nevertheless, even the construction of such a grammar can be very difficult, if its grammar class is not large enough. Obviously, the grammar class must be large, if there is to be a high probability that the grammatical construction, deviced by a language designer to describe some language feature, does not violate the definition of the grammar. Thus it actually is the combination of two features, a large grammar class and a comprehensive definition, that distinguishes the partitioned chain grammars from all the other wellknown classes of grammars used for parser-generators.

Section 2 of this paper gives a formal definition of the partitioned chain grammars. If furthermore states some interesting properties of this grammar class and compares it to other grammar classes wellknown in syntax analysis. Section 3 contains the most interesting results about partitioned chain languages. Section 4 deals with a parsing-method for partitioned chain grammars.

The reader is assumed to be familiar with basic concepts of context-free grammars and parsing as described in [Aho.Ullman 72].
A context-free grammar (abbreviated cfg) is denoted by G=(N,T,P,S), where
- N is the set of <u>nonterminals</u> (denoted by A,B,C,D,...)
- T is the set of <u>terminals</u> (denoted by a,b,c,d,...)
- P is the set of <u>productions</u>
- S N is the <u>startsymbol</u>

N ∪ T is denoted by V , the elements of which will be denoted by X,Y,Z. Elements of T* will be denoted by u,v,w,x,y,z; elements of V* by $\alpha,\beta,\gamma,\delta,\ldots$. The symbol ε is reserved for the empty word.
In addition note, that

- $_1(\alpha)$ denotes the first symbol of α
- the <u>left-corner</u> of a production $A \rightarrow \alpha$ is $_1(\alpha)$
- a cfg G=(N,T,P,S) is called ε-free if P contains no ε-productions (not even $S \rightarrow \varepsilon$)
- every cfg in this paper is reduced.

2. PARTITIONED CHAIN GRAMMARS

Chains, as they are defined here, differ from the definition given by A.Nijholt in that a chain may contain a nonterminal or ε as its last element. The reason for this difference is discussed in chapter 4 (see Remark 4.1).

DEFINITION: (chain)

Let G=(N,T,P,S) be a cfg.

If $X_0 \in V$, then CH(X_0), the set of chains of X_0, is defined by

$$CH(X_0) = \{<X_0,\ldots,X_n> \mid n \geq 0,\ X_0 \ldots X_{n-1} \in N^*, X_n \in (N \cup T \cup \{\varepsilon\}) \text{ and } X_0 \underset{L}{\Rightarrow} X_1\sigma_1 \underset{L}{\Rightarrow} \ldots \underset{L}{\Rightarrow} X_n\sigma_n,\ \sigma_i \in V^*, 1 \leq i \leq n\}$$

Note, that $\langle\varepsilon\rangle$ is not a chain.

A very important notion in connection with the definition of partitioned chain grammars is that of a k-follow set of a chain.

DEFINITION: (k-follow set of a chain)

Let G=(N,T,P,S) be a cfg and let $\equiv$ be an equivalence relation on N. Furthermore let $A \to \rho X \sigma$ be a production in P and let $\pi = <X_0,\ldots,X_n>$ be a chain in CH(X). Then

$$f_k(\pi,\sigma,follow_k(A)) = \{y \mid y \in first_k(\sigma_n\, \sigma\, follow_k(A))\ X_0 \underset{L}{\Rightarrow} X_1\sigma_1 \underset{L}{\Rightarrow} \ldots \underset{L}{\Rightarrow} X_n\sigma_n,\ \sigma_i \in V^*, 1 \leq i \leq n\}$$

is called the k-follow set of chain π with respect to $A \to \rho \underline{X} \sigma$, where the underlined symbol marks the beginning of chain π.

Although this definition might seem a little complicated at first sight, it actually describes a quite simple relationship between a lookahead of k symbols and a chain. This relationship is depicted in the following figure

Figure 2.1

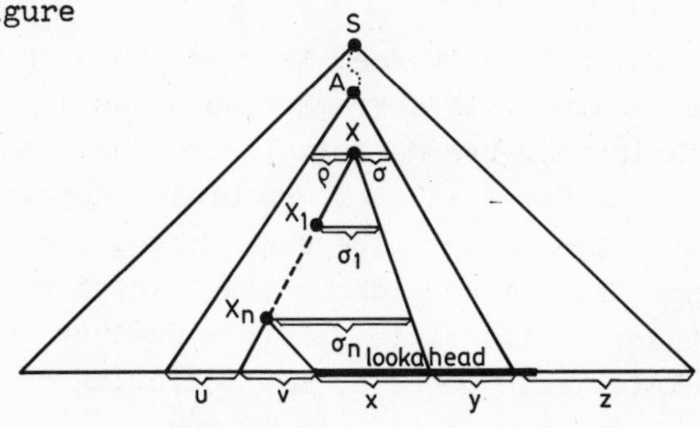

where $\rho \overset{*}{\Rightarrow} u$, $X_n \overset{*}{\Rightarrow} v$, $\sigma_n \overset{*}{\Rightarrow} x$, $\sigma \overset{*}{\Rightarrow} y$, $z \in follow(A)$ and

lookahead = $_k(xyz) \in f_k(<X,X_1,\ldots,X_n>,\sigma, follow_k(A))$.

Different chains, which may appear in a similar context, must, to a certain extend, be distinguishable on account of the lookahead. The following definition describes exactly which differences have to be recognized.

DEFINITION: (conflict chain)

Let $G=(N,T,P,S)$ be a cfg and let $\equiv$ be an equivalence relation on N. Two chains $\pi_1 = \langle X_o,\ldots,X_n\rangle \in CH(X_o)$, $\pi_2 = \langle Y_o,\ldots,Y_m\rangle \in CH(Y_o)$, $X_o,Y_o \in V$, are called conflict chains (with respect to $\equiv$) of type

a) iff $n,m>o$ and $X_n = Y_m$ and $X_{n-1} \not\equiv Y_{m-1}$

b) iff $n=o$, $m>o$ and $X_n = Y_m$

c) iff $X_n \in T$ and $Y_m = \varepsilon$

DEFINITION: (PC(k)-grammar)

Let $G=(N,T,P,S)$ be a cfg and let $k \geq o$ be an integer.
The augmented grammar for G is defined to be the grammar $G_a = (N\cup\{S'\}, T\cup\{\Delta\}, P\cup\{S'\to\Delta S\}, S')$, where Δ is not in T and S' is not in N.
G is a partitioned chain grammars with k symbols lookahead (abbreviated PC(k)-grammar) if any only if there is an equivalence relation $\equiv$ on $N\cup\{S'\}$, such that the following conditions hold for G_a:

1) if $A\to\varrho X\sigma$, $B\to\varrho Y\bar{\sigma}$ $\in (P\cup\{S'\to\Delta S\})$, $\varrho\neq\varepsilon$ and $A\equiv B$ then

a) $f_k(\pi_1,\sigma,\text{follow}_k(A)) \cap f_k(\pi_2,\bar{\sigma},\text{follow}_k(B)) = \emptyset$
for any two conflict chains $\pi_1 \in CH(X)$, $\pi_2 \in CH(Y)$ of type a) or b)

and

b) $\text{first}_k\ (a\ \ f_k(\pi_1,\sigma,\text{follow}_k\ (A))) \cap f_k(\pi_2,\bar{\sigma},\text{follow}_k(B)) = \emptyset$
for any two conflict chains $\pi_1 \in CH(X)$, $\pi_2 \in CH(Y)$ of type c),
where $\pi_1 = \langle X,\ldots,a\rangle$, $a \in T$.

2) if $A\to\varrho$ and $B\to\varrho\sigma$, $A\equiv B$, are different productions in P then
$\text{follow}_k\ (A) \cap \text{first}_k\ (\sigma\text{follow}_k\ (B)) = \emptyset$.

This definition may initially seem to make sense only for non left recursive grammars, since, if a grammar does contain left recursive nonterminals, chains can become infinitely long. This, however, is only true for k = 0. For k = 1 left recursive nonterminals may very well occur in a PC(k)-grammar. The main reason for this is, that one actually does not have to consider chains, which contain some nonterminal more than k+1 times, to find out whether a grammar is PC(k). This is a immediate consequence of the following two lemmas.

LEMMA 2.1

All PC(k)-Grammars, $k \geq 0$, are cycle-free.

Proof:

The proof is ommitted here. It is quite simple for ε-free PC(k)-grammars (see [Schlichtiger1 79]).

□

LEMMA 2.2

Let $G=(N,T,P,S)$ be a cycle-free cfg and $k \geq 1$ an integer. If there is a chain $\pi \in CH(X), X \in N$, in G which contains some nonterminal $A \in N$ more than k+1 times, then there has to be a chain $\pi' \in CH(X)$ in G which contains that nonterminal A at most k+1 times and for which the following holds:

1) $f_k(\pi', \sigma, follow_k(A)) = f_k(\pi, \sigma, follow_k(A))$
   with respect to any production $A \to \varrho \underline{X} \sigma \in (P \cup \{S' \to \Delta S\}), \varrho \neq \varepsilon$,

and

2) the last two elements of π and π' are equal.

Proof:

As G is cycle-free every left recursive leftmost derivation in G is of the form $A \overset{+}{\underset{L}{\Rightarrow}} A\sigma$, where $\sigma \overset{*}{\not\Rightarrow} \varepsilon$.

Hence every leftmost derivation belonging to a chain $\pi = \langle X_0, \ldots, X_n \rangle$ in $CH(X_0), X_0 \in N$, which contains some nonterminal $A \in N$ $k+\ell$ times, $\ell > 1$, has to be of the form

$$X_0 \overset{*}{\underset{L}{\Rightarrow}} A\gamma \overset{+}{\underset{L}{\Rightarrow}} A\sigma_1\gamma \overset{+}{\underset{L}{\Rightarrow}} A\sigma_2\sigma_1\gamma \overset{+}{\underset{L}{\Rightarrow}} \ldots \overset{+}{\underset{L}{\Rightarrow}} A\sigma_{k+\ell-1}\cdots\sigma_1\gamma$$
$$\overset{*}{\underset{L}{\Rightarrow}} X_n\beta\sigma_{k+\ell-1}\cdots\sigma_1\gamma$$

where $\beta, \gamma \in V^*$ and $\sigma_i \in V^+$ for $1 \leq i \leq (k+\ell-1)$.

So for any production $A \to \varrho \underline{X_0} \sigma \in (P \cup \{S' \to \Delta S\}), \varrho \neq \varepsilon$,

$f_k(\pi, \sigma, follow_k(A)) = \{y \mid y \in first_k(\beta\sigma_{k+\ell-1}\cdots\sigma_1\gamma\sigma\, follow_k(A))$ and $X_0 \overset{*}{\underset{L}{\Rightarrow}} A \overset{+}{\underset{L}{\Rightarrow}} A\sigma_1\gamma \overset{+}{\underset{L}{\Rightarrow}} \ldots \overset{+}{\underset{L}{\Rightarrow}} A\sigma_{k+\ell-1}\cdots\sigma_1\gamma \overset{*}{\underset{L}{\Rightarrow}} X_n\beta\sigma_{k+\ell-1}\cdots\sigma_1\gamma$ is a leftmost derivation belonging to

Now consider the chain $\pi' \in CH(X_0)$ which results from π by eliminating the first ℓ-1 occurences of A in π.

Obviously every leftmost derivation belonging to π' must be of the form

$$X_0 \overset{*}{\underset{L}{\Rightarrow}} A\gamma \overset{+}{\underset{L}{\Rightarrow}} A\sigma_\ell\gamma \overset{+}{\underset{L}{\Rightarrow}} \ldots \overset{+}{\underset{L}{\Rightarrow}} A\sigma_{k+\ell-1}\cdots\sigma_\ell\gamma \overset{*}{\underset{L}{\Rightarrow}} X_n\beta\sigma_{k+\ell-1}\cdots\sigma_\ell\gamma$$

where $\beta, \gamma \in V^*$ and $\sigma_j \in V^+$ for $\ell \leq j \leq (k+\ell-1)$

and hence we have for every production $A \to \varrho \underline{X_0} \sigma \in (P \cup \{S' \to \Delta S\}), \varrho \neq \varepsilon$:

$f_k(\pi', \sigma, follow_k(A)) = \{x \mid x \in first_k(\beta\sigma_{k+\ell-1}\cdots\sigma_\ell\gamma\sigma\, follow_k(A))$ and $X_0 \overset{*}{\underset{L}{\Rightarrow}} A\gamma \overset{+}{\underset{L}{\Rightarrow}} A\sigma_\ell\gamma \overset{+}{\underset{L}{\Rightarrow}} \ldots \overset{+}{\underset{L}{\Rightarrow}} A\sigma_{k+\ell-1}\cdots\sigma_\ell\gamma$

$\overset{*}{\underset{L}{\Rightarrow}} X_n \beta \sigma_{k+\ell-1} \cdots \sigma_\ell \gamma$
is a leftmost derivation belonging to π' }

As G is assumed cycle-free no σ_i, $1 \leq i \leq (k+\ell-1)$, can generate the empty word. Consequently each word in $first_k(\beta \sigma_{k+\ell-1} \cdots \sigma_\ell)$ has to be at least k terminals long, which proves that $f_k(\pi', \sigma, follow_k(A)) = f_k(\pi, \sigma, follow_k(A))$ for any production $A \rightarrow \rho \underline{X_0} \sigma \in (P \cup \{S' \rightarrow \Delta S\})$, $\rho \neq \varepsilon$. Moreover the tail of chain π beginning with the ℓ'th A in π equals the tail of chain π' which begins with the first A in π'. As this tail contains exactly k+1 A's and as $k \geq 1$, π and π' must at least agree in their last two elements.

□

<u>THEOREM 2.1</u>

To decide if a cfg G=(N,T,P,S) is a PC(k)-grammar for some integer $k \geq 1$ only chains which do not contain any nonterminal more than k+1 times have to be considered.

<u>Proof:</u>

Let π_1, π_2 be conflict chains and let π_1 contain some nonterminal more than k+1 times. According to lemma 2.2 there has to be another chain π_1', which contains that nonterminal at most k+1 times, such that π_1', π_2 are conflict chains too.

□

Mainly as a consequence of theorem 2.1 it suffices to look at chains up to a maximal length of $(k+1) \cdot |N| + 1$ links, to decide if a given grammar is a PC(k)-grammar for a certain $k \geq 0$. Looking at grammars for programming languages one will however find, that the chains that actually have to be considered in such grammars are much shorter than $(k+1) \cdot |N| + 1$. An average length of 3 or 4 links should be realistic.

The following theorems show, that the class of PC(k)-grammars is indeed quite large compared to other grammar classes used in parser-generators. Unfortunately most of the corresponding proofs are rather lengthy. Therefore they had to be omitted in this paper. Detailed proofs of all the theorems can be found in [Schlichtiger 1 79] for an ε-free version of PC(k)-grammars.

THEOREM 2.2

Every strong LL(k)-grammar is PC(k)

Proof: (Sketch)

Let G=(N,T,P,S) be a cfg, $k \geq o$, and assume G is not PC(k).
Then G in particular cannot be a PC(k)-grammar with respect to the equivalence relation = on $N \cup \{S'\}$.

1) A violation of condition 2) for PC(k)-grammars with respect to = quite immediately causes a conflict with the definition of the strong LL(k)-grammars.
2) If there is a violation of condition 1) for PC(k)-grammars respecting = , then there are productions $A \rightarrow \varrho \underline{X} \sigma$, $A \rightarrow \varrho \underline{Y} \overline{\sigma}$ in $P \cup \{S' \rightarrow \Delta S\}$, where $\varrho \neq \varepsilon$ and $\pi_1 = \langle X_o, \ldots, X_n \rangle \in CH(X)$, $\pi_2 = \langle Y_o, \ldots, Y_m \rangle \in CH(Y)$ are conflict chains for which $first_k\ (X_n\ \ f_k\ (\pi_1, \sigma, follow_k(A))) \cap first_k(Y_m\ \ f_k(\pi_2, \sigma, follow_k(A))) \neq \emptyset$.
If $A \rightarrow \varrho X \sigma$ and $A \rightarrow \varrho Y \sigma$ are different productions, a violation of the definition of strong LL(k)-grammars is evident.
If these productions are equal, then a LL(k)-conflict cannot be shown that easily. Nevertheless one has to exist.

□

THEOREM 2.3

Every PC(k)-grammar is LR(k).

Proof:

The proof, which is rather difficult and lengthy, is omitted in this paper.

□

An analogous theorem is not true for LALR(k)- and SLR(k)-grammars. Instead the following theorem holds.

THEOREM 2.4

There are

1) PC(k)-grammars, which are not LALR(k)

and

2) SLR(k)-grammars, which are not PC(k).

Proof:

1) The grammar $G_1 = (\{S,A,B,C,D,E\},\{a,b\},P_1,S)$, where
$P_1 = \{S \rightarrow aA,\ S \rightarrow bB,\ A \rightarrow Ca,\ A \rightarrow Db,\ B \rightarrow Cb,\ B \rightarrow Da,$
$C \rightarrow E,\ D \rightarrow E,\ E \rightarrow \varepsilon\}$,
is a LL(1)-grammar. According to theorem 2.2 it is also a PC(1)-grammar. However, it is not LALR(1) (the set of LALR(1)-items valid for the viable prefixes aE and bE $\{(C \rightarrow E., a|b], D \rightarrow E., a|b]\}$ is inconsistent).

2) The grammar $G_2 = (\{S,A\},\{a,b\},P_2,S)$, where
$P_2 = \{S \to aaab,\ S \to aAa,\ A \to aa\}$,
is SLR(1). However, it is not PC(1) (Consider the productions $S \to a\underline{a}ab$, $S \to a\underline{A}a$. There are two conflict chains of type b) $\langle a \rangle$ and $\langle A,a \rangle$ which violate condition 1), because
$f_1\ (\langle a \rangle, ab, follow_1\ (S)) \cap f_1\ (\langle A,a \rangle, a, follow_1\ (S)) = \{a\} \neq \emptyset$). □

The following theorem compares PC(k)-grammars with a number of other efficiently parsable grammar classes which have been developed in the past few years. Among these simple chain grammars (see [Nijholt 1 79]) are of particular interest in that they also use chains instead of derivations as their central structure. (However note, that the notion of a chain used here slightly differs from the one used by A. Nijholt).

THEOREM 2.5

1. The class of simple chain grammars is equal to the class of all ε-free PC(0)-grammars with respect to the equivalence relation = .
2. PC(k)-grammars can easily be extended to a grammar class which properly contains the predictive LR(k)-grammars (see [Soisalon, Ukkonen 76]). (This is achieved by replacing the global follow sets by socalled context-dependent follow sets. For details see [Schlichtiger 1 79] and [Schlichtiger 3 80] .)
3. The partitioned LL(k)-grammars (see [Friede 79]), which are an extension of the wellknown strict deterministic grammars (see [Harrison, Havel 73]), form a proper subset of the class of PC(k)-grammars.

3. PARTITIONED CHAIN LANGUAGES

Theorem 2.2 to theorem 2.5 show, that the class of PC(k)-grammars is a large grammar class. The same is true for the class of context-free language (cfl) described by PC(k)-grammars.

THEOREM 3.1

The PC(0)-grammars generate exactly all deterministic prefix-free context-free languages.

Proof:

According to theorem 2.3 PC(0)-grammars can at most generate all the LR(0)-languages (which are exactly all the deterministic prefix-free cfl's).

According to theorem 2.5 the class of PC(0)-grammars generates at least all the partitioned LL(0)-languages. The partitioned LL(0)-grammars, however, are exactly the strict deterministic grammars, which are known to describe all deterministic prefix-free cfl's.

□

THEOREM 3.2

The PC(1)-grammars generate all deterministic cfl's.

Proof:

According to theorem 2.3 PC(1)-grammars cannot describe more than LR(1)-grammars can. That is to say, they cannot generate more than all deterministic cfl's.

According to theorem 2.5 the PC(1)-grammars must at least describe all the partitioned LL(1)-languages, which are all deterministic cfl's.

□

REMARK:

For $k > o$, the PC(k)-grammars with respect to the equivalence relation = generate exactly the LL(k)-languages (which are a proper subset of the deterministic cfl's). This shows that partitions must be considered a powerful tool in language description.

4. THE PARSING OF PARTITIONED CHAIN GRAMMARS

The parsing method for PC(k)-grammars will only be discussed rather informally here. A precise description of a PC(k)-parsing-algorithm can be found in [Schlichtiger 2 79].

Let $G=(N,T,P,S)$ be a PC(k)-grammar with respect to some equivalence relation $\equiv$ and let W be the partition induced on $N \cup \{S'\}$ by $\equiv$.

Assume that the parser has reached a configuration, which describes the following structure

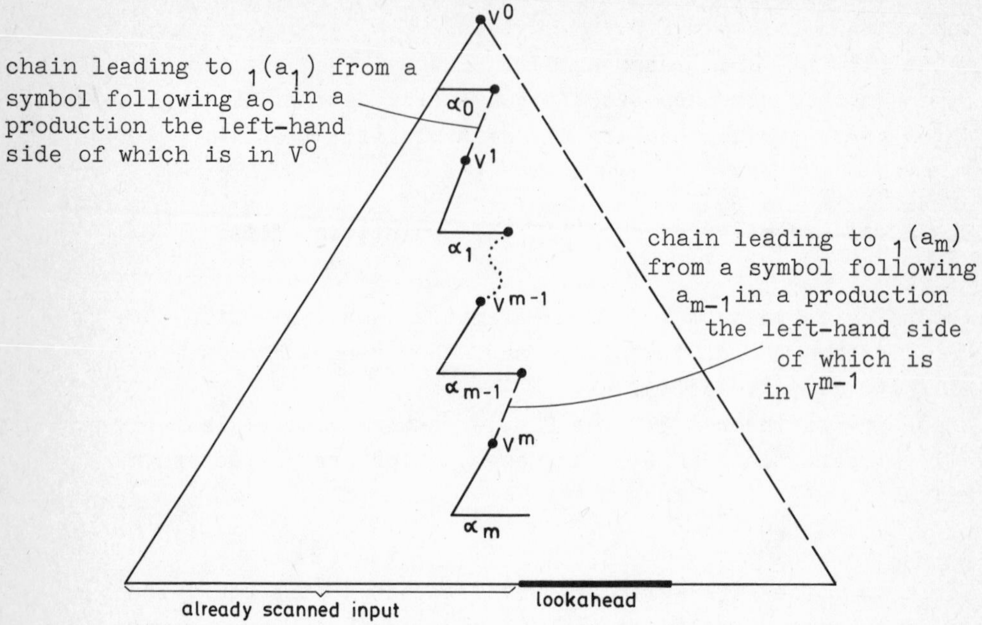

where

- $V^i \in W$ for $0 \leq i \leq m$
- $\alpha_i \neq \varepsilon$, $0 \leq i \leq m$, is a nonempty prefix of the right-hand side of a not yet completely recognized production, the left-hand side of which is in V^i
- $S' \in V^0$ and $\alpha_0 = \Delta$

Note that at the beginning $m = o$.

The parser proceeds as follows:
First of all he has to find out, if α_m is a proper prefix of the right-hand side he is presently trying to recognize, or if α_m already is that whole right-hand side. On the basis of condition 2) for PC(k)-grammars this can be decided by simply looking at the lookahed.

a) If α_m is a proper prefix, the parser will have to compute the symbol immediately right to α_m in this right-hand side. This is achieved by trying to recognize the chain, which begins with the symbol next to α_m and leads to either ε or the next input symbol. For this purpose the parser looks at all chains (with

less than k+2 repetitions) which end with either ε or the next input symbol, and which begin with any symbol that can immediately follow α_m in a production, the left-hand side of which is in V^m. If there are such chains ending with ε as well as chains ending with the next input symbol, condition 1b) guarantees that by inspecting the lookahead it can be determined which kind of chain is correct in the present context. After this decision, the last element of the chain presently under consideration is known. If it is the next input symbol, this symbol is scanned, thereby of course changing the lookahead. If it is ε , then because of condition 1a) for conflict chains of type a), the parser can determine the equivalence class of the predecessor of ε in the chain, again by examining the lookahead. Since this predecessor must be the left-hand side of an ε-production, then by condition 2), it is moreover possible to decide exactly which nonterminal in this equivalence class is the correct one. Let X denote the next input symbol or this nonterminal as the case may be.
If there is a chain of length 1 among the chains leading to X from some symbol to the right of α_m, then the only element of this chain may be the symbol next to α_m the parser has been trying to find. On the basis of condition 1a) for conflict chains of type b) the parser can decide this question by inspecting the present lookahead. If X really is the symbol following α_m, then α_m is extended by X and the parser has apparently reached a situation similar to the one this description started with.
If only chains longer than 1 have to be considered, condition 1a) for conflict chains of type a) guarantees, that by looking at the lookahead, the class V^{m+1} of the predecessor of X in the chain the parser is presently trying to recognize can be determined. Note, that V^{m+1} actually is the class of the left-hand side of a production with left-corner $X = \alpha_{m+1}$. Before being able to continue with recognizing the chain, this production has to be recognized completely. This again leaves the parser in a situation similar to the one we started with.

b) If the parser, by examing the lookahead, finds that α_m is the right-hand side he has been looking for, his next step will be to determine the left-hand side of this production exactly. Condition 2) requires that, dependent on the lookahead, it must be possible to decide which nonterminal in V^m is the left-hand side of α_m. Let $A \in N$ denote this nonterminal.

That completes the recognition of this production.
Apparently, A has to be the last but one elemente in a chain leading to $_1(\alpha_m)$ from a symbol immediately right to α_{m-1}. In order to recognize this symbol next to α_{m-1} exactly, the parser must now look at all chains (with less than k+2 repetitions) that end with A and start with some symbol following α_{m-1} in a production whose left-hand side is in V^{m-1}.
Now, one of these chains can of course contain A as its sole element, which means that A may itself be the symbol next to α_{m-1} for which the parser is looking. As before this can be decided on the basis of condition 1a) for conflict chains of type b) by inspecting the present lookahead and if it turns out to be the next symbol of the right-hand side beginning with α_{m-1}, then α_{m-1} is extended by A, leaving the parser in a situation analogous to the one we started off from.
If on the other hand the present lookahead only permits chains longer than 1 , condition 1a) for conflict chains of type a) demands that, dependent on the lookahead, the class (call it V^m again) of the predecessor of A in the chain to be recognized can be determined. As before, this is the class of the left-hand side of the production (with left-corner A), which must be recognized next. So the parser once again has come to a situation, which resembles the initial one.

The parser goes on recognizing the parse-tree in this manner node by node until the production $S' \rightarrow \Delta S$ is recognized, If at that time all the input has been scanned, then the input word will be accepted.

REMARK 4.1:
In contrast to the parsing of simple chain grammars, which on having scanned a new input symbol requires to be able to recognize the whole chain leading to that input symbol (see [Nijholt 2 79]), PC(k)-parsing only requires to be able to recognize the class of the last but one element of this chain (see step a) of the above description).

As soon as the last but one element has been recognized exactly (see step b) of the above description), this chain will be shortened by its last element, leaving a chain which, unlike the chains considered in simple chain grammars, ends with a nonterminal. Thus instead of recognizing the chain leading to the next input symbol immediately after this input symbol has been scanned, PC(k)-parsing recognizes this chain link by link in a bottom-up fashion.

For this very intuitively presented parsing method an efficient parsing-algorithm has been developed, which works in linear time and for $k < 2$ will generally use less space than a LALR(k)-parser.

5. CONCLUSION

PC(k)-grammars prove to be very well suited for parser-generators. This is so for three reasons:

1) Efficient parsers can be constructed for PC(k)-grammars
2) PC(k)-grammars form a large class of grammars and languages
3) The definition of PC(k)-grammars can be understood and verified easily.

PC(k)-grammars differ from other wellknown grammar classes used for parser-generators in that 2) and 3) usually do not occur together. Nevertheless this is a desirable combination which leads to significant improvement in the constructibility of grammars. Ease of construction, which is a very inportant argument in favour of making practical use of parser-generators, can be increased even further for partitioned chain grammars by making use of various possibilities to support their construction (see[Schlichtiger 1 79] and [Schlichtiger 3 80]).

6. REFERENCES

[Aho, Ullman 72] A.V.Aho, J.D.Ullman: The Theory of Parsing, Translation and Compiling I,II (1972), Prentice Hall, Inc.

[DeRemer 71] F.L.DeRemer: Simple LR(k)-Grammars, CACM 14 (1971) , 453-460

[Friede 79] D.Friede: Partitioned LL(k)-Grammars , Lecture Notes in Computer Science 71 (1979), 245-255

[Ginsburg,Greibach 66] S.Ginsburg,S.A.Greibach: Deterministic Context-Free Languages, Information and Control 9 , 620-648

[Harrison,Havel 73] M.A.Harrison,I.M.Havel: Strict Deterministic Grammars, JCSS 7 (1973) , 237-277

[Mayer 78] O.Mayer: Syntaxanalyse, Bibliographisches Institut Mannheim (1978)

[Nijholt 77] A.Nijholt: Simple Chain Grammars, Lecture Notes in Computer Science 52 (1977), 352-364

[Nijholt 78] A.Nijholt: On the Parsing and Covering of Simple Chain Grammars, Lecture Notes in Computer Science 62 (1978), 330-344

[Nijholt 1 79] A.Nijholt: Simple Chain Grammars and Languages,Theoretical Computer Science 9 (1979), 282-309

[Nijholt 2 79] A.Nijholt: Structure Preserving Transformation on Non-Left-Recursive Grammars, Lecture Notes in Computer Science 71 (1979), 446-459

[Rosenkranth,Lewis 70] D.J.Rosenkrantz,P.M.Lewis II: Deterministic Left Corner Parsing, IEEE Conf. Rec. of the 11'th An. Symp. on Switching and Automata Theory (1970), 139-152

[Schlichtiger 1 79] P.Schlichtiger: Kettengrammatiken - ein Konzept zur Definition handhabbarer Grammatikklassen mit effizientem Analyseverhalten, Doctorial Thesis,University of Kaiserslautern (1979)

[Schlichtiger 2 79] P.Schlichtiger: On the Parsing of Partitioned Chain Grammars, Interner Bericht 21/79 (1979),University of Kaiserslautern

[Schlichtiger 3 80] P.Schlichtiger: On How to Construct Efficiently Parsable Grammars, Interner Bericht 22/80 (1980), University of Kaiserslautern

[Soisalon, Ukkonen 76] E.Soisalon-Soininen,E.Ukkonen: A A Characterisation of LL(k)-Languages, Proc. of the 3rd Coll. on Automata, Languages and Programming (1976), 20-30

AN IMPROVED PROGRAM FOR CONSTRUCTING OPEN HASH TABLES

Jeanette Schmidt and Eli Shamir

Department of Applied Mathematics
The Weizmann Institute of Science
Rehovot, Israel

1. OVERVIEW

The introduction to an important recent article of Gonnet and Munro, "Efficient ordering of hash tables" [1], is the most suitable one for the present article. We treat the same problem, and we shall show that our construction yields hash tables which perform better in every respect (especially in the "worst case"). It is also simpler and quicker to implement.

An w-loaded table is a map from a set K of keys into the set of table locations, $w = |K|/N \leq 1$ is the load factor. ($|K|$ denotes the cardinality of K.) Hashing is a design of a direct access from keys to locations, in order to enter and retrieve information quickly, practically irrespective of the table size (at least for average performance). The ensemble of potential keys is much larger than the number N of table location, so there must be a mechanism to resolve collisions. **Chaining** of colliding keys is a commonly used method, if permanent retention of pointers in the table is acceptable.

In open addressing, which concerns us here, a hashing technique is used to define and compute, for each potential key k , a probe sequence ps(k) which is a sequence of distinct table locations. To retrieve a key k , one looks up the locations given by ps(k) one by one until $ps(k)_q$ is the location where k is found, or else if k is not in the table, until a ceiling position q is reached where we can ascertain that k is absent. This position q is cost(k,L) . Set

$$a(L) = \frac{1}{|K|} \sum_{k \in K} cost(k,L) \quad \text{(average over the set K of keys in the table)}$$

$$m'(L) = \max_{k \in K} cost(k,L)$$

$$m(L) = \max\{cost(k,L), \text{max over all potential } k\} \ .$$

How to load a table using the ps ? In simple open addressing [5,4,12] the insertion is completely dual to retrieval. Given k , one looks up ps(k) for the first empty location ℓ and inserts k there. In this method, which was extensively analysed, the costs deteriorate rapidly as the table fills up.

The map $k \to L(k)$ is an assignment of a location to the key k , and cost(k,L) is the position of L(k) in ps(k) . Reordering the keys in the table provides an alternative assignment, and so we are faced with an optimal-cost assignment problem [3,8,10]. This may help to reduce the cost a(L) or m'(L) , but not m(L) in which we consider answers to retrieval requests for all potential keys, most of which are absent from the given table. In fact m(L) is O(N) , the table size, in all the open hasing method proposed before; this liability is presumably the reason for prefering chained methods whenever possible.

First-order reordering schemes were discussed by Donath [8] and Brent [2]. This is an on-line method, where the key k to be inserted may displace a key k' occupying $ps(k)_i$ if k' has shorter distance to go up to an empty location. This simple scheme already brings down the expectation of a(L) to 2.49. It is further reduced to 2.13 in the Gonnet-Munro [1] reordering scheme, which allows an unlimited order displacement. This is already quite expensive in terms of the number of displacements involved in loading a table, and no analysis is given for the value of m'(L) . For strictly optimal reordering, displacement down the ps may be necessary and as noted in [1,3], this requires a vast effort with little benefit.

We present here a rather inexpensive hash-table loading algorithm which produces tables with close to optimal performance with respect to all costs. Even m(L) is tightly controlled for fully loaded tables. The algorithm is also useful for the purpose of storing compactly a sparse table [9].

2. PROBABILITY ASSUMPTIONS

The loading procedure in open hashing techniques should depend only on the probe sequences. The performance is determined by the probability distribution of the ps encountered; those are obtained by applying the hashing mechanism to the universe of keys.

The assumption of uniform hashing

(1) A key arriving for insertion has a ps y ; all possible ps have equal probability to occur as values of y .

(2) For distinct key insertions, the ps occurrences constitute independent events.

In terms of the assignment problem, this assumption corresponds to taking the probability space of all $N \times N$ matrices, every row of which is a permutation of $\{1,\dots,N\}$ and all $(N!)^N$ possible matrices are equiprobable. Solution of the assignment problem in other spaces can often be reduced to the solution in the space we described [8,10].

Actually the clauses (1) and (2) in the assumption are used in a weaker form, just for limited initial segments of the ps ; we shall see that a ceiling of 2 Log N will suffice on these prefixes. It was established [4] that a double hashing mechanism generates ps which for all practical purposes satisfy the uniform hashing assumption (for quite long prefixes). Double hashing is the standard generation technique for problem-instances in experiments carried out to test the performance of various open hashing loading methods.

Provided with a probability distribution on the input space and a way to sample it, one should analyze and test the retrieval cost performance of various methods and the complexity of the construction. For the expectation of $a(L)$, sample averages give an unbiased estimate. As for $m(L)$, sample averages are virtually impossible. Even for $m'(L)$, taking their sample average as done in [1] is not very significant. The valuable information is provided by estimating the probability of tail events of the form

$\{m(L) \geq d\}$ and also $\{a(L) \geq e\}$,

which we do for our algorithm. Its description is given in the next section and in Section 7, its performance is analyzed in Sections 4, 5 and summarized in 6. Experimental results are described in Section 8.

3. INFORMAL DESCRIPTION OF THE ALGORITHM JSES

There are two parts to JSES. In the first part we load the table up to load factor $w = .79$ in the following way: The inserted key k_1 hashes up its probe sequence. If the location ℓ is hashed in to be occupied by k_2, both keys check locations ℓ_1, ℓ_2, which are their next probe positions. If one of these is empty, the corresponding key is placed there, the other key retains ℓ. If both ℓ_1, ℓ_2 are occupied, then the key which is in a higher position in its ps retains ℓ, while the other keeps searching up its ps.

For the second part we define $\varphi(w)$ and w_k :

$$\varphi(w) = w^{-1} \operatorname{Log} \frac{1}{1-w} ,$$

w_k is the solution of $\varphi(w_k) = k$, $k \geq 2$.

Part 2. The second part of the algorithm takes over at $w = w_2 = .79$. Insertion block j, $j \geq 2$, starts when $w = w_j$, terminates when $w = w_{j+1}$. Within block j the lookup range of all ps has a ceiling $2\varphi(w_j)+1 = 2j+1$ (thus the ceiling increases by 2 from block j to block $j+1$).

The inserted key k looks up its ps up to the ceiling. If no empty location is found for it, it is placed in the location given by its first probe position, displacing k_1. Now k_1, which was in position t of its ps, resumes its look-up to the ceiling. If no empty location is found, it is placed in the location given by position shift (t) of its ps (shift is defined below), displacing k_2. Now k_2 proceeds as k_1, and this chain of displacements terminates if finally the last displaced key finds an empty location. (The probability of non-termination, which results in a failure to construct the table, will be estimated.)

The shift sequence of a key k within a block depends on the initial position t_0 of $L(k)$ in $ps(k)$:

If $t_0 = 1$: $t_0 = 1 \to 2 \to 3 \to 4 \to 5 \to 1 \to \ldots$ (cycle thru first five positions)

if $t_0 \geq 1$: $t_0 \to 1 \to 2 \to \ldots \to t_0 - 1 \to t_0 + 1 \to \ldots \to 5 \to 1 \to \ldots$ (" " " " ")

Thus $\{\text{shift}^i(t_0), 0 \leq i \leq 4\} = \{1,\ldots,5\}$. Formal listing of the algorithm JSES is given in Section 7. See also Remark 5.1.

At this point we give the idea behind this algorithm in a nut-shell: The ceiling on the blocks controls the cost $m(L)$ to be $2\varphi(w)+1$ (2 Log N for full table), this ceiling is chosen just so that success (termination) is highly probable. The shift backward controls effectively the average cost $a(L)$.

4. PERFORMANCE OF THE ALGORITHM

LEMMA 1. (a) The expected number of look-up positions needed to insert Nw keys is $Nw\varphi(w)$. The expected number per block is about N .

(b) $\text{Prob}\{\frac{3}{2} Nw\varphi(w)$ look-up positions do not suffice for insertion of Nw keys$\} = O(N^{-\frac{1}{2}})$, $N \to \infty$.

(c) Prob{the algorithm JSES fails} $= O(N^{-\frac{1}{2}})$, $N \to \infty$.

REMARK 4.1. Replace $w\varphi(w)$ by Log N (natural logarithm) for full tables ($w = 1$). If the ceiling of the ps in JSES is increased to $C\varphi(w_j) = Cj$ in block j , then the tail estimates are $O(N^{1-3/4\,C})$.

PROOF. Looking up M positions on the ps in order to find Nw table locations is precisely like purchasing M items in order to collect Nw coupons in the classical coupon-collector problem [5,6,11], for which the expected value of M in (a), and the tail estimates in (b), are standard facts.

The algorithm fails to load a table if upon trying to insert a new key, say the Nw one, it exhausts all possible displacements obtained by shifting within the fixed range of the first five ps positions, and if it could not find, among the looked up positions, enough empty locations to accomodate all Nw keys. This means:

(i) There is a set K of keys and a set L of $|K|-1$ locations which form a reference cycle in the sense that the first 5 positions in $ps(k)$, $k \in K$, cover precisely L (L is the set of locations of K minus one key at the time Failure is detected) and

(ii) The $|K| \cdot 2\varphi(w)$ looked up positions do not supply Nw locations.

Now if $|K| \geq \frac{3}{4} Nw$ then by (b) the event in (ii) has probability $O(n^{-\frac{1}{2}})$. Technically we could add a termination when we reach $|K| = \frac{3}{4} Nw$. If $|K| < \frac{3}{4} Nw$, then

$$\text{Prob}\{\text{event in (i)}\} \leq \sum_{t \leq (3/4)N} \binom{N}{t}^2 \left(\frac{t}{N}\right)^{5t} . \quad (*)$$

The terms in the sum decrease with t , the largest terms, for small t , are $O(N^{-3t})$.

If t is at least, say, 3, the whole sum is $O(N^{-8})$.

REMARK 4.2. If we restrict the shift in JSES to the first 3 proble positions, we have to replace 5 by 3 in (*) above, the sum is still $O(N^{-2})$, so all the statements of the lemma remain true.

REMARK 4.3. FAILURE of the algorithm JSES in an event in the space of all problem instances. It is important to emphasize that FAILURE has nothing to do with a "failure" to find a key in a successfully constructed hash table. A key k to be retrieved from an w-loaded table is <u>absent</u> if it is not located up to ps-position $2\varphi(w)$ (or $2 \text{ Log } N$ for full table).

REMARK 4.4. In practice JSES does not fail. In theory, one can pass to another table-construction method in the event of failure. A theoretically satisfying solution is to repeat JSES (or the block where failure occurred) with extended look-up range $3\varphi(w)$, $4\varphi(w)$, ... , N . This will be called the extended JSES. Failure probabilities with look-up range $C\varphi(w)$ is already $O(n^{1-3/4\,C})$,while max cost rises slowly, being $C\varphi(w)$. Expectations, of $a(t)$ say, taken over the whole space differ negligibly from expectations conditioned by the event {JSES succeeds}.

THEOREM 1. <u>The hash tables</u> L <u>constructed by the extended</u> JSES <u>algorithm have the following retrieval cost performance</u>:

1. $\text{Prob}\{m(L) \geq \frac{2}{w} \text{ Log } \frac{1}{1-w}\} = O(N^{-\frac{1}{2}})$ <u>for</u> w-<u>loaded tables</u>,
2. $\text{Prob}\{m(L) \geq 2 \text{ Log } N\} = O(N^{-\frac{1}{2}})$ <u>for full tables</u>,
3. $\text{Prob}\{a(L) \geq 5.5\} = O(N^{-\frac{1}{2}})$,
4. $\text{Exp } a(L) \leq 5.5$.
5. <u>If we restrict the shift in</u> JSES <u>to</u> 3 <u>probe positions</u>, <u>statements</u> 3 <u>and</u> 4 <u>are valid for</u> 4.1 <u>instead of</u> 5.5.

PROOF. The results follow from Lemma 1 and the remarks following it. The inequalities in 1 and 2 are violated only if the original JSES fails and we have to use extension. For 3, we note that the look-up ceiling is > 5 only for block $k \geq 3$. Thus at most 6% of the elements can be inserted beyond position 5 in their ps . Their contribution to $a(L)$ is at most

$$\sum_{k \geq 3} (2k+1)(w_{k+1} - w_k) = 7(1-w_3) + 2\,\frac{1-w_4}{w_4} \approx .44 \quad . \quad (*)$$

Thus

$$\text{EXP}(a(L) \,|\, L \text{ is constructed by JSES}) \leq 5.5$$

and as noted above, the same value will be good for $\text{EXP}(a(L))$.

If we restrict the shift to 3 ps, then we saw in Remark 4.2 that the lemma about termination remains true. The bound we obtain on the average is $3 + .44$ (from (*)) +

the contribution of the two half block $k = 2, 2.5$, which place the incoming keys at position 4 and 5 at most (see Remark 5.1 below). The last addition is .65 so the bound is 4.1.

5. REALISTIC ESTIMATES OF EXPECTED PERFORMANCE

Extensive experiments for $N = 500$ up to $N = 20.000$ show that about $N/3$ keys are displaced (move) in each block, and that the average $a(L)$ for wN rises slowly up to about 2.1 for $w \to 1$ (full table). To account with precision for this behavior, we need some working assumption about the shifting and displacement process, or else derive cruder estimates rigorously (like 4.1 for $a(L)$ we already obtained).

For block 1, up to $w_2 = .79N$, we used just one position look-up, and analysis of this block follows the lines of [2,1], to obtain expected positioning of the keys in their ps by the end of the block.

REMARK 5.1. It is useful to divide block 2 into two half-blocks (indexed 2 and 2.5), running from .79 to .89 with ceiling = 4, and from .89 to .94 with ceiling = 5. Separate analysis is needed for them, and actually also for blocks 3 and 4, along the lines described below for a typical late block $k \geq 5$.

Let D be the set of locations loaded by the end of block 2, $|D| = .89N = n$. Let S = complement of D. All the looked-up positions of keys loaded in D also belong to D, most of these keys looked up to position 3, and many up to position 4 in their ps. So the locations in D appear again and again in displacements in later blocks, whereas a location $\ell \in S$ is probably introduced after some key settles in ℓ in some block $k > 2$. The analysis of movements of keys in a block will be done for the dynamic part D. Contribution of the static part S to $a(L)$ will be estimated separately.

<u>Analysis of a block</u>. Let

dn = EXP(number of keys moving in a block)
$d_i n$ = EXP(" " " " i times in a block)
$f_j n$ = EXP(number of keys in position of their ps at the start of a block)
$f'_j n$ = EXP(" " " " " " " " " " end " " ") .

We neglect $\sum_{i \geq 5} d_i$ — it is highly improbable that the same key move 5 times in a block. Then we can write

$$f' = f \cdot B \quad , \quad B = (b_{ij}) \quad , \quad f = (f_1, \ldots, f_5) \quad , \quad f' = (f'_1, \ldots, f'_5) \quad .$$

Here $b_{ij} n$ is the expected number of keys starting at position i and winding up in position j of their ps. Each b_{ij} is a linear expression in d_i, $0 \leq i \leq 4$. The <u>balance</u> transformation given by B has a fixed point f^*. If the initial f, by the end of block 2, is sufficiently close to f^*, successive blocks will push f

toward f^* , the limiting (expected) distribution of positions, and $a^* = \sum_{j=1}^{5} jf_j$ is the expected average on D .

The values of d and d_i will determine B , f^* and a^* . Which values to take? We assume that the table location of the next displaced key is a random choice out of D , independent of the past and of the event {k is in position j} . This is obviously true for a first displacement in a chain, caused by a new incoming key. For the following displacements the shift $t \to t'$ is defined solely in terms of positions of the displacing key k and the location $ps(k)_{t'}$ seems completely random.

Knowing d , we can now compute d_i using the coupon-collector model. For $d = .4$, $d_0 = .6$ and

$(d_1,d_2,d_3,d_4) = .4*(.767,.195,.033,.005)$

$\sum id_i = .511$ (total number of moves)

$f^* = (.44,.38,.16,.02,.002)$, $a^* = 1.77$,

$f^{(2)} = (.48,.33,.13,.06\ ,-)$, $a^{(2)} = 1.77$,

$f^{(2)}$ is the initial vector for the balance equation, by the end of block 2. It is very close to f^* , and $a^{(2)}$ happens to coincide with a^* . This means that the average on the dynamic part D is practically unchanged, and the increase of the average as $w \to 1$ is due to the contribution of the static part S . This contribution is computed separately for some early blocks and the result is summarized in the following table:

blocks	1 and 2	≤2	≤2	3	≤3	4	≤4	5+6	≤6
percent	89	5	94	4	98	1.3	99.3	.6	99.9
aver. position	1.77	3.2	1.85	5	1.98	7	2.04	10	2.07

The experiments match this table almost perfectly.

Calculating the value of d . In each block $dn = .89dN$ keys move in order to compile an N new look-up position (Lemma 1). The residual look-up is at least 2 for each key. From this we already have $d \leq .55$. With $d = .55$ the resulting value of a^* (on D) is about 2, and a(L) is about 2.3. Let

$r = \text{Prob}\{k \text{ moves in block } j+1 \mid k \text{ moves in block } j\}$. (*)

The true value of a depends on r , which measures the movement dependence between successive blocks. If $r < 1$, then in block j many keys with residual look-up > 2 move (the average residual look-up is $j+1$). For late blocks, where displacement chains are long, there is indeed a strong dependence but a simple estimate (which we omit here) shows that $r = .8$ and then $d < .4$.

Expected number of steps in loading. The toal number of displacements in a block has expectation of about .5N , so $.5N\varphi(w)$ for w-loaded table, and .5N Log N for full table. The expected number of look-ups is N per block, a total of $N\varphi(w)$ if we keep track of how far each element looked-up. If we simply look-up any key all the way in each block, we have $\frac{1}{2} N\varphi^2(w)$ or $\frac{1}{2}$ N Log^2N for full tables, which fits the experimental data.

6. CONCLUSION

We presented and analyzed an on-line algorithm for constructing open hash tables with high load factor, even full. The most serious objection to open hashing technique is that retrieval may sometimes be very costly, especially for absent keys. Our algorithm resolves this difficulty completely for the first time. The maximal cost for retrieval of all keys is $O(\mathrm{Log}\,\frac{1}{1-w})$ for w-loaded tables, O(Log N) for full tables of size N. The average cost has a universal bound, around 4, and its expected value is about 2, the same as in [1], however compared to [1], the effort invested in constructing the table is much smaller, about $N\,\mathrm{Log}^2\,\frac{1}{1-w}$ operations. Extensive experimental results are in very good agreement with the theoretical predictions. The algorithm can be used to construct efficient solutions to the assignment problem [8,10,3] with average and max cost.

7. FORMAL PRESENTATION OF THE ALGORITHM

Part 1 of the algorithm

```
MAIN PROGRAM
BEGIN
  TABLE(I,I=1,N)=0
  LIMIT=N*0.79
  FOR I=1,LIMIT
  BEGIN
    GET(KEY)
    COST=1
    NEXTADR=PROBE(KEY;COST)
    NEXTKEY=TABLE(NEXTADR)
    UNTIL NEXTKEY=0 DO
    BEGIN
      NEXTC=COST(NEXTADR)
      CHOOSE(KEY;COST;NEXTKEY;NEXTC)
      COST=COST+1
      NEXTADR=PROBE(KEY;COST)
      NEXTKEY=TABLE(NEXTADR)
    END
    TABLE(NEXTADR)=KEY
    COST(NEXTADR)=COST
  END
END
```

```
SUBROUTINE CHOOSE(KEY  ;COST1;KEY2;COST2)
BEGIN
  IF COST1>COST2 AND COST2<=4 THEN
    EXCH(KEY1;KEY2)  , EXCH(COST1;COST2)
  IF COST1>=4 THEN
  BEGIN
    NEXTADR:=PROBE(KEY1,1)
    EXCH(KEY1,TABLE(NEXTADR))
    EXCH(COST1,COST(NEXTADR))
  END ELSE
  BEGIN
    NEXTADR1=PROBE(KEY1;COST1+1)
    NEXTADR2=PROBE(KEY2;COST2+1)
    IF TABLE(NEXTADR1)>0 THEN
    IF TABLE(NEXTADR2)=0 AND COST2<4 THEN
    BEGIN
      EXCH(KEY1;KEY2),EXCH(COST1;COST2)
    END
    ADR=PROBE(KEY2;COST2)
    TABLE(ADR)=KEY2,COST(ADR)=COST2
  END
END
```

Subroutines

1) exch(a,b)   : exchanges the values of a and b
2) get(key)   : generates a random key
3) probe(key,cost): calculates position "cost" of key in its probesequence. In our simulations : probe(K,cost)=mod{[K+(cost-1)*mod(K,N-1)],N}+1
4) choose(key1,cost1,key2,cost2)
   - input : key1 hashes to position cost1 in its probesequence.The correspondent location is occupied by key2,in its cost2 probe position.
   - action: choose determines which one of the 2 keys continues the search and inserts the other one in the location fought for.
   - output: key1=the key to continue the search
     cost1= its position in its probe-sequence.

Part 2 of the algorithm

```
MAIN PROGRAM
 BEGIN
  DO K=2,LN(N)
  LIM=2K+1
  wK=BETA(K)
  BIT(I;I=1,N)=0
  FOR I=Nwk,Nw(k+1)
  BEGIN
    GET (KEY)
    COST=0 ,  BIT=0
    UNTIL KEY=0 DO
    BEGIN
      LOOKUP(KEY,COST,BIT,LIMIT,NEXTADR)
      EXCH(KEY,TABLE(NEXTADR))
      EXCH(COST,COST(NEXTADR))
      EXCH(BIT,BIT(NEXTADR))
    END
  END
END
```

```
SUBROUTINE  LOOKUP(KEY;COST;BIT;LIMIT;ADR)
 BEGIN
   IF BIT=0 THEN
   BEGIN
     FOR I=COST+1,LIMIT DO
     BEGIN
       NEXTADR=PROBE(KEY,I)
       NEXTKEY=TABLE(NEXTADR)
       IF NEXTKEY=0 THEN
       BEGIN
          COST=I
          RETURN
       END
     END
     BIT=COST
     COST=1
   END
   ELSE COST=COST+1
   IF COST=BIT THEN COST=COST+1
   IF COST>MIN(5,LIMIT) THEN
   BEGIN COST=1 , BIT=-1 END
   NEXTADR=PROBE(KEY,COST)
 END
```

Subroutines

1) lookup(K1,cost1,bit,limit,adr):

input: K1 was displaced by some key from its cost1 probe position,and is to check its probe sequence up to position limit . Bit is the initial position of K1 before the current block was started,or -1 if K1 reached position 5 of it's ps (i.e. was moved 4 times).

action: lookup checks K1's probe-positions from cost1 to limit; then determines the location K1 is to occupy,and memorizes the initial position of K1 before the current block was started.

output: cost1=the new position K1 is to occupy in its probesequence.

8. EXPERIMENTAL RESULTS

To carry out our simulations we chose the method of double hashing. This means choosing the table size ,N, to be prime and making the primary hash location the key (binary number represented by the bit pattern of the key) modulo N.Subsequent locations are determined by repeatedly adding (modulo N) the key (modulo N-1)+1.

We present first the results of the simulation of Gonnet and Munro's algorithm, and the results of our algorithm at the loadfactors used in Gonnet's and Munro's simulations. Then we present the results of our algorithm at the loadfactors which correspond to the block-structure of our algorithm.

	GONNET AND MUNRO SAMPLESIZE: 250 TABLESIZE: 997		JSES SAMPLESIZE: 100 TABLESIZE: 997	
OCCUP	AVER. ACCESS	AVER. STEPN.	AVER. ACCESS	AVER. STEPN.
80% = 798	1.579	2563.1	1.668+- 0.039	1674.4
90% = 897	1.751	4206.3	1.779+- 0.034	2503.6
95% = 947	1.880	6365.1	1.875+- 0.035	3504
99% = 987	2.050	14250.	2.013+- 0.035	6083.3
100% = 997	2.135	31587.	2.088+- 0.088	13166.6

The following table shows the results of our algorithm on tables of size 997 and 499 , at the loadfactors which correspond to the block-structure of our algorithm.

	TABLESIZE : 499 SAMPLESIZE: 150			TABLESIZE : 997 SAMPLESIZE: 100		
OCCUP	OCCUP	AVER.ACCESS	AV.STEPN.	OCCUP	AVER.ACCESS	AV.STEPN.
79%	394	1.660+- 0.051	809.2	788	1.662+- 0.039	1623.8
89%	444	1.768+- 0.49	1195.2	887	1.768+- 0.032	2394.1
94%	469	1.854+- 0.048	1617.5	937	1.855+- 0.034	3267.5
98%	489	1.983+- 0.053	2367.2	977	1.983+- 0.037	4887.7
99.3 %	496	2.05 +- 0.058	3332.86	990	2.036+- 0.037	6767.2
99.7 %	498	2.074+- 0.063	4324.3	994	2.052+- 0.039	8612.9
99.9 %	-	-	-	996	2.066+- 0.042	10755.9
100 %	499	2.095+- 0.078	5341.3	997	2.088+- 0.088	13166.6

The following table shows the results of our algorithm on tables of size 4999 , 10567 and 19997 at the loadfactors which correspond to the block-structure of our algorithm.

		TABLESIZE :4999 SAMPLESIZE: 50		TABLESIZE :10567 SAMPLESIZE:50			TABLESIZE :19997 SAMPLESIZE:20		
OCCUP	OCCUP	AVER.ACCESS	AV.STEPN.	OCCUP	AVER.ACCESS	AV.STEPN.	OCCUP	AVER.ACCESS	AV.STEPN.
79%	3949	1.664+-0.02	8145.	8348	1.662+-0.012	17196.	15798	1.663+-0.01	32555.
89%	4449	1.769+-0.01	12037.	9405	1.770+-0.01	25336.	17797	1.767+-0.009	47965.
94%	4699	1.859+-0.01	16533.	9933	1.856+-0.009	34558.	18797	1.856+-0.007	65423.
98%	4899	1.987+-0.01	24781.	10356	1.987+-0.012	51892.	19597	1.986+-0.009	98678.
99.3 %	4964	2.039+-0.01	34591.	10493	2.041+-0.013	73035.	19857	2.041+-0.012	40084.
99.7 %	4984	2.053+-0.01	45068.	10535	2.053+-0.011	95168.	19937	2.051+-0.009	81875.
99.9 %	4994	2.082+-0.03	59974.	10556	2.076+-0.018	25623.	19977	2.076+-0.017	42214.
99.97%	4998	2.095+-0.03	77899.	10564	2.089+-0.032	63325.	19991	2.088+-0.018	18334.
99.99%	-	-	-	10566	2.087+-0.030	98051.	19995	2.084+-0.028	95194.
100 %	4999	2.092+-0.05	91628.	10567	2.096+-0.066	31567.	19997	2.113+-0.097	90106 .

The following table presents the values of Pi for the above simulations.The same results were obtained for all simulations.(Pi = ratio of keys in position i).

	Loadfactor of the table							
	0.79	0.89	0.94	0.98	0.993	0.997	0.999	1
P1	50	48	46	43	42	42	41	41
P2	36	33	33	33	34	34	35	34
P3	12	13	13	13	13	13	13	14
>P3	2	6	8	11	11	11	12	11

REFERENCES

1. Gonnet, G., and Munro, I. Efficient ordering of hash tables. SIAM S. Comput. 8, 3, 1979, pp. 463-478.
2. Brent, R.P. Reducing the retrieval time of scatter storage technique. Comm. ACM 16, 2, 1973, pp. 105-109.
3. Rivest, R.L. Optimal arrangement of keys in a hash table. JACM 25, 2, 1978, pp. 200-209.
4. Guibas, L.J., and Szemeredi, E. The analysis of double hashing. J. Comput. System Sci. 16, 1978, pp. 226-274.
5. Knuth, D.E. Mariage stable. Les presses de l'Universite de Montreal, Quebec, Canada, 1976.
6. Kolchin, V.F., Sevast'yanov, B.A., and Chistyakov, V.P. Random Allocations, V.H. Winston & Sons, Washington, D.C., 1978.
7. Ajtai, M., Komlos, J., and Szemeredi, E. There is no fast single hashing algorithm. Information Processing Letters 7, 6, 1978.
8. Donath, W.E. Algorithm and average-value bounds for assignment problems. IBM J. Res. Develo., 1969, pp. 380-386.
9. Tarjan, R.E. and Yau, A.C.C. Storing a sparse table. Comm. ACM 22, 11, 1979, pp. 606-611.
10. Walkup, D. On the expected value of a random assignment problem. SIAM J. Comput. 8, 3, 1979, pp. 440-442.
11. Feller, W. An Introduction to Probability Theory and its Application. Vol. 1, 2nd Ed., Wiley, New York, 1951.
12. Knuth, D.E. The Art of Computer Programming, Vol. III, Sorting and Searching. Addison-Wesley, Don Mills, 1973.
13. Gonnet, G.H. Interpolation and Interpolation Hash Searching. University of Waterloo, Computer Science Dept. Research Report 77-02.
14. Knuth, D.E. Computer science and its relation to mathematics. Am. Math. Monthly 8, 1974, pp. 323-343.

ON THE POWER OF COMMUTATIVITY IN CRYPTOGRAPHY

Adi Shamir*
Department of Mathematics
Massachusetts Institute of Technology
Cambridge, Massachusetts 02139 U.S.A.

and

Department of Mathematics
The Weizmann Institute of Science
Rehovot, Israel

ABSTRACT

Every field needs some unifying ideas which are applicable to a wide variety of situations. In cryptography, the notion of commutativity seems to play such a role. This paper surveys its potential applications, such as the generation of common keys, challenge-and-response identification, signature generation and verification, key-less communication and remote game playing.

1. INTRODUCTION

The science of cryptography can be subdivided into subareas in many ways, but the one I find most useful distinguishes between the analysis of the security of cryptographic functions and the analysis of the applications of these cryptographic functions. The two subareas are fairly independent, since one can usually combine any strong cryptographic function with any novel cryptographic application (under a few compatibility constraints) to get concrete implementations.

Historically, the first subarea dominated the field since the only application of strong cryptographic functions used to be secret communication, but in the last few years most of the exciting new ideas (such as digital signatures, public-key cryptography, or login authentication via one-way functions) have been in the second subarea.

The long range goal of any kind of cryptographic research is to change the status of the field from a heuristic art into an exact science. However, the mathematical analysis of the security of cryptographic functions seems to be an extremely difficult challenge. The two approaches tried so far are information theory and complexity theory, but each one of them has serious deficiencies.

*This research was supported by the Office of Naval Research under contract no. N00014-76-C-0366.

Information theory (developed by Claude Shannon [1948]) has been an active research area for the last three decades, and its main cryptographically related consequences are fairly well understood. Its ideas, methods and results are ideally suited to simple pencil-and-paper cryptosystems (e.g., monoalphabetic substitutions or one-time-pads), and the main question they answer is whether the cryptanalyst can in principle recover the original cleartext from a given piece of cyphertext.

However, in practice the important distinction is not between the doable and the undoable, but between the easy and the difficult. With the advent of cypher machines and computers, a new breed of cryptographic functions has emerged. Typically, these functions encrypt by performing a long sequence of operations whose aggregate effect is extremely difficult to analyse (e.g., mixtures of substitutions and permutations or repeated shifts with nonlinear feedbacks). All these functions are breakable in Shannon's idealized model once the cryptanalyst obtains enough cyphertext, but from the practical point of view their security is well established.

Complexity theory, on the other hand, seems to be more relevant to modern day cryptography but less well understood. It attempts to quantify and analyse the inherent difficulty of computational tasks, and cryptography is one of its most natural applications. Its most powerful tool at this stage is the notion of NP-completeness, but even if we assume that $P \neq NP$ we cannot claim that cryptographic functions based on NP-complete problems are secure (see Shamir [1979] and Even and Yacobi [1980]). In fact, the area of cryptocomplexity currently lacks a sound theoretical basis, and we cannot use it in order to prove the security of any practical cryptographic function.

The second subarea (applications and protocols) seems to be in a much better shape. Here we can assume the existence of strong cryptographic functions, and proceed to analyse what can be done with them and how they should be used. Most of the problems in this direction are technical rather than conceptual. The field lends itself to a precise axiomatic treatment, but it lacks a formal language in which assumptions can be expressed, applications can be specified, and security can be proved. One of the goals of this paper is to introduce a simple notational system which can be the basis for such a formal "security logic".

To be a mature science, cryptography must identify a set of fundamental principles which give it structure and uniformity. The literature on cryptographic applications is full of clever ideas and elegant techniques, but most of them are ad-hoc solutions to unrelated problems with very few unifying ideas. Among the few exceptions is the notion of commutativity, which seems to be useful in a wide variety of applications.

Commutativity simply means that the order in which the various parties encrypt or decrypt messages does not affect the final computed value. To understand why it is such a powerful notion, we have to remember that in cryptography the cooperation between parties is severely restricted by the existence of the eavesdropper. Each party can operate freely within its own premises, but any information transfer over the insecure communication channel must be protected by heavy cryptographic shields. A commutative set of encryption functions enables the two parties to proceed independently (with a minimum of information transfer) along two different paths in the commutative diagram, and yet converge at the end towards the same value.

The main purpose of this paper is to survey in a systematic way the potential applications of commutativity in cryptography. In Section 2 we define our model and describe the commutative family of encryption functions based on modular exponentiation. In Sections 3, 4, and 5 we consider three different types of commutative diagrams, and explore their potential uses. The last section summarizes the paper and poses some open problems.

2. THE MODEL

The purpose of this Section is to develop a simple cryptographic environment that can support a wide variety of applications. The emphasis is on simplicity and uniformity rather than on generality, and thus some of the following assumptions may be unnecessarily strong for certain applications.

ASSUMPTION 1: The cleartexts, the cyphertexts and the keys are atomic objects taken from a common universe U. This uniformity enables us to use messages as keys or to iterate the application of encryption functions, and the indivisibility of the objects eliminates the conceptual difficulties posed by partial cryptanalysis of the cleartext or key bits.

ASSUMPTION 2: For each key $y \in U$, the encryption function f_y is a permutation on U, and thus has an inverse decryption function f_y^{-1} which satisfies:

for all $x, y \in U$, $f_y^{-1}(f_y(x)) = f_y(f_y^{-1}(x)) = x$.

ASSUMPTION 3: Any two permutations in this family commute:

for all $x, y, z \in U$, $f_y(f_z(x)) = f_z(f_y(x))$.

The users of these cryptographic functions are denoted by a, b, c,... . In communication applications, we refer to a as the sender, to b as the receiver, and to c as the cryptanalyst. In more symmetrical applications we refer to a and b as the legitimate users and to c as the intruder. Unless we specify otherwise, we assume that c is an active eavesdropper -- he can read, alter or jam messages between a and b and he can inject his own messages into the communication channel.

In our axiomatic approach, we recognize only two types of computations -- those which are everywhere easy and those which are everywhere difficult. By eliminating the gray area between the two levels, we can bypass many of the problems of complexity theory and yet capture the essential features of cryptographic systems.

Easy computations are denoted by $T_1 \underset{S}{\rightarrow} T_2$, where T_1 and T_2 are sets of terms and S is a set of users. The semantics of this notation is that any one of the users in S can easily compute any term in T_2 if he knows all the terms in T_1. If T_1 and T_2 contain variables, they are assumed to be universally quantified. The dual notation for difficult computations is $T_1 \underset{S}{\twoheadrightarrow} T_2$, and it means that none of the terms in T_2 can be computed by members of S if all they know are the terms in T_1 (note, however, that additional knowledge can make a difficult computation easy). Pure knowledge can be represented by arrows with an empty left-hand side, since a value can be computed from scratch if it is already known. Since variables are meaningless in this context, we use letters from the middle of the alphabet (k,l,m,...) to represent fixed (but randomly chosen) elements in U which are known to the various users.

<u>EXAMPLE:</u> We illustrate the arrow notation by axiomatizing a simple secret communication system:

(i)	$x,y \underset{a,b,c}{\longrightarrow} f_y(x)$	(any one who knows the key can encrypt)
(ii)	$x,f_y(x) \underset{a,b,c}{\longrightarrow} x$	(any one knows the key can decrypt)
(iii)	$f_y(x) \underset{a,b,c}{\twoheadrightarrow} x$	(the cleartext cannot be extracted from the cyphertext)
(iv)	$x_1,f_y(x_1),\ldots,x_i,f_y(x_i) \underset{a,b,c}{\twoheadrightarrow} y$	(the key cannot be extracted from a collection of cleartext/cyphertext pairs)
(v)	$\underset{a,b}{\longrightarrow} k$	(the sender and the receiver know a common key)
(vi)	$\underset{a}{\longrightarrow} m_1,\ldots,m_j$	(the sender knows all the cleartexts)

(vii) $\underset{c}{\twoheadrightarrow} k, m_j$ (the eavesdropper does not know the key or the last cleartext)

Note that the first j-1 cleartexts are not explicitly mentioned in (vii), and thus in the worst case scenario the cryptanalyst knows them. Similarly, any computation which is not declared difficult may be easy. One of the most important goals of formal proofs of security is to identify the minimal set of complexity axioms that can carry them through. In our example, we have made enough assumptions in order to infer that if a sends $f_k(m_1),\ldots,f_k(m_j)$ to b and c intercepts them, then b knows $m_1,\ldots,m_j$ but c still does not know m_j. To prove the security of this scheme against active intruders, further assumptions (or better protocols) are needed. □

The only example of cryptographically strong commutative family of encryption functions discovered so far is based on modular exponentiation. Let n be a fixed natural number, and let U be the set of integers in [0,n). For each x and y in U we define

$$f_y(x) = x^y \pmod{n} \quad .$$

These functions are permutations over U whenver n is square-free and y is relatively prime to $\phi(n)$ (see Blakley and Blakley [1978]), and thus a careful choice of n can make f_y a permutation for almost all the odd values of y. Whenever f_y is a permutation, its inverse is equal to f_z for some key $z \in U$ (i.e., this subfamily of permutations is closed under inversion). The commutativity property follows directly from the definition.

Two kinds of cryptanalytic attacks can be mounted against these functions- the extraction of x from n, y and $x^y \pmod{n}$ (the root problem), and the extraction of y from n, x and $x^y \pmod{n}$ (the log problem). The complexity of these problems is still an active research area, but the state of the art is:

(i) For large values of n, efficient algorithms for the root problem exist only when all the factors of n are known (see RSA [1978]).

(ii) For large values of n, efficient algorithms for the log problem exist only when all the factors of $\phi(n)$ are known and small (see Pohlig and Hellman, [1978]).

(iii) Large values of n can be factored only in specialized cases (e.g., when all the factors of n are small). (See Knuth [1969] for a survey of factoring algorithms).

By choosing an appropriate modulus n and by controlling the dissemination of information about its factorization, we can support with these functions the wide variety of applications described in the rest of this paper.

3. THE FIRST COMMUTATIVE DIAGRAM

The simplest application of commutativity in cryptography uses the natural commutativity of functions and their inverses:

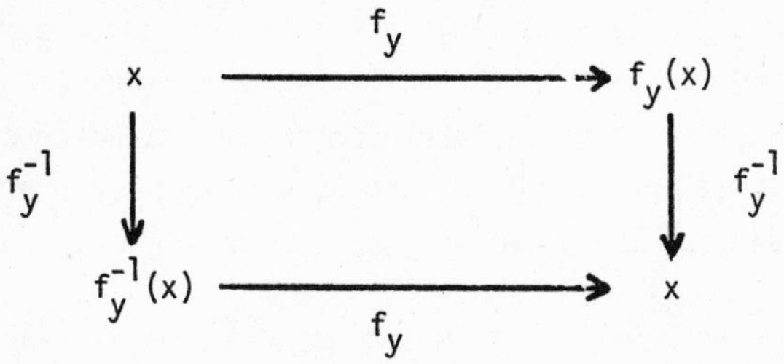

FIGURE 1

Assuming that f_y and f_y^{-1} are easy to compute if and only if the key y is known, we can use either path from x to x in Figure 1 as the encrypt/transmit/decrypt sequence of operations in a secret communication system.

Diffie and Hellman [1976] were the first to observe that by eliminating the symmetry between the complexities of f_y and f_y^{-1}, exciting new types of cryptographic systems can be obtained. The revised set of assumptions is:

(i) $\xrightarrow[a,b,c]{} k$

(ii) $x,y \xrightarrow[a,b,c]{} f_y(x)$

(iii) $x,y \xrightarrow[b]{} f_y^{-1}(x)$

(iv) $x,y \underset{a,c}{\twoheadrightarrow} f_y^{-1}(x)$.

Under this axiomatization, the two paths in Figure 1 are not equivalent -- any one can proceed along the horizontal f_k arrows, but only b can proceed along the vertical f_k^{-1} arrows. Rivest, Shamir and Adleman [1978] have shown that these assumptions can be satisfied by the modular exponentiation function if b generates n as the product of large randomly chosen primes which he keeps secret.

The upper-right path from x to x in Figure 1 represents a public-key cryptosystem. To encrypt a cleartext m, a uses b's publicly available key k to compute $f_k(m)$, and sends this cyphertext to b (who is the only one capable of decrypting it). This scheme is particularly useful in large communication networks, since it eliminates the need for secrecy in key exchange protocols and reduces the number of keys per user to 1.

The lower-left path from x to x in Figure 1 represents a signature generation/verification scheme. To sign a cleartext m, b computes $f_k^{-1}(m)$. To verify b's signature on m, a applies the publicly known function f_k to $f_k^{-1}(m)$ and compares the result with m. This signature cannot be forged or attached to a different cleartext even by its recipient a, and thus it can replace hand-written signatures in banking, business, and legal applications.

Both applications are completely secure against passive eavesdroppers, but they can be compromised by active eavesdroppers who pretend to be b during the key distribution phase. It is clear that without knowing anything about b, a cannot possibly distinguish between b and c, and thus any solution must assume the existence of some piece of information whose authenticity is guaranteed. Under this assumption, safe key distribution protocols can be easily constructed (see, e.g., Needham and Schroeder [1978]).

4. THE SECOND COMMUTATIVE DIAGRAM

The second commutative diagram we consider is based on the commutativity of arbitrary pairs of functions in our model:

$$\begin{array}{ccc} x & \xrightarrow{\;f_y\;} & f_y(x) \\ {\scriptstyle f_z}\downarrow & & \downarrow{\scriptstyle f_z} \\ f_z(x) & \xrightarrow[\;f_y\;]{} & f_z(f_y(x)) = f_y(f_z(x)) \end{array} .$$

FIGURE 2

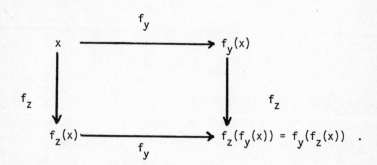

This diagram can support the following applications:

4.1 Public-key distribution system (Diffie and Hellman [1976]):

A public-key distribution system enables pairs of users to generate common secret values (which can be later used as keys for other applications) by communicating over the insecure communication channel. The assumptions for this application are:

(i) $\xrightarrow[a,b,c]{} s, f_k(s), f_l(s)$

(ii) $\xrightarrow[a]{} k, \qquad \twoheadrightarrow_{b,c} k$

(iii) $\xrightarrow[b]{} l, \qquad \twoheadrightarrow_{a,c} l$

(iv) $x,y \xrightarrow[a,b,c]{} f_y(x)$

(v) $x, f_y(x) \twoheadrightarrow_{a,b,c} y$

Here we assume that three points (a seed and two encrypted forms of the seed) in the commutative diagram are publicly known, but only a can proceed along the horizontal arrows and only b can proceed along the vertical arrows. If c cannot extract the keys from the cleartext/cyphertext pairs, he cannot compute the fourth point in the commutative diagram, but both a and b can converge on the common value $f_k(f_l(s)) = f_l(f_k(s))$.

The modular exponentiation function can support this application with prime or composite values of n, since f_k and f_l should be protected against extraction of the key rather than against inversion.

4.2 Identification via challenge-and-response

In this application, user b wants to verify the authenticity of user a by asking him to perform a task that no one else can perform. The task cannot be fixed since the eavesdropper c can record and replay a's response, but on the other hand the tasks cannot be completely unrelated since b cannot store a large table of a's potential answers. Commutativity can solve this problem in the following way:

(i) $\xrightarrow[a,b,c]{} s, f_k(s)$

(ii) $\xrightarrow[a]{} k, \quad \twoheadrightarrow_{b,c} k$

(iii) $x, f_y(x) \twoheadrightarrow_{a,b,c} y$

(iv) $x, y \xrightarrow[a,b,c]{} f_y(x)$.

In this case everyone has one authentic $(s, f_k(s))$ pair generated by a, but only a can apply f_k to arbitrary arguments. To challenge a, b chooses a random key l, computes $f_l(s)$, and asks a to apply f_k to it. The result is easily verifiable since b can compare it with $f_l(f_k(s))$, but it cannot be produced by c unless he knows k or l. Note that this is not a signature scheme, since b himself can compute a's expected response to a challenge, and thus cannot use it as evidence in court. This application can be supported by the same modular exponentiation functions as the previous application.

4.3 Another signature scheme

To get a message-dependent signature, we use the message itself as one of the keys in our commutative diagram. The assumptions we make are:

(i) $\xrightarrow[a,b,c]{} k, f_k(s)$

(ii) $\xrightarrow[a]{} s, \quad \twoheadrightarrow_{b,c} s$

(iii) $x, y \xrightarrow[a,b,c]{} f_y(x)$

(iv) $y_1, f_{y_1}(x), \cdots, y_i, f_{y_i}(x) \twoheadrightarrow_{b,c} x$.

To sign a message m, a applies f_m to his secret seed s and sends m and $f_m(s)$ to b. The receiver now has two encrypted versions of s, and thus he can close the commutative diagram by applying f_m to the published value $f_k(s)$ and f_k to the signature $f_m(s)$. The signature is verified if the two computed values are indeed the same. If b or c want to forge a's signature on m, they have to find an element whose f_k is equal to the known value of $f_m(f_k(s))$, but assumption (iv) implies that this inversion of f_k is difficult.

This scheme is an excellent example of the potential subtlety of formal proofs of security. If we replace assumption (iv) by

$$\text{(iv)}' \quad y, f_y(x) \underset{b,c}{\twoheadrightarrow} x,$$

we get an axiomatic system which is satisfied by the modular exponentiation functions. However, it is easy to show that these functions have a curious property which leads to a totally insecure implementation of our scheme:

Lemma: If k and m are two relatively prime numbers, then c can easily compute s from a's signature on m in an implementation based on modular exponentiation.

Proof: If k and m are relatively prime, c can easily compute two integers d and e such that

$$dk + em = 1.$$

By raising the published value to the d-th power, the signature to the e-th power, and by multiplying the results mod n, c can compute:

$$(s^k)^d \cdot (s^m)^e = s^{dk+em} = s \pmod n \quad . \qquad \text{Q.E.D.}$$

Once c finds s, he can forge a's signature on any message. To protect against such a disaster, we have to replace (iv)' by the stronger assumption (iv), but at present we do not have any example of a commutative family of functions that satisfy it.

5. THE THIRD COMMUTATIVE DIAGRAM

The first commutative diagram did not use the commutativity of f_y and f_z, while the second commutative diagram did not use their invertibility. By combining the two assumptions, we get the third commutative diagram:

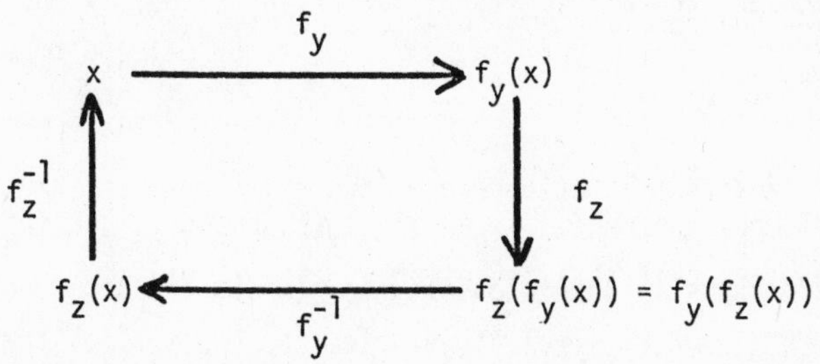

FIGURE 3

Shamir, Rivest and Adleman [1979] describe an interesting key-less communication scheme which can be based on this diagram. Its complexity assumptions are completely symmetrical with respect to a, b and c:

(i) $x,y \xrightarrow[a,b,c]{} f_y(x)$

(ii) $y,f_y(x) \xrightarrow[a,b,c]{} x$

(iii) $x,f_y(x) \xrightarrow[a,b,c]{} y$.

To encrypt a message m, a picks a random key k, and sends $f_k(m)$ to b. The receiver also picks a random key l, and returns the doubly encrypted cyphertext $f_l(f_k(m))$ to a. Due to the commutativity of f_k and f_l, a can compute $f_l(m)$ by applying f_k^{-1}, and send it back to b who computes m by applying f_l^{-1}.

Michael Rabin has suggested a nice mechanical analog for this scheme in which encryption corresponds to the addition of a padlock to a box with clasp rings, and decryption corresponds to its removal. By adding padlock k, adding padlock l, removing padlock k and removing padlock l, m can be physically transmitted from a to b in such a way that it is always protected by at least one padlock.

This scheme is secure against passive eavesdroppers, but without additional information about b, a cannot distinguish between b and an active eavesdropper c. In other words, user a can communicate with someone in complete privacy, but he cannot know for sure who this someone is! If active eavesdropping is a threat, an authentication procedure should be added to the protocol.

Modular exponentiation functions can be used in this application whenever the factorization of n is universally known (e.g., when n is a prime) since both a and b can then invert their encryption functions. The cryptographic security of the scheme depends on the difficulty of extracting either k or l from cleartext/cyphertext pairs, and this computation seems to be difficult even when the factorization of n is known.

This key-less communication scheme can solve a number of seemingly unsolvable cryptographic problems. One of them (described in Shamir, Rivest and Adleman [1979]) involves two mutually suspicious parties (which are not assumed to be honest) who want to play mental poker. The main problem is how to deal the imaginary cards in a fair way by communicating over a telephone line. More specifically, we want a and b to get five cards each from a deck of 52 cards without the assistance of a trusted third party so that:

(i) Each party knows its five cards
(ii) Each party knows nothing about the opponent's five cards
(iii) The two hands are guaranteed to be disjoint
(iv) All the possible hands are equally likely
(v) Cheating can be detected.

To achieve these seemingly contradictory goals, user a chooses a random key k and encrypts the 52 card names "two of clubs", ..., "ace of spades" under f_k. The 52 scrambled names are sent to b in a randomly permuted order, so that b cannot tell which cleartext corresponds to which cyphertext. Five of the cyphertexts are chosen at random by b and returned to a, who can decrypt them and read his hand. Five other cyphertexts are re-encrypted by b under a randomly chosen key l, sent back to a for decryption of f_k, and returned to b for final decryption of f_l. The remaining 42 cards are not disclosed by b unless further cards are requested.

This protocol clearly satisfies conditions (i) and (ii), since each party has access only to the cleartexts of its own hand. Condition (iii) is satisfied by the fact that only one party (b) chooses all the cards. Condition (iv) may not be satisfied if a permutes or b chooses the cyphertexts under a non-uniform probability distribution, but any consistently skewed behaviour can only help the opponent adapt his own moves in order to improve his hand, and thus cannot be a logical strategy. Finally, condition (v) is satisfied if a and b reveal k and l at the end of the game (but before the payoffs!) and check the legality of the opponent's moves.

The mental poker application can be supported by the moduluar exponentiation functions, but it demonstrates an interesting behaviour with respect to partial cryptanalysis. Dick Lipton has pointed out to us that modular exponentiation functions which are permutations preserve the quadratic residue/non-residue status of their argument. Since the 52 card names are known in advance and about half of them are of each type, each party can compare their status with the status of the encrypted version of the opponent's five cards in order to gain approximately five bits of information about their real identity. To fix this problem, user a has to equalize the status of all the card names before encryption by slightly augmenting some of them.

6. SUMMARY

This paper demonstrates that almost any way of looking at commutative diagrams is likely to be cryptographically useful. The examples surveyed here may be just the tip of the iceberg, with many more applications (possibly based on more complicated diagrams) waiting to be discovered.

The emphasis in this paper is on the role of commutativity in the subarea of applications, but this notion seems to be useful even in proofs of cryptographic strength. For example, it is possible to prove that for certain types of pseudo-random sequence generators based on commutative functions, even complete knowledge of n-1 of the n sequence elements does not make the computation of the remaining element any easier (see Shamir [1980]).

Another interesting research area which was only briefly alluded to is the information-theoretic aspect of the various applications (i.e., what the cryptanalyst could know if his computational resources were unbounded). For example, Shamir, Rivest and Adleman [1979] prove that in this model it is impossible to play mental poker, and Lempel and Ziv use the same proof technique to show that any key-less communication scheme is inherently unambiguous.

The cryptocomplexity of the modular exponentiation functions is still an open research problem. In this paper we have mentioned a number of minor cryptographic weaknesses (like the invariance of quadratic residues and the possible extraction of cleartexts from pairs of cyphertexts) but it is not clear whether this is an exhaustive list. The complexities of the root problem and the log problem should also be looked at very carefully.

One of the most important open problems in this area is whether there are other commutative families of cryptographic functions. The modular exponentiation functions are extremely versatile but they are too slow for many real-time applications and thus the discovery of a faster family can have a major impact on the field.

ACKNOWLEDGEMENTS

I would like to thank Ron Rivest, Len Adleman, Michael Rabin and Avraham Lempel for many fruitful discussions.

BIBLIOGRAPHY

1. B. Blakley and G. Blakely [1978], "Security of Number Theoretic Public-Key Cryptosystems Against Random Attack", Cryptologia, October 1978.

2. W. Diffie and M. Hellman [1976], "New Directions in Cryptography", IEEE Trans. Info. Theory, November 1976.

3. S. Even and Y. Yacobi [1980], "Cryptocomplexity and NP-Completeness", Seventh ICALP, July 1980.

4. D. Knuth [1969], The Art of Computer Programming, Vol 2, Addison-Wesley, 1969.

5. S. Pohlig and M. Hellman [1978], "An Improved Algorithm for Computing Logarithms Over GF(P) and Its Cryptographic Significance", IEEE Trans. Info. Theory, January 1978.

6. R. Rivest, A. Shamir and L. Adleman [1978], "A Method for Obtaining Digital Signatures and Public-Key Cryptosystems", CACM, February 1978.

7. A. Shamir [1979], "On the Cryptocomplexity of Knapsack Systems", Proc. Eleventh ACM Symposium on the Theory of Computing, May 1979.

8. A. Shamir [1980], "A Pseudo-Random Sequence Generator Whose Cryptocomplexity is Provably Equivalent to that of the RSA", in preparation.

9. A. Shamir, R. Rivest and L. Adleman [1979], "Mental Poker", MIT/LCS/TM-125, February 1979.

10. C. Shannon [1948], "The Mathematical Theory of Communication", Bell System Technical Journal, July and October 1948.

CHARACTERIZATIONS OF THE LL(k) PROPERTY

(Extended Abstract)

Seppo Sippu
Department of Computer Science
University of Helsinki
Tukholmankatu 2
SF-00250 Helsinki 25, Finland

and

Eljas Soisalon-Soininen†
Department of Mathematics
University of California at Santa Barbara
Santa Barbara, Ca. 93106/USA

Abstract. Characterizations of the LL(k) property for context-free grammars are given, which lead to efficient algorithms for testing an arbitrary context-free grammar for the LL(k) property. The characterizations are based on succinct nondeterministic representations of a finite-state automaton used for constructing a canonical LL(k) parser. The resulting testing algorithms are usually of the same order to time complexity as their LR(k) counterparts. For example, one characterization (the LR(k) counterpart of which has been used by Hunt, Szymanski and Ullman for obtaining the fastest known algorithm for LR(k) testing) implies an $O(n^{k+2})$ algorithm for LL(k) testing, where n is the size of the grammar in question and k is considered to be a fixed integer. This time bound for LL(k) testing has previously only been obtained indirectly, by a linear time-bounded reduction of LL(k) testing to LR(k) testing. Moreover, it is shown that the LL(k) property allows an especially convenient characterization, one which allows an $O(n^{k+1})$ algorithm for LL(k) testing. This new time bound suggests that the LL(k) property might be strictly easier to test than the LR(k) property.

---

† On leave from the University of Helsinki as an ASLA Fulbright Research Scholar. The work of this author was additionally supported by the National Science Foundation under Grant No. MCS77-11360.

1. INTRODUCTION

The construction of LR(k) parsers is usually based on the well-known canonical LR(k) parser construction technique involving the "canonical collection" of sets of valid LR(k) items (e.g., [1]). The canonical collection is a deterministic finite-state automaton accepting the viable prefixes of the grammar, i.e., the grammar strings corresponding to the contents of the stack of an LR(k) parser. The parser construction technique also provides an automata-theoretic characterization of the LR(k) property and, accordingly, an algorithm for testing an arbitrary context-free grammar for the LR(k) property. The time as well as space complexity of this algorithm is, however, exponential with respect to the size (i.e., the sum of the lengths of productions) of the grammar in question because exponential space is required even to store the whole canonical collection.

It is possible to obtain, for each fixed integer k, a polynomial time-bounded algorithm for LR(k) testing by using a characterization of the LR(k) property based on an essentially more succinct representation of the canonical collection, one requiring only polynomial space. One such representation is the nondeterministic version of the canonical collection, in which the states are single LR(k) items rather than sets of LR(k) items. The size (i.e., the number of states and transitions) of this nondeterministic automaton is only $O(|G|^{2k+2})$, where $|G|$ is the size of the grammar G in question and k is considered to be a fixed integer. Moreover, the automaton can be constructed in $O(|G|^{2k+2})$ steps. Testing the automaton for possible LR(k) conflicts is somewhat more difficult than in the deterministic case, because the pairs of conflicting LR(k) items are now split into different states. Therefore, all pairs of states mutually accessible by some viable prefix must be determined. This can be performed in time proportional to the square of the size of the automaton by using the algorithm presented by Hunt, Szymanski and Ullman in [4]. The whole LR(k) test can therefore be carried out in $O(|G|^{4k+4})$ steps.

The fastest known algorithm for LR(k) testing, presented by Hunt, Szymanski and Ullman in [5], has been obtained by using an even more succinct representation for the canonical collection. This representation consists of <u>several</u> nondeterministic finite-state automata of size $O(|G|)$ instead of a single nondeterministic automaton of size $O(|G|^{2k+2})$. There is one automaton, denoted by M(G,u), in the representation for each terminal string u of length k or less. The number of different automata M(G,u) is thus bounded by $|G|^k$. Each automaton M(G,u) characterizes the LR(k) property for the particular lookahead string u, and is, accordingly, only tested for LR(k) conflicts caused by u. Since each M(G,u) can be tested for conflicts in time proportional to the square of its size, i.e., in $(|G|^2)$ steps, the whole LR(k) test can be carried out in $O(|G|^{k+2})$ steps.

As pointed out in [5], the time bound $O(|G|^{k+2})$ for testing a grammar G for the inclusion in the class of LR(k) grammars carries over to LL(k) grammars as well as to many other parameterized classes of grammars, since it has been shown that a grammar G can in $O(|G|)$ steps be transformed into a grammar G_T such that the original grammar G is LL(k) if and only if the transformed grammar G_T is LR(k). (This fact was first observed by Brosgol [2]; also see [6].) Thus any algorithm for LR(k) testing automatically implies an algorithm for LL(k) testing with time complexity of the same order. In fact, no means for efficient LL(k) testing other than this <u>indirect</u> method based on the linear time-bounded reduction to LR(k) testing has been proposed. <u>Direct</u> testing algorithms have so far only been designed for special cases such as the class of strong LL(k) grammars [1,4,7]. In particular, no better time bound for general LL(k) testing than the best bound $O(|G|^{k+2})$ for LR(k) testing has been established yet.

In the present paper we develop characterizations of the LL(k) property which can be considered as <u>duals</u> of those characterizations of the LR(k) property based on succinct representations of the canonical collection. This is made possible by a recently presented technique for constructing canonical LL(k) parsers, which is a dual of that for constructing canonical LR(k) parsers [8]. The counterpart of the canonical collection of sets of valid LR(k) items is called the canonical collection of sets of valid LL(k) items, and it has representations similar to those of its LR(k) counterpart. The resulting dual characterizations of the LL(k) property yield <u>direct</u> algorithms for LL(k) testing, the time complexities of which are, as might be expected, of the same order as those for LR(k) testing. For example, the representation of the canonical collection of sets of valid LL(k) items as a single nondeterministic finite-state automaton yields an $O(|G|^{4k+4})$ algorithm for testing a grammar G for the LL(k) property.

The representation involving $|G|^k$ nondeterministic finite-state automata of size $O(|G|)$ in turn yields an $O(|G|^{k+2})$ algorithm for LL(k) testing (see Section 2). It can be argued that this algorithm in itself is more efficient in practice than that obtained through the reduction to LR(k) testing, even though the asymptotic time bound remains the same. Moreover, it suggests how the time bound for LL(k) testing might be sharpened. Namely, it turns out that the underlying representation of the canonical collection can be modified so that the time-consuming task of determining the pairs of mutually accessible states in each automaton becomes unnecessary. This means that each of the automata of size $O(|G|)$ can be tested for LL(k) conflicts in $O(|G|)$ steps instead of $O(|G|^2)$ steps. Thus, an $O(|G|^{k+1})$ algorithm for LL(k) testing is obtained (see Section 3).

The existence of the modified representation allowing the LL(k) property to be tested in $O(|G|^{k+1})$ steps originates from the greater simplicity of the grammatical characterization of the LL(k) property over that of the LR(k) property. Our automata-theoretic characterizations of the LL(k) property and the resulting direct testing algorithms faithfully preserve the nature of this original grammatical characterization. Notice that in an indirect LL(k) testing algorithm obtained through the LR(k) test, all traces of the original characterization of the LL(k) property are destroyed. The corresponding modified representation in the LR(k) case does not, on the contrary, yield any better time bound for LR(k) testing. This suggests that the LL(k) property is essentially easier to test than the LR(k) property.

2. A CHARACTERIZATION YIELDING AN $O(|G|^{k+2})$ TEST

We make free use of the notation and definitions given in [1] concerning strings and (context-free) grammars. We recall the convention that (1) A, B, and C denote nonterminals, (2) a, b, and c denote terminals, (3) X, Y, and Z denote either nonterminals or terminals, (4) terminal strings are represented by u, v, ..., z, whereas general strings are represented by $\alpha, \beta, \ldots, \omega$, and (5) the empty string is denoted by ε. As usual, we assume that every nonterminal can be used in the derivation of some terminal string.

We now present a succinct representation of the canonical collection of sets of valid LL(k) items [8] for a grammar G by at most $|G|^k$ nondeterministic finite-state automata of size $O(|G|)$. This representation implies characterizations of the strong LL(k) and general LL(k) properties which allow the strong LL(k) property to be tested in $O(|G|^{k+1})$ steps and the general LL(k) property in $O(|G|^{k+2})$ steps. We begin with definitions which are analogous to those given in [5].

Let $G = (N,\Sigma,P,S)$ be a grammar, $G' = (N \cup \{S'\}, \Sigma \cup \{\$\}, P \cup \{S' \to S\$\}, S')$ the \$-augmented grammar for G and u a terminal string of G'. If α is a general string then we denote by $L_u(\alpha)$ the set of all suffixes z of u such that z is a prefix of some terminal string derivable from α. A pair $[A \to \alpha.\beta, z]$ is an LL(u) item of G if $A \to \alpha\beta$ is a production of G' and z is a suffix of u. For convenience, we also call a pair [A,z] an LL(u) item of G if A is a nonterminal of G' and z is a suffix of u. A general string γ is a viable suffix of G if there exists a terminal string x, a production $A \to \alpha\beta$ of G' and a general string η such that

$$(1) \qquad S' \underset{lm}{\Rightarrow}^* xA\eta \underset{lm}{\Rightarrow} x\alpha\beta\eta = x\alpha\gamma^R$$

holds in G'. (Here γ^R denotes the reversal of γ defined by $\varepsilon^R = \varepsilon$ and $(\beta X)^R = X\beta^R$ where β is a general string of G' and X is a nonterminal or terminal of G'.) In particular, a viable suffix γ is said to be complete if (1) holds for $\alpha = \varepsilon$. An LL(u) item of the form $[A \to \alpha.\beta, z]$ is valid for a viable suffix γ if z is in $L_u(\gamma^R)$ and (1) holds for some x and η. An LL(u) item of the form [A,z] is valid for γ if z is in $L_u(\gamma^R)$ and $S' \underset{lm}{\Rightarrow}^* xA\gamma^R$ holds in G' for some terminal string x. (Notice that an LL(u) item of the form $[A \to \omega., z]$ is valid for γ if and only if [A,z] is valid for γ.)

Instead of a nondeterministic finite-state automaton which accepts all viable prefixes which can be followed by a terminal string u [5], we construct for the terminal string u an automaton which accepts all complete viable suffixes γ for which u is in $L_u(\gamma^R)$. Formally, we define $M_u(G)$ to be the nondeterministic finite-state automaton $(Q_u, N \cup \Sigma \cup \{\$\}, \delta_u, [S',\varepsilon], F_u)$ where the set Q_u of states consists of all LL(u) items of G, the set F_u of final states consists of all LL(u) items of the form $[A \to .\omega, u]$, and the transition function δ_u is defined by the conditions

(a) $\delta_u([A,z], \varepsilon) = \{[A \to \omega., z] \mid A \to \omega$ is a production of $G'\}$,
(b) $\delta_u([A \to \alpha X.\beta, z], X) = \{[A \to \alpha.X\beta, v] \mid v$ is in $L_u(Xz)\}$,
(c) $\delta_u([A \to \alpha B.\beta, z], \varepsilon) = \{[B,z]\}$.

Notice that, unlike in the LR(k) case, the dot is first placed after the string ω in the type (a) transitions and is then moved to the left in the type (b) transitions. Moreover, the lookahead string z in the type (b) transitions is changed to v, whereas in the type (c) transitions the lookahead string z is left unchanged.

A reader who is familiar with the work of Hunt, Szymanski and Ullman [5] may notice that our definition for the automaton $M_u(G)$ is not completely analogous to the definition of the corresponding automaton $M(G,u)$ of [5], because in $M(G,u)$ the transitions are, without loss of generality, restricted such that the lookahead string z is always monotonically nondecreasing. (This property of $M(G,u)$ is used in [5] for obtaining certain nondeterministic time bounds.) We have, however, resorted to the definition given here because it is more concise and because the construction to be presented in Section 3 (which is, after all, the actual contribution of the present paper) does not depend on which of the two alternative approaches is used.

We shall prove that $M_u(G)$ can be constructed in $O(|G|)$ steps. For this purpose we need the following lemma.

Lemma 2.1. For every grammar $G = (N,\Sigma,P,S)$ there exists a grammar $G_T = (N_T,\Sigma,P_T,S_T)$ of size $O(|G|)$ such that the following three conditions are satisfied.

(1) G_T is in Chomsky normal form (e.g., [3]) except that it may contain productions of the form $A \to B$, where B is in N_T.

(2) G_T is loop-free, i.e., no nonterminal in N_T can nontrivially derive itself.

(3) For each nonterminal A in N there are nonterminals A' and A'' in N_T such that A' generates exactly the nonempty sentences in the language $L(A)$ and A'' generates exactly the nonempty prefixes of the sentences in $L(A)$.

Moreover, G_T can be constructed from G in $O(|G|)$ steps.

In what follows it will be most important that the transformed grammar G_T of Lemma 2.1 is only of size $O(|G|)$. Therefore, we have not required G_T to be in true Chomsky normal form because the elimination of chain productions may result in a grammar of size $O(|G|^2)$ [3].

Lemma 2.2. $M_u(G)$ can be constructed in $O((|u|+1)^3|G|)$ steps.

Proof. First, the number of type (a) and (c) transitions in $M_u(G)$ is clearly $O((|u|+1)|G|)$ and they can be constructed in $O((|u|+1)|G|)$ steps. (Notice the role of $LL(u)$ items of the form $[A,z]$ in obtaining these space and time bounds.) The number of type (b) transitions is $O((|u|+1)^2|G|)$ and their construction involves the computation of the sets $L_u(Xz)$. This can be done efficiently by applying a modified version of the general Cocke-Kasami-Younger recognition algorithm (e.g., [3]) to the transformed grammar G_T of Lemma 2.1. Recall that the original Cocke-Kasami-Younger algorithm, when applied to a string $u =$

$a_1 \ldots a_k$ computes a $k \times k$ matrix t such that an entry t_{ij} contains exactly those nonterminals that can derive the substring $a_i \ldots a_j$. The underlying grammar is required to be in Chomsky normal form. However, the algorithm can be modified to work also for such grammars as G_T by topologically sorting the list of possible chain productions of G_T with respect to the partial order induced by the chain productions on the set of nonterminals of G_T. (Recall that G_T is loop free.) The modified algorithm computes an entry t_{ij} in the recognition matrix by first initializing it by the original algorithm and then adding zero or more nonterminals to it by a single traversal of the topologically sorted list of chain productions. It is clear that the order of the complexity of the modified algorithm remains the same, i.e., $O(|u|^3|G_T|)$. By the construction of G_T and t, an entry t_{ij} contains a nonterminal A' of G_T if and only if the nonterminal A of G can derive $a_i \ldots a_j$, and a nonterminal A'' of G_T if and only if $a_i \ldots a_j$ is a prefix of some terminal string derivable from A. This makes it then trivial to compute the collection of sets $L_u(Xz)$. We can thus conclude that $M_u(G)$ can be constructed in $O((|u|+1)^2|G| + |u|^3|G_T|)$ steps, which is $O((|u|+1)^3|G|)$, since $|G_T|$ is $O(|G|)$. □

The next lemma states that the set of states in $M_u(G)$ reachable from the initial state $[S',\varepsilon]$ upon reading a viable suffix γ equals the set of those $LL(u)$ items which are valid for γ. The lemma corresponds to Lemma 2.3 in [5].

<u>Lemma 2.3</u>. If γ is a viable suffix of G and q is a valid $LL(u)$ item for γ, then q is a state in $\delta_u([S',\varepsilon], \gamma)$. Conversely, if γ is a general string and q is a state in $\delta_u([S',\varepsilon], \gamma)$, then γ is a viable suffix of G and q is a valid $LL(u)$ item for γ.

Lemma 2.3 implies in particular that the strings accepted by $M_u(G)$ are exactly those complete viable suffixes γ for which u is in $L_u(\gamma^R)$. It is easy to see that a grammar G is <u>not</u> strong $LL(k)$ if and only if there exist viable suffixes $\beta_1 A$ and $\beta_2 A$ of G, two productions $A \to \omega_1$ and $A \to \omega_2$ of G' and a string u in $FIRST_k(\Sigma^*\$)$ such that u is both in $L_u(\omega_1\beta_1^R)$ and in $L_u(\omega_2\beta_2^R)$. (Notice the role of \$ in the "if" part of this statement.) Thus we get by Lemma 2.3 the following characterization of the strong $LL(k)$ property.

<u>Theorem 2.4</u>. A grammar G is not strong $LL(k)$ if and only if there exists a string u in $FIRST_k(\Sigma^*\$)$ and accessible final states $[A \to .\omega_1, u]$ and $[A \to .\omega_2, u]$ in $M_u(G)$ such that $\omega_1 \neq \omega_2$.

We can now prove that the strong $LL(k)$ property can be tested in $O(|G|^{k+1})$ steps. The same time bound appears (without proof) in [4].

Theorem 2.5. A grammar G can be tested for the strong LL(k) property in $O((k+1)^3|G|^{k+1})$ steps.

Proof. First, construct G_T from G in $O(|G|)$ steps. Then for each string u in $FIRST_k(\Sigma^*\$)$ construct $M_u(G)$ and test it for the property stated in Theorem 2.4. For each u this test takes $O((|u|+1)^2|G|)$ steps since the accessible states in $M_u(G)$ can certainly be determined in time proportional to the size of $M_u(G)$. Since, by Lemma 2.2, eacn $M_u(G)$ can be constructed in $O((|u|+1)^3|G|)$ steps, and there are at most $|G|^k$ different strings u in $FIRST_k(\Sigma^*\$)$, we conclude that the whole test for the strong LL(k) property can be performed in $O((k+1)^3|G|^{k+1})$ steps. □

As an example, consider the grammar G_1 with productions $S \to AB$, $A \to \varepsilon \mid a$, and $B \to ab \mid bc$. The automaton $M_{ab}(G_1)$ is presented in Figure 1. Clearly, G_1 is not a strong LL(2) grammar since there are accessible final states $[A \to .a, ab]$ and $[A \to ., ab]$ in $M_{ab}(G_1)$. Of these the former is accessible by the viable suffix \$Ba and the latter by the viable suffix \$B. In this case there even are states [A,b] and [A,ab] both accessible by <u>the same</u> viable suffix \$B such that $[A \to .a, ab]$ is a final state in $\delta_{ab}([A,b], a^R)$ and $[A \to .,ab]$ is a final state in $\delta_{ab}([A,ab], \varepsilon^R)$. In fact, this means that G_1 does not even possess the general LL(2) property. Indeed, it is not hard to see that a grammar G is a non-LL(k) grammar if and only if there exists a viable suffix βA of G, two productions $A \to \omega_1$ and $A \to \omega_2$ of G' and a string u in $FIRST_k(\Sigma^*\$)$ such that u is both in $L_u(\omega_1\beta^R)$ and in $L_u(\omega_2\beta^R)$. By Lemma 2.3 we then get the following characterization of the general LL(k) property. The theorem corresponds to Lemma 2.6 in [5].

Theorem 2.6. A grammar G is a non-LL(k) grammar if and only if there exists a string u in $FIRST_k(\Sigma^*\$)$, (not necessarily distinct) states $[A,z_1]$ and $[A,z_2]$ in $M_u(G)$ mutually accessible by some viable suffix β, a final state $[A \to .\omega_1, u]$ in $\delta_u([A,z_1], \omega_1^R)$ and a final state $[A \to .\omega_2, u]$ in $\delta_u([A,z_2], \omega_2^R)$ such that $\omega_1 \neq \omega_2$.

The following theorem states that the general LL(k) property can be tested in $O(|G|^{k+2})$ steps. The theorem corresponds to part (b) of Theorem 2.9 in [5].

Theorem 2.7. A grammar G can be tested for the LL(k) property in $O((k+1)^3|G|^{k+2})$ steps.

Proof. The proof is similar to that of the strong LL(k) test given in Theorem 2.5. The increase in the time bound by a factor of $|G|$ is due

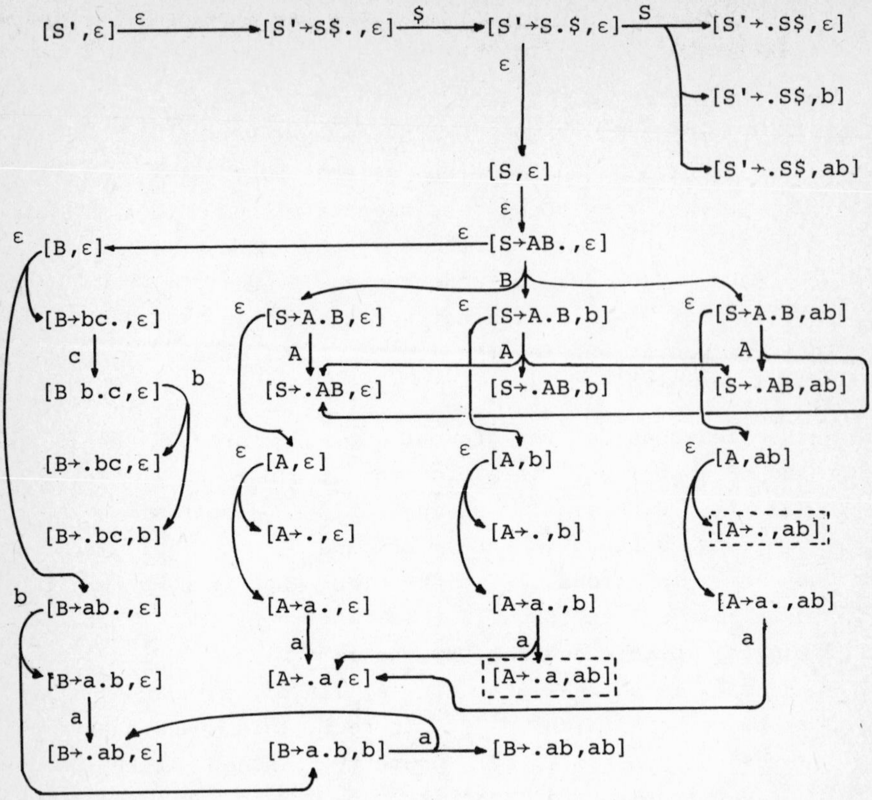

Figure 1. The automaton $M_{ab}(G_1)$ for the grammar G_1 with productions $S \to AB$, $A \to \varepsilon \mid a$, and $B \to ab \mid bc$. (Only the accessible states are visible.)

to the necessity of determining all those pairs of states $[A,z_1]$ and $[A,z_2]$ in $M_u(G)$ which are mutually accessible by some viable suffix. Using a similar reasoning as in the proof of Lemma 2.8 in [5], it can be shown that this takes at most $O((|u|+1)^3|G|^2)$ steps. The set of states of the form $[A\to\omega.,z]$ in $M_u(G)$ for which $\delta_u([A \to \omega.,z], \omega^R)$ contains the final state $[A \to .\omega, u]$ in turn can be determined in time proportional to the size of $M_u(G)$. This makes it then easy to find the pairs of conflicting states in $M_u(G)$. We therefore conclude that the whole $LL(k)$ test can be carried out in $O((k+1)^3|G|^{k+2})$ steps. □

3. A CHARACTERIZATION YIELDING AN $O(|G|^{k+1})$ TEST

In the previous section we showed that an arbitrary context-free grammar G can be tested for the $LL(k)$ property in time $O((k+1)^3|G|^{k+2})$. The result itself is not new; it has already been established by Hunt, Szymanski and Ullman [5]. In the present section we develop further our method of direct $LL(k)$ testing and show that the above time bound can in fact be sharpened by a factor of $|G|$ by eliminating the necessity of finding the mutually accessible pairs of states in the automata $M_u(G)$. The fact that this elimination is possible in the case of $LL(k)$ testing (but not, we feel, in the case of $LR(k)$ testing) reflects the simplicity of the $LL(k)$ property over the $LR(k)$ property. The desired effect is achieved by removing nondeterminism from $M_u(G)$ in the case of non-ε-transitions. The cost of this modification is an increase in the size of $M_u(G)$ by a constant factor depending exponentially on k.

The states of the modified automaton $M'_u(G)$ will be <u>sets</u> of $LL(u)$ items of the forms $\{[A \to \alpha.\beta, z] \mid z \in W\}$ and $\{[A,z] \mid z \in W\}$ where $A \to \alpha\beta$ is a production of the \$-augmented grammar G' for G and W is a set of suffixes of u. We abbreviate these sets to $[A \to \alpha.\beta, W]$ and $[A,W]$, respectively. The concept of validity of $LL(u)$ items is extended to these sets of $LL(u)$ items as follows. An $LL(u)$ item set $[A \to \alpha.\beta, W]$ is <u>valid</u> for a viable suffix γ of G if $W = L_u(\gamma^R)$ and there exists a terminal string x and a general string η such that

$$S' \underset{lm}{\Rightarrow}^* xA\eta \underset{lm}{\Rightarrow} x\alpha\beta\eta = x\alpha\gamma^R$$

holds in G'. An $LL(u)$ item set $[A,W]$ is <u>valid</u> for γ if $W = L_u(\gamma^R)$ and $S' \underset{lm}{\Rightarrow}^* xA\gamma^R$ holds in G' for some terminal string x.

We then define $M'_u(G)$ to be the nondeterministic finite-state automaton $(Q'_u, N \cup \Sigma \cup \{\$\}, \delta'_u, [S',\{\varepsilon\}], F'_u)$ where the set Q'_u of states consists of all $LL(u)$ item sets of the forms $[A \to \alpha.\beta, W]$ and $[A,W]$, the set F'_u of final states consists of all states of the form $[A \to .\omega, W]$ where u is in W, and the transition function δ'_u is defined by the following conditions:

(a) $\delta'_u([A,W], \varepsilon) = \{[A \to \omega., W] \mid A \to \omega$ is a production of $G'\}$,
(b) $\delta'_u([A \to \alpha X.\beta, W], X) = \{[A \to \alpha.X\beta, L_u(XW)]\}$,
(c) $\delta'_u([A \to \alpha B.\beta, W], \varepsilon) = \{[B,W]\}$.

Here $L_u(XW)$ means the union of all sets $L_u(Xz)$ where z is in W.

Corresponding to Lemma 2.2 and Lemma 2.3 we have the following lemmas.

Lemma 3.1. $M'_u(G)$ can be constructed in $O(|u|^3 \cdot 2^{|u|+1} \cdot |G|)$ steps.

Proof. The proof is similar to that of Lemma 2.2. Notice that the size of $M'_u(G)$ is $O(2^{|u|+1} \cdot |G|)$. □

Lemma 3.2. If γ is a viable suffix of G and q is a valid LL(u) item set for γ, then q is a state in $\delta'_u([S', \{\varepsilon\}], \gamma)$. Conversely, if γ is a general string and q is a state in $\delta'_u([S', \{\varepsilon\}], \gamma)$, then γ is a viable suffix of G and q is a valid LL(u) item set for γ.

Using Lemma 3.2 we can prove the following characterization of the general LL(k) property.

Theorem 3.3. A grammar G is a non-LL(k) grammar if and only if there exists a string u in $\text{FIRST}_k(\Sigma^*\$)$, an accessible state [A,W] in $M'_u(G)$, a final state $[A \to .\omega_1, W_1]$ in $\delta'_u([A,W], \omega_1^R)$ and a final state $[A \to .\omega_2, W_2]$ in $\delta'_u([A,W], \omega_2^R)$ such that $\omega_1 \neq \omega_2$.

Notice that according to Theorem 3.3 the "origin" of an LL(k) conflict can always be traced back to a single state of the form [A,W]. This is a natural consequence of the fact that in the grammatical characterization of the LL(k) property (e.g., [1]) there is a single left sentential form with respect to which the nonterminal A in question is tested for possible conflicting alternatives. The lookahead set W in [A,W] contains exactly the legal followers of A in this single left sentential form (which are suffixes of u).

We are now ready to state the main result of the present paper.

Theorem 3.4. A grammar G can be tested for the LL(k) property in $O(k^3 \cdot 2^{k+1} \cdot |G|^{k+1})$ steps.

Proof. The reasoning is similar to that presented in the proof of Theorem 2.7 except that we only need to determine, for each u, the set of accessible states in $M'_u(G)$ and the set of states $[A \to \omega., W]$ in $M'_u(G)$ for which $\delta'_u([A \to \omega., W], \omega^R)$ contains a final state of the form $[A \to .\omega, W']$. This can certainly be performed in time proportional to the size of $M'_u(G)$. □

The automaton $M'_{ab}(G_1)$ for our example grammar G_1 is presented in Figure 2. Notice that the conflicting states $[A \to .a, \{\varepsilon,ab\}]$ and $[A \to ., \{\varepsilon,b,ab\}]$ are both reachable (by a^R and ε^R, respectively) from the same accessible state $[A, \{\varepsilon,b,ab\}]$.

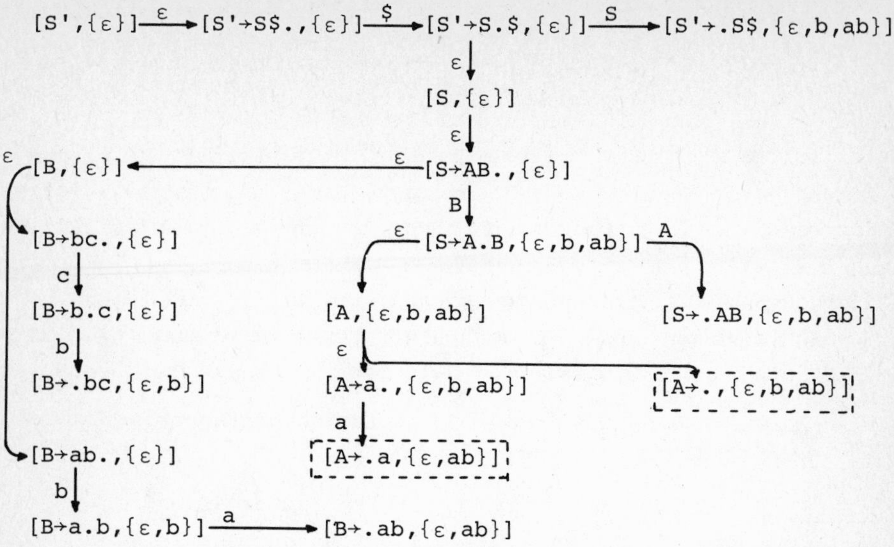

Figure 2. The automaton $M'_{ab}(G_1)$ for the grammar G_1 with productions $S \to AB$, $A \to \varepsilon \mid a$, and $B \to ab \mid bc$. (Only the accessible states are visible.)

REFERENCES

1. Aho, A.V., and J.D. Ullman, The Theory of Parsing, Translation and Compiling. Vol. 1: Parsing. Prentice-Hall, 1972.
2. Brosgol, B.M., Deterministic Translation Grammars. TR 3-74, Center for Research in Computing Technology, Harvard University, 1974.
3. Harrison, M.A., Introduction to Formal Language Theory. Addison-Wesley, 1978.
4. Hunt, H.B., III, T.G. Szymanski and J.D. Ullman, Operations on sparse relations and efficient algorithms for grammar problems. IEEE 15th Annual Symposium on Switching and Automata Theory, 1974, 127-132.
5. Hunt, H.B., III, T.G. Szymanski and J.D. Ullman, On the complexity of LR(k) testing. Comm. ACM 18 (1975), 707-716.
6. Hunt, H.B., III, and T.G. Szymanski, Lower bounds and reductions between grammar problems. J. ACM 25 (1978), 32-51. (Corrigendum: J. ACM 25 (1978), 687-688.)
7. Johnson, D.B., and R. Sethi, Efficient Construction of LL(1) Parsers. Technical Report No. 164, Computer Science Department, The Pennsylvania State University, 1975.
8. Sippu, S., and E. Soisalon-Soininen, On constructing LL(k) parsers. Automata, Languages and Programming, Sixth Colloquium, Graz, July 1979 (H.A. Maurer, ed.). Springer-Verlag, 1979, 585-595.

COMPUTABILITY IN CATEGORIES

M.B. Smyth

Dept. of Computer Studies
University of Leeds
Leeds, England

-Extended Abstract-

O. INTRODUCTION

Questions of effectiveness have been considered in connexion with several of the special categories of domains studied in denotational semantics. Let us mention Tang [28] vis-a-vis Scott's "classical" category CL of continuous lattices [21],[22]; Egli and Constable [5] for the category ACPO of algebraic bounded-complete cpo's; Smyth [23] for the cateogry CCPO of continuous bounded-complete cpo's; Kanda [11] for Plotkin's SFP [19]. Each of these categories could lay some claim to being *the* category of interest in semantics. Recently, however, it has become clear that we cannot limit ourselves in advance to a small fixed set of categories of domains. Current work on parallelism, sequentiality and concrete domains, especially, gives rise to a proliferation of categories ([1], [4], [8]). Even apart from this proliferation, explicitly categorical constructions are playing an increasing role, especially in connexion with data types [6], [15]. The question arises, whether we can treat effectiveness itself in a categorical setting, so that the effectiveness of domains and functions can be defined in a uniform way, and - beyond that - the effectiveness of categorical notions themselves, especially that of a functor. In this paper we propose an affirmative answer, using (mainly) the notion of an *effectively given O-category*.

Why should we give so much attention to effectiveness? One reason has to do with the systematic study of the power of specification techniques. We cannot require of a general purpose programming language that it be able to specify (define) all number-theoretic functions, but only (at most) those which are partial recursive. A corresponding distinction must be made for all the "data types" which one may wish to handle. And the problem is not simply that of picking out the computable functions over a given data type; we have the problem of specifying the data types themselves, and thus of determining the "computable", or effectively given, data types (i.e. the types which should in principle be specifiable). For data types considered simply as sets with operations, the discussion has reached a fairly advanced state (see [29] and references there given). For data types with *domains* as carriers (with which we are concerned here), the problems are much more complex. Little is known about the completeness or adequacy of specification methods for these types.

The requirements that all semantic constructs be effective can be a useful discipline, both negatively (thus, the power-domain construction of [14] remains suspect, since we cannot see how to make it effective), and as a positive aid in finding suitable constructs (see the remarks on "finite elements" in Sec. 1).

As our final reason for insisting on effectiveness, let us just cite the connexion between computing and mathematical constructivism, argued by Bishop [2] and Constable [3], and recently asserted in a very strong form by Martin-Löf [17].

Some of the proofs missing from this extended abstract can be found in [27].

1. OVERVIEW

The guiding principle of our work is a very simple one: in every system (domain, category, etc.) with which we have to deal, there is a clearly identifiable subsystem of finite elements, whose properties completely determine the whole system. The infinite elements have as it were a secondary existence as limiting processes applied to the finite elements (more concretely, as rules for the production of finite elements), all their properties being derivative from those of the finite elements. One naturally defines a *computable* (infinite) element as one which is given as an effective limit of finite elements (relative to a suitable enumeration of the finite elements).

This concentration on the finite elements was the main factor in the simplification of the power-domain constructs [24], and has also been fruitful in developing the theory of concrete domains [10]. Its main application in the present work is the characterization of the computable arrows/objects of a category as limit of chains of "finite" arrows/objects. Unfortunately we lapse from our principle in regard to effective(ly given) categories and functors themselves: we do not here build them from chains of finite categories and functors. On this point, see the concluding remarks of the paper.

In Section 2 we introduce the class of "admissible" categories, which forms the frameowrk of our investigation. An admissible category is essentially an O-category in which the subcategory of embeddings is algebraic (in the terminology of [24]). Some important properties of admissible categories are proved. In Section 3 we define the notion of *effective basis* of an admissible category, and characterize the *effectively given* objects and arrows in a category with effective basis. We indicate that these abstractly defined notions reduce to the usual ones when we specialize to the particular concrete categories in which effectiveness has been studied previously (we verify it in detail only for the case of ACPO). In Section 4 we introduce "frames" of functors as a counterpart to graphs of functions, and in terms of them define *computable* functors. We show that, for suitable indexings of our categories, this notion of computability of functors agrees with Kanda's in [11]; this means that we can use Kanda's results to get "fully effective" solutions of domain equations. The concluding section treates some miscellaneous topics: O-categories versus ω-categories; effective versions of the adjoint functor theorem; continuous versus algebraic domains; and a possible refinement of the notion of an effectively given category that seems to be required if we are able to construct functor categories effectively.

We have just alluded to Kanda's work on effective categories. The relationship between our work and that of Kanda has been discussed in [26]. Briefly, Kanda is not concerned with developing a unified theory of computability; rather, he assumes that we have a countable category (thought of as a category of effective domains and computable functions), suitably indexed, already given to us. In terms of such indexed categories, the effectiveness of various categorial constructions (functors, initial fixpoints) can be handled straightforwardly. Our theory can be considered as an account of how the "suitably indexed" categories come about. The direct verification that given categories and functors are effective in Kanda's sense tends to be very complex; but, for categories/functors build up in the way we describe here, such verification is usually trivial.

2. ADMISSIBLE CATEGORIES

We begin with some definitions as in [30], [24], [26]:

DEFINITION 1. An O-*category* is a category in which (i) every hom-set is a partial order in which every ascending ω-chain has a lub, and (ii) composition of morphisms is ω-continuous with respect to these partial orders. If $A \xrightarrow{f} B \xrightarrow{g} A$ are arrows in an O-category K such that $g \circ f = Id_A$ and $f \circ g \sqsubseteq Id_B$, then we say that $\langle f,g \rangle$ is a *projection pair* of K.

The category having the same objects as K, but having as arrows the projection pairs of K (with the obvious definition of composition) is denoted KPR. If p is any projection pair, we denote by p^L the left part (the *embedding*) and by p^R the right part (the *projection*) of p. Similarly for chains, cones, etc.: thus if Δ is an ω-chain in KPR, Δ^L will be the ω-chain in K obtained by dropping the second components of the arrows of Δ. It will occasionally be useful to consider the category KP having the same objects as K, in which an arrow from A to B is just a pair $\langle f: A \to B, g: B \to A \rangle$ of K (composition as in KPR). KPR is of course a subcategory of KP.

DEFINITION 2. An object A of a category L is *finite* in L provided that, for any ω-chain $\Delta = \langle A_n, f_n \rangle_{n \omega}$ in L with colimit $\mu: \Delta \to V$, the following holds: for any arrow $v: A \to V$ and for any sufficiently large n, there is a unique arrow $u: A \to A_n$ such that $v = \mu_n \cdot u$. We say that L is *algebroidal* (= *algebraic* in [24]) provided (1) L has as initial object and at most countably many finite objects, (2) every object of L is a colimit of an ω-chain of finite objects, and (3) every ω-chain of finite objects has a colimit in L.

We shall be interested in O-categories K for which KPR is algebroidal. "Finiteness" of objects should always be understood relative to KPR. Notation: KPR_O (resp. K_O) is the full (O-) subcategory of KPR (K) with objects restricted to be finite. The following (new) definition is the cornerstone of this paper:

DEFINITION 3. An O-category K is *admissible* provided

(i) KPR has at most countably many finite objects.

(ii) If A, B are finite in KPR then Hom(A,B) is a finite set.

(iii) For every object A of K there is an ω-chain $\Delta = A_0 \to A_1 \to \ldots$ in KPR_0 and a cone $\mu: \Delta \to A$ in KPR such that $\bigsqcup_i \mu_i^L \circ \mu_i^R = Id_A$. - A cone μ satisfying this condition will be called an *approximating* cone for A; we will also say that μ (or sometimes just A) is an O-*limit* of Δ.

(iv) Every ω-chain in KPR_0 has an O-limit.

The principal definitions and results of this paper concern admissible categories. However, in order to capture more fully the idea of a category of *domains*, in which Scott's D_∞ constructions can be carried out, we need to specialize as follows:

DEFINITION 4. A *domain-category* is an admissible category K in which:

(i) Every Hom(A,B) has a least element $\perp_{A,B}$;

(ii) There is an object E such that $Id_E = \perp_{E,E}$;

(iii) For any arrow f: A $\to$ B and object C,

$$\perp_{B,C} \circ f = \perp_{A,C} .$$

An arrow f: A $\to$ B is called *strict* if $f \circ \perp_{E,A} = \perp_{E,B}$. The domain-category K is *strict* if every arrow K is strict.

The clauses of Definition 4 can be seen as extending the defining properties of admissible categories from ω-chains and sequences to finite (in particular, empty) chains and sequences . Thus, clause (i) says that in each hom-set the empty sequences has a lub; (ii) says that the empty chain in KPR_0 has the O-limit E; (iii) gives one-solid distributivity ("continuity") over the empty sequence, while in the strict category we have full distributivity (it is easy to see that if f is strict we have $f \circ \perp_{C,A} = \perp_{C,B}$ for all C).

All the usual categories of algebraic domains with continuous functions are domain-categories (we are excluding the more general "continuous" domains; see Sec. 5), provided that isomorphic finite domains are identified. Cutting down to the strict functions (in the usual sense) gives a strict domain-category. A simple example of a strict domain-category is obtained by taking as objects the sets of natural numbers and as arrows the partial functions, the ordering of hom-sets being the usual inclusion of partial functions.

FACT. If K is a domain-category, then: E is terminal in K; E is initial in KPR; every embedding and projection is strict; if K is strict then E is initial in K; finally, the category KS obtained from K by cutting down to the strict arrows is a strict domain-category, and KSPR = KPR.

THEOREM 1. *Let* K *be an admissible* O-*category, and* $\mu: \Delta \to A$ *an approximating cone for*

A *in* K. *Then* μ *is colimiting in* KPR *and* μ^L *is colimiting in* K.

For the proof, see [26] Lemma 5.

COROLLARY. *If* K *is admissible and* KPR *has an initial object then* KPR *is algebroidal.*

The following result is relevant to the computability of the $\rightarrow$- functor (of type $K^{Op} \times K \rightarrow K$):

LEMMA 1. (i) K *is admissible iff* K^{Op} *is admissible.* (ii) *The product of two admissible* O-*categories is admissble.*

PROOF. (sketch). (i) Define a (1,1)-correspondence $X \rightarrow \bar{X}$ between entities (objects, arrows, w-chains,...) of KPR and entities of K^{Op}-PR by:

$$A \mapsto \bar{A} \qquad (\text{i.e.}\ \bar{A} = A)$$

$$\langle f,g\rangle: A \rightarrow B \mapsto \langle g,f\rangle: A \rightarrow B$$

$$A_0 \overset{P0}{\rightarrow} A_1 \overset{P1}{\rightarrow} \ldots \mapsto A_0 \overset{\bar{P}0}{\rightarrow} A_1 \overset{\bar{P}1}{\rightarrow} \ldots$$

and similarly for cones. Using this correspondence, verify that: A is finite in KPR iff A ($=\bar{A}$) is finite in K^{Op}-PR; and $\mu: \Delta \rightarrow A$ is an approximating cone in KPR iff $\bar{\mu}: \bar{\Delta} \rightarrow A$ is an approximating cone in K^{Op}-PR. The result follows at once.
(ii) Routine verification.

Projection pairs give us our notion of "approximation" between objects. We need also a notion of approximation for morphisms:

DEFINITION 5. Let K be an O-category. Then the *arrow-category* of K, K_{arr}, has as objects the arrows of K and as arrows from f to g (where $f: A \rightarrow A'$, $g: B \rightarrow B'$ in K) the pairs $\langle p: A \rightarrow A', q: B \rightarrow B'\rangle$ ($p,q \in$ KPR) such that

$$f \sqsubseteq q^R \circ g \circ p^L.$$

Assume now that K is admissible. Let $\Delta = A_0 \overset{f_0}{\rightarrow} A_1 \rightarrow \ldots$, $\Gamma = B_0 \overset{g_0}{\rightarrow} B_1 \rightarrow \ldots$ be ω-chains in KPR_0 with limits $\mu: \Delta \rightarrow A$, $\nu: \Gamma \rightarrow B$, and assume that arrows $h_i: A_i \rightarrow B_i$ satisfy

$$h_i \sqsubseteq g_i^R \circ h_{i+1} \circ f_i^L \qquad (i = 0,1,\ldots)$$

(so that we have an ω-chain H in K_{Arr}). Then a O-*limit* of H is a cone $\xi: H \rightarrow \bar{h}_i$ in K_{Arr}, where $\xi_i = \langle \mu_i, \nu_i\rangle$, $\mu: \Delta \rightarrow A$ and $\nu: \Gamma \rightarrow B$ are O-limits, and $\bar{h}_i: A \rightarrow B$ is given by $\bar{h}_i = \nu_i^L h_i \mu_i^R$ (we also say that ξ is an *approximating* cone for $h = \bigsqcup_i \bar{h}_i$). We will often omit the prefix O- of O-limit.

It is easily checked that $\langle \bar{h}_i \rangle$ is increasing, so that this definition is sound, and a limit for an ω-chain H as described always exists; furthermore, limits are unique up to isomorphism of cones, so that we may as well write *the* limit. By an abuse we will also write, for example, "$\bar{h}_i$ is a limit of the h_i", the connecting arrows and cone being understood.

Various elementary properties of the category K_{Arr} can at once be established: for example, the "limit" just defined is actually the colimit in K_{Arr}, and K_{Arr} has as finite objects exactly the finite arrows of K (that is, the arrows f: A → B, A, B finite in KPR). But we shall not need these in the present work.

<u>THEOREM 2</u>. *In an admissible* O*-category* K, *every arrow can be expressed as the limit of some* ω*-chain of finite arrows.*

<u>PROOF</u>. Let h: A → B be any arrow in K, and let $\mu: \Delta \to A$, $\nu: \Gamma \to B$ be limits, where $\Delta = A_0 \overset{f_0}{\to} A_1 \to \ldots$, $\Gamma = B_0 \overset{g_0}{\to} B_1 \to \ldots$ are chains in K_0. Put $h_i = g_i^R \circ h_{i+1} \circ f_i^L$. Further

$$\bigsqcup_i \nu_i^L \circ h_i \circ \mu_i^R = \bigsqcup_i \nu_i^L \circ \nu_i^R \circ h \circ \mu_i^L \circ \mu_i^R = (\bigsqcup_i \nu_i^L \circ \nu_i^R) \circ h \circ (\bigsqcup_i \mu_i^L \circ \mu_i^R) = h.$$

So h is the limit of $\langle h_i \rangle_i$.

Notice that the sequence $\langle h_i \rangle_i$ constructed here has the strong property that $h_i = g_i^R \circ h_{i+1} \circ f_i^L$, where only $\sqsubseteq$ is required for an "approximating" cone in K_{Arr}. Intuitively, the difference is that the strong sequence $\langle h_i \rangle_i$ gives the *best* approximation to h that is available at stage i. It might be asked why we do not work with the strong sequences which have this (apparently) attractive property. The main reason has to do with effectiveness: even when h is computable, in an appropriate sense, we cannot (in general) *effectively* list the h_i (more precisely: list explicit indices for the h_i, see Sec. 3.2).

An important point in our investigation is that the operations / relations over objects and arrows which we want to discuss can be all expressed in terms of operations / relations over the finite entities in the approximating cones for those objects and arrows. Example:

<u>LEMMA 2</u>. *Let* $\langle h: A \to B,\ p: B \to A \rangle$ *be a pair of arrows in the admissible category* K. *Let* $\mu: \Delta \to A$, $\nu: \Gamma \to B$ *be approximating cones for* A, B, *where* $\Delta = A_0 \overset{f_0}{\to} A_1 \to \ldots$, $\Gamma = B_0 \overset{g_0}{\to} B_1 \to \ldots$, *and let* $\langle h_i: A_i \to B_i \rangle_i$, $\langle p_i: B_1 \to A_i \rangle_i$ *be* ω*-chains of arrows having* h, p *as limits (via* μ, ν*). Then* ⟨h,p⟩ *is a projection pair iff*
(i) *for all* k, *and for all sufficiently great* i (≥ k), $f_{ik} \circ p_i \circ h_i \circ f_{ki} = Id_{A_k}$, *and*
(ii) *for all* k, $h_k \circ p_k \sqsubseteq Id_{A_k}$.

<u>PROOF</u>. Only if:

(i) $$\mathrm{Id}_{A_k} = \mu_k^R \circ p \circ h \circ \mu_k^L = \mu_k^R \circ (\bigsqcup \mu_i^L \circ p_i \circ \nu_i^R) \circ (\bigsqcup \nu_i^L \circ h_i \circ \mu_i^R) \circ \mu_k^L$$

$$= \bigsqcup \mu_k^R \circ \mu_i^L \circ p_i \circ h_i \circ \mu_i^R \circ \mu_k^L = \bigsqcup_{i \geq k} f_{ik} \circ p_i \circ h_i \circ f_{ki} .$$

Since there are only finitely many terms in this (increasing) sequence (Def. 3, (ii)), all of them from some point on must be Id_{A_k}.

(ii) $$h_k \circ p_k \sqsubseteq \nu_k^R \circ h \circ \mu_k^L \circ \mu_k^R \circ p \circ \nu_k^L \sqsubseteq \nu_k^R \circ h \circ p \circ \nu_k^L \sqsubseteq \mathrm{Id}_{B_k} .$$

If: Straightforward.

An alternative formulation is: $\langle h,p\rangle$ is a projection pair iff, for all k and for all sufficiently great i ($\geq$k), $\langle h_i \circ f_{ki}, f_{ik} \circ p_i\rangle$ is a projection pair. From this in turn we can get a simple characterization of *isomorphism* pairs h, p.

Simple characterizations of $f \sqsubseteq f'$ and of $f = f'$, in the same style, may be obtained. A particularly important example is *composition*: this is just given by pointwise composition in the approximating chains. That is, if f, g are given as limits of $\langle f_i: A_i \to B_i\rangle$, $\langle g: B_i \to C_i\rangle$ then $g \circ f$ is the limit of $\langle g_i \circ f_i: A_i \to C_i\rangle$. Note that this does not work if "strong" approximating sequences are used: the strong commuting property does not carry over to the composed diagram. This technical difficulty - which becomes quite troublesome when we come to consider effective sequences - is another reason for preferring the weak sequences.

3.1. Effectiveness

DEFINITION 5. An *effective basis* for an admissible O-category K consists of an enumeration $O_0, O_1, \ldots$ of the finite objects (of KPR) and an enumeration $m_0, m_1, \ldots$ of the finite arrows of K, satisfying the following:

(i) The predicate $O_m = O_n$ is recursive in indices.

(ii) The predicate "m_n is an identity" is recursive.

(iii) There are recursive functions D, C such that

$$O_{D(n)} = \mathrm{dom}(m_n) \quad \text{and} \quad O_{C(n)} = \mathrm{cod}(m_n).$$

(iv) There is a partial recursive function Comp such that $m_k \circ m_n = m_{\mathrm{Comp}(k,n)}$, where Comp is defined iff the composition exists.

(v) The predicate $m_k \sqsubseteq m_n$ is recursive in indices (false if m_k, m_n are not in the same hom-set).

Informally: Equality of (finite) objects is decidable, as are the orderings of the hom-sets; whether an arrow is an identity is decidable; and the domain, codomain and composition of arrows are computable (in indices).

In the following work we make heavy use of recursive sequences of objects/arrows in an effective basis, given as, say, $\langle O_{e(i)}\rangle_i$, $\langle m_{f(i)}\rangle_i$ (e, f recursive functions). To spare the notation we will often just write the index e(i) (f(i)) in place of $O_{e(i)}$ ($m_{f(i)}$).

DEFINITION 6. An *effectively given* O-category is an admissible category K together with an effective basis of K (Notation K^E). An *effective finitary projection sequence* (or *basic sequence*) in K is an effective ω-chain in KPR_O, that is, an ω-chain in KPR_O of the form $e(0) \xrightarrow{f(0)} e(1) \to \ldots$, e, f recursive. An *effectively given* object of K is an object A of K together with an approximating cone $\mu: \Delta \to A$ for A, where Δ is basic. An *effectively given* (or *computable*) arrow in K is an arrow h together with an approximating cone $\Phi: \;\; \to h$ for h, where Γ is basic (i.e. Γ is of the form

$$
(1) \qquad \begin{array}{ccccc}
e(0) & \xrightarrow{f(0)} & e(1) & & \ldots \\
g(0)\downarrow & & g(1)\downarrow & & \\
e'(0) & \xrightarrow{f'(0)} & e'(1) & & \ldots
\end{array}
$$

e, f, e', f', g recursive).

This definition is in the spirit of Kanda and Park [13], where it is shown that an effectively given basis of a domain must be understood to include a particular enumeration of the basis, and an effectively given domain must be taken as a domain D *together with* an effective basis for D (not just: for which *there exists* some effective basis).

We still have to explain the exact relation between our categorical formulation of effectiveness and the familiar formulations in terms of domains. To be specific, let us take K = ACPO (bounded-complete algebraic cpo's, continuous maps). We will show in the next subsection that, relative to suitable indexings of the finite objects of ACPO-PR (i.e. the finite domains) and of the finite arrows of ACPO, the effectiveness of objects and arrows given by Definition 6 coincides with that studied in [5], [23].

3.2. Effectively given domains

We are going to require that the finite domains (in ACPO) and maps between finite domains be enumerated by a system of *explicit* indices. An explicit index for a finite structure is an index from which we can recover the whole structure in a "time" (number of steps) bounded in advance. The term "explicit" is borrowed from Myhill and Shepherdson [18]; it corresponds to Rogers' "canonical" [20]. Explicit indices for domains might be constructed, say, as follows: Suppose that c is an explicit index of a finite set C, and that r is an explicit index of a binary relation

R on C which gives the structure of a finite domain; then $\langle c,r\rangle$ is an *explicit index* of this domain. This gives only a partial indexing, of course; we suppose it made total in some obvious way. Explicit indices for the maps are constructed similarly. It is obvious that enumerations of the finite objects and arrows of ACPO, using explicit indices, yield an effective basis for ACPO (Definition 5).

We claim that, given an effective basis built in this way (a *standard* effective basis, we shall say), the notions of effectively given object and arrow obtained from Definition 6 agree with the usual notions of effectively given domain and computable functions. (For reasons of space, we omit all details here; see [27].)

4. COMPUTABLE FUNCTORS

Corresponding to the notion of a graph of a function we introduce *frames* of a functor. A frame of a locally continuous functor $F: K \to K'$ (K, K' admissible) is an O-functor $F_0: K_0 \to \bar{K}'_0$ such that for each finite object A (finite arrow f) of K, $F_0(A)$ ($F_0(=f)$) is an approximating chain for F(A) (F(f)). In case K, K' are effectively given, we have the notion of a *recursive* frame F_0: the object and morphism maps of F_0 are given by recursive index maps. Of course, functors do not have unique frames; but we shall find that computability of functors can be defined in terms of frames in much the same way as computability of functions in terms of graphs.

DEFINITION 7. Let K, K' be effectively given O-categories. A *computable* functor from K to K' is a locally continuous functor $F: K \to K'$ which has a recursive frame.

THEOREM 3. *A computable functor* $F: K \to K'$ *preserves computability of objects and morphisms. More precisely, if* D *is effectively given then a basic sequence can be given for* F(D)*, and similarly for morphisms. Moreover, the object and morphism maps so defined are recursive in indices.*

In practice the basic functors used in semantics (+,×,→,p,...) always map finite domains/functions to finite domain/functions, and the computability of these functors is immediate. Theorem 3 assures us that application of these functors does not take us outside the realm of the computable. More interesting is the question of the computability of initial fixpoints (algebras) of such functors. This can, indeed, be ensured by restricting to domain-categories which are effectively given (as admissible categories). Probably the easiest way to handle this topic is to begin by showing that, for effectively given categories, our computable functors are essentially the same as Kanda's *effective* functors ([11], [12]) - something which follows easily from Theorem 3 - and then borrow the results of [12]. It is intended to publish the details on another occasion.

In connexion with Kanda's work, let us mention, finally, his exhaustive study (in [11]) of effectiveness in Plotkin's category SFP. Kanda finds that the definition of effectiveness of an SFP object in terms of suitable conditions on the basis of finite elements is very troublesome to work with, especially in connexion with the function space construction. Purely on grounds of simplicity of the resulting theory, he is led to a definition in terms of colimits of ω-chains of finite domains, in close agreement with our abstract Definition 6.

5. MISCELLANEOUS

(1) O and ω. A striking feature of the category-theoretic treatment of data types ([16], [26]) is the interplay between "O-notions", deriving from the ordering of hom-sets, and "ω-notions", having to do with colimits of ω-chains. O-notions are appropriate to categories of (domains and) continuous functions, ω-notions to categories of projection pairs. Both types of notion seem to be necessary to get a satisfactory theory of data types, and so it is perhaps useful to have an independent set of definitions of effectiveness for the ω-notions. We say "perhaps" since in fact it is nearly always most convenient to establish ω-properties via corresponding O-properties (see [26] for examples), so that effectiveness of the O-properties may be sufficient. In any case it is easy to give direct definitions of *effectively given* ω-category, *computable* ω-functor, and so on. For the effectively given ω-category, for example, we just incorporate some effectiveness conditions into the definition of an algebroidal category; this is similar to, but simpler than, Definitions 2, 4 above.

(2) Adjoint functors. Much use of adjoint functor theorems has been made in, for example, [8] and [15]. This is suspect from our point of view, since the "constructions" given in the usual proofs of these theorems are highly non-effective. One could look for restricted versions of these theorems that could readily be made effective. For example we note that, often, the functors for which we wish to construct adjoints preserve finiteness (of objects and arrows); they may be regarded as functors between "bases" K_0 of admissible categories K. Let us then restrict attention to countable O-categories in which no two distinct objects are isomorphic and in which all hom-sets are finite. Let us say that such a category is *finitely powered* if every object has only finitely many subobjects. For these categories we have the following version of the Special Adjoint Functor Theorem of [9]:

<u>THEOREM 4</u>. *Suppose that* K *is finitely powered, finitely complete, and has a coseparator. Then an* O*-functor* $G: K \to X$ *has a left adjoint iff* G *preserves finite limits.*

One can immediately write down an *effective* version of this theorem (relative to suitable indexings of K, X).

We doubt that such theorems are really very useful. It seems that it is usually just as easy to construct the adjoint for a "basis" functor G directly, as to appeal to general theorems. What is, perhaps, more useful is to extend adjointness from functors between "bases" K_0, L_0 to functors between the completed (admissible) cateogries K, L:

<u>THEOREM 5</u>. *Let* F: K→L *be a computable functor which preserves finiteness, so that* F *has in effect a recursive frame* F_0: $K_0 \to L_0$. *Suppose that* F_0 *has a recursive left (right) adjoint* G_0: $L_0 \to K_0$. *Then* F *has a computable left (right) adjoint* G: K→L *with* G_0 *as frame.*

Our construction of the power-domains in [24] can - by taking into account [8] - be seen to fit this pattern (it would have done so still more closely had we followed the "first variant" mentioned in Sec. 4 of [24]).

(3) The definitions we have given above are appropriate only to categories of "algebraic" domains. An abstract treatment capable of handling continuous domains can be developed using a construction of Freyd [7], p. 51. The construction yields, for any category K, a canonical extension of K in which all idempotents split. The extended category might be called the *category of retracts* over K ([25], Ch. 3, Sec. 2.2); given a category of algebraic domains such as ACPO it yields in effect the corresponding category of continuous domains (here, CCPO). However, such a development seems more trouble than it is worth, especially it is still not clear whether non-algebraic domains are really needed in computer science.

(4) A weakness of our notion of effectively given category is that it is not closed under the formation of functor categories. (Functor categories are useful in the theory of data types: [16] Sec. 4.) The situation is analogous to that obtaining in the theory of domains. As is well-known, the class of countably-based algebraic cpo's is not closed under function space formation; we have to restrict at least to SFP to achieve closure. The same solution is, we believe, appropriate here: to restrict to categories which may be considered as limits of finite categories (so eliminating the "lapse" mentioned in Section 1). This is currently under investigation.

REFERENCES

1. Berry, G., Modeles completement adequats et stables des lambda-calculus types, These, Universite Paris VII, 1979.
2. Bishop, E., *Foundations of Constructive Analysis*, McGraw-Hill (N.Y.), 1967.
3. Constable, R., Constructive mathematics and automatic program writers, IFIP (1972), 229-233.
4. Curien, P., Algorithmes sequentiels sur structures de donnees concretes, These de 3e cycles, Universite Paris VII, 1979.
5. Egli, H. & R. Constable, Computability concepts for programming language semantics, *Theor. Comp. Sci.* 2 (1976).
6. Ehrich, H.-D. & V. Lohberger, Parametric specification of abstract data types, parametric substitution, and graph replacements, Proc. of workshop on "Graphentheoretische Konzepte in der Informatik", ed. - J. Mühlbacher, Hanser-Verl., München, 1977.

7. Freyd, P., *Abelian Categories*, Harper and Row, 1964.

8. Hennessy, M. & G. Plotkin, Full abstraction for a simple parallel programming language, MFCS '79, LNCS 74, 1979.

9. Herrlich, H. & D. Strecker, *Category Theory*, Allyn and Bacon, 1978.

10. Kahn, G. & G. Plotkin, Domaines concrets, Rapport No. 336, IRIA Laboria, 1978.

11. Kanda, A., Thesis, University of Warwick, 1979.

12. Kanda, A., Fully effective solutions of recursive domain equations, MFCS '79, LNCS 74, 1979.

13. Kanda, A. & D. Park, When are two effectively given domains identical?, *Proc. 4th GI Conf. in T.C.S.*, Aachen, LNCS 67, 1979.

14. Lehmann, D., Categories for fixpoint semantics, Theory of Computation Report No. 15, University of Warwick, 1976.

15. Lehmann, D., On the algebra of order, Mathematics Institute, Hebrew University, Jerusalem.

16. Lehmann, D. & M. Smyth, The algebraic specification of data types; a synthetic approach, Report No. 119, Dept. of Computer Studies, University of Leeds, 1978 (also to appear in Math. Syst. Theory).

17. Martin Löf, P., Constructive mathematics and computer programming, 6th Int. Congress for Logic, Methodology and Phil. of Science, Hannover, 1979.

18. Myhill, J. & J. Shepherdson, Effective operations on partial recursive functions, *Zeitschr. f. math. Logik u. Grundl. d. Math.*, 1956.

19. Plotkin, G., A power-domain construction, *SIAM J. Comput.* 5 (1976), 452-487.

20. Rogers, H., *Theory of Recursive Functions and Effective Computability*, McGraw-Hill, 1967.

21. Scott, D., Continuous lattices, *Lecture Notes in Math.* 274, Springer, 1974.

22. Scott, D., Data types as lattices, *SIAM J. Comput.* 5 (1976), 522-587.

23. Smyth, M., Effectively given domains, *Theor. Comp. Sci.* 5 (1977), 257-274.

24. Smyth, M., Power Domains, *J. Comp. Syst. Sci.* 16, (1978), 23-26.

25. Smyth, M., D. Phil Thesis, University of Oxford, 1978.

26. Smyth, M. & G. Plotkin, Category-theoretic solution of recursive domain equations, D.A.I. Report 60, University of Edinburgh, 1978.

27. Smyth, M., Computability in Categories, Theory of Computation Report, University of Warwick, 1979.

28 Tang, A., Recursion theory and descriptive set theory in effectively given T_0 spaces, Ph.D. Thesis, Princeton University (1974).

29. Bergstra, J. & J. Tucker, Algebraic specifications of computable and semi-computable data structures, Dept. of Computer Science Report 1W115, Math. Cent., Amsterdam, 1979.

30. Wand, M., Fixed-point constructions in order-enriched categories, TR 23, Computer Science Dept., Indiana University, 1975.

On the Size Complexity of Monotone Formulas

Marc Snir
Computer Science Department
Edinburgh University
Edinburgh, Scotland.

Abstract

"Monotone" formulas, i.e. formulas using positive constants, additions and multiplications are investigated. Lower bounds on the size of monotone formulas representing specific polynomials (permanent, matrix multiplication, symmetric functions) are achieved, using a general, dynamic programming approach. These bounds are tight for the cases investigated. Some generalizations are suggested.

1. Introduction

A long standing goal of the research in the area of computational complexity is to give a precise estimation on the number of operations needed to compute specific arithmetic functions. Whereas for certain problems (as polynomial evaluation) such estimation has been achieved, other cases, for example matrix multiplication, escape analysis, despite continuous efforts.

One approach used to cope with this situation is to restrict the family of allowed algorithms in some sensible way, such that within this family tight bounds can be proved. Thus Miller [Mi], by requiring that computations fulfil some formal "numerical stability" requirements, and Schnorr [Sc], by considering "monotone" computations, i.e. computations using only additions and multiplications (a restriction which implies Miller's one) were able to prove that the straightforward algorithm for the multiplication of matrices which uses $O(n^3)$ operations is optimal.

A numerical algorithm (producing one output) can be represented by a formula involving constants, variables (inputs) and operations. Different algorithms computing the same function over some fixed field are represented by equivalent formulas, so that given one such formula one can get all the others by applying transformations corresponding to the standard axioms of the ring of polynomials over this field. Restricting the family of allowable algorithms amounts to restricting the set of allowable transformations, i.e. using only a partial system of axioms. Thus, use of monotone computations only is tantamount to prohibition of the use of the cancellation axiom $x + (-x) = 0$. Under such approach, the problem of finding the shortest restricted algorithm conputing a given function is equivalent to the problem of finding the "simplest" formula equivalent to a given one under a restricted set of axioms.

This level of abstraction achieved, it is easy to see that results obtained for monotone arithmetic computations are in fact valid for other algebras as well: + can be interpreted as minimum and * as addition, yielding the min, + semiring which is often used to formulate and solve optimization problems (see [AHU], p.195), or + can be union and * concatenation, leading to the consideration of star free regular expressions.

Two different ways of achieving this level of generality can be found in [ShS], where bounds are obtained on the depth complexity of formulas, and in [JeS], where the number of multiplications in straight line algorithms is measured.

In this paper we shall be concerned with the size complexity of formulas. In order to simplify the presentation, we shall state our results for monotone arithmetic formulas only. Nevertheless, it should be borne in mind that all results proven in section 3 applies to the above mentioned systems as well.

One of the results is that the shortest monotone formula for the permanent of a $n \times n$ matrix has size $2^{2n-0.25\lg^2 n+O(\lg n)}$. This result implies a lower bound of $2n - 0.25\lg^2 n + O(\lg n)$ steps for a parallel monotone computation of the permanent (this bound is tight). The minimal length of a monotone straight line computation of the permanent is $O(n2^n)$. When subtraction is used without restrictions the upper bounds can be improved to $n^2 2^{n-1}$ for size, $n + O(\lg n)$ for depth, and $O((n-1)2^n)$ for s.l.a. complexity, using the inclusion exclusion formula of [Ry]. No non trivial lower bounds are known in this case, although the results of [Va2] and [Va3] lead us to expect for exponential complexity. We remark that in the min, + algebra the permanent function represents the value of a minimal matching in a bipartite graph and is thus related to the "minimal assignment" optimization problem.

Two other problems considered in this paper are multiplication of p $n \times n$ matrices (formula size $(2n)^{\lg p}$), and evaluation of symmetric functions on n variables (formula size $n^{0.25\lg n + O(1)}$ in the worst case). For both problems we are not aware of any significant reduction in formula size complexity when subtraction is used, although subtraction can be used to generate shorter straight line computations of these functions.

2. Main Result

Let $S = \langle R^+, +, * \rangle$ be the semiring of positive real numbers with the operations of addition and multiplication; let X be a fixed (infinite) set of variables. We denote by P the semiring $R^+[X]$ of monotone polynomials over S. Each polynomial $p \in P$ has an unique canonical representation $p = \sum_{i=1}^{k} r_i m_i$, where m_i are different monomials, and $r_i \in R^+$. We denote by $Mon(p)$ the set of monomials appearing in this representation, and define $w(p)$, the weight of p, to be the cardinality of $Mon(p)$. The degree of p, $d(p)$ is defined as usual.

Polynomials in P are represented by (monotone) formulas: F is a formula if

$F = a$, where $a \in R^+ \cup X$, or

$$F = (F_1 \text{ op } F_2), \quad \text{where } F_1, F_2 \text{ are formulas, and } \text{op} \in \{+,*\}.$$

We shall omit subsequently superfluous parentheses when writing down formulas.

To each formula F we associate a polynomial $\text{poly}(F)$ in the usual way. The degree of a formula F, $d(F)$, the set of its monomials, $\text{Mon}(F)$, and its weight $w(F)$ are defined exactly as $d(\text{poly}(F))$, $\text{Mon}(\text{poly}(F))$, $w(\text{poly}(F))$ respectively.

The formula F is a <u>subformula</u> of G if

$F = G$, or

$G = (G_1 \text{ op } G_2)$ and F is a subformula of G_1 or G_2.

We denote by $\text{Sub}(G)$ the set of subformulas of G.

A formula is <u>atomic</u> if it consists of an unique constant or variable (i.e. has no operation symbols within it). The <u>size</u> of a formula F, $s(F)$, is the number of occurrences of variables in F; the <u>height</u> of F, $h(F)$, is defined inductively by

$h(F) = 0$ if F is atomic,

$h(F_1 \text{ op } F_2) = 1 + \max[h(F_1), h(F_2)]$.

Clearly, $h(F) \geq \lg s(F)$ (we denote by $\lg x$ the logarithm to basis 2 of x).

Since

$$\text{Mon}(F_1 + F_2) = \text{Mon}(F_1) \cup \text{Mon}(F_2) \tag{2.1}$$

and

$$\text{Mon}(F_1 * F_2) = \text{Mon}(F_1) * \text{Mon}(F_2) = \{m_1 * m_2 : m_i \in \text{Mon}(F_i),\ i = 1,2\}, \tag{2.2}$$

the weight function fulfils

$$w(a) = 1 \text{ if } a \text{ is a variable, } 0 \text{ if } a \text{ is constant} \tag{2.3}$$

$$w(F_1 + F_2) \leq w(F_1) + w(F_2); \tag{2.4}$$

and

$$w(F_1 * F_2) \leq w(F_1) * w(F_2). \tag{2.5}$$

For the degree function we have

$$d(a) = 1 \text{ if } a \text{ is a variable, } 0 \text{ if } a \text{ is constant} \tag{2.6}$$

$$d(F_1 + F_2) = \max[d(F_1), d(F_2)]; \tag{2.7}$$

$$d(F_1 * F_2) = d(F_1) + d(F_2). \tag{2.8}$$

A simple, but crucial fact is provided by the next lemma.

<u>Lemma 2.1</u>: <u>If G is a subformula of F then there exist polynomials $p,q,p \neq 0$; such that</u>

$$\text{poly}(F) = p.\text{poly}(G) + q.$$

<u>In particular</u>

$$\text{Mon}(F) \supseteq \text{Mon}(G) * \text{Mon}(p). \tag{2.9}$$

This last relation (which breaks down as soon as cancellation is allowed) puts severe limitations on the structure of formulas representing a given polynomial. We shall use these limitations (or more exactly a quantitative formulation of them) in order to prove lower bounds on formula size.

Let us introduce the following definitions:

The complement of a monomial m with respect to the polynomial p is

$$\mathrm{Comp}(m,p) = \{n : m*n \in \mathrm{Mon}(p)\};$$

The growth function of a polynomial p is defined by

$$\mathrm{Gr}(k,p) = \max_{d(m)=k} \; \max_{n \in \mathrm{Comp}(m,p)} |\mathrm{Comp}(n,p)|$$

($\mathrm{Gr}(k,p) = -\infty$ if maximum is taken over an empty set.)

We shall denote by $\mathrm{Comp}(m,F)$ and $\mathrm{Gr}(k,F)$ the functions $\mathrm{Comp}(m, \mathrm{poly}(F))$ and $\mathrm{Gr}(k, \mathrm{poly}(F))$ respectively.

If G is a subformula of F then, according to lemma 2.1, $\mathrm{Mon}(G) * n \subseteq \mathrm{Mon}(F)$ for some monomial n. If $m \in \mathrm{Mon}(G)$, then $n \in \mathrm{Comp}(m,F)$. Also, $\mathrm{Mon}(G) \subseteq \mathrm{Comp}(n,F)$. It follows, from the definition of the growth function, that $w(G) \le \mathrm{Gr}(d(m),F)$. We have shown that

Lemma 2.2: If G is a subformula of F containing a monomial of degree k, then $w(G) \le \mathrm{Gr}(k,F)$.

In particular $\mathrm{Gr}(k,F)$ is an upper bound on the weight of a subformula of F of degree k.

It is also easy to check that

$\mathrm{Gr}(n,p) = w(p)$, if p contains a monomial of degree n, (2.10)

$\mathrm{Gr}(0,p) = 1$, provided that no monomial of p is a factor of another, and (2.11)

$\mathrm{Gr}(k,p)$ is a monotonic non decreasing function of k. (2.12)

We can now view the task of building a minimal size formula representing a polynomial p as a dynamic programming problem of building a formula of weight $w(p)$ and degree $d(p)$ under the constraints provided by lemma 2.2. and those implicit in 2.3 - 2.8. Using this approach we obtain lower bounds for formula size which depends only on the behaviour of the growth function $\mathrm{Gr}(\cdot,p)$. We ignore of course by such a quantitative approach, many of the restrictions applying to the original problem, but are still capable in some cases to achieve tight lower bounds.

Let F be a fixed formula. Define $w(i,j)$ to be the maximal weight of a subformula of F of degree i and size j ($w(i,j) = -\infty$ if there is no such subformula). We have the following relations:

(i) $w(i,1) = 1$ if $i = 1$, $-\infty$ otherwise; (2.13)

(ii) If $j > 1$ then either $w(i,j) = -\infty$ or there exist numbers i_1, i_2, j_1, j_2 such that

$j_1, j_1 \geq 1,\ j_1 + j_2 = j,$ and either

$$i = \max[i_1, i_2] \text{ and } w(i,j) \leq w(i_1,j_1) + w(i_2,j_2) \quad (2.14)$$

(addition case), or

$$i = i_1 + i_2 \text{ and } w(i,j) \leq w(i_1,j_1) \,.\, w(i_2,j_2) \quad (2.15)$$

(multiplication case).

(iii) $w(i,j) \leq Gr(i,j)$ (2.16)

Indeed, (i) and (ii) are immediate consequences of relations 2.3 - 2.8, whereas (iii) follows from lemma 2.2.

Define now the function $W(i,j)$ on the integers inductively by

$$W(i,1) = 1 \text{ if } i = 1, -\infty \text{ otherwise}$$

and for $j > 1$

$$W(i,j) = \min\{Gr(i,F), \max[\max_{j_1+j_2=j} (W(i,j_1) + W(i,j_2)), \max_{i_1+i_2=i, j_1+j_2=j} (W(i_1,j) . W(i_2,j_2))]\}.$$

We have

<u>Lemma 2.3</u>: (i) <u>The Function $W(i,j)$ is monotonic non decreasing in its first variable.</u>

(ii) $w(i,j) \leq W(i,j)$ <u>for all $i,j > 0$.</u>

<u>Proof</u>: Claim (i) follows easily by induction on j, using the fact that the function $Gr(\cdot,F)$ is monotonic non decreasing; claim (ii) is proved by induction on j :

If $j = 1$ then $w(i,j) = W(i,j)$ from 2.13 and the definition of W ;

If $j > 1$ then either according to 2.14 $w(i,j) \leq w(i_1,j_1) + w(i_2,j_2)$, with $i = \max[i_1,i_2]$ and $j = j_1 + j_2$, in which case, using the inductive assertion and (i) we have

$$w(i,j) \leq W(i_1,j_1) + W(i_2,j_2) \leq W(i,j_1) + W(i,j_2) \quad (2.17)$$

or according to 2.15 $w(i,j) \leq w(i_1,j_1) \cdot w(i_2,j_2)$, with $i = i_1 + i_2$, and $j = j_1 + j_2$, so that

$$w(i,j) \leq W(i_1,j_1) \cdot W(i_2,j_2). \quad (2.18)$$

The claim now follows by comparing inequalities 2.16, 2.17, 2.18 to the equations which define the function W .

□

The value of $W(i,j)$ is an upper bound on the weight of a subformula of F of degree i and size j . In particular we have that $W(d(F),s(F)) \geq w(F)$, from which it follows that $s(F) \geq \min\{j : W(d(F),j) \geq w(F)\}$. We have obtained a lower bound on the size of F which value hinges on the values of $w(F), d(F)$, and on the behaviour of the function $W(i,j)$, which in its turn hinges on the behaviour of the growth function $Gr(\cdot,F)$, which is just the growth function $Gr(\cdot,p)$ where p is the polynomial represented by F .

Since $w(F) = Gr(d(F),F)$ we can rephrase this result as follows:

Theorem 2.4: Let F be a formula representing the polynomial p; Let the function $W(i,j)$ be defined by

$$W(i,1) = 1 \text{ if } i = 1, -\infty \text{ otherwise}$$

and for $j > 1$

$$W(i,j) = \min\{Gr(i,p), \max[\max_{j_1+j_2=j}(W(i,j_1) + W(i,j_2)), \max_{i_1+i_2=i, j_1+j_2=j}(W(i_1,j_1)\cdot W(i_2,j_2))]\}$$

Let the threshold function t be defined by

$$t(1) = \min\{j : W(i,j) = Gr(i,p)\}$$

Then

$$s(F) \geq t(d(F)).$$

Thus our strategy for proving lower bounds on the length of any formula representing a given polynomial is to find a closed definition of its growth function, and then a closed definition for the related threshold function. It turns out that in the interesting cases a direct inductive definition can be provided for a function that closely bounds from below the threshold function. Indeed, the dynamic programming problem we consider is interesting only when the boundary constraint provided by the growth function comes into play. This turns out to be the case when this function is submultiplicative, i.e. fulfils

$$Gr(i+j,F) \geq Gr(i,F) \cdot Gr(j,F) \quad \text{for all } i,j > 0 .$$

When such is the case, the product of two maximal weight formula results in a formula with less than maximal weight, and additions must be intertwined between multiplications.

Theorem 2.5: Let $Gr(\cdot,p)$ be submultiplicative.

Let the functions $W(i,j)$ and $t(i)$ be defined as in theorem 2.4, and let the function $T(i)$ be defined by

$$T(1) = 1$$

and for $k > 1$ $\quad T(k) = \min_{i+j=k} [T(i)\cdot Gr(i,p)+T(j)\cdot Gr(j,p)]/[Gr(i,p)\cdot Gr(j,p)]$

Then

(i) $j \geq T(i)\cdot W(i,j)$ for all $i,j \geq 0$.

(ii) $t(i) \geq T(i)\cdot Gr(i,p)$ for all $i > 0$.

The idea behind the definition of T, and the assertion of the theorem is that an (almost) optimal way of building formulas, according to our dynamic programming model, is to build for each k a maximal weight formula of degree k by repeatingly adding to itself a subformula of degree k with a minimal size to weight ratio.

This subformula is built by multiplying two subformulas of degree i and j, with $i + j = k$, of maximal weight (and minimal size to weight ratio). $T(i)$ is the minimal size to weight ratio for a formula of degree i. The discrepancy between $t(i)$ and $T(i)\cdot G(i,p)$ is due solely to the impossibility of adding "fractional" formulas, i.e. to the replacing of an integer valued programming problem by a real valued one.

Proof of theorem 2.5: (i) is proved by induction on $\langle i,j\rangle$ (in lexicographic order). It is clearly sufficient to prove the assertion for $j \le t(i)$. If $i = 1$ then $W(1,j) = j$, and the claim follows. Suppose $i > 1$; if $W(i,j) = -\infty$ the claim is trivial; if $W(i,j) \le W(i,j_1) + W(i,j_2)$, with $j_1 + j_2 = j$, then, using the inductive assertion

$$j = j_1 + j_2 \ge T(i)W(i,j_1) + T(i)W(i,j_2) \ge T(i)W(i,j);$$

If $W(i,j) \le W(i_1,j_2)\cdot W(i_2,j_2)$, where $i_1 + i_2 = i$, $j_1 + j_2 = j$, then

$$\begin{aligned} T(i) &\le T(i_1)/Gr(i_2,p) + T(i_2)/Gr(i_1,p) \quad \text{by the definition of } T, \\ &\le T(i_1)/W(i_2,j_2) + T(i_1)/W(i_1,j_1) \\ &= [T(i_1)W(i_1,j_1) + T(i_2)W(i_2,j_2)]/[Wi_1,j_1)\cdot W(i_2,j_2)] \\ &\le [j_1 + j_2]/[W(i_1,j_1)\cdot W(i_2,j_2)] \quad \text{by the inductive assertion} \\ &\le j/W(i,j) \end{aligned}$$

So that $\qquad j \ge T(i)\cdot W(i,j)$

(ii) Follows from the relations

$$t(i) \ge T(i)\cdot W(i,t(i)) = T(i)\cdot Gr(i,p).$$

□

3. Applications

We shall apply now the results of section 2 to specific functions. The first case we consider is the permanent polynomial which is defined on the matrix (x_{ij}), $1 \le i, j \le n$ by

$$per = \sum_{\sigma\in Sn} x_{1\sigma(1)}\cdot\ldots\cdot x_{n\sigma(n)},$$

where Sn is the group of permutations over $\{1,\ldots,n\}$.

Claim: The growth function of per is $Gr(k,per) = k!$

Proof: Let m be a monomial of degree k. If $r \in Comp(m,per)$ then r is a monomial of degree $n - k$ with no row index or column index in common with m, and $Comp(r,per)$ is in fact the set of monomials of the permanent of the $k \times k$ submatrix which row and column indices are those of m.

Theorem 3.1: If F is a formula representing the permanent polynomial then

$$s(F) \ge 2^{2n-0.25\lg^2 n + O(1/n)}$$

Proof: the factorial function is submultiplicative, so that theorem 2.5 applies. In order to prove our theorem it is sufficient to show that the function

$L(n) = 2^{2n - 0.25 \lg^2 n + O(1/n)}$ fulfils the inequalities

$L(1) \le 1$

$L(i + j) \le [L(i) + L(j)] \cdot Gr(i + j, per)/[Gr(i, per) \cdot Gr(j, per)]$

Indeed, in such a case $L(k)/Gr(k,per)$ is a lower bound to $T(k)$, and $L(n)$ a lower bound to $t(n)$, which in turn, is a lower bound to the size of a formula representing per.

The first inequality can be fulfilled by a suitable choice of the O term. It remains to prove that for $n = i + j$

$$L(n) \le \binom{n}{i} [L(i) + L(j)] .$$

We assume w.l.g. that $i \le n/2$. It is easily checked that the function $g(i) = \binom{n}{i} [L(i) + L(n - i)]$ is unimodal in the interval $1 \le i \le n/2$, and the inequality holds at both extremities of the interval. □

The above result is almost optimal. Indeed, using the Laplace method to compute the permanent (see [ShS]), one gets a formula of length $2^{2n - 0.25 \lg^2 n + O(\lg n)}$.

Let us turn now to another example - multiplication of matrices.
Define

$$mat = \sum_{1 \le i_1, \dots, i_{p-1} \le m} x^1_{1 i_1} \cdot x_{i_1 i_2} \cdot \dots \cdot x^p_{i_{p-1} 1}$$

The polynomial mat is one of the coefficients of the product of p $m \times m$ matrices.

<u>Theorem 3.2: If F is a formula representing the polynomial mat then</u>

$$s(F) \ge (2m)^{\lg p}$$

<u>Proof</u>: The growth function of mat is given by $Gr(k,mat) = m^{k-1}$. This function is submultiplicative. So, we use the same method as in the previous proof, and set to prove, for $n = i + j$, the inequality

$$(2m)^{\lg n} \le [(2m)^{\lg i} + (2m)^{\lg j}] m^{n-1} / [m^{i-1} . m^{j-1}]$$

or

$$(2m)^{\lg n} \le m[(2m)^{\lg i} + (2m)^{\lg j}]$$

Since the expression on the right is minimal when $i = j$ it is sufficient to prove that

$$(2m)^{\lg n} \le m[(2m)^{\lg(n/2)} + (2m)^{\lg(n/2)}]$$

and both sides of this last inequality are in fact equal. □

The standard binary splitting method yields a formula representing the polynomial mat of length $(2m)^{\lceil \lg p \rceil}$, so that above bound is tight.

Although theorems 2.3 - 2.5 have been stated for the weight function and growth function as defined in section 2 it should be obvious that these theorems hold true for any pair of functions fulfilling relations 2.3 - 2.5, 2.10 - 2.12, and lemma 2.2. (In fact in 2.3 equality can be replaced by inequality). We shall use this approach to analyse the complexity of the symmetric polynomials, and more particularly of the middle one,

$$\text{sym} = \sum_{I\subset\{1,\ldots,2n\},|I|=n} \prod_{i\in I} x_i$$

Theorem 3.3: If F is a formula representing the polynomial sym then

$$s(F) \geq n^{0.25\lg n + O(1)}$$

Proof: Let $v(G)$ be the number of different variables occurring in the formula G. We use the "weight" function defined by

$$\bar{w}(G) = w(G)\cdot 2^{[d(G) - v(G)]}$$

and the "growth" function defined by

$$G(k) = \binom{2k}{k} 2^{-k} .$$

(The rationale lying behind these seemingly gratuitous definitions is the wish to "penalize" subformulas where high weight and low degree is achieved at the expense of many variables occurring in them; such subformulas are not subsequently useful.)

We have

$$v(G_1 + G_2) \leq v(G_1) + v(G_2) .$$

Moreover, since the polynomial sym is linear in each variable, if $G_1 * G_2$ is a subformula of F then

$$v(G_1 * G_2) = v(G_2) + v(G_2) .$$

Also, since this polynomial is homogeneous, if $G_1 + G_2$ is a subformula of F, then $d(G_1) = d(G_2)$. Using these facts it is easily verified that the function $\bar{w}$ fulfils relations 2.3 - 2.5. Also, the function G fulfils relations 2.10 - 2.12. It remains to be shown that the "growth" function indeed provides an upper bound on the "weight", i.e. that if $d(G) = k$ then $\bar{w}(G) \leq G(k)$. But if G is a subformula of F of degree no greater than k then $w(G) \leq \binom{v(G)}{k}$, so that $\bar{w}(G) \leq \binom{v}{k}2^{k-v}$ with $v = v(G)$. We are left with the easily checked inequality.

$$\binom{v}{k} 2^{k-v} \leq \binom{2k}{k} 2^{-k} \qquad (\text{for } v \geq k).$$

Since the function G is submultiplicative, we can apply theorem 2.5, and, as before the proof is reduced to the verification of the inequality

$$n^{0.25\lg n + O(1)} \leq [i^{0.25\lg i} + j^{0.25\lg j}]\binom{2n}{n}/[\binom{2i}{i}\cdot\binom{2j}{j}]$$

where $i + j = n$. This inequality is verified using the same argument as in theorem 3.1. □

Here also using the binary splitting method, a formula for sym of length $n^{0.5\lg n + O(1)}$ can be constructed. This result can be improved to $n^{0.25\lg n + O(1)}$ when addition is idempotent (as in the case it is interpreted as union).

4. Conclusion

Tight lower bounds on the size of formulas representing certain functions have been proven, when only addition and multiplication are used. As hinted at in the introduction, these results are valuable for other settings as well. For example, the lower bound proved for the permanent applies as well to the determinant which formal definition is similar: any formula representing the determinant of a matrix of rank n, such that no terms cancel when parentheses are opened, has length at least $2^{2n - 0.25\log^2 n + O(1/n)}$. On the other hand, we know that when this limitation is removed, a formula of length $2^{O(\log^2 n)}$ can be built. (Valiant, in [Va1], has given an example of a similar gap for a polynomial with positive coefficients.)

From our bounds on formula length, bounds on formula height (i.e. the number of steps in a parallel algorithm) can be directly derived. Indeed, $h(F) \geq \lg s(F)$, for any formula F. Thus, a parallel "monotone" algorithm for permanent computation takes at least $2n - 0.25\lg^2 n$ steps, an algorithm for the multiplication of p $m \times m$ matrices takes $\lg p \cdot (\lg m + 1)$ steps, an algorithm for the computation of the middle symmetric function on n variables takes $0.25\lg^2 n$ steps. (These results were directly proven in [ShS].)

As said before, our results apply to star free regular expressions. New results can be achieved by taking into account the non-commutativity of multiplication (concatenation). This is done by redefining in an obvious way the complement and growth functions. The remaining results of section 2 carry through, without modification. Using this approach we can prove that the minimal size of a regular expression representing the set of all permutations on n symbols is $2^{2n - 0.25\lg^2 n + O(\lg n)}$; the minimal size of a regular expression representing the set of all paths of length $p+1$ in an arc-labelled complete graph on m nodes is $(2m)^{\lg p}$. These two results match, and can in fact be directly inferred from, the results on the permanent and matrix multiplication. Related results can be found in [EhZ].

Any extension of the results of this paper to less restricted systems (arithmetic with subtraction, monotone Boolean formulas) is likely to be an arduous task, and for the permanent, would be of major significance (see [Va2] and [Va3]).

Acknowledgements

I would like to thank Professor Eli Shamir for his important contribution in the shaping of this work.

References

[AHU] A.V. Aho, J.E. Hopcroft and J.D. Ullman. The design and analysis of computer algorithms. Addison-Wesley, 1974.

[EhZ] A. Ehrenfeucht and P. Zeiger. Complexity measures for regular expressions. Proc. 6th ACM Symposium on Theory of Computing (1974) 75-79.

[JeS] M. Jerrum and M. Snir. Some exact complexity results for straight line computations over semirings. University of Edinburgh Technical Report CSR-58-80 (1980).

[Mi] W. Miller. Computational complexity and numerical stability. SIAM J. Computing, 4 (1975) 97-107.

[Ry] H.J. Ryser. Combinatorial Mathematics. The Carus Mathematical Monographs 14, 1963.

[Sc] C.P. Schnorr. A lower bound on the number of additions in monotone computations. Theoretical Computer Science, 2 (1976) 305-315.

[ShS] E. Shamir and M. Snir. On the depth complexity of formulas. Mathematical System Theory (to appear).

[Va1] L.G. Valiant. Negation can be exponentially powerfu. Proc. 11th ACM Symposium on Theory of Computing (1979) 189-196.

[Va2] L.G. Valiant. The complexity of computing the permanent. Theoretical Computer Science (to appear).

[Va3] L.G. Valiant. Completeness classes in algebra. Proc. 11th ACM Symposium on Theory of Computing (1979) 249-261.

REVERSIBLE COMPUTING

Tommaso Toffoli

MIT Laboratory for Computer Science
545 Technology Sq., Cambridge, MA 02139

Abstract. The theory of reversible computing is based on invertible primitives and composition rules that preserve invertibility. With these constraints, one can still satisfactorily deal with both functional and structural aspects of computing processes; at the same time, one attains a closer correspondence between the behavior of abstract computing systems and the microscopic physical laws (which are presumed to be strictly reversible) that underly any concrete implementation of such systems.

According to a physical interpretation, the central result of this paper is that *it is ideally possible to build sequential circuits with zero internal power dissipation.*

1. Introduction

This is an abridged version of a much longer report of the same title[27], to which the reader may turn for further details, most proofs, and extended references. Here, the numbering of formulas, figures, etc. reflects that of the original version.

Mathematical models of computation are abstract constructions, by their nature unfettered by physical laws. However, if these models are to give indications that are relevant to concrete computing, they must somehow capture, albeit in a selective and stylized way, certain general physical restrictions to which all concrete computing processes are subjected.

One of the strongest motivations for the study of reversible computing comes from the desire to reduce heat dissipation in computing machinery, and thus achieve higher density and speed. Briefly, while the microscopic laws of physics are presumed to be strictly reversible, abstract computing is usually thought of as an irreversible process, since it may involve the evaluation of many-to-one functions. Thus, as one proceeds down from an abstract computing task to a formal realization by means of a digital network and finally to an implementation in a physical system, at some level of this modeling hierarchy there must take place the transition from the irreversibility of the given computing process to the reversibility of the physical laws. In the customary approach, this transition occurs at a very low level and is hidden—so to speak—in the "physics" of the individual digital gate;* as a consequence of this approach, the details of the work-to-heat conversion process are put beyond the reach of the conceptual model of computation that is used.

On the other hand, it is possible to formulate a more general conceptual model of computation such that the gap between the irreversibility of the desired behavior and the reversibility of a given underlying mechanism is bridged *in an explicit way* within the model itself. This we shall do in the present paper.

*Typically, the computation is logically organized around computing primitives that are not invertible, such as the NAND gate; in turn, these are realized by physical devices which, while by their nature obeying reversible microscopic laws, are made *macroscopically* irreversible by allowing them to convert some work to heat.

An important advantage of our approach is that any operations (such as the clearing of a register) that in conventional logic lead to the destruction of macroscopic information, and thus entail energy dissipation, here can be planned at the whole-circuit level rather than at the gate level, and most of the time can be replaced by an information-lossless variant. As a consequence, *it appears possible to design circuits whose internal power dissipation, under ideal physical circumstances, is zero.* The power dissipation that would arise at the interface between such circuits and the outside world would be at most proportional to the number of input/output lines, rather than to the number of logic gates.

2. Terminology and notation

A function $\phi: X \rightarrow Y$ is *finite* if X and Y are finite sets. A *finite automaton* is a dynamical system characterized by a transition function of the form $\tau: X \times Q \rightarrow Q \times Y$, where τ is finite. Without loss of generality, one may assume that such sets as X, Y, and Q above be explicitly given as indexed Cartesian products of sets. We shall occasionally call *lines* the individual variables associated with the individual factors of such products. In what follows, we shall assume *once and for all* that all factors of the aforementioned Cartesian products be identical copies of the *Boolean* set $\mathbf{B} = \{0, 1\}$. A finite function is *of order* n if it has n input lines.

The process of generating multiple copies of a given signal must be treated with particular care when reversibility is an issue (moreover, from a physical viewpoint this process is far from trivial). For this reason, in all that follows we shall restrict the meaning of the term "function composition" to *one-to-one* composition, where any substitution of output variables for input variables is one-to-one. Thus, any "fan-out" node in a given function-composition scheme will have to be treated as an explicit occurrence of a fan-out *function* of the form $\langle x \rangle \mapsto \langle x, \ldots, x \rangle$. Intuitively, the responsibility for providing fan-out is shifted from the composition rules to the computing primitives.

Abstract computers (such as finite automata and Turing machines) are essentially function-composition schemes. It is customary to express a function-composition scheme in graphical form as a *causality network*. This is basically an acyclic directed graph in which nodes correspond to functions and arcs to variables. By construction, causality networks are "loop-free," i.e., they contain no cyclic paths. A *combinational* network is a causality network that contains no infinite paths. Note that a finite causality network is always a combinational one. With certain additional conventions (such as the use of special markers called *delay elements*), causality networks having a particular iterative structure can be represented more compactly as *sequential* networks.

A causality network is *reversible* if it is obtained by composition of invertible primitives. Note that a reversible combinational network always defines an invertible function. Thus, in the case of combinational networks the structural aspect of "reversibility" and the functional aspect of "invertibility" coincide. A sequential network is *reversible* if its *combinational part* (i.e., the combinational network obtained by deleting the delay elements and thus breaking the corresponding arcs) is reversible.

We shall assume familiarity with the concept of "realization" of finite functions and automata by means of, respectively, combinational and sequential networks. In what follows, a "realization" will always mean a *componentwise* one; that is, to each input (or output) line of a finite function there will correspond an input (or output) line in the combinational network that realizes it, and similarly for the realization of automata by sequential networks.

3. Introductory concepts

As explained in Section 1, our overall goal is to develop an explicit realization of computing processes within the context of reversible systems. As an introduction, let us consider two simple functions, namely, FAN-OUT (3.1*a*) and XOR (3.1*b*):

$$\text{(a)}\quad \begin{array}{c} x \\ 0 \\ 1 \end{array} \rightarrow \begin{array}{c} y_1\,y_2 \\ 0\;0 \\ 1\;1 \end{array} \qquad\qquad \text{(b)}\quad \begin{array}{c} x_1\,x_2 \\ 0\;0 \\ 0\;1 \\ 1\;0 \\ 1\;1 \end{array} \rightarrow \begin{array}{c} y \\ 0 \\ 1 \\ 1 \\ 0 \end{array}. \tag{3.1}$$

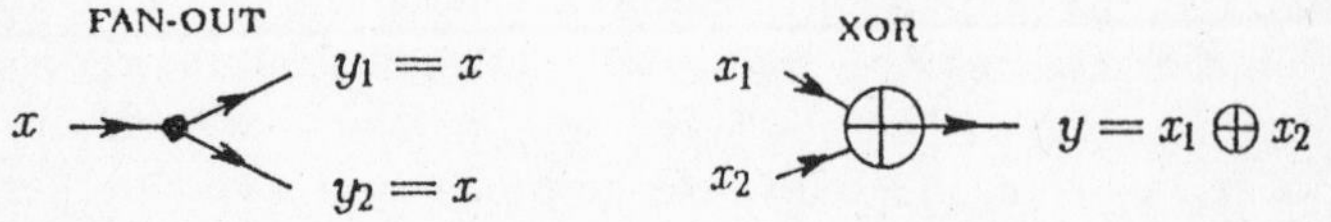

Neither of these functions is invertible. (Indeed, FAN-OUT is not *surjective*, since, for instance, the output $\langle 0,1\rangle$ cannot be obtained for any input value; and XOR is not *injective*, since, for instance, the output 0 can be obtained from two distinct input values, $\langle 0,0\rangle$ and $\langle 1,1\rangle$). Yet, both functions admit of an invertible realization.

To see this, consider the *invertible* function XOR/FAN-OUT defined by the table

$$\begin{array}{c} 00 \\ 01 \\ 10 \\ 11 \end{array} \rightarrow \begin{array}{c} 00 \\ 11 \\ 10 \\ 01 \end{array}, \tag{3.2}$$

which we have copied over with different headings in (3.3a), (3.3*b*), and (3.6*b*). Then, FAN-OUT can be realized by means of this function* as in (3.3a) (where we have outlined the relevant table entries), by assigning a value of 0 to the auxiliary input component c; and XOR can be realized by means of the same function as in (3.3*b*), by simply disregarding the auxiliary output component g. In more technical terms, (3.1a) is obtained from (3.3a) by componentwise *restriction*, and (3.1*b*) from (3.3*b*) by *projection*.

$$\text{(a)}\quad \begin{array}{cc} c & x \\ 0 & \boxed{0} \\ 0 & \boxed{1} \\ 1 & 0 \\ 1 & 1 \end{array} \rightarrow \begin{array}{cc} y_1 & y_2 \\ \boxed{0} & \boxed{0} \\ \boxed{1} & \boxed{1} \\ 1 & 0 \\ 0 & 1 \end{array} \qquad\qquad \text{(b)}\quad \begin{array}{cc} x_1 & x_2 \\ \boxed{0} & \boxed{0} \\ \boxed{0} & \boxed{1} \\ \boxed{1} & \boxed{0} \\ \boxed{1} & \boxed{1} \end{array} \rightarrow \begin{array}{cc} y & g \\ \boxed{0} & 0 \\ \boxed{1} & 1 \\ \boxed{1} & 0 \\ \boxed{0} & 1 \end{array} \tag{3.3}$$

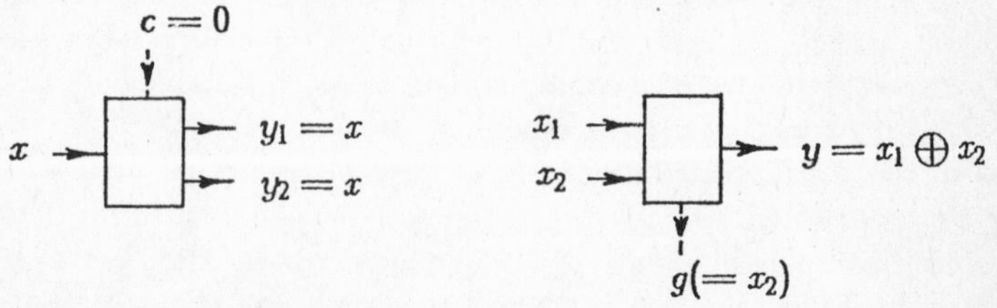

*Ordinarily, one speaks of a realization "by a network." Note, though, that a finite function by itself constitutes a trivial case of combinational network.

In what follows, we shall collectively call *the source* the auxiliary input components that have been used in a realization, such as component c in (3.3*a*), and *the sink* the auxiliary output components such as g in (3.3*b*). The remaining input components will be collectively called *the argument*, and the remaining output components, *the result.*

In general, both source and sink lines will have to be introduced in order to construct an invertible realization of a given function.

$$
\text{(a)}\quad \begin{array}{cc} x_1\,x_2 \\ 0\;0 \\ 0\;1 \\ 1\;0 \\ 1\;1 \end{array} \rightarrow \begin{array}{c} y \\ 0 \\ 0 \\ 0 \\ 1 \end{array} \qquad\qquad \text{(b)}\quad \begin{array}{c} x \\ 0 \\ 1 \end{array} \rightarrow \begin{array}{c} y \\ 1 \\ 0 \end{array} \tag{3.4}
$$

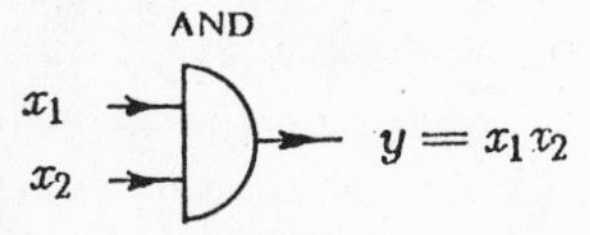

For example, from the *invertible* function AND/NAND defined by the table

$$
\begin{array}{c} 000 \\ 001 \\ 010 \\ 011 \\ 100 \\ 101 \\ 110 \\ 111 \end{array} \rightarrow \begin{array}{c} 000 \\ 001 \\ 010 \\ 111 \\ 100 \\ 101 \\ 110 \\ 011 \end{array}, \tag{3.5}
$$

the AND function (3.4a) can be realized as in (3.6a) with one source line and two sink lines.

$$
\text{(a)}\quad \begin{array}{ccc} c & x_1 & x_2 \\ 0 & \boxed{0} & \boxed{0} \\ 0 & \boxed{0} & \boxed{1} \\ 0 & \boxed{1} & \boxed{0} \\ 0 & \boxed{1} & \boxed{1} \\ 1 & 0 & 0 \\ 1 & 0 & 1 \\ 1 & 1 & 0 \\ 1 & 1 & 1 \end{array} \rightarrow \begin{array}{ccc} y & g_1 & g_2 \\ \boxed{0} & 0 & 0 \\ \boxed{0} & 0 & 1 \\ \boxed{0} & 1 & 0 \\ \boxed{1} & 1 & 1 \\ 1 & 0 & 0 \\ 1 & 0 & 1 \\ 1 & 1 & 0 \\ 0 & 1 & 1 \end{array} \qquad\qquad \text{(b)}\quad \begin{array}{cc} x & c \\ 0 & 0 \\ \boxed{0} & 1 \\ 1 & 0 \\ \boxed{1} & 1 \end{array} \rightarrow \begin{array}{cc} y & c' \\ 0 & 0 \\ \boxed{1} & 1 \\ 1 & 0 \\ \boxed{0} & 1 \end{array} \tag{3.6}
$$

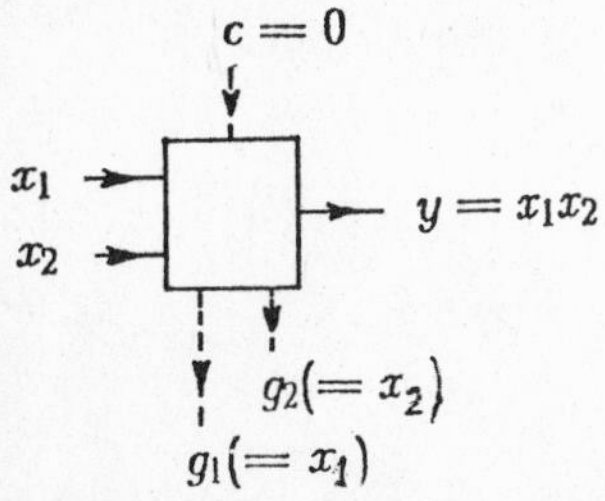

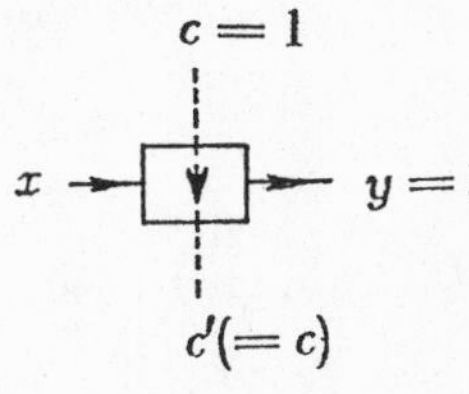

Observe that in order to obtain the desired result the source lines must be fed with specified *constant* values, i.e., with values that do not depend on the argument. As for the sink lines, some may yield values that do depend on the argument—as in (3.6a)—and thus cannot be used as input constants for a new computation; these will be called *garbage* lines. On the other hand, some sink lines may return constant values; indeed, this happens whenever the functional relationship between argument and result is itself an invertible one. To give a trivial example, suppose that the NOT function (3.4*b*), which is invertible, were not available as a primitive. In this case one could still realize it starting from another invertible function, e.g., from the XOR/FAN-OUT function as in (3.6*b*); note that here the sink, c', returns in any case the value present at the source, c. In general, if there exists between a set of source lines and a set of sink lines an invertible functional relationship that is independent of the value of all other input lines, then this pair of sets will be called (for reasons that will be made clear in Section 5) a *temporary-storage channel.*

Using the terminology just established, we shall say that the above realization of the FAN-OUT function by means of an invertible combinational function is a realization *with constants,* that of the XOR function, *with garbage,* that of the AND function, *with constants and garbage,* and that of the NOT function, with *temporary storage* (for the sake of nomenclature, the source lines that are part of a temporary-storage channel will not be counted as lines of constants). In referring to a realization, features that are not explicitly mentioned will be assumed not to have been used; thus, a realization "with temporary storage" is one *without* constants or garbage. A realization that does not require any source or sink lines will be called an *isomorphic* realization.

4. The fundamental theorem

In the light of the particular examples discussed in the previous section, this section establishes a general method for realizing an *arbitrary* finite function ϕ by means of an *invertible* finite function f.

In general, given any finite function one obtains a new one by assigning specified values to certain distinguished input lines (*source*) and disregarding certain distinguished output lines (*sink*). According to the following theorem, *any* finite function can be realized in this way starting from a suitable *invertible* one.

THEOREM 4.1 *For every finite function* $\phi: \mathbf{B}^m \to \mathbf{B}^n$ *there exists an invertible finite function* $f: \mathbf{B}^r \times \mathbf{B}^m \to \mathbf{B}^n \times \mathbf{B}^{r+m-n}$, *with* $r \leq n$, *such that*

$$f\langle \overbrace{0,\ldots,0}^{r}, x_1,\ldots,x_m\rangle = \phi_i\langle x_1,\ldots,x_m\rangle, \qquad (i = 1,\ldots,n). \tag{4.1}$$

Thus, whatever can be computed by an arbitrary finite function according to the schema of Figure 4.2a can also be computed by an *invertible* finite function according to the schema of Figure 4.2*b*.

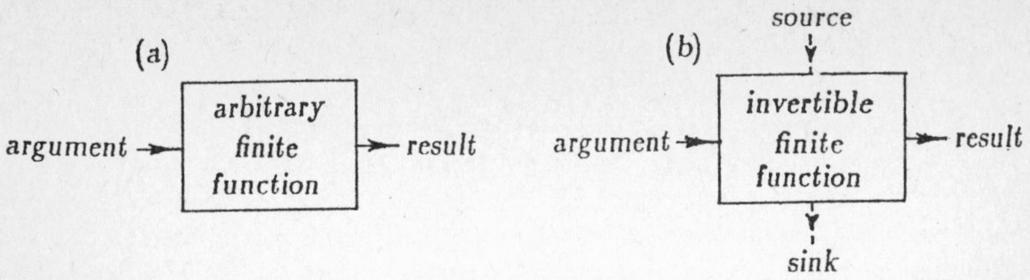

FIG. 4.2 *Any finite function (a) can be realized as an invertible finite function (b) having a number of auxiliary input lines which are fed with constants and a number of auxiliary output lines whose values are disregarded.*

5. Invertible primitives and reversible networks

In the previous section, each given ϕ was realized by a reversible combinational network consisting of a single occurrence of an *ad hoc* primitive f. In this section, we shall study the realization of arbitrary finite functions by means of reversible combinational networks constructed from given primitives; in particular, from a certain finite set of very simple primitives.

It is well known that, under the ordinary rules of function composition, the two-input NAND element constitutes a universal primitive for the set of all combinational functions.

In the theory of reversible computing, a similar role is played by the AND/NAND element, defined by (3.5) and graphically represented as in Figure 5.1c. Referring to (3.6a), observe that $y = x_1x_2$ (AND function) when $c = \mathbf{0}$, and $y = \overline{x_1x_2}$ (NAND function) when $c = \mathbf{1}$. Thus, as long as one supplies a value of $\mathbf{1}$ to input c and disregards outputs g_1 and g_2, the AND/NAND element can be substituted for any occurence of a NAND gate in an ordinary combinational network.

In spite of having ruled out fan-out as an intrinsic feature provided by the composition rules, one can still achieve it as a *function* realized by means of an invertible primitive, such as the XOR/FAN-OUT element defined by (3.2) and graphically represented as in Figure 5.1*b*. In (3.3a), observe that $y_1 = y_2 = x$ when $c = \mathbf{0}$ (FAN-OUT function); and in (3.3*b*), that $y = x_1 \oplus x_2$ (XOR function).

Finally, recall that finite composition always yields invertible functions when applied to invertible functions (cf. Section 2).

Therefore, using the set of invertible primitives consisting of the AND/NAND element and the XOR/FAN-OUT element, any combinational network can be immediately translated into a reversible one which, when provided with appropriate input constants, will reproduce the behavior of the original network. Indeed, even the set consisting of the single element AND/NAND is sufficient for this purpose, since XOR/FAN-OUT can be obtained from AND/NAND, with one line of temporarty storage, by taking advantage of the mapping $\langle \mathbf{1}, p, q\rangle \mapsto \langle \mathbf{1}, p, p \oplus q\rangle$.)

In the element-by-element substitution procedure outlined above, the number of source and sink lines that are introduced is roughly proportional to the number of computing elements that make up the original network. From the viewpoint of a physical implementation, where signals are encoded in some form of energy, each constant input entails the supply of energy of predictable form, or *work*, and each garbage output entails the removal of energy of unpredictable form, or *heat*. In this context, a realization with fewer source and sink lines might point the way to a physical implementation that dissipates less energy.

Our plan to achieve a less wasteful realization will be based on the following concept. While it is true that each garbage signal is "random," in the sense that it is not predictable without knowing the value of the argument, yet it will be correlated with other signals in the network. Taking advantage of this, one can augment the network in such a way as to make correlated signals interfere with one another and produce a number of *constant* signals instead of garbage. These constants can be used as source signals in other parts of the network. In this way, the overall number of both source and sink lines can be reduced.

In the remainder of this section we shall show how, in the abstract context of reversible computing, destructive interference of correlated signals can be achieved in a systematic way. First, we shall prove that any invertible finite function can be realized *isomorphically* from certain generalized AND/NAND primitives. Then, we shall prove that any of these primitives can be realized from the AND/NAND element possibly with temporary storage but with *no garbage*.

DEFINITION 5.1 Consider the set $\mathbf{B} = \{0, 1\}$ with the usual structure of Boolean ring, with "$\oplus$" (*exclusive*-OR) denoting the addition operator, and juxtaposition (AND) the multiplication operator. For any $n > 0$, the *generalized* AND/NAND *function of order* n, denoted by $\theta^{(n)}: \mathbf{B}^n \to \mathbf{B}^n$, is defined by

$$\theta^{(n)}: \begin{pmatrix} x_1 \\ x_2 \\ \vdots \\ x_{n-1} \\ x_n \end{pmatrix} \mapsto \begin{pmatrix} x_1 \\ x_2 \\ \vdots \\ x_{n-1} \\ x_n \oplus x_1 x_2 \cdots x_{n-1} \end{pmatrix}. \tag{5.1}$$

We have already encountered $\theta^{(1)}$ under the name of the NOT element, $\theta^{(2)}$ under the name of the XOR/FAN-OUT element, and $\theta^{(3)}$ under the name of the AND/NAND element. The generalized AND/NAND functions are graphically represented as in Figure 5.1*d*.

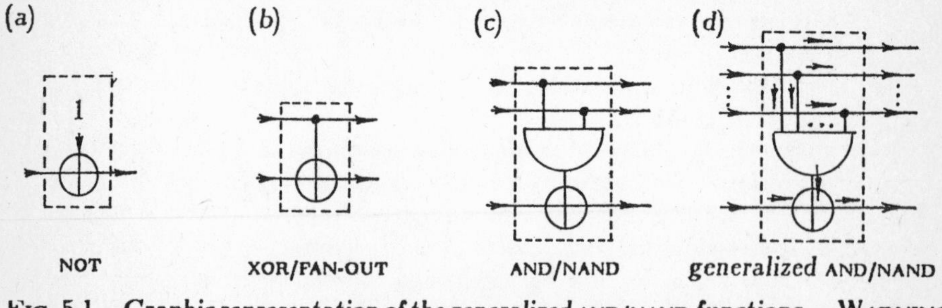

FIG. 5.1 *Graphic representation of the generalized* AND/NAND *functions.* WARNING: This representation is offered only as a mnemonic aid in recalling a function's truth table, and is not meant to imply any "internal structure" for the function, or suggest any particular implementation mechanism. *(a)* $\theta^{(1)}$*, which coincides with the* NOT *element; (b)* $\theta^{(2)}$*, which coincides with the* XOR/FAN-OUT *element; (c)* $\theta^{(3)}$*, which coincides with the* AND/NAND *element; and, in general, (d)* $\theta^{(n)}$*, the generalized* AND/NAND *function of order* n*. The bilateral symmetry of these symbols recalls the fact that each of the corresponding functions coincides with its inverse.*

THEOREM 5.1 *Any invertible finite function of order n can be obtained by composition of generalized* AND/NAND *functions of order* $\leq n$.

Remark. Note that the realization referred to by Theorem 5.1 is an *isomorphic* one (unlike that of Section 4, which makes use of source and sink lines).

THEOREM 5.2 *There exist invertible finite functions of order n which cannot be obtained by composition of generalized* AND/NAND *functions of order strictly less than n.*

Remark. According to this theorem, the AND/NAND primitive is not sufficient for the *isomorphic* reversible realization of arbitrary invertible finite functions of larger order. This result can be generalized to any *finite* set of invertible primitives Thus, one must turn to a less restrictive realization schema involving source and sink lines.

THEOREM 5.3 *Any invertible finite function can be realized, possibly with temporary storage,* [but with no garbage!] *by means of a reversible combinational network using as primitives the generalized* AND/NAND *elements of order* ≤ 3.

Proof. In view of Theorem 5.1, it will be sufficient to realize (possibly with temporary storage) all $\theta^{(i)}$ for $i \leq n$, where n is the order of the given function. We shall proceed by recursion; namely, given $\theta^{(n-1)}$, $\theta^{(n)}$ can be realized with one line of temporary storage as follows.

Construct the network of Figure 5.3, which contains two occurrences of $\theta^{(n-1)}$ and one occurrence of $\theta^{(3)}$. Observe that $c' \equiv c$, since every generalized AND/NAND element coincides with its inverse (and thus the second occurrence of $\theta^{(n-1)}$ cancels the effect of the first). Therefore, the pair $\langle\{c\},\{c'\}\rangle$ constitutes a temporary-storage channel. When $c = \mathbf{0}$, the remaining variables behave as the corresponding ones of $\theta^{(n)}$. ∎

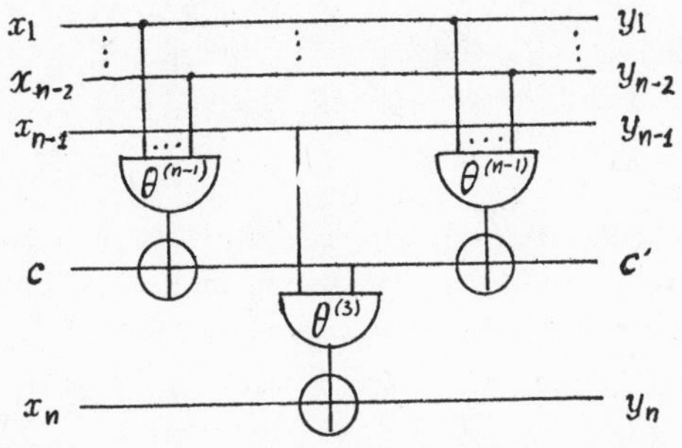

FIG. 5.3 *Realization with temporary storage of $\theta^{(n)}$ from $\theta^{(n-1)}$ (and $\theta^{(3)}$). In this network, when $c = \mathbf{0}$, also $c' = \mathbf{0}$, and the remaining components behave as the corresponding ones of $\theta^{(n)}$.*

The proof of Theorem 5.3 establishes a general mechanisms for bringing about destructive interference of garbage. With reference to Figure 5.3, which can serve as an outline for the general case, observe that the left portion of the network is accompanied by its "mirror image" on the right. The left portion computes an intermediate result (on the line running from c to c') that is needed as an input to the lower portion and is returned by it unchanged. Having performed its function, this intermediate result is then "undone" by the right portion, so that no garbage is left.

The reader may refer to [7] for more specific examples of destructive interference of garbage.

The following list (cf. Figure 5.5) sums up in a schematic way the input/output resources of which a reversible network must avail itself in order to be able to compute a finite function ϕ.

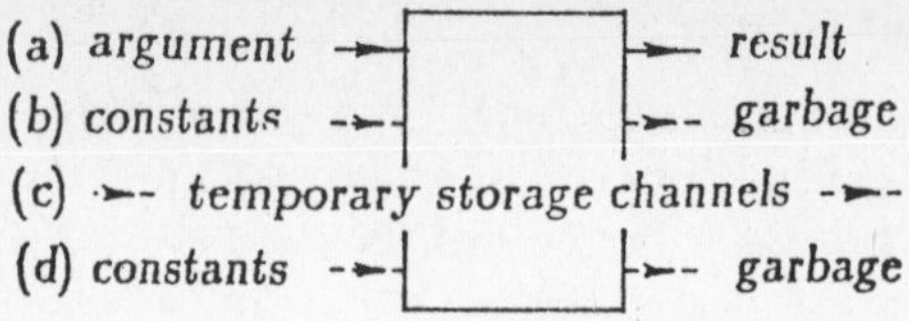

FIG. 5.5 *Classification of input and output lines in a reversible combinational network, according to their function. (a) Argument and result of the intended computation. (b) Constant and garbage lines to account for the noninvertibility of the given function. (c) "Temporary storage" registers required when only a restricted set of primitives is available. (d) Additional constant and garbage lines required when in designing the network one chooses not to take full advantage of the correlation between internal streams of data, and thus looses opportunities to bring about destructive interference of garbage.*

6. Conservative logic

Universal logic capabilities can still be obtained even if one restricts one's attention to combinational networks that, in addition to being reversible, conserve in the output the number of **0**'s and **1**'s that are present at the input. The study of such networks is part of a discipline called *conservative logic* [7] (also cf. [11]). As a matter of fact, most of the results of Sections 4 and 5 were originally derived by Fredkin and associates in the context of conservative logic.

In conservative logic, all data processing is ultimately reduced to *conditional routing* of signals. Roughly speaking, signals are treated as unalterable objects that can be moved around in the course of a computation but never created or destroyed.

The basic primitive of conservative logic is the *Fredkin gate*, defined by the table

$$\begin{array}{ccc} c & x_1 & x_2 \\ \mathbf{0} & \mathbf{0} & \mathbf{0} \\ \mathbf{0} & \mathbf{0} & \mathbf{1} \\ \mathbf{0} & \mathbf{1} & \mathbf{0} \\ \mathbf{0} & \mathbf{1} & \mathbf{1} \\ \mathbf{1} & \mathbf{0} & \mathbf{0} \\ \mathbf{1} & \mathbf{0} & \mathbf{1} \\ \mathbf{1} & \mathbf{1} & \mathbf{0} \\ \mathbf{1} & \mathbf{1} & \mathbf{1} \end{array} \quad \rightarrow \quad \begin{array}{ccc} c' & y_1 & y_2 \\ \mathbf{0} & \mathbf{0} & \mathbf{0} \\ \mathbf{0} & \mathbf{1} & \mathbf{0} \\ \mathbf{0} & \mathbf{0} & \mathbf{1} \\ \mathbf{0} & \mathbf{1} & \mathbf{1} \\ \mathbf{1} & \mathbf{0} & \mathbf{0} \\ \mathbf{1} & \mathbf{0} & \mathbf{1} \\ \mathbf{1} & \mathbf{1} & \mathbf{0} \\ \mathbf{1} & \mathbf{1} & \mathbf{1} \end{array} . \tag{6.1}$$

This computing element can be visualized as a device that performs conditional crossover of two *data* signals a and b according to the value of a *control* signal c (Figure 6.1a). When $c = \mathbf{1}$ the two data signals follow parallel paths, while when $c = \mathbf{0}$ they cross over (Figure 6.1b).

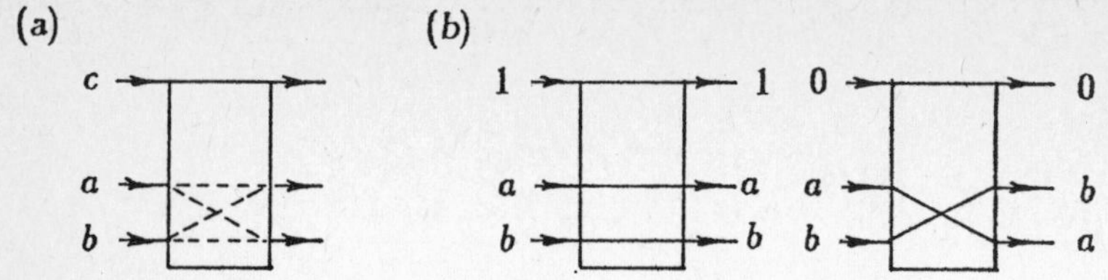

FIG. 6.1 *(a) Symbol and (b) operation of the Fredkin gate.*

In order to prove the universality of this gate as a logic primitive for reversible computing, it is sufficient to observe that AND can be obtained from the mapping $\langle p, q, \mathbf{0}\rangle \mapsto \langle p, pq, \bar{p}q\rangle$, and NOT and FAN-OUT from the mapping $\langle p, \mathbf{1}, \mathbf{0}\rangle \mapsto \langle p, p, \bar{p}\rangle$.

In a conservative logic circuit, the number of 1's, which is conserved in the operation of the circuit, is the sum of the number of 1's in different parts of the circuit. Thus, this quantity is an additive "integral of the motion," and can be shown to play a role analogous to that of energy in physical systems. Other connections between conservative logic and physics will discussed in more detail in [7], where, in particular, we describe a physical realization of the Fredkin gate based on elastic collisions.

7. Reversible sequential computing

In Sections 4 and 5, we started from a certain computing object (viz., a finite function), and we discussed the conditions for its *reversible* realization first (a) as an object of the same nature (viz., an invertible finite function) treated as a "lumped" system, thus stressing *functional* aspects, and then (*b*) as a "distributed" system (viz., a reversible combinational network), thus stressing *structural* aspects and paving the way for a natural physical implementation.

By and large, we shall follow a similar plan in dealing with the more complex computing objects that constitute the paradigms of sequential computing, namely, *finite automata* (in the present section), *Turing machines* (Section 8), and *cellular automata* (Section 9).

By definition, a finite automaton is *reversible* if its transition function is invertible. Thus, in order to realize a finite automaton by means of a reversible sequential network, it will be sufficient to take its transition function, construct a reversible realization of it, and use this as the combinational part of the desired sequential network. The problem of reversibly realizing an arbitrary finite function has been solved in Section 4. Thus, we have the following theorem.

TEOREM 7.1. *For every finite automaton $\tau: X \times Q \to Q \times Y$, where $X = B^m$, $Y = B^n$, and $Q = B^u$, there exists a reversible finite automaton $t: (B^r \times B^m) \times B^u \to B^u \times (B^n \times B^{r+m-n})$, with $r \leq n+u$, such that*

$$t_i\langle \overbrace{\mathbf{0}, \ldots, \mathbf{0}}^{r}, x_1, \ldots, x_m, q_1, \ldots, q_u\rangle = \tau_i\langle x_1, \ldots, x_m, q_1, \ldots, q_u\rangle, \quad (i = 1, \ldots, u+n).$$

In other words, whatever can be computed by an arbitrary finite automaton according to the scheme of Figure 7.3a can also be computed by a *reversible* finite automaton according to the schema of Figure 7.3*b*.

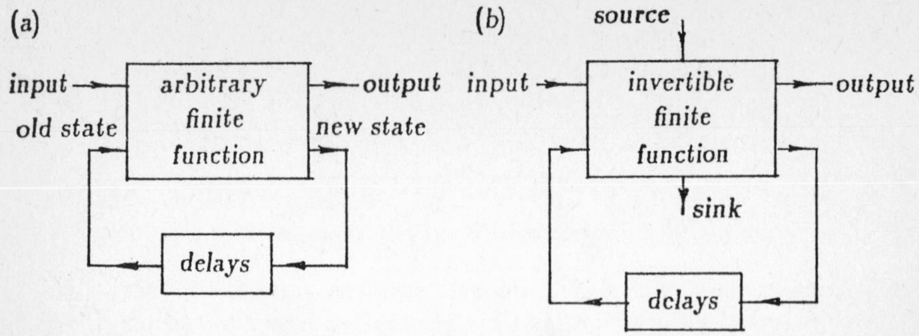

Fig. 7.3 *Any finite automaton (a) can be realized as a reversible finite automaton (b) having a number of auxiliary input lines (source) which are fed with constants and a number of auxiliary output lines (sink) whose values are disregarded.*

Having discussed the realization of finite automata by means of reversible finite automata, we turn now to the realization of finite automata by means of reversible finite sequential networks based on given primitives.

It is clear that all the arguments of Sections 5 and 6 concerning finite functions immediately apply to the transition function of any given finite automaton. In particular, every finite automaton can be realized by a finite, reversible sequential network based on, say, the AND/NAND primitive. With reference to Figure 5.5, one can visualize such a realization by feeding back, via delay elements, some of the result lines to some of the argument lines, and *all* all of the temporary-storage outputs to the corresponding inputs. In order to insure the desired behavior, the delay elements associated with the temporary-storage channels must be initialized *once and for all* with appropriate values (typically, all **0**'s), while the source lines must be fed with appropriate constants (typically, all **0**'s) *at every sequential step.*

In a conventional computer, power dissipation is proportional to the number of logic gates. On the other hand, the number of constants/garbage lines in Figure 7.4 is at worst proportional to the number of input/output lines (cf. Theorems 4.1 and 5.3). From the viewpoint of a physical implementation, where signals are encoded in some form of energy, the above schema can be interpreted as follows: *Using invertible logic gates, it is ideally possible to build a sequential computer with zero internal power dissipation.* Power dissipation might arise outside the circuit, typically at the input/output interface, if the user chose to connect input or output lines to nonreversible digital circuitry. Even in this case, power dissipation is at most proportional to the number of argument/result lines,* rather than to the number of logic gates (as in ordinary computers), and is thus independent of the "complexity" of the function being computed. This constitutes the central result of the present paper.

8. Reversible Turing machines

We shall assume the reader to be familiar with the concept of *Turing machine.* From

*According to Theorem 4.1, the number of constant lines need not be greater than that of result lines, and the number of garbage lines need not be greater than that of argument lines.

our viewpoint, a Turing machine is a closed, time-discrete dynamical system having three state components, i.e., (*a*) an infinite *tape*, (*b*) the internal state of a finite automaton called *head*, and (*c*) a *counter* whose content indicates on which tape square the head will operate next. Let T, H, and C be the sets of tape, head, and counter states, respectively. A Turing machine is *reversible* if its transition function $\tau: T \times H \times C \rightarrow T \times H \times C$ is invertible.

It is well known that for every recursive function there exists a Turing machine that computes it, and, in particular, that there exist computation-universal Turing machines. Are these capabilities preserved if one restricts one's attention to the class of *reversible* Turing machines?

The answer to the above question is positive. In fact, in [4] Bennett exhibits a procedure for constructing, for *any* Turing machine and for certain quite general computation formats, a reversible Turing machine that performs essentially the same computations.

In order to obtain the desired behavior, Bennett's machine is initialized so that all of the tape is blank except for one connected portion representing the computation's argument, and the head is set to a distinguished "initial" state and positioned by the argument's first symbol. At the end of the computation, i.e., when the head enters a distinguished "terminal" state, the result will appear on the tape alongside with the argument, and the rest of the tape will be blank. Thus, a number of tape squares that are initially blank will eventually contain the result. These squares fulfill a role similar to that played by the constants/garbage lines in Section 5, in the sense that they provide a sufficient supply of "predictable" input values (blanks) at the beginning of the computation, and collect the required amount of "random" output values (in this case, a copy of the argument—cf. the first row of (4.2)) at the end of the computation. Moreover, during the computation a number of originally blank tape squares may be written over and eventually erased. These squares fulfill a role similar to that played by the temporary-storage lines in Section 5.

It is clear that, like the constants in the reversible combinational networks of Section 5, the blanks in Bennett's machine play an essential role in the computation, since without their presence one could not achieve *universality* and *reversibility* at the same time. Intuitively, computation in reversible systems requires *a higher degree of "predictability" about the environment's initial conditions* than computation in nonreversible ones.

9. Reversible cellular automata

We shall assume the reader to have some familiarity with the concept of *cellular automaton*—in essence an array of identical, uniformly interconnected finite automata[21]. From a physical viewpoint cellular automata are in many respects more satisfactory models of computing processes than Turing machines[22], and for this reason the question of whether there exist reversible cellular automata that are computation- and construction-universal is of particular interest (and has been long debated).

The answer to the above question is positive. In fact, in [20] Toffoli exhibits a procedure for constructing, for *any* cellular automaton (presented as an infinite, space-iterative sequential network), a reversible cellular automaton that realizes it. As in the case of reversible Turing machines, also in reversible cellular automata the predictability of a computing structure's environment plays an essential role in making the computation proceed as intended.

It is well known that any Turing machine can be embedded in a suitable cellular automaton. Thus, according to the foregoing discussion, any Turing machine can be realized by an infinite *reversible* sequential nework.

10. Conclusions

We have shown that the choice to use reversible mechanisms in describing functional and structural aspects of computing processes is a viable one. What can be gained from this choice?

In the synthesis of an abstract computing system, the requirement that the system be reversible can in general be met only at the cost of greater structural complexity. This "logical" overhead is quite slight; on the other hand, the system's very reversibility promises to be a key factor in leading to a more efficient physical realization, since, at the microscopic level, the "primitives" and the "composition rules" available in the physical world resemble much more closely those used in the theory of reversible computing than those used in traditional logic design.

Acknowledgments

Many ideas discussed in the present paper were originated by Prof. Edward Fredkin, to whom I also owe much useful advice and encouragment.

This research was supported by the Advanced Research Projects Agency of the Department of Defense and was monitored by the Office of Naval Research under Contract No. N00014-75-C-0661.

List of references

[4] Bennett, C. H., "Logical Reversibility of Computation," *IBM J. Res. Dev.* **6** (1973), 525-532.

[7] Fredkin, Edward, *and* Toffoli, Tommaso, "Conservative Logic," (in preparation). Some of the material of this paper is tentatively available in the form of unpublished notes from Prof. Fredkin's lectures, collected and organized by Bill Silver in a *6.895 Term Paper,* "Conservative Logic," and in the form of another *6.895 Term Paper,* "A Reversible Computer Using Conservative Logic," by Edward Barton, both at the MIT Dept. of Electr. Eng. Comp. Sci. (1978).

[11] Kinoshita, Kozo, *et al.*, "On Magnetic Bubble Circuits," *IEEE Trans. Computers* **C-25** (1976), 247-253.

[12] Landauer, Rolf, "Irreversibility and Heat Generation in the Computing Process," *IBM J.* **5** (1961), 183-191.

[20] Toffoli, Tommaso, "Computation and Construction Universality of Reversible Cellular Automata," *J. Comput. Syst. Sci.* **15** (1977), 213-231.

[21] Toffoli, Tommaso, "Cellular Automata Mechanics" (Ph. D. Thesis), *Tech. Rep. no. 208*, Logic of Computers Group, Univ. of Michigan (1977).

[22] Toffoli, Tommaso, "The Role of the Observer in Uniform Systems," *Applied General Systems Research* (ed. G. J. Klir), 395–400 (Plenum Press, 1978).

[23] Toffoli, Tommaso, "Bicontinuous Extensions of Invertible Combinatorial Functions," *Tech. Memo MIT/LCS/TM-124*, MIT Lab. for Comp. Sci. (1979) (to appear in *Math. Syst. Theory*).

[27] Toffoli, Tommaso, "Reversible Computing," *Tech. Memo MIT/LCS/TM-151*, MIT Lab. for Comp. Sci. (1980).

THE USE OF METASYSTEM TRANSITION IN THEOREM PROVING AND PROGRAM OPTIMIZATION

Valentin F. Turchin, The City College, The City University of New York

Compare proving a theorem in an axiomatic system with the computation process when we are dealing with recursive function definitions. The former is nondeterministic and requires either an exhaustive search or an heuristic technique to set subgoals which are likely to lead to the desired end. The latter is deterministic and straightforward. Obviously, we should try to substitute the proof by computation for the proof by constructing a demonstration if our aim is to facilitate computerization. The purpose of the present paper is to introduce a technique which, as we believe, crucially increases the power of the proof by computation.

1. Metasystem transition in formal arithmetic

We shall illustrate our idea by examples from formal arithmetic. In the axiomatic arithmetic, 0 is a constant, x, y, etc. are variables, and x' denotes the number which immediately follows x . The axioms are those of the predicate calculus with equality, the axiom of induction, and a number of specific axioms, which may be, e.g., as follows:

(1) $x=y \Rightarrow x'=y'$

(2) $x'=y' \Rightarrow x=y$

(3) $\neg\, x'=0$

(4) $x+0 = 0$

(5) $x+y' = (x+y)'$

(see [1]; universal quantifiers are implied; we will not use multiplication.)

In the recursive arithmetic the numbers are: 0, 01, 011, etc. The predicate of equality and the function of addition are recursive functions defined in some algorithmic language. Our formalism is based on Refal (see [2-4]). The definition of equality and addition in Refal is:

#1.1 $k=(0)(0) \Rightarrow T$

#1.2 $k=(e_x 1)(e_y 1) \Rightarrow k=(e_x)(e_y) \perp$

#1.3 $k= e_x \Rightarrow F$

#2.1 $k+(e_x)(0) \Rightarrow e_x$

#2.2 $k+(e_x)(e_y 1) \Rightarrow k+(e_x)(e_y) \perp 1$

Essentials of Refal can be seen here even without reading the description of the language. Functions are defined on expressions , meaning by an expression any string of symbols and parentheses having correct structure with respect to parentheses. A function definition is a sequence of sentences, which are replacement rules, with $\Rightarrow$ separating the right side from the left. A function call is represented by $k \mathcal{F} \mathcal{E} \perp$, where $\mathcal{F}$ is a function symbol and $\mathcal{E}$ is the argument. Concretization brackets k and $\perp$ obey the bracket syntax, the sign $\Rightarrow$ serves as $\perp$ for the initial k in the left side of a sentence. e_x, e_y, etc. are free e-variables, which can take any expressions as values. Free s-variables: s_x, s_y, etc. take only symbols as their values. In concretizing (evaluating) a function call, the first applicable sentence is used in each replacement step. The applicability of a sentence and the values of the free variables are determined in matching the function call with the left side. The Refal machine transforms workable expressions in its view-field , step by step, using sentences until there are no k-signs in the view-field.

Consider the theorem

(6) $0'' + 0''' = 0'''''$

of the axiomatic arithmetic. To prove it,we start from the axiom (5) with x=0'', and y=0 :

(7) $0'' + 0' = (0''+ 0)'$

Using axiom (4) with x=0'', we have:

(8) $0'' + 0 = 0''$

From (7), (8), and the axioms for equality we derive:

(9) $0'' + 0' = 0'''$

Proceding in this manner, we obtain a demonstration of (6) in two more steps.

The analogue of theorem (6) in the recursive arithmetic is the statement that the result of the evaluation of the function call $k+(011)(0111)\perp$ is 011111 . To prove this statement we only have to put the former into the view-field of the Refal machine, to start the machine, and to check that when it stops, the contents of the view-field is the latter.

Consider now a statement with (implied) universal quantifiers:

(10) $\neg x' = 0$

which is an axiom in the axiomatic arithmetic. In the recursive arithmetic it is equivalent to the statement that the concretization of

(11) $k{=}(e_x 1)(0)\bot$

is F with any e_x .

To formalize this statement, we introduce the function (predicate)

#3 $kP^1 e_x \Rightarrow k{=}(e_x 1)(0)\bot$

Our statement now is: the definition #3 is functionally equivalent to the following definition:

#4 $kP^1 e_x \Rightarrow F$

(to be referred as an F-identity).

We say that a program (algorithm) $\mathcal{A}'$ in Refal is functionally equivalent to an algorithm $\mathcal{A}$ with respect to function $\mathcal{F}$, iff for every expression $\mathcal{E}$ from the domain of $\mathcal{F}$ according to $\mathcal{A}$, the concretization of $k\mathcal{F}\mathcal{E}\bot$ according to $\mathcal{A}'$ produces the same result as according to $\mathcal{A}$. The transformation of $\mathcal{A}$ into $\mathcal{A}'$ will be called an equivalence transformation. We note that the relation between $\mathcal{A}'$ and $\mathcal{A}$ is not symmetric, thus it is not a "relation of equivalency" in the usual mathematical sense. The domain of a function may be extended as a result of an equivalence transformation.

A system of rules for equivalence transformations in Refal has been formulated (see [3]). We shall not reproduce these rules in the present paper, but will use them in an informal manner. In addition to the rules of equivalence transformations, a strategy of applying these rules has been also formulated in [3], which results in an algorithm of equivalence transformation. We denote this algorithm Q without its formal definition. Instead we shall show in examples what it can, and what it cannot do.

It is easy to transform #3 into #4. We have only to "drive" through the Refal machine a set of workable expressions represented by a general Refal expression, which may include, unlike a workable expression, free variables. We call this procedure driving . To drive expression (11), we notice that neither #1.1, nor #1.2 will be found applicable for concretization, whatever the value of e_x is. Hence #1.3 will be used, which gives F as the result.

This was one of the simplest cases of driving. Generally, the Refal sentence used in concretization step will depend on the values of the free variables, which leads to branching. The branches will correspond to certain subsets of the set of all possible values of each variable involved. We call this subsets <u>contractions</u> of the original full set, and represent them as substitutions for variables. For example, the contraction $(e_x \rightarrow Ae_x)$ defines:(1)the subset of the set of all expressions comprising all expressions which start with A; (2)the corresponding branching condition depending on the value of the variable e_x;(3)the new value of the variable e_x, which is the old value less the initial A . The set of all possible values of the new variable e_x will again be the full set of all expressions.

Consider the theorem:

$$0 + x = 0$$

which is proved by induction in the axiomatic arithmetic. In the recursive arithmetic, this is equivalent to the transformation of

#5 $\quad kP^2e_x \Rightarrow k{=}(k{+}(0)(e_x)\bot)(e_x)\bot$

into the <u>T-identity</u>: $kP^2e_x \Rightarrow T$.

Let us put

(12) $\quad kP^2e_x\bot$

into the view-field of the Refal machine. In one step we will have:

(13) $\quad k{=}(k{+}(0)(e_x)\bot)(e_x)\bot$

Apply driving to (13). The concretization of the function + call leads to the branching:

$$\begin{cases} (e_x \rightarrow 0)\text{: sentence \#2.1 will be used} \\ (e_x \rightarrow e_x)\text{: sentence \#2.2 will be used} \end{cases}$$

If the first branch is taken, we easily come to T as the final result of concretization. Taking the second branch, we have

(14) $\quad k{=}(k{+}(0)(e_x)\bot\ 1)(e_x\ 1)\bot$

in the view-field as the result of the substitution for e_x and the subsequent step of the Refal machine using #2.2 .

Now we use #1.2 to concretize (14), which gives:

$$k{=}(k{+}(0)(e_x)\bot)(e_x)\bot$$

We have come to exactly the same configuration in the view-field as it was at an earlier stage (13). The graph of states of the Refal machine which operates according to #5 is:

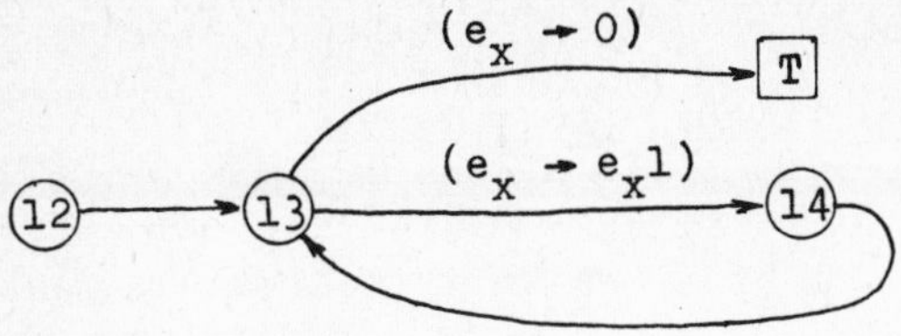

It is not difficult to recognize the structures of this kind, and transform them into:

which corresponds to a T-identity.

The equivalence transformation Q does it. In fact, it does only a little more: it knows how to produce simple generalizations representable in the form of pattern expressions. For example, two expressions: (ABC) and (AXYZ), may be generalized as (Ae_x). Using this generalization technique, Q performs a transformation which is equivalent to a one-time application of the induction principle to a hypothesis produced by generalization.

As our next example, consider the statement:

(15) $\quad x + y = y + x$

expressing the commutativity of addition. In recursive arithmetic it corresponds to the transformation of the predicate

#6 $\quad kP^c(e_x)(e_y) \Rightarrow k{=}(k{+}(e_x)(e_y)\bot)(k{+}(e_y)(e_x)\bot)\bot$

into a T-identity.

Applying Q , we drive the function P^c call, and get

(16) $\quad k{=}(k{+}(e_x)(e_y)\bot)(k{+}(e_y)(e_x)\bot)\bot$

in the view-field. The next step of driving produces the branching:

(17) $\quad (e_y \rightarrow 0){:} \quad k{=}(e_x)(k{+}(0)(e_x)\bot)\bot$

(18) $\quad (e_y \rightarrow e_y1){:}\ k{=}(k{+}(e_x)(e_y)\bot\ 1)(k{+}(e_y1)(e_x)\bot)\bot$

Configuration (17) is transformed into T by Q , as we saw in the preceding example. But configuration (18) causes trouble. The algorithm Q will drive the second + call at the next step, which will lead to a branching on the value of e_x . The branch ($e_x \to 0$) will produce a configuration which is transformed by Q into T , like (17); the branch ($e_x \to e_x 1$) will produce the configuration:

(19) $$k=(k+(e_x 1)(e_y)_\perp\ 1)(k+(e_y 1)(e_x)_\perp\ 1)_\perp$$

which after one more step of driving using #1.2 transforms to:

(20) $$k=(k+(e_x 1)(e_y)_\perp)(k+(e_y 1)(e_x)_\perp)_\perp$$

This configuration is not identical to (16). If we try to continue the transformation of (2) by Q, we only receive new configurations:

$$k=(k+(e_x 11)(e_y)_\perp)(k+(e_y 11)(e_x)_\perp)_\perp$$

etc., but never come back to the original configuration (16). But the only way for Q to transform a definition using induction is to loop to the same configuration in the course of generalized computation -- driving. Thus Q fails to prove the commutativity of addition.

Turning to the axiomatic arithmetic, we can see that the failure of Q to prove theorem (15) stems from the fact that a double induction loop is needed to prove it. Configuration (18) is:

(21) $$(x + y)' = y' + x$$

We first prove by induction an auxilliary theorem:

(22) $$y' + x = (y + x)'$$

and then combine (22) and (21) by the transitivity of equality into

$$(x + y)' = (y + x)'$$

Using axiom (2), we come back to (15), which allows to close the second induction loop. Thus we have a loop nested in loop. The interaction of these two loops leads to the proliferation of new configurations in the straightforward computational approach,which dooms Q to failure.

The fact that statement (22) can be proved as a theorem, and that it will be useful, must be guessed somehow, and (22) must be set as a subgoal if we use the axiomatic approach. In our approach, we look for a different solution.

Suppose one of the free variables in the configuration (16), say e_y, is given a certain value. Then only one induction loop will be needed for transformation, and Q will be able to do the job. We have already seen it for $e_y \to 0$, configuration (17). Giving to e_y the values 01, 011,... etc., we reduce (16) to the configurations:

(23) $$k=(e_x 1)(k+(01)(e_x)_\perp)_\perp$$
$$k=(e_x 11)(k+(011)(e_x)_\perp)_\perp \quad \ldots \text{ etc.}$$

each of which can be transformed by Q into T , as the reader can easily verify.

To prove the commutativity of addition for the case when both variables in P^c are arbitrary, we make a metasystem transition: we formalize Q as a recursive function in Refal (this will become a metasystem with respect to recursive arithmetic) and consider statements about Q . Our idea is to prove that the application of Q to any of the configurations (23) will produce T .Should we succeed in proving this, we have proved that configuration (16) can be replaced by T also. As the instrument of proof we choose the same algorithm Q which is applied to arithmetic statements. The big question is: will the new algorithm resulting from this self-application be more powerful than the original algorithm Q ? In particular, is it possible to prove the commutativity of addition in this way?

It is shown in [3] that the answer to this question is positive. In Sec. 2 we define the basic concepts which serve to formalize metasystem transition, and which lead, in particular,to the desired proof.

2. MST-formulas

The concept of metasystem transition was introduced and taken as the basis for the analysis of evolutionary processes in the author's book [5]. It was the philosophical background exposed in [5]that gave a push to the work on the Refal project in the mid-1960s. The language Refal was designed as the means to facilitate the formalization of metasystem transition. It finds a compromise between the complexity necessary to write non-trivial algorithms, and the simplicity necessary to formulate effective rules of equivalence transformations.

Metasystem transition is one of the main instruments of creative human thinking. To solve a problem, we first try to use some standard system of operations, rules, etc.If we fail we start to analyze why did we fail, and for this purpose we examine the process of applying our rules and operations. We construct a metasystem with respect to the ground-level system of rules and operations which would give us some new, more elaborate, rules and operations to solve the problem. If we fail once more, we analyze the processes on the first metasystem level, which means that we make a second metasystem transition. This time we create instruments which would help us, on the first metasystem level, create instruments to solve the ground-level problem. This transition from the use of an instrument to the analysis of its use and creation of instruments to produce instruments may be repeated again and again; it stands behind the two and a half millennia of the development of contemporary mathematics. For a computer system to match the human being, it must model this process.

Since functions in Refal may be defined only on object expressions (i.e. not including free variables and concretization brackets), the representation of function definitions to be used in metasystem transition must transform sentences (and their parts: free variables, pattern expressions, function calls) into object expressions. We call this representation metacode .

We need not describe the metacode in full (although it is very simple); let us only show how free variables are encoded. Note that metasystem transition may be repeated many times, thus generating a multilevel system. The original functions, such as + , = , P^c , etc., will be referred to as functions of the ground (zero) metasystem level. Functions applied to transform (or generate) these functions, such as Q , will be referred to as being on the first metasystem level. Functions transforming the functions of the first metasystem level are said to be on the second metasystem level, and so on.

Variables of the ground metasystem level, like e_x, s_1, etc. represent sets of object expressions. In metacode (i.e. on the first metasystem level) they turn into non-terminals of the first order E_x, S_1, etc., which are not variables, but just regular symbols. The first metasystem level has, of course, its own free variables, which have again the usual form: e_x, s_1, etc. When we make a metasystem transition to the second level, they turn into first-order non-terminals, while first-order non-terminals E_x, S_1, etc. turn in metacode into second-order non-terminals E^2_x, S^2_1, etc.

The formalism which exploits the idea exposed in Sec.1 rests on the concept of integral metafunction, or metaintegral. In our case we are interested in the metafunction which will be denoted as:

$$k\int P^c(E_x)(e_y)\perp$$

We read it: the metaintegral of P^c over e_x. This is a function which depends on one variable e_y . For any value $\mathcal{E}$ of e_y, the value of this function is the metacode representation of the definition of function

(24) $\quad kP^x(e_x) \Rightarrow kP^c(e_x)(\mathcal{E})\perp$

of one argument e_x .This function, of course will be different for different values of $\mathcal{E}$ (a family of functions).

We introduce now the Refal-interpretation function R, whose definition is: if $[\underline{def}(\mathcal{F})]$ is the metacode of the definition of a function $\mathcal{F}$, and $\mathcal{E}$ is an expression from the domain of $\mathcal{F}$, then

$$kR([\underline{def}(\mathcal{F})])\mathcal{E}\perp \quad = \quad k\mathcal{F}\mathcal{E}\perp \tag{25}$$

Consider an equivalence transformation function Q. It is a metafunction which has the set of all correct metacodes of function definitions as its domain. By the definition of equivalence,

$$kR(\ kQ[\underline{def}(\mathcal{F})]\perp)\mathcal{E}\perp = kR(\ [\underline{def}(\mathcal{F})])\mathcal{E}\perp \tag{26}$$

Combining (25) and (26) we have:

$$k\mathcal{F}\mathcal{E}\perp \ = \ kR(\ kQ[\underline{def}(\mathcal{F})]\perp)\mathcal{E}\perp \tag{27}$$

By the definition of metaintegral,

$$kR(k\textstyle\int P^{c}(E_x)(e_y)\perp)(e_x)\perp \quad = \quad kP^{c}(e_x)(e_y)\perp \tag{28}$$

Therefore, if we redefine function P^c in this way:

$$kP^{c}(e_x)(e_y) \ \Rightarrow \ kR(k\textstyle\int P^{c}(E_x)(e_y)\perp)(e_x)\perp \tag{29}$$

this new definition will be equivalent to the old one. We call such definitions as (29) <u>MST-formulas</u> (MST standing for MetaSystem Transition). An MST-formula defines an equivalence transformation using one or more metasystem transitions.

Using (26) we obtain from (29) another MST-formula:

$$kP^{c}(e_x)(e_y) \ \Rightarrow \ kR(kQk\textstyle\int P^{c}(E_x)(e_y)\perp\perp)(e_x)\perp \tag{30}$$

The algorithm of evaluating P^c according to (30) is this:

<u>Step 1</u>. Take the definition of P^c with a specific e_y, but with an arbitrary e_x. It will be a function of e_x; e.g., if e_y = 011, this function will be

$$kP^{x}(e_x) \ \Rightarrow \ k{=}(k{+}(e_x)(011)\perp)(k{+}(011)(e_x)\perp)\perp \tag{31}$$

<u>Step 2.</u> Translate this function definition into metacode and transform by function Q. A new function definition results.

<u>Step 3</u>. Interpret this last definition with the specified e_x.

We know from Sec.1 that the function resulting from step 2 will always be identical T, because configurations (23) are successfully transformed by Q. But it is only our knowledge, and not yet a fact proven by machine. To have it proved, we must make one more metasystem transition. Let us define:

$$kI^{x}(e_y) \ \Rightarrow \ kQk\textstyle\int P^{c}(E_x)(e_y)\perp\perp \tag{32}$$

and apply to this function transformation Q again. The metacode of (32) is denoted as $k\int I^x(E_y)\perp$. According to (27):

$$(33) \qquad kI^x(e_y)\perp \quad = \quad kR(kQk\int I^x(E_y)\perp\ \perp)(e_y)\perp$$

From (30), (32), and (33) we obtain this MST-formula:

$$(34) \qquad kP^c(e_x)(e_y) \ \Rightarrow\ kR(kR(kQk\int I^x(E_y)\perp\ \perp)(e_y)\perp)(e_x)\perp$$

Together with (32), it defines an equivalence transformation, but it is not yet the final form of the transformed definition. To get the final form, we use an equivalence transformation once more: to simplify the definition (34). This last procedure transforms (34) into a T-identity. The same function Q may be formally used, but even a much simpler technique will suffice on this stage. The essential part of it is just a computation: that of the value of $kQk\int I^x(E_y)\perp\ \perp$. The result will be:

$$(35) \qquad [kI^x(e_y) \ \Rightarrow\ [\, kP^x(e_x) \ \Rightarrow\ T\,]\,]$$

where by bracketing a sentence we denote its metacode.(compare with (32) and (24)). This result is a formal proof by Q that Q proves any definition of type (31) to be a T-identity. It is interesting to note that theorem (22), which in the axiomatic approach must be guessed as a useful subgoal, in our approach appears automatically in the course of computation (and, of course, is easily proven by Q, since it requires only one induction loop).

Using (35) in the right side of (34), we first obtain:

$$kR(\,[\,kP^x(e_x) \ \Rightarrow\ T\,]\,)(e_x)\perp$$

by virtue of the definition of R, and then - by the same definition - T , which completes the formal proof of the commutativity of addition.

It should be stressed that after function Q has been once defined, the use of MST-formulas like (34) is a purely mechanical process: we just write the formula and apply Q to it. One can write many different MST-formulas splitting variables in different ways between two, three,etc. metasystem levels and returning to the ground level by using the interpretation function R .

The algorithm Q must be of certain minimal complexity in order to deal successfully with itself. When this level of complexity is achieved, we have a good reason to believe that the second, third, etc. metasystem transition will also be successful (i.e.provide more and more powerful algorithms), because at each next step of this stairway Q is still applied to itself. It seems plausible that the number of metasystem transitions we have to make in the computational approach is equal to the number of nested loops of induction, but it has not been demonstrated in a rigorous manner.

Theorem proving and program optimization are indistinguishable in our approach, they are two applications of the same functional equivalence transformation. The algorithm Q, although not very strong in proofs by induction, is strong enough to ensure some important types of optimization (see [3]). Coupled with metasystem transition, it should become a powerful instrument of program optimization.

3. System approach to mathematical knowledge

Our approach to theorem proving is not based on mathematical logic in its traditional form. It should be viewed as constituting first steps toward creation of a system of mathematical knowledge, the general plan of which is represented below:

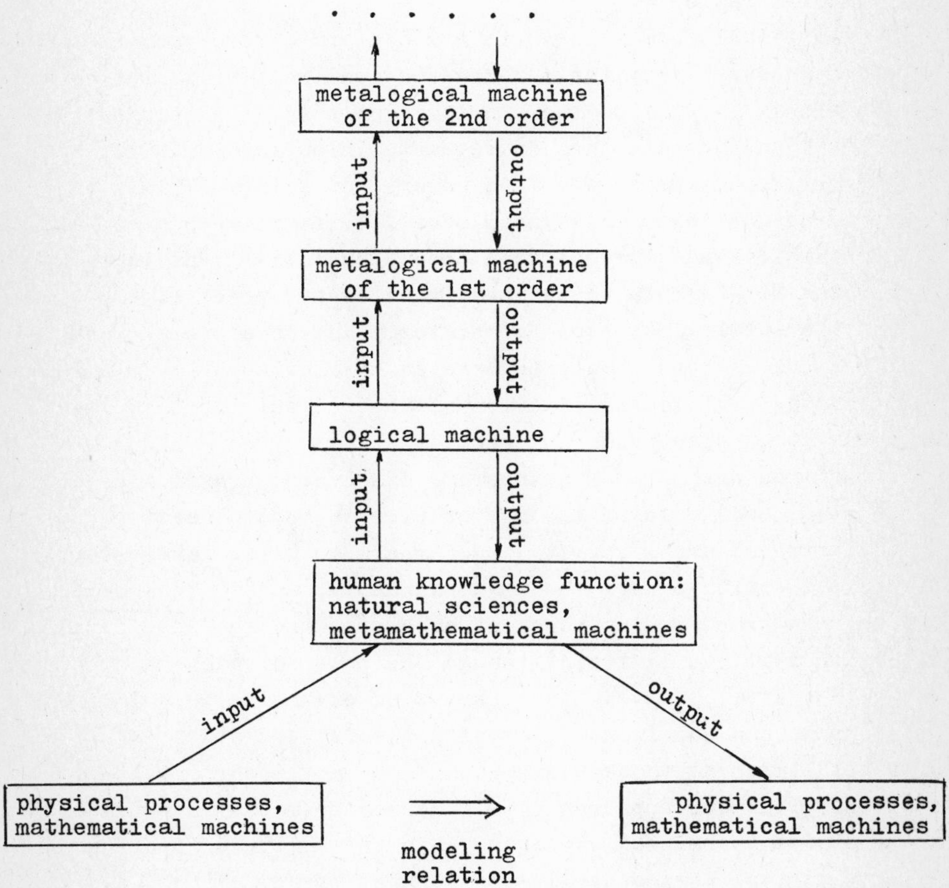

Human knowledge at any moment of time can be seen as a function which receives a material process as its input, and produces (or does not produce) its model as the output. Mathematics is the part of human knowledge which models special type of processes: mathematical machines. Arithmetic functions may serve as example of mathematical machines. They are used by the human knowledge function to create models of physical processes; at the same time they are an object of study of mathematics, and the result of this study is a metamathematical machine.

Our function Q is an example of a metamathematical machine. Equivalence transformation is a conctruction of a model. Metamathematical machines are created and improved using logic. We used logic when obtained a new Q from the old one. Logic, generally, creates new knowledge, makes the human knowledge function evolutionize. Formalization of logic creates a logical machine, which can be deterministic or nondeterministic.

Traditional formal logic is a nondeterministic machine which generates demonstrations; the metamathematical machine in this approach is trivial: it just keeps the knowledge created (the theorems proven) up to date, and outputs them on request. In our approach all the machines will be deterministic, and we are not going to limit the hierarchy by any definite metasystem level. We start with an intelligent metamathematical machine Q ; then create an intelligent logic, which chooses the MST-formula to be used; then create a metalogic, which tries different logics; etc. No metalogic may be supreme, because a more powerful one can always be created by a metasystem transition. There exists no ultimate criterion of the reliability of a logic or metalogic other than proof in practice.

Starting with Goedel's theorem, metasystem transition has been extensively used in logic and mathematics to obtain negative results (incompleteness, unsolvability). We embark on using metasystem transition in a positive way: to expand actually, and in the needed direction, the transforming power of each specific machine, not only to show that it has limits. Although the power of each machine remains, of course, limited, the process of expansion is unlimited -- as far as we can see it now. Goedel's theorem and other negative results set limits to those systems which do not incorporate metasysten transition. Our approach does incorporate metasystem transition as one of its formalized elements. This is why it is free from Goedel's limits. What other limits it has, if any, is not easily seen at the present time.

****

REFERENCES

1. Kleene, S.C., Mathematical Logic, J.Wiley & Sons, 1967.

2. Turchin, V.F., A supercompiler system based on the language Refal, SIGPLAN Notices, 14, No 2, pp.46-54, Febr. 1979.

3. Turchin, V.F., The Language Refal -- The Theory of Compilation and Metasystem Analysis,Courant Computer Science Report #20, February 1980, New York University, 1980.

4. Turchin, V.F., Semantic definitions in Refal and automatic production of compilers, Proc. of the Workshop on Semantics-Directed Compiler Generation, Aarhus University, Denmark, January 14-18 1980, Springer Verlag, 1980.

5. Turchin, V.F., The Phenomenon of Science, Columbia Univ. Press, New York, 1977.

ON THE POWER OF REAL-TIME TURING MACHINES UNDER VARYING SPECIFICATIONS*

(Extended abstract)

Paul M.B. Vitányi
Mathematisch Centrum
2e Boerhaavestraat 49
Amsterdam, The Netherlands

ABSTRACT

We investigate the relative computing power of Turing machines with differences in the number of work tapes, heads pro work tape, instruction repertoire etc. We concentrate on the k-tape, k-head and k-head jump models as well as the 2-way multihead finite automata with and without jumps. Differences in computing power between machines of unlike specifications emerge under the real-time restriction. In particular it is shown that k+1 heads are more powerful than k heads for real-time Turing machines.

1. INTRODUCTION

Since the first Turing machine appeared in 1936, there have been many advances in the field. In the late 1950's the *multitape* Turing machine was introduced, often equiped with a separate read-only input tape. Since then we saw the arrival of the *multihead* Turing machine, Turing machines with a *fast rewind square* (also called limited random-access machines) and Turing machines with *head-to-head jumps*, and many others. One common feature in this abundance of models is that they all have a finite control and an unrestricted read-write storage facility. This allows each model, whatever its specification, to compute all recursive functions. Differences in capabilities become apparent if we impose time limitations, and in particular when we demand the machines to operate in *real-time*. As a standard in this area we may take the class of *real-time definable languages* R, which is the class of all languages accepted by multitape Turing machines in real-time, ROSENBERG [1967]. It has been shown that all of the above mentioned variations of Turing machines accept in real-time precisely R. Hence we observe that, within the world of real-time Turing machine-like devices, R plays somewhat the same role as the class of recursively enumerable languages in the world of computability at large. Like in this wider setting, we shall impose restrictions on the machines and observe what happens. In the province of real-time computations, differences in computing power amongst unlike Turing

---

*

The results in sections 2 and 3 are taken from VITÁNYI [1979]. The present paper is registered as Mathematical Centre Technical Report IW 132.

machines may come out under variations in instruction repertoire, amount or type of storage devices, in short, under different *specifications*.

The class of real-time definable languages is remarkably extensive (e.g. the set of unmarked palindromes is in R, GALIL [1978]). To prove that a given language is not in R is often hard. Proofs usually rely on an information-capacity argument, see HARTMANIS & STEARNS [1965] and ROSENBERG [1967].

Real-time computations of Turing machines are especially interesting because of their intrinsic feasibility. Originally, they were defined relative to the multitape Turing machines. Most algorithms, however, are more naturally stated in terms of computing models which allows faster memory access. A k-head tape unit consists of a Turing machine with a single storage tape on which k read-write heads operate. P. FISCHER, MEYER & ROSENBERG [1972] proved that one can simulate a k-head tape unit in real-time by a multitape Turing machine with 11k-9 tapes. Later, LEONG & SEIFERAS [1977] improved this to 4k-4 tapes. RABIN [1963] has observed that 2-tape Turing machines are more powerful in real-time than 1-tape Turing machines. (Recall that a 1-tape Turing machine has one input tape and one storage tape with a single head.) AANDERAA [1974] demonstrated that k+1 tapes are more powerful than k tapes in real-time. Together with the LEONG & SEIFERAS' result this shows that more heads will yield additional power in real-time. Specifically, it follows that a (4k-3)-head tape unit is more powerful in real-time than a k-head tape unit. We shall show that AANDERAA's result implies that a (k+1)-head tape unit is more powerful than a k-head tape unit in real-time, section 2.

In ROSENBERG [1967] several closure properties of R are investigated. We investigate such questions for the classes R(k) (languages recognized by k-tape real-time Turing machines), $R^H(k)$ (languages recognized by k-head real-time Turing machines) and $R^J(k)$ (languages recognized by k-head real-time Turing machines with head-to-head jumps). Furthermore, we shall consider the relations between R(k), $R^H(k)$ and $R^J(k)$, sections 3 and 5.

In SAVITCH & VITÁNYI [1977] it was shown that a k-head jump Turing machine can be simulated in linear time by an (8k-8)-tape Turing machine. KOSARAJU [1979] has claimed a proof that jump Turing machines can be simulated in real-time by multitape Turing machines at the cost of many tapes in the latter pro head in the former machine. In section 4 we show that the analog of this result does not hold if we restrict ourselves to 2-way multihead finite automata. The sample languages we use to prove this result are interesting in their own right, since they give once more an indication how wrong our intuition can be with respect to which languages belong to R and which languages do not.

But for RABIN's and AANDERAA's results, all results in the area of models of real-time Turing machines are about feasibility of simulating one type of machine by another one. Virtually nothing is known about the nonfeasibility of certain computations, which are possible on a machine of specification A, by a machine of specification B. Obvious open problems in this area of specified Turing machines are, for instance:

$R(2) \subset R^H(2)$; $R^H(k) \subset R^H(k+1)$; $R^J(k) \subset R^J(k+1)$; $R(k) \subset R^H(k)$; $R(k) \subset R^J(k)$; $R^H(k) \subset R^J(k)$? Some of these questions we shall decide, or alternatively, show some interdependence among seemingly unrelated questions.

For formal definitions and so on concerning multitape- and multihead Turing machines, real-time computations, etc. we refer to ROSENBERG [1967], FISCHER, MEYER & ROSENBERG [1972] and LEONG & SEIFERAS [1977]. In this paper we do not give all proofs; complete proofs and additional results shall be provided in a final version to appear elsewhere.

2. k+1 HEADS ARE BETTER THAN k HEADS IN REAL-TIME

AANDERAA [1974] proved by a very complicated argument that there is, for each $k \geq 0$, a language A_{k+1} which can be recognized by a (k+1)-RTTM but not by a k-RTTM. For completeness we define A_{k+1} below by a real-time algorithm which accepts it using k+1 pushdown stores. The input alphabet is $\Sigma_{k+1} = \{0_i, 1_i, P_i \mid 1 \leq i \leq k+1\}$. The algorithm is as follows:

```
"ACCEPTENABLED := TRUE;
Initialize k+1 stacks to empty;
REPEAT FOREOVER
  CASE NEXTINPUTLETTER OF
  0_i: Push 0 in stack i
  1_i: Push 1 on stack i
  P_i: IF stack i empty
       THEN ACCEPTENABLED := FALSE and reject input
       ELSE BEGIN
             pop stack i;
             IF element popped was 1
             AND ACCEPTENABLED
             THEN accept input
             ELSE reject input
             END
  ENDCASE"
```

The strategy used to prove that k+1 heads are more powerful in real-time than k heads (on a single tape) is, by a judicious choice of input, to force the heads so far apart that for a given recognition problem the k-head unit must act like a k-tape Turing machine since the heads will never read each others writing.

<u>THEOREM 2.1</u>. *There is a language which is recognized by a* k+1 *head real-time Turing machine but not by any* k *head real-time Turing machine.*

PROOF. By induction on the number of heads. (k=0 is obvious).

k=1. The language A_2 cannot be recognized by a 1-tape (= 1-head) real-time Turing machine, but can be recognized by a 2-tape (and hence by a 2-head) RTTM. Set $H_2 = A_2$.

k > 1. Suppose the theorem is true for all j < k. Hence, in particular there is a language H_k such that H_k is recognized by a k-head RTTM but not by a (k-1)-head RTTM. Define H_{k+1} as follows:

$$H_{k+1} = H_k \cup H_k * A_{k+1}$$

where * is a special symbol not in the alphabet of A_i, $i \geq 2$.

Let M_k be a k-head RTTM claimed to recognize H_{k+1}. Present M_k with strings of the form

$$w = a_1^{(2)} a_2^{(2)} \ldots a_{n_2}^{(2)} * a_1^{(3)} a_2^{(3)} \ldots a_{n_3}^{(3)} * \ldots * a_1^{(k+1)} a_2^{(k+1)} \ldots a_{n_{k+1}}^{(k+1)}$$

$$= w_2 * w_3 \ldots * w_{k+1}$$

such that w_i is over the alphabet of A_i, $2 \leq i \leq k+1$. During the processing of w_2, M_k must recognize A_2. Since A_2 cannot be recognized by a 1-head RTTM, the distance between the outermost heads on the storage tape of M_k must grow larger than any given constant c_2 for a suitable choice of w_2. Hence, subsequent to the processing of w_2, we can single out a tapesegment of length at least c_2/k tape squares, contained by the tapesegment delineated by the outermost heads, such that no tape square of the former segment is scanned by a head. Choose c_2 later so that $c_2/k > 2 \Sigma_{i=3}^{k+1} (n_i+1)$. Therefore, for the remainder of the computation on w, M_k consists in effect of at best a $k_1^{(1)}$-head and a $k_2^{(1)}$-head tape unit, $k_1^{(1)}, k_2^{(1)} \geq 1$ and $k_1^{(1)} + k_2^{(1)} = k$, where $k_1^{(1)}$ is the number of heads left of the unscanned tapesegment and $k_2^{(1)}$ is the number of heads right of it, at the end of processing w_2. Now M_k is presented with w_3. Since $w_3 \in A_3$ cannot be decided in real-time by 2 single-headed tapes, M_k must use one, or both, of its remaining tape units in an essential way during the processing of w_3. I.e., for at least one of the tape units (and one containing more than one head), say the $k_1^{(1)}$-head unit, the distance between the outermost heads must grow larger than any given constant c_3 for a suitable choice of w_3. Hence, subsequent to the processing of w_3, we can single out a tapesegment, no square of which is scanned by a head and of length at least $c_3/k_1^{(1)}$, which is in between the outermost heads of this $k_1^{(1)}$-head tape unit. Now choose c_3, and hence w_3, later so that $c_3/k_1^{(1)} > 2 \Sigma_{i=4}^{k+1} (n_i+1)$. Similar to before, we now divide the $k_1^{(1)}$ heads into $k_1^{(2)}$ and $k_2^{(2)}$ heads to the left and right, respectively, of the latter nonscanned tapesegment, and we observe that, for the remainder of the computation on w, M_k now consists in effect of a $k_1^{(2)}$-head-, a $k_2^{(2)}$-head- and a $k_3^{(2)}$-head tape unit, $k_1^{(2)}, k_2^{(2)}, k_3^{(2)} \geq 1$, $k_1^{(2)} + k_2^{(2)} + k_3^{(2)} = k$, $k_1^{(2)} + k_2^{(2)} = k_1^{(1)}$ and $k_3^{(2)} = k_2^{(1)}$.

Repeating the argument we can choose $w_4, \ldots, w_k$ such that after the processing of

w_k we are left in effect with a k-tape RTTM which is required to determine whether $w_{k+1} \in A_{k+1}$. According to AANDERAA [1974], for each k-tape RTTM claimed to recognize A_{k+1} we can construct a word v which fools the machine. Let w_{k+1} be such a word, and choose $c_k, w_k, c_{k-1}, w_{k-1}, \ldots, c_2, w_2$, in that order, so that the above inequalities and conditions are satisfied. Hence w is accepted by M_k iff $w \notin H_{k+1}$ which contradicts the assumption that M_k recognizes H_{k+1}. (The above argument seemingly contains a circularity which might invalidate it. The word v which fools the machine trying to recognize A_{k+1} does not only depend on the finite control but *also* on the initial tape contents. Thus the argument seems to become circular: w_{k+1} depends on $w_2 * w_3 * \ldots * w_k *$, while $w_2, w_3, \ldots, w_k$ depend on the length of w_{k+1}. As it happens, AANDERAA's argument does not need to make any assumptions about the initial tape contents of the k-RTTM assumed, by way of contradiction, to accept A_{k+1}. Hence he proves in fact that for all k-RTTM M there exists a positive integer n such that for all initial tape contents of M there exists a word v of at most length n which fools M. The existence of such a bound n eliminates the apparent circularity from the above argument.) It is easy to see that k+1 pushdown stores can recognize H_{k+1} in real-time. □

Surprisingly, an argument like "H_k is not accepted by a (k-1)-head RTTM and hence $H_{k+1} = H_k \cup H_k * A_{k+1}$ is not accepted by a k-head RTTM" does not work, since we cannot assume a priori that in a k-head RTTM recognizing H_k all heads get pairwise arbitrarily far apart for some input. We could only conclude that all k heads are necessary, but it might very well be that for each time t some heads are near to each other. Then we could be stuck with a set of tape units, one of which is a multihead one, for which AANDERAA's proof might not work.

The situation we have in mind is exemplified by, e.g., the languages E_k, $k \geq 4$, in section 5 (although AANDERAA's proof technique fails there for another reason, as shall be pointed out). As an example of a language which can be recognized by a 4-head RTTM in which there are always 2 heads together, and which probably cannot be recognized by a 4-RTTM, or a 3-head RTTM, we give the language L below. Clearly, we cannot conclude from $L \notin R^H(3)$ (if that is the case) that $L \cup L * A_5 \notin R^H(4)$ just because $A_5 \notin R(4)$. We would need to show at least that A_5 cannot be recognized by a RTTM with one 2-head tape and 2 1-head tapes as storage.

$$L' = \{u_1 ww^R u_2 vv^R u_3 2\ 0^{|u_1 w|} 2\ 0^{2|w|} 2\ 0^{|u_3 v|} 2\ 0^{|v|} \mid u_1 w u_2 v u_3 \in \{0,1\}^*\};$$

$$L = \{x \in \{0,1,2\}^* \mid x \text{ is a prefix of a word in } L'\}.$$

For suppose we want to recognize L by a 3-head or a 4-head RTTM. Essentially, up to reading the marker 2 on the input tape, it would seem that we can do nothing more than record the input prefix over {0,1} on the storage tape.

Now if we take $|w|, |v| \in \Theta(n^{2/3})$, $|u_2| \in \Theta(n)$, $|u_1|, |u_3| \in \Theta(n^{2/3})$, where n is the length of the input word, we need 2 heads to check ww^R (since to check ww^R with 1 head takes time $\Theta(n^{4/3})$) and 2 heads to check vv^R (for the same reason). To cross

u_2 with some head takes time $\Theta(n)$, but upon meeting the first letter 2 we have only time $\Theta(n^{2/3})$ left. Hence 4 heads seem necessary, although there always are 2 together. If this conjecture is true, then $L \in R^H(4) - R^H(3)$. But in this case $L \in R^H(4) - R^H(3)$ together with $A_5 \notin R(4)$ does not, without additional considerations, imply $L \cup L * A_5 \notin R^H(4)$.

By the proof method of Theorem 2.1 we precluded this flaw in the argument. Due to the form of A_{k+1}, the line of reasoning works also for A_{k+1} itself. Hence, $A_{k+1} \in R(k+1) - R^H(k)$.

<u>COROLLARY 2.2</u>. *There is a language which can be recognized by* k+1 *pushdown stores in real-time (and hence by a* (k+1-RTTM)) *but not by any* k-*head* RTTM.

The relation between tapes and pushdown stores is direct; clearly 2k pushdown stores can simulate k tapes in real-time. Hence from AANDERAA's result we have: (if $R^P(k)$ denotes the class of languages recognizable by k pushdown stores in real-time)

$$R^P(k+1) - R(k) \neq \emptyset;$$
$$R^P(k) \subset R^P(k+1) \quad ;$$
$$R(k) \subset R(k+1) \quad ;$$
$$R(k) \subset R^P(2k) \quad .$$

By the result above it follows that we can replace R by R^H in the first formula above. It also follows that

$$R(k+1) - R^H(k) \neq \emptyset;$$
$$R^H(k) \subset R^H(k+1).$$

By using LEONG & SEIFERAS' [1977] result we obtain

<u>LEMMA 2.3</u>. $R(k) \subseteq R^H(k) \subset R(4k-4)$.

3. CLOSURE PROPERTIES OF R(k)

In ROSENBERG [1967] several closure properties of the class R of languages accepted by real-time Turing machines were investigated. It appeared that R is closed under union as well as intersection, complementation, suffixing with a regular set, inverse real-time transducer mapping, and minimization. R is not closed under concatenation, Kleene star, reversal, (nonerasing) homomorphism, inverse nondeterministic sequential machine mapping, quotient with a regular set, maximization and prefixing with a regular set.

When we restrict the number of tapes the picture gets different: R(k) is closed under complementation, union as well as intersection with regular sets, suffixing with regular sets, inverse gsm mapping and minimization. R(1) is not closed under union or intersection, nor under inverse real-time transducer mapping.

In this section we will investigate some more closure properties of (number of) tape restricted real-time languages. It will e.g. appear that R(k) is closed under several marked operations; furthermore it often happens that the closure under certain operations of R(k) is in R(2k) but not in R(2k-1). (Proofs to be provided later).

LEMMA 3.1. R(k) *is closed under marked union, marked concatenation and marked Kleene star.*

LEMMA 3.2. *Let* k_1, k_2 *be positive integers such that* $k_1 + k_2 \geq 1$.

(i) R(k) *is not closed under union or intersection, for* $k > 0$. *If we take* $A \in R(k_1)$ *and* $B \in R(k_2)$ *then* $A \cup B, A \cap B \in R(k_1+k_2)$, *but not necessarily* $A \cup B, A \cap B \in R(k_1+k_2-1)$.

(ii) *If* $A \in R(k_1)$ *and* $B \in R(k_2)$ *and the alphabets of* A *and* B *are disjoint, then shuffle* (A,B) $\in R(k_1+k_2)$ *but shuffle* (A,B) *does not need to belong to* $R(k_1+k_2-1)$. *Hence* R(k) *is not closed under shuffle over disjoint alphabets.*

(iii) R(k) *is not closed under inverse real-time transducer mapping. The closure of* $R(k_1)$ *under inverse* k_2-RTTM *mapping is contained in* $R(k_1+k_2)$ *but not in* $R(k_1+k_2-1)$.

(iv) (i)-(iii) *hold also if we replace everywhere* "R" *by* "R^H".

The results in Lemma 3.2 are obtained by reducing the problems to the recognition problem of $A_{k_1+k_2}$.

LEMMA 3.3. *If* $A \in R(0)$ *and* $B \in R(1)$ *then shuffle* (A,B) *does not need to belong to* R. *I.e.,* R *is not closed under shuffle.*
($L = \{\Sigma^* x \Sigma^* 2 x^R \mid \Sigma = \{0,1\}, x \in \Sigma^*\} \notin R$ *and an isomorphic language can be obtained as a shuffle of languages in* R(0) *and* R(1).)

According to FISCHER, MEYER & ROSENBERG [1972], the family of multihead RTTM languages equals R and hence the (non) closure properties mentioned before apply. If we look at multihead RTTM languages in $R^H(k)$ the situation is different. Here not more was known than we could readily deduce from the results on R(k) and simulations like LEONG & SEIFERAS [1977]. With the preceding results we obtained more. Also, $R^H(k)$ is closed under complementation, union and intersection with regular sets, suffixing with regular sets, inverse gsm mapping and minimization. Lemma 3.2 holds even if we denote by k only the total number of heads on the storage tapes, and don't take into account the way in which the heads are distributed.

Clearly, $R^H(k)$ is closed under marked union. The markers in an input, due to marked concatenation or marked Kleene star, serve to indicate the beginning of a new task. Accordingly, it seems reasonable to assume that recognizing RTTMs *ignore*, subsequent to reading such a marker, the garbage left on the storage tapes by the preceding computation segment. Under this assumption we can prove Conjectures 3.4 and 3.5.

CONJECTURE 3.4. $R^H(k)$ is closed under marked concatenation iff $R^H(k)$ is closed under marked Kleene star iff $R^H(k) = R(k)$.

A k-head jump Turing machine (cf. SAVITCH & VITÁNYI [1977]) is a k-head Turing machine where at each step the k heads may be redistributed over the scanned tape squares. In SAVITCH & VITÁNYI [1977] it was shown that a k-head jump Turing machine can be simulated in linear time by a (8k-8)-tape Turing machine. KOSARAJU [1979] has claimed that, by a complicated simulation, a k-head jump Turing machine can be simulated in real-time by a multitape Turing machine. It is at present unresolved whether k heads are more powerful than k tapes in real-time. A possibly easier problem is to show that k heads with jumps are more powerful than k tapes in real-time. We will show that these matters are related.

It is easy to see that $R^J(k)$ (the class of languages accepted in real-time by k-head jump Turing machines) is closed under marked concatenation and marked Kleene star. By first feeding A_k, we can always reduce a k-head RTTM to a k-tape RTTM. This, however, is not the case for a k-head jump RTTM. Hence, k jump heads are more powerful than k tapes iff k jump heads are more powerful than k heads. Similarly, if k heads are more powerful than k tapes then k jump heads are more powerful than k heads. Hence we have

CONJECTURE 3.5.
(i) $R(k) \subset R^J(k)$ *iff* $R^H(k) \subset R^J(k)$;
(ii) *if* $R(k) \subset R^H(k)$ *then* $R^H(k) \subset R^J(k)$.

4. REAL-TIME 2-WAY MULTIHEAD FINITE AUTOMATA WITH AND WITHOUT JUMPS

Recall that we saw before that KOSARAJU [1979] has shown that the jump Turing machine as defined in SAVITCH & VITÁNYI [1977] may be simulated in real-time by multitape Turing machines. Hence $R^J = R$ (where $R^J = \bigcup_{k=1}^{\infty} R^J(k)$). In this section we show that for 2-way multihead finite automata the head-to-head jump facility does extend the class of languages accepted in real-time. Incidentally, this shows also that the class of languages accepted by real-time 2-way multihead finite automata is strictly included in R. To obtain the result, we give several example languages which are acceptable in real-time by 2-way 2-head finite automata with jumps, but not by any real-time 2-way multihead finite automaton without jumps. Hence these languages belong to R, and constitute nontrivial examples of the power of the head-to-head jump option. Let in the following $h: \{0,1,\bar{0},\bar{1}\}^* \to \{0,1\}^*$ be a homomorphism which is defined by $h(\bar{a}) = h(a) = a$ for $a \in \{0,1\}$.

$$L_1 = \{\overline{wva}av^R \mid \overline{wv} \in \{0,1,\bar{0},\bar{1}\}^*,\ v \in \{0,1\}^*,\ a \in \{0,1\},\ h(\bar{v}) = v\};$$

$$L_2 = \{\bar{w}b\bar{u}cva \mid \overline{wu} \in \{0,1,\bar{0},\bar{1}\}^*,\ v \in \{0,1\}^*,\ c \in \{\bar{0},\bar{1}\},\ |\bar{u}| = |v|,$$
$$a \in \{0,1\},\ b \in \{0,1,\bar{0},\bar{1}\},\ h(b) = a\}.$$

The reader will easily figure out more complicated examples along these lines.

Note that L_1, L_2 are linear context free but not deterministic context free.

LEMMA 4.1. L_1, L_2 *are accepted by real-time 2-way 2-head finite automata with jumps.*

PROOF. Let M be a 2-way 2-head finite automaton with jumps as follows. The front head reads from left to right one letter at a time. Whenever this first head reads a barred letter it calls the second head to its present position. This second head starts reading from right to left one letter at a time. So M is able to recognize L_1. A minor variation of M can recognize L_2. □

LEMMA 4.2. L_1, L_2 *are not accepted by any real-time 2-way multihead finite automaton.*

PROOF. Along the same lines as the proof of Theorem 2.1. □

Hence we have:

THEOREM 4.3. (i) *There are languages accepted by real-time 2-way 2-head finite automata with jumps which are not accepted by any real-time 2-way multihead finite automaton without jumps.*
(ii) *The class of languages accepted by real-time 2-way k-head finite automata with jumps properly includes the class of languages accepted by such automata without jumps.*

Computations of 1-way multihead finite automata have been considered by YAO & RIVEST [1978]. They show that k+1 heads are better than k heads for both the deterministic and the nondeterministic versions of the machine. Furthermore, they show that the k-head nondeterministic variety is strictly more powerful than the k-head deterministic one. Recently, JANIGA [1979] studied the analog questions for 2-way real-time multihead deterministic (resp. nondeterministic) finite automata, from now on called 2DRTFA and 2NRTFA, respectively. He obtained, mutatis mutandis, the same results for the 2-way real-time machines as did YAO and RIVEST for the 1-way (no time limit) variety. Whereas the latter used "palindromes" of $\binom{k}{2}$ strings to obtain their result, for the 2-way real-time case the former employed strings of k palindromes. E.g., let PALM be the set of palindromes in $\{0,1\}^*\{2\}\{0,1\}^*$. Let $P_k = (\text{PALM}\{*\})^k$. Then P_k is recognized by a (k+1)-head 2DRTFA but not by any k-head 2NRTFA. $\{0,1,2,*\}^* - P_k$ is accepted by a 2-head 2NRTFA but not by any k-head 2DRTFA. Now consider the language $P = \bigcup_{k=1}^{\infty} P_k$. It is easy to see that P is recognized by a 2-head 2DRTFA with jumps, but that P is not accepted by any multihead 2NRTFA without jumps because of JANIGA's result. Therefore we have:

THEOREM 4.4. *The class of languages accepted by* k-*head* 2NRTFA *with jumps properly includes the class of languages accepted by* k-*head* 2NRTFA *without jumps*, $k \geq 2$. *The same holds for* 2DRTFA's (*i.e. Theorem* 4.3).

Another matter which we would like to decide is the power of jumps versus nondeterminism for the machines.

THEOREM 4.5. *There is a language acceptable by a 2-head* 2NRTFA *which is not acceptable by any multihead* 2DRTFA *with jumps.*

PROOF. The language L in the proof of Lemma 3.3 was not in R, and hence, by KOSARAJU's [1979] result, is not acceptable by any multihead 2DRTFA with jumps. It is easy to see how L can be accepted by a 2-head 2NRTFA. □

The only question remaining seems to be whether (k+1)-head 2DRTFA's with jumps are more powerful than k-head 2DRTFA's with jumps, and the same matter for the non-deterministic versions. For a proof we might use the language J_k over the alphabet

$$\Sigma = \{0,1\} \times F \times M \times Q,$$

where

$$F = \{f \mid f \text{ is a total function } f\colon \{0,1\}^k \times Q \to \{0,1\}\},$$

$$M = \{m \mid m \text{ is a total function } m\colon \{1,2,\ldots,k\} \times Q \to$$
$$\to \{\text{left},\text{right},\text{no move}\} \text{ and } m(1,q) = \text{right}$$
$$\text{for all } q \in Q\}.$$

The interpretation is as follows. J_k is recognized by a k-head 2DRTFA M with state set Q. Suppose M has an input $s_1s_2\ldots s_is_{i+1}\ldots s_n$ on its tape, $s_i = (a_i,f_i,m_i,q_i) \in \Sigma$, $1 \le i \le n$. At the i-th step the vanguard head 1 of M reads s_i in state $q_{i-1} \in Q$ and outputs $f_i(a_{j1},a_{j2},\ldots,a_{jk},q_{i-1})$ where a_{jh} is the first element of the symbol read by the head h at that moment, $1 \le h \le k$. Subsequently, M repositions head h according to $m_i(h,q_i)$, $1 \le h \le k$, and enters state q_i.

THEOREM 4.6. J_{k+1} *is accepted by a* (k+1)*-head* 2DRTFA *but not by any* k*-head* 2NRTFA *with jumps. Hence* (k+1)*-head* 2DRTFA (2NRTFA) *with jumps are strictly more powerful than* k*-head* 2DRTFA (2NRTFA) *with jumps.*

If we take J'_k equal to J_k but without "left" in the range of $m \in M$ we can similarly prove:

COROLLARY 4.7. J'_{k+1} *is accepted by a* (k+1)*-head* 1DRTFA *but not by any* k*-head* 1NRTFA *with jumps. This implies that all inclusions according to the number of heads in the* 1XRTFA *are proper, where* X ∈ {D,N,D *with jumps,* N *with jumps*}.

All results in this section hold whether or not we assume end markers, or that the heads can detect coincidence.

We think that Theorem 4.3 also holds for the corresponding Turing machine versions which are allowed to modify the contents of each square on the storage tapes but a bounded number of times, for some fixed constant bound.

5. ON THE RELATIVE POWER OF TAPES, HEADS AND JUMP HEADS IN REAL-TIME TURING MACHINES

One of the major drawbacks in the game of showing a difference in power between two very similar machine types A and B such as considered in this paper, apart from the difficulties involved in giving a proof, is to find some likely candidates for showing a difference between type A and type B. RABIN's [1963] language in $R(2) - R(1)$ did not generalize in an obvious way to show a difference between $R(k+1)$ and $R(k)$, $k > 1$. AANDERAA [1974] provided a uniform construction for a language in $R(k+1) - R(k)$, $k \geq 1$. No likely candidates for showing the difference between, e.g., $R(k)$ and $R^H(k)$ or $R^H(k)$ and $R^J(k)$ have been proposed, except possibly $\{xy2x \mid xy \in \{0,1\}^*\}$ for showing a difference between $R^H(2)$ and $R(2)$. In the present section we propose to fill this gap, besides proving some facts about the candidates. The only languages known to be in $R - R(k)$ are $A_{k'}$, $k' > k$, put unfortunately these languages are not in $R^H(k)$ either. SEIFERAS [personal communication] claims to have proven that $A_{k'} \notin R^J(k)$, and we will proceed on this assumption. Hence the only candidates of which we have negative results are not acceptable either by placing all heads on the same tape nor by adding the jump option. From the existing simulation results it is also clear that there cannot be a single language L which is acceptable by some k-head (jump) RTTM but not by any multitape (multihead) RTTM, thus proving the required results by a single example as in section 4. Now consider a language which is like A_k but with the extra requirement that at all times during the processing of the input w by a k stack machine at least 2 of the stacks are of equal length for w to be accepted. More formally, if $|v|_i$ denotes the number of 0_i's and 1_i's subtracted by the number of P_i's in v, then:

$$E_k = \{w \in \Sigma_k^* \mid w \in A_k \ \& \ \forall v \in \text{prefix}(w) \ \exists i,j (i \neq j \text{ and } 1 \leq i,j \leq k) \ [|v|_i = |v|_j + \delta, -1 \leq \delta \leq +1]\}.$$

<u>LEMMA 5.1</u>. $E_k \notin R(k-2)$, $R^H(k-2)$, $R^J(k-2)$.

<u>PROOF</u>. Suppose, by way of contradiction, that the (k-2)-RTTM M accepts E_k. Now change M to a (k-2)-RTTM M^* which accepts A_{k-1} by having the finite control of M, for every letter $0_{k-1}, 1_{k-1}, P_{k-1}$ read $0_{k-1}0_k, 1_{k-1}1_k, P_{k-1}P_k$, respectively, and speed up the storage handling as much as required. Then A_{k-1} is accepted by the (k-2)-RTTM M^* contradicting known results. $E_k \notin R^H(k-2)$ then follows by Theorem 2.1 and for $E_k \notin R^J(k-2)$ see the introduction of this section. □

(The case k = 2 above is obvious since E_2 is not regular.) Note that AANDERAA's proof does not show that $E_k \notin R(k-1)$ since the subset $S\Sigma_k^*$ used in AANDERAA's proof (which in fact shows that no k-RTTM can distinguish between $S\Sigma_k^* \cap A_k$ and $S\Sigma_k^* \cap (\Sigma_k^* - A_k)$) is disjoint from E_k.

<u>LEMMA 5.2</u>. $E_2 \in R(1)$, $E_3 \in R^H(2)$.

PROOF. $E_2 \in R(1)$ is obvious. $E_3 \in R^H(2)$: keep the 3 stacks on different tracks of the recognizing 2-head RTTM M. Whenever there is a change in pairs of equal size stacks, all 3 stacks must be of equal length, otherwise we reject the input. Both heads of M therefore come together with everything to the right of them blank, and therefore the role of the "fat" head, maintaining 2 tracks, can change. □

We conjecture that $E_3 \notin R(2)$. To prove this conjecture would also prove that $R(2) \subset R^H(2)$, a well-known open problem. In general we conjecture that $E_k \notin R(k)$, $k \geq 3$, which for the case $k = 3$ would show that the LEONG-SEIFERAS simulation is optimal for 2 heads. By Lemma 5.1 and the fact that a multihead machine can detect coincidence we have that

LEMMA 5.3. $E_k \in R^H(k) - R^H(k-2)$.

LEMMA 5.4. $E_k \in R^J(k-1)$ *for all* $k > 1$.

COROLLARY 5.5. $E_k \in R^J(k-1) - R^J(k-2)$.

We conjecture that E_k cannot be recognized by a (k-1)-head RTTM for $k \geq 4$. A proof of this fact would show that $R^H(k) \subset R^J(k)$ for $k \geq 3$, leaving open the case $k = 2$. Although we have an upper bound on the recognition of E_k by multihead RTTM's (with respect to the number of heads needed) we have not yet a good upper bound for recognition by multitape RTTM's, except by the crude $E_k \in R(4k-4)$ offered by Lemma 5.3 and the LEONG-SEIFERAS' result.

LEMMA 5.6. $E_2 \in R(1)$; $E_3 \in R(4)$; $E_k \in R(2k-2)$, $k \geq 3$.

We can generalize the above approach in several directions. For instance, by requiring that i of the k stacks have the same height at all times during the processing of the input, Formally,

$$E_{\binom{k}{i}} = \left\{ w \in \Sigma_k^* \mid w \in A_k \ \& \ \forall v \in \text{prefix}(w) \ \exists j_1, j_2, \ldots, j_i \in \{1,\ldots,k\} \atop j_1 < j_2 \ldots < j_i \right.$$
$$\left. [\, \big| |v|_{j_\ell} - |v|_{j_m} \big| \leq 3 \text{ for all } j_\ell, j_m \in \{j_1, j_2, \ldots, j_i\}] \right\}.$$

These languages are especially suited to jump Turing machines since it is easily seen that:

LEMMA 5.7. $E_{\binom{k}{i}} \in R^J(k-i+1)$.

Furthermore, we can easily show that $E_{\binom{k}{i}} \in R^H(k-i+1)$ provided $i > k/2$; $E_{\binom{k}{i}} \notin R(k-i), R^H(k-i), R^J(k-i)$; and $E_{\binom{k}{i}} \in R^H(k)$ for $i < k/2$. (Some border cases for $i \geq k/2$: $E_{\binom{5}{3}} \in R^H(3)$ and $E_{\binom{5}{4}} \in R^H(2) \subset R(4)$.)

Looking at the above we see there is a relation between the optimality of the real-time simulations of jump heads by heads and heads by tapes and how many tapes or heads are needed to recognize $E_{\binom{k}{i}}$. Let f(k) be the minimum number of tapes (heads) needed for simulating k jump heads in real-time. Then, if we need at least k tapes (heads) for accepting $E_{\binom{k}{i}}$, $i < k/2$, then

$$f(k-i+1) \geq k.$$

Hence the conjecture that we need k or more tapes (heads) to recognize $E_{\binom{k}{i}}$ for $i < k/2$ can be dissolved if we can improve KOSARAJU's result to "less than 2 k tapes (heads) are necessary for the real-time simulation of k jump heads". From the real-time simulation of heads by tapes it follows that $E_{\binom{k}{i}} \in R(4(k-i))$ for $i > k/2$, and therefore e.g. $E_{\binom{k}{3k/4}} \in R(k)$.

Yet another language sequence we might consider is $A_k - E_k$, $k \geq 1$. Since $A_k - E_k$ contains AANDERAA's subset $A_k \cap S\Sigma_k^*$, it follows that $A_k - E_k \notin R(k-1), R^H(k-1), R^J(k-1)$. We also see that $A_k - E_k \in R^H(k), R^J(k)$. With respect to acceptance by k-RTTM's the same upper bounds apply as argued for E_k. This is not so for the languages $A_k - E_k'$, where E_k' is like E_k but the condition of two stack heights being equal only holds at the end of the processing of the input word, i.e.,

$$E_k' = \{w \in \Sigma_k^* \mid w \in A_k \ \& \ \exists_{i \neq j} i,j \in \{1,\ldots,k\}[\,||w|_i - |w|_j| \leq 3]\}.$$

Here we have that $A_2 - E_2' \in R(3)$ but, presumably, that $A_2 - E_2' \notin R(2)$. By the now familiar reasoning, if the latter case is affirmative then $A_2 * (A_2 - E_2') \in R^J(2) - R^H(2)$, settling the question whether or not $R^H(2) \subset R^J(2)$.

Some of the candidates to try for solving the various questions met are given in the table below.

	$R(k) \subset R^H(k)$?	$R^H(k) \subset R^J(k)$?
k = 2 :	$L = \{xy2x \mid xy \in \{0,1\}^*\}$ E_3, $A_2 - E_2'$	$A_2 * (A_2 - E_2')$
arbitrary $k \geq 3$:	E_k, $A_k - E_k'$	E_{k+1}

Acknowledgements. *J. SEIFERAS pointed out to me that the earlier version of the proof of Theorem* 2.1 *may have been prone to circularity of the argument. Discussions with W. SAVITCH were valuable for section* 4.

REFERENCES

AANDERAA, S.O. (1974), *On k-tape versus (k-1)-tape real time computation*, SIAM AMS Proceedings, Vol. 7 (Complexity of Computation), 75-96.

FISCHER, M.J. & A.L. ROSENBERG (1968), *Limited random access Turing machines*, Proceedings 9-th IEEE-SWAT, 356-367.

FISCHER, P.C., A.R. MEYER & A.L. ROSENBERG (1972), *Real-time simulation of multihead tape units*, JACM 19, 590-607.

GALIL, Z. (1978), *Palindrome recognition in real time on a multitape Turing machine*, J. Comp. Syst. Sci. 16, 140-157.

HARTMANIS, J. & R.E. STEARNS (1965), *On the computational complexity of algorithms*, Trans. AMS 117, 285-306.

JANIGA, L. (1979), *Real-time computations of two-way multihead finite automata*, in: Fundamentals of Computation Theory (FCT '79) (L. Budach ed.), Akademie Verlag, Berlin, 214-218.

KOSARAJU, R. (1979), *Real-time simulation of concatenable double-ended queues by double-ended queues*, Proceedings 11-th ACM-STOC, 346-351.

LEONG, B. & J. SEIFERAS (1977), *New real-time simulations of multihead tape units*, Proceedings 9-th ACM-STOC, 239-248.

RABIN, M.O. (1963), *Real-time computation*, Israel Journal of Mathematics 1, 203-211.

ROSENBERG, A.L. (1967), *Real-time definable languages*, J. ACM 14, 645-662.

SAVITCH, W.J. & P.M.B. VITÁNYI (1977), *Linear time simulation of multihead Turing machines with head-to-head jumps*, Lecture Notes in Computer Science (ICALP 4) 52, Springer-Verlag, Berlin, 453-464.

VITÁNYI, P.M.B. (1979), *Multihead and multitape real-time Turing machines*. Technical Report IW 111, Mathematisch Centrum, June 1979.

YAO, A. & R.RIVEST (1978), k+1 *heads are better than* k, J. ACM 25, 337-340.